Second Edition

EMPLOYMENT RELATIONS

ED ROSE

Prentice Hall

FINANCIAL TIMES

An imprint of **Pearson Education**

Harlow, England • London • New York • Boston • San Francisco • Toronto
Sydney • Tokyo • Singapore • Hong Kong • Seoul • Taipei • New Delhi
Cape Town • Madrid • Mexico City • Amsterdam • Munich • Paris • Milan

Pearson Education Limited
Edinburgh Gate
Harlow
Essex CM20 2JE
England

and Associated Companies throughout the world

Visit us on the World Wide Web at:
www.pearsoned.co.uk

First published 2001
Second edition published 2004

ISBN 0273 68259 8

British Library Cataloguing-in-Publication Data
A catalogue record for this book is available from the British Library

10 9 8 7 6 5 4 3
08 07 06 05

Typeset in 9.5/12pt Sabon by 35
Printed and bound by Ashford Colour Press Ltd., Gosport

The publisher's policy is to use paper manufactured from sustainable forests.

CONTENTS

Website Resources

For Students:

• Learning outcomes for each chapter
• Links to relevant sites on the web
• Glossary to explain key terms

For Lecturers:

• A secure, password protected site with teaching material
• Complete, downloadable Instructor's Manual
• PowerPoint slides that can be downloaded and used as OHTs
• Answers to exercise material from the book
• Additional case studies

ACKNOWLEDGEMENTS

We are grateful to the following for permission to reproduce copyright material:

Tables 2.1, 6.2, 6.3, 6.4, 8.1, 8.2 and 9.4 from Millward, N., Bryson, A. and Forth, J., *All Change at Work*, 2000, Taylor & Francis Books Ltd, reproduced with the kind permission of Taylor & Francis Books Ltd; Table 5.2 from Procter, S. and Ackroyd, S., 'Flexibility' in Redman, T. and Wilkinson, A., *Contemporary Human Resources Management*, 2000, Pearson Education; Table 7.4 from Cully, M., Woodland, S., O'Reilly, A. and Dix, G., *Britain at Work*, 1999, Routledge, reproduced with the kind permission of Routledge.

We are grateful to the Financial Times Limited for permission to reprint the following material:

Exhibit 6.3 Union vows to oppose wholesale export of jobs, © *Financial Times*, 12 February 2003; Exhibit 12.5 Pay gap widens between sexes, © *Financial Times*, 18 October 2002; UK firefighters set to walk out as talks fail, © *Financial Times*, 13 November 2002; One in two trains could be halted by strikes, © *Financial Times*, 19 February 2003; Activists warned of firefighter strikes, © *Financial Times*, 16 April 2003; Teachers threaten 'old union' action on workload, © *Financial Times*, 23 April 2003.

Whilst every effort has been made to trace the owners of the copyright material, in a few cases this has proved impossible and we take this opportunity to offer our apologies to any copyright holders whose rights we may have unwittingly infringed.

PREFACE TO THE SECOND EDITION

The book is intended for use by undergraduate and postgraduate students who study employment/industrial relations on courses leading to social science, business studies and other degrees with a strong HRM component, MBA, and other employment relations and HRM-specific postgraduate courses. The book is extremely useful for those studying for CIPD qualifications at postgraduate and professional levels (see relevant CIPD professional standards below). Independent learners such as those embarked on Open University courses will also find the book helpful in its approach.

The prime justification for a second edition of this book is to do with the sheer pace of change, particularly in the legislative areas affecting employment relations. Since the publication of the first edition in 2001, there has been a considerable amount of legislative 'catching up' as a result of the first Blair government's 'opt in' to the Social Chapter of the European Union. This meant that the government was obliged to adopt and 'transpose' European Union Directives concerning discrimination, parental leave, equality of treatment for part-time workers on a par with full-time workers and a range of other employment protection provisions, the outcome of which was the 2002 Employment Act. By 2008, the UK will have an equality legislative framework in place which embraces not only race, gender and disability discrimination, but also age and religious discrimination, and will, in this respect, fall in line with many other European Union member states.

However, the themes of 'partnership', 'stakeholder society' and the 'third way', which optimistically heralded the inception of the first New Labour government in 1997, have now been tempered by a more critical and sober evaluation. Critics point to the further encroachment of market forces within the public domain; euphemisms such as 'modernisation', it is argued, mask a process (or may even be a byword for) privatisation by stealth. Trade union opposition to what has become known as 'marketisation' has firmed up in recent years and points to a more confrontational phase of employment relations, particularly within the public sector, following the disillusionment with the government's handling of the firefighters' dispute.

After 1999 trade union membership stabilised and has latterly shown a slight increase, this being attributed to the effects of the trade union recognition provisions in the 1999 Employment Relations Act. However, the trade union movement overall remains weak, and the prospects for a sustained renewal, not only of membership but also of influence within both the collective bargaining sphere and nationally via the Trades Union Congress (TUC), seem to be as distant in 2004 as they were in 1999. HRM (human resource management), however, whether at workplace level or, more strategically, at corporate level, has never been more popular in its many guises and manifestations. On the one hand HRM continues to extol the worthy virtues of 'involvement', 'commitment' and 'empowerment' while on the other it deals with the realities of global and national competitive forces and provides rationalisations for higher rates of work intensification, the increasing use of non-standard contracts and greater flexibilisation of work.

The second edition of this book additionally traces the changes that have taken place within the employment relationship since 1999, mainly within the UK, but also, where relevant, in relation to the European Union member states. The structure of the book remains essentially the same as the first edition but with the inclusion of separate chapters dealing with employee participation and industrial action. There is comprehensive updating of legislative developments and statistical data, while data from the latest Workplace Employee Relations Survey (WERS), which reported in 1999 and 2000, is disseminated and referred to throughout.

2003

Ed Rose

INTRODUCTION

RATIONALE AND MAKE-UP OF THE BOOK

One of the most important considerations in producing an academic text is that it should be written in a way which is easily understandable to the reader but without making the content appear simplistic. The presumption that the reader has no prior knowledge of the subject area suggests that relevant theoretical insights, historical and contemporary developments and institutional characteristics concerning employment relations be treated as fully and carefully as space permits. Employment relations is not generally regarded as a 'pure' academic discipline; it utilises theories and concepts from a range of social science disciplines such as economics, sociology, political science and psychology. The subject matter of the book reflects these varied interdisciplinary inputs and most chapters contain theoretical insights where appropriate.

Employment relations is frequently grounded in organisational and workplace practice, whether it comprises the day-to-day activities of employee and employer representatives concerning, for example, pay determination, or the implementation and consequences of strategic decisions unilaterally or jointly determined by corporate management. One of the main features of the book is the emphasis, particularly from Chapter 10 onwards, upon practices governing the management of workplace relations such as discipline, redundancy, discrimination and other related aspects. The changing national, international (the European Union particularly) and political contexts of employment relations have a direct bearing upon the activities of both trade unions and their members, and upon employers. For example, government policy and political ideology has always influenced, by legislative and other means, the complexion of employment relations; it is not an

understatement to argue that employment relations in this sense is a 'movable feast'.

The first main theme of the book is concerned with continuity and change; continuity referring to the persistence and presence over time of the traditional parties to the employment relationship – employers and management, employees and trade unions and the state, with their roles and functions largely unchanged within a capitalist society. The theme of change refers to the social, political, legislative and economic developments which have affected the traditional roles of the parties to the employment relationship, many of these changes having been instigated by one party exerting influence over the others as, for example, the influence and legacy of Thatcherism upon employers, trade unions and employment relations generally. Other changes concern the transformation of the industrial landscape and the labour market which has implications and consequences for the nature of workplace employment relations and its management. The transition to an economy dominated by services and information technology has indeed altered traditional images of the collective nature of the employment relationship – images epitomised by cloth-cap metaphors, adversarialism and strike-prone traditional industries, prompting evocations concerning the 'end of organised labour', 'the demise of collectivism' and of industrial relations itself. Collective aspects of the employment relationship nevertheless continue to be a dominant feature within the vast majority of unionised and, more importantly, non-unionised organisations. The changing focus is upon how these relationships are managed, the shifts in balance of power between employers and employees and the extent to which employers either exploit or value their workers within a generally employer-supportive legislative framework.

Many analyses concerning the 'decline' of collectivism point to the progressive downturn in trade union membership from 1979 to 1999, with the subsequent stabilisation of membership regarded as insignificant, and the weakening of collective forms of regulation and representation involving trade unions, such as the decline of collective bargaining and employee voice mechanisms during the 1980s, 1990s and early 2000s. Many explanations have been advanced in order to account for the alleged shift in emphasis from 'collectivism' to 'individualism' within the employment relationship, ranging from the 'anti-union' government policy of previous Conservative governments to the adoption of HRM strategies, policies and practices which focus upon the individual employee to the detriment of collective representation.

Equally, however, much debate also focuses upon the continuity of the collective 'voice' within the employment relationship. Rather than witnessing (for example) the death throes of trade unions, we may well be embarking upon a period of readjustment and consolidation as unions come to terms with structural changes within industry, occupations and the labour market, the 'globalising effect' upon labour and work, and adopt more proactive approaches to recruitment and organisation in areas traditionally considered difficult to organise.

The book reflects debates in relation to these and other changes relating to the demography of the labour market, the restructuring of industry and work, new technologies, the proliferation of HRM practices (however imperfect), government policy and legislation and their impact upon the nature and conduct of the employment relationship at industry, organisation and workplace levels.

A second theme, both distinct and related, is that of policy and practice, with the latter highlighted from Chapter 9 onwards. Policy refers to both government and employer policy, particularly with regard to employment protection, and is also flagged up from Chapter 9 onwards. The book, then, is not content merely with identifying and assessing the implications of change for the parties to employment relations. Insofar as these changes impinge upon management practice and the quality of the employment relationship, the development of effective policies and practices is seen as crucial in attempting to ensure enhanced levels of equity, equality and justice in the workplace.

STRUCTURE AND CONTENT OF THE BOOK

The overall aim of this book, then, is to provide the reader with an introduction to, and analysis of, the main problems and issues concerning continuity and change, policies and practices appertaining to employment relations in Britain. Chapter 1 examines the nature and context of employment relations and provides an overview of the main institutions and processes governing the employment relationship. Various theoretical approaches relevant to the analysis of employment relations are considered in some detail and are referred to where appropriate throughout the book. Chapter 1 also considers the problem of defining the subject matter. Essentially, the term 'industrial relations' is, nowadays, too constraining, and arguably should be restricted to the collective nature of the employment relationship. The term 'employment relations' is used to embrace all facets of the employment relationship, both collective and individual, which are dealt with in the book. Changes in the nature of the employment relationship are also considered in some detail, particularly with reference to the post-Second World War period.

Chapters 2–9 deal with the collective aspects of the employment relationship. The major institutional 'parties' (managers and employers, trade unions, government and the state) to the employment relationship are examined in some detail in Chapters 2–4, with particular attention being focused upon their historical development and contemporary patterns of change. Relevant theoretical approaches are used in order to explain strategies, policies and practices. For example, in Chapter 4 the evolution of government policy, insofar as it influences employment relations, is explained by the use of appropriate theoretical frameworks. This is particularly so in relation to economic policy where a familiarity with Keynesian economic theory proves invaluable to an understanding of incomes policies within the context of full employment. Similarly, an appreciation of monetarist economic theory will explain the motives and rationale of the Conservative governments' employment relations policies during the period 1980–97.

Developments in workplace industrial relations are considered in Chapter 5 and elsewhere throughout the book. Workplace change is put within the context of the Fordist and post-Fordist paradigm, using the example of the call centre workplace to illustrate the latter. Chapter 5 also considers the contentious debate concerning the problematic relationship between HRM and industrial relations. Chapter 6 provides an exploration of the central processes of collective bargaining, Theoretical approaches to collective bargaining, its historical development and contemporary trends are examined, the latter with particular reference to the public sector. The increase in the number of workplaces and organisations whose managements refused to recognise trade unions for collective bargaining purposes, derecognised trade unions and ensured that employees did not join unions in the first place has generated much interest in the phenomenon of the 'union-free' workplace and organisation. This, together with employee involvement, is looked at in Chapter 7. Chapter 8 is concerned with the decline in union voice and the diversity of employee representation and participation mechanisms. The vexed issue of formal machinery to promote information and consultation is addressed, particularly in view of the transposition of the European Union Information and Consultation Directive. European, and specifically EU, initiatives over the years are also considered. Patterns of industrial action and stoppages are analysed in Chapter 9. Strikes are the most prominent manifestation of industrial action and much of the chapter is taken up with an examination of the strike phenomenon. While some academics would argue that the declining incidence of strikes no longer necessitates a dedicated textbook chapter, longer-term evidence suggests that there is a cyclical nature to the phenomenon and occasional upsurges in strike activity involving firefighters, postal workers and railway staff during the course of 2002 and 2003 is justification enough for including a chapter.

Chapter 10 is the first of the skills-oriented chapters and its subject, negotiation, straddles both collectivist and individualist camps. The collective aspects of negotiation are concerned with collective bargaining, while the individual elements deal with areas such as individual grievance processing.

Chapters 11–13 consider individual elements of the employment relationship, but not exclusively so. As with Chapter 10, the main focus of these chapters is upon practical skills which are required by both managers and employees in order to resolve common workplace-related problems associated with disciplinary matters, grievances (Chapter 11), and unfair dismissal and redundancy (Chapter 13). Of increasing significance within the area of employment relations is that of gender and ethnic inequalities within the workplace, and Chapter 12 provides an analysis of the main problem areas and how they should be tackled. Many of the issues dealt with in these chapters are subject to both EU and national employment protection legislation which is referred to where necessary. A brief overview of individual employment legislation is provided at the beginning of Chapter 11. Chapter 14 is speculative and very briefly attempts to extrapolate from the main data sets available what employment relations might be like during the course of the next decade, in possible anticipation of the next Workplace Employee Relations Survey (WERS).

USING THE BOOK

Within higher education there is an increased emphasis upon activity-based applications of learning within tutorials and workshops, particularly in courses and modules within business studies, and students are correspondingly required to assume greater responsibility for their learning. This text facilitates learning of this nature in a number of ways.

Firstly, each chapter, after a short introduction, starts with a series of learning outcomes, which will enable readers to check understanding of the subject matter of a chapter.

Secondly, and more importantly, each chapter contains a variable number of learning activities which are termed self-evaluation activities or SEAs. The SEAs encourage the reader to be an active participant in the learning process and provide the opportunities to develop summarising, analytical and problem-solving skills. They therefore serve a number of purposes:

- Some SEAs are of an exploratory nature and ask the reader to produce examples and cite instances of employment and industrial relations phenomena which are derived from experience or have been gleaned from various media sources such as newspapers.
- Many SEAs require summarising of material read in a preceding section of a chapter.
- A number of SEAs invite analysis of theory and practice, ensuring an understanding of theoretical issues and how some of these are relevant to everyday employment/industrial relations situations.
- Some SEAs tackle practical, 'how to do it' problems which practitioners confront on a regular basis.
- Some SEAs assist the reader to 'experience' problems through cases and other examples and invite problem-solving approaches to them.

Readers are encouraged to develop responses to questions posed by SEAs. In the majority of instances, responses can be downloaded from the book's website, while other responses are found within the text itself, because it is not advisable to separate the response from sequential development of the text itself.

Thirdly, in addition to SEAs each chapter contains exhibits, mini cases and main cases. Exhibits provide examples of good practice and highlight aspects of policy or procedure at relevant points in the chapter. Specific examples of organisations which demonstrate or do not demonstrate good practice and which exemplify the various themes within and between chapters are provided by both short or mini cases and longer or main cases. Attempts have been made to ensure a clear and logical progression of themes within each chapter. Cases and other examples introduced within each chapter are intended to assist this process. Most cases and exhibits are intentionally relatively short 'snapshots' of actual everyday problems or good/bad practice which help illustrate the chapter themes and provide opportunities for analysis and developing understanding.

CIPD PROFESSIONAL STANDARDS FOR EMPLOYEE RELATIONS

The following CIPD operational and knowledge indicators are covered by various chapters of the book as indicated.

Employee Relations Professional Standards   *Chapter(s)*

Operational indicators – practitioners must be able to:

1. Contribute to setting the strategic direction for an organisation's policy and practice.	3
2. Provide advice on the appropriateness of adopting different forms of employee involvement/participation and how to implement them.	8, 7
3. Supply appropriate advice on the basic rights and obligations of employers and employees arising from the contract of employment and associated legislation.	11, 12, 13
4. Draft policies and procedures dealing with employee grievances, discipline, redundancy, harassment and bullying and ensure their effective implementation and management.	11, 12, 13
5. Participate in the preparation of a case at employment tribunal on behalf of an employer.	13
6. Advise on the contemporary developments in employee relations and their potential impact on the organisation's policies and practices.	All

Knowledge indicators – practitioners must understand and be able to explain:

1. The various means and methods available for effective workplace decision-making and management policies and approaches to gain commitment, co-operation and empowerment of the workforce.	3, 7, 8
2. The organisational, regional, national and international (EU) context and their potential impact on current employee relations policies, issues and practices.	All

3. The range of internal factors within an organisation that may affect the
   management of employee relations in the public and private sectors.   **All**
4. The mechanisms in both non-union and unionised enterprises designed to
   reconcile the different interests of employees and employers for mutual gain.   **All**
5. The skills managers need for grievance handling, discipline in the workplace
   and negotiation.   **10, 11, 12, 13**

Source: Adapted from CIPD, 'Professional Standards for Employee Relations', 2003: www.cipd.co.uk

PART 1

OVERVIEW OF EMPLOYMENT RELATIONS

CHAPTER 1

SETTING THE SCENE

INTRODUCTION

Employment relations is a compelling and complex area of study which involves the interaction of employees, employers, trade unions and government on a regular basis. Employment relations is never dull: we often hear or read about industrial disputes, negotiations concerning the latest pay round or other work-related issues and cases dealing with discriminatory practices on the part of employers and employees. In order to appreciate the nature of everyday employment relations, it is crucial to understand the relevant theoretical contributions underpinning it. It is also important to understand the environment or context which influences industrial relations. This chapter provides a general understanding of the nature and theoretical aspects of industrial relations and how employment relations in Britain has developed over the years. We start with the problem of definition and then go on to identify the parties to employment relations. We then trace the development of British employment relations and this is followed by a consideration of the main theoretical approaches to employment relations and an examination of the economic context. Finally, we look briefly at the extent to which employment relations has changed during the post-war period from 1950 to 2004.

Learning outcomes

When you have read this chapter, you should be able to:

1. Define employment relations, distinguish between the terms 'industrial relations' and 'employee relations' and identify the different disciplinary inputs which comprise the study of employment relations.

2. Identify the parties to employment relations and explain the important functions of each party to employment relations.

3. Trace the development of British employment relations and Identify the main changes that have affected employment relations during the post-war period.

4. Explain in basic terms the meaning of each of the theoretical approaches to employment relations.

5. Describe the main contexts (economic, political, legal) within which employment relations operates and explain how each of these contexts has influenced, and continues to influence, employment relations.

DEFINING EMPLOYMENT RELATIONS

We begin by looking briefly at some of the characteristics inherent within the employment relationship, including main themes, issues and disciplines
which comprise and contribute to our understanding of that relationship. We have chosen the term
employment relations rather than *industrial relations*
as the latter term denotes an exclusively collective
orientation to the employment relationship while
certain chapters in this book concentrate upon the
relationship which employees as individuals have
with employers. This reflects the (not necessarily
irreversible) changes that have taken place in British
employment and industrial relations since 1979 and
which are considered later in the chapter. Certainly
there is an influential view that 'In order to survive,
industrial relations needs to change its focus to
"employment relations", examining not just institutions but how the employment relationship operates
in practice' (Blyton and Turnbull, 1998, quoting
Edwards, 1995). Indeed, in the latest edition of
Industrial Relations Theory and Practice, Edwards
(2003) asserts that 'if we were starting from scratch,
this [employment relations] might be the best label'
(p. 10).

NATURE AND DEFINITION OF THE EMPLOYMENT RELATIONSHIP

While employment relations is an academic subject area which is studied at undergraduate and
postgraduate levels, it is also concerned with practical issues and processes which affect employers
and employees, the government and other important institutions such as the Trade Union Congress
(TUC) and the Confederation of British Industry
(CBI). Many of the collective aspects of employment relations have a certain popular appeal and
often hit the headlines when there are, for example,
strikes, redundancies or discrimination cases. Self-
Evaluation Activity (SEA) 1.1 is concerned with
a number of 'high profile' industrial disputes and
reactions to them which took place in 2002–2003,
during the term of the second New Labour
government.

Self-Evaluation Activity 1.1

Getting a feeling for employment relations
The response is given below

Read the scenarios in Exhibit 1.1 and spend a few
minutes to identify:

1. groups of employees and trade unions involved;
2. the issues concerning the disputes.

The scenarios in Exhibit 1.1 will give you some idea of
what the employment relationship is concerned with
even though it does not yet provide you with the complete picture.

1 Groups of employees and unions involved
The employment relationship is partly concerned with
groups of employees who are represented by trade
unions. The nature of this representation is collective.
Employees who are collectively represented by trade
unions arguably have greater power to influence
decisions concerning, for example, levels of pay and
working conditions than those employees who do not
belong to trade unions. The scenario identifies the
following groups of workers who are collectively represented by trade unions:

- The main rail employee groups identified are the
  drivers, most of whom belong to Aslef, the train
  drivers' union, guards and conductors who belong
  to the RMT (Rail, Marine and Transport).
- The firefighters are members of the FBU (Fire
  Brigades Union). The FBU has strong, semi-
  autonomous area organisation.
- The school teachers belong to one of three main
  teaching unions. In this case, the NUT (National
  Union of Teachers), which is the largest, is in dispute with government.

2 The issues concerning the disputes
The majority of disputes concern pay and pay-related
issues such as those involving the firefighters and
Aslef. However, an increasing number of disputes are
about multiple issues other than or including pay. The
firefighters are concerned about 'modernisation' which
involves changes to shift patterns and methods of
working, while the NUT is campaigning against a workload agreement which includes the introduction of
unqualified teaching assistants in classroom sessions.
The disputes within the rail network are more complex,

Exhibit 1.1

Three industrial disputes

One in two trains could be halted by strikes

Half of train services could be halted by strikes after the country's largest rail union announced a ballot of thousands of guards. Intercity, regional services and outer commuter services from London, which have guards on their trains, would be heavily affected by the RMT's dispute. The union yesterday threatened industrial action over its complaint that guards were not being given an appropriate role in ensuring safety on trains. The announcement marked a worsening of labour relations, which are already in a poor state, between unions and the rail industry. Mick Rix, general secretary of Aslef, the train drivers' union, said last month (March 2003) that he would ballot members for industrial action if the principle of national pay and conditions was not agreed by May. Bob Crow, general secretary of RMT, endorsed Mr Rix's call. The RMT has complained about the switch of responsibility for safety from guards to drivers during the 1990s, claiming it reduces overall passenger security. The union is to ballot 5000 guards. In a separate dispute, strike action took place on Arriva Trains Northern in the dispute over pay.

Postscript: The RMT guards' initial industrial action took place during the Easter weeks of 2003.

Activists warned of firefighter strikes

Union activists representing firefighters have warned of the risk of local strikes after a substantial minority opposed a compromise proposal put forward by the national leadership to end the long-running dispute. At a special conference in Brighton, the Fire Brigade Union's executive council managed to push through its proposal for a compromise solution that envisages increases in pay in return for local agreement on changes to working practices, by a 2–1 majority. But local representatives speaking for more than 15 000 members voted against the national leadership's motion. The motion was based on a proposal by Frank Burchill, an industrial relations expert and designated peacemaker between firefighters and employers, which had suggested changes in working practices, including shift systems, in return for a 16 per cent increase in the pay bill over three years. While all representatives are to consult the membership over the motion, and employers would also consult locally, London representatives have already voted against the motion. One London activist added after the motion was carried that if the management of the London Fire Brigade insisted on alterations to shifts that the local firefighters found unacceptable, strikes could follow. These comments confirmed employers' fears that any national agreement that was not absolutely watertight could shatter the national dispute into numerous local disputes, making the 'modernisation' of the fire service difficult to achieve

Teachers threaten 'old union' action on workload

The biggest teaching union promised the government 'traditional, old trade union industrial action' if it pressed ahead with its £1bn workload agreement which the National Union of Teachers (NUT) believes undermines the profession. Delegates cheered as Doug McAvoy, general secretary, told its annual conference that it should brush aside ministers' pleas for it to join other 'modern progressive' unions in signing the pact and instead threatened some 'old time religion' instead. In a swingeing attack on the refusal of Charles Clarke, Education Secretary, to speak at the conference, Mr McAvoy produced documents that he said showed civil servants had been instructed to 'pull the plug' and seek ministerial advice before allowing any contact between government and the dissident union. Mr McAvoy was speaking after militant delegates won a majority for an even tougher campaign of action over the agreement than had been recommended by the leadership. The leadership wants to avoid any action that is too disruptive and which would make it unpopular with parents. Instead it is likely to keep its powder dry and see if the workload agreement survives, and then time action to cut to the core of its real concern, that unqualified teaching assistants will undermine an all-graduate qualified teaching profession.

Source: *Financial Times*: 19 February 2003; 16 April 2003; 23 April 2003

owing to the number of rail companies each having separate pay and conditions agreements, and are concerned with ongoing pay and safety issues.

The scenarios in Exhibit 1.1 focus upon the collective nature of the employment relationship which Blyton and Turnbull (1998) and Kelly (1998) characterise in the following way:

> *The employment relationship is the context within which intricate interactions between employees, who may be unionised or non-unionised, and employers are conducted, both collectively and individually.*

Edwards (2003) suggests that the focus is upon employment: 'all forms of economic activity in which an employee works under the authority of an employer and receives a wage in return for his or her labour' (pp. 1–2). Gospel and Palmer (1993) provide a fairly general definition of the employment relationship as being 'an economic, social and political relationship in which employees provide manual and mental labour in exchange for rewards allotted by employers' (p. 3). The rewards from employment can be economic, social and psychological, while the effort (the contribution the employee makes in his or her job) can range from skilled to unskilled, and can be tightly controlled or left free to initiative and individual creativity. The employment relationship can be short term, as with casual labour, or long term and all-embracing, as with employees in larger Japanese companies. These variations exist in both private sector firms and public sector organisations, and within unionised and non-unionised contexts. Following Blyton and Turnbull (1998) and Kelly (1998), we may identify certain characteristics of the employment relationship:

- The extent to which workers define their interests is at the same time crucial and problematic. Worker interests include the pursuit of higher pay, job security, career progression and training, while employer interests within the private sector of the economy are focused upon the pursuit of profitability by means of attempting to secure greater employee productivity and efficiency. Furthermore, the employment relationship

is often characterised by the conflict of worker and employer interests which may result in industrial disputes as exemplified above. There is no assumption of equality of interests since workers typically are in a subordinate position within the employment relationship and 'are subject to repeated challenges by employers as they try to redefine and realign worker interests with corporate goals' (Kelly, p. 4).

- The subordinate position of workers within the employment relationship is formalised in two main but related ways; firstly, through the employment contract which specifies the duties of workers in return for payment of wages. In other words, there is an (unequal) exchange relationship whereby the worker agrees to sell his or her labour power in order to contribute towards the production of goods and services. Secondly, the worker submits himself or herself to the authority of the employer, as Blyton and Turnbull (1998) put it: 'The employment relationship is necessarily an *authority relationship* between super- and subordinate where the employee agrees to accept and follow the "reasonable" instructions of those in positions of authority' (p. 29).

- The employment relationship is characterised by its continuous, dynamic and 'open-ended' nature whereby employers, for example, are in a position, through the exercise of their 'rights' or managerial prerogative, to determine and redefine employee obligations and duties in relation to job content and work effort.

- The employment relationship is also characterised by power relationships between employer and worker. At its simplest the relationship comprises two aspects. Firstly, workers organise themselves collectively by joining trade unions since collectively workers have greater power than individuals. Hence, workers organised within a trade union 'meet the employer on a more equal footing than the individual, and confront the employer with collective power' through collective bargaining (Kelly, 1998, p. 9). Secondly, there is the power of the employer ('power' being defined as the extent to which one party to a relationship can compel the other party to do something he or she otherwise would not do voluntarily) over the worker whereby the former seeks to achieve the compliance to the organisation of the latter. The arbitrary exercise of power by the employer can engender employee resistance and result in conflict. On the other hand, the judicious exercise of power can result in mutual accommodation and employee co-operation.

- Finally, the employment relationship is also concerned with the nature of the individual employee's association with the employer in relation to, for example, contracts of employment, discipline, individual grievance, individual redundancy and discrimination.

Arriving at a definition of employment relations

We are now in a position to go beyond the rather simplistic media representation of employment relations which tends to see the subject within the narrow confines of the rather dramatic events exemplified in the above scenarios. However, arriving at a definition is not a simple matter, as employment relations involves complex patterns of interaction between different occupational groups, trade unions and employers at organisational level, and the state and its agencies, the TUC and CBI, at national level. Identified below are a number of important aspects which, taken together, will inform our definition.

The rule-making process

A traditional approach to employment and industrial relations has been to regard it as 'the study of the rules governing employment, and the ways in which the rules are changed, interpreted and administered' (Bain and Clegg, 1974). Trade unions, management, employers' associations and the government are all concerned with regulating the terms and conditions of employment, and within the work context Flanders (1965) argued that work is governed by a mass of rules and regulations covering criteria for recruitment, effort, performance, pay, hours, holidays and numerous other details of employment. According to this traditional approach, the primary focus of industrial relations tended to be upon the institutions that take part in rule-making, the processes of interaction between the parties, and

the rules that result from this. Ultimately, it is managers who attempt to enforce rules, and the extent to which rules are applied depends upon the procedures such as those governing discipline or equal opportunities, whether a union is recognised for purposes of representing employees, and the enforcement of legislation governing employment protection.

Levels of analysis

Employment and industrial relations operates at four main levels. The first is the level of the workplace, office or factory. It is here that the individual employee, manual or non-manual, has direct contact with his or her union representative, the shop steward or convenor. Any disagreement or local dispute can be resolved *informally* at this level by the convenor and local management. The second level is that of the organisation. A large organisation such as Toyota or ICI has a number of factories or workplaces nationally and globally. At this level, many of the larger unionised private sector organisations conduct important negotiations concerning pay and pay-related issues and hours of work for all their manual and many of their non-manual employees. Many negotiations are conducted *formally* at company headquarters by senior management and senior trade union officers. The third level is industry or national level. Traditionally, in some industries such as the engineering industry, many small and medium-sized firms form employers' associations. In the engineering industry, for example, the employers' associations based on geographical areas have for many years been affiliated to the Engineering Employers' Federation (EEF). The EEF comprises a number of local associations each with its own member firms, covering up to a million manual and staff employees in many thousands of establishments. The EEF, in representing employer interests in their relations with trade unions, negotiates and concludes agreements relating to wages, hours and other conditions of employment. The fourth level we may call the societal. A great deal of industrial relations is concerned with the way in which wider social factors such as class, property ownership, political ideologies and economic variables influence what takes place within industries and organisations. We shall be dealing with some of these contextual factors later in this chapter.

Intertwined with the societal is the global and the globalisation process whereby national systems are increasingly influenced by international economic forces.

The employment relationship

Discussed earlier in the chapter, see pp. 4–7.

Industrial relations issues

The final aspect is concerned with issues in industrial relations. We can distinguish between two types of issues. These are:

- substantive issues and
- procedural issues

Substantive issues cover the details of the reward–effort exchange and include pay, holidays, overtime arrangements and 'fringe benefits' such as pensions, company cars and personal use of company equipment and resources. Also included are training and promotion prospects. Procedural issues focus upon the question of *how* the substantive issues are decided and deal with the following questions:

- What people or groups control the substantive issues and decisions?
- Are decisions to be taken unilaterally by the employer or jointly by employer and employees?
- What influence should employee institutions such as trade unions and professional associations have?
- What rules should the state lay down in legislation?
- What procedures jointly or unilaterally determined should an organisation have to regulate its industrial relations? In this respect, the most common procedures concern disputes, disciplinary matters, grievances, sexual harassment and equal opportunities.

With these aspects in mind, we can now arrive at a broad working definition of employment relations as follows:

> *Employment relations is the study of the regulation of the employment relationship between employer and employee, both collectively and individually, and the determination of substantive and procedural issues at industrial, organisational and workplace levels.*

Self-Evaluation Activity 1.2

What 'employment relations' includes
Response on website

In order to consolidate your knowledge about the essence of employment relations so far, spend a few minutes to identify what the subject includes under the following headings:

- Institutions
- Actors (individuals and groups)
- Procedures
- Topics

Summary: employment relations, industrial relations and employee relations

So far we have examined the definitional issues relevant to employment relations, and have demonstrated that the subject is more complex than its media representation. Employment relations is a rule-making process which is concerned with different levels of analysis, with the employment relationship and with substantive and procedural issues both collectively and individually and within union and non-union contexts. The term *industrial relations*, which we use frequently throughout this book, is concerned largely with the collective aspects of the employment relationship. In addition, the term *employee relations* adopted by professional bodies such as CIPD and by some textbook authors (Blyton and Turnbull, 1994, 1998; Farnham, 1997, 2000; Gennard and Judge, 1997, 2002; Hollinshead *et al.*, 2002) is often indistinguishable from *industrial relations* although there are some differences in emphasis and content. Gennard and Judge devote much space to individual aspects of the employment relationship, while Blyton and Turnbull look almost exclusively at collective relationships, but focus upon non-unionism. *Employee relations* may be considered by some to be a more 'acceptable' term than *industrial relations* – as it avoids the negative connotations associated with the latter, which is sometimes referred to as 'old industrial relations', exemplified by the 1984 coal dispute and the 'Winter of Discontent' (1979) – and is more acceptable to those advocating human resource management strategies, policies and practices. Beardwell (1997) unintentionally makes the case for adopting the *employment relations* label in stating:

> *Perhaps for the first time in a century, it is possible to reconstruct the central problem of industrial relations as being not so much the role of the trade union in the market economy as the role of the individual within the employment relationship, and in this way recast the framework of industrial relations so that the traditional collectivism we have been accustomed to is greatly reduced.* (p. 7)

We now turn to a consideration of the parties to employment relations.

THE PARTIES TO EMPLOYMENT RELATIONS: AN OVERVIEW

The parties to be considered are:

- Management and employer
- Management organisations
- Employee organisations
- The state and state agencies

Management and employer

Management and employers are dealt with in greater detail in Chapter 2. In general, the term *management* may be used in two ways. In the first sense management comprises activities carried out by those with decision-taking and executive responsibilities in organisations and focuses on the jobs, tasks and activities which managers do. This view of management incorporates three aspects of managing:

- what managers do;
- how they do it; and
- how they are grouped in organisations, vertically or horizontally.

The second way the term is used is to describe the group of people in organisations who are collectively responsible for the efficient and effective running of their organisations.

Managements are concerned not only with profits and efficiency or with 'value for money' in the public sector, but also with being socially responsible to the wider communities with which they interact. They may also want good working relationships with their employees. Employment and industrial relations is, however, only one important concern of management, and there are significant variations in how managements in different organisations interpret their industrial relations roles. At one extreme, managements may devise sophisticated industrial relations strategies, policies and procedures and attempt to develop 'best' employment practices. At the other extreme, any industrial relations policies and practices that might exist are crude, and meet only the minimum employment standards required by law and local labour market pressures.

Employment and industrial relations management

Nowadays, most managements in medium and larger organisations who are concerned with promoting 'best practice' in employment relations use employment and industrial relations specialists. These specialists are variously described as personnel officers, industrial relations advisers, employee relations managers, or, since the mid-1980s, as human resource managers. However, there are significant variations by which managements interpret their industrial relations functions of which we can distinguish three different types. These are:

- The traditional management function.
- The sophisticated management function.
- The human resource management function.

We will briefly consider each of these in turn.

The traditional management function
According to Farnham (2000, p. 28), the traditional management function 'has been a disinterested, reactive and fire-fighting one'. Top management choose to ignore industrial relations and do not regard it as part of corporate strategy. It is left to relatively junior managers to react to industrial relations problems by treating their symptoms rather

than their causes. Farnham then goes on to identify more specifically the characteristics of these functions as being:

- separate from an organisation's corporate strategy;
- short term;
- of no interest to the board of directors;
- focused mainly on unionised, lower-status groups of workers.

The sophisticated management function

From the late 1960s we have witnessed a substantial increase in the number of personnel and industrial relations specialists, many of whom are in senior positions and are therefore capable of viewing industrial relations strategically as well as operationally (Legge, 1995). These specialists are also in a position to advise senior line management in the following activities:

- taking part in negotiating with employee and union representatives;
- helping to draft collective agreements which cover substantive and procedural issues;
- providing advice on employment legislation;
- providing advice on grievance and disciplinary cases;
- handling redundancies;
- helping to devise equal opportunities policies; and
- assisting in the making of personnel policy.

While there is *some* input into corporate strategy, the main emphasis is upon providing advice, expertise and technical know-how to line management.

The human resource management function

The term 'human resource management' (HRM) became popular during the 1980s (HRM is also referred to below and examined in Chapter 2). HRM incorporates industrial relations and personnel management within an overall organisational strategy which emphasises the 'human' aspects of management and concern with people in organisations. HRM therefore has a much broader scope than the management of industrial relations and often includes the following aspects:

- it stresses the development of the talents and capacities of each individual employee;

- it seeks to communicate directly with employees rather than through the medium of a trade union;
- it is concerned with individually negotiated reward packages which reflect the individual's personal skills, experience, efforts and performance;
- it may involve individual employees in making a larger contribution towards decision-making in relation to their jobs; and
- it may provide individual employees with the opportunity to influence, and in some cases to negotiate, their own terms and conditions of employment rather than leaving them to the outcome of some distant negotiations between employers and trade unions.

In seeking to involve employees and to communicate with them directly, employers may bypass the traditional channels of communication with employee representatives and trade unions. In unionised organisations this often means a decline in trade union influence upon these processes and a shift away from 'collectivism' to 'individualism'.

Self-Evaluation Activity 1.3

The three management industrial relations functions
Response on website

In order to test your understanding of the three management industrial relations functions, read the short case scenario given in Mini case 1.1, and answer the questions that follow.

Mini case 1.1
A company stuck in time?

Company X has been established for some 50 years and employs 1500 people, 900 of whom are manual workers. The personnel function, if that is what it could be called, came under the company's transport director who had a small clerical section to look after these matters and who mainly kept personnel records. Training and development of employees was minimal.

The company reluctantly recognised trade unions for its manual employees only and there was no negotiating or consultative committee that met on a regular basis. Any industrial relations activity was conducted on an ad hoc basis by the transport director, and from what he said this consisted mainly of annual pay negotiations that invariably came close to a stand-up fight. Unionisation of non-manual staff was actively discouraged, and it was made clear to any potential staff employee that this was the case.

The only procedure which was operational was a rather antiquated disciplinary procedure which was liberally interpreted. Any disputes and grievances which occurred were arbitrarily dealt with by line managers in 'fire-fighting' fashion. However, as a result of the 2002 Employment Act, the company is compelled to revise and formalise such procedures in line with the majority of larger organisations in the private sector.

1. Which of the industrial relations management functions do you think this case demonstrates, and why?
2. What improvements to Company X's industrial relations management would you suggest?

Management organisations

There are a number of organisations which represent management interests in industrial relations. In this section we shall concentrate briefly on three of them. They are:

* Employers' associations.
* The Confederation of British Industry (CBI).
* The Union of Industrial and Employers' Confederations of Europe (UNICE).

Employers' associations

Employers' associations emerged parallel to trade unions and can be defined as associations of firms in a particular industry which provide various services for member firms. In 1994, there were 228 associations with a total company membership of 275 331. The number of employers' associations has been steadily declining over the years – to 187 associations at the end of 2002 (Certification Office, 2002) – for reasons which are explained in Chapter 2.

The functions of employers' associations
The functions of employers' associations include:

* the representation of members in negotiations with trade unions at industry level;

* the collection of information and data for members concerning industrial relations and non-industrial relations issues;
* assisting members in operating procedures in order to avoid disputes;
* the provision of policy guidelines and advice on industrial relations;
* the provision of consultancy and training for managements;
* representing employers at industrial tribunals; and
* protection for employers taking part in trade disputes against the trade unions in their industry.

In acting as specialist centres of industrial relations knowledge and expertise, employers' associations are staffed by full-time officers who liaise with elected representatives from member companies in order to devise policy and represent employer interests at company level.

The Confederation of British Industry (CBI)

The CBI, the employers' equivalent to the TUC, was formed by Royal Charter in 1965. The CBI was formed as a result of the amalgamation of three existing national bodies which represented employers. The three national bodies were:

* The Federation of British Industry formed in 1916.
* The National Association of British Manufacturers.
* The British Employers' Confederation.

The CBI currently represents manufacturing industries, commercial organisations, public sector corporations and around 150 employers' associations. Not all organisations are represented by the CBI, many small firms and employers' associations prefer to remain outside membership, along with all local authorities (who have separate national associations).

Functions and objectives of the CBI
The objectives of the CBI are set out in its Royal Charter and include the following:

* to provide for British industry the means for formulating, making known and influencing general policy in regard to industrial, economic, fiscal,

commercial, labour, social, legal and technical questions, and to act as a national point of reference to those seeking industry's views;

- to develop the contribution of British industry to the national economy; and
- to encourage the efficiency and competitive power of British industry to the national economy, and to provide advice, information and services to British industry to that end.

The CBI has, since 1977, had an annual conference which provides a wider forum for its members to discuss policy issues and for it to publicise its policies. It does not directly negotiate as a body with trade unions and does not involve itself in disputes. The CBI is not attached to any political party, although some of its member firms traditionally contribute to party funds (notably the Conservative Party). There is, however, a strong correlation between CBI policy and Conservative Party policy although relations between the two organisations became strained during the 1980s' period of Thatcher governments and have fared little better since.

The CBI is run by a council comprising 400 members from the constituent organisations. Detailed policy formulation is undertaken by 26 standing committees which cover areas such as employment policy, industrial relations and manpower, health and safety and economic policy. There is a permanent staff headed by a Director General, and the organisation is split into Directorates covering economics, education, social affairs, administration, information, company affairs, regional and small firms. There is a regional structure involving 12 regions, each of which has its own Council. The CBI also acts as a source of nominees for various tripartite bodies such as the (now defunct) National Economic Development Council and quangos like the Health and Safety Commission, and it provides a panel of employer representatives for industrial tribunals.

The Union of Industrial and Employers' Confederations of Europe (UNICE)

UNICE was formed in 1958 and consists of over 30 central employers' federations (like the CBI) from over 20 European countries. UNICE's main contacts are with the European Union, the European Parliament, the Council of Ministers and the Economic and Social Committee. It also works with other European-level governmental organisations and international non-governmental organisations such as the European Trade Union Confederation (ETUC).

Priorities, purposes and activities of UNICE
Priorities include:

- creating a favourable climate for enterprise;
- promoting European research and development, and technology;
- strengthening European economic and social cohesion;
- developing a dialogue between UNICE and ETUC; and
- liberalising world trade on the principles of reciprocity and fair competition.

Purposes and activities include:

- promoting the common professional interests of the firms represented by its members;
- providing the framework through which member organisations can co-ordinate their European policies;
- ensuring that European decision makers take UNICE's policies and views into account;
- maintaining effective contacts with all European institutions;
- organising members into working groups and committees to examine European policies and proposed legislation; and
- promoting UNICE's policies and opinions at European Union and national level.

The growing importance of the European dimension (see Chapter 4) upon British employment and industrial relations means that organisations such as UNICE have an increasingly significant role to play in the employment relations arena.

Employee organisations

We now turn to a brief consideration of employee organisations. These are:

- Trade unions.
- Staff associations and professional bodies.
- Trades Union Congress (TUC).

- European Trade Union Confederation (ETUC).
- International Confederation of Free Trade Unions (ICFTU).

Trade unions

Trade unions are considered in greater detail in Chapter 3. Here we confine ourselves to a definition and an overview of their main functions and objectives.

According to Webb and Webb (1920, p. 1), a trade union is:

a continuous association of wage earners for the purpose of maintaining or improving the conditions of their working lives.

This is the classic definition of trade unions that is still relevant today. A more contemporary definition is provided by the Trade Union and Labour Relations (Consolidation) Act 1992 which states that a trade union is:

an organisation (whether permanent or temporary) consisting wholly or mainly of workers of one or more descriptions whose principal purpose includes the regulation of relations between workers of that description and employers or employers' associations.

The main characteristics which define a trade union are derived from Blackburn (1967). The organisation is a 'whole-hearted' trade union if it incorporates the following characteristics:

- a statement that the organisation is a trade union (this is similar to the statement a company makes in order for it to become a plc (public limited company));
- registration with the Certification Officer as a trade union which accords it a special legal status;
- independence from the employer, which may be evidenced by a Certificate of Independence from the Certification Officer;
- affiliation to the TUC, Labour Party or joining a confederation of unions;
- its principal aim being that of maintaining and improving the conditions of its members; and
- the possible use of sanctions to further its aims, as, for example, by taking industrial action.

The concept of unionateness is used by Blackburn and others to identify the extent to which a union

manifests these characteristics. It is important to note at this stage that not all unions will include every one of these characteristics. For example, some unions are not affiliated to the TUC.

Main aims and functions of trade unions

Trade unions organise by occupation or industry. An example of an occupational union is the National Union of Teachers (NUT) which recruits primary and secondary school teachers. An example of an industrial union is the greatly depleted National Union of Mineworkers (NUM) which recruits solely from the coal mining industry. As with employers' associations, trade unions exist to safeguard the interests of their members within the labour market (market relations) and within the employment context involving management (managerial relations). Unions do this through collective organisation and strength, based on an ideology of collectivism or worker solidarity as summarised by the slogan 'Unity is Strength'.

The aims and objectives of the trade union movement are best summarised by the TUC, in its evidence to the Royal Commission on Trade Unions and Employers' Associations (known as the Donovan Commission, as it was chaired by Lord Donovan), which reported in 1968. These are:

1. to improve the terms of employment;
2. to improve the physical environment at work;
3. to achieve full employment and national prosperity;
4. to achieve security of employment and income;
5. to improve social security;
6. to achieve fair shares in national income and wealth;
7. to achieve industrial democracy;
8. to achieve a voice in government;
9. to improve public and social services;
10. to achieve public control and planning of industry.

Self-Evaluation Activity 1.4

Have all these objectives been achieved?
The response is given below

Some of these objectives remain to be achieved. Identify which of the above objectives you think have not been achieved and give some reasons for this.

There was consistent improvement throughout the twentieth century in relation to objectives 1 and 2, but this varied according to occupational group, skill factors and other economic conditions. There was some progress with objective 3 during the post-war years, but with current, relatively high unemployment levels and periodic recession, there have been significant setbacks. With regard to 4, the 1990s witnessed a decline in employment security in many occupations, partly because of economic factors such as unemployment and partly because of technological change. Objectives 5, 6 and 7 have seen little, if any improvement, again owing to economic factors such as unemployment, recession and low pay. Britain has not adopted a national system of worker participation and democracy such as exists in many European Union countries, and public and social services have generally deteriorated owing to cash limits placed on many local authorities.

Moreover, we could argue that, within the context of the 1990s and 2000s one or two objectives (such as achieving public control and planning of industry) are quite unrealistic. The TUC influenced Labour governments during the post-war period but since 1979 the TUC has had no input into government economic policy (although this situation has changed somewhat under the later Labour government – see Chapter 3) not only because of the political complexion of government, but also because of the decline in *corporatism* (dealt with below). Finally, objective 10 appears particularly elusive in the context of the 1980s, 1990s and 2000s. Conservative governments have never countenanced it and New Labour government does not endorse it.

We now turn briefly to the specific functions of trade unions. These can be found in individual trade union rule books, but they can be summarised under six headings:

Collective bargaining. This is a central function of a trade union and Chapter 6 deals with this in detail. Collective bargaining is concerned with the determination of wages, hours and working conditions of union members.

Safeguarding jobs. Keeping members in their jobs and protecting these jobs is a prime function. During times of redundancy, unions attempt to counter job loss, often with little success. In many instances

there are agreements on redundancy procedure and, additionally, there is a legal requirement for unions to be consulted on redundancies.

Co-operation with employers. This function varies from union to union and from employer to employer. While there is a basic difference of interest between unions and employers, the economic and political climate of the 1980s and 1990s, together with the spectacular decline in union membership (see Chapter 3) has resulted in a re-evaluation of the role of trade unions by the movement itself (this was dubbed the 'new realism' in the 1980s and the 'new unionism' in the 1990s) and a reinforcement of this function.

Political activities. Traditionally, unions have played an important role as a political pressure group in the area of reform through legislation. Many unions are still affiliated to the Labour Party and provide a significant proportion of party funds.

Provision of social services. Some unions provide financial assistance for sickness, unemployment, retirement and death. Unions can provide strike pay for official strikes but this can be negligible if funds are low. Convalescent and retirement homes may be provided and legal services are available to members.

Provision of friendly services. This traditional function which provided facilities for leisure in clubrooms still exists but again varies according to size of union.

Staff associations and professional bodies

Staff associations are:

- specific to single employers and their membership comprises non-manual employees;
- not regarded as trade unions;
- found in private sector companies, more particularly in financial services such as banks, insurance and building societies.

While staff associations may be representative of a company's non-manual staff, and may even be encouraged by the employer, they do not normally negotiate with the employer on equal terms. Employers may even encourage the formation of staff associations in order to keep trade unions out of the organisation. Staff associations are rarely an acceptable alternative to trade unions, but some employees, in the face of employer hostility towards a trade union presence, may prefer the type of collective representation that staff associations offer to none at all.

Professional bodies are only peripherally concerned with industrial relations issues. Their primary functions are:

- to limit entry to the profession to those who achieve the appropriate qualifications;
- to enhance the status of the profession and its members; and
- to maintain and improve professional standards of members.

There is a wide variety of professional associations (the Law Society and the Chartered Institute of Personnel and Development (CIPD) are examples) but only a few of them, concerned with public sector professionals, such as doctors, teachers and midwives, have specific industrial relations functions such as pay determination or collective bargaining.

The Trade Union Congress (TUC)

The TUC is the representative body for all affiliated trade unions, in much the same way as the CBI is representative of employers and their associations, and was formed in 1868. Affiliated unions pay an annual affiliation fee based on size of union membership. The number of TUC affiliates is steadily declining. It had 69 affiliated unions in 2002 (TUC, 2002) compared with 108 affiliates in 1981. The main objectives of the TUC are:

- to help resolve disputes between members of affiliated organisations and their employers, between affiliated organisations and their members and between affiliated organisations themselves;
- to assist in the unionisation of all workers eligible for union membership;
- to promote the interests of its members;
- to help any organisation which has similar objectives to the TUC;
- to improve the economic and social conditions of workers globally; and

- to promote the interests of all or any of its members.

These objectives are put into practice in a number of ways which include:

- devising policies concerning industrial, economic and social matters and campaigning actively for them;
- providing services to members;
- regulating relations between members and promoting inter-union co-operation;
- nominating representatives on statutory and consultative bodies;
- assisting unions in dispute; and
- taking part in international trade union organisation.

The TUC has an annual congress which discusses policy and is attended by more than 1000 delegates. The governing body of the TUC is the General Council, membership of which is determined by size of union and which is elected by congress. The General Council has nine standing committees which deal with matters such as economic issues, education and training, employment policy and organisation, equal rights and trade union education. Since the TUC 'relaunched' itself, there have been further changes to its structure, administration and mission (see Chapter 3).

The European Trade Union Confederation (ETUC)

The ETUC, based in Brussels, is the umbrella organisation of the major trade union confederations in Europe. It is made up of 39 organisations in 21 Western European countries (including, of course, the TUC) and represents over 45 million workers. The major objectives of the ETUC are:

- to represent and promote the social, economic and cultural interests of workers at European level; and
- to safeguard and strengthen democracy in Europe.

These objectives are achieved by:

- negotiating within a number of European bodies where it is officially recognised;
- statutory rights of consultation on specific matters;

- engaging in policy discussions with heads of government and ministers; and
- taking direct action jointly with unions in different countries.

The International Confederation of Free Trade Unions (ICFTU)

The ICFTU has 141 members. It is a worldwide organisation, representing 97 national trade union centres, with headquarters in Brussels and New York. Its objectives include:

- reducing the gap between rich and poor;
- working for rising living standards, full employment and social security;
- promoting the interests of working people throughout the world;
- working for international understanding, disarmament and world peace;
- helping workers to organise themselves and secure the recognition of their organisations as free bargaining agents;
- fighting against oppression, dictatorship and discrimination of any kind; and
- defending fundamental human and trade union rights.

The ICFTU has a very close relationship with the International Labour Organisation (ILO) which is the only international body made up of government, employer and worker representatives.

We now turn to the final category of parties to employment relations, that of state agencies. For the purposes of this chapter the terms 'state' and 'government' are used interchangeably.

The state and state agencies

The state itself exerts a major influence upon employment relations. Government enacts legislation, devises and executes economic policy and acts as employer, directly or indirectly within the public sector. The role of the state is dealt with in Chapter 4 and certain aspects dealing with government policy are considered later in this chapter. We will confine our attention here to looking at the agencies set up by the state and which have a direct influence upon industrial relations. These are:

- employment tribunals (ETs) and the Employment Appeals Tribunal (EAT);
- the Advisory Conciliation and Arbitration Service (ACAS);
- the Central Arbitration Committee (CAC);
- the Commissioner for the Rights of Trade Union Members (CROTUM); and
- Certification Officer.

Employment tribunals and the Employment Appeals Tribunal

Employment tribunals (ETs) are independent judicial bodies set up to hear matters of dispute quickly, informally and cheaply – see Chapter 13 for more detail. The types of matters the ETs deal with include:

- claims for unfair dismissal – Chapter 13 for more detail;
- cases of alleged discrimination on the grounds of race, gender and disability – Chapter 12 for more detail;
- cases concerning equal pay issues – Chapter 12 for more detail;
- health and safety issues; and
- redundancy issues – Chapter 13 for more detail.

There are about 50 ETs that sit daily in England and Wales hearing around 12 500 cases annually. ETs have a legally qualified chairperson and two other members who are chosen from panels appointed by the Secretary of State for Trade and Industry after consultation with both employee and employer organisations. Anyone may present cases at ETs, which deal with a variety of appeals, applications and complaints concerning the issues identified above and which determine questions of compensation delegated to them. About 60 per cent of cases relate to claims for unfair dismissal.

The Employment Appeals Tribunal (EAT) was established by the Employment Protection Act 1975 and sits regularly in London and Edinburgh. It consists of appointed judges and lay members with specialist knowledge of industrial relations. The EAT hears appeals from the decisions of ETs on questions of law only. It is *not* the function of the EAT to rehear the facts of the case as they were put to the ET, and the EAT cannot interfere with the judgment reached by ETs on those facts. Any appeal to the EAT must show that in reaching its decision the ET made an error in its interpretation or application of the law. As with ETs, any individual may appear before the EAT, including employer and union representatives. The EAT hears hundreds of cases annually.

The Advisory Conciliation and Arbitration Service

ACAS, which is independent of government, unions and employers, was formed in 1975 by statute (Employment Protection Act 1975), and its primary statutory duty is to promote the improvement of industrial relations. The main activities which ACAS undertakes relating to its statutory duties are:

- resolving disputes;
- providing conciliation services for individuals; and
- giving advice, assistance and information on industrial relations and employment issues.

The resolution of disputes is the function for which ACAS is best known. The means whereby ACAS attempts to resolve disputes are through:

Collective conciliation. This is the process whereby an ACAS conciliation officer helps employers and trade unions to reach mutually acceptable settlements of disputes through neutral intervention. It is a purely voluntary process and agreements so reached are determined by the parties themselves and only after all agreed procedures are exhausted.

Voluntary arbitration. This is provided when the employer and union(s) involved in the dispute invite one or more impartial persons to make a decision which both parties agree to accept in advance. Voluntary arbitration is viewed as a last resort method for determining a peaceful settlement where disputes cannot be resolved by other methods.

Mediation. This is where a third party, appointed by ACAS, assists the parties to reach their own negotiated settlement, by making appropriate suggestions to both sides. These recommendations are similar to an arbitrator's award, but the parties do not agree in advance to accept them. Mediation tends to constrain the parties more than conciliation does, but is more flexible and decisive.

ACAS also has a statutory duty to encourage settlements of complaints by individuals (such as complaints of unfair dismissal), which have been, or could be made to an employment tribunal. In addition, ACAS provides advisory and information services concerned with:

- orderly, dispute-free collective bargaining;
- the orderly and voluntary resolution of individual employment issues;
- effective and fair payment and reward systems;
- improved communication, consultation and employee involvement practices; and
- the effective use of human resources at work, including participative approaches to change.

Self-Evaluation Activity 1.5

Dispute resolving services of ACAS
Response on website

This activity is concerned with the dispute resolving offered by ACAS. Read the scenario in Mini case 1.2 and then answer the questions which follow.

Mini case 1.2
A breakdown

You are a director of human resource management at Strikes plc, a manufacturer of matches. Company industrial relations is fairly sophisticated: you have personnel and industrial relations specialists and adequate procedures for resolving internal disputes. On this occasion, however, negotiations with the union representatives have broken down. You have exhausted the disputes procedure and have decided, with the agreement of the union, to involve ACAS.

1. Distinguish briefly between arbitration, conciliation and mediation.
2. Which of these methods of resolving disputes would you choose and why?

Central Arbitration Committee (CAC)

Established in 1976, but independent of government, the CAC will arbitrate directly in an industrial dispute if requested to do so by the parties involved, as well as receiving arbitration requests from ACAS. It also deals with complaints under the legislation concerning the duty of employers to disclose, and trade unions' rights to, information at all stages of collective bargaining. The CAC is empowered to make a ruling on all complaints made to it concerning non-disclosure of information. Over the years the workload of the CAC declined, particularly since the 1980s when its powers were severely curtailed. However, with the passing of the Employment Rights Act 1999, the CAC has additional powers to make decisions concerning the statutory trade union recognition rights on receiving applications by unions. Accordingly, the CAC has been 'restructured and reinforced' in relation to its role in the recognition procedures – see Chapter 3. Its members are 'only persons experienced in industrial relations' and will include both those with experience of representing employers and trade unions. The Secretary of State appoints CAC members, including the chairperson.

Commissioner for the Rights of Trade Union Members (CROTUM)

CROTUM was created by the Employment Act 1988 in order to enforce the rights of individual trade union members, which include the right of a trade union member to require a ballot before industrial action and the right of a union member to inspect union accounts. If a union member alleged that the union had breached that member's statutory union membership rights then CROTUM would provide assistance to that member. CROTUM would also help an individual member if there were an alleged breach of the rules of a trade union or one of its branches or sections. Following its establishment CROTUM assisted, on average, only nine applicants each year. CROTUM was finally abolished under provisions contained in the Employment Relations Act 1999 (ERA99), section 28, and most of its powers transferred to the Certification Officer.

Certification Officer

The post of Certification Officer was established in 1975 and its functions are contained in the Trade Union and Labour Relations (Consolidation) Act 1992 (see Exhibit 1.2). The Officer is responsible for maintaining separate lists of trade unions and

employers' associations. If a union is on the list it is entitled to a certificate that it is 'independent'. The requirements for being on the list are that a union is free from domination or control of an employer or employers' association/organisation, and that it should not run the risk of interference as a result of financial or other powers an employer might have. Not all organisations are able to satisfy these requirements, particularly smaller employer-financed staff associations. Certification is important for collective bargaining purposes because it confers significant bargaining rights such as:

- time off for employees to take part in union activities;
- information needed by union representatives for collective bargaining purposes;
- information and consultation when there is a transfer of the employer's business;
- government financial assistance for holding ballots relating to strike action, elections of representatives and other union purposes;
- details and supplementary information about pensions;
- time off for representatives to have industrial relations training; and
- notification and consultation rights in the event of collective redundancies.

The Certification Officer's Annual Report is an indispensable source of data concerning union numbers and membership, trade union accounts and information concerning unions' finances and political funds. Its data is used selectively in Chapter 3.

Summary points

- The parties (or actors) to employment relations comprise management and employer; management and employer organisations; employees and employee organisations; the state and state agencies.
- The basic industrial relations functions of management are termed 'traditional', sophisticated and HRM, each of which is based on different views or ideologies concerning how to manage the employment relationship.
- Management/employer organisations include employers' associations, the CBI and UNICE,

Exhibit 1.2

Functions of the Certification Officer

1. For maintaining a list of trade unions and for determining the independence of trade unions.
2. For dealing with complaints by members that a trade union has failed to maintain an accurate register of members; for seeing that trade unions keep proper accounting records, have their accounts properly audited and submit annual returns; for the investigation of the financial affairs of trade unions.
3. For dealing with complaints by members that a trade union has failed to comply with statutory provisions requiring a trade union to hold secret postal ballots for electing members of its executive committee, president and general secretary.
4. For ensuring observance of the statutory procedures governing the setting up, operation and review of political funds; and for dealing with complaints about breaches of political fund rules or about the conduct of political fund ballots.
5. For seeing that the statutory procedures for union amalgamations, transfers of engagements and changes of name are complied with and for dealing with complaints by members about the conduct of merger ballots.
6. For maintaining a list of employers' associations; for ensuring that the statutory requirements concerning accounting records, auditors, annual returns, financial affairs, political funds and statutory procedures for amalgamations, and transfers of engagements in respect of employers' associations are complied with.

Source: Annual Report of the Certification Office, 2002

while employee organisations include trade unions, staff/professional associations, the TUC, the ETUC and ICFTU.

- The state is an important influence upon employment relations. The agencies set up by government are considered to be independent and include employment tribunals, the EAT, ACAS, CAC, CROTUM (now abolished) and the Certification Officer.

We now briefly consider the development of industrial relations in Britain from the nineteenth century to the present day.

THE DEVELOPMENT OF BRITISH INDUSTRIAL RELATIONS

British employment and industrial relations has developed in a rather haphazard way over the past 130 years, and in this section we will trace that development using a broadly chronological approach. Since 1980, workplace employment relations has been well documented by the longitudinal Workplace Industrial Relations Survey series (WIRS)

of which there have been four major ones, the last survey being completed in 1998, entitled the *Workplace Employee Relations Survey* (Cully *et al.*, 1999; Millward *et al.*, 2000). Taken together, these surveys provide the most reliable evidence we have of changes in workplace employment relations since 1980. We first of all look at the early development of industrial relations.

Early development of industrial relations

Nineteenth-century development

The early growth of industrial relations was linked to the growth of trade unions themselves. Trade unions are largely a consequence of the factory system which developed during the industrial revolution. Trade union growth was hindered by the Combination Acts of 1799 and 1800, and until these Acts were replaced with the Combination Laws in 1825 most trade union activities were illegal. Until 1825, all that working people could do on a collective basis was to form mutual benefit or 'friendly societies' (Pelling, 1987). With the repeal of the Combination Acts, trade unions were allowed to exist and pursue their objectives in a free way, but they could not engage in strike activity which was still illegal.

The early unions were very locally based and confined solely to skilled craftsmen, and became known as craft unions. However, in 1851 the first forerunner of a national trade union as we know them today was formed. This was the Amalgamated Society of Engineers from which developed the present Amalgamated Engineering and Electrical Union (AEEU). This form of national union became known as 'New Model Unionism' and spread rapidly to other unions. During the latter part of the nineteenth century trade unionism and collective bargaining were still largely confined to skilled trades and then to 'piecework' industries where pay was related to output. Although many trade unions became organised on a national basis, early collective bargaining was still locally based, workers' common interests being centred upon the immediate geographical locality.

Twentieth-century development

The late nineteenth and early twentieth centuries witnessed unprecedented growth of trade unions and the formation of employers' associations. This corresponded with the growth of traditional manufacturing and extractive industries such as engineering, shipbuilding and coal mining. The main impetus for the development of national or industry level collective bargaining, however, did not come until the First World War period. The reasons for this were that:

- some industries became nationalised and unions could negotiate with a single employer;
- other industries experienced labour shortages which led some employers to seek national agreements in order to retain labour;
- inflation growth, together with the introduction of compulsory arbitration, resulted in greater uniformity in wage claims and wage settlements; and
- the Whitley Committee, set up in 1916, recommended the establishment of joint industrial councils (JICs) with written constitutions which

functioned at national, district and work levels. JICs provided a formal forum in which employers and unions could negotiate.

The 1920s and 1930s experienced economic depression and high unemployment. These conditions were characterised by:

- a significant decline in trade union membership from a high of 8.3 million in 1920 to a low of 4.4 million in 1932–3;
- hostile employer attitudes towards trade unions;
- government economic policies detrimental to trade unions; and
- abolition of half the JICs.

Since the First World War, industrial relations in Britain, according to Salamon (1998, p. 55):

has developed through a number of overlapping phases: increased pressure, particularly on the industry-level part of the system; voluntary reform; increased governmental and legislative intervention; confrontation; and possibly a new realism.

We will now look at these phases in greater detail.

Increased pressure on post-war British industrial relations

The immediate post-war period saw the establishment of the welfare state and government policy geared towards full employment and economic growth. At this time it was thought that industry-wide collective bargaining, established as we have seen during the course of the late nineteenth and early twentieth centuries, would be the basis for orderly and peaceful industrial relations. However, this was not to be; there were new pressures from employees and management which threatened the stability of the industrial relations system.

Employee pressures included:

- rising aspirations for greater monetary and other material rewards;
- union expectations for greater involvement in managerial decision-making; and
- expansion of trade union membership at a time of full employment and scarcity of labour.

Employer pressures included:

- the need to change working practices; and
- the need to improve productivity to cope with increased demand and competition.

Increasingly these pressures could not be accommodated by the traditional industry-wide bargaining mechanisms and agreements. As we have seen, industry-wide bargaining established relatively uniform wage rates for employees across the industry. This system worked well when labour was plentiful during the inter-war years and agreed industry-wide wage rates were accepted as the maximum that could be achieved. However, because of the pressures identified above, individual employers were compelled to negotiate locally at organisation level and agree on pay rates and other substantive issues which breached the industry-wide agreement.

Self-Evaluation Activity 1.6

Pay pressures
Response on website

In order to illustrate and understand this important trend read the short scenario in Mini case 1.3 and answer the question which follows. You should take about five minutes on this activity.

Mini case 1.3
Pay problems

ABC Engineering employs 2000 people on two sites and has been established for 80 years. Until 1962, ABC was a member of a local employers' association federated to the EEF. All pay rates were negotiated at industry level and the system worked well until the late 1950s. Full employment, increased scarcity of skilled labour and full order books eventually created strains and tensions within the company, particularly upon its industrial relations. ABC had problems retaining labour at existing pay rates and increased competitive pressures meant that working practices needed to be changed and productivity increased.

In view of the changing pressures upon employers, what should ABC management do about this changing situation?

The Donovan Commission Report (1968)

The switch to organisational and local bargaining in the private sector during the 1960s tended to result in a two-tier system of industrial relations which was characterised by the conflict between organisational and industry-level bargaining. There was a feeling that industrial relations in Britain was becoming increasingly fragmented and uncontrollable as a result of what Flanders (1965) calls 'the challenge from below':

> *What stands out about the workplace bargaining of recent years is first that it has developed on a much greater scale than ever before, except under special conditions of war. But it has also been a spontaneous development with its own independent momentum, so that it lies largely outside the control of trade unions and employers' associations. Far from being subservient to the system of external job regulation, it appears rather to threaten its stability. In other words it has assumed a form which is not so much an extension of the system as a challenge to it.* (p. 109)

It was under these circumstances that the Donovan Commission was charged by the Labour government to analyse and recommend changes to the British industrial relations system. The Commission made certain assumptions about industry-level bargaining on the one hand, and the informal system of organisational and workplace bargaining on the other. We will now briefly identify these conflicting assumptions.

The formal system of industry-level bargaining assumed that:

- it was possible to negotiate and resolve all industrial relations issues in a single written agreement which could then be applied throughout the industry;
- trade unions and employers' associations could ensure that the terms of any agreement were observed by their members; and
- the function of the industrial relations system at organisational level was primarily one of interpreting and applying the industry agreement and providing a basis for joint consultation between management and employees.

The informal system of organisational bargaining assumed that:

- many industrial relations issues were specific to the organisation and could be regulated by informal arrangements or 'custom and practice' at the workplace;
- both management and union members at the workplace had a relatively high degree of autonomy to reach decisions independently of their central organisations; and
- the distinction between the processes of joint consultation and collective bargaining, and therefore between which issues were appropriate for which process, was blurred.

In the opinion of the Commission, the informal system at organisational level tended to undermine agreements reached in formal industry-level bargaining, especially as far as pay determination was concerned. The Commission suggested that the resolution of the conflict between the formal (industry) and informal (organisational/workplace) could be achieved on a voluntary, not statutory, basis through managements and trade unions accepting the reality and importance of the organisational level and developing it on more formal and orderly lines.

The voluntary reform of British industrial relations

The Commission's main recommendation that there should be more formal and orderly industrial relations at organisational level, on a voluntary basis, was eventually implemented, but in a rather sporadic and piecemeal fashion. The responsibility for initiating change tended to be placed upon management and success in this area depended upon the agreement of the relevant trade unions. Most larger companies and all public sector organisations, including local authorities, initiated reforms, the most important of which was the systematic development of formal substantive and procedural agreements at organisational level.

The development of formal substantive agreements included the following aspects:

- reform of payment structures and systems;
- removal of piecework and bonus systems;
- reduction in the number of grades and jobs; and
- linking these and other reforms to changes in working arrangements.

The development of formal procedural agreements included:

- written disciplinary procedures;
- written grievance procedures;
- written redundancy procedures; and
- written disputes procedures.

The onus for initiating these reforms was placed, as we have seen, mainly upon management. At the same time, the Donovan Commission provided the impetus for trade unions to reform themselves. We will now look briefly at this.

Trade union reform: simplifying trade union structure

As we shall see in Chapter 3, the structure of British trade unions is rather complex and it is not the intention here to examine trade union structure. Suffice it to say that during the post-war period, trade union structure has, to some extent, been simplified as a result of a number of well-publicised mergers. For example, within the public sector, three large unions, the National Association of Local Government Officers (NALGO), the National Union of Public Employees (NUPE) and the Confederation of Health Service Employees (COHSE) merged in 1993 to form UNISON, Britain's largest union. There are many examples of smaller-scale mergers. The merger process has:

- reduced the number of trade unions;
- simplified collective bargaining arrangements (managements find it simpler to negotiate with one union rather than two); and
- made the introduction of new working arrangements easier by reducing the boundaries between work groups and eliminating demarcations (as with the merger of the electricians' and plumbers' unions to create the Electrical, Electronic, Telecommunications and Plumbing Union (EETPU)).

Government legislation and intervention

The voluntary reform of industrial relations as recommended by the Donovan Commission did not proceed fast enough, even for a Labour government.

This prompted both political parties to produce proposals to introduce, for the first time in the history of British industrial relations, a comprehensive legal framework with the intention of compelling reform. The incoming Conservative government quickly enacted their own proposals which gave rise to the Industrial Relations Act (1971) but, for reasons which we shall consider in Chapter 4, the Act failed and was repealed by the Labour government's Trade Union and Labour Relations Act in 1974.

This was followed by a period of positive legislative support for trade unions in exchange for union support to moderate wage claims. This accord became known as the Social Contract, which endured with varying degrees of success until 1979. The main legislative support took the form of the Employment Protection Act (1975), which established a number of employee and union rights. Other positive government support for unions was reflected in the terms of reference of the Bullock Committee on Industrial Democracy (1977) (see Chapter 8), which were concerned with the extension of industrial democracy to include worker representation on company boards. The recommendations of Bullock were subsequently shelved and never implemented.

Confrontation and 'new realism'

In 1978/9 there was a wave of industrial disputes, mainly in the public sector, after three years of voluntary wage restraint. This episode became known as the 'Winter of Discontent', and the subsequent election heralded a period of successive Conservative governments. The Conservatives were committed to an ongoing programme of legislation which imposed, in incremental fashion, increasingly greater legal constraints on the activities and affairs of trade unions. Examples of the main pieces of Conservative legislation are listed below:

1980	Employment Act
1982	Employment Act
1984	Trade Union Act
1986	Wages Act
1988	Employment Act
1989	Employment Act
1990	Employment Act

1992	Trade Union and Labour Relations (Consolidation) Act
1993	Trade Union Reform and Employment Rights Act

We shall be examining the legislation in greater detail in Chapter 4. The net effect of the Conservative legislation has been to weaken trade union power and influence in industrial relations. At the same time managements' influence in industrial relations increased during the 1980s, and there are numerous examples of employers asserting themselves in rather extreme ways, as for example with:

- Rupert Murdoch's News International at Wapping in 1986 where unions were deliberately excluded by management; and
- the more recent dispute in 1997 concerning the sacking of over 300 dockers employed by the Mersey Docks and Harbour Company.

The 1980s also witnessed a new development in British industrial relations, the so-called 'new realism', which has the following characteristics.

Management

This, according to Salamon (1998), involves 'taking a more proactive approach to industrial relations to ensure that it supports and is integrated with the achievement of business objectives (be it improved competitiveness, quality or customer care)' (p. 24).

Process relationship

This means:

- a move from negotiation and agreement to communication and consultation, thereby strengthening management's right to manage (managerial prerogatives);
- a move from 'disclosure' of information to unions for bargaining purposes to 'dissemination' of information to employees; and
- a move from employee 'participation' to employee 'involvement' to secure the individual employee's identification with and commitment to the organisation and its goals.

Structure of bargaining

This involves:

- a continuation of the shift from industry-level (multi-employer) to organisational-level (single-employer) bargaining thereby taking advantage of local labour market conditions;
- rationalisation of union recognition for bargaining purposes to a 'single-table' or 'single-union' basis (see Chapter 6); and
- less commonly, replacing industrial action with 'pendulum' arbitration (see Chapter 9).

Workplace

This is concerned with employees becoming more flexible in numerical (differentiating between core and periphery workers), task and time terms.

Basis of pay

This means placing greater emphasis on organisational or individual performance, as with performance-related pay, and less on the uniform rate for the job.

Union response

Unions have responded to the changed conditions of the 1980s by:

- focusing their recruitment in employment growth areas (women, part-timers, service sector) in order to reverse the decline in union membership (see Chapter 3);
- developing individual member services such as issuing credit cards; and
- selling themselves to the employer and competing with each other in 'beauty contests' in order to secure employer recognition, as with the AEEU and Nissan/Toyota.

The 'new realism', therefore, largely represented a reaction on the part of unions to the changed economic circumstances of the 1980s and 1990s and to government policies which have curtailed their influence.

Self-Evaluation Activity 1.7
Summarising
Response on website

Attempt the following questions which are intended to enable you to summarise and assist your understanding of what you have just read:

1. Identify some of the major developments in British industrial relations during the twentieth century.
2. Why was the reform of industrial relations considered necessary during the late 1960s?

Social partnership, 'new unionism' and New Labour

With the election of the first Blair New Labour government in 1997, there was a general expectation that there would be a reversal of Conservative employment relations policies and the development of a substantial industrial relations reform agenda. By 2003, the extent of that agenda has become clear; there has been no radical departure from Conservative industrial relations policies. The employment legislation enacted during the 1980s and 1990s remains largely intact and is still the most restrictive on trade unions of all western economically developed countries. Conservative governments' enthusiasm for encouraging a flexible workforce within a largely deregulated labour market has been endorsed by Labour, albeit tempered by the rhetoric of 'social partnership' and 'fairness'. Relations with the TUC are lukewarm at best; there is no close, 'special' relationship with the Labour government which characterised the corporatist years of previous Labour administrations. The TUC itself, under the modernising influence of John Monks and to a lesser extent under his successor Brendan Barber, has committed itself to fostering a partnership relationship with government and employers and an increased willingness to work closely with the CBI on issues of mutual interest. However, during the early 2000s, both government and CBI have been increasingly reluctant to endorse co-operation and partnership at national level. Moreover, many trade unions have become increasingly disaffected with New Labour policy regarding the 'modernisation' of public services and other matters, this situation being compounded by the election of union leaders of a more left-wing persuasion, dubbed 'the awkward squad'. During 1997 the TUC developed its 'new unionism' strategy (see Chapter 3).

The Labour government has introduced legislation that aims to encourage 'greater adaptability at work, to deepen the sense of partnership between employers and employees and to achieve "fairness at work" for all' (Taylor, 1998). The ERA99 was the most significant piece of legislation during Blair's first government, and this was followed by the Employment Act of 2002 (EA02) with subsequent legislation to enact certain provisions. The main elements of both pieces of legislation, apart from the union recognition proposals within ERA99, comprised elements of employment protection which set in motion various European Union Directives which were not transposed owing to the Conservative veto of the European Union Social Chapter (see Chapter 4). Some of the more important legislative developments included:

- The establishment of a national minimum wage as a result of the National Minimum Wage Act 1998 and National Minimum Wage Regulations 1999 (see Chapter 4).
- The Employment Relations Act 1999, which includes provisions concerning individual employee rights and statutory procedures concerning trade union recognition.
- The Employment Act 2002 which contains provisions dealing with statutory disputes, discipline and grievance procedures, employment tribunals and further improvements to parental leave and payments.
- A supportive stance and a more co-operative relationship with the European Union which has resulted in the ending of Britain's opt-out from the Social Chapter of the EU's 1991 Maastricht Treaty and the acceptance of the EU's Employment Chapter agreed at the 1997 Amsterdam summit as part of the Treaty of Amsterdam (see Chapters 4 and 8). The immediate consequences of this are:
  - adoption of the European Works Council Directive, implemented in the UK at the end of 1999; and
  - the implementation of various EU Directives such as the Working Time Directive which

for most categories of employees limits the length of the working week to a maximum of 48 hours; the Part-Time Workers Directive which seeks to ensure that part-time workers are not treated any less favourably than full-time employees and will benefit from the same statutory and contractual terms and conditions of employment.

THEORETICAL APPROACHES TO EMPLOYMENT AND INDUSTRIAL RELATIONS

Employment relations is not only a matter of description and prescription. As we have seen, prescription is important because governments and other policy makers, trade union leaders, the TUC and CBI make statements of policy which seek to prescribe 'remedies' to problems or recommend possible solutions, in much the same way as the Donovan Commission did. Academic analysis of the employment relationship and industrial relations generally involves the use of a number of competing theoretical perspectives. For example, an academic study of government industrial relations policy will assume that the policy is based upon some sort of coherent theoretical analysis of the role of the state, of the economy and the political system. Different governments will use contrasting and possibly conflicting theoretical analyses in operationalising their political agendas. Labour government politicians and their advisers in the 1970s had a view of industrial relations based upon a degree of legislative support for trade unions and their members, whereas the Conservative governments and politicians of the 1980s had a negative view of trade unions which informed their policies. We can therefore argue that the policies of both Labour and Conservative governments were based on conflicting theoretical perspectives and analyses of the role of the state and political economy.

By the same token theoretical analysis is extremely valuable in explaining the actions, statements and behaviours of employers and trade unionists. As these actions, behaviours and statements often conflict, it would be reasonable to assume that the theoretical assumptions on which they are based also conflict. The following quote taken from Gospel and Palmer (1993) reinforces what we have argued up to now:

> Prescriptions and descriptions often purport to be based on pragmatic, non-theoretical common sense, for any discussion of social behaviour requires that some assumptions and generalisations be made. In industrial relations, the existence of contentious and conflicting proposals from the different participants suggests that whatever the assumptions are, they are certainly not 'common' to all. For example, while some people assume that employers always have the real power in industrial relations, others assume that employees, when organised into trade unions, can be as powerful or more so. While some assume that government adopts a neutral stance on industrial matters, others assume the government is always active, but disagree over whether governments usually act primarily in the interests of employers or employees. If we try to sort out the theoretical generalisations and assumptions behind different public policy proposals we find ourselves faced with a great range of different approaches. As they are usually not presented as clearly differentiated theories, we can best speak of the existence of a number of broad theoretical perspectives on the processes of control over the employment relationship, the organisation of work, and relations between employers and their employees. (p. 11)

We now go on to examine broad theoretical perspectives on industrial relations. More specifically, we shall look at a number of different prescriptions, assess the assumptions that lie behind these prescriptions and indicate the different views or value judgements linked to certain perspectives.

Traditional organisational perspectives concerning employment relations

The unitary perspective

The unitary perspective is based upon the assumption that the organisation is, or should have:

- an integrated group of people;
- a simple authority or loyalty structure; and
- a set of common values, interests and objectives.

Management's prerogative (that is, its right to manage and make decisions) is regarded as legitimate, rational and accepted, and any opposition to it internally or externally is seen as irrational. The underlying assumption of this view, then, is that 'the organisation exists in perfect harmony and all conflict, not only industrial relations conflict is both unnecessary and exceptional' (Salamon, 1992, p. 31).

There are two important implications stemming from this. The first is that conflict as the expression of employee dissatisfaction and differences with management is perceived as an irrational activity. Here, conflict is regarded as 'bad' for the organisation and should be suppressed through coercive means. The second is that trade unions are regarded as an intrusion into the organisation from outside, competing with management for the loyalty of employees. Therefore, trade unions should be denied a presence within the organisation. In some cases, however, managements may be 'forced' to accept a trade union presence for the purposes of determination of pay and conditions of employment (that is, market relations). Under no circumstances, according to this perspective, should unions have a part to play in the exercise of authority and decision-making within the organisation (that is, managerial relations), as this would represent a violation of managerial prerogative.

Relevance of the unitary perspective

As a simple theoretical device, the unitary perspective can be used to identify the industrial relations climate within specific types of organisation, both historically and currently. We shall now look briefly at these types:

- During the nineteenth century many firms adopted an 'aggressive' unitary perspective, with authoritarian employers actively excluding trade unions. Employees, including women and children, were poorly treated and worked long hours for subsistence level wages.
- During this period there were also 'good' employers who, while resisting any trade union presence, treated their workforces relatively well by, for example, providing works outings and excursions and housing. These employers concerned themselves with their employees'

well-being and were regarded as benevolent and paternalistic (this means taking a 'fatherly' interest in the workforce). Early examples included the Cadburys and Rowntrees.

- Even in the 2000s there are many examples of organisations whose managements adopt a modified unitary view. Many firms still exclude trade unions and of these a high proportion may not be particularly 'good' employers. Others, such as Marks & Spencer, treat their employees well, and it is firms within this category that are often described as neo-paternalist.

Allan Fox (1966), who first made the distinction between the unitary and pluralist perspectives, argues that the unitary perspective, where it exists, is found primarily among managers and is therefore often regarded as a management ideology. The ideology still exists today for the following reasons:

- It enables management to legitimise its authority by regarding the interests of management and employees as being the same and that managers manage in the best interests of the entire organisation.
- It reassures management by confirming that the blame for conflict can be placed with employees rather than management.
- It may be projected to the outside world as a means of persuading them that management's decisions and actions are right and that any challenge to them is misguided or even subversive.

The unitary perspective, therefore, remains an important theoretical device for examining the attitudes and perceptions of managers in some organisational contexts. Fox argues that the importance of this perspective is declining and has been superseded by the pluralist perspective to which we now turn.

The pluralist perspective

The pluralist perspective is regarded as being more congruent with developments in contemporary society, while the unitary perspective would seem to be more appropriate to nineteenth-century capitalism. The changes that have given rise to the pluralist perspective during the twentieth century include:

- a widespread distribution of authority and power in society;
- a separation of ownership from management;
- a separation of political and industrial conflict; and
- an acceptance and institutionalisation of conflict in both spheres.

Given these and other changes, the principal assumption of the pluralist perspective is that the organisation comprises groups of individuals and that these groups have their own aims, interests and leadership. These aims and interests often conflict and compete with those of other groups and give rise to tensions which have to be managed. Unlike the unitarist assumption of only one source of loyalty and authority which resides in management, the pluralist organisation has many sources of loyalty and authority in groups, trade unions and other sectional interests and is in a constant state of dynamic tension arising from conflicts of interest and loyalty which require to be managed through a variety of procedures. We will now look briefly at how the pluralist perspective deals with conflict between management and employees and the role of trade unions within the organisation.

Management–employee conflict

According to the pluralist perspective, conflict is both rational and inevitable and stems from the different roles of managerial and employee groups. The causes of such conflict are examined in Chapter 9 and need not concern us here. Pluralist managers recognise that these conflicts exist and that they can only be resolved by the establishment and use of appropriate procedures. This involves collective negotiation and bargaining and shared decision-making which leads to compromise. Management's role is therefore a 'balancing act' which recognises the legitimacy of the organisation's conflicting interests and requires the consent of the parties, groups or sections involved in the resolution of conflicts. The only legitimate basis for managing industrial relations is, therefore, through consent and not (as with the unitary perspective) through the exercise of prerogative.

The role of trade unions in the organisation

The pluralist perspective accepts that trade unions are legitimate representative organisations which enable groups of employees to influence management decisions. It also accepts that employees have loyalties to organisations other than their own management and that trade unions are a legitimate source of these loyalties. While the pluralist perspective would seem to be much more relevant than the unitary perspective in the analysis of industrial relations in many large unionised organisations within the private and public sectors, some theorists such as Hyman (1975) argue that given the nature of capitalist society industrial relations can be analysed from a more radical perspective.

Before we consider the radical perspective, attempt the following activity which tests your knowledge of the unitary and pluralist perspectives.

Self-Evaluation Activity 1.8

Summarising unitary and pluralist perspectives
Response on website

Read the brief statement given in Exhibit 1.3 and attempt the question which follows.

Which of the categories, unitarist or pluralist, do you feel is most reflected in the statements in Exhibit 1.3?

The radical perspective: Marxist analysis

The radical perspective is broader in scope than either the unitary or the pluralist perspective and incorporates a Marxist analysis of the employment relationship. The radical perspective also emphasises the importance of collective action and organisation explained in terms of mobilisation theory. Additionally, the radical perspective differs from both unitarism and pluralism in a number of fundamental ways:

- Both unitary and pluralist perspectives are views or ideologies which academics such as Fox have attributed to managers and employers.
- These ideologies change as organisations and society itself change. Put simplistically, the unitary ideology could be regarded as being representative of views held by the nineteenth- and early twentieth-century employer, while the pluralist ideology reflects organisational and societal changes taking place during the course of the mid- to late twentieth century and extending into the twenty-first century.
- Both unitarist and pluralist ideologies are reflections of an organisational and societal status quo. They both accept and endorse the capitalist economic and political system and are therefore not critical of it.

Exhibit 1.3

Unitarist or pluralist?

We deplore the use of the terms 'industrial relations' and 'labour relations'. We prefer 'human relations', by which we mean a recognition of the essential dignity of the individual.

An employee, at whatever level, must be made to feel that he or she is not merely a number on a payroll but a recognised member of a team: that he or she is part of the company and an important part; and 'company', not in the sense of some inanimate thing possessing no soul, but rather in the sense of goodly fellowship.

We reject the idea that amongst the employees of a company there are 'two sides', meaning the executive directors and managers on the one hand and the weekly-paid employees on the other. Executive directors are just as much employees of the company as anyone else. We are all on the same side, members of the same team. We make no secret of the belief that any employee, from executive director to admin assistant, who does less than his or her best, while drawing his or her full salary or wages, is morally indistinguishable from a thief who helps himself or herself to petty cash.

We recognise that the tone of any organisation depends primarily on one person, on the executive head of it: on his or her philosophy, on his or her outlook, on the standards he or she sets, on his or her example: in short on his or her leadership.

- On the other hand, the radical perspective is deeply critical of capitalist society and its system of production, distribution and exchange.
- The level of analysis of the radical perspective embraces the social, political and economic structures of society of which the organisation of work is only one small part. This perspective, therefore, views and analyses industrial relations not only in organisational job regulation terms but also in social, political and economic terms.

The radical perspective owes much to the Marxist analysis and critique of capitalist society. According to this perspective economic inequalities manifest themselves in wider social conflict and more specifically within the industrial relations arena, industrial conflict. There are certain assumptions underlying the radical perspective:

1. Change in society is the result of class conflict and without this conflict, society would stagnate.
2. Class conflict arises from the inequalities in the distribution of economic power in society.
3. The basic economic inequality is between those who own capital (entrepreneurs, big business, etc.) and those who supply and sell their labour (employees).
4. The nature of society's social and political institutions is derived from this basic economic inequality. Inequality is maintained and reinforced by selective recruitment and differential access to education, government employment, legal professions, the media and other establishment institutions.
5. Social and political conflict in its many manifestations is merely an expression of the underlying economic conflict (based on inequality) within society.

Following on from these assumptions, contemporary capitalism exhibits three main characteristics. Firstly, capitalism requires continued economic growth in order to ensure its survival, as economic growth guarantees profitability and capital accumulation. Secondly, economic growth is realised through the extraction of surplus value which accrues to the employer when the workers' costs of subsistence have been extracted from the value of what he or she produces. This does not mean that workers only live on the barest minimum for survival as the worker is also a consumer of capitalist goods and services.

Consequently, a relationship of mutual dependence is established between capitalist and worker, and the support of the latter is required in order to achieve the goals of profitability through the purchase and consumption of the former's products. One of the main methods of ensuring such support is through employer control of the labour process in the workplace (see Chapter 2) and control of patterns of consumption and exchange in the market place through advertising to promote consumer demand. Thirdly, capitalism requires continuous technological and organisational change in order to perpetuate itself and satisfy the criteria of efficiency, labour productivity and profitability.

Example of industrial conflict

Industrial conflict, which is the focus of Chapter 9, manifests itself in strikes and other forms of collective action short of striking (working to rule, go-slows, sit-ins, etc.). These forms of collective action are regarded not only as reflecting tensions within the organisation, but also and perhaps more importantly as stemming from the unequal division within society between those who own or manage the means of production and those who have only their labour to sell. Because of this inequality and division, industrial conflict is continuous and unavoidable, and is synonymous with political and social conflict. In similar vein the radical perspective sees the growth of trade unionism as an inevitable response to capitalism. Trade unions:

- enhance their collective industrial power by reducing competition between individual employees;
- provide a focus for the expression and protection of the interests of the working classes; and
- are part of the overall political process for achieving fundamental changes in the nature of economic and social systems.

Self-Evaluation Activity 1.9

Summarising

Response on website

Take a few minutes to consider the following question:

To what extent do you think the radical perspective presents a 'negative' view of capitalism, industrial conflict and trade unions?

Mobilisation theory

Industrial relations is concerned with the nature of collective action and the conditions under which individuals organise collectively. Mobilisation theory, of which there are several versions, attempts to provide an explanatory framework within which these questions are considered. Tilly's (1978) mobilisation theory, considered by Kelly (1998), is essentially Marxist in orientation, encapsulating the argument that in theorising about collective action it is necessary to identify its components and different forms of action in relation to each. The five components are summarised as follows:

Interests and the way in which these are defined, together with what factors identify the collective interest(s) of employees from those of employers. One important factor concerns the extent to which an individual sense of injustice (say, a grievance) can be translated into a collective interest.

Organisation 'refers to the structure of a group, and in particular those aspects which affect its capacity for collective action' (Kelly, 1998, p. 25). This is basically concerned with the trade union movement and the extent to which union members identify with their organisation.

Mobilisation is 'the process by which a group acquires collective control over the resources needed for action' (Tilly, 1978, quoted by Kelly, 1998). This requires a cost–benefit analysis of collective action and a consideration of the role of the leadership function in mobilising workers for collective action.

Opportunity is concerned with 'the balance of power between the parties, the costs of repression by the ruling group and the opportunities available for subordinate groups to pursue their claims' (Kelly, 1998, p. 25). An analysis of the extent of employer 'repression' during the 1980s and 1990s together with a consideration of the concept and balance of power is relevant here.

Counter-mobilisation represents the degree to which 'ruling groups', such as employers, seek to alter employees' interests and discourage the emergence of collective organisation (trade unions) and collective action.

Collective action itself takes many forms including strike action and action short of strikes.

Kelly (1998) summarises the essence of mobilisation theory in relation to industrial relations in the following terms:

> *Mobilisation theory argues that collective organisation and activity ultimately stem from employer actions that generate amongst employees a sense of injustice or illegitimacy. Employees must also acquire a sense of common identity which differentiates them from the employer; they must attribute the perceived injustice to the employer; and they must be willing to engage in some form of collective organisation and activity. This whole process of collectivisation is heavily dependent on the actions of small numbers of leaders or activists.* (p. 44)

Mobilisation theory is therefore useful in attempting to explain the origins and rise of collective organisation and action. The dramatic decline in collective organisation as a result of 'a wide-ranging hostility to union presence, activity and organisation on the part of employers' (ibid., p. 63) during the 1980s and 1990s is explained by mobilisation theorists in relation to:

- 'a far-reaching employer and state offensive against trade unionism, as employers have sought both to increase profitability and to reassert their managerial prerogative against joint regulation with trade unionism' (ibid., p. 61); and
- the decline in union recognition (see Chapter 3), negative attitudes towards collective bargaining, derecognition of unions and the bypassing and marginalisation of unions are all expressions of employer militancy.

To conclude, mobilisation theory provides us with a suitable framework for analysing contemporary industrial relations, and is an effective antidote to the employer-supporting ideologies underpinning unitarism, pluralism and HRM, and to a lesser extent systems theory and postmodernism (see below). We now consider certain theoretical perspectives which, at different stages in the post-war development of industrial relations, have attempted to explain and/or justify the actions of government, employers and trade unions.

Perspectives underpinning industrial relations developments up to 1979

There are three major theoretical contributions which seek to analyse and explain industrial relations processes and developments during the post-war period until 1979. These are:

- Liberal collectivism.
- Systems and action approaches.
- Corporatist perspectives.

It should be noted at the outset that there are varying degrees of overlap between each of these perspectives, and, where necessary, these will be indicated.

Liberal collectivism

The liberal collectivist perspective forms the basis of much academic analysis of British employment relations during the post-Second World War period. The term 'liberal' denotes a limited role for government and a 'laissez-faire' approach to the use of legislation in industrial relations which gives negotiators a high degree of freedom to negotiate without statutory intervention. The term 'collectivist' or 'collective' describes the legitimate right of employees to form collective organisations to increase their bargaining power when negotiating agreements. This theoretical perspective emphasises:

- the benefits of freedom of association to organise collectively;
- collective bargaining freely undertaken and without interference by government; and
- negotiated agreements between conflicting parties.

Liberal collectivism and collective bargaining
The main focus of liberal collectivism is upon collective bargaining (see also Chapter 6) which Gospel and Palmer (1993) define as:

> the process by which trade unions and similar associations, representing groups of employees, negotiate with employers or their representatives with the object of reaching collective agreements. (p. 15)

Collective bargaining enables conflicts to be aired and resolved, and it entails negotiations concerning procedural and substantive issues; it is essentially a process which seeks to regulate the labour market and prevent a competitive 'free-for-all'. Its successful operation requires:

- a political system that allows employees freedom of association and action to organise independently of employers and the state;
- the mutual recognition of different and often conflicting interests by employers and employees;
- the willingness of both employers and employees to accept the compromise of jointly agreed terms; and
- a market system which allows the price of labour and of goods and services to fluctuate according to supply and demand.

Liberal collectivists strongly support the case for collective bargaining. Essentially, they argue that:

- collective bargaining creates a form of industrial democracy by enabling employees to influence pay determination and conditions of employment; and
- collective bargaining contributes to and promotes social stability by resolving conflicts which could otherwise be politically disruptive. In this sense, collective bargaining is seen as a 'safety valve'.

Liberal collectivism, therefore, encapsulates the view that collective bargaining is a flexible and democratic method for the satisfactory resolution of conflicts at work. There are, however, a number of criticisms that have been made of the liberal collectivist view of collective bargaining. These are now briefly summarised.

Criticisms of liberal collectivism
Some critics from the political right argue that collective bargaining is too disruptive because:

1. The level of industrial action is too high and costly for a nation competing in global markets.
2. Employers and employees collude to push up wages and prices without due regard for consumers.
3. Collective bargaining gets in the way of individual rights thereby complicating the employee–employer relationship.

Other critics from the political left argue that:

1. Unions are too weak.
2. Employee participation in decision-making is too limited under collective bargaining.

Self-Evaluation Activity 1.10

Government action

The response is given below

Having noted the criticisms of liberal collectivism, suggest one proposal for action within the employment relations sphere which a government of the political right could make, and one proposal for action which a government of the political left could make which would satisfy the critics.

Some on the political right have advocated government action to reduce the power of trade unions by adopting tight economic policies and introducing industrial relations legislation.

The political left would suggest a strengthening of collective bargaining and legislation to support trade unions in their various activities.

Systems and action approaches

While liberal collectivist assumptions tended to dominate much British thinking within the industrial relations field, systems theory originated in the United States and became a major school of sociological thought derived from the work of von Bertalanffy (1951) and Talcott Parsons (1951). The basic idea of systems theory is that the whole is greater than the sum of the parts. Systems theory can be applied to society viewed as a whole system which contains economic, political, religious and other subsystems. It is also possible to analyse subsystems of society as whole systems, enabling us to consider a variety of organisations and institutions in this way, industrial relations being no exception, as we shall see. For example, work organisations analysed as whole systems draw our attention to their subsystems (or parts) and the relationships between these parts. The major principles of the systems approach include:

Subsystems, parts or components. A system by definition is composed of interrelated parts or subsystems which are interconnected.

Holism. The whole system is not just the sum of the parts; the system itself can be explained only as a totality. Holism is the opposite of *reductionism* which views the total as the sum of its individual parts and concentrates on the properties of the subsystem without reference to the whole system (this would be equivalent to looking at trade unions without reference to the rest of the industrial relations system).

Open-system view. Systems can be considered as either closed or open. Open systems are viewed as exchanging information with their environments and this is the preferred way of analysing systems. Open systems analysis uses an *input-process/ transformation-output model*. It receives various inputs, transforms these inputs in some way, and exports outputs. Figure 1.1 provides an example of the model for an organisation; it converts human activity, energy, information resources and components of raw materials into products and services, usable information, by-products and waste.

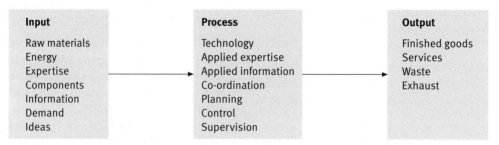

Figure 1.1 An organisational system

System boundaries. Systems have boundaries which separate them from their environment. The same is true of subsystems which interact with other subsystems without losing their identity as they maintain their boundaries.

Entropy and equilibrium. Closed systems have a tendency towards disorder and collapse due to a lack of resources and interaction with the environment. Open systems tend more towards a level of greater elaboration and differentiation, eventually reaching a steady state or equilibrium with the environment.

Feedback/'feedback loop'. The concept of feedback is essential in understanding how a system maintains a steady state. Information concerning the outputs or the process of the system is fed back as an input into the system, perhaps leading to changes in the transformation process and/or future outputs.

Social action

In general terms, the systems approach has been criticised for failure to examine the attitudes and views or orientation of individual members to the organisation, the different expectations people have of, and reactions to work, union organisation and management or ways in which the environment influences these expectations. The social action approach considers the organisation from the position of the individual members or actors who will each have their own goals, and interpretation of their work situation in terms of satisfaction sought and the meaning that work has for them. The goals of the individual and the means selected and actions taken to achieve these goals are affected by the individual's perception and definition of the situation and this also provides a basis for explaining behaviour. The action approach also regards conflicts of interests as normal behaviour and part of organisational life and is best understood as 'a method of analysing social relations within organisations' (Silverman, 1970, p. 147). An example of a social action perspective applied to industrial relations is Fox's unitary/pluralist approach considered above.

Subsequent contributions to the debate concerning social systems and action approaches argue that the two may actually complement each other (Bowey, 1976) and that it is possible to redefine certain concepts borrowed from systems theory so that they are congruent with an action approach. Bowey identifies four such concepts:

Role. The concept of role explains the similar action(s) of different people in similar situations within the organisation and the expectations held by other people. For example, it is useful to explain the role of the shop steward in these terms.

Relationships. This concept focuses on the patterns of interaction among people and the behaviours displayed towards one another. An example of this is the interaction of the two parties in a collective bargaining and negotiation situation.

Structure. The relationships and interactions between members of an organisation give rise to temporary and transitory social and behavioural structures. In an employment relations context, these social interactions occur in relation to non-social factors such as employee reactions to changes in payment systems, methods of production and the role of the union.

Process. Employee behaviour can be analysed in terms of processes or interdependent sequences of action.

The industrial relations subsystem

John Dunlop was the first academic to apply systems thinking to industrial relations in his book *Industrial Relations Systems* (1958). Dunlop's contribution is highly significant as he was the first to argue that systems theory provided the analytical and theoretical basis to make industrial relations an academic discipline in its own right. Although the approach can be generalised to all national industrial relations systems, it was more applicable without adaptation to the US industrial relations system of the 1950s. Much of the systems terminology has become a familiar part of the language of employment relations.

Dunlop's general definition of an industrial relations system is:

> *An industrial relations system at any one time in its development is regarded as comprised of certain actors, certain contexts, an ideology which binds the industrial relations system together, and a body of rules created to govern the actors at the workplace and work community.* (p. 7)

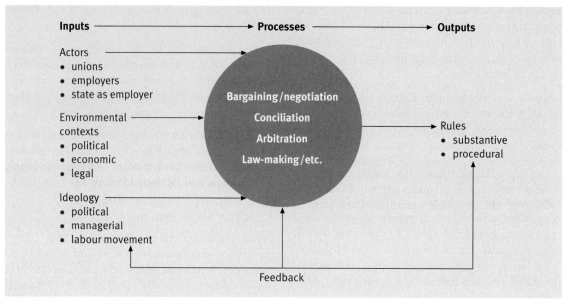

Figure 1.2 An industrial relations system
Source: Adapted from Dunlop, 1958

Figure 1.2 represents a simple model of an industrial relations system and we shall now look at its various components under the headings inputs, processes and outputs.

Inputs
There are three sets of independent variables here: the actors, environmental contexts and ideology:

1. **Actors.** The actors or active participants consist of:
   - managers and their representatives;
   - non-managerial employees and their representatives; and
   - specialised third-party agencies, governmental or private (such as ACAS).
2. **Environmental contexts.** These play an important part in shaping the rules of an industrial relations system (see below). Dunlop identifies three environmental contexts:
   - the technological characteristics of the workplace and the work community;
   - the market or budgetary constraints which affect the actors; and
   - the locus and distribution of power in the larger society.

3. **Ideology.** The ideology of an industrial relations system is the set of ideas or beliefs held by the actors which binds the system together. As Dunlop put it:

   > *The ideology of an industrial relations system is a body of common ideas that defines the role and place of each actor and that defines the ideas which each actor holds towards the place and function of the others in the system.* (p. 16)

   While each of the main sets of actors in an industrial relations system might have its own ideology, it is, according to Dunlop, more usual to have a common ideology and therefore a common set of ideas concerning important traditions within the system. For example, Dunlop cites the ideology of legal abstentionism (the absence of direct government statutory intervention) as being the one traditionally accepted by the parties within the British system of industrial relations.

Processes
This simply relates to how the various inputs affect and influence industrial relations processes within an industrial relations system. Examples of major processes are provided in Figure 1.2.

Outputs

Every industrial relations system, such as the British system, has a network of rules which are the outputs of the system. These rules consist of:

- procedures for establishing the rules;
- the substantive rules themselves; and
- the procedures for deciding their application to particular situations, which are the products of the system.

Dunlop contends that, 'The establishment and administration of these rules is the major concern or output of the industrial relations subsystem of industrial society' (p. 13). These rules, of which there are various kinds, may be written, oral or custom and practice and include:

- managerial decisions;
- trade union regulations;
- laws of the state;
- awards by government agencies;
- collective agreements; and
- workplace traditions.

Having considered the main concepts described by Dunlop in his systems theory of industrial relations, we now turn to some basic criticisms of it. These criticisms do not invalidate systems theory which has had a major impact on industrial relations theorising and research since the 1960s. However, they do highlight the limitations of the theory.

Some criticisms of Dunlop's systems theory

These criticisms are made by both supporters of systems theory on the one hand, and by those who reject, on an ideological basis, systems theory altogether. The supporters argue that Dunlop's theory:

- is not analytical enough;
- has a static view of industrial relations since Dunlop has omitted to provide a framework for analysing sufficiently the processes or dynamics of industrial relations decision-making; and
- does not give sufficient weight to:
  - influencing action and the actors' definition of industrial relations: the social action approach provides a corrective to this;
  - its notion of a unifying ideology; and
  - the difficulties in analysing change and conflict.

The 'rejectionists' consider systems theory as being, like pluralist theory, too concerned with defending the political and economic status quo. For them, the relevance of pluralism and systems thinking is that:

> *It provides a plausible explanation of reality in that it recognises conflicts which are visibly apparent yet it is as protective of the status quo, and as unquestioning about existing relationships, as the purely static unitary approach.* (Farnham and Pimlott, 1995, p. 52)

Validity of the systems approach

Those such as Clegg (1979) who advocated collective bargaining in the liberal collectivist tradition have also been closely associated with Dunlop's ideas and framework. Free collective bargaining is advocated on the grounds that it satisfactorily resolves conflicts at work and removes economic/industrial relations conflicts from the political arena. These assumptions appeared valid during the post-war period until the 1970s, and it was argued by its supporters that collective bargaining within the industrial relations system 'provided a stable, self-adjusting system of conflict resolution buttressed by the ideological support of different groups' (Gospel and Palmer, 1993, p. 19).

During the 1980s and 1990s, however, collective bargaining was increasingly undermined as a result of government policy, and the systems-based assumptions that industrial relations can be largely divorced from the wider political system, or that there is consensus support for collective bargaining, became much more suspect and less valid.

Corporatist perspectives

Both liberal collectivist and systems approaches do not see industrial relations being influenced very much by the state and the political system. This is not true of corporatist perspectives which emphasise active state intervention in industrial relations together with the involvement of government, employer representatives (such as the CBI) and employee representatives (such as the TUC) in tripartite decision-making at national level and often in the 'national interest'.

The case for corporatism
During the late 1960s and 1970s, Britain adopted some aspects of corporatism on the following grounds:

- that the influence and power of interest groups (trade unions, employers) had grown so much during the post-war years as to be disruptive in terms of strikes and wage inflationary pressures;
- that because of this the state had to take the responsibility of intervening to regulate the activities of these powerful groups and to harness their potential for the national economic good; and
- that this would, in turn, lead to the control of wage and price inflation and to the encouragement of economic efficiency.

There are three main assumptions which support the case for corporatism. These are:

1. That there are two dominant interests in society: capital and labour.
2. That there is sufficient equality of power between capital and labour to prevent the state from 'favouring' one group over another.
3. That the state must therefore take an 'umpire' role of neutrality in relation to capital and labour.

Corporatism was an influential perspective upon industrial relations in Britain up to 1979. Both the Conservative and Labour Parties endorsed corporatist policies and the TUC and CBI advocated forms of corporatist state intervention. It was a Conservative government, for example, which established the National Economic Development Office (NEDO) in 1961. NEDO was a tripartite body, comprising government, TUC and CBI representatives, which periodically discussed matters of economic and industrial policy.

The case against corporatism
Many critics of the corporatist perspectives believe that the interests of capital and labour are based on real or perceived inequalities of power and that the state will intervene either to bolster the power of capital or to support labour in order to redress the power imbalance. According to the critics the state can never be neutral as far as industrial relations is concerned. A change of government in 1979 with the election of Mrs Thatcher resulted in the rapid decline of corporatism as the more fundamentalist

doctrine of liberal individualism became dominant. Before examining this doctrine, attempt the activity below.

Self-Evaluation Activity 1.11
Can the state be neutral?
Response on website

By reference to the theoretical perspectives outlined in the text, do you think that the state is always neutral in industrial relations?

Summary points

- Liberal collectivism assumes that the role of government in industrial relations is relatively limited while endorsing the view that the collective regulation of the employment relationship is desirable but best left to the parties directly involved in the relationship, with collective bargaining as the main method for resolving conflicts of interest.
- Systems theory provides a framework for analysing the component parts (or subsystems) of a particular social system (such as the industrial relations system) and the extent to which they interact with each other. Open systems approaches adopt an input-process/transformation-output model.
- Social action approaches are critical of systems theory for neglecting the attitudes, orientations and role of individuals (actors) within an organisational context, and attempt to rectify this.
- Dunlop's industrial relations systems approach is useful in identifying the contribution of the 'parts' to the industrial relations system, but suffers the same limitations as general systems theory.
- Corporatist perspectives focus upon the active role of the state, involving the TUC and CBI in decision-making at national level.

Perspectives of the 1980s, 1990s and 2000s

Here we shall briefly look at two major perspectives which have dominated British employment relations during the 1980s, 1990s and 2000s together with one other which has gained some currency during this period. These are:

- liberal individualism and neo-laissez-faire;
- human resource management; and
- postmodernism.

The advent of the Conservative governments of the 1980s and 1990s heralded an era of liberal or laissez-faire individualism more reminiscent of the early nineteenth century but adapted to late twentieth-century conditions. The characteristics of liberal individualism are:

- that economic conflicts of interest should be freely entered into by individual employees and employers operating in competitive markets;
- that in order to ensure the greatest benefit for all, individual workers should bargain with individual employers over the contract of employment and any conflicts arising between them at that stage should be resolved;
- that once agreeing the employment contract, the employment relationship should be entirely free of conflict and the employee should accept the authority of the firm in the best interests of all (this is part of a unitary perspective as described earlier in this chapter);
- that any combination by trade unions or employers' associations to influence the terms of the employment contract was to be deplored because this would upset competitive market forces which determine a fair price for labour and ensure the greatest efficiency in terms of production and allocation of resources; and
- that it is best for individuals, in a free society, to take responsibility for their own actions and not to rely on others such as trade unions and the state.

In this context, the term liberal is used to mean a society of individuals who are capable, without state and other interference, of pursuing their best interests by freely entering into contracts with others. The term individualist is used to mean that the state follows a laissez-faire doctrine and that the individual is paramount: pressure groups, monopolies and other combinations are to be deplored. Mrs Thatcher's famous (or infamous) statement

that 'there is no such thing as society' encapsulates this doctrine.

Relevance of liberal individualism to the 1980s and 1990s

Gospel and Palmer (1993) argue that:

The economic and ideological shifts which led to the election of President Reagan in the US and of Mrs Thatcher in the UK, both relying on neo-laissez-faire economic policies, brought new life to this perspective. In Britain the change in direction was striking. The industrial relations policy of the Conservative governments after 1979 displayed a suspicion and distrust of trade unionism often expressed in liberal individualist terms by questioning the process of collective bargaining. (p. 25)

Contemporary liberal individualism is characterised by:

- non-intervention by the state in private sector collective bargaining where market forces should dominate;
- no unnecessary intervention in the labour market which would hinder labour flexibility and efficiency;
- deregulation of labour markets by doing away with legal and other restrictions;
- privatisation of many public sector industries thereby 'liberating' them from state control and exposing them to market forces; and
- 'contracting out' local authority services to private companies.

No longer were trade unions seen as 'joint managers' with government of the industrial and economic system, but rather a barrier to the achievement of government objectives and therefore needing to be curtailed through legislation progressively reducing union rights and power. All these aspects will be considered in more detail in Chapter 4. The swing of the ideological pendulum also led to a revival of unitarist type ideas amongst employers and an increased emphasis upon individual relations within industry. These ideas have been put into practice as a result of the application of 'human resource management' techniques which we shall now consider.

Human resource management

As we shall see in Chapter 2, human resource management (HRM) became increasingly practised in Britain during the 1980s, and the growth in the uptake of HRM has coincided with a steady decline in the importance of industrial relations and collectivism as significant features in the management of the employment relationship. It also coincided with a decline in the membership and influence of trade unions. HRM has been applied to a diverse range of management practices and strategies and the term is often used by many managements as a more acceptable substitute for personnel or industrial relations management. The importance of HRM for our understanding of industrial relations and industrial relations change 'lies in its association with a strategic, integrated and highly distinctive managerial approach to the management of people' (Salamon, 1998, p. 19).

Storey (1995), along with others, makes a distinction between 'hard' and 'soft' versions of HRM:

- 'hard' HRM focuses on human resource strategy and employee utilisation; and
- 'soft' HRM focuses on the 'human' aspects of management and concern with people in organisations.

Both these versions are more fully discussed in Chapters 2 and 5. We should stress at this stage, however, that HRM approaches emphasise the individual rather than the collective regulation of the employment relationship and the direct relationship between management and its employees.

HRM therefore questions the collective regulation basis of traditional industrial relations and it could be argued that an important part of the HRM approach is that negotiations with trade unions and other collective industrial relations activities are to be avoided, removed or at least minimised. A central question stemming from this, which we shall consider in Chapter 5, is whether HRM equates to a non-union 'individualistic' model of industrial relations or whether there can be a form of complementary 'dualism' within the organisation where HRM co-exists with industrial relations (Boxall and Purcell, 2003).

Self-Evaluation Activity 1.12

Filling in the gaps
Response on website

In Figure 1.3 you will find a summary of the views or *value judgements* associated with each major theoretical perspective which we have considered omitted. Your task, either individually or within a small group, is to fill in the gaps under and across each heading. You will notice that the pluralist perspective does not appear in this table; this is because many pluralist assumptions are made in relation to the liberal collectivist and corporatist perspectives.

Postmodernism

The concept of postmodernity is a valuable 'problematic' that alerts us to key questions

Likely judgement on	Unitarist	Liberal collectivist	Corporatist	Liberal individualist	Radical
Conflict					
Co-operation					
Management role					
Trade union role					
The state's role					

Figure 1.3 Views associated with different perspectives

concerning contemporary social changes. I see it as a concept that invites participation in a debate over the nature and direction of present-day societies, in a globalised context, rather than one describing an already existing state of affairs. Quite unprecedented social and cultural shifts are occurring; whether or not 'postmodernity' is the best term to sum them up is a moot point. The important thing is to understand what is happening, not to agree on a concept to capture it with. 'Postmodernity' will do fine for now.
(Lyon, 1995, p. 85)

'Postmodernism' embraces the notion that advanced capitalist societies are experiencing monumental and significant changes, and movements away from the previous 'modernist' era. In order to understand the nature of postmodernism it is important to turn briefly to 'modernist' assumptions.

The nature of modernism

The modernist era has its roots in the Enlightenment of the seventeenth century and the philosophical belief that human beings are not only capable of achieving a rational understanding of social reality but can also use their understanding to create a more rational and fair society. Modernist thinking is both optimistic about the 'human condition' and rationalistic in the process of knowledge accumulation. A rational understanding of society can only be achieved by deriving knowledge based on deductive reasoning. Deductive reasoning (also known as 'positivism') involves the construction of general and universal laws or theories, the validity of which is confirmed or invalidated by observation and experimentation. The positivist approach therefore entails the generation of assumptions or hypotheses which are capable of being empirically tested by the use of scientific method. Hypotheses can be either confirmed or falsified and theories altered as a result. Positivism became the most influential method of accumulating knowledge and dominated the social and natural sciences during the course of the twentieth century. All of the theories attempting to explain industrial and employment relations (with the exception of some elements of 'social action' approaches) are based on positivist/modernist assumptions. Legge (1995) identifies some of the

institutions of modernity which we summarise below.

Industrialism is characterised by 'the social organisation of production [and] by a division of labour within a factory system, urbanisation and the geographical concentration of industry and population and changes in occupational structure . . . it is imbued with the spirit of scientific rationalism and is the engine of material progress via the technical and social innovation associated with economic growth' (p. 291).

Capitalism, while assuming different forms, is essentially defined as the system of private ownership and control of the means of production, directing economic activity towards making profits within a market framework and is subject to a Marxist analysis (see above).

The nation state (see Chapter 4).

Fordism refers to the system of mass production and assembly-line technology which developed during the early twentieth century within an organisational context based on rational principles of management – such as 'scientific management' (see Chapters 2 and 5).

Old, adversarial industrial relations usually associated with the period prior to 1980.

The nature of postmodernism

The postmodernist critique of the academic foundation of modernism is persuasive and comprehensive but, as we shall see in connection with industrial relations, seriously flawed. For Lyotard (1992) knowledge in the modernist era meant science, and science, with its universal laws/theories needed to be justified in terms of a 'grand story' or metanarrative. The modernist justification for science – that science would lead to human emancipation – has been questioned and undermined. As no metanarrative can be 'objectively' proved or rejected, it is necessary to be sceptical of all metanarratives. While the importance of knowledge is recognised, the postmodern view is that knowledge is fragmented and can be reduced to a series of 'language games' where truth and falsity are relative, and relatively meaningless. Moreover, in view of the fact that there are no indisputable foundations to knowledge or firm bases to meaning, it is extremely arrogant of us to put forward general theories which pretend to reveal *the* truth or *the* meaning of things. We need to abandon attempts to produce theories which seek to depict the structure and dynamics of society as a whole and tolerate the co-existence of a diversity of more limited theories: knowledge is therefore relative rather than universal.

Postmodernism also conceptualises certain fundamental changes affecting western societies in particular. The most important are summarised as follows:

- The transition from industrialism to post-industrialism (Bell, 1973; Touraine, 1974; Castells, 1989). Bell, for example, argues that the general direction of change in western societies is towards a service economy where the majority of people are employed within the service sector which is driven by the dynamic forces of knowledge and information; the generation of knowledge and the processing of information stimulate economic growth. 'Knowledge work' therefore becomes more important than manufacturing goods and manual work.

- The change from Fordist to post-Fordist production methods (explored in more detail in Chapter 5) meant that 'the giant mass production plant, with its standardised products, dedicated equipment, narrow job descriptions and semi-skilled workers is said to be giving way to a quite different type of workplace – smaller in size, with small runs of customised products manufactured by a multi-skilled and "flexible" workforce' (Kelly, 1998, p. 113).

- The change towards a consumer society also reflects the declining importance of the workplace in the economy. Lyon (1995) contends that:

> Most sociology (and of course, industrial relations) has chosen to pursue questions of capitalism as productive (and class) relations involving labourers, managers and so on. Today's postmodern challenge returns the spotlight to the ideals, values and symbols of economic life as they appear in the lives of consumers and in consumerism. Taste and style, far from being marginal reflexes of production, are now viewed as centrally significant. (p. 74)

- Postmodernism revels in fragmentation, ephemerality and discontinuity, preferring difference over uniformity. This contrasts with modernism which emphasises uniformity, continuity and wholeness. Modern mass technologies of communication facilitate a great expansion of service and leisure industries and for 'mushrooming simulations of reality' (Lyon, 1995).

- In the postmodernist context high-brow authority over cultural taste collapses, and the distinction between high and mass culture is replaced by 'popular culture' and the juxtaposition of, for example, musical styles with radio programmes mixing folk, rock and classical music, loosening the boundaries between them. The term 'popular music' is beset by recurrent waves of nostalgia and 'retro' and belies the continuing process of fragmentation into rock, ambient and dance, and differentiation within them. Dance music, for example, is further fragmented into 'house', 'rave', 'techno', 'jungle' and 'hip-hop' (to name but a few).

- There is a growing emphasis in postmodernist thinking on looking for 'local' factors or partial explanations such as the micro-politics of power relations in different social contexts. This would emphasise, for example, multi-issue community politics and local pressure group campaigning.

- The transition to postmodernism implies the decline of class-based politics and the traditional party political system and the increasing importance of 'new' social movements such as peace campaigners and environmentalists.

Implications of postmodernism for employment/industrial relations

We have noted that the societal transformations identified above are relatively profound and comprehensive, directly affecting the economy, politics, work, consumption and culture. Industrial relations, according to postmodern analysis, is affected in a number of ways and the outlook is extremely pessimistic. Kelly (1998), for example, argues that a postmodern perspective suggests that industrial disputes are likely to diminish with the move away from Fordism, with an increasing emphasis upon work which is flexible (see below), more skilled and challenging. Conflicts of interest will decline 'as there will be fewer issues that divide workers and employers and provide the fuel for conflict and more interests in common as employers come to value the contribution of a skilled and committed workforce' (p. 116). As a result of the permanent decline in conflict, employees will find union membership increasingly irrelevant, prompting a further decline in union membership reinforced by changes in the composition of the workforce away from those traditionally well-organised groups (full-time male manual workers) and towards groups that have proved historically to be difficult to organise and sometimes unreceptive to trade unionism (part-timers, women, non-manuals, service workers). As a movement, the trade unions will no longer represent a 'distinct working class constituency based in Fordist industry'; the 'working class' will become increasingly fragmented and this will make it difficult for the union movement to represent these disintegrated interests and 'its role as a political actor is therefore likely to diminish'. Postmodern analysis therefore suggests that the trade union movement is in terminal decline. In addition, it has been suggested that the term 'employee relations' and the 'individualistic' preoccupation of HRM are both part of a postmodernist project (Nichols, 2002).

However, the criticisms of the postmodern account of union and labour movement decline made by Kelly and others are arguably more coherent than postmodern theory itself. The postmodern prognosis can be largely discounted in favour of more convincing analyses such as mobilisation theory. Kelly (1998) summarises the critique in the following way:

> What we have been offered [by postmodernism] is an untenable philosophical relativism; an incoherent attack on meta-narratives; a view of the decline of mass production that does not accord with the evidence; ideas about consumption and production that lose sight of the intimate links between the two; a vision of the manufacturing workplace of the future that sounds more like a unitarist fantasy than a well-grounded depiction and which is practically silent on the new-found power of the employer; . . . claims about the decline of the labour movement that take no account of historical precedents; and assertions about 'new social movements' and the end of

class politics based on superficial and incoherent categories and on sloppy use of evidence. There are so many holes in the postmodernist case that there is genuine puzzle as to why it was ever taken so seriously. Its prognosis for the labour movement is not only bleak (that at least would be a legitimate point of view), but is ill-informed in the extreme. (p. 125)

In conclusion, the postmodernist prognosis provides a justification for those who argue that industrial relations as a collective phenomenon is in terminal decline.

Summary points

- Liberal individualism, adopted by the Conservative governments from 1980 to 1997 emphasises, within the employment relations context, the primacy of market forces together with a rejection of collective regulation of the employment relationship. Government intervention is minimal, except where required to restore the balance of market forces, and this provides the justification for employment relations legislation.
- HRM approaches complement liberal individualism with its emphasis upon the individualisation of the employment relationship.
- Postmodernist perspectives criticise both the 'grand theories' associated with modernism and Fordist systems of production and, within the industrial relations context, underline the fragmentation of the employment relationship and the flexibilisation of labour.

THE ECONOMIC CONTEXT OF INDUSTRIAL RELATIONS

The economic context comprises the most important set of influences upon employment relations. First, we shall consider national economic management which includes both Keynesian and monetarist economic policy and their impact upon industrial relations during the post-war period. We shall then look at the British labour market and how changes in the labour market have caused problems for employment/industrial relations, particularly in the 1990s and early 2000s.

NATIONAL ECONOMIC MANAGEMENT

Economic management may be defined as the **policies and action which governments take in order to influence economic performance**. For our purposes, the post-war period can be divided into two periods. During the first period, from 1945 until the mid-1970s, economic management was dominated by Keynesian economic policy, while the latter period, from the mid-1970s to the mid-1990s was characterised by monetarist economic policy which in turn gave way to a hybrid policy under New Labour which was neither monetarist nor Keynesian. Both types of policy have implications for almost every aspect of British industrial relations.

Keynesian economic policy

Keynesian economic policy is based upon the seminal work of John Maynard Keynes (1936) and is often referred to as Keynesianism. In basic terms, Keynes argued that:

- levels of unemployment are determined by the total demand for goods and services within the economy – what economists call *aggregate demand*;
- during periods of high unemployment, aggregate demand should be stimulated by government;
- government can stimulate aggregate demand by increasing government expenditure within the public sector by, for example, spending on road construction and other 'public works';
- this will create extra employment and thereby increase individual spending power;
- this, in turn (other things being equal), will increase aggregate demand for goods produced in the private sector;
- as a result of this, firms within the private sector will take on more labour, thereby increasing spending power and aggregate demand once again; and
- this process is then repeated throughout the economy and in this way unemployment is reduced.

Keynes also argued that changes in levels of aggregate demand can only be achieved by government intervention through the operation of fiscal policy. The objectives of Keynesian fiscal policy are:

- full employment;
- incomes policy;
- price stability;
- balance of payments equilibrium; and
- economic growth.

We consider two of these objectives (full employment and price stability) in more detail as they impact directly upon industrial relations.

Full employment

One major Keynesian policy aim is to achieve a level of aggregate demand which is compatible with full employment. This means that should unemployment rise the government can 'inject' spending power into the economy by cutting taxes and/or increasing public expenditure. This will, as we have seen above, increase aggregate demand and lead to a higher demand for labour by employers, thereby reducing unemployment. Full employment has a number of industrial relations consequences, not all of them necessarily beneficial. These include:

- increased collective bargaining power of trade unions within the labour market;
- increases in wages which may or may not be accompanied by increased labour productivity or decline in unit labour costs;
- the start of a 'wage-price spiral' where employers seek to offset pay increases by increasing the price of their goods and services;
- trade union negotiators in the public sector taking note of 'benchmark' pay increases in the private sector and attempting to secure pay increases comparable to those in the private sector; and
- if pay increases are conceded in the public sector, the increases are funded by government (as the government is the employer) through increased taxes or the public sector borrowing requirement (PSBR).

Self-Evaluation Activity 1.13

The downside of maintaining full employment
The response is given below

It was stated above that not all of the consequences of maintaining full employment as a government policy objective are beneficial. Which of the above consequences are not beneficial to either the employee, the employer or to the government?

Increased bargaining power is beneficial to the employee as it can result in increased pay. In the private sector the employer will have to foot the bill for increased wages, and if this cannot be paid for by improved labour productivity or increases in sales, then the employer will have to increase prices of goods and services. This is not a good situation for the employer and eventually the employer may have to shed labour in order to maintain competitiveness. If the employer resorts to labour shedding, then some employees will also suffer.

A 'wage-price spiral' is inflationary or potentially so. If a high proportion of private sector employers have to make some of their employees redundant, then this can result in an increase in aggregate unemployment and, for the government, this would be detrimental to maintaining the full employment objective.

In the public sector pressures to increase wages of public sector employees in line with the increases within the private sector could lead to government increasing taxes to fund the pay bill. In the medium term this cannot be beneficial either to the government, as tax increases are politically unpopular, or to the individual taxpayer. The other government option to fund the wage bill is to increase public borrowing, but this is also potentially inflationary, especially if it involves increasing the supply of money in the economy.

As a result of the possible disbenefits we have outlined to employee, employer and to the government itself, the government will need to be very careful in its Keynesian management of demand. If there is inflationary pressure, then the government will have to deflate the economy through fiscal measures such as:

- reducing purchasing power through raising taxes; and
- reducing purchasing power through reductions in public spending.

On the other hand, if the economy is sluggish, it may need to be stimulated by reflating the economy. Reflation may lead to:

- increased government spending;
- revived economic growth;
- rising wages and prices; and eventually to
- renewed attempts by government to deflate the economy to ensure price stability.

Keynesian economic policy, in order to maintain the full employment policy objective, is geared towards balancing inflationary and deflationary pressures by adopting deflationary measures when the economy is 'speeding up', and reflationary measures when the economy is slowing down. This type of policy is also known as the 'stop-go' economic cycle.

Incomes policy

Incomes policy, considered in greater detail in Chapter 4, is a broadly Keynesian measure whereby the government attempts to control wage inflation by intervening in the collective bargaining process between employers and trade unions. Governments have used four types of incomes policy during the post-war period. These are:

- the pay freeze;
- the statutory norm;
- the voluntary norm; and
- pay review bodies.

We now briefly consider each of these types of incomes policy.

The pay freeze
This is where, for relatively short periods, the government passes legislation which effectively prevents employers and employees implementing pay settlements during the period specified by the legislation. The aim here is to halt the rate of increase in pay.

The statutory norm
After the period of the pay freeze, the government may impose a statutory pay norm in the form of a 'pay ceiling' which allows for very small overall increases in pay. The aim here is to reinforce the pay freeze by limiting pay increases: again, this is an anti-inflationary measure. The pay freeze and statutory pay norm were measures introduced by Labour governments during the 1960s with varying degrees of success.

The voluntary norm
This is where government specifies maximum permissible pay increases either across the board

nationally (as with the pay freeze and the statutory norm) or within a particular sector of the economy such as the public sector. The voluntary norm, as the term suggests, has no legal force and employers and employees need not comply with it. Private sector firms usually only pay lip-service to it. But in areas where government can exert direct control over wage levels, as amongst public sector employees, the policy can be quite effective.

Pay review bodies

Pay review bodies were set up during the 1980s as a means of determining pay levels. The bodies cover certain groups of public servants such as the armed forces, doctors, dentists, senior civil servants and teachers. They make recommendations to government about pay levels for each of these groups on an annual basis, although the government is not obliged to accept them. This method of pay determination circumvents collective bargaining although union evidence may be taken into consideration.

In the short term, incomes policies can be effective in reducing the rate of wage inflation. Over the longer term, however, the benefits of incomes policy are not so evident as employees and unions seek to 'catch up' on lost ground during the post-statutory pay period. For a discussion of the advantages and disadvantages of incomes policy, see Chapter 4.

Monetarist economic policy

As we have seen, the period from 1979 witnessed the introduction of liberal individualism with a change of government. Liberal collectivism declined as the 'enterprise culture' grew and market mechanisms and market forces would henceforth determine supply and demand for goods and labour, economic prosperity and the level of employment.

The central task of government was to control the supply of money and its rate of increase and to reduce central government expenditure. Keynesianism had become associated with interventionism and corporatism, with its concentration on the 'demand side' of the economy. Monetarism was concerned with the 'supply side' and dominated economic management from 1979 until 1997.

The monetarist argument

Monetarists such as Milton Friedman (1991) have argued that if the monetary system is well regulated, then the rest of the economy could be left to 'self-regulating' market forces and economic prosperity would follow, but only as long as measures were taken to ensure that the supply side of the economy worked more efficiently. Friedman and others have identified inflation as being the main economic problem of governments during the 1970s, while Keynesian economists as we have seen, identify unemployment as one of the major problems. Monetarists argue that:

- the causes of inflation lie in historically high levels of government expenditure which lead to a rapid growth in the supply of money circulating in the economy;
- if the amount of money expands more rapidly than the growth in the production of goods and services, then inflation will result;
- a major cause of excessive monetary growth is government borrowing, or the PSBR being used to finance budget deficits;
- if inflation is to be controlled, then government must control its public expenditure and balance its budget, or at least reduce its budget deficit; and
- incomes policies and similar policies aimed at getting the agreement of trade unions to reduce their wage demands and so achieve lower unemployment do not work because government expansion of the money supply is a cause of inflation and trade unions naturally react to this by increasing their wage demands in the longer term.

Monetarist and supply-side measures

The main objective of monetarist and supply-side policies is derived from the arguments set out above, and is to create and develop the economic conditions which are necessary to achieve rapid growth, low inflation and full employment. The measures taken by the Conservative governments during the 1980s and 1990s to achieve this objective involved increasing aggregate supply to match demand without creating inflation, and included:

- reducing levels of personal and corporate taxation to create incentives for individuals to work and corporations to invest;
- placing public sector industries into private ownership (privatisation); and
- enacting legislation to control and restrict trade union bargaining power within the labour market.

These and other measures and how they impact upon industrial relations are considered in greater detail in Chapters 4 and 5. It is sufficient to state here that as far as industrial relations is concerned, monetarist and supply-side policies have resulted in a 'market-led' situation where trade unions and individual employees have lost a great deal of traditional collective influence over managerial decision-making concerning the employment relationship.

During the 1990s, the Conservative government of John Major pursued a more pragmatic economic policy which consisted of a revised form of monetarism, often called neo-monetarism, and a revised version of Keynesian policy usually termed neo-Keynesianism. With the onset of worldwide recession during the early 1990s the government pursued neither full-blooded Keynesian demand management nor rigid monetarism. However, privatisation and labour market deregulation measures continued, albeit at a more leisurely pace than before.

Self-Evaluation Activity 1.14

Summarising monetarism and Keynesianism
Response on website

We have looked briefly at monetarist and Keynesian policies. From what you have learnt so far, produce a list of contrasting policy statements which summarise the two approaches and compare your statements with those in the figure on the website which summarises a selection of Keynesian and monetarist policy statements.

THE BRITISH LABOUR MARKET

We will now identify the main features of the labour market insofar as they influence industrial relations institutions and practices. It is important to note at the outset that the labour market influences a whole range of activities and institutions related to industrial relations. These include:

- working practices;
- personnel management;
- collective bargaining;
- wage levels and structures;
- terms and conditions of employment; and
- recruitment, selection and retention policies of employers.

On the other hand, the labour market itself is affected by:

- the general level of economic activity;
- changes in the level of unemployment;
- technological change;
- the birth rate;
- the number of people willing to work and seeking work; and
- the output of educational and training establishments.

The changing structure of the labour market

The labour force comprises all those aged 16 and over in civilian jobs who are either in work or seeking work. In 1991 there were 25.6 million people in work and 2.4 million unemployed and in 2002 there were around 27.8 million workers. Labour force projections for the period 1998–2011 suggest that the labour force will increase slowly, reaching 29.8 million by spring 2011 (LMT, 1999). Women are projected to make up 46.1 per cent of the total labour force in 2011 compared with 45.9 per cent in 2002. The gender composition of the labour force has changed during the post-war period. While the number of men in employment has been fairly stable on average, the number of women in employment has increased year on year as Table 1.1 indicates. There has also been an overall shift from full-time employment to part-time employment, this trend being much more marked with women than with men. In 2002, 78.7 per cent of all people of working age who worked part-time were women, and around 43.6 per cent of women in employment worked part-time, up from 42 per cent in 1988. The

Table 1.1 Women and men in employment in the UK: 1988–2002

	Thousands			Change %
	1988	1993	2002	1988–2002
Women 16–59				
In employment	10 613	10 958	12 793	17.0
Full-time	6 159	6 245	7 214	14.6
Part-time	4 434	4 711	5 580	20.5
Men 16–64				
In employment	14 561	13 780	15 019	3.1
Full-time	13 856	12 910	13 510	–2.6
Part-time	675	867	1 509	44.7

Source: LMT, 1999, 2003

proportion of men working part-time is extremely small, but rose from 5 per cent in 1988 to 10 per cent in 2002.

Other developments affecting the labour market concern industrial and occupational changes, the most significant of these being the steady decline in manufacturing and some extractive industries, and particularly within the 'traditional' industries such as engineering, shipbuilding, coal and textiles which provided long-term and fairly secure manual employment. On the other hand, the service sector of the economy has expanded. During the 1960s and 1970s there was considerable growth in white-collar employment within public sector services including education, health and government departments such as the Civil Service. Private sector services such as financial, insurance and leisure services have witnessed considerable growth during the past 25 years and newer industries associated with information technology have also contributed to employment growth. Nevertheless, employment in some of these services, such as leisure services, is increasingly of a part-time, short-term or subcontracting nature.

The dual labour market

The changes identified above have prompted considerable discussion concerning the state of the labour market in the 1990s. Watson (1995) and Fevre (1992) argue that the contemporary labour market is characterised by a dualism which on the one hand exposes workers to the vicissitudes of the laws of supply and demand and on the other protects workers from these competitive pressures. Watson defines dualism as:

The effective division of an economy into two parts: typically a prosperous and stable 'core' sector of enterprises and jobs and a peripheral sector which is relatively and systematically disadvantaged. (p. 185)

The first part is known as the primary sector and the second as the secondary sector. In the primary sector, work is characterised by:

- relatively good working conditions and pay levels;
- opportunities for advancement;
- fair treatment at work; and
- stability of employment.

In the secondary sector, workers are worse off in all the respects identified for the primary sector and their work is associated with considerable instability of employment, usually of a part-time nature, together with a high labour turnover rate. They tend to be people who:

- are easily dispensed with;
- possess clearly visible social differences;
- are little interested in training or gaining high economic reward; and
- tend not to organise themselves into trade unions.

Given these features and the social and cultural characteristics of the wider society, we tend to find recruitment to the secondary labour force drawing to a disproportionate extent on women, blacks, immigrants, unqualified teenagers, students seeking part-time work and disabled persons. Within the secondary sector such as cleaning services, hotels and catering, retail, non-teaching education and health services women and ethnic minorities tend to be over-represented. On the other hand, much of the increase in labour market participation over the last decade has been concentrated among women with higher qualifications and in professional and managerial occupations where women are traditionally under-represented (LMT, 2003).

A flexible labour market?

The notion of 'flexibility' in relation to the labour market is usually considered within the context of general changes in the technology of production, the product market, the labour process and the nature of the employment relationship as exemplified in the shift from Fordism to post-Fordism, and is part of the postmodern condition (see Chapter 5 for a more detailed discussion). Piore (1988) argues that flexibility and flexible specialisation allowed by the new technologies increases the skills needed by the workforce and, unlike industries where scientific management techniques are used, workers may actually co-operate with management in organising the labour process. According to this view, flexible specialisation may be regarded as a new form of skilled craft production made easily adaptable by programmable technology to provide specialist goods which can supply an increasingly fragmented and volatile market.

This optimistic view of flexibility is reinforced by Atkinson (1988), who argues that economic recessions, the weakening of trade union powers and technological changes have encouraged employers to make their firms more flexible, thereby securing

lower unit labour costs and increasing productivity. According to Atkinson, the 'flexible firm' comprises:

- **core** employees who are multi-skilled, employed full-time and have considerable job security; and
- **peripheral** employees drawn from the external labour market who are unskilled, many of whom work part-time, on short-term contracts, under temporary contracts or under 'welfare to work' schemes. These employees can be quickly called in and disposed of in response to market fluctuations. They can be regarded as 'labour on call', providing a 'buffer' stock of resources enabling the organisation to expand and contract 'organically'.

While Atkinson argues that peripheral workers are disadvantaged because of the nature of their employment, he nevertheless believes that core workers benefit from the trend towards flexibility in terms of greater variety of skills and greater opportunity to participate in decision-making. Some organisations, however, appear to go one stage further by employing the bulk of their workforce on a peripheral basis as the example in Exhibit 1.4 illustrates.

The McDonald's example is replicated throughout that part of the service sector of the economy where organisations require relatively unskilled labour of a temporary or seasonal nature in order to meet cyclical or daily fluctuations in demands for products or services. The trend towards 'McDonaldisation' has been accentuated by Conservative governments. Farnham and Pimlott (1995), for example, assert that:

> As pay is relatively low for both the peripheral and the temporary employees of the flexible firm, the importance of government measures aimed at freeing the lower end of the labour market, by reducing the value of the floor of social benefits and by the abolition of the wages councils, can be clearly seen. (p. 97)

The trend has undoubtedly been encouraged by the New Labour government's stated commitment to the flexible labour market. The balance of research evidence relating to the flexibility debate suggests that while organisations have made efforts to increase flexibility in numerical and/or functional

Exhibit 1.4

The example of McDonald's

McDonald's secret recipe for success comes not from the Big Mac sauce, but from a new production process, using a combination of the Fordist conveyor belt with a Japanese emphasis on flexibility.

Each store is a factory where workers' skills have been kept to a bare minimum. No chefs, no apprentices are wanted on this burger-line; everyone has been levelled down to the uniform 'crew member' rushing between stations to perform tasks learnt in a day. From Oxford Street to Manila, McDonald's workers follow identical steps to produce identical burgers.

Labour costs should never exceed 15% of an outlet's sales. 'It is very tight' said one manager. 'If sales are down, labour costs must come down. You have to cut the staff and make those remaining work harder.' Workers hired for busy sessions are later shown the door.

Such flexible working practices are as contagious on the high street as on the industrial estate. By employing part-timers, stores can cover unsocial hours without paying overtime, and adjust workers' hours on a weekly, or even daily basis as sales and staff numbers fluctuate. As one manager put it: 'We don't have full and part-timers here. Everyone at McDonald's works flexible hours.'

The new tribe of so-called 'peripheral workers' is becoming increasingly central to the economy. Today, one in four British workers are part-time and 90% of them are women.

Source: Adapted from Lamb and Perry, 1987

respects, these efforts do not often conform very closely to the model of the flexible firm (Pollert, 1988; Wood, 1989; Millward *et al.*, 1992; Claydon, 1994; Millward *et al.*, 2000). In particular, there is little evidence that core and periphery strategies are being systematically employed by organisations. Government policies aimed at increasing general labour market flexibility together with recession may encourage some organisations to cut costs by reducing standards of employment and taking advantage of workers' vulnerability to work intensification. While this may be presented within the context of the flexibility thesis, it is debatable whether such actions contribute to the long-term health of organisations or that of the economy.

Employment relations implications of labour market change: concluding comments

The labour market changes identified above have had a number of consequences for industrial relations

over the past 20 years, and some of these are summarised below:

1. The decline of long-established industries such as engineering, coal, docks and railways in terms of employment has led to an erosion of the importance of national, industry-wide collective bargaining and a decline in trade union membership. The growth in employment in newer sectors of British industry has been accompanied by a small but significant trend towards a 'new style' of collective bargaining and industrial relations, mainly in small to medium sized companies and plants. These new-style agreements are often, but not exclusively, focused upon greenfield sites which also attract inwardly investing companies. Within these companies, there tends to be greater emphasis upon the individual nature of the employment relationship, including employee involvement, single-status employment, job security, labour flexibility and direct employer–employee communication.

2. Within the public sector where employment has declined in recent years as a result of privatisations,

cost and efficiency drives and contracting out of services, trade unions are experiencing membership losses and an erosion of their collective bargaining power.

3. More generally, the changing nature of the labour market which governs the supply of and demand for labour, the peripheralisation of work within parts of the service economy and labour flexibility 'have greatly reduced the ability of trade unions to protect their members' jobs and conditions of work' (Farnham and Pimlott, 1995, p. 21).

4. Against the backdrop of post-industrialism and post-Fordism, together with the advent of the so-called 'information society', it could be argued that the nature and context of employment relations has changed considerably during the past 50 years or so.

So why read on? Employment relations continuity and change in an 'information society'

The label 'information society' is subject to unscientific and ambiguous interpretative controversy, and for this reason this term, together with that of 'globalisation', is rarely used in this book. Moreover, if there were enough space and scope for justificatory argument, the concept of 'information society' in particular could be debunked altogether. This is not to devalue the extent and pace of societal changes that have been taking place during the past 50 years or so and the consequences of these developments for work, non-work and other activities. It is often a matter of ideological and pedagogic convenience to attach labels such as 'post-industrial society' or 'information society' to describe changes in work, social relations and political economy, but to do so uncritically is to deny that these changes may provide excuses for legitimising and re-legitimatising the continued survival of capitalist society.

Indeed, some may argue whether there is any qualitative difference, apart from the product, in a workplace such as a factory, which mass produced goods ('industrial society') and a workplace such as a call centre, which mass produces services using deskilled labour (post-industrial/post-Fordist/information society). Employment relations, with its traditions of conflict and compromise, steeped in

the necessity of economic survival, job protection and security of past workforces, has much to offer present and future workforces, and should not, therefore, be regarded as part and parcel of this legitimising process. Rather, the domain of the subject should be seen within the context of a challenging, continuous and constructive critique both of the management of the employment relationship, and of those who maintain that 'old' collective industrial relations with its conflict imagery is a thing of the past and hence not relevant to the contemporary and future management of the human resource, and/or human capital in organisations and workplaces.

The truth of the matter is that, using 'exploitation' as an example, there are as many if not more instances of gross exploitation of workers in terms of pay, conditions of work, discrimination and unfair dismissal in the early twenty-first century as compared with the mid-twentieth century (albeit the nature of that exploitation is currently more covert and 'individualised' than in the past). It is for this reason, and others which will become apparent during the course of reading this book, that we seek to understand contemporary issues and challenges facing the parties to employment relations by tracing appropriate historical developments and antecedents. In the same vein, we may also argue that knowledge of relevant theoretical underpinnings will assist in the critical appreciation of contemporary issues affecting the employment relationship. For the same reason, we also focus upon the management of the employment relationship, identifying areas of good practice for managers in order to avoid the mismanagement of the workforce or 'human resource' – still so endemic in the 2000s – in areas such as dismissal, discrimination, redundancy and grievance.

The following chapters develop many of the issues identified in this chapter. As described in the introductory section of this book, the text adopts an approach based on the theme of continuity and change which includes historical and theoretical perspectives incorporating arguments relevant to the nature of individualism and collectivism within the employment relationship on the one hand, together with practical, policy-related issues concerning the appropriate management of the employment relationship on the other.

RELEVANT WEBSITES

www.cbi.org.uk (Confederation of British Industry) Not as useful as the TUC site for employment relations issues, although more comprehensive as not exclusively devoted to employment relations.

www.dti.gov.uk (Department of Trade and Industry) A comprehensive and informative website detailing government policy, legislation and statistics concerning many aspects of the employment relationship.

www.eiro.eurofound.ie (European Foundation for the Improvement of Living and Working Conditions) Comprehensive information, research and data relating to social and employment relations developments within the EU and specific member states.

www.ilo.org (The International Labour Organisation) International data dealing with employment relations issues.

www.statistics.gov.uk (Office for National Statistics) Access to a vast range of government statistics including *Labour Market Trends* and Labour Force Survey.

www.tuc.org.uk (Trades Union Congress) An impressive site which covers a comprehensive range of issues covering employment, TUC and government policy, information about membership and individual trade unions, press releases, publications and a special section for students.

REFERENCES

Atkinson, J. (1988) *Flexibility, Uncertainty and Manpower*. IMS Report No. 189. Brighton, Institute of Manpower Studies

Bain, G.S. and Clegg, H.A. (1974) 'Strategy for industrial relations research in Great Britain'. *British Journal of Industrial Relations*, 12, 1, 91–113

Beardwell, I.J. (1997) 'How do we know how it really is?: An analysis of the new industrial relations', in Beardwell, I.J. (ed.) *Contemporary Industrial Relations: A Critical Analysis*. Oxford, Oxford University Press

Bell, D. (1973) *The Coming of Post-Industrial Society*. New York, Basic Books

Bertalanffy, L. von (1951) 'Problems of general systems theory: A new approach to the unity of science'. *Human Biology*, 23, 4, 302–12

Blackburn, R.M. (1967) *Union Character and Social Class*. London, Batsford

Blyton, P. and Turnbull, P. (1994) *The Dynamics of Employee Relations*. London, Macmillan

Blyton, P. and Turnbull, P. (1998) *The Dynamics of Employee Relations*, 2nd edn. London, Macmillan

Bowey, A.M. (1976) *The Sociology of Organisations*. London, Hodder & Stoughton

Boxall, P. and Purcell, J. (2003) *Strategy and Human Resource Management*, Houndmills, Palgrave Macmillan

Bullock Committee of Inquiry (1977) *Report on Industrial Democracy*. London, HMSO

Castells, M. (1989) *The Informational City*. Oxford, Blackwell

Certification Office (2002) *Annual Report 2001–2002*. London, Certification Office

Claydon, T. (1994) 'Human resource management and the labour market', in Beardwell, I. and Holden, L. (eds) *Human Resource Management: A Contemporary Perspective*. London, Pitman

Clegg, H.A. (1979) *The Changing System of Industrial Relations in Great Britain*. Oxford, Blackwell

Cully, M., Woodland, S., O'Reilly, A. and Dix, G. (1999) *Britain at Work*. London, Routledge

Donovan (1968) *Report of the Royal Commission on Trade Unions and Employers' Associations 1965–1968*, Cmnd 3623. London, HMSO

Dunlop, T. (1958) *Industrial Relations Systems*. New York, Holt

Edwards, P. (1995) 'The employment relationship', in Edwards, P. (ed.) *Industrial Relations: Theory and Practice in Britain*. Oxford, Blackwell

Edwards, P. (2003) 'The employment relationship and the field of industrial relations', in Edwards, P. *Industrial Relations Theory and Practice*, 2nd edn. Oxford, Blackwell

Farnham, D. (1997) *Employee Relations in Context*. London, IPD

Farnham, D. (2000) *Employee Relations in Context*, 2nd edn. London, IPD

Farnham, D. and Pimlott, J. (1995) *Understanding Industrial Relations*. London, Cassell

Fevre, R. (1992) *The Sociology of Labour Markets*. Hemel Hempstead, Harvester Wheatsheaf

Flanders, A. (1965) *Industrial Relations: What is Wrong with the System?* London, Faber

Fox, A. (1966) *Industrial Sociology and Industrial Relations.* Royal Commission Research Paper No. 3. London, HMSO

Friedman, M. (1991) *Monetarist Economics.* Oxford, Blackwell

Gennard, J. and Judge, G. (1997) *Employee Relations.* London, IPD

Gennard, J. and Judge, G. (2002) *Employee Relations*, 3rd edn. London, CIPD

Gospel, H.F. and Palmer, G. (1993) *British Industrial Relations.* London, Routledge

Hollinshead, G., Nicholls, P. and Tailby, S. (2002) *Employee Relations*, 2nd edn. Harlow, Financial Times/Prentice Hall

Hyman, R. (1975) *Industrial Relations: a Marxist Introduction.* London, Macmillan

Kelly, J. (1998) *Rethinking Industrial Relations: Mobilisation, Collectivism and Long Waves.* London, Routledge

Keynes, J.M. (1936) *The General Theory of Employment, Interest and Money.* London, Macmillan

LMT (Labour Market Trends) (1999) 'Women in the labour market'. *Labour Market Trends*, March

LMT (Labour Market Trends) (2003) 'Labour market trends'. *Labour Market Trends*, March

Lamb, H. and Perry, S. (1987) 'Big Mac is watching you'. *New Society*, 9 October

Legge, K. (1995) *Human Resource Management: Rhetorics and Realities.* London, Macmillan

Lyon, D. (1995) *Postmodernity.* Buckingham, Open University Press

Lyotard, J.F. (1992) 'Abandoning the metanarratives of modernity' in Hall, S., Held, T. and McGrew, T. (eds) *Modernity and its Futures.* Cambridge, Polity Press

Millward, N., Bryson, A. and Forth, J. (2000) *All Change at Work?* London, Routledge

Millward, N., Stevens, M., Smart, D. and Hawes, W.R. (1992) *Workplace Industrial Relations in Transition.* Aldershot, Dartmouth

Nicholls, P. (2002) 'Context and theory in employee relations', in Hollinshead, G., Nichols, P. and Tailby, S. (eds) *Employee Relations*, 2nd edn. Harlow, Financial Times/Prentice Hall

Parsons, T. (1951) *The Social System.* New York, The Free Press

Pelling, H. (1987) *A History of British Trade Unionism.* Harmondsworth, Penguin

Piore, M. (1988) 'Perspectives on labour market flexibility'. *Industrial Relations*, 45, 2

Pollert, A. (1988) 'Dismantling flexibility'. *Capital and Class*, 34, 3

Salamon, M. (1992) *Industrial Relations: Theory and Practice.* London, Prentice Hall

Salamon, M. (1998) *Industrial Relations: Theory and Practice*, 3rd edn. London, Prentice Hall

Silverman, D. (1970) *The Theory of Organisations.* London, Heinemann

Storey, J. (1995) *Human Resource Management: A Critical Text.* London, Routledge

Taylor, R. (1998) 'Annual review article 1997'. *British Journal of Industrial Relations*, 36, 2, 293–311

Tilly, C. (1978) *From Mobilisation to Revolution.* New York, McGraw-Hill

Touraine, A. (1974) *The Post-Industrial Society.* London, Wildwood

TUC (Trades Union Congress) (2002) *Annual Report.* London, TUC

Watson, T.J. (1995) *Sociology, Work and Industry.* London, Routledge

Webb, S. and Webb, B. (1920) *The History of Trade Unionism 1866–1920.* London, Longman

Wood, S. (1989) (ed.) *The Transformation of Work?* London, Unwin Hyman

PART 2

EMPLOYMENT RELATIONS: MOVERS, SHAKERS, PARTIES AND INSTITUTIONS

CHAPTER 2

EMPLOYERS AND THE MANAGEMENT OF INDUSTRIAL RELATIONS

INTRODUCTION

In Chapter 1 we considered in general terms the nature and functions of management concerning industrial relations, and the extent to which management ideologies determine both the climate and practice of employment relations within organisations. These aspects will be examined in greater detail.

The chapter commences with an overview of the employer and management contexts, and this is followed by a discussion of the nature of managerial control over the labour process. We then examine in some detail management styles, ideologies and strategies and how these impact upon industrial relations in particular organisational settings within both the public and private sectors. The relationship between personnel management, human resource management and employment relations is then considered at workplace and organisational levels. As the quality of employment relations within smaller firms is to some extent influenced by the advice they receive from employers' associations, the role of the latter within this context is finally examined.

Learning outcomes

When you have read this chapter, you should be able to:

1. Explain the distinction between the terms 'employer' and 'management' and account for the rise of 'managerialism'.

2. Explain the central issues concerning the management of the labour process.

3. Distinguish between management styles, management ideologies and management strategies.

4. Explain the impact of management styles, ideologies and strategies upon industrial relations in both public and private sector organisations.

5. Differentiate between personnel management and human resource management approaches to industrial relations.

6. Explain the changing nature of employers' associations.

OF EMPLOYERS AND MANAGEMENT

'Management' and 'employer' are terms assumed, often wrongly, to be synonymous, largely because they are generic categories that overlap with and complement each other. The term 'employer' applies equally to a small business where the owner of the business is the employer of labour (employees), a large company where the employer is equated with the name of that company and its legally registered status ('limited' or 'public limited' company) and large areas of the public sector where the government is either 'direct' employer (as in central government) or indirect employer (as in the National Health Service and education). On the other hand, the term 'management', as defined in Chapter 1, is a process concerned with the functions of planning, co-ordinating, organising, staffing, directing and controlling the various activities and resources of an organisation in order to ensure its efficient operation and to achieve its relevant goals. In larger organisations, professional managers are employed to undertake these functions within their various specialisms (for example, in finance, sales, production, marketing, personnel and human resource management) and, as such, form a distinct employee elite within the organisation.

The managerial occupation

During the eighteenth and early decades of the nineteenth centuries, enterprises tended to be owned and managed by the owners themselves. Owner-managers, in attempting to survive and prosper within a competitive product market, would, according to classical economic theory, seek to minimise labour costs while attempting to maximise the effort and productive capabilities of their employees. To be sure, many employers were highly exploitative of their workforces as the following example taken from the textile industry illustrates:

The worst situation is that of those workers who have to compete against a machine that is making its way. The price of the goods which they produce adapts itself to the price of the kindred product of the machine, and as the latter works more cheaply, its human competitor has but the
lowest wages. . . . Of all the workers in competition with machinery, the most ill-used are the hand-loom cotton weavers. They receive the most trifling wages, and, with full work, are not in a position to earn more than ten shillings a week. One class of woven goods after another is annexed by the power-loom, and hand weaving is the last refuge of workers thrown out of employment in other branches, so that the trade is always overcrowded. Hence it comes that, in average seasons, the hand-weaver counts himself fortunate if he can earn six or seven shillings a week, while to reach this sum he must sit at his loom fourteen to eighteen hours a day. (Engels, 1892, pp. 172–3)

On the other hand, many employers sought to treat their workers more humanely within the constraints of competitive markets. Gospel and Palmer (1993) cite the example of Quaker employers, drawing upon research derived from Child (1964).

Self-Evaluation Activity 2.1

The notion of a 'good employer'

Response on website

In Chapter 1 we considered the unitary perspective which, in its nineteenth-century form, embraced both 'good' and 'bad' employers. The example of the exploitative nature of employers in the textile industry has just been given. In what ways do you think the Quakers as 'good' employers differ from this example?

The rise of managerialism

Watson (1995) defines managerialism as:

A belief that the people who manage or 'direct' the corporations of modern societies have taken control away from those allegedly separate interests who own wealth. (p. 203)

During the course of the nineteenth and twentieth centuries, many firms became larger and more complex, and with the advent of the joint stock company share ownership became diffuse, eventually giving rise to the formation of a separate category of employee – the salaried, professional manager concerned with the successful running of large, complex business organisations and public bureaucracies. This development represented nothing less than a managerial revolution (Burnham, 1945) through which the specialist knowledge and skills of managerial experts have undermined the dominance of the owners. The managerialist assumptions then are, firstly, that managers, because of their expertise and separation from shareholder interests have greater freedom in running the business either in their own, sectional interests or, in a broader sense in the interests of the wider community. Secondly, as employees, managers may have a shared, common interest with other employees in the survival of the business, and that should the business fail then their situation is no different from that of other employees. Thirdly, as a separate group within the business, managers have the authority to make decisions on behalf of the owners, the consequences of which could conflict with other employee interests. Managers, then, according to the managerialist thesis, comprise a neutral 'buffer zone' between the conflicting interests of capital and labour within the organisation.

Criticisms of managerialism

Self-Evaluation Activity 2.2

Are managers neutral?

The response is given below

Read the extract in Mini case 1.1 concerning the long-running Liverpool docks dispute, which came to an end in December 1997. To what extent can we criticise the managerialist assumption of manager neutrality?

Mini case 1.1
Liverpool docks dispute

On 25 September 1995, 22 workers employed by the Torside docks company in Liverpool were informed by managers that they would have to work overtime to get a ship ready for sailing. Although the notice was short the dockers had become increasingly used to such demands. What they were not used to was the news that 'normal overtime arrangements' would not apply. The short notice and the payment arrangements both breached existing agreements between the Mersey Docks and Harbour Company (MDHC), Torside Ltd and the Transport and General Workers Union (TGWU). Taken aback, the dockers decided to discuss the situation with their shop stewards (who were working elsewhere). As the working day finished, the men left the ship and went to the canteen to wait for the stewards. As the first group of five dockers arrived they were met by the Managing Director of the Torside company who sacked them for leaving the ship. Bewildered, they wandered out to meet the others and tell them what had happened. When they in turn went into the canteen they were informed that they should go back to the ship, without their five sacked colleagues, or they would suffer the same fate; they refused to go back on such terms and were sacked.

The next morning the remainder of the Torside workforce gradually heard what had happened and a quick meeting with the stewards was arranged at 8 a.m. Over the previous evening the MDHC Port Stewards had advised the Torside stewards and workforce to go to work and let the senior stewards and the TGWU Docks Officer deal with the sackings via negotiation and the 'normal' grievance procedures. However, the situation was further inflamed by the Managing Director of Torside Ltd who appeared at the canteen meeting and sacked the entire workforce. On the morning of 27 September the Torside workforce mounted a picket of the Nelson Freight Company (a part-owned subsidiary of MDHC). The Torside men regularly worked side-by-side with dockers from Nelson Freight and the dockers (11 in all) refused to cross the picket line. As a consequence they were sacked by MDHC. The main workforce was now in the Royal Seaforth docks giving the stewards a further day to resolve the dispute. MDHC refused to discuss the issue because they claimed it was an internal dispute at an independent company. Frustrated and angry, the sacked workers informed the Seaforth workforce of their intention to picket the Seaforth docks. On the morning of the 28th the pickets were in place and the Seaforth workforce refused to cross the lines. In response the entire workforce was sacked by MDHC who proceeded to use casual labour thereafter.

Source: Lavalette and Kennedy, 1996, pp. 1–2

The example of the origins of the Liverpool docks dispute graphically demonstrates that the interests of MDHC management contrasts markedly with those of the sacked workforce and that the managerialist assumption of a neutral management buffer is not valid in this case. Watson (1995) suggests counter-arguments to the managerialist thesis and cites research by Nichols (1969) and Pahl and Winkler (1974) in making the following criticisms of managerialism:

- Senior managers tend to internalise profit-related values and priorities and act as long-term profit maximisers and cost minimisers. Whether or not MDHC management had a hidden agenda to weaken the union, isolate rank-and-file militants and casualise the workforce we may never know for certain, but the cost-minimising strategy of pursuing the employment of a casualised workforce has, from the company's point of view, been successful.

- Research evidence from the USA and other countries (Zeitlin, 1989) supports the assertion that managers' and owners' interests are virtually identical. Maintaining corporate profitability is an aim shared by owners/shareholders and managers alike. Moreover, corporate profits are essential determinants of high managerial income and status and this establishes a 'dependency relationship' between managers and owners in which the owners depend upon managerial expertise to generate profits and efficiency-driven cost-minimising strategies and managers depend upon owners for high status and rewards.

- Child (1969) argues that top managers and owners have similar socio-economic origins and backgrounds; correspondingly, they share the same or similar values, attitudes, ideologies and objectives.

- Research by Poole *et al.* (1981) concerning a survey of over 1000 managers suggests that managers do not simply share owner interests or act as agents of capital. Managers' concerns are often more pragmatic than this and are related to their own career and immediate interests. For example, opposition to trade unionism and industrial democracy, Watson suggests, is:

> less a matter of principled class action (in the interests of the owners) than a matter of defending their own freedom to manoeuvre in their everyday work as is strongly suggested by the evidence that personnel specialists within

> management hold distinctive attitudes (for or against) in these two areas. (p. 205)

MANAGEMENT CONTROL AND THE LABOUR PROCESS

The related concepts of 'control' and 'power' are central to our understanding of how the labour process is 'managed'. We are concerned here with the control over the production process in determining how employees within organisations perform their work. The extent to which this control can be exercised depends upon the possession of power. Before examining the ramifications of the debate concerning control of the labour process, we look briefly at the power concept.

The concept of power

Power is a complex concept in its own right and is the subject of broad philosophical and sociological debate. Within the industrial relations arena inequalities of power sometimes result in conflict, but more often compromise is the order of the day, as we shall see when we consider collective bargaining in Chapter 6. Fox (1985) identifies two strategies that managements could adopt in order to ensure employee compliance. The first is through coercion and the second is through consent. At one extreme, a manager could rely on the exercise of naked power (coercion) to force employees to do his will, while at the other extreme a manager could exercise power in less obvious and direct ways to engineer voluntary compliance with a decision or policy. Many forms of coercive power are derived from dependency relationships. An employer needs workers and uses managers to control that labour and workers depend upon employers to pay their wages, but, as Fox argues, dependence is rarely one-sided and the important issue is always concerned with the balance of power and where it lies. To a certain extent, the balance of power within a unionised context is determined by the perceptions of power which each party – management or union – may have of the other and by assessing which party holds the advantage at a given point in time (Gennard and Judge, 1997, p. 31). In practice management strategy represents a 'mix' of coercion and consent. The 'mix' usually reveals relatively more coercion towards the bottom of the organisational hierarchy and relatively more consent towards the top.

While coercive power was undoubtedly used by managements and employers in the nineteenth century in order to cajole workers into submitting to certain systems of rules and patterns of behaviour, the more common basis upon which power is exercised by contemporary managements within the employment relationship is consent. In this situation workers regard management's rule as legitimate and offer full consent to it and to the policies and decisions through which it is expressed so that management no longer needs to coerce. By giving full consent, workers 'authorise' management to govern them, 'thereby giving a special significance to the term "authority". Management can govern without this authorisation by employing coercion, but it faces at best passive indifference and at worst militant hostility. The value to management of consent is therefore apparent' (Fox, 1985, p. 67).

Self-Evaluation Activity 2.3

Power bases at the disposal of management
Response on website

Having identified the nature of power by coercion and consent, we are now in a position to consider the different bases of power at the disposal of management. Give examples of each and state which are more relevant to the management of industrial relations today. French and Raven's (1960) analysis of power suggests the following six categories:

1. **Rewards.** Reward power refers to the number of positive incentives that the employee thinks or perceives management has to offer.
2. **Punishment.** Punishment power has to do with the negative things which employees think management can do.
3. **Information.** Information can be a source of power. If employees think that management controls information that employees want, then management has power.
4. **Legitimacy.** Legitimate power as a resource stems from employees feeling that management has a right to make a given request. Legitimate power is

normally described as authority and stems from the position or status which a manager has in the organisational hierarchy.
5. **Expertise.** A manager may have expertise within a certain area of his responsibility, or on some topic or issue. If so, employees may often comply because 'management knows best'.
6. **Referent power.** In some cases an employee will look up to and admire a manager as a person. In this situation the employee may comply with the manager's demands because the employee identifies with the manager and wants to achieve whatever goals and objectives the manager wants to achieve.

The bases of social power managers draw on to exert influence in organisations are therefore dependent upon their access to organisational resources, their location within the communication network and formal organisational structure, who they are trying to influence, their own personal characteristics, the characteristics of the organisation itself and their control over the production and labour process, to which we now turn.

MANAGERIAL CONTROL OF THE LABOUR PROCESS

As we noted earlier, control over the production process in the sense of determining how employees of an organisation perform their work depends on the possession of power that in turn is derived from the differential access to the power bases we have identified. Huczynski and Buchanan (1991) define this type of control as 'the process through which obedience, compliance and conformity to predetermined standards of behaviour are achieved through interpersonal and group processes and is thus a property of the *relationship* between controller and controlled' (p. 595).

Self-Evaluation Activity 2.4

Examples of management control over the workforce
Response on website

Identify two or three examples of management control over the workforce.

As long ago as 1947, Warner and Low argued that mechanisation and division of labour facilitates management control:

> Control problems are simplified on two counts through mechanisation: (1) machines are easier to control than human beings, and (2) mechanisation tends to disrupt the social solidarity of the workers, who thereby become easier to control than they would if they were to maintain close social relations during working hours ... these factors tend to increase the subordination of the individual worker to management; from the management's viewpoint they are valuable means of social control over workers. .... The routinisation of jobs also simplifies control of workers in another way. The individual operative today does not have the feeling of security that the old-time craftsman derived from his special technical abilities. In most cases, today's operative is aware that only a comparatively brief training period protects him in his job from a large number of untrained individuals. The members of the supervisory hierarchy are also well aware of this fact. The psychological effect of this result of the division of labour is to intensify the subordinate position of the individual operative and to make him submit more readily to the limitations of his behaviour required by the supervisory group. (pp. 78, 80, 174)

However, control is rarely one-sided and may be concerned with some issues on which there is consensus between management and employees, and with other issues on which there may be conflict (Child, 1984). Child goes on to argue that:

> An increase in control achieved by workers over an issue that is in dispute will be at the expense of the amount of control available to management; and vice versa. Control then takes on a 'win-lose' character. An example might be control over the level of manning in a department. Where there are issues on which the different parties agree, perhaps such as safety, this win-lose character disappears. It is then possible to share control and for an increase in the devolution of control to employees not to mean a loss in control by management. (p. 139)

At the strategic level of the organisation, however, it is management that makes decisions concerning the objectives and policies of the organisation as a whole simply because control over strategic resources such as financial resources resides solely with management. The absence of any input into, or influence of, the strategic control process on the part of the non-managerial workforce may lead to collective resistance to managerial control over issues such as:

- **the employment contract,** whereby the balance between employee effort or work input contractually required by management and payment contractually offered is mediated through collective bargaining and ultimately through the withdrawal of labour sanction;
- **competitive pressures** faced by many organisations due to global economic factors such as the decline of the Far Eastern 'tiger' economies and over-valued national currencies may oblige managers to exercise more stringent control in an attempt to reduce costs, increase productivity, threaten redundancies and respond more swiftly to market changes.

The labour process debate

Labour process theory has its origins in the work of Marx. Essentially, Marx presents us with a critique of the political economics of capitalism, an economic system which creates two broad social classes: the capitalists, or bourgeoisie, who own and control the means of production, and the working class, or proletariat, who sell their labour power to capitalists in order to survive. Both classes, Marx argues, need each other and are mutually dependent upon each other, but their interests conflict. Capitalists aims to make profits in order to accumulate capital and so make more profits, whereas workers' interests are concerned with increasing wages and improving working conditions. The manager in a capitalist organisation cannot, therefore, depend upon the voluntary and willing co-operation, loyalty and commitment of the workforce and has to seek employee compliance through the exercise of control.

Self-Evaluation Activity 2.5

Employee compliance
The response is given below

Given that managers cannot rely on a willing workforce and therefore need to exercise control in order to obtain employee compliance, such employee compliance is not necessarily guaranteed. In other words, there are **limits** to compliance. Suggest examples of situations where such compliance may be regarded as unreasonable by employees.

Compliance in itself presents problems, as Hyman (1980) points out:

> Yet the acceptance of a generalised obligation to follow managerial instruction does not entail that a worker will accept without question every specific order which any manager may issue. There is a logical gap between generalised social values and specific rules in concrete situations. . . . Skilled toolmakers are normally conservative and stolid members of an engineering labour force, unlikely to contest in general terms the right of management to manage; but a supervisor who instructed a toolmaker to sweep the floor would be likely to be told to fuck off. . . . Yet precisely because most workers' customary obedience reflects no more than low-key acquiescence, the limits of obedience are easily tested. . . . There tends to be a 'zone of acceptance' where workers will, for example, normally perform without question tasks which are clearly technically necessary and which come within the customary range of their functions; but as soon as these limits are exceeded, their conformity becomes problematic. (p. 314)

Expressed in a different way, the problem of compliance becomes a 'problem of motivation'. Citing the case of 'Chemco', a large multinational corporation, Nichols (1980) argues that workers' low expectations of work reflects the low trust status of and relatively high levels of control over the workforce. Therefore attempts to change the low expectancy culture by introducing job enrichment and flexibilisation could well fail as workers may regard these changes in terms of replacing one form of control by another, and in any event they have been 'socialised' into accepting this culture and the high levels of compliance that go with it. As Nichols states:

> It is arguable that their [the workers'] problem is not so much that Chemco workers have high expectations of work but rather that they expect so little . . . they do not expect their work to be satisfying and have entered into a grudging bargain with their employers. Part of just one more generation of working class men and women, well used to being denied

meaning and control over their lives, like industrial whores they do enough to get enough. 'It's a job' they say. (p. 294)

A further example which demonstrates the limits of compliance concerns air stewardesses and other 'pink-collar' workers such as supermarket checkout staff who must exercise 'emotional labour at work' (Blyton and Turnbull, 1998). Emotional labour is defined as 'the management of feelings to create a publicly observable facial and bodily display' (ibid., p. 75). Since emotional labour involves 'putting on a front' and acting according to the dictates of others over long periods, many workers may experience strain and tensions. A study of supermarket checkout staff reveals that if employees do not exercise emotional labour they are reprimanded by supervisors, using discipline as control: 'We are able to detect when a checkout operator is not smiling or even when she is putting on a false smile . . . we call her into a room and have a chat with her' (ibid., p. 82, citing Ogbonna, 1992).

Labour process theory concerns itself with the imperatives of managerial control and its effects upon workers themselves and the process whereby work becomes deskilled and degraded. The influential work of Braverman (1974) follows the tradition of Marxist critique. His central argument is that the pursuit of capitalist interests has led to a general trend towards deskilling, routinising and mechanising of jobs across the employment spectrum, from manufacturing to retailing and from design to clerical work. Braverman critically evaluates the work of F.W. Taylor in order to support his arguments, and it is his work to which we now turn.

Taylorism and control

The ideas concerning 'scientific management' originated and developed by Taylor (1947) in the late nineteenth and early twentieth centuries became widely disseminated and used by engineers and work study practitioners in Britain, Japan, and, interestingly in the Soviet Union under Lenin, but had only a limited influence upon the USA (Grint, 1991). For Taylor, the problem of work is the problem of managerial control and the issue for management is to ensure the maximum degree of effort for the minimum amount of reward. The solution, according to Taylor was to extend the division of labour, separate the conception (thinking) of work from its execution (doing) and make the workforce less skilled. This would result not only in higher levels of productivity per worker and cheaper labour, but also a more compliant workforce. Having worked as a labourer, clerk and machinist himself, Taylor was well aware of the problems of production at shop-floor level and suggested three reasons for this:

- Management lacked the knowledge to maximise production; their ignorance left them at the mercy of workers' wisdom.
- The workers themselves had a reason and rationale for restricting output which included the real fear of underpayment and redundancy.
- The existing payment systems did not include sufficiently sophisticated incentive schemes, where they existed at all.

Taylor blamed management, not the workforce, for these problems and insisted they drop their conventional 'rule of thumb' schemes and use his 'scientific management' techniques. These involved a number of discrete changes which included:

- technical improvements to machinery;
- extension of the division of labour so that each task was fragmented into its smallest constituent units which would be timed and measured;
- a piece-rate system that was individually rather than collectively organised (to avoid encouraging collective action and trade unions) involving accelerating rewards and punishment should the relatively high targets be exceeded or not met; and
- deskilling of jobs to facilitate the employment of cheaper labour and to eliminate the restrictive practices previously used by employees on the basis of their monopoly over knowledge.

Taylorism therefore enabled employers to transfer work which involved planning, design and other 'cerebral' work activities from the shop floor to new production engineering and work study departments. The remaining tasks which were simple, routine and unskilled could then be undertaken by cheap, substitutable and easily available labour. These tasks required little training and, through work study techniques, the input required from workers could

be easily and accurately calculated and workers' output could therefore be measured against output targets. Individual workers' output would then be rewarded through payment-by-results incentive schemes. Because tasks were simplified and measurable, worker performance could be easily checked and this facilitated management control.

Braverman and the critique of Taylorism

Braverman makes the assumption that there is a fundamental conflict underlying the relationship between capital and labour, and that the relations between management and workforce and the question of technological change need to be seen in this light. For Braverman, the employment relationship begins when the employer buys the services of an employee in the labour market. In entering into a contract of employment, the employer and employee have only agreed the terms and conditions of the employment relationship. The details of what work employees do, when they do it, and how it is done have to be resolved day by day in the workplace. Braverman argues that, in order to get maximum return on their 'investment' in human labour, employers have to maximise their control over the behaviour of employees, whatever the type of technology currently in use. Moreover, management control systems, according to Braverman, were one aspect of the wider class conflict between capital and labour.

Braverman also argued that the need for management control to cope with uncommitted workers led to the degradation of work skills and workers. He claimed that although science and technology were demanding more education, training and exercise of mental effort, work was increasingly subdivided into routine and easy-to-learn fragments as Taylor had suggested. The need for managers to maintain a disciplined workforce led them into a continuing process in which approaches to control were perpetually refined and intensified. These extensions of management control erode craft skill, reduce workers' independence and reduce the importance of their knowledge of the craft. In addition, workers are excluded from decisions about methods and the pace of work; technology reduces worker skill and discretion, fragmenting tasks as Taylor recommended, stifles individual development, reduces wages and enhances management status.

Self-Evaluation Activity 2.6

Illustration of Braverman's thesis

Response on website

Read the following extract about the electrical equipment industry. Does this example illustrate Braverman's thesis?

> *Electrical employers transformed the work of making lamps. The jobs were simplified and divided into minute segments with the former skills built into specialised machines. This allowed the companies to cut costs, increase production, and eliminate skilled workers. The craftsmen, who had used their own specialised skills and knowledge to produce the lamps, were replaced by workers, predominantly women, who performed only one special operation and required little training to do the job.* (Thompson, 1990, p. 32)

Labour process control and employment relations issues

Management control over the labour process is also an important manifestation of management's assumed right to manage (the exercise of managerial prerogatives). The way management does this is just as much a matter of form, or style, as of content and this is explored further in the following section.

Summary points

- Owner-managers who were often highly exploitative of labour during the eighteenth and early nineteenth centuries were replaced by the 'managerialism' of the twentieth century as the dominant control ideology and mechanism within the employment relationship.
- 'Managerialism' itself has been criticised, mainly because of its inherent and erroneous assump-

tion of managerial 'neutrality' which, for example, pervades the HRM literature.
- The concept of power itself and the 'bases of power' model are vital to our understanding of the inequalities inherent within the employment relationship, as is the body of theory concerning managerial control over the labour process which stems from a critique of Taylorism by Braverman.

STYLES OF MANAGEMENT AND INDUSTRIAL RELATIONS

In general terms, 'style', as Legge (1995, p. 31) points out, is simply 'a way of doing something'. As we have seen, managers direct and control labour and the style adopted in enabling them to do so is at its most observable on a day-to-day basis. Gospel and Palmer (1993) suggest that the articulation of a particular management style is best understood within the context of broader ideologies and beliefs held by managements. An ideology is essentially a set of beliefs held by a specific group having the same or similar interests in common, while beliefs refer to those ideas that people hold to be right and true, which provide not only guides and rules for action, but also justifications for actions by which behaviour is made accountable to the self and to others. Beliefs are therefore used as a means of persuasion 'whereby the employer seeks to persuade employees to act in a certain way' (ibid., p. 63). Management style, seen within the context of management ideology and belief systems, has been defined as 'a set of proposals and actions that establishes the organisation's approach to its employees and acts as a reference point for management' (Brewster *et al.*, 1983, p. 62).

The contribution of Fox and Purcell

Fox (1966, 1974) identified three contrasting 'frames of reference', two of which typify managements' industrial relations style and are termed unitary and pluralist, while the third, which Fox labels radical, draws upon Marxist theory concerning unequal power relationships and is not considered here. The unitary and pluralist frames of reference or perspectives were considered in Chapter 1, and you should now reread these. Marchington and Parker (1990) argue that there are three essential differences between these two perspectives 'in relation to management's acceptance and recognition of unions, their views about management prerogatives and employee participation, and in the perceived legitimacy of and reactions to conflict at work' (p. 77). Fox (1974) elaborated on his basic unitary/pluralist dichotomy and identified six variations or subcategories of patterns of industrial relations management that represent combinations of unitary and pluralist perspectives. These are:

- the **traditional** variant where managers and employees both hold unitary frames of reference;
- the **sophisticated modern** where pluralist views are held by managers and employees;
- **sophisticated paternalism** which represents a combination of pluralist employers and unitary employees;
- **classical conflict** representing variants of unitary employers and pluralist employees;
- **continuous challenge**, again representing variants of unitary employers and pluralist employees;
- the **standard modern** 'was the result of ambivalent frames of reference within both management and worker groups; this could occur because of splits within the managerial hierarchy, for example, or as a result of experience, with individual managers' frames of reference varying from one event to another over time' (Marchington and Parker, 1990, p. 78).

Purcell and Sisson (1983) further elaborated upon Fox's categorisation and developed five ideal-typical styles of industrial relations management which are identified below:

Traditionalist, similar to Fox's traditionalist pattern, is characterised by hostile and negative stances to trade unions and a highly exploitative approach to the workforce. This is accompanied by a strong belief in management's right to manage, and that the exercise of its managerial prerogative is legitimate.

Sophisticated paternalist/human relations, differs from Fox's category in that management holds strong unitary views even though there is concern for employee welfare and development. Sophisticated paternalists are similar to traditionalists in that

they refuse to recognise or negotiate with trade unions, but will not necessarily use coercive power to keep them out. Rather they would prefer to offer employees incentives such as better pay and conditions of work and use appropriate recruitment and selection methods in order to provide disincentives to unionisation. Through these methods they aim to encourage employee commitment, loyalty and dependency. Companies identified as typifying this style are Marks & Spencer, Hewlett-Packard, John Lewis Partnership and, before its major restructuring, IBM. Marchington and Parker (1990) argue that 'although most of the enterprises in this category do not recognise unions, their approach to management is substantially different from the traditionalists [and] this group spans the unitary/pluralist distinction, exhibiting elements of both in their management styles' (p. 78).

Sophisticated modern is similar to Fox's category in that pluralist views dominate. There is an acceptance of a trade union presence, even though this might limit the perceived freedom of managerial decision-making. The union presence and voice is seen to contribute in a positive way towards facilitating communication and change and maintaining stability of relationships. There is a strong emphasis upon the development and operation of formal and informal procedures in order to handle and resolve conflicts of interest. Purcell and Sisson propose two subcategories of the sophisticated modern type. These are:

Consulters: similar to sophisticated paternalist except that unions are recognised. 'The attempt is made to build "constructive" relationships with the trade unions and incorporate them into the organisational fabric. Emphasis is also placed on techniques designed to enhance individual employee commitment to the firm and the need to change (share option schemes, profit sharing, briefing or cascade information systems, joint working parties, quality or productivity circles/councils' (Blyton and Turnbull, 1994, p. 80). Companies tending to approximate to this subcategory are large, fairly successful and have substantial market share, and would include ICI and Cadbury-Schweppes.

Constitutionalists: unions have been recognised for some time and are accepted as inevitable. Policies emphasise the need for stability and control. 'Management prerogatives are defended through highly specific collective agreements. The importance of management control is emphasised with the aim of minimising or neutralising union constraints on both operational (line) and strategic (corporate) management.' (ibid., p. 80). Companies most likely to demonstrate characteristics of this subcategory include those single industry companies with mass production technologies selling products within a highly competitive international market. Examples include General Motors and Ford.

Standard modern, where a pragmatic approach to industrial relations is adopted and trade unions are recognised. This is by far the largest group in which industrial relations is considered the responsibility of line or operational management and 'fire-fighting' is often resorted to. The importance attached to industrial relations policies varies from time to time both within and between organisations, and also between different levels within the organisational hierarchy. This type is most commonly manifested in larger multi-product companies that have had a growth history characterised by takeovers and mergers, particularly within heavy engineering and manufacturing. Examples include Rover Cars and Lucas Industries.

Self-Evaluation Activity 2.7

Relating style to particular cases
Response on website

This exercise is concerned with management styles based on the contributions of Fox and Purcell and Sisson. Consider Mini cases 2.2 and 2.3 and identify the appropriate industrial relations style together with your justification.

Mini cases 2.2 and 2.3

Case 2.2 Garibaldi Supermarket Chain

Garibaldi (UK) Ltd is a major supermarket chain with stores predominantly in England and Wales. It is one of the newer supermarkets on the scene that have the policy of 'piling them high and selling them cheap', no frills shopping. Its stores compare in size with those of its competition: Netto, Lidl and Kwiksave. Recruit-

ment is the responsibility of the general managers of individual stores and staff are expected to function in any area of the store from shelf stacking to checkout work. Competition is fierce and Garibaldi runs a lean operation with an average of ten staff per store. This means that there is a minimum of personnel for any situation, and only at peak times are the relatively few checkouts fully staffed.

Company policies are highly centralised and determined at national level. There is no personnel or human resource department and responsibility for personnel matters lies with the Purchasing Director who has a small secretarial section whose main responsibility in the personnel area is to keep employee records. Apart from 'on site' training for store staff, which is the responsibility of the store manager, there is no formal provision for training and development of employees. Pay levels are determined centrally for full- and part-time staff. Interestingly, the pay of store staff is rather higher than most of the competitor supermarkets which reflects the intensification of work, the flexibility demanded of staff and the fact that checkout work involves the committing to memory of the prices of the relatively limited range of products (there is no bar-coding of products). There is a policy of non-recognition of trade unions. However, Garibaldi's UK management have been advised that, owing to government legislation concerning trade union recognition, this policy will be subject to review in 2003. Procedures concerning grievances, redundancy and equal opportunities do not exist, but these issues are under review. The only formal procedure that operates is the company disciplinary procedure which was introduced after a highly publicised 'unfair dismissal' case.

Case 2.3 A Division of the Home Office

Manager 1
'For nearly ten years in the Home Office there were two unions. One was the CPSA (now the CPSU), which nearly all of the administrative grades belonged to. The other was NUCPS, which the management grades belonged to. CPSA was the more militant union whilst NUCPS was nigh on dormant. Generally, senior management grudgingly admit to the necessity for unions in the Home Office. Some will argue that it is yet another mechanism by which to monitor bad practice in the office. It is indisputable that the different agendas, when combined in a constructive fashion, do

produce a better working environment. . . . In management terms, a union that requests too many meetings over innocuous subjects just wastes valuable time and is not taken as seriously as the union which "picks its battleground", and its moment! In conclusion, unions are a vital element in good industrial relations and provide an essential safety net for staff from target-conscious managers. The union, however, has to acknowledge its responsibilities across the office and should be seen to act responsibly at all times.'

Manager 2

'In a workplace where management liaises with unions, the working environment will only be enriched if, of course, its reps represent the views of its workplace and not their own political views. Sometimes unions can attract individuals who are politically motivated and members feel they are not represented by these people and do not get involved. This is sad. Anyway, unions in my opinion are necessary, people fought vigorously for the right to belong to unions and without them who knows what injustices may have occurred. They still do even with unions present. I would encourage all new staff to join and, if they want to, to get involved.'

Home Office management's approach to trade unions:

1. Encourages trade union membership by including a paragraph in all new entrant letters which recommends they join their recognised trade union.
2. Encourages trade union membership by including a paragraph in the Home Office Staff Handbook which recommends staff join their recognised trade union.
3. Signed a departmental facilities agreement which allows:
   (a) Trade union representatives paid time off in order to undertake trade union activity
   (b) Trade union representatives access to accommodation, telephones, photocopying, fax, information technology and other facilities
   (c) Staff paid time off to attend trade union meetings
   (d) An organised Whitley joint negotiating structure which allows for regular meetings at a local, departmental and national level between management and trade union representatives on a whole host of issues relating to the pay and conditions of staff.

4. Signed other agreements covering disciplinary matters which allow staff access to trade union representatives whenever they need advice or at any meeting with their manager and trade union representation before, during and after any disciplinary hearings.
5. Signed agreements with the trade unions on issues such as:
   (a) promotion/recruitment procedures
   (b) probation procedures
   (c) flexible working hours
   (d) part-time/jobshare arrangements
   (e) sick/special/maternity/paternity leave arrangements
   (f) equal opportunities
   (g) retirement/re-employment
   (h) redundancy arrangements

There is some evidence to suggest that many organisations adopt a 'mix and match' approach to pluralist and unitarist assumptions (Cully *et al.*, 1999). For example, while the sample of managers for the Workplace Employee Relations Survey (WERS) were either neutral (54 per cent) or in favour of union membership (29 per cent) thereby indicating a pluralist orientation, 72 per cent of managers preferred to consult directly with employees than with unions, revealing a unitarist approach (Cully *et al.*, 1999). In order to test the 'mix and match' approach, a group of the author's students gave a summary of Purcell and Sisson's model to a senior manager of the Tesco supermarket chain whose response is given in Mini case 2.4.

Mini case 2.4
Tesco manager's view of Tesco management style

'Looking at your various models, I would say that Tesco, in the main, uses a "sophisticated modern" approach to the employment relationship in the form of being "consulters". I think we have built a constructive relationship with trade unions and Tesco regard trade unions as a body to work with because they want to and not because they have to. . . . Tesco is a pluralist organisation that works closely with trade unions. There are in a number of stores that I am aware of at least one and sometimes two USDAW representatives who help to handle disputes and other people problems in a fair manner. In terms of the employment relationship the use of trade unions indicates a collective aspect. This is the case. However, we also use individual approaches concerning employees. This means that we can resolve group and individual problems. It also gives us a better chance to train, develop and appraise individuals. In practice this means that Tesco can motivate employees through their management approaches. It also means that employees have a higher commitment to the organisation. This helps to achieve the overall aims and objectives of Tesco as an organisation.'

Commentary: It is clear from this view of Tesco management style that a pluralist (collective) perspective of the employment relationship is taken which recognises the legitimate authority of trade unions as the main employee voice mechanism. However, this exists alongside a more 'individualistic' approach identified by Purcell and Gray (1986) – see below – which is characterised, amongst other things, by a commitment to training, development, appraisals and feedback as part of the day-to-day administration of employees within the organisation.

Individualist and collectivist styles and policies

A further approach devised by Purcell and Gray (1986) and Purcell (1987) identifies two broad categories of approach that overlap with the style categories considered earlier. The first category represents an individualistic approach to the relationship between employer and employee and relates to 'policies based on the belief in the value of the individual and his or her right to advancement and fulfilment at work' (Purcell and Gray, 1986, p. 213). Employee motivation is encouraged by the development of effective direct communications with individual employees, providing opportunities for personal development and advancement within the organisation; monitoring and evaluating performance; and the devising of rewards that recognise individual effort and performance – and 'with their emphasis on equality of treatment between employees,

the trade unions could well be seen as a major constraint on the possibilities of implementing the new principles of effective management' (Gallie et al., 1996, p. 14). Bacon and Storey (1996) also assert that 'the new emphasis upon the individual employee in management strategies suggests that any notion of a standardised group of workers pursuing similar interests has become increasingly difficult to sustain' (p. 43). The individualist approach, then, has the following characteristics:

- The right of employers to offer financial incentives to an employee covered by a collective agreement in order that the employee may accept a personal contract, this right being granted to employers by the Trade Union Reform and Employment Rights Act 1993. In this context, Kessler and Purcell (1995) argue that 'personal contracts represent a reassertion of the managerial prerogative and unilateral control' (p. 339).
- Individualism is often closely associated with certain personnel techniques such as individual performance pay and direct communication with employees which may result in the marginalisation of trade unions within unionised organisations.
- Individualism is closely associated with the ideas of human resource management (HRM) with its emphasis upon developing the talents and capacities of each individual employee and thereby securing the commitment of the employee to the organisation.

Individualism is as much a subject of political rhetoric as it is of HRM. The Conservative White Paper, *People, Jobs and Opportunity* (DoE, 1992) stated that 'there is a new recognition of the role and importance of the individual employee', while Conservative industrial relations legislation has made it easier for employers to adopt individualistic styles and practices. The rhetoric of individualism erroneously assumes that individualism and collectivism are mutually exclusive categories, but it is a compelling argument, the essence of which is captured by Kessler and Purcell (1995):

The force of the rhetoric of 'new individualism' is not easily challenged. An emphasis on common goals, flexibility and personal performance which allows individuals to achieve commitment to their job and firm is intuitively attractive.

Here, management control is achieved via employee commitment – the ultimate dream of the self-managed workforce. The assumption is that what was previously covered by collective regulation is now both unilaterally determined by the employer and focused on or targeted to each employee. The worker is assumed to have neither the interest nor the ability to combine with others, but will strive to maximise his or her own interests which coincide with, or are complementary to, those of the employer. (p. 31)

Individualism and collectivism are not mutually exclusive categories

As we have seen in Chapter 1, the focus of industrial relations is upon collective labour organisations (trade unions and employers' associations) and the institution and process of collective bargaining as determining and regulating the employment contract. Purcell and Gray (1986) define collectivism as 'the recognition by management of the collective interests of groups of employees in the decision-making process' (p. 213). Marchington and Parker (1990) add that this definition 'needs to incorporate not only the structures for employee participation and collective bargaining, but also the approach of management towards these institutions' (p. 80).

However, while it is important to define individualism and collectivism, they should not be regarded as dichotomous or mutually exclusive. Examples of both can be found to operate in any one workplace since they concern different aspects of the employment relationship where the employee may be treated both as an individual worker and as part of a collective organisation such as a trade union or works council. Essentially, individualism indicates a non-union and/or HRM style approach to employees and includes a cost-minimisation approach to employees, a 'paternalist' stance for employee welfare, and an employee development approach (Storey and Sisson, 1993), while collectivism is concerned with adversarial conflict relations with unions, a partnership/co-operative approach with unions and, less frequently, a non-union but representative stance (Bacon, 2001).

Self-Evaluation Activity 2.8

Mapping individualism and collectivism
The response is given below

Going back to the typology of management styles based on Purcell and Sisson (1983) and by reference to Figure 2.1, identify which of these are predominantly individualist, which are predominantly collectivist, and

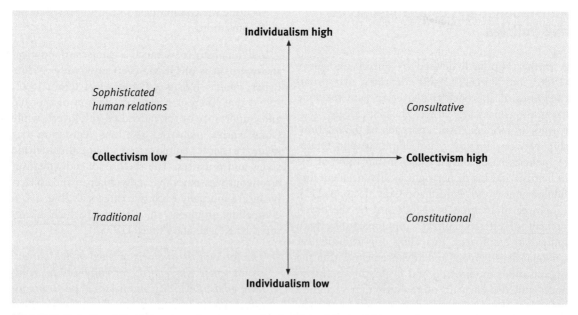

Figure 2.1 Purcell and Gray's typology of management industrial relations styles
Source: Purcell and Gray, 1986

which are both equally individualist and collectivist, giving examples of each.

The traditional style is manifested by extremely low scores for both individualism and collectivism. As we have seen with this style, labour is unashamedly exploited and unionism is opposed and often vilified. Casual labour is often used for labour intensification and cost-minimising purposes. If there is an example of the less unacceptable variant of traditionalism, then it would probably be the high street burger chain of the McDonald's organisation. Sophisticated paternalism/ human relations as described above exists in organisations where individualism is high, and collectivism, which may exist in the form of consultative committees, is low and sometimes non-existent. In addition to the examples of this type already given, other companies identified as typifying this style are to be found in high technology/professional service firms operating on greenfield sites. The consultative and constitutional as we have seen, are two sophisticated modern styles and are contrasted in terms of their sympathy with individualism:

- The consultative style features highly on both collectivist and individualist dimensions and is similar to sophisticated paternalism/human relations, except that unions are recognised. Management attempts both to treat unions almost as partners in order to discuss a whole range of issues and to place great emphasis on securing individual commitment and loyalty through, for example, profit sharing, training and development, joint working parties and team briefing exercises.

- The constitutional style occurs in organisations where collectivism is high and individualism is low: 'Unions are recognised, but grudgingly as unavoidable rather than welcomed into a constructive dialogue. Management prerogatives are jealously guarded through highly specific collective agreements which are carefully administered and monitored on the shop floor' (Legge, 1995, p. 37).

The fifth style, the standard modern, represents the pragmatic approach as described above, and falls outside the individualism/collectivism matrix. There is no consistent policy concerning union recognition, the union presence either having established itself due to historical factors, or been inherited through company takeover and acquisition. Union bargaining power may be high or low and managerial prerogatives may be in the ascendancy or waning.

The individualism/collectivism dimension was further elaborated by Purcell (1987) and, in relation to the styles already considered, can be depicted as shown in Figure 2.2.

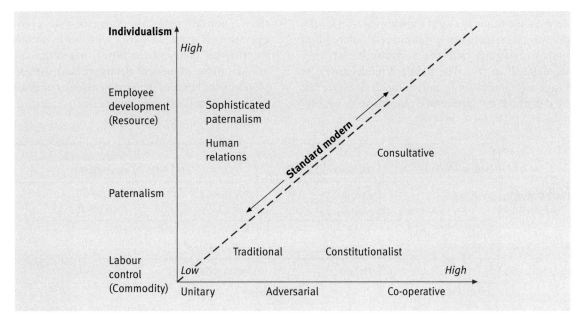

Figure 2.2 Mapping management industrial relations styles
Source: Based on Purcell, 1987

The following points concerning Figure 2.2 need to be emphasised:

- 'High' individualism is concerned with treating employees as a resource with a strong emphasis upon employee training and development.
- 'Low' individualism exists in situations where the employee is treated as an expendable commodity, is highly exploited and is subject to tight control over his or her labour.
- The mid-point represents a situation where the employee's actions are limited by well-intended regulations and actions on the part of the employer.
- 'High' collectivism is concerned with co-operative relationships with employees' collective organisations, whether they be trade unions, staff associations or other collective bodies.
- 'Low' collectivism is characterised by a unitary frame of reference or perspective with no union presence allowed.
- The mid-point between 'high' and 'low' collectivism is often typified by conflict and adversarial relations between employer and collective organisations (normally trade unions).

Legge (1995) points out that if the five management styles are superimposed on the graph (see also the Purcell and Ahlstrand (1994) modification in Figure 2.3), 'the similarities, on the one hand, between the traditional and constitutional style and, on the other, between sophisticated paternalism/human relations and the consultative style is highlighted' (p. 39). The standard modern style as Legge also points out is more difficult to locate 'as, by definition, its appearance changes with circumstances [and probably] is best located as a dotted diagonal line, with the potential to span the range of possibilities' (p. 39).

Purcell and Ahlstrand's revised typology of management styles is shown in the matrix in Figure 2.3 using the individualism/collectivism dimensions as adapted by Kessler and Purcell (1995). As with Purcell's typology, management styles are identified according to the degree of individualism and collectivism they exhibit. Kessler and Purcell point out that some firms may have no real style, 'being essentially opportunistic in reaction to events' (p. 347). This corresponds to the attempted definition of the standard modern style which Purcell and Ahlstrand omit altogether. In relation to the two boxes showing ??, it should be noted that:

- the type of individualistic policies developed by the firm will influence the nature of the collective relationship with a union or other collective body;
- the type of collectivism in action may well influence the nature of the firm's policies towards, and expectations of, individual employees;
- it is highly improbable, however, that a firm with well-established employee development policies representing considerable investment in employees would engage in and sustain high levels of conflictual and adversarial relations with trade unions, hence the ?? top central box; and
- the ?? bottom right box suggests that a co-operative relationship exists with trade unions but that the policy of the firm is based on cost minimisation, numerical flexibility and the exploitation of labour. The incompatibility of these approaches makes this an unrealistic scenario.

(Resource)

	Employee development	Sophisticated human relations	??	Sophisticated consultative
Individualism	Paternalism	Paternalist	Bargained constitutional	Modern paternalist
	Cost minimisation	Traditional	Bargained constitutional	??
		None	Adversarial	Co-operative

(Commodity)   **Collectivism**

Figure 2.3 Purcell and Ahlstrand's management styles matrix as adapted by Kessler and Purcell (1995)
Source: Kessler and Purcell, 1995

The names of the style categories within the matrix differ slightly from the earlier formulations in Figure 2.2, and for purposes of clarification the following points are made:

- The traditional category remains the same according to the original definition.
- The sophisticated paternalist/human relations also remains the same.
- The sophisticated consultative style of Figure 2.3 is identical to the consultative style of Figure 2.2.
- The bargained constitutional style of Figure 2.3 is identical to the constitutionalist style of Figure 2.2.
- The two categories within Figure 2.3 not specifically mentioned in previous formulations are the paternalist and modern paternalist.

The paternalist projects a welfare and caring image with an emphasis upon loyalty and downward communication. There are fixed grades determined through job evaluation with a high proportion of lower grade employees being women, for whom promotion is a rarity. Everyone knows his or her place within a fixed hierarchy which emphasises stability and order. Conflict is seen as a failure of communication and unions are avoided. This type is often found in firms within financial and service distribution sectors. The modern paternalist emphasises constructive relationships with trade unions and dissemination of information through a network of collective consultative committees. The image projected is one of caring and concern for employee welfare, but as with the paternalist context there are fixed grades based on job evaluation (allowing input in their determination from union representatives). Pay is average and the overall emphasis is upon stability and order with employees knowing their place. This type is most usually found in stable process industries such as foods and oil.

The style typologies we have considered in this section all stem from Fox's original unitary/pluralist classification. The more recent individualist/collectivist dimensions assist our analysis and understanding of managerial approaches to industrial relations during the course of the twentieth century. During the 1970s the approach of managements to industrial relations veered more towards a greater acceptance of pluralism and collectivism, and there was a detectable trend towards adoption of the sophistic-

ated consultative style. During the 1980s and 1990s, we witnessed a reversal of this trend with a move towards the unitary and individualistic approach and towards an approximation of the sophisticated paternalist model on the one hand and towards a cost minimisation approach on the other.

Management industrial relations styles do not operate independently of other organisational concerns and are clearly related to industrial relations policies and strategies to which we now turn.

MANAGEMENT AND INDUSTRIAL RELATIONS STRATEGIES, POLICIES AND PROCEDURES

Industrial relations strategies and policies are concerned with influencing and directing the employment relationship in the medium to long term. However, the management of industrial relations has traditionally been low in the order of organisational priorities and smaller firms generally have an unstructured and day-to-day approach to industrial relations management. The Donovan Commission (1968) argued that much of the industrial unrest of the 1960s could be attributed to the inadequate conduct and management of industrial relations at corporate and workplace level, with management at corporate headquarters frequently ignorant or out of touch with what was going on at the workplace. The Commission therefore recommended that corporate industrial relations should be reviewed and appropriate strategies and policies devised and implemented which would reconstruct workplace industrial relations through the operation of positive personnel policies, the formalisation of industrial relations procedures concerning dispute, discipline and grievance handling, the creation of orderly collective bargaining machinery and the formal incorporation of the shop steward within the negotiation process.

The traditional antipathy of British management to the formation and formalisation of effective policies, procedures and practices in industrial relations can be explained in terms of the following:

- Fear of sharing power with trade unions as this may threaten management's decision-making authority and legitimacy:

Even where trade unions are recognised, much managerial time is spent in attempting to preserve management's traditional prerogatives rather than in developing new areas of joint regulation with the trade unions with which it negotiates. (Farnham and Pimlott, 1995, p. 72)

- Lack of managerial expertise in industrial relations is indicative of a lack of commitment to the management of industrial relations at senior levels. 'Even now, board and senior managerial appointments continue to be dominated by accountants, lawyers and others of the more traditional professional groups' (ibid., p. 72).
- Even though multi-employer industry-wide or national agreements are in decline, 'there is little incentive for line managers to be involved in day-to-day industrial relations' in industries where they operate (ibid., p. 71). Conversely in those organisations where industrial relations has been devolved (as, for example, within NHS trust hospitals), managers may lack the necessary skills required for the efficient and effective management of industrial relations and for dealing with trade unions at plant or operational levels.
- Weaknesses inherent in industrial relations management are often a reflection of poor education and training of British management generally (Handy, 1993) and an absence of expertise and sophistication can lead to production failures, productivity problems and industrial disputes (Nichols, 1986).
- Finally, the low priority accorded to industrial relations on the part of British management is partly due to the consequences of their actions, specifically their failure to secure the active co-operation of the workforce as opposed to mere compliance or enforced consent, and this arises from the fundamental tension that exists, and persists, between employer and employee. Inevitably there is no 'one best way' to manage these conflicts, only different routes to partial failure. It is on this basis that managerial strategy can best be conceptualised 'as the pragmatic choice among alternatives none of which can prove satisfactory' (Blyton and Turnbull, 1994, p. 94, quoting Hyman, 1987, p. 30).

In recent decades managements, particularly within the larger multiple-plant companies, have become more sophisticated in their approaches to industrial relations, mostly where industrial relations policy and practice is incorporated within HRM strategies (see below).

Strategies

In general terms, according to Miller (1993), strategic management is concerned with:

- assessing the organisation's internal competencies and capabilities;
- assessing environmental threats and opportunities;
- deciding the scope of the organisation's activities;
- creating and communicating a strategic vision; and
- managing the process of change in an organisation.

The main purpose of strategy is to influence and direct an organisation as it conducts its activities, and 'may be described as the attempt by those who control an organisation to find ways to position their business and organisational objectives so that they can exploit the planning environment and maximise the future use of the organisation's capital and human assets' (Gennard and Judge, 1997, p. 91). Gennard and Judge consider the main issues concerning strategy (following Johnson and Scholes, 1993).

Firstly, strategy concerns itself with the full range of an organisation's activities.

Secondly, strategy is concerned with the nature of the external environment in which an organisation operates. An environment can be static, where, for example, the product market is stable and decisions are routine and predictable. Many local authorities, for example, have operated in situations where demand for their services was highly predictable and could be met on the basis of fairly accurate estimates of government subsidy together with local revenues. However, sudden changes in the external environment can cause problems. Changes in government funding and alternative methods of raising local income (such as the change from income based on rateable value to other methods such as the 'poll tax') have influenced strategic decisions concerning the efficiency of service provision, which services to retain and which services to 'contract out'.

An environment can also be very dynamic, subject to rapid and often unpredictable change, as with organisations operating within the information technology and computing industry. Environments also exhibit varying degrees of complexity where some organisations operate in multiple product markets, which may also be extremely competitive and volatile.

Thirdly, strategy is concerned with the match between the activities of an organisation and its resources. 'These resources can be physical (equipment, buildings) or they can be people. Strategies in respect of physical resources may require decisions about investment or even about the ability to invest. Strategies in respect of people might require decisions about the type of competencies needed for future development and where such resources are to be found' (Gennard and Judge, 1997, p. 92).

Conventional definitions of strategy normally identify and differentiate between different strategic levels. For example, we can distinguish between:

- **first-level or first-order** strategy which deals with the long-term direction of the organisation and the scope of its activities, market positioning and penetration, where to locate, how much to invest, etc.;
- **second-order or business** strategy which is concerned with the operating procedures and relationships between the different parts of the organisation; and
- **third-order or functional** strategy which involves decisions concerning the different functions of the organisation, which includes personnel, HRM and industrial relations functions; devising broad strategies to support business strategy and achieve functional performance objectives.

In relation to these strategic levels, Legge (1995) points out that the assumption inherent in identifying them is that the strategy process is a 'cascade', where the top of the waterfall is the corporate level, and subsequent levels are logically 'downstream' or dependent on directions established at corporate level. Hence, Chandler's (1962) classic dictum that structure – how a firm is organised to achieve its goals: a second-order strategy – follows strategy – the type of business undertaken at present and in the future: a first-order strategy (p. 97).

Industrial relations strategy

Industrial relations strategies may be defined as 'long-term goals developed by management to preserve or change the procedures, practice or results of industrial relations activities over time' (Farnham and Pimlott, 1995, p. 75). The existence of such strategies is based on assumptions that:

- corporate management determine overall strategies to achieve their organisational goals;
- strategic thinking is a prerequisite for organisational success;
- top management have some choice in the matter; and
- choice of industrial relations strategies and policies 'rationally implies they be linked to other objectives and policies' (Thurley and Wood, 1983).

Gennard and Judge (1997) argue that there should be a direct relationship between industrial relations strategies and business strategy:

[They] need to be imaginative, innovative and action-oriented. They need to be formulated by a continuing process of analysis to identify what is happening to the business and where it is going. In this context, the relevance of clear business objectives, as expressed through the medium of a mission statement, cannot be overstated. The key is to develop an employee relations strategy which is responsive to the needs of the organisation, which can provide an overall sense of purpose to the employee relations specialist, and which assists employees in understanding where they are going, how they are going to get there, why certain things are happening, and most importantly, the contribution they are expected to make towards achieving the organisational goals. Another key feature is to ensure that the employee relations policies and strategies do not stand alone but integrate with other employment policies and strategies. (p. 96)

It is also important to realise that industrial relations strategy formulation is not only a matter of choice, but also of constraints. Poole (1980) argues that the constraints upon strategy formulation arise from environmental pressures upon the organisation, particularly economic and political. These pressures limit strategic choices and may stifle initiative. Major constraints which Poole identifies stem from the nature of the free enterprise market ideology, which limits managerial discretion by implementing strategies which favour the satisfaction of economic and production needs of the organisation rather than meeting the needs and aspirations of employees (minimising wage costs while maintaining or increasing productivity). Another significant constraint concerns the role of the state in managing the economy which 'through a corporatist political ideology or indirectly through a laissez-faire one, may constrain managerial freedom and initiative at organisational level' (Salamon, 1998, p. 217).

Self-Evaluation Activity 2.9

Changing industrial relations strategies: the ongoing case of Rover
Response on website

Read Main case 2.1 and attempt the question which follows.

Main case 2.1
Rover Cars

In the spring of 1994, British Aerospace sold its 80 per cent share of Rover to BMW for £800 million. The sale of Britain's last volume manufacturer to a German company provoked an outcry, but this has begun to subside as BMW provide assurances as to the future of the Rover factories and the Rover badge, and settle their differences with Honda who owned the other 20 per cent of Rover. These events come at the end of a remarkable story of strategic change in a company written off just a few years ago as incompetent, out of date, riddled with bad industrial relations and poor working practices, and producing second-rate motor vehicles. The chief negotiator for the MSF Union at Rover commented: 'Over a decade ago, Rover managed workers by fear and intimidation.'

Rover manufactures cars at its principal sites at Longbridge and Solihull, near Birmingham, and at Cowley, Oxford. These sites were typical British 'brownfield' sites with competing unions and poor productivity, but with considerable engineering experience and innovation. The Cowley plant was opened by

Lord Nuffield in 1913 to house Morris Motors. Today 3500 workers at Cowley turn out the 600 and 800 models, amongst other models, and annual productivity has risen to 34 cars per employee.

Land Rover is based at Solihull. Fifteen years ago it was a ponderous sprawling business, overmanned and inefficient, and with two products, the Land Rover and Range Rover, which were long in the tooth. Today, Land Rover has also been transformed; it took 115.9 hours per man to make a Land Rover in 1991, and by 1993 this was down to 86.4 hours, and progressively reducing. The relatively new model, the Discovery, is helping to push up sales. Remaining models, including the 200/400 series, are built at Longbridge, the former Austin Car Company headquarters.

In order to understand the culture change that has transformed Rover, it is important to understand its past history, and the transformation that has taken place. The Austin Car Company dates back to 1905, Morris to 1912, Rover to 1904 and Leyland to 1896. In 1968 British Leyland was created to run the British-owned vehicle industry, incorporating these and other once famous names. In 1975 the Labour government bought out British Leyland's private shareholders. In 1977 Michael Edwardes was appointed Chairman to turn the company around. Edwardes was successful in gaining new investment, taming the power of the union barons, and reforming working practices. However, the company was still making losses, and producing cars with a quality inferior to those of the Japanese and Germans. In 1986 Graham Day was appointed Chief Executive. Under Day the car business was reshaped, cutting production to viable levels while moving the range upmarket with the help of Honda. Honda became the dominant partner in engineering design. BL, as British Leyland was now termed, was sliced up – trucks were sold to DAF of the Netherlands, buses to a management group, Unipart – the spare part operations – to a group of financial institutions, and the remains of BL, renamed Rover, to British Aerospace in 1989 (adapted from Lundy and Cowling, 1996, pp. 361–2).

From an industrial relations perspective, perhaps the most important change in BL/Rover over the years has been the transformation of union-management relations from one of almost perennial conflict to one of mutual accommodation. This in turn suggests a transformation of power relationships particularly during the 1980s at Rover. As Rose and Woolley (1992, p. 263) suggest: 'What seems clear from much of the research dealing with the past relationships between employees and employers in the car industry is that, until the 1980s it was one founded manifestly on inequality of power, differing needs and aspirations and a history characterised by the often crude use of power by both parties.' Terry and Edwards (1988), for example, examine such events and provide a retrospective analysis and perspective concerning employers often in the person of entrepreneurial 'tycoons' such as William Morris and Herbert Austin who used their power to obtain a reduction in union influence.

The Edwardes era within the company was characterised by aggressive assertions of managerial prerogatives, dilution of (overt) union power and major changes in working practices. In retrospect, it can be argued that such developments were considered necessary and desirable, albeit unpopular with much of the workforce. The view that the Edwardes' initiative represented 'an important unblocking of a logjam', but that the methods used to dilute union power were 'unfortunate' and unsustainable in the long term was one that many managers held. The period following the departure of Edwardes was one of growing confidence at Rover and provided the impetus for a change of strategy and the initiation of a new management style.

Rob Meakin, who became Personnel Director of the Rover Group in 1989, 'sold' the notion of 'Roverisation' and the Total Quality Initiative (TQI). This has been described as a process by which the workforce of some 40 000 employees will become dedicated out of self-interest to the welfare of the firm, multi-skilled, flexible, committed to quality and 'with us all the way'.

The previous ideology (of the Edwardes' period and earlier) based on 'conflict of interest' and structured in terms of 'antagonistic' trade unions matched by 'hard-nosed' combative management is no longer the policy. To be sure, there do appear to be a minority of those who still advocate adversarial styles of industrial relations, but despite this, there is general endorsement of the radical and fundamental change from overt conflict to mutuality (adapted from Rose and Woolley, 1992, pp. 260–1).

The degree of change since 1989 has been remarkable, given this past history, and a culture developed over many years embodying hostility between management and workers. Strategic change at Rover has succeeded in combining essential ingredients of social and technical change. Rover could only hope to survive if it adopted the 'lean production' methods of the Japanese

successfully, and achieve a social change amongst its employees whereby they willingly contributed to the goals of the organisation of survival and profit, and adopted the new working practices now needed. Alongside lean production had to come a commitment to total quality. The basic ingredients of the human resource strategy (incorporating the industrial relations strategy) had to include a change of culture, a shared vision for the future, a major investment in retraining, a customer focus, team working, flexibility and an end to demarcation and continuous improvement. The seven basic principles of TQI were:

- prevention not detection
- management-led
- everyone responsible
- cost of poor quality
- right first time
- company-wide
- continuous improvement

Rover employees were organised in teams under team leaders, with teams operating like quality circles. Previously spans of control had about 30 hourly-paid employees under a foreman, who was in turn responsible to a senior foreman, who answered in turn to a superintendent. An assessment centre was used to select the new team leaders. The new teams consisted of about 40–50 employees. No extra supervising jobs were created, and ex-foremen not selected as team leaders became trained facilitators or took voluntary redundancy. On the production line teams were empowered to stop the process when a fault occurred, and to work out the best way to solve the problem.

In 1991 Rover proposed a new industrial relations deal. This proposal was made two weeks before the implementation of the second stage of a two-year pay deal and its provisions included:

- single-status terms and conditions
- greater emphasis on team working and continuous improvement; full flexibility
- streamlined trade union arrangements
- an updated procedure agreement.

Following negotiation with the unions and a ballot of workers, the agreement accepting these principles took effect in April 1992. As a result, 'clocking' has been abolished, single status has been implemented, regular health checks are provided and payment is by weekly credit transfer. In the event of layoffs, for so long the bugbear of the car industry, all employees continue to be paid their standard salary, provided they undertake other work. The grading structure comprising a five-grade hourly and six-grade staff structure is being replaced by a scheme with a reduced number of occupational classifications. Teams are now responsible for quality, routine maintenance, housekeeping, plant and office layout, process improvements, cost reduction, control of tools and materials, work allocation, job rotation, and training each other.

In conclusion, one can argue that the turnaround at Rover and the co-operation of the unions only came about because Maggie Thatcher made it quite clear that she was not going to bail the company out again. Faced with the prospect of massive unemployment and layoffs, a sense of realism took over. However, to achieve levels of quality and productivity which match the Japanese and Germans, as Rover has done, required a change in attitudes and working practices of major proportions. The human resource strategy (incorporating the industrial relations strategy) was an essential ingredient in the total corporate strategy and the turnaround at Rover (adapted from Lundy and Cowling, 1996, pp. 361–2).

Postscript: Subsequent events affecting Rover up to 2004 are provided in the response to this SAE.

Comment on the changes to the industrial relations strategy that have been made by successive managements at BL/Rover.

Summary points

- Typologies of styles of industrial relations management are based upon the basic unitarist/pluralist distinction of Fox (1966).
- Fox (1974) elaborated upon the basic distinction which in turn was refined by Purcell and Sisson (1983). This typology is the one which is still referred to most frequently in industrial relations texts. The typology comprises:
  - traditionalists;
  - sophisticated paternalists/human relations;
  - sophisticated moderns (consulters/constitutionalists); and
  - standard moderns.

- Purcell and Gray (1986) and Purcell (1987) have positioned management industrial relations styles within the broad categories of 'individualism' and 'collectivism' (which are not mutually exclusive categories).
- The 'individualism/collectivism' dimension was further elaborated upon by Purcell (1987) and Purcell and Ahlstrand (1994).
- During the 1980s and 1990s, there was a reversal of the trend towards adopting 'sophisticated consultative' styles of industrial relations management as the 'sophisticated paternalist' (HRM) and 'cost minimisation' approaches gained ground.
- Within a growing number of larger companies industrial relations policies and practices are subsumed under and incorporated within their HRM strategies.

METHODS OF MANAGING THE EMPLOYMENT RELATIONSHIP

The example of BL/Rover/Rover MG demonstrates, amongst other aspects, how industrial relations management strategies and styles can change over a relatively short period of time. We now turn our attention to the question of **how** senior management actually manage the employment relationship with particular reference to personnel management and HRM. The basic methods whereby managers deal with industrial relations and personnel matters has been summarised by Gospel and Palmer (1993):

1. Firstly, senior management often depend upon **line management**, who comprise junior and middle managers, to deal with various personnel matters such as recruitment and working with employee representatives. One important advantage in devolving these matters to line management is its familiarity with the immediacy of the work situation and 'being there' to deal with problems as they arise. The tendency to decentralise collective bargaining arrangements and procedures in some organisations in recent years has tended to increase the importance of line management's role in this area. However, undue reliance upon line management has certain

disadvantages. Gospel and Palmer (1993, p. 72) point out that:

- if line managers spend too much time dealing with industrial relations problems, then this 'takes line managers away from their main task which is the management of production';
- 'different line managers can take different decisions and this can lead to inconsistencies which cause industrial relations problems'; and
- 'line managers are prone to take a short-term view of personnel matters'.

2. The problems encountered with line management may be minimised, particularly in larger organisations, by the use of **staff specialists** such as personnel managers. We will consider the role of personnel management in the next section, but suffice it to say here that the allocation of responsibility for industrial relations and related matters between staff and line is not clearly defined and changes over time. Gospel and Palmer (1993) point out that:

    Through the 1960s and 1970s the personnel function grew in power and influence, in part reflecting growing trade union power, increasing legislative intervention, and the institutionalisation of industrial relations. In the 1980s, however, there has been a shift back from managing through the personnel function towards giving line managers more responsibility for personnel matters, especially in such areas as selection, appraisal and training. In more complex areas such as design of pay and benefit systems, many firms are also using specialist external consultants. This sometimes leaves personnel departments with a mixture of more strategic planning functions and lower-level administrative functions. (p. 73)

3. As we have seen in Chapter 1, **employers' associations** play a part in the management of industrial relations, and their functions will be considered in greater detail later on.

4. A final method of industrial relations management identified by Gospel and Palmer is through the medium of various forms of **subcontracting** which has become increasingly important in recent years. Subcontracting is a method of employing the labour force indirectly through an agent or subcontractor who also deals with recruiting the workforce, monitoring production and paying workers. Subcontracting arrangements were fairly common in the nineteenth century, particularly in industries such as coal mining, iron manufacture, shipbuilding, cotton and pottery, but declined in importance as competitive and technological pressures increased. There has, however, been a resurgence of subcontracting in recent years, particularly in clerical, catering and maintenance work, in services provided by the NHS and by local authorities. This development has resulted in many instances in the creation of a so-called 'two-tier workforce' within the public services (see Chapter 6). Gospel and Palmer (1993) point out that:

Subcontracting has the advantage that labour matters are handed over to someone else, the firm does not need to take on a large staff directly, and it is easier to lay workers off if necessary. It has the disadvantages, however, that organisations using subcontracted labour have less direct control over labour costs and over the effort and compliance of workers. (p. 74)

Subcontracting has caused a number of disputes including that concerning cleaners at Hillingdon Hospital, as related in Mini case 2.5.

Mini case 2.5
Subcontracting at Hillingdon Hospital

A private cleaning company which cut the wages of Asian women cleaners at Hillingdon Hospital in Uxbridge, West London, by up to £30 a week also demanded that they hand over their passports for photocopying to prove that they were legally entitled to work. Many of the women had worked in the hospital for more than 15 years. Yesterday, 56 workers began to picket the hospital after they were sacked for refusing to agree to new terms and conditions, including the salary cuts, reduced payments for weekend working, and cuts in holiday pay. Mal Kiab Bilko said: 'In June when they tried to give us the new contracts they started asking for our passports and photocopying them. It was the timing of it. They were trying to scare people into signing the new contracts.' Pall Mall, the company which employed the women, yesterday said it would not comment on the passport demands. Hillingdon Hospital, which granted the cleaning contract to Pall Mall, has washed its hands of the dispute, saying that the women 'now belong to Pall Mall' and it will not interfere with the working of a 'perfectly reputable company'. The firm is, however, under union attack for allegedly driving down conditions and forcing other private contractors to follow suit. The women also claimed that Pall Mall had used heavy-handed tactics to persuade the women to sign. The head of Unison's health section said: 'It is outrageous in this day and age that people should be forced to take a £25 to £30 pay cut. Our campaign aim is to point out just what bad employers Pall Mall are.' The union was in dispute with Pall Mall in two other hospitals in England and Scotland.

Source: Adapted from *The Guardian*,
3 September 1997

Personnel management

In many larger public and private sector organisations the traditional personnel department assumed responsibility for the management of industrial relations amongst other functions, with a minority having dedicated industrial relations departments. Many smaller firms do not have personnel departments and some dispense with personnel managers altogether (Cully *et al.*, 1999). Additionally, as Legge (1995) points out, there would appear to be a credibility gap affecting personnel management, one of the causes of which must be the lack of consensus concerning the meaning of the term 'personnel management' since there are in existence at least four defining models of the term.

Model one: The normative model

The term 'normative' refers to what 'ought' to be. Personnel management is therefore defined in terms of what it should aspire to. The model is prescriptive, although the definitions actually tend to equate

what 'is' with what 'ought to be'. Legge (1995) summarises the approach thus:

> *It seems that personnel management is about selecting, developing, rewarding and directing employees in such a way that not only will they achieve satisfaction and 'give of their best' at work, but by so doing enable the employing organisation to achieve its goals. Furthermore, personnel management is the task of all managers, not just of personnel specialists alone.* (p. 4)

Model two: The descriptive-functional model

This model defines personnel management in terms of the functions it actually serves rather than what these functions should be and is concerned with the regulation of employment relationships. According to Legge:

> *Neither [definition] assumes that the regulation is directed towards some fixed God-given set of organisation goals, but rather implies (or explicitly states) that the goals as well as the means to achieve them are open to negotiation. ... The existence of different stakeholders within an organisation identifies the necessary function of regulation. If an organisation is to survive, regulation is necessary – and hence is the prime function of personnel management.* (p. 5)

Model three: The critical-evaluative model

Legge identifies just one definition – that of Watson (1986) – as being the unique exemplar of this model:

> *Personnel management is concerned with assisting those who run work organisations to meet their purpose through the obtaining of the work efforts of human beings, the exploitation of those efforts and the dispensing of those efforts when they are no longer required. Concern may be shown with human welfare, justice or satisfactions but only insofar as this is necessary for controlling interests to be met and, then always at least cost.* (Watson, 1986, p. 176)

Watson's definition is critical from a radical (or Marxist) perspective as personnel management is deemed to be exploitative rather than regulatory.

Model four: The descriptive-behavioural model

If personnel management can be defined in terms of what it should do (normative) and what function or functions it actually serves, how do personnel people behave in order to achieve all of this? Definitions based on what personnel specialists actually do 'at best convey an air of disappointment and at worst are positively disparaging, even insulting' (Legge, 1995, p. 6). Drucker's (1961) view of personnel management still holds good:

> *Personnel administration . . . is largely a collection of incidental techniques without much internal cohesion. As personnel administration conceives the job of managing workers and work, it is partly a file clerk's job, partly a housekeeping job, partly a social worker's job and partly fire-fighting to head off union trouble or to settle it. . . . The things the personnel administrator is typically responsible for – safety and pension plans, the suggestion system, the employment office and union's grievances – are necessary chores. I doubt though that they should be put together in one department for they are a hodge podge . . . They are neither one function by kinship of skills required to carry out the activities, nor are they one function by being linked together in the work process, by forming a distinct stage in the work of the managers or in the process of the business. (pp. 269–70)*

Self-Evaluation Activity 2.10

Definitions and models of personnel management
Response on website

Given below are two definitions of personnel management. Identify which definition approximates to which model, and justify your decision.

1. Personnel management is a responsibility of all those who manage people, as well as being a description of the work of those who are employed as specialists. It is that part of management which is concerned with people at work and with their relationships within an enterprise. Personnel management aims to achieve both efficiency and justice, neither of which can be pursued successfully without the other. It seeks to bring together and develop into an effective organisation the men and women who make up an enterprise, enabling each to make his or her own best contribution to its success both as an individual and as a member of a working group. It seeks to provide fair terms and conditions of employment, and satisfying work for those employed (IPM, 1963).

2. Personnel management is a series of activities which: firstly enables working people and their employing organisations to agree about the nature of their working relationship and, secondly, ensures that the agreement is fulfilled (Torrington and Hall, 1987).

Typologies of personnel management

The most well-known typology is that of Tyson and Fell (1986). Using a 'low-discretion/high-discretion' continuum and metaphors from the construction industry, they identify three main types:

- *'Clerk of the works'*. Is mainly concerned with routine matters such as record keeping, preparing letters and documents on instruction, first interviewing of some applicants for employment and welfare matters. The clerk reports to a senior line manager or personnel manager.
- *'Contracts manager'*. This type is most likely to be found in organisations with a strong trade union presence and a traditional industrial relations background. There is involvement in policy-making, but not normally of a strategic nature. The main activity is likely to be the making and interpretation of procedures and agreements. In some organisations this type may exercise considerable power and authority which comes from the ability to resolve day-to-day problems, and from intimate knowledge and personal relationships with shop stewards and trade union officers as well as senior line managers.
- *'Architect'*. This type is likely to be extensively involved in policy-making as a member of the

senior management team and/or to have a seat on the board of directors. The architect will see himself or herself as 'business manager' first and personnel manager second and will have a broad portfolio which encompasses not just dealing with trade unions but with the organisation's entire human resources. He or she is also likely to be involved in the design of the structure of the organisation. The architect is probably qualified, both academically and vocationally, although he or she may not be a member of the IPD, and may well have considerable experience as a line manager or consultant at some stage of his or her career.

As a result of survey and case study work, Storey (1992) proposed an alternative two-dimensional classification based, firstly, upon the extent to which personnel managers intervene in decision-making and, secondly, the extent to which the type of intervention which does prevail is strategic or tactical. Figure 2.4 locates the types of personnel management on these dimensions.

Type 1: Advisers

Advisers act as 'internal consultants' and are knowledgeable about current developments but prefer to leave everyday things to line and general managers. The adviser role is compatible with devolved management structures which place more responsibility upon line managers. Advisers arguably have a more strategic focus.

Type 2: Handmaidens

More subservient than advisers, but like the adviser adopts a mainly non-interventionary stance, 'but the kind of contribution made is more of a service provider at the behest of the line' (Storey, 1992, p. 172). Handmaidens act out an imposed role rather than one they want to play and are responsive to customer requirements. The handmaiden role is often the result of organisational restructuring, itself a result of 'prolonged buffeting in the shape of reorganisations, shifts in priorities and culture, budget cuts and similar threats to traditional, and relatively stable, personnel and IR roles' (ibid., p. 172). More specifically, they:

- service the routine requirements of the line;
- fulfil a clerical and welfare function (maintain records for absence, sickness and pay; visiting sick employees); and
- explain rules and regulations and procedures to line managers who are faced with a grievance from a unionised workforce.

The handmaiden role differs from the adviser type in that the service offered is more routine and administrative and more tactical than strategic.

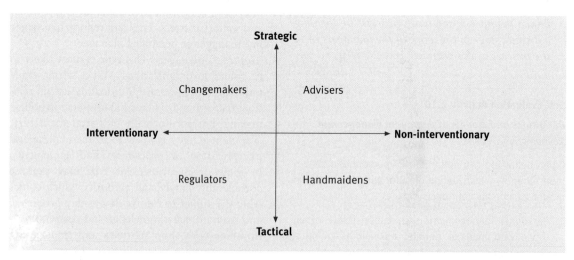

Figure 2.4 Types of personnel management
Source: Based on Storey, 1992

Type 3: Regulators

Regulators are more interventionist in the conduct of managing the employment relationship, but these interventions rarely concern wider strategic policies of the organisation. Storey states (1992, pp. 175–6):

> In many regards they represent the classic IR manager – responsible for devising, negotiating and defending the procedural and substantive rules which govern employment relations. They are to be found at both company and establishment level. Some of their rule-making activity may appear to have 'strategic' character in that it occasionally involves such 'big' decisions as union recognition and membership or non-membership of employers' associations. But these sorts of decisions are rarely recognised as of a corporate strategy nature by senior business managers. . . . In a company or plant where the personnel specialist plays a regulatory role the line manager may feel displaced and upstaged or, in time, readily abdicate managerial responsibility in labour matters to this specialist.

Type 4: Changemakers

> This role type denotes the natural location of the human resource manager proper. These personnel specialists make a highly proactive, interventionary and strategic contribution. The orientation is away from bargaining, away from ad hocery, and away from 'humble advice'. It is, in fact, the antithesis of all these. The integration of the different aspects of resourcing, planning, appraising, rewarding and developing and the further integration of all this into the business plan are the characteristic features of this type of personnel approach. (Storey, 1992, p. 176)

The changemaker role is however more ideal than real and may encompass both types of HRM, the 'hard' and the 'soft' (see below).

Self-Evaluation Activity 2.11

Types of personnel practitioner
This SEA has no commentary

In order to appreciate the nature of Storey's typology, read the four statements given below and identify which of these approximate to the four types of personnel practitioner:

1. 'Personnel is part of the total management system and shares with line managers in running the business – contributing from vision to results, and operating in the forefront of change management. It acts in partnership with line management and provides expert advice on all aspects of manpower management. These include not only traditional personnel areas such as training and employee relations but also the most fundamental issues of company business policy and philosophy.'

2. 'I try to ensure that discussions are between line managers and their opposite numbers on the trade union side. Me and my people are not to be seen as go-betweens or, still less, as people who make the line managers roll over. The line managers have to have the commitment to the solution. I like to see them getting on with it and I like to keep out of their hair.'

3. 'It is only a few years ago that the production managers here would pass all their IR problems on to us. More than once I have come into this very room [a conference room] to find a plant manager facing a group of stewards whose lads had already walked off the job. As soon as I came through that door the so-called manager would stand up and say "Ah I'm glad you've arrived to sort this out" and then he'd head off out!'

4. 'I basically deal with the production managers and as far as I'm concerned the personnel managers serve them. However, what I do want is definitely more "say" on the types of services offered by the RGMs [regional general managers] and naturally much of this relates to what Personnel are doing. It means I want to look at job descriptions, I want to look at management development . . . yes I really want to know what it is that I am paying for.'

Personnel as contradiction?

The diversity of definitional models reflects the inconsistency and ambiguity of approach adopted by personnel managers to their organisational status and role, and this has resulted in a crisis of credibility. The problem not only concerns the mismatch between the pious aspirations articulated by the normative model and the reality of what personnel managers actually do, but also stems from a chequered history of the profession and the consequences of its role within a capitalist society.

The quality of industrial relations and personnel policies and practices is largely a reflection of the quality of British management. If these policies are not particularly successful (as in the case of the Edwardes' era at British Leyland) as a result, for example, of adopting inappropriate strategies or styles, then personnel management often has to shoulder the blame. The following factors help to explain the contradictions inherent within the personnel management function.

Historical

Personnel management had its origins in the larger paternalist firms of the nineteenth century with the emphasis upon employee welfare and well-being. With the advent of the First World War, large numbers of women were employed for the first time in munitions, and the government and other employers recruited personnel or welfare officers, most of whom were also women, in order to deal with recruitment and other labour-related issues. Many firms dispensed with personnel managers and departments as an expensive luxury during the inter-war depression years, but in those firms which retained personnel departments, the gender profile changed and personnel management became increasingly male-dominated as they assumed responsibility for industrial relations matters. The Second World War provided an impetus to the growth of personnel management as once more women were recruited to war-related industries and by 1946 there were around 5000 personnel managers in Britain. However, up to the end of the 1950s personnel management was considered to be a low-status occupation with little professional credibility. Gospel and Palmer (1993) state:

> Overall, the majority of personnel managers in Britain lacked formal qualifications and personnel management remained relatively low-status in the management hierarchy. Their role was usually administrative and reactive rather than strategic or proactive and, in dealings with trade

> unions, much was still left to employers' associations. (p. 75)

During the 1960s and 1970s, with the increasing complexity and volume of individual and collective employment legislation and the higher profiling of employment-related problems and issues, the number of personnel managers increased from 15 000 in the 1960s to 50 000 by the late 1970s. Numbers continue to increase as does membership of the IPD. However, as we have previously noted, many small firms still do not have personnel specialists, and even during the early 1980s, more than half of all personnel managers did not belong to the IPM (now IPD). Sisson (1995, p. 89) reinforces the point that 'many personnel managers did not see themselves as "professional" in the sense of owing their prime loyalty to the occupation'. Most were 'managers first and personnel people second' (Mackay and Torrington, 1986, pp. 161–2). Other relevant points in recent historical context made by Sisson include:

- Personnel management, as we have already seen, is not a single homogeneous occupation but involves 'a variety of roles and activities which differ from one organisation to another and, perhaps more importantly, from one level to another in the same organisation', and this can be seen in relation to Tyson and Fell's (1986) and Storey's (1992) typologies.
- The 'balkanisation' of personnel management. 'Not only was there a variety of roles and activities, but these tended to be relatively self-contained, with little passage between them. Many of the architects [in relation to Tyson and Fell's typology] came from the ranks of line managers, rather than personnel managers' (p. 89).
- Personnel management was highly structured on gender lines. Women made up the great majority of personnel managers, yet they tended to be employed in lower-level and less well-paid jobs than their male counterparts, which helped to reinforce the 'Cinderella' image of the function as a whole.

Within a capitalist market economy

As Legge (1995) states: 'The fact that personnel specialists oscillate between the "personnel" and "management", between "caring" and "control" aspects of the function, can be attributed to their role in mediating a major contradiction embedded in capitalist systems: the need to achieve both the control *and* consent of employees' (p. 14). The control issue has been dealt with in an earlier section of this chapter. In relation to personnel management, the following issues are relevant:

- Personnel management helps to realise surplus value. 'Surplus value' is a Marxist concept which Giddens (1989) defines thus: 'In the course of the working day, workers produce more than is actually needed by employers to repay the cost of hiring them. This surplus value is the source of profit, which capitalists are able to put to their own use' (p. 210).
- Personnel managers help to create surplus value by ensuring that control systems are in place. Edwards (1979) identifies three aspects of control relevant to personnel management:
  - direction and specification of work tasks;
  - evaluation, monitoring and assessment of performance; and
  - discipline and reward systems designed to encourage co-operation and compliance.
- As we have seen, control systems often engender employee resistance which takes the form of absenteeism, labour turnover and various forms of industrial action which in turn may impede surplus value and profit. Personnel managers also ameliorate the more adverse consequences of control systems by emphasising the caring/welfare function.
- The personnel manager is therefore a mediator between 'the formally rational criteria of productivity, profit, effectiveness and the rest, [and] the human needs, interests and aspirations of employees' (Watson, 1977, p. 63). This may cause credibility problems as managers oscillate between satisfying the competing demands of 'control' and 'care'.

Within a patriarchal society

A further source of contradiction and ambiguity within the personnel specialism is the legacy of patriarchy. Essentially, patriarchy refers to male dominance, and is 'a set of hierarchical relations between men, and solidarity among them, which enables them to control women. Patriarchy is thus the system of male oppression of women' (Hartmann, 1982, p. 138). Traditionally, because of their role as mothers and carers, women are primarily absorbed in domestic activities and become the 'second sex' because they are excluded from the more 'public' activities in which males are free to engage (de Beauvoir, 1972). The existence of patriarchy has given rise to gender inequalities at work and elsewhere.

Initially, personnel was dominated by women, and up to the 1930s the vast majority of personnel managers were women. The Quaker concern for employee welfare (often regarded as a female concern) was regarded as low in the order of priorities for most enterprises in the first half of the twentieth century. As Legge (1995) points out:

> This early development of personnel management with female welfare activities in a patriarchal society inevitably meant that the function would carry a legacy as being of low status and unimportance, at least in comparison to central male activities, such as production, finance and so on. . . . It is not surprising, then, that personnel management has an enduring problem of establishing credibility. In its task of managing the contradictions of capitalism, personnel specialists become prey to a series of ambiguities and double-bind situations, from which extraction is difficult, if not to say impossible. In the decade of the enterprise culture and into the 1990s, human resource management is being presented as a model of managing people at work that is more credible than personnel management. (p. 20)

We now consider the nature of human resource management (HRM) and its relationship to personnel management within the employment relationship.

HUMAN RESOURCE MANAGEMENT: OLD WINE IN NEW BOTTLES?

Chapter 5 contains a fuller discussion of HRM and workplace industrial relations. In this section we explain the meaning of HRM and how it differs from traditional personnel management. HRM arguably incorporates more strategic approaches to managing industrial and employee relations

(Farnham, 1997) within larger organisations and in response to changes in product market competition, market structure and technology.

HRM and related developments are well documented (Storey, 1992; Storey and Sisson, 1993; Legge, 1995; Storey, 1995). HRM emerged in Britain during the mid-1980s after originating in the United States and could be described as 'the Americanised version of "Japanese" methods' (Storey, 1992). Its development has been somewhat haphazard and eclectic, there being no single, consistent approach to HRM in most organisations which have, by their own admission, adopted such practices. The main reason for this, as Storey goes on to argue, is that HRM is subject to different interpretations both theoretically/strategically, and operationally. For example, HRM is often taken to be synonymous with personnel management; a label change is often considered sufficient, but this merely masks the same old practices and policies. Many organisations go further and attempt to integrate the various personnel management techniques (including elements of industrial relations) in a systematic way. With this in mind, we can identify a general definition and two important HRM categories or models.

Definition

Storey's (1995) definition of HRM is fairly specific in orientation:

> Human resource management is a distinctive approach to employment management which seeks to achieve competitive advantage through the strategic deployment of a highly committed and capable workforce, using an integrated array of cultural, structural and personnel techniques. (p. 5)

On the other hand, Boxall and Purcell (2003) opt for an all-inclusive definition in which the term 'human resource management' is equated with the terms 'employee relations' and 'labour management':

> Human resource management (alternatively 'employee relations' or 'labour management') includes the firm's work systems and its models of employment. It embraces both individual and collective aspects of people management. It is not restricted to any one style or ideology. It engages the energies of both line and specialist managers (where the latter exist) and typically entails a blend of messages for a variety of workforce groups. (p. 23)

The main components of HRM are represented in summary form in Exhibit 2.1.

The first element concerns beliefs, assumptions and values about the importance of the human resource above all other factors of production. If the organisation is to be competitive, then the human resource must be developed as a valued asset in order to secure employee commitment, adaptability and continuous improvement. The second element is to do with strategy and the strategic importance of HRM in securing competitive advantage. The third element concerns line management. As we have seen in our discussion of personnel management, line management often assumes greater importance in dealing with operational IR and related issues, and Storey (1995) states:

> If human resources are so critical for business success, then HRM is too important to be left to operational personnel specialists. Line managers are seen as crucial to the effective delivery of HRM policies: conducting team briefings, holding performance appraisal interviews, target setting, encouraging quality circles, managing performance-related pay, and so on. (p. 7)

The fourth element concerns key levers used in the implementation of HRM, particularly the emphasis upon the 'management of culture'. Storey notes: 'Corporate culture management has generated much excitement because it is perceived to offer a key to the unlocking of consensus, flexibility and commitment. These are self-evidently prized objectives' (ibid., p. 8).

Within the broad definition of HRM, we have two important subcategories based on Storey's (1987) distinction between 'hard' and 'soft' models which are described below.

The 'hard' model

The 'hard' model emphasises the importance of integrating human resources policies, systems and activities with business strategy, and is a response to internal and external pressures during the 1980s

Exhibit 2.1

The HRM model

1. *Beliefs and assumptions*
   - That it is the human resource which gives competitive edge.
   - That the aim should be not mere compliance with rules, but employee commitment.
   - That therefore employees should be very carefully selected and developed.
2. *Strategic qualities*
   - Because of the above factors, HR decisions are of strategic importance.
   - Top management involvement is necessary.
   - HR policies should be integrated into the business strategy – stemming from it and even contributing to it.
3. *Critical role of managers*
   - Because HR practice is critical to the core activities of the business, it is too important to be left to person-nel specialists alone.
   - Line managers need to be closely involved both as deliverers and drivers of the HR policies.
   - Much greater attention is paid to the management of managers themselves.
4. *Key levers*
   - Managing culture is more important than managing procedures and systems.
   - Integrated action on selection, communication, training, reward and development.
   - Restructuring and job design to allow devolved responsibility and empowerment.

Source: Storey, 1995, p. 6

which required organisations to be more competit-ive nationally and globally and adopt an increas-ingly market-led stance. These pressures affected both private and public sector organisations and concerned technological change, 'quality' initiatives and customer-oriented services. Organisational changes including mergers and 'rationalisations', decentralising and delayering strategies and the devolution of routine responsibilities to line man-agers within cost centres reflected a desire to create a performance-oriented culture. It is assumed that personnel policies, systems and practices are con-sistent with and supportive of business objectives. Specifically, the 'hard' model emphasises:

- that the human resource is no more and no less than a factor of production together with land and capital and is an 'expense' rather than a potential for turning production into wealth;
- that human resources are passive and reactive rather than creative and proactive; and
- that there is an emphasis upon the 'quantitative, calculative and business strategic aspects of man-aging the headcount in as "rational" a way as for any other economic factor' (Storey, 1987, p. 6).

The 'soft' model

The 'soft' model also stresses the importance of integrating HR policies with business objectives. Specifically, the model has certain assumptions embedded in it (paraphrasing Legge, 1995, p. 36):

- employees are treated as valued assets;
- employees are a source of competitive advantage through their commitment, adaptability and high quality of performance and skills;
- employees are proactive and capable of 'develop-ment', worthy of 'trust' and 'collaboration', to be achieved through 'participation' and 'informed choice';
- management generates employee commitment through communication, motivation, and lead-ership; and
- greater employee commitment will result in improved economic performance and so assist in employee development and training.

Apart from the 'hard' and 'soft' models of HRM, Storey (1992) distinguishes two different HRM approaches identified as 'strong' and 'weak'. The 'strong' approach assumes a distinctive package which encompasses both strategic and operational aspects of HRM, while the 'weak' approach assumes that organisations can get by through changing the name 'personnel' to 'HRM', as with 'old wine in new bottles' (see Figure 2.5).

Self-Evaluation Activity 2.12

'Strong' commitment: hard or soft?

The response is given below

Given in Exhibit 2.2 is an example of an organisation with a 'strong' commitment and approach to HRM. Indicate whether this is also an example of the 'soft' or 'hard' model.

The example indicates a distinctive 'strong' approach to HRM strategy and practice which is characteristic of the 'soft' model. Moreover, Legge (1995) argues that the 'hard' and 'soft' models are not incompatible with each other or mutually exclusive, and many organisations will contain elements of both; it is the combination of the 'strategic' and 'commitment' elements

which provides organisations with the opportunity and means to develop competitive strategies based on value added, quality and flexibility rather than on cost alone. It is doubtful, however, whether in practice the take-up of 'soft' HRM is particularly widespread, as Legge (1995) argues:

> [HRM practices and policies] are adopted to drive business values and are modified in the light of changing business objectives and conditions. It is a thinking pragmatism. Insofar that any one model is being implemented, the evidence would suggest more support for the 'hard' rather than the 'soft' model. There is little evidence for the widespread implementation of the long-term developmental 'soft' model, yet it is the latter that is supposed to be distinctly different from the stereotypes of personnel management practice, not the former. Is what we are seeing in reality the implementation of the old-style 'standard modern' personnel management, asserting an opportunistic exercise of managerial prerogative, but dressed up in a 'soft' HRM rhetoric? (p. 47)

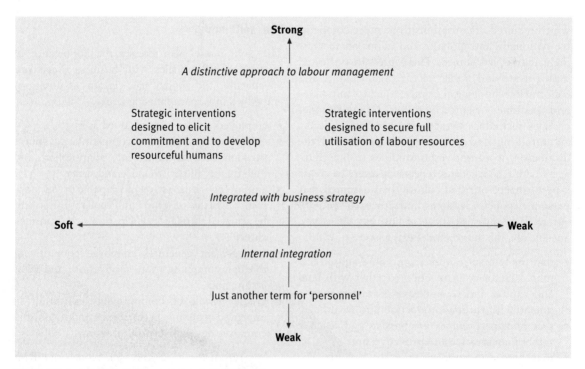

Figure 2.5 Approaches to the management of labour
Source: Storey, 1992, p. 27

Exhibit 2.2

An organisation with a strong commitment to HRM

1. The firm competes on the basis of product quality and differentiation as well as price.
2. Human resource considerations weigh heavily in corporate strategic decision-making and governance processes. Employee interests are represented through the voice of the human resource staff professionals and/or employee representatives consult and participate with senior executives in decisions that affect human resource policies and employee interests. In either case, employees are treated as legitimate stakeholders in the corporation.
3. Investments in new hardware or physical technology are combined with the investments in human resources and changes in organisational practices required to realise the full potential benefits of these investments.
4. The firm sustains a high level of investment in training, skill development and education, and personnel practices are designed to capture and utilise these skills fully.
5. Compensation and reward systems are internally equitable, competitive and linked to the long-term performance of the firm.
6. Employment continuity and security is an important priority and value to be considered in all corporate decisions and policies.
7. Workplace relations encourage flexibility in the organisation of work, empowerment of employees to solve problems, and high levels of trust among workers, supervisors and managers.
8. Worker rights to representation are acknowledged and respected. Union or other employee representatives are treated as joint partners in designing and overseeing innovations in labour and human resource practices.

Source: Beaumont, 1995, p. 40

HRM and personnel management

Can HRM be distinguished from personnel management, or is it a case of the 'emperor's new clothes'? Is it the same old personnel management dressed up in the verbiage and rhetoric of market-led managerialism with a social conscience? As long ago as 1987, Fowler argued that what is new about HRM is not what it is, but who is saying it: 'In a nutshell, HRM represents the discovery of personnel management by chief executives.' Fowler's statement at least recognises the strategic focus of HRM, but seems to imply that HRM is 'strategic' personnel management. Armstrong (1987) reinforces this argument:

It could indeed be no more and no less than another name for personnel management, but, as usually perceived, at least it has the virtue of emphasising the need to treat people as a key resource, the management of which is the direct concern of top management as part of the strategic

planning process of the enterprise. Although there is nothing new in the idea, insufficient attention has been paid to it in many organisations. The new bottle or label can help to overcome this deficiency. (quoted in Legge, 1995, p. 69)

If HRM is similar to personnel management, what is the nature of these similarities? Legge identifies four similarities:

- Both emphasise the importance of integrating personnel/HRM practices with organisational goals.
- Both vest personnel/HRM practice firmly in line management.
- Both, in the main, stress the importance of individuals developing their abilities fully for their own personal satisfaction to make their 'best contribution' to organisational success.
- Both identify placing the 'right' people into the 'right' jobs as an important means of integrating personnel/HRM practice with organisational goals, including individual development.

Given the variety of HRM and personnel categories and models, however, it would be inappropriate to infer that there were no differences between the two. As Legge (1995) argues, 'Perhaps the sharpest contrasts may be found in comparing British personnel management models with US HRM models, or paradoxically, the "hard" and "soft" versions of the HRM model' (p. 72). Farnham (1997) identifies five areas of difference between HRM and personnel management:

- HRM focuses on employees as resources which, like other resources, need to be used efficiently.
- HRM views employees as a key resource, with employers actively pursuing employee commitment to corporate goals and values. Only through a systematic set of policies on recruitment, rewards for performance, staff appraisal, training and development and effective communication, it is argued, can commitment and excellence be achieved.
- HRM assumes that personnel management is the responsibility of all line managers rather than of personnel specialists.

- With HRM there is a preference for individual management communication with employees, rather than relying on collective forms of information exchange through trade unions.
- HRM assumes a neo-unitary model of employee relations, in contrast with the pluralist model underpinning traditional personnel management.

Figure 2.6 identifies variations and differences between the main personnel models and HRM.

The paternalist welfare model is largely unitary, equating with the sophisticated paternalist subcategory, while the professional personnel model is pluralist and incorporates the consultative, constitutionalist and standard modern categories. Both paternalist and professional models are grounded in the traditional 'culture' of personnel management in Britain. The HRM model is largely neo-unitary with emphases just as much upon the individualism as upon the collectivism inherent within the employment relationship. In addition, HRM, it could be argued, has a strategic orientation which personnel management often does not have, as Legge (1995) points out:

Selected characteristics	Dominant models of the personnel function		
	Paternalist welfare model	**Professional personnel model**	**HRM model**
Orientation	Welfare, moral and humanist	Occupational, service and manpower control	Managerial, market and HR utilisation
Ideology	Paternalist	Collectivist	Individualist
Role of personnel management	Person management	System management	Resource
Relationship with line management	Administrative	Advisory/executive	Strategic
Generic activity relations	Human relations	Industrial relations	Employee
Status of workforce	Workers	Employees	Professionals
Contract with workers	Social	Legal	Psychological
Role of unions	Marginal	Adversarial	Collaborationist/absent
Change	Slow	Moderate	Continuous
Market position	Protected	Stable	Competitive
Attitude to workforce	Cost containment of labour	Cost-effectiveness of workforce	Investment in human resources

Figure 2.6 Differences and similarities between personnel and HRM
Source: Farnham, 1997

[HRM is], in theory, a more central strategic management task than personnel management in that it is experienced by managers as the most valued company resource to be managed; it concerns them in the achievement of business goals and it expresses senior management's preferred organisational values. (p. 75)

In smaller firms where both personnel and HRM functions are not as well developed, employers will often turn to employers' associations (which are examined below) for assistance.

Changes in the management of employment relations: evidence from WIRS/WERS

Much of the information we have concerning the management of employment relations emanates from the Workplace Industrial Relations Survey (WIRS) series comprising four longitudinally-linked national surveys which took place in 1980, 1984, 1990 and 1998 (see Chapter 5 for a general overview of workplace change). The main findings from the 1998 Workplace Employee Relations Survey (WERS98) are summarised below (see also Millward *et al.*, 2000):

- The survey confirms the major demographic change concerning the increasing proportion of women in employment relations management – the 'feminisation of personnel' phenomenon referred to earlier in the chapter.
- Also plotted by the survey is the steady rise of the employment relations specialist (see Table 2.1), due mainly to the greater prevalence of specialists in newer workplaces. Millward *et al.* comment that 'the rise of the ER specialist, and the increased likelihood that they will hold employee relations qualifications, mark a significant departure in the way that a growing minority of workplaces manage employee relations [and where] . . . the conduct of employee relations is treated as a professional pursuit requiring formal credentials' (p. 81).
- The work content of employment relations specialists has remained remarkably consistent since 1984 with considerable majorities ranging from 61 to 95 per cent dealing with the 'traditional' responsibilities relating to pay and conditions of employment, recruitment/selection, training, payment systems, grievance handling and staffing. However, there has been a slight but perceptible increase in the proportion of non-specialist employee relations managers having functional responsibility for these areas.

Table 2.1 Job titles of workplace employee relations managers: 1980–8

	1980 %	1984 %	1990 %	1998 %
Employee relations specialists	15	16	17	23
Personnel manager	14	14	16	22
Employee/industrial/staff relations manager	1	2	1	1
Line managers	10	14	28	28
Accountant/finance function	6	7	11	10
Marketing/commercial/sales function	2	1	2	2
Professional/technical	2	6	15	16
Generalists	75	64	51	46
General management	49	49	24	34
Production/works/factory/plant manager	5	5	5	2
Branch/depot/establishment manager	21	11	22	10

Source: Millward *et al.*, 2000, p. 52

- The explosion of HRM titles is in evidence in newer workplaces and in existing ones where there has been a name change from ER specialist to HR manager.
- The survey reveals that within multi-site private sector organisations, board-level representation of employment relations fell from 1984 onwards and fewer head offices were employing ER specialists, thereby revealing a contradiction between the latter trend and the increase in ER workplace specialists.
- Evidence indicates that the job of the ER manager within multi-site organisations has become more complex since 1984 owing to a diffusion of ER practices throughout the organisation and the reduction of facilities enabling ER mangers to perform their tasks.
- These developments affect all sectors, but during the 1990s, the public sector was most affected, while the non-unionised private sector was least affected.

With regard to the corporate personnel/ER/HR (PEH) function in multinational and hence multi-site companies, there is much evidence in addition to WERS (Millward *et al.*, 2000) to suggest that there is indeed a decline in the role of PEH at corporate level as a result of decentralisation of organisational structures, and even the decline of collective industrial relations itself (Purcell and Ahlstrand, 1994). However, others would argue that there has been a resurgence of the PEH strategic role in multinational companies (MNCs) associated with the dynamics of the multi-divisional company – or dominant global M-form company structure and its variant the N-form company (M-form organisations are those organisations having many or multiple divisions; the N-form variant is based around networks) which is based around global information or knowledge economy networks (both types being defined as having structures based on multiple divisions) (Scullion and Starkey, 2000). There is also clear evidence that MNCs are innovators in HR and PEH practice at local as well as national/international level. The popular mantra 'think global, act local' means adapting PEH practice to local circumstances while pushing for performance and market leadership (Boxall and Purcell, 2003). Yet a third approach suggests a 'steady growth' thesis of the

PEH function's power and influence arising from the Donovan Report's (1968) recommendation that companies appoint directors responsible for industrial relations (Kelly, 2001). This is reinforced by the work of Kelly and Gennard (2001) whose research indicates that the PEH role continues to be increasingly important in the formulation and implementation of corporate business and HR strategies.

Employers' associations

The legal definition of an employers' association is provided in section 122 of the Trade Union and Labour Relations (Consolidation) Act 1992, the essence of which is that:

> Employers' associations are organisations which consist wholly or mainly of employers or individual owners of undertakings of one or more descriptions and whose principal purposes include the regulation of relations between employers of that description or those descriptions and workers or trade unions.

This definition implies that employers' associations exist mainly for industrial relations purposes, so it is important to note that non-industrial relations activities concerning commercial matters, for example, feature prominently for most associations.

Their origins

Early employers' associations which formed during the eighteenth century became widespread and fairly influential, and, like trade unions which formed much later into the nineteenth century, were locally based. During this early period there was little effort to co-operate with each other, although individual associations often used to influence rates of pay and some agreed standard wage rates and/or piecework rates. Where there was collaboration, then this would be of a commercial and not industrial relations nature. The growth of trade unions in the nineteenth century, however, provided an impetus to the growth of employers' associations as they responded to the threat of organised labour. Many associations became national federations representing employers in particular industries, examples of which include the Engineering Employers' Federation, the Building Trades Federation and the Shipbuilding Federation. The development of national federations was accompanied during the early twentieth century by a move towards industry-wide bargaining, which became the dominant form of collective bargaining until the 1960s.

During this period, employers, either individually or increasingly through the employers' associations, attempted to counter the growing power of trade unions by adopting oppositionary strategies, which Gospel and Palmer (1993) identify as:

- the use of blackleg or replacement labour in industries such as docks and shipping;
- the use of the so-called 'Document' which 'was a signed undertaking in which a worker accepted, as a condition of employment, that he would leave, or not join, a trade union' (p. 77) and which helped to overcome attempts at unionisation; and
- the use of blacklists of 'militants' compiled by the associations themselves.

During the course of the twentieth century outright opposition to trade unions declined and collective bargaining mechanisms were set up which sought to regulate, jointly with unions, external matters such as pay across the industry, while seeking to minimise union influence within the organisation in an attempt to retain employers' assumed 'right to manage', or managerial prerogative.

Their structure

Employers' associations are heterogeneous in their structure. Gennard and Judge (1997) identify three types. The first is the national federation to which local employers' associations belong, such as the Engineering Employers' Federation (EEF) which comprises 15 independent organisations. The second is the single national body, such as the British Printing Industries Federation (BPIF) 'which is divided into six regions for administrative and representational purposes (until 1982 this was a federated body like the engineers, but a serious national dispute in 1980 caused it to re-invent itself)' (p. 69). The third type is the single association with a national membership, such as the British Ceramic Federation. Associations are made up of companies of different sizes and the largest of them (the National Farmers' Union is the largest) are organised into autonomous local associations (engineers) or non-autonomous district associations (printers). The number of employers' associations has declined dramatically since the late 1960s, from around 1350 in 1968, to 228 in 1994, to 187 (comprising 94 'listed' and 93 'unlisted') in 2002, and this is indicative of a steady decline in their importance (Certification Office, 2002).

Their traditional functions

1. *Multi-employer bargaining.* A typical response to union demands was for employers within one industry to act collectively. This had the advantage of uniting the strength of the employers against the unions and ensured some degree of uniformity in basic wage rates.
2. *Limiting the scope of collective bargaining.* Although many employers eventually recognised trade unions, they succeeded in limiting the scope of bargaining to industry and external labour market issues, including wages, hours and overtime rates. All issues concerning managerial control within the workplace were left for management itself to determine and included supervision, manning of machines, discipline, hiring and firing and promotion, as the following example of the engineering industry demonstrates:

> *In the engineering industry, the protection of managerial prerogatives came to dominate employer association policy and lay behind major confrontations with the unions in 1851–2, 1897–8 and 1922. The skilled engineering workers formed the first central, national union in the UK. In the latter half of the nineteenth century they felt that their traditional craft status and job control was threatened by new technology which enabled once-skilled metal-working jobs to be accomplished by unskilled machine minders. They used their union to demand that the new machine-tools be manned by craftsmen at skilled rates and they resisted the introduction of piecework. On their side, the employers were eager to take advantage of the new technology to increase their control over work and reduce the power of craft groups. They sought to cheapen the labour process by employing less skilled labour and to manage the deskilled*

work by introducing piecework systems. The battles over managerial prerogative did not occur simply because unions were challenging employers' controls of the labour process, but because employers themselves were tightening and centralising their control of workplace activity. The engineering union lost the confrontation and was forced to sign agreements accepting management's right to operate machines and manage labour as management chose. (Gospel and Palmer, 1993, p. 80)

The above example was typical of what Goodrich (1975) described as the struggle between management and workers over the 'frontier of control'.

3. *Disputes procedures.* In common with the establishment of industry-wide collective bargaining, employers' associations adopted industry-wide disputes procedures as a means of resolving disputes. Only when the procedure was exhausted could constitutional strike action take place.

4. *Industry-wide agreements.* The increase in the number of employers' associations in particular industries not only facilitated the development of employers' federations, but also the establishment of industry-wide bargaining.

Their decline and reasons for it

The dramatic decline in the numbers of employers' associations has been accompanied by some decline in their power and influence, particularly within the industrial relations area. Some of the reasons for this decline lie within the area of collective bargaining, including the following:

- The decline in industry-wide, multi-employer bargaining has meant that employers' associations have become increasingly less attractive to larger organisations in particular, and smaller employers may be reluctant to pay a joining fee if national agreements cannot be sustained. According to the IRS (2002) survey of 50 employers' associations, 28 per cent of them still represent employers in national negotiating forums.
- Larger firms from the 1960s onwards increasingly preferred to negotiate their own agreements independently of employers' associations. This meant that, in effect, industry-agreed wage rates were

being undermined so that 'by 1989, only minimum rates of pay and working time remained live issues at national level (for example, in the engineering industry)' (Gennard and Judge, 1997, p. 70).

- Increasingly, larger organisations have their own specialist personnel/HRM departments for managing employment policy and so rely less, or not at all, upon the employers' association for help and advice.
- Some organisations left, or did not join, because of their policy towards trade unions; for example, some organisations may have adopted a 'non-recognition' policy towards trade unions.

Are there exceptions?

Gospel and Druker (1998) examine the electrical contracting industry which is one of the few cases where multi-employer national bargaining has remained strong (see also Chapter 6). Within engineering, national bargaining is also fairly resilient. For example, the Engineering Construction Industry Association (ECIA) continues to engage in industry-level pay bargaining with trade unions and believes that such arrangements continue to bring benefits for all parties concerned in the particular circumstances of the engineering construction industry (see Mini case 2.6).

Mini case 2.6
The ECIA

The ECIA is the national employers' organisation representing companies in the UK engineering construction industry. In 1996, membership rose to 280 companies, representing a net addition of 28 new members on the previous year. The UK engineering construction industry is the third largest in the world after the USA and Japan.

The activities of member companies include design and procurement, project management, construction, installation, erection commissioning and decommissioning, dismantling and re-erection, together with the repair and maintenance of power plant; steelwork structures and bridges; steel production and other primary production plant; pipework; process, chemical and petrochemical plant; erection of steel plates, tanks and pressure vehicles; pumps, compressors, switchgear, instrumentation and associated engineering construction activities onsite.

Member firms range in size from those with less than 10 employees to others with more than 3000 and they employ a total of some 60 000 employees (including head office as well as site staff). Collectively, annual turnover exceeds £8 billion. While the majority of employer members are small and medium-sized enterprises (SMEs), the organisation also covers over 50 multinationals. 'Every major company active in the UK engineering construction industry is a member' according to ECIA.

Predecessor organisations to the ECIA have operated in the industry since 1918. The ECIA itself was formed in April 1994 through the amalgamation of two associations, the National Engineering Construction Employers' Association (NECEA) and the Oil and Chemical Plant Constructors' Association (OCPCA).

The ECIA is an autonomous organisation whose policies are controlled by a council elected by its members. The association is a member of the CBI and EEF (Engineering Employers' Federation). It is the main employer signatory to the National Agreement for the Engineering Construction Industry (NAECI), and any changes are negotiated through the industry's National Joint Council (NJC).

The ECIA also represents the interests of member companies within the industry's Engineering Construction Industry Training Board (ECITB) and to government departments, the European Commission, the Health and Safety Executive and the Client's Group. The association's committees, on which many companies are represented, play a 'vital role' in identifying members' interests.

Professional staff based at the association's regional offices aim to provide practical advice and assistance on all employment issues, and to maintain expertise in specific local issues that can be of assistance to members 'before, during and after they undertake work in the particular region'. The association's regional offices are based in Belfast, Glasgow, Newcastle, Manchester, Sheffield, Oakham and Bristol. The regional staff are backed up by the ECIA's Westminster-based head office staff, including specialists in health and safety, employment and contractual law and other commercial services.

Source: IRS, 1998

Their future

Not every employers' association declined in importance, and some larger firms have remained members for reasons other than collective bargaining. For example, a growing number of associations have broadened their advisory services in relation to disciplinary, dismissal and redundancy procedures. These services have become more important to members with the growth in employment legislation since the 1970s concerning unfair dismissal, discrimination on grounds of race and gender, health and safety and equal pay issues. One area in which employers' associations are featuring more prominently is in representing the views of members to other organisations, including political lobbying (Gennard and Judge, 2002, p. 167). If there is a future for employers' associations, then it lies in the extent to which they diversify their services to accommodate the needs of an increasingly volatile membership. However, with the continuing decline in industry-wide bargaining, it appears unlikely that employers' associations will regain their former importance in respect of their industrial relations functions and that 'employers' associations were a far less important part of the institutional structure of industrial relations in 1990 than they were a decade or more earlier' (Millward *et al.*, 1992, p. 351). The WERS survey (Millward *et al.*, 2000), points to a continuing and sustained decline in the reliance upon the provision of information and advice to members, although it is still an important function (see IRS survey below), and in multi-employer bargaining concerning pay and other terms of employment. The IRS (2002) study of 50 employers' and trade associations confirms at least some of these trends (see Exhibit 2.3).

Although the advent of New Labour has had little impact upon employers' associations so far, most of the IRS survey's panel of associations expected the role of associations or members' perceptions of associations to change over the next four years. One response highlighted the latter:

Our role has not changed, but the members' perceptions of the importance of that role has increased – due in no small measure to the increased complexity of employment legislation. (IRS, 2002, p. 13)

Exhibit 2.3

Findings from the IRS 2002 survey of 50 employers' and trade associations

- With regard to the provision of free advice, this was still an important function in 2002. The main areas on which advice is provided by number of employers' associations include: health and safety (45), training and education (45), employment law (35), industrial/employment relations (30), discipline (27), equal opportunities (26), pay (22), employee welfare (20), recruitment (18).
- Lobbying and campaigning is an important role undertaken by employers' associations acting as pressure groups, providing a voice for members. Lobbying and campaigning targets include central government – the most popular with 45 out of the 50 associations acting in this capacity, followed by the European Union (25). Other areas include local government (13), trade unions (8) and the general public (7).
- Concerning the decline of multi-employer bargaining, the main traditional function of employers' associations, only 14 out of 50 associations are actively involved, and even where they are negotiated, many members do not follow the terms of the agreement. Moreover, only seven associations reported that a joint industry board or other third party exists to administer agreements.
- Only 13 of the 50 associations operate a disputes procedure that allows for the interpretation of the multi-employer pay and conditions agreement and disputes outside this agreement. In general, there has been very little change in the numbers of employers making use of the procedure, the main issue of contention over the past year being redundancy and recognition.
- Nearly all associations provide newsletters and other forms of communications for members and 35 have a members-only website. 39 associations provide networking opportunities via a members-only website.

Summary points

- Four models of personnel management have been identified, and comprise:
  - the normative model;
  - the descriptive functional model;
  - the critical evaluative model; and
  - the descriptive behavioural model.
- In addition, a number of typologies of personnel management have been devised by Tyson and Fell (1986) and Storey (1992). These typologies are not mutually exclusive as they reflect the entire range of personnel practice.
- Personnel management has been dogged by contradictions stemming from different interpretations of the personnel management role (often by practitioners themselves), the historical development of personnel management, the nature of the market economy and assumptions of patriarchy within capitalist society.
- There is a continuing debate concerning the relationship between HRM and ER on the one hand, and HRM and personnel management on the other. With regard to the latter relationship, it could be argued that while there are similarities and differences between the two, HRM has, at least in theory, a stronger strategic orientation than personnel management.
- Employers' associations have declined in both numbers and importance as industry-wide, multi-employer bargaining itself has declined in favour of single-employer bargaining.

RELEVANT WEBSITES

www.cbi.org.uk (Confederation of British Industry) An important site for the organisation representing UK employers. More general in scope than most websites cited in this book with employment relations issues not featuring too prominently.

www.cipd.co.uk (Chartered Institute of Personnel and Development) An extremely useful site for members, but limited access for non-members. The professional association for HR managers.

www.dti.gov.uk (Department of Trade and Industry) A comprehensive and useful site which contains plenty of information relevant to business and employers.

REFERENCES

Armstrong, M. (1987) 'Human resource management: a case of the emperor's new clothes?' *Personnel Management*, August

Bacon, N. (2001) 'Employee Relations', in Redman, T. and Wilkinson, A. *Contemporary Human Resource Management*. Harlow, Financial Times/Prentice Hall

Bacon, N. and Storey, J. (1996) 'Individualism and collectivism and the changing role of trade unions', in Ackers, P., Smith, C. and Smith, P. *The New Workplace and Trade Unionism*. London, Routledge

Beaumont, P.B. (1995) *The Future of Employment Relations*. London, Sage

Beauvoir, Simone de (1972) *The Second Sex*. Harmondsworth, Penguin

Blyton, P. and Turnbull, P. (1994) *The Dynamics of Employee Relations*. London, Macmillan

Blyton, P. and Turnbull, P. (1998) *The Dynamics of Employee Relations*, 2nd edn. London, Macmillan

Boxall, P. and Purcell, T. (2003) *Strategy and Human Resource Management*. Houndmills, Palgrave Macmillan

Braverman, H. (1974) *Labour and Monopoly Capital: The Degradation of Work in the Twentieth Century*. London, Monthly Review Press

Brewster, C., Gill, C. and Richbell, S. (1983) 'Industrial relations policy: a framework for analysis', in Thurley, K. and Wood, S. (eds) *Industrial Relations and Management Strategy*. Cambridge, Cambridge University Press

Burnham, J. (1945) *The Managerial Revolution*, Harmondsworth, Penguin

Certification Office (2002) *Annual Report of the Certification Office*. London, HMSO

Chandler, A.D. (1962) *Strategy and Structure: Chapters in the History of the American Industrial Enterprise*. Cambridge, Mass., MIT Press

Child, J. (1964) 'Quaker employers and industrial relations'. *Sociological Review*, 12, 3, 293–315

Child, J. (1969) *The Business Enterprise in Modern Society*. London, Harper and Row

Child, J. (1984) *Organisation: A Guide to Problems and Practice*. London, Harper and Row

Cully, M., Woodland, S., O'Reilly, A. and Dix, G. (1999) *Britain at Work*. London, Routledge

DoE (Department of Employment) (1992) *People, Jobs and Opportunity*. London, HMSO

Donovan (1968) *Report of the Royal Commision on Trade Unions and Employers' Associations 1965–1968*, Cmnd 3623. London, HMSO

Drucker, P. (1961) *The Practice of Management*. London, Mercury Books

Edwards, R. (1979) *Contested Terrain: The Transformation of the Workplace in the Twentieth Century*. London, Heinemann

Engels, F. (1892) 'The condition of the working class in England', in *Marx and Engels on Britain*. Moscow (1953), Foreign Languages Publishing House

Farnham, D. (1997) *Employee Relations in Context*. London, IPD

Farnham, D. and Pimlott, J. (1995) *Understanding Industrial Relations*. London, Cassell

Fowler, A. (1987) 'When chief executives discover HRM'. *Personnel Management*, January

Fox, A. (1966) *Industrial Sociology and Industrial Relations*. Royal Commission Research Paper No. 3. London, HMSO

Fox, A. (1974) *Beyond Contract: Work, Power, and Trust Relations*. London, Faber & Faber

Fox, A. (1985) *Man Mismanagement*. London, Hutchinson

French, J.R.P. and Raven, B. (1960) 'The bases of social power', in Cartwright, D. and Zander, A.F. (eds) *Group Dynamics: Research and Theory*, New York, Harper and Row

Gallie, D., Penn, R. and Rose, M. (eds) (1996) *Trade Unionism in Recession*. Oxford, Oxford University Press

Gennard, J. and Judge, G. (1997) *Employee Relations*. London, IPD

Gennard, J. and Judge, G. (2002) *Employee Relations*, 3rd edn. London, CIPD

Giddens, A. (1989) *Sociology*. Oxford, Polity Press

Goodrich, C.L. (1975) *The Frontier of Control: A Study in British Workshop Politics*. London, Pluto Press

Gospel, H. and Druker, J. (1998) 'The survival of national bargaining in the electrical contracting industry: a deviant case?' *British Journal of Industrial Relations*, 36, 2, 249–67

Gospel, H.F. and Palmer, G. (1993) *British Industrial Relations*. London, Routledge

Grint, K. (1991) *The Sociology of Work*. Oxford, Polity Press

Handy, C. (1993) *Understanding Organisations*. London, Penguin

Hartmann, H. (1982) 'Capitalism, patriarchy and job segregation by sex', in Giddens, A. and Held, D. (eds) *Classes, Power and Conflict: Classical and Contemporary Debates*. London, Macmillan

Huczynski, A. and Buchanan, D. (1991) *Organisational Behaviour*. London, Prentice Hall

Hyman, R. (1980) 'Trade unions, control and resistance', in Esland, G. and Salaman, G. (eds) *The Politics of Work and Occupations*. Milton Keynes, Open University Press

Hyman, R. (1987) 'Strategy or structure? Capital, labour and control'. *Work, Employment and Society*, 1, I, 25–55

IPM (1963) 'Statement on personnel management and personnel policies'. *Personnel Management*, March

IRS (1998) 'Back to the future: a new role for employers' associations'. *IRS Employment Trends*, No. 647

IRS (2002) 'Stormy waters ahead for employers' associations?' *IRS Employment Trends*, No. 743

Johnson, G. and Scholes, K. (1993) *Exploring Corporate Strategy*. London, Prentice Hall

Kelly, J. (2001) 'The role of the personnel/HR function in multinational companies'. *Employee Relations*, 23, 6

Kelly, J. and Gennard, J. (2001) *Power and Influence in the Boardroom: The Role of the Personnel Director*. London, Routledge

Kessler, I. and Purcell, J. (1995) 'Individualism and collectivism in theory and practice', in Edwards, P. (ed.) *Industrial Relations: Theory and Practice in Britain*. Oxford, Blackwell

Lavalette, M. and Kennedy, J. (1996) *Solidarity on the Waterfront: The Liverpool Docks Lock Out of 1995/96*. Liverpool, Liver Press

Legge, K. (1995) *Human Resource Management: Rhetorics and Realities*. London, Macmillan

Lundy, O. and Cowling, A. (1996) *Strategic Human Resource Management*. London, Routledge

Mackay, L. and Torrington, D. (1986) *The Changing Nature of Personnel Management*. London, IPM

Marchington, M. and Parker, P. (1990) *Changing Patterns of Employee Relations*. London, Harvester Wheatsheaf

Miller, S. (1993) 'The nature of strategic management', in Harrison, R. (ed.) *Human Resource Management, Issues and Strategies*. Wokingham, Addison-Wesley

Millward, N., Bryson, A. and Forth, J. (2000) *All Change at Work?* London, Routledge

Millward, N., Stevens, M., Smart, D. and Hawes, W.R. (1992) *Workplace Industrial Relations in Transition*. Aldershot, Dartmouth

Nichols, T. (1969) *Ownership, Control and Ideology*. London, Allen and Unwin

Nichols, T. (1980) 'Management, ideology and practice', in Esland, G. and Salaman, G. (eds) *The Politics of Work and Occupations*. Milton Keynes, Open University Press

Nichols, T. (1986) *The British Worker Question*. London, Routledge

Ogbonna, E. (1992) 'Organisational culture and human resource management: dilemmas and contradictions', in Blyton, P. and Turnbull, P. (eds) *Reassessing Human Resource Management*. London, Sage

Pahl, R.E. and Winkler, J.T. (1974) 'The economic elite', in Stanworth, P. and Giddens, A. (eds) *Elites and Power in British Society*. Cambridge, Cambridge University Press

Poole, M. (1980) 'Management strategies and industrial relations' in Poole, M. and Mansfield, R. (eds) *Managerial Roles in Industrial Relations*. London, Gower

Poole, M., Mansfield, R., Blyton, P. and Frost, P. (1981) *Managers in Focus*. Farnborough, Gower

Purcell, J. (1987) 'Mapping management styles in employee relations'. *Journal of Management Studies*, 24, 5, 533–48

Purcell, J. and Ahlstrand, B. (1994) *Human Resource Management in the Multi-Divisional Company*. Aldershot, Dartmouth

Purcell, J. and Gray, A. (1986) 'Corporate personnel departments and the management of industrial relations'. *Journal of Management Studies*, 23, 2, 205–23

Purcell, J. and Sisson, K. (1983) 'Strategies and practice in the management of industrial relations', in Bain, G.S. (ed.) *Industrial Relations in Britain*. Oxford, Blackwell

Rose, E. and Woolley, T. (1992) 'Shifting sands? Trade unions and productivity at Rover Cars'. *Industrial Relations Journal*, 23, 4, 257–67

Salamon, M. (1998) *Industrial Relations: Theory and Practice*, 3rd edn. London, Prentice Hall

Scullion, H. and Starkey, K. (2000) 'In search of the changing role of the corporate human resource function in the international firm'. *International Journal of Human Resource Management*, 11, 6, 1061–81

Sisson, K. (1995) 'Human resource management and the personnel function', in Storey, J. (ed.) *Human Resource Management: A Critical Text*. London, Routledge

Storey, J. (1987) *Developments in Human Resource Management: An Interim Report*. Warwick Papers in Industrial Relations, no. 17. Coventry, University of Warwick

Storey, J. (1992) *Developments in the Management of Human Resources*. Oxford, Blackwell

Storey, J. (1995) *Human Resource Management: A Critical Text*. London, Routledge

Storey, J. and Sisson, K. (1993) *Managing Human Resources and Industrial Relations*. Milton Keynes, Open University Press

Taylor, F.W. (1947) *Scientific Management*. New York, Harper and Row

Terry, M. and Edwards, P.K. (eds), (1988) *Shopfloor Politics and Job Controls*. Oxford, Blackwell

Thompson, P. (1990) *The Nature of Work*. London, Macmillan

Thurley, K. and Wood, S. (eds), (1983) *Industrial Relations and Management Strategy*. Cambridge, Cambridge University Press

Torrington, D. and Hall, L. (1987) *Personnel Management: A New Approach*. London, Prentice Hall

Tyson, S. and Fell, A. (1986) *Evaluating the Personnel Function*. London, Hutchinson

Warner, W. and Low, J.O. (1947) *The Social System of the Modern Factory*. New Haven, Yale University Press

Watson, T.J. (1977) *The Personnel Managers: A Study in the Sociology of Work and Industry*. London, Routledge

Watson, T.J. (1986) *Management, Organisation and Employment Strategy. New Directions in Theory and Practice*. London, Routledge

Watson, T.J. (1995) *Sociology, Work and Industry*. London, Routledge

Zeitlin, M. (1989) *The Large Corporation and Contemporary Classes*. Oxford, Polity Press

CHAPTER 3

TRADE UNIONS AND THE EMPLOYMENT RELATIONSHIP

INTRODUCTION

The main focus of this chapter is upon the collective organisation of employees. Trade unions are still, by far, the most common form of collective organisation, and these will now be considered in greater detail. The eminent labour historian, Henry Pelling, stated that 'for better or for worse, the structure of present-day British trade unionism can be understood only in terms of its historical development' (1992, p. 1). The chapter, therefore, begins by tracing the development of trade unions and examining their significance in both historical and contemporary contexts. We then look at trade union structure and government, together with the role of shop stewards and this is followed by a review of the changing nature of trade unions in the late twentieth and early twenty-first century. Finally, we consider the importance of the role of the TUC and the European context of trade unionism. It should be noted that collective and other forms of representation in non-union settings are examined in Chapter 8.

Learning outcomes

When you have read this chapter, you should be able to:

1. Understand how trade unions have evolved.

2. Identify the functions, role and significance of trade unions in historical and contemporary contexts.

3. Appreciate the importance of trade union structure, government and democracy.

4. Explain the functions and roles of shop stewards.

5. Explain the changing nature of trade unions and the problems faced by them in the twenty-first century.

THE DEVELOPMENT OF BRITISH TRADE UNIONS

We have defined trade unions, outlined their characteristics, aims, objectives and functions in Chapter 1, and it would be useful to review these before reading on. Trade unions in Britain are in a state of continuous evolution with their development spanning three tumultuous centuries. According to Hyman (2003, p. 45), the evolutionary longevity of British trade unionism explains three important and distinctive features associated with unionism:

- 'structural complexity and fragmentation' (variations in size, nature of representation, variety of structure, recruitment patterns etc.);
- 'an ambiguous orientation to political action' (this embraced revolutionary socialism prior to 1926, syndicalism through to political incorporation and 'legitimation' via the Labour Party); and
- 'the potent moral value attached to the principle of "free collective bargaining"'.

Organisational beginnings

Consider the following quote:

Historically, they [trade unions] came into being as a response to capitalism, a form of social and economic organisation where the ownership of the means of production is in private hands, where the object of production is the competitive pursuit of profit in a free market and where the majority, excluded from the ownership of the means of production, are compelled to sell their labour power in order to live. For workers, a reasonably paid, secure job is an essential basis for a decent life. But their wages are a cost to their employers, an important item to be set against profit, and thus to be minimised and dispensed with entirely where labour is insufficiently profitable. Trade unions, therefore, take the stage in order to redress the bargaining imbalance between employer and employee and render the conflict between capital and labour a more equal one, replacing individual competition for

jobs by collective organisation as a means to protect wage levels and the conditions and security of employment. (McIlroy, 1988, p. 1: a modified form of the above quote appears in McIlroy, 1995, p. 2)

McIlroy's quote is instructive for the following reasons. Firstly, trade unionism represents an organisational reaction to the development of capitalism and the process of industrialisation, a dialectical relationship of opposition to, and dependency upon, capitalism. Secondly, the conflict of interest between buyers and sellers of labour power can only be resolved by collective organisation of workers into trade unions engaging in the process of collective bargaining. According to Webb and Webb (1898, p. 173):

Instead of the employer making a series of contracts with isolated individuals, he meets with a collective will and settles, in a single agreement, the principles upon which, for the time being, all workmen of a particular group, or class, or grade will be engaged.

This establishes the 'common rule' of collectively agreed standards (rates of pay, working hours) governing the employment of groups of workers. Thirdly, the need to protect wage levels was guided by the Webbs' doctrines of *supply and demand* and *a living wage*. The doctrine of supply and demand underlined the importance of wage costs being linked to the price of the product or service. However, employers could use this as a justification for reducing wage costs should the product price fall, thereby giving rise to wage-cutting. The doctrine of a living wage was partly a response to endemic wage-reduction strategies of employers and partly due to the resistance of semi-skilled and unskilled workers within the 'new unionism' of the late nineteenth century (see below) to employer wage-cutting.

Self-Evaluation Activity 3.1

A 'living wage'
Response on website

What, in your opinion, do you think is meant by the term 'a living wage'?

From trade clubs to the 'new unionism'

The first chapter of the Webbs' *History of Trade Unionism, 1866–1920* (1920) provides an interesting description of the origins of trade union organisation in Britain. Trade unions did not grow out of the medieval craft guilds (although some point to a possible association (Hyman 2003, p. 44)), but can be traced to the local trade clubs of the eighteenth century (Flanders, 1972). Whereas the Webbs could point to evidence of temporary associations of wage earners meeting to 'take a social pint of porter together' (1920, p. 23), trade clubs were local associations of skilled craftsmen in many trades whose aims were to protect the wages and status of the craft and their members and to reinforce the tradition of apprenticeship. Some of the trade clubs evolved into what became known as friendly societies which were:

> *societies of skilled tradesmen whose members formed an 'aristocracy of labour' . . . best able to build their organisation on traditions of apprenticeship and the defence of the craft against the unqualified. This they did with the help of a system of friendly benefits. . . . Out of work benefit . . . was most important in preventing men from transgressing the rules of the trade. Accident, sickness, superannuation benefits, even emigration grants, were also provided with the same end in view.* (Flanders, 1972, pp. 12–13)

This 'method of mutual insurance' (a term coined by the Webbs) provided an impetus to the growth of national unions in the latter half of the nineteenth century. All this took place within a national environment uniquely hostile to the development of trade unions. At a time of rapid industrialisation and the emergence of large, unskilled urban workforces, the Combination Acts of 1799 and 1800 ushered in an era of outright repression of trade union activity. Despite this, trade unionism took root, albeit under the guise of friendly societies, and when the Combination Acts were repealed in 1824, workers could organise openly and new unions were formed.

Geographically, trade union development was uneven and intermittent during this period and tended to be localised on an urban or regional basis rather than being focused upon nationally-based institutions.

Exhibit 3.1 illustrates the temporary nature and uneven development of unionisation within the rapidly growing coal industry.

The repeal of the Combination Acts and the passing of a new Act in 1825 gave trade unions limited protection, but they remained legally vulnerable. There were many prosecutions and heavy sentences culminating in the most celebrated case of the 'Tolpuddle Martyrs', six agricultural labourers who were sentenced to seven years' transportation in 1834 on the charge of administering 'illegal oaths'. Attempts were made to overcome the problems of local and regional unions and associations, culminating in the establishment of one general union for

Exhibit 3.1

The example of the coal industry

A few attempts at organisation had been made in the Scottish and South Wales fields as early as the 1820s, but these proved largely unsuccessful. However, by the 1840s, 'county unions' had been formed in the coal mining communities in Durham, Northumberland, Lancashire, Yorkshire and Staffordshire as well as in Scotland. In 1842, delegates from these areas formed a Miners' Association of Great Britain and Ireland, which by 1844 claimed to represent some 70 000 miners, about a third of the total labour force in the industry at that time. . . . Union organisation in the mining industry was then set back by economic slump and unsuccessful strikes. By the late 1840s, the Association had all but collapsed, although mining unions survived in several of the coal mining counties.

Source: Martin *et al.*, 1996, p. 43

Exhibit 3.2

How the ASE was formed

Following the repeal of the Combination Laws, several societies of millwrights, machinists and other engineering craftsmen were formed in the north of England . . . and in the 1840s, workers in the industry endeavoured to amalgamate all the skilled engineering societies into a single over-arching organisation. The result was the ASE, the first national union, created in 1851 from more than a hundred local associations. Apart from its formation by the amalgamation of numerous local associations, the ASE also combined a central financial administration based in London with a devolved organisational structure of local branches and districts.

Source: Martin *et al.*, 1996, p. 43

all workers. There was a rapid rise and decline in 1834 of Robert Owen's Grand National Consolidated Trades Union. The union failed owing to the cumbersome nature of its organisational structure, limited funds and because the employers in the building trades, where it had most support, retaliated by insisting on their employees signing 'the Document', an undertaking to leave or not to join a trade union.

By the 1850s, many local or regional societies of craftsmen amalgamated to form what became known as new model unions, the first of which was the Amalgamated Society of Engineers (ASE) which was formed in 1851. The case of the ASE is an interesting one and Exhibit 3.2 is an account of how it came into being.

The trend towards amalgamation and national organisation became widespread during the second half of the nineteenth century, which witnessed an unprecedented growth in trade unionism and other representative bodies such as trades councils. A number of factors specific to this period accounted for the growth of trade unions. These include:

- the increasing scale of industry;
- the widening of the market for labour and goods;
- improved transport;
- blurring of occupational boundaries;
- the greater mobility of workers; and
- the growth of employers' associations.

By 1869, membership of unions affiliated to the newly formed Trades Union Congress (TUC) had grown to around 250 000 and by the mid-1870s membership stood at over 500 000. Also during the 1870s, the legal status of trade unions became established through legislation in 1871, 1875 and 1876. The Trade Union Act of 1871, which was amended in 1876, stated that trade unions were no longer unlawful simply because their objectives were 'in restraint of trade'. The Act also gave unions a large measure of freedom from legal proceedings in the conduct of their internal affairs. The Conspiracy and Protection of Property Act of 1875 made collective bargaining and peaceful picketing lawful.

The next phase of development was the most important one because it involved the unionisation of semi- and unskilled workers on a permanent basis and laid the foundations of the modern trade union movement; it became known as the new unionism.

From new unionism to the General Strike

The success of the London dockers' strike in 1889 gave an added impetus to union-organising activity in much the same way as the formation of the ASE did earlier. In that year the dockers' union (the forerunners of the Transport and General Workers' Union) and the gas workers' union (the precursor of the General, Municipal, Boilermakers' and Allied Trades Union) were formed. We now look in more detail at the gas industry which is a notable example of the rise of new unionism.

Mini case 3.1
The gas industry

Hobsbawm (1974) provides an insightful analysis of the explosive growth of unionisation within this nineteenth-century public utility. Space does not permit much detail. We start with a short quote which is followed by summary points.

The British gas industry presents a remarkable and extreme example of the rise of trade unionism. Gas workers were – in common with others who were conventionally thought of as 'unskilled' – believed to be incapable of strong and stable trade unionism; and indeed, with short-lived and local exceptions, they had never formed important and lasting organisations before 1889. For 17 years before that date they possessed no traceable unions at all. Yet when in 1889 they demanded concessions which, it was generally held, would raise the industry's wage-bill by one-third, their demands were conceded virtually without a struggle. Moreover, the new unions maintained themselves against subsequent counter-attack. Over a large part of the country, therefore, the industry changed overnight from a wholly unorganised into an exceptionally unionised one; with important effects on its structure and policy. Why did it change? Why did it remain changed? What effects had the rise of the union? (p. 158)

The following summary points attempt to throw some light upon these questions. For a fuller appreciation of the issues, however, you should read Hobsbawm (1974), Chapter 9.

1. The gas industry was municipally owned and immune from competition. There was no incentive to technological change and labour costs were relatively low. Technical change was therefore sluggish and gas making in the 1880s was substantially similar to what it had been at the beginning of the century. The gas-making process involved carbonisation (the work of making and stoking fires), filling retorts with coal, spreading it and drawing the coke.
2. Stokers and firemen, the key workers in the whole process, had an exceptionally strong bargaining position. But the work was casual, semi-skilled at best, and there were extreme seasonal fluctuations in demand which resulted in pools of surplus labour.
3. 'A considerable impetus was therefore needed to overcome this deadweight of tradition and irregular labour' (p. 162). Gas was an expanding industry and a labour-intensive one, and the labour force had scarcely grown during the 1880s. The impetus for change therefore lay in:
   (a) the intensification of work (increased output using the same number of workers) owing to the expansion of demand for gas;
   (b) increased worker effort for the same wage.
4. By 1888 there were signs of unrest, and in 1889 separate unions were formed in Birmingham, London and Bristol. With the formation of a national union organisation later that year and the dispute which followed, the employers gave way: 'Yet between June and December 1889 most of the important gasworks in the country yielded, hardly even testing the men's strength' (p. 165). The workforce gained important concessions (higher rates of pay; an eight-hour day) and the union consolidated its new-found strength.
5. 'The effect of the union on the industry was striking and wholly beneficial . . . (and) . . . gas embarked on a programme of major technical reorganisation and re-equipment' (p. 166). There is no doubt that the explosion of unionisation in the gas industry shook the employers out of their complacency, but the unions, throughout the remainder of the nineteenth century 'succeeded, even in a period of depression, in safeguarding their status against the machine' (p. 171).

In summary, the history of the unionisation of the gas workers is significant in three respects. Firstly, we are provided with a neat and elegant model of 'trade union explosion': unions, previously almost unknown, become universal overnight. Secondly, gas presents a notable example of an industry which has been modernised almost entirely because of the pressure of labour and the beneficial effects of labour militancy. Finally, gas illustrates the considerable strength of groups of indispensable workers in a situation of technological innovation, especially when this takes place within an already old, well-established and heavily capitalised industry.

The new unionism of unskilled and semi-skilled workers was now firmly established and expanding. From 1900 to 1914, trade union membership increased from 2 to 4 million, with most of the increase coming after 1910. This period also witnessed the beginnings of non-manual or white-collar unionism amongst teachers, clerks and local authority (municipal) workers.

Political development

An alliance between some trade unions and socialist political groupings emerged in 1900 and became known as the Labour Representation Committee which, in 1906, changed its name to the Labour Party. This political development indirectly influenced legislation during this period (an Education Act, 1907; the Old Age Pensions and Coal Mines [Eight Hours] Acts, 1908; trade boards for fixing legal minimum wages in the 'sweated' trades in 1909 and the National Health Insurance Act of 1912).

The Taff Vale and Osborne Judgments

More direct assistance to unions was given by the fledgling Labour Party in relation to decisions made by the law courts against certain unions. One of the most infamous was a judgment given by the House of Lords in the case of the *Taff Vale Railway Company* v *Amalgamated Society of Railway Servants* (1901) which appeared to violate the provisions of the 1871–6 legislation. In this case, the Taff Vale Railway Company sued the union for damages as a result of financial loss through strike action and the verdict was given in favour of the company. The judgment had serious implications for trade unions generally because any strike action would then put union funds at risk. The Trade Disputes Act of 1906 removed this liability and defined the law concerning industrial action until the 1980s. More specifically the Act:

- protected union funds from civil claims for damages;
- legitimised acts done in contemplation or furtherance of a trade dispute so that they were no longer regarded as 'civil conspiracy';

- ended the liability for inducing a breach of contract of employment by persons acting in a trade dispute; and
- made peaceful picketing lawful.

Following this parliamentary success, the political activities of trade unions were next threatened by the Osborne Judgment of 1909 (*Osborne* v *Amalgamated Society of Railway Servants*) in which the House of Lords held that 'it was illegal for a trade union to spend its funds on other purposes than the industrial objects specified in previous Acts' (Flanders, 1972, p. 17). The judgment had serious implications for the Labour Party which relied heavily on the unions for financial support. Eventually, in 1913, the Trade Union Act reversed the Osborne Judgment and permitted trade unions, with the consent of their members, to set up a separate political fund in order to pursue political objectives.

The only other major piece of legislation affecting trade unions until 1971 was the Trade Disputes and Trade Union Act of 1927, repealed in 1946.

Self-Evaluation Activity 3.2

Trade union rights
The response is given below

Britain is the only country where trade unions do not have a positive right to strike, organise or to engage in collective bargaining. Why do you think this has come about?

The following quote from Hyman (1995) explains this unique situation:

The method by which trade unions and collective bargaining were eventually legalised was not, as in many other countries, by establishing a positive right to organise, to negotiate and to strike, but by defining an area of industrial relations 'immunities'. The key legislative initiatives – the Trade Union Act of 1871, the Conspiracy and Protection of Property Act of 1875 and the Trade Disputes Act of 1906 – were designed to remove the specifically legal obstacles to collective action. But while workers were thus free to organise collectively, the employer was equally free to dismiss a worker for joining a trade union; while unions were entitled to bargain collectively, employers were equally at liberty to refuse to negotiate; and while a union could lawfully call a strike 'in contemplation or furtherance of a trade dispute', striking workers were in breach of their contracts of employment and might therefore be dismissed (or even sued individually for damages). This is in marked contrast to many other national labour law regimes, which oblige employers to respect workers' right to unionise, to bargain 'in good faith' with representative unions, and to impose no penalty (beyond withholding pay) on those who legally strike.

The absence of statutory regulation, a condition known as voluntarism or collective laissez-faire, was long celebrated as an index of maturity and sophistication. The Royal Commission on Labour in 1894 concluded its lengthy deliberations by insisting that strong organisations of workers and employers, and voluntary agreement between the two parties, offered the most stable and desirable basis for regulating employment. For almost a century thereafter, a major policy commitment of governments of every political complexion was to encourage the institutions and processes of collective self-regulation. (pp. 29–30)

The rise of the shop stewards

Shop stewards are unpaid representatives of trade unions at the workplace and are fairly prominent and widespread within most contemporary unionised work organisations. However, 'there is no evidence that shop stewards achieved any widespread significance much before the First World War' (Coates and Topham, 1988, p. 144). Workplace representation did exist in some nineteenth-century industries such as coal mining and engineering. The first major manifestation of shop steward organisation came with the First World War, a period during which there was considerable co-operation between many unions and government in the interests of prosecuting the war. The policy of co-operation was not accepted so readily by many politically-minded workers who regarded employers as profiteering from the war while keeping wages down. There were many unofficial stoppages of work in

industries such as munitions, organised by local shop stewards combining to form 'Shop Stewards' Committees', 'Workers' Committees' and the like. These local organisations amalgamated to form the Shop Stewards' Movement (also known as the National Workers' Committee Movement).

The Shop Stewards' Movement articulated the dissatisfaction with wartime conditions and gave political expression to the socialist aims of syndicalism and workers' control of industry. After a brief interval of optimism spanning a period up to 1920, during which there was a strong belief in the power of the labour movement to change the social order, the great post-war depression gave rise to a harsher reality, and the years up to 1926 were punctuated by a number of national disputes spearheaded by the 'Triple Alliance' of unions representing railwaymen, transport workers and miners. All this activity culminated in the nine-day General Strike, 'the most momentous event in the development of British trade unionism' (Flanders, 1972, p. 19). According to Flanders, the strike demonstrated both the solidarity of the organised workforce and the failure of syndicalism to change society through direct action. The victory of the government, the ongoing depression and falling trade union membership, from a peak of 6.5 million in 1920, signalled a sober reality for both unions and employers.

From the General Strike to 1945

The remainder of the 1920s and 1930s witnessed a more constructive period of industrial relations based on co-operation rather than conflict. It was a time of consolidation and amalgamation for trade unions. The trend towards fewer and larger unions became established, and many of the large unions of today, such as the TGWU, were formed at this time. The unions and the TUC worked more closely with the Labour Party in order to secure change through the ballot box rather than on the picket line. Trade union membership reached its lowest point in 1933, but thereafter membership increased yearly to reach 8 million in 1945 and this tended to reflect, amongst other things, the changed perception of trade unionism as a willing partner in the conduct of national economic and industrial affairs.

Self-Evaluation Activity 3.3

The development of the trade union movement
Response on website

We have concentrated on the history and development of the trade union movement up to 1945. Identify
the main factors which you think account for this
development.

Postscript: unions in contemporary perspective: 1945–2003

This brief section summarises some of the main
developments affecting trade unions during the second half of the twentieth century. These developments will be considered in more detail either in this
chapter or in subsequent chapters to which reference will be made.

- The number of trade unions has continued to
  decline: in 2002 there were 199 (70 TUC-
  affiliated) unions while in the 1920s there were
  more than 1300 (see Table 3.3, p. 129).
- Much of this decline can be attributed to mergers
  and the disappearance of smaller unions.
- Trade union membership rose steadily in 1945
  from around 8 million to a peak of 13.289 million in 1979: thereafter, membership fell steadily
  to 7.801 million in 1997, picked up slightly and
  levelled at 7.897 in 2001 and 7.779 in 2002 (year
  beginning figures; see also Table 3.3, p. 129).
- During the 1980s and 1990s, non-manual union
  membership declined only very slowly and now
  makes up around 50 per cent of total membership, much of this being concentrated within the
  public sector (see below).
- Since 1979 trade union bargaining power has
  declined quite substantially for a number of
  reasons which will be considered in Chapter 6.
- During the 1980s trade union government and
  democracy were affected by legislation concerning secret ballots, election of union officials and
  rights of union members (see below).
- Workplace representation and shop steward
  organisation, despite setbacks in the 1980s,

continues to play an integral part in the conduct
of industrial relations at workplace level (see
below).

Summary points: historical development

- Trade unions developed as a response to the
  development of capitalism and the realisation
  that conflicts of interest between employees and
  owners could only be resolved collectively.
- During the latter part of the eighteenth and early
  decades of the nineteenth centuries, trade unions
  evolved from trade clubs/friendly societies having
  purely local organisational roots to 'new model'
  unions of craftsmen, some of which became
  regionally based.
- The second half of the nineteenth century saw
  many union amalgamations and moves towards
  national organisation. In recognition of this
  trend, the TUC was formed as a national co-
  ordinating body for affiliated trade unions.
- During this period, unions representing interests
  of semi-skilled and unskilled workers developed,
  a phenomenon known as the 'new unionism'.
  Workplace unionism became more widespread
  and with it the increased importance of the shop
  steward.
- After the collapse of the General Strike, there
  was a period of consolidation with unions and
  the TUC working closely with the Labour Party.

TRADE UNION STRUCTURE, ORGANISATION AND DEMOCRACY

To a large extent the contemporary structure of
British trade unions reflects its uneven development
over the years, as described in an earlier section. As
we shall see, classification of unions into general
categories or types has its problems as Coates and
Topham (1988) point out: 'unions come in a wide
variety of sizes, shapes and "types": their classification is no longer the simple matter it used to
seem' (p. 41). A definition of trade union structure
would need to take into consideration the following
factors:

- the recruitment patterns to reflect the occupational and skills profile of a union's membership;
- the geographical concentration or dispersion of actual and potential membership; and
- the recruitment strategies adopted by unions.

Trade union organisation and democracy (also referred to as trade union government) is concerned with the internal structure of unions and the extent to which they are representative of their members. It is also concerned with how a union is managed or administered. Efficient and professional administration is equally as important as the effective and democratic representation of the membership, particularly in the larger, more complex unions with composite memberships.

Trade union structure

As we have mentioned, trade union structure is a fairly complex affair, and for many years there was a reliance upon what has become known as the simple or traditional classification which takes a broadly chronological approach to the issue. The problems with this approach resulted in an alternative approach (although it may also be regarded as complementary) which looks at unions on a continuum ranging from open to closed (Turner, 1962; Hughes, 1968). A third typology considers union structure in terms of recruitment of membership on vertical or horizontal principles. Again, this approach may be seen as complementing rather than supplanting the traditional classification.

Before we examine these approaches to union structure, it is important to note that:

- trade unions, in common with most other organisations, are dynamic in the sense that they are continually changing (evolving, declining or amalgamating) and are responsive not only to their memberships but also to the wider society, both reactively and proactively; given this propensity for unions to change, then any method of classification is, at best, arbitrary; and
- it is more appropriate to regard the approaches to structure as conceptual constructs, assisting our analysis of trade unions in the 'real' world rather than presenting us with neat categories into which unions can be fitted.

The traditional classification

The traditional classification presents us with a number of ideal types which for our purposes may be regarded as simplified conceptual constructs or abstractions providing a set of characteristics enabling us to identify each union with each type.

The first type is that of the craft union. The craft union is characterised by:

- the principle of recruiting members from a specific skilled trade usually entered through a system of apprenticeship in order for apprentices to qualify as unionised tradesmen;
- the control of the numbers of apprentices entering the trade and the regulation of the length and nature of apprenticeship; and
- the generation of 'fraternity' amongst the members based on a sense of shared skills and similar levels of earnings.

Industrial, technological and other changes have rendered craft unions virtually obsolete. In the face of such changes, the craft union that seeks to preserve its 'pure' form would experience a damaging loss of membership and inevitable extinction. In order to survive, some craft unions have either broadened their membership base or amalgamated to form multi-craft unions. These have proved to be short-term solutions for most craft unions which, at best, have only served temporarily to delay their further decline. Another problem for craft unions in a changing economy was the absence of any political influence within the TUC and Labour Party and the very limited financial services they could offer because of their small membership.

Self-Evaluation Activity 3.4
Craft bypass
Response on website

Can you think of one example of a craft being by-passed as a result of technological change?

A second category is the industrial union, defined as one which aims to recruit all workers within a particular industry, regardless of occupation. In theory, industrial unionism assumes a more orderly system of trade union organisation (as it does in

Germany) and the claimed advantages for industrial unions are based on this assumption. For example:

- an industrial union, being larger than a cluster of occupational/craft unions would represent the united strength of all the industry's workers;
- it eliminates the problem of multi-unionism (more than one union per industry); and
- it simplifies the collective bargaining process.

In practice, however, industrial unionism has not been a successful means of organisation and, in terms of the definition given above, it can be argued that no union today can claim to be exclusively industrial. One example of a union which approximated to this definition was the National Union of Mineworkers (NUM) before the miners' strike of 1985, but even here supervisory grades and colliery managers had a separate union (NACODS and BACM respectively). After 1985, the supremacy of the NUM was challenged by the Nottinghamshire-based Union of Democratic Mineworkers (UDM).

Self-Evaluation Activity 3.5

Industrial representation
Response on website

Can you think of one other industry which had its workers represented on an industrial basis?

The third category is the general union which recruits across occupational and industrial boundaries and in theory has no restrictions on potential membership. In practice, however, because of their historical development, the memberships of general unions tend to be focused upon specific industries and occupations. Nevertheless, the main reason for their survival and growth has been their ability to maintain and consolidate membership within their traditional catchment areas and to recruit within non-traditional growth areas. Consider the examples of the TGWU and the GMB, traditionally the largest general unions in Britain:

Both the two largest general unions began life in the late 1880s, organising particular groups of unskilled workers. The main parent of the Transport and General Workers' Union was the Dock, Wharf, Riverside and General Labourers'

*Union, and the chief forerunner of the General and Municipal Workers' Union was the National Union of Gasworkers and General Labourers of Great Britain and Ireland. We should note the significance of the phrase 'and general labourers' in the titles of both these pioneering organisations. It tells us that, **from the outset**, these unions deliberately intended that their recruitment should not be restricted to specific industries or occupations. The reason for this is not hard to find; unlike the craftsmen, dockers and gasworkers were in no position to construct a tightly exclusive barrier around their occupations. Because their jobs were casual and relatively unskilled, all 'general labourers' were potential blacklegs threatening effective trade unionism anywhere unless all could be enrolled in the union. Thus the general unions felt it necessary to construct organisations having all the flexibility which other forms of union denied to themselves. It is small wonder that they have flourished and grown to their present dominant size.* (Coates and Topham, 1988, p. 47)

Self-Evaluation Activity 3.6

Advantages and disadvantages of general union structure
Response on website

With the extract from Coates and Topham in mind attempt to identify some advantages and disadvantages of the general union type.

The general union category is certainly appropriate for the GMB and TGWU, and Table 3.1 (p. 112) demonstrates their supremacy in the membership stakes. Falling membership has provided an impetus for mergers and amalgamations (see below) and this has resulted in increased concentration of membership within the largest unions, of which Amicus and UNISON are probably the best examples to date.

As most contemporary unions do not fit neatly into craft, industrial or general types, other typologies have been used (Salamon, 1998). These include:

1. **The occupational union.** This category comprises unions which organise workers in a particular occupation or occupations which are related

to each other. The Union of Shop, Distributive and Allied Workers (USDAW) which recruits its membership from related occupations within the retail sector is an example.

2. **The white-collar union**. White-collar, or non-manual unions comprise a sector of the trade union movement which has expanded considerably since 1945. They can be regarded as part of the occupational category, but not exclusively so and recruit from a particular non-manual occupation or profession such as the National Union of Teachers (NUT). Apart from unions that concentrate exclusively on white-collar occupations, the large general and quasi-industrial unions often incorporate white-collar sections of their own, such as the Association of Clerical, Technical and Supervisory Staffs (ACTSS) which is part of the TGWU. In addition, some professional associations such as the British Medical Association (BMA) perform some trade union functions, particularly within the area of collective bargaining.

3. **Federations**. Federations of trade unions have arisen as a result of multi-unionism (the existence of several unions within one industry) in a multi-employer context (where there are several employers within the same industry). The need to present a common approach to employers in national industry-wide negotiations made some kind of joint organisation essential. The federation, then, is a rather loose-knit structure which facilitates collective bargaining in an industry with many employers. Federations which have existed in the past include the Confederation of Shipbuilding and Engineering Unions, the National Federation of Building Trade Operatives, and the Printing and Kindred Trades Federation. With the decline of multi-employer bargaining in recent years, the role of federations has also declined.

The problems we have identified in relation to the traditional method of classification of unions has resulted in two other main attempts to explain trade union structure which are known as the 'vertical' and 'horizontal' structure and the 'open' and 'closed' structure which are now briefly considered.

Vertical and horizontal structures

This method of classification assumes that unions are organised along either 'vertical' or 'horizontal' lines. The horizontally-organised union recruits from one of several grades of workers across industry boundaries – all managers in a managers' union, all electricians in an electricians' union. This type of union corresponds loosely to craft organisations. The vertical union, on the other hand, aims to recruit all workers, whatever their grade or occupation, with a common industrial background, and therefore corresponds to the industrial union type. These categories are useful in helping to explain, particularly in a historical context, trends and tendencies in union organisation and recruitment and they also reveal the complexity of the existing and changing union organisation in Britain.

Open and closed structures

This method of classification, originated by Turner (1962), adopts a more dynamic approach which assumes that unions are constantly changing in response to changes in their external environments. It also assumes that unions can influence events in a proactive way. A useful way of looking at unions as open structures is provided by open systems theory. The key for viewing organisations as open systems, argues Luthans (1992, p. 532) 'is the recognition of the external environment as a source of significant input. In systems terminology, the boundaries of the organisation are permeable to the external environment (social, legal, technical, economic and political)'.

An open union as an open system actively recruits and/or seeks mergers with other unions in new occupational or industrial sectors and is not able to control entry into a trade or occupation. It is expansionist in orientation, relies on the numerical strength of its membership to provide and reinforce its bargaining power and corresponds more or less to the general union type. A closed union, to all intents and purposes, is a closed system in that it is minimally responsive to changes in its external environment; it 'concentrates on its existing territory, aiming to make that a strongpoint of organisation and bargaining strength' (Coates and Topham, 1988, p. 54). A closed union is analogous to a craft union, restricting entry to the trade or occupation and adopting an 'exclusive' approach to membership recruitment. The open and closed categories may be regarded as two extremes on an open–closed continuum rather than a dichotomy of mutually exclusive types. At the one extreme we have the completely closed, single-craft or occupational union and, at the other, we have the completely general, open union. The approach is useful because it enables us to assess the extent to which a particular trade union changes over time. During the course of its history, a union may be closed at one time and open at another. For example, the former Amalgamated Society of Engineers (ASE) was a pure craft union and therefore closed. Over time, the union, partly owing to its strong occupational base, transformed itself into the near general unionism of the Amalgamated Engineering Union (AEU) with its engineering, foundry and construction sections. In 1993 the AEU merged with the Electrical, Electronic, Telecommunications and Plumbing Union (EETPU) to form the Amalgamated Engineering Electrical Union (AEEU), making the union even more open. The union has since merged with MSF to form a two-divisional organisation called Amicus, comprising Amicus MSF and Amicus AEEU. The trend ever since the 1960s has been towards a more open strategy resulting in intense inter-union competition for membership regardless of structural considerations. As aggregate union membership fell during the 1980s and 1990s so the pace of amalgamations and mergers speeded up (see below).

Summary points: trade union structure

We may summarise our consideration of trade union structure as follows:

- The traditional classification of craft, industrial and general categories of union together with the refinements of the occupational and white-collar categories contains serious flaws which have been identified.
- The most significant weakness of the traditional classification worth reinforcing here is that it presents us with a largely static view of structure (the 'snapshot in time' view) and therefore ignores the dynamics of external change and the internal (to the union) pressures which influence a union's policies and decision-making.
- The vertical–horizontal analysis of union structure is an improvement upon the traditional classification, but has the disadvantage of placing unions into an 'either/or' category, while the general union may well possess both characteristics.

- The open–closed continuum is, arguably, the most useful as it assumes a dynamic relationship between a union and its complex external environment.

Self-Evaluation Activity 3.7
Identifying structural types
Response on website

Figure 3.1 is a simple matrix with examples of four trade unions identified in the left-hand column. Simply place a cross in the box or boxes which you think adequately describes the structural type of each of these unions. When you have done this, attempt a brief explanation of your reasoning.

	Open	Closed	Vertical	Horizontal
GMB				
UNISON				
NUM				
NUT				

Figure 3.1 Trade union structural types

Trade union strategy

One of the main assumptions underlying the identification of structural typologies is the rather determinist one that structure influences union behaviour. In recent years attention has focused upon strategy and the impact of strategic choices made by individual unions and by the union movement as a whole. With regard to membership recruitment, for example, strategy may be focused upon particular areas of potential membership, with unions in the banking and finance sector, for instance, targeting workers in call centres (Taylor and Bain, 1999). One of the most recent attempts to categorise unions in terms of their strategic interests and identification is that of Hyman (1996) who suggests five types:

- **the exclusive guild** which safeguards the interests of an occupational elite;

- **the friendly society** which offers consumer services to individual members, partly as a means of recruitment;
- **the company union** which co-operates with management on productivity issues;
- **the social partner** which aims to secure a dialogue with government; and
- **the social movement** which attracts widespread support by campaigning about popular issues.

It is important to note that the strategies associated with four of these categories (with the exception of the 'exclusive guild' strategy) are also associated with the TUC after its 'relaunch' in 1994 (see below).

Trade union mergers

At the beginning of the twentieth century there were approximately 1300 unions in Britain. By 1989 there were 314 unions, reducing to 268 in 1992 and to 226 in 2001/2 of which 69 are affiliated to the TUC (TUC, 2002). Much of the decline is the result of smaller, craft-oriented unions simply disappearing, while a smaller proportion of the decline in numbers can be attributed to mergers between small and large and medium and large unions. In fact, McIlroy (1995) contended that we had, by the 1980s, entered upon a period of 'merger mania' (p. 18). In retrospect, it is possible to identify certain merger trends and patterns over the past 35 years or so. During the 1970s, the main merger trend was for large unions to take over smaller unions. In the 1980s, the trend for medium sized unions merging with unions of similar size became established while from the late 1980s onwards, the 'super-union' trend became established which was characterised by large unions combining together to form large conglomerates. The term 'merger' is commonly used to include a takeover by a larger union of a smaller union and amalgamation to form a new organisation. As Waddington (2003) points out, mergers raises the problem of a growing diversity or heterogeneity of membership, which in the case of the main merged unions of UNISON and Amicus, for example, 'is associated with attempts to develop new forms of cohesion and articulation among heterogeneous memberships' (p. 224). Examples of mergers since 1980 include:

- Boilermakers with the General and Municipal Workers to form the GMB in 1982.
- National Association of Theatrical, TV and Kine Employees and ABS to form BETA in 1984.
- POEU and CPSA (Posts and Telecommunications section) to form the NCU in 1985.
- Amalgamated Textile Workers to GMB in 1986.
- ASTMS with TASS to form MSF in 1988.
- GMB with APEX (still known as GMB) in 1988.
- Civil Service Union with the Society of Civil and Public Services to form the National Union of Civil and Public Servants in 1988.
- NUR and NUS to form the RMTU in 1990.
- NGA and SOGAT to form the GPMU in 1990.
- BETA and ACTAT to form BECTU in 1990.
- NALGO, NUPE and COHSE to form UNISON (not an acronym) in 1992.
- AEU and EETPU to form AEEU in 1992.
- UCW and NCU to form CWU in 1995.
- IRSF and NUCPS to form PSTCU in 1996 which then through further amalgamation with the Civil and Public Services Association (CPSA) became known as the Public and Commercial Services Union (PCSU) in 1998.
- BIFU, UNIFI and NatWest Staff Union to form UNIFI in 1999.
- Engineers and Managers Association (EMA) and the Institution of Professionals, Managers and Specialists (IPMS) to form Prospect.
- AEEU and MSF to form Amicus in 2002.

Figure 3.2 depicts the trend in the decline of both numbers of trade unions and trade union membership (the two generally tend to go together) for the period 1976–2002, and Table 3.1 provides membership figures for the 'top ten' unions for 1989, 1996, 1997 and 2002. It is important to note that there are differences in how the Labour Force Survey (LFS) and the Certification Office report membership, with the latter including the entire UK showing aggregate higher membership levels. For comparative purposes, particularly where back time series go beyond 1989, and as a basis for comparison of more recent data, Certification Office data is used. Where sectoral and occupational membership figures are presented, LFS data is used.

Reasons for merger

Undy *et al.* (1981) analysed union mergers in the 1960s and 1970s and provided a threefold

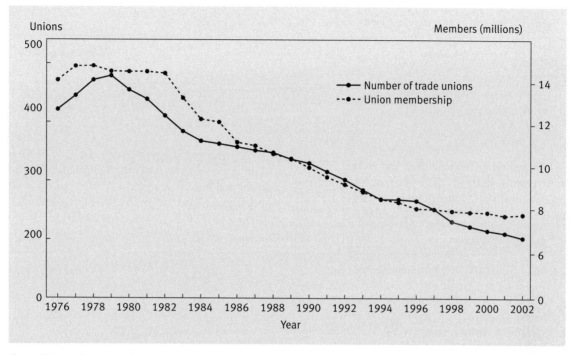

Figure 3.2 Decline in numbers of trade unions and fluctuations in trade union membership: 1976–2002
Source: Labour Market Trends and Certification Officer's reports, various years

explanation for them. According to Undy *et al.*, there are three reasons for merger. The first is defensive where a smaller union can escape the problem of its decline through falling membership and faltering finances by merging with a larger union. The second is consolidating where the larger union reinforces its dominant role within an industry, and the third is expansionist where a major union seeks to grow further, often into new industrial and/or occupational sectors as a matter of policy even if it means competing aggressively with a rival union. Mergers may also be prompted by the need to introduce economies of scale, improve organisational efficiency and to enable the merged union to expand into new and existing areas of employment growth (Waddington, 2003).

The accelerated pace of union mergers of the late 1980s and 1990–2000s involving larger organisations may be seen as part of an unplanned process towards rationalisation of the trade union movement, and as a TUC review of 1991 predicted, the merger process has grown 'and will continue to grow over the next ten years' (p. 20). The consequent fall

in numbers of unions and growing rate of mergers suggest a greater concentration of membership within the larger unions as Table 3.2 indicates.

Self-Evaluation Activity 3.8

The birth of UNISON and Amicus MSF
Response on website

Exhibit 3.3 is a description of the merger that spawned UNISON and the history of Amicus MSF together with a summary of their membership groupings. The UNISON merger was a unique event in the history of trade union mergers as it involved the amalgamation of three medium to large sized organisations while the Amicus MSF merger is the culmination of many previous mergers. Read the summary now and attempt the question which follows. (Note that UNISON was the 'newest' union in 1993.)

If you were a member of the UNISON or Amicus MSF National Executive, what would be your priorities for membership expansion for the next ten years?

Table 3.1 Membership of 'top ten' unions: 1989, 1996, 1997, 2002

	Top ten unions	Membership (000s) (to nearest 000)
1989	Transport and General Workers' Union	1 271
	GMB	823
	National and Local Government Officers' Association	751
	Amalgamated Engineering Union	742
	Manufacturing, Science and Finance Union	653
	National Union of Public Employees	605
	Union of Shop, Distributive and Allied Workers	376
	Electrical, Electronic, Telecommunications and Plumbing Union	367
	Royal College of Nursing of the United Kingdom	286
	Union of Construction, Allied Trades and Technicians	258
1996	UNISON: The Public Service Union	1 375
	Transport and General Workers' Union	885
	Amalgamated Engineering and Electrical Union	725
	GMB	718
	Manufacturing, Science and Finance Union	425
	Royal College of Nursing of the United Kingdom	307
	Union of Shop, Distributive and Allied Workers	290
	Communication Workers' Union	275
	National Union of Teachers	271
	National Association of Schoolmasters and Union of Women Teachers	238
1997	UNISON: The Public Service Union	1 300
	Transport and General Workers' Union	881
	Amalgamated Engineering and Electrical Union	720
	GMB	710
	Manufacturing, Science and Finance Union	416
	Royal College of Nursing of the United Kingdom	312
	Union of Shop, Distributive and Allied Workers	293
	National Union of Teachers	277
	Communication Workers' Union	274
	National Association of Schoolmasters and Union of Women Teachers	246
2002	UNISON: The Public Service Union	1 272
	Amicus	1 078
	Transport and General Workers' Union	858
	GMB	683
	Royal College of Nursing	334
	Union of Shop, Distributive and Allied Workers	310
	National Union of Teachers	286
	Communication Workers' Union	284
	Public and Commercial Services Union	267
	National Association of Schoolmasters and Union of Women Teachers	255

Source: Annual Reports of the Certification Officer, 1990, 1997, 1998 and 2002

Table 3.2 Trade union distribution by size: 2002

Number of members	Number of unions (listed and unlisted)	Membership (000s)	Number of unions		Membership of all unions	
			%	Cumulative %	%	Cumulative %
Under 100	50	1.7	22.1	22.1	–	–
100–499	41	11.9	18.1	40.2	0.2	0.2
500–999	21	14.2	9.3	49.5	0.2	0.4
1000–2499	28	46.5	12.4	61.9	0.6	1.0
2500–4999	21	74.0	9.3	71.2	1.0	2.0
5000–9999	12	85.7	5.3	76.5	1.1	3.1
10 000–14 999	4	48.1	1.8	78.3	0.6	3.7
15 000–24 999	12	222.8	5.3	83.6	2.9	6.6
25 000–49 999	15	515.1	6.6	90.3	6.6	13.2
50 000–99 999	6	361.0	2.7	92.9	4.6	17.8
100 000–249 999	5	764.8	2.2	95.1	9.8	27.6
250 000 and over	11	5 633.0	4.9	100.0	72.4	100.0
Total	226	7 779.4	100.0		100.0	

Source: Annual Reports of the Certification Officer, 1998, 2002
Note: Membership data is compiled both by the Certification Officer's Annual Reports and the annual Labour Force Surveys of trade union membership. The Certification Office data covers the membership of all trade unions known to the Certification Officer and since 1975 includes all organisations falling within the definition of a trade union under section 28 of the Trade Union and Labour Relations Act 1974. Details of unions are maintained on an official list. Membership of listed trade unions includes home and overseas members and some people who are self-employed, unemployed or retired. The Labour Force Survey data includes only those trade union members in employment.

Exhibit 3.3

UNISON and Amicus MSF

UNISON is Britain's newest and largest union and remains the largest and most complex merger in British union history (Dempsey and McKevitt, 2001). Its members provide services to the public in both the private and public sectors and it is firmly committed to the public service ethos. Two-thirds of its members are women and UNISON's organisation and constitution reflect the importance of equal opportunities and fair representation. The amalgamation will lead to improvements in an already highly developed system of collective bargaining and workplace representation. The two traditions of party political independence and Labour Party affiliation are maintained through the existence of separate political funds. UNISON came into being on 1 July 1993 through an amalgamation of three partners, the Confederation of Health Service Employees (COHSE) representing around 200 000 health service staff, the National and Local Government Officers Association (NALGO) representing some 700 000 white-collar staff in a range of public services and the National Union of Public Employees (NUPE) which represented about 600 000 manual staff in the public services. The amalgamation was accomplished after more than three years' intensive negotiation and agreement. Throughout this process, there was widespread consultation with the three unions' members, detailed reports were taken to each union's conferences, and information was provided to the negotiators from educational meetings and research. Arrangements for membership ballots were agreed with the Certification Officer and a motion to amalgamate was put to a secret, individual postal vote of each union's members. The results of the ballots were declared in December 1992. Each union returned a substantial majority in favour of amalgamation. UNISON's membership groups comprise:

- **Local government:** around 800 000 members comprising manual and non-manual workers belong to this group and about 50 per cent of all local government staff are UNISON members.
- **Healthcare:** UNISON has 440 000 members in this group which includes the NHS. Almost three-quarters of the membership are women, a significant proportion is black, and many work part-time.
- **Electricity:** UNISON has about 20 000 members in the electricity supply industry. About 60 per cent of the membership are women and they work primarily in administration and clerical jobs. There is also some representation in electrical retailing.
- **Gas:** There are approximately 20 000 members in the gas industry covering staff and senior officers, and UNISON is the largest non-manual union.
- **Water:** UNISON is the largest union in the water industry, with around 25 000 members, the majority of whom work for the water companies.
- **Transport:** There are about 5000 transport members who work for Passenger Transport Executives, the British Waterways Board and private and municipal bus companies.
- **Higher education:** Membership is concentrated within non-academic groups.

Amicus MSF

MSF stands for Manufacturing, Science, Finance and recruits skilled and professional employees in all parts of manufacturing including engineering, electronics, aerospace, cars, chemicals and pharmaceuticals, tobacco and food and drink. MSF also recruits from the finance sector and from the health service and universities etc.

Structure: The basis of the union's work is members in the workplace which is the foundation of union activities undertaken by workplace representatives elected by members and supported by a network of professional regional officers located throughout the UK. Regional officers are the workplace reps' link to specialist services provided by MSF head office departments such as Communications, Research, Legal and Health and Safety. Work at national level is co-ordinated by national secretaries under the leadership of the General Secretary. The union also has a structure of branches, regional councils and an annual conference. Branches are represented at regional councils and form the basis for the election of delegates to annual conference which is the union's policy-making body. Between annual conferences, the national executive council is responsible for the union's government.

History: MSF was formed in January 1988 when two unions, ASTMS (Association of Scientific, Technical and Managerial Staffs) and TASS (Technical, Administrative and Supervisory Staffs) merged. The membership of the two founding unions complemented each other. TASS members were skilled and professional staff and were employed mainly in the engineering industry, and TASS had its origins in DATA, the Draughtsmen and Allied Technicians' Association. ASTMS had developed into a white-collar union with members in all sectors of industry and services and had itself been created by a merger in 1969. ASTMS had a phenomenal record of growth following its formation and expanded rapidly into new industries and services, particularly the finance and insurance sector.

Trade union government and democracy

Here we look at how trade unions are internally structured in relation to two areas:

- the management and authority structure (or organisational structure) of unions; and
- the democratic process within unions.

In practice there is considerable overlap between these two areas as much emphasis is placed upon representation of members' interests, and this may naturally impede the efficiency by which decisions are made.

Organisational structure

Despite the heterogeneous nature of British trade unions, we can discern a basic, common structural pattern which includes the following elements:

1. The branch is the first point of contact which a rank-and-file member has with his or her union and 'provides him with an opportunity to participate in the government and administration of the union' (Flanders, 1972, p. 50). The branch may be workplace or factory-based on a single employer, or it can be based on a particular trade group. Branches vary in size, and within the TGWU, for example, branches range in size from a minimum of 50 to as many as 5000. They also vary in frequency of meetings: the TGWU stipulates that branches must meet at least monthly, while others may only meet annually.

   The branch provides the opportunity for members to attend its meetings. However, the many studies of membership participation at branch meetings (ranging from the early research of Roberts (1956) to that of Undy and Martin (1984)) indicate that attendance is routinely low and within the 5–10 per cent range. A study of London Transport bus workers (Rose, 1974), a sector where the TGWU branches are based on individual garages, confirms the low attendance figures of previous studies and suggests possible reasons for this including:
   - general apathy and disinterest of members;
   - work patterns based on shifts;
   - male-dominated meetings discourage women members;
   - location of meetings (e.g. in public houses);
   - perceived domination of branch meetings by cliques of 'activists', and unrepresentative of the membership as a whole.

   A more general reason for low branch member participation noted by Hawkins (1981) is 'that for most of them [the members] the union as an institution is not a salient feature of day-to-day life in the workplace. Motivated by instrumental collectivism, they see the union simply as a means of achieving tangible improvements in pay and conditions and as long as it meets their expectations they are not unduly disturbed if the union is led by individuals whose political outlook is at variance with their own' (p. 115).

2. The next level of a trade union's organisational structure is variously called the area, district, division or region. There are formal links between branches at this intermediate level based either on direct representation of each branch or indirectly by, say, the regional membership. The power and influence of the area, district, division or region varies with different unions, but as a general rule, the regional influence may have assumed greater importance with the shift in collective bargaining from industrial to organisational level, particularly within the private sector (including the recently privatised industries and utilities). The full-time union officer is either appointed by the union or elected by lay members and features prominently at the intermediate level and above. The duties of officers vary, but the vast majority represent members in formal negotiations at organisational and industry levels. A small proportion has specialist functions in the areas of recruitment, health and safety, research, finance and public relations. The number of officers nationally is relatively small. In 1968, the Donovan Commission estimated that there were about 3000 officers (one for every 3800 members) and according to Kelly and Heery (1994) this number has remained unchanged but with a ratio of one for every 3229 members.

3. The third formal level within the trade union organisational hierarchy is the National Executive Committee (NEC) which is responsible for

carrying out the policies agreed at delegate conferences and for the efficient administration of the union between conferences. The delegate conference itself enables branch representatives and other delegates to discuss policy issues and make the decisions to be carried out by the NEC. Conferences vary in size and in frequency of meeting; for some unions, an annual conference will suffice, while others will hold two or even three per year. All members of the NEC, the General Secretary and President are directly elected by the membership, via postal ballot as required by the Trade Union Act (1984) and the Employment Act (1988). NECs generally attempt to ensure adequate representation of the variety of interests and sections within the union, and efforts are being made to encourage greater representation of women and black members on the NEC.

The democratic process

In order to determine the nature of union democracy we need to be aware of the problems associated with the definition of the concept of democracy. (A fuller discussion of the concept is provided in Chapter 8.) There are two main types of democracy, known as direct and representative democracy. The direct form assumes situations whereby everyone has a direct input into the decision-making process – as in the city states of Ancient Greece in which all citizens participated in taking decisions. The early craft unions developed a form of direct democracy which enabled ordinary members to have access to the unions' meetings and determine decision-making. However, in all but the smallest organisations, the direct form of democracy is considered to be unwieldy, impracticable and unworkable, and is irreconcilable with the criteria for administrative efficiency in larger, more complex and bureaucratically structured organisations. The Webbs were the first to point out this paradox and advocated a more practical system of democracy based upon greater representation of members' interests – hence the term representative democracy.

Critics of organisations which purport to be democratic – such as trade unions and political parties – have argued that these organisations, in an attempt to reconcile the demands for democracy on the one hand, and efficiency on the other, are neither particularly democratic nor efficient. Indeed, Michels (1959) asserted that in trade unions, as in other organisations, an 'iron law of oligarchy' operated. Within the trade union context this means, according to McIlroy (1988, 1995), that 'full-time union officials developed a monopoly of expertise – and used their control over resources and the prestige their position gave them to impose their own goals on the members whose ignorance and apathy facilitated this process. Unions were ruled, not by their members, but by small groups of bureaucrats' (p. 158).

In reality, the relationship between the leadership of a trade union and its members is complex. As the example of UNISON demonstrates, the membership of that union is fairly diverse and sectionalised and there are many membership interests to be represented, a process which may be called vertical representation. By the same token, the leadership role within UNISON is both multifaceted and diffuse and the democratic process additionally implies decision-making between various sections of the leadership – a process of horizontal representation. This situation is understandable in UNISON and other large federated unions such as Amicus. In the former case there were considerable cultural, organisational and democratic differences between the three constituent unions and to a certain extent these differences still remain (Dempsey and McKevitt, 2001). Studies of trade union democracy reflect the complexities of organisation, sectionalism and diversity of membership interests, and the following points will assist in clarifying the debate:

1. Studies which support the view that at least some **trade unions are inherently oligarchic in nature** include those of Turner (1962) and Edelstein and Warner (1975). Turner provides a threefold classification of union types:
   - the first union type is the **exclusive democracy** whose membership is homogeneous and cohesive with high participation rates, the typical example being the traditional craft unions;
   - the second union type is the **aristocracy** whose membership is more heterogeneous and sectionalised, and in which one group or section has much higher participation rates than the

other groups and which consequently dominates the union through full-time officers drawn from that group; and

- the third union type is the **popular bossdom** whose membership is extremely heterogeneous and largely unskilled or semi-skilled, with very low participation rates, and whose leadership, based on full-time officials, is firmly in control.

Edelstein and Warner in their comparative study of union democracy in the USA and Britain argue that oligarchic tendencies within unions have beneficial effects of maintaining unity provided that countervailing interests within the membership are properly organised and represented, thereby preventing any abuse of power on the part of the leadership.

2. Studies which emphasise the **existence of opposition** and therefore of choice for the membership as being a vital element of the democratic process include the classic examination of the TGWU by Goldstein (1952) and the study of the American International Typographical Union (ITU) by Lipset *et al.* (1956). Put simply, if there is no opposition, there is no democracy, bearing in mind the analogy of the one-party state. The nature of the 'opposition' varies from the formalised, seemingly permanent 'party system' of the ITU to more transient groups pursuing short or medium-term goals as Blackwell's (1990) examination of the Bakers' union indicates. Hawkins (1981) considers the example of the (then) AUEW in this context:

> If an elaborate system of constitutional checks and balances reinforced by the general principle of accountability through the ballot box, was synonymous with membership control then the AUEW would be a model of democracy. In practice, however, the main result has been the development of a unique system of two-party conflict. Over the last twenty years union elections have been closely contested by two highly organised and ideologically opposed electoral organisations which, having many of the trappings of parties, are worthy of the title. The parties concerned represent respectively the 'establishment' and the 'opposition'. Until the late 1960s the

> establishment party controlled the main constitutional organs of the union at national level and held the principal offices. Ideologically it has usually been identified with orthodox Labour Party policy. Between 1967 and 1974, however, the more left-wing opposition party (or 'progressives') gained ground by intense campaigning. . . . Their most notable achievement was the capture of the presidency of the union in 1967 by Hugh Scanlon, a former communist who won with communist support. (p. 118)

Other unions such as CPSA, the former NALGO, NUT and UCATT saw the growth of 'rank-and-file' opposition movements, committed to a programme of militant confrontation with employers and the expansion of activist democracy during the 1960s and 1970s.

3. A third area of study considers **size of union and the diversity of membership**. The basic proposition is that as a union grows in size, either by increasing its traditional membership base or by amalgamation, 'the administrative subsystem is likely to become more formalised and bureaucratic, and the representative system will face increased difficulties in ensuring that the differing views of disparate groups are brought to bear on decision making' (Salamon, 1998, p. 140). The recent focus upon trade union renewal and organising (see below) has brought into greater contention the representation of women and other marginalised groups and how their voices can be articulated (Colgan and Ledwith, 2002). Many unions have sought to tackle this problem by decentralising their decision-making and policy formulation processes. A relevant example of how one union attempted to come to terms with the problem of representing different groups during the 1970s and 1980s is the old 'popular bossdom', the TGWU which we now briefly consider.

From popular bossdom to popular democracy?

When Jack Jones was General Secretary of the TGWU, his vision for the highly centralised, officer-dominated union was to commit it to the 'concept of democratic trade unionism, under rank and file control' (Coates and Topham, 1988, p. 190).

Jones himself described the objective in the following way:

> *I am working for a system where not a few trade union officials control the situation but a dedicated, well-trained and intelligent body of trade union members is represented by hundreds of thousands of lay representatives – every one of whom is capable of helping to resolve industrial problems and assisting in collective bargaining and the conclusion of agreements.* (Taylor, 1978, p. 133)

Under Jones, as Heery (1997) points out, 'the union leadership both endorsed and encouraged participation by members in union decision making and activities and promoted self-reliance, such that policy objectives, workplace organisation, collective bargaining and representation rested increasingly in the hands of members themselves and their shop stewards' (p. 177). The research by Undy *et al.* (1981) identifies the reforms undertaken by the TGWU in order to achieve these objectives:

- reducing the power of national trade groups (the centralised 'old guard');
- extending lay participation by encouraging the appointment of shop stewards, decentralising collective bargaining and supporting the ratification of collective agreements by the membership;
- promoting a switch from officer to lay representation;
- decentralising the union's internal financial system, giving regions greater responsibility for financial and administrative decisions; and
- tighter control over appointments to ensure that the strategy of participative unionism was implemented and the culture of the organisation changed.

Self-Evaluation Activity 3.9

The new unionism of the GMB

Response on website

The 2003 structure of the GMB is described in Main case 3.1, and this is followed by a brief account of the reforms to the union instigated by John Edmonds, its former General Secretary. Read through the passage and attempt the following question (a diagrammatic representation of the GMB structure is provided in Figure 3.3). Comment on the nature of the GMB's democratic structure.

Main case 3.1
The GMB

The GMB is a general union of over 683 000 people. The structure of the union consists of:

The Branch: The Branch is the basic unit of the union's organisation. Branches consist of all the members of a given area or, in cases where enough members are concentrated in one Branch of industry, it can be industrial or workplace based. Each GMB Branch has its Officers: the Secretary, President, Auditor, Branch Youth Officer and Branch Equality Officer. All Branch Officers are elected every two years. In the workplace there are over 30 000 Shop Stewards and Staff Representatives who are directly elected by the membership. Many workplaces also have a Health and Safety Representative and an Equal Opportunities Officer. Large workplaces often have a senior shop steward known as the Convenor. These people are men and women who are elected by their workmates and are the front-line of the union.

Regions: The GMB keeps in close touch with its members through its ten regional offices and over 60 sub-offices. There are ten regions of approximately equal size of membership and they are responsible for membership servicing. The senior official in each region is the Regional Secretary and is responsible to the regional council for the workings of the union and its officers, staff and administration. The councils are made up of active members of the union who are elected every two years and in turn elect a committee to oversee the business of the region. There are over 300 Regional Organisers in the GMB who are paid, full-time employees of the union. Their job is to help negotiations and back-up our workplace representatives. They are experts in their industries as well as holding experience and knowledge in employment law, pensions and other vital areas of concern to our members.

National Level: Like all trade unions, the GMB belongs to its members. In practical terms this expresses itself through the union's annual Congress. Each year the union brings together around 500 delegates from around the country – any member of the union can put themselves forward as a delegate and seek election in the regional ballot. The Congress, subject to the law, can make any decision on behalf of the union and its policies become the goals for everyone in the organisation.

Central Executive Council: Notwithstanding Congress, the Central Executive Council is the supreme body of the union. The 'CEC' as it is known, meets every two months or so and consists of about 80 members of the

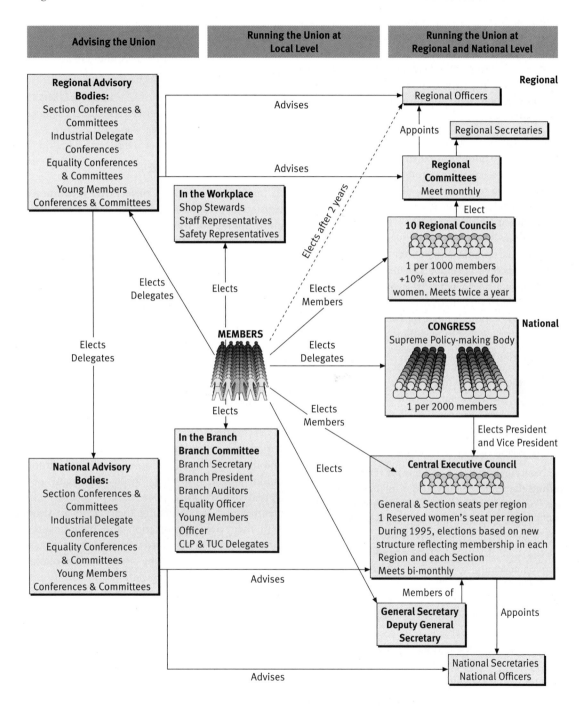

Figure 3.3 Structure of the GMB

union. It is elected by secret ballot of the whole union every four years. For practical reasons its business is run by sub-committees such as Finance, Organisation, Services and Training.

National Office: The senior officials of the union are the General Secretary, and his deputy. Both positions are elected every five years by a secret ballot of the union's 683 000 members giving them enormous democratic credibility to represent working people. They have responsibility for the union's industrial and policy work as well as being the senior executive managers of the GMB.

Sections of the Union: As industry and technology has changed, so too has the nature of work. The blue collar/white collar distinction is disappearing in many industries whilst Human Resource Management has revolutionised working practices for many. In the 1990s the GMB created a new structure to reflect these changes in the economy. Eight Sections were created to cover the whole of the union's membership. So instead of looking at a single company or single employer, we are now able to take a strategic view across a whole sector. Each Section has its own National Committee of lay members elected from within the industry and its own annual Conference. Each Section is headed by a National Secretary and, with the support of National Officers, they lead the negotiations at national level, backed up by Regional Organisers. The Sections include the Apex Partnership which provides union representation to administrative, clerical and technical staff at all grades.

The New Agenda: The GMB has led the way in modernising the trade union world. Our New Agenda is based on the premise that our first job is to strive to achieve what it is that our members want from their work. Launched in 1990, the New Agenda stated: 'It is essential that Britain's Unions abandon traditional, reactive stances and set an agenda which confronts the new issues of the 1990s. Britain's performance in the last twenty years has not been impressive. Trade unions should wish to work together with employers and Government to create a successful industry, a strong economy and a caring, sharing society. Doing so successfully requires that we adjust to the changing contours of the economic and social landscape. The task ahead demands that we take collective bargaining into territory that we have barely explored before.'

Since the launch of the New Agenda, which was accepted by the TUC in 1991, trade unions, led by the GMB, have begun to win through on childcare, training packages, employee consultation and many other areas of employment. Perhaps the biggest impact, however, has been the influence on Europe. In 1992 we became the first UK union to open an office in Brussels and in 1994 became the first UK union to sign up to a European Works Council.

Source: GMB 1998

Legislation for democracy

A major part of the Conservative governments' legislative programme dealing with trade unions and employment was concerned with internal union affairs and in particular with providing statutory underpinning to and reinforcement of the representational concept of democracy. The political slogans mouthed by Conservative ministers and particularly by Norman Tebbitt, erstwhile Employment Secretary, such as 'we must return the union to its members and protect the individual member against union tyranny' were intended primarily for conference consumption, but also had wider credibility. The Conservatives convinced themselves that the minority of 'activist extremists' was manipulating the majority of the 'passive' membership. McIlroy (1995) argues that 'what has been involved . . . is a qualitative increment to state regulation of trade unionism and a diminution of self-regulation by union members' (p. 42). To be sure, many of the legislative provisions appear to have benefited union members by strengthening their rights in dealing with their own organisation and have ensured a formal, common standard of representation across the union movement. The first New Labour government endorsed the legislation and had no intention of repealing it (apart from the 'check-off' requirement identified below). The main provisions are:

- The provision of public financial support for expenditure incurred by unions in the conduct of secret ballots and elections (Employment Act 1980) but withdrawn by the Trade Union Reform and Employment Rights Act 1993.

- The provision in the Trade Union Act 1984 that unions' NECs must be directly elected by the membership, extended by the Employment Act 1988 to include the General Secretary, President and non-voting members of the NEC, and that all elections must be conducted by postal ballot subject to independent scrutiny.
- The provision of legal rights for union members (Employment Act 1988).
- The provision in the Employment Act 1988 to establish a new Commissioner for the Rights of Trade Union Members (CROTUM) to help union members who wish to take legal proceedings against their union concerning their new statutory rights.
- The requirement for the employee to provide prior written consent, renewed every three years, to the employer who automatically deducts union subscriptions from earnings (known as the 'check-off'). By 1998, around two-thirds of unionised establishments practised the check-off (Cully *et al.*, 1999). Nevertheless, a campaign by the TUC resulted in the Labour government repealing the requirement.

Some of the advantages and disadvantages of legislated democracy in relation to postal ballots are identified in Exhibit 3.4.

The closed shop: no democracy at the point of entry?

Prior to 1988, the closed shop – defined as 100 per cent union membership (of which there were two types: pre-entry, where the employee joined prior to signing the contract of employment, and post-entry, where the employee joined after signing the contract of employment) – was considered to be an enduring feature of the employment relationship for many employees and employers, albeit highly undemocratic at the point of entry. The employer could not use the criterion of union membership for dismissing employees and in 1988 dismissal owing to union or non-union membership was deemed unfair while in 1990 it became unlawful for employers to refuse to hire workers based on their union membership status. This effectively spelt the demise of the closed shop in Britain, so much so that by 1998 only 2 per cent of workplaces were identified by WERS98 where employees had to be union mem-

bers to keep their jobs (Cully *et al.*, 1999), contrasted with 23 per cent of workplaces which had a closed shop in operation in 1980 (Millward and Stevens, 1986). The decline of the closed shop cannot be entirely attributed to the Conservative legislation. Pencavel (2001), for example, argues that the pre-entry closed shop proliferated in the old craft industries such as printing, newspapers, docks and shipping which have been greatly affected by technological change, giving rise to the probability that 'many closed shops would have been swept aside anyway by the onslaught of the new technology' (p. 23).

Summary points

- The number and frequency of trade union mergers has increased in recent decades. Mergers are seen as necessary in order to cope with falling membership and to ensure that the necessary financial and other resources are devoted to implementing recruitment strategies and service provision.
- The typical union representative structure comprises the branch (shop stewards); area, district, divisional and regional departments and sections (full-time officers); a national executive committee and delegates' conference.
- In theory, members' interests are represented within a formal democratic structure which reflects sectional and membership diversity. Studies of union democracy, however, have been critical of union representative structures and, in common with most non-union representative structures, have assumed that:
  - unions, in common with other democratically structured organisations, have a tendency towards oligarchy;
  - the existence of opposition or factionalism is essential for the health and effectiveness of the democratic process; and
  - increasing diversity of union membership creates tensions between the administrative (bureaucratic) and the representative (democratic) subsystems.
- Many unions (such as the GMB) have undergone a certain amount of organisational restructuring, in order to encourage broad-based participation in decision-making.

Exhibit 3.4

Advantages and disadvantages of legislated union democracy in relation to postal ballots

Arguments for

1. Unions are involved in activities vital to the economy and society and, left to themselves, their decision-making mechanisms are profoundly unsatisfactory. In 1980, more than 40 per cent of General Secretaries were unelected and never had to face the voters.

2. The 'closed shop' inhibits the democratic process by interfering with the freedom of the individual, the right to work, and the efficiency of the enterprise. Those press-ganged into membership are unlikely to become loyal, let alone active members.

3. Participation cannot be improved by cajoling members to attend mass meetings which are open to intimidation and making decisions on the basis of a 'show of hands'. There are risks of manipulation under these circumstances. Workplace ballots are also unsatisfactory if members are not given sufficient privacy when recording votes.

4. The secret postal ballot overcomes these difficulties and it is in the interests of unions to compile a register of members and use the services of an independent scrutiniser.

5. The advantages of the postal ballot outweigh the disadvantages, making the unions more democratic and producing more moderate leadership.

6. Individuals wishing to exert their democratic right not to participate in industrial action require specific protection from union leaders. The Commissioners (CROTUM) are essential to help intimidated members in pursuing their legal rights against unions.

Arguments against

1. Postal ballots produce decreased turnout compared with workplace ballots; there is no evidence that postal ballots produce more moderate leaders.

2. The closed shop is justified by imbalance of power between employer and employee. This argument is somewhat academic as closed shops have virtually ceased to exist.

3. Governments have produced no evidence of intimidation or manipulation, and postal ballots are not necessarily immune to manipulation.

4. Unions' vitality depends upon members acting collectively. Postal balloting can minimise the quality of participation. Members are in a better position to take decisions when they have listened to the arguments. If workers vote in the workplace, they are in a better position to consider collective interests than if they vote as isolated individuals at home.

5. Rights to ignore strike decisions arrived at by state-imposed ballots emphasise that the purpose of legislation is to disorganise and demobilise trade unionism, not make it more democratic.

6. State intervention weakens the roots of democracy in society by restricting the scope of legitimate self-government of social organisations.

Source: Adapted from McIlroy, 1995, pp. 170–2

SHOP STEWARDS AND WORKPLACE ORGANISATION

The main channels for a collective representative voice have shown a considerable decline since the 1980s. WERS98 confirmed that this is a continuing trend involving union and non-union forms, particularly in new workplaces. However, as far as actual workplace representatives are concerned, 40 per cent of workplaces employing more than 25 people had both union and non-union representatives (Cully *et al.*, 1999), down from 54 per cent in 1984 (Millward *et al.*, 1992). Terry (2003) reports that the number of shop stewards has declined only fairly gradually since 1978, from 250 000 to 218 000 in 1998. They exist in around 75 per cent of unionised workplaces, with a higher concentration and density within the public services, the privatised utilities and services, in large manufacturing workplaces and less so in finance and banking. In all other sectors, the shop steward phenomenon is an unusual one (Terry, 2003, p. 259). The main decline in 'on-site' representation during the time span of the WIRS series happened in the latter half of the 1980s; between 1984 and 1990 the proportion of union representatives within unionised workplaces fell from 82 per cent to 71 per cent with no further reduction during the 1990s. Millward *et al.* (2000) conclude that 'if unions were losing their organizational strength in the 1990s, then we might have anticipated a continuation in the decline of on-site representation that had begun in the latter half of the 1980s. In fact the evidence from the 1998 [survey] clearly indicates that on-site representation stabilized in the 1990s' (p. 152).

The role and function of stewards

Employee representatives are elected by fellow employees and in the case of shop stewards, by union members only, within a specific constituency whose average size is around 29 union members. There is a 'representational weighting' towards the professions, with professional representatives comprising 33 per cent of all union representatives even though they comprise only around 13 per cent of union members (Cully *et al.*, 1999). The main reason for this degree of 'professional over-representation' may be that professionals generally have more immediate access to communications media than, say, their manual counterparts.

Traditionally, many union rulebooks made sparse reference to the definition of a steward's function and responsibilities, although the larger unions and the TUC have recognised for some time that training and education provision is essential if stewards are to perform these functions efficiently on behalf of their members. The concept of role suggests that the steward is in a continuing dynamic relationship with others (his other role set) both within and outside the workplace. Within the workplace, we have an internal role set which comprises:

- Management (personnel, industrial relations, human resource and line management).
- Steward's membership.
- Other shop stewards.

Outside the workplace, the external role set comprises:

- The trade union.
- Shop stewards from other workplaces within the same organisation.
- The full-time union officer.

Within the internal and external role sets (or the role network) there are both formal and informal expectations or perceptions of what the steward should do. In addition, the steward will have his or her own subjective expectations of the role which may, at times, differ from those of the role set. Where different expectations of role behaviour clash, this can result in role conflict.

Self-Evaluation Activity 3.10

Expectations of the steward's role
Response on website

Provide examples of the sort of expectations the members of a steward's role network may have with regard to the steward's role. Exhibit 3.5 is an example of how UNISON defines the shop steward role.

Exhibit 3.5

The Steward's tasks

Below is an ideal list of tasks a Steward could be asked to undertake. No one Steward could do everything included here, but it will serve as a reference and reminder of what needs to be done.

(a) Recruitment

- finding out who the members and non-members are
- helping keep the members interested in and informed about the union
- trying to get non-members to join the union and
- trying to get members to become Stewards or safety reps

(b) Relations with management

- talking to members about what their problems at work are and discussing how they can best be dealt with
- getting advice and help from senior Stewards or branch officers
- meeting with supervisors/management to sort out members' grievances and problems
- representing members in disciplinary cases
- attending joint consultative meetings with management and Stewards from other unions
- reporting back to members
- ensuring that collective agreements are implemented and kept
- reporting any breaches of agreements to the branch officials or full-time officer
- negotiating and reaching local agreements (this depends on the degree of devolution of local bargaining)
- referring health and safety problems to the Safety Rep. or if there isn't one, raising these issues with management

(c) Representing members

- finding out your members' views on union and work issues
- putting your members' views at relevant meetings such as Stewards' committees (if you have one)
- reporting back from those meetings to members.

One of the main requirements of a good Steward is to be accessible to members. This accountability includes representing members' views and interests on the departmental Stewards' committee and branch executive and telling them what has happened. Make sure all your constituents know that you are their Steward – make sure members isolated by where or when they work or the job they do are kept fully informed. Let members know when and where you can be contacted.

(d) Constituency

The constituency is the workplace and should have been defined so that you know whom you are responsible for. If you are not sure, check with other Stewards in your department and agree on an appropriate division of responsibilities.

(e) Negotiation

The vital element in the duties of a Steward is often that of negotiation with management on behalf of members. The link with the rest of the branch structure is still crucially important but is combined with being the first point of contact between member and union in all matters affecting employment. There are limits to your responsibility and authority and the sort of problems you should attempt to solve.

(f) Explaining the union's policies

- finding out UNISON's policies on important issues from UNISON publications, from meetings or from other Stewards/branch officers
- talking to members about these policies
- giving out information/leaflets from the union to your membership
- holding meetings with members

(g) Organisation

- finding out who the branch officers and other reps are
- finding out about how the branch works and how members can take a part in it
- discussing how to improve the organisation of the branch so that it can best help your members

Source: *UNISON Stewards' Handbook*

Shop stewards: The current situation

During the 1960s and 1970s, the trend towards workplace-based industrial relations, together with the growth in the numbers of shop stewards, became firmly established in a large proportion of manufacturing and public sector establishments and organisations (see also Chapter 6). While some of the factors contributing to this development have been considered in Chapter 1, those specific to the growth in numbers of shop stewards include the following:

- the steady growth in trade union membership and, in particular, of white-collar and public service workers;
- the tendency for trade unions to decentralise their structures, thereby encouraging the involvement of members and shop stewards at the workplace, as exemplified by the TGWU in the previous section of this chapter;
- the introduction of training and education provision for shop stewards under the auspices of the TUC and the Workers' Education Association;
- the acceptance by employers of the recommendations of the Donovan Commission concerning the formalisation of collective bargaining at plant and company level (which also hastened the decline of industry-wide national bargaining in many industries);

- the need for employers to introduce new technology at the workplace, together with payment systems which rewarded local productivity gains, facilitated the development of plant and workplace bargaining and encouraged employer support for workplace union organisation; and
- the role of the state in supporting collective bargaining (active support from Labour governments; passive or grudging support from Conservative governments) and shop steward organisations through health and safety legislation and statutory rights for shop stewards to take time off work in order to perform their duties.

The growth and spread of shop stewards' organisation during the 1970s was not wholly beneficial to managers or to employees. The continuing high level of unofficial disputes involving workplace representatives during this period was problematic and reinforced media perceptions of 'poor' industrial relations and 'militant' shop stewards. Moreover, labour productivity gains were limited (testifying to the failure of local 'productivity bargaining') and wage inflation remained buoyant throughout the period. There was a growing perception amongst employers that workplace bargaining was a hindrance rather than a help and that shop stewards 'had not come up with the goods'. Furthermore, Terry (1995) asserts that:

*Even at their peak, shop steward power and influence were limited and constrained by ideological factors, in particular the decentralisation and relative autonomy of steward organisations and the associated focus of their attention on the short-term bargaining of pay and conditions. This 'narrowness' of activity was in turn reinforced by a continuing managerial refusal to widen the scope of formal bargaining and consultation, in particular to issues of 'managerial relations'. On matters such as work organisation, staffing levels, the speed and intensity of working, managers continued to resist formalisation, being unwilling to concede **de jure** rights to unions.* (p. 211)

The 1980s and 1990s

The 1980s witnessed a dramatic decline in trade union membership, and with it a decline in the number of shop stewards and an erosion of their power base. To some extent the decline can be attributed to macroeconomic factors such as recession and growth of unemployment, particularly in manufacturing industry. The 1990 WIRS survey, covering the period 1984–90, identifies significant changes (some of which have already been referred to) associated with this trend:

- in establishments in which trade unions are recognised, 38 per cent of them had stewards in 1990 as opposed to 54 per cent in 1984;
- most of the decline in steward representation in private manufacturing took place in those establishments where the proportion of trade union members (or union density) was already low;
- there was a decline in the support given by employers to workplace representation, particularly in the area of shop steward training; and
- the stabilisation in the incidence of on-site union representatives from 1990 onwards (WERS98).

Other surveys and case study evidence point to the growing 'marginalisation' of shop stewards as managers make changes and take decisions without negotiation, replacing negotiation with consultation and assuming an increasing reliance upon 'direct' forms of communication (Marchington and Parker, 1990). The 'marginalisation thesis' is given further support from case study evidence of unionised Japanese transplants (inwardly investing multina-

tional companies establishing on 'greenfield' sites). Where transplants are unionised, Grant (1997) argues:

Their approach to employee relations will have generally led to their signing of new-style agreements with a single union. These agreements are based on a spirit and intention which seeks to move industrial relations from a conflictual process to one based on cooperation and trust. In this context, new-style agreements can be seen as attempting to facilitate reductions in 'them and us' (that is in adversarial relations between management and workforce). (p. 209)

However, Grant's analysis of the Japanese manufacturing transplant which he calls 'RENCO' indicates that not only do adversarial relations persist, but also that 'what occurred at RENCO does not suggest that new-style agreements offer trade unions a strategy with which to halt the perceived decline in their influence and power since the early 1980s. Instead, it appears to give credence to the argument that the agreements are symptomatic of, and may even contribute to, this decline' (p. 230).

There is evidence that on-site shop steward representation is becoming progressively ineffective in influencing major outcomes such as negotiating pay and pay differentials and negotiation per se. The enduring ability of union representatives to negotiate effectively to reduce pay differentials (the gap between those on high and low earnings) has finally disappeared (Millward *et al.*, 2000). Moreover, in around 50 per cent of workplaces with union representatives, there was no negotiation on any issue, while in 17 per cent there was negotiation on pay alone – a conjunctive bargaining situation (see Chapter 6). Hence the empirical evidence of WERS98 suggests that the traditional picture of the convenor being locked in negotiation with local management over a wide range of issues is no longer sustainable. Therefore, the declining effectiveness of steward representation is consistent with other established trends concerning the marginalisation of unions and their representatives, the bypassing of union communication channels, the use of 'negotiation' – where it is used – as a consultative mechanism and the imposition of organisational change without recourse to the use of any form of representation whatsoever.

Shop steward decline and workplace unionism: the growing 'representation gap'

Terry (1995, 2003) attributes the decline of shop steward influence in the 1990s to four sets of factors: economic and industrial changes, the roleof the state, new approaches by employers and the contribution of shop-floor unions. These factors have created an ever-widening collective 'representation gap' which is most marked in non-union firms, but which is now becoming increasingly evident in unionised organisations and workplaces.

Economic, industrial and structural

Low levels of unemployment and the relative scarcity of labour, particularly skilled labour, in the 1960s and 1970s resulted in 'tight' labour markets and situations both locally and nationally where the demand for certain types of labour exceeded their supply. This tended to increase both the bargaining power of unions and workplace representatives at shop-floor level, particularly in larger workplaces, and the potential for industrial action. The different circumstances prevailing during the 1980s and 1990s which contributed to the decline in the influence of shop stewards included:

- high levels of unemployment and changes in product markets which weakened bargaining power;
- a decline in the average size of the 'employing' unit and in the number of employees per unit weakened shop steward organisation;
- the displacement effect of new technologies and the introduction of flexible production systems have tended to increase employer control over the work process and the employment relationship; and
- the increase in the incidence of non-standard forms of employment and the outsourcing of employment such as call centre work.

The role of the state

Government policy, including those of the New Labour governments, towards employment relations

and market-led initiatives, particularly in the public sector, has been detrimental to shop steward organisation. More specifically:

- much of the legislation concerning industrial action (see Chapter 4) has placed restrictions upon unions and workplace representatives and affected the stability of workplace union organisation;
- the decentralisation and reorganisation of public services has, at least in some sectors such as the National Health Service, restricted local bargaining as a result of 'a managerial desire to exert effective unilateral control over pay and conditions' (Terry, 1995, p. 220);
- the policy of compulsory competitive tendering within local authorities has often resulted in a deterioration in terms and conditions of employment; and
- public sector 'modernisation' programmes, together with public–private funding initiatives and the creation of a two-tier workforce, fragment representation and dilute representational effectiveness.

New approaches by employers

As we have seen in Chapter 2, there has been an increase in employers' bargaining power partly through their greater control of the production process and through increased reliance upon alternative forms of communication and representation which bypassed the traditional trade union representation channels. This, in turn, has 'individualised' the employment relationship and 'marginalised' both shop steward influence and collective bargaining over non-pay issues. These developments are underpinned by the evolution and increased sophistication of HRM techniques, policies and strategies (see Chapters 2, 6, 7 and 8).

The contribution of workplace union organisation

Terry (1995) states that:

The events of the 1980s raised serious problems for stewards and their organisations of a qualitatively different kind from those encountered earlier. Rarely did they take the form of all-out attack; rather, they reflected a managerial determination to reduce or eliminate steward influence over certain issues, and to construct alternative channels of communication to and from the workforce. Shop stewards were confronted by employers arguing in detail the need not only for job loss but for the rapid introduction of new technology, the development of functional flexibility (multi-skilling), the introduction of new forms of employment (part-time, temporary employees, subcontracting), more intensive working patterns . . . , and other changes associated with a drive for increased labour productivity. Frequently, the need for radical change was driven home by managerial propaganda direct to employees, emphasising the seriousness of the problems faced by the company and the urgency of such change. (p. 222)

In conclusion

The nature of the response of shop stewards and trade unions to these developments is problematic, and is considered in the following section. What is contentious is the effect of what Terry calls 'the growth of a statutory system of employee representation', particularly as far as the proposed implementation of the EU Information and Consultation Directive is concerned, the likely consequence of which could well be a significant increase in non-union forms of representation. The already well-established European Works Council system (see Chapter 8) does not consider national or workplace matters and appears to have marginal impact upon union representation. The advent of 'social partnership' (see Chapters 6 and 8) brings with it representational problems for shop stewards. For example, the partnership approach, which is based on consultation, corporate success and efficiency-driven criteria, suggests a union input based more on expertise than collective interest and therefore begs the question, 'from where is the expertise to come?' (Terry, 2003, p. 280). It is likely that, given these contemporary developments, the steady erosion of the effectiveness of union representational influence at the workplace will continue.

Self-Evaluation Activity 3.11
Summarising shop steward organisation
This SEA has no commentary

Identify the factors which contributed to the growth of shop steward organisation in the 1960s and 1970s, and those factors which influenced the decline in shop steward influence during the 1980s and 1990s.

TRADE UNIONS: MEMBERSHIP AND RECOGNITION

The 1980s and 1990s witnessed a serious weakening of the trade union movement nationally, and a persistent and continuing decline in union membership. It is interesting to note that industrial relations texts published during the 1970s (a period of seemingly irreversible membership growth), often did not countenance the possibility that union membership could conceivably decline. In this section we shall attempt to identify the main challenges facing British trade unions with respect to the current situation of membership decline, the issue of recognition and derecognition of trade unions, and the role of the TUC in responding to these and other related issues and problems.

The challenge of trade union membership

The current decline in membership is not unique in the later twentieth and early twenty-first centuries. During the 1920s, for reasons already identified earlier in this chapter, membership fell significantly (see Table 3.3). For the remainder of the period until 1979, and particularly from 1945, membership grew substantially. Trade union membership is no longer in free-fall and there is some reason to believe that membership will remain stable, or even increase over the next several years.

Membership growth: 1945–79

While aggregate membership grew throughout the period, density of union membership actually

Table 3.3 Trade union membership: 1979–2002

Year	Number of unions at end of year	Total membership at end of year (000s)	Percentage change in membership since previous year
1979	453	13 289	1.3
1980	438	12 947	−2.6
1981	414	12 106	−6.5
1982	408	11 593	−4.2
1983	394	11 236	−3.1
1984	375	10 994	−2.2
1985	370	10 821	−1.6
1986	335	10 539	−2.6
1987	330	10 475	−0.6
1988	315	10 376	−0.9
1989	309	10 158	−2.1
1990–1	287	9 947 (8 835)	−2.1
1991–2	275	9 585 (8 602)	−3.6
1992–3	268	9 048 (7 956)	−5.6
1993–4	254	8 700 (7 767)	−3.8
1994–5	243	8 278 (7 530)	−4.9
1995–6	238	8 089 (7 309)	−2.3
1996–7	233	7 938 (7 244)	−1.9
1997–8	224	7 801 (7 154)	−1.7
1998–9	224	7 851 (7 152)	+0.9
1999–2000	221	7 898 (7 257)	+0.9
2000–1	206	7 779 (7 321)	−1.4
2001–2	196	7 751 (7 340)	(neg.)

Note: Membership figures in brackets from 1990–1 onwards refer to the Labour Force Survey/Labour Market Trends series (ONS). The other source is the Certification Office (see note to Table 3.2 concerning statistical discrepancy between ONS and Certification Office).

declined slightly in most years until 1967. Union density, or density of union membership, is a useful measure as it relates aggregate membership to the size of the labour force nationally, expressed as a percentage. It can also be usefully applied to particular industries or sectors, to an organisation and to a workplace. Union density can therefore be used as a measure of union penetration over a period of time at any, or all, of these levels. The reasons for fluctuations in union density from 1948 to 1967 include the following:

- Those industries with highest union densities (coal, railways) declined in relation to employment (and

therefore in relation to aggregate membership) while retaining or increasing measures of density.

- Those industries or sectors where union density was traditionally low, such as financial, banking, insurance, professional, scientific, distribution and leisure services, have expanded and, with one or two exceptions, union membership and density increased.

- The increase in white-collar employment in most manufacturing and service sectors was accompanied by increased white-collar union membership and from 1964 the rate of increase in white-collar membership outstripped the increase in white-collar employment.

Hawkins (1981) has identified a number of factors affecting union growth during this period, and these are now briefly summarised:

1. In general terms, **fluctuations in aggregate membership** could traditionally be explained by upswings and downswings in the economic cycle. During periods of economic expansion, membership would rise and vice versa. However, this 'prosperity theory' of union membership growth is only a partial explanation and does not account for periods of economic decline where membership has not correspondingly declined.

2. More specifically, the **rate of changes in prices and wages or inflation** may exert a positive influence on trade union membership. Hawkins (1981), for example, argues, 'to the extent that unions succeed in negotiating increases in money wages and salaries which keep pace with or exceed the rate of inflation, the lesson is not likely to be lost on non-unionists' (p. 82). However, Bain and Elsheikh (1976) suggest that prices do not have a constant effect on union growth and that once inflation exceeds 4 per cent growth tails off.

3. Concern over the restoring of **pay differentials** and the maintenance of the status of certain occupations, particularly during periods of incomes policy, has acted as a spur to union membership growth. The increase in white-collar union membership may be partially explained by white-collar workers' resentment aroused as a result of compression of differentials between themselves and manual workers.

4. **Unemployment and the threat of unemployment** may, in certain circumstances, have a positive influence upon trade union membership. For example, in the case of white-collar workers, organisational and technological changes may generate fears of redundancy and feelings of job insecurity. This sense of uncertainty, Hawkins (1981) argues, 'may have induced many white-collar staff to join a union for basic self-protection. If they feel threatened by technological and organisational change then at the very least they will see that collective representation could be needed if they are to obtain the best possible severance terms' (pp. 84–5).

5. **Employer recognition of trade unions** is an important determinant of membership growth and decline. The hostility of many employers towards trade unions in past years proved to be a powerful obstacle to the expansion of membership, but during the 1970s more active intervention of governments in encouraging the extension of collective bargaining, reinforced by the statutory recognition procedure established by the Employment Protection Act of 1975, exerted some influence on employers to recognise trade unions.

6. Structural factors such as **size of establishment** tend to have an influence upon union membership and density. Research by Bain and Elsheikh (1976) and the later WIRS surveys confirm that the larger the establishment the greater the union presence and 'voice'. Bain and Elsheikh conclude that 'the larger the establishment the more interested its employees are likely to be in joining trade unions. For the larger the number of employees the more likely they are to be treated not as individuals but as members of groups, to have their terms and conditions of employment determined by collective rather than individual bargaining' (p. 142).

7. The growth in employment within much of the **public sector** during this period, particularly in the health, education and local authority areas, together with the legal obligation placed upon public corporations to recognise appropriate trade unions and engage in collective bargaining, resulted in increased union membership and density, especially amongst white-collar staffs.

8. Finally, the traditional **reluctance of women** to join trade unions had been gradually replaced by a more receptive attitude towards unionisation, particularly amongst white-collar employees.

In addition to the factors identified above, Pencavel (2001, pp. 9–14) points out that there was considerable *indirect support* for collective bargaining by the state during this period (see Chapter 6), thereby contradicting the view that the regulation of the employment relationship was best left to the parties (unions and employers, for example) concerned. In fact, according to Pencavel, considerable support for collective bargaining was provided by the state as employer within the public sector, with the nationalisation programme immediately after the Second World War creating public corporations that were legally required to recognise unions and to set up collective bargaining machinery. Other state support, which contributed towards a favourable climate for trade unions, included the setting of minimum wages in wage council industries, requiring government contractors to pay union-negotiated wages and discouraging product market competition.

Self-Evaluation Activity 3.12

Membership decline during the 1980s and 1990s
Response on website

We have considered some aspects of industrial relations change in Chapter 1 and more specific issues of relevance to trade unions in this chapter. In relation to membership decline, try to identify the factors you think caused the decline in membership during the 1980s and 1990s. Compare your list with the analysis presented by the GMB, which is summarised on the website.

The nature of membership and 'union voice' decline

Waddington and Whitson (1995) provide a fairly detailed overview of the nature and dimensions of membership decline, the main elements of which are summarised below.

Aggregate unionisation
Although there have been fluctuations in the rate of decline during the 1980s and 1990s, much of the membership gains made during the 1970s had been wiped out by 1987. Moreover, the fall in membership and union density since 1979 represents the longest period of continuous decline recorded.

Male and female unionisation
During the 1970s a large proportion of the increase in total membership was the result of increased unionisation of women. During the 1980s, however, there was a much faster rate of decline in the unionisation of men as compared with that for women, and this trend continued into the 1990s. Waddington and Whitson (1995) assert that 'The decline in employment during this period (1989–92)

was almost entirely due to the employment of fewer men. Over the same period the number of men trade union members fell by almost 700 000, and the number of women in membership decreased by about 200 000. In other words, between 1989 and 1991 both potential union membership and actual union membership became relatively more feminised' (p. 159).

Manual and white-collar unionisation
The number of white-collar workers continued to grow during the 1980s and comprised the majority of the total labour force, while manual employment continued to decline. But from 1979 to 1987 there were declines in total membership for both groups, with a much faster rate of decline for manual workers. By 1987, 'white-collar members comprised 48 per cent of total membership, compared to 41 per cent in 1979 and a mere 24 per cent in 1951. After 1987, constant employment density for white-collar workers and further declines among manual workers continued this trend' (ibid., p. 161).

Unionisation by sector
By 1987 public sector trade union members outnumbered those in manufacturing, with union densities of 80 per cent and 60 per cent respectively. Trade union membership declined rapidly in the agriculture, forestry and fishing sectors with resultant falls in density. Union membership grew more slowly than employment in the private services revealing a decline in union density for this sector. After 1987, union density in manufacturing, agriculture, forestry and fishing, and in construction fell more rapidly than in the non-manufacturing sectors.

Unionisation by industry
In industries where unions are well entrenched (cotton and man-made fibres, printing and publishing, coal mining, gas, electricity, water, post and telecommunications, railways, sea transport and air transport), employment contracted during the 1980s and 1990s. Conversely, in many industries where unionisation is relatively sparse (entertainment and miscellaneous services, distribution, construction, timber and furniture), employment was expanding.

More recent analysis (WERS98 – Machin, 2000; Millward *et al.*, 2000; Pencavel, 2001; Verma *et al.*,

2002; Waddington, 2003) examines in greater detail the nature of the decline. Machin, by reworking the WERS98 data concludes that the patterns of decline witnessed during the 1980s continued into the 1990s with much lower union recognition, membership and density rates in newer establishments being a continuing phenomenon. In addition, the research confirms the continuation of the sectoral pattern with sharpest falls in membership and union recognition within private manufacturing and to a lesser extent in private services. Furthermore, age of establishment or workplace is associated with aggregate membership and recognition decline, with older workplaces more likely to be unionised than younger ones. Union decline is by no means a UK phenomenon as Verma *et al.* (2002) point out. It is a global phenomenon and, as such, a global problem. It would appear that those countries that have adopted neo-liberal approaches and policies are amongst the ones that have witnessed the steepest declines. For example, New Zealand experienced a 56.6 per cent decline in union density between 1980 and 1995, while density in France declined by 65.3 per cent. Both countries compare unfavourably with the UK where union density declined by 46.1 per cent (all figures from ILO, 1998).

In summary, the overall picture is one of decline in both union membership and density since 1979. While there are industrial and sectoral variations in both membership and density, the decline in employment in well-organised industries has been amongst the most persistent of trends during this period. However, Blyton and Turnbull (1998) point out that 'while the net outcome has been an overall decline in membership levels, unions continue to attract new members. Hence, a picture depicting only a scene of dwindling membership, with employees unwilling to become union members, is, in reality, a gross over-simplification' (p. 111).

Reasons for decline in union membership since 1979

It is generally acknowledged that there are many explanatory factors to be taken into consideration and therefore that no one single-cause explanation of membership decline can suffice (Mason and Bain, 1993). Metcalf (1991) suggests that union membership and density are determined by a combination of factors including the macroeconomic climate, the composition of jobs and of the workforce, government policy, the attitude and actions of employers, and the position taken by trade unions. A major problem for researchers adopting a multi-causal framework is that of quantification: the extent to which a measurable proportion of membership decline can be attributed to each causal factor or to the interaction of more than one factor. Notwithstanding these and other methodological problems, we can identify a number of reasons for decline (based on Metcalf, 1991; Waddington and Whitson, 1995; Machin, 2000; WERS98 – Millward *et al.*, 2000; Pencavel, 2001).

Employer policies

Employer policies have been considered in Chapter 2 and briefly in this chapter in relation mainly to union recognition–derecognition and we have noted that:

- during the 1980s employers began to depart from a policy of collaboration with unions to one of bypassing them in favour of direct links with employees and that this could constitute a threat to union density (Beaumont, 1987);
- that the rapidly changing technical and product market environment encouraged at least some employers to seek greater flexibility in the use of labour;
- the advent of HRM conflicted with many of the assumptions of traditional industrial relations; and
- the failure of unions to establish themselves in newly-formed workplaces (Millward *et al.*, 2000) is at least partly due to employers' attitudes towards collective bargaining; compared with the pre-1970s' decades, 'the new breed of employers is less altruistic in their dealings with their own employees and this has manifested itself in the view that unions are irrelevant or, worse, damaging to the enterprise' (Pencavel, 2001, p. 19).

However, Gallie *et al.* (1996) in their study of workplace unionism in a number of organisations argue that 'the evidence adduced for such a profound change in employer strategies is often little more than anecdotal . . . [and that] there was no evidence of widespread anti-unionism among employers and those employers that had unions present emphasised the continuity rather than change in their policies' (p. 14). They go on to argue on the basis of their case evidence that: 'Employers have maintained their relationship with trade unions within the workplace rather than trying to undermine them. The explanation for this is primarily that they consider unions play a valuable role in mediating their relations with the workforce' (p. 19). There is, nevertheless, some tangible survey evidence (Millward *et al.*, 1992; Smith and Morton, 1993) of some employers derecognising trade unions, which may have contributed to some decline in union membership (recognition and de-recognition are considered in more detail later on), and of some unions failing to secure recognition at some newer greenfield sites, which may partly explain the absence of membership growth, particularly between 1983 and 1998 (Millward *et al.*, 1992; Millward *et al.*, 2000).

Business cycle explanations

We have referred to the work of Bain and Elsheikh (1976) in relation to the earlier period of membership growth. Subsequent research in this area (Booth, 1983; Carruth and Disney, 1988; Disney, 1990) tends to support the argument that increases in real wages for a sustained period, as that from 1980 to 1991, may reduce incentives for employees to join trade unions. This is particularly the case with white-collar workers who were motivated to become union members in the 1970s as a result of the narrowing of their pay differentials vis-à-vis manual workers. During the 1980s the white-collar/manual differential steadily increased to such an extent that the incentive to join on the part of white-collar workers was correspondingly reduced. Business cycle explanations also tend to support the argument that as unemployment rises, so trade union membership falls. During the 1980s and early 1990s, chronically high levels of unemployment 'provide[d] employers with an opportunity to resist unionisation' (Blyton and Turnbull, 1994, p. 108), thereby restricting opportunities for employees to unionise.

There is another economic argument linked to productivity and organisational performance. During the 1980s the issue of the relationship between unions and productivity/performance became highly politicised and to a much greater extent than previously (Pencavel 2001; Nolan and O'Donnell 2003). The untested and highly ambiguous assumption that trade unions adversely affect productivity and performance, which received a great deal of publicity during the 1980s, conceivably provided extra ammunition for those employers who were antagonistic towards unions and singled them out as scapegoats for all productivity and performance woes. However, while some small, if not marginal, measure of union decline could be attributed to employers endorsing this untested hypothetical assumption – and current research remains equivocal (Addison and Belfield, 2001) – a consensus could focus upon the results of Pencavel's statistical reworking of selected WERS98 data which concluded that 'average union-non-union differences in labour productivity appear to be negligible [and that] unionism may serve as an agent permitting employees to participate in shaping their work environment without productivity suffering' (p. 36).

Legislative effects

The impact of industrial relations legislation upon union membership is rather less quantifiable and should be seen within the context of the 'neo-liberal assault' (see Chapter 4) of the Conservative governments, 1980–1997 (Waddington, 2003). Freeman and Pelletier (1990) undertook a comprehensive analysis of the effects of labour legislation upon union density for the period 1948–86 and concluded that the unfavourable (to trade unions) legislation of the 1980s adversely affected union density and membership. Notwithstanding the criticisms levelled at Freeman and Pelletier's analysis and claims, there can be no doubt that, in combination with the other causal factors, the legislation has permitted employers to restrict trade union influence and 'prevent any membership growth during the mid-1980s when employment expanded' (Waddington and Whitson, 1995, p. 167). This argument is reiterated by Pencavel (2001) who argues that the legal framework of the 1980s gave *new* firms greater flexibility in tailoring employment relations processes and procedures to suit their circumstances without the 'hindrance' of a trade union presence, but more generally it was the abandonment of full employment goals and the 'harsher competitive environment that complemented the new legal setting and produced unionism's decline' (p. 41).

Employment composition

The changing composition of employment during the 1980s and 1990s in relation to trade union membership is marked by:

- a decline in employment where union membership was concentrated;
- an increase in employment where union membership was sparse, scattered or negligible, accompanied by a sectoral shift from manufacturing to services;
- increases in the employment of women from 38 to 40 per cent from 1980 to 1998 in workplaces with 25 or more employees, and increases in the numbers of white-collar workers and part-time workers (WERS98 – Millward *et al.*, 2000);
- the proliferation of non-standard forms of employment contracts in relation to part-time, temporary, subcontracted and agency employees; and
- the growth of self-employment.

As we have noted, some of these changes were also a feature of the employment pattern during the 1970s, when trade union membership was rising, and so cannot be considered as the only explanation of the current membership decline. At best, therefore, employment changes account for a proportion of membership decline.

Employees themselves

Falls in union membership, accompanied by a decline in employee voice, suggest that there is a 'withering of support' for union membership amongst the existing workforce and that the reduced support or 'appetite' appears to be the main source of union decline (Millward *et al.*, 2000, pp. 92, 180). This not only affects the private sector but also the public sector, where membership density declined from 80 per cent in 1980 to 62 per cent in 1998 (WERS98 – Cully *et al.*, 1999; Millward *et al.*, 2000). If the 'reduced appetite' explanation is valid, then this could indicate an increasingly pay and conditions orientation or 'instrumental' commitment to trade unions on the part of public sector workers. Current research in this area is sparse and recent contributions appear to contradict the reduced

appetite explanation, suggesting that improved union representation and a more proactive approach to organising could have a positive affect upon recruitment and membership (Prowse, 2003).

Self-Evaluation Activity 3.13

Explanations of union membership decline
Response on website

Do you think that these explanations of membership decline are of equal importance?

Derecognition and recognition of trade unions: two sides of the same coin?

The overall incidence of derecognition from 1984 to 2003 has been slight. According to earlier data assembled by Claydon, there were four cases nationally in 1984, with a significant increase to 22 in 1988, an increase which was sustained, albeit with minor fluctuations, in subsequent years. An earlier study (Claydon, 1989) reveals that grade-specific derecognitions, which comprised the highest proportion of derecognitions during the mid-1980s, affected white-collar workers primarily, while later research covering 1989–93 indicates that the incidence of total derecognition involving all grades of employee increased substantially (Claydon, 1997). Even more recent research (Gall and McKay, 1999, 2001) indicates that derecognition cases have declined substantially (see below). What is, perhaps, of greater significance is the distribution of derecognition cases by industry sector from 1984 to 1993. The heaviest and most consistent concentration of cases during this period has been in publishing, paper and print and in petroleum and chemicals; wholesale and retail distribution and engineering featured prominently during 1989–93 and this trend seems to have continued up to 2003.

Against the backdrop of union decline, an underlying trend of persistent decline in union recognition can be discerned, and to this end, WIRS and WERS98 provide an impressive time series of data dealing with the extent of union presence in Britain (see Table 3.4 and also Chapter 7).

Table 3.4 Union presence in Britain: 1980–98

	1980 %	1984 %	1990 %	1998 %
Aggregate changes				
Establishments with any union recognised for collective bargaining purposes	64	66	53	42
Workers who are union members	62	58	48	36
Workers covered by collective bargaining	–	71	54	41
Sectoral changes				
Establishments with any union recognised for collective bargaining purposes, private sector manufacturing	65	56	44	30
Establishments with any union recognised for collective bargaining purposes, private sector services	41	44	36	23
Establishments with any union recognised for collective bargaining purposes, public sector services	94	99	87	87

Source: Cully *et al.*, 1999, p. 85; Millward *et al.*, 2000

In commenting upon the data, Machin (2000) confirms that the pronounced decline in recognition was due to a failure to organise in new workplaces throughout the period, noting that there are sectoral differences with the greatest falls in recognition occurring in private manufacturing and in younger workplaces (Millward *et al.*, 2000). However, despite the persistent decline in recognition, Machin's reworking of WIRS and WERS98 data demonstrates that derecognition in existing workplaces was relatively infrequent during the 1980–98 period, with 7.5 per cent of panel workplaces derecognising unions. Gall and Mackay's (1999, 2002) review of reported cases of derecognition from 1989–2000 reveals that the yearly rate of reported cases of derecognition peaked in the early 1990s – with 79 cases in 1992 – and then declined, with only four cases of total derecognition reported in 1998, six in 1999 and one in 2000.

The nature of derecognition

The decline in trade union membership, representation and influence which we have commented upon has more ominous implications for trade unions themselves. Claydon (1997), for example, asserts that since the mid-1980s, 'it has become increasingly

apparent that this decline does not simply reflect structural change in the economy and the growth of unemployment, but also the conscious intent of key industrial relations actors, notably the State and employers, to exclude trade unions from control of the employment relationship' (p. 151). The process of exclusion may take one of two forms:

- **marginalisation** of unions, or partial derecognition, where unions are excluded from negotiating over pay and related issues and are confined to negotiating over non-pay issues; and
- **total derecognition**, where unions have no collective negotiation rights whatsoever.

Derecognition may encompass the entire organisation, entailing the withdrawal of collective bargaining rights from all employees. Alternatively, narrower forms of derecognition may entail either withdrawing bargaining rights from specific grades of employee or withdrawing bargaining rights from all employees at specific plants or workplaces. Whether derecognition is total (or general), or partial may depend upon one or more factors. It may be that the ownership of the business had changed or that there had been changes to the employee relations policies and objectives of a company.

Other factors may include the continued depletion of union membership within a company, the move towards other forms of collective agreement such as single-union agreements and a management preference for dealing with employees individually rather than collectively. A survey of 30 British firms undertaken by Brown *et al.* (2001) revealed that the nature of derecognition varied considerably between the surveyed firms, particularly in terms of coverage and scope:

Coverage: In multi-union firms, employers were often selective, the most common practice being to derecognise unions representing managerial staffs, but with some firms this was only the first phase of a staged derecognition strategy ultimately covering all unionised employees, and still other firms would derecognise by function (for example, by derecognising store but not distribution staff).

Scope: Derecognising unions does not mean banishing them from the workplace, since employees have a statutory right to join or not to join a trade union. Derecognising a union for the purpose of negotiating over the entire range of issues, both individual and collective is relatively rare. Some organisations will confine derecognition to collective issues and allow individual representation in disciplinary and grievance cases, while others will confine union activity to consultation on one or more committees. In this sense derecognition is partial for pragmatic reasons and it is clear to see the extent to which unions have become marginalised in one or more ways (Brown *et al.*, 2001). Claydon (1997) additionally identifies two general approaches to both partial and total derecognition that could be adopted by employers:

1. The first approach Claydon calls 'reactive' in that 'it represents a management response to a weakening of union power brought about largely by changes in the organisation's industrial relations environment rather than resulting from purposive management action' (p. 169). One important environmental influence upon the propensity to derecognise is existing Conservative legislation which, Smith and Morton (1993, 1994) argue, has weakened trade union power and made unions themselves more susceptible to individualist approaches which undermine col-

lective control over the employment relationship. Claydon points out that 'reactive' approaches are more likely to be appropriate to the weaker unionised and more peripheral areas of the unionised workforce, at least in the first instance.

2. A second approach to derecognition is called 'purposive', 'reflecting a long-term effort by management to eliminate unionised industrial relations' (Claydon, 1997, p. 169). This approach, more strategic than spontaneous, assumes a staged process as mentioned above, directed initially at 'specific groups of workers who are seen as offering least resistance or small groups occupying strategic positions in the production process' (p. 169). The whole process is a gradual one, may take a number of years to complete, and is instigated by larger organisations which have the financial and managerial resources to undertake such an exercise.

Mini case 3.2
The example of Esso

The process of derecognition within the petrochemical industry can be illustrated by reference to the example of Esso's Fawley refinery where a long-term approach involving stage-by-stage targeting of successive groups was adopted by management. The first group to be identified were warehousemen who were transferred to staff status in 1974 and whose collective bargaining rights were withdrawn. Other groups were then targeted:

on the basis of their size and their strategic position in the production process. Thus instrument fitters were taken out of bargaining in 1979, followed by the boilermakers in 1982. In 1983, management attempted to extend staff status to welders, but at this point, union-led resistance involving industrial action (temporarily) put an end to the process. . . . In 1989 the remaining refinery craftsmen were transferred to staff status, and in 1993 the process was completed when the TGWU's bargaining rights on behalf of 700 process operators at Fawley were withdrawn. Esso maintained membership check-off arrangements, and unions retain the right to represent individual members in discipline and grievance proceedings. They have, however, ceased to have a role as collective representatives of the Fawley workforce. At the same time, moves to end collective bargaining have been extended to other areas of Esso's operations. Airport technicians employed by Esso were transferred to staff status in 1989, and in 1991 tanker drivers were similarly transferred and the TGWU derecognised for collective bargaining.

Source: Claydon, 1997, p. 164

Self-Evaluation Activity 3.14

Responses to derecognition

Response on website

How do you think trade unions could respond to the derecognition threat?

The recognition conundrum

As the number of derecognitions, never high, diminishes, the number of recognitions in recent years has increased significantly, resulting in a net increase of 49 000 workers covered by union recognition agreements between 1997 and 1998 (Gall and McKay, 2002). The number of recognitions in 2001 reached 264, covering some 85 000 workers (IRS, 2002a). The growth in the number of recognitions may be explained by the activities of trade unions, the reactions and responses of employers and the impact of the recognition procedures contained within the ERA99 (Gall and McKay, 2002).

Trade union activity is focused upon the TUC relaunch under the banner of 'new unionism' in 1995 and the subsequent creation of the 'Organising Academy' in 1997 (see below). According to Gall and McKay (2002), TUC and union efforts to recruit new members is paying off, and 'it would be reasonable to suggest that there has been a substantial increase in the number and extent of recognition and organising campaigns since the mid 1990s [and this] has led to more new recognition agreements' (p. 5). Drawing upon data from employers, unions and the CAC, Wood *et al.* (2002) conclude that unions are proactive in seeking to gain members before approaching employers or 'relying on employers to initiate discussions' (p. 232), and while

the ERA procedures are used, the main increase in recognition is voluntary rather than statutory. However, increases in the *scope* of recognition are more likely to be union rather than employer-led (see below).

Employer reactions to recognition claims, the evidence suggests (CBI annual *Employment Trends*; Brown *et al.*, 2001; Wood *et al.*, 2002) means not only that employers are increasingly compelled to confront recognition issues, but also that there are difficulties with some employers in actually conceding recognition claims. Nevertheless, many employers, if only reluctantly, accede to the 'business case for trade unionism' and that 'overwhelmingly, employers and trade unions have taken a non-confrontational, voluntary approach to reaching agreement on recognition in preference to using the new statutory powers' (IRS, 2002b).

The recognition provisions of the ERA have acted as a stimulus to both trade unions and employers, instilling a sense of urgency and a 'reorientation towards existing recognition campaigns' (Gall and Mckay, 2002, p. 5). Nevertheless, if the statutory procedure is to be effective, it should result in changes in behaviour of both unions and employers, and it may still be too premature to form any firm conclusions (Wood *et al.*, 2002).

The recognition procedure

Statutory procedures for recognition are not new to the UK, although the past two attempts are confined to the 1970s. The first statutory procedure was operated by the now defunct Commission for Industrial Relations (CIR) between 1972 and 1974, while the second was operated by ACAS under the 1975 Employment Protection Act and although a considerable number of recognitions were granted, the employers complained that the procedures were biased towards the unions while the unions argued that the procedure was too unwieldy and cumbersome (Wood, 1997). The statutory procedure contained within the ERA99, and introduced on 6 June 1999, is the third such attempt to operate a statutory procedure and was designed to deal with the alleged weaknesses of the former attempts. It is described in Exhibit 3.6.

Exhibit 3.6

The procedure for recognition: ERA99: introduced June 2000

The procedure applies only where an employer refuses to recognise a trade union and provides the employer and union (the 'social partners') every opportunity at each stage to reach an agreement. For example, once a union has been awarded recognition by the Central Arbitration Committee (CAC), the employer and union are given 30 working days to negotiate their own recognition agreement. It is only if they fail to do so that the specified method of collective bargaining is imposed. Unions are unlikely to make a claim unless they feel reasonably confident of success (see below, main text). Unions usually have 'hit lists' of businesses that they will initially target and are geared up for the process, so employers also need to be prepared for when the campaigning starts in earnest.

1. **Voluntary union recognition (30 working days):** A union makes a formal, written claim for recognition in respect of a specified bargaining unit. The employer then has 10 working days in which to decide whether it will negotiate over recognition or reject it outright. If it decides to negotiate, the employer and union are given a further 20 working days to try to reach an agreement. If an agreement has not been reached, or the employer refuses to negotiate, then the union can refer its claim to the CAC.

2. **Identification of the bargaining unit (30 working days):** Once the CAC has decided the union's claim is admissible, the employer and union have 20 working days to agree a bargaining unit (comprising a definable group such as all hourly-paid workers, or those in certain grades, or one particular department across one or more different sites). The union must persuade more than half of those voting to back recognition and the number of votes must represent at least 40 per cent of the bargaining unit. So the union will seek a bargaining unit where this level of support is achievable. If agreement on the bargaining unit cannot be reached, the CAC will decide on the unit within 10 working days. Should employers encourage a large bargaining unit with the aim of diluting the union's influence so that it cannot achieve the requisite level of support in the ballot? (This could backfire and result in the employer having to recognise the union for a wider group of employees.) Or should employers agree a smaller bargaining unit in the hope that support for the union can be contained? (This would give the union a 'foot in the door' from which it could raise a more generalised degree of interest amongst other groups of employees.) Unions are more likely to adopt the incremental approach, if only for the reason that, if they are not successful, they face a three-year moratorium on putting forward another recognition claim for the same bargaining unit.

3. **Campaign and ballot (30 working days):** Once the bargaining unit has been decided and a ballot is due to take place the employer and union have 10 working days to reach an access agreement which establishes the circumstances and times the union can communicate with employees in the bargaining unit to persuade them to vote in favour of recognition. If no agreement is reached, during a 20-day access period when both union and employer can campaign for and against recognition respectively, CAC will make the order. The recognition ballot has to be overseen by 'a qualified independent person' such as a solicitor or specified organisation such as the Electoral Reform Society. If the ballot achieves the requisite majority, CAC awards recognition and the process moves to the next stage. If the majority is not achieved the union cannot make another statutory recognition claim for the same bargaining unit for three years.

4. **Setting of bargaining structure (30 working days):** The employer and union have the opportunity, over a period of 30 working days to negotiate their own collective bargaining structure. If they fail to do so the CAC will impose the specified method of collective bargaining as identified in the procedure.

Can a claim proceed? Before the CAC sets the recognition process in motion, it has to be satisfied that the claim is admissible. Situations in which the claim will be thrown out include those where:

- the employer has 20 or fewer employees in the UK;
- the union has previously made an application for union recognition for the same bargaining unit and has been rejected by CAC in the preceding three years;
- the union's membership is less than 10 per cent of the proposed bargaining unit; and
- another trade union is recognised for collective bargaining for any part of the proposed bargaining unit.

The current state of recognition

Some of the new recognition agreements are called partnership agreements (see Chapter 8 for a detailed overview and assessment). The term itself is general enough to subsume any number and type of activity as long as it is, in formal terms, agreeable to the 'partners' and that there is equality of power-sharing so that unions' and employers' areas of influence are mutually respected. The TGWU, for example, is prepared to endorse partnership agreements where 'partnership is fine so long as the union retains the ability to kick the other in the nuts' (Gall and McKay, 2002, p. 15). Some recognition agreements may not give pride of place to collective bargaining and may permit other non-union forms of representation. This could well reflect employers' intentions to create and retain consultative committees, either as an exclusive forum for non-unionised staff or as an all-inclusive forum, which support collective bargaining as one of several consultative mechanisms. An increase in the number of such committees is to be expected in advance of the adoption in 2005 of the EU Information and Consultation Directive. A further consequence of the statutory recognition procedures is the greater impetus given to single-union agreements, probably further hastening the decline of multi-union representation.

The IRS 2002 survey of full-recognition deals notes that the great majority of employers and unions have taken a non-confrontational, voluntary rather than statutory approach to reaching agreement on recognition and this is borne out by the evidence: ACAS, unlike the CAC, does not play any formal role in determining or adjudicating upon recognition but assists in the voluntary aspects of recognition and in 2001–2002, only 49 cases involved the triggering of the statutory recognition process out of some 264 cases completed (ACAS, 2002). The IRS (2002a) survey comes up with the following important findings:

- the main sectors of the economy in which recognition deals are occurring are paper and printing (113 cases, comprising 43 per cent of the total), transport and communication (31 cases, 12 per cent of total), general manufacturing (26, 10 per cent), general services (25, 9.5 per cent) and engineering/metals (23, 9 per cent);
- the typical number of employees covered by a new recognition agreement is 65, although the mean figure is 322. The largest agreement is that between the broadcasting and entertainment union BECTU and the real estate company Land Securities Trillium covering 15 000 workers. The smallest deal covered four workers only;
- most employees covered by the new agreements are manual or craft workers (65 per cent), non-manual are in a minority with 18 per cent, while 'mixed' manual–non-manual comprise 18 per cent;
- unions with the best success rates include the print union – GPMU with 36 per cent of the deals covered in the IRS survey, followed by GMB and Amicus;
- the trend in recognition deals is upwards, with the existence of the legal procedure being, arguably, the most important factor in the ability of unions to secure voluntary deals; and
- the **main criticisms** of the legal framework for recognition have focused on:
  - the exclusion of employers with fewer than 21 employees;
  - the narrow range of issues covered by collective bargaining;
  - the criteria for defining the bargaining unit;
  - the general complexity of the procedures;
  - the use of ballots as opposed to membership audit;
  - the availability of employer challenge through judicial review;
  - the exclusion of jurisdiction where recognition already exists; and

– the thresholds for admissibility and awarding recognition.

Factors to consider in membership recruitment, recognition and retention

In the light of statutory recognition procedures, the supportive role of the TUC is essential in providing unions, particularly smaller ones, with appropriate guidance and information (see below). Larger unions have a part to play in this respect, as the case of the GMB illustrates (Main case 3.2).

Main case 3.2
Trade union recruitment and recognition: the case of the GMB

The analysis of causes of membership loss undertaken by the GMB also contains survey data concerning the needs of membership and how the union should respond to them. Four broad analytical categories were identified:

(i) **Analysis of reasons for being in the GMB.** The reasons given, in order of importance, include support if a problem arises at work; improved pay and conditions; a belief in trade unionism; GMB industrial benefits; most people at their workplace are union members; GMB membership services; GMB financial services; GMB public campaigning.

(ii) **The support required most at the workplace.** This includes advice and representation on disciplinary and grievance matters; advice and representation on health and safety matters; legal assistance on accidents and problems at work.

(iii) **Bargaining priorities.** These differed between the sexes, women tending to rank equal pay for work of equal value higher than pensions, while men generally place pensions ahead of equal pay. Both sexes rank equal pay in front of other equalities like nursery or crèche facilities and paid paternity leave. The top six bargaining priorities were: improvements in pay; better pensions and retirement rights; equal pay; protection against unfair dismissal; improvements in health and safety; a legal minimum wage.

(iv) **The scope for improvements in workplace support members receive from GMB.** The main observations were:

- most members say that they want more contact with full-time officials. Many members feel that contact with their shop steward or staff representative is already well organised and say the same about contact with their full-time officer;
- three-quarters want more information on union affairs and on pay and conditions negotiations. They also want the GMB to listen more to their views on workplace issues; and
- over two-thirds say they want branch meetings at more convenient times or more appropriate locations.

From survey analysis and other investigations, the GMB report comes up with certain recommendations for action: 'There can be no concealing the need to boost organisation and recruitment and to win recognition in new sites. That must mean steering more resources towards recruitment activities in areas offering the best prospects of success.'

- **Where?** East Anglia, the East Midlands, the South West, Yorkshire and Humberside, and the South East outside Greater London – because those are the parts of the country where most new jobs are expected to appear.
- **Which industries?** The service sector of the economy – public services and private services, notably business areas covered by GMB Commercial Services Section – because that is where recruitment potential is greatest and where most new jobs are being created.
- **Which occupations?** White-collar jobs – especially in the personal and protective occupations and associate professional and technical jobs like nurses, social workers and technicians – rather than craft and skilled manual jobs, because the former are gradually replacing the latter.
- **Which age groups?** Those aged about 30–45 in particular, because their numbers are rising rapidly and there will be four times as many in this age group in five years' time as the numbers of non-students aged below 25. We should use new information technology to encourage young people to become more aware of the world of work and what the GMB does for its members.
- **Men or women?** Increasingly women, because most new jobs are likely to be taken by women.
- **Full-time or part-time jobs?** Increasingly part-time jobs, because they already account for one job in four and this proportion is rising. But probably not self-employed people because only 10 per cent of

them appear to join any union, though special circumstances may apply in the construction industry.

- **Promoting which union services?** Emphasising the terrific deal that the GMB service package represents – support if a problem arises at work, including advice and representation on job security, grievance and disciplinary matters, health and safety issues, training and personal development opportunities and pay, especially equal pay and low pay; specialist legal support; other specialist services including help in improving pensions entitlements and retirement rights and dealing with human resource management initiatives.

- **Championing which issues?** Whichever ones matter most according to the relevant workplace health check but, in general, the top six among most people who join the GMB are: low pay, equal pay, protection against unfair dismissal, better pension and retirement rights, health and safety, and a national minimum wage.

- **How?** In five main ways:

  1. By more workplace contact with members and potential recruits, using the workplace health check system and prioritising officer time.

  2. By establishing GMB organisation on new sites, using the new law that the Labour government is committed to bringing in, obliging employers to recognise a union where the majority of workers want it to represent them.

  3. By acting on the principle of 'follow the work' and winning recognition from major employers who are new to traditional areas of GMB activity, like private contractors to local authorities and new competitors in the energy sector.

  4. By breaking into new recruitment fields, like employment agencies and private residential care homes, with the aim of building genuine partnerships with responsible companies, to the benefit both of employees and employers.

  5. By steering GMB resources towards organisation and recruitment and away from routine administration and low value activities of any kind. The CEC (Central Executive Committee) has already earmarked an initial £0.5 million for a recruitment fighting fund to allow regions to appoint temporary recruiters, and several regional initiatives are going ahead.

Source: GMB, 1998

Self-Evaluation Activity 3.15

Extent to which recruitment aims are achieved
Response on website

To what extent do you think that trade unions in Britain today are able to achieve the recruitment aims established by the GMB?

THE FUTURE OF UK TRADE UNIONS

We have identified many aspects of union decline, which, taken together, point to a fairly persistent trend of decline from 1980 onwards. There is nothing to suggest that this trend will either suddenly, or over a short period of time, be thrown into reverse. Probably the very best we can hope for is a stabilisation of membership in the short term as indicated by membership figures for 1998–2003, with marginal increases in membership as more recognition agreements are processed. The initiatives identified in the following pages will undoubtedly have a positive effect on membership, but membership gains can easily be cancelled out by recruitment inertia, employer policies and membership turnover, to name but a few factors. At the present time, the analogy with attempting to run up a quickly descending escalator would seem to be appropriate for the union movement.

So what can be done? Some light upon this dilemma is shed by the recent contributions of Hyman (2002), Heery (2002) and Kelly (2002). Kelly contends that unions should take advantage of 'power resources' when negotiating with employers and government. This probably assumes that unions are not using latent bargaining power (see Chapter 6) and other influences to their fullest extent. Secondly, unions should identify and exploit the weaknesses inherent in multinational companies to their own advantage and, finally, collective action from within may not be 'sufficient to defeat powerful opponents' and this may necessitate the support and use of additional resources such as other workers, government, public sector organisations, organised consumers, campaigning groups and social movements. Hyman (2002), on the other hand offers more specific prescriptions and argues that unions in the twenty-first century 'confront old dilemmas, but in new forms' (p. 10). In essence, unions must tackle three issues:

- *Whose* interests do trade unions represent? Relevant constituencies include 'the qualified elite'; the core workforce; peripheral employees and those outside employment.
- *Which* interests of those represented are of primary interest and relevance to trade unions? Interests may include basic collective bargaining over pay and benefits; more rights limiting employers' 'arbitrary authority' by improving employment protection (p. 11); the role of the state and its policies; and interests external to work and union such as environmental, consumer protection and community.
- *How* are interests represented? The main issues are structure of unions and which is the most effective; the organisational capacity of the union, involving a proactive rather than reactive approach to membership and policy generally; the 'complex dialectic between leadership and democracy' (p. 12) in terms of the extent to which union members can influence and shape priorities and programmes of their unions; and how unions balance 'contradictory modes of action: mobilisation and struggle on the one hand, compromise on the other' (p. 12).

Heery (2002) considers the way ahead in the uneasy and often contradictory relationship between 'partnership' and 'organising' strategies which 'are often presented as alternative options for revitalising British labour' (p. 21). In fact, partnership and organising may be regarded as complementary, constituting a combined union renewal strategy (see below). In the first instance, we look at the pragmatic issue of what unions in general should focus upon for the purpose of recruitment and bringing recognition claims.

Which areas should unions target for the purpose of bringing recognition claims?

Three sources amongst many (TUC, 1999, 2002), IRS (1998, 2002a) and the Labour Force Survey

(reported in LMT, 2002), identify the areas which are thought to have an influence on trade union membership levels. These are:

- **personal characteristics** of the employee such as gender, ethnicity, age, education, political ideology and area of residence;
- **features of employment** such as occupation, manual or non-manual work, part-time or full-time work, permanence of job, earnings and size of establishment;
- **attitudes to work** such as satisfaction with, and commitment to employment; and
- **macroeconomic conditions,** including the level of employment and the inflation rate.

We have considered some of these factors earlier in the chapter and you should review the appropriate section before reading on. We shall now concentrate upon membership influences identified under the five sub-headings below, but before doing so, it is important to point out that, according to the TUC trends analysis of trade union membership (2002), and the Labour Force Survey (LFS) of 2002, the interim membership figures for 2002 suggest that trade union membership, apart from minor fluctuations, has stabilised and that trade unions' increased commitment to recruitment is paying off. Unions are signing up new members in areas where unionisation has been traditionally low and are recruiting more women, part-time and Asian workers (TUC, 2002). Some unions, such as the GMB, are attempting to organise workers in non-traditional occupations where labour is dispersed, where there is no history of unionisation and where employers may be hostile. Examples of atypical occupations as targets for recruitment include lapdancers and minicab drivers (GMB), childcare workers in private nurseries (TGWU) and clergy, mostly drawn from the Church of England (Amicus MSF). Nevertheless, trade union density remains at a post-war low, the proportion of employees belonging to a union in 2001 being 29.1 per cent (UK figures), having fallen from the 1979 high of 55 per cent.

Men and women (2001 data)

Women traditionally have been less likely than men to join trade unions, although the rate of decline in membership amongst men has been more dramatic:

between 1989 and 2001 membership among men fell by around 13 per cent to just below 30 per cent, while the corresponding decline among women has been 4 per cent to 28 per cent. The main reason for this difference is the lower unionisation rate in part-time jobs and the over-representation of women in part-time work. The disproportionately low unionisation rate for women can also be explained with reference to their employment in certain sectors, such as the service sector which has traditionally low density rates, and the fewer opportunities for women to unionise as compared with men (WERS98). However, the LFS data reveals that there has been a modest increase in the number of women union members for 2001.

Age and ethnicity (2001 data)

Unionisation increases rapidly with age. The highest union density recorded for any age group is for employees aged between 40 and 49 years, at 38 per cent. Low rates of unionisation among young employees can be partly explained by the proliferation of part-time and temporary work in sectors which are traditionally under-unionised.

Older women employees are less likely to be union members than male employees. Explanations for these variations are tenuous and speculative and await further research.

Overall, black employees are as likely to be in a trade union as the workforce generally with 30 per cent of black, and 29 per cent of white employees. There are, however, gender and ethnic group differences. Afro-Caribbean women have a higher rate of membership than all other female groups at 33 per cent, and black women employees are more likely to be unionised (27 per cent) than black male employees, while mixed, Asian and other ethnic groups have lower densities, varying from 22 to 25 per cent.

Geographical and occupational variations (2001 data)

Table 3.5 shows the distribution of unionisation on a regional basis. To a large extent the differences in unionisation rates across the regions are due to the industrial distribution of employment, with some areas having more sectors with a history of high union density than others. There is evidence of a north/south divide with employees in the north more

Table 3.5 Union density by region and occupation: 2001

Unionisation in the regions Employees in union and staff associations (%)		Union density by occupation Employees in unions (%)	
South East	22	Managers and senior officials	17
Eastern	23	Professional	48
London	26	Associate professional/technical	42
South West	26	Administrative and secretarial	24
East Midlands	28	Skilled trades	30
West Midlands	30	Personal service	29
Yorks and Humberside	31	Sales and customer service	13
North West	34	Process, plant and machine operatives	37
North East	39	Elementary	22
Wales	39		
Scotland	35		
Northern Ireland	40		
England	28		
All employees	29		

Source: Labour Force Survey, Autumn 2001

likely to be union members. Table 3.5 also shows the extent of union density by occupation, and confirms that more trade union and members are employed in non-manual occupations, and that the most highly unionised occupations are those held by professionals.

Sectoral and industrial distribution (2001 data)

Union membership is fairly evenly divided between public and private sectors (LFS includes higher and further education within the public sector). However, union density in the public sector is much higher (60 per cent) than in the private sector (19 per cent). The gender breakdown of union membership in the two sectors is very different as more men than women work in the private sector. Hence 60 per cent of men belonging to a union are private sector employees, while 66 per cent of women belonging to a union are public sector employees. Union density rates are highest in public administration, education and health, energy and water, and transport, while retail, hotels and catering, agriculture, forestry and fishing, and real estate reveal the lowest

densities. Union density among women employees is lower in all industrial sectors apart from financial and business services and hotels and catering (see Table 3.6).

Workplace size, length of service and flexible labour (2001 data)

The larger the establishment, the more likely it is to be unionised. Clearly, it is easier for unions to organise in larger workplaces, and where the workforce is large it is more likely that employees will regard themselves as a collectivity rather than individuals, which will make them more amenable to unionisation (Bain and Elsheikh, 1976). In workplaces with fewer than 25 employees, union density stood at only 15 per cent, compared with 36 per cent among larger establishments (LMT, 2002). The LFS report confirms the direct correlation between union density and length of service. Unionisation rates for employees who have been in their current job for less than one year is 12 per cent, rising to 32 per cent for those who have been in their current job for between five and ten years, and for those

Table 3.6 Union density by industry: 2001

Industry	Percentage of employees in unions		
	All	Private sector	Public sector
Agriculture/forestry/fishing	9	6	–
Mining/quarrying	25	25	–
Manufacturing	27	27	61
Energy and water	53	53	–
Construction	19	14	69
Wholesale and retail trade	12	12	–
Hotels and restaurants	5	4	32
Transport and communication	42	37	75
Financial intermediation	27	27	–
Real estate and business services	11	8	54
Public administration	59	33	61
Education	53	29	57
Health	45	16	62
Other activities	22	11	49

Source: *Labour Force Survey*, 2001

in their current job for over 20 years the figure is 60 per cent. The report also provides a breakdown of union membership in different types of 'flexible' employment, including temporary employment, flexitime, job sharing arrangements, term-time working, annualised hours, 4.5-day weeks, nine day fortnights and zero hours contracts. Temporary work includes fixed term contracts as well as agency temping, casual and seasonal employment, and employees within this category, unsurprisingly, are less likely to be unionised, with 19 per cent union members compared to 30 per cent of employees in permanent jobs. Other forms of flexible working, with the exception of those on zero hours contracts, show relatively high unionisation rates.

Self-Evaluation Activity 3.16

Recruitment strategies
This SEA has no commentary

From the information provided above, identify those categories of employee on which unions should focus their recruitment strategies.

Recruitment strategies and the 'relaunch' of the TUC

Clearly, the TUC has a crucial role in shaping strategies to counter union decline, recognising the limits to what individual unions can achieve without the assistance and guidance of a concerted overarching strategy. The TUC, of necessity, sought out a new role for itself during the early 1990s, prompted by the weakening of unions as a result of the 'neo-liberal assault' of Thatcherism (Waddington, 2003); continuing employer resistance to unionism in growth sectors of the economy, including attempts by employers to minimise union influence where unions are recognised; the considerable and progressive weakening of links between the union movement and the Labour Party (the 'end of traditionalism' thesis) and restricted access to government. These adverse developments not only encouraged an organisational rejuvenation of the TUC, but also helped to widen and deepen links

with the EU in terms of supporting European integration and social policy, and facilitated the development of 'social partnerships' with employers (see Chapter 8). Perhaps the most significant initiative was the adoption of an organising model and strategy to tackle union membership decline, as part of the TUC 'relaunch' and 'new unionism' slogan.

In its analysis of the LFS membership data, the TUC (2002) asserts, rather optimistically, that 'this latest report shows an encouraging stabilisation in trade union membership in 2001 with the employee unionisation rate remaining at around 30 per cent' (p. 21). The TUC goes on to state:

> There are also positive indications that the 'New Unionism' campaign of recent years, focusing on attracting new members (especially among women and ethnic minority employees) is beginning to bear fruit. Specific examples of this include the increases in union density between 1997 and 1998 among two particular groups of employees – women part-timers and black women. (p. 21)

The TUC 'relaunch'

In 1994 the TUC reinvented itself by restructuring its administrative and decision-making system and by attempting to generate a 'new ethos and sense of mission' (Heery, 1998). Internally the TUC has reformed its representative machinery which involved:

- The elimination of the standing committees of the General Council and the TUC industry committees while retaining the General Council itself which meets less frequently and delegating some of its activities to an Executive Committee and other joint committees.
- The setting up of Task Groups comprising General Council members and other representatives to develop policy on a range of issues 'including stake holding, full employment, representation at work, human resource management, part-time workers and union organising' (Heery, 1998, p. 341).

The TUC also reformed its management practice and structure which was considered to be unwieldy and bureaucratic, in order to reflect the functioning of the newly created task groups. Heery (1998) states:

> There has been a new emphasis on project work across department boundaries; posts have been redesigned and redesignated and their incumbents encouraged to act with greater autonomy; there has been a deliberate attempt to renew the organisation through external appointments; and TUC staff have been granted formal membership of Task Groups, alongside representatives from affiliates, and encouraged to participate openly in decision making. These developments, in turn, have been supported by greater investment in staff development, including a successful attempt to secure the Investors in People standard. (p. 342)

A further development has been to make the TUC more broadly representative, not only of trade unions but also of labour as a whole. The TUC has attempted to become a more broadly-based pressure group reflecting the diversity of employee interests within a 'world of work' context. For example, the broadening of the TUC's constituency included encouraging employees to contact the TUC 'Bad Bosses Hotline' in order to expose employer malpractices and focusing upon hitherto marginal concerns such as gays, young workers and home workers.

The next stage of the TUC relaunch was the inauguration of the TUC's Organising Academy in 1998 which offers training for union officers in recruitment and organising skills (see p. 148). The relaunch not only focuses upon the TUC as an organisation in relation to its internal structure and constituents, but also, in line with its mission statement to adopt a high profile in campaigning nationally, emphasises links external to the labour movement. Heery (1998) identifies four important changes which typify this alliance-building and networking approach:

1. Initiating contacts with political parties other than the Labour Party, by, for example, establishing a presence at the annual conference of all the main parties. There has also been a 'greater emphasis on lobbying members of Parliament in both Houses of Parliament and seeking to identify cross-party support for TUC policy' (p. 343).

2. Strengthening links with the CBI by encouraging reciprocal invitations to both organisations' conferences and establishing contacts with employers' associations, the Association of British Chambers of Commerce, the Institute of Directors, the Institute of Personnel and Development and other bodies. The TUC is also keen to establish and maintain contacts with employers and attempt to influence employer behaviour by, for example, promoting the idea of 'social partnership' whereby unions co-operate with employers concerning 'the modernisation of British industry on the basis of flexible working and investment in skills' (p. 344).

3. Facilitating contacts with voluntary sector organisations including churches, single-issue campaigning organisations, professional bodies and public agencies and using their specialist knowledge and skills to enrich TUC campaigns. For example, campaigns concerning occupational pensions have embraced organisations such as various pensions bodies, the Consumers' Association, Age Concern and the Police Federation.

4. Developing a new Campaigns and Communications Department to encourage greater professionalism in campaigning on a variety of issues, 'engaging a non-traditional union audience through non-traditional media [such as] the personal finance and women's pages of newspapers like the *Daily Mail* and *Daily Express*, women's magazines and local press and radio' (p. 345). Heery (1998) summarises the TUC relaunch below:

> The relaunch of the TUC can be viewed as an attempt both to change trade union methods and to promote a substantive shift in trade union strategy. The changes in methods fall into two broad categories. First, there has been the attempt to promote 'strategic' action by the TUC in which key goals and attainable objectives are identified and a plan is set in train for their realisation. The manifestation of this shift has been the transposition of the TUC's work into a series of campaigns, each conducted through its dedicated Task Group. Second, there has been an emphasis on 'partnership' and the building of supporting coalitions for each campaign, which has been seen in the changed orientation to political parties,

employers and third sector organisations. The TUC has become a networking organisation, and in certain respects the relaunch amounts less to the renewal of the labour movement and more to its submersion in a diffuse network of progressive alliances and campaigns. The key substantive change echoes these themes of partnership and coalition, in its concern to develop an encompassing trade union movement based on recognising and responding to diversity within the workforce. Since the relaunch, the question of union organising has moved to the forefront of TUC policy and has found expression in a dual concern to promote sustained recruitment by member unions and to draw an increasing proportion of women, young, contingent and service-sector workers into trade union membership. (p. 346)

The 'new unionism' and recruitment: 'organising' v 'servicing'

The 'organising' approach, strategy or model, which is described in more detail below, is counterposed by the 'servicing' model, both of which are intended to reinforce and extend union organisation. The servicing approach, which was initiated by the TUC in 1987, is concerned with providing support and services to union members. The source of such support is external to the workplace and comes typically from full-time union officers and from the union itself, examples of which include a range of financial services packages comprising discounted insurance on holidays, cars etc., credit card facilities, personal loans and mortgage arrangements, with the object of attracting potential membership. Research undertaken by Waddington and Whitson (1997) and Waddington and Kerr (1999) suggests that the servicing approach used on its own would appear to have had little success in influencing the rate of unionisation, hence the move towards the organising approach (see also Waddington, 2003). The organising approach, the main elements of which are summarised below, complements rather than excludes the servicing approach and seeks to cultivate a proactive culture of organising and recruitment based on the activities of workplace union representatives.

Launched in 1996, the 'new unionism' is based on a number of organising principles which the TUC argues are needed to guide successful organising campaigns. They include:

- **Put organising first:** recruitment and organisation must become the top priority for the whole union movement.
- **Invest real resources:** organising does not come cheap, and only a significant commitment of resources – money and people – to recruitment and organisation can reverse membership decline.
- **Develop a strategic approach:** properly thought-out and resourced organising campaigns which set realistic targets are more likely to deliver results – and boost morale.
- **Cut out wasteful rivalries:** unions must be encouraged to focus on the rise of the non-unionised sector and the threat this poses to the whole union movement.
- **Reflect the diversity of the workforce** and those groups traditionally under-represented in unions.
- **Increase the use of dedicated organisers – and boost their training and status:** the AFL-CIO Organising Institute (USA) and ACTU Organising Works (Australia) programmes have brought new blood into the movement, upskilled the job of organising – and paid for themselves through recruitment success.
- **Build lay representatives' confidence and skills:** investing in building lay representatives' organisation helps strengthen existing bases and frees up full-time officers to organise in new areas.
- **Communication is the key:** imaginative campaigning and use of the mass media are key to getting the union message across to working people.
- **Government sympathy does not guarantee growth:** union membership can continue to slide even where the government in power is sympathetic to union values and, as in Australia, a social partnership accord is in place.

Based on these organising principles, a number of objectives were identified by the new unionism task group. These include promoting organising as top priority together with a shift towards an organising culture; increasing investment of union resources in recruitment and organising; strengthening lay structures and developing new training packages for both lay and full-time organisers; setting up special projects for unions to build their existing bases and break into new areas, winning recognition rights; sharpening unions' appeal to 'new' workers, including women, youth and those at the 'rough end' of the labour market, through campaigns and the media; promoting debate and disseminating information on successful organising approaches; and assessing the feasibility of launching an organising academy (see right) to train up – mainly young – specialist union organisers.

The TUC has also been informed by research into why people join unions during a period of membership decline (Waddington and Whitson, 1997). The responses to a questionnaire survey of new recruits' reasons for joining a union were placed into one of two broad categories comprising:

- **collective reasons** such as mutual support, improved pay and conditions, peer group pressure and a belief in the principle of union organisation; and
- **individual benefits** including training and education, industrial benefits and professional services, free legal advice and financial services.

Waddington and Whitson found that collective factors are by far the most important reasons why people join trade unions, thereby emphasising the importance of collective forces which underpin union membership and the support amongst new recruits for what are regarded as 'traditional' trade union activities. There is, therefore, little support for the argument that 'individualisation' has dissolved the labour movement since 1979. Indeed, collective reasons for joining a trade union remain as strong as ever, and this is repeated across most industries and occupations. But the fact that employers have found it easy to resist recognition claims, or even an effective union presence, has made unions unavailable to vast numbers of potential members. The lessons to be drawn from this research are that there are two main strategic activities that unions should concentrate on: firstly, deepening recruitment in organised workplaces; and secondly, extending membership in unorganised areas rather than offering financial and other services. Waddington and Whitson's research therefore provides support for

the view that trade unions should develop organising strategies rather than concentrate upon 'service' aspects. In adopting organising strategies, the TUC has also been learning from the experiences of unions overseas, particularly Australia and the USA.

The Organising Academy

In 1996 the TUC task group agreed to develop an organisers' academy modelled on the US AFL-CIO's Organising Institute and the Australian 'Organising Works' programme. The TUC gave the Organising Academy the go-ahead in 1997. In commenting upon the rationale for the Academy, the TUC (1998) states:

> The Organising Academy stresses that successful organising involves not only recruiting members but building strong sustainable workplace organisation. In this way members can win more power and practical improvements in their working lives – and they are more likely to stay in membership. The old recruitment model, in its extreme form, uses numbers as the main (and sometimes the only) criterion; it makes no allowance for the value of recruiting, say 100 members in a hostile environment compared with 200 in easier recruitment grounds. Nor is any special value attached to using innovative techniques, to making inroads into new jobs or categories of workers, or to putting the brakes on membership throughput. The Academy does not under-estimate the importance of the old adage 'strength through numbers'. The success of many campaigns hinges on winning new members fast and in volume as the best means to achieve real workplace change. What distinguishes the organising model from the old recruitment approach is that organisers aim to achieve success both in numbers and strong organisation. The organising model can deliver numbers plus. This approach underpins our evaluation of organising success and, if we succeed, will help guarantee our future. (p. 15)

Other main features of the Academy include:

- carefully structured arrangements for recruitment, training, coaching, mentoring and placement of predominantly young organisers who will also reflect the gender (at least half the trainees are women) and racial diversity of the workforce the unions aim to attract;

- an active partnership between the national centre and participating unions in shaping, overseeing, managing and delivering the programme;
- a TUC Organising Academy steering group comprising representatives of each sponsoring union

– along with appropriate TUC personnel – to oversee all aspects of the initiative;

- recruitment to the programme through an agreed process involving the TUC and participating unions; and
- a rigorous and independent evaluation of the pilot programme.

The US and Australian examples are given in greater detail in Exhibit 3.7.

Exhibit 3.7

Lessons from overseas

USA: a recipe for success?

The success of the recruitment campaigns conducted by the American trade union federation, the AFL-CIO, provides hard evidence that the labour movement can organise its way out of decline. Forty years ago American unions represented 35 per cent of the workforce, but that figure has fallen to around 15 per cent. In the face of corporate hostility, changes in the labour market, and a legal framework that is loaded against them, the American trade union movement has begun to reverse decades of sliding membership by conducting a major recruitment drive to attract new workers in emerging industries. The organising drive has targeted workers at the sharp end of the labour market including women, ethnic workers, health care workers, etc. Strategies have included a blitz of nationwide company chains; a sharp rise in the use of specialist union organisers; and high profile popular protests, using the media and improved communication techniques, that draw heavily on community campaign tactics. Using aggressive recruitment techniques and backed by substantial financial resources, the campaign has helped to turn the AFL-CIO into what US magazine *Business Week* has called 'a lean, mean recruiting machine' – the process reversing decades of membership decline. In 1996, for the first time in 30 years, the AFL-CIO reported an increase in membership to 13 million.

Central to the campaign is the commitment to increase the level of investment in organising and recruiting. Working with national unions, regions and locally, the AFL-CIO is helping affiliates restructure so they can organise more effectively, switching funds away from servicing declining membership bases to recruitment in new jobs and industries.

Main aims

A vitally important part of the AFL-CIO's recruitment initiative is the launch of its Organising Institute (OI), which the federation call 'the engine of the US organising drive'. Set up in 1989, the Institute's stated aims are to:

- highlight the importance of organising within the labour movement
- examine and disseminate information on successful organising approaches
- advise union organising departments on their own strategies
- help unions recruit and train organisers
- coordinate apprenticeships for new organisers.

A key feature of the OI is the partnership approach between the union centre and affiliates in the funding, shaping, resourcing, delivery and evaluation of programmes.

Australia: the 'wisdom of Oz'

Faced with a similar pattern of long-term membership decline, employer hostility, labour market change and anti-union laws, Australian trade unions have also tried to learn from their American counterparts by prioritising organising and recruitment. They have adopted a two-pronged strategy to try to reverse the cycle of decline.

First, the unions undertook a radical reorganisation of their structures through a series of strategic amalgamations. Begun in the late 1980s, the merger programme resulted in 95 per cent of affiliated union members belonging to just 20 Australian Congress of Trade Unions (ACTU) 'super unions'. But the mergers failed to halt membership decline and the key to the survival and growth of the union movement in Australia was a coordinated recruitment campaign, with new young trainee organisers to the fore.

In 1994 ACTU set up its 'Organising Works' programme, under the banner 'Strength in Numbers'. Organising Works is a nine-month traineeship for union activists, involving two weeks of formal residential training and an average of two days per fortnight in the classroom, delivered and assessed by the staff of Organising Works and the Trade Union Training Authority. For the rest of the nine months, trainees receive on-the-job training from officers of their host union, with the expectation that, after graduation, they will be provided with employment from the sponsoring unions in an organising role.

Source: IRS, 1997

Concluding comments: is organising working?

The relaunch of the TUC against the backdrop of declining membership, economic recession and, until 1997, right-wing government, 'reinforced by the increased competitive pressures in world markets and the internationalisation of production and corporate organisation' (Kelly, 1998, p. 60) could be regarded not only as a 'modernisation' process but also as a means of accommodating employers by trading benefits to employers (many of whom are hostile to a union presence). One such benefit is co-operation in changing work arrangements and flexibility in return for concessions such as recognition for purposes of collective bargaining; this is the 'social partnership' theme, which is part of the rhetoric of new unionism (Kelly, 1996). Social partnership (see Chapter 8) replaces (or deconstructs) 'traditional' methods since 'the adverse balance of power (in favour of the employer) appears to rule out the feasibility of unions recovering membership and influence by threatening uncooperative employers with sanctions' (Kelly, 1998, p. 59). However, given the 'growing tide of employer hostility' to unions (ibid., p. 63) throughout the 1990s, perhaps despite the efforts of the TUC to renew itself,

the appropriateness of union collaboration and social partnership is brought into question. As Kelly suggests: 'It is, after all, difficult for a union to construct a partnership with an employer who would prefer that the union simply did not exist' (ibid., p. 63). Elsewhere, Kelly (1996) argues that militancy often pays off and 'is a better guarantor of union survival and recovery' than moderation which yields no significant benefits for the union and increases its dependency upon the employer. This critical view of the employment relationship accords with mobilisation theory (see Chapter 1) with its emphasis upon conflicts of interests within that relationship.

The 'servicing' model of trade unionism (see Figure 3.4) is consistent with the moderate, collaborative and partnership-oriented approach, and is now rejected as a model of recruitment by the TUC. However, the organising model eschews 'traditionalist' terms such as 'militancy', although as Blyton and Turnbull (1998) point out: 'militancy is a method rather than an aim with the emphasis first and foremost on *solidarity* as opposed to *strike* action'. They go on to point out:

*While the servicing union expects its members to ask no more than 'What can the union do **for***

Element	Militancy–Organising	Moderation–Servicing
Goals	Ambitious demands (scale and scope) with few concessions	Moderate demands with some or many concessions
Membership resources	Strong reliance on mobilisation of union membership	Strong reliance on employers third parties or law
Institutional resources	Exclusive reliance on collective bargaining	Willingness to experiment with or support non-bargaining institutions
Methods	Frequent threat or use of industrial action	Infrequent threat or use of industrial action
Ideology	Ideology of conflicting interests	Ideology of partnership
Recruitment	Members own the campaign to unionise their workplace	The union is seen as a third party It enters the workplace to increase membership or solve problems
	Members identify their own issues and organise to solve them together	Unions tell members how they can solve their problems
	Mapping the workplace and staff attitudes are crucial; names and information are provided by workers	Relying on the employer to provide a list of the names of workers to the union official
	Initial organising can be done outside work – in workers' homes and other places	Relying on workplace access and employer co-operation
	Establishing initial contacts and finding natural leaders to help recruit	Cold-selling union membership by organisers
	Workers empowered to act for themselves through education and support	Selling the union for services and insurance protection
	An internal organising committee formed and workers encouraged to build the union through one-to-one organising	Relying on full-time officials to recruit and solve problems
	Recruitment and organising are integrated	Recruiting is seen as a separate activity
	Results obtained through sustained efforts – more likely to be permanent	Results are achieved but likely to be short term
	Members share decisions and solve problems together with union leaders	The union is blamed when it cannot get results
	Members make a real contribution to union struggles and identify with the union An attack on the union is an attack on themselves	Members complain when they pay fees and the union does nothing
	The image of the union is positive and active	Organisers resent members not attending meetings or participating
	The union has its own agenda with members involved and it keeps management 'off-balance'	Management acts, while the union reacts and is always on the defensive

Figure 3.4 Servicing and organising recruitment patterns within the framework of 'militancy' and 'moderation'
Source: Adapted from Organising Works, 1995; Blyton and Turnbull, 1998; Kelly, 1998

me?, the organising union asks 'What can we achieve with the union?'. The organising union depends upon membership being of value in itself: members should be able to identify their own issues, organise to solve their own problems and satisfy their aspirations on a collective basis. If all union members defined their own interests in isolation and then simply looked to 'the union' to service their needs, not only would the costs be prohibitive, but the very basis of organisation and unity would be precarious and ultimately ephemeral. In short, there would be no union. (p. 137)

Despite certain criticisms of the new unionism campaign and the modernisation of the TUC, the response to the campaign and the relaunch amongst affiliates has been generally positive. The TUC has a new mission, logo and style; its internal structure has been transformed in order to facilitate the re-focusing upon its external relationships with government, employers and other significant pressure groups. Above all, its Organising Academy has instilled a more proactive approach to recruitment according to the organising principles identified in Figure 3.4. The TUC which remains optimistic about the prospects for organising (see Exhibit 3.8)

Exhibit 3.8

Some organising successes: the TUC version

Over the last four years (1998–2002), the TUC has helped train 150 (mainly young) organisers through the Organising Academy, while more individual unions are hiring specialist organisers, setting up organising units and targeting non-union companies in their determination to adapt and survive. There are many lessons to be learnt from this union renaissance of which the main ones are:

- Specialist lead organisers have been crucial, using their planning and organising skills to mount successful campaigns in a range of different settings. The Organising Academy and associated initiatives in individual unions have helped develop a body of organising expertise that was almost certainly lacking in the movement five years ago (1997).
- Building the union on the ground has been done by the workers themselves, with organisers and other 'external' union contacts providing support, expertise and resources. All the campaigns have relied on reps, shop stewards and activists to recruit members, lead worker opinion and, in many cases, plan strategy through organising committees.
- Every campaign has been built on the issues the workers themselves care most about, and unions have often shown great sensitivity about tackling problems without appearing to undermine an industry or employer. Through practical, concrete help, they've shown that collective organisation is the most effective method for winning at work.

But organising is not an easy option. It may be expensive, difficult and time-consuming, and spreading the message in small companies, flexible workforces and high turnover industries requires long-term commitment.

Two success stories

The NUJ

The last two decades have been tough for newspaper journalists as proprietors have torn up recognition agreements with the NUJ, slashed pay rates and given their managers free rein to play the bully boy. But the NUJ is on its way back. Since June 2000, it's clocked up more than 55 new recognition deals (most of them voluntary) and extended the protection of collective bargaining to 5000 newspaper and magazine journalists. And where bosses have dragged their feet, they've more than not simply been putting off the inevitable. The CAC backed the union's case for recognition at the *Bristol Evening Post* earlier this year – the first crucial victory of the most anti-union regional group, Northcliffe Newspapers. The union's been careful throughout to present recognition not as an end in itself but as a way to claw back the fall in relative earnings. To boost its chances, the NUJ has appointed a new assistant organiser to build up membership in magazines and book publishing and is sponsoring a trainee at the Organising Academy, who will be helping members secure recognition in new media including at Ananova, the first stand-alone, online news service where the NUJ has established chapel organisation.

The ISTC

It's an inspired moment that has since passed into organising folklore: community union ISTC handing out condoms at a night club, to hard-pressed staff at a Scottish computer hardware firm FCI with the message: 'There's more than one form of protection – join a union.'

This was the beginning of a three-year campaign, and it all started when a former ISTC member of the non-union plant contacted the union complaining about the intolerable conditions and management style back in 1998. The union handed the FCI brief to two of its Academy-trained organisers and launched phase one of the campaign – taking the union message to the company's sites and identifying staff who could wage the organising battle from the inside. They used housecalls to track down opinion formers on the shop floor who were interested in becoming activists; they formed the core of a large organising committee, mapping and re-mapping the workplace and systematically approaching non-members. With the union established by the workforce themselves, helped by the ISTC organisers (and sometimes the entire organising team), it was the threat of a major redundancy programme that triggered the final phase of the recognition campaign. The non-union staff forum declared it could not cope, and its entire membership not only joined the ISTC, but urged the 750-strong workforce to do the same as well. And when the union's organisers were bundled out of a car park meeting the very next day, there was another surge in recruitment. Despite management's tough anti-union campaign, the ISTC won the backing of the workforce, gained recognition – and have proved their worth protecting the workforce ever since. When another 150 redundancies were announced in the wake of recognition, the new branch managed to negotiate that down to 90, and reduced the impact of another restructuring by securing the transfer of workers between sites. Membership has continued to rise, currently standing at around 75 per cent, and management style has grown a little less confrontational, while negotiations continue to draw up a full set of procedures for grievance, discipline, equal opportunities, harassment and redundancy.

Source: Adapted from TUC documents 2002

can, with some justification, point to the general stabilisation of union membership during the period 1998–2003, and in particular to the slight increases in membership amongst groups who are traditionally resistant to unionisation, especially in the face of sustained employer hostility. A barometer of the future success of organising campaigns will be the extent to which density of unionisation increases in 'non-traditional workplaces', such as call centres which cut across a variety of industry sectors. However, Heery (2002) points out that organising unionism 'remains a minority trend within the British movement' (p. 29), partly owing to resource limitations, to a shortage of trained, committed organisers and to inadequate facilities

(Waddington, 2003). Another related issue is the extent to which employees, with the labour market increasingly fragmented and segmented, are able or willing, despite the commitment of organisers, to generate a 'mobilisation consciousness' appropriate to unionising. The organising initiative, while it has clearly secured the endorsement of the union movement, has been subject to fluctuating fortunes. To be sure, the statutory recognition procedures have provided an impetus, but the danger here is of a 'free for all', which ultimately may well be counterproductive to union organisation in the longer term. The measure of the efficacy of organising is the strength of commitment of workplace organisers to motivate employees to join a union, and on this issue it is still too early to judge whether the organising initiative is a success.

TRADE UNIONS, THE TUC AND POLITICS

As we noted in Chapter 1, the industrial and political role of trade unions has declined significantly since 1979. The Conservative governments were committed to trade union reform and to market rather than corporatist solutions to economic problems, and this had implications 'for the relationship between government, unions and the TUC. We now explore in more detail the nature of this changed relationship.

Access to government

The role and functions of the TUC were briefly described in Chapter 1. We now concentrate upon the extent to which access to government changed during the 1980s and the effect this has had upon the influence of the TUC as a pressure group. Mitchell (1987) provides an interesting and insightful analysis concerning the extent and consequences of TUC access to government, based on an examination of the reports by the General Council of the TUC to each annual conference, during the period 1976–84. Mitchell's analysis has been extended by Marsh (1992). The main conclusions of the analysis are as follows:

- The number of contacts between government and unions did not decrease, but the pattern and quality of those contacts changed significantly as there were fewer meetings, less personal contact and a decline in the number of contacts initiated by government.
- There was a decline in the effectiveness of these contacts as government hostility to the TUC's various policy positions grew more intense and the TUC's influence over the Conservative governments waned.
- The number of tripartite contacts (TUC, CBI and government) became more important to the TUC after 1979. Mitchell (1987) comments that this in itself is not surprising 'as tripartite contacts

are institutionalised, not impromptu, and inherently less susceptible to partisan or ideological change than bipartite contacts, as long as tripartite institutions themselves survive' (pp. 514–15).

TUC influence upon government legislation

Prior to 1979 the TUC had considerable influence upon government legislation, but during the 1980s and 1990s TUC influence was minimal, despite the more accommodating strategy adopted by the TUC at the 1983 Annual Conference which subsequently became known as the 'new realism'. There was only one major example of government making a concession to trade unions when it agreed to drop its commitment to 'contracting in' from the 1984 Trade Union Act. We now consider this example in greater detail.

The political funding of trade unions

Prior to the 1984 Act, trade unions' political finance was based on the 1913 Trade Unions Act. This Act established the principle that unions could establish a political fund out of members' subscriptions, provided that any union member who did not want to pay that part of their subscription to the political fund could contract out. The only exception to this was during the period 1927–46 when the government introduced a requirement that those who wished to pay the political levy should contract in. The difference which contracting-in made to unions' political funds was significant, as Marsh (1992) points out: 'when contracting-out was reintroduced in 1947 those paying the political levy increased from 39 per cent to 60 per cent in eighteen months' (p. 115). Marsh goes on to state:

The government's overall strategy in the 1984 Act was clear. They wished to depoliticise the trade union movement; to weaken its link to the Labour Party and force it to concentrate on economic, not political activity. It claimed a mandate for reform, especially as public opinion polls indicated widespread antipathy to the political levy and union political, particularly party political, activity. Soon after the election, Norman

Tebbit, the Employment Secretary, announced that the political levy would be reformed so that, once again, contracting-in replaced contracting-out. However, when the Trade Union Bill was published, it didn't include any such provision, rather it contained a redefinition of political objects and a requirement that ballots be held for the continuation of political funds. (p. 116)

Uncharacteristically, the government had negotiated the issue with the TUC and made the concession to retain contracting-out.

The European dimension

During the 1970s and early 1980s the attitude of the TUC towards the European Community (EC) varied from open hostility to grudging acceptance. From the mid-1980s onwards, there was a more positive and permanent endorsement of Europe, partly because the TUC came to regard the EC (or the European Union as it became known after the Maastricht Treaty of 1992), as a possible alternative means whereby to influence government policy, and partly because the unions and the TUC regarded the Social Charter as a radical programme of reform to extend, protect and promote the rights and interests of workers and which the Labour government finally endorsed in 1997. TUC links with European trade union organisations and the ETUC have also been strengthened. The extent to which the TUC now actively endorses its links with the EU is illustrated by the following extract taken from a recent (1997) policy document:

The European agenda will require immediate attention, and the new Government will also need to prepare for the UK's Presidency in the first half of 1998. The TUC looks forward to a new constructive approach to EU matters during the UK Presidency, and indeed during the lifetime of the new Government. A decision on Economic and Monetary Union will need to be taken, on which a referendum will be necessary. The TUC's discussions with fellow trade union organisations in the European Union, the European Commission and other European Governments have reinforced its view that Britain must engage in the debates, and cannot afford to opt out of European developments such as the extension of the competence of the Union to act and the introduction of a single currency. In order to ensure the greatest possible understanding of the issues involved, as well as working towards a national consensus, the TUC has suggested a Task Force on the single currency, involving the CBI and Bank of England as well as the TUC. More generally, the TUC will be playing an active part in the European social partner discussions designed to put the European Union on the road to full employment and, along with its ETUC counterparts, will be urging all governments of the member states to make this a priority and will be pressing for [the adoption of the] Employment Chapter. (TUC, 1997, p. 4)

The TUC, as a supporter of the EU's social policy, was pleased that the Labour government had signed up to the Social Chapter in 1997 (see Chapter 4) and welcomed transposition of the European Works Council Directive and initiatives concerning information and consultation of employees. As an active member of the ETUC, the TUC was playing a significant role in the social dialogue procedure as an EU-supported means for developing directives affecting social policy. Hence, the TUC was playing an important part within the EU tripartite system of 'bargained corporatism', a role that it lacks under the Labour government in the UK, and in addition the TUC has the opportunity to pursue legislative changes resisted by Labour. From 1997 to 2003 the content and transposition of EU directives was subject to a considerable amount of lobbying by the TUC and CBI. The CBI was successful in deferring the progress of the Information and Consultation Directive while the TUC was urging a more positive approach by government to strengthening the European Work Councils and resisting any derogations which would weaken the Working Time Directives. In the main, however, the TUC has had little influence and involvement in Labour decision-making in this and many other respects. Perhaps the elevation of the former General Secretary of the TUC, John Monks, to the presidency of the ETUC will lead to the TUC itself playing a more effective lobbying role both within the EU and in the national arena.

Trade unions and the Labour Party

Since 1979 the relationship between the trade union movement and the Labour Party has been subject to re-evaluation, prompted largely by the transformation of the party that began in 1983 (McIlroy, 1998). The modernisation programme initiated by Blair (see Chapter 4) was, to varying degrees, supported by the major unions and the TUC, exemplified by the TUC's enthusiastic support of 'social partnership' (see Chapter 8) and the 'stakeholder' notion – later abandoned by Labour. However, subsequent policy shifts involving 'partnership with business', developing a flexible labour market and what some saw as a flirtation with the CBI conspired gradually to widen the ideological interests of organised labour and government to such an extent that John Monks, the former General Secretary of the TUC, admitted that trade unions and New Labour were not the 'senior partners of old' (Monks, 1998, p. 126). Unions and the TUC responded with pragmatism to union decline with the new unionism approach, which was concerned not only with 'organising' but also with social market policies and enterprise-level social partnership. It could also be argued that the twin-track approaches of new unionism and social partnership were accommodatory responses to the modernisation and increasingly market-led policies of New Labour as the TUC 'sought to re-brand British trade unions as "part of the solution" to Britain's problems' (Undy, 2002). The quid pro quo for unions was the expectation that New Labour in government would work with the TUC in initiating and supporting substantive improvements to both employment protection and collective aspects of the employment relationship. Procedurally, New Labour eschewed formal partnership with unions at national level for its entire period of government up to 2003 and this, according to Undy (2002), prompted unions to attempt to reinforce their 'traditional' relationship with government which comprised:

- the relatively informal relationship between the TUC as pressure group and the Labour Party; and
- the formal but indirect relationship between individual unions and the Labour Party.

However, the relationship at both levels continued to weaken, particularly in recent years, although it is the second-level relationship that has proved to be the most contentious. With regard to the second level, a majority of unions, and in particular the larger unions, affiliate to the Labour Party. In 1990, for example, the Labour Party had 5.3 million affiliated union members secured through the political levy. However, the relationship between the 'political' and 'industrial relations' functions of unions is complex and often contradictory. Despite the fact that the union share in the Labour Party's finances decreased from 90 per cent in the early 1980s to 50 per cent in 1995 and has declined even further in 2003, unions have been potentially influential within the Labour Party in three ways:

- unions sponsor many Labour Members of Parliament;
- based on the number of affiliated members, union leaders control 50 per cent of the votes at the annual Labour Party conference; and
- unions still have significant say in policy forums and the National Executive Committee of the Labour Party, having 12 of 32 seats on the Executive.

Symptomatic of the decline in influence over government policy is the diminished impact of unions at Labour Party conferences. In 1990 the unions controlled 80 per cent of votes at conference, reducing to 70 per cent in 1994, with the four largest unions alone holding 60 per cent, and then to 50 per cent up to 2003. Between 1997 and 2001 the procedural relationship between the union movement and Labour was at once competitive and co-operative as described above. In terms of substantive outcomes, however, there was much greater dissent and discontent, particularly from 2001 to 2003. The chief areas of contention are:

- **In the field of employment legislation.** While there was support for the recognition procedures and the right to be accompanied in discipline and grievance interviews within the ERA99, together with the restoration of trade union rights at GCHQ, there were contentious issues to which the TUC objected, including the substitution of the term 'accompanied' rather than 'represented' in discipline and grievance procedures; the requirement that the union at the 'admissibility' stage of the formal recognition process should demonstrate that it was likely to win support in a subsequent recognition ballot; and the need for the CAC to ensure an imposed bargaining unit was compatible with 'effective management'. These changes had the support of the CBI. Furthermore, the TUC was disappointed with issues arising from the transposition of EU Directives by Labour (see above) which 'systematically minimize the effect of the EU instruments at the stage of transposition into UK law' (Undy, 2002).

- **In relation to privatisation** the main issues focus upon Labour's private finance initiative (PFI) inherited from the Conservatives, the public private partnership (PPP) and the private sector provision of public services (see Chapters 4 and 6). The TUC found it problematic to confront the government on the basis of a long-term campaign and, indeed, to decide how it should approach the government. The line of least resistance was to emphasise the need to protect terms and conditions of all employees affected by these measures (McIlroy, 2000). There have been a number of high-profile controversies concerning the issue, including the part-privatisations of the National Air Traffic Services, London Underground and the National Health Service. The government's commitment to greater private involvement in the Health Service provoked stern opposition from unions such as UNISON and threats by affiliated unions to suspend financial contributions to Labour. Campaigns such as UNISON's 'Positively Public' have contributed to a growing public awareness of the implications of PFI and the creation of a 'two-tier workforce' in relation to the transfer of staff to a private sector contractor, thereby widening the rift between government and unions in this area.

It is clear that the relationship between New Labour and the union movement is undergoing a period of difficulty which could not be entirely foreseen in 1997. The successes in terms of procedural and substantive issues and outcomes, such as the stress upon the partnership ideology at workplace level that equated with the 'new unionism', are outweighed in many instances by the raft of unpopular (with the unions) policies identified above, together with the absence of any major involvement by the TUC in government decision-making. All

of this contributes to the widening ideological gap between New Labour, which has relegated collectivism as a core value, and new unionism, which still accords collectivism a high value.

Self-Evaluation Activity 3.17
Weakening ties with the unions
Response on website

Why in your opinion do you think the Labour Party has sought to weaken ties with the trade union movement?

Summary and conclusion: rejuvenation, steady state or retirement?

Throughout their history, trade unions have metamorphosed and adapted to change, sometimes reactively, as with their reaction to the failure of the 1926 General Strike, and sometimes proactively, as with some elements of organising and partnership. However, certain enduring characteristics of the union movement have either impeded or hastened change. One important characteristic remains the high degree of organisational fragmentation concerning type, structure and size of unions, as we have seen earlier in the chapter. One consequence of this is that the largest unions mostly formed by mergers and takeovers after periods of intense union rivalry over membership, and currently representing the vast majority of trade union members, dominate decision-making and resource allocation within the TUC. Diversity of political ideology amongst trade union leaderships is a fact of any democratically structured organisation and ensures a measure of competition and conflict concerning strategic decisions affecting a wide range of matters, from European and national government policies down to workplace matters. A change of leadership, therefore, may also mean a change of policy concerning one or more strategic policy issues. During 2002, for example, the election of 'left-wing' union leaders such as Mark Serwotka of PCSU and Andy Gilchrist of the FBU meant that there was likely to be a more polemic relationship between these and other trade unions and the government, as acknowledged by the General Secretry of the TUC: The new leaders 'reflect the impatience I feel sometimes too, that they've not got the relationship with the Labour government on the basis that we want to see' (Brendan Barber, General Secretary of the TUC, quoted in *Financial Times*, 30 January 2003).

The TUC itself remains a loose coalition of affiliated unions whose claim to represent all UK unions is weakened by the fact that a large number of unions are not affiliated. In addition, since 1980 the TUC has all but lost its influence over government decision- and policy-making while consolidating its role within the EU. An even more daunting prospect amidst employer hostility and government indifference is how to deal with the seemingly intractable and ongoing problem of union decline, both nationally and at the workplace, and which was also a consequence of the neo-liberal offensive of Thatcherism of the 1980s and 1990s. The efficacy of the 'organising' approach has yet to be tested, while partnership initiatives at organisational and workplace level may yet prove to be a transitory phenomenon and possibly to be jettisoned in the same way as other disposables such as the 'third way' and 'stakeholding'. If the UK were to adopt wholesale the Information and Consultation Directive, incorporating fully-fledged and effective works councils at workplace level which currently exist in most social market member states, then there would be in all probability no need for formal partnership agreements. This development, coupled with a reinvigorated workplace 'organising and mobilising' union presence, again at workplace level, together with more clout for European works councils would do much to rejuvenate union organisation and unions themselves.

As was pointed out earlier in the chapter, union decline is a global phenomenon and a number of prescriptions have been mooted to reverse the decline which may apply to more than one country. Part of the solution may reside in a re-examination of the 'who', 'what' and 'how' questions posed by Hyman (2002), referred to earlier in this chapter, and articulated more specifically by Verma *et al.* (2002) in relation to seven areas:

Demand for representation. Charlwood (2002) argues that 40 per cent of non-union employees in

the UK would be willing to join a union if they were given a choice to do so. This positive assessment should, arguably, provide an incentive towards increasing and improving organising activities in UK workplaces.

Method of organising. According to Verma *et al.* (2002), given the latent demand for union membership, concentrating on organising groups of employees who are dissatisfied with their jobs and see union involvement in purely instrumental terms may not be enough to increase membership. It may well be that unions need to make far more effort with peripheral groups of employees, for example, and to appeal to diverse constituencies of employees with an 'agenda that must reflect the far more differentiated ways in which work connects to life – or in which workers *wish* it to relate' (Hyman, 2002, p. 13). This means looking at individualism and collectivism as mutually inclusive rather than antagonistic, combining also the 'instrumental' (pay conditions, choice, opportunity, flexibility) with the 'affective' (solidarity, commitment).

The retention challenge. Membership turnover or 'churn' means that unions are losing almost as many members (or in many cases more) than they are recruiting. The prescriptions mentioned above may help reduce turnover, but fail to address the problem of membership loss when moving from job to job. One solution mooted is to move towards a system which facilitates lifelong union membership, whereby members are recruited at the start of their careers and are provided with all services and benefits relevant to particular stages of work and non-work life. The TUC has proposals for lifelong membership of the TUC with a range of benefits etc., which would be supplemented by optional membership of a particular affiliated trade union.

Targeting youth.

Overcoming employer opposition. As far as the future is concerned, Verma *et al.* (2002) identify a number of scenarios applicable to the UK and other countries, including:

Continued decline on the basis of past trends. This scenario is probably the safest to make if present trends are extrapolated to the future, other things being equal, and assuming that unions continue to be 'sclerotic' in adapting to change. At best, unions can hope for a 'downward stabilisation' of membership, although density will continue to decline.

Fragmented growth on the basis of existing strengths. Not a scenario recommended for the UK as the traditional union industrial enclaves continue to decline and existing strengths which reside mainly in the public sector are too concentrated. According to this scenario 'the labour movement could maintain its current base and, with continuous adaptation, become stronger and more effective in some sectors or occupations with little growth or even presence in others' (p. 381).

Rejuvenation through crisis. Taking a longer-term view of history, it is argued that the confluence of certain events such as the Great Depression in the USA and the defeat of Nazism and Fascism at the end of the Second World War bolstered trade union membership – although simple cause-effect is not good methodology and very unreliable as predictor. Multi-causal factor independent variables such as those that account for union decline are less reliable as predictors.

New organisational forms: the cyber union?
Unions, as we have mentioned in the British context, have metamorphosed in the past, transforming themselves from local to national, craft to industrial organisations in the nineteenth century, and from manual to professional and then to the emergence of 'super-unions' in the twentieth century The assumption that unions will change again in the twenty-first century while retaining their organising essence is a reasonable one. Hyman (2002) for example, suggests that in addition to the implications of union modernisation, information technology offers some possibilities of reducing the hierarchical levels while introducing more interactive and open communication and opening the scope more for effective participation in decision-making. A 'new' cyber-oriented e-union would be expected to provide individual representation and customised services while continuing to bargain collectively for workers with management. The differences between traditional unionism and e-unionism are identified in Table 3.7.

Whether trade unions reinvent themselves as 'virtual social movements' in cyberspace or elsewhere

Table 3.7 Traditional unions into e-unions

	Pre-internet activities of unions	Additional activities after internet
Primary business	Collective bargaining	Individual representation and advice
Delivery of services	Workplaces	Web
	Services delivered by reps/leaders	Digital AI services
	Outcomes depend on collective bargain with employer	Services provided directly to workers
Method of dispute	Strikes	Web communication
		Cyber picketing
	Pre-internet membership	**Post-internet membership**
Locale	Workplace	Differentiated membership
	Members with employer recognition	Members, subscribers
		Visitors to website
		Virtual presence at workplaces
Free-rider problems	Collective bargain creates incentive to free ride	Customised services to members only
Internal democracy	Elected leaders and bureaucracy	Decentralised; internet plebiscites
		Activists operate independently

Source: Diamond and Freeman, 2002

depends very much upon the nature of the current and potential problems they have to deal with. In any event, the more responsive unions become to the needs of the membership – actual and potential – and the more proactive and inventive unions are in taking up the new opportunities and challenges, the more likely they will survive well into the twenty-first century as rejuvenated and vibrant organisations.

RELEVANT WEBSITES

www.acas.org.uk (The Advisory, Conciliation and Arbitration Service) Useful all-round information.

www.dti.gov.uk/er/emar (Department of Trade and Industry) Up-to-date information on unions and other employment relations matters. Provides access to government statistics website for information on trade union membership etc. Also details of research, publications, European Union Directives and workplace partnership.

www.etuc.org (European Trades Union Confederation) Provides information on constituent union organisations and other relevant statistics.

www.eurofound.ie (European Foundation for the Improvement of Living and Working Conditions) A very informative website created by the EU which considers policy issues concerning social and work-based matters as well as research and publications at EU, country and sector levels.

www.lrd.org.uk (Labour Research Department) A trade union-oriented research body which researches and regularly publishes across the whole employment relations range. Union members can obtain a password through their union for free access to online material.

www.tuc.org.uk (Trades Union Congress) The website of the TUC provides a wealth of material and information on all aspects of the employment relationship. Contains a good section for students.

www.unions21.org.uk (Unions 21) A website which provides valuable material concerning trade unions and the TUC.

Individual trade unions: website addresses of the larger unions are to be found in the Appendix.

REFERENCES

ACAS (2002) *Annual Report 2001–2002*. London, ACAS

Addison, J. and Belfield, C. (2001) 'Updating the determinants of firm performance using the 1998 UK Workplace Employee Relations Survey'. *British Journal of Industrial Relations*, 39, 3, 341–66

Bain, G.S. and Elsheikh, F. (1976) *Union Growth and the Business Cycle*. Oxford, Blackwell

Beaumont, P. (1987) *The Decline of Trade Union Organisation*. London, Croom Helm

Blackwell, R. (1990) 'Parties and factions in trade unions'. *Employee Relations*, 12, 1, 12–23

Blyton, P. and Turnbull, P. (1994) *The Dynamics of Employee Relations*. London, Macmillan

Blyton, P. and Turnbull, P. (1998) *The Dynamics of Employee Relations*, 2nd edn. London, Macmillan

Booth, A. (1983) 'A reconsideration of trade union growth in the United Kingdom'. *British Journal of Industrial Relations*, 21, 3, 379–91

Brown, W., Deakin, S., Hudson, M. and Pratten, C. (2001) 'The limits of statutory trade union recognition'. *Industrial Relations Journal*, 32, 2, 94–113

Carruth, A. and Disney, R. (1988) 'Where have two million trade union members gone? *Economica*, 55, 1, 1–19

CBI (1998) *Employment Trends Survey: Measuring Flexibility in the Labour Market*. London, CBI

Charlwood, A. (2002) 'Why do non-union employees want to unionise?' *British Journal of Industrial Relations*, 40, 3, 463–91

Claydon, T. (1989) 'Union derecognition in Britain during the 1980s'. *British Journal of Industrial Relations*, 27, 2, 214–23

Claydon, T. (1997) 'Union recognition: A re-examination', in Beardwell, I.J. (ed.) *Contemporary Industrial Relations: A Critical Analysis*. Oxford, Oxford University Press

Coates, K. and Topham, T. (1974) *The New Unionism*. Harmondsworth, Penguin

Coates, K. and Topham, T. (1988) *Trade Unions in Britain*. London, Fontana

Colgan, F. and Ledwith, S. (2002) 'Gender and diversity: Reshaping union democracy'. *Employee Relations*, 24, 2, 167–89

Cully, M., Woodland, S., O'Reilly, A. and Dix, G. (1998) *The 1998 Workplace Employee Relations Survey*. London, DTI

Cully, M., Woodland, S., O'Reilly, A. and Dix, G. (1999) *Britain at Work*. London, Routledge

Dempsey, M. and McKevitt, P. (2001) 'Unison and the people side of merger'. *Human Resource Management Journal*, 11, 2, 4–16

Diamond, W.J. and Freeman, R.B. (2002) 'Will unionism prosper in cyberspace?' *British Journal of Industrial Relations*, 40, 3, 569–96

Disney, R. (1990) 'Explanations of the decline in trade union density in Britain: An appraisal'. *British Journal of Industrial Relations*, 28, 2, 165–78

Donovan (1968) *Report of the Royal Commission on Trade Unions and Employers Associations 1965–1968*, Cmnd 3623. London, HMSO

Edelstein, J.D. and Warner, M. (1975) *Comparative Union Democracy*. London, Allen and Unwin

Flanders, A. (1972) *Trade Unions*. London, Hutchinson

Freeman, R. and Pelletier, J. (1990) 'The impact of industrial relations legislation on British trade union density'. *British Journal of Industrial Relations*, 28, 2, 141–64

Gall, G. and McKay, S. (1999) 'Developments in union recognition and derecognition in Britain, 1994–1998'. *British Journal of Industrial Relations*, 37, 4, 601–11

Gall, G. and McKay, S. (2001) 'Facing fairness at work: Union perception of employer opposition and response to union recognition'. *Industrial Relations Journal*, 32, 2, 94–113

Gall, G. and McKay, S. (2002) *Trade Union recognition in Britain; The Dawn of a New Era*, London, LRD

Gallie, D., Rose, M. and Penn, R. (1996) 'The British debate on trade unionism: Crisis and continuity', in Gallie, D., Penn, R. and Rose, M. (eds) *Trade Unionism in Recession*. Oxford, Oxford University Press

GMB (1998) *Changing Job Patterns and GMB Recruitment Prospects*. London, GMB

GMB (2002) *A Brief Guide to a Modern Union*. London, GMB

Goldstein, J. (1952) *The Government of a British Trade Union*. London, Allen and Unwin

Grant, D. (1997) 'Japanisation and the new industrial relations', in Beardwell, I.J. (ed.) *Contemporary Industrial Relations: A Critical Approach*. Oxford, Oxford University Press

Hawkins, K. (1981) *Trade Unions*. London, Hutchinson

Heery, E. (1997) 'The new new unionism', in Beardwell, I.J. (ed.) *Contemporary Industrial Relations: A Critical Approach*. Oxford, Oxford University Press

Heery, E. (1998) 'The relaunch of the Trades Union Congress'. *British Journal of Industrial Relations*, 36, 3, 339–60

Heery, E. (2002) 'Partnership v organising: Alternative futures for British trade unions'. *Industrial Relations Journal*, 33, 1, 20–35

Hobsbawm, E.J. (1974) *Labouring Men: Studies in the History of Labour*. London, Weidenfeld & Nicolson

Hughes, J. (1968) *Trade Union Structure and Government, Part 1*. Donovan Commission Research Paper no. 5. London, HMSO

Hyman, R. (1995) 'The historical evolution of British industrial relations', in Edwards, P. (ed.) *Industrial Relations: Theory and Practice in Britain*. Oxford, Blackwell

Hyman, R. (1996) 'Changing union identities in Europe', in Leisink, P., Van Leemput, J. and Lilrokx, J. (eds) *The Challenges to Trade Unions in Europe: Innovation or Adaptation*. Cheltenham, Edward Elgar

Hyman, R. (2002) 'The future of unions'. *Just Labour*, 1, 7–15

Hyman, R. (2003) 'The historical evolution of British industrial relations', in Edwards, P. *Industrial Relations Theory and Practice*, 2nd edn. Oxford, Blackwell

ILO (1998) *World Labour Report, 1997–1998*. Geneva, ILO

IRS (1997) 'Organising the unorganised'. *IRS Employment Trends*, November, No. 644

IRS (1998) 'Predicting union membership'. *IRS Employment Trends*, December, No. 667

IRS (2002a) 'Gaining recognition'. *IRS Employment Trends*, February, No. 745

IRS (2002b) 'Part of the union'. *IRS Employment Trends*, November, No. 764

Kelly, J. (1996) 'Union militancy and social partnership', in Ackers, P., Smith, C. and Smith, P. (eds) *The New Workplace and Trade Unionism*. London, Routledge

Kelly, J. (1998) *Rethinking Industrial Relations: Mobilisation, Collectivism and Long Waves*. London, Routledge

Kelly, J. (2002) 'Decline and revival of the international union movement'. *TUC Pamphlet*. London, TUC

Kelly, J. and Heery, E. (1994) *Working for the Union: British Trade Union Officers*. Cambridge, Cambridge University Press

LMT (Labour Market Trends) (2002) 'Trade union membership: An analysis of the data from the Autumn 2001 LFS'. *Labour Market Trends*, July, 343–55

Lipset, S.M., Trow, M.A. and Coleman, J.S. (1956)*Union Democracy*. New York: The Free Press

Luthans, F. (1992) *Organisational Behaviour*. New York, McGraw-Hill

Machin, S. (2000) 'Union decline in Britain', *British Journal of Industrial Relations*, 30, 4, 631–45

Marchington, M. and Parker, P. (1990) *Changing Patterns of Employee Relations*. Hemel Hempstead, Harvester Wheatsheaf

Marsh, D. (1992) *The New Politics of British Trade Unionism: Union Power and the Thatcher Legacy*. London, Macmillan

Martin, R., Sunley, P. and Wills, J. (1996) *Union Retreat and the Regions: The Shrinking Landscape of Organised Labour*. London, Jessica Kingsley

Mason, B. and Bain, P. (1993) 'The determinants of trade union membership in Britain: A survey of the literature'. *Industrial and Labour Relations Review*, 46, 2, 332–51

McIlroy, J. (1988) *Trade Unions in Britain Today*. Manchester, Manchester University Press

McIlroy, J. (1990) *A History of British Trade Unionism*. Manchester, Manchester University Press

McIlroy, J. (1995) *Trade Unions in Britain Today*, 2nd edn. Manchester, Manchester University Press

McIlroy, J. (1998) 'The enduring alliance? Trade unions and the making of New Labour'. *British Journal of Industrial Relations*, 36, 4, 537–64

McIlroy, J. (2000) 'The new politics of pressure: The Trade Union Congress and New Labour in government'. *Industrial Relations Journal*, 31, 1, 2–16

Metcalf, D. (1991) 'British unions: Dissolution or resurgence?'. *Oxford Review of Economic Policy*, 7, 1, 18–32

Michels, R. (1959) *Political Parties*. Dover, Constable

Michels, R. (1970) 'Oligarchy', in Grusky, O. and Miller, G.A. *The Sociology of Organisations*. New York: The Free Press

Millward, N. and Stevens, M. (1986) *British Workplace Industrial Relations 1980–1984*. Aldershot, Gower

Millward, N., Bryson, A. and Forth, J. (2000) *All Change at Work?* London, Routledge

Millward, N., Stevens, M., Smart, D. and Hawes, W.R. (1992) *Workplace Industrial Relations in Transition*. Aldershot, Dartmouth

Mitchell, N. (1987) 'Changing pressure group politics: The case of the TUC, 1976–1984'. *British Journal of Political Science*, 17, 2, 261–74

Monks, J. (1998) 'Trade unions, enterprise and the future', in Sparrow, P.R. and Marchington, M. (eds) *Human Resource Management: The New Agenda*. London, Financial Times/Pitman Publishing

Nolan, P. and O'Donnell, K. (2003) 'Industrial relations, HRM and performance', in Edwards, P. (ed.) *Industrial Relations: Theory and Practice*, 2nd edn. Oxofrd, Blackwell

Organising Works (1995) Organising Works, no. 2. Melbourne, Organising Works

Pelling, H. (1992) *A History of British Trade Unionism*. Harmondsworth, Penguin

Pencavel, J. (2001) 'The surprising retreat of union Britain'. *Stanford Institute for Economic Policy Research*, SIEPR Discussion Paper No. 00-31

Prowse, P. (2003) 'Recruitment and representation amongst nurses in hospital trusts'. Research Paper, University of Bradford School of Management

Roberts, B.C. (1956) *Trade Union Government and Administration*. London, Bell

Rose, E. (1974) 'On the nature of work and union involvement: the case of London Busmen'. *Industrial Relations Journal*, 5, 2, 12–23

Salamon, M. (1998) *Industrial Relations: Theory and Practice*, 3rd edn. London, Prentice Hall

Smith, P. and Morton, G. (1993) 'Union exclusion and the decollectivisation of IR in contemporary Britain'. *British Journal of Industrial Relations*, 31, 1, 97–114

Smith, P. and Morton, G. (1994) 'Union exclusion in Britain: Next steps'. *Industrial Relations Journal*, 25, 1, 22–35

Taylor, R. (1978) *The Fifth Estate: Britain's Unions in the Seventies*. London, Routledge

Taylor, P. and Bain, P. (1999) 'An assembly line in the head: work and employee relations in the call centre'. *Industrial Relations Journal*, 30, 2, 27–42

Terry, M. (1995) 'Trade unions: shop stewards and the workplace', in Edwards, P. (ed.) *Industrial Relations: Theory and Practice in Britain*. Oxford, Blackwell

Terry, M. (2003) 'Employee representation: The shop stewards and the new legal framework', in Edwards, P. (ed.) *Industrial Relations: Theory and Practice*, 2nd edn, Oxford, Blackwell

TUC (1991) *Annual Report*. London, TUC

TUC (1997) *Annual Report*. London, TUC

TUC (1998) *Focus on Recognition: Trade Union Trends Survey on Union Recognition and Derecognition*. London, TUC

TUC (1999) *Trade Union Trends: Today's Trade Unionists*. London, TUC

TUC (2002) *Annual Report*. London, TUC

Turner, H.A. (1962) *Trade Union Growth, Structure and Policy*. London, Allen and Unwin

Undy, R. (2002) 'New Labour and New Unionism, 1997–2001: But is it the same old story?' *Employee Relations*, 24, 6, 638–55

Undy, R. and Martin, R. (1984) *Ballots and Trade Union Democracy*. Oxford, Blackwell

Undy, R., Ellis, W., McCarthy, W. and Halmos, A. (1981) *Change in Trade Unions*. London, Hutchinson

Verma, A., Kochan, T.A. and Wood, S. (2002) 'Union decline and prospects for revival'. *British Journal of Industrial Relations*, 40, 3, 373–84

Waddington, J. (2003) 'Trade union organisation', in Edwards, P. (ed.) *Industrial Relations: Theory and Practice*, 2nd edn. Oxford, Blackwell

Waddington, J. and Kerr, A. (1999) 'Membership retention in the public sector'. *Industrial Relations Journal*, 30, 2, 151–65

Waddington, J. and Whitson, C. (1995) 'Trade unions: Growth, structure and policy', in Edwards, P. (ed.) *Industrial Relations: Theory and Practice in Britain*. Oxford, Blackwell

Waddington, J. and Whitson, C. (1997) 'Why do people join unions during a period of membership decline?' *British Journal of Industrial Relations*, 35, 4, 515–46

Webb, S. and Webb, B. (1898) *Industrial Democracy*. London, Longman

Webb, S. and Webb, B. (1920) *The History of Trade Unionism 1866–1920*. London, Longman

WERS (1998) See Cully, M. *et al.* (1998)

Wood, S. (1997) *Statutory Union Recognition*. London, IPD

Wood, S., Moore, S. and Willman, P. (2002) 'Third time lucky for statutory union recognition in the UK?' *Industrial Relations Journal*, 33, 3, 215–33

CHAPTER 4

GOVERNMENT POLICY AND EMPLOYMENT RELATIONS

INTRODUCTION

Government is the third and most important 'actor' within the industrial relations 'system' (see Chapter 1). In general terms government may be defined as the political machinery or apparatus within which officials make policies and decisions either as elected representatives or by civil servants. Government can be regarded as both a process involving public policy-making to include legislation, policy directives and legislative proposals contained in green and white papers, and a formal structure responsible for the administrative policy-making process. Capitalist societies or states usually (but not always) have governments based on representative multi-party democracy and are termed liberal democracies. In Britain, the ideologies of the two main political parties, particularly when they have been in opposition, have traditionally operated to serve the different and opposing interests of the actors within the industrial relations system but, as we saw in Chapter 1, from 1946 until 1979, parties in government adopted liberal collectivist and corporatist policies which served the interests of both trade unions and employers to varying degrees. However, from 1979 until 1997 the succession of Conservative governments adopted the more radical policies of liberal individualism and neo-laissez-faire (see Chapter 1), with the emphasis upon market forces, and on individualism rather than collectivism. The succeeding New Labour governments chose not to revert to the corporatism of the 1970s, shedding the mantle of 'old Labour' in the process, and veering at times towards the individualism of the Conservatives.

There is some semantic confusion concerning the terms state and government in the industrial relations literature. Gospel and Palmer (1993) declare that 'the state is not synonymous with government' (p. 154) and that the government is part of the state and acts as its representative. A distinction is made, therefore, between government and state, where government is regarded as part of a range of state institutions that include the judiciary, the Civil Service, armed forces and police. While we would accept the validity of this distinction, it is the government of the day, whatever its political complexion, which is the active and only legislator and which, therefore, plays the most important part in influencing economic, political and social processes and institutions, including, of course, industrial relations. We therefore prefer, wherever possible and appropriate, to use the term 'government' rather than 'state', although occasionally both terms will be used where this is unavoidable.

The traditional role of government and the state in industrial relations embodies the view that government should be non-interventionist. Theoretically, this means that government should remain neutral between employers and employees and should intervene only in order to:

- protect the employment interests of employees when no other means of doing so are available;
- protect the wider interests of society as a whole when these are threatened by particular industrial pressure groups; and

- maintain an even balance of bargaining power between the interests of the buyers and sellers of labour.

While many still subscribe to this view, the approach of government to industrial relations has varied over time, as we shall see. At this stage, we need only point out that in reality the government has, and does, intervene in industrial relations in a variety of ways of which the following are examples:

- minimum employment rights and wage levels (minimum wage);
- economic policies, particularly in relation to prices and incomes;
- legislation to regulate the conduct of industrial disputes, collective bargaining and the activities of trade unions;
- conciliation and arbitration in industrial disputes; and
- activities to stimulate and improve the quality of the labour market.

Many of these interventions, which can take the form of statutory legislation and policy guidelines, have been relatively non-controversial as, for example, concerning the role of ACAS (see Chapter 1 for an overview of the role of ACAS which we will consider in greater detail in this chapter), which is a government agency whose role in the resolution of disputes is still highly valued by trade unions and employers alike. In other areas, however, government intervention can be highly controversial and unpopular with either trade unions or employers. For example, some of the employment legislation of the 1980s and 1990s is widely regarded as being ideologically motivated and contrary to the interests of trade unions.

In this chapter we start by looking briefly at the main theories underpinning the role of government generally and then go on to examine the historical and contemporary role of government as it affected industrial relations during the course of the twentieth century, and particularly during the post-Second World War period. We then go on to consider the effects of both economic policy and incomes policy upon the parties to industrial relations, together with the arguments concerning the desirability of minimum wage legislation. The legislative framework of industrial relations will be examined in some detail, again with regard to the changing role of government as legislator during the 1980s and 1990s, and this is followed by a review of the role and function of government agencies. The industrial relations agenda of the New Labour governments will then be examined and critically assessed, and the chapter ends with a consideration of the European Union, the 'Europeanisation' of employment relations and the impact upon UK industrial relations.

Learning outcomes

When you have read this chapter, you should be able to:

1. Describe the main theories underpinning government policy and account for the traditional and contemporary role of government in employment relations.

2. Trace the development of economic and incomes policy and the impact of these upon employment relations since 1945.

3. Explain the nature of statutory intervention and the role and functions of government agencies.

4. Critically examine the impact of New Labour's employment relations policies.

5. Understand the EU context of policy-making and evaluate its impact upon UK employment relations.

THEORETICAL OVERVIEW OF THE ROLE OF GOVERNMENT

As was mentioned in the introduction to this chapter, government in most capitalist societies is based upon representative multi-party democracy, and such societies are termed liberal democracies. There are, however, a number of competing and conflicting perspectives which seek to explain the role of government in liberal democratic societies. We will now consider these perspectives as they are crucial to our understanding of government policies which impact upon industrial relations.

The Marxist perspective

Basically, the Marxist argument is that the distribution of power in capitalist society is a reflection of the relationships of domination and subordination, which are determined primarily by the economic arrangements and mode of production of society. Marx terms this the relations of production, where production is organised socially in ways which have always created classes with opposed interests and unequal resources of power, so that one class will dominate others through economic exploitation. The social class that dominates the economic relations of production will also wield political power over other classes and by doing so maintains and enhances its dominant position in society. Hence the concentration of political power in one class enables that class to dominate others through economic exploitation and the extraction of maximum surplus value from the labour force. According to this analysis, government and the state represented the interests of the dominant capitalist class (also called the bourgeoisie) and were linked to the satisfaction of the economic interests of that dominant class. Thus Marx and Engels (1967) asserted that in capitalist society 'the executive of the modern state is but a committee for managing the common affairs of the whole bourgeoisie' (p. 26).

According to the Marxist analysis, therefore, the state and government in capitalist society are not an impartial referee in the power game, but a vehicle for the realisation of the interests of the bourgeoisie – an agency of class domination which provides the

illusion of serving the general or national will, while in reality acting as a cloak for class interests. Attempts by the bourgeoisie or dominant capitalist class to cultivate a picture of the state as being above particular group or class interests constitute an ideological strategy to legitimise its own dominant position. The state in turn, through government policies, agencies and institutions, is engaged in a constant exercise to legitimate the existing order. Furthermore, while the economic relations of capitalism give the dominant class control over material forces and political power in society, they are also able to control ideas and beliefs. That is, they possess ideological power, whereby a set of dominant values may be disseminated through major social institutions which justify or legitimise existing socio-economic and political arrangements, and hence their own dominant position. As Marx and Engels (1967) state: 'The ideas of the ruling class are, in every age, the ruling ideas. . . . The class which has the means of material production at its disposal has control at the same time over the means of mental production.'

Government and the state, according to this analysis, are not neutral but serve the interests of the bourgeoisie and legitimise their dominant position within society. The other classes subject to this degree of domination and exploitation Marx collectively termed the proletariat. The emergent proletariat of the Industrial Revolution soon came to realise that while their interests conflicted with those of the bourgeoisie, individually they were powerless against the employer within the employment relationship and that collective organisation could serve to redress some of the imbalance of power (see Chapter 6).

Self-Evaluation Activity 4.1

Redressing the power imbalance
Response on website

In what ways, according to a Marxist perspective, do you think the proletariat could redress the power imbalance within the capitalist state?

However, as we have seen (Chapter 3), economism has been the dominant motivation behind trade unions' theory and practice, and only rarely has trade union industrial action been geared towards control. The pursuit of financial improvements and better working conditions has been the guiding principle for action, which, while often involving bitter conflicts and protracted disputes, has essentially entailed working within the existing structure of capitalism and not systematically questioning its fundamental assumptions. Economistic trade unionism, then, generates an essentially parochial consciousness, and a collectivism limited in its scope by its lack of independence from the dominant value system of government, ownership and production.

Economistic orientations are reinforced and intensified by the sectionalism inherent in a trade union movement comprising organisations whose individual role is the representation of the interests of workers in specific occupations rather than those of a whole class. This generates what has been termed occupational consciousness, with trade unions – particularly of the craft variety – traditionally being concerned with guarding their status and maintaining differentials in reward in relation to other occupational groups at the expense of any massive class-based assault on capitalism.

In summary, then, the Marxist perspective considers the role of the state and government as serving the interests of the dominant capitalist bourgeoisie class. To the extent that the working class, or proletariat, did not provide the revolutionary opposition spearheaded by the trade union movement, the current Marxist argument is that the state and government have merely incorporated the union movement into the capitalist system by conceding certain economistic demands, thereby attracting criticism that the unions have 'sold out' to capitalism.

Democratic elitism

One of the most influential views of the nature and limits of democracy and government was propounded by Max Weber (1978), one of the 'founding fathers' of sociology, and modified by the economist Joseph Schumpeter (1976). In essence, Weber argued that representative multi-party democracy helps to defend society against both arbitrary decision-making on the part of political leaders and the appropriation

of power by bureaucrats. However, in both respects government and other democratic institutions have been less effective than the 'ideal' situation simply because political parties, as with other large institutions and organisations such as large trade unions, develop bureaucratic party machines and structures which threaten the autonomy of government. If a governing party with a large majority is simply able to dictate what is decided, and if the decision-making process is obscured, reducing Parliament to a mere 'talking shop', then the democratic process is much diluted.

In order for democratic systems to be effective, Weber argues that two conditions must be fulfilled. Firstly, there must be parties that represent different interests and have different outlooks. If the policies of competing parties are more or less the same, voters are denied effective choice. Secondly, there must be political leaders who are not caught up in the bureaucratic machinery and who are able to demonstrate leadership within a democratic context. Weber emphasises the importance of leadership within democratic government decision-making contexts, arguing that rule by leadership elites is inevitable and that the best we can hope for is that those elites effectively represent our interests. Multi-party democracy is valued more for the quality of leadership it generates than for the mass participation in politics that it makes possible.

Like Weber, Schumpeter argued that democracy is more important as a method of generating effective and responsible government than as a means of providing significant power for the majority. According to Schumpeter, democracy is the rule of the politician, not the people, and in order to achieve voting support, politicians must nevertheless be at least minimally responsive to the demands and interests of the electorate. Mechanisms of political democracy should be kept largely separate from economic life as the competitive market place provides a measure of consumer choice, just as a competitive system of parties provides at least a small measure of political choice.

Democratic elitism may, in part, explain why in liberal democracies any one political party in government at least minimally purports to represent the interests of those sections of the electorate which provide that party with ideological support. However, the electorate generally is portrayed by democratic elitists as being relatively passive and unenlightened; should, for example, a Labour government enact legislation supportive of workers' rights and trade union interests, it will do so on the assumption that individual citizens can have little or no direct influence on political decision-making and would have little motivation to exert such influence. Democratic elitism also assumes that the process and quality of governmental decision-making requires the expertise of professionals. The mass of the electorate, it is argued, cannot master the intricacies of the decisions which governments constantly have to take, but civil servants and elected members of representative bodies have the time to acquire specialist knowledge of issues. While 'experts' need to be constrained by the views of those affected by policies they formulate, they can make decisions on an informed basis. Nevertheless, democratic elitists reject the notion that groups representative of the electorate can be active partners or have a dynamic input on governmental decision-making.

Pluralism

The pluralist perspective is concerned with the diffusion of power within society, buttressed and safeguarded by a number of important mechanisms and institutions. The pluralist theorists such as Dahl (1961) were strongly influenced by the ideas of Weber and Schumpeter and recognise the existence of elites in modern liberal democracies. Unlike supporters of the Marxist analysis of the capitalist state and the role of government within it, pluralists argue that interests in modern society have become progressively diversified, so that a greater number of groups with particular interests and political demands to be satisfied have come to make their presence felt in the political arena and compete for power. For pluralists, the distinctive feature of a liberal democracy is that it is a political system of 'open' power groups, participating in the power game. The various groups are located in such institutional areas as business, government administration, parliamentary politics, labour, education and culture, and draw their membership from various social strata on the basis of merit and regardless of class, gender and ethnicity.

Liberal democracy, then, is characterised as a system of competing interest groups and elites where no single group is able to secure a monopoly of power and manipulate the system consistently to its exclusive advantage. One important assumption underlying the pluralist analysis is that different interest groups have influence only over a narrow range of issues of concern to themselves and therefore no one group's interests will prevail. This runs contrary to the Marxist emphasis on the prime importance of economic power residing in the hands of a small dominant economic class. According to pluralists, certain developments during the twentieth century strengthened their position and considerably weakened the Marxist analysis. These include:

- the greater role played by government in the economic affairs of the state and the growth of public ownership and nationalisation of public services and industries (now reversed by the privatisations of the 1980s and 1990s and maintained by New Labour);
- the increasing separation of ownership and control in private industry (see Chapter 2); and
- the growth of joint stock companies with an increase in and more diffuse shareholdings. This development was given a major impetus as a result of the privatisations of the 1980s–early 2000s (see Chapter 6 for details of privatisations).

Finally, pluralists argue that government policies within liberal democracies are influenced by continual processes of bargaining between numerous groups representing different interests; these competing interests may have some impact upon policy but none of them dominates the actual mechanisms of government. Government is therefore the neutral arbiter of different interests (more like a weather vane subject to the vagaries of wind speed and direction).

Self-Evaluation Activity 4.2

Summarising pluralism and Marxism
Response on website

Attempt a summary of the pluralist and Marxist perspectives on the role of government.

Concluding comments

Both the Marxist view that government is a tool of capitalism and is therefore ideologically motivated in all it does, and the pluralist perspective that the state is the neutral arbiter deciding between the claims of competing interest groups such as the TUC and CBI may be regarded as simplistic abstractions, and in many instances these conceptions of the role of government do not necessarily correspond to the reality of government decision-making within a complex society such as Britain's. We have already pointed out in the introduction to this chapter that the government in Britain has been and can be highly interventionist in all areas and industrial relations is no exception in this regard. Both Marxist and pluralist arguments accept that government intervenes; what is contentious is the nature of that intervention. From a largely pluralist perspective, for example, Gospel and Palmer (1993) state that:

> From the late 1960s . . . industrial relations became more intertwined [than in previous periods] with politics and politics with industrial relations. All recent governments have been concerned to introduce major changes in industrial relations law and practice. Both the TUC and CBI have favoured legislative changes that have provoked opposition from the other side. Fundamental differences in policy towards industrial relations have never been far from the centre of political debate. (p. 154)

Ideally, therefore, government should take the views of both the TUC and the CBI into consideration before acting upon policy decisions or legislating. During the 1960s and 1970s (the era of liberal collectivism and bargained corporatism) various governments, with some exceptions, managed to maintain a balance of power between the competing interest groups of the TUC and CBI within policy forums such as the National Economic Development Council (NEDC) set up by a Conservative government in 1962.

The opposing (Marxist) argument is that the purpose of government intervention is to protect the interests of capital from the encroachments of trade unions upon management's right to manage. Within the context of early 'Thatcherism' Hyman (1984) asserts:

> While Thatcherite anti-unionism is embedded in a visceral ideological hostility, it also reflects an integrated economic analysis. The succession of anti-union laws, the attacks on public welfare, the privatisation of state industries and services, the deliberate creation of mass unemployment, are all logical reflections of a passionate faith in the virtues of competitive capitalism. (p. 222)

Furthermore, government 'non-intervention' cannot be regarded as government neutrality if by not intervening capitalist interests are protected. Edwards (1994), in his analysis of the role of the state, argues that capitalist states in justifying the accumulation of capital (and profits) attempt to legitimise the exploitative nature of the capitalist system of production as manifested within the workplace. Beaumont (1992) and others, however, steer an intermediate path and argue that government neither supports and protects the capitalist mode of production nor is a 'slave' to capitalism. On the other hand, they argue that the state is rarely, if ever, a neutral arbiter of conflicting interests. Neither the Marxist nor the pluralist view may be 'correct', and as Farnham and Pimlott (1995) point out, the economic and social commitments and role of government have actually increased over the past 50 years and 'the pressures for State intervention in industrial relations have been both cumulative and inevitable' (p. 211).

ROLE OF GOVERNMENT IN HISTORICAL CONTEXT TO 1979

The role of government in British employment relations can be divided into five main phases:

1. The period of *laissez-faire* based on the liberal individualist ideology of the nineteenth century.
2. The period of *collective laissez-faire*, prevalent throughout the first half of the twentieth century.
3. The period of *bargained corporatism* of the post-Second World War era from 1945 to 1979.
4. The period of *neo-laissez-faire* of the Conservative governments from 1980 to 1997.
5. The period of *post-laissez-faire* of New Labour which we consider later in this chapter.

In this section, the first three periods only are considered.

The laissez-faire period

Laissez-faire embodied the principle of non-interference or non-intervention by government during the nineteenth century. This was accompanied by the development of a 'voluntary' system of industrial relations referred to as voluntarism, which is defined as the **preference of employers, trade unions and the government to decide of their own free will on matters concerning the regulation of the employment relationship and the conduct of industrial relations.** Laissez-faire meant that the primacy of free markets, and, in particular, the labour market, determined the process and outcomes of procedures and agreements. Hobsbawm (1974) provides an amusing and illustrative description of the laissez-faire ideology:

> The orthodoxy of laissez-faire economic liberalism had the force of natural law: a world in which, as in Newtonian physics, prices like water found their natural level; wages, like stones, when unnaturally raised, must come down, and pint-pots did not hold quarts. It was an orthodoxy which made virtually no provision (at least in the all-important field of production) for 'state interference', whose effects, when not directed to 'the sole purpose of disestablishing state interference' must be ruinous. (p. 260)

Laissez-faire, then, was concerned with the pursuit of self-interest unfettered by any constraints upon the actions of both employees and employers who were free to enter into individual contracts. This led to the unregulated growth of industry and the factory system together with increasingly intolerable levels of economic exploitation. As was pointed out in Chapter 3, the paradoxical consequence of this was the development of a more organised trade union movement during the latter half of the nineteenth century and a growing collectivist orientation towards regulating the employment relationship.

Collective laissez-faire

The legal doctrines of 'restraint of trade' (see Chapter 2), which prohibited workers organising collectively and taking industrial action, were finally removed and trade unions were finally granted legal immunities. Hyman (2003) states that: 'The method by which trade unions and collective bargaining were eventually legalised was not, as in many countries, by establishing a positive right to organise, to negotiate and to strike, but by defining an area of industrial relations immunities where the effect of the common law [law made by judges] was inhibited' (p. 39). While the Trades Disputes Act 1906 removed the legal impediments to collective bargaining and industrial action (within limits), this Act and subsequent legislation did not give trade unions the legal right to organise workers or to take industrial action. McIlroy (1991) comments that:

> The legal acceptance of trade unionism, crucially in 1871, 1875 and 1906, did not take the form of a bill of rights, or a developed legal code or a transformation of the judiciary. The armistice the cautious conservative union leaders sought involved no direct assault on the legal framework. Instead the trade unions sought exemption from the common law – not its replacement by a system of positive rights to organise, bargain and strike. If the social, political and economic role of trade unions is fully accepted, then it can be seen that the consequent system of immunities by which unions were granted protection from common law doctrines of restraint of trade, conspiracy and inducement to breach of contract were not 'privileges' which 'placed trade unions above the law'. The system of immunities simply constituted the method by which unions were given basic rights to exist, organise and bargain. (p. 3)

The government tradition of legal abstentionism, or non-intervention, was therefore not compromised and the principle of voluntarism remained largely intact. There was an acceptance of the principle of collective organisation and bargaining which distinguished this period from the previous one, but the fact that there was no statutory endorsement of collective bargaining and no notion of a legal collective contract made Britain unique in this respect, as other European governments have legislated in this area giving European trade unions the positive collective rights which British trade unions do not have. Governments during this period have generally been 'reluctant legislators' and, despite acting on the Whitley Reports' recommendations (see Chapter 6), legislation on individual employment conditions, for example, has been much weaker in Britain than in other European countries. As Hyman (2003) points out: 'When governments assumed an industrial relations role, this was most often restricted to providing assistance to collective bargainers' (p. 40).

The main areas where government did legislate with regard to the employment relationship included:

- the introduction of health and safety requirements in particular industries or processes;
- the regulation of the employment of women and young persons;
- minimum wage regulation in certain trades; and
- machinery for conciliation and arbitration in industrial disputes.

Bargained corporatism: the beginning of the end of voluntarism

'Corporatism' is the term used to describe a society dominated by large organisations whose activities and relations are co-ordinated and planned rather than being determined by competition in the market or by conflict (see also Chapter 1).

Self-Evaluation Activity 4.3

Becoming a corporatist state
Response on website

Can you think of any trends and developments since 1945 which suggested that Britain was becoming a 'corporatist' state? You can refer back to Chapter 1 if you wish.

The post-war governments built upon the experience of direct intervention in the economy, which became necessary during the Second World War. The period from 1945 until 1979 witnessed a number of fundamental changes in the way government managed the economy, and, with the possible exception of the Conservative government of 1971–4, government policy was fairly consistent in its attempts to achieve a consensus on economic and industrial relations issues. Governments remained committed to free collective bargaining which represented a continuation of the laissez-faire approach that dominated previous periods, but at the same time increasingly favoured direct intervention to regulate incomes in the form of incomes policies (considered later in this chapter) while making concessions to trade unions in other areas of social, industrial and economic policy. This 'trade-off' approach, which involved tripartite decision-making within the various quasi-governmental bodies referred to above, became known as bargained corporatism.

The nature of the changes in the way governments managed the economy were both fundamental and complex. Firstly, Keynesian methods of intervention with government managing effective demand – expanding it in a slump and dampening it in an upturn (derisively known at present as the economics of 'boom and bust') – became the new and relatively successful conventional wisdom. One important policy aim was the maintenance of full employment. The guarantee of full employment gradually gave trade unionists greater confidence and increased bargaining power. Pressures to maintain full employment and expand the welfare state resulted in increases in taxation and public (government) borrowing which in turn produced pressures for increased wages, higher prices and a declining national competitive edge.

Secondly, awareness of declining economic growth rates and the resurgence of wage and price inflation led to attempts from the mid-1960s to introduce prices and incomes policies. The attempted regulation of prices and incomes and to relate pay increases more directly to productivity increases failed primarily because of the decentralised nature of collective bargaining (see Chapter 6), which gave shop stewards considerable power and leeway to bargain over pay and conditions independent of national union leaderships and unfettered by legal constraints.

Thirdly, the failure of state intervention concerning the incomes policies of the 1960s led to a greater emphasis on the reform of industrial relations and trade union structures which resulted in the Donovan Commission Report of 1968 (see Chapters 1 and 6). White papers produced by both the Labour government (*In Place of Strife*) and the Conservative opposition (*Fair Deal at Work*) expressed both parties' intentions to legislate in order to curb industrial action and reform industrial relations. However, none of the legislative proposals contained any provision to put collective bargaining on a legal footing by making collective agreements legally binding, although there was a presumption within the 1971 Industrial Relations Act that collective agreements were presumed to be legally binding upon the parties unless the parties stated their intention to the contrary. The repeal of the Conservative Industrial Relations Act in 1974 restored the status quo ante but the British economy continued to decline during the 1970s.

Fourthly, continued economic decline, rising inflation and a sustained high level and incidence of industrial disputes encouraged a consensus amongst politicians of all major parties that trade unions must be reformed if relative economic decline was not to become absolute and that free collective bargaining was incompatible with full employment and price stability. This encouraged the Wilson and Callaghan governments to introduce the Social Contract, probably the best example of bargained corporatism during the post-war period. In return for the maintenance of full employment, welfare state expenditure and greater state intervention on prices, the trade union leaders would control incomes growth. The policy of non-intervention or legal abstentionism was put in doubt by the provisions of the Trade Union and Labour Relations Acts (1974, 1976), the Employment Protection Acts (1975, 1978) and the Health and Safety At Work Act (1974) which 'sought to placate the unions and stimulate both employers and unions to introduce many of the procedural and institutional reforms recommended by the Donovan Report – rather than relying on the voluntaristic tradition of prodding and exhortation' (McIlroy, 1991, p. 6).

By 1978 there was more legislation than ever before affecting employment relations either directly or indirectly. It dealt with both 'individual' issues such as unfair dismissal and redundancy, and 'collective' matters concerning union recognition, the closed shop and shop steward facilities. McIlroy (1991) points out that these developments meant that the government 'had carried out a quiet revolution in legal abstention and this, combined with incomes policy, heralded the wake of voluntarism' (p. 7). All this, however, did little to solve the 'union problem'. From 1974 to 1979, unemployment increased to 1.3 million, there were cuts in the welfare state and real living standards fell. By 1978 it became clear that the Social Contract had failed to alleviate Britain's economic problems; it had become a policy of wage restraint aimed at lowering unit labour costs.

Postscript: 1979 and the end of voluntarism

By 1979, successive attempts to solve Britain's economic problems had failed. The use of legislation to curb trade union activity in some areas and encourage it in others was by now nothing new as witnessed by the 1971 Industrial Relations Act and the 1974–8 legislation. However, the failure of some of this legislation and the economic and industrial relations problems besetting the government, culminating in the so-called 'Winter of Discontent', resulted in electoral defeat and the first Conservative government led by Mrs Thatcher.

Self-Evaluation Activity 4.4

Summarising
Response on website

Summarise the distinguishing features of both collective laissez-faire and bargained corporatism. (Use one sentence for each.)

ALL CHANGE: NEO-LAISSEZ-FAIRE: 1980–97

The political approach which emerged with the election of the first Thatcher government in 1979, marked a return to laissez-faire individualism in many respects reminiscent of the nineteenth century. The extract in Exhibit 4.1 from Will Hutton's book, *The State We're In*, seeks to explain why 1979 was such a watershed date, not only for industrial relations but for the whole British economy and society; while Mrs Thatcher's policies were highly retrograde and divisive, there could nevertheless be no return to what, in comparison with the Thatcher years, seemed like the Golden Age of Keynesian economics.

Exhibit 4.1

1979: The crucial year?

1979 . . . was a crucial year. It was the moment when Conservative England reclaimed its institutions and traditions from the attempt to bend them to a social democratic cause. Labour's weakness had made the 1974 government a dismal affair. . . . But Labour's inadequacies were only part of the story. . . . More and more businessmen, officials and opinion-formers began to line up behind Mrs Thatcher and her programme. This was partly because the credit boom gave it the illusion of success; but also because the language of free markets, sound money and individual choice had a profound resonance. Mrs Thatcher was speaking for a set of values that had existed long before the post-war consensus.

Sound money and limits on public spending implied no more than a return to the orthodoxies of the 'Treasury view' that Keynes had mocked in the 1930s, while the promotion of competition, free trade and low taxation drew on a tradition that reached back to the eighteenth century. Moreover, the teachings of neo-liberal economics, with the emphasis that the general good can only result from the free interplay of supply and demand, now seemed to be in harmony with the thinking of a straight-talking politician. . . . Resources were best allocated where there was more competition; government regulation did stand in the way of market forces; and trade unions did force up the price of labour.

But something deeper was also at work. The British state had not been designed actively to intervene in economic management at either national or local level. The Civil Service tradition that officials should not engage in private sector activity remained strong [and] the accent was still placed on administration rather than intervention; on high policy rather than commercial strategy. So the state had no apparatus for making British industrial policies work and its efforts were undermined by a latent value system always ready to return to an earlier relationship between state, society and economy. Once Keynesianism had been discredited, Mrs Thatcher's job was more to disinter laissez-faire than to reinvent it. The England of Adam Smith, John Stuart Mill and Herbert Spencer had been submerged by the rise of Keynes, the welfare state and the attempt at government direction of the economy, but it had not been extinguished.

Once uncovered, these foundations supported fifteen years of building Conservative hegemony. But the theory was to prove a poor master and the results disappointing. . . . Yet the clock cannot be put back – nor should it be. The post-war settlement may have stopped the rot, but it did not solve the basic British problem. Keynesian economics as practised in the UK had its limits. Industrial policy was not a success; incomes policies were an ignominious failure. The welfare state was creaking at the seams, unable to meet the new demands placed upon it. Productivity growth was poor. It is true that income inequality narrowed and wealth became more equitably distributed and that, compared with what went on before and what was to follow, the period can appear like a Golden Age. But even within its own terms it was unsustainable. If Britain cannot go back, to continue on the present path offers little but social polarisation, political authoritarianism and economic weakness.

Source: Hutton, 1995, pp. 52–5

The essential characteristics of the Thatcher and Major years of neo-laissez-faire or the new liberalism were:

- a resurgence of capitalist values (free enterprise, open markets, deregulation, individualism, privatisation) and abandonment of Keynesian 'mixed economy' economics;

- avid pursuit of monetarist supply-side economics;

- a concerted attempt to weaken the fabric of collective bargaining in order to allow market forces much greater impact on pay and conditions of employment; and

- the gradual dismantling of tripartism (Crouch, 2003).

Some of the main features of this period were, firstly, the introduction of government statutory interventions and legislation to reduce the influence and bargaining power of trade unions; a succession of statutes introduced further legal constraints on the freedom of unions to organise and on their ability to use industrial action in the bargaining process. Secondly, the government used high interest rates and financial control of the public sector, rather than incomes policies, to control inflation which helped to sustain the consistently high levels of unemployment. Thirdly, the government introduced legislation which enabled the privatisation of major nationalised industries and services with important industrial relations consequences (see Chapter 6).

In other ways, however, the period of new liberalism significantly reduced the level of intervention consistent with government adherence to the basic policies of both Friedman (1962, 1968) and the Chicago School and Hayek (1978) and the Austrian School of monetarist economics. Measures affecting the employment relationship were justified by government using the argument that existing laws imposed outdated restrictions upon employment opportunities; the effect of many of these measures, however, was to reduce the statutory protection and rights of individual employees. These measures included:

- the reduction of employee rights in relation to unfair dismissal;
- the curtailment of the role and functions of wages councils and their ultimate abolition; and
- the repeal of certain of the protective statutes relating to the employment of women and young persons.

Crouch (1995) summarises the effect of the legislation:

> *The post-1979 Conservative governments have had a strong neo-liberal ideology. This has predisposed them: to reject Keynesian demand management and the search for full employment; to oppose policy deals with trade unions that would involve taking action incompatible with neo-liberal principles; and to reject relations with organisations of interests – on both sides of business but especially on the labour side – that interfered with neo-liberal policy priorities.* (p. 238)

The Conservative programme

The Conservative programme was thus founded on a combination of the political ideology of laissez-faire individualism or neo-liberalism and the monetarist policy of Hayek and Friedman (see the next section). The main areas of policy affecting industrial relations were concerned with:

1. The control and eventual elimination of inflation.
2. The control of public expenditure.
3. The strengthening of market forces.
4. The curbing of trade union power.
5. The abandonment of tripartism.

The control of inflation

The Conservative governments endorsed the argument that the elimination of inflation should be the main economic policy objective which displaced the post-war consensus policy of maintaining full employment. Keynesian-inspired inflation hindered the operation of the free-enterprise market system by encouraging unions to exploit their bargaining power in order to keep wages artificially high. By controlling inflation, the constraints upon the labour and product market (trade unions and employers) could be overcome, and markets would operate more efficiently. The control of inflation (and therefore of prices and incomes) could not be achieved without dismantling many of the controls which inhibited the operation of free markets, imposed by previous 'corporatist' governments. MacInnes (1987) points out that:

> *The inertia of too much state control, the lack of commitment to enterprise, the assumption that extra wage demands or profits or public spending could be passed on through higher prices or taxes and mopped up by general inflation; all these would be 'squeezed out' of the system along with inflation.* (p. 50)

The attempt to control inflation had not been wholly successful during the period of Conservative government. One important problem as Crouch (2003) argues was the tendency for wages of skilled workers to rise during periods of economic recovery, which was 'largely a result of the neglect of training and other elements of skill provision during recessions, leading to skill shortages which firms seek to resolve through wage rises' (p. 242). The effect of counter-inflationary policies as far as industrial relations was concerned was that government took the TUC and CBI out of the pay determination equation. Both bodies were no longer consulted by government and negotiators were left to their own devices in the knowledge that high unemployment, high interest rates and exchange rates, as market mechanisms, would facilitate pay settlements more in line with government counter-inflation targets.

The control of public expenditure

Closely related to the control of inflation by restricting the supply of money is the problem of controlling public expenditure. Monetarists such as Friedman argue that any effort to control inflation requires a reduction of government deficits (basically, the difference between what a government spends and what it receives in revenue), but whereas Friedman and his associates argue that the main reason for reducing budget deficits is to enhance individual freedom, Minford and the now defunct 'Liverpool School' of monetarism argued that inflation would never be brought under control unless budget deficits are significantly reduced as a matter of priority (Minford, 1985). Conservative governments therefore believed that public expenditure should decline in relation to private expenditure both in order to 'set the market free' and to control inflation. Another related strand of policy was that of tax reductions as an antidote to large pay increases, the assumption being that if workers were paying fewer taxes they would accept lower pay increases.

However, in real terms, public expenditure did not come down until the end of the 1980s, and by the 1990s it had resumed its upward course. Attempts to reduce expenditure through the imposition of 'cash limits' within the public and local authority sectors meant that employers in these sectors had to settle pay claims either above the cash limit or 'ceiling', in which case the excess expenditure had to be met by increased efficiencies or unemployment (or both), or within the limit, which would prevent unemployment but also depress wage increases.

If local authorities pursued the latter course, both employers and union representatives could accuse the government of endorsing a public sector pay policy. Indeed, during the 1990s there were more determined efforts by the Major governments to impose a pay ceiling upon the public sector.

The strengthening of market forces

It was the declared intention of the Conservative governments to 'roll back the frontiers of the state' and significantly reduce state intervention in the economy. New liberals were very critical of the general direction of industrial policy since the 1930s, which was characterised by freely available government subsidies, grants and loans, controls on the movement of foreign exchange, on the labour market and employment. All these controls, monetarists argued, interfered with the 'evolutionary process of the market whereby consumers' interests are served' (Green, 1987, p. 197), and in particular tended to eradicate or distort the price mechanism. The measures put into effect included the following:

- Along with controls on prices and wages, all controls on foreign exchange movements were abolished which gave companies the opportunity to move capital and revenue overseas. This enabled British companies to take advantage of product and labour markets overseas with possible adverse consequences for local labour.
- A new Industry Act did away with the provision for planning agreements and cut public subsidies to industry, including regional aid.
- Enterprise zones, in which firms were to be exempt from tax and 'red tape' constraints, were established in a number of depressed regions even though they were criticised by the right-wing Adam Smith Institute for becoming 'subsidy islands'. The Institute favoured a strategy whereby all small business should be treated as a 'general experimental zone' of the economy.
- The transfer of state-owned assets to the private sector (privatisation) was pursued in order to reduce the size of the public sector, to extend the 'property-owning democracy' by providing windfall gains for small investors, to introduce market forces and restructure industrial relations

and to provide the government with a one-off source of revenue which the former Conservative Prime Minister Harold Macmillan criticised as 'selling off the family silver' (see Chapter 6).

- Withdrawal of the state from the labour market meant the abolition of industry training boards which introduced training opportunities for companies to take advantage of, and which monitored training standards.
- Measures were introduced in order to increase competition within the newly privatised industries, a policy which New Labour governments have since endorsed. Many examples abound, including the deregulation of bus transport and the break-up of British Rail into constituent rail companies.
- The Enterprise Allowance Scheme was introduced in order to encourage unemployed people to become self-employed.

All of these measures had an indirect effect upon industrial relations. The free-play of the market mechanism favoured by the Conservative governments also included measures which directly influenced industrial relations and which we will consider in a later section of this chapter.

The curbing of trade union power

New liberals have been severe critics of 'trade union privileges'. Hayek (1984) argued that trade unions contributed to Britain's economic decline and attributed their (in his opinion) unwarranted power to legal privileges, and that the immunity from civil liability, initially granted by the 1906 Trade Disputes Act, is the chief culprit:

> These legalised powers of the unions have become the biggest obstacle to raising the living standards of the working class as a whole. They are the chief cause of the unnecessarily big differences between the best and worst paid workers. They are the prime source of unemployment. They are the main reason for the decline of the British economy in general. (p. 52)

Hayek was, of course, a staunch advocate of individualism and the freedom of the individual worker to decide whether he or she wishes the conditions of

his or her employment to be determined individually or collectively. Trade unions, Hayek argued, have now become the 'open enemies of the ideal of freedom of association by which they once gained the sympathy of true liberals. Freedom of association means the freedom to decide whether one wants to join an association or not' (ibid., p. 61). Hayek, therefore, attached great importance to trade union reform and stated that 'there can be no salvation for Britain until the special privileges granted to trade unions three-quarters of a century ago are revoked' (ibid., p. 58). Hayek was writing in the late 1970s, and the Thatcher and Major governments introduced a number of measures purportedly to remove some of the most 'damaging' trade union 'privileges', as we shall see later in the chapter. What is not in doubt is that from being 'centre stage' in tripartite decision-making, as far as pre-1979 corporatist government was concerned, trade unions became sidelined and peripheral to the decisions of the Conservative governments.

Kessler and Bayliss (1998) identify five reasons why the new liberals found trade union power objectionable:

1. Unions were too powerful in relation to pay determination: 'They pushed up pay beyond what was compatible with effective performance in the international economy. They protected practices which prevented increases in productivity. They stood out against changes which managers proposed in the interests of efficiency. They usurped managerial authority where they could, especially in the public services' (ibid., p. 60).
2. The very existence of trade unions was antithetical to the workings of the 'unfettered' labour market. While, of course, even the Conservative governments would not want to legislate for union derecognition, their very presence contradicted everything new liberalism stood for. It may be reasonably inferred, therefore, that government would not stand in the way of any employer who wished to derecognise unions. Kessler and Bayliss argue that: 'the banning of trade unions at GCHQ [Government Communication Headquarters] Cheltenham in 1984, though brought about for other reasons, showed that the government was prepared to practice what it preached' (ibid., p. 60).

Mini case 4.1
The GCHQ affair

From its establishment in 1947, employees at GCHQ were encouraged to join trade unions. In Mrs Thatcher's second term things changed. In January 1984 the Minister for the Civil Service, acting under powers given to him, issued an instruction which changed the terms and conditions of employment of those working at GCHQ. From now on they would be prohibited from being members of a trade union and would only be entitled to belong to a staff association. This body required the approval of the Director of GCHQ and its rules prohibited industrial action and affiliation to other union bodies. At the same time the legal right of GCHQ staff to take a case to industrial tribunal was withdrawn.

The issue was fought through the courts, but GCHQ workers had little chance of victory as in English law there is no positive right to belong to a trade union. They argued that on broad grounds of *natural justice* there had been no consultation with the unions before the decision was taken. The House of Lords agreed with the view that the unions had a right to be consulted before their members' terms and conditions were drastically revised. But the Law Lords decided that this right was outweighed by the interest of the state in national security – and the government was custodian of that interest. What the government saw as required *was* required by national security. The ban on union membership was, the Law Lords accepted, genuinely motivated by government fears over the national security issue, and it was acting within its legal rights.

The European Court of Human Rights decided that the case was inadmissible as the international convention allows governments to impose non-trade unionism on the army, police force and certain categories of state employee. In November 1988, 25 000 workers took some form of action in support of the 18 remaining trade unionists at GCHQ, another four of whom were threatened with the sack. Despite heroic tenacity on the part of many workers, by 1989 trade unionism had all but been uprooted in GCHQ.

Source: Adapted from McIlroy, 1991, p. 78

In 1997, the New Labour government fulfilled its pledge to restore recognition rights to GCHQ employees.

3. The new liberal Conservative governments swept away consensus politics and the bargained corporatism associated with it in order both to minimise union influence in government decision-making and to confine unions' activities to bargaining with employers.
4. Government hostility towards collectivism was reinforced by the idea of putting the individual employee first and the belief that employees should not be coerced into joining unions if they did not wish to do so. 'The coercion to which they were subjected could be removed by putting an end to the closed shop, by limiting picketing and the extent of lawful strike action, and by the introduction of ballots which would enable individuals to assert themselves against the small group of activists who dominated the affairs of unions' (Kessler and Bayliss, 1995, p. 62).
5. There was opposition towards the accumulated legislative protection given to trade unions and their members during the period of Labour government from 1974 to 1979. As Kessler and Bayliss point out, the Conservative Party manifesto endorsed the party view that unions were dominated by a small minority of 'extremists' and the Labour government had given unions privileges 'without responsibility'.

Unions were therefore to be 'cut down to size', as McIlroy (1991) argues:

> Changes in employment legislation dealing with union recognition and the closed shop would enable members to leave trade unions. They would be denied political purchase and their leaders would no longer be consulted by Cabinet or treated to 'beer and sandwiches' by the Prime Minister. Legislation on strikes and picketing would mean that unions would find it harder to deliver. Members would in consequence find membership less attractive. Wider policies such as privatisation would also undermine union power by depriving them of the fertile breeding ground of a complacent monopoly employer. Management would be freer to operate according to the dictates of the market rather than the whims of shop stewards and union leaders. This would be particularly important given the changing pattern of industry. If the blitz on manufacturing industry

of the early 1980s had the beneficial side-effect of decimating many of the strongholds of trade unionism, it was vital that the poisonous weed of the old trade unionism should not take root in the new hi-tech industries. A key purpose of legislation was the restriction of trade unionism in the industries of the year 2000. (p. 16)

The abandonment of tripartism

Trade unions, the TUC and, to a large extent, the CBI were sidelined by government as we have noted, together with the other corporatist baggage of tripartite co-operation. When the first Conservative government was elected, there were basically six tripartite channels:

- The National Economic Development Council (NEDC).
- The Manpower Services Commission (MSC).
- The Advisory, Conciliation and Arbitration Service (ACAS).
- The Health and Safety Commission.
- The Equal Opportunity Commission (EOC) and the Commission for Racial Equality (CRE) (see Chapter 12).
- The wages councils.

The NEDC was established in 1961 and provided a regular discussion forum for government, unions (TUC) and employers (CBI) in considering both general and specific matters relating to the economy. The administration of these matters was conducted by the National Economic Development Office (NEDO) which provided the three parties with evaluations of issues and statistical data and analysis. The NEDC was not abolished immediately; it was rather a slow death, with government having 'neither industrial policy nor tasks for the union and employer organisations that could provide a serious agenda' (Crouch, 1995, p. 248). The death knell was finally sounded in 1987 and the NEDC was abolished in 1992 after being virtually moribund for the previous five years.

The MSC was formed in 1973 in order to revitalise training and manpower policy, and to take over other Department of Employment functions of manpower forecasting together with the administration of local employment offices and job centres in providing a placement service and employment advice. The first Conservative government significantly reduced its functions, but between 1983 and 1987 the MSC assumed a higher profile by undertaking the controversial task of securing 'changes in the education system that the Department of Education and Science seemed reluctant to pursue' (ibid., p. 249). Basically, this involved the devising of training schemes and the provision of vocational education and even the devising of parts of the school curriculum. While there was an input into the MSC by both TUC and CBI, government largely ignored TUC arguments opposing the policy of securing reductions in the wages of trainees and increases in the pressures on the young unemployed to opt for training rather than unemployment pay. In 1987 the role of the MSC changed again; its functions were diluted, trade union representation was reduced while employer representation increased, and in 1988 the MSC was renamed the Training Commission and placed under the direct control of the Department of Employment. The Employment Act of 1989 abolished the Commission and replaced it with a Training Agency under the direct control of government; by 1991 the Training Agency itself was abolished to be replaced by a national network of Training and Enterprise Councils (TECs) run by unelected local business leaders, co-opted trade union leaders and senior educational personnel.

ACAS lost many of its functions during the 1980s (for an overview of the functions of ACAS, see Chapter 1). The Health and Safety Commission continued its work largely unhindered during the period. The various inspectorates were co-ordinated and grouped into a Health and Safety Executive, responsible for the administration of the health and safety regulations backed up by union-appointed workplace safety representatives. Finally, wage councils were the longest standing of the tripartite bodies set up in 1945 to deal with the problem of low pay; it was not until 1986 that there was a serious attempt to abolish the councils which did result in a diminution of their powers, rendering them virtually ineffective until they were finally abolished in 1993. As Crouch (2003) points out, the 1977 New Labour government 'made virtually no changes to this policy of gradually disappearing tripartism' (p. 121).

Self-Evaluation Activity 4.5

Summarising

Response on website

Summarise the main elements of the new liberal programme as it affected industrial relations.

Concluding comments

The monetarist era is now over, but its legacy remains: the industrial relations map is considerably redrawn since 1979 and, for the time being at least, no substantial change to the legislative framework introduced by the Conservatives is envisaged by the New Labour government whose agenda we will consider later in the chapter. Given the political ideology of the Conservatives, legislation and policy initiatives reflecting that ideology were inevitable. All that was considered sacrosanct under the corporatist era was attacked; the 'market' now led and the march towards unleashing its forces would create many casualties in its wake, ranging from the growing number of unemployed to the trade unions suffering from ignominious defeats, as with the NUM in 1984.

GOVERNMENT ECONOMIC AND INCOMES POLICY: 1945–99

Government economic policy – which we considered briefly in Chapter 1 – has important and fundamental consequences for industrial relations, and may be defined as **the strategy and measures adopted by government to manage the economy as a means of achieving its economic objectives**. In general terms, governments at the macro level are concerned with securing the objectives of:

- full employment;
- price stability (that is, a low rate of inflation);
- economic growth; and
- balance of payments equilibrium.

In practice, given the complexities of the economy and its exposure to international influences, the simultaneous achievement of all these objectives is virtually impossible, so that a degree of prioritising is necessary. Inevitably, political as well as economic considerations will influence this process. Of the economic policy objectives, it is, perhaps, full employment and price stability which have the most immediate impact upon industrial relations, and in view of the fact these two objectives tend to conflict with each other, what is important from an industrial relations viewpoint is where a government puts the emphasis.

Self-Evaluation Activity 4.6

Economic objectives

The response is given below

The priority accorded to different economic objectives will reflect the ideology of the government of the day. Can you expand on this in general terms? Why do you think that full employment and price stability conflict with each other?

Put simply, governments with a broadly left-wing ideology tend to favour widespread state ownership of the means of production and detailed intervention in the economy as a means of achieving their economic objectives, while governments with a broadly right-wing ideology tend to favour limited state ownership and minimum government intervention in the economy, relying instead on the market mechanism.

Full employment enhances the bargaining power of workers and their unions and thus enables them to force up wages and salaries. Pay increases may lead in turn to price increases and hence to inflation. It follows that unemployment, as we have seen over the past 20 years or so, helps to keep the rate of inflation down. (We examine this in greater detail in this chapter.) It is possible to achieve the aims of full employment and price stability at the same time, but only if government, employers and unions can reach some consensus on a prices and incomes policy – which they have not been able to achieve, at least not for long! It is difficult to achieve such a consensus because such policies, even with a system of bargained corporatism in operation, are difficult to administer; the problem of how to agree a 'norm', how to deal with justified exceptions to the norm, and the means of enforcement is a very complex one. Perhaps the main reason for not arriving at a consensus is because conceptions of what would be a 'fair' prices and incomes policy differ. For example, there is no agreement as to the relative worth of different industries and occupations. There is usually agreement that there should be exceptions, such as the low-paid groups which are 'seriously out of line', or groups where it is in the 'national interest' to encourage growth. But there is always argument as to which groups actually fall into – or outside – these categories. We shall be considering this aspect later.

At the macroeconomic policy level, various general measures can be used by governments operating in mixed economies to achieve their objectives, including fiscal policy (the manipulation of tax rates and government expenditure), monetary policy (the control of the money supply and interest rates), prices and incomes policy (controls on costs and prices), and the management of the exchange rate. These policies are augmented at a more specific level by measures designed to encourage industrial investment, research and development and to protect consumer interest. Fiscal and monetary policies are the main measures used by governments in Britain since 1945.

Approaches to the management of the economy

We shall look in some detail at three basic approaches to the management of the economy as they affect employment relations (the first two of these were briefly considered in Chapter 1):

- Keynesian demand management;
- monetarism and supply-side economics; and
- the rational expectations model.

Initially, however, it is important to understand what is meant by the inflation phenomenon.

Inflation and deflation

We had a brief look at inflation in Chapter 1 when we described inflation as an increase in prices or the cost of living. One 'explanation' of the cause of inflation is related to the level of demand in the economy, and it is here that the terms deflation and reflation come in. Any policy that results in a fall

in the level of demand can be described as a deflationary policy, and anything that leads to a rise in demand as a reflationary policy. It is possible that a reflationary policy may also be inflationary, but this is not always the case. Inflation can be caused by changes in aggregate (total) demand and by changes in aggregate supply.

As far as changes in aggregate supply are concerned, one of the main determinants of the price of a commodity, good or service is the cost of supplying it. An increase in the costs of production often takes the form of increased wage costs brought about by a situation in which groups of workers bid up wages, and this is called cost- or wage-push inflation. In the international context these cost increases could be increases in the cost of essential raw materials brought about by producers' cartels flexing their political and economic muscle (such as the rise in price of OPEC oil in the 1970s). Alternatively, these increases in costs may be attributable to natural causes such as late frosts ruining the coffee bean harvest.

Inflation is also caused by shifts in aggregate demand so that an increase in the aggregate price level can be caused by an increase in aggregate demand. For example, titanium is an essential but rare metal used in the construction of some aircraft and the supply of titanium is fixed for a certain period. If the demand for titanium increases (maybe because the demand for new aircraft is increasing, or different uses have been found for titanium), then the price of titanium will rise because buyers are competing against each other to secure larger proportions of the fixed supply. This relationship between demand and supply affects all commodities and services, including, of course, labour. This type of inflation is called demand-pull. It has been argued that cost-push inflation is the main type that occurred in the 1970s when unions made use of their bargaining strength to push up wages, and employers passed on the additional costs by raising the prices of their products. Demand-pull inflation was in evidence during the credit boom of the 1980s. The control of inflation has been one of the overriding concerns of governments during the post-war period and particularly from the 1960s onwards. The effects of this aspect of government economic policy upon industrial relations are extremely important, as the example in Exhibit 4.2 demonstrates.

Exhibit 4.2

The effects of controlling inflation

This is a hypothetical example relating to the production of widgets in order not to give offence to any particular category of workers or their unions.

As a result of industrial action on the part of the Widgetworkers' Union, wage rates rose in that industry. Note that we are considering wage increases which result not from *demand* pressure in the labour market but from autonomous increases in wage costs (that is, increases in wages which are independent of the state of demand in the labour market). Will this spark off pure *cost-push* inflation? There are several possible outcomes:

- the increased wages could all be offset by increases in labour productivity, such that wage costs did not rise;
- the increase in wage costs could all be paid out of profits, so that profits fell but widget prices did not rise; or,
- if we assume neither of these two things happens, then the result will be that widget prices start to rise.

Suppose that the government senses this, and in an effort to control inflation it introduces policies which increase the amount of tax revenue taken out of the system (assume increases in income tax and or VAT). It therefore succeeds in keeping the level of total spending at its pre-existing level. In other words, aggregate demand is fixed and in such a situation an increase in the price of widgets can only result in one of the following scenarios:

- The amount of widgets purchased falls by exactly the same amount as the price rose, leaving total expenditure on widgets unchanged. In this scenario, the widget workers are 'pricing themselves out of the market'. Demand for their product falls in direct proportion to the increase in price. The demand for widget workers' labour will, therefore, fall as the demand for the product which they produce falls. In all probability, this would lead to unemployment among widget workers.
- The amount of widgets purchased does not fall, but spending on other commodities does fall. In this scenario the demand in other sectors of the economy falls, creating depressed labour markets and possibly unemployment in those sectors. The widget workers have benefited at the expense of workers in other industries and have 'grabbed a larger share of the national cake' for themselves.
- The price of other commodities falls. In this scenario there is a change in relative prices, widgets becoming more expensive relative to other commodities. The overall price level has remained unchanged, however.

The most likely outcome of the widget workers' action is some combination of the first and second scenarios. This represents a fall in the volume of production, accompanied by a rise in unemployment.

We could, therefore, describe the scenario in Exhibit 4.2 as a *deflationary* situation (this is another meaning of the term *deflation*, which here means a fall in output). Paradoxically, however, what we have here is both a fall in output and employment (deflation) coupled with a rise in the price level (inflation). Thus by restricting aggregate demand in a situation in which cost increases are occurring, the government has produced the worst possible outcome. That is why many post-war governments have – at least until 1979 – preferred to act in an accommodating fashion, allowing the level of aggregate demand to rise so that the same volume of goods can be bought at the new higher prices. By allowing demand to rise they prevent the fall in sales – and therefore the fall in output and employment – that would otherwise have occurred. If the government acts in this consensual fashion it is evidence that, even though it may be capable of restricting demand, it is unwilling to do so, preferring the evil of inflation to what it regards as the greater social evil of unemployment.

However, such a policy may encourage inflation in the longer term, because the widget workers by their action appear to have gained increases in wages without suffering any fall in employment. This will have a 'demonstration effect' on workers in other industries who will also push for wage increases which, if granted, will result in increases in the price of those commodities. Inflation, therefore proceeds and, as it does people develop expectations that the government will continue to act in an accommodating fashion by allowing demand to rise. Thus, cost inflation and demand inflation reinforce one another.

The control of inflation, whichever economic policy is adopted, affects prices and incomes; governments influenced by Keynesian economics used incomes policies in their attempts to control cost or wage-push inflation and hence indirectly curb collective bargaining. The unemployment effects of monetarist anti-inflation policy has led to a decline in trade union membership and a weakening of trade union bargaining power. It is for these reasons that the relationship between inflation, unemployment and incomes is examined in greater depth later on.

Keynesian demand management

Keynesian demand management strategies, as we have noted earlier, dominated macroeconomic policy from the 1950s through to the late 1970s. The simple precept of Keynesian economics is that it is the role of the government to manage aggregate demand, through budgetary and fiscal measures, in order to ensure a level of economic activity which maintains full employment.

Self-Evaluation Activity 4.7

The Keynesian model

This SEA has no commentary

The Keynesian model was summarised in Chapter 1. Reread the relevant section and then summarise the approach in your own words.

Here, we shall look at those aspects which Keynesian economists and policy makers consider most relevant to industrial relations, namely, the nature of demand, the determinants of aggregate demand and the manipulation of aggregate demand.

But first we build upon the Keynesian model we introduced in Chapter 1. The basic model derives from a theoretical view of the economy as a circular flow of income. The simple economy (see Figure 4.1) comprises two economic units – firms and households, and also comprises two flows:

- 'real' flows of goods and services (the continuous line); and
- money flows of income and expenditure (the dotted line) in the opposite direction.

With reference to Figure 4.1, firms pay incomes to households in the form of wages, rent, interest and profits in return for the use of labour services, land and capital owned by households. Households in turn spend their income on goods and services produced by firms. The real economy is rather more complex, and in the Keynesian model it is the level of aggregate demand which is responsible for determining the values of most other variables in the macroeconomic system. As we have seen, aggregate demand influences the rate of inflation; it will also influence the level of output, the level of employment, and hence of unemployment, the level of investment, of savings, the rate of growth, spending on imports and so on. Using our basic 'firms' and 'households'

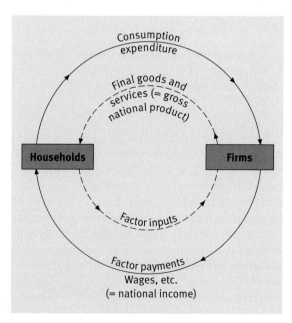

Figure 4.1 The circular flow of income

dichotomy we can represent this figuratively (see Figure 4.2).

The level of demand in the economy determines the volume of production, investment and so on; but what determines the level of aggregate demand itself? Crucial to the Keynesian paradigm is the concept of macroeconomic equilibrium:

- Spending is assumed to flow around the economy in a circular fashion – from households to firms as payment for goods and services and back again to households as payment for the factor services (labour, capital, etc.) which were used in production.
- The economy is said to be in equilibrium when spending which has 'leaked out' of the system or withdrawals in the form of savings, spending on imports and tax payments, is matched by an exactly equal volume of injections – investment, government spending and export sales.

Self-Evaluation Activity 4.8

Effects on employment
Response on website

According to the model, what would be the effect on employment of a reduction in the amount of income in the circular flow, for example, as a result of increased taxation?

The manipulation of aggregate demand

The final element of the Keynesian model is, perhaps the most obvious, and is concerned with the extent to which the level of aggregate demand can be manipulated by the government. We saw in Chapter 1 how government can reduce people's disposable income and therefore their ability to spend through higher taxation. On the other hand, an increase in government spending, say on education, roads and pensions, will increase incomes of teachers, road builders and pensioners and therefore lead to an increase in spending. The following terms are important when considering government expenditure:

- The overall level of government spending relative to its revenue from taxation is known as its **budget stance**.
- If government spending exceeds government tax revenue, this is said to be a **budget deficit** as the government takes out of the economy (in the form of taxation) less than it puts back (in the form of government spending). Such a budget is sometimes described as reflationary.
- When government spending equals total tax revenue, this is said to be a **balanced budget,** and when tax revenues exceed government spending, the budget is in surplus. A budget surplus is described as deflationary in the sense that it reduces aggregate demand.

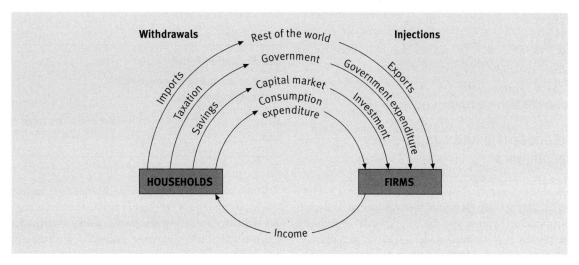

Figure 4.2 Dynamics of circular flow

Self-Evaluation Activity 4.9

Maintaining full employment
The response is given below

As we have seen, the maintenance of full employment was a key objective for governments in the post-war period up to the late 1970s. Describe how this was done, using some of the terms introduced above.

It was seen as the accepted task of governments, whatever their political persuasion, to use budgetary measures to stimulate or deflate the economy as circumstances required, in order to keep the level of unemployment as low as possible without causing cost-push inflation. If the level of unemployment began to rise, and economic activity declined, the government would stimulate demand either by reducing taxation or by increasing government (public) expenditure. If necessary, the government would borrow in order to do so. Prior to 1939, a budget deficit was considered the road to economic and financial disaster. In Keynesian economics, deficit budgeting became an acceptable method of ensuring relative prosperity, steady economic growth and very low levels of unemployment. By the 1970s, governments were finding it increasingly difficult to maintain full employment, cope with increasing and escalating budget deficits and contain inflation. What began to emerge in the late 1970s was a high-taxation economy, with rising public expenditure, increasing trade union power, and the phenomenon known as stagflation – sharply rising prices (inflation) and unemployment at the same time. Many economists and politicians began to have doubts about the validity of Keynesian demand management, and this heralded a new approach by the first Conservative administration.

Monetarism and supply-side economics

We looked at monetarism briefly in Chapter 1. Here we shall consider monetarism in relation to inflation and unemployment and the 'supply-side' economics to which it is related. A definition of monetarism (Pass and Lowes, 1998, p. 92) would comprise the following:

Monetarism is a body of analysis relating to the influence of MONEY in the functioning of the economy. The theory emphasises the importance of the need for a 'balanced' relationship between the amount of money available to finance purchases of goods and services, on the one hand, and the ability of the economy to produce such goods and services, on the other.

The theory provides an explanation of inflation centred on excessive increases in the money supply. Simply defined, money supply is that amount of money in circulation in the economy at any given point in time. The size of the money supply is an important determinant of the level of spending in an economy and its control is a particular concern of monetary policy. However, the monetary authorities have a problem because, given the number of possible definitions of the money supply (see Figure 4.3), it is difficult for them to decide which is the most appropriate money supply category to target for control purposes.

In the 1980s, the UK government, as part of its medium-term financial strategy, set 'target bands' for the growth of initially sterling M3 and later M0. Towards the end of the period of Conservative government, formal targeting of the money supply had been abandoned, although the authorities continued to 'monitor' M0, together with M4 as 'indicators' of general monetary conditions in the economy. One of the main contentions of monetarism is that inflation stems from the excessive growth of the money supply.

Self-Evaluation Activity 4.10

Inflation according to monetarists
Response on website

What type of inflation do you think monetarists have in mind?

Monetarists also argue that if the government spends more than it receives in taxes (there is a budget deficit), increasing the public sector borrowing requirement (defined as the excess of government expenditure over tax receipts, requiring the government to make good the difference by borrowing

Initials	Definition	Amount £bn July 1996
	'Narrow' money (money held predominantly for spending)	
	Bank notes and coin in circulation	22
M0	Currency plus banks' till money and operational balances at Bank of England	24
M1	M0 plus UK private sector bank deposits	325
M2	M1 plus UK private sector deposits in banks and building societies	452
	'Broad' money (money held for spending and/or as a store of value)	
M3	M1 plus UK private sector time bank deposits and UK public sector sterling deposits	537
M4	M3 plus net building society deposits	652
M5	M4 plus UK private sector holdings of money market instruments (e.g. Treasury Bills plus national savings)	682

Figure 4.3 Money supply definitions
Source: Bank of England *Quarterly Bulletin*, October 1996

money from the banking system (Treasury Bills) or from the general public (long-dated bonds)) to finance the shortfall, then the increase in the money supply which results from financing the increase in the public-sector borrowing requirement will increase the rate of inflation. The 'pure' quantity theory of money (MV = PT – see Exhibit 4.3) suggests that the ultimate cause of inflation is excessive monetary creation (that is 'too much money chasing too little output') – thus it is seen as a source of demand-pull inflation.

Monetarists suggest that 'cost-push' is not a truly independent theory of inflation – it has to be 'financed' by money supply increases. For example, assume a given stock of money and given levels of output and prices. Assume now that costs increase (for example, higher wage rates) and this causes suppliers to put up prices. Monetarists argue that this increase in prices will not turn into an inflationary process (that is, a persistent tendency for prices to rise) unless the money supply is increased. The given stock of money will buy fewer goods at

Exhibit 4.3

The quantity theory of money

This theory posits a direct relationship between the money supply and the general price level in an economy. The basic identity underlying the quantity theory was first developed by Irving Fisher (1911). The Fisher equation states that:

$$MV = PT$$

where M is the money stock; V is the velocity of circulation of money (the average number of times each pound or dollar changes hands in financing transactions during a year); P is the general price level; and T is the number of transactions or the total amount of goods and services supplied.

the higher price level and real demand will fall; but if the government increases the money supply – as Keynesians recommend – then this enables the same volume of goods to be purchased at the higher price level. If this process continues, cost-push inflation is validated.

Monetarists therefore argue that it is the responsibility of government to:

- maintain 'sound money' by pursuing a fixed level of money supply increase, departing from it only with great caution;
- reduce government borrowing; and
- reduce the overall level of government spending.

The financing of government spending through taxation or by borrowing from the public is not 'sound money' and has, according to monetarists, undesirable side effects even if this does not contribute to an increase in the money supply. Some of these undesirable consequences include the disincentive effect of raising taxes; reducing people's ability to purchase goods and services which leads to a fall in consumption and eventually in society's welfare. A further undesirable consequence is that the money which the government borrows could have otherwise been spent on consumption, or they may be funds which could otherwise have been lent to some other sector, such as private industry. 'Sound money' is supposed to keep inflation down and the goals identified above are intended to ensure that the government does not itself inject unnecessary money into the economy.

Monetarists go on to argue that if the monetary system is well-regulated and controlled, the rest of the economy can safely be left to self-regulating market forces. This approach may mean high unemployment in the short term, but in the longer term it will lead to improved productivity and competitiveness and thus to sustained economic growth.

Monetarist views on the determinants of unemployment

Unlike Keynesian economists, monetarists are not committed to the maintenance of full employment if this interferes with the workings of markets. They believe that real wage and employment levels are determined in the labour market and that the market is in equilibrium. They distinguish between short-run

and long-run equilibrium. Short-run equilibrium is a situation in which expectations are incorrect and hence are unfulfilled, whereas in long-run equilibrium the expectations of all the parties involved are correct anticipations of future events. The suppliers of labour (the unions, say) will be interested in the real wage. At the same time firms will take on labour only as long as the wage they have to pay is less than the value of what that labour can produce. In other words, they also will be interested in the real wage (the money wage relative to the money value of the extra output that the labour can produce).

Monetarists believe that this real wage is flexible in the long run and that this flexibility will ensure full employment (or rather, no involuntary unemployment) in a market equilibrium situation. Any registered unemployment that remains will be 'natural' since the economy will be at the 'natural level' of unemployment.

The natural level of unemployment explained

Assume that the government undertakes expansionary policies designed to reduce the level of unemployment. The effect will be first of all to increase demand in the market for goods and services, pushing up prices. The demand for labour, therefore, increases because each employee becomes more productive in the sense that the *value* of the goods which they produce per hour will rise. The disequilibrium situation in the labour market caused by the increased demand for labour causes money wages to rise and this results in an expansion of labour supply as more individuals opt voluntarily for labour rather than leisure. Thus employment levels increase, along with money wages and prices.

Note, however, that this short-run effect will occur only if workers can be fooled into supplying more labour by an increase in money wages alone, in a situation in which real wages remain unchanged, prices and wages having increased at the same rate. Workers in this case are said to suffer from money illusion. In the longer run, however, they realise that increased prices have completely offset the increase in money wages and they therefore revert to their former behaviour. Those who have recently entered employment drop out again, preferring leisure to labour at this real wage. This fall in the supply of labour results in labour shortages and consequently a further rise in money wages. This increase in money wages, which may also be a temporary increase in real wages, leads to a fall in demand for labour, the net result being that the economy falls back to the natural level of unemployment.

Supply-side economics and the 'rational expectations' hypothesis

Closely linked with monetarism, supply-side economics emerged during the 1970s, and policies based on supply-side economics were aimed at improving the competitive efficiency of markets, particularly the labour market. Not only had inflation to be 'squeezed out' of the economy by monetary discipline, but also the economy had to be freed from obstacles inhibiting the efficient working of the market mechanisms.

Self-Evaluation Activity 4.11

Obstacles to the market
Response on website

What do you think are the main obstacles to 'the efficient working of market mechanisms'?

However, supply-side economists also advocate a range of positive measures to improve the efficiency of product and labour markets such as:

- increased competition between producers;
- better education and training of the labour force; and
- the introduction of new technologies.

Rational expectations

In the Depression years of the 1930s, Keynes argued that demand should be increased in order to reduce unemployment. The classical economists (those who came before Keynes) resisted, arguing in favour of balanced budgets and action to reduce wages. In the post-war era Keynesian economics dominated and became the 'conventional wisdom', but during the mid-1970s the conventional wisdom was under attack and by 1980 Keynesian economics was in the wilderness. New-style monetarism is the absolute

negation of the Keynesian belief that demand management was capable of raising output and reducing unemployment. The first part of the attack on Keynesianism came with the so-called 'crowding out' hypothesis (discussed earlier) whereby it was argued that the government was incapable of raising demand because any increase in government spending would displace an equivalent amount of private investment spending. This hypothesis lost support by the mid-1980s and was replaced by a much more sophisticated and damaging critique of Keynesian views.

The new critique (also related to supply-side economics) was based on the rational expectations hypothesis (REH) and gave new impetus to the debate about the causes of unemployment. The debate itself was called the real wage debate which concerned the question of whether unemployment was the result of real wages being too high. Had workers priced themselves out of jobs and would unemployment fall if workers accepted lower real wages? Would an expansion of demand engineered by the government succeed in reducing unemployment or would it merely lead to wage inflation without any impact on employment levels?

What is REH?

REH suggests that firms and individuals predict future events without bias and with full access to relevant information at the time the decision is to be made. Only 'new' information will have an effect on expectations or behaviour. Expectations play an important part in pay determination and bargaining, whereby each side (employers and employees) have to anticipate future events such as the rate of inflation; by doing this, employment would be based on real wages at all times. The rational expectations model is perhaps more applicable to 'perfect' markets and is rather less successful when applied to modern 'real world' macroeconomic problems. The controversy which surrounded this seemingly innocuous hypothesis is based on the view that when REH is combined with a certain view of the labour market it appears to offer a theoretical justification for the sort of policy stance which right-wing governments like to adopt. That is, REH provides radical right-wing governments with a justification for abandoning any sort of reflationary actions to reduce unemployment since it forms a vital part of an analysis which concludes that such reflationary policies are ineffective and damaging. If REH is true, and if the labour market works in ways that monetarists believe, then expansionary (Keynesian) fiscal and monetary policies cannot alleviate unemployment. Reflation brings inflation without any increase in real output. Demand management, in a Keynesian sense, is dead and the way is open for 'supply-side' policies – 'making markets work better'.

Monetarism and Keynesianism: summary and conclusion

As we have noted, Keynesianism became the economic conventional wisdom with its largely optimistic outlook, as Dunnett (1998) points out:

> The message of Keynesianism was one of hope; governments could spend their way out of a recession and thereby eliminate the scourge of unemployment. There is absolutely no doubt that the Keynesian medicine worked. And it was easy for Keynesianism to win the hearts and minds of the people, for the medicine was pleasant to take. Just inject more spending into the economy and prosperity will follow with no nasty side effects – or so it seemed at the time. (p. 61)

During the 1960s and 1970s inflation was becoming a major concern, and the Keynesian prescription in the form of deflation accompanied by a slowdown in economic growth and a rise in the level of unemployment, was rather more unpalatable. The treatment was painful but largely ineffective. Critics argued that the existence of both unemployment and inflation demonstrated the inability of Keynesian economics to deal with these 'twin evils', and it was under these circumstances that the monetarists started to gain intellectual and ideological support. The government policy of increasing public spending was, of course, criticised by monetarists and had, according to Dunnett (1998), four main consequences:

- It became increasingly costly and difficult for government to service the increasingly burdensome national debt.
- Increasing public borrowing had 'crowded out' private sector investment and had therefore hindered the growth of the private sector.

- Increasing government expenditure led to monetary expansion and therefore to inflation which resulted in the raising of inflationary expectations amongst both employees and employers which in turn made the reduction of monetary expansion more difficult to achieve.
- The increasingly active role of the state in supporting both individuals, through generous state benefit payments for example, and firms, from 'bailing out' of financial trouble through to providing generous regional incentives, had led to a decline in traditional values of self-advancement and self-help and 'this moral degeneration had manifested itself at the personal level in a belief that the individual had the right to be maintained by the state (the "nanny state"), and at the company level by the belief that the state should cushion the firm from the unpleasant effects of market forces' (ibid., p. 62).

From the late 1970s to the mid-1980s, monetarism held sway. But towards the end of that decade disillusion with monetarist policy, because of its apparent failure to control aggregate demand by controlling the money supply, resulted in the displacement of monetarism by specific supply-side policies, some of which were based on the rational expectations model.

Incomes policy

Inflation, arguably, is fuelled by expectations of unions and firms. Unions **expect** that an increase in wage rates will not result in a decline in demand for its labour as increased wage costs will be passed on to the consumer in the form of higher prices. The employer expects that as a result of increased costs, which have been passed on to customers in the form of higher prices, the demand for the firm's product will not fall because there will be an increase in purchasing power and because the firm's competitors are also announcing similar price increases. These expectations could be dampened in the longer term by deflationary demand management policies, but this was deemed to be politically and socially unacceptable during the Keynesian post-war period. The alternative policy option would be to introduce a period of pay restraint; these incomes policies were an important part of government counter-inflation policy up until 1979.

The rationale for incomes policies (also called prices and incomes policies, as some governments sought to place some curbs on prices as part of a two-pronged strategy for reducing inflation) was that if wage costs could be held down in the short run, this would bring down the rate of inflation. This would, in turn, reduce the expected rate of inflation and hence the wage increases negotiated in the following time period would be more modest, the hoped-for result being the progressive reduction in the rate of inflation consistent with full employment, price stability and economic growth.

Incomes policies have proved to be fairly complex and varied, ranging from statutory to voluntary and involving price constraints and a whole complex of administrative bodies such as the old Prices and Incomes Board. There are six broad types of incomes policy:

1. Efforts to inform or influence 'public opinion' on the need for restraint. These may influence the general level of expectations concerning wages and prices.
2. Implementation of more formal guidelines for restraint on a voluntary or mandatory basis.
3. Attempts to restrain cost pressures in specific sectors, especially 'key sectors' such as the public sector where wage and price decisions are highly visible.
4. Short-term government intervention to freeze or severely restrain wage and price increases, either to buy time or influence inflation expectations.
5. The operation of a longer-term co-ordinated system of income determination with or without government involvement.
6. 'Institutional engineering', including the long-term reform of bargaining structures to lessen the pressure from competitive wage bargaining; labour market policies to improve mobility and ease inflationary bottlenecks; and reform of the legal framework to control strikes, improve mediation and arbitration, or limit union power.

The last type (6) is, perhaps, not immediately identifiable as a form of incomes policy, but its objectives are those normally identified and associated with incomes policy. The first four types of policy are typical of the various forms of incomes policy adopted in Britain during the 1960s and 1970s, while the sixth is identified with the type of policy pursued during the 1980s and 1990s. The fifth type, the operation of a longer-term system of pay restraint, has never been successfully achieved in Britain, although the 'Social Contract' of the 1970s had some short-term success, the policy being largely administered by the parties themselves.

Elements of an incomes policy

There are two main elements to an incomes policy. Firstly, there are the rules which guide or constrain the behaviour of parties, that is the norm and the criteria for any exceptions to the norm. Secondly, there are the mechanisms of compliance; that is, the enforcement policies and procedures and the administrative machinery, if any, through which the policy is managed and/or enforced – the main choice is between voluntary and statutory or mandatory policies (as we identified above) – and the extent to which statutory policies are backed up by appropriate sanctions. Whatever the objectives and type of policy, there are three basic criteria which should be observed:

- the rules and the administrative machinery should make economic sense and have some sort of economic rationale;
- the objectives and rules must be simple enough to be easily understood; and
- policies, if they are to be in place for any length of time, must be flexible enough to encompass broadly accepted notions of fairness; this is particularly important if the policy is to achieve any kind of consensus about its operation.

Most incomes policies include, as an essential component, some sort of 'norm' for pay increases. The most straightforward is an outright pay 'freeze' which, however, lacks flexibility and is difficult to sustain in the long term. Most incomes policies specify a wage 'target', 'guiding light', or 'norm' together with a list of exceptions. In Britain, norms have been set in relation to the underlying increase in productivity in the economy, or in relation to the rate of inflation. The problem of how the norm should be 'stated' is important, and in the past it has been expressed as a percentage, a percentage with lower and/or upper limits, as a flat rate, as a combined flat rate and percentage, and as 'averages' and 'ceilings'.

Self-Evaluation Activity 4.12

The norm

The response is given below

1. What do you think are the possible side effects of expressing the norm as a percentage?
2. What do you think is the main problem of expressing the norm as an average?

1. Percentages and flat rates can both have awkward side effects. It is argued, for example, that flat-rate increases depress or 'squeeze' differentials, although there are associated problems concerning how differentials are measured. Percentage increases, on the other hand, will consistently increase the gap between lower and higher paid workers. The combination of a flat rate and a percentage norm, as in the Conservative government's counter-inflation policy (1971–3) represented an attempt to balance these problems.
2. The obvious problem with the norm as an average is that some people have to get less than the average in order that others might exceed it. In any event, what usually happens is that the norm becomes the standard and gains by the exceptional cases are not offset by 'losses' elsewhere. In other words, the norm becomes the minimum.

With most incomes policies, particularly of the statutory type, there are exceptions to them. Any attempt to restrain the growth of incomes in the longer term must provide for a range of exceptions broad enough to allow for some flexibility and the correction of anomalies. However, the range should not be so broad as to undermine the objectives of the policy in the first place. One of the most comprehensive statements of exceptions was that provided under the Labour government's 1965 incomes policy which allowed four exceptions to the 3–3.5 per cent norm. These comprised:

- **the low paid:** where there was a general recognition that existing levels of remuneration were too low to maintain a reasonable standard of living;
- **productivity:** where the employees concerned had made a direct contribution towards increasing productivity;
- **comparability:** where there was widespread recognition that certain groups had fallen seriously out of line with the level of remuneration for similar work; and

- **manpower shortages:** where it was essential in the national interest to secure a change in the distribution of manpower and a pay increase was necessary for the purpose.

Self-Evaluation Activity 4.13

The exceptions

Response on website

Can you think of any likely problems concerning the application of these exceptions?

Securing compliance with incomes policies

Because of the inherent difficulties with policies which attempt to restrain pay in a formal, statutory way, governments have often opted for voluntary incomes policies. They are 'voluntary' in the sense that no legislation has been placed on the statute book, though governments have attempted to ensure compliance with these policies by a variety of means. During the 1970s this took the form of tripartite agreements between government, TUC and CBI. However, since neither the CBI nor the TUC had any power to compel their members to abide by the agreements, the effectiveness of the agreements depended to a large extent on the degree to which a consensus existed about the desirability of wage and price restraint. Within the British context, there is often insufficient consensus for agreements to have much effect. Hence, consensus and compliance can only be achieved and maintained if the policy is acceptable to all parties, based on the perceived need for, and fairness of, the policy in the first place (for example, that the policy covers all forms of income, including prices and profits).

The main problem with statutory policies is what action to take when particular groups refuse to comply. With most of the UK's statutory policies there has been some form of third party agency or institution, typical of the corporatist approach, such as the National Board for Prices and Incomes in 1964–70, to whom the government can refer borderline cases or claims for exception. Referral decisions of this nature have not always been perceived as fair, with powerful groups receiving more favourable treatment than less powerful ones. The same argument applies if the policy includes penal sanctions, but with all the attendant problems of the use of courts in industrial relations. As a result, where sanctions have been imposed to support an incomes policy, they have been directed primarily at employers rather than employees and trade unions. Overall, however, there has been a marked tendency to avoid direct prosecution. Under phases 3 and 4 of the Social Contract (1977–9), for example, the government threatened sanctions against firms in breach of the policy in the form of the loss of export credit guarantees and the removal of government contracts, rather than directly prosecuting those firms.

Administrative machinery and incomes policy: chronological details

A feature of British incomes policies has been the variety of different types of administrative machinery set up either to advise the government or to administer the policy. These have included the Council on Prices, Productivity and Incomes – also known as the 'Three Wise Men' (1957), and the National Incomes Commission (1962). The first to play a fully active role in the operation of a comprehensive incomes policy was the National Board for Prices and Incomes (or Prices and Incomes Board) which was established as an advisory and consultative body to help administer the Labour incomes policy of 1965–9. Later bodies included the Pay Board (1972), the Price Commission (1973), and the Standing Commission on Pay Comparability (1974–9). Details of post-war incomes policies are given in Table 4.1.

Why have incomes policies had limited success?

Since 1947 there have been over 30 attempts to institute an incomes policy of one sort or another (see Table 4.1 for details of the main ones), and none of them has lasted for more than two years. The reason for this is that there are too many institutional and political constraints upon the long-term effectiveness of incomes policies.

Self-Evaluation Activity 4.14

Institutional and political constraints
Response on website

Can you identify some of these institutional and political constraints?

The success of an incomes policy may also be determined by the extent to which that policy reduces the rate of price inflation (and inflation generally). For this purpose it is not sufficient merely to compare the rate of inflation in those years when the policy was in operation with those years when it was not, since incomes policies have only been introduced when the inflation rate was high. What is needed is an analysis to estimate what the rate of inflation would have been in the absence of incomes policy and compare this with the rate of inflation that actually occurred with the policy in operation. The difference between the two could then be ascribed to the effects of incomes policy. The Phillips curve has been used to illustrate this possibility.

Phillips's analysis, published in 1958, was concerned with the rate of change of money wages and the level of unemployment. Phillips found that as a result of his analysis there appeared to be a fairly stable relationship between the level of unemployment and the rate of wage inflation in Britain. If we look at Figure 4.4, we see that a fall in unemployment from A to B due to an increase in aggregate demand brings about an increase in the rate of money wages from C to D, reflecting employers' greater willingness to grant wage increases as the demand for their product expands. By contrast, rising unemployment and falling demand leads to a slowing down in the rate of increase in money wages. The 'curve' suggests, then, that there is a 'trade-off' between unemployment and demand-pull inflation. We can see, therefore, that if the level of unemployment is, say, 1 per cent, the Phillips curve model predicts that the rate of inflation will be 7 per cent.

We can use this as a way of measuring the effectiveness of incomes policies in moderating the rate of inflation. If, for example, in a particular year in which an incomes policy was in operation, the average level of unemployment were 2 per cent, we could predict from the Phillips curve that the rate of wage inflation would be 3 per cent. If the actual rate of wage inflation was, say, only 2.5 per cent, then the difference between the two could be the result of the moderating influences of the policy. In other words, the policy would have succeeded in reducing the rate of wage inflation by 0.5 per cent.

While there has been strong empirical support for the Phillips curve relationship in the past, in recent decades unemployment and inflation have tended

Table 4.1 Post-war UK incomes policies: 1948–2003

Year	Type of policy	Co-ordinating bodies
1948–50: Labour	'No increase of individual money incomes'	National Arbitration Tribunal
1956: Conservative	'Price plateau' policy	Council on Prices, Productivity and Incomes: 'Three Wise Men'
1961–2: Conservative	'Pay pause' followed by 'guiding light' norm of 2.5%	National Incomes Commission
1965: Labour	3.5% norm with exceptions	National Board for Prices and Incomes (NBPI)
1966: Labour	Six months' incomes standstill Six months' 'severe restraint' with 'nil norm'	NBPI
1968–9: Labour	3.5% 'ceiling' with exceptions for justified productivity agreements (no cash limit)	NBPI
1969: Labour	2.5–4.5% voluntary norm with exceptions for productivity	NBPI (abolished by Conservatives, 1970)
1970: Conservative	Public sector pay restraint (N-1)	No overseeing body
1972–3: Conservative	Stage 1: complete freeze on pay, prices, dividends and rents Stage 2: £1 a week plus 4% up to a maximum of £250 per year Stage 3: 7% maximum or £2.25 a week up to £350 per year. Plus 40p for each 1% increase in RPI	 Pay Board Price Commission
1974: Labour	TUC and government agreement to limit increases to cost of living (RPI)	
1975–6: Labour	£6 per week, and nothing for those earning over £8500 per year	Social Contract Phase 1
1976–7: Labour	5% increases with minimum of £2.50 and maximum of £4 per week	Social Contract Phase 2
1977: Labour	Unilateral government imposition of 10% plus 'self-financing productivity agreements'. TUC acquiescence	Social Contract Phase 3
1978–9: Labour	Government-imposed 5% limit. No TUC support and exceptions for productivity	Social Contract Phase 4
1980s and 1990s: Conservative	Severe financial constraints on public sector pay. 1992–3, maximum permitted increase was 1.5%. For 1993 onwards, a freeze on public sector pay, but 2.5% permitted No formal pay policy, however	
1997–2003: 'New' Labour	Continued pay restraint in public sector, but no formal pay policy	

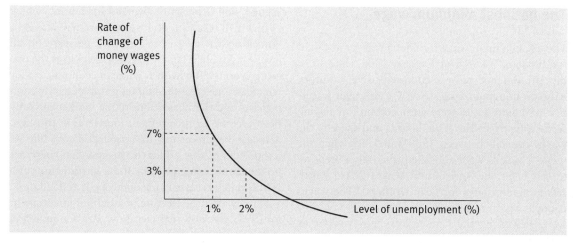

Figure 4.4 The Phillips curve: inflation and unemployment
Source: Phillips, 1958

to co-exist. This has led to attempts to reformulate the Phillips curve by Friedman and other monetarists who argue that there is no trade-off between inflation and unemployment. For them (for reasons which are outside the remit of this book), the Phillips curve is vertical and incomes policy is unnecessary as the economy will always return to the natural level of unemployment.

Summary points

- Prices and incomes policy is concerned with controlling inflation by *directly* attempting to halt or slow down the inflationary spiral of price-wage rises. The basic rationale for an incomes policy is that whereas deflationary monetary and fiscal policies can only control inflation by increasing the rate of unemployment, a prices and incomes policy, if applied rigorously, can check inflation and maintain high levels of employment.

- An incomes policy can be operated on a voluntary or statutory (compulsory) basis. In the former case, an appeal is made to the collective responsibilities of firms not to increase their prices 'unduly' and for trade unions to 'moderate' their demands for wage increases. These exhortations have often proved to be too vague and have been given short shrift by the parties concerned.

- A statutory policy has greater chance of success, particularly in the very short term as in the case of a 'pause' or 'freeze', and also in the medium term (the British experience suggests two years) if it is backed by strong penalties for non-compliance.

- Typical elements of the statutory approach include:
  - an initial, brief (six months to a year) standstill or freeze on all prices, wages, dividend, etc. increases; and
  - a following period (usually phased to allow for a progressive relaxation of controls), in which either general 'norms' are laid down for permitted wages and prices, for example by limiting them to say, 3 per cent per annum; or, more specifically, the establishment of formulas for linking permitted price and wage increases to, for example in the case of a wage rise, increases in productivity.

- The introduction of pay formulas and the creation of exceptional cases requires the establishment of some regulatory body (such as the NBPI) to ensure that the proposed price and wage increases are indeed justified.

- Supporters of a prices and incomes policy (usually Keynesian economists) see it as a useful way of 'defusing' inflationary expectations, thereby removing the danger of accelerating inflation rates. Opponents (usually monetarists) argue that such a policy would interfere with the operation of market forces.

The national minimum wage

The UK minimum wage for adults was set at £4.50 for 2003 and £4.85 from October 2004. Until 1999 the UK did not have a comprehensive statutory national minimum wage (NMW), although statutory minimum wages were set in certain low paying sectors, firstly by the trade boards and then by the wages councils between 1909 and 1993 when the wages councils were abolished (the only exception to this being the Agricultural Wages Board which sets minimum rates for farm workers). The wages councils began to be dismantled in the 1980s; they were viewed by the Conservative government as being riddled with anomalies and an unnecessary interference with the workings of the 'free' market. At the same time, the Labour Party adopted a policy of introducing a statutory NMW to replace the wages councils. Both political parties agreed that wages councils were no longer appropriate to a modern economy ('by the time they were abolished there was a Council setting minimum wages in the Ostrich and Fancy Feather and Artificial Flower industry but none in the private security industry' (Lourie, 1997)).

The opposition of Conservative governments to the idea of a NMW are based upon the economic premises of monetarism discussed previously. Essentially, using the assumption of the competitive labour market, wage levels will be determined by factors such as inflation and unemployment in such a way that the supply of, and demand for, labour correspond to set a 'labour market clearing wage'. The introduction of a NMW set above the market-clearing rate, it is argued, will depress the demand for labour, which in turn will result in job losses. There will also be a 'knock-on' effect exerting upward pressure on all levels of pay. In contrast to this argument is the one more synonymous with Keynesian economic policy which assumes that the market is not 'perfectly competitive' and that distortions to the market can only be overcome by government intervention through, amongst other measures, the introduction of a NMW. Supporters of this argument suggest that there are no inevitable consequences of the introduction of a NMW and increases in unemployment and inflation.

Shortly after the election of a Labour government in 1997, the now defunct Low Pay Commission (LPC) was set up with a brief to:

- recommend the initial level at which the national minimum wage might be introduced;
- make recommendations on lower rates or exemptions for those aged 16–25; and
- consider and report on any matters referred to it by ministers.

The report of the LPC made 24 recommendations, most of which were accepted by the government, but with the following modifications:

- that the rate for young people is 20p lower than that proposed by the LPC;
- that workers aged 21 will be covered by the 'development rate' (see Exhibit 4.4), though the LPC recommended that this should apply only to 18–20 year olds; and
- that no undertaking be given that the full rate will be automatically increased.

Exhibit 4.4

The LPC recommendations

Defining the wage

1. The NMW should apply to the gross amount of those earnings that are defined as included in its scope. The amount should be calculated before tax, N.I. and other appropriate authorised deductions are made.
2. Incentive payments should be included in the earnings that count towards the NMW. All pieceworkers must, whatever the piece rate set and output achieved, be paid no less than the NMW on average for the pay reference period.
3. Homeworkers and others paid by output, rather than by time, must be paid at least the NMW on average for the pay reference period.

4. Incentive payments should only count in the pay period in which they are received, which may not necessarily be the period in which they are earned.

5. Any service charge or centrally organised system of distributing tips and gratuities whereby workers receive their share through the payroll, such as the 'tronc', should be included in the NMW.

6. Cash tips paid directly by customers to staff should be excluded from calculation of the NMW.

7. Premium payments for overtime and shifts should be excluded from the definition of earnings for the NMW . . . only standard pay for overtime and shift hours should be counted.

8. Allowances and supplements should be excluded from the definition of the NMW.

9. With the exception of accommodation, benefits should be excluded from the calculation of the NMW.

10. An 'offset' should be allowed where accommodation is provided as a benefit-in-kind . . . but should be phased out in the longer term.

11. The actual working time definition should define what constitutes working time for the purposes of the NMW. The NMW should also apply to all working time when a worker is required by the employer to be at the place of work and available for work, even if no work is available for certain periods.

12. For hours when workers are paid to sleep on the work premises, workers and employers should agree their allowance, as they do now. But workers should be entitled to the NMW for all times when they are awake and required to be available for work.

13. The pay reference period over which eligible earnings may be averaged for the NMW should be the normal pay period, as agreed between worker and employer, up to a maximum of one calendar month.

Training and development

14. All those aged 16 and 17 should be exempt from the NMW.

15. All those on apprenticeships should be exempt from the NMW.

16. A minimum development rate should be available for 18-to-20-year olds.

17. A development rate for those aged 21 or over should be available for a maximum of six months for workers beginning a new job with a new employer and who are receiving accredited training.

Choosing the rate

18. We advise that the appropriate rate for the NMW should be £3.70 per hour in June 2000. Consistent with introducing the rate at an earlier date and our aim to proceed with prudence, however, we recommend that the initial rate of £3.60 per hour should be introduced in April 1999.

19. We recommend that an initial development rate of £3.20 per hour should be introduced in April 1999. Our advice is that the appropriate development rate in June 2000 should be £3.30 per hour.

Implementing and enforcing

20. The NMW should commence in April 1999.

21. Employers should be obliged to display on pay slips both the NMW and details to enable workers to confirm readily whether they have received the statutory minimum.

22. An existing government agency should be asked to take on the responsibility of verifying employers' compliance with the NMW.

23. Employers should be encouraged to display details of the NMW prominently in the workplace.

24. There should be a review of the NMW, in the first instance, within two years of its introduction, to examine its initial impact and to assess its future level, definition and possible exceptions.

Source: Low Pay Commission, 1998

The LPC's role was limited; its main task post-NMW was to monitor the impact of the NMW with a view to any future uprating or variation of the NMW level(s). The LPC has been disbanded now that it has completed the tasks set for it by government.

The National Minimum Wage Act 1998

The Act provided for the introduction of the NMW in April 1999 covering every region of the UK and all sectors of the economy. Agriculture, however, remains outside the scope of the legislation, although agricultural wage boards will continue to fix statutory minimum wage rates for agricultural workers. The Act closely follows the recommendations of the LPC (with the exceptions noted earlier) and its main points are:

- The introduction of a statutory NMW at the rate of £3.60 an hour before deductions (£3.00 an hour for 18–21 year olds and £3.20 an hour for accredited trainees aged 22 or over in the first six months of a new job with a new employer), in April 1999. Regulations under the Act may vary the rate from time to time.
- The Act applies to all 'workers' over school-leaving age in the UK other than 'voluntary workers'. It also excludes servicemen and women, prisoners and sharefishermen and women, and Regulations under the Act exclude 16 and 17 year olds and those on formal apprenticeships.
- The Act also applies to homeworkers and agency temps without contracts which make them 'workers', civil servants, parliamentary staff, merchant seamen and women, and the Act may be extended to offshore workers and others whom it does not expressly exclude.
- The Act rules out the possibility of providing a modified rate for the NMW for, or of excluding, workers according to the region, sector, size of business or occupation in which they work or, if they are over 25, on the basis of their age.
- Regulations under the Act will prescribe how to calculate a worker's hourly rate of remuneration for the purposes of determining if that is at least the NMW.
- The Act places duties on employers to pay their workers no less than the NMW, to give them a NMW statement and to keep records. In addition to their rights to receive at least the NMW and a NMW statement, the Act also gives workers a right of access to records, a right not to suffer detriment in certain circumstances and, if they are employees, a right not to be unfairly dismissed in the same circumstances.
- Workers may enforce their right to be paid at least the NMW by complaining to an employment tribunal of an unauthorised deduction from their wages or by bringing a civil action for breach of contract. Their other rights under the Act are enforceable before employment tribunals only.
- The other enforcement mechanisms under the Act are a range of powers exercisable by enforcement officers, who will come from an existing government agency, and six new criminal offences, each punishable by a fine of up to £5000.
- In any civil proceedings to recover the difference between what a person has been paid and the NMW, the presumption will be that the person was paid less than the NMW and that he or she qualifies for the NMW. The burden of proof will therefore be upon the employer who will need to prove otherwise.

Economic, social and regional impact of the NMW

At the outset it was possible to make some generalisations by extrapolating from the set statutory level of £3.60. With regard to the workforce, it is clear that women workers and particularly those employed on a part-time basis would benefit from the NMW. For example, the adult and development rates covered around 1.4 million female employees and 1.3 million part-time workers. In its report the LPC identified those sectors which experienced the greatest changes, in terms of coverage of employees affected, as a result of the NMW, including:

- **Retail:** Around 500 000 employees, mainly in smaller stores were covered.
- **Hospitality:** 340 000 workers affected, around 20 per cent of whom were under 21 and so were covered by the development rate.
- **Cleaning and security:** 900 000 workers received the NMW.

- **Social care:** Private nursing and residential homes were affected with some 80 000 employees in receipt of the NMW.
- **Clothing and footwear:** Around 40 000 workers were affected.

In terms of labour costs, the LPC estimated that the NMW would increase the national wage bill by 0.6 per cent. However, Philpott (1997) argues that the indirect impact of the NMW, via the restoration of pay differentials, would be greater, particularly in sectors – such as the public sector – with flat pay structures and a concentration of pay rates just above the minima. Some employers, whose main cost is the increase in the wage bill, may devise strategies to mitigate any such increase by cutting back on labour-related costs such as fringe benefits and training. Later evidence reported by Rubery and Edwards (2003) suggests that the NMW has had some impact in reducing wage inequality, but this appears marginal. Nevertheless there is what Rubery and Edwards call a 'clear pay spike at the NMW level suggesting that wages are being concentrated at this point and hence that there has been an equalisation of pay and that differential effects have been small' (p. 465). The impact of the NMW on prices depends upon the ability of employers to pass on increased labour costs in increased prices and the degree of competition in the markets in which they operate. Low-wage sectors tend to be in very competitive markets and this may inhibit the impact on inflation. Garrard and Martin (1996) estimated that a NMW of £3.80 accompanied by a restoration of pay differentials would increase the inflation rate (other things being equal) by 1.1 per cent. However, by 2004 it became clear that such estimates of higher inflation rates due to the inception of the NMW have been exaggerated.

The effects of a minimum wage on employment depend critically on its level. As we have pointed out, standard economic theory suggests that if the cost of labour increases, the demand for it must fall. Simulations of the impact of a NMW on employment through macroeconomic models of the economy yield a wide range of results, depending on the assumptions made by the modellers. Fernie and Metcalf (1996) summarise available simulations which suggest employment losses associated with a NMW set at half male median earnings ranging from 9000 to 259 000 with an average of around 80 000. Machin

(1997) in a review of the employment effects of minimum wage setting in wages councils' industries concluded that:

> *Evidence from the past experience of minimum wages in Britain suggests the employment effects then were moderate or non-existent. One should be somewhat cautious about generalising this to the case of a national minimum wage but, nevertheless, the previous experience of minimum wages in Britain was not detrimental to jobs and unemployment.* (p. 152)

The current and previous NMW levels did not necessarily mean that employers, despite CBI reservations, would inevitably react by cutting jobs, particularly as employment growth is determined by a variety of factors. The existence of a NMW in other countries such as the USA has not prevented them experiencing rapid job growth over the longer term.

In terms of social justice the NMW can be regarded as one component of New Labour's social policy. More specifically, the NMW has slowed, further widening the gap between the lowest and the highest paid (chief executives of large corporations are not included in the latter category), alleviating some in-work poverty but barely improving work incentives. The impact of the NMW across the regions of the UK varies owing to different employment structures and other local factors. For example, the LPC estimated that around 14 per cent of the employed workforce (130 000 employees) in the North East, which has the lowest level of average full-time earnings in Britain, are affected. In addition, around 13 per cent of employees (130 000) in Wales are covered, particularly in the hospitality and tourism sectors, while in London and the South East 400 000 workers are eligible. Finally, four areas can be identified directly concerning industrial relations where there has been some 'NMW effect'. These are:

Pay differentials: In many organisations pay structures, particularly at the lower end, are relatively tight. The introduction of the NMW has in some cases led to the consolidation of pay into fewer pay bands, despite opposition from a few trade unions and managers eager to encourage employees to take on more responsibilities through greater work flexibilisation and intensification.

The 'going rate': There is no perceptible 'NMW effect' upon re-establishing the importance of the 'going rate'. The 'going rate' is that amount the employer should be prepared to pay as a result of comparisons with levels of wages paid in other organisations. Since the NMW attempts to create a minimum 'wage floor', employers may be discouraged from offering wages below the rate for similar jobs in other organisations as this may 'squeeze' differentials and result in union opposition. Nevertheless, in recent years, many employers have, in typical HRM style, been able to persuade their employees that pay increases should be determined more by the success of the individual company (e.g. profit-sharing) than by any external factors such as the inflation rate or pay increases elsewhere. It is, therefore, probable that the more substantial the annual increase in the NMW, the more likely it is to reinforce 'going rate' comparisons. However, this assumes a much higher NMW level than the 2003 level of £4.50.

Pay structures: Pay structures have changed significantly in recent years, with a move away from basic rates to more incentive payments, bonuses and fringe benefits (such as pension contributions). As the NMW is set as an hourly rate, some employers have been encouraged to consolidate incentive payments into that rate.

Contracted-out services: The main impetus behind the explosion in contracting out non-core services since the 1980s has come from the fact that such services (typically, cleaning, catering and security) can be provided more cheaply in this way as employees tend to be paid less. However, the introduction of the NMW has not significantly eroded let alone removed this cost differential.

International comparisons

Other countries having a statutory minimum wage include France, Luxembourg, the Netherlands, Portugal, Spain and the USA. Most other developed nations have some form of minimum wage. Belgium and Greece, for example, have a national minimum wage set by legally binding collective agreement, while Japan and Canada have statutory minimum wages which vary from sector to sector and from region to region. In Germany, Italy and the Scandinavian countries, national industrial relations systems provide for legally binding, industry-level collective agreements which set minimum wages across almost all sectors of the economy. Research dealing with the economic impact of European minimum wages concludes that there is scant evidence that minimum wages have any particular effect on employment levels in Europe (Dolado *et al.*, 1996). The authors point out:

> The evidence on the employment effects of minimum wages is very mixed. We have found evidence that higher minimum wages reduced employment in some cases (particularly for young workers) and raised it for others (particularly for total employment). But it is surprisingly hard to find strong evidence of any adverse employment effects of minimum wages in situations where many commentators are firmly convinced (rightly or wrongly) that the job losses exist: France in the 1980s is a good example of this. As the employment effects of minimum wages on the youth labour market do seem to be worse, there is a strong case for having a lower minimum wage for young workers. We should emphasise that none of our results suggests that the effects (good or bad) on the economy of current levels of minimum wages are particularly large. The presence or absence of a minimum wage will not be the difference between economic success and failure. (p. 31)

Table 4.2 provides a comparison of key features of European minimum wage systems, and a more detailed overview of the NMW structure in the USA and France is given in Exhibit 4.5.

Policing the minimum wage

Policing or enforcement of the NMW is the responsibility of the Inland Revenue, which responds to all complaints made about employers suspected of not paying the NMW. The enforcement approach is via a confidential helpline and a network of 16 teams of six NMW compliance officers per team, located throughout the country. There are five key aspects of the compliance team's work, which are:

- responding to all complaints from workers and third parties, referred by the helpline, that the minimum wage has not been paid;

Exhibit 4.5

Minimum wage systems in the USA and France

USA

The USA has had a federal minimum wage since the passage of the *Fair Labor Standards Act* (FLSA) in 1938. Many individual states also set their own minimum wage level which is, in some cases, higher than the federal rate. The federal rate in 1997 was $5.15 an hour. Overtime pay at a rate not less than 1.5 times regular rates of pay is required after 40 hours of work a week. There is no formula for increasing the minimum wage: every increase requires a bill amending the FLSA to be passed by Congress and signed into law by the President. The FLSA applies to enterprises that have employees who are engaged in interstate commerce, producing goods for interstate commerce, or handling, selling or working on goods or materials that have been moved in or produced for interstate commerce. For most firms, an annual dollar volume of business test of $500 000 applies (those enterprises under this dollar amount are not covered).

The following are covered by the Act regardless of their dollar volume of business: hospitals, institutions primarily engaged in the care of the sick, aged, mentally ill or disabled who reside on the premises; schools for children who are mentally or physically disabled or gifted; preschools, elementary and secondary schools and institutions of higher education; and federal, state and local government agencies.

Some groups of employees are exempt from the federal minimum wage. These include executive, administrative and professional employees, employees of certain seasonal amusement and recreational establishments and employees engaged in newspaper delivery. Employees under 20 years of age may be paid a minimum wage of not less than $4.25 an hour during the first 90 consecutive calendar days of employment with an employer. Employers may not displace any employee to hire someone at the youth minimum rate. Employers may pay employees on a piece-rate basis, as long as they receive at least the equivalent of the required minimum hourly wage rate.

France

The French introduced a statutory minimum wage, known as the SMIG (*Salaire Minimum Interprofessionnel Garanti*) by an Act in 1950. This was an hourly rate designed to cover the basic needs of a single unskilled worker as assessed by special survey. A subsequent Act in 1952 linked the SMIG to changes in the cost of living, which protected the minimum wage against inflation but failed to ensure that it kept pace with the general level of wages. In 1970 an Act replaced the SMIG with the SMIC (*Salaire Minimum Interprofessionnel de Croissance*) with a view to guaranteeing the lowest paid workers a share in economic growth. SMIC is a basic hourly rate applicable throughout industry, the service sector and agriculture. It takes into account regular bonuses, tips and the value of board and lodging where provided. The hourly rate was increased to 1083 euros in 2000 comprising 49 per cent of average earnings. There are lower rates for young workers. There are three principles governing the revision of the SMIC:

1. Protection against inflation: as soon as the retail price index (RPI) shows a rise of 2 per cent since the last increase, the SMIC must be increased by 2 per cent on the first day of the following month.
2. Those on the SMIC must share in the nation's economic growth: the government can at any time raise the SMIC by more than the RPI would merit, for example at a time of particularly rapid rises in general wage levels.
3. The SMIC must be revised annually. A committee (the *Commission Nationale de la Negociation Collective*) made up of relevant government ministers, an equal number of representatives of the Employers' Confederation and the main trade unions, and the Chairman of the Social Section of the Conseil d'État examines the level of the SMIC each year in the light of reports on the country's economic situation and recommends any changes. The Council of Ministers takes the final decision.

Ministry of Labour inspectors (*Inspecteurs du Travail*) carry out random checks to ensure that employers comply with the law and investigate complaints. The present (2004) government intends to make changes to the administration of the wage.

Table 4.2(a) Countries with a statutory minimum wage (SMW): October 2000

	Name and coverage	How SMW established	Updating mechanisms	Current level	Other government intervention
Belgium	*Revenue minimum mensuel moyen garanti* (RMMMG) applies to employees aged 21+ outside scope of agreed industry minima. Reduced youth rates. Covers c. 8% workforce. Excludes apprentices, trainees, sheltered workshops	By legally binding national collective agreement (No. 43 for adults, No. 50 for youth rates)	RMMMG, like all pay, is index-linked to consumer prices. Rates increased when central agreement renegotiated, usually every 2 years	11.48 euros in 2000 comprising 39% of average earnings. Rates reduced by 6% for each year under 21. Includes regulatory contractual bonuses	Collectively-agreed sectoral minima may be extended to non-signatory parties by royal decree; c. 85% private sector covered by industry or company CAs
France	*Salaire minimum interprofessionnel de croissance* (SMIC) applies to private/semi-public employees aged 18+ outside scope of agreed industry minima. Reduced youth/trainee rates. Covers 11.2% workforce. Disabled covered by separate regulations	By statute	SMIC is index-linked to consumer prices. Also reviewed annually by National Collective Bargaining Board	10.83 euros in 2000 comprising 49% of average earnings. 16/17 year olds receive 89–90% full rate. Includes all reg. contractual bonuses	Collectively-agreed sectoral minima may be extended to non-signatory parties by Ministry of Labour. Covers c. 80% private sector workforce
Greece	Binding legal minimum wage rates (depending on marital status + service) for wage and salary earners in private and public sectors. Covers est. 10% wage earners	As part of national collective agreement	Rates increased when central agreement renegotiated every 1–2 years, most recently in 2000	4.58 euros in 2000 comprising 41% of average earnings	Collectively-agreed minima can be extended to non-signatory parties by Ministry of Labour

Luxembourg	*Salaire social minimum* (SSM) applies to private sector employees aged 18+ outside scope of agreed industry minima. Reduced youth rates. Covers 15% workforce	By statute	Index-linked to consumer prices. Parliament reviews biennially in line with economic and pay growth	12.59 euros in 2000 comprising 42% of average earnings	Collectively-agreed sectoral minima can be extended. Majority of workforce covered by co/sector CAs
Netherlands	*Minimumloon* covers employees aged 23+ outside scope of agreed industry minima. Reduced youth rates. Covers 200 000 (3.7% workforce including part-timers and some home workers)	By statute	Link with collectively-agreed wage rate index abolished in 1991. Government usually increases annually	1154 euros in 2000 comprising 44% of average earnings. Includes all reg. contractual bonuses. Youth rates between 30–85% full rate	Collectively-agreed sectoral minima can be extended to non-signatory parties. CAs cover c. 70% private sector workforce
Portugal	*Remuneração minima mensal garantida* (RMMG) covers employees aged 18+. Reduced rates for youth, + trainees under 25. Covers c. 6.9% workforce. Disabled under separate regulations	By statute	Updated annually by law after tripartite consultation, taking into account economic growth, inflation and productivity	3.90 euros in 2000 comprising 57% of average earnings. Includes regular pay elements. Youths 75% full rate, trainees under 25, 80%	Collectively-agreed minima can be extended to non-signatory parties. Covers c. 80% private sector workforce
Spain	*Salario minimo interprofesional* (SMI) covers employees aged 18+. Reduced youth rates. Covers 500 000. Apprentices excluded (rates specifed in CAs usually between 70–90% SMI)	By statute	Updated annually by law after tripartite consultation, taking forecast inflation and economic performance into account	5.06 euros in 2000 comprising 34% of average earnings	Extension of collectively-agreed rates possible but rarely occurs

Note: Belgium and Greece are included, even though the SMW originates in a ntaional collective agreement in both cases.

Table 4.2(b) Countries with alternative minimum wage mechanisms

	Mechanisms to protect low paid	How rates are fixed	How rates are expressed	How/when rates updated	Groups covered
Austria	Binding collectively-agreed (or decreed) minimum rates by sector, (union-proposed AS 10 000 monthly minimum now widely met)	Mostly by collective bargaining	Minimum hourly/ monthly rates by sector	Mostly annually	90% of employees
Denmark	Most collective agreements use 'minimum wage system' setting one minimum rate (lower minima for under 18s and trainees). 'Normal wage system' fixing effective rates for all categories now rarer. No extension mechanism	By collective bargaining	Minimum or effective hourly/monthly rates by sector/wage category	Agreement sets minima for each year it covers (usually biennial). Pay progression may be guaranteed when qualifications obtained	70–80% employees covered directly or indirectly by CAs. Non-signatory employers often apply items of appropriate CA
Finland	Collectively-agreed minimum rates by sector binding on signatory employers can be extended if union density +50%	By collective bargaining	Hourly/monthly rates by sector	Agreement sets own revision date, usually 2 yearly. Often contains revision clause if inflation exceeds a pre-set limit	c. 80% of employees
Germany	Collectively-agreed minimum rates by sector binding on signatory employers. Can be extended by Ministerial Order, if 50% + employees signatories. (In construction, from 1996 binding rate for non-signatories.) Courts have limited power to raise pay rates but rarely used	By collective bargaining	Minimum hourly/monthly rates depending on the job category/sector. Trainees paid special allowances	Agreement sets own revision date, normally annual but may be longer	80–85% employees covered directly/indirectly by CAs. Non-signatory employers often apply terms of CA but less so in the former East Germany. Of total 4.4m employees in the former West covered by extended CAs, only 700 000 affected by pay rates

Irish Republic	A legally-binding Employment Regulation Order (ERO) issued for sectors with low union density. A Registered Employment Agreement (REA) may be negotiated where density higher, and is legally binding on signatories when registered with the Labour Court	ERO rate set by consultation in Joint Labour Committees, under auspices of Labour Court. REA rate negotiated in Joint Industrial Councils – independent bargaining bodies	Minimum weekly rates at 9.63 euros in 2000	ERO/REA rates updated annually. Current pay policy, PCW, provides for guaranteed minimum weekly rises	EROs and REAs together cover 150 000 employees (c. 10% workforce)
Italy	Collectively-agreed minimum pay rates by sector, binding on non-signatory employers	By collective bargaining	Minimum hourly/monthly rates by job category and sector. Some trainee rates	Pay indexation system formally abolished July 1992. Pay rates updated once in every bargaining cycle (every two years) but new rate set for each year of agreement	Virtually 100% of employees since all sectors of the economy establish minimum rates
Sweden	Binding collectively-agreed minimum rates. No extension mechanism	By collective bargaining	Minimum hourly/monthly wage (trainees, under 18s lower minima)	Minima negotiated for each year covered by CA	90% of workforce. Employers seek complete devolution of pay bargaining
United Kingdom (until 1998)	Wages councils which set binding minimum rates for some sectors (2.5 million employees) abolished August 1993, except in agriculture	n/a	n/a	n/a	n/a

> **Exhibit 4.6**
>
> **NMW arrears: some 'real life' examples**
>
> **Case one:** A complaint was received from a former worker of a mortgage advice company because she had worked some weekends and not been paid. The employer had kept no records and denied that weekends had been worked. Evidence was gathered that supported the worker's claim and the employer eventually agreed to pay the wage arrears identified as being paid below the minimum wage as a result of the legislation.
>
> **Case two:** A part-time car driver and car cleaner was paid £50 per week for working 16 hours. When enquiries were made of the employer he confirmed this was the case, saying that he was unaware of the existence of a minimum wage.
>
> **Case three:** Six workers who had been employed as sales representatives for a building hardware retailer complained that they had not been paid for all the hours they worked. The employer was not able to produce any records of pay for hours worked and was keen to pay the arrears identified without recourse to employment tribunal.
>
> *Source*: Low Pay Commission, 2002, pp. 20–2

- carrying out inspections of employer's records to check employers are meeting their obligations to pay the minimum wage;
- helping employers understand their obligations under minimum wage law;
- securing pay arrears (see Exhibit 4.6); and
- regularly presenting cases to employment tribunals on behalf of workers.

Alongside the helpline is the Central Information Unit, which collates statistical data concerning enforcement performance and helps to publicise the NMW to a variety of organisations such as Citizen's Advice Bureaux, trade unions, large employer groups, community and voluntary organisations. From 1999 to 2003 the helpline handled over 7500 complaints about non-payment of the minimum wage and up to £10 million in pay arrears for workers, with £5 million arrears identified in 2001–2002 alone, an increase of almost £2 million on the previous year. These figures indicate that, contrary to more optimistic views (Rubery and Edwards, 2003, pp. 461–462), minimum wage arrears is an important issue which the government feels compelled to act upon, with support from the TUC: 'TUC welcomes Government's £10m crackdown on scrooge bosses' (September 2002 Press Release). The TUC is also campaigning for a substantial increase in the minimum wage level to £5 or £5.30 per hour by 2005, with the adult rate paid from age 18, arguing that to date the NMW has had a negligible effect on employment levels.

GOVERNMENT AS LEGISLATOR

Before 1980, and particularly during the 1950s and to a lesser extent the 1960s, there was very little legislation which had a direct impact upon industrial relations. Kahn-Freund (1954), a prominent labour law specialist, commented of this period:

> *There is, perhaps, no major country in the world in which the law has played a less significant role in shaping of these relations than in Great Britain and in which today the law and legal profession have less to do with labour relations . . . British industrial relations have, in the main, developed by way of industrial autonomy. This notion of autonomy is fundamental . . . it means that employers and employees have formulated their own codes of conduct and devised their own machinery for enforcing them.* (p. 44)

Contrast this with the 1980s and 1990s. McIlroy (1991) comments of this period:

> *Since 1979 Britain's trade unions have been hit by wave after wave of trade union legislation. Not a year has passed without new proposals*

being aired, new bills being introduced into Parliament, new Acts receiving the Royal Assent. The trade union problem has scarcely been declared to have been solved by Conservative politicians before a new Green Paper proposing further measures to deal with it is up and running. After the great Acts of 1980, 1982 and 1984 had apparently, at least in Conservative eyes, dealt with the important abuses once and for all, we have had further important statutes in 1988, 1989 and 1990 dealing with new problems – as well as a host of ancillary measures and still more promised. Britain has moved from a system of industrial relations whose legal framework was minimal to one where law progressively reaches into every nook and cranny of relations between employers and trade unions. (p. 1)

Before 1980, then, and particularly before 1970, legislation on strikes and picketing, for example, aimed to keep the law out of industrial relations and gave trade unionists a great degree of freedom to withdraw their labour. Employers and unions were expected to deal with matters concerning the employment relationship through collective bargaining within only a minimal framework. Terms and conditions of employment and the procedure for their agreement were jointly regulated through collective bargaining by employers and trade unions, not by Parliament and the courts. This is the system which was characterised by voluntarism, collective laissez-faire, state abstentionism and statutory non-intervention, terms which refer to the same phenomenon. It is through the significant pieces of legislation of 1871, 1875 and 1906 that trade unions gradually became exempt from the common law rather than having to operate within a framework of positive rights to organise, bargain and strike. Unions were granted immunities by which they were given protection from common law doctrines of restraint of trade, conspiracy and inducement to breach of contract. This did not prevent individuals taking unions to court over various issues and in cases such as *Rookes* v *Barnard* (1964) the courts sought to limit the immunities of trade unions which were invariably restored by statutory intervention. The situation changed dramatically from 1980 onwards.

Functions of labour law

Kahn-Freund (1977) has suggested that the law has three distinct functions which affect industrial relations to varying degrees. These are:

- **The auxiliary function:** whereby the law can support the autonomous system of collective bargaining by providing norms and sanctions to stimulate the bargaining process itself. It can also strengthen the operation of collective bargaining by promoting the observance of concluded agreements.
- **The regulatory function:** whereby the law can provide a code of substantive rules to govern the terms and conditions of employment. These would be designed to supplement the substantive rules provided by the parties themselves.
- **The restrictive function:** whereby the law can provide the 'rules of the game' of what is allowed and what is forbidden in the conduct of industrial hostilities. This, Kahn-Freund argues, is necessary in order to protect the parties from each other, and to protect the interests of the community at large.

The essence of Kahn-Freund's argument is that compared with other industrialised countries, Britain in the 1960s had experienced minimal intervention in relation to these functions. He suggests that this peculiarly British experience can be attributable to, firstly, a steadfast and determined refusal to use the direct sanctions of the law to assist either the collective bargaining process or the operation of concluded agreements. Secondly, an almost complete failure to provide anything even remotely deserving the name of a 'code of rules' governing the mutual rights and duties of employers and employees in their individual relationship. Thirdly, and much the most conspicuous characteristic, was the conflict between the traditions of the common law as interpreted by judges and the needs of society as interpreted by Parliament. As a result of this conflict, all the statutes concerned with trade unions and labour relations were negative. Their main purpose had been to remove obstacles which the courts had erected (such as restraint of trade and conspiracy), which threatened to impede the operation of industrial relations. In other words, the law had created 'negative' immunities rather than 'positive' rights.

Self-Evaluation Activity 4.15

Functions of labour law
Response on website

To what extent do you think these functions have been developed in Britain during the 30 or so years since Kahn-Freund put forward these ideas?

The extent of employment legislation until 1979

As we have already indicated, there had been relatively little legislation directly affecting the conduct of industrial relations – with the major exception of the 1971 Industrial Relations Act. Legislation concerning aspects of the individual's relationship with his or her employer did, of course, exist, and the volume of this grew during the 1970s. Long-standing examples include safety regulations applied in most industries and statutory bodies such as wages councils which regulated pay in some industries and occupations. But, basically, employees' rights were derived primarily from their contracts of employment, while the law, particularly prior to 1970, made little attempt to regulate collective labour relations except to give trade unions immunity from civil actions for damages.

A chronology of legislation affecting industrial relations and trade unions from 1721 until 1979 in relation to Kahn-Freund's three functions is given in Table 4.3. Note that the list is selective with the

Table 4.3 The law and industrial relations, 1721–1979

Date	Legislation or case	Description
1721	*Journeymen Tailors of Cambridge*	Judges declared trade unionism a criminal conspiracy
1797	Unlawful Oaths Act	With the Combination Acts this made all collective agreements enhancing wages or conditions criminal and trade unionism illegal
1799	Combination Act	See above
1800	Combination Act	See above
1813	Statute of Artificers (Repeal) Act	Abolished some of the powers of magistrates to fix wages in favour of freedom of contract
1823	Master and Servant Act	Updated earlier legislation making breach of contract a criminal offence for *the employee*
1824	Combination of Workmen Act	Repealed Combination Acts and granted unions limited legality. But they were still liable to criminal offences when striking/picketing
1825	Combination Laws Repeal Act	As above
1859	Molestation of Workmen Act	Limited unions' criminal liabilities
1867	*Hornby v Close*	Judges declared union rules to be unenforceable
1871	Criminal Law Amendment Act	Gave unions greater protection against the criminal law and restraint of trade – granted them a limited civil status
1871	Trade Union Act	As above
1872	*R v Bunn*	Restricted policy of acceptance of unions by making strikes common law conspiracies and still criminal offences
1875	Conspiracy and Protection of Property Act	Reversed *Bunn*'s case: protected strikes against criminal conspiracy if 'in contemplation or furtherance of a trade dispute'

Table 4.3 (Cont'd)

Date	Legislation or case	Description
1875	Repeal of Master and Servant Legislation	
1901	*Quinn* v *Leathem*	The judges developed *civil law* liability for conspiracy, opening unions to attacks the 1875 Act had sought to minimise by excluding the criminal law
1901	*Taff Vale*	Landmark decision which allowed the new civil law remedies to be pursued against unions as legal persons
1906	Trade Disputes Act	Reversed *Taff Vale* and protected unions from civil law liabilities such as conspiracy and including breach of contract in contemplation or furtherance of a trade dispute
1910	*Osborne Judgment*	House of Lords limited trade union political activities on birth of Labour Party
1913	Trade Union Act	Reversed *Osborne* decision and introduced balloting for political funds and right to 'opt out'
1924	*Reynolds* v *Shipping*	The courts went some way to accepting trade unionism as a legitimate social activity and recognising boycotting and closed shop
1927	Trade Disputes and Trade Union Act	After General Strike, it limited picketing and secondary action, stopped civil service unions affiliating to TUC and changed 'opting out' of political levy to 'opting in'
1942	*Crofter*	Further acceptance by judges of trade union purposes
1946	Trade Disputes and Trade Union Act	Repealed the Act of 1927
1964	*Rookes* v *Barnard*	House of Lords judgment which opened trade unionists to tort of intimidation
1965	Trade Disputes Act	Protected trade unionists from *Rookes* v *Barnard*
1965	Prices and Incomes Act	Criminal enforcement of incomes policy
1969	*In Place of Strife*	Labour government unsuccessfully sought to legislate to control industrial action
1970	Equal Pay Act	Attempt to end pay discrimination against women
1971	Industrial Relations Act	Comprehensive Conservative legislation to restrict strikes and picketing, etc.
1972	Counter Inflation Act	Criminal offence to breach incomes policy
1974	Trade Union and Labour Relations Act	Repealed Industrial Relations Act. Legislated in firmer form the immunities in the 1965 Act
1975	Employment Protection Act	Extended the floor of rights for individual workers and also dealt with union recognition and rights for officials
1975	Sex Discrimination Act	Legislated against discrimination at work
1976	Trade Union and Labour Relations (Amendment) Act	Strengthened position on dismissal and union membership
1976	Race Relations Act	Legislated against discrimination at work
1978	Employment Protection (Consolidation) Act	1974–9 legislation consolidated

main statutes and cases identified, although individual employment law cases are not identified at all as they would be far too numerous to detail.

As we can see from the cases and legislation in Table 4.3, the traditional emphasis by governments on 'voluntarism' did not imply or preclude the complete absence of statutory intervention. Action to legalise fundamental trade union activities through the granting of immunities in the face of common law liabilities was part of the essential nature of the voluntary system. The auxiliary function of legislation which included the supporting and supplementing of collective bargaining (such as the wages councils to support low-income groups), the establishment of health and safety standards and the protection of individual employees within the employment relationship, was regarded as being consistent with the tradition of voluntarism. From 1979, as Dickens and Hall (2003) point out, it was 'the nature and function of the legislation enacted which has transformed the legal environment in which relations between employers, employees and trade unions are conducted . . . and which constituted a decisive shift away from voluntarism' (p. 127). We now turn to the post-1979 legislation.

Post-1979 legislation

The period of continuous Conservative government from 1979 was characterised by frequent, often controversial changes to the framework of labour law. The sequence of 'step-by-step' legislation significantly increased the extent of legal regulation to which industrial relations is subject and, according to Dickens and Hall (2003) 'the period has seen the final death of voluntarism, under which law was essentially an adjunct to an autonomous, self-regulated system of industrial relations' (p. 127). The legislation has been motivated, in the view of Wedderburn (1986), by a need to dilute trade union power, to emphasise individualist rather than collectivist values, and to reinforce employer prerogative. The ideologically inspired reasons for the legislation have already been referred to in the context of the influence of the Hayek school of monetarism.

The legislation is concerned with three broad areas which we now consider in more detail:

- the relationship between employer and employee;
- the relationship between employer and union; and
- the relationship between the union and its membership.

The relationship between employer and employee

As part of the strategy for focusing upon the individual employee and asserting the primacy of market forces, the Conservative governments aimed to reduce or even remove employees' statutory rights where these hitherto had constrained the labour market as a result of the protective legislation of the 1960s and 1970s, and so encourage 'flexibility' of labour within a climate in which entrepreneurial initiatives could flourish. It was felt that the scales in the employment relationship were too heavily weighted in favour of the employee and that the employer was faced with unnecessarily high labour costs and a heavy burden of 'red tape'. Government was therefore committed to a programme of 'deregulation' within the labour market, although in some areas, employment rights were actually increased in order to meet certain EU requirements (even though Britain had 'opted out' of the Social Chapter). Nevertheless, at the end of the Conservative period of government in 1997, employees retained most of the statutory rights that the 1960s and 1970s legislation had granted them, and some areas, for example, those concerning sex and race discrimination, remained virtually unaffected by deregulation. Deregulation even had some positive benefits, as Dickens and Hall (2003) point out:

> *Employees benefited from the enactment of individual employment rights in that many sought and gained redress at industrial tribunals in circumstances where previously none would have been available. Arbitrary 'hire and fire' approaches to discipline were curbed; 'due process' and corrective procedures were instituted. Those losing their jobs through no fault of their own are compensated. Pay structures have been revised and de-sexed with the use and threat of equal pay actions providing a lever to reform. The gender pay gap has narrowed. Discrimination legislation has curbed the most overt discriminatory*

practices, especially in recruitment; has indicated how less overt, taken for granted, practices can be discriminatory; and has given a push to the development of equal opportunity policies. Maternity rights facilitate mothers' interaction with the labour market. (p. 135)

The adverse impact of deregulatory measures upon employees, however, more than cancel out the benefits referred to above. Some of these include:

- Adverse effects upon women employees as a result of the abolition of wages councils in 1994, which at the time covered around 2.5 million workers who were mainly women.
- Many part-time workers and to a lesser extent, full-time workers, were excluded from the protections offered concerning unfair dismissal as a result of the hours and length of service qualifications (see Chapter 13); deregulation removed certain legal safeguards from employees who were not unionised or covered by collective bargaining.
- Generally, employment protection rights were curtailed and some protections were abolished altogether; by 1997, the employment relationship remained relatively unregulated by law, hence there was 'little left to deregulate' (ibid., p. 137).

The relationship between employer and union

The relationship between employer and union changed considerably during the 1980s and 1990s. The legislation influenced this process in two ways: firstly, collective bargaining was severely undermined as a result of the legislation promoting the rights of the individual, and secondly, the scope for unions taking industrial action was considerably curtailed.

The undermining of collective bargaining

Since 1979 collective bargaining has been undermined by the repeal of the legislative supports for collective bargaining, compulsory trade union membership and trade union recognition granted by the legislation of the 1970s, and in particular by the Employment Protection Acts. The Conservative governments also sought to protect the interests of non-unionists by the incremental legal undermining of the closed shop and the eventual abolition of the 'pre-entry' closed shop in 1990, making it unlawful

for employers to refuse job applicants on the grounds that they were not union members. Furthermore, the 1993 Trade Union Reform and Employment Rights Act considerably modified the 'check-off' arrangements whereby most union members had union subscriptions deducted from pay by the employer who then gave them to the union. This measure, together with other measures such as ballot financing, threatens the financial viability of unions. All in all, as Dickens and Hall (1995) suggest, there has been a legislative shift to individualist relations as witnessed by a decline in the proportion of workers covered by collective agreements and the decline in trade union membership itself (see Chapter 3). The absence of any legislative obstacle in the way of employers wishing to derecognise unions has not only encouraged the spread of non-unionism, but also more individualist managerial approaches as typified by some forms of HRM. Dickens and Hall conclude:

> *Overall, we can see that at a time when sectoral and labour-market change increased the unions' need for positive legal support to aid organisation, such support was removed. At a time when unions are weakened by recession and declining membership, their economic and organisational security is reduced by legislative change. In a context where some employers are questioning the appropriateness or functional value of collective bargaining, some of the tactics which in the past have been part of the unions' legitimate armoury of persuasion have been made unlawful, and non-unionism is increasingly supported by law.* (p. 279)

Curtailment of industrial action

This is examined in greater detail in Chapter 7 and is summarised only here. The legislation has restricted the scope for taking 'lawful' industrial action in the following ways:

- the withdrawal of immunities from specific types of industrial action, for example, picketing away from pickets' own workplace was made unlawful (Employment Act 1980);
- restricting the areas subject to industrial action by redefining 'lawful' industrial action: lawful industrial action can only be taken 'in contemplation or furtherance of a trade dispute';

- unions became liable for taking 'unlawful' industrial action, whereas previously individuals who were organising the action were liable;
- lawful industrial action became subject to progressively stringent balloting requirements; and
- the range of potential litigants was extended from employers, to union members who had complaints about balloting procedures (1988) to members of the public who are adversely affected by industrial action.

The relationship between the union and its membership

The main concern of the legislation in this area has been to provide for the introduction of secret ballots by unions in union elections. For example, the 1984 Trade Union Act required secret ballots every five years in order to elect union executive councils and this was extended to the election of all union general secretaries and presidents in 1988. Government concern about balloting requirements extended not only to industrial action but also to unions' political funds which became subject to 'review' ballots every ten years (1984).

A summary of the legislation concerning the collective nature of employer-union and union-membership relationships is given below. For an overview and details of the legislation concerning the employer and individual employee, please refer to the separate chapters dealing with this (Chapters 11, 12 and 13). In addition, the provisions in the legislation which deal with industrial action are dealt with in detail in Chapter 9.

A summary of the legislation concerning employer–union and union–membership relationships

The 1980 Employment Act
The Act focused mainly upon industrial action, picketing and the closed shop.

(a) **Industrial action**
   The Employment Act introduced a distinction between *primary* and *secondary* industrial action for the first time in British law. **Before 1980,** any industrial action was immune from civil action provided it related to *someone's* trade dispute – not necessarily your own. **After 1980,** immunity was removed unless:
   - the purpose of the secondary action was to interfere directly with the flow of goods or services to or from the employer in dispute;
   - its purpose was to interfere directly with the flow of goods of an 'associated employer' and the goods or services were in substitution for those normally supplied to or by the employer in dispute.

   Any employer who considered that action was being taken 'unlawfully' could start legal proceedings against individuals (but not against the trade union until measures introduced in the 1982 Employment Act) who were 'inducing' the action. This was normally against the person organising the strike (for example, the General Secretary or national officer of the relevant union). The employer could seek an injunction stopping the action and could sue the individual named for damages.

(b) **Picketing**
   Peaceful picketing for a trade dispute had been lawful since the 1906 Trades Disputes Act. The 1980 Employment Act restricted this right to picket by laying down new rules on where and when workers can 'lawfully' picket. Any picketing outside these limits is unlawful and employers can take legal action to stop it. **Before 1980,** therefore, picketing was lawful virtually anywhere providing it was in furtherance of a trade dispute. **After 1980,** immunity from prosecution for picketing was removed unless:
   - employees are picketing their own place of work; or
   - they are union officials joining members they represent in lawful picketing; or
   - they are dismissed workers of the company concerned.

(c) **The closed shop**
   The closed shop was the result of agreement between an employer and the relevant trade union whereby 100 per cent union membership was enforced on signing the contract of employment. However, **before 1980,** specific exceptions did apply:

- an individual could be expelled from, or refused admission to, a trade union where a closed shop operated; and
- an employee could refuse to join a trade union only on the 'grounds of religion' which prevented him or her from joining any union.

After 1980, an individual could not be 'unreasonably' expelled from or refused admission to a union where a closed shop was in operation. If an individual were to be 'unreasonably' expelled, the Employment Appeal Tribunal could order the union to contribute to a compensation award. Furthermore, the statutory religious conscience clause has been widened to include objections on other grounds of conscience or deeply held personal belief concerning union membership. In addition, non-union members at the time any new closed shop agreements came into force are now exempt from compulsion to join the trade union concerned.

The 1982 Employment Act

The 1982 Employment Act introduced a new definition of a 'trade dispute', new limitations on trade union immunity, and further restrictions on the closed shop.

(a) **New definition of a trade dispute**
  Strikes are only immune from legal action if they fall inside the legal definition of a 'trade dispute'. The 1982 Act substantially reduced the protection by changing and narrowing the definition of a trade dispute. **Before 1982**, a trade dispute was defined as any dispute 'connected with' terms and conditions, discipline, dismissals or bargaining machinery, whether between 'employers and workers' or 'workers and workers'. **After 1982**, for industrial action to be lawful the dispute must now relate 'wholly or mainly' to the issues identified above, but with the following exclusions:
  - disputes which are merely 'connected with' rather than related 'wholly or mainly' to the issues previously identified;
  - disputes between 'workers and workers';
  - disputes which are not between an employer and that employer's own employees; and
  - international action unless it directly affects the terms and conditions of the UK workers taking action.

(b) **New limitations on trade union immunity**
  Individuals could invariably be prosecuted if they stepped outside the area of immunity, but union funds have been protected since the 1906 Trade Disputes Act so that **before 1982**, no action was possible against the union (as opposed to individual members) for what its members did, whether they acted officially or unofficially, legally or illegally. **After 1982**, unions can now be sued for damages and their funds sequestrated where 'unlawful' industrial action organised by their officials is 'authorised or endorsed' by a responsible person or body within the union. The upper limit for damages which can be awarded against unions is £250 000 for unions with over 100 000 members.

(c) **Further restrictions on the closed shop**
  Before 1982, a worker could be 'fairly' dismissed for refusing to become a union member in a closed shop situation as a result of an agreement between employer and union (except for non-union workers in closed shop agreements concluded after 1980 who were exempted from compulsion to join a union as a result of the 1980 Employment Act). **After 1982**:
  - it is unfair for an employer to sack a non-unionist where there is a closed shop unless this closed shop (now renamed union membership agreement) has been 'approved' in a ballot during the preceding five years. In this ballot, 80 per cent of the employees covered, or 85 per cent of those voting must vote in favour of the union membership agreement;
  - damages are substantial for individuals who complain to industrial tribunals about their dismissals and the complaint is upheld, with a minimum basic award of £2000; and
  - the union can be 'joined' as a party (in addition to employers) in the dismissal case and the tribunal can award compensation against the union instead of or as well as the employer.

The 1984 Trade Union Act

The 1984 Trade Union Act was concerned with reforming trade union structure with the aim of making trade unions more accountable to their members together with further restrictions upon industrial action. The main provisions of the Act concerned the legal requirements for union elections, legal requirements for industrial action ballots, and legal requirements for political fund ballots.

(a) **Union elections**

Before 1984, unions decided their own form of democratic participation and their own rules and methods of voting. **After 1984**, unions have had to change their rules and procedures to comply with the law. Voting members of union executive councils must be elected by secret ballot every five years from a members' register.

(b) **Industrial action ballots**

Before 1984, industrial action and its various forms was decided upon by union members in a variety of ways such as mass meetings, secret ballot, or by spontaneous reaction to events. **After 1984**, it became unlawful to take industrial action without a ballot. Hence for unions to retain immunity from being sued a secret ballot approving industrial action must be held, and members must be informed that by taking part in the ballot and voting for industrial action they would be breaking their contracts of employment.

(c) **Political fund ballots**

Before 1984, unions could have political funds and engage in political activity. **After 1984**, unions must hold a political fund secret ballot every ten years, and should a union lose a political fund ballot, it would not be able to hold a political fund or engage in political activities.

The 1988 Employment Act

There were four main provisions concerning the 1988 Employment Act. These were the removal of a union's right to discipline members who fail to take industrial action, further restrictions on union membership agreements, further legal requirements for union elections and the introduction of a Commissioner for the Rights of Trade Union Members.

(a) **Membership discipline**

Before the 1988 Act unions could discipline members for ignoring a call for industrial action after a ballot in favour of such action. **After 1988**, it became unlawful for unions to discipline members for ignoring a call for industrial action after a ballot in favour of such action. If a union member is disciplined by the union, he or she can take his or her case to industrial tribunal and be compensated. Moreover, union members now had a right to seek court orders to restrain unballoted industrial action.

(b) **Membership agreements**

Before the 1988 Act:

• industrial action could be taken in an effort to create or maintain a 100 per cent union membership agreement; and

• dismissals for non-membership of a union could be lawful provided it was within an 'approved' union membership agreement context as laid down by the 1982 Act in which 85 per cent of members had voted in favour of a union membership agreement.

After the 1988 Act:

• it became unlawful to undertake industrial action designed to create or maintain a 100 per cent union membership agreement; and

• all dismissals for non-membership of a union are unlawful even where there is an 'approved' union membership agreement.

(c) **Union elections**

Before 1988, voting members of union executive councils had to be elected every five years from a members' register. **After the 1988 Act** union general secretaries and presidents are subject to the same electoral arrangements and term of office requirements as voting members of the executive council and all ballots must now be postal.

(d) **Commissioner for the Rights of Trade Union Members (CROTUM)**

Before 1988, trade unions conducted their own internal enquiries into complaints of malpractice from members. **After the 1988 Act** the appointment of Commissioner was made, with the power to assist union members taking or contemplating legal action against their union for any breach of the law concerning union elections, industrial action, political fund ballots and union accounts.

The 1990 Employment Act

The 1990 Employment Act contains four major provisions concerning the pre-entry closed shop, further restrictions on secondary industrial action and unofficial industrial action and an extension of the role of CROTUM.

(a) **Abolition of pre-entry closed shop**

Before 1990, a minority of closed shop agreements (traditionally within some crafts such as printing and within engineering) stipulated that an individual had to be accepted as a union member before starting work in a job covered by such an agreement. **After the 1990 Act** a worker cannot be refused a job on the grounds of non-membership or membership of a union. This effectively abolishes the pre-entry closed shop.

(b) **Further restrictions on secondary industrial action**

Before the 1990 Act there was immunity from civil action for inducing industrial action by workers at the premises of an 'associated employer' (a separate firm related to the actual firm in dispute) of an employer in dispute, or at the associated employer's customers or suppliers, if certain conditions were met. **After 1990,** it became unlawful to induce industrial action by workers of an employer not party to a trade dispute, except where such action meets the lawful picketing requirements.

(c) **Severe restrictions on unofficial action**

Before 1990:
- those taking unofficial action did not need to ballot before taking such industrial action and the union was not liable for such action; and
- employers could dismiss strikers taking unofficial action, but, in order to avoid unfair dismissal claims, employers had to dismiss all those taking such action and not rehire any dismissed worker for at least three months.

After 1990:
- unions became automatically liable for all industrial action, including unofficial action, unless the union concerned has taken specific measures to 'repudiate' the action;

- employers could select for dismissal any employees taking unofficial action and those employees have no right to claim unfair dismissal; and
- any industrial action, whether official or balloted upon or not, is deemed unlawful where it is called in support of workers dismissed for taking unofficial action.

(d) **An extension of the role of CROTUM**

Before 1990, CROTUM could assist union members taking or considering taking legal action against their union for any breach of the law concerning union elections, industrial action, etc. **After the 1990 Act** the Commissioner could be named as a party to an action against unions, and could also assist in legal proceedings over complaints about union rulebooks.

The Trade Union and Labour Relations (Consolidation) Act 1992

This Act consolidated all existing provisions concerning collective labour law and trade union law provision.

The 1993 Trade Union Reform and Employment Rights Act (TURER)

The last major piece of Conservative legislation concerning the collective aspects of the employment relationship again focuses upon industrial action. The Act also creates the Commissioner for Protection Against Unlawful Industrial Action. There are also measures concerning the payment of union subscriptions.

(a) **More restrictions on industrial action**
- **Before 1993,** separate ballots for industrial action were required for each workplace involved (Employment Act 1988), and balloting could take place at the workplace without the union being required to give notice of the ballot to the employer.
- **After the 1993 Act** a trade union now has to ensure that the ballot is conducted by post in order to have immunity from any legal repercussion. In addition, the union must give the employer concerned seven days' notice of the ballot. Further, the union must give the employer seven days' notice prior to calling industrial action, assuming that a majority of those balloted voted in favour of taking industrial action.

(b) **Creation of Commissioner for Protection Against Unlawful Industrial Action**

After the 1993 Act any individual who as a result of unlawful industrial action is likely to be prevented from receiving goods and services can apply to the High Court for an order to prevent further industrial action. The Commissioner for Protection Against Unlawful Industrial Action was set up in order to assist members of the public with legal advice and representation, thereby enabling them to stop unlawful industrial action via the High Court.

(c) **Payment of union subscriptions and union membership**

Before the 1993 Act:

- in common with other organisations, union members were required to provide their authorisation for the check-off once only. (The 'check-off' system allowed employers to deduct union subscriptions from employees' pay.) Union members could then terminate their authorisation as and when they saw fit; and

- as a result of the long-standing Bridlington Agreements, unions were discouraged from 'poaching', and therefore had some measure of control over their membership.

After 1993:

- union members must now give their written consent every three years if they wish to pay their union subscriptions by the 'check-off' system; and

- unions cannot take any disciplinary action against a member who leaves his or her union, nor can a union refuse membership to a member of another union who wishes to join that union.

In conclusion

It is highly unlikely that there will be a return to the largely autonomous voluntarist system which characterised government approaches to employment relations up to 1979. In addition to the Employment Relations Act 1999, there have been a number of other measures which have added to employment protection (see Chapters 11, 12 and 13), including the Employment Act 2002. However, the framework established by the Conservative governments is likely to remain intact, for the foreseeable future at least.

NEW LABOUR POLICIES AND LEGISLATION: 1997–2003

The ideological direction of the 'New' Labour government elected in May 1997 remains problematic, although Smith and Morton (2001) maintain that in some areas New Labour has 'taken over New Right Conservative policy' (p. 121). During the first New Labour period of government, financial 'prudence', relying to some extent upon the 'supply-side' economics practised by previous Conservative administrations appeared to be one of the cornerstones of economic policy. New Labour had no plans to increase public expenditure during the first two years in office, and any increases in spending, at least initially, would be accounted for by increases in indirect and corporate taxation. The overriding concern of the first New Labour government was to sustain the steady pattern of economic growth inherited from the previous government, although growth targets were being revised downwards as a result of the global turbulence in money markets prompted by the downturn in the Far Eastern, South American and Russian economies during the mid–late 1990s. The control of inflation so as not to undermine business confidence was also a major policy aim; low inflation was seen as a precondition for long-term economic growth. The 1997 manifesto proposals included:

- more efficient use of public expenditure, in partnership with the private sector where necessary, and adhering to planned public spending for at least two years of a New Labour government;
- fair taxes to encourage work and reward effort;
- encouraging small businesses and local economic growth; and
- reducing long-term unemployment.

In addition, and in contrast to the previous Conservative governments of the 1980s and 1990s, New Labour believed that to be economically successful Britain must harness the talents of the workforce to the full, that economic success is dependent upon partnership and not confrontation between employees and employers, and that the way to achieve this is 'through trust, consultation, teamworking and offering people real security' (DTI, 1997). By 2003, the reality belied the rhetoric.

There is no doubt that the New Labour governments' approach to the economy and to employment issues is different from that of the *new liberal* approach of its predecessors, but the degree to which it does differ in offering a coherent 'third way', by claiming to combine social justice with economic efficiency, still awaits a verdict. However, by 2003, evidence of government handling of the firefighters' dispute 2002–2003 suggested a growing polarisation of interests between government and organised labour. In examining some of the recent developments and policy initiatives in the following sections, you may well reach such a verdict.

The evidence from 1997–2003

In its election manifesto directed at the business community, *New Opportunities for Business*, it was stressed that Labour would not bring about a 'blanket repeal of the main elements – on ballots, picketing and industrial action – of the 1980s employment and industrial relations legislation' (DTI, 1997). A Labour government would help to create a 'fair and flexible labour market' through the development of 'an adaptable, flexible and skilled workforce' and through the establishment of partnerships in industry. A Labour government would not 'be held to ransom by the unions . . . [and] unions will get no special favours under a Labour government' (Tony Blair, *The Sun*, 12 April 1997). It was clear that there would be no return to the corporatist days of the 1960s and 1970s or to the days of 'beer and sandwiches' at 10 Downing Street; business leaders rather than trade union leaders were to be invited to see the Prime Minister in the first instance. Nevertheless, national trade union leaders were invited to join a range of advisory bodies such as the newly formed Low Pay Commission, the 'welfare to work' programme concerned mainly with the long-term unemployed, a body to examine obstacles to competitiveness, and a standing committee on preparing for European economic and monetary union. One of the first decisions by the New Labour government was to restore trade union recognition at the government's communications centre in Cheltenham

(GCHQ) which was seen as a welcome indication of a more receptive mood by government towards trade unions.

New Labour, in opposition, had committed itself to developing a programme of employment relations reform which had three objectives:

- to encourage greater adaptability at work;
- to deepen the sense of partnership between employers and employees; and
- to achieve 'fairness at work'.

To this end, a Department of Trade and Industry minister made it clear that:

> These three objectives are interlinked and none can be achieved in isolation. . . . We believe every individual should have the right to decent minimum standards of fairness at work which are enforceable by law. It is not merely a moral right but makes sound economic sense. Our primary aim is to bring a sensible and fair balance to the world of work between the rights and responsibilities of employers and employees. (Ian McCartney at the 'Unions 21' Conference, November 1997)

We now turn to the *Fairness at Work* white paper (1998) as this contains the most comprehensive overview of New Labour's employment relations philosophy during Blair's first government. This was followed by the Employment Relations Act 1999 which implemented the white paper proposals in stages.

Fairness at Work and the Employment Relations Act

> There will be no going back. The days of strikes without ballots, mass picketing, closed shops and secondary action are over. Even after the changes we propose, Britain will have the most lightly regulated labour market of any leading economy in the world. (Tony Blair, 1998)

The above quote expresses some elements of the government's political ideology relevant to employment relations. What is particularly clear and unambiguous is the rejection of corporatism and the implicit perseverance with previous Conservative policies and legislation. For trade unions, the most important Labour pledge was the promise of legislation which would provide them with the legal right to recognition. The recognition proposals of the Act and their consequences are detailed in Chapter 3. The outcome of discussions held with both the TUC and CBI resulted in recognition proposals contained in the *Fairness at Work* white paper of May 1998, and this was followed by the Employment Relations Act of 1999. Predictably, the CBI had reservations about the whole idea, arguing that recognition legislation would have adverse effects on business, and suggesting specific amendments, including:

- proof by trade unions that they enjoyed at least 40 per cent support from relevant employees in a bargaining unit before a recognition ballot could be heard;
- exemption from recognition proposals for small companies;
- acceptance that individual employees should be free to agree their own terms and conditions with their employers even if they worked in units covered by union recognition;
- a ban on strikes concerning recognition; and
- a right for employers to call a union recognition ballot where 50 per cent of employees demonstrated that they wanted one.

Most importantly, the CBI was convinced that 'it had secured an assurance from 10 Downing Street that companies need not have to recognise trade unions for collective bargaining purposes unless they secured the consent of 50 per cent plus one of those employed in the proposed bargaining unit and entitled to vote, and not just a majority of those who actually voted in the ballot as the TUC had maintained' (Taylor, 1998). The TUC argued that few, if any, workplaces would manage to secure recognition rights if the CBI position were upheld.

The Employment Relations Act (ERA) 1999

The legislation (see Exhibit 4.7), based upon the white paper proposals as outlined above, represented an attempt to modernise employment relations in Britain with the aim of promoting a new culture of 'partnership' at work. Taken together with the signing of the social protocol and adoption of the Social Chapter as part of the Maastricht Treaty, endorsement of the EU Working Time Directive and implementation of the £3.60 national minimum

wage, it would have been reasonable to argue at the time that there was potential for a distinct shift in the 'balance of power' in favour of employees – a move welcomed as long overdue by many unions. However, it was also argued that far from being radical and revolutionary the legislative provisions were cautious and unambitious and that 'the government did not alter its [White Paper] proposals significantly in response to criticism from unions as to their inadequacy from the perspective of promoting and strengthening workers' collective organisation or individual rights' (Smith and Morton, 2001, p. 123). The legislative provisions were the result of extensive consultation with the TUC and CBI which inevitably, given New Labour's new found 'employer friendliness' led to a 'watering down' of some clauses which the CBI found contentious. Concessions to employers ranged from the adoption of similar procedures for derecognising unions as for recognising them, to the small firms exemption, which excludes organisations with fewer than 21 employees from statutory union recognition. An IRS (1999b) survey of employers' reactions to the white paper proposals and legislative provisions suggests that, despite criticisms made by the CBI and Institute of Directors:

What is surprising from our mini-case studies is not how much, but how little the legislation will impact on companies as a whole. This lends support to the view that the Fairness at Work legislation will act as something of a minimum 'safety net' rather than bringing about major change in the majority of workplaces. In the area of improved individual rights, for instance, many employers already have written disciplinary and grievance procedures which entitle employees to some form of representation. On the subject of union recognition, 44 of the UK's 50 largest companies already recognise unions for collective bargaining purposes. And many firms currently operate some family-friendly policies, including provision for maternity, paternity and emergency leave. . . . In many organisations, Fairness at Work will thus not undermine management in the way some commentators fear. Our mini-case studies suggest that while there will be an increase in time-consuming bureaucracy, the autonomy of management in strategic decision making will not be challenged. (p. 26)

Other points arising from the IRS survey concerning the implications of the legislation upon industrial relations include:

- the employer view that the legislation is unlikely to change the course of British industrial relations or the employment relations structures in organisations in any drastic way;
- that many larger companies have consultative machinery such as company councils or joint consultative committees for resolving workplace issues and, given their relative popularity, it is almost certain that, in the event of unions being recognised for collective bargaining, these consultative forums will be retained; and
- the view that the core objectives of *Fairness at Work* in terms of promoting both social partnership (see Chapter 8) and greater employee commitment and productivity 'are unlikely to be achieved'; the legislation is unlikely, on its own, to create cultural change or 'create the conditions conducive to the kind of cultural change the government would like to see'.

The IRS report concludes:

Employer responses to Fairness at Work – in terms of individual firms and their representatives such as the CBI and IoD – perhaps reflect how dramatically the industrial relations landscape has changed since 1979. Any attempt to legislate against the power of employers is seen as turning the clock back to the 'bad old days' of the corporatist 1970s. Companies, it seems are suspicious of regulation, intervention and the 'nanny state', and – in an age of direct consultation, flatter management structures and financial participation – some perceive unions as being less and less relevant to the real needs of employees. If the long-term success of Fairness at Work rests in part on the attitudes of employers, the omens are not looking good at this early stage. Labour may believe it can dismantle parts of the Conservative industrial relations architecture through legislation, but addressing its apparently embedded cultural legacy will be more of a challenge. (p. 28)

Exhibit 4.7

The Employment Relations Act: an overview

The ERA99 sets out the main provisions of the government's *Fairness at Work* white paper. The main changes are:

Individual rights (see also Chapter 11)

The qualifying period for unfair dismissal is reduced from two years to one with effect from 1 June 1999, and the maximum unfair dismissal compensatory award is raised from £12 000 to £50 000 from 25 October 1999 and is index-linked from that date. Employees on fixed term contracts are no longer able to agree with an employer to waive their unfair dismissal rights (but can still waive their redundancy rights).

Employees taking lawful industrial action have the right not to be unfairly dismissed, irrespective of their length of service. For the employee to be protected, the dismissal must occur within eight weeks from the start of the industrial action. The employer's right to dismiss employees for participating in 'unofficial' industrial action remains.

Where an employee has been invited to a disciplinary or grievance hearing, he or she is entitled to be accompanied by one companion who may be a trade union official or colleague of choice. That person can address the meeting and consult with the employee during the hearing, but will not be able to answer questions on behalf of the employee.

Employment protection rights are also extended to workers other than employees by means of Regulations, in response to the growing number of 'atypical' workers.

Family rights

As part of New Labour's family-friendly agenda, the Act creates new rights relating to parental and maternity leave. Final Regulations implementing the EU Parental Leave Directive came into force on 15 December 1999. According to the Directive, employees who have 'responsibility for a child' are entitled to 13 weeks' unpaid leave if they satisfy the one-year qualifying period.

Pregnant employees benefit in full from the changes in maternity leave regulations from Spring 2000. The ordinary leave period is increased from 14 to 18 weeks and employees may choose the date on which this period is to start. The Regulations lower the qualifying period of service for the entitlement to extended maternity leave of up to 40 weeks from two years to one. There is now compulsory maternity leave of 2 weeks following childbirth. An employee who exercises her right to ordinary maternity leave is entitled to the benefit of all the terms and conditions of her employment during her absence, other than those entitling her to remuneration.

There is a new right to a reasonable amount of time off during working hours for reasons related to a dependant, such as to make arrangements for the provision of care for a dependant who is ill or injured.

Collective rights (see also Chapter 3 for more detail)

The Act sets out a new regime for the recognition of trade unions by employers and the rights that trade unions can enjoy once recognised. Although encouraging a voluntary approach, the Act allows for compulsory recognition for collective bargaining purposes under certain circumstances. One or more unions can obtain an order from CAC that it or they be recognised. This new right will depend on various detailed procedures being followed and will only affect those employers who employ at least 21 employees. The union will have to demonstrate that it has the support of at least 40 per cent of the relevant workforce and a majority of those voting. A ballot may be avoided if the majority of workers are members of the union and there is no industrial relations or other reason why recognition should not be awarded automatically. The CAC may also specify a legally enforceable method by which the parties should conduct collective bargaining if the parties are unable to agree a method themselves.

Once recognised, trade unions have the right to be consulted under the usual statutory rights concerning redundancy programmes, health and safety issues and transfers of undertakings as well as matters they have agreed in a collective bargain. A union recognised under the statutory procedure will in some circumstances also have the right to be consulted on training.

Self-Evaluation Activity 4.16

Practical consequences of ERA99

The response is given below

What do you think are the practical consequences of ERA99 for employers?

As can be seen the Act covered much ground, and much of the detail is contained in subsequent regulations which have now been implemented. Employers without recognised unions need to assess their approach to employee consultation and involvement if union support is likely to be significant and to consider agreeing to recognition where it might otherwise be imposed. Employment handbooks and procedures should be updated to take account of the new parental leave, domestic incidents and maternity provisions, and the right to be accompanied to disciplinary and grievance procedures. The lifting of the ceiling to £50 000 and subsequently to £52 600 concerning unfair dismissal compensation has, on balance, provided enough incentive not to be complacent. Managers need to realise that bad disciplinary decisions will be costly, and the cheap (and all too easy) option of a cost-effective compromise agreement following a termination without procedures will be a thing of the past as ensured by the Employment Act 2002.

The National Minimum Wage 1999

The national minimum wage, which came into effect in 1999, constitutes a wage floor that removes the gross exploitation of many employees such as casual and part-time workers. However, the relatively low level at which the wage was set and the continuing low level (£4.50 in 2003 and a lower rate for 18–21 year olds called the development rate) has incurred the opposition of the TUC which seeks to establish a much higher rate by 2005 and an automatic uprating of the wage. A fuller discussion of the national minimum wage is to be found in an earlier part of this chapter.

Employment protection

The first Blair government opted in to the Social Chapter of the European Union, and many of the new employment protection rights since 1997 have been the result of a transposition of relevant European Union Directives into UK law (see below), either within the ERA99, the Employment Act 2002 or by Regulations. A summary of these employment protection rights up to and including 2003 is given in Exhibit 4.8 (see also Chapter 11).

In addition, there will be some concessions, which do not incur the wrath of the CBI, to the Information and Consultation Directive (see Chapter 8) and to the 'two-tier' workforce in local government (see below).

Employment Act 2002 and other developments

The Employment Act 2002 is described in greater detail in Chapter 11. In essence the Act concerns itself with the revision of disputes procedures, incorporating disciplinary and grievance procedures the statutory versions of which are already in place; reforms to the employment tribunal system; and more generous provision regarding parental leave and payments. Provisions concerning maternity/paternity/adoption leave and pay, dispute resolution, equal pay questionnaires, union learning representatives,

---

Exhibit 4.8

Employment protection rights: 1997–2004 (for legislation preceding 1997 see Chapter 11)

Existing rights have been improved upon and new ones introduced:

1. National minimum wage
2. Right to be accompanied in grievance and disciplinary hearings
3. Working time
4. Urgent family leave
5. Parental leave
6. Part-time workers' right to equal treatment
7. Protection and equal treatment for fixed-term contract workers
8. Public interest disclosure ('whistle-blower') protection
9. Paid paternity leave
10. Paid time off for union representatives
11. Adoption leave
12. Right to request a flexible working arrangement
13. Equal pay questionnaire
14. Maternity leave
15. Reform of the Transfer of Undertakings (Protection of Employment) Regulations
16. Reform of the ERA99 (pending)
17. Anti-discrimination measures
18. Extension of Working Time Regulations
19. Employment tribunal reforms
20. Dispute resolution – new ACAS code on disciplinary and grievance procedures

dismissal procedures, fixed term and flexible working and tribunal reform have all been implemented.

Public sector employment relations reform

While reforms to employment rights attracted varying degrees of approval, it is in the area of public sector reform and 'modernisation' that the second Blair government has encountered considerable opposition from the TUC and others. This is despite substantial increases in public expenditure arising from the second public spending review 2001–4 which reversed the first Blair government's parsimony in adhering to the Conservative public spending guidelines. The reform of public services has been central to New Labour's agenda for a variety of reasons, incorporating the government argument that state intervention and investment in the public sector are integral to enhanced competitiveness in world markets. This line of reasoning has a number of strands as identified by Bach (2002):

- the emphasis upon a 'strong' interventionist state with an increase in regulatory and audit activity (Kirk and Wall, 2002) has involved the use of performance management systems and new inspectors to 'direct and monitor performance against a plethora of centrally defined targets' (Bach, 2002, p. 326);
- regulation rather than ownership is the important criterion to ensure improved delivery of services which logically should involve a 'mixed economy' approach, utilising the private sector to provide some public services as exists within many EU economies; and
- a strong 'networking' approach involving trade unions and private organisations in discussions about public sector modernisation: specific issues include establishing networks to increase patient involvement in the NHS.

While there is broad consensus amongst trade unions concerning the aims of government policy, there remains considerable opposition to the means and methods proposed and employed to finance public services and the role of the private sector in their provision under the banner of 'public private partnerships'. The separate issue of pay determination within the public sector is also problematic and is considered in Chapter 6.

Private sector involvement and the Private Finance Initiative (PFI)

The first Blair government continued with its predecessor's privatisation policies, endorsing the view that improvements in the quality and efficiency of service provision would ensue even if this resulted in job losses and deterioration of conditions of service for those employed by the newly privatised companies. The partial privatisation of the National Air Traffic Service and the initial refusal to renationalise Railtrack after its poor management record confirmed this policy – although subsequently Railtrack collapsed and the government in this exceptional case was compelled to renationalise. Furthermore, New Labour accepted the PFI policy of the Conservatives aimed at utilising private sector funds to finance public sector capital expenditure without increasing the public sector borrowing requirement. The PFI policy was introduced in 1992 and Exhibit 4.9 provides an explanation of its workings.

There are a number of objections to PFI which are central to the employment relationship within the public sector. The first objection concerns the 'value for money' issue which now assumes precedence over public spending and borrowing concerns. As a result of the stance taken by the ASB (Accounting Standards Board) there has been an increase in documentation and consultancy fees as a result of lengthier negotiations and an increased rate of return demanded by SPVs. Both these factors have led to an increase in costs, which have fuelled the debate as to whether PFI really does represent 'value for money'. Secondly, the TUC and trade unions generally have viewed PFI as an antecedent of privatisation and expressed concern about consequences that this development would have upon union membership and influence. Thirdly, there has been concern about the impact upon terms and conditions of employment of workers transferred to private sector employers as part of the PFI process, that those workers not covered by TUPE Regulations would, upon transfer to the private sector, experience inferior pay and working conditions compared with those they enjoyed in the public sector. This has prompted unions such as UNISON to mount campaigns to highlight the problem and to publicise the creation of the so-called 'two-tier' workforce. However, in a rather surprising move which to some extent placated the unions, but at the same time aggravated 'business

Exhibit 4.9

PFI explained

Under PFI the private sector enterprise (referred to as the 'operator') usually undertakes to design, build, finance and operate a property in order to provide the required service demanded by the public sector body (referred to as the 'purchaser') responsible for the ultimate delivery of the service. For larger contracts the private sector side of the partnership can be a Special Purpose Vehicle (SPV), which is a consortium of companies involved in construction, finance and other disciplines relevant to the particular public sector project. The policy of privatisation was regarded as an important step towards restoring the private sector's role within the economy. PFI, however, has swung the pendulum back even further. Instead of being a provider of services, a streamlined public sector has transferred many of its functions to private companies. The state now contracts out both construction of capital assets and the provision of services to a new breed of organisation, enabling the constructors to become both operators and builders of new facilities such as schools and hospitals. McKendrick and McCabe (1997) argue that the main aims of PFI are:

- accelerating investment in the infrastructure through providing access to private capital;
- improving the way in which facilities are designed and procured;
- enabling a better balance between capital and current spending; and
- constraining public expenditure in favour of private sector expenditure.

Most public sector departments have used PFI to improve and upgrade their infrastructure, including health (Norfolk and Norwich General Hospital), prisons (Fazakerley, Liverpool), education (Avery Hill student village), culture (Royal Armouries Museum) and defence (Defence Helicopter Flying School). Since coming into power in 1997, New Labour has endorsed the idea with enthusiasm, so much so that it is almost impossible to detect any policy difference from the previous Conservative government.

leaders' (*Financial Times*, 14 February 2003), the government endorsed a code of practice covering all workers transferred as a result of PFI within the local authority context. These workers are now to enjoy 'fair and reasonable' terms and conditions 'which are, overall, no less favourable' than those of their colleagues who were working for the public sector and were simply transferred. Whether the code actually eliminates the 'two-tier' workforce, however, remains to be seen.

Conclusion

Apart from a renewed commitment to the European Union and its social policy objectives which are ongoing (see the following section which deals with European Union social policy), the establishment of a statutory minimum wage and the Employment Relations Act define the extent of New Labour's intervention within the employment relations arena during

its first term of government. During the second Blair government, despite further legislation considered above, a great deal of ambiguity regarding its political ideology vis-à-vis employment relations remains. New Labour apparently seeks to placate employers by attempting to strike a balance between employment protection on the one hand, and employer prerogative on the other (Dickens and Hall, 2003). Sensitivity to the concerns of employers manifests itself in the modest national minimum wage levels from 1999 to 2004, the modest proposals for trade union recognition (see Chapter 3) and the rejection of TUC proposals for improving the ERA99, as evidenced by the white paper (2003) review of the ERA99:

Commenting on the review of the Employment Relations Act, Brendan Barber the TUC General Secretary said: 'While there are some useful advances in this White Paper that will make a real difference to people at work, unions will find the Government's rejection of many TUC

*proposals extremely disappointing. The government would be unwise to ignore the real anger in unions today. Our call for people at work to be represented by a union when a majority back it, irrespective of the size of the business, is a basic human right. Our call for an end to rigged votes in recognition ballots where abstentions count the same as votes against is a simple matter of democracy. Our call to end the right of employers to sack staff after eight weeks on strike would enshrine the basic human right to withdraw your labour. Of course we welcome the measures that will help people at work and the technical improvements in employment law and union recognition procedures, **but on balance the White Paper has been too influenced by business lobbying.'***
(TUC Press Release, 27 February 2003)

New Labour continues to heed CBI views concerning the impact of regulation upon business performance and the effect of this upon employment costs. The government acknowledgement that the 'regulatory burden' is a sensitive employer issue may explain 'light touch' regulation and commitment to 'soft touch' legislation and codes of practice. These amount to relatively little in practice. Examples are employer-friendly amendments to the Working Time Directive, which reduce the record-keeping requirements on employers enabling employees to 'opt out' of the statutory 48-hour limit (Dickens and Hall, 2003), and in the area of equality where government rejected EOC proposals for the introduction of mandatory employer pay reviews. Within the area of individual employment protection, while there have been some improvements prompted by EU Directives, progress has been slower than in many other EU countries, and at best could be described as 'constrained expansion' (Dickens, 2002), which is better than no expansion at all. However, the verdict of Smith and Morton (2001) is less kind:

The devil in Labour's employment law programme is its commitment to a particular form of employer domination of the employment relationship. From this flows its support for a minimalist regulation of the employment relationship and hostility to the politics and practice of trade unionism conceived as the mobilisation of workers' collective power. Devlish details flow from devlish values. (p. 135)

This view reinforces the argument that New Labour employment relations policies are geared more towards continuity with the policies of previous Conservative governments than with promoting radical change. To be sure, the first Blair government put an end to the overt hostility between the labour movement and government; trade unions and the TUC were encouraged to endorse the new 'social partnership' culture (subsequently ignored by government) in which they had a theoretical and rhetorical part to play, together with the CBI and employers whom Labour courted so fervently before and after being elected into government. The balance of power between employers and employees in the workplace even where unions are recognised hardly changed as a result of legislative developments; employers are likely to remain in the ascendancy and continue to dominate the employment relations agenda for the foreseeable future (Kessler and Bayliss, 1998; IRS, 1999a; Smith and Morton, 2001; Dickens and Hall, 2003). This view is also reinforced by TUC suspicion of the government's motives in resisting, with reservations and qualifications, the draft EU Information and Consultation Directive (see Chapter 8) which would make works councils mandatory for firms with 50 workers or more. The draft directive was resisted by government on the grounds that its implementation would impede the scope for employers to decide what was the most appropriate system of information and consultation for their organisation. But the logical position for government to adopt 'would have been to be supportive of the draft directive. Information and consultation is an essential part of a partnership arrangement between employers and employees' (Gennard, 2002, p. 593). In that context, John Monks, the former TUC General Secretary, has stated that 'the employers are more afraid of this [works councils] than they are of trade union recognition because they think it will be a Trojan horse for unions to get into every company' (*The Guardian*, 24 May 1999). It appears, therefore, that continuity rather than change has characterised government policy towards employment relations during the period 1997–2004, and we would still agree with Kessler and Bayliss (1998) who argued some years ago that the 'present balance of forces' in which employers are dominant will remain: 'the unions may retreat no further, but employers will remain firmly in the ascendancy' (p. 301).

THE EUROPEAN UNION AND EMPLOYMENT RELATIONS

There can be no doubt that the influence of the European Union upon member states through its institutions, 'social partners', treaty provisions and directives has assumed much greater importance during the 1990s than in previous decades as a result of moves towards a common currency and eventual political union, together with attempts to co-ordinate social and economic policy across a whole range of substantive and procedural issues. Our main concern here is with the 'social' dimension of EU policy – the term 'social' being used in treaty provisions and directives to include employment and employment relations matters. In order to understand the process of social policy-making it is necessary to consider the main policy-making institutions and decision-making processes of the EU insofar as they impinge upon employment relations issues. Before doing so, it is important to note that there are two main methods that are employed by the EU in its attempts to develop an 'integrated' system of European employment relations (Hall, 1992, 1994). These are:

- the adoption of regulatory measures, usually in the form of directives aiming to 'harmonise' or align more closely the laws and practices of member states or to regulate transnational employment relations matters; and
- the use of 'procedural' initiatives 'such as the promotion of "social dialogue" between European-level employer and trade union organisations and their inclusion into a network of sectoral or advisory bodies which feed into the Commission's policy development work' (Hall, 1994, p. 284).

The process of policy- and decision-making within the European Commission (EC) is far from smooth. The Council of Ministers which is responsible for decision-making has often curtailed the wider ambitions of the Commission within the social policy field. Moreover, the presidency of the Council of Ministers, which is held on a six-monthly rotating basis by a member state government, can exert a major influence upon the direction of EC social policy. The pace and direction of social policy can also be heavily influenced by certain key member states (France,

Germany and the UK) which can either encourage or impede its development – the UK Conservative governments of the 1980s and 1990s for example, blocked a range of proposed directives within the Council leading to an 'impasse' over EC labour law initiatives (Hall, 1994), while the West German government under Brandt adopted a more facilitative and proactive approach to policy-making during the 1960s. To a certain extent, policy-making has become a more complex affair in recent years as a result of the enlargement of the European Union.

The institutions of the EU relevant to social policy-making

All EU policy- and decision-making involves four main institutions. These are the European Commission, the Council of Ministers, the European Parliament (EP) and the European Court of Justice (ECJ). Other institutions relevant to social policy generation comprise the Social Partners representing national union and management/employers' bodies and the Economic and Social Committee.

The European Commission is the principal body for initiating policy, and will comprise 38 Commissioners, provisionally one from each of the 18 smaller member states and two each from the ten larger ones. Each Commissioner has responsibility for one administrative department, known as a Directorate-General and for one set of issues. Hence, there is a Commissioner for Social Affairs who is responsible for 'employment, industrial relations and social affairs'. The most important function of the Commission is to initiate policy to form the basis of European legislation. Other functions include:

- The responsibility for ensuring that the provisions of the various treaties (such as the Treaty of Rome), policy and legislative decisions are actually put into effect and that member states comply with these.
- The responsibility to act as 'power broker' should there be disagreement between member states within the Council of Ministers in order to reach a compromise.
- The responsibility to take action against member states should they fail to fulfil a treaty obligation by bringing the matter before the ECJ.

The Council of the European Union (Council of Ministers and the European Council) is the most important law-making institution. Membership of the Council varies according to what is being discussed, and there are a number of constituent bodies, each of which will consider particular issues. The Social Affairs Council, for example, is responsible for all employment relations issues; it comprises Employment Ministers (or equivalent) from each of the 28 member states and makes decisions on draft proposals put forward by the Commission.

The European Parliament (EP) comprises 732 (maximum from 2004 according to the Treaty of Nice) representatives who are Members of the European Parliament (MEPs), elected by universal suffrage. Each member state has an allocation of MEPs proportionate to its population, with Germany having the greatest number of seats (99) with Luxembourg and Malta having the least (six and five respectively). The EP, unlike national parliaments, has limited power and influence, although subsequent to the Maastricht and Amsterdam Treaties it acquired limited powers of veto which now extends to many social policy areas. The traditional functions of the EP include:

- a consultative role; the Council of Ministers must consult with the EP on all aspects of EU legislation;
- a supervisory role with power to dismiss the European Commission on passing a vote of no confidence (such action was taken successfully for the first time in 1999); and
- the power to reject the entire draft annual budget of the EU by majority vote, enabling individual modifications to be negotiated.

The European Court of Justice comprises 28 judges, one from each member state, and deals with two categories of cases. Firstly, it makes decisions concerning whether member states have complied with their treaty obligations; it also monitors the legality of the acts of the Council of Ministers and of the Commission. Secondly, it makes judgments on cases originating within individual member states concerning the interpretation of EU directives and legislation. For example, cases involving sex discrimination can be referred to the ECJ if they are not resolved to the satisfaction of one party by the judicial system of a member state. The ECJ will make preliminary judgments or rulings which are ultimately binding upon member states.

The Social Partners

The main Social Partners are the European Trade Union Confederation (ETUC) and the Union of Industrial and Employers' Confederations of Europe (UNICE). These were described in Chapter 1. In addition to these, another employers' organisation, the European Centre of Public Enterprises (CEEP), representing public sector employer interests, plays a less significant part in social policy determination. The Commission's aim 'to develop the dialogue between management and labour at European level which could, if the two sides consider it desirable, lead to relations based on agreement' (Article 118b, Single European Act 1987) has been only partially successful. The 'dialogue' was intended to result in social policy initiatives upon which the Social Partners could agree. While there were some successes, the interests and values of the ETUC and UNICE, whereby the former is more receptive to social policy developments and interventions and the latter is predisposed to oppose such initiatives, were not conducive in helping to create a climate of co-operation. Moreover, the aim of developing Europe-wide collective bargaining machinery with the Social Partners being the major actors has encountered serious problems and obstacles apart from the ideological incompatibility of the Partners. Some of these problems are identified by Leat (1999) citing Schulten (1996):

- There are no institutional or organisational underpinnings and machinery, and no political mandate which would enable the Partners to negotiate at this level.
- Political interests of the actors are still predominantly national and relatively narrowly focused.
- European-level bargaining ideally requires the commitment of member states to political union, thereby subordinating national interests to those of the European state.

Nevertheless, the Maastricht Treaty and the Treaty of Amsterdam give much greater prominence to the roles of the Social Partners in consultation and negotiation of collective agreements in areas of social policy (see Exhibit 4.10).

Exhibit 4.10

The legislative process in Europe

There are four different routes by which EU proposals on employment issues can become law. These are:

The consultation procedure: a proposal is submitted to the Council of Ministers by the Commission. Following consultation of the European Parliament and the Economic and Social Committee, the Council may adopt the proposal on a unanimous vote.

The co-operation procedure: here the Council adopts a 'common position', by qualified majority voting, which is then put forward to the European Parliament for a second reading. The European Parliament then either approves or takes no decision on the common position; either of these positions leads to the automatic adoption of the proposal by the Council. Alternatively, it can reject the proposal – in which case the Council can adopt it only on a unanimous vote – or it may propose amendments, which will lead to a new proposal by the Commission. Adoption by the Council is by qualified majority voting.

The co-decision procedure: the European Parliament has a right to veto proposals where a common position has been reached by the Council. This right was established by the Treaty of European Union, which came into force on 1 November 1993, and was reinforced by the Treaty of Amsterdam.

The Social Partners: can reach an agreement under the social policy Protocol and Agreement (Social Chapter) annexed to the Treaty of European Union. The Commission is required to consult the Partners on social legislation, as well as the content of the measure, before a proposal is submitted. The UK's 'opt-out' of the Social Chapter has meant that it has not been covered by legislation adopted via this route. However, as a result of the Labour government's decision to sign up to the social policy Agreement, the UK is formally covered under the relevant provisions of the Treaty of Amsterdam (1999).

The employers' and trade unions' representatives that comprise the Social Partners should forward an opinion or recommendation on the proposal to the Commission. If they wish to negotiate, they have nine months to reach agreement, though this may be extended by a joint decision of the Commission and the Partners. Agreement resulting from this process can be implemented either 'in accordance with the procedures and practices specific to management and labour of the member states' or, where requested by the Social Partners, by a Council decision on a proposal by the Commission. The issue concerned determines whether the Council's decision can be taken by qualified majority voting or only on a unanimous vote.

Where the Partners cannot reach agreement, or either side refuses to discuss the subject matter, then the Commission may submit a proposal to proceed under either the co-operation or consultation procedure. For example, following the refusal by the private sector employers to engage in negotiations, the Commission has advanced its own proposal on national-level employee information and consultation.

When adopted at European level, the two key ways EU employment measures are incorporated into UK law are by the passing of a new statute or by the introduction of regulations.

Source: Adapted from IRS, 1999a

Economic and Social Committee

The Economic and Social Committee comprises representatives from those involved in the main areas of social and economic activity such as businesses, employees, professional organisations and agriculture. Membership composition is in proportion to the size of the member states. The Committee has a right to be consulted and also provides advice on economic and social matters.

EU law, treaties and social policy

EU law is in two parts; primary law comprises legal provisions contained in treaties and related documents which define the obligations of the parties, while secondary law contains legal provisions derived from primary law which are incorporated into regulations, directives, decisions, recommendations and opinions.

Regulations are rarely used but are directly applicable to and binding upon member states. Regulations do not require any intervention from the member state to give them legal force. Regulations take precedence over and supersede national law.

Directives are also binding upon member states, but require member states to take some action in order to incorporate them into legislation. Directives usually have an implementation date. For example, the UK endorsed the European Works Council Directive and the date for UK implementation was 31 December 1999. This means that a directive becomes law for member states by a certain date and is part of the EU legal framework.

Decisions are made by the Council and occasionally by the Commission and are binding on those parties to whom they are addressed.

Recommendations and opinions are not legally binding, and together with resolutions, solemn declarations and codes of practice have a moral rather than a legal imperative. The Community Charter of Fundamental Social Rights for Workers (known as the Social Charter) is one such example.

Treaties and the social policy framework

The treaties governing the establishment and continuing development of the EU have also established certain social policy initiatives and frameworks. However, social policy has been dogged by the debate between advocates of the 'free market' and those who consider intervention is necessary for the social well-being and protection of individuals and groups within the labour market and the employment relationship.

The Treaty of Rome 1957, created a customs union and common market and gave the European Economic Community (EEC), as it was then known, a distinct legal personality. Certain 'articles' within the Treaty established the basic principles of social policy as then conceived. These are:

- equal pay between women and men (Article 119);
- free movement of labour (Article 48 and others); and
- help with relocation and retraining of individuals affected by the integration of Community countries into a common market. Article 123 'provided the basis for the creation of the European Social Fund (ESF) which has been the main mechanism for achieving improved employment opportunities and enhancing geographic and occupational mobility' (Leat, 1999, p. 231).

The period up to 1985 saw the enlargement of the EEC and a number of directives on workers' rights concerning redundancies and equal opportunities. There was little consensus on other issues, the most notable being the Fifth Directive concerning employee participation and information (see Chapter 8). The era of Conservative governments from 1979 ensured that, as a result of persistent blocking of directives, very little progress was made on the social policy front. The period since 1985, notable in its earlier years for the appointment of the social interventionist Jacques Delors as President of the European Commission, saw a number of important developments in, and a more systematic approach to, social policy which would enable member states, with or without the co-operation of the UK, to apply the directives under, for example, the Social Charter Action Programme of 1989.

The Single European Act (SEA) 1987

The Act introduced institutional changes in order to establish the basis for the single European market by the end of 1992. It also introduced qualified majority voting within the Council of Ministers in order to speed up decision-making on measures necessary to achieve the single market. Article 118(b) opened the possibility for European-level social dialogue between the Social Partners; this had no immediate impact on the development of free-standing agreements, but was followed later by the Agreement on Social Policy under the Maastricht Treaty. The creation of a single market provided the impetus for the development of social policy.

Exhibit 4.11

The Social Charter: a summary

The proposals enshrining the rights of all EU citizens are:
- the freedom of movement for workers and self-employed persons across all countries of the EU;
- adequate protections for employment and remuneration;
- improvement of living and working conditions;
- adequate social protection and social security;
- freedom of association – including the right to join or not to join trade unions;
- adequate and continuing vocational and job training;
- equality of treatment for men and women;
- information, consultation and participation of workers on key workplace issues;
- health, protection and safety at the workplace;
- protection of children and adolescents at work;
- the access of elderly persons to labour markets; and
- the access of disabled persons to labour markets.

The Social Charter

The proposed establishment of the single market involving the removal of physical barriers to trade implied an intensification of competition between firms and attempts on the part of employers to reduce labour costs by moving investment to other member states with lower labour costs and relatively deregulated labour markets – a practice which became known as social dumping. Fear of worsening employment relations and deterioration of conditions of employment as a result of social dumping and other factors led the Commission to propose a Community Charter of Fundamental Social Rights for Workers (Social Charter), as summarised in Exhibit 4.11, which laid down minimum conditions and rights which should be incorporated into the employment legislation of member states. The Social Charter proposals were acceptable to all member states with the exception of the UK. Since the Charter proposals required a unanimous vote amongst Council members, the UK had effectively vetoed the Charter which consequently was not legally binding upon member states, remaining a 'statement of intent'. The Charter was supported by a Social Action Programme (SAP) which contained 47 proposals, including 17 draft directives, ten of which concerned health and safety issues. The SAP excluded some important areas such as specifying minimum pay levels, the right to strike,

the right of freedom of association which includes the right to join a trade union or employers' association, and imposing or constraining the process and status of collective bargaining. The UK veto therefore considerably weakened the impact of the Social Charter and the accompanying SAP but nevertheless it formed the basis of a draft Social Chapter of the Maastricht Treaty, 1991.

The Maastricht Treaty 1992

Also known as the Treaty of European Union, the Treaty established the European Union and introduced a number of major changes in the scope for regulating social and employment policy across the community of member states. During negotiations in 1991 leading up to the Treaty, attempts were made to amend Articles 117–122 (the 'social' clauses of the Treaty of Rome as amended by the Single European Act) in order to facilitate and broaden the scope of decision-making on employment matters, and to allow for greater qualified majority voting on employment-related matters. The UK government's refusal to co-operate with and agree to a revised Treaty that contained the draft Social Chapter – the infamous 'opt-out' – compelled the other (then) 11 member states to find an alternative solution which was annexed to the Treaty under a mechanism known as the Social Policy Protocol and Agreement (see below).

The Social Policy Protocol and Agreement

This provides a legal mechanism for implementing social policy, giving employers and unions the right to negotiate binding European framework agreements. The Protocol stated that member states (with the exception then of the UK) wished to continue developing social policy in line with the 1989 Social Charter and had therefore adopted an Agreement to this end. The Protocol authorises member states to make use of the institutions, procedures and mechanisms of the Maastricht Treaty in order to give effect to the Agreement. The Protocol thus enshrined the UK 'opt-out', while the Agreement constitutes the so-called Social Chapter. The agreement on social policy attached to the Social Protocol provides for qualified majority voting (QMV) by member states in the following areas:

- working conditions;
- information and consultation of employees;
- equal opportunities between men and women; and
- integration of people excluded from the labour market.

Proposals may be blocked where a sufficient number of member states form a blocking majority under QMV rules (26 out of 77 votes). Policy areas where unanimity is still required include:

- social security and protection of employees;
- protection of employees whose contract is terminated;
- collective representation;
- conditions of employment for third world country nationals legally resident in the EU; and
- financial provision for job creation schemes

Policy areas outside the scope of the EU are: pay; the right of association; the right to strike; and the right to impose lockouts. The Social Policy Agreement gives a wide role to the EU-level Social Partners. Where the Commission wishes to propose a measure, it is required to consult the Partners firstly, on the need for action at European level and, secondly, on whether it should be introduced by legislation or by collective agreement. Where the Partners choose to negotiate a collective agreement this must be done within nine months and it then passes to the Council for adoption as a directive without alteration.

The Treaties of Amsterdam and the Nice summit

The Treaty of Amsterdam (1999) to which the UK under New Labour is party, provides a legal framework for the EU to pursue objectives and take action in a number of social and employment areas that were not possible before. The main provisions affecting employment relations, and which incorporate revised Articles 118 and 119, include:

- The incorporation of the Social Policy Protocol and Agreement (see above) in the main text of the Treaty with Article 118 providing the legal basis for EU action.
- The introduction into the Treaty of a specific Chapter on employment issues (the Employment Chapter) which for the first time requires governments to co-ordinate their strategies for creating employment and promoting a skilled, trained and adaptable workforce. It also requires the member states to produce an annual report on the employment situation in the EU, detailing the effectiveness of actions taken.
- A renewed commitment to take action to 'combat discrimination based on sex, racial or ethnic origin, religion or belief, disability, age or sexual orientation' under a new Article 6a which enables the Council unanimously to take such action.
- A renewed obligation upon each member state, under the new Article 119, to ensure that the principle of equal pay and equal pay for equal value is applied (see Chapter 12).

The Nice summit (2000) gave rise to yet another Charter, that of Fundamental Rights of the European Union, which, while separate from the Social Charter, incorporates similar rights and will enable individuals to refer to the Charter in the determination of legal cases arising from national and EU contexts. The Charter is summarised in Exhibit 4.12.

New Labour's European agenda

The election of the Labour government signalled a more positive approach towards the EU. As we have already noted, a most significant development in the UK's relationship with the EU was the decision to end the 'opt-out' from the Social Chapter of the Maastricht Treaty, accept the Employment Chapter

Exhibit 4.12

Charter of Fundamental Rights of the European Union

The Charter includes the following Articles relevant to the employment relationship. For a more detailed description, consult the website www.europa.eu.int

Article 12: Freedom of assembly and of association
Includes the implied right of everyone to form and join trade unions.

Article 21: Non-discrimination
Any discrimination based on any ground such as sex, race, colour, ethnic or social origin, genetic features, language, religion or belief, political or any other opinion, membership of a national minority, property, birth, disability, age, or sexual orientation shall be prohibited.

Article 23: Equality between men and women
Equality between men and women must be ensured in all areas, including employment, work and pay. The principle of equality shall not prevent the maintenance or adoption of measures providing for specific advantages in favour of the under-represented sex.

Article 27: Workers' right to information and consultation within the undertaking
Workers or their representatives must, at the appropriate levels, be guaranteed information and consultation in good time in the cases and under the conditions provided for by Community law and national laws and practices.

Article 28: Right of collective bargaining and collective action
Workers and employers, or their respective organisations, have, in accordance with Community law and national laws and practices, the right to negotiate and conclude collective agreements at the appropriate levels and, in cases of conflicts of interest, to take collective action to defend their interests, including strike action.

Article 30: Protection in the event of unjustified dismissal
Every worker has the right to protection against unjustified dismissal, in accordance with Community law and national laws and practices.

Article 31: Fair and just working conditions
Every worker has the right to working conditions which respect his or her health, safety and dignity. Every worker has the right to limitation of maximum working hours, to daily and weekly rest periods and to an annual period of paid leave.

Article 33: Family and professional life
The family shall enjoy legal, economic and social protection. To reconcile family and professional life, everyone shall have the right to protection from dismissal for a reason connected to maternity and the right to paid maternity leave and to parental leave following the birth or adoption of a child.

of the Amsterdam Treaty and in due course the Charter of Fundamental Rights agreed at the Nice Summit in 2000. The transposition into UK domestic legislation of the various EU Directives (see below) is having and will have important consequences for employers, trade unions and individual employees, particularly as Britain traditionally had considerably less legal regulation in the areas of employment

and social policy than most other member states. The government, in line with the majority of member states, now endorses the concept of a social market economy which aims to provide sustainable economic growth 'underpinned by a social dimension characterised by a commitment to a strong welfare state, a partnership between government, employers and workers, and minimum standards at work' (IRS,

1997). However, the government also has reservations concerning any social regulation that might add to the cost burdens of industry and which would impair business competitiveness. The expectation is, therefore, that the government has not, and will not adopt Directives indiscriminately, and will temper its enthusiasm for the social market with a concern for economic efficiency.

The Directives which have been adopted by the government are:

Posted Workers Directive: this aims to ensure fair competition and provide minimum standards of employment for workers temporarily moved to another EU member state. All member states, including the UK, implemented the Directive by 24 September 1999.

Parental Leave Directive: gives parents the right to three months' unpaid time off work. The Directive had to be implemented in the UK by 15 December 1999; the Employment Relations Act 1999 together with separate regulations gave effect to the Directive.

European Works Councils: companies with more than 1000 employees in the participating states and at least 150 workers in each of two or more of these countries must set up a European Works Council or another appropriate procedure to inform and consult employees on key organisational issues. The UK gave effect to the Directive by the end of December 1999.

Directive on part-time work: this provides for equal treatment of part-timers with full-time employees, except where 'justified by objective reasons'. The UK implemented the Directive on 1 July 2000.

Directive on the burden of proof in sex discrimination cases: this places a greater onus on the employer to prove that discrimination did not take place in such cases. The Directive was implemented in the UK on 12 October 2001.

Part-time workers: fixed-term work: the Social Partners had been negotiating on the use of fixed-term contracts since March 1988. The ensuing Directive was transposed on 1 October 2001.

Working Time Directive: sets maximum 48 working hours per week and was transposed by the UK on 17 December 1999. Certain 'excluded' sectors, such as road, rail, air and sea, are now covered.

Directive on Information and Consultation of workers: employers are required to inform and consult employees on specific issues concerning the organisation, including its activities and economic and financial situation. The Directive was adopted in 2002 and in the UK a phased implementation is proposed, dependent on the size of the employer, starting from March 2005.

Young Workers Directive: protection for young or adolescent workers, above minimum school leaving age but below 18, not to be employed for more than 40 hours a week (8 hours a day). Implemented in UK on 6 April 2003.

Working Time Directive – excluded sector amendments: now to include those employed in road, rail, sea, inland waterway and lake transport, sea fishing and 'other work at sea' and the activities of doctors in training. Changes operational from 1 August 2003.

Acquired Rights Amendment Directive: allows for the inclusion of pensions within TUPE. UK implementation set for late 2003–2004.

Race Directive: covers discrimination on grounds of race or ethnic origin and required changes to the Race Relations Act 1976. Changes implemented on 19 July 2003.

Equal Treatment Framework Directive: covers discrimination on grounds of religion or belief, disability, age and sexual orientation based on proposals in government consultation document *Towards Equality and Diversity* (2001–2002). Implementation of proposals for religion or belief and sexual orientation by 2 December 2003; and for age and disability, 2 December 2006.

Temporary Agency Workers Directive: providing for same treatment of agency workers compared with permanent workers. The consultation period ended on 18 October 2002. No set date for implementation.

Takeover Directive (draft): to guarantee employee consultation regarding informing and consulting workers and shareholders on takeover bids. No set date for implementation.

Summary points

- EU social policy is influenced by the political complexion of member state governments and the nature of the presidency of the Council of Ministers.
- Social policy decision-making originates from proposals by the European Commission. The main decision-making bodies are the Council of Ministers, the European Parliament and the European Court of Justice, together with the Social Partners and the Economic and Social Committee.
- The legal instruments which put social policy into effect comprise regulations, directives and decisions. Instruments which are not legally binding include recommendations, opinions, resolutions and codes of practice.
- The procedures giving legal effect to proposals on directives, etc. at supranational level consist of the consultative procedure, the co-operation procedure, the co-decision procedure and agreements made by the Social Partners.
- The main Acts and treaties which govern social and economic policy are the Treaty of Rome; the Single European Act (which gave rise to the Social Charter); the Maastricht Treaty (which contains the original Social Chapter and Social Policy Protocol and Agreement); the Treaty of Amsterdam (which incorporates the 'new' Social Chapter endorsed by the UK), and the Nice Summit which agreed the Charter of Fundamental Rights.
- A more positive approach towards the EU on the part of the UK government has led to the adoption of a number of directives which are in the process of being implemented by incorporation either into new legislation such as the Employment Relations Act or by separate Regulations.

RELEVANT WEBSITES

www.acas.org.uk (Advisory, Conciliation and Arbitration Service) Provides information not only on disputes resolution but also on government initiatives in the area of general employment relations.

www.dti.gov.uk/er (Department of Trade and Industry) Contains a plethora of detail on government initiatives and policy.

www.eurofound.ie (European Foundation for the Improvement of Living and Working Conditions) Contains information on research projects directed and commissioned by the EU across a range of issues.

www.europa.eu.int (European Union On-Line) Full of factual information about the European Union, its institutions, legislative procedures and employment relations.

www.lowpay.gov.uk (Low Pay Commission) Annual reports on the operation of the National Minimum Wage.

www.statistics.gov.uk (Office for National Statistics) A wide variety of topics, including the labour force and the economy.

REFERENCES

Bach, S. (2002) 'Annual review article, 2001'. *British Journal of Industrial Relations*, 40, 2, 319–39

Beaumont, P.B. (1992) *Public Sector Industrial Relations*. London, Routledge

Crouch, C. (1995) 'The state: Economic management and incomes policy', in Edwards, P. (ed.) *Industrial Relations: Theory and Practice in Britain*. Oxford, Blackwell

Crouch, C. (2003) 'The state: Economic management and incomes policy', in Edwards, P. (ed.) *Industrial Relations Theory and Practice*, 2nd edn. Oxford, Blackwell

Dahl, R. (1961) *Who Governs? Democracy and Power in an American City*. London, Yale University Press

Dickens, L. (2002) 'Individual statutory employment rights since 1997: constrained expansion'. *Employee Relations*, 24, 6, 619–37

Dickens, L. and Hall, M. (1995) 'The state: Labour law and industrial relations' in Edwards, P. (ed.) *Industrial Relations: Theory and Practice in Britain*. Oxford, Blackwell

Dickens, L. and Hall, M. (2003) 'Labour law and industrial relations; a new settlement? In Edwards, P. (ed.) *Industrial Relations Theory and Practice*, 2nd edn. Oxford, Blackwell

Dolado, J., Kramarz, F., Machin, S., Manning, A., Margolis, D. and Teulings, C. (1996) 'The economic impact of minimum wages in Europe'. *Economic Policy*, No. 23

DTI (Department for Trade and Industry) (1998) *Fairness at Work*, Cm 2968. London, HMSO

Dunnett, A. (1998) *Understanding the Economy: An Introduction to Macroeconomics*. London, Longman

Edwards, P.K. (1994) 'Discipline and the creation of order' in Sisson, K. (ed.) *Personnel Management*, 2nd edn. Oxford, Blackwell

Farnham, D. and Pimlott, J. (1995) *Understanding Industrial Relations*. London, Cassell

Fernie, S. and Metcalf, M. (1996) *Low Pay and Minimum Wages: The British Evidence*. LSE: Centre for Economic Performance

Fisher, I. (1911) *The Purchasing Power of Money*. New York, Macmillan

Friedman, M. (1962) *Capitalism and Freedom*. Chicago, University of Chicago Press

Friedman, M. (1968) 'The role of monetary policy'. *American Economic Review*, 58, March, 1–17

Garrard, A. and Martin, W. (1996) *Labour's Economics: Can Mr Blair do it?* London, UBS Global Research

Gennard, J. (2002) 'Employee relations and public policy developments, 1997–2001'. *Employee Relations*, 24, 6, 581–94

Gospel, H. and Palmer, G. (1993) *British Industrial Relations*. London, Routledge

Green, D.G. (1987) *The New Right: The Counterrevolution in Political, Economic and Social Thought*. Brighton, Wheatsheaf Books

Hall, M. (1992) 'Behind the European Works Council Directives: the European Commission's legislative strategy'. *British Journal of Industrial Relations*, 30, 4, 547–66

Hall, M. (1994) 'Industrial relations and the social dimension', in Hyman, R. and Ferner, A. (eds) *New Frontiers in European Industrial Relations*. Oxford, Blackwell

Hayek, F.A. (1978) *The Road to Serfdom*. London, Routledge

Hayek, F.A. (1984) *1980s' Unemployment and the Unions*. Hobart Paper 87. London, IEA

Hobsbawm, E.J. (1974) *Labouring Men: Studies in the History of Labour*. London, Weidenfeld & Nicolson

Hutton, W. (1995) *The State We're In*. London, Jonathan Cape

Hyman, R. (1984) *Strikes*. London, Fontana

Hyman, R. (2003) 'The historical evolution of British industrial relations, in Edwards, P. (ed.) *Industrial Relations Theory and Practice*, 2nd edn. Oxford, Blackwell

IRS (1997) 'Labour's European agenda'. *IRS Employment Review*, No. 639

IRS (1999a) 'Employment law update: What's next from Brussels?'. *IRS Employment Review*, No. 671

IRS (1999b) 'New ground rules for employment relations'. *IRS Employment Review*, No. 674

Kahn-Freund, O. (1954) 'The legal framework', in Flanders, A. and Clegg, H.A. (eds) *The System of Industrial Relations in Great Britain*. Oxford, Blackwell

Kahn-Freund, O. (1977) *Labour and the Law*. London, Stevens

Kessler, S. and Bayliss, F. (1995) *Contemporary British Industrial Relations*. London, Macmillan

Kessler, S. and Bayliss, F. (1998) *Contemporary British Industrial Relations*, 2nd edn. London, Macmillan

Kirk, R. and Wall, A. (2002) 'The private finance initiative'. *Public Management Review*, 1, 4, 529–47

Leat, M. (1999) 'The European Union', in Hollinshead, G., Nicholls, P. and Tailby, S. (eds) *Employee Relations*. London, Financial Times/Pitman Publishing

Lourie, J. (1997) *National Minimum Wage Bill*. Research Paper 97/133. House of Commons

Low Pay Commission (1998) *The National Minimum Wage: First Report of the Low Pay Commission*. Cmnd 3976, London, HMSO

Low Pay Commission (2002) *National Minimum Wage Annual Report (2002)*. www.lowpay.gov.uk

Machin, S. (1997) 'A national minimum wage: who would be affected and the effect on employment', in Philpot, J. (ed.) *Implementing a National Minimum Wage*. London, Employment Policy Institute

MacInnes, J. (1987) *Thatcherism at Work*. Milton Keynes, Open University Press

Marx, K. and Engels, F. (1967) *The Communist Manifesto*. London, Penguin

McKendrick, J. and McCabe, W. (1997) 'An observer's tale: Stonehaven Community Hospital'. *Public Money and Management*. 17, 3, 17–20

McIlroy, J. (1991) *The Permanent Revolution? Conservative Law and the Trade Unions*. Nottingham, Spokesman

Minford, P. (1985) *Unemployment, Cause and Cure*, 2nd edn. Oxford, Blackwell

Pass, C. and Lowes, B. (1998) *Collins Dictionary of Economics*. Glasgow, HarperCollins

Phillips, A.W. (1958) 'The relation between unemployment and the rate of change of money wage rates in the United Kingdom, 1816–1957'. *Economics*, vol. 25, pp. 283–99

Philpott, J. (ed.) (1997) *Implementing a National Minimum Wage in the UK: Key Issues for the Low Pay Commission*. London, Economic Policy Institute

Rubery, J. and Edwards, P. (2003) 'Low pay and the national minimum wage', in Edwards, P. (ed.) *Industrial Relations Theory and Practice*, 2nd edn. Oxford, Blackwell

Schulten, T. (1996) 'European Works Councils: prospects of a new system of European industrial relations'. *European Journal of Industrial Relations*, 2, 3, 303–24

Schumpeter, J. (1976) *Capitalism, Socialism and Democracy*. London, Allen and Unwin

Smith, P. and Morton, G. (2001) 'New Labour's reform of Britain's employment law: the devil is not only in the detail but in the values and policy too'. *British Journal of Industrial Relations*, 39, 1, 119–138

Taylor, R. (1998) 'Review article 1997'. *British Journal of Industrial Relations*, 36, 2, 293–331

Weber, M. (1978) *Economy and Society: An Outline of Interpretive Sociology*. Berkeley, University of California Press

Wedderburn, K. (1986) *The Worker and the Law*. London, Penguin

PART 3

EMPLOYMENT RELATIONS: PATTERNS, PROCESSES AND OUTCOMES

CHAPTER 5

THE CHANGING WORKPLACE

INTRODUCTION

Having considered the role of trade unions and management as principal actors within the industrial relations system, we are now in a position to examine in more detail some of the central issues concerning workplace employment relations in Britain. Developments affecting employment relations and HRM within the workplace context are examined with reference to appropriate examples.

The chapter begins by considering the relationship between HRM and industrial relations, focusing on the extent to which the two are compatible. We look at the debate concerning the status of employment relations in the light of economic and structural changes that have taken place in Britain during the past 30 years or so, and how these developments have affected the nature of workplace employment relations as described and analysed in surveys and other empirical investigations. The transformation of workplaces as a result of changing production technologies and the impact of this upon workplace employment relations is examined, again by reference to examples of inwardly investing companies and contemporary forms of work organisation such as the call centre workplace.

Learning outcomes

When you have read this chapter, you should be able to:

1. Explain the association between employment relations and the 'hard' and 'soft' versions of HRM.

2. Explain the extent to which employment relations is compatible with HRM practice and strategy.

3. Differentiate between 'Fordist', 'neo-Fordist' and 'post-Fordist' production systems and the extent to which they have influenced the nature of workplace industrial relations.

5. Explain, by reference to specific examples, the impact of technological and other changes upon workplace employment relations.

EMPLOYMENT RELATIONS AND HRM

The association between employment relations and HRM is both uneasy and problematic. It is difficult to marry 'traditional' or 'orthodox' industrial relations with HRM since traditional industrial relations has a mainly collective orientation while HRM's concerns in its 'hard' and 'soft' aspects are largely individualistic. It should be noted that the contrast between traditional industrial relations and personnel management is more clear-cut, with traditional industrial relations focusing upon the organised relationship between trade unions and management (collective bargaining being the central institution and process binding this relationship), while personnel management attends to (amongst other things) recruitment and training issues (Edwards, 2003). To be sure, the 'individualist' components of employment relations such as disciplinary matters, grievance and redundancy procedures, and rules governing unfair dismissals and harassment, can often be relatively easily integrated, but their incorporation within HRM remains partial and potentially conflictual, as Exhibit 5.1 illustrates.

Does 'hard' and 'soft' HRM breed confrontation?

The interface between HRM and industrial relations is, therefore, problematic. One of the main issues concerns the *impact* of HRM upon workplace industrial relations and the internal labour market, and specific chapters of this book examine this in relation

Exhibit 5.1

Uneasy bedfellows

It is easy to see that the hard faces of HRM will often place it in confrontation with trade unions – especially in those settings where unions still retain some strength. For example, London Underground's wide-ranging plan consists of a package of measures which include staff reductions, salary status for all employees, the abolition of premium pay for weekend working, a reduction in the number of separate grades of staff from 400 to 70, and the replacement of promotion based on seniority to one based on assessed merit. A central plank in its attempted reform of working practices is the tackling of 'split shifts' where drivers work the morning and evening rush hours, take the middle part of the day off but are paid for 12 hours. The Rail, Maritime and Transportation Union (RMT) had planned an indefinite strike in response to a breakdown in negotiations on this package.

But even the 'soft' aspects – increased communication with employees, team participation techniques, harmonisation of terms and conditions, appraisal and reward – can lead to difficulties between management and unions. The basic reason for this is that whether hard or soft aspects are being activated, HRM in broad terms represents, or is seen as, a departure from the 'joint procedure' formula. To this extent, Guest's (1989) summation would seem to be correct: HRM and trade unionism are incompatible.

But under competitive conditions some sort of modus vivendi between industrial relations and HRM (between collectivism and individualism) would appear to be necessary. In some situations managers may choose to take the route of trying to dispense with the unions and thus clear the way for human resource management methods without the need for compromise. Certain greenfield site start-ups and certain NHS Trusts have taken this path. But in the latter cases there are examples where the reality of continuing union membership and the lack of trust emanating from management's refusal to recognise trade unions has eventually led to a decision to recognise the union – albeit on terms relatively more favourable to management than hitherto.

The implication is that in the larger number of cases in the British context some degree of balance between individualism and collectivism will have to be struck. This will clearly involve compromises on both sides. The precise nature of that balance and the way it can be managed is currently something of an open question. This issue is at the cutting edge of contemporary practice in the management of human resources and industrial relations.

Source: Adapted from Storey and Sisson, 1993, pp. 17–18

to non-unionism (Chapter 7) and representation (Chapter 8). The overall message of human resource policy is clear enough, according to Beaumont (1991):

> The key messages in the HRM literature are a strategic focus, the need for HRM policies and practices to be consistent with the nature of the overall business strategy, the need for individual components of a HRM package to mutually reinforce each other and be consistent with corporate culture; teamwork, flexibility, individual employee involvement and commitment are the leading watchwords of this approach. (p. 300)

Self-Evaluation Activity 5.1

Commitment and HRM

Response on website

Many models of HRM identify commitment as the main distinguishing feature between HRM and traditional personnel management/industrial relations. Why do you think this is? Table 5.1 puts this in context.

Both the 'hard' and 'soft' HRM models do not, therefore, have much in common with 'traditional' industrial relations as described in Chapters 1 and 3, with its collectivist orientation and corporatist structure. Legge (1995) identifies the contradictions between the two by posing a number of rhetorical questions:

> Can an employee be committed to both organisation and trade union simultaneously, particularly if workplace employee relations are adversarial rather than collaborative? How does functional flexibility square with multi-unionism and associated demarcation lines between jobs with union territoriality? Can numerical flexibility ever be compatible with union positions on job security, and how does the unitaristic stance of HRM sit with the pluralism of 'traditional' industrial relations? Can HRM and 'traditional' British industrial relations cohabit? (p. 247)

In relation to the issue of employee commitment to the employing organisation referred to above, we also have the issue of commitment to the trade union by the same employees (assuming they are trade union members). At first sight high levels of commitment shown by the same employees to both union and organisation could demonstrate that the goals and values of the union and organisation are similar if not compatible, but is probably an unrealistic situation. It is more likely that within a traditional industrial relations context employees would show a 'dual commitment' which would oscillate between high and low levels according to certain events or situations, such as during and after a strike. Guest (1995) suggests three models of industrial relations where dual commitment (to both union and organisation) may be identified.

The first is derived from the example of some Japanese organisations where the trade union at workplace level is regarded as an adjunct of the company. This model assumes a high degree of congruence between the aims of union and company. The second typifies those countries whose industrial relations is integrated within the political and legislative framework. In Germany, for example, rates of pay are determined by collective bargaining at national or industry level, while at local workplace level other issues are dealt with by works councils which are part of a structure of employee

Table 5.1 HRM's key dimensions

Dimension	Industrial relations	Human resource management
Psychological contract	Compliance	Commitment
Behaviour referent	Norms, custom and practice	Values/mission
Relations	Low trust, pluralist, collective	High trust, unitarist, individual
Organisation and design	Formal roles, hierarchy, division of labour, managerial controls	Flexible roles, flat structure, teamwork/autonomy, self-control

Source: Guest, 1995, p. 112

participation legislated for by the state. Works councils comprise both union and non-union members and commitment to the union may be variable, as traditionally there is relatively little involvement by remote union representatives in the affairs of the company. The third model approximates to the British system as described in Chapter 1, and 'the absence of legislative or cultural forces encouraging dual commitment makes its presence more fragile and more susceptible to the choices and actions of the key stakeholders (such as management) . . . The important point about this system is that it is inherently less stable and provides a less predictable basis for dual commitment' (Guest, 1995, p. 116).

THE OLD GIVES WAY TO THE NEW?

As HRM became, at least in its rhetoric, increasingly dominant during the 1980s and 1990s, so industrial relations rhetoric also began to change. The term 'new realism' was adopted by the media to denote attempts by trade unions to come to terms with the market-led ideology of Thatcherism (liberal individualism) and the decline in union membership. Academics noticed that the old leopard was changing its spots and used the term 'new industrial relations' to encompass some of the individualistic concerns of HRM. As Beardwell (1997) asserts:

> It is possible to reconstruct the central problem of industrial relations as being not so much the role of the trade union in the market economy as the role of the individual within the employment relationship, and in this way recast the framework of industrial relations so that the traditional collectivism we have been accustomed to is greatly reduced. (p. 7)

The context of change

Self-Evaluation Activity 5.2

Industrial relations change
Response on website

In Chapters 1, 2 and 3 we identified a number of significant changes to British industrial relations since 1979. Attempt to list the main ones.

The reasons for these changes are both structural and political/economic. Rose (1994) suggests the following structural reasons (based on Lash and Urry, 1987):

1. There is a continuing trend towards globalisation of markets and an increase in the scale of large, multinational organisations on the one hand, and a lessening concentration of capital in national internal markets on the other. For Britain and western countries generally, this implies a continuing erosion of the traditional manufacturing and extractive base with the well-documented industrial relations consequences such as the decline in union membership and density.

2. The fragmentation and eclipse of 'class' politics and 'working class solidarity'. In an industrial relations sense this means the increasing 'individualisation' of the employment relationship and the decline of collectivism.

3. A rapid decline in the manual 'core' working class as economies are de-industrialised. This has been a particularly significant ongoing trend during the 1980s, and has two consequences: first, the development of a permanently unemployed and increasingly unemployable underclass; and second, the condemnation of employed labour to an industrial diaspora of low-paid, under- or non-unionised and casualised work.

4. The decline in the number of people employed in, and the importance of, extractive and manufacturing industry, together with the growing prominence of service industries. The result has been the restructuring of social/industrial relations within smaller plants using, in particular, flexible labour processes and a labour force which is increasingly feminised and casualised.

5. The decline of 'occupational communities' (local communities dependent upon a single traditional industry such as coal mining and shipbuilding) and regional economies based on relatively few centralised extractive/manufacturing industries. This trend is also associated with the complementary decline in average plant size, together with the advent of labour-saving investment, subcontracted activities and the export of labour-intensive activities to world-market factories in the Third World and to rural (greenfield) sites in the First World.

Political/economic factors include:

1. Unemployment and recession which, as we have seen in Chapter 3, correlates with membership decline.
2. Changes in collective and individual legislation, referred to in Chapter 4, which represents the first systematic attempt to impose a legal framework upon industrial relations. Collective legislation has resulted in a progressive diminution of trade union power bases, while individual legislation has deregulated employment laws by, for example, removing statutory and administrative protection of terms and conditions of employment, the abolition of wage councils, repeal of Truck Acts and the removal of statutory restrictions on the employment of women and young people. Labour market deregulation proceeded apace, not only as a result of removal of statutory restrictions, but also by government determination to encourage the move towards decentralisation of pay bargaining and the projected dismantling of national collective bargaining machinery in the public sector.
3. The consequences of privatisation and contracting out of local authority services include job losses and the substitution of full-time jobs in a unionised sector for part-time jobs in non-unionised companies.

What happened to the 'new' industrial relations and is it 'neo' unitarist?

The term 'new' industrial relations (NIR) was topical for a period in the 1990s, so why continue to use the term in the early 2000s? Is it a legitimising term used not only to tease out the differences between the 'new' and the 'old' but also to make it more readily assimilated under the HRM banner? Boxall and Purcell (2003) would subscribe to that view as their definition of the subject area of HRM makes perfectly clear. Painting with a broad brush, they contend that HRM incorporates industrial, employment and work relations. In more critical vein, Clark (1997) offers the following interpretation of NIR:

New industrial relations represents three ideological images propagated by the contemporary state: first the promotion of the managerial prerogative, employee compliance and a low strike level; secondly, a rejection of collective bargaining and trade union recognition as public policy and their replacement with managerially determined regulation and individualism in the employment relationship; thirdly, a prescription for management labour use strategies centred on flexibility and extra-contractual commitment through human resource management. Each image evokes the formative influences of libertarian laissez-faire . . . and rejects influences centred on pluralism, collective bargaining and trade unions. (p. 42)

The above statement by Clark makes NIR virtually synonymous with an individualist unitary ideology (see Chapter 2). In addition, the ideological agenda of government as reflected in the definition above has some basis in practice (see also Chapter 4). The practices that came to be associated with NIR are diverse, although it is possible to identify three distinct patterns of arrangements comprising:

- the 'Japanese model';
- union avoidance and derecognition; and
- the challenge of HRM.

The 'Japanese model'

This is exemplified by the original Toshiba Consumer Products factory set up in Plymouth in 1981 and contains the following elements (Trevor, 1988, pp. 221–42):

- sole bargaining rights for a single trade union;
- a 'no-strike' agreement with binding 'final offer' arbitration as a last resort in disputes of interest;
- a broadly-based forum for consultation and employee participation;
- 'single status' conditions of employment; and
- complete freedom on the part of management to organise work.

The proliferation of single-union representation and agreements within 'greenfield' sites since the early 1980s is not a uniquely inspired Japanese phenomenon. As we have seen (Chapter 3), many trade unions such as the TGWU and the EEPTU, in the face of declining membership, have with varying degrees of enthusiasm encouraged such developments. The claimed advantages of a single union are that bargaining and consultation are simplified, that disputes are less likely and that introducing flexible working arrangements is made easier. According to Bevan (1987):

> The fact that agreements are single union, at a stroke, removes many of the potential obstacles to flexibility. Inter-union demarcation lines are a thing of the past and flexibility depends on nothing more than receiving the necessary training to carry out the task required. (p. 9)

WERS98 points to the decline in multi-unionism against the backdrop of union decline during the period 1990–8. While more than half of all unionised workplaces had two or more unions present, over half of the unionised workplaces in wholesale and retail, financial services and other community services had a single-union agreement and 43 per cent of all workplaces had single-union representation in 1998, up from 34 per cent in 1990 (Cully *et al.*, 1999; Millward *et al.*, 2000). A further impetus to the spread of single unionism is provided by the modest growth of partnership agreements (see Chapter 8).

Another characteristic of the Japanese model new-style agreements concerns the 'no-strike' clause with dispute resolution in the last resort through 'pendulum arbitration'. Although by the end of 1987 some 28 companies in Britain were known to have strike-free agreements (Oliver and Wilkinson, 1992), Millward (1994) found that these deals were extremely rare in British industry, while WERS98 did not even give them a mention. Millward states:

> A mere 1 per cent of workplaces with recognised trade unions had pendulum arbitration and in workplaces with a sole union agreement the figure was less than half of 1 per cent. In fact, pendulum arbitration was somewhat more common in multi-union workplaces. It was therefore by no means a distinctive element of 'new-style' agreements, as much of the literature has portrayed. Nor was it especially a feature of younger workplaces or of the industries, regions and trade unions in which the well-documented 'single union deals' have occurred. We concluded

> that pendulum arbitration was a rare practice, probably not increasing dramatically in its incidence and probably of longer standing than the single union deals of the mid to late 1980s. As a distinctive development in British industrial relations, pendulum arbitration has yet to reach the point of take off. (pp. 123–4)

A third characteristic of the Japanese model of NIR is the company advisory board or company council. These boards, which should be differentiated from the more traditional joint consultative committee (see Chapter 8), are often regarded as necessary to provide further stability and predictability in workplace industrial relations. The boards comprise elected representatives who are not necessarily shop stewards or trade union members and are chosen by non-union as well as unionised employees, providing a forum for negotiations on pay and conditions where traditional demarcations between consultation and negotiation are eliminated. Companies adopting this system often experience conflicts of interest as a result of the shift of responsibilities from shop stewards to the boards. In relation to Nissan's long-standing deal with the AEU, for example, Crowther and Garrahan (1988) claim that:

> It allows virtually no independent role for shop stewards, and whilst it appears that the company does not intend to actively obstruct union activities, the mechanism for representation is highly supportive of non-union participation. (p. 56)

An argument in support of the company board is, that as a consultative mechanism, it disseminates company information on important matters that most UK companies have tended to keep secret – but even this concession is dependent on the goodwill of management. According to the WIRS analysis conducted by Millward (1994), company boards are neither as popular nor as frequent as is often assumed. A mere 17 per cent of workplaces having a single-union agreement bothered to set up boards, and there was little difference between single-union workplaces *without* an agreement and workplaces without any recognised unions. However, the impact of the European Works Council Directive implemented in the UK in December 1999 has resulted in an increase in the proportion of workplaces having 'higher level' boards or committees (see Chapter 8). In 1998, 56 per cent of workplaces belonging to a wider organisation reported a higher level committee, up from 48 per cent in 1990. In addition, there can be no doubt that the adoption of the Information and Consultation Directive from 2005 will provide further impetus to the development of representative committees and boards.

A fourth characteristic of the model concerns single status employment conditions. Based on examining differences between manual and non-manual employees, Millward found that only around one in eight workplaces had equality of employment conditions and that 'workplaces with sole union agreements were no different from the generality of workplaces in this respect' (Millward, 1994, p. 125). By 1998, there appeared to be a significant increase in the proportion of workplaces with single-status entitlements covering pension schemes, company car or car allowance, private health insurance, four weeks' or more paid annual leave and sick pay in excess of statutory requirements, with 41 per cent of workplaces qualifying (Cully *et al.*, 1998).

A final feature of Japanese-style NIR within the single-union representation context (but not exclusively so) concerns the freedom of management to organise work at the establishment in any way it thought fit. Millward (1994) found that:

management flexibility . . . was widespread. Nearly three-quarters of workplaces with recognised trade unions were reported to have complete management flexibility. It was hardly something unique to workplaces with 'single union deals'. In fact, workplaces with sole union agreements were no more and no less likely to have management flexibility. They simply reflected the common reality of the widespread lack of union influence upon issues of work organisation. Management flexibility was more widespread in younger workplaces and . . . in those with lower levels of union membership. When we looked at single union workplaces . . . it appeared that sole union agreements were associated with less management flexibility, not more as the stereotype of the 'single union deal' had suggested. (p. 124)

Management/worker flexibility is therefore far more widespread and diffuse within British industry and certainly not confined to single-union contexts. It is, perhaps, the single most important factor which characterises and distinguished NIR and is as common in multi-union, as in single-union organisations; in British-owned, as in foreign-owned companies. The content of flexibility agreements varies around a common core as exemplified in the abstracts from the Komatsu-AEU and the Hitachi-EEPU agreements given in Exhibit 5.2.

Exhibit 5.2

Flexibility deals in Komatsu and Hitachi

In *Komatsu* there is complete flexibility and mobility of employees; changes in processes and practices will be introduced to increase competitiveness and . . . these will improve productivity and affect manning levels. To achieve such change, employees will work as required by the company and participate in the training of themselves or other employees as required. The company using appropriate industrial engineering and manpower planning techniques will determine manning levels.

In *Hitachi* all company members will agree the complete flexibility of jobs and duties. When necessary to fit the needs of the business all company members may be required to perform whatever jobs and duties are within their capability. The company accepts its responsibility to train, retrain and develop company members to broaden their skills, grow their potential and meet the needs of rapid technological change. The company also accepts that in the instances where more competitive manning levels can be achieved by agreed flexibility . . . manning levels will be achieved without compulsory redundancy.

Source: Oliver and Wilkinson, 1992, pp. 293–4

More established companies on 'brownfield' sites with established unions and agreements may have greater problems in introducing such arrangements, and although the UK motor industry has made considerable progress in implementing Japanese-style manufacturing techniques, it has not so readily changed its industrial relations. One notable exception to this was the former Rover car company, considered as a case example in Chapter 2, which introduced its 'New Deal' in a multi-union, multi-site context (Rose and Woolley, 1992). Following Guest's 'stronger' version of HRM, it appeared that Rover had adapted this distinctive approach to industrial relations management which incorporated the following principles:

- strategic interventions designed to elicit commitment and to develop 'resourceful' employees;
- strategic interventions designed to secure full utilisation of labour resources; and
- both interventions identified above to be integrated within the business strategy.

The outcome of this strategic approach to HRM was the 'New Deal', which was summarised in Chapter 2. The New Deal arrangements at Rover represented the culmination of its Total Quality Initiative (TQI) which began in 1987. After initial resistance from the shop floor, a survey of managers and convenors revealed a general endorsement of the TQI (Rose and Woolley, 1992). The New Deal thus built upon the TQI and was the result of extensive consultation and negotiation between management and senior convenors. While HRM assumptions and the 'Japanisation' elements are important constituents of the New Deal policy, the company's multi-union structure remains intact and collective industrial relations, despite moves towards 'single-table' bargaining, had not been eroded. Rover's somewhat improved performance during the 1990s, together with the relative absence of industrial disputes, appeared to vindicate this policy. The New Deal also represented a further stage of the organisational cultural change process and an unfolding human resource strategy which emphasised co-operation rather than conflict, and which contrasted starkly with the conflict-ridden years of Rover's past.

Union avoidance and derecognition

The second component of NIR concerns the complete and continuing avoidance of trade union involvement. Millward (1994) states:

> Union avoidance at new workplaces was far less controversial and thus attracted much less public attention. In many private sector industries, particularly those dominated by small independent firms, the absence of trade unions has always been the common pattern. But as yet we do not know whether union avoidance has become a more common feature of newer workplaces or if the processes of maturation that sometimes led to unionisation have been attenuated. (p. 2)

As we saw when the issue was discussed in greater detail in Chapter 2, there is growing evidence that trade union derecognition intensified during the 1990s and support for trade unions weakened amongst employees in unionised organisations (Millward et al., 2000).

The challenge of human resource management

There is, to be sure, a wide gap between the rhetoric of HRM-speak and the reality of the workplace. While at strategic level HRM is often espoused in accommodatory terms, emphasising the treatment of employees as 'assets', fostering a broadly-based communications system, and involving employees in the organisation and planning of work, the workplace experience of employees, and in particular unionised employees, sometimes suggests otherwise (see Legge, 1995, for a fuller discussion). According to the latter perspective, HRM is associated with union derecognition and a systematic attempt to undermine the union role, and to some extent the WIRS survey and analysis confirms this view. However, there is one significant caveat here which concerns company *size* and HRM. A large proportion of companies within the *Financial Times* Top 50 recognise trade unions and implement at least some 'industrial relations-friendly' HRM policies focusing on information, consultation and employee involvement. Conversely, going down the size scale, the *smaller* the company the more likely it is to be union-free and, where there is a union presence, the more hostile the employer is to that presence. The latest comprehensive empirical evidence from WERS98 concerning the growing prevalence of HRM is presented in Exhibit 5.3.

Notwithstanding the evidence already presented – and most certainly more empirical evidence is still required – the unavoidable conclusion is that within both unionised companies, and more especially non-unionised companies, employers have at best been only partially successful in developing a positive HRM agenda and developing more sophisticated HR practices. WERS98, for example, confirms that sophisticated HR practices are confined mainly to larger workplaces and in the public sector. The reasons for this may lie in the absence of a formal statement of strategy (Hunter and MacInnes, 1994) owing to short-term financial pressures on British managers which prevent them from implementing long-term strategies to develop employee skills and attributes (Sisson, 1993), and to 'widespread managerial incompetence in both technical and organisational matters' (Procter and Ackroyd, 2001).

Implications of these developments for employment relations issues

The developments identified above have affected employment relations issues in the following ways:

- In organisations where HRM is well established and which demonstrate high levels of management involvement and employee commitment, then it is more likely that elements of the NIR will be incorporated into HRM and be operated relatively successfully, and will manifest themselves as 'high commitment management practices'. High-commitment practices include: the use of personality tests, performance tests, formal off-the-job-training, regular appraisals, group-based team briefings with feedback and participation in problem-solving groups. Within unionised contexts, it has already been established that individual unions are modifying their approaches on both individualistic and collectivist dimensions (Bacon and Storey, 1993, 1996; Boxall and Purcell, 2003; Kessler and Purcell,

---

Exhibit 5.3

WERS98 and HRM: the rise of human resource managers

1. In 1990, 1 per cent of respondents bore the 'human resources' title, but by 1998 7 per cent of managers responsible for workplace employment relations were HR managers, comprising 30 per cent of all employment relations specialists.

2. The increase in HR managers accounts for the increase in specialists between 1990 and 1998. HR managers were not confined to head office in a strategic sense, but were diffused throughout the organisation. The incidence of HR managers increased with workplace size although this is no simple correlative association.

3. Of the very smallest workplaces, for example, there was a disproportionate number of employment relations specialists in 40 per cent of such workplaces. The human resource title was very much in evidence in the privatised services.

4. The growth in HR managers can be partly attributed to the increased penetration of foreign-owned workplaces where HR managers accounted for 64 per cent of employment as compared with 26 per cent in UK-owned workplaces.

5. HR managers were less common in the public sector where 20 per cent of employment relations specialists were HR managers compared with 35 per cent in the private sector.

6. HR managers are not confined to new workplaces; 32 per cent of employment relations specialists in workplaces aged ten years or more were HR managers with the corresponding proportion in workplaces aged under ten years being 29 per cent. Millward *et al.* (2000) conclude that 'it seems likely that human resource managers will become more prevalent if more continuing workplaces change the type of employment relations specialist they employ and new workplaces continue to introduce them' (p. 55).

2003). Within non-unionised contexts, most UK organisations do not have well-developed HRM (Millward *et al.*, 2000) but within the sample enterprises which Guest and Hoque (1994) examined, there was a sizeable minority of UK greenfield site operations which did, and whose industrial relations were largely integrated within HRM. The deficiency of HRM may also be explained by reference to factors other than the absence (or presence) of the collective union voice. In addition, WERS98 indicates that sophisticated HRM practices are to be found alongside union recognition and workplaces with higher densities of unionisation, and that 'an active and strong union presence is compatible with the broad suite of high commitment management practices' (Cully *et al.*, 1999, p. 111).

- Insofar as collective bargaining is concerned, the evidence of the 1980s and 1990s indicates that, according to Brown (1993):

> the coverage of collective bargaining has contracted substantially, that the scope of bargaining has narrowed, that the depth of union involvement has diminished and that organisational security offered to unions by employers has deteriorated. (p. 195)

Moreover, Millward *et al.* (1992) also demonstrate how much worse off are those employees who do not enjoy the protection of collective bargaining in terms of pay, health and safety, labour turnover, contractual security, compulsory redundancy, grievance procedures consultation, communication and employee representation. Therefore, the erosion of collective bargaining as a result of union substitution practices and/or marginalising the bargaining process has indeed resulted in a deterioration of conditions associated with the employment relationship. The contraction of collective bargaining continued throughout the 1990s and into the 2000s to such an extent that Brown *et al.* (2003) conclude that 'the reality for the vast majority of employees who work in the private sector in Britain is that managements, not trade unions, determine their pay' (p. 204).

- The issue as to whether trade unions and, more recently, HRM and NIR have or have not had an impact upon organisational performance has been part of a long-running debate in labour

economics. The accumulated evidence summarised by Rose and Woolley (1992) suggests that far from hindering productivity and competition, high levels of unionisation actually encourage it, particularly when associated with well-developed human resource strategies as within the Rover context. The assumption, therefore, that by encouraging the 'free play' of market forces and by discouraging union involvement and representation this can somehow result in a more highly competitive and performing organisation, is seriously flawed. The new and often non-unionised labour market, where it has emerged, has in general terms not supported improved organisational competitiveness. Nolan and O'Donnell (2003), in their latest review of the literature, argue that by resisting crude forms of exploitation in production and campaigning for higher wages for their members, 'unions may have a transforming impact on the nature of production and business strategies' (p. 492). With regard to HRM, research by Guest *et al.* (2000) revealed that productivity and financial performance had been lifted by extensive use of HR practices. However, as WERS98 also demonstrates, the application of HR practices has been more prevalent in establishments and workplaces in which there is also a union presence, and the argument therefore shifts as to whether either HR or union presence or both singly and/or in combination have a positive influence upon performance and productivity (Ramsay *et al.*, 2000).

- Finally, the impact of NIR in the public sector has been far more limited than within the private sector. This view must, however, be qualified by acknowledging, as Bach and Winchester (2003) do, that by the end of the 1980s:

(a) the privatisation of public corporations removed entire groups of employees from the public sector;

(b) the introduction of compulsory competitive tendering for many ancillary public services resulted in substantial job losses, a downward pressure on wages and benefits, and more intensive patterns of work; and

(c) the introduction of controls over public expenditure affected traditional 'comparability' arguments in pay negotiations and replaced this with 'ability to pay' argument in the face of strict cash limits.

Despite these developments, Bach and Winchester (1994) argue that Conservative governments achieved only limited success in encouraging decentralised industrial relations and pay determination in the public services, even though national agreements became more flexible. They go on to conclude that:

> Advocates of decentralised market-sensitive pay determination will be disappointed to find no evidence that the government intends to withdraw from the active and inconsistent involvement in public sector pay determination that has characterised its predecessors' policies for the last thirty years. (p. 280)

The changes, the reasons behind them and the impact of them upon employment relations have helped to create a new climate in which industrial relations operates. They have undoubtedly encouraged managements to take HRM initiatives and adopt human resource strategies geared towards improving employee productivity and commitment and fostering a more harmonious and co-operative employee-oriented organisational culture. However, the HRM rhetoric, as suggested earlier, belies the reality in many instances. This must be a cause for concern to all parties in the employment relationship, and as Storey and Sisson (1993) state:

> In the light of the rhetoric one would expect to find impressive evidence of an upturn in the amount of training and development, in the utilisation of appropriate performance management techniques, in the integration of human resource practices and business strategy, and not least in the economic performance outcomes of British industry. However, Britain still has a long way to go. Senior managers are either not practising what they espouse or they are installing new initiatives in an incompetent and ineffective way. (p. 50)

The example in Exhibit 5.4 illustrates this in a vivid way.

Exhibit 5.4

'Union unwraps Cadbury's secret strategy'

Over the years Cadbury has won the respect of trade unions and workforce as well as peers who rate it seventh most admired company. But this reputation only increased the damaging impact of an internal management document on 'manufacturing human resource strategy'. The strategy embraces many of the elements of present-day HRM: the emphasis on communication and feedback, training and development, 'performance-focused culture' backed up by reward for skills and competencies, and employee involvement.

However, for the union a different and more sinister slant is put on all these programmes by the final part of the strategy which calls for the union to be 'marginalised by greater focus on direct communication and consultation, but without an overt statement to this effect'. It speaks of the 'likelihood of downsizing' and adds: 'For those groups where the trade union has already been de-recognised . . . it is important that they are not exploited by the company as this would lead to pressure for renewed trade union involvement.'

The union (TGWU) describes the approach as 'fundamentally dishonest', and Cadbury workers are reported to have instructed shop stewards to halt co-operation with such key parts of the people strategy as Quality Improvement Teams and NVQ skills programmes. . . . Far from being willing to be innovative and creative on the company's behalf, the Cadbury unions are explicitly advising members to 'take care about giving ideas to management', since it could lead to job cuts, and to refuse co-operation with attempts to individualise pay.

Now there is no reason why union membership should be incompatible with individual development – see Rover, for example. But this implies a recognition and negotiation of different, legitimate interests which Cadbury's human resource managers were not prepared to admit. The final irony is that because of the leak the matter is now out of the hands of the professionals and in the court of top management and the trade unions – which is where the HRM project came from in the first place.

Source: The Observer, December 4, 994

Having read the previous sections, you should be able to identify the main alleged differences between 'traditional' and 'new' industrial relations. Attempt this now and also comment on the degree to which you think HRM is, or is not, compatible with industrial relations, new or otherwise. (The following section may be helpful.)

The British context: peaceful co-existence or open warfare?

The human resource strategy models such as the best-practice models of Beer *et al.* (1985) and Kochan *et al.* (1986) and the contingency models of Fombrun *et al.* (1984) and Schuler and Jackson (1987) rest on the basic assumption that HRM requires a more *strategic* orientation to the management of employees than do traditional personnel management or industrial relations models. While it is not the intention to describe these models in any greater detail than that which is summarised below, they do present problems in their implementation within the British context (since all the models referred to above are American) where research still points to an endemic *absence* of strategy in British HRM/industrial relations together with the failure to incorporate HRM/industrial relations within existing business strategies. Storey and Sisson (1993), moreover, challenge the assumptions upon which both best-practice and contingency theorists build their cases.

Assumption one: 'That HR/IR managers have easy access to a business strategy'

This assumption is largely invalid, at least in an operational sense, since access to such a strategy requires HR/IR managers to have a range of knowledge of the practical implications of the exercise of numerous strategic choices within non-HR/IR

areas. Moreover, the reality of strategy formulation and planning is rarely as neat as some of the models suggest. Too often, short-term or even day-to-day considerations impinge on that process: effectively the process is deconstructed and atomised, making it difficult for HR/IR managers to respond meaningfully in a strategic sense. There is also, as Storey and Sisson (1993) suggest, little evidence that, in normative terms, the 'grand' strategy is better than having no strategy at all. In practice, the assumed link between HRM policies (however sophisticated) and elements of 'grand' strategy is, at least, tenuous. Indeed, in the British context 'pick and mix' and 'fire-fighting' may still be the HR/IR operational order of the day. Storey and Sisson quote Marginson *et al.* (1988) in support of this latter assertion:

> It is difficult to escape the conclusion that, although the great majority of our respondents claim that their organisations have an overall policy or approach to the management of employees, with the exception of a number of companies which are overseas owned, or financially centralised or operating in the service sectors, it would be wrong to set very much store by this . . . the general weight of evidence would seem to confirm that most UK owned enterprises remain pragmatic or opportunist in their approach. (p. 120)

Assumption two: 'That managers have a genuine free choice of strategic stance'

This assumption is too naive and raises the philosophical notion of 'free will' and 'determinism'. In practice, organisations and their participants – including the most senior managers – operate within a set of circumscribed constraints, as any student who has studied the political, economic and social environment of organisations will readily acknowledge. The absence of such choice goes a long way towards explaining the tenuous link between corporate and HR/IR strategy (where such a strategy exists). However, various strategy models have been developed, of which two of the more important – best-practice and contingency, as mentioned above – are described in Exhibit 5.5.

Exhibit 5.5

Strategy models

Best-practice models

Beer *et al.* (1985), and Kochan *et al.* (1986) are concerned with influences upon HRM policy choices exerted by stakeholders and by 'situational' factors. Appropriate decisions made on this basis will result in beneficial human resource outcomes. An industrial relations-oriented variation has been developed by Kochan *et al.* Their basic argument is that industrial relations practices and outcomes are the result of environmental forces interacting with the strategic choices and values of managers, union leaders, employees, etc. Strategic choice, therefore determines the type of industrial relations system that emerges at the three main levels of decision-making: collective bargaining at divisional, organisational, and workplace levels.

Kochan *et al.* use this framework to track the fundamental changes in American industrial relations over a 50-year period. This enables them to identify the current and prevailing industrial relations orthodoxy, which they label as the 'new industrial relations' model. This model largely displaces the traditional conflict-oriented model, and emphasises the involvement of unions at business strategy levels. Unlike the situation in the UK, union involvement means nothing less than 'union engagement' by senior union personnel in strategic business decisions. These decisions concern new investment, new technology, workforce adjustment strategies and new forms of work organisation. In order to facilitate this new level of involvement, new attitudes involving a high degree of attitudinal restructuring were required by both unions and management. It is important to note that these shifts in union–management co-operation go far beyond what has happened in the UK and required 'a blending of traditional representation and newer participatory processes along with, perhaps, additional, more individualised forms of voice and representation' (Kochan *et al.*, 1986, p. 225).

Contingency models

These models assume that policy choices vary according to changing business conditions. Kochan and Barocci (1985), for example, argue that the type of HRM strategies and priorities an organisation selects are contingent upon the life-cycle stage of an organisation. Fombrun *et al.* (1984) posit a contingency model which is concerned with identifying particular strategies and structures, and with linking these to appropriate HR policy choices concerning selection, appraisal, rewards and employee development. A further refinement to the contingency approach is made by Schuler and Jackson (1987) whose model builds upon Porter's (1985) 'competitive advantage' paradigm. Essentially, Schuler and Jackson identify three sets of *strategic options* (innovation, quality enhancement and cost-reduction) each of which gives rise to associated 'employee role behaviours'. HRM policy choices are required to foster and maintain these behaviour patterns.

Are HRM and IR strategies truly incompatible and does it matter?

It is likely that NIR, which places greater emphasis upon 'individualist' aspects of the employment relationship together with a correspondingly lower priority to collective and conflictual aspects, will be more congruent with HRM and its strategies provided the latter genuinely reconciles the aims of greater employee commitment, investment in long-term training and development and security of employment with a 'pluralist' orientation towards employee representation and all that this entails. However, should employers continue to espouse contradictory values clothed in the rhetoric of HRM (for example, by reiterating the importance of 'quality' and 'customer care' while at the same time precariously cutting costs and 'casualising' the workforce), then the prospects for any reconciliation between the two seem rather poor. This is, of course, particularly true of the British context where strategic HRM is still regarded by some as an ideological movement, the aim of which is to disaggregate labour and marginalise trade unions.

Guest's approach (1989) to this problem is to argue that there is indeed a basic incompatibility between unitarist HRM and the pluralist traditions of British industrial relations, particularly within multi-union 'brownfield' sites. It may seem obvious to argue that a fundamental prerequisite for compatibility/incompatibility is that within an organisational context the two systems should be extant. Where strategic HRM is well developed – and within the British context this is still a relatively rare phenomenon – perhaps on the lines suggested by contingency theory, then industrial relations may well be incorporated within the human resource strategy. Arguably, therefore, compatibility will depend upon the extent to which industrial relations is included as a major component of an organisation's human resource strategy. Where, however, the human resource strategy is imposed arbitrarily within a unionised organisation, and where little thought is given to the industrial relations consequences, then the two systems will be in conflict with each other and even mutually exclude each other. In the UK, the problem of incompatibility arises as the consequence of the latter scenario, where senior managers on the one hand and senior convenors on the other each fear encroachment upon their prerogatives. Senior managers may also perceive themselves as having the upper hand and will take advantage of the weakened position trade unions are in nationally to further weaken them in the workplace. The 'softening-up' process, which includes introducing individualised forms of pay determination, thereby diluting collective bargaining, and excluding unions from other forms of decision-making, is seen as a necessary condition for the implementation of 'full-blown' strategic HRM.

There can be little doubt that incorporation of the 'best' elements of an organisation's industrial relations system into its HRM strategy is the way forward. Given the paucity of such human resource strategies and the piecemeal way HRM policies have been introduced within British organisations, the task remains daunting. The combined HRM/IR strategy (which should contain elements of NIR

examined earlier) must, according to Storey and Sisson (1993) satisfy three criteria:

> *The first of these is that the business strategy must be capable of being translated into operational action plans. Second, it must be made absolutely clear to whom the responsibility for developing the strategy actually belongs: does it rest, for example, at corporate headquarters, the divisional office or at each business unit? Third, some decision has to be taken about the overall thrust of the approach – will it, for example, aspire to match up to one of the 'best practice' models or will it reflect in contingency fashion, the particular needs of the organisation?* (p. 79)

The ongoing conundrum concerning individualism and collectivism in relation to management style (see Chapter 2 and Kessler and Purcell, 2003), the growing literature in relation to HR strategy (summarised by Boxall and Purcell, 2003), the accommodation of union voice mechanisms (see Chapters 3 and 8), and the extent to which high commitment and performance HR systems, either in concert with a union presence or not, affect performance and productivity (Nolan and O'Donnell, 2003), will ensure that this debate and its contradictions will continue to run.

Summary points

- Insofar as NIR encompasses new-style agreements, flexibility agreements and other new employment practices such as employee involvement, TQM, teamworking and empowerment, then it could be argued that NIR is more compatible with HRM strategies than 'traditional' industrial relations. The evidence for this, as we have noted, is still relatively sparse and should be related, amongst other things, to industrial relations outcomes such as wage levels, productivity and investment in new technology.
- Moreover, there appears to be some convergence between a modified collectivist approach, as evidenced by NIR, and an HRM strategy which is more 'pluralist' in orientation, of the 'soft' rather than the 'hard' variety and which can develop in the context of a well-established union presence. This is the argument adopted by Legge (1995):

It would appear that the greater the extent to which unions adhere to a liberal collectivist (or 'traditional') view of employee relations the more likely it is that in theory they will regard HRM as a threat undermining the institutions of collective bargaining. If 'soft' HRM undermines via co-optation and marginalisation, 'hard' HRM undermines via marginalisation, non-recognition and, in extreme cases, de-recognition. . . . Whereas traditional British industrial relations and 'hard' HRM appear ideologically incompatible with any 'practical' accommodation based on the exercise of managerial prerogative over weakened unions, both ideologically and practically, 'new' industrial relations and 'soft' model HRM appear compatible, even if the weaker partner runs the risk of being absorbed by the more dominant one, or of a breakdown occurring through disappointed expectations. (p. 282)

- We end this section on a cautionary note. While the 'take-up' of HRM has been partial and sporadic, Pemberton and Herriot (1994) have argued that there is growing evidence of some faltering of the HRM project and that some workforces are showing signs of mutiny. They cite BT and Cadbury-Schweppes as organisations whose remaining employees express anger concerning increased job insecurity, distrust about employers' motives and loss of pride in working for their companies. More recently, deep suspicions concerning employers' motives with regard to pensions and the continuing and increased use of non-standard employment contracts have done little to convince employees of the authenticity of HR spin and rhetoric. There can be little confidence that those employees who remain will wish to deliver what the organisation requires, particularly within what some employees perceive as a 'culture of fear' which is undermining the effective implementation of business changes because of a focus on short-term results. Pemberton and Herriot go on to state:

  The willingness to improve customer care through building long-term relationships is likely to be undermined by the [employee's] desire to get out the minute an alternative job opportunity arises. The exhortation to grow with the job and embrace multi-skilling is being undermined by a desire to get even; digging in and resisting overtly or covertly the organisation's agenda.

- While this may be a rather pessimistic scenario, it does suggest that as far as some organisations are concerned, playing 'hard-ball' has not produced the business results expected, or sold the case for HRM. In those organisations, NIR remains elusive and illusory.

SURVEY EVIDENCE OF WORKPLACE INDUSTRIAL RELATIONS: 1968–2002

The number of workplaces in Britain runs to many thousands of varying sizes. They may be on established urban sites ('brownfield' sites) or increasingly on new purpose-built 'greenfield' sites. It is at the workplace where much of the day-to-day industrial relations activities take place, involving local management and workplace representatives and shop stewards (see Chapter 3). However, while there is a growing amount of case study and survey evidence, relatively little is known about industrial relations at this level. This is due largely to the limitations of case-study research which provides in-depth knowledge of one or two workplaces but which cannot be generalisable to the totality of all workplaces. Case-study research, nevertheless, is useful in that it may provide information about a specific subject, such as 'flexibility', thereby enhancing our knowledge of it. Surveys, on the other hand, are much more wide-ranging than case-study research, as the example given in Exhibit 5.6 of the design of the 1998 Workplace Employee Relations Survey (WERS) demonstrates.

General findings of the pre-1990 surveys

The first important survey of workplace industrial relations was undertaken by the Donovan Commission in 1968. Additional workplace surveys were conducted in 1973 and 1978, but were not very comprehensive. This brings us on to the WIRS/

Exhibit 5.6

The 1998 Workplace Employee Relations Survey

Throughout the 1980s the reform of British industrial relations was high on the agenda of politicians, managers, workers and their trade unions. The Workplace Employee Relations Survey (known as WERS) series was designed to contribute to these continuing debates by making available large-scale, systematic and dispassionate evidence about a broad range of industrial relations and employment practices across almost every sector of the economy. The reports on the first three surveys, conducted in 1980, 1984 and 1990, known as WIRS 1, 2, and 3 respectively, were widely welcomed as providing the most comprehensive bank of material on such matters yet available for any developed economy. Not only were the findings much discussed by policy makers and practitioners within and outside government, but also the data was subject to secondary analysis by academic and other researchers in a range of disciplines.

The design of the 1998 survey

Like its predecessors, the 1998 survey was a representative national survey of establishments, with the respondents being the key role-holders in those establishments. Again like its predecessors, it contained predominantly factual questions about the formal structures and practices of industrial relations at the sampled workplace. To maximise the potential for comparisons it had to have the same comprehensive coverage of sizes and types of establishment as the earlier surveys but, as a departure from earlier surveys, very small workplaces were included for the first time.

The sample

The sampling frame was as similar as possible to the 1980 and 1984 surveys, using the most recent Census of Employment on each occasion. The original surveys were limited to workplaces with 25 or more employees and their industrial coverage was all manufacturing and services (Divisions 1 to 9 of the Standard Industrial Classification) in both public and private sectors. The 1998 survey dropped the threshold from 25 employees to ten. Overall, the workplaces represented by each of the surveys are estimated to account for around 70 per cent of all employees in Britain in each of the survey years.

The survey analyses are based on time series and panel data. The time series data extending from 1980 to 1998 was formed from interviews with the main management respondent or 'senior person dealing with employee relations' and makes the most of the continuity present within the survey series by providing direct comparisons of employment relations practice at four specific points in time over the past two and a half decades. It is therefore possible to investigate the degree of change or stability in the incidence of specific practices over time, both in aggregate and within particular sectors of the economy or types of workplace. It is also possible to assess the extent to which historical relationships – such as that between workplace size and union presence, for example – have changed over the period of observation.

Three categories of workplace are identified:

1. The panel survey looks at change in a random sample of continuing workplaces – those workplaces which continue in operation over the period of observation: 1980–98.
2. The second category, referred to as leavers, comprised those establishments that closed down during 1980–98.
3. The third category comprises those establishments that joined the population since 1990.

WERS series of surveys as described above, the 1980 survey being published in 1983, the 1984, 1990 and 1998 surveys being published in 1986, 1992 and 1999–2000 respectively. Clearly, the findings of these surveys tend to explode a few tabloid myths and conventional wisdoms concerning workplace industrial relations, and the main conclusions of the pre-1990 surveys are identified below:

1. Nationally, since 1979 trade union membership, influence and bargaining power have declined, and these trends can be identified statistically (see Chapter 3). Also, nationally, it is accepted wisdom that managers recovered some of the power they apparently 'lost' in the 1960s and 1970s. The workplace survey evidence reveals that while there may have been a shift in the balance of power, this was by no means a uniform trend and its more extreme manifestation of 'aggressive' macho management cropped up in a statistically insignificant number of workplaces.

2. It is also conventional wisdom that national decline in trade union influence was mirrored in the workplace where employees, workplace representatives and shop stewards have embraced the 'new realism' (if not the NIR) of some of their trade union leaders and 'acknowledged the realities of comparatively high unemployment, substantial redundancies, the importance of new technologies and the need for the organisations employing them to improve their competitiveness' (Farnham and Pimlott, 1995, p. 394). The surveys do confirm that managers have attempted to improve competitiveness by introducing elements of flexible specialisation, numerical flexibility and employing more part-time workers and contract workers: subcontracting and utilisation of self-employed labour has also grown. An important ACAS survey (1987) of the extent to which employers had introduced flexible working noted that:

> Overall two-thirds . . . said they employed some part-time employees. . . . Larger firms, those in the service and public sectors, and those in the South East, were especially heavy users of part-time labour. Particularly interestingly we found substantial use of part-timers in manufacturing industry, where until recently they were a relatively small part of the workforce, suggesting here too that the practice is spreading. We also found extensive and growing use of subcontractors.

The issue of flexibility in relation to the 'new' workplace will be dealt with in greater detail in the next section.

Findings of the 1990 Survey

Some of the main findings of the 1990 WIRS survey included:

- A continuing decline in the extent of trade union representation, particularly in the latter half of the 1980s.
- Both private and public sectors showed falls in trade union density, and the closed shop showed the sharpest fall.
- The late 1980s saw fewer lay union representatives (such as shop stewards): 'The fall was widespread, affecting workplaces of all types, but particularly smaller workplaces and those with low levels of union membership. . . . But, in the much smaller number of workplaces where lay union representatives still operated, stability rather than change prevailed. On average, there was the same number of union members per lay representative as before. In workplaces where local organisation traditionally had been strong, it remained so' (Millward *et al.*, 1992, p. 143).
- Trade union officials outside the workplace played a larger part in workplace matters than previously and contacts between lay representatives and the union at national level increased.
- Managements used an extensive range of channels to communicate with their employees, and they consulted their workforces about a wide range of issues and 'there was substantial growth since the mid-1980s in the overall reporting of a wide range of new initiatives for employee involvement, particularly in the service sector' (ibid., p. 180).
- Formal disciplinary and dismissal procedures 'became almost universal in all but the smallest workplaces during the 1980s. . . . Procedures for resolving individual grievances were also widely introduced and health and safety procedures became commonplace' (ibid., p. 212).

- There was a widespread decline in the extent to which basic rates of pay were determined by multi-employer industry-wide bargaining and 'where basic rates of pay were not subject to collective bargaining, it was increasingly the case that local management, rather than head offices, took the decisions' (ibid., p. 215).
- Basic pay amongst non-manual workers was increasingly supplemented by performance-related components and there was a spread in the growth of profit sharing and employee share ownership.
- The level and rate of occurrence of workplace industrial action had fallen away significantly during the 1980s.

It must be borne in mind that the survey evidence can only reveal general trends. Within that framework, however, individual case research can highlight and detail certain characteristics and factors concerning a workplace or workplaces within a particular locality, even if the findings of the research 'buck the trend'. For example, research into the changing position of trade unions in Rochdale during the 1980s (Penn and Scattergood, 1996) reveals that within Rochdale workplaces, across all industries in both the public and private sectors, 'there occurred no major significant gains in union strength yet, conversely, there was no strong evidence of union decline' (p. 282). They go on to state:

> No concerted effort was mounted by employers in the locality to weaken trade unions or to rearrange the fundamentals of collective bargaining. . . . The general pattern of collective bargaining remained locally based within manufacturing and focused overwhelmingly on wages. . . . There occurred no significant collapse of union membership and most trade unionists belonged to a small number of conglomerate unions. . . . We uncovered no evidence of single-union deals or of the other, widely publicised panoply of the 'new collective bargaining' (or 'new' IR). We concluded that such developments were being, and continue to be, exaggerated and related to a small number of atypical examples – albeit widely cited by commentators. . . . We found little direct evidence of any effects of the new industrial relations legislation. However it had affected the attitudes of trade union officials and

> had made them more cautious in the escalation of industrial grievances. (pp. 283–4)

Self-Evaluation Activity 5.4

Extrapolating

Response on website

WERS98 contains an extensive analysis of employment relations change. Based on what you have read so far, attempt to predict what might occur within the UK employment relations arena during the next five years.

Some comments on the 1998 WERS Survey

As we have noted where appropriate elsewhere in this book, findings of the Workplace Employee Relations Survey (WERS98 – Cully *et al.*, 1998; Cully *et al.*, 1999 and Millward *et al.*, 2000) have been described at length. WERS98 is the latest survey in the WIRS series, and reflects the changing contours of British workplace industrial relations. Some of the important points emerging from the survey are identified in Exhibit 5.7.

CHANGES IN THE NEW WORKPLACE: FROM FORDISM TO POST-FORDISM

The changes in employment relations, including the alleged emergence of NIR, cannot be seen only as the consequence of a shift in political ideology and economic policy at national level important though these are. Changes in production technologies such as the shift from mass production (Fordism) to flexible specialisation (post-Fordism) are regarded as crucial in determining the nature of emerging patterns of industrial relations. Ackers *et al.* (1996) cite Kenney and Florida (1993) who:

> use Fordist and post-Fordist neologisms to suggest that unions which are locked within a Fordist paradigm remain reactionary in the face of the new demands of work in what they call 'innovation mediated production', [and] Wickens [1993] argues that just as Fordism created a type

Exhibit 5.7

Some findings of WERS98

1. There has been a further contraction of collective industrial relations. In the 1990 survey, it was found that union recognition had fallen from 66 per cent in 1984 to 53 per cent, and by 1998 this had fallen a further eight percentage points to 45 per cent. Moreover, the proportion of workplaces with no union members has increased from 27 per cent in 1984, to 36 per cent in 1990, to 47 per cent in 1998. This signals clearly a transformation in the landscape of British employment relations, particularly when contrasted with the relative stability and continuity that has characterised the system for much of the post-war period.

2. A substantial proportion of workplaces operate a large number of 'new' management practices and employee involvement schemes. 'A preliminary investigation of these practices and schemes showed a number of clusterings.' (p. 52)

3. 'Overall, harmonious employment relations are very much the norm. The level of overt conflict is low, and a majority of managers, worker representatives and employees rated relations as being very good or good. However, there is a very substantial gap between the proportion of workplace managers who hold this view, and worker representatives and employees. Part of this might be explained by some discontent about the true extent of consultation and involvement in decision making. Many worker representatives, as agents of recognised unions, appear to have a role that is narrow in scope and, in many instances, management would rather go direct to employees than deal with unions. Employees, however, are sceptical about the extent of consultation, with more rating management as poor than good in this area.' (p. 81)

4. Satisfaction at work (not considered in previous surveys) is also widespread, with many employees satisfied or very satisfied across various dimensions of their job. 'There is, however, a good deal of dissatisfaction with levels of pay. More importantly, a significant minority of employees feel that the overall deal they have – their implicit, or psychological contract – is a poor one.' (p. 93) Lower levels of job satisfaction are particularly evident among some occupational groups and among those who feel they have been inadequately consulted and, to a lesser extent with those who do not have access to training and flexible working arrangements.

5. 'The ability of managers to adjust the size of their workforces in line with requirements and demand (numerical flexibility) appears to be quite widespread.' (p. 98) It has also increased over the past five years in each of the following categories:
   - employees on fixed-term contracts
   - temporary agency employees
   - contractors
   - part-time employees

6. The ability to move workers from one task to another (functional flexibility) where those workers have received formal training was surveyed. 'In more than half of all workplaces this form of flexibility is either non-existent or negligible, but in around a quarter of workplaces, most employees in the largest occupational group are trained to be adaptable.' (p. 121) There are negative associations between the use of 'non-standard' workers – particularly, the use of temporary agency workers – and the proportion of employees who are trained to be functionally flexible.

Source: Cully *et al.*, 1999

of adversarial trade unionism, the new manufacturing system of lean production (or neo/post-Fordist) will favour a more co-operative partnership. (p. 7)

The transition from Fordism to post-Fordism is also accompanied by new ideas about the organisation of work and the notion of flexibility (Procter and Ackroyd, 2001; Boxall and Purcell, 2003; Geary,

2003). Before considering important elements of workplace change, we examine the nature of the 'paradigm shift' from Fordism to post-Fordism.

The emergence of Fordism

Fordism is based on the premise of a linkage between the division of labour and mass markets. As early as the eighteenth century, Adam Smith (1776) realised that the division of labour depends on the desired volume of output which, in turn, depends on the size of the market. The 'Scientific Management' principles of Taylor (1911) assumed a breakdown of jobs into measurable and relatively unskilled tasks. If a type of technology could be developed to exploit the division of labour in order to maximise production, then markets could be developed to take advantage of the increased production. Henry Ford was among the first to take advantage of this relationship. His name was given consequently to the large-scale, assembly-line industrial system which he developed and others copied. 'Fordism is the name used to designate the system of mass production, tied to the cultivation of mass markets which Henry Ford himself developed' (Hounshell, 1984, p. 34). Fordism, then, concerns manufacturing carried out in large plants, producing mass market materials using assembly-line processes.

The nature of the system

Ford established his first plant at Highland Park, Michigan, in 1913. It made only one product – the Model T Ford car. The model of production worked out by Ford in order to service the potential mass market involved the transfer of traditional skills from workers to specialised machines. By 1914 about 15 000 machines had been installed and company policy was to scrap machines as fast as improved types could replace them. In addition, Ford perfected the flow-line principle of assembly work which meant that 'instead of workers moving between tasks, the flow of parts is achieved as much as possible by machines (conveyors and transporters) so that assembly-line workers are tied to their work position and have no need to move about the workshop. A crucial consequence is that the pace of work is controlled mechanically and not by the workers and supervisors' (Littler and Salaman, 1985, p. 88). Associated with the new fixed-speed, moving assembly line was an accelerated division of labour and short task-cycle times. Ford pushed job fragmentation to an extreme and records a survey of jobs in his plants:

> *The lightest jobs were again classified to discover how many of them required the use of full facilities, and we found 670 could be filled by legless men, 2637 by one-legged men, two by armless men, 715 by one-armed men and ten by blind men. Therefore out of 7882 kinds of job . . . 4034 did not require full physical capacity.* (Ford, 1922, p. 108, cited in Littler and Salaman, 1985, p. 88)

Being associated with scientific management and the diffusion of Taylorist principles, Fordist production systems which depended to a great extent on scientific management became the dominant mode of production within much of British manufacturing industry from the mid-1940s until the late 1970s. The multinational corporation facilitated the spread of Fordist production. For example, Ford established subsidiaries in Britain, Germany, Japan and other countries, as did Ford's main competitor – General Motors. Factories were designed by engineers, invoking the metaphor of large engines comprising cogs and wheels rationally linked together which denies humanity and human emotion. Work was deskilled through task fragmentation and detailed division of labour 'and as workers no longer owned their own means of production, being reliant, as wage slave, on the owner and his management agents, individuals were dehumanised' (Boxall and Purcell, 2003, p. 94).

Self-Evaluation Activity 5.5

The Ford workplace
Response on website

Mini case 5.1 is an extract from Beynon's *Working for Ford* (1975) which describes the conditions at the former Ford Halewood plant during the late 1960s. After you have read it attempt the question that follows.

Mini case 5.1
Working for Ford

Working in a car plant involves coming to terms with the assembly line. 'The line never stops you are told. Why not? . . . Don't ask. It never stops.' The assembly plant itself is huge and on two levels, with the paint shop on the one floor and the trim and final assembly departments below. The car shell is painted in the paint shop and passed by lift and conveyor to the first station of the trim assembly department. From this point, the body shell is carried up and down the 500-yard length of the plant until it is finally driven off, tested and stored in the car park. Few men see the cars being driven off the line. While an assembly worker is always dealing with a moving car it is never moving under its own steam. The line stands two feet above floor level and moves the cars monotonously, easily along. Walking the floor of the plant as a stranger, you are deafened by the whine of compressed air spanners, you step gingerly between and upon the knots of connecting air pipes which writhe like snakes in your path and you stare at the moving cars on either side. This is the world of the operator. In and out of the cars, up and over the line, check the line speed and model mix. Your mind restlessly alert, because there's no guarantee that the next car will be the same as the last. But still a blank – you keep trying to blot out what's happening. 'When I'm here my mind's a blank. I make it go blank.' They all say that. They all tell the story about the man who left Ford to work in a sweet factory where he had to divide the reds from the blues, but left because he couldn't take the decision making . . .

The history of the assembly line is a history of conflict over speed-up – the process whereby the pace of work demanded of the operator is systematically increased. This can be obtained in a number of ways, the simplest involving a gradual increase in the speed of the line during a shift. The worker gets suspicious after a bit because he finds he can't make time on the job. He can't get those few stations up the line which allow him a break and half a ciggie now and then. The long-serving stewards and workers at Halewood insist that plant management made frequent use of this type of speed-up in the early days of the plant. Production managers out to make a name for themselves can only do it through figures – through their production and their costs. They abuse their supervision to this end. To service the god of production is also to serve yourself, and in this climate a few dodges are part of the game. (Beynon, 1975, pp. 109, 138–9)

A senior manager

'We are here to make a profit and that's the bottom line. If we don't succeed, we all go down. The assembly line is efficient and the workers know the score. We need close supervision to ensure production targets.'

Source: Beynon, 1975, pp. 109, 138–9

Comment on the nature of workplace industrial relations at the plant.

The limitations of Fordism and the 'neo-Fordist' alternative

There have been a number of criticisms of Fordism which expose its limitations. The nature of these limitations are economic, technological and social, and are now examined:

- The economic limits are basically concerned with the extent to which it is economically viable to continue fragmenting jobs and transferring skills to specialised machinery. As we have seen, mass production depends upon demand, and if that demand is not forthcoming then further specialisation is not economically justifiable. Furthermore, Fordism can only be developed in industries producing standardised products for large markets, and to set up mechanised production lines is enormously expensive.
- Once a Fordist system is established it is quite rigid. In order to alter a product, for example, substantial reinvestment is needed.
- The further subdivision of jobs and labour is dependent upon the further development or transformation of production technology.
- Fordist production systems are relatively easy to copy if sufficient funding is available to set up the plant, and firms in countries in which labour power is expensive find it difficult to compete with those in areas where wages are cheaper.

This was a factor involved in the first successes of the Japanese car industry and more recently that of South Korea.

- The limits to the direct control methods of Fordism are set by increasing the costs to the employer of securing the co-operation of the workforce. Generally, in Fordist organisations workers are neither trained to show, nor are rewarded for, initiative, and there is little scope for creative involvement of employees (Salaman, 1984). Workers may not be motivated beyond the prospect of the pay packet, and it is difficult under these circumstances to encourage workers to do more than the bare minimum necessary to get by. Littler and Salaman (1985) provide an account by an American worker (quoted from Douglas, 1980):

> I am – or was – an American autoworker. I built GM cars for 16 years. Then, in March (1980) I was laid off indefinitely. . . . It was not the worker who determines the quality of the car, but the executives in Detroit and the plant supervisors. The worker who performs a certain task 320 times a day, 5 days a week, knows more about the specifics of this particular job than anyone else. Yet in 16 years, I have never been consulted on how to improve a job qualitatively or quantitatively. There are suggestion programmes but their main concern is always 'how to save the company's money'. The autoworker can only build as good a car as he is instructed or permitted to build. We on the line take our cue from those in head office. If they don't really care about the quality, they can't expect us to either.

According to Sabel (1982), the high point of Fordism is long past but nevertheless, despite the substantial drawbacks, we must also recognise that Fordism had its advantages, particularly for the firm and the consumer in terms of economies of scale. This means that the larger the unit of production, the greater the potential output of goods at cheaper unit costs. In order to take full advantage of these economies, the factory must produce to maximum, or near maximum capacity. This in turn means that there must be a ready market for the goods. The consumer is, therefore, part of this equation, and the consumer also derives benefits from Fordism by being able to afford to buy the goods produced in this way. Those who contend that, despite its limitations, Fordism has not had its day nevertheless concede that there has been a movement from 'traditional' Fordism of the type we have considered, to 'neo' Fordism, which 'is often regarded as representing the alternative production system in which the stultifying rigidities of Fordism were eased apart to allow some degree of flexible production using new technologies to expand the range of products without modifying the tight managerial control structures' (Grint, 1993, p. 296). Neo-Fordism, then, looks at workplace change in relation to the labour process, the introduction of new technologies, automation, new methods of employment and changes in working practices. Horton (1997) describes the neo-Fordist project as being led by technological innovations such as computer-integrated manufacturing systems and electronic offices which in turn 'have led to reductions in the labour force, employment of more multi-skilled technicians, greater flexibility in production methods and diversification in types of product. At the same time, new working practices and the introduction of participative working groups, such as quality circles, have introduced flexibility into the socio-technical systems in the workplace' (pp. 162–3). Grint (1993), however, sounds a note of caution:

> It is not axiomatic either that neo-Fordism should be regarded as a solution to pre-existing problems or that it is prevalent in itself. Even where it does exist . . . there are many who doubt that neo-Fordism is the solution to the problem. For these people the problems lie much deeper than simply at the level of technology and reflect rather the very nature of Fordism as an organisational form, replete with its large-scale and cumbersome bureaucracies, its over-concentrated control structures and its over-centralised decision making. (p. 296)

Post-Fordism

By the 1970s, new ideas about the way work should be organised as a reaction to Taylorism, scientific management and a failing Fordist system began to take root, partly as a result of social changes that had taken place in the 1960s and partly as a result of episodic crises, such as the 'oil crisis' of the mid-1970s, which in turn focused thinking upon competitiveness and productivity.

Post-Fordism represents a movement beyond Fordism, and signifies a qualitative shift in the organisation of production and consumption. As an ideology, post-Fordism is essentially optimistic as it postulates the apparent long-term solution to the assembly-line blues: the breakdown of the assembly line and the introduction of new work technologies are seen as creating opportunities for re-skilling the workforce and offer the prospect of a multi-skilled labour force operating flexibly in a less hierarchical work environment. The assembly line is assumed to be a thing of the past, skill and flexibility levels are increased, teamwork structures are devised and specialised niche markets for high-quality, high-value products and services are sought out. In essence, then, the production changes over the past few decades associated with post-Fordism can be summarised as:

- changes in product life and product innovation, with shorter flexible runs and a wide range of products on offer;
- changes in stock control, with just-in-time methods removing the need to hold large amounts of costly stock;
- changes in design and marketing, such as the development of niche marketing, in response to an increasingly diverse pattern of consumer demand;
- changes in consumption with increased emphasis upon niche markets, market segmentation and rapidly changing consumer tastes.

Post-Fordism is characteristic of, and incorporates the notion of 'flexible specialisation' (see pages 266–7) which focuses on the move away from mass production to batch production and the manufacture of a wide variety of custom-made goods and services using flexible labour and skilled, adaptable workers. The example in Exhibit 5.8 of the retail sector provides the essence of what post-Fordism represents.

Exhibit 5.8

Post-Fordism: the example of retailing

Since the 1950s retailers have been using computers to transform the distribution system. All mass producers have the problem of forecasting demand. If they produce too little they lose market share. If they produce too much they are left with stocks which are costly to hold or have to be sold at a discount. Retailers face this problem not just for a few products but for thousands. Their answer has been to develop information and supply systems which allow them to order supplies to coincide with demand.

Every evening, Sainsbury's receives details of the sales of all 12 000 lines from each of its shops; these are turned into orders for warehouse deliveries for the coming night, and replacement production for the following day. With computerised control of stocks in the shop, transport networks, automatic loading and unloading in warehouses, Sainsbury's flow-line make-to-order system has conquered the Fordist problem of stocks.

They have also overcome the limits of the mass product. For, in contrast to the discount stores which are confined to a few fast-selling items, Sainsbury's, like the new wave of high street shops, can handle ranges of products geared to segments of the market. Market niching has become the slogan of the high street. Market researchers break down the market by age (youth, young adults, 'grey power'), by household types (dinkies, single-gender couple, one-parent families), by income, occupation, housing and increasingly by locality. They analyse lifestyles, correlating consumption patterns across commodities, from food to clothing and health and holidays.

The point of this new anthropology of consumption is to target both product and shops to particular segments. In modern shops, the emphasis has shifted from the manufacturer's economies of scale to retailer's economies of scope. The economies come from offering an integrated range from which customers can choose their own basket of products. There is also an economy of innovation, for the modern retail system allows new product ideas to be tested in practice, through shop sales, and the successful ones then to be ordered for wider distribution. Innovation has become a leading edge of the new competition. Product life has become shorter, for both fashion goods and consumer durables.

A centrepiece of this new retailing is design. Designers produce the innovations. They shape the lifestyle. They design the shops. With market researchers, they have steered the high street from being retailers of goods to retailers of style. These changes are a response to, and a means of shaping, the shift from mass consumption. Instead of keeping up with the Joneses there has been a move to be different from the Joneses. Many of these differences are vertical, intended to confirm status and class. But some are horizontal, centred around group identities linked to age, or region or ethnicity. Whatever our responses, the revolution in retailing reflects new principles of production, a new pluralism of products and a new importance for innovation. As such it marks a shift to a post-Fordist/postmodernist age.

Self-Evaluation Activity 5.6

Differences between Fordism and post-Fordism
The response is given below

Summarise the main differences between Fordism and post-Fordism

Figure 5.1 summarises the main differences between Fordist and post-Fordist systems. It is also important to emphasise that post-Fordism and neo-Fordism may be compared and contrasted apart from the basic distinction between them referred to earlier. For example, both

emphasise the importance of flexible production systems to cater speedily for changing market tastes and demand, and to ensure high quality products and services. One important difference, as Horton (1997) puts it, is:

. . . in how they perceive technology. Neo-Fordists see technology as being used primarily to save labour and improve productivity, and argue that although task structures and modes of management may deviate from conventional Taylorism, they are not significantly different. Neo-Fordism is capitalism's

	Fordist	Post-Fordist
1. Technology	Fixed, dedicated machines	Micro-electronically controlled multi-purpose machines
	Vertically integrated operations	Subcontracting
	Mass production	Batch production
	For a mass consumer market	Diverse, specialised products
2. Products	Relatively cheap	Price variable
	Variable quality	High quality
3. Labour process	Fragmented	Integrated
	Few tasks	Many tasks for versatile workers
	Little discretion	Some autonomy
	Hierarchical authority and technical control	Group control
4. Contracts	Collectively negotiated rate for the job	Payment by individual performance
	Relatively secure	Dual market, secure core; highly insecure periphery

Figure 5.1 Fordist and post-Fordist systems contrasted

response to the effects of overproduction and saturated domestic markets and the falling rate of profit. It is exploiting new product and labour markets and reconstructing itself, but the classic characteristics of Fordism are still in evidence. (p. 163)

The division between neo-Fordism and post-Fordism extends beyond the workplace to encompass consumer–producer relations, such that neo-Fordism is still premised upon Fordist mass production for international mass markets, whereas post-Fordism implies a large degree of product specialisation for specialised, and often localised, markets.

Summary points: Fordism, neo-Fordism, and post-Fordism

Although, as our analysis revealed, there is some overlap between the three systems, we may attempt to summarise them (following Grint, 1993, p. 297):

- **Fordism** represents the archetypal assembly-line production system with extensive division of labour and isolated workers using limited skills.
- **Neo-Fordism** represents a transitional form in which workers are required to become flexible with the use of multiple skills and multiple tasks.
- **Post-Fordism** occurs when multi-skilled and flexible workers are engaged in production systems which depend on teamworking rather than isolated individuals, and involve a reduction in the division of labour and some flattening of hierarchical authority, that is, devolved responsibility for decision-making. This method of working is also known as flexible specialisation.

IMPORTANT ELEMENTS OF WORKPLACE CHANGE

Ackers *et al.* (1996, p. 2) focus upon three areas of change affecting the new (neo and post-Fordist) workplace. Firstly, there is the impact upon the workplace of foreign investment in Britain (also termed *inward investment*). These companies which are mostly multinational corporations (or MNCs) have their own trade union and industrial relations agendas. Secondly, there is the impact of new technologies, especially computer-based information systems, and thirdly, there is the issue of flexibility of labour, of work and the workplace.

Inward investment

Hutton (1995) in examining the state of the British economy during the 1980s and 1990s declared that:

By 1995 the Japanese will be boosting the UK trade balance by £4 billion. British regions engage in unseemly attempts to outbid each other in attracting the foreign multinationals that bring jobs and wealth; 25 per cent of UK manufacturing capacity is now owned by foreigners who employ 16 per cent of British workers. (p. 8)

Much of the inward investment in recent decades has taken place in the manufacturing sector of British industry. What was happening was that the UK was specialising in fewer sectors – such as chemicals and aerospace – while giving up ground in others like textiles and mechanical engineering. In high growth sectors there was virtually no British representation, while in areas such as consumer electronics and cars the turnaround was wholly due to inward direct investment, notably from Japan.

Japanese foreign direct investment (FDI) into the UK began in 1969 with the opening of a manufacturing facility for zip fasteners in Runcorn, Cheshire. However, Japanese FDI did not start to make an impact until the mid-1980s onwards when it increased at annual rates of between 22 and 36 per cent (Morgan *et al.*, 2002) and during the period 1985–94 almost 40 per cent of all Japanese FDI in Europe was within the UK (Dickens, 1998).

At the same time as foreign MNCs increased their share of investment, jobs and exports, employment in manufacturing fell by around 50 per cent. Apart from the Japanese and, more recently, South Koreans, the other main investors are European and US MNCs. The significant area for research into workplace industrial relations focuses upon the transfer of industrial relations traditions and practices from one country to another, and much of the recent research concerns Japanese 'transplants', although US firms have featured in empirical work concerning issues as diverse as employee involvement, payment systems and HRM (Purcell and Sisson,

1983; Storey, 1992; Rose, 1996; Boxall and Purcell, 2003). Relatively little research has been undertaken in European transplants (Guest and Hoque, 1994):

- Research into workplace industrial relations and related areas in Japanese transplants and other non-Japanese firms which hoped to emulate Japanese practices are based on the notion of Japanisation. Ackroyd *et al.* (1988) identify three types of Japanisation:
  - the first of these is 'direct' Japanisation which refers to the arrival in Britain of Japanese firms who bring Japanese practices with them. Procter and Ackroyd (2001) point out that the Japanese-owned sector in the UK is relatively small, employing 9 per cent of the total employed in the foreign-owned manufacturing sector, and that there 'is little evidence to suggest that Japanese-owned plants offer an example to their British counterparts in terms of efficiency or effectiveness in management and organisation' (p. 236);
  - the second type Ackroyd *et al.* call 'mediated', which describes the imitation of Japanese practices by non-Japanese firms including indigenous UK companies; and
  - the third type is 'full' or 'permeated', depicting the unlikely scenario of Britain attempting to mirror Japan's economic and social structure.

The main findings of empirical research into the so-called 'Japanisation of British industry' and its industrial relations consequences at workplace level are as follows:

- The Japanese have embraced trade unions and collectivism to a much greater extent than other inward investors, particularly US investors (firms such as IBM, Hewlett-Packard, Mars and Motorola are all non-union).
- Most inwardly-investing Japanese companies use greenfield sites and half of these are unionised. Research into regional patterns of investment suggest that those greenfield workplaces in areas having strong trade union and industrial relations traditions, such as South Wales and the North East, have higher levels of trade union recognition than those sites established in areas having few or no such traditions, such as new towns.
- Of the Japanese workplaces which are unionised, 85 per cent 'are single union, with the AEEU

being the most favoured organisation, regardless of sector [and] in single union deals, density rates vary considerably, with some of the celebrated cases, such as Nissan's Sunderland plant having membership coverage variously put at 33 and 45 per cent of employees' (Ackers *et al.*, 1996, p. 10).

- Japanese firms have been the real and symbolic movers behind a more widespread adoption of single unionism, no-strike deals, new arbitration agreements, company councils and other forms of management-directed reforms of British industrial relations which have capitalised on union weakness and inter-union competition for declining members. They have also broken with custom and practice in certain areas, such as the use of temporary labour by Nissan, the first time it had been used in the British motor industry since the 1940s (ibid., p. 11).
- Regarding the role trade unions actually play within the single-union, NIR post-Fordist workplace, Grant's study (1997) of a unionised Japanese transplant reveals that the workplace union membership can have very traditional expectations of a union's role and that these expectations conflict with the provisions of a new-style agreement based on co-operation and trust.
- A research survey by Danford (1998) of 15 Japanese-owned manufacturing transplants in the electronics and auto components sectors, located in South Wales, concluded that the transplants did not:

> display fundamentally different characteristics from their market competitors because even if their managements were disposed to experiment with different work organisational forms in unfamiliar environmental conditions, intense global market pressures do not provide the necessary space for such innovation. ... The logic of their capital accumulation strategies in these circumstances will always be to efficiently exploit these markets to the full rather than venture into new 'empowering' labour processes and employment relations. (p. 60)

Moreover, Danford argues that the lean production systems within these transplants leads to the complete subordination of the employee to supervisors, the machine and to the intensified pace of production. The extent of inward investment in Britain also demonstrates the extent to which the importation of different models of capitalism can impact upon the workplace. Hutton (1995) identifies four such models: the US model, the European social market model, the East Asian model, and the British model. Figure 5.2 provides a comparative analysis of the four models in relation to the labour market and workplace.

The decline of the Japanisation effect: the era of post-Japanisation?

Geary (1995), however, questions the degree of penetration of the Japanese model (and by implication, the other models). Considering evidence from a study of personnel policies and manufacturing practices in a representative sample of non-Japanese manufacturing plants and a comparable sample of Japanese-owned transplants (Wood and Mundy, 1993), Geary concludes that:

> In sum, then, the evidence would suggest that certain Japanese practices have become quite common, with a trend towards common patterns, with few – albeit some significant – UK-Japanese differences. Caution is required here, however: the industrial relations practices of Japanese firms in the UK are a variant of a home-country approach, and while UK firms have copied certain techniques, any deeper Japanisation is highly questionable. (p. 386)

Interestingly, Procter and Ackroyd (2001) suggest that Japanisation has created a form of organisation and/or workplace which may be called 'the high surveillance firm' whereby just-in-time production (JIT) and total quality management (TQM), together with the ability of computer systems which record and provide information on work performance, enable managers to control employees by continuously monitoring, measuring and reporting their performance (p. 237).

More recent research points to a decline and change in emphasis of Japanese FDI as a result of changing conditions in Japan and the world economy more generally. After 1996 the number of foreign affiliates opened by the Japanese worldwide declined from 1062 in 1995 to 316 in 1998 (MITI, 2000), and within Europe the number opened fell from 84 to 61. A more disturbing trend is that the number of Japanese companies withdrawing from overseas business increased fourfold between 1995 and 1998 and has been increasing to such an extent that the number of those now withdrawing exceed the number of those opening. The reasons for the withdrawal lie not only with the collapse of the Japanese 'bubble economy' but also with changes in the strategies and structures of Japanese companies, increased competition in areas where Japanese expertise seemed invincible – such as electronics and cars – together with the opening up of central and Eastern Europe and the entry of China into the global economy.

Characteristic	American capitalism	Japanese capitalism	European social Market	British capitalism
Labour market and workplace				
Job security	low	high	high	low
Labour mobility	high	low	medium	medium
Labour/management	adversarial	co-operative	co-operative	adversarial
Pay differential	large	small	medium	large
Turnover	high	low	medium	medium
Skills	medium	high	high	poor
Union structure	sector-based	firm-based	industry-wide	craft
Strength	low	low	high	medium

Figure 5.2 A comparison of four capitalist models
Source: Hutton, 1995

The implications for these developments within the UK market and for UK employment relations are likely to focus upon the well-known assumptions held about Japanese-style working methods and the longevity of Japanese subsidiaries in the UK. In relation to the former assumption, there is the received wisdom that Japanese managers had discovered the 'holy grail' to economic success via their working methods and practices such as *kaizen* and *kanban*, which some saw as a form of neo-Taylorism (see Chapter 2) involving a systematic extension of the principles of rationalisation both inside and outside the firm, leading to increased work intensification and increased exploitation of supplier firms (Delbridge, 1998). On the other hand, some argued that Japanese-style working practices provided greater scope for employee involvement leading to more efficient supply chain management practices (Oliver and Wilkinson, 1992). The second assumption – that of Japanese subsidiaries having a certain, stable and even permanent place within the plans of Japanese companies, has been severely dented by the net exit rates of Japanese FDI. Despite some examples of considerable investment within, for example, the car industry (Nissan, Toyota), the growing emphasis upon cost-effectiveness and global competition within the auto industry makes 'rationalisation' inevitable and thereby exposes the vulnerability of 'long-term' investment, the example of the UK Nissan plant cited below (pp. 271–4) being a case in point. Morgan *et al.* (2002) argue that the Japanisation debate overlooked or underestimated the uncertainties inherent within Japanese firms and their subsidiaries and assumed a degree of permanence of Japanese FDI which belied what was in fact 'a temporary position of competitive advantage' (p. 1030).

How will these developments affect the UK workplace?

Firstly, in relation to the strategic decisions Japanese MNCs are now required to take, they are now faced with a much wider range of possible locations for their production of standardised, mass products. For example, the second Toyota plant is located in France and the threat to the continued survival of Nissan Sunderland has been resolved. Closures are more common – such as that of the Fujitsu semiconductor plant in the North East. For

those plants and workplaces that remain, particularly within the production domain of standardised commodities such as consumer electronics, there is likely to be increased pressures upon costs which will affect both employees and suppliers. These pressures are unlikely to disappear should Britain join the euro-zone.

Secondly, as a consequence of cost pressures, wages are likely to be closely scrutinised and employment levels will be subject to tight control with possible short-term reductions in workforces as part of cost-cutting strategies; Sony and Hitachi, for example, reduced their payroll owing to adverse market conditions. There will be greater intensification of work and the attendant consequences in the form of greater labour unrest, absenteeism and labour turnover. It is likely that increasingly standardised production models will be imposed requiring less monitoring by head office and so leaving local mangers to assume responsibility for emerging labour problems The emergence of more adversarial employment relations may well lead to higher quit rates by Japanese companies to areas of more docile labour, either in other parts of Europe, or within Asia itself. Suppliers and their employees will feel similar 'knock-on' effects.

Perhaps the only growth area attracting Japanese FDI in future will be the trend to research and development within scientific and general knowledge areas taking advantage of scientific and technological excellence in the electronics and software industry, biotechnology, medical appliances and optics. However, even here the UK is competing globally, particularly with the USA and Germany.

Information technology

There is nothing novel about the notion of information technology. McLoughlin and Clark (1994), citing research by Friedman and Cornford (1989), identify three phases in the development of computer systems:

- *Phase 1* concentrated on the development of large mainframe computers used in defence and university research applications and spanned the period from the 1940s until the mid-1960s.
- *Phase 2* focused on improvements in software as the hardware became more reliable. The

information technology revolution became a media catchphrase. This phase lasted until the mid-1980s.

- *Phase 3* lasting from the mid-1980s to date is concerned with the problem of matching the supply of computer hardware and software with the needs of users.

Information technology (IT) is the term now used for all types of computer hardware (machines) and software (programs that tell computers what to do), telecommunications and office equipment, and is the science of collecting, storing and processing information. IT has had a wide impact on all sectors, and as far as the employment relationship is concerned there are a number of issues to be considered, albeit briefly:

1. *To informate and automate*: The distinction between informating and automating of information and computing technologies is made by Zuboff (1988). On the one hand, the technology can be seen as a replacement for less efficient technology and/or for workers – a process which has been ongoing since the nineteenth century – in order to maintain and improve the performance of existing processes with greater continuity and control. This is the automating function. On the other hand, the same technology simultaneously generates information about the underlying productive and administrative processes through which an organisation accomplishes its work, and 'provides a deeper level of transparency to activities that have been either partially or completely opaque. In this way, IT supersedes the traditional logic of automation. The word . . . to describe this unique capacity is informate. Activities, events, and objects are translated into and made visible by information when a technology informates as well as automates' (Zuboff, 1988, p. 25). In other words, IT greatly increases the amount of information available to workers and managers. The informating function of IT enables information to be captured, stored, manipulated and distributed. In summary, the automating effects involve the substitution of technology for human labour, while the informating effect involves the generation of new and deeper levels of information about work operations.

2. *Replacement or compensation*: The human replacement effects of new technology conjures up the popular image that new devices will increase productivity, and is based on the assumption that as machines do more and more, people will be required to do less and less. This type of productivity increase will therefore reduce job opportunities and create unemployment. In order to offset the potentially undesirable human consequences of replacement there are, it may be argued, certain compensatory and limiting mechanisms which may function at any given time. For example, technical innovation generates new products and services which can change the pattern of demand, i.e. increase demand which in turn encourages new investment and new employment opportunities. Additionally, higher productivity means producing the same output with fewer resources or more output with the same or fewer resources, and the lower unit costs can (theoretically) be passed on to the consumer in the form of lower prices. Consumers will then have more disposable income which may increase demand for goods and services within the economy.

3. *Action-centred and intellective skills*: Skilled manual workers had traditionally used skills based on the physical experience of manipulating things and they developed 'experience-based knowledge'. These skills have meaning only within the context in which the associated physical activities can occur and through the act of physically performing the task. Action-centred skills are therefore closely associated with the physical performance of work tasks. On the other hand, the automating effects of information and computing technologies involve computerising tasks based on action-centred skills thereby making labour of this type redundant. In this changed situation employees work with information provided by these new technologies, that is, the 'data interface', and input information into the new system. Work with a data interface requires new and more abstract 'intellective' skills which involve:
   - the performance of mental tasks or 'procedural reasoning';
   - an understanding of the internal structure of the information system and its functional capabilities;

- an understanding of what actions at the data interface lead to appropriate outcomes; and
- an ability to interpret new data as feedback on the results of responses.

4. *Upskilling or downgrading?*: It has been argued that successive changes in technology have resulted in a progressive deskilling of the production of existing products and services. This is the argument of Braverman (1974), encountered in Chapter 2. However, if we accept, to some extent at least, the informating potential of IT, then we could also infer from this that economic development involves a process of increased differentiation and efficiency. This process of change invariably requires a broader variety of skills and a higher average level of skills from the workforce. The downgrading view draws on studies of the labour process to argue that capitalist industrialisation has involved a steady fragmentation and narrowing of tasks and a separation of the planning and conceptual aspects of work from its implementation and 'doing'. Workplace industrial relations has been affected by all these changes, and often adversely. Some of the high-profile disputes of the 1980s have concerned, in no small measure, the introduction of new information technologies and the replacement effects of these. Consider the classic case concerning Rupert Murdoch's News International in Mini case 5.2.

Mini case 5.2
News International

Throughout 1984 Rupert Murdoch who owned the *Sun*, the *News of the World*, *The Times* and *The Sunday Times* negotiated with the print unions to transfer printing and production of his papers from Fleet Street to a new plant at Wapping. Murdoch wished to take advantage of developments in technology and communications, reduce staffing levels and union work controls. Murdoch was willing to go through the process of talking to the unions. But this was on the basis of presenting them with his terms on a take-it-or-leave-it basis, using 'negotiation' as a stalling mechanism whilst preparing pre-emptive action. If the unions were going to Wapping then, as far as News International was concerned, they were not going on the old terms. As it became clear that this would be unacceptable to

the unions, the company began to plan for a union-free Wapping. . . . By autumn 1985, with a sophisticated direct input system installed at Wapping by leading US computer specialists, Murdoch was ready to move. The unions were presented with extremely harsh terms which News International claimed were necessary if they were to compete with Eddie Shah's *Today* newspaper. In future there would be no recognition of chapels and branches and no negotiations at local level. The unions must sign a 'no strike-no industrial action whatsoever' agreement and accept instant dismissal for every worker breaking it. There would be no closed shop, no union recognition for white collar and management grades, complete flexibility and freedom for management to change working methods – and no demarcations. Not surprisingly, there was a failure to reach agreement and the unions balloted their members on industrial action. The move to Wapping was on and the unions called out their members from 24th January 1986.

Source: McIlroy, 1991, pp. 109–10

Ackers *et al.* (1996) point out that IT has been investigated for its impact upon industrial relations in three respects: 'First, for its potential to increase direct forms of communication and therefore side-step union channels and networks; second, for its use in increased monitoring and surveillance of employees; and, third, for its capability of integrating employees into the company ethos and interests through the use of video and visual communications' (p. 12). They also point out that IT has the potential to disperse a workforce through teleworking practices and home working.

Flexibility

Flexibility has often been synonymous with labour market deregulation, contracting in and out of services, multi-skilling, and creating different categories of employees. The post-Fordist workplace may be characteristic of a move towards flexible specialisation. Piore (1986) identified four primary features of flexible specialisation:

1. **Greater specialisation.** According to Piore, manufacturers have used new technology to make

manufacturing more flexible. For example, computer numerical-controlled machine tools can be reprogrammed to perform different tasks which enable manufacturers to make goods in small batches economically, which means that it no longer costs vast amounts to shift from the production of one product to another. Piore suggests that this process helps industry to meet changing demands as consumers are increasingly demanding more specialised products.

2. **Changed patterns of work and management.** The developments identified above have resulted in changes in patterns of work and management. As companies become more flexible, they require more flexible and skilled workers, and as a new employment structure evolves, low-skilled repetitive tasks are reduced.

3. **More flexible organisation structures.** More flexible working requires a more flexible organisation structure which is less hierarchical, with more communication between departments.

4. **Different training needs.** Workers in companies which are changing along these lines need to be more broadly trained as their work becomes increasingly varied. This core group of workers enjoys more job security and management makes greater attempts to enlist their co-operation through, for example, quality circles, worker representation on company boards and profit-sharing schemes.

Piore (1986) and Piore and Sabel (1984) postulate an overly optimistic view of flexible specialisation which has been criticised by Pollert (1988) and Wood (1989). These criticisms are summarised in Exhibit 5.9. Moreover, Lane (1995) argues that within the British context, although greater functional flexibility (another term for flexible specialisation) of labour and upskilling is practised, the pursuit of numerical flexibility and the greater casualisation of the workforce appears to be the more widely adopted alternative. Although numerical flexibility can successfully cope with uncertainties in demand of a quantitative type, it is doubtful whether a casualised labour force can handle other aspects of market uncertainty, such as frequent product changes or product diversification, and the demand for customised high-quality goods.

Self-Evaluation Activity 5.7
Flexibility in three contexts
Response on website

In Chapter 1 reference was made to the Atkinson (1984) model of the flexible firm. As we have seen, this model suggests that flexibility takes the two forms already referred to: functional flexibility or flexible specialisation refers to the employment of multi-skilled workers forming the core of an organisation's workforce who are employed full-time and who have considerable job security, while numerical flexibility is provided by peripheral groups comprising less-skilled, often part-time and temporary workers. Look at the two short cases of the retail firms Barton and Asla and the example of rail companies in Mini case 5.2, then consider the implications for workplace industrial relations of the changes made by these organisations in seeking greater workforce flexibility.

Mini case 5.2
Flexibility in three contexts

The Barton Group
The Barton retail group dismissed some 2000 full-time sales staff in their shops and offered them redeployment on part-time contracts. They have also offered 'nil hours' contracts to some workers whereby they are offered work as and when required. This is to enable staffing levels to be adjusted in line with customers' shopping patterns.

Asla Supermarkets
As an experiment, full-time and part-time posts have been dispensed with, to be replaced by 'key timers', workers available to cover peak times or absences and called in at two hours' notice.

The rail companies
Rail operators have been planning for months to defeat threatened widespread strikes by training managers to do the jobs of guards.

Nevertheless, cases such as Barton and Asla do present problems for trade unions as recruitment of part-time workers is traditionally more difficult than recruiting full-time workers. Specific criticisms of flexibility theories are provided in Exhibit 5.9.

Exhibit 5.9

Criticisms of theories of flexibility

Arguments in favour of flexibility such as those put forward by Piore (1986) have been criticised by those who support the deskilling argument based on Braverman (1974). Some critics such as Pollert (1988) have attempted to 'dismantle' flexibility theories, believing they are inaccurate and oversimplified. The criticisms we examine are concerned with six areas:

1. Production methods

Pollert (1988) does not believe that Fordist production methods have ever been as dominant as flexibility and post-Fordist theories imply. She therefore refutes the 'displacement' argument that flexible working and post-Fordist technology are superseding Fordist production. Specifically:

- Small batch production has been important throughout the twentieth century and companies with the flexibility to produce specialised products are nothing new.
- Pollert does not believe that there has been any marked reduction in the importance of mass production.
- She points out that the success of Japanese business is largely the result of producing cheap, well-designed and reliable products rather than specialist products in small numbers.
- The spread of new flexibility in industry is, she argues, in any case limited by the cost of new technology.

2. Flexibility and skill levels

Pollert questions the views that flexibility, where it has been introduced, has led to the workforce acquiring more skills. Basing her argument on a number of empirical studies, she claims that flexibility can have a wide variety of effects upon work. She argues that more flexible production may lead to a continuing dependence on traditional skills and/or on deskilling, and in some instances on skill increases and skill polarisation (widening the gap or 'skill differential' within the workforce between the highest and the lowest skilled). She also argues that management and workers may come into conflict as a result of the introduction of new technology or management proposals for the introduction of new working practices. In her study of teamworking (a form of flexibility) that was introduced within a large unionised workplace site of a large company, she concluded that not only was teamworking 'not working' but that there were considerable tensions between the shop floor and management as a result of its introduction (Pollert, 1996). More recent evidence within the UK context (Procter and Ackroyd, 2001) suggests that there is little indication of a sharp divide between a core of highly trained multi-skilled workers and a less-skilled dispensable periphery (see also Cully *et al.*, 1999, p. 38). In addition, 'the idea of a fully functional flexible "core" worker taking the form of a polyvalent super-craftsperson has proved to be a wildly optimistic one' (Procter and Ackroyd, 2001, p. 231).

3. Skill levels and new technology

Wood (1989) also questions the view that changes associated with flexibility have led to workers needing greater skills. His study of two British steel rolling mills found that new technology did help to increase the product range, but it did not increase significantly the skills needed by workers. This is partly because workers who are highly skilled to start with (as most of the steel workers were) did not have their skills increased, and partly that in other cases flexibility for workers meant little more than having to move between semi-skilled jobs which require little training. Wood criticises Piore and Sabel (1984) for ignoring the negative consequences of changes in work for the British workforce in recent decades. These include job losses, unemployment, tightening of performance standards, labour intensification, changing employment contracts and reduction of the power of trade unions and other worker representatives – developments confirmed by WERS98.

4. Costs to the employer

Organisations often perceive that there are significant costs attached to the use of non-standard labour. A survey conducted by Hunter and MacInnes (1994) for the Department of Employment reveals that temporary workers are seen to be less committed and reliable than permanent staff and that part-time workers employed on a permanent basis are seen as reliable but more difficult to manage than full-time workers because they spend less time at work. There is, as Claydon (1994) points out, a possible paradox: the inflexibility of the flexible workforce! He goes on to state: 'This not only restricts the uses to which non-standard workers are put: it has also meant that some organisations have moved away from non-standard contracts. This is because initial cost savings were seen to be outweighed by additional costs arising from lower commitment' (p. 109).

5. Training, integration and other problems

The extensive use of non-standard labour can also pose other problems for organisations. A study of US-owned electronic plants in Ireland (Geary and Roche, 2001) found that local managers were keen to minimise their use of temporary labour despite certain advantages they provided in terms of the exercise of managerial control. The reasons for this are:

- problems in providing necessary training for temporary workers within the period of their employment;
- widespread use of temporary workers led to reduced commitment from permanent staff and they suffer lower morale and motivation;
- conflicts between permanent and temporary staff impede the development of good working arrangements;
- difficulty of terminating temporary workers once they become integrated within the workforce and the organisation; and
- a fear that being seen to operate different standards of treatment for temporary and permanent staff, for example in terms of non-wage benefits such as sick pay, might undermine management's claim to be following enlightened HRM policies for the workforce as a whole. This in turn could threaten the basis of trust and co-operation between managers and permanent staff.

The study concluded that 'management would have preferred to attain a requisite level of control over their labour force by engendering their co-operation and commitment to the organisation' (p. 267). Other evidence (Gospel, 1995; Poole and Jenkins, 1997; Keep and Rainbird, 2003), suggests that little additional upskilling or even reskilling can be attributed to functional flexibility owing to the dissolving of traditional demarcations between different crafts, production and maintenance work. In addition, the decline in training and apprenticeships and the dilution of training in many organisations represents a failure of both government and individual organisations investing in and embarking upon a sustained programme of skills training.

6. Conflicts with existing agreements and other arrangements

In other cases, management's efforts to increase labour flexibility may conflict with other work arrangements and with existing agreements between management and trade unions. This is illustrated by the classic example of the introduction by British Rail (as it was then known) of 'flexible rostering' (Pendleton, 1991). Flexible rostering was an attempt to increase the proportion of the time on their shift that train drivers actually spent driving trains. While management succeeded in moving from fixed eight-hour shifts to a work rota which provided for shifts varying from seven to nine hours, this increase in labour flexibility actually obstructed flexibility in both work scheduling and day-to-day labour deployment. This was because of the need to reconcile management's aim of flexibility with existing agreements with trade unions regarding working hours and arrangements. The nature of the compromise was such that while flexibility of hours worked was increased, this detracted from, rather than improved, operational flexibility.

Research by Ackroyd and Procter (1998) claims to identify 'a new distinctive pattern for the organisation of manufacture at plant level' (p. 171), which they term 'the new flexible manufacturing firm'. This is contrasted with the original flexible firm model of Atkinson (1984) and that of the high-surveillance firm mentioned above (Procter and Ackroyd, 2001). These contrasts are brought out in Table 5.2. Looking at large British manufacturing companies, Ackroyd and Procter (1998) identify the following characteristics of such firms:

- production organised through the arrangement of machines and workers as cells capable of producing 'families' of components or products;

- advanced manufacturing technology is little used, except as additions to existing configurations of equipment;
- employed labour contributes to flexibility as teams of semi-skilled workers performing a range of specific tasks are given on-the-job training;
- employees do not enjoy privileged status or high employment security, but compete with subcontracted labour and alternative suppliers;
- production operations are considered as dispensable separate 'segments', about which calculations of cost are regularly made; and
- management takes the form of intensified indirect control based on the allocation of costs.

Table 5.2 Three models of flexibility

	Labour	Technology in use	Sources of flexibility	Management	Network	Problems/sector
Original flexible firm (OFF)	*Requirements*: High-skill and low-skill groups. *Policy*: Segmentation	Little or nothing specified	Labour	*Objective*: Rapid changes in direction and scale of production *Strategy*: Labour segmentation	Little or nothing specified; independent producer	Does it exist anywhere?
High-surveillance firm (HSF)	*Requirements*: Semi-skilled *Policy*: Progressive training	Medium to high investment in productive technology	Mix of technical and labour flexibility	*Objective*: Medium to large batch production *Strategy*: High quality/ low price	Japanese parent	Electronics and automotives
New flexible firm (NFF)	*Requirements*: Mostly unskilled/ semi-skilled *Policy*: Limited on-the-job training	Low to medium technology; cell working	Labour and selection of product markets	*Objective*: Medium batches of related products for specific niches *Strategy*: Short-term profit	Specialist provider to supply chains	General manufacturing

Source: Procter and Ackroyd, 2001, p. 239

They go on to argue that the 'new flexible firm' (apparently confined to British manufacturing firms rather than foreign-owned transplants) has a distinctive approach to utilisation of labour at plant level, and that 'in this sector of the economy at least, corporate changes make sense of changes in workplace industrial relations' (p. 170). The 'new flexible firm' model proposed by Ackroyd and Procter (1998) contrasts in many of its characteristics with the flexible firm model of Atkinson (1984).

WORKPLACE RELATIONS AT NISSAN: 1986–2003

Self-Evaluation Activity 5.8

Characteristics of post-Fordist workplaces

This SEA has no commentary

Before reading the case example below, identify the significant characteristics of 'new' post-Fordist workplaces and consider the extent to which 'new' industrial relations practices are appropriate to them. While you will obviously find 'pointers' to an answer in previous sections, you will also find evidence within the Nissan case.

As a result of inward investment the Nissan car manufacturing plant in Washington, near Sunderland, opened in 1986. Nissan chose to locate its production site in Britain partly because the British market was Nissan's largest export market and partly because the combined effects of legislation and recession had weakened the traditional trade union power bases. Large numbers of union members were lost in the North East as traditional industries declined, and this made it easier for Nissan to negotiate the best possible deal for trade union recognition. In addition to the Washington plant, Nissan has created links with many suppliers nationally, and the company claims to have created over 8000 permanent jobs in the North East alone. The Nissan plant has been well researched by its former Director of Personnel, Peter Wickens (1987, 1993), and by academics (Garrahan, 1986; Crowther

and Garrahan, 1988; Garrahan and Stewart, 1991, 1992; Stephenson, 1996).

In 1999, the French car company Renault bought 44.4 per cent of Nissan's shares and now has a considerable interest and influence over Nissan's fortunes. At the same time Carlos Ghosn, the Brazilian-born Frenchman nicknamed 'Le Costcutter', became President and Chief Executive of Nissan and made it clear that the Sunderland plant's future could be at risk if the UK did not adopt the euro in the short-term future. This is despite the decision to invest, with the help of EU regional investment aid of £40 million, in the manufacture of the new Micra which commenced in November 2002, and the fact that the workforce at Sunderland was ranked Europe's most productive plant for the sixth year running (with workers producing 95 cars each in 2002, up from 73 cars each in 1996). Around 4500 production line workers are employed, of which 1200 work on the manufacture of the Micra. Other cars produced at Sunderland include the Primera and Almera. In January 2003, the threat of what would have been Nissan Sunderland's first strike was averted. During the course of the dispute, which was concerned with pay issues, the company participated for the first time in talks at ACAS and Amicus/AEEU.

The nature of production and working practices

Wickens (1987) identified the triad of working practices which Nissan would follow: teamwork, quality consciousness and flexibility. According to Oliver and Wilkinson (1992), supervisors would work as 'team leaders' and were central to the production process with overall responsibility for whatever happened in their area. They go on to state:

Supervisors act as mini-managers of their areas, and team leaders are taught every function of their team in considerable detail. Supervisors typically attend courses on leadership, problem solving, organisation, communication and quality. Job flexibility and delegation of responsibility for inspection and minor maintenance are made feasible by the use of only two job titles for manual workers, with no grade numbers and no job specifications. Manual workers are classified simply as 'manufacturing staff' or 'manufacturing technicians'. There are daily work area meetings at the beginning of each shift. The content of these meetings often concerns quality issues, but matters such as schedules, work distribution, training and social events are also raised . . . most of the discussion concerns matters of relevance, and only occasionally is there 'a great message from on high'. (p. 217)

Quality is maintained, it is claimed, by a system of vehicle evaluation which details any defects which can then be traced back to work teams and individual workers, who are awarded points for quality performance. However, as Garrahan and Stewart (1992) point out, this actually constitutes a system of employee peer surveillance which could encourage 'competitive individualism' rather than efficient teamworking. At the same time, there is considerable work intensification as the pace of work is extremely rapid. Research undertaken by Stephenson (1996) considered Nissan's emphasis upon work performance, and the following observations are made:

- Workers who were interviewed confirmed the existence of peer group pressure within the team to maintain quality standards and speed.
- While Nissan claim that their workforce enjoy the same wages and conditions, individual workers are appraised annually by supervisors and rewarded.
- The monitoring of workers' attitudes by shop-floor managers 'is most clearly illustrated in what the team leader called "willingness to change", i.e. to flexibility, to participation in *Kaizen* (the Japanese term for continuous improvement in "total quality"). In order to qualify for good appraisals, workers have to make their attitude to the Nissan way of working *visible* through an active commitment to quality monitoring and *Kaizen*' (p. 223).
- Interviews with workers indicated a code of social conduct within Nissan which embraced competitiveness, individualism, ambition and total commitment to the company.

The agreement with Amicus-AEEU

Prior to recruiting its workforce, Nissan concluded an agreement with the AEEU (as it was then known) in 1985, the objectives of which were:

> To develop and maintain the prosperity of the company and its employees, to promote and maintain mutual trust and co-operation between the company, its employees and the union [and] to establish an enterprise committed to the highest levels of quality, productivity and competitiveness using modern technology and working practices and to make such changes to this technology and working practices as will maintain this position. (Crowther and Garrahan, 1988, p. 54)

Stephenson (1996) argues that 'the agreement left no meaningful role for the trade union; there was to be no shop steward representation and no role for the union in negotiation or in representation of its membership' (p. 218). The AEEU and its full-time officials acknowledge that the agreement is restricting, but at least it ensures a union presence and a means whereby the union could consolidate and enhance its power base within the company. There has, however, been little progress in improving the original agreement in favour of the union, although the company has agreed to allow just one shop steward within the plant even though that steward has no recognised role in terms of negotiation for, or representation of, AEEU members within the plant. 'None of the Nissan workers interviewed knew the shop steward or had any contact with him' (Stephenson, 1996, p. 218). Other findings raised by Stephenson's research include:

- The AEEU's estimate of union density is 33 per cent, while Nissan claim membership is 45 per cent.
- Some 'pro-union' members retained membership through previous employment, while others did not join AEEU on principle as the union was regarded by some as having 'sold out'.
- The traditional functions of trade unions, particularly within the car industry, have been usurped within Nissan by the team leader, the Company Council and the *kaizen* meeting.

- The team leaders pass shop-floor information to senior managers and send information down to shop-floor workers.
- The Company Council [which now (2003) includes five Amicus convenors but which remains predominantly non-union], conducts communication, negotiation and problem-solving activities which previously would have been the responsibility of shop stewards and other representatives.
- A central part of the Nissan 'philosophy' is *kaizen* (see Exhibit 5.10), and in Nissan this is achieved by employees forming teams to develop projects in order to improve any aspect of the work process, the best proposals being put into operation.

Employee involvement

On the shop floor successful employee involvement and commitment starts with recruitment. Nissan ensured that the most suitable people were recruited so maximising the extent to which the workforce endorsed the company's philosophy. Commitment was reinforced by teamworking and *kaizen* as described in Exhibit 5.10. The more formalised structure of employee involvement is the Company or Works Council whose functions are described within the single-union agreement. Its terms of reference include the aim of 'promoting effective communication and harmonious relations between the Company, its employees and the Union', within 'a forum in which elected members can discuss with representatives of the Company those matters which directly affect them', in recognition 'that all concerned have a mutual interest in ensuring the prosperity of the company'. The Council has ten elected members representing the main areas of the plant's activities (Paint Shop, Body and Press Shops, Trim Lines and Assembly, and so on). Other members are nominated by management and include the chairperson and secretary, the managing director, personnel director and production director. The Council carries out three primary functions:

Exhibit 5.10

Kaizen

'For many, *kaizen* is the distinguishing feature between Japanese and Western organisations and the belief in the possibility and desirability of continuous improvement has been held out as underpinning Japanese production methods.' The emphasis on continuous improvement derives from Buddhism because 'the idea of perfection is far more present in this way of thinking than in that of the West. It is associated with a pessimism which is typically Buddhist and which is grounded on the fact that one knows one will never get there – in contrast to the optimism of the Westerner who can reach his goal because he is happy with less' (Kolm, 1985, p. 20). The assumption here is that there is no limit to possible improvement.

Eliminating waste in Japanese companies through *kaizen* involves an attempt to harness the mental as well as the manual skills of shopfloor workers. 'Individuals are encouraged to make suggestions – through quality circles, suggestion schemes and so on – as to how savings can be made. Such participation is not mandatory, though failure to make suggestions will result in criticism and may mean smaller bonuses' (Oliver and Wilkinson, 1992, p. 35).

Kaizen allowed managers to access workers' knowledge of the production process. Garrahan and Stewart (1992) noted that workers have suggested changes which have led to the speeding up of work. They also acknowledge that through *kaizen* workers learn how to participate in the Nissan way of working in a way which is acceptable to their employers. In addition to this, it is important to note that the legitimacy of *kaizen* has been maintained as projects are not narrowly defined or directed towards improvements in the labour process or other areas which directly affect the accumulation of profit.

1. There are discussions about most aspects of the business during its three-monthly meetings, including production and productivity levels, market share and penetration, profitability and investment. These discussions are essentially consultative, and there is no direct employee input into the decision-making process.
2. The Council is the ultimate decision-making corpus for resolving both individual and collective grievances.
3. The Council conducts negotiations concerning pay, and terms and conditions of employment, and a union official may ratify the agreement. If there is no basis for an agreement reference is made to ACAS to resolve the dispute via pendulum arbitration. The Company Council effectively bypasses the formal union channels, thereby marginalising the trade union which has no formal collective bargaining rights. Blyton and Turnbull (1998) identify an important paradox here:

> *In effect, what the Company Council structure allows . . . is for management to locate all its dealings with the workforce within an essentially consultative relationship. This presents something of a dilemma for management: if union organisation and representation is emasculated, and the company's own consultative procedures perceived as a sham, then employee discontent could lead to the formation of autonomous shop floor organisation. Not surprisingly, then, management have actively encouraged employees to join the AEEU. Thus, where management draws the line between consultation and negotiation, and the extent to which such activities are complementary or competing processes of regulation, will be a key determinant of both management control and employee resistance.* (p. 221)

In conclusion

Work processes at Nissan are based on a combination of Taylorist and post-Fordist work practices, relying on standard operations and standard time calculations. In addition, workers were offered financial incentives through the yearly appraisal programme. Workers were involved in the intensification of their own labour through the monitoring of their own quality standards and those of others. Workers were also concerned with other activities such as *kaizen* and the monitoring of a variety of activities by workmates in accordance with the participative corporate philosophy. *Kaizen* also partly assumed the role and function of workplace unions and in doing so tended to legitimate the absence of workplace unions and their representatives while promoting the image of Nissan as a responsive, listening employer.

CALL CENTRES: THE NEW WHITE-COLLAR FACTORIES?

Handy (1995) has argued that the growth of the service economy (also referred to in Chapter 1) has been characterised by an expansion of 'knowledge work' within areas as diverse as local government, libraries, banking and insurance. However, much of this type of work 'requires little more of workers than information transfer' (Warhurst and Thompson, 1998), particularly in the largest growth area of recent years – that of telesales or call centres – and is often characterised by a process 'likely to be governed by scripted interactions, and monitored for deviance by supervisors' (p. 5). The call centre phenomenon is remarkable for its rapid expansion in recent years and warrants further consideration in relation to workplace organisation and the employment relationship (Exhibit 5.11).

The call centre is a relatively recent phenomenon which has changed the complexion of the British (and indeed global) workplace. The growth and application of telecommunications and computerised systems in the field of customer services, sales and information has been nothing short of spectacular during the past eight years, and it has been suggested that the sector in 2002 employed 420 000 people nationwide, from front-line centre agents and operators (73 000) to telephone salespersons (79 000) and customer care occupations (268 000) (ONS, 2002). The 2002 figure represents a slight drop from the 2001 figure of 424 000 positions. Forecasts for future growth are contradictory, with the IDS report (2003) citing the consultancy

Exhibit 5.11

Call centres: a chronology of events

1998: Call centre to create 2000 jobs

Barclays Bank is to set up a call centre in Sunderland to cope with its rapidly growing demand for its telephone banking service. The centre will open in the first quarter of next year [1999] and is expected to employ 2000 people over the next three years, more than tripling Barclay's telephone banking workforce. Barclaycall, the bank's specialised telephone service was set up in 1994 and has more than 6 000 000 customers. It employs 650 staff in Coventry, the site of its first call centre, and another 200 at a centre opened in Manchester last year. (*Financial Times*, 6 February 1998)

1998: Ear-bashed operatives can find they are working the aural equivalent of Bentham's perfect prison

'I couldn't take it any more – it was driving me mad', says Pete after a year of quickfire phone calls starting and ending with a monotonous compulsory formula – 'Good morning, welcome to Barclaycall, my name is Pete . . . Is there anything else I can help you with? Thank you for calling. Good-bye'. He began to think he would wake up at night screaming that patter. 'I found it all right for most of my time, but at this time of the month, when everyone's just been paid, it was peep, one call, finish that, then peep, another one, all the time.' Pete's worked on sales and service advice for eight-hour shifts, usually with spells of a maximum two hours' phone work. Any 'walkaway' – hanging up to stop calls – was logged and required an explanation. 'There was no problem if you needed walk-away to go to the lavatory, say, but they needed to know how long you were off and why.' Calls are also monitored for quality and length. Calls that drag on mean fewer customers served.

Pete has no criticism of Barclaycall's running of the system. 'There's a career structure and salary rises on performance.' The starting rate of £10 310 rises to £12 129 (with most staff at Pete's call centre on the top rate). The stress of the job in such regulated circumstances becomes hugely increased at the 'cowboy' end of the trade, according to bank unions. According to an officer with the Banking Insurance and Finance Union 'the worst places are dominated by fear – complain and you're out – and that's where the total control which the computer system allows leads to abuse. People get burned out and they're employing a constant stream of new ones. No one's happy and it's not efficient.'

Professor David Metcalf, of the London School of Economics, warned of the 'Orwellian potential' of such closely monitored work and said LSE studies of 100 call centres showed an eerie parallel with Jeremy Bentham's nineteenth-century 'perfect prison', the Panopticon. 'His principle was complete visibility of all prisoners from a central control centre, and that is what we have here.' (*The Guardian*, 9 February 1998)

1999: Women in teleservices 'frustrated' by routine

First findings from a new European study of work opportunities for women in the fast-growing call centre industry reveal widespread frustration with routine work, frequent reports of employee 'burn-out', training that is too often focused on the product rather than skills development, and limited opportunities for promotion. (IRS, 1999)

2001: Extreme monitoring and lack of breaks top TUC call centre complaints

Extreme monitoring by supervisors and not being allowed to take adequate rest breaks, were the top two concerns of call centre workers calling the *It's your Call* hotline, according to a TUC report *Calls for Change*. The report features a 'league table' of complaints from call handlers. One in four complained about extreme monitoring of work and most of these (53 per cent) said they were monitored over when they went to the toilet and the length of time they spent there. Some had to ask permission to go and others complained of being hauled up in front of bosses to explain why they were going so often. 15.5 per cent said they were not given adequate breaks at work and some of these said they were given no breaks at all even though they were working more than a six-hour shift – against the rules of the Working Time Directive. The report also revealed that call centre workers' salaries amount to only 60 per cent of average earnings. (TUC, 2001)

2002: Call centre recruitment policies are contradictory

Callaghan and Thompson (2002) argue that personnel policies are unsuitable in a call centre context because of the dichotomy between the sort of people that call centre managers 'think' they want and the sort of people more suited to call centre work practices. Only one in seven of job applicants was accepted within the case-study organisation, yet staff turnover was high. Callaghan and Thompson argue that this problem is endemic in the selection process where the focus was on identifying good communicators with 'personality', or 'naturals', but once employed and trained, recruits were 'reprogrammed' and instilled with a sense of conformity, told how to behave and given scripts to follow. The result, unsurprisingly, was high levels of frustration on the part of staff who had been selected for their outgoing personalities, but who found themselves unable to use them. Call centre managers emphasised achieving staff uniformity and hitting target numbers, rather than providing customers with a high-quality service. While managers talked in terms of 'building rapport with the customer', they failed to recognise that this was frequently at odds with their emphasis on hitting numerical targets.

Management and Business Development which predicts growth in number of agent positions to be less than 15 per cent a year, and Datamonitor (2002) forecasting growth to well over 500 000 agent positions by 2005. In contrast, Mitial Research (2002) has predicted that the industry will shrink over the next couple of years, partly as a result of the transfer of work to other countries, most notably India. Areas where call centres are expected to grow are local government and the outsourcing sector.

Call centres (or contact centres as they are also known) integrate computer and telephone technology, designed to provide fast and accurate services to clients, and also to monitor, tape record and measure staff performance. Centres are turning increasingly to 24-hour, seven-day operations as they compete with each other for customers and customer loyalty. Call centres are the consequence of companies across a whole range of services (banking, insurance and other financial services are probably the most visible) focusing more sharply on the needs of individual customers. In order to gain a competitive edge, and in order to offer this level of 'individual' service, the call centre was created to centralise all customer activities:

In today's highly competitive marketplace it is vital that companies build relationships with cus-tomers that are lasting and loyal by offering consistent quality of service and brand values. The call centre is central to this objective. (Customer Service Management, May 1998)

Most call centres are located outside London and the South East. The supply of greenfield sites, coupled with regional grants and lower wages, make migration of large 'tele' operations like British Airways ticket sales and London Electricity enquiries inevitable. Regional accents are also important; studies show that the public perceives the Scottish accent to convey reliability, while other accents such as the Brummie twang may convey criminal tendencies! (Fernie and Metcalfe, 1998).

The call centre workplace

Call centres are far from uniform and have many differentiating features which are summarised in Exhibit 5.12.

The majority of call centres deal with incoming calls; the employee or agent answers the call which is automatically directed or routed to him or her (calls are 'force-fed' where the agent has no control over whether or not to answer a call and as soon as one call is dealt with another is put through) and

Exhibit 5.12

Differentiating features of call centres

1. **In house:** The call centre is part of a larger organisation and handles calls for that organisation only
2. **Outsourced:** Usually a company in its own right which handles work from a variety of clients. An increasing number of UK companies outsource their work to companies in India and other countries.
3. **Type of work:** Inbound (receive) or outbound (solicit) call handling or a combination of the two.
4. **Degree of service:** Will embrace single function (outbound sales soliciting) or multiple functions such as sales, service, enquiries and technical matters.
5. **Unionisation:** Smaller call centres which are often outsourced are more likely to be union free.
6. **Size:** Call centres vary in size from very small with ten or so handlers to very large with hundreds of handlers, depending upon nature of the business and volume of work.
7. **Type of employment:** Non-standard employment is common in call centres, which may employ predominantly agency workers (common in outsourced call centres) who may also be part-time. Many call centres employ a mix of permanent and temporary full-time and part-time handlers.

any relevant information required is computer processed. All time is monitored – whether the agent is actually dealing with calls, in between calls or unavailable for whatever reason. The technology that makes this possible is called 'automatic call distribution' (ACD). The new technology behind the centres enables management to wring every last ounce of productivity out of the workforce. Not a moment is wasted. For outward calls the computer does all the dialling and can detect and automatically drop calls if there is no reply. Sophisticated 'predictive software' allows computer-generated judgements concerning the length of the average call and calculates how many calls it needs to make in order to provide potential customers for the available workforce. Calls, whether outbound or inbound, are completely scripted; the computer prompts the operator through a series of questions to ask a customer. Supervisors can listen in at any time to check whether an employee – who will be expected to deal with several hundred clients a day – is adopting the correct (cheerful) tone and displaying enthusiasm for the job, sometimes referred to as 'emotional labour'.

The monitoring of behaviour and measurement of output, according to some research, at least equals if not exceeds the worst supervisory excesses of the Fordist assembly line. Fernie and Metcalfe (1998) describe the control process in the following terms:

The tyranny of the assembly line is but a Sunday school picnic compared with the control that management can exercise in computer telephony. Indeed, the advertising brochure for a popular call centre is titled TOTAL CONTROL MADE EASY. Critics refer to them as new sweatshops and battery farms. Agents' activities are monitored in real time by the supervisor. Real time screens display status information such as the number of existing calls in queue, how long the oldest call has been waiting, how many agents are on calls and how many are logged out or unavailable. Schedule adherence monitoring allows the supervisor to see whether agents are adhering to what they are scheduled to be doing at any given moment. There is also, in most centres, the large LED display looking down on agents as a further reminder of their aims; the number of calls waiting to be answered in 6-inch high red letters is a big brother from which no-one can hide. (p. 7)

Fernie and Metcalfe use the analogy of Bentham's Panopticon (mentioned earlier) which Foucault (1979) adopts as a metaphor for the emergent workplace and which describes the sort of supervisory control process within workplaces which is evident in call centres:

All that is needed, then, is to place a supervisor in a central tower and to shut up in each cell . . . a

worker. They are like so many cages, so many small theatres, in which each actor is alone, perfectly individualised and constantly visible . . . visibility is a trap. . . . Each individual is securely confined to a cell from which he is seen from the front by the supervisor; but the side walls prevent him from coming into contact with his companions. He is seen but does not see; he is the object of information, never a subject in communication . . . this invisibility is the guarantee of order . . . there are no disorders, no theft, no coalitions, none of those distractions that slow down the rate of work, make it less perfect . . . power should be visible and unverifiable.
(Foucault, 1979, p. 53)

The research by Fernie and Metcalf (1998) and others (Arkin, 1997; Baldry *et al.*, 1998; Belt, 1999) provides support for the 'sweatshop' view of call centres as being 'a contemporary version of the 19th century sweatshop or those dark satanic mills' (Knights *et al.*, 1999) or some sort of Orwellian construct. Most of these contributions adopt the Foucauldian perspective, emphasising the disciplinary implications of call centre work and the subservience of employees to the 'electronic panopticon'. Bain and Taylor (1999) provide another description of this type of work:

For many employed in the sector, the daily experience is patently of repetitive, intensive and frequently stressful work, based on Taylorist principles, which can result in employee 'burnout'. These pressures are exacerbated through the performance of 'emotional labour'. Individual employee performance is measured and monitored to an unprecedented degree by means of electronic surveillance, augmented by more traditional supervisory methods. Involvement and communication techniques, particularly teamworking, are more concerned with the exercise of managerial control, productivity improvements and social objectives than with any meaningful commitment to developing employee empowerment. Flat organisational structures severely constrain opportunities for promotion and further contribute to the sector's high labour turnover. (p. 2)

The negative effects of call centre work may be greater for some types of worker than others and be more evident in some types of work situation than others (Deery *et al.*, 2002). It is important to note,

however, that not all researchers share the pessimistic views of those cited above espousing what we may collectively label the 'sweatshop view'. An alternative perspective suggests that the relationship between call centre staff and the customer means that the employer is highly dependent on the social skills and emotional labour of staff to ensure that customers are treated well. This implies that the employment relationship has to be managed with care (Frenkel *et al.*, 1998, 1999; Knights *et al.*, 1999) and that management need to balance the requirements of productivity and performance with a concern for customer satisfaction, focusing upon the quality of interaction between staff and customer. To that end, employers may well utilise the rhetoric, if not the application, of HRM policies in order to emphasise employee commitment and initiative through, for example, 'empowerment' techniques (Rose and Wright, 2003). This alternative perspective, therefore, emphasises a more positive image of call centre work, embracing 'the idea of a semi-professional, empowered worker who uses information technology as an opportunity to tailor services to the client whilst simultaneously using and developing their own skills [and arises] as a consequence of management wanting to customise the product or service to the requirements of the customer' (Simms *et al.*, 1999, p. 6). Frenkel *et al.* (1998, 1999) suggest that this approach, therefore, contains elements associated with professional identity and a knowledge of what the customer needs, and this has to be reconciled with standardised and bureaucratically imposed performance and productivity criteria. The type of organisational model Frenkel *et al.* advocate under these circumstances is called mass customised bureaucracy (MCB). Both the 'sweatshop' and the MCB models have implications for trade union recruitment within call centres (see below).

Self-Evaluation Activity 5.9
Employment relations in call centres
Response on website

Having read the descriptions of call centres and working conditions within them, try to come to some conclusion about the nature of employment relations within these workplaces.

Are call centres a threat to union organisation?

The apparently hostile working environment and the fact that workers are not always unhappy with it presents a challenge to those unions seeking to recruit within call centres. Some employers (and the size of employer, the work and the HRM practices adopted vary considerably) adapt personnel policies to suit the circumstances, often on an ad hoc basis. Flexible and casual working arrangements, a heavy emphasis on teamworking and regular performance reviews are usual methods of binding the employee's interests to those of the company, and for employees there is some degree of stability and certainty in a situation where targets are simple and clearly defined, however difficult they may be to achieve.

At first sight it might be assumed that recruiting employees to the relevant union would be relatively easy as employees are working in close proximity to each other, will have similar interests and will be in constant communication with each other. The reality for most centres is that staff have very little time to communicate with each other and that discussion about collective issues is very difficult, as is identifying an individual to act as workplace representative. Constant monitoring and surveillance prevent agents from giving much, if any, time to union activities. Labour turnover and the extent to which casual staff are employed also hamper union recruitment efforts and activities.

However, the nature of unionisation is patchy, and while union density figures are difficult to ascertain in such a rapidly growing industry there is much to be done to increase the proportion of union members within it. Many of the smaller workplaces are not unionised, while the finance sector is notorious for treating unions with disdain. A senior Amicus-MSF officer (Liverpool branch) contends that: 'Employee relations in call centres are polarised. Where unions are recognised and staff consulted, terms and conditions and the working environment can be very good. However, if not, then working life can be very unpleasant.'

Nevertheless, there are indications that unionisation within the larger call centres is becoming more widespread. The influential annual Incomes Data Services (IDS) survey of pay and conditions in call centres reveals that of the 133 organisations in the survey, 47 per cent recognised a trade union for pay bargaining and a further 5 per cent recognised a union for individual representation only. The increase in recognition since 2000 has been slight but positive. IDS confirms that larger employers are more likely than smaller employers to recognise a union – hence the overall proportion of employees covered by collective bargaining arrangements is around 66 per cent, with a further 8 per cent covered by individual representation. Bain and Taylor (1999) point out that 'in Scotland, for example, just over one half of all employees worked in call centres with either a trade union or staff association' (p. 2). One tendency which we have already noted is that some companies such as Virgin and Barclays have not extended recognition to their call centre operations (although there are signs that Barclays is conceding recognition to its call centres). A review of pay and benefits in call centres (IRS, 1998) within organisations formerly in the public sector reveals that unions had retained recognition in most of the call centres which had opened within the previous three years. However, unions had been excluded from several greenfield sites where alternative employee consultation machinery was in place (London Electricity, Northumbrian Water and Vertex).

Further grounds for optimism include evidence from a TUC report (1999) of a slight increase in trade union membership, particularly within the service sector during 1998, partly as a result of more proactive recruitment methods adopted by unions and partly due to the recognition provisions contained in the ERA99 (see Chapter 3). The TUC has, as part of its 'new unionism' approach (TUC, 1998) and Organising Academy initiative, considered the recognition opportunities within call centres in the face of employer hostility in the sector and argued that the determination of some employers to exclude unions demanded not only resilience, but also the development of more imaginative ways of making contact with call centre staff. However, the realisation of the potential for union recruitment in call centres 'will depend in part on a wider understanding of the attitudes of call centre employees, both to the experiences of work and to union's representation and recruitment activities' (Bain and Taylor, 1999, p. 8).

In considering a range of union recruitment experiences within call centres, Bain and Taylor (1999, 2002) identify the following approaches.

'Official' union activity, with employer agreement

In instances where the union has an existing agreement with the employer, representatives may gain access to new call centres in order to encourage recruitment. Eagle Star, Abbey National and BT are examples of organisations which permit this type of approach. Occasionally, unions have successfully attempted to recruit and negotiate terms and conditions before the opening of a new call centre within organisations as diverse as First Direct and the Inland Revenue. A more recent development has been the establishment of formal partnership agreements, for example with the Co-operative Bank and BIFU, and Scottish Widows and Amicus-MSF. In addition, as mentioned above, the call centre division of Barclays, Barclaycall, which previously resisted all attempts by UNIFI to recruit its call centre employees, apparently shifted its stance in early 1999 towards acceptance of a partnership approach which has provided union access to its Salford, Coventry and Sunderland centres.

Union activity, without employer agreement

In the face of employer resistance and hostility to union recognition within companies such as IBM, Kwik-Fit, BSkyB, Midland Bank (owned by HSBC) and Direct Line, unions have covertly attempted to organise with varying degrees of success. Bain and Taylor (2002) provide examples of tactics union activists have employed to attract new members in hostile environments (see Exhibit 5.13).

Joint union activity

There is evidence of growing co-operation between unions in various sectors concerned with call centre representation. For example, the Finance Sector Direct Staff Forum (FSDF) is a union organisation concerned solely with call centre matters and meets on a regular basis. It comprises the major unions within the sector, such as BIFU and Amicus-MSF, and many staff associations, many of which have affiliated to the TUC. In 1999, BIFU, UNIFI and the NatWest Staff Union made a decision to merge to create a new union (UNIFI) with around 200 000 members. Bain and Taylor (1999) point out that:

> *Whilst it would be starry-eyed idealism to suggest that elements of inter-union rivalry no longer exist, nevertheless, it is clear that the finance unions have made a hard-headed judgement based on the logic of developments in the sector. The result is far-reaching collaboration.*

Exhibit 5.13

Recruiting members in hostile environments

At a recent seminar discussing union recruitment, while acknowledging the continuing prioritisation over pay, hours of work, etc., by potential recruits, union activists and officials described particular tactics they had employed to attract new members in hostile environments [Finance Sector Unions (FSU) seminar, Bishop's Stortford, 18 February 1999]. These included consciously targeting non-union members in the course of the union rep carrying out workplace health and safety inspections and audits and taking a strong stand in defence of employees on disciplinary charges. In one call centre no less than three-quarters of the staff were facing disciplinary action and representation in these cases clearly enhanced the union's credibility. In other centres activists have compiled lists of new employees from information supplied by existing union members. Company logos and colours have been successfully and strategically placed on union recruitment material. At other centres special subscription rates have been offered to new staff. Colourful reports testify to the creative and varied methods employed to enhance the unions' profile. In one centre representatives utilised local electronic mail to reach beyond the ranks of existing members. In workforce activists adopted a philosophy of 'stick your nose in everywhere' leading to a small but no less significant achievement where the union negotiated the relaxation of a strict dress code imposed by the employer.

Source: Bain and Taylor, 2002, p. 252

The regular meetings provide a constructive forum for the collective discussion of problems and union successes. There can be no doubt that this co-operation is perceived to be of general benefit, perhaps particularly for the smaller unions, and seems likely to encourage further moves towards formal mergers. (p. 254)

Bain and Taylor (2002), in their analysis of the finance sector call centre, demonstrate that despite uneven rates and extent of union presence and voice, 'research indicates some growth in both union membership and recognition' (p. 258). This is due partly to the provision of personal services by the unions involved, partly to the diminishing extent of inter-union rivalry and partly as a consequence of union recognition provisions of the ERA99.

Targeting recruitment: some successes and failures

Self Evaluation activity 5.10

Organising and servicing approaches
Response on website

In Chapter 3 we identified two approaches which could be adopted by unions in shaping their recruitment strategies – the organising approach and the servicing approach. Briefly summarise these approaches and indicate how these might be applied to the call centre contexts.

Some union successes

- Over 1800 members were recruited by the CWU in two of BT's new call centres at Doncaster and Newcastle. BT has three other unionised call centres, the largest of which is at Warrington employing over 1700 people. The vast majority of new recruits were agency staff who do not work on a BT contract.
- In the finance sector, the First Direct call centre in Leeds was set up in 1989. Of the 3500 staff now employed in First Direct, about one-third have joined BIFU. After initial refusal of recognition, the union secured a collective agreement

whereby office representatives have successfully negotiated above-inflation pay deals and fended off performance-related-pay in relation to salaries.
- The Norwich Union Direct operation in Sheffield has been open for two years and employs around 350 staff of which 150 are members of Amicus-MSF. Call centre union representatives have access to management and take up issues which arise, including salary levels, rosters and the distribution of overtime. Difficulties for Amicus-MSF stem from the high staff turnover rate, currently 33 per cent annually, and this raises problems for organisation and continuity of workplace representation.

One problem ultimately resolved

Barclays Bank call centres, or Barclaycall centres, presented a difficult problem. At Barclaycall Coventry, Barclay's in-house union UNIFI recruited almost half the 300 workers, but only after sustained campaigning and despite the fact that unions were not recognised within Barclaycall. UNIFI's National Officer, Sarah Messenger stated that:

Staff at Barclaycall are undoubtedly exploited compared to other Barclays employees. Recognition has been denied to the union for Barclaycall even though a full recognition agreement operates in the rest of the bank. The reality is that staff are not too unhappy and attempts to convince them that they work in a sweatshop tend to turn them off. Management have been very clever in making staff feel as if they belong, by providing a gym, a good restaurant, and involving themselves in the local community. The staff have a consultation forum which is effectively excluded from any power. Our challenge is to pitch criticisms of management at the right level and portray UNIFI and its activities in a positive light. The staff must understand that we have a crucial contribution to make and that we will fight for their interests at the same time as having a regard for the health of the business. (Quoted in UNIFI's Annual Report, 1999)

Organising efforts at Barclaycall were rendered more difficult by the following factors:

- there is a 40 per cent yearly staff turnover rate;
- there were no identifiable workplace representatives; and

- Barclays was disinterested in 'social partnership' despite union overtures.

However, there has been a change of heart at Barclays which now endorses the 'partnership' model. This development and the greater clout of the merged finance unions to form UNIFI in 1999 will facilitate union recognition within Barclaycall itself.

The threat from India

Some insurance companies and banks are amongst those companies outsourcing their call centre activities to India. Prudential announced its intention to transfer 1000 jobs but agreed to delay this after union pressure for a ban on compulsory redundancies. Norwich Union (parent company Aviva) decided in February 2003 to open a new call centre in India for 1000 employees. Amicus-MSF is involved in resisting these developments, mainly by attempting to secure guarantees of no redundancies. HSBC bank is already processing UK-originated calls in centres in Asia, as is Lloyds TSB. BT is to open two Indian call centres – in Bangalore and Delhi – employing 2200 people by 2004. This development is part of plans which will see BT's UK-based centres drop from around 100 to 31, with the number of call centre workers falling from 16 000 to 14 000. Despite assurances of no permanent UK employees being made redundant, and no compulsory lay-offs amongst agency staff, the union involved (CWU) is suspicious of BT's motives and is resisting the move.

The allure of India for British companies includes the wage bill. Research by Adecco (2003) suggested that British companies would create up to 100 000 call centre jobs in India by 2008. As the wage bill of an up-and-running call centre comprises two-thirds of its operating costs, and with Indian call centre workers earning around £1200 a year – less than one-tenth of the earnings of their British equivalents – companies would be able to reduce their costs substantially. In addition, India has a surplus of skilled and highly educated workers, many of them graduates, who find that the wages in call centres compare extremely favourably or even exceed those wages paid in their chosen occupations. Apart from the relatively routine call centre operations, Indian advisers are provided with training in accents and briefed on the weather, football scores and even latest TV soap story lines in order to hold conversations with British customers.

As far as future developments are concerned, larger UK companies may well continue to outsource to India, despite the risks inherent in such moves such as the distance involved, the control and quality issues and possible political instability. Smaller firms are less likely to take the plunge as the risk of things going wrong tends to increase. Despite the outsourcing trend which Datamonitor predicts will increase, especially for financial services firms, growth in the UK market will also increase, but less rapidly than hitherto at around 4 per cent annually. Indeed, IDS (2003) found that only 6 per cent of the firms surveyed expected to cut jobs in the next 12 months while 60 per cent had intentions of hiring new staff.

Concluding remarks

Notwithstanding the 'threat from India', UK call centres have now established themselves as major employers and more people work in call centres than in coal, steel and vehicle production put together. Within these new workplaces, which vary in size, there is strict computer-operated monitoring and supervisory processes and an intensification of work which exceeds that of the traditional assembly line. Despite this, the limited evidence available suggests that call centre workers, or 'agents' are not unhappy with their lot. Suggested reasons for this concern age (a relatively young workforce), response to challenges pertaining to 'customer care', and the benefits of teamworking. Salary levels are also higher than in other parts of the core business (the financial sector, for example). Unionisation is patchy, the problems of organising and recruiting exacerbated by high staff turnover rates and employer union recognition problems. There is a need for more research on union and non-union patterns of organisation within call centres, pay structures and employee attitudes which impinge upon job-related and industrial relations contexts. The call centre provides an opportunity to study emerging forms of workplace industrial relations which contrast with those in the traditional Fordist, mainly manual, full-time and unionised workplaces.

REFERENCES

ACAS (1987) *Occasional Paper 41: Labour Flexibility in Britain.* ACAS, London

Ackers, P., Smith, C. and Smith, P. (1996) 'Against all odds? British trade unions in the new workplace', in Ackers, P., Smith, C. and Smith, P. *The New Workplace and Trade Unionism.* London, Routledge

Ackroyd, S. and Procter, S. (1998) 'British manufacturing organisation and workplace industrial relations: some attributes of the new flexible firm'. *British Journal of Industrial Relations,* 36, 2, 163–83

Ackroyd, S., Burrell, G., Hughes, M. and Whitaker, A. (1988) 'The Japanisation of British industry'. *Industrial Relations Journal,* 19, 1, 11–23

Adecco (2003) *Best Locations for Contact Centres.* Oxfordshire, Omis Research

Arkin, A. (1997) 'Hold the production line'. *People Management.* February

Atkinson, J. (1984) 'Manpower strategies for flexible organisations'. *Personnel Management,* August

Bach, S. and Winchester, D. (1994) 'Opting out of pay devolution? The prospects for local pay bargaining in UK public services'. *British Journal of Industrial Relations,* 32, 2, 263–82

Bach, S. and Winchester, D. (2003) 'Industrial relations in the public sector', in Edwards, P. (ed.) *Industrial Relations Theory and Practice,* 2nd edn. Oxford, Blackwell

Bacon, N. and Storey, J. (1993) 'Individualisation of the employment relationship and implications for trade unions'. *Employee Relations,* 15, 1, 5–17

Bacon, N. and Storey, J. (1996) 'Individualism and collectivism and the changing role of trade unions', in Ackers, P., Smith, C. and Smith, P. (eds) *The New Workplace and Trade Unionism.* London, Routledge

Bain, P. and Taylor, P. (1999) ' "An assembly line in the head": work and employee relations in the call centre'. *Industrial Relations Journal,* 30, 2

Bain, P. and Taylor, P. (1999) 'Employee relations, worker attitudes and trade union representation in call centres'. Paper for the 17th Annual International Labour Process Conference, University of London

Bain, P. and Taylor, P. (2002) 'Union recognition and organisation in call centres'. *Industrial Relations Journal,* 33, 3, 246–61

Baldry, C., Bain, P. and Taylor, P. (1998) 'Bright satanic offices: intensification, control and team Taylorism', in Thompson, P. and Warhurst, C. (eds) *Workplaces of the Future.* London, Macmillan

Beardwell, I.J. (1997) 'How do we know how it really is? An analysis of the new industrial relations', in Beardwell, I.J. (ed.) *Contemporary Industrial Relations: A Critical Analysis.* Oxford, Oxford University Press

Beaumont, P.B. (1991) 'Trade unions and HRM'. *Industrial Relations Journal,* 22, 4, 300–8

Beer, M., Spector, B., Lawrence, P.R., Mills, D. and Walton, R. (1985) *Managing Human Assets.* New York, The Free Press

Belt, V. (1999) 'Are call centres the new sweatshops?'. *The Independent,* 3 January

Bevan, W. (1987) 'Creating a no-strike environment: the trade union view'. Paper to Confederation of British Industry Conference, London

Beynon, H. (1975) *Working for Ford.* Wakefield, EP Publishing

Blyton, P. and Turnbull, P. (1998) *The Dynamics of Employee Relations,* 2nd edn. London, Macmillan

Boxall, P. and Purcell, J. (2003) *Strategy and Human Resource Management.* Houndmills, Palgrave Macmillan

Braverman, H. (1974) *Labour and Monopoly Capital.* New York, Monthly Review Press

Brown, W. (1993) 'The contraction of collective bargaining in Britain'. *British Journal of Industrial Relations,* 31, 2, 189–200

Brown, W., Marginson, R. and Walsh, J. (2003) 'The management of pay', in Edwards, P. (ed.) *Industrial Relations Theory and Practice,* 2nd edn. Oxford, Blackwell

Callaghan, G. and Thompson, P. (2002) ' "We recruit attitude": the selection and shaping of routine call centre labour'. *Journal of Management Studies,* 39, 2, 233–55

Clark, I. (1997) 'The state and new industrial relations', in Beardwell, I.J. (ed.) *Contemporary Industrial Relations: A Critical Analysis.* Oxford, Oxford University Press

Claydon, T. (1994) 'Human resource management and the labour market' in Beardwell, I. and Holden, L. (eds) *Human Resource Management: A Contemporary Perspective.* London, Pitman

Crowther, S. and Garrahan, P. (1988) 'Invitation to Sunderland: corporate power and the local economy'. *Industrial Relations Journal,* 19, 1, 51–9

Cully, M., Woodland, S., O'Reilly, A. and Dix, G. (1998) *The 1998 Workplace Employee Relations Survey*. London, DTI

Cully, M., Woodland, S., O'Reilly, A. and Dix, G. (1999) *Britain at Work*. London, Routledge

Danford, A. (1998) 'Work organisation inside Japanese firms in South Wales: a break from Taylorism?', in Thompson, P. and Warhurst, C. (eds) *Workplaces of the Future*. London, Macmillan

Datamonitor (2001) *Customer Relationship Outsourcing in Europe*. London, Datamonitor

Datamonitor (2002) *Call Centres in Europe*. London, Datamonitor

Deery, S., Iverson, R. and Walsh, J. (2002) 'Work relationships in call centres; understanding emotional exhaustion and employee withdrawal'. *Journal of Management Studies*, 39, 4, 471–96

Delbridge, R. (1998) *Life on the Line in Contemporary Manufacturing*. Oxford, Oxford University Press

Dickens, P. (1998) *Global Shift*. London, Paul Chapman Publishing

Donovan (1968) *Report of the Royal Commission on Trade Unions and Employer' Associations 1965–68*, Cmnd 3623. London, HMSO

Douglas, M. (1980) 'Autoworker can only do as well as Head Office permits'. *Albuquerque Journal*, 24 July, A5

Edwards, P. (2003) 'The employment relationship', in Edwards, P. *Industrial Relations Theory and Practice*, 2nd edn. London, Routledge

Farnham, D. and Pimlott, J. (1995) *Understanding Industrial Relations*. London, Cassell

Fernie, S. and Metcalfe, D. (1998) '(Not hanging on the telephone): payment systems in the new sweat shops'. *Centre for Economic Performance*. London, LSE

Fombrun, C.J., Titchy, M. and Devanna, M.A. (1984) 'Linking competitive strategies with human resource management practices'. *Academy of Management Executive*, 1, 209–13

Ford, H. (1922) *My Life and Work*. New York, Doubleday Page

Foucault, M., (1979) *Discipline and Punish*. Harmondsworth, Penguin/Peregrine Books

Frenkel, S., Korczynski, M., Shire, K. and Tam, M. (1998) 'Beyond bureaucracy? Work organisation in call centres'. *The International Journal of Human Resource Management*, 9, 6, 957–79

Frenkel, S., Korczynski, M., Shire, K. and Tam, M. (1999) *On the Front Line*. Ithaca, New York, ILR Press

Friedman, A. and Cornford, D. (1989) *Computer Systems Development: History, Organisation and Implementation*. Chichester, John Wiley

Garrahan, P. (1986) 'Nissan in the North East'. *Capital and Class*, 27, 5, 5–13

Garrahan, P. and Stewart, P. (1991) 'Nothing new about Nissan', in Law, C. (ed.) *Restructuring the Automobile Industry*. London, Routledge

Garrahan, P. and Stewart, P. (1992) *The Nissan Enigma*. London, Mansell

Geary, J.F. (1995) 'Work practices: the structure of work', in Edwards, P. (ed.) *Industrial Relations: Theory and Practice in Britain*. Oxford, Blackwell

Geary, J.F. (2003) 'New forms of work organisation: still limited, still controlled, but still welcome?' in Edwards, P. (ed.) *Industrial Relations Theory and Practice*, 2nd edn. Oxford, Blackwell

Geary, J. and Roche, B. (2001) 'Multinationals and human resource practices in Ireland'. *International Journal of Human Resource Management*, 12, 1, 109–27

Gospel, H. (1995) 'The decline in apprenticeship training in Britain'. *Industrial Relations Journal*, 26, 1, 32–44

Grant, D. (1997) 'Japanisation and new industrial relations', in Beardwell, I.J. (ed.) *Contemporary Industrial Relations*. Oxford, Oxford University Press

Grint, K. (1993) *The Sociology of Work*. Oxford, Polity Press

Guest, D. (1989) 'Human resource management: its implications for trade unions and industrial relations', in Storey, J. (ed.) *New Perspectives in Human Resource Management*. London, Routledge

Guest, D.E. (1995) 'Human resource management, trade unions and industrial relations', in Storey, J. (ed.) *Human Resource Management: A Critical Text*. London, Routledge

Guest, D. and Hoque, K. (1994) 'The good, the bad and the ugly: employment relations in new non-unionised workplaces'. *Human Resource Management Journal*, 5, 1, 1–14

Guest, D., Michie, J., Sheehan, M., Conway, N. and Metochi, M. (2000) *Human Resource Management and Performance'*. Birkbeck College, University of London School of Management and Organisational Psychology

Handy, C. (1995) *The Future of Work*. W.H. Smith Contemporary Papers, No. 8

Horton, S. (1997) 'The employee relations environment', in Farnham, D. (ed.) *Employee Relations in Context*. London, IPD

Hounshell, D.A. (1984) *From the American System to Mass, Production, 1800–1932: The Development of Manufacturing Technology in the United State*. Baltimore, MD, Johns Hopkins University Press

Hunter, C. and MacInnes, J. (1994) 'Employees and labour flexibility: the evidence from case studies'. *Employment Gazette*, June

Hutton, W. (1995) *The State We're In*. London, Jonathan Cape

Hyman, R. (1980) 'Trade unions, control and resistance', in Esland, G. and Salaman, G. (eds) *The Politics of Work and Occupations*. Milton Keynes, Open University Press

IDS (Incomes Data Services) (2003) *Pay and Conditions in Call Centres, 2002*. London, IDS

IRS (1998) *Employment Review*, No. 650

IRS (1999) 'Women in teleservices frustrated by routine'. *IRS Employment Trends*, No. 675

Keep, E. and Rainbird, H. (2003); 'Training', in Edwards, P. (ed.) *Industrial Relations Theory and Practice*, 2nd edn. Oxford, Blackwell

Kenney, M. and Florida, R. (1993) *Beyond Mass Production*. Oxford, Oxford University Press

Kessler, I. and Purcell, J. (2003) 'Individualism and collectivism in industrial relations', in Edwards, P. (ed.) *Industrial Relations Theory and Practice*, 2nd edn. Oxford, Blackwell

Knights, D., Calvey, D. and Odih, P. (1999) 'Social managerialism and the time-disciplined subject: quality-quantity conflicts in a call centre'. Paper for the 17th Annual International Labour Process Conference, University of London

Kochan, T.A. and Barocci, T. (eds) (1985) *Human Resource Management and Industrial Relations*. Boston, Little Brown

Kochan, T.A., Katz, H.C. and McKersie, R.B. (1986) *The Transformation of American Industrial Relations*. New York, Basic Books

Kolm, S.C. (1985) 'Must one be a Buddhist to grow? An analysis of the cultural basis of Japanese productivity', in Koslowski, P. (ed.) *Economics and Philosophy*. Tubingen, J.C.B. Morh

Lane, C. (1995) 'The pursuit of flexible specialisation in Britain and West Germany', in Heap, N., Thomas, R., Einon, Mason, R. and Mackay, H. *Information Technology and Society*. London, Sage

Lash, S. and Urry, J. (1987) *The End of Organised Capitalism*. London, Polity Press

Legge, K. (1995) *Human Resource Management: Rhetoric and Realities*. London, Macmillan

Littler, C.R. and Salaman, G. (1985) 'The design of jobs', in Littler, C.R. (ed.) *The Experience of Work*. Aldershot, Gower

Marginson, P., Edwards, P. and Martin, R. (1988) *Beyond The Workplace: Managing Industrial Relations in Multi-establishment Enterprises*. Oxford, Blackwell

McIlroy, J. (1991) *The Permanent Revolution? Conservative Law and the Trade Unions*. Nottingham, Spokesman Books

McLoughlin, I. and Clark, J. (1994) *Technological Change at Work*. Milton Keynes, Open University Press

Metcalf, D. (1993) 'Industrial relations and economic performance'. *British Journal of Industrial Relations*, 31, 2, 255–83

Millward, N. (1994) *The New Industrial Relations*. London, Policy Studies Institute

Millward, N., Bryson, A. and Forth, J. (2000) *All Change at Work?* London, Routledge

Millward, N., Stevens, M., Smart, D. and Hawes, W.R. (1992) *Workplace Industrial Relations in Transition*. Aldershot, Dartmouth

MITI (Ministry of International Trade and Industry) (2000) *Summary of the 1999 Survey of Overseas Business Activities*. Tokyo, MITI

Mitial Research (2002) 'UK 2001 call and contact centre study'. Mitial Research, www.mitial.com

Morgan, G., Sharpe, D.R., Kelly, W. and Whitley, R. (2002) 'The future of Japanese manufacturing in the UK'. *Journal of Management Studies*, 39, 8, 1023–44.

Nolan, P. and O'Donnell, K. (2003) 'Industrial relations, HRM and performance', in Edwards, P. (ed.) *Industrial Relations Theory and Practice*, 2nd edn. Oxford, Blackwell

Oliver, N. and Wilkinson, B. (1992) *The Japanisation of British Industry*. Oxford, Blackwell

ONS (Office for National Statistics) (2002) *Labour Force Survey*, Spring 2002

Pemberton, C. and Herriot, P. (1994) 'Inhumane resources'. *Observer*, 4 December

Pendleton, A. (1991) 'Workplace industrial relations in British Rail: change and continuity in the 1980s'. *Industrial Relations Journal*, 22, 3, 209–21

Penn, R. and Scattergood, H. (1996) 'The experience of trade unions in Rochdale during the 1980s', in Gallie, D., Penn, R. and Rose, M. (eds) *Trade Unionism in Recession*. Oxford, Oxford University Press

Piore, M.J. (1986) 'Perspectives on labour market flexibility'. *Industrial Relations*, 25, 2, 146–66

Piore, M.J. and Sabel, C.F. (1984) *The Second Industrial Divide*. New York, Basic Books

Pollert, A. (1988) 'The flexible firm: fact or fiction?' *Work, Employment and Society*, 2, 3, 281–316

Pollert, A. (1996) 'Team work on the assembly line: contradiction and the dynamics of union resilience', in Ackers, P., Smith, C. and Smith, P. (eds) *The New Workplace and Trade Unionism*. London, Routledge

Poole, M. and Jenkins, G. (1997) 'Developments in HRM in manufacturing in modern Britain'. *International Journal of Human Resource Management*, 8, 3, 841–56

Porter, M.E. (1985) *Competitive Advantage: Creating and Sustaining Performance*. New York, The Free Press

Procter, S. and Ackroyd, S. (2001) 'Flexibility', in Redman, T. and Wilkinson, A. (eds) *Contemporary Human Resource Management*. Harlow, Financial Times/Prentice Hall

Purcell, J. and Sisson, K. (1983) 'Strategies and practice in the management of industrial relations', in Bain, G.S. (ed.) *Industrial Relations in Britain*. Oxford, Blackwell

Ramsay, H., Scholarios, D. and Harley, B. (2000) 'Employees and high performance work systems; testing inside the black box'. *British Journal of Industrial Relations*, 38, 4, 501–31

Rose, E. (1994) 'The disorganised paradigm: British industrial relations in the 1990s'. *Employee Relations*, 16, 1, 27–40

Rose, E. and Woolley, E. (1992) 'Shifting sands? Trade unions and productivity at Rover cars'. *Industrial Relations Journal*, 23, 4, 257–67

Rose, E. and Wright, G. (2003) 'Skill, control and satisfaction amongst call centre customer service representatives'. Research paper, School of Management, Liverpool John Moores University

Rose, M. (1996) 'Still life in Swindon: case studies in union survival and employer policy in a "sunrise" labour market', in Gallie, D., Penn, R. and Rose, M. (eds) *Trade Unionism in Recession*. Oxford, Oxford University Press

Sabel, C.F. (1982) *Work and Politics: The Division of Labour in Industry*. Cambridge, Cambridge University Press

Salaman, G. (1984) *Working*. London, Ellis Horwood/Tavistock

Schuler, R.S. and Jackson, S. (1987) 'Linking competitive strategies with human resource management practices'. *Academy of Management Executive*, 1, 209–13

Simms, M., Stewart, P., Delbridge, R. and Heery, E. (1999) 'Unionising call centres'. Paper for the 17th Annual International Labour Process Conference, University of London

Sisson, K. (1993) 'In search of HRM'. *British Journal of Industrial Relations*, 31, 2, 201–10

Smith, A. (1910) *The Wealth of Nations*. London, Dent and Sons (first published 1776)

Stephenson, C. (1996) 'The different experience of trade unionism in two Japanese transplants', in Ackers, P., Smith, C. and Smith, P. (eds) *The New Workplace and Trade Unionism*. London, Routledge

Storey, J. (1992) *Developments in the Management of Human Resources*. Oxford, Blackwell

Storey, J. and Sisson, K. (1993) *Managing Human Resources and Industrial Relations*. Buckingham, Open University Press

Taylor, F.W. (1911) *The Principles of Scientific Management*. New York, Harper and Row

Trevor, M. (1988) 'Toshiba's new British company: competitiveness through innovation'. Unpublished paper, University of Cardiff, Wales

TUC (1998) New Unionism Seminar: Organising Telephone Call Centres, November. London, TUC

TUC (1999) *Today's Trade Unionists: Trade Union Trends Analysis of the 1998 Labour Force Survey*. London, TUC

TUC (2001) *It's Your Call*. London, TUC

Warhurst, C. and Thompson, P. (1998) 'Hands, hearts and minds: changing work and workers at the end of the century', in Thompson, P. and Warhurst, C. (eds) *Workplaces of the Future*. London, Macmillan

Wickens, P. (1987) *The Road to Nissan*. London, Macmillan

Wickens, P. (1993) 'Lean production and beyond: the system, its critics and its future'. *Human Resource Management Journal*, 3, 4, 75–90

Wood, S. (ed.) (1989) *The Transformation of Work? Skill, Flexibility and the Labour Process*. London, Unwin

Wood, S. and Mundy, J. (1993) 'Are Human Resource Practices in Japanese Transplants Truly Different?' Paper presented at the BUIRA Conference, York

Zuboff, S. (1988) *The Age of the Smart Machine: The Future of Work and Power*. Oxford, Heinemann

CHAPTER 6

COLLECTIVE BARGAINING AND PAY DETERMINATION

INTRODUCTION

Collective bargaining, some would argue, is the very essence of industrial relations and an important institution in all democratic societies where freedom of association is common. In previous chapters we recognised, at least implicitly, that collective bargaining is the main method whereby unionised workforces and their managements jointly determine matters such as pay and conditions of work, and our introductory chapter (Chapter 1) provided us with a brief overview of the topic. In Britain and elsewhere, collective bargaining is in decline and its influence is declining, although the percentage of employees whose pay is affected by collective bargaining remained fairly constant during the period 1996 to 2001 within the 34.5–36.4 range (LMT, 2002). However, the growing number of recognition and partnership agreements (see Chapters 3 and 8) may well reverse these trends, albeit marginally.

In this chapter we consider collective bargaining and pay determination as related topics, but in the light of the decline of collective bargaining in recent decades alternative forms of pay determination are also considered. Given the central importance of collective bargaining to industrial relations, we begin by defining and justifying its significance both as a process and as an institution within the British context. An understanding of the essential theoretical underpinnings of collective bargaining is important as this will assist our appreciation of the variety of levels, circumstances and issues with which collective bargaining is involved. After taking into account the historical development of collective bargaining in Britain, we consider some of the notable trends that have taken place in collective bargaining during the past 60 years, focusing particularly upon decentralised bargaining patterns evident during the latter decades of last century and continuing into the twenty-first century. As most of our attention will have been upon the private sector, we devote a section to public services such as the National Health Service, local authorities and the privatised industries. Finally, we consider the extent to which collective bargaining over pay has been either replaced or supplemented by other methods of pay determination.

Learning outcomes

When you have read this chapter, you should be able to:

1. Describe the theoretical underpinnings and explain the historical development of collective bargaining.

2. Explain the trends in the patterns of collective bargaining.

3. Distinguish between different collective bargaining arrangements within the public and private sectors.

4. Identify alternative methods of pay determination.

THE SIGNIFICANCE OF COLLECTIVE BARGAINING

The term 'collective bargaining' was originated by Webb and Webb (1920), to describe the process of agreeing terms and conditions of employment through representatives of employers (and possibly their associations) and representatives of employees (and probably their unions). As we shall see, collective bargaining was regarded by the Webbs mainly as a substitute for the employer bargaining individually with each employee and establishing such terms and conditions for each through the contract of employment. A major factor behind collective organisation has been the recognition that the balance of bargaining power between the employer and single individual was uneven, and that even on a representative and collective basis bargaining power is rarely equalised, being skewed either towards the employer or the employees collectively. We may define collective bargaining in the following way:

> Collective bargaining is the process whereby representatives of employers and employees jointly determine and regulate decisions pertaining to both substantive and procedural matters within the employment relationship. The outcome of this process is the collective agreement.

Collective bargaining, then, is a representative process in which representatives of capital reach agreements or compromises with representatives of labour. It is not a discrete process whereby agreements are arrived at on a periodic basis. Rather, it should be seen as a continuous process 'which calls for the maintenance, regulation and supplementation of such agreements day by day' (Burchill, 1992, p. 77). Collective bargaining is, therefore, a dynamic method and process of joint determination which displays a vast diversity of form and content between different industries, different organisations and even different workplaces. It is also an evolving institution, changing its character and structure and its relationships with other institutions over a period of time.

Collective bargaining is a major determinant of the rules which govern the relationships between the parties at the workplace and as such is a form of joint regulation. However, it is only one method of decision-making amongst several which include the following:

- **Unilateral employer regulation** where the decisions and rules are made by one side only. This is an important form of regulation as it may well be the dominant form in organisations which do not have any collective bargaining arrangements whatsoever and where the management ideology is basically unitarist.
- **Individual bargaining** which we have referred to above, where the individual bargains with his or her employer concerning wages and conditions, working arrangements and other matters, is relatively common in non-unionised organisations or where previously unionised employees (usually at management levels) are de-unionised. As with unilateral employer regulation, individual bargaining takes place within a unitarist framework.
- **Joint consultation** provides a mechanism whereby employees are given a voice in decision-making via a number of forms of representation and formal mechanisms. The process varies from largely informal, regular or daily meetings to the more formal consultative committees and works councils (the latter being voluntary and sparse in Britain, but compulsory in many EU countries – see Chapter 8). Joint consultation has a long history in Britain and more than one-third of workplaces have it in some form or other. Some consultative arrangements exist in non-union workplaces and, from a union perspective, joint consultation may have an 'anti-union' connotation. The decisions subject to consultation may be fairly trivial and consultation may even take place after the decision is actually made. From the employer's perspective, however, 'joint consultation has the advantage that management retains ultimate discretion and control, but simultaneously joint consultation can give employees a voice and perhaps thereby increase employee commitment' (Gospel and Palmer, 1993, p. 176).
- **Unilateral employee regulation** is where employees themselves devise workplace rules through the medium of formal and informal work groups, trade unions or professional associations, or some other formalised mechanism. There are four broad traditional categories of employee regulation:

- The first is custom and practice rules which are not introduced by management or written down, and not formally created by collective bargaining. They can cover a whole variety of matters such as breaks, starting times, finishing times, regulation of output, transfers and work allocation. For example, London bus crews would tend to rush early journeys to and from destinations in order to ensure longer morning breaks. The culture of custom and practice has led to industrial relations problems and conflicts, as managements may see them as examples of restrictive practices.
- The second has taken the form of craft regulation of labour supply, wage and output levels. Printers used to confine entry to their craft to union or 'chapel' members.
- The third is related to the second, but involves professional employees such as doctors and solicitors who regulate entry to their profession.
- The fourth includes more formal methods of worker regulation such as worker co-operatives, worker self-management and, at its furthest extreme, workers' control.

Self-Evaluation Activity 6.1

Methods of decision-making
This SEA has no commentary

By way of review, summarise the main methods of decision-making governing the employment relationship.

Dubin (1954) famously described collective bargaining as 'the great social invention that has institutionalised industrial conflict' (p. 52). This is an important point because Dubin is suggesting that without collective bargaining, industrial conflict would threaten not only the industrial order but also social stability. The term 'institutionalised' basically means both _contained_ and _formalised_ within a societally recognised structure, a structure that is legitimised by all members of society, and certainly within the industrial relations context by both employers and employees. In the words of Dubin:

Collective relations between management and union are grounded in the conscious and deliber-

ate use of power and force. Power is marshalled and force is used to gain the immediate ends of the contending parties as they are formalised in the collective agreement. The union agreement sets forth that final resolution of the current conflicts in a body of policies and rules that govern the management-men relationships. It is not of central significance that these rules be arrived at by peaceful means. More important is the fact that the collective agreement represents a compromise between what management wants and what the union wants. It is the fact of both the expectation of compromise and its actual achievement that is most relevant in delineating collective bargaining as a mode for institutionalising industrial conflict. (p. 52)

Collective bargaining is a pluralist concept in that it is encouraged by those who share a pluralist perspective and who argue that collective bargaining not only provides a mechanism whereby potentially destructive conflict can be dealt with, but also contributes an economic method of dealing with the workforce. The Donovan Commission report (1968) argued that in a democratic, civilised society workers had a right to be represented in any decisions affecting their working lives and that collective bargaining was the most effective means of achieving this. From a unitarist perspective, collective bargaining and pay determination distorts the free market mechanisms by restraining the free flow of labour in response to those forces and prevents the proper use of incentives, thereby limiting motivation and productivity. These two arguments feature prominently in attempting to explain the changes that affected collective bargaining and industrial relations generally during the 1980s and 1990s, and the decline in the coverage of collective bargaining during the same period. Table 6.1 shows the extent to which the coverage of collective bargaining declined up to 1998.

As Table 6.1 indicates, 70 per cent of all employees in all establishments, unionised and non-unionised, were covered by collective bargaining arrangements in 1984, but this fell to 54 per cent in 1990 and 40 per cent in 1998. However, the proportion is much higher when non-unionised establishments are taken out of the equation. If collective bargaining coverage is broken down by sector, as the table shows, the private services witnessed the

Table 6.1 Proportion of employees covered by collective bargaining: 1984, 1990, 1998

	Proportion of employees covered by collective bargaining (%)			Average annual change (%)	
	1984	1990	1998	1984–90	1990–8
All workplaces	70	54	40	−2.9	−3.3
Broad sector					
Private manufacturing	64	51	46	−2.6	−1.3
Private services	60	33	21	−2.3	−4.7
Public sector	95	78	62	−2.3	−2.6
Any recognised union	90	81	69	−1.3	−2.1

Source: Millward *et al.*, 2000, p. 197

steepest rate of decline in coverage and had the lowest degree of coverage, while the public sector had the highest level of coverage at 62 per cent. It should be emphasised that the coverage of collective agreements is wider than union membership since in most workplaces there are numerous non-union workers whose basic pay and conditions are fixed by collective agreements. Collective bargaining as a process and also as an institution is therefore extremely important, even though there have been important changes in recent decades and considerable turbulence created by the demise of national bargaining and the rise of domestic bargaining during the 1960s and 1970s, which resulted in government attempts to inject some order into the system. Before looking at these developments we shall consider some of the main theoretical contributions which assist our understanding of collective bargaining. WERS98 provides a fuller analysis of collective bargaining coverage and scope which will be considered below.

COLLECTIVE BARGAINING: THEORETICAL BACKGROUND

It would be erroneous to suggest that there is a body of 'collective bargaining theory' which is either critical or coherent. The industrial relations orientation to the debate is fairly specific as it focuses largely upon the functions of collective bargaining rather than the societal context in which bargaining takes place. The contributions are mainly pluralist and systems theory oriented and rarely challenge or present a critique of capitalist society. The reason for this lies largely in the uncritical acceptance of collective bargaining as a form of institutionalised problem-solving, the purpose of which is to avoid conflict which threatens social stability. In this, collective bargaining has been hugely successful. Much of the theory concerning collective bargaining is fairly self-contained, although each contribution builds to some extent upon its predecessor (usually by criticising what has been omitted by the previous theory) and some of the more important contributions are based on the US system of industrial relations. The main contributors are Sydney and Beatrice Webb, Flanders, Chamberlain and Kuhn, and Walton and McKersie.

The contribution of the Webbs

The Webbs regarded collective bargaining as one of three main methods used by trade unions to achieve their basic aim of improving the conditions of their members' working lives. The other two methods they called mutual insurance and legal enactment, which we will now briefly describe.

The method of mutual insurance was not only a system of formal insurance to provide cash benefits for sickness, industrial injury, retirement or death, but also involved the use of trade union funds to provide 'out of work' benefit and travelling allowances to individual workers to enable them to refuse jobs offered at below the rate agreed amongst union members. Coates and Topham (1988) comment on this method:

> Obviously the method of mutual insurance, which required no formal recognition of trade unions by employers, and indeed no necessity for a bargaining process, was a response to a time when industrial relations were rudimentary and undeveloped, when employers insisted successfully on their prerogatives, and when trade unions were small and confined to defined crafts and particular occupational skills. (p. 173)

Legal enactment is another method of creating employment rules and could also be called 'statutory regulation'. It involves state regulation of wages, conditions and other aspects of the employment relationship, and trade unions would lobby for legislative changes in favour of their members. To a great extent we already have 'legal enactment', that is, a body of legislation covering individual (health, safety, unfair dismissal) and collective (strikes, trade union matters) aspects of the employment relationship.

The Webbs did not consider **collective bargaining** other than as a trade union method, and their interpretation of collective bargaining can be illustrated by the following example which they provide in their book, *Industrial Democracy* (1902):

> In organised trades the individual workman, applying for a job, accepts or refuses the terms offered by the employer without communication with his fellow-workmen, and without any other consideration than the exigencies of his own position. For the sale of his labour he makes, with the employer, a strictly individual bargain. But if a group of workmen concert together, and send representatives to conduct the bargaining on behalf of the whole body, the position is at once changed. Instead of the employer making a series of separate contracts with isolated individuals, he meets with a collective will, and settles, in a single agreement, the principles from which, for the time being, all workmen of a particular group, or class, or grade, will be engaged. (p. 173)

For the Webbs, collective bargaining was the collective equivalent of individual bargaining, and where workmen were able and willing to combine they preferred it to bargaining as individuals with their employer as it enabled them to secure better terms of employment by controlling competition amongst themselves. The larger the size of the bargaining unit (the workplace, the organisation, or the whole industry) the greater the advantage secured by the union and workers.

The critique and contribution of Flanders

Allan Flanders (1970a) has criticised the Webbs' view of collective bargaining. He argues firstly, that the Webbs 'ignored any positive interest (in collective bargaining) on the part of employers' (p. 215). Employers would only have an interest in collective bargaining if there were some sort of compensatory outcome favourable to them, but this was not an issue which the Webbs considered. They assumed that collective bargaining was 'forced' upon employers, and that as a method of trade unionism collective bargaining overlooked the role of employers and their associations. A second criticism is that the Webbs assumed that collective bargaining was merely the collective equivalent of individual bargaining, and to that extent they were not comparing 'like with like'. According to Flanders, the individual bargain 'provides for an exchange of work for wages and . . . adjusts for the time being conflicts of interest between a buyer and seller of labour' (p. 216). A collective agreement, on the other hand, does not commit anyone to buy or sell labour: 'It is meant to ensure that when labour is bought and sold, its price and other transactional terms will accord with the provisions of the agreement' (p. 216). These provisions comprise a 'body of rules' intended to regulate the terms of employment contracts, and, therefore, according to Flanders, collective bargaining is itself essentially a rule-making process which has no equivalent or counterpart in individual bargaining. A third and final criticism made by Flanders is that the Webbs ignored another characteristic feature of collective bargaining, 'namely that it is a "power relationship" between organisations' and that 'negotiation is best described as a diplomatic use of power', and that bargaining power is an important factor in influencing the outcome of the bargaining or negotiating process itself. We deal with bargaining power in more detail later in this chapter, but a basic definition of this important concept would be that **bargaining power is the ability of one party or the other to influence the outcome of negotiations in such a way that the outcome is favourable to the more influential party.**

As far as the rule-making aspect of collective bargaining is concerned, Flanders stresses that the parties negotiate procedural as well as substantive agreements. (For a definition of 'substantive' and 'procedural', see Chapter 1, p. 8.) Procedural agreements regulate the conduct of the parties in settling disputes and grievances as well as other matters concerning redundancies, equal opportunities and disciplinary matters, and 'the fact that the joint making of procedural rules is normally an integral part of collective bargaining means that everything appertaining to the resolution of conflict between the parties . . . must be considered as belonging to its institutions' (p. 222).

Self-Evaluation Activity 6.2

Webbs' view and criticism of Flanders
Response on website

As a review exercise, attempt to summarise the Webbs' view of collective bargaining together with the criticisms of Flanders.

The contribution of Chamberlain and Kuhn

The distinction between collective bargaining as an economic process (the Webbs) and collective bargaining as a political/power-based process (Flanders) does not imply that there are two self-contained types of collective bargaining. Chamberlain (1961), joined later by Kuhn, argued that collective bargaining could be considered from three perspectives which represent three different stages in the development of collective bargaining. These perspectives, or 'theories' are complementary to each other and do not necessarily conflict, reflecting different stages

in the historical development of collective bargaining. They are (1) a means of contracting for the sale of labour, (2) a form of industrial government, and (3) a method of management, and are better known as the marketing theory, the governmental theory and the managerial or decision-making theory. These are now considered in turn:

1. The **marketing theory** is similar to the Webbs' view of collective bargaining and is 'the process which determines under what terms labour will continue to be supplied to a company by its existing employees and by those newly hired as well' (Chamberlain, 1961, p. 121). It therefore views collective bargaining as the means by which labour is bought and sold in the market place, and therefore as an economic and exchange relationship. The theory assumes that industrial relations is, at least initially, a labour market activity which addresses the bargaining inequalities between the strong position of the employer and the weak position of the individual employee in the buying and selling of labour. Chamberlain is more concerned about the contractual aspect whereby the collective agreement is regarded as a formal contract and the collective bargaining process is basically concerned with determining the substantive terms on which people are to be employed.

2. The **governmental theory** holds that collective bargaining is essentially a political process which can be compared with a constitutional or law/rule-making institution (or legislature), determining the relationship between management and union representatives. There is a mutual dependency (involving power-sharing) between the two parties in that trade unions are sharing sovereignty with management and in so doing trade unions attempt to use their power to fulfil their members' aspirations and protect their work-based interests. Flanders (1970a) states that:

   > The principle underlying the governmental view is 'the sharing of industrial sovereignty' which, according to Chamberlain, has two facets. The one is that employers should divide their power with unions so as to produce 'mutually acceptable' laws of industrial self-government; the other that they should engage in a joint defence of their autonomy. (p. 232)

The sharing of power between management and union means that only rules concerning employment which are acceptable and have the consent of employees can be legitimised and enforced. The content of collective bargaining is concerned just as much with procedural issues involving the distribution of power and authority as it is with substantive issues and the distribution of money (Salamon, 1998).

3. The **managerial theory** stems from the governmental theory and 'allows workers, through their union representatives to participate in the determination of the policies which guide and rule their working lives' (Chamberlain and Kuhn, 1965, p. 30). Decisions are reached mutually by the parties on matters vital to their interests, and collective bargaining involves union representatives in decision-making roles and even in management roles; they are 'actually *de facto* managers' (Chamberlain, 1961, p. 95). The managerial view is supported by the principle of mutuality which 'holds that those who are integral to the conduct of an enterprise should have a voice in decisions of concern to them' (ibid., p. 135). It recognises that the ownership of property is not an exclusive entitlement to the exercise of authority in industry and that 'responsibility towards other constituent groups of a business enterprise gives grounds for insisting that managerial authority should be shared with their representatives in the manner collective bargaining can achieve' (Flanders, 1970a, p. 232).

In summarising these three theoretical perspectives, the market perspective sees the trade union acting as a labour alliance or cartel in collective bargaining more or less as the Webbs conceived, while the governmental perspective introduces an autonomous and agreed rule of law into industrial relations, and the managerial perspective emphasises the contribution of the trade union towards making management more democratic or furthering industrial democracy.

As we have stated, these three perspectives are not mutually exclusive categories and in the 'real world' the collective bargaining process contains elements of all three but in different proportions to reflect the diversity and uniqueness of different bargaining situations. We also argued earlier that the three perspectives could be seen as stages in the development of the collective bargaining process and of the bargaining relationship between employer and trade union. The developmental aspect is well illustrated by Flanders (1970a):

> They [the perspectives] reflect different stages in the historical development of collective bargaining. Early negotiations were mainly a matter of fixing terms for the sale of labour; the agreements might consist of no more than standard piecework price lists [the marketing perspective]. Later came the need for procedures for settling disputes on these and other issues between the parties, which sometimes took the form of setting up joint bodies possibly with an independent chairman; this provided a foundation for the governmental theory. Only when eventually agreements were made on subjects that entered into the internal decision-taking process of a business enterprise was there a basis for the managerial theory of collective bargaining. (p. 231)

Furthermore, each perspective emphasises a different guiding principle and each influences the actions taken by the parties (Farnham, 1998, p. 294). Farnham provides the example of data required for the purpose of collective bargaining (for example, financial data, sales figures, productivity figures and so on). Under the marketing perspective data may be withheld or facts may be distorted – but these actions will be considered legitimate tactics in negotiations. Under the governmental theory it may be problematic to decide whether specific data should be accessible to both parties or only to one. Under the managerial perspective all relevant data is essential in order to make informed, joint decisions (ibid., pp. 294–5).

Self-Evaluation Activity 6.3

Which perspective is most useful?

Response on website

Which of the three theories/perspectives would you, as either a trade union negotiator or a management negotiator, prefer to use in a 'real life' bargaining situation?

Co-operative and conjunctive bargaining relationships

Chamberlain and Kuhn (1965) argue that the collective bargaining relationship is governed by the implicit requirement that some agreement must be reached between the parties. They go on to assert:

> However prolonged the strike to settle disputes over divergent interests, some agreement must ultimately be forthcoming if collective bargaining continues. Thus neither party is independent under collective bargaining. Neither can perform its function without the other. Only by ridding itself of collective bargaining, which allows workers to participate in negotiations and to resist managerial demands, can a company be said to gain an independence of operation. When collective bargaining is accepted, however, the great change which takes place is the creation of two organisations, in one sense independent of each other, but in another sense mutually dependent. For each, the achievement of its own function is dependent upon a working relationship with the other. Where collective bargaining is the prescribed system of industrial relations, neither company alone nor union alone has any functional significance; rather they acquire significance only in relation to each other. This fact of mutual dependence cannot be overstressed, for it is perhaps the most fundamental aspect of modern industrial society. (pp. 424–5)

This highly significant quote emphasises that the collective bargaining relationship is founded upon mutual dependence, that the degree to which the parties depend upon each other will vary according to a number of factors, such as density of unionisation, supply and demand for labour and other labour market considerations, and the extent to which management emphasises employee commitment and involvement within the organisation. The collective bargaining relationship acknowledges the fact of mutual dependence and recognises the extent to which conflicting interests can be reconciled. To this end Chamberlain and Kuhn have devised two basic models of the collective bargaining relationship which they call conjunctive bargaining and co-operative bargaining.

Conjunctive bargaining

This type of bargaining relationship takes place in situations where union and management come to agreement through sheer functional necessity. 'It arises from the absolute requirement that some agreement – any agreement – be reached so that the operations on which both [parties] are dependent may continue' (Chamberlain and Kuhn, 1965, p. 425). The following characteristics of conjunctive bargaining are relevant:

- Conjunctive bargaining is a working relationship between the parties where each party agrees to provide certain services, accept certain responsibilities and recognise certain authority relationships. Without such agreement there would be no collective bargaining. 'Such bargaining may, therefore, be thought of as the minimum basis for organisation of the company and union into a going concern' (ibid., p. 425).
- Coercion is the main component of conjunctive bargaining power, and the resolution of different interests through conjunctive bargaining 'provides a basis for operation of the enterprise – and nothing more' (ibid., p. 426).

Conjunctive bargaining, therefore, provides no incentives to the parties to do more than carry out the minimum terms of the agreement which has temporarily resolved their divergent and conflicting interests. Mutual obligations and any advantages accrued from business performance are fixed. 'Conjunctive bargaining allows the minimum required co-operation of each with the other, which tends to become the maximum actual co-operation as well' (ibid., p. 426). Chamberlain and Kuhn also argue that conjunctive bargaining limits the ability of each party to achieve its objectives. But if a better relationship between the parties can be established whereby each recognises that the other shares, or can share, more than the minimum of obligations, then business performance and the quality of industrial relations can be improved.

Co-operative bargaining

The rationale for achieving a bargaining relationship that extends beyond conjunctive bargaining is persuasively argued:

> Neither a union nor a management feels free to establish a more fruitful bargaining relationship

unless it believes that it will gain something from the added benefits which the improved business performance will make possible. This amounts to saying that neither will gain additional advantages unless the other gains too. Neither party will expect the other to give up something for nothing. Realistically, we may expect that the effort of one party to better the other will never be abandoned, but this does not rule out the possibility that intelligent union and management officials will observe that the mutual relationship can be improved, to the advantage of each, by holding out the promise of benefit to the other party too. This appears to be a prima-facie case for co-operation based on personal benefit rather than altruism. (ibid., p. 428)

The basis for co-operative bargaining acknowledges the fact of mutual dependency and that each party can achieve its objectives more effectively if it wins the support of the other. This means that when one party is seeking improvements (be it to pay, conditions or any other issue), it can do so if it anticipates what objections may be raised by the other party 'on whose co-operation in the matter the degree of its own success depends' (ibid., p. 429). In order to win the necessary co-operation, one party (usually the one that starts the process) may have to make concessions, perhaps over and above the minimum that it considers fair or just. Concessions are, therefore, made because the subsequent joint bargaining effort produces a greater advantage to the initiating party than would have been possible without them. For example, if management, as the initiator, seeks greater flexibility from its workforce, it may have to make greater concessions than would be considered 'fair' (for example, by reducing the overall weekly working hours) in order to secure the co-operation of the union representatives, and this would ultimately secure a better agreement than would have been possible under conjunctive bargaining. Seeking and making concessions does not mean that the parties are pursuing a common interest, but that their different and diverging interests are better achieved if each party is prepared to permit the other to move towards its objective.

Chamberlain and Kuhn point out that reaching and maintaining co-operative agreements is no easy task and that there are certain dangers to both

parties in pursuing the transition from conjunctive to co-operative bargaining. These include the following:

- For managers there may be a perceived decline in their 'right to manage' or managerial prerogatives. For union representatives there may be a loss of function, possibly making their role unnecessary, and for employees, there is a fear of the possibility of increased job insecurity as a result of efficiency and productivity improvements in turn resulting in job reduction.
- If unions have a say in business decisions, it is argued, this would dilute the powers of owners of businesses and thereby reduce the power of managements to make decisions on the owners' behalf. Co-operation thus poses a threat to the authority structure within the enterprise.
- 'By refusing co-operation for fear that it will widen the union's area of participation in business decisions, management may be gaining no greater long-run protection from the dilution of its authority, and at the same time may be losing the fruits of co-operation' (ibid., p. 434).
- If co-operative bargaining is considered successful (by creating a spirit of common interest between worker and company in important areas) trade union members may be 'robbed' of their union's militancy in pursuing pay demands.
- Employees may fear that a union which accepts co-operative bargaining may become little more than an adjunct of management, stressing efficiency to the detriment of employee welfare.

Despite these perceived dangers, the benefits of co-operative bargaining probably outweigh its disadvantages, and in any event, the two models are not meant to be mutually exclusive but complementary.

The contribution of Walton and McKersie

Walton and McKersie (1965) make a similar distinction to that of Chamberlain and Kuhn, but use different terms. They identify two types of bargaining relationship: distributive bargaining, which is similar to conjunctive bargaining, and integrative bargaining, which is comparable to co-operative bargaining.

Distributive bargaining entails conflict whereby one party seeks to achieve gains and advantages at the expense of the other. The term for one party seeking a bargaining advantage which entails an equivalent loss for the other party is a fixed or zero-sum game. If we assume that the size of the bargaining 'cake' is constant, then if one party's share of it increases the other party's share decreases in exact proportion. This process involves a great deal of threats, bluffs and counter-tactics, with bargaining power being a strong determinant of the outcomes pursued and achieved. In a wage negotiation, for example, what the management party wins, the union party loses; and what management concedes, the union side gains. Both sides neither gain nor lose at the same time as the bargaining relationship is not based upon reciprocity.

Integrative bargaining seeks to ensure mutual gains in areas where the parties have common interests; it is a joint problem-solving process, which results in a 'win-win' situation (as contrasted with the 'win-lose' situation under distributive bargaining). By analogy with the collective bargaining 'cake',the size of the cake is not fixed and mutual gains will be influenced by factors such as the willingness of the parties to share information and the level of trust between them. It is, in other words, a varying sum game. For example, in a situation where management and union agree that productivity gains and cost savings should be made, perhaps through the introduction of more efficient and flexible working practices, the gains in cost savings would be shared amongst both management and workforce. This means that higher profits for the company would be reflected in higher wages for the workforce and (perhaps) lower prices for the customer. Integrative bargaining is concerned with the whole range of bargaining issues; it covers both monetary and managerial issues and would include ensuring job security while improving efficiency and joint decision-making about investment, relocation and downsizing. The prerequisites for successful integrative bargaining include:

- the extent to which the parties are motivated to share in decision-making;
- the possession of adequate skills to communicate and evaluate relevant information;
- adequate access to all relevant information by the parties; and
- a mutually supportive and trusting relationship between the parties.

The observation made by Chamberlain and Kuhn (1965) that in the United States it is conjunctive bargaining which traditionally dominates can also be applied to distributive bargaining, not only in the United States but also in the British contexts. But as with conjunctive and co-operative bargaining, distributive and integrative bargaining do not necessarily exclude each other and many bargaining contexts display elements of both models.

Self-Evaluation Activity 6.4

Frod Motors

Response on website

Exhibit 6.1 is an abbreviated record taken from the minutes of the Joint Negotiating Committee Meeting of 18 September 2003 within Frod Motors Ltd. Attempt the questions that follow.

1. What issues identified above fall into the market, governmental and managerial models of collective bargaining?
2. Comment on the nature of the collective bargaining relationship at Frod Motors.

Exhibit 6.1

Frod Motors Ltd

Pay and conditions

As confirmed by recent meetings of the joint union pay negotiation group and corporate human resources and industrial relations management:

1. Pay increases over the next two years to be one percentage point above the going rate of inflation
2. Team bonus payments to be introduced in January 2004
3. Following the introduction of continuous shift working, all remaining shift premium rates to be abolished.

Management could not agree to any reductions in the working week hours until the new shifts had been consolidated. The union joint negotiating committee and the joint shop stewards' committee reserved the right to bring the matter up at a later date.

Proposed procedural agreements

The JSSC representing the South Wales plants were registering concern about the health and safety aspects of teamworking and submitted draft agreements to cover areas such as training for zero defects and monitoring of health and safety in the workplace. The union side also submitted draft procedures concerning re-grading problems subsequent to the consolidation of the original seven grades into three.

The management side agreed to consider the union documentation and an early response before the next meeting in December was promised. Management conceded that the 'rounding up' and 'rounding down' formulas needed revising in the light of re-grading grievances and would be acting promptly to deal with the situation.

Total Quality Initiative

Management has circulated a consultative paper *Towards High Commitment and High Performance* (HCHP) stating that TQI has been in operation for some ten years and now needed revising. The union raised some concern that management suggestions for improving flexibility agreements to make workers more productive would be at the expense of sacrificing certain skills which were proved to increase productivity. Management responded by reminding the union side that exports were static and all could not be blamed on the 'strong pound', which was now considerably weaker than two years ago. Management would welcome proposals from the union team to make 'HCHP' more efficient.

Redundancies

This is a highly contentious issue. The proposed shedding of some 550 employees company-wide was not met with enthusiasm by the union team despite assurances by management that this would not affect the lifelong employment guarantee as all the redundancies would be voluntary. The union team requested a detailed breakdown of the proposals before responding formally.

Communication

There was some discussion about the best way of disseminating information about the content of discussions at joint consultative and negotiating committee meetings. Management proposed that jointly agreed content could be inserted in the 'house' bulletin distributed weekly and the more serious issues could be communicated in short workplace meetings provided stewards and supervisors were thoroughly briefed. The union team accepted this proposal.

Smoking policy

Management put forward proposals for a policy on smoking. The main issue was whether the company should be a 'non-smoking' organisation and, recognising the sensitive issues concerning individual rights, it was felt that health issues were more important than issues concerning the freedom of the individual. The union representatives agreed this was a good idea but said there would be opposition from the membership. It was therefore agreed that a questionnaire be distributed to all employees without exception and that the matter would be discussed further when the results were analysed.

Summary points

- Collective bargaining is a process of joint determination of substantive and procedural matters, the outcome of which is the collective agreement.
- Collective bargaining is the dominant method of joint decision-making. Other types of decision-making relevant to the employment relationship include:
    - unilateral employer regulation;
    - individual bargaining;
    - joint consultation; and
    - unilateral employee regulation.
- There has been a marked decline in the numbers and proportion of employees covered by collective bargaining arrangements since 1979.
- Theoretical contributions towards our knowledge and understanding of collective bargaining include those of the Webbs (1902), Flanders (1968), Chamberlain and Kuhn (1965) and Walton and McKersie (1965).
- Chamberlain and Kuhn distinguish between conjunctive bargaining (minimalist) and co-operative bargaining, the scope of which extends, by agreement of the parties, far beyond that of conjunctive bargaining.
- Walton and McKersie identify distributive bargaining and integrative bargaining which are similar to conjunctive and co-operative bargaining respectively.

BARGAINING POWER

Bargaining power is central to the bargaining relationship in determining the outcome of the collective bargaining process and 'the final outcome of a collective bargaining situation is determined in some way by the relative bargaining power of the parties involved' (Levinson, 1966, p. 92). To put it simply:

> Workers join unions in order to overcome their weakness as individuals in the employment relationship. A group of workers organised in a trade union meets the employer on a more equal footing than the individual, and confronts the employer with collective power. When union and employer engage in collective bargaining their relationship involves the threat or deployment of power and the outcomes of bargaining reflect the balance of power. Workers' power, however, is fragile and is particularly susceptible to the corrosive effects of high unemployment. (Kelly, 1998, p. 9)

For a more detailed overview of power relationships, see Chapters 1, 2 and 10. Here, we confine ourselves to a relatively basic approach to defining bargaining power, which is to consider it in terms of the costs to each party of agreement relative to the costs to each of them of disagreement. This may be expressed in the following way:

The bargaining power of A =

$$\frac{\text{the costs to B of disagreement with A's terms}}{\text{the costs to B of agreement with A's terms}}$$

The bargaining power of B =

$$\frac{\text{the costs to A of disagreement with B's terms}}{\text{the costs to A of agreement with B's terms}}$$

In other words, the greater the costs to the employer of disagreeing (for example, in sustaining a strike) as opposed to the costs of agreeing (conceding the union claim), the greater will be the bargaining power of the union. Conversely, the greater the costs to the union of disagreeing (calling a strike) as opposed to the costs of agreeing (accepting management's offer), the greater will be the bargaining power of the employer. Before and during the bargaining process, demands are formulated and concessions made on the basis of each party's estimates of its own and of its opponent's power functions. The intention is either progressively to reduce the costs of agreement by making concessions (possibly during or after a strike) or gradually to increase the costs of disagreement to the point where the bargaining power of each party is equalised, thereby enabling an agreement to be reached.

Bargaining power is not a static property. In general terms bargaining power is, according to Dunlop (1993), determined by the bargaining preferences and priorities of both parties, labour and product market conditions, the quality of negotiating skills of each party and the ability to coerce the other party.

Self-Evaluation Activity 6.5

Factors influencing bargaining power

The response is given below

Apart from the factors identified above there are other factors, both internal to the workplace and external to it, that influence the bargaining power of each party. Try to identify as many of these factors as you can.

Examples of factors internal to the workplace include:

- *Density of unionisation*: although there is no inevitable correlation between union density and bargaining power, it is often assumed that the higher the density of unionisation the greater the degree of union bargaining power.
- The *number of unions* representing workers in a workplace (that is, multi-unionism) could dilute bargaining power as it may disaggregate the workforce and result in competing factions or inter-union rivalry for membership.
- *Skill levels and technology* may influence union bargaining power if groups of skilled workers control crucial areas of the work process (such as electricians within generating stations).
- Successful *attempts to marginalise* trade unions and collective bargaining itself would tend to increase management's bargaining power.

Examples of factors outside the workplace include:

- *Government economic policies*, such as the Conservatives' market-oriented policies, have influenced the bargaining power of both parties. For example, wage deregulation within former wages council industries has tended to increase management bargaining power where unions exist.
- *Industrial relations and employment legislation* has tended to increase the bargaining power of management by, for example, legislating to make it more difficult to take industrial action.
- *Local labour market factors* governing, amongst other things, the supply of and demand for labour will affect union bargaining power positively if labour is scarce and demand for such labour is high; and union bargaining power negatively if labour supply is plentiful and demand is relatively low.

The bargaining model described by Levinson (1966) can be used to illustrate both union and management bargaining power. It can provide help

and direction for both union and management negotiating teams. In the example which follows (adapted from Farnham, 1998), the management response to the union's pay claim are considered. The following factors are important:

- the union is claiming a 4 per cent pay increase;
- the union is claiming a 2.5 hour reduction in the working week to 35 hours;
- the 'going rate' for wage increases locally is 2 per cent;
- unemployment locally is low and is now slowly increasing; and
- the union has balloted its members concerning a 'work-to-rule' should the pay claim not be met.

The disadvantages to management of disagreeing and agreeing with the union's claims are illustrated in Figure 6.1.

In examples such as this one, Farnham (1998) states:

> *Agreement by management with the union's bargaining proposal is likely to incur more weighting (or costs) to management than disagreement. This indicates that bargaining power rests with management for this proposal. In this case, however, the balance of bargaining power is relatively marginal* [21 as against 18]. (p. 302)

The Levinson model (1966) in common with most models of power relationships has its drawbacks and advantages. One of the most obvious drawbacks is the problem of measuring 'bargaining power'. Because there are so many subjective elements involved, including attitudes and perceptions of the parties, and because collective bargaining is a process rather than a discrete event, power becomes difficult to quantify accurately. An important advantage of the model is that within the bargaining context bargaining positions can be analysed as can the determinants of bargaining power at different stages of the bargaining process.

THE DEVELOPMENT OF COLLECTIVE BARGAINING

The course of collective bargaining in Britain has been anything but smooth, and in order to understand the present structure of collective bargaining it is necessary to consider its historical development.

Disadvantages to management of agreeing with the union's claim			
Element	*Cost*	*Likelihood*	*Total*
Increased unit costs of production	10	1.0	10.0
Settlement higher than 'going rate'	7	1.0	7.0
Could set a precedent	8	0.5	4.0
			21.0

Disadvantages to management of disagreeing with the union's claim			
Element	*Cost*	*Likelihood*	*Total*
Work-to-rule	8	1.0	8.0
Lost orders	8	0.9	7.2
Some workers might leave firm	7	0.4	2.8
			18.0

Figure 6.1 The use of bargaining power by management
Source: Farnham, 1998, p. 302

A little history

Over the past 200 years, collective bargaining, according to Coates and Topham (1988), went through five stages of evolution:

- The first stage represented the evolution of basic workplace bargaining reinforced by the method of mutual insurance.
- The second stage saw the development of district or local agreements in particular industries, mostly prior to 1914.
- The third stage concerned the development of national, industry-wide bargaining and agreements after 1914, which established the 'common rule' on wages and hours whereby the agreement applied to the whole industry.
- The fourth stage saw national agreements, particularly in the private sector, being supplemented by widespread plant or 'domestic' bargaining undertaken by local managers and shop stewards during the 1960s and 1970s.
- Finally, we have the development of more formalised types of company-level bargaining during the 1980s and 1990s.

As we saw in Chapter 3, trade unions were often too weak to enforce their rights to negotiate. Before the First World War, most workers either were not unionised or were conducting their negotiations with individual employers or groups of employers at local level only, and this led to a wide variety of pay rates throughout the country in each industry. However, up to the outbreak of the First World War there were increased pressures exerted by many trade unions for national-level industry-wide bargaining. The war itself provided an impetus to the development of industry-wide bargaining, and with increased government intervention in industrial relations and in those industries important to the war effort, such as mining and railways, national bargaining became a permanent feature of British collective bargaining. One of the most important examples of government intervention during this period was the establishment of a wide-ranging inquiry dealing with 'the relations between employers and employed' under the chairmanship of J.H. Whitley. The findings of the Whitley Committee were contained in the Whitley Reports, and were to have an enduring impact upon collective bargaining and British industrial relations generally. The Whitley Reports (1916–17) recommended the following:

1. Joint Industrial Councils (JICs) should be established. The Councils, comprising employer and

trade union representatives, were empowered to make industry-wide agreements in particular industries.

2. District committees, below the level of JICs, were to be set up.

3. Works committees were to be established for consultative purposes in particular companies and plants.

4. The Trades Boards system of statutory wage regulation in industries where collective organisation was inadequate to sustain collective bargaining was to be extended. These became known as Whitley Councils and were the forerunners of the wages councils (abolished in 1993) which set minimum wage rates for low-paid workers in particular industries and services.

5. There was to be recourse to government-appointed courts of inquiry to facilitate settlement of major industrial disputes.

At the end of the war the Whitley recommendations were implemented, and 73 JICs were established between 1918 and 1921 which covered both private and public sector industries. The Whitley proposals did not make much difference to the major industries, such as engineering, textiles and coal mining, as these were industries where collective bargaining had already become established. However, the proposals were significant for the public sector, both within central and local government, where Whitley Councils were established to help encourage collective bargaining amongst manual and non-manual staff.

The period from the early 1920s until the mid-1930s was one of recession and decline in trade union membership as unemployment rose and unions suffered the consequences of defeat in a number of major industrial disputes (the 1926 General Strike being the most prominent). JICs in a number of industries collapsed as employers withdrew their support and in one or two industries, such as coal mining, industry-wide national negotiations reverted to district level as employers refused to bargain nationally. There was, then, some reversal of the trend towards national bargaining during this period, but it did prove resilient and survived well into the post-Second World War period. Coates and Topham (1988) argue that while the advance towards a coherent system of national industry-wide bargaining was not uniform, with a number of setbacks as well as advances:

> [y]et, the creation by mergers of the two large general unions in the 1920s added weight to the pressure on employers to concede the principle of national machinery; the TGWU and GMWU became the most active propagandists for Joint Industrial Council machinery in the trade union world. The changing character of industrial organisation assisted the growth of national agreements – the appearance of large combines in such industries as chemicals, flour milling, and cement was one sign of a general shift away from small family business towards large-scale enterprise, managed along professional lines. Trade union professionalism, concentrated at national level, became the counterpart, the two sides converging on national agreements. (p. 177)

The 'formalisation of collective bargaining at national levels implied, at least for many employers, that no significant negotiation should occur at the level of the company, plant, or workshop' (Gospel and Palmer, 1993, p. 202). However, because national agreements were only 'framework' ones which established the very basic rates of pay and conditions, it was inevitable that there would be forms of workplace-based collective bargaining which would augment the industry agreement. The main inspiration for the development of early workplace bargaining was the shop stewards' movement of the early decades of the twentieth century, described in Chapter 3. Shop steward workplace bargaining became common in the munitions industries during the First World War, but because the Whitley Committee wanted to encourage national bargaining structures development of this type of bargaining was erratic, and in any event declined drastically during the inter-war recession.

The Second World War stimulated government intervention which in turn revived national bargaining, and wartime conditions also proved favourable to the development of workplace bargaining. As far as national bargaining was concerned, 56 new JICs were created during the period 1939–45 and the wages council system of national negotiating machinery was extended 'in the belief that this would protect the industry-level bargaining system if there were a post-war recession similar to that following the First World War' (ibid., p. 204). At the end of the war, the Nationalisation Acts establishing the nationalised industries contained clauses compelling the newly-created authorities to set up negotiating machinery with the appropriate trade unions. By 1946, some 15.5 million workers in industrial and service occupations were covered by collective machinery, or by statutory wages councils, and since the war around 70 per cent of the working population have had their wages and working conditions regulated by these means. Much of this growth can be attributed to the growth of education, health and social services where collective bargaining for white-collar professional employees expanded, this being reflected in the substantial increase in white-collar trade union membership (see Chapter 3).

National bargaining during the post-Second World War period was the dominant form of collective bargaining until the late 1960s, but it should be emphasised that shop-floor, workplace bargaining (also called 'domestic' bargaining, a general term often preferred by academics and practitioners as it covers a whole variety of different bargaining contexts where shop stewards are the principal negotiators) was once again on the increase during the 1950s and 1960s to the point where it became the main source of anxiety about 'disorder' in British industrial relations.

Domestic (workplace) bargaining comes of age

From the mid-1950s onwards, then, there was a reassertion of workplace bargaining activity which gained further momentum during the 1960s. The increase in shop steward activity associated with domestic bargaining progressively undermined the legitimacy of national collective agreements, and the reasons for this are identified below.

The first reason concerns the relative weakness of industry-wide national bargaining under postwar conditions of full employment which were placing national agreements under some strain. British national agreements traditionally cover a much narrower range of bargaining issues than their European counterparts, and this has meant that local collect-ive bargaining 'developed a more substantial and independent role, filling larger gaps left by the national settlements' (Blyton and Turnbull, 1998, p. 198). The relative weakness of national industry agreements therefore provided shop stewards with considerable leeway to bargain at local level, and this 'left individual employers faced with the need to establish rules and agreements in those areas insufficiently covered by the industry agreement' (ibid., p. 198).

The second reason concerns local labour market conditions. Labour scarcity, and shortages of skilled labour in particular, together with improved workplace union organisation 'provided a power base and a means for unions and work groups to mobilise that power base to force wage concessions' (ibid., p. 183). This has resulted in the phenomenon known as wage drift. Wage drift represents the gap between take-home earnings and the nationally negotiated pay rates which had gradually increased from the inter-war period until the 1960s, mainly because of the spread of piecework and bonus schemes, overtime and other local additions to national rates which contributed an increasing proportion of actual earnings. Gospel and Palmer (1993) consider piecework, overtime and factory additions in greater detail:

- **Piecework earnings** 'were seen as evidence that piecework schemes, originally introduced as a means for motivating workers and giving employers tighter control over effort, had degenerated and were being used by workgroups and shop stewards to increase earnings by presenting claims based on comparability and precedent at every job change. Constant domestic negotiations over piecework prices and times served, in the context of tight labour markets and soft product markets, to weaken managerial control over labour costs' (ibid., p. 209).
- **Overtime** was problematic because the increasingly high levels of overtime worked reflected not so much the need on the part of the employer to have his employees work longer hours, but rather the perceived need on the part of workgroups to increase their earnings to such an extent that 'the control and distribution of overtime opportunities formed a significant part of the shop steward's bargaining role' (ibid., p. 209).

- **Factory additions** 'to nationally agreed rates, in the form of supplements, productivity payments and conditions allowances, mushroomed and most employers' associations turned a blind eye to the problem' (ibid., p. 209).

Allan Flanders (1970b) contended that domestic workplace bargaining during the 1960s was 'informal, largely fragmented and autonomous' (p. 169). Informality essentially means that in many instances workplace agreements were unwritten and unsigned. Fragmentation 'means simply that [bargaining] is conducted in such a way that different groups in the works get different concessions at different times. Within the plant, however, in the absence of any common and comprehensive system of negotiation, an inadequately ordered pay structure encourages separate work groups to press their own advantage and exploit its anomalies and inequities' (ibid., p. 169). Much domestic bargaining was autonomous in that neither trade unions nor employers' associations had any real control over or knowledge of it. Flanders goes on to argue:

Because of the traditional reliance on national industry-wide agreements to settle the main terms of employment and to provide disputes procedures, domestic bargaining had developed, not as a deliberate policy, but haphazardly and as a result of the pressures of the moment. It has been forced upon employers and unions, at first largely against their will, by the logic of the prevailing industrial situation. Hence its autonomous growth and their reluctance to formalise it and integrate it into the industrial relations system. . . . This mixture of realism and pretence, of being forced to yield to bargaining power on the shop floor while denying it any legitimacy is the most fundamental cause of the weakening of managerial control and the growing anarchy in workplace relations. The paradox, whose truth managements have found it so difficult to accept, is that they can only regain control by sharing it. . . . To bring together what has already been said about this growing anarchy in workplace relations, they are to be seen: in unofficial strikes and earnings drift; in under-utilisation of labour and resistance to change; in the growth of systematic overtime and the demoralisation of incentive pay schemes; in inequitable and unstable factory pay structures; in a general decline in industrial discipline; in an undermining of external regulation by industry-wide and other agreements; and in a weakening of control by trade unions and employers' associations over their members. (pp. 169, 170, 196; emphasis added)

Finally, Flanders argues that the 'informal system' of domestic bargaining, being fragmented, uncodified, dependent on work-group custom and practice and 'generally incapable of serving as the necessary replacement to the formal structure of industry-wide agreements' (p. 241) leads to 'disorder' in the informal system and in British industrial relations generally. The restoration of 'order' was the principal motive behind the setting up of the Donovan Commission which reported in 1968.

The Donovan Commission and its aftermath

As we saw in Chapter 1, the Donovan Commission was set up to examine the consequences of the 'formal' industry-wide and the 'informal' domestic systems of British industrial relations manifested in the two types of collective bargaining levels that we have already considered, and to make recommendations concerning the 'disorder' and 'anarchy' that the informal system apparently generated. The Commission found widespread evidence that ad hoc workplace bargaining had indeed created an 'informal' system of industrial relations alongside the 'formal', industry-wide and JIC method of determining pay and conditions. The principal recommendation of the Commission was that all the informal, fragmented and autonomous ad hoc activities which characterised workplace, domestic bargaining and the activities of shop stewards should be formalised in plant or company-level agreements covering procedures and standards for these bargains, to bring the informal arrangements into line with formal arrangements at higher levels. Other specific observations and recommendations made by the Donovan Commission (1968) included:

- that top managements should take the initiative to reform collective bargaining within their own organisations;
- that such company-based reform should include:
  - developing authoritative and formal collective bargaining machinery;

- formulating comprehensive procedural agreements concerning discipline, grievance and disputes; and
- determination of measures to promote health and safety.
- the negotiation of productivity agreements concerning pay and output with the aim of lowering unit production costs, stabilising prices, increasing pay and improving profitability;
- the passing of an Industrial Relations Act which would, amongst other things, require larger companies, the nationalised industries and the public services to register procedural agreements with the Department of Employment and Productivity; and
- the establishment of a Commission for Industrial Relations (CIR) which would consider procedural and other cases stemming from the registration of agreements, analysing and making recommendations concerning company-specific industrial relations problems.

The emphasis of the majority of recommendations was upon voluntary rather than statutory procedural reform, with legislation to be used as a method of last resort. Allan Flanders's assertion (1968) that management 'should regain control by sharing it' was shared by certain members of the Donovan Commission, as it rather optimistically assumed that management were prepared to do so and, additionally, prepared to change their attitude towards shop stewards and trade unions in general so as to incorporate them in joint regulation and decision-making as part of a move towards co-operative bargaining. Unfortunately, the experience of the 1980s and 1990s belies the Commission's optimistic expectations as managements did not seek to share control, but to reassert their prerogatives.

Growth of formal workplace and company-wide bargaining

The formalisation of company and workplace bargaining as recommended by Donovan gradually spread throughout industry during the 1970s, encouraged by the CIR and by successive Labour and Conservative governments (see Chapter 4). By the late 1970s, 68 per cent of manual employees in 53 per cent of establishments had their pay determined by formalised company bargaining at various levels within the organisation. And, as we have seen in Chapter 2, shop steward organisation also developed to match the formalisation of company bargaining. The growth of formalisation was seen to favour employers rather than trade unions. Employers, in the face of increasing inflationary and competitive pressures and internationalisation of markets, saw formalisation as a means to achieve the workplace changes they preferred in order to cut costs and increase productivity, and to rationalise payment systems and structures by replacing piecework systems with measured day-work schemes (payment by time and not by individual output in order to achieve the requisite production targets usually determined by job evaluation).

Despite arguments supporting the view that formalisation generally favoured management and employers, trade unions and their shop stewards 'for the most part did not resist moves in this direction' (Gospel and Palmer, 1993, p. 212). To be sure, many shop stewards and shop-floor groups wanted to retain their informal control over working practices ('custom and practice', restrictive practices, and so on), but as Gospel and Palmer go on to argue:

> [Shop] stewards sought more bureaucratic arrangements as a means to greater effectiveness. The traditional fragmentation of workplace bargaining had disadvantages for employees and the move to more structured steward organisation was thought to be essential if stewards were to retain or increase their influence in the face of more sophisticated managerial policies or were to affect decisions made [in the higher echelons] of company management. Thus, plant-wide and sometimes company-wide joint shop stewards committees were established to co-ordinate strategy and to engage in the new collective bargaining arrangements. (p. 213)

It is important to note that formal domestic bargaining during the 1970s usually occurred at individual plant or establishment level rather than covering all the plants within a uniform company-wide agreement. Uniform multi-plant agreements were confined largely to companies which had broken away from employers' associations within the industry-wide bargaining machinery, and to inwardly-investing foreign companies. Gospel and

Palmer also point out that 'the aim of many large firms through the 1970s and 1980s was to relocate and formalise collective bargaining. This meant somewhere **below** the level of the industry, but **above** the level of the shop floor. The intention was to internalise industrial relations and reduce the number of bargaining units thereby tailoring agreements to the firm's needs and strengthening management's position' (ibid., p. 213; emphasis added).

By the end of the 1970s the two-tier structure of collective bargaining, commented upon so extensively by Donovan, was still in evidence, but had evolved into a system comprising industry-wide agreements still common in industries with a large number of smaller firms, and formal company bargaining structures which contrasted substantially with the informal system of the previous decade. Collective bargaining structures remained complex with varied patterns of union-management interaction. The complexity and variety of collective bargaining can be identified on a number of dimensions:

1. **Levels of bargaining**, as we have seen, range from national or industry level down to regional and district level and to organisational or company level, including single or multiple plants, factories and workplaces. The terms that we have used so far to denote the different bargaining levels (industry-wide/national bargaining; organisational/company bargaining; and domestic/workplace/shop-floor/plant bargaining) were the conventional terms used to describe bargaining levels during the 1960s and 1970s and are still in current usage. More recently, other terms have become popular and help to clarify the increased complexity of bargaining levels in Britain. These are:
   - **Multi-employer bargaining:** this is equivalent to industry-wide/national bargaining.
   - **Single-employer bargaining:** this is equivalent to organisational or company bargaining where all terms and conditions are negotiated at employer level in either single-site or multisite organisations.
   - **Enterprise bargaining:** this is equivalent to plant, factory, shop-floor or workplace bargaining.
   - **Two-tier bargaining:** this is where some components of the collective agreement are deter-

mined at one level, and others are decided at a lower level. For example, multi-employer agreements determine minimum pay rates nationally, while company agreements determine actual earnings including bonuses and overtime payments. Another example is where, within the single-employer bargaining context, basic conditions are settled at the centre while pay is determined at plant or workplace level.

2. **Bargaining unit coverage** means that in any given organisation or industry the groups of employees covered by a particular collective agreement (or bargaining unit) will vary. In one organisation, for example, all white-collar workers may be covered by the same collective agreement, while in another organisation, different categories of white-collar workers will have their own separate agreements.

3. **Bargaining form** includes those collective agreements which range from entirely formal and highly comprehensive agreements to fully informal and fairly parochial agreements.

4. **Bargaining scope** refers to the extent of bargaining issues ranging from extremely limited, as in conjunctive bargaining, to fairly extensive, as in co-operative bargaining.

5. **Bargaining depth** refers to the degree of influence that union or employee representatives have on the outcome.

Self-Evaluation Activity 6.6
Bargaining structures
Response on website

For each of the examples in Mini cases 6.1, 6.2 and 6.3, identify the level of bargaining, the nature of the bargaining unit, the scope and, where possible, the form of bargaining undertaken.

Mini cases 6.1–6.3
Case 6.1 A multinational corporation

BritChem is a British-owned multinational chemical company with five major plants in Britain. The company used to be part of an employers' federation which negotiated national agreements, but withdrew from these arrangements some 30 years ago. The company employs 15 000 people comprising 800 managers, 4500 salaried staff and 9700 skilled manual workers. All staff, including managerial grades, are unionised, there are three separate negotiating committees for these three categories of employee and there are separate agreements for each category. At organisational level, basic rates of pay, procedural and policy agreements concerning disputes and collective grievances are jointly determined centrally, while locally these agreements concerning the above and other issues may be supplemented in separate negotiation with each of the unions representing each of the three categories of employee.

Case 6.2 A small engineering company

BritEng is a small, well-established engineering company which has always been a member of the Engineering Employers' Federation (EEF). There are some 260 employees comprising 25 managers, 35 non-manual workers and 203 skilled manual workers. The managers and non-manual workers do not belong to a trade union, but 96 per cent of the manual workers belong to the AEEU. Negotiations on pay and conditions are conducted at industry level by the EEF on behalf of the employer. There is some enterprise bargaining, but it is very limited and will not include any other issue apart from pay and very few local conditions.

Case 6.3 Building Cleaning Services

Building Cleaning Services (BCS) is a private contractor providing cleaning services for local authorities and hospitals. It employs around 400 cleaning staff in 'Locality A' and has observed the Transfer of Undertakings (Protection of Employment) Regulations of 1981 (TUPE). BCS is a large national contractor and was awarded the 'Locality A' contract in 1991 through the Compulsory Competitive Tendering (CCT) process. Under TUPE, BCS must retain the existing workforce from the start of the contract period, on existing pay and conditions. All existing arrangements concerning trade union recognition and collective agreements and bargaining arrangements including disciplinary and grievance procedures are transferred to the new employer. The new employer and trade unions can set new terms and conditions if both parties agree but these cannot affect continuity of employment for all transferred staff. TUPE applies to transferred staff and not to new starters. The TUPE Regulations do not

alter the fact that at the time under existing UK law, employers may terminate collective agreements and derecognise trade unions.

BCS, however, did not derecognise trade unions or end collective bargaining. There was, however, some considerable staff turnover for various reasons, and of the original 400 staff, some 150 are new starters. BCS therefore operates a two-tier pay and conditions structure, one for the transferred staff and one for the new staff. While recognising UNISON and representation rights for transferred staff, BCS does not recognise unions for new staff at the moment. The 250 transferred staff still enjoy their original pay and conditions and the same bargaining rights as previously, but there is no 'in house' negotiation. Inferior pay and conditions for new staff are imposed by BSC without consultation.

Bargaining trends and tendencies from the 1980s onward

The emerging trend which has come to dominate British collective bargaining, notably in the private sector, is the move away from multi-employer bargaining, particularly as far as pay is concerned, and the growing absence of collective pay determination at workplace level as demonstrated by WERS98 (Cully *et al.*, 1999, Millward *et al.*, 2000). There have also been significant changes in the coverage and scope of collective bargaining during this period, both of which are considered below.

Levels of bargaining

As we have seen, in the 1960s most employees in the private sector were covered by multi-employer (industry-wide) agreements, but during the 1970s, single-employer arrangements became important. Brown *et al.* (1995), by reworking the WIRS survey data, confirm an intensification of this trend for private sector bargaining, and in particular the continuing decline of multi-employer agreements. They go on to state:

> *At the time of Donovan it had been possible to speculate that multi-employer agreements might*

come to provide the base of a 'two-tier' bargaining system, such as has been successful elsewhere in Europe, with industry-wide agreements being explicitly supplemented by single employer additions. This has not happened. Both CBI and WIRS surveys confirm that, during the 1980s, most firms that had earlier adopted two-tier arrangements decided to abandon them. (p. 137)

Table 6.2 identifies the changes that have taken place in the patterns of pay bargaining during the period of the WIRS and WERS98 from 1984 to 1998, between the three main bargaining levels – multi-employer, single employer and workplace within private manufacturing and services, the public sector and overall. The table also looks at the proportion of workplaces where pay bargaining is absent, and at what level of the wider organisation

and where, if applicable, outside the organisation decisions about pay are taken. The latest data confirms some previous trends, and overall the picture is one of a considerable decline of around 50 per cent in the proportion of workplaces where collective bargaining was the dominant method of pay determination over the period 1984–98. The trend away from multi-employer bargaining continued apace, but there was no discernable decline in the proportion of workplaces whose wider organisation bargained as a single employer over multiple sites, and there was a further decline in the proportion of workplaces where pay was determined at that level. As collective determination of pay declined the proportion of workplaces whose organisations' pay determination was not subject to collective bargaining increased to 71 per cent overall in 1998. In most instances, collective bargaining has not been replaced by individual bargaining but by unilateral

Table 6.2 Changes in the pattern of pay bargaining, 1984–98: percentage of workplaces

	1984				1990				1998			
	overall	psm	pss	pub	overall	psm	pss	pub	overall	psm	pss	pub
Collective bargaining	60	50	36	94	42	33	29	71	29	23	14	63
Most distant level of negotiation												
Multi-employer bargaining	41	21	17	82	23	12	8	58	13	6	3	39
Multi-site, single employer												
bargaining	12	11	14	11	14	6	19	12	12	5	10	23
Workplace bargaining	5	17	3	–	4	14	2	–	3	12	1	1
Don't know	1	2	1	1	1	1	–	1	–	–	–	–
Not collective bargaining	40	50	64	6	58	67	71	29	71	77	86	37
Most distant level of												
decision-making												
External to organisation												
(e.g. central government, pay												
review body, industry body)	7	4	13	3	9	7	5	16	14	3	10	29
Management at a higher level												
in organisation	11	11	19	1	16	11	24	6	25	24	36	6
Management at workplace level	21	33	31	–	30	47	41	–	30	48	39	2
Don't know	1	1	1	–	3	2	1	6	2	2	2	0

Source: Based on Millward *et al.*, 2000, pp. 186, 188, 191, 194

Notes: **psm** = private sector manufacturing   **pss** = private sector services   **pub** = public sector management determination either at workplace level or higher up in the organisation (Brown *et al.*, 2002).

There was a steep decline in the proportion of workplaces experiencing multi-employer bargaining in both private services and manufacturing and, by 1998, the manufacturing sector 'contained only a small proportion of workplaces where collective bargaining was the dominant form of pay setting [while] unilateral determination by management became the dominant mode of pay determination' (Millward *et al.*, 2000). Within private services in particular, there were significant differences in patterns of pay determination shown by 'leavers' and 'joiners', with the former category having considerably higher incidences of collective pay determination than the latter. Within the public sector there were similar trends to those in the private sector, with the decline in multi-employer bargaining, which started from a higher base than in private manufacturing and services, being quite drastic: from 82 per cent to 39 per cent of workplaces. This was somewhat compensated for by the rapid increase in multi-site bargaining, reflecting a significant degree of decentralisation of bargaining affecting 23 per cent of workplaces in 1998 compared with 11 per

cent and 12 per cent for 1984 and 1990 respectively. These changes, and indeed the rate of change, are remarkable departures from past practice and are more significant than those in the private sector, mainly because they have occurred over a much shorter time-span.

Overall, then, collective bargaining as a system of pay determination had become confined to a minority of all workplaces (25 per cent), and in the increasing proportion of workplaces where pay was determined without negotiation (almost 75 per cent), decisions determining pay were made at workplace level, usually unilaterally by local management.

Self-Evaluation Activity 6.7

Collective bargaining: main trends and patterns
Response on website

Looking at the data contained in the above tables, summarise the main trends and patterns in collective bargaining in Britain during the 1980s and 1990s.

The example of the docks industry given in Exhibit 6.2 demonstrates the decline in multi-employer bargaining.

Exhibit 6.2

The docks

The National Dock Labour Scheme (NDLS), established in 1947, was introduced to end the casual nature of dock employment, and this was finally achieved in 1967. This enabled the separate collective bargaining machinery to ensure greater national consistency of basic terms and conditions of employment. In common with most industry-wide bargaining in other industries such as engineering, national negotiations provided a minimum framework for pay and conditions, with regional or local negotiations usually, but not always, resulting in agreements in excess of these rates. The dockers had a long tradition of collective solidarity extending back to the nineteenth century, and the industry was one of the most strike-prone in Britain. Technological change in the form of containerisation and 'roll-on, roll-off' ferries eventually resulted in many redundancies, and ports outside the NDLS, such as Felixstowe, using casual labour began to develop. The NDLS was abolished in July 1989. The effects of abolition were most marked within Associated British Ports (ABP), the former nationalised ports group, which was the largest employer of registered dockworkers prior to abolition.

Out of a total of approximately 1700 dockers, fewer than 700 remained in 1990. In five ABP ports no registered dockers (RDWs) remained. At King's Lynn, 38 former RDWs took severance payments, leaving 12 dockers to handle all throughputs at the port. At Hull, compulsory weekend overtime coupled with a lengthening of the working week was introduced. ABP also brought in 'auxiliary manual workers' to augment shortfalls in the workforce, and a specific 'no-strike' clause was included in a contract imposed on 80 former RDWs employed at Immingham and Grimsby. At ABP's major ports of Southampton and Hull, alterations to employment practices were implemented on a more measured basis than elsewhere. In the general cargo area of Southampton docks, for example, former registered labour force reductions were less drastic than elsewhere, but nevertheless had been reduced from 306 to 140 by 1990.

During the early 1990s average wages in Invergordon had fallen to £2 an hour and in Aberdeen to £4 an hour, compared with the average wage of around £6 an hour in the ABP ports. In Aberdeen, four new companies replaced the former NDLS employers, all eventually employing casual labour. At Clydeport, all 150 former RDWs opted for severance payments, and at Glasgow all former RDWs were dismissed for refusing to accept new contracts. With most of the Welsh ports ridding themselves of former RDWs, 80 dockers employed at Barry formed their own co-operative. The Port of London witnessed a 50 per cent reduction in the workforce to 500 and dismissal of over 150 shop stewards and trade union activists who were involved in the national strike which preceded the abolition of NDLS. The Port of London Authority also refused to recognise the TGWU.

Ultimately, Associated British Ports derecognised trade unions for purposes of collective bargaining and placed all its employees on individual contracts. The situation at the Port of Liverpool in the aftermath of abolition was considerably different from the pattern of events at other former NDLS ports as described above. Uniquely, relations between the TGWU and the Mersey Docks and Harbour Company (MDHC) were traditionally good, but the TGWU did not receive the support of the majority of shop stewards or the dockers themselves who accused the TGWU of colluding with management in undermining the NDLS by permitting casual, non-union labour to handle dock work. However, after abolition of the NDLS, MDHC continued to recognise the union for purposes of collective bargaining and all redundancies were voluntary. A local TGWU Docks District Secretary conceded that:

> MDHC's labour relations track record shines in comparison with other British port employers. I honestly believe that the company would rather make changes through negotiation than through confrontation. Unlike some of the cowboy firms in other docks, they also don't try to offload ships using one man and a dog, and I respect them for that. (*Management Today*, March 1990)

Nevertheless, developments in the port indicated that the company would, albeit at a more gradual pace, eventually emulate the post-NDLS rationale adopted by all of its competitors. During the 1980s parts of the port's non-dock activities were privatised, 'joint venture' companies were established and bulk-handling operations were already staffed by non-union, often casual labour. This process accelerated somewhat after abolition of the NDLS, and was eventually to trigger off one of the most acrimonious disputes in British labour history, the Liverpool docks dispute of 1996–7. The following extract from a local newspaper demonstrates the extent of the growing gulf between management and the 'rank-and-file' union representatives and dockers:

We were too soft with dockers
The chief of the Mersey docks says his company should have sacked all its dockers years ago. Trevor Furlong, chief executive of Mersey Docks and Harbour Company says the firm made a mistake when it did not take advantage of the abolition of the National Dock Labour Scheme in 1989. The move led to MDHC's rival ports, Hull, Southampton and London sacking all their dockers and ceasing to recognise trade unions. But MDHC kept their workers and a relationship with the Transport and General Workers Union. In an interview with shipping magazine IFW, Mr Furlong said: 'I suppose, in hindsight, we were too soft in 1989. We should have got rid of the lot and recruited non-union labour, but we didn't believe it was right. We felt we could work with the TGWU. Other ports got out, we didn't.' (Liverpool Echo, 17 July 1996)

Reasons for the move away from multi-employer bargaining: 1980s onward

Unlike the informal, fragmented and autonomous domestic bargaining of the 1950s and 1960s, which was largely initiated by workplace representatives taking advantage of full employment and local labour scarcity to 'bid up' the price of labour, the move away from multi-employer bargaining in the private sector and from centralised bargaining in the public sector from the 1980s was encouraged by management and government rather than by workplace representatives. The following factors are relevant:

1. Many larger companies have undergone changes to their organisational structures which favour decentralisation and diversification of activities. A common distinction between larger organisational forms within the private sector is that between the majority of organisations having many or multiple divisions (these organisations are termed M-form), the minority (around 20 per cent) which do not have divisions and which are centrally controlled with highly centralised structures (these can be termed C-form), together with those organisations which are loosely co-ordinated holding companies (termed H-form) (Hill and Pickering, 1986). Clearly the highest degree of decentralised bargaining takes place in M-form organisations, where managers in individual operating units, often called 'profit centres', take day-to-day operational decisions and are accountable to the centre for their financial performance. These organisational changes, and accompanying changes to business strategy and devolved financial accountability to smaller profit centres, have, according to Purcell and Ahlstrand (1989), been the most important factor in the decentralisation of bargaining down from the centre (corporate level) to the other organisational levels.

2. Developments in HRM (see Chapters 2 and 5) both in terms of strategy and of securing employee commitment to that strategy, have been instrumental in encouraging flexible working arrangements, development of the 'human resource' and in linking pay to performance. Devolved bargaining over these issues can help to achieve HRM objectives as, for example, in linking pay to productivity on a teamwork basis with team-based bonus systems. In addition, the desire of managements to reform working practices, concerning the introduction of new technology for example, has facilitated local bargaining with reference to these changes.

3. Operating divisions and units in 'M-form' organisations are accountable for their financial performance and therefore may concentrate efforts to secure greater control over labour costs. Increasing competition on a local, national and global scale, recession and declining profit margins, will all contribute to pressures to cut costs and increase productivity, hence the importance of local issues being negotiated locally. Brown *et al.* (1995) argue that:

   > *The positive reasons for adopting enterprise bargaining come less from any benefits on the wages front than from the potential it offers employers to improve labour's productivity in the light of their own business circumstances. It allows employers to cultivate internal labour markets. When much skill acquisition is on-the-job and when technological change is constant and incremental, there are advantages in having fluid job titles, predictable career trajectories, and stable internal salary structures. Enterprise bargaining fits in with the more individualistic treatment of employees which is associated with the decline of manual employment and it provides a ready base for enterprise related incentive schemes.* (p. 138)

4. From management's perspective, decentralised bargaining has the advantage that unions may find it more difficult to organise industrial action at enterprise level because of the need to arrange ballots for each workplace. In addition, workers in at least some decentralised units may not wish to take industrial action. Furthermore, bargaining devolution fits in with the employer's quest to maximise production, optimise wage costs and encourage labour flexibility (Salamon, 2003, p. 356).

5. The decline in the importance of employers' associations has also been accompanied by the decline in multi-employer bargaining and the rise

of single-employer bargaining, and as such can be implicated in the development of decentralised bargaining during the 1980s and 1990s. As we have commented, some major organisations have withdrawn from national bargaining arrangements and have set up their own arrangements.

6. Conservative governments of the 1980s and early 1990s regarded industry-wide, national multi-employer bargaining as potentially inflationary which, because pay settlements did not take into account local labour market situations, could contribute to unemployment. Local pay determination, on the other hand, stresses the 'ability to pay', is more able to relate pay to performance and is more responsive to local labour market conditions.

7. As we shall see, some of the privatised industries have devolved bargaining arrangements and multi-employer bargaining has been completely abandoned as in the railway companies, water industry and the ports. Within the public sector itself, privatisation and compulsory competitive tendering removed collective pay determination and within teaching, health care and central government a growing market orientation has resulted in greater decentralisation of pay determination (Millward *et al.*, 2000).

Self-Evaluation Activity 6.8

Advantages and disadvantages of different types of bargaining activities
The response is given below

Identify what you consider to be important advantages and disadvantages of multi-employer, single-employer bargaining, and enterprise or workplace bargaining.

Advantages of multi-employer bargaining include:

- fair treatment of all employees within the industry or sector;
- prevention of pay leapfrogging by unions;
- local management left to concentrate on business matters;
- making best use of employers' association or federation negotiation resources;
- focus union bargaining power and bargaining skills;
- all union members benefit from collective bargaining outcomes; and

- the union role is legitimised within the industry and within a union confederation where it exists.

Disadvantages of multi-employer bargaining include:

- reduces the opportunity for individual employers to negotiate local deals to take into consideration local labour market variations;
- national pay deals may not motivate employees to work more efficiently without extra financial bonuses;
- some employers would prefer to pay less than the industry agreed rate; and
- reduces the potential for the union to bargain locally in order to secure a better deal for the workforce.

Advantages of single-employer centralised bargaining include:

- uniformity and consistency of pay for employees doing similar jobs;
- greater predictability of labour costs for management;
- stable relationships between the different negotiating groups;
- stable pay differentials amongst the different bargaining groups within the company;
- common approach for handling grievances and resolving disputes within the company; and
- pay leapfrogging avoided and pay parity claims minimised across the organisation.

Disadvantages of single-employer centralised bargaining include:

- differentiation in product markets, production systems, labour markets and technology can make it difficult for this type of bargaining to accommodate differences of this nature, and therefore bargaining inflexibility and rigidities are encouraged;
- organisational decision-making tends to be centralised and therefore remote from 'local' situations, and this may reduce management and employee commitment to these decisions;
- requires effective in-company communications systems;
- can weaken the status and power of shop stewards as focus of negotiation is not at the workplace; and
- can be expensive because of the requirement to have a centralised employee relations structure.

Advantages of single-employer decentralised bargaining (enterprise bargaining) include:

- takes into consideration local factors in collective bargaining;
- line and operational managers in divisions and profit centres become closely involved in industrial relations decision-making;
- is suitable for large companies with divisions that specialise in different types of work or product, therefore necessitating the employment of different categories of employee according to skill, expertise, qualifications, etc.;
- unit-level performance-related pay can be more easily introduced;
- the company's most highly valued groups of employees can be properly rewarded;
- local communications between unit-level manage-ment and employee representatives are facilitated;
- increases employee commitment through locally determined agreements; and
- consolidates shop steward power.

Disadvantages of single-employer decentralised bar-gaining (enterprise bargaining) include:

- can weaken the authority of full-time trade union officers;
- in situations of labour scarcity and skill shortages, this would encourage inflationary pay settlements and higher production costs;
- changes in working methods and terms and con-ditions of employment might be introduced in an unco-ordinated and haphazard way;
- issues discussed at local level may be too parochial, ignoring matters concerned with corporate strategy, planning and investment; and
- makes the control of labour costs more difficult.

Coverage and scope of collective bargaining: evidence from WERS98

The extent of the declining coverage of collective bargaining in unionised workplaces and more gen-erally has been referred to earlier in the chapter. The scope of bargaining, excluding pay determination, however, has not altered significantly, if at all from the 1990s onwards. We now examine coverage and scope in more detail in relation to the WERS find-ings (Millward *et al.*, 2000).

Bargaining coverage

Bargaining coverage varies widely within unionised organisations and workplaces. The categories least often represented include managerial groups and members of the secondary labour market such as part-time and agency employees. WERS98 reports that coverage has fallen consistently since 1984, when collectively-determined pay covered 86 per cent of workers in unionised workplaces, falling to 67 per cent in 1998. A significant development in this respect is the 'sudden appearance' (Millward *et al.*, 2000) of a large number of workplaces where no workers were covered by collective bargaining even though unions were recognised. Typically in these situations, union density is low – hence estab-lishing an association between low union density and low bargaining coverage – and there is a notice-able absence of trade union organisation at work-place level. Organisations in this category tend to be small, with fewer than 100 employees, and in sec-tors such as certain private services where unions experience perennial difficulties in organising and recruiting members. A further finding reveals that there is little evidence of any positive association between workplace union representation and higher bargaining coverage, which declined from 87 per cent in 1984 to 68 per cent in 1998. Finally, decline in coverage is common to all three industrial sectors, with decline in the public sector equalling that of private manufacturing for 1998 (70 per cent in 1998 from 94 per cent in 1984). However, nearly half the unionised workplaces in the public sector retained 100 per cent coverage, accounting for 70 per cent of all unionised workplaces with 100 per cent coverage.

There can be no doubt that there are serious implications for trade unions should coverage con-tinue to decline, or even remain at the present (2003) level. Unions' strength and influence at the work-place is at least in part dependent upon a respect-able level of bargaining coverage. Ongoing decline in coverage into the first decade of the twenty-first century is likely to marginalise further the level of union influence in determining terms and condi-tions for their members.

Bargaining scope

Scope refers to the range of substantive and pro-cedural issues that may be subject to collective bargaining – using either conjunctive or co-operative methods. Wider bargaining scope may mean that the union within the workplace is firmly established and that the bargaining relationships between employer and employees, assuming a relatively high union density level, is routine. The WERS98 evidence shows that while the number of non-pay issues negotiated declined in unionised workplaces during the 1980s, there was 'relatively little change in the scope of bargaining among continuing establishments recognising unions in 1990 and 1998' (Millward *et al.*, 2000, p. 168) as Table 6.3 shows. There was a very slight but insignificant increase in the proportion of unionised workplaces where none of the items shown in Table 6.3 was negotiated.

Across industry sectors, the most significant finding was that the scope of bargaining concerning non-pay issues, in terms of mean number of items negotiated, declined somewhat in private manufacturing from 3.7 to 3.0, in private services there was a marginal increase from 2.9 to 3.3 items, while the public sector experienced a statistically insignificant decline from 4.3 to 4.1. To conclude, it appears that there has been very little change in the coverage of non-pay items subject to negotiation, at least from 1990 to 1998. This contrasts with the situation concerning pay whereby joint determination frequently gave way to unilaterally imposed pay levels. The nature of the management of pay is considered in more detail in the next section.

Table 6.3 Bargaining scope in unionised workplaces: 1990, 1998

Items subject to negotiation	1990 %	1998 %
Physical working conditions	80	79
Staffing levels	57	51
Recruitment	44	34
Redeployment within the establishment	70	66
Size of redundancy payments	46	57
Reorganisation of working hours	88	75
None of these	5	7
Mean number of items	3.8	3.6

Source: Millward *et al.*, 2000, p. 168

Summary points

- The concept of bargaining power is central to the bargaining relationship, and is basically concerned with the costs to each party of agreement relative to the costs to each of them of disagreement.
- Factors internal to the workplace which influence bargaining power include the density of unionisation, the number of unions in a workplace, skill levels and technology. Factors external to the workplace include economic policy, employment legislation and local labour market factors.
- The historical development of collective bargaining includes a number of phases, the most important of which are:
  - the development of national, industry-wide bargaining after 1914 until the 1950s;
  - the spread of local, 'domestic' bargaining during the 1960s and 1970s;
  - the development of company-level bargaining during the 1980s and 1990s.
- Levels of bargaining in Britain are complex, but include:
  - multi-employer bargaining;
  - enterprise bargaining;
  - single-employer bargaining; and
  - two-tier bargaining.
- The emerging trend now dominating British collective bargaining is the tendency towards single-employer bargaining (see summary points in relation to SEA 6.8).
- The coverage of collective bargaining has declined quite considerably, while bargaining scope concerning non-pay issues has remained much the same overall. Pay itself is increasingly determined by unilateral (employer) imposition.

PAY DETERMINATION AND ITS MANAGEMENT: THE NEW REALITIES

The substantial change in the method of determining pay from joint collective regulation to unilateral imposition by management as recorded by the WERS98 raises some important issues concerning the equitable determination and management of pay. In order to understand the economic rationale behind pay determination, we look briefly at the market mechanism for determining wages before going on to consider the implications for employers and trade unions of the retreat of collective bargaining over pay.

The labour market mechanism

Labour as a factor of production will command a price, which must ultimately depend on its scarcity, and which in a market context will be an equilibrium price determined by the forces or laws of supply and demand. In the long run, therefore, although there may be short-term variations, the reward that any particular type of labour receives will depend upon the forces of supply and demand (Hicks, 1932). Hence, we have an economically-based pattern of wage differentials across jobs and occupations, according to this neo-classical market economics approach. If we look at examples of three occupations, pilots, surgeons and nurses, how can neo-classical economics explain the earnings of these three groups?

Taking the example of the pilot, the equilibrium wage will equal the actual wage for a given level of supply and demand (see Figure 6.2) which is *We*. If

the actual wage is less than *We*, say *WL*, there will be an excess demand for pilots. The airlines will find that they cannot service all their schedules with their existing staff and they will try to hire more staff, attracting them away from other employers by offering them higher wages – so the actual wage will tend to move up towards the equilibrium. In the same way, if the actual wage is higher than the equilibrium wage (WH) there will be an excess supply of pilots, and in wage bargaining pilots will be in a weak position since there are now more people seeking pilots' jobs than there are jobs available, resulting in a decline in pilots' wages relative to other workers.

So what factors influence the demand and supply of pilots? Obviously demand for air travel will influence demand for pilots who are an essential factor of production. This goes some way toward explaining why pilots are paid more than other crew members since it is impossible to provide flights without pilots. On the supply side, certain attributes and qualifications are needed, making the supply of pilots fairly inelastic. The professional association operates in a similar way to a traditional craft trade union, restricting entry to the 'profession' thereby pushing the supply curve to the left and

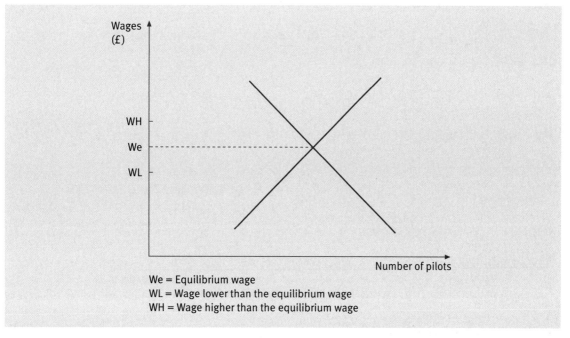

We = Equilibrium wage
WL = Wage lower than the equilibrium wage
WH = Wage higher than the equilibrium wage

Figure 6.2 The market for pilots

raising the equilibrium wage from We (1) to We (2) (Figure 6.3).

In the case of doctors within the NHS, the demand for doctors does not yet depend upon market forces despite the increased extent of marketisation within the NHS. Because health care is, in the main, provided publicly by the NHS, the government in effect decides when it allocates spending, and how much health care will be produced and consumed. In so doing the government also determines the demand for doctors. Should doctors' services become very expensive, there is the possibility of substituting other factors of production, such as technicians and nurses (already in force with general practitioners), in order to minimise the cost of producing a given amount of health care. In theory, the degree to which doctors can be substituted will determine the elasticity of demand for doctors. However, in reality, as with pilots, the demand for doctors is relatively inelastic because of the essential role they play in providing health care. On the supply side, again the supply of doctors, as with pilots, is relatively inelastic owing to qualifications required and the lengthy training period. The existence of a professional association can restrict supply still further by imposing minimum entry requirements. The

supply and demand factors will therefore ensure a high equilibrium wage.

The wages of nurses, on the other hand, are relatively low and if the level of nurses' wages is the equilibrium wage, then this must be because demand for nurses is low in relation to supply. But is this actually the case? As with doctors, demand for nurses is not dictated by market forces but by administrative decisions, and demand elasticity will depend upon how easily nurses' services can be substituted by other factors of production such as ancillary staff etc. As many nurses' tasks can be substituted, nurses will be less essential and face a far more elastic demand for their services than pilots or doctors. On the supply side, entry requirements and levels, together with length of training, are much lower in quality and duration, while there is a high elastic supply of overseas-trained nurses. In addition, with a split trade union affiliation, and no effective organisation to impose entry requirements or restrictive codes of conduct, the supply of nurses is highly elastic. Hence a small increase in wages calls forth a generally increased supply, thus ensuring that the equilibrium wage remains low. The neo-classical market analysis therefore explains *why* some occupations earn more than others and does

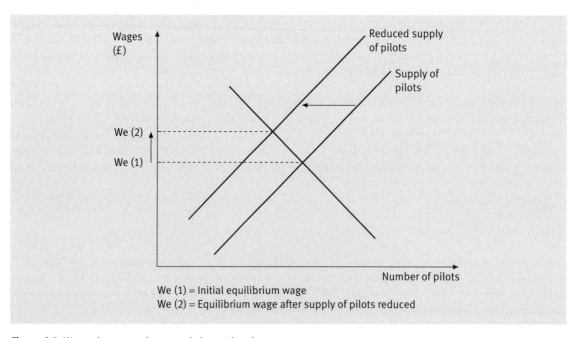

We (1) = Initial equilibrium wage
We (2) = Equilibrium wage after supply of pilots reduced

Figure 6.3 Wages increase when supply is restricted

not attempt to pass judgement on what differentials *ought* to exist (as we may agree that nurses should be more highly paid and that if nurses had more effective trade union organisation, the equilibrium wage might be raised).

Self-Evaluation Activity 6.9

The trade union effect

The response is given below

What effect do you think trade unions might have upon equilibrium wage levels?

An important assumption of the neo-classical approach to wage determination is that there is ultimately a competitive wage level at which all firms eventually pay their workers. If employers pay above the rate, they will become uncompetitive, and if they pay below the rate they will not be able to recruit or retain labour. However, the 'union effect' departs from the competitive model in that wage levels are distorted upwards owing to the pressure of collective bargaining caused by the monopoly that unions allegedly have over the supply of labour, so forcing firms out of business and eventually resulting in the contraction of the unionised workforce (Hicks, 1932). The union effect is one cause of pay dispersion whereby different employers tend to pay different rates of pay to those performing similar jobs (a major exception being the public sector, particularly before 1980, which is dealt with from p. 321 – see below). There are, of course, other economic reasons for the prevalence of pay dispersion which are discussed in greater detail by Brown *et al.* (2003, pp. 190–4). In considering this question, sight must not be lost of the fundamental role of collective pay determination which underpins the employment relationship and which seeks to address the essential inequalities of economic exchange between employer and employee whereby 'the concentrated economic power of capital confronts the far more vulnerable sellers of labour power' (Hyman, 1980, p. 308). The 'union effect' upon income distribution has been patchy over the past 60 years, and up to 1980 certain groups of employees benefited appreciably from the exercise of bargaining power, while many other groups were marginally better off. After 1980, however, the neo-liberal onslaught strove to restore market forces by weakening unions in the labour market (see Chapter 4) and diminishing their influence over pay through a con-

traction of collective bargaining, the net result of which was 'a marked growth in wage inequalities, reversing moves towards greater equality in the distribution of earnings that characterised the post-war period up to the late 1970s' (Brown *et al.*, 2003, p. 208).

Factors influencing pay outcomes

So far we have considered the role of market forces in pay determination, together with the 'union effect'. We have also noted the growing inequalities in the distribution of pay during the 1980s and 1990s, due in no small part to the diminished impact of collective pay determination and other factors associated with 'supply-side' economics (see Chapter 4). In this section we consider, albeit briefly, the factors which have a bearing upon pay outcomes in unionised and non-unionised contexts by reference to the WERS98. We then examine the role of the employer as the manager of pay and the types of payment systems most commonly encountered.

Influences on pay outcomes

The WIRS/WERS series provides information concerning the factors affecting pay outcomes, and in particular pay increases of unionised or 'covered', and non-unionised or 'uncovered' employees in every sector of the economy. Given that many workplaces have different pay systems and structures in place that affect different categories of employee, the surveys examine arrangements impacting upon the largest group of employees in each workplace, whether it be a bargaining unit or the largest group of 'uncovered' employees. Owing to difficulties in comparing data as a result of recoding data and recasting questions from the first (1984–90) to the latter half of the series (1990–8), we consider the latter period only.

In relation to the most recent pay settlement for the largest group of employees covered by collective bargaining in both the public and private sectors, it should be reiterated that only a minority of private sector workplaces are covered. The major findings are given in Table 6.4 and represent management responses.

Table 6.4 Factors influencing size of most recent pay settlement for largest groups: 1990, 1998

	Private sector		Public sector	
	1990 %	1998 %	1990 %	1998 %
Cost of living	60	53	43	40
Labour market conditions	37	23	23	4
Comparisons with other employers	31	22	18	3
Recruitment or retention	6	1	4	0
Economic factors	32	63	6	17
Ability to pay	16	16	2	3
Performance of workplace or organisation	14	28	2	11
General economic conditions	3	19	1	2
Linkage to other settlement	11	6	20	18
Other influences	19	31	51	49
Productivity improvements	6	7	5	10
Limits set by higher authority	1	6	16	33
Individual employee performance	3	2	5	3
Changes in pay systems	0	9	6	2
Industrial action or threat of it, bargaining power	2	0	12	0
Other answers	7	6	7	2
Don't know, not stated	8	6	2	11

Source: Millward *et al.*, 2000, p. 209

Table 6.4 shows that the 'cost of living' factor featured most prominently in workplaces for groups where collective bargaining was dominant, both in the public and private sectors; it was more prominent in the private sector, where it declined in importance from 60 per cent to 53 per cent over the period. Labour market conditions and comparisons with other employees were also important, but less so in 1998 than in 1990; fewer employers mentioned the 'going rate' and external comparabilities as being important in 1998 than in 1990. Economic factors became more significant in 1998 than in 1990, with improved economic conditions, ability to pay and financial performance featuring strongly, reflecting not only the improved economic performance of the UK economy, but also a greater awareness amongst firms that competition in product markets became more acute and had a bearing upon wage determination. Many of the changes within the private sector are reflected in the public sector, where comparisons with other employers were not as frequent and where workplace/organisational performance and limits set by higher authority (such as pay review bodies) became more important. Changes to payment systems (see below) were made more frequently (Millward *et al.*, 2000).

In workplaces where collective bargaining over pay was either non-existent or a minority activity, fewer employers mentioned labour market conditions in 1998 than in 1990, but a much higher proportion mentioned workplace/organisational performance (19 to 35 per cent). An increasing proportion of respondents mentioned setting of levels and pay limits by higher-level management and an increasing centralisation of decision-making about pay in larger organisations. Again, changes to payment systems featured more prominently in 1998.

Pay justifications and payment systems

The retreat, temporary or otherwise, of collective pay determination at workplace and other organisational levels has provided many managements within the private sector with unprecedented opportunities to impose pay levels and revise payment systems. This may suggest that employers have a free hand unilaterally to decide the levels and amounts they pay their employees, but in practice there are certain constraints upon this theoretical freedom, two of which are now considered. The first constraint is that even in the absence of collective bargaining pay is often part of a package of measures, many of which are designed to be motivational in order to increase employee productivity. The contention that pay is more important to employees if the work itself is intrinsically unrewarding has prompted attempts by some employers to increase job interest. For example, in some call centres where pay is a critical issue for employers and where the work of customer service representatives (CSRs) is frequently pressurised, some attempts have been made to emphasise 'quality of CSR/customer interaction' rather than frequency and number of calls processed (Rose and Wright, 2003). The interplay between product and labour markets constitutes a second constraint in that 'the influences of the product market are in contest with those of the labour market in determining pay, and employers have to mediate between them' (Brown *et al.*, 2003).

Employers should, of course, consider the external labour market since if pay for a certain skill is not broadly in line with that of the external labour market consequences such as labour turnover could ensue. However, as we have seen, the external labour market is becoming increasingly globalised and advances in communication and information technologies has meant that a growing number of financial sector organisations such as banks and insurance companies have transferred customer service facilities to India and other parts of South-East Asia. In these locations call centre labour is cheaper and often more highly educated than that of the UK, thereby reinforcing the influence of market forces in pay determination, albeit in a global context (see Exhibit 6.3).

To conclude, partly because of the contraction of collective pay determination, managements are able to exercise greater discretion not only in unilateral pay determination but also in employment and working practices. With this in mind, firms of all sizes need to develop and review the coherency and fairness of their reward structure and payment systems, to which we now turn.

Payment systems

It is not the intention here to describe the numerous and complex payment systems that exist; most HRM texts contain descriptive chapters, while Thorpe and Homan (2000) provide a comprehensive yet detailed analysis of the nature of strategic reward systems. Instead reference will be made to those payment systems which have been systematically surveyed by WIRS and WERS98 and from which realistic assessments may be made. Millward *et al.* (2000), identify

---

Exhibit 6.3

'Union vows to oppose wholesale export of jobs'

Union leaders were yesterday seeking assurances over jobs after Aviva, the country's largest insurer, announced plans to open a call centre in India, employing 1000 staff. Amicus, the UK's second largest union, said it would oppose the 'wholesale' export of jobs. Dave Fleming, Amicus's national officer, said: 'This announcement and the recent trend of finance sector companies outsourcing jobs to lower-cost employment areas suggest that tight regulations affecting the insurance sector are having a serious impact on UK jobs.'

Source: Financial Times, 12 February 2003

three types of payment systems which have been subject to longitudinal analysis, namely incentive pay, profit-related pay schemes and share-ownership schemes.

Incentive pay: In 1990, the WIRS identified two forms of incentive payment – payment by results and merit pay. The former linked some element of employees' pay to a measurable increment of output and the latter is dependent upon subjective assessment by managers. WERS98 utilises the same payment categories, which have for some years been generically labelled *performance-related pay* (PRP). The diversity of PRP schemes includes the following instances:

- where individual performance criteria are established so that actual individual performance can be judged and assessed against the performance criteria established;
- where links are established between the level of individual performance assessed and the level of reward received by the individual;
- where the actual relationship between pay and performance is established by managerial assessment of performance which may be used on either objective or subjective criteria;
- where it is assumed that these links will lead to increased organisational performance through improved individual performance which arises from higher rewards for improved performance; and
- where a formal performance management system is used to establish the linkage between the performance of the individual and the performance of the organisation.

In terms of the incidence of incentive pay, there was little change in the proportion of workplaces covered – 62 per cent in 1990 and 58 per cent in 1998. There was no significant change in the incidence of PRP/incentive pay across the three sectors, with just under 50 per cent take-up in the public sector, 66 per cent in private services and 75 per cent in manufacturing. Large workplaces and workplaces with no recognised union tended to make greater use of incentive pay. While individual incentive pay was more common than group or team pay throughout the period, more non-manual employees were covered by such pay systems than manual

grades in 1998, while the opposite applied in 1990. Overall, then, there was little change in the frequency of application and incidence of PRP systems throughout the 1990s.

Profit-related pay schemes: These were first introduced in the nineteenth century and then reintroduced by the Conservative government in the 1980s, being one of the few cash profit-sharing schemes to attract tax concessions. The intention was to encourage greater pay flexibility in the hope that employees would see part of their pay contingent upon the fortunes of the company. The considerable tax advantages to employees were thought to be additional motivators. Such schemes became popular during the 1980s; by 1990 44 per cent of workplaces belonged to organisations which operated them, and this increased imperceptibly to 46 per cent in 1998. Profit-related pay (PRP) schemes are more prevalent in manufacturing workplaces, up from 33 to 50 per cent during the period, and more common in UK multinationals. From 1990 onwards most workplaces with 1000 or more employees had employees who benefited from PRP schemes. WERS98 also established a link between non-financial participation and PRP schemes. Hence, during 1990–8, workplaces having arrangements for non-financial participation, or employee voice, were more likely to also operate a profit-sharing scheme for their employees than those workplaces with no such voice arrangements. All in all, there was, therefore, no significant change in the incidence of profit-related pay during the course of 1990–8.

Share-ownership schemes: Until the introduction of profit-related pay, most new profit-sharing schemes took the form of 'approved profit-sharing', which was introduced in 1978. Part of the profits (up to 5 per cent) are used to purchase shares in the employing company on behalf of employees, and are placed in trust for two years. If they remain in trust for a further year (three years before 1995), the employee is exempt from income tax. Employees may also elect to receive a cash profit share in place of shares, but no tax benefits are secured. From 1980 to 1990, the incidence of such schemes in the WIRS workplaces increased from 13 per cent to 30 per cent with a subsequent decline to 24 per cent in 1998. Such schemes remain more common in workplaces where there is a combination of union representation and other employee-management communication channels.

COLLECTIVE BARGAINING IN THE PUBLIC SECTOR

Public sector industrial relations has experienced considerable upheaval since 1979 under both the Conservatives and New Labour. Successive Conservative governments sought to introduce far-reaching changes. These included the privatisation of former nationalised industries and public services, the 'contracting out' of services such as cleaning and catering within both the local authority sector and the NHS, and the establishment of NHS trusts and Civil Service agencies (a more thorough examination of the public sector is provided in Chapter 4). These changes took place largely as a result of the Conservatives' conviction that an injection of market forces would promote competition and increase efficiency of service provision while at the same time curtailing the growing proportion of government expenditure consumed by the public sector. Government criticism was directed at public sector trade unions for insulating their members from competitive forces and acting as labour cartels, and also at public service managers for being inefficient and not providing 'value for money'. New Labour has endorsed much of the agenda of the Conservatives, consolidating many of the Conservatives' policies and redirecting others in pursuit of 'modernisation' of public services (see Chapter 4).

Public sector employment comprises:

- employees within **central government** such as departments of state, regional health authorities, national museums and art galleries and various national research councils;
- employees within the **Civil Service** which comprises the home Civil Service and the diplomatic service, government agencies such as the Employment Service and Benefits Agency;
- employees within the **local authority sector** such as all local authorities, the police, fire and probation services; and
- employees within **public corporations** including bus companies and airports, NHS trust hospitals,

and nationalised industries, most of which have been privatised. Royal Mail remains the most significant public corporation.

The size of the public sector is still relatively large, as Table 6.5 indicates, despite the changes and employee reductions in the Civil Service, the pressure on the NHS and local authorities to contract out services and the privatisation of most of the public corporations. Nevertheless, as a proportion of the entire workforce, public sector employment has declined by around 10 per cent from 7.445 to 5.163 million during the period 1979–2001. The pattern of employment, however, conceals significant changes to the composition of the workforce. Firstly, there has been a steep reduction in the numbers of ancillary staff employed in the public sector as a result of the competitive tendering process where employees compete for their jobs against external competition. Secondly, over the past 15 years or so there has been an appreciable increase in the proportion of women and part-time employees within the public sector workforce, from 50 to 60 per cent, and from 25 to 36 per cent respectively (Bach and Winchester, 2003). Thirdly, there has been an increase in the number of temporary workers in public service employment to around 10 per cent of all staff, most of whom are on fixed-term contracts. Finally, it appears that over the years, as temporary employment and other forms of 'contingency' contractual employment have increased, the risk of job loss has also increased and experience of deteriorating conditions of work has become more widespread (Bach and Winchester, 2003).

Collective bargaining within the public sector was traditionally undertaken at national and industry-wide level, assisted in its development by 'Whitleyism' (see p. 325) after the First World War, and by the Nationalisation Acts after the Second World War. The collective bargaining machinery for most employees within the public sector operates 'within clearly defined and sometimes large bargaining units . . . often divided into manual, craft, professional and technical and other specialist groups typified, for example, by British local authorities' (Farnham and Pimlott, 1995). The greater part of collective bargaining arrangements in the public sector take the form of what has long been termed 'Whitleyism' (Bailey, 1997). The Whitley recommendations, as

Table 6.5 Public sector employment: 1979–2001

	1979 (000s)	1985 (000s)	1991 (000s)	1997 (000s)	2001 (000s)
Central government					
HM forces	314	326	297	210	204
NHS	1 152	1 223	1 098	78	75
Other	921	811	783	645	595
TOTAL	2 387	2 360	2 178	933	874
Local authorities					
Education	1 539	1 429	1 416	1 187	1 349
Health and social services	344	376	414	403	376
Construction	156	125	106	65	57
Police and civilians	176	187	202	207	214
Other	782	774	809	726	736
TOTAL	2 997	2 958	2 947	2 593	2 732
Public corporations					
Nationalised industries	1 849	1 131	497	242	229
Other	216	120	102	128	134
NHS trusts			124	1 121	1 194
TOTAL	2 065	1 251	723	1 491	1 557
General government	5 385	5 318	5 125	3 463	3 606
Total public sector	7 449	6 569	5 848	4 954	5 163
Total workforce in employment	27 059	26 231	27 992	28 135	28 424
Public sector as percentage of the workforce in employment	28	25	21	18	18

Source: *Economic Trends Annual Supplement*, November 2002

we have already noted, stressed the need for negotiations at a jointly agreed level which resulted in national bargaining machinery, and pay structures which were uniform and applied nationally to specific occupational groups. Bailey points out that:

> By the time the successive Conservative Governments of the 1980s came to demand decentralisation of bargaining, Whitleyism had become for unions (and some managers) all that was good and fair about public sector industrial relations. For government ministers and some senior public service managers, Whitleyism does not allow pay to respond to service needs, leading in some

> cases to underpayment of employees [and also] to overpayment in many instances. (p. 126)

National or industry-wide bargaining continued as the prevailing system of pay determination more or less until the early 1980s but since then, as we point out here and in Chapter 4, the reorganisation of the public sector started by the Conservatives has had a significant impact on collective pay determination. National pay bargaining is no longer paramount as privatisation and compulsory competitive tendering (CCT) have removed these activities, and elsewhere pay is determined by pay review bodies as with teaching. Commercialisation or 'marketisation' of large chunks of the public sector have further eroded the status of national bargaining, generating a decentralisation of pay setting and increasing local autonomy in bargaining, reflecting the earlier trend in private industry. These developments are uneven, and have 'led to unprecedented fragmentation of pay setting arrangements within the sector' (Millward *et al.*, 2000). Overall, the trends identified above have contributed to a decline in the coverage of collective pay determination in the public sector, down from 71 per cent in 1990 to 63 per cent in 1998 (WERS98). Since the early 1980s decentralisation of bargaining within the public sector has been problematic for a number of reasons:

- public service managers were divided on the pace and direction of reform;
- trade unions wanted but failed to retain many centralised agreements and bargaining machinery;
- government policy has been inconsistent with ministerial utterances and rhetoric often undermined by Treasury strictures for tight budgetary control; and
- there are also significant variations in the form and substantive content of national agreements, and these arrangements 'have been shaped by past conflicts between central government, public employers and trade unions, and they also reflect the diverse labour market characteristics of different occupations in public service employment' (Bach and Winchester, 2003, p. 299).

The onward march of the pay review bodies

The previous centralised and national system of pay bargaining, whereby every occupational grade enjoyed the same national pay level, ratings and structures, at least guaranteed consistency of approach to pay and conditions of employment and enabled fair comparisons to be made with pay levels and pay increases in the private sector. It was commonplace to invoke comparability arguments in support of wage claims and offers, and arbitration procedures were widespread and well established. Two major groups, the firefighters and the police, enjoy indexation formulas, established in 1977 and 1979 respectively after actual and threatened industrial action.

The formulas link annual increases in pay to the top quartile of male manual earnings in the case of firefighters, and to the median increase in private sector non-manual settlements in the case of the police. Different criteria for determining pay were introduced by the Conservatives. Comparabilities and 'fair comparison', together with the Comparabilities Commission established during the 1978/9 'Winter of Discontent' dispute season, gave way to employer 'affordability' and market-led pay determination. The Conservatives also established independent pay review bodies – for nurses, midwives and other NHS and medicine-related professions in 1983, and for teachers in 1991 – which removed around 1 million staff from collective pay determination.

The membership of pay review bodies (PRBs) consists of a relatively small number of members appointed by government and serviced by an independent secretariat within the Civil Service. PRBs receive submissions from all interested parties, both orally and in writing; they also visit workplaces and commission their own research before making recommendations on pay increases which, nevertheless, are not binding upon government. Bach and Winchester (2003) point out that PRBs, while they have been successful in preventing manifest conflict over pay, have also impeded the progress of decentralised bargaining and 'limited the erosion of the principle of "fair comparison"' (p. 298). PRBs have often been critical of government intentions to 'phase' pay awards and they have also recommended increases above government's intended spending levels for pay. Notwithstanding this PRBs have, in comparison with more traditional forms of pay bargaining, formulated their recommendations on the basis of fairly rigorous research on the internal and external labour markets of the professions concerned, alongside the basic function of assessing the validity of the parties' arguments (government, employer, unions and others). It is likely that PRBs will remain the primary pay determining machinery for the medical and teaching professions for the foreseeable future, but any future effort to extend these bodies to incorporate other public service occupations would in all likelihood be strongly opposed by the parties concerned.

It is difficult to generalise concerning the extent and scope of pay determination mechanisms within the public sector as a whole. This is owing to the uneven pace of change, heterogeneity of organisational forms, occupations and traditions of industrial relations within each occupational sector. Reference is therefore made separately to the Civil Service, the NHS, and to local authorities and teachers.

The Civil Service

Until 1981 the terms and conditions of employment of the half a million or so civil servants were determined centrally, and national negotiations between the Treasury and trade unions 'produced a detailed pay and conditions code which had to be applied uniformly throughout the service' (Winchester and Bach, 1995, p. 318). Pay determination within the Civil Service was based on the recommendation of the Priestley Commission (1955) that pay levels should be guided by the principle of 'fair comparability', that 'the primary principle for determining the pay of civil servants should be fair comparison with the current remuneration of outside staffs employed in broadly comparable work'. From 1981 until 1987, two important factors influenced Civil Service pay determination:

- Because of the desire by government to introduce efficiencies and cost savings throughout the public sector, a specific pay 'factor' or 'assumption' was introduced which acted as a benchmark for pay increases, whereby any actual pay increase in excess of the pay 'factor' could be clawed back in the form of staff economies resulting in deteriorating quality of services.
- The government withdrew from the Civil Service pay agreement, effectively ending the principle of 'fair comparability' in 1981, and this resulted in a bitter 20-week dispute and the setting up of an independent committee. The subsequent report (the Megaw Report, 1982) recommended some modification of the comparability principle consistent with the need to 'recruit, retain and motivate by increasing pay flexibility and introducing forms of performance-related (or merit) pay'. The new structure of pay determination would be defined by cash limits and 'affordability'. However, it was not until 1987 that the Megaw recommendations were acted upon.

The 1988 report entitled *Improving Management in Government: the Next Steps,* by the head of the Efficiency Unit, Sir Robin Ibbs, was highly critical of the size of the Civil Service and the quality of management and service delivery. Specifically it pointed to the incompatibility of a policy-oriented focus with efficient management of service delivery, and recommended the restructuring of Civil Service departments into a series of executive agencies to resolve this problem. It was expected that these agencies would be more businesslike in their outlook and practice. Each would have a chief executive, often recruited externally, and would be given more freedom to manage financial and personnel matters, more in the style of the private sector. Chief executives would also have some freedom to determine pay levels and systems. By 1993 there were 92 agencies employing around 60 per cent (or 350 000) of the Civil Service. During the 1990s the trend towards local, agency-based pay determination continued, and by 1996 the process was complete, with most agencies, particularly the larger ones having specific pay agreements and procedures. These agencies included Customs and Excise, HM Prison Service, the Inland Revenue and HMSO.

Two further developments have influenced pay determination within the Civil Service. Firstly, the Civil Service (Management Functions) Act permitted the Treasury and Cabinet Office to delegate their responsibility for setting civil servants' pay and conditions to the agencies. To all intents and purposes the Act formalised existing decentralised pay determination systems within many agencies. The Treasury does retain the right to change conditions and withdraw delegated authority, as well as maintaining overall budgetary control. Secondly, the Next Steps Review, 1993, confirmed the government's intention to regard executive agencies as transitory vehicles on the road to full privatisation or contracting out of services. As for the future, while the speed and direction of change according to the size, activities and financial control characteristics of delegated agencies will vary between agencies, the trend towards decentralisation of pay determination is set to continue, despite a change in government.

During the mid-1990s, individual performance-related pay (PRP) became widespread under a system of 'delegated bargaining' and progression through pay scale increments was abolished and replaced by performance appraisal linked to pay. The individual PRP system provoked union opposition, despite attention being paid to dealing with low pay and recruitment problems, equal pay and diversity management problems. Finally as a result of the recommendations of the Makinson report (2000), which looked at the problems of PRP within Civil Service departments, some departments have been examining the application of team rather than individual performance which could be related to operational targets, and other departments have revised the operation of existing PRP schemes.

The National Health Service

There are three-quarters of a million people (2001 figures) within diverse occupational categories employed by the government-funded National Health Service. The main occupations are doctors and dentists, nurses, paramedics, technicians, clerical and administrative, managerial, ancillary workers and ambulance workers. Before 1991 NHS staff were employed by Regional and District Health Authorities. However, since 1991 increasing numbers have been employed by self-governing trusts and by 1998 nearly all employees were employed by trusts. From inception in 1948 until the early 1980s, and in common with the Civil Service, the NHS pay determination system was based on the tradition of 'Whitleyism' and had ten Whitley Councils in which terms and conditions of employment were negotiated. As with the Civil Service, the collective bargaining machinery was centralised at national level and external pay comparators were used to determine the pay of health service employees. There were entrenched problems concerning collective pay determination due to the size and complexity of the workforce and the multi-layered and bureaucratic organisational structure of the NHS. Winchester and Bach (1995) point to the following issues:

- 'The enormous diversity of occupational groups was reflected in the multiplicity of staff organisations, about forty of which had national recognition.' (p. 322)
- 'Staff-side representation was divided between TUC-affiliated unions, often competing for health

service membership as well as members outside the service, and non-affiliated professional associations which recruited mainly health care staff.' (p. 322)
- 'Intense organisational rivalry and conflict over bargaining objectives and tactics in defence of narrow occupational or professional interests complicated both national negotiations and local consultation.' (p. 322)
- 'These difficulties were exacerbated by the representational problems on the "management side" . . . [which] has been dominated by Health Department civil servants and regional NHS managers, "employers who do not pay and pay-masters who do not employ" in the words of McCarthy (1976).' (p. 322)

The government's view of pay determination in the NHS was virtually identical to that of the Civil Service, and was prompted by the criterion of 'ability to pay' and not comparability criteria, the former of which was applied to the 1982 pay negotiations. The breakdown of these negotiations resulted in industrial action, the outcome of which was the establishment of two new pay review bodies for nurses and midwives and other health service professionals. As a consequence, over half of the NHS staff (doctors, nurses and allied professions) had their pay determined by the review bodies. The pay review system, particularly for nurses, has been associated with real improvements in their pay, relative to other health service employees. However, the nurses' pay review system created a problem as this method of pay determination was not consistent with demands by politicians and some senior health service managers, who argued that pay determination should be more responsive to local labour market conditions.

Other developments affecting pay determination, directly or indirectly included, firstly, the appointment of general managers as the chief executives of health authorities as a result of the recommendations of the Griffiths Report (1983). The new breed of general manager had their pay determined individually and incorporated performance-related pay for all general managers. Most managers' pay is now determined individually, and performance-related pay in general has become much more widespread within the NHS in recent years. A second development has been the pursuit of 'efficiency savings' by government, to be achieved by the 'contracting out' of ancillary services, more efficient management, improved working methods and reduction in staff costs. A third development was that, from April 1991, certain NHS hospitals have been encouraged to set themselves up as self-managing trusts, as a result of the National Health Service and Community Care Act 1990, and subsequent applications for trust status meant that by 1994 trusts were providing 95 per cent of all hospital and community care services. The trusts are local employers and have responsibility for providing both health care and financial viability in addition to responsibility for pay and conditions of all trust employees. Although only a minority of trusts up to 1993 had adopted some form of local bargaining, the coverage of employees by local bargaining was estimated to be in the region of 10 per cent, or 50 000 in that year. Practical arrangements for local pay arrangements were given an impetus by a letter from the Chief Executive which 'requested all trusts to prepare action plans by October 1994 in order to have pay machinery set up by February 1995' (Thornley, 1998). The nurses' PRB played an important part in facilitating the localisation process by allowing for locally determined 'top-ups' to basic national pay recommendations for the 1995/6 and 1996/7 pay awards. However, the body's recommendations for 1997 criticised the conduct of the local pay process and provided for a fully national award in recognition of the extensive resistance to local pay determination by NHS staff. By the end of the 1990s progress towards pay devolution was still sluggish, and since 1997 the PRB has recommended national pay increases only. The New Labour government, whose report *Agenda for Change* advocated a comprehensive modernisation of the NHS pay systems, initiated a series of discussions with unions, employers and occupational groups with a view to firming up a set of proposals which would underpin the new pay system. These are:

- three new pay spines to replace disparate pay structures: one for doctors and dentists; one for nurses and allied professions and one for all other staff;
- grades within the three pay spines to be subject to an NHS-wide job evaluation scheme;

- incremental progression to be based on new competencies and responsibilities, linking staff development and pay; and
- basic conditions of service to be determined nationally, with others to be determined locally.

These proposals are to be implemented during the period 2003–5.

Local government

The main characteristics of the developments in pay determination and collective bargaining generally within the NHS and Civil Service are at least partly repeated in the case of local government and with particular regard to local authority professional and clerical staff (known as 'APT&C' or 'APTC' staff, specifically including local government administrative, professional, technical and clerical employees), and schoolteachers.

Pre-1979

Around 2.5 million people are employed by local authorities with some 700 000 manual workers and 600 000 APTC grades, the remainder comprising police, firefighters and teachers. Local authorities take up over one-third of total public expenditure (Kessler and Bayliss, 1995), and as with the NHS and the Civil Service, government preoccupations with reducing public expenditure, introducing market forces and providing 'value for money' services had important ramifications for the local authority sector. In short, government pressure took three forms (Kessler, 1989):

- the government stressed that local authorities were overmanned, and must therefore shed labour;
- local authorities needed to be efficient service providers, hence exhortations and then legal compulsion to put out to tender many local authority services; and
- local authorities needed to operate within a different financial framework with a shift from central government to local authority financing of local services as government reduced its share of the central grant from 61 per cent in 1979 to 39 per cent in 1990. This was accompanied by

strict controls over local authority expenditure in the form of cash limits and capping.

The traditional forms of pay determination and collective bargaining adopted by the local authority sector are similar to the old centralised model of the NHS and Civil Service, with approximately 20 national pay determination agreements varying in size and complexity. Winchester and Bach (1995) assert that the future of national bargaining – as seen at the time – within the local authority sector is uncertain despite the support given by employers to a national framework. They go on to state:

> The research conducted by Kessler (1991) suggested that particular groups within the main bargaining groups may be moving away from nationally agreed terms, whereas for the majority of staff, national agreements retain an important regulatory effect, subject to the same modification. He argued that this had led to 'the emergence of more dynamic and sophisticated forms of workplace industrial relations', rooted in broader managerial and organisational changes, and in which 'the scope of the unions had either been incorporation into the management process or restriction to a consultative role' (1991, p. 29). This marginalisation of unions has taken an extreme form in some of the 40 councils which have opted out of national bargaining and developed local pay determination systems in which unions play only a consultative role. (p. 327)

Research by Jackson et al. (1993) confirms the trend identified above and determined that 30 local authorities in England and Wales (under 10 per cent of all local authorities in England and Wales) had adopted local bargaining for their APTC staff, the majority of the local authorities being located in the South East. In this context, Bailey (1997) points out that:

> While national agreements were only framework agreements beyond which authorities could apply some discretion in the use of pay scales, incremental points and annual increases (upwards), this was inadequate in the South East in terms of resolving relative pay problems. National bargaining had been ineffective, as most annual increases negotiated by NALGO (which became part of UNISON) tended to

> benefit their lower paid members, rather than professionals. (p. 120)

Post-1997

However, in 1997, as part of New Labour's public sector pay modernisation policy, a new agreement (the Local Government Agreement) proposed reforms to the national agreement such as single status, a single pay spine, a standard 37-hour week and the merging of APT&C, craft and manual negotiating machinery within a single-table arrangement to be implemented by April 1999. The new national pay spine, subject to a jointly agreed job evaluation scheme, 'was designed to provide a framework within which each local authority could seek local agreement on a grading structure covering all staff' (Bach and Winchester, 2003, p. 304). However, there had been delays in implementation owing to the difficulties in incorporating two groups of diverse occupations into a single pay spine, together with a lack of funding to defray the cost of moving to single-status pay and conditions.

The teachers

Schoolteachers' pay had been subject to government restrictions during the 1980s and 1990s, and up to 1987 national negotiations between employers and the main teaching unions took place annually within the Burnham Committee, negotiating machinery set up by the Remuneration of Teachers Act in 1965. The Burnham Committee was a negotiating forum which brought together representatives of six teachers' unions, over 100 local education authorities and central government. The history of teachers' pay reflects the history of public sector pay generally, in that periods of pay erosion were followed by 'catching-up' exercises such as the Houghton Committee awards in 1974 and the Clegg Report awards in 1980. In 1987, the Teachers' Pay and Conditions Act abolished collective bargaining for teachers for at least three years allowing the government to take over direct control of teachers' pay, assisted by an Interim Advisory Committee. In 1991 the government announced that the pay and conditions of teachers henceforth would be determined by a review body, the School Teachers' Review Body. Another development affecting the determination of teachers' pay was the establishment of Local Management of Schools (LMS) introduced as a result of the Education Reform Act of 1988. LMS devolves responsibility for school budgets and the teaching wage bill to head teachers, although heads are bound by the implementation of the review body recommendations (assuming acceptance of these by government). An accompanying funding formula permits schools to receive money calculated according to the cost of an 'average' teacher's salary (according to criteria of age and grade). Bailey (1997) points out that 'no allowance is made where "above average" staff profiles exist' (p. 140).

More recently, the New Labour government, in line with pay modernisation initiatives elsewhere in the public sector, advocated an overhaul of teachers' pay with the intention of making the profession more attractive to new entrants and providing 'good' teachers with substantial pay increases. The main mechanism used to achieve this is a system of performance-related pay (PRP) to 'top up', sometimes substantially, the nationally determined rate. In essence, the policy to link pay with performance would permit fast-track progression through the main pay scale for those teachers whose performance was 'excellent'. In addition, on reaching the top of the pay scale, teachers could apply to cross a 'performance threshold' and, if successful, they would receive a £2000 pay increase immediately by moving to the new upper scale. The PRP system met with intense opposition from the teachers' unions, particularly the NUT which criticised criteria for assessment such as inclusion of 'pupil progress' and the assessment process itself as being too complex and subject to head-teacher bias. Nevertheless, almost all teachers who had applied were told they had met the requisite criteria and received the £2000 threshold payment and scale progression in 2001. This outcome muted union criticism and revealed the NUT as the main critic to be out of step with the other teachers' unions.

Concluding comments

The public services have undergone considerable upheavals during the course of the past three decades. The legacy of years of underfunding, rigid and complex bargaining structures, management

inefficiencies and sheer diversity of occupational patterns and types have all contributed towards current and ongoing problems, many of them related to pay, expenditure and resource allocation. Increased government spending from 2002 onwards may help alleviate some of the problems, but within the specific area of pay determination there are some lessons to be learnt as identified by Bach and Winchester (2003). These include the fact that we are dealing with a hugely diverse and heterogeneous sector which requires adequate resources to improve systems of pay determination subject to considerable delays in implementation. Inter-union agreement for implementation is required, as is extra government funding. Furthermore, as Bach and Winchester point out, pay schemes such as PRP can have short life cycles unless they are constantly maintained and, in the longer term, 'changes in market conditions and public expenditure growth interact with service-specific pay problems in ways that may undermine the rationale of reforms or their later impact' (p. 306).

THE PRIVATISED INDUSTRIES

In general, the process of decentralised bargaining has been more pronounced within the privatised industries and services that make up the former nationalised industries, than within the public sector organisations that we have already considered. The reasons for this are often specific to particular industries or services, but may include factors such as financial and market constraints and opportunities, the traditions and climate of industrial relations within specific industries, and the longer timescales within many privatised industries which enabled decentralised bargaining to evolve over a longer period. Table 6.6 illustrates the extent of privatisation. Amongst the few organisations remaining under public ownership in 1998 were Royal Mail, London Transport (partial privatisation in 2003), nuclear power (now privatised) and the BBC. We now go on to look at a selection of industries in more detail.

Few industries have transformed themselves more dramatically than **British Steel** (now known as Corus). During the 1970s, British Steel (BS) had around 269 000 employees. By the late 1970s and into the 1980s, BS was operating in a global market

Table 6.6 The extent of privatisation: 1982–2003

Organisation	Year	Employees
National Freight Co.	1982	28 000
Britoil	1982	14 000
Associated British Ports	1983	–
Enterprise Oil	1984	–
British Telecom	1984	250 000
British Shipbuilders	from 1984	–
British Gas Corporation	1986	89 000
National Bus Co. Subsidiaries	1986–8	30 000
British Airways	1987	36 000
Royal Ordnance Factories	1987	17 000
British Airports Authority	1987	7 000
British Steel	1988	53 000
Passenger Transport Executives	from 1988	8 000
Regional Water Authorities	1989	40 000
Girobank	1990	6 700
Area Electricity Boards and National Grid Company	1990	119 000
National Power and Powergen	1991	26 400
Scottish Power	1991	9 800
N. Ireland Electricity service	1993	5 000
British Rail including the former Railtrack and various rail companies	from 1995	–
British Coal	from 1994	15 000
British Energy	from 1996	
Air traffic control; PFI and PPP	from 1998–2004	

Source: Adapted from Kessler and Bayliss, 1998, p. 148, plus author's own addition

which, because of intense competition and a global situation where supply outstripped demand, resulted in serious overcapacity, particularly in the domestic market. The new integrated steel plants were under-producing and so could not take advantage of economies of scale in the production of sheet steel. This contributed to high production costs and low productivity. The result was a process of rationalisation which included the closure of uneconomic steel plants, manpower reductions and decentralisation of management functions, including industrial relations, to product divisions in 1989. Manpower reduction in the wake of the 1979–80 three-month national strike was dramatic, with 42 000 employees remaining in 1998. An IRS survey comments:

The company may be smaller now, but it is fitter: with a turnover of over £8 billion, British Steel is the UK's fourth largest exporter. Serving different marketplaces – and making everything from drinks cans to coating steels for cars to railway lines – British Steel has evolved into a complex, diversified firm. Investment in high-technology process equipment such as the continuous anneal and pickle line at Port Talbot is critical if the company is to remain competitive. (IRS, 1998)

Collective bargaining at company level has ended, with complete decentralisation of bargaining to the separate businesses.

The **water industry** comprised ten Regional Water Authorities (RWAs) and a National Water Council to regulate their activities as a result of the 1973 Water Act. Until the 1980s collective bargaining was conducted at multi-employer level, with well-established bargaining machinery and three negotiating bodies for manual production, craft and white-collar staff and one for senior managerial grades. The Water Act of 1983 limited the core activities of the RWAs to the supply of water and the treatment of sewage, and this eventually provided the RWAs with the opportunity to act like private companies in the run-up to privatisation in 1989. Thames Water was the first (and largest) RWA to break away from the industry-wide bargaining machinery in 1986, followed by Northumbrian Water (the smallest RWA) in 1988. By 1989, the whole industry-wide bargaining structure had collapsed and all the water companies conducted their own single-employer bargaining. A similar pattern emerged within the **electricity supply industry** which was privatised in 1990–1. The structure of the industry was established by the 1957 Electricity Act which set up 12 area boards and the Central Electricity Generating Board (CEGB), and prior to privatisation the national collective bargaining machinery remained intact. After privatisation national collective bargaining ceased, and the generating companies (PowerGen) and the regional distribution companies introduced their own bargaining arrangements, often excluding senior managerial grades.

Self-Evaluation Activity 6.10

Main changes influencing collective bargaining in the public sector

Response on website

Identify the main changes that have influenced the pattern and structure of collective bargaining within the public sector.

While the many changes that we have identified can be criticised for being ideologically motivated, it may be that the cumbersome, Whitley-inspired multi-employer bargaining machinery was no longer a suitable basis for determining the pay and conditions of an increasingly heterogeneous workforce. Indeed, Bailey (1997) in arguing in support of decentralised bargaining machinery suggests that

decentralisation could resurrect Whitleyism with regard to one of its original aims, 'namely that co-operation between employers and employees could be channelled towards making the changes required to make everyone better off, and rewarded accordingly, rather than shying away from change' (p. 136). Following Bailey's logic we might be tempted to conclude that the public services present us with a unique opportunity to preserve what is best of the 'old' Whitley system and incorporate this within the (now dominant) decentralised bargaining context, recognising that the demands being made on past practices suggest an increasingly fragile basis upon which to sustain national collective bargaining machinery. Whether this prospect leads to more or less coherence in public sector industrial relations remains to be seen. In truth the decentralisation of bargaining and other practices we have seen so far has caused greater fragmentation rather than coalescence of patterns of industrial relations, and this, according to Winchester and Bach (1995), is set to continue given the 'variations in organisational resources, management strategies and the individual and collective responses of employees' (p. 332).

NEW AND RECENT DEVELOPMENTS IN COLLECTIVE BARGAINING

As we have seen, collective bargaining takes place at different levels and agreements cover bargaining units of varying size. In addition, substantive and procedural issues subject to collective bargaining have widened, and in some organisations this may manifest itself in moves towards co-operative bargaining/integrative bargaining. The following are examples of recent developments in this area, and some of these will have been identified briefly in previous sections and chapters.

Single-union agreements

At both multi-employer and single-employer level, managements traditionally have negotiated with more than one union. At multi-employer (industry) level, an employers' federation may negotiate with a confederation of trade unions, as in the engineering industry, while at single-employer (company) level, managements may negotiate with representatives of each of the unions within their organisation (Ford UK and ICI, for example). At both multi-employer and single-employer levels, therefore, we have the classic multi-union situation. Multi-unionism is common in Britain and may be defined as **the process of concluding separate agreements with individual trade unions representing specific groups of employees differentiated by skill and/or occupation.** Multi-unionism in Britain has often been based on traditional skill or occupational demarcations and trade unions have fiercely defended their right to represent particular groups of employees. In the process of doing so they have, in the past, fostered intense inter-union rivalry in attempting to recruit employees sharing similar skill or occupational attributes (known as 'poaching'). The Bridlington Agreements (see Chapter 3) to some extent alleviated the problem. Multi-unionism also tended to encourage demarcation and demarcation disputes, particularly in the 'traditional' industries such as shipbuilding, which were costly to the employer. The sheer complexity of negotiating agreements with different unions (or bargaining agents) representing different groups of workers (or bargaining units), often at different times of the year, and the time-consuming nature of the exercise, resulted in some employers and unions attempting to simplify the entire process. In addition, technological change, employers' preference for greater flexible specialisation and multi-skilling, have eroded traditional skill and occupational demarcations and hence the rationale for multi-unionism. Employer responses to the problems created by multi-unionism range from outright derecognition of unions (difficult) to clarifying bargaining arrangements in the form of 'single-table' bargaining (see pp. 332–3). A more radical solution for employers would be to wipe the slate clean and start with one recognised bargaining agent for one company-wide bargaining unit and opt for a 'single-union agreement'.

A single-union agreement (SUA), whereby management formally recognises only one union for the purpose of collective bargaining for all or part of an organisation's employees, may be more appropriate for companies on greenfield rather than brownfield locations and would therefore favour inwardly-investing companies (see chapter 5). Indeed, during the 1980s when SUAs were introduced, their spread was confined largely to Japanese and some other foreign-owned companies. While there was a signi-

ficant increase in greenfield SUAs, their penetration into other areas of industry has been relatively limited, despite most of the larger unions having concluded such agreements. Recent developments in statutory union recognition (see Chapter 3) may rejuvenate the single-union agreement.

Self-Evaluation Activity 6.11

Advantages of and problems with single-union agreements

The response is given below

Describe some of the advantages of and problems with single union agreements.

Claimed advantages include:

- simplification of bargaining machinery for both parties;
- increase in employee commitment to the company's objectives and less resistance to change by the workforce, although this may also be due to specific employee involvement practices within such firms as Nissan (see Chapter 5);
- reduces the potential for conflict over demarcation;
- enables full-time union officials to acquire expertise and specialist knowledge of the company's operations; and
- having a SUA is better than having no union representation whatsoever and unions' acceptance of SUAs may well be a reflection of their weakened situation during the 1980s and 1990s.

Claimed disadvantages/problems include:

- workplace unionism is not truly independent and is more prone to management control where management sets the agenda for bargaining;
- a single union may not be the most appropriate for representing all grades of workers;
- the ability of the union to defend and promote members' interests is weakened where there are no effective sanctions for the union to impose; and
- introduction of SUAs may increase competition and conflict between unions concerning matters of recognition (the 'beauty contest' phenomenon), representation where other unions are representing employees to be covered by an SUA and recruitment where one other union has secured a recruitment base within the company but is not the one selected by the company for single-union representation.

SUAs may also contain other mutually agreed clauses or sub-agreements concerning pendulum arbitration, no-strike agreements and flexibility agreements which we will now briefly consider.

Pendulum arbitration (see also Chapter 4), also called final offer arbitration, is a method of determining the level of pay increase by an ACAS-appointed third party where there is disagreement between the parties. Unlike conventional arbitration, where the arbitrator makes an award after considering the merits of each case, arriving at a compromise figure between management's offer and the union's claim, under pendulum arbitration the arbitrator must decide upon either the claim or the final offer; there is no further negotiation and the settlement is binding upon both parties.

No-strike agreements incorporate the principle that during the course of negotiations and arbitration there is to be no recourse to industrial action. The union therefore eschews in advance the right to withdraw labour. However, because collective agreements in the UK are not legally binding, no-strike clauses within such agreements do not carry any legal force and so the effectiveness of these agreements depends upon the commitment of the parties to settle disputes by means other than industrial action.

Flexibility agreements concern the modification of traditional working practices, elimination of demarcations and the introduction of functional flexibility, flexible specialisation and multi-skilling (see Chapter 5).

Single-table bargaining, single status and partnership agreements

Single-table bargaining (STB) is the process whereby there is one set of negotiations between employer and recognised unions in a multi-union situation, covering most of an organisation's or an establishment's workforce (management grades are often excluded), including manual and non-manual employees. Pay and conditions for all eligible workers comprising the organisational bargaining unit are determined around the table in a single set of negotiations. Bargaining arrangements are harmonised, usually within a single-status context where all workers enjoy the same holiday, pension, sick leave and hours entitlements. There are fewer than 200 instances of STBs in Britain, but there are signs that STB is gradually increasing in popularity as the impetus towards single status gains momentum. In general, trade unions prefer STB to single-union agreements as they do not appear to pose a threat to unions' representational or recognition concerns. The claimed benefits of STB include the following:

- the bargaining process is made more cost- and time-effective;
- bargaining outcomes are achieved more efficiently;
- it facilitates workplace changes, particularly concerning working practices; demarcations are avoided and flexibility is enhanced; and
- opportunities are created for discussion concerning issues of strategic importance which go beyond negotiation of pay and conditions.

The problems of STB include:

- it may be inappropriate for organisations which retain status differences between manual and non-manual groups as separate negotiations would have to be pursued;
- it requires unions to present a united bargaining strategy, and this means reconciling differences between them, which in practice may be difficult to achieve;
- there is a problem of representation around the single table if there are several unions with varying sizes of membership: if representation is allocated on a pro-rata basis, then the largest union is likely to dominate negotiations; if representation is allocated equally irrespective of size of membership, then the larger unions may object to management giving undue attention to the concerns of the smaller unions;
- it should not be considered as a replacement for existing bargaining arrangements, as there are specific and parochial bargaining issues which may affect one union's membership only, but as the 'top tier' of the organisation's bargaining structure which provides the framework for negotiations concerning company-wide issues; and

- managements may not be able to reward specific groups of employees who, in the opinion of management, are making an above average contribution to the organisation's activities.

STB works most effectively within single-status organisations in which managers and all other employees share the same canteen, use the same car park, have equal entitlements to superannuation schemes and so on. Apart from making it easier for STB to operate, there are a number of reasons why an organisation should practise single status. Firstly, it is argued that status differences makes it difficult for management to get the most out of employees and for employees to be committed to the extent that management requires (Storey and Sisson, 1993). Secondly, it is often difficult, owing to technological change and other factors, to distinguish between manual and non-manual jobs, and related to this is the argument that technological changes may require new or revised working practices which straddle traditional occupational boundaries. Thirdly, Storey and Sisson point out that 'as the non-pay items increase in cost, management want greater returns from them . . . in the attempt to draw attention to the costs and benefits of these elements, employees are encouraged to choose between different combinations of non-pay benefits instead of taking them for granted (the so-called "cafeteria principle")' (p. 53). Fourthly, as all employees are supposed to contribute to client or customer satisfaction, there is the normative assumption that they should all enjoy good terms and conditions of employment. Throughout the 1980s and beyond there were moves to harmonise some of the terms and conditions within many organisations, but current examples of complete harmonisation are relatively limited. Perhaps the incremental approach adopted by some organisations is in response to problems in moving towards single status, which include cost to the employer and trade union opposition mainly from non-manual unions who are afraid that their members may lose out on certain advantages.

Single status for all employees is also sometimes part of a more wide-ranging partnership agreement which may also include mutually acceptable pay review formulas and 'co-operation between management and union(s) as an obligation within the partnership arrangements' (Farnham, 1998, p. 321). An examination of partnership and partnership agreements is provided in Chapter 8.

Technology agreements

The issue of technological change is central to the employment relationship, and the consequences of introducing new technology were considered in Chapter 5. These include negative effects such as the displacement and progressive deskilling of jobs and workers, resulting in unemployment. More positive effects include the opportunities for retraining and reskilling which the introduction of new technology provides and the removal of mundane tasks as a result of the introduction of robotics in manufacturing, as, for example, in the car industry. Technological change and its impact on production systems and working arrangements has inevitably incurred the wrath and opposition of trade unions representing workers who are directly affected by these changes and who have legitimate fears for their jobs and job losses generally, possible deskilling of jobs and enhanced management control over work processes. Collective bargaining and agreements should address these issues and the responsibilities of management in this area should be clearly understood by all parties to the change. As Gennard and Judge (1997) argue:

> The skill of the employee relations specialist lies in understanding these concerns and seeking ways of mitigating them. Personnel specialists should have a vested interest in the management of change, not just the imposition of change . . . The Rover New Deal is one example of a management seeking to take its employees with it when change is required. (p. 61)

Given management concern about the impact of technological change – and not all technological change has adverse consequences (Daniel, 1987) – it would seem appropriate for managements within unionised organisations to negotiate, in the spirit of co-operative bargaining, about issues arising from, and problems concerning, the whole process of change from its conception to its implementation. To this end, the TUC report *Employment and Technology* (1979) identifies negotiating guidelines for union representatives including: full involvement of unions before technological change is imposed; the establishment of joint arrangements between the parties to monitor the effects of technological changes; access to relevant information, including financial information and consultation with unions concerning company strategy and policy; and the training of all those affected by change. With regard to the last point the TUC (1998) argues that 'those employers that involve unions in training decisions are the most successful in managing change and that employees in unionised workplaces are more likely to receive training than those in non-unionised enterprises' (pp. 16–17).

The substantive content of a technology agreement clarifies the terms and arrangements to be introduced and includes:

- the distribution and sharing of savings generated by technological change amongst management and workforce (methods by which increases in productivity as a result of such change can be shared include higher pay and bonuses, revised working hours and shifts, and improved pensions and retirement conditions);
- how any redundancies are to be managed as a result of technological change;
- the extent of the impact of change upon terms and conditions of employment and upon health and safety;
- possibly a statement of management's commitment to avoiding compulsory redundancies; and
- the extent to which management information is to be revealed to employee representatives, and its nature.

Many technology agreements concentrate upon procedural aspects and issues such as:

- the extent to which retraining, re-grading and redeployment policies are required;
- arrangements for discussing problems caused by technological change;
- the extent to which existing procedures are affected by technological change concerning trade union recognition, discipline and grievance, health and safety, disputes and possibly equal opportunities procedures;
- training needs identified and acted upon, covering areas such as job training of employees and the employee representative role; and

- monitoring of change jointly by management and employee representatives and possibly by outside consultants.

Given the pace of technological change and management imperatives to improve employee productivity and efficiency by other non-technological means, it may be difficult to disentangle those areas attributable to technology alone and those brought about by a wide range of other related factors. Moreover, in view of the relative weakness of trade unions during the 1980s, 1990s and early 2000s, technology agreements may not deal adequately with the substantive issues governing the introduction of new technology.

Summary points

- Collective bargaining in the public sector, which comprises central government, the Civil Service, local authorities and public corporations, has been affected by changes in market-led government policies resulting in privatisation and contracting out of services.
- National or industry-wide bargaining continues as the most important level of collective pay determination, but there are some notable exceptions such as the Civil Service. Since the 1980s, the trend towards local autonomy in pay determination has accelerated, and within the Civil Service national pay machinery has been almost completely replaced by agency-based pay determination. Similar trends towards localisation of some elements of the pay package are evident within the NHS.
- National pay arrangements, although modified substantially, remain the main level of bargaining within the local authority context, and also, despite the inception of 'local management of schools' and PRP, within the teaching profession. However, the proposed introduction of PRP for teachers will, if adopted, introduce a significant element of local pay determination.
- Developments in collective bargaining over the past 20 years or so include the advent of single-union agreements, single-table bargaining, partnership agreements and technology agreements.

RELEVANT WEBSITES

www.acas.org.uk (Advisory, Conciliation and Arbitration Service) Good overall coverage including pay and bargaining issues.

www.cbi.org.uk (Confederation of British Industry) Coverage on pay-related matters for members.

www.incomesdata.co.uk (Incomes Data Services) Provides information on pay-related matters.

www.lowpay.gov.uk (Low Pay Unit) A useful site concerned with aspects of low pay, even though the Unit is no more.

www.lrd.org.uk (Labour Research Department) Provides information on all matters relating to bargaining and trade union matters (subscription only).

www.tuc.org.uk (Trades Union Congress) Comprehensive coverage including information on bargaining and pay.

REFERENCES

Bach, S. and Winchester, D. (2003) 'Industrial relations in the public sector', in Edwards, P. (ed.) *Industrial Relations Theory and Practice*, 2nd Edn. Oxford, Blackwell

Bailey, R. (1997) 'Public sector industrial relations', in Beardwell, I. (ed.) *Contemporary Industrial Relations: A Critical Analysis*. Oxford, Oxford University Press

Blyton, P. and Turnbull, P. (1998) *The Dynamics of Employee Relations*, 2nd edn. London, Macmillan

Brown, W., Marginson, P. and Walsh, J. (1995) 'Management: pay determination and collective bargaining', in Edwards, P. (ed.) *Industrial Relations: Theory and Practice in Britain*. Oxford, Blackwell

Brown, W., Marginson, P. and Walsh, J. (2003) 'The management of pay as the influence of collective bargaining diminishes', in Edwards, P. (ed.) *Industrial Relations Theory and Practice*, 2nd edn. Oxford, Blackwell

Burchill, F. (1992) *Labour Relations*. Basingstoke, Macmillan

Chamberlain, N.W. (1961) 'Determinants of collective bargaining structure', in Weber, A.R. (ed.) *The Structure of Collective Bargaining*. New York, The Free Press

Chamberlain, N.W. and Kuhn, J.W. (1965) *Collective Bargaining*. New York, McGraw-Hill

Clegg Report (1980) *Standing Commission on Pay Comparability Report No. 9, General Report*, Cmnd 7995. London, HMSO

Coates, K. and Topham, T. (1988) *Trade Unions in Britain*. London, Fontana

Cully, M., Woodland, S., O'Reilly, A. and Dix, G. (1998) *The 1998 Workplace Employee Relations Survey*. London, DTI

Cully, M., Woodland, S., O'Reilly, A. and Dix, G. (1999) *Britain at Work*. London, Routledge

Daniel, W.W. (1987) *Workplace Industrial Relations and Technical Change*. London, PSI

Donovan (1968) *Report of the Royal Commission on Trade Unions and Employers' Associations, 1965–1968*, Cmnd 3623. London, HMSO

Dubin, R. (1954) 'Constructive aspects of industrial conflict', in Kornhauser, A., Dubin, R. and Ross, A.M. (eds) *Industrial Conflict*. New York, McGraw-Hill

Dunlop, J.T. (1993) *Industrial Relations Systems*. Boston, Harvard Business School Press

Farnham, D. (1998) *Employee Relations in Context*. London, IPD

Farnham, D. and Pimlott, J. (1995) *Understanding Industrial Relations*. London, Cassell

Flanders, A. (1968) 'Collective bargaining: a theoretical analysis'. *British Journal of Industrial Relations*, 6, 1, 1–26

Flanders, A. (1970a) 'Collective bargaining: a theoretical analysis' (essay dated 1968), in Flanders, A. (ed.) *Management and Unions: The Theory and Reform of Industrial Relations*. London, Faber and Faber

Flanders, A. (1970b) 'Collective bargaining: prescription for change' (essay dated 1967), in Flanders, A. (ed.) *Management and Unions: The Theory and Reform of Industrial Relations*. London, Faber and Faber

Gennard, J. and Judge, G. (1997) *Employee Relations*. London, IPD

Gospel, H.F. and Palmer, G. (1993) *British Industrial Relations*. London, Routledge

Griffiths Report (1983) *NHS Management Inquiry: Report*. London, DHSS

Hicks, J. (1932) *The Theory of Wages*. London, Macmillan

Hill, C.W.L. and Pickering, J.F. (1986) 'Divisionalisation, decentralisation, and performance of large UK companies'. *Journal of Manpower Studies*, 22, 3, 34–45

Houghton, D. (1974) *Report of the Committee of Inquiry into the Pay of Non-University Teachers*, Cmnd 5848. London, HMSO

Hyman, R. (1980) 'Trade unions, control and resistance', in Esland, G. and Salaman, G. (eds) *The Politics of Work and Occupations*. Milton Keynes, Open University Press

Ibbs, R. (1988) *Improving Management in Government: The Next Steps*. London, HMSO

IRS (1998) 'British Steel survey'. *IRS Employment Trends*, No. 662

Jackson, M.P., Leopold, J.W. and Tuck, K. (1993) *Decentralisation of Collective Bargaining*. London, Macmillan

Kelly, J. (1998) *Rethinking Industrial Relations: Mobilisation, Collectivism and Long Waves*. London, Routledge

Kessler, I. (1989) 'Bargaining strategies in local government' in Mailly, R., Dimmock, S.J. and Sethi, A.S. (eds) *Industrial Relations in the Public Services*. London, Routledge

Kessler, I. (1991) 'Workplace industrial relations in local government'. *Employee Relations*, 13, 2, 1–31

Kessler, S. and Bayliss, F. (1995) *Contemporary British Industrial Relations*. London, Macmillan

Kessler, S. and Bayliss, F. (1998) *Contemporary British Industrial Relations*, 3rd edn. London, Macmillan

LMT (Labour Market Trends) (2002) 'Trade union membership: an analysis of the data from the autumn 2001 LFS'. *Labour Market Trends*, July, 343–55

Levinson, H.M. (1966) *Determining Forces in Collective Wage Bargaining*. New York, John Wiley

Makinson, J. (2000) *Incentives for Change: Rewarding Performance in National Government*. London, The Treasury

McCarthy, W. (1976) *Making Whitley Work*. London, HMSO

Megaw Report (1982) *Inquiry into Civil Service Pay: Report*, Cmnd 8590. London, HMSO

Millward, N., Bryson, D. and Forth, J. (2000) *All Change at Work?* London, Routledge

Priestly Report (1955) *Royal Commission on the Civil Service: Report*, Cmnd 9613. London, HMSO

Purcell, J. and Ahlstrand, B. (1989) 'Corporate strategy and the management of employee relations in the multidivisional company'. *British Journal of Industrial Relations*, 27, 3, 396–417

Rose, E. and Wright, G. (2003) 'Skill, control and satisfaction amongst call centre customer service representatives'. Research paper, School of Management, Liverpool John Moores University

Salamon, M. (1998) *Industrial Relations: Theory and Practice*. London, Prentice Hall

Salamon, M. (2003) 'Collective bargaining' in Hollinshead, G., Nichols, P. and Tailby, S. (eds) *Employee Relations*. Harlow, Financial Times/Prentice Hall

Storey, J. and Sisson, K. (1993) *Managing Human Resources and Industrial Relations*. Milton Keynes, Open University Press

Thornley, C. (1998) 'Contesting local pay: the decentralisation of collective bargaining in the NHS'. *British Journal of Industrial Relations*, 36, 3, 413–34

Thorpe, R. and Homan, G. (eds) (2000) *Strategic Reward Systems*. Harlow, Financial Times/Prentice Hall

TUC (1979) *Employment and Technology*. London, TUC

TUC (1998) *Partners for Progress: Next Steps for the New Unionism*. London, TUC

Walton, R.E. and McKersie, R.M. (1965) *A Behavioural Theory of Labour Negotiations*. New York, McGraw-Hill

Webb, S. and Webb, B. (1902) *Industrial Democracy*. London, Longman

Webb, S. and Webb, B. (1920) *The History of Trade Unionism, 1666–1920*. London, Longman

WERS (1998) See Cully, M. *et al.* (1998)

Whitley, J.H. (1918) *Relations Between Employees and Employed* Reports 1916–1918. London, HMSO

Winchester, D. and Bach, S. (1995) 'The state: the public sector', in Edwards, P. (ed.) *Industrial Relations: Theory and Practice in Britain*. Oxford, Blackwell

CHAPTER 7

UNION ABSENCE AND MARGINALISATION

INTRODUCTION

The extent of union derecognition (see Chapter 3) and the general decline in collectivised employment relations in recent years has drawn attention to the growing phenomenon of non-unionism which, until recently, had been neglected by industrial relations researchers and text-book authors – a notable exception of the latter being Blyton and Turnbull (1994 and 1998). It could be argued that the non-union phenomenon has always been with us, and even when trade union membership was at its height in 1979 almost half of the workforce was non-unionised. Perhaps, given the changing economic and political climate, a greater understanding of non-union organisations and workplaces is now even more necessary (Dundon, 2002; Colling, 2003). The focus of this chapter is on organisations, both small and large, which are totally non-union. There is no overall unified explanation which accounts for the growth in non-union organisations and much recent research reveals a complex of factors explaining the phenomenon. What is clear, however, is that organisational size is an important factor that determines employer strat-egies designed to exclude unions. Larger non-union companies, many of which are well-known, have well-developed strategies designed to avoid union recognition by providing their employees with working environments, pay and conditions superior to those of their unionised counterparts – the so-called union substitution effect. Employees within these organisations may therefore regard union membership as unnecessary.

While larger non-union companies may represent the 'acceptable' face of non-unionism – although there are prominent exceptions such as the certain fast food chain – the same cannot be said of smaller companies, many of whom, as we shall see, manifest the 'ugly' face of non-unionism. There are two important caveats to bear in mind, however. Firstly, we should be wary of making generalisations based on the limited amount of research available, although in some instances this may be unavoidable. Secondly, while we identify size as an important variable, it is contingent upon other factors such as technology, local and regional variations, the nature of the workforce such as gender and skill profiles, management ideology and product markets (Blyton and Turnbull, 1998).

We begin the chapter by looking at some of the approaches adopted in the study of non-unionism, and then consider the extent of non-unionism in Britain. We then go on to consider the reasons for the growth in non-unionism and employer strategies towards it, taking organisational size as an important but dependent variable. Small, medium and large firms and organisations are examined in some detail, taking into account some of the available research evidence. Finally, we consider some of the union substitution methods employed in larger non-unionised companies, with particular emphasis upon employee involvement and downward and upward communications.

Learning outcomes

When you have read chapter, you should be able to:

1. Understand the main approaches to the study of the non-union phenomenon.

2. Explain the extent of union absence.

3. Distinguish between different management styles and strategies in non-union organisations.

4. Appreciate the importance of organisational size as a major explanatory variable in association with other factors such as technology, product and labour markets and industry sector.

5. Describe the main union substitution methods adopted by many larger companies.

APPROACHES TO THE STUDY OF NON-UNIONISM

Kelly (1998) identifies four main, analytically distinct approaches to the study and evaluation of the growth of non-unionism. These approaches do not necessarily mutually exclude each other and may co-exist, as demonstrated in the researches of Guest and Hoque (1994), McLoughlin and Gourlay (1994) and Flood and Toner (1997). The first approach uses raw data generated by the Workplace Industrial Relations Surveys (WIRS) of 1980, 1984 and 1990, and the Workplace Employee Relations Survey (WERS) of 1998. In addition, information from the Labour Force Survey and the Inter Departmental Business Register provides valuable material relating to enterprises of all sizes. This method of analysis is useful in establishing certain correlations over time. For example, the data will reveal any correlates of concentration of non-unionism with size of enterprise, with age of enterprise and with the industrial sector in which the enterprise is located. Time series also indicate trends in relation to these three variables which, for example, enable comparisons to be made with previous surveys (Millward *et al.*, 1992; Millward, 1994; Millward *et al.*, 2000).

The second approach identified by Kelly (1998) comprises 'studies of managerial practices in non-union firms, and is premised on the idea that such practices play a critical role in keeping unions out' (p. 43). Usually, the examples chosen are the 'high

profile' ones of Marks & Spencer (Turnbull and Wass, 1998) and IBM (Dickson 1988), which look at the characteristics of the organisation as a whole. One difficulty with this case study-oriented approach is that it becomes difficult to generalise from the specifics of Marks & Spencer to other non-union organisations even within the same sector, such as the John Lewis Partnership. Allied to this approach is the survey method which attempts to elicit opinions of management, employees or both within a number of non-union firms (Guest and Hoque, 1994; Flood and Toner, 1997), ranging from small to medium-sized enterprises (SMEs) on 'greenfield' sites (Guest and Hoque) to large, non-union companies within electronics (Flood and Toner). This research is useful in that it purports to reveal certain consistent characteristics and attributes common to the companies surveyed and may even 'generate typologies based on the multiple dimensions of managerial behaviour' (Kelly, 1998, p. 43) such as Guest and Hoque's 'the Good, the Bad, and the Ugly'. More unusually, we have a few studies of enterprises within a specific geographical location which seek to compare and contrast a number of enterprises or subsidiaries, both unionised and non-unionised, across a range of characteristics such as ownership, type of employment relationship, dominant management style, pay determination, and so on. (Rose, 1996). As Rose points out, case study approaches have their limitations, one of the main ones being constraints upon the number of workplaces that can be examined owing to limited financial and other research resources, not to mention the time involved in producing in-depth analyses. This makes it very important to ensure that 'the cases chosen are appropriate for examining the theoretical and policy issues' relevant to the aims of the research (p. 71).

The third approach considers survey evidence on union recruitment both from the WIRS series the TUC (1998, 2002) and individual trade unions and from other academic sources such as Heery (1997) and Machin (2000). In this respect, Kelly (1998) argues:

> This research is useful in documenting just how few resources unions devote to recruitment and recognition, a fact which perhaps explains some of the failure to penetrate the growing ranks of non-unionism. On the other hand, we have no reliable, contemporary evidence on organising drives per se, on the way they come about, the issues involved and the responses of the workforce and of management . . . Consequently we know virtually nothing about the differences between successful and unsuccessful union campaigns. (p. 43)

The fourth approach identified by Kelly (1998) is that which is based upon employee attitude surveys using data from the Labour Force Survey, British Social Attitudes surveys and the Employment in Britain Survey, results of which often appear in *Labour Market Trends* (the monthly publication of the Office for National Statistics). WERS98 for the first time incorporated employees within the scope of the survey. This involved managers in each workplace reviewed distributing a short questionnaire to 25 randomly chosen employees, and if there were fewer than 25 employees in the workplace all employees were surveyed. In addition to these sources, there are, as Kelly calls them, 'one-off surveys' of national samples and other smaller-scale evidence from particular groups such as gender groups and young people. Gallie (1996), for example, looks at the relative importance of individual and structural factors in accounting for union membership levels together with the examination of the motives of those who have left trade unions.

A fifth approach not identified by Kelly is regional and area analyses of union decline. Given the theoretical and statistical analyses of union membership decline since 1979 (as considered in Chapter 3), it is somewhat surprising that the regional dimensions of this retreat of organised labour has not been greatly researched. Gallie *et al.* (1996), in examining the reasons for membership loss and the implications of this for workplace unionism and non-unionism, set their research in six different localities (Aberdeen, Coventry, Kircaldy, Northampton, Rochdale and Swindon):

> with the aim of studying both employers and the labour force. At the same time, it made it possible to assess arguments about the implications of different local labour market contexts for employment experience. The localities selected differed both in terms of their experiences of unemployment and of their history of industrial development. Both factors could have had important implications for the organisational strength of trade unions with the onset of severe recession in the 1980s. (p. 9)

Other industrial relations studies not focusing specifically upon non-unionism that have examined inter-regional differences in unionisation are few and far between, but include Knowles (1952), Phelps-Brown (1959) and Beaumont and Harris (1988). Perhaps the most rigorous analysis of union decline within a regional context is that of Martin *et al.* (1996). They argue that differences in employment structures across the British regions 'have long been a topic of recurring interest amongst geographers and regional economists [and where] a region's industrial mix has been seen as a key determinant of its economic and labour market characteristics' (p. 92). This line of reasoning suggests that (other things being equal) regional differences in unionisation should be closely correlated with regional differences in industrial composition. For example, regions with above-average proportions of their employment in industries which nationally are heavily unionised will have high overall union densities and recognition rates, and the converse will be evident for regions more reliant on industries which nationally are less unionised. Martin *et al.* support their analysis by referring to a wide variety of national and regional data sources.

THE EXTENT OF UNION ABSENCE AND REASONS FOR IT

In Chapter 3, we considered the extent of union derecognition and noted that there were significant increases in the derecognition process (Claydon, 1997; Gall and McKay, 1999, 2001; Machin, 2000; Brown *et al.*, 2001). Derecognition has undoubtedly contributed towards the increase in the proportion of all establishments with no union members at all. Millward *et al.* (1992) contend that: 'It is likely that some of this increase arose from compositional changes, but there are indicators elsewhere in the survey that some of it was where workplaces with low levels of density changed to having none' (p. 61). Results from WERS98 reveal a further increase in the number of workplaces with no union members from 36 per cent in 1990 to 47 per cent in 1998 which represents a 'substantial change' (Cully *et al.*, 1998), confirming the trend since 1984; this is incorporated in Table 7.1.

There is also a strong correlation between employee size of enterprise and rates of non-unionism – hence the smaller the enterprise the greater the rate of non-unionisation. Table 7.2 provides the picture. Moreover, there are also significant correlations for organisation size, similar to those of workplace size, while other variables such as public/private and industry sectors provide significant variations (see Table 7.3)

One significant development indicated by Table 7.2 is that the gap between non-unionisation rates by company size appears to be narrowing, with the medium to large establishments showing considerably higher rates of non-unionisation in 1998 than in 1984, while the non-unionisation rates for establishments of up to 99 employees have been

Table 7.1 Union absence for all employees: 1984, 1990, 1998

Proportion of establishments with no unions (%)		
1984	1990	1998
27	36	47

Source: Millward *et al.*, 1992; Cully *et al.*, 1998

Table 7.2 Non-unionism rates in private sector establishments by establishment size: 1984, 1990, 1998

Size of establishment	1984 %	1990 %	1998 %
25–49 employees	74	81	77
50–99 employees	70	75	73
100–199 employees	61	67	68
200–449 employees	53	51	62
500 or more employees	34	46.5	52

Source: Millward *et al.*, 1992; Cully *et al.*, 1998
Note: The category *500 or more employees* appears in WERS98 and WIRS (Millward *et al.*, 1992) and includes two categories of *500–999 employees* and *1000 or more employees*. In order to ensure comparability the percentages for both categories for 1984 and 1990 have been averaged.

Table 7.3 Union absence by sector including manual and non-manual employee categories: 1980, 1984, 1990

	1980 %	1984 %	1990 %
No union members among:			
Manual employees	36	32	42
Non-manual employees	45	42	49
All employees	27	27	36
No recognised unions present			
Private manufacturing	35	44	56
Private services	59	56	64
Public sector	6	1	13
All establishments	36	34	47
No recognised manual unions			
Private manufacturing	35	45	56
Private services	67	62	69
All establishments	52	45	38

Source: Millward *et al.*, 1992; McLaughlin and Gourlay, 1994, p. 12

relatively stable. This may be due to a variety of factors, one of which may be changing attitudes towards union membership on the part of managements. WERS98 includes associated surveys of managers in all workplaces concerning their attitudes towards union membership. Over one-third of employees do not belong to unions in the 29 per cent of workplaces where managements are in favour of union membership. In workplaces where managements have neutral attitudes towards union membership, union density is relatively low, and in the 17 per cent of workplaces where management are unfavourably disposed towards membership, union density is extremely low. It is arguably more appropriate to consider employee size of establishment and management attitudes of favourableness or unfavourableness towards unions as independent variables. Gallie (1996), for example, in the study cited earlier, comments that:

> It is notable that size made very little difference to membership levels where employers were pro-union. Where employers were favourable to unions, 87 per cent of employees in large establishments were members; however, this was also the case for 79 per cent of employees in the smallest size of establishment. It is mainly where the employers are unfavourable to unions that size of establishment had a clear independent effect, raising the proportion of members from 6 per cent in the small establishments to 35 per cent in the largest. (p. 151)

Another important variable to be taken into consideration together with employee size of establishments is the age of workplaces. Predictably, older workplaces are more likely than younger workplaces to recognise trade unions. According to Cully et al. (1998), '28 per cent of those [workplaces] at their current address for less than 10 years recognise trade unions, compared with 53 per cent which have been at their current address for 10 years or more' (p. 16). In addition, of all workplaces that are five or more years old, 14 per cent recorded a fall in the number of recognised unions, including 3 per cent which had completely derecognised unions. Millward et al. (1992) reveal, paradoxically, that in the 1990 survey the youngest workplaces in the survey had slightly higher union density levels than those in the five- to nine-year range and that 'this reveals something distinctive about workplaces that were established in the early part of the 1980s' (p. 63) but is quite possibly an aberration! However, in the newer workplaces of the 1990s, Millward et al. (2000) report that there was a 'greater propensity than in earlier periods for new private sector workplaces to have low membership levels or no members at all' (p. 86)

There are also significant differences in union absence rates, as we may expect, between the public and private sectors, and to a lesser extent between private manufacturing and services. Table 7.3 indicates the extent of non-unionism within these sectors while Table 7.4 provides data concerning the above variables and others for 1998 showing that the trends established in Table 7.3 have continued throughout the 1990s.

Table 7.3, therefore, confirms the trend away from unionisation within the private sector by indicating a significant increase in the proportion of non-union workplaces. The public services, however, remain fairly heavily unionised.

In considering the extent of union absence nationally, we can be guilty of making sweeping generalisations. It is, therefore, important to draw upon research which establishes whether there is a 'north/south divide' in the concentration of unionisation and union density which may give us some idea of the existence or otherwise of regional variations in patterns of non-unionisation. One approach, adopted by Martin et al. (1996), was to consider the question as 'to what extent the decline of British trade unionism since the end of the 1970s has erased the regional pattern of union organisation that has dominated the development of the union movement since the middle of the nineteenth century' (p. 81). Their research methods included a reworking of WIRS data and an analysis of the experience of individual unions by region. Their tables indicate the extent of union recognition and density by region for manual and non-manual workers, full and part-time workers. Table 7.5 is shown in adapted form to demonstrate the regional extent of non-recognition.

In 1980, the proportion of private sector manual workers in establishments not recognising unions was low almost everywhere except for the four southern regions of London, the outer South East, East Anglia and the South West. Non-recognition was highest in the outer South East and lowest in the two Midlands regions and the North. Although

Table 7.4 Union presence and absence rates by main classifications: 1998

	No union present %	Union present but no recognition %	Recognised union %
Workplace size			
25–49 employees	54	7	39
50–99 employees	48	11	41
100–199 employees	34	9	57
200–499 employees	23	10	67
500 or more employees	14	8	78
Organisation size			
Less than 100 employees	75	11	13
100–999 employees	60	11	29
1000–9999 employees	36	6	58
10 000 employees or more	21	7	73
Sector			
Private	64	11	25
Public	3	3	95
Organisational status			
Stand-alone workplace	70	11	19
Part of a wider organisation	38	7	54
Industry			
Manufacturing	60	10	30
Electricity, gas and water	2	0	98
Construction	55	8	37
Wholesale and retail	70	8	22
Hotels and restaurants	88	5	7
Transport and communications	41	7	52
Financial services	33	1	65
Other business services	74	7	19
Public administration	1	0	99
Education	5	9	86
Health	29	14	57
Other community services	51	8	45
All workplaces	47	8	45

Source: Cully *et al.*, 1999, p. 92

by 1990, non-recognition had risen throughout Britain, the relative differential between the southern and northern regions had widened substantially: the proportion of private sector manual employees working in establishments not recognising unions had risen to almost 60 per cent in the three southern regions, but remained below 40 per cent in the northern half of the country. A similar pattern also

Table 7.5 Union non-recognition (or absence) by region for manual and non-manual workers in the private sector: 1980–90

| | Percentage of employees in workplaces not recognising unions | | | | | |
| | 1980 | | 1984 | | 1990 | |
	Manual	Non-manual	Manual	Non-manual	Manual	Non-manual
London	24	45	32	60	59	71
Outer South East	30	56	41	57	57	64
East Anglia	18	32	50	61	59	53
South West	21	33	36	49	44	64
East Midlands	7	26	37	35	40	48
West Midlands	8	32	14	41	38	50
Yorks-Humberside	13	43	14	44	38	57
North West	11	31	15	33	36	45
North	8	28	15	35	35	46
Wales	14	27	27	28	31	58
Scotland	15	37	33	53	38	48

Source: Adapted from Martin *et al.*, 1996, using WIRS data

emerges for private sector non-manual workers. Non-recognition rates for this group are consistently higher than those for manual employees, but while a broad north/south pattern was discernible, it was much less clear-cut than for manual workers. Despite these trends, Martin *et al.* contend that northern regions still constitute 'union heartlands' and have displayed remarkable resilience in the face of general union membership decline. It is not surprising, therefore that non-unionism is more prevalent in the southern regions.

Within regions, there are local variations in degrees of unionisation and non-unionisation but these might be minimised by what Martin *et al.* (1996) describe as the regional externality effect. The argument here is that the union and industrial relations traditions of key groups of workers, firms and industries in a region are not self-contained but:

generate spillovers to other workers, firms and industries in the region through the course of time. . . . Hence the whole employment structure in the region becomes characterised by the forms of industrial relations systems, traditions and conventions found in the (once) leading or dominant sector(s), thus producing high (or low) levels of

union density, recognition, collective bargaining, shop steward representation, industrial militancy and community activity relative to the average levels found in these and other industries nationally. (p. 119)

The externality effect may be reproduced locally, which might explain union resilience in Rochdale, for example (Penn and Scattergood, 1996), and the lack of unionisation in new towns such as Milton Keynes and other areas of recent industrial growth. Bassett (1988), for example, found that approximately 80 per cent of companies based in Milton Keynes were non-union.

The characteristics and composition of the workforce may indicate the extent of non-unionisation, in that non-unionised firms are more likely to employ female workers, part-time workers and fewer manual workers than unionised firms (Millward *et al.*, 1992). Low paid employment is also a characteristic of non-union firms, but not exclusively so. The Low Pay Commission report (LPC, 1998), for example, points out that:

Certain groups of workers are much more likely to be low paid than others; these include women (particularly those who work part-time) as well as young, ethnic minority and disabled workers. Temporary workers and male part-time workers are also more likely to experience low pay. . . . Several of the lowest-paying business sectors – for example the retail and wholesale trades, and hotels and restaurants – have very low union representation. These industries employ a significant number of part-time or seasonal employees, frequently women and young people who for a number of reasons are less likely to become union members. (pp. 15–16)

Moreover, the pattern of low pay in smaller businesses in the retail and social care sectors demonstrates a trend within industry generally: a clear link between the incidence of low pay and size of business. Although many small businesses pay higher wages, small firms generally pay lower wages than large firms. This is partly influenced by the greater concentration of small firms in lower paying sectors. Evidence from the WERS98 survey indicates that 17 per cent of all workplaces surveyed had between 10 per cent and over 25 per cent of their employees earning below £3.50 an hour. The survey also confirms that low pay is 'overwhelmingly a private sector phenomenon' (Cully *et al.*, 1998, p. 24), but within the private sector, low pay is concentrated in the hotels and restaurants sector (48 per cent of workplaces with 25 employees or more), health and community services (36 per cent), 'other business services' (10 per cent) and wholesale and retail (8 per cent). Workplaces of 25 and over employees were 'much less likely than workplaces without union members to have a quarter or more of the workforce earning below £3.50 per hour' (ibid., p. 25).

A note concerning small businesses

According to a national DTI survey (2002), small businesses (defined by the DTI as employing 0–50 employees) including those without employees, accounted for 99 per cent of private sector businesses, 44 per cent of non-government employment and 37 per cent of turnover. Most of the moderate growth in the small business population between 1995 and 2001 has been in the number of 'micro' businesses employing fewer than ten people and in the number of one-person companies. Small busi-

nesses in terms of share of employment are well represented in most industry sectors with only finance and mining sectors well below 25 per cent; agriculture, fishing, construction and other services have shares well above 50 per cent. Other relevant sectors include manufacturing (above 25 per cent) and hotels and restaurants (above 40 per cent). For the first time, WERS98 incorporated data from very small workplaces with between ten and 24 employees and define small businesses as 'stand-alone private sector workplaces with fewer than 100 employees' (ibid., p. 26). The following characteristics were identified by analysing data from 250 workplaces:

- Over half of the small businesses are family run and 43 per cent have a full-time owner-manager on site.
- The typical small business is characterised by relative informality of the employment relationship; few new management practices and employee involvement schemes are in place; procedures are less formal than in larger establishments and relatively few had joint consultative committees.
- Just over 20 per cent had some employees who were union members, and only 10 per cent recognised trade unions but rarely had union representatives or other employee representatives.
- 'Taking this in tandem with the relative lack of formal mechanisms for indirectly or directly consulting with the workforce, it might be thought that the opportunity for employees in small businesses to give voice to their concerns is slight. Though that might be the case, employees were no more or less likely to rate managers as poor or very poor in consulting them about workplace changes' (ibid., p. 27).
- 'The indicators of a healthy employment relationship are mixed. Employees in small businesses had relatively high levels of job satisfaction, but at the same time they were more likely to find themselves low paid and industrial tribunal applications were relatively high' (ibid., p. 27).

The extent to which it is assumed that the small non-union firm is characterised by harmonious relationships is, therefore, at least partly erroneous as the WERS98 findings imply. Furthermore, as Blyton and Turnbull (1994) suggest, 'the appearance of industrial harmony begins to appear somewhat suspect once the reality of [authority] relations between employer and employee within small non-union firms are analysed more closely' (p. 247). However, the 'happy family' cliché does, of course, have a literal connotation as indicated above with over 50 per cent of the WERS98 sample being family run. Research cited by Blyton and Turnbull suggests that at best close affective ties between bosses and workers in many cases is mere tokenism and that more often than not conflicts simmer below the surface only to be revealed when change threatens these relationships. An example of this type of dysfunctional relationship revealed by Scott *et al.* (1989) and referred to by Blyton and Turnbull indicates that:

> Even the 'happy family' owner/manager will change his tune when confronted by external pressures or internal dissent. Scott et al. (1989), for example, refer to one manager who boasted of his caring, paternalistic approach which he illustrated by reference to two older workers allowed to stay on at the firm beyond their retirement age. At a subsequent interview, however, these two workers were referred to in less than affectionate terms. In the interim period, profits had fallen and the company had gone into the red for the first time. The result had been redundancies, including the two older workers who were now referred to in terms of 'getting rid of the shit'. (p. 248)

Another example which exposes the hypocrisy of the 'happy family' is the small hotel workplace. The 'family' of waiters and head waiter is governed by the whims of the latter in a work situation characterised by low pay and high staff turnover. A waiter is particularly vulnerable to the power of his head waiter not only because a head waiter has control over hiring and firing, but also because he is able to provide and withdraw support for subordinates. 'Keeping in' with head waiters is, therefore an important part of the work relationship. In a classic study of hotel pilferage and fiddles, Mars (1973) comments:

> Head Waiters vary as to their 'hardness' or 'softness'. A 'hard' Head Waiter asks for and obtains an accepted upper maximum of 50 per cent of fiddles; a 'soft' Head Waiter may receive much less. In return for his kickback, a Head Waiter is expected to allocate chance punters, provide services facilitating fiddles and 'cover' any waiter if things go wrong, that is, he must use his office to defend subordinates against higher management. In one instance, the Head Waiter was dissatisfied with his kickback from one waiter who was promptly told to 'sod off' and dismissed. (p. 206)

Self-Evaluation Activity 7.1

The employment relationship in small, non-unionised businesses
Response on website

Summarise the main characteristics of the employment relationship in small, non-unionised businesses. (For more recent research, see below.)

Reasons for the extent of non-unionisation

Self-Evaluation Activity 7.2

Factors discouraging trade union membership
The response is provided below

Many of the factors which discourage trade union membership and which account for the national decline in membership and density of unionisation have been dealt with in a number of chapters under different headings (Chapters 3, 4, 5 and 6). Identify as many of these factors as you can and compare your list with the headings which appear below.

Given that it is sometimes difficult to distinguish between cause and effect, throughout this book so far we have identified major changes affecting Britain's industrial relations system. Many of these changes have taken place since 1979 and have been documented by the WIRS surveys. Working from the general to the more specific, the following factors, taken together are likely to account for most of the increase in non-unionism from 1979–98:

1. *Fundamental changes during the 1980s and 1990s*
   - Political and economic changes incorporating the shift towards free market economics and a

rejection of Keynesian economics and 'corporatism' created the appropriate climate in which small enterprises could flourish.

- The move away from a generalised ideology of 'collectivism' to one which emphasises individualist attitudes and values.
- Government labour market policy based on the Hayekian premise that trade unions are a hindrance to the efficient functioning of the labour market together with government pronouncements that 'good' working relationships are facilitated in small (non-union) companies (see Chapter 5).
- Legal reforms which have sought to make it more difficult for unions to pursue their collective activities by imposing restrictions upon the exercise of industrial action, by requiring changes to the 'check-off' system making it more difficult for unions to retain membership and by ending the 'statutory supports and political encouragement for the extension of collective bargaining' (McLoughlin and Gourlay, 1994). For a further discussion of these issues, see Chapters 4 and 6.

2. *Trade union membership and density*

The decline in trade union membership and density since 1979 would seem to indicate a decline in collective industrial relations (McLoughlin and Gourlay, 1994) and therefore an increase in non-unionism. Whether this decline is terminal or just part of the downswing in the 'long wave' cycle is debatable, and mobilisation theory in any event suggests a less pessimistic scenario for the future of collectivism (Kelly, 1998). What is certain is that there has been an increase in the number of non-union workplaces revealed by the empirical evidence which we have already considered in this chapter. Our discussion in Chapter 3 looks at decline in union membership and density in greater detail.

3. *Union substitution and derecognition*

The extent and pace of union derecognition, again documented by the various workplace surveys such as WERS and other research by Gall and McKay (1994, 1999, 2001), Brown *et al.* (2001) and Claydon (1997), would tend to have the predictable effect of increasing the proportion of firms and workplaces with no recognised trade unions for the purposes of collective bargaining. In addition to the decline in recognition, we should also consider the willingness or reluctance of existing non-union firms and recently

formed establishments to grant recognition. Gall and McKay (1999) do, however, declare that 'the previous pattern of cases of derecognition exceeding those of new recognition agreements has now been reversed' (p. 602). The recognition proposals within the Employment Relations Act 1999 (ERA99) now provide an opportunity for union members to secure union recognition through statutory means and there is evidence that the number of new recognitions is on the increase (Gall and McKay, 2001). In any event, the evidence to date suggests that new establishments and workplaces are considerably less likely to recognise unions than older establishments (Millward *et al.*, 1992, 2000; Cully *et al.*, 1998). For a more detailed discussion of the recognition/ derecognition issue, see Chapter 3.

4. *Recent trends in collective bargaining*

We have examined the recent and ongoing trends and developments in collective bargaining in Chapter 6. In that chapter we noted that there had been a decline in the number and proportion of employees covered by bargaining arrangements and machinery during the 1980s and 1990s, so much so that by 1990 a minority of employees in the private sector had their pay and conditions determined by such arrangements (Millward *et al.*, 1992). In fact, according to Brown (1993) and Milner (1995), collective bargaining now covers a substantial minority of the workforce as a whole (47 per cent). We also looked at the trend towards decentralisation of collective bargaining from multi-employer to single-employer arrangements. It has been argued that the decentralisation trend is indicative of a 'dominant de-collectivist policy' on the part of employers (Smith and Morton, 1993). Kelly (1998) also contends that the evidence concerning employer attempts to bypass or marginalise trade unions and unilaterally to impose new terms and conditions of employment, together with the questioning of the continued relevance of collective bargaining by the CBI, 'demonstrates a wide-ranging hostility to union presence, activity and organisation on the part of employers and suggests that the scale and intensity of such hostility gathered pace in the late 1980s and early 1990s' (p. 63). This argument, however, is not conclusive as we may attribute mixed motives on the part of employers for decentralising collective bargaining (Marchington and Parker, 1990; Jackson *et al.*, 1993). There is also evidence that companies in which unions are recognised for the purposes of collective bargaining have reduced the range of issues subject to bargaining (the move towards 'conjunctive' bargaining as noted in Chapter 6) and that this could be the start of a process towards marginalisation of bargaining and, ultimately, de-recognition. That the decline in collective bargaining remains an ongoing phenomenon is underlined by the WERS finding that 'the proportion of workplaces where bargaining was the dominant mode of pay determination fell in all sectors of the economy' (Millward *et al.*, 2000 pp. 196–7).

5. *Employer motivation*

Employers may be motivated to de-unionise not only as a response to the structural and institutional changes referred to above, but also if they perceive that non-union firms perform better than unionised firms in relation to certain outcomes such as labour productivity, investment and general economic per-formance. If this perception on the part of employers is supported by evidence, then employers will have a greater incentive to derecognise. However, much of the academic research in this area either contradicts these assumptions or is ambivalent. Economists at Harvard, for example, have sought to demonstrate that American trade unions have been good for pro-ductivity in that they may 'shock' management into adopting 'best practice' techniques in the organisa-tion of production (Freeman and Medoff, 1984). Unions can provide channels of communication and methods of conflict resolution which encourage co-operation with management over technological change and the organisation of work itself and this, in turn, will 'encourage more effective implementa-tion and operation of new technologies and working methods' (McLoughlin and Gourlay, 1994, p. 18). Moreover, unions may also contribute to increased employee morale (Freeman and Medoff, 1984) and employee perceptions of fairness (Millward *et al.*, 2000). A main conclusion of the Harvard studies is that 'unionism per se is neither a plus nor a minus to productivity. What matters is how unions and man-agement interact at the workplace' (Freeman and Medoff, 1984, p. 179, cited in Nolan and O'Donnell, 1995). Some of the empirical evidence (for example, Gregg and Yates, 1991) is assessed by Nolan and O'Donnell and the results are somewhat contradictory. On the one hand, during the 1980s, and particularly for the period 1985–9, unionised firms are said to have outperformed non-unionised firms, but also 'there is further evidence that the process of union derecognition gave a further fillip to productivity' (p. 421). Nolan and O'Donnell add:

> Presumably the authors [Gregg and Yates] would argue that the growth of productivity will be higher in unionised firms because there is more scope for improvement. But that was also the implication of the results of the earlier studies for the first half of the decade. In short, we are asked to accept that throughout the entire duration of Thatcherism, non-union firms performed less well on average than their unionised counterparts. (p. 421)

If there is a productivity advantage in non-union firms, it may not necessarily be due to an absence of unions but to the quality of management's approach to employees and the firm as a whole. However, pro-ductivity advantages in unionised firms may well depend upon the nature and quality of the union's interaction with management (Metcalfe, 1989).

6. *Injustice at work*

One possible, but not particularly credible, explana-tion for the rise of non-unionism 'is that fewer and fewer employees experience work-related injustices that are sufficiently serious to encourage unionisa-tion' (Kelly, 1998). Kelly uses evidence of the num-ber of workplace related complaints reported to the Citizens' Advice Bureau from 1983–97 to argue that there has been a significant upward trend, with the number of grievances almost doubling by 1997. The Low Pay Commission reveals widespread dissatis-faction with pay levels, and the TUC's 'Bad Bosses Hotline' reveals a rich variety of employer instigated injustices across the board, but mainly within smaller private sector firms (see Chapter 10). It may be that the existence of grievances per se do not necessarily encourage workers to become trade union members and Kelly contends:

> As mobilisation theorists argue, grievances are necessary but not sufficient for employees to become collectivised. What is also essential is that workers blame the employer or manage-ment for their problems; after all, if aggrieved employees believed they could resolve their problems through discussion with management, then their incentive to unionise would be dimin-ished correspondingly. (p. 45)

Further evidence from British Social Attitudes surveys reveals a steady deterioration in workers' opinions of the quality of management and of the employment relationship, and Kelly therefore concludes that:

> *Taken as a whole this evidence suggests that we cannot account for declining unionisation in Britain by reference to improvements in worker attitudes to, and trust in, management. The growing mistrust of management is potentially good news for trade unions because it implies that recruitment literature focused on managerial deficiencies is likely to fall on receptive ears. Yet even if this point were to be accepted, it does not necessarily follow that employees will join unions.* (p. 48)

Summary points

- Approaches identified to the study of non-unionism include:
  - studies using raw data generated by various workplace and labour force surveys;
  - studies of managerial practices in non-union firms;
  - examination of union recruitment and recognition;
  - attitude surveys; and
  - regional and area analysis of union decline.
- There has been a steady increase in the number of workplaces with no union members since 1984, but there are variations depending upon size and age of establishment, public and private sectors, regional and local variations, and characteristics and composition of the workforce.
- Small, non-unionised enterprises are characterised by the degree of informality within the employment relationship.
- Reasons for the extent of non-unionism include:
  - fundamental political and economic changes during the 1980s and 1990s;
  - changes in trade union membership and density;
  - union substitution and derecognition;
  - recent trends in collective bargaining;
  - employer motivation; and
  - injustice at work.

EMPLOYER AND MANAGEMENT STRATEGIES AND STYLES

Non-union firms obviously do not constitute one homogeneous category. In terms of size they range from the very small family firm to the large multinational company. They also differ by product and service market, industry sector, 'high or low technology', employment characteristics and organisational structure. Non-union firms are, therefore, extremely diverse in these respects and this makes generalisation difficult, if not impossible. After much deliberation, the size variable was selected in order to identify the nature of any common characteristic that could be determined by size alone, such as the degree of formality within the employment relationship and all that this entails. Most importantly, organisational size can, to a large extent, be a determinant of management style although this is not always the case (for example, 'paternalism' is a characteristic style in some larger organisations as well as many smaller ones). As we have seen (Chapter 2), management styles of industrial relations vary considerably between organisations and also within organisations over time. We have also discussed the nature and role of HRM (Chapters 2 and 5) and whether it acts as a form of 'union substitution' by providing employees with opportunities to communicate directly with management, make individual decisions about pay, and involve themselves generally in the activities of the organisation without requiring the services of trade unions. Less sophisticated methods such as 'outright opposition might also come to the fore in attempts to avoid unionisation' (McLoughlin and Gourlay, 1994, p. 23).

Self-Evaluation Activity 7.3
Review excercise
This SEA has no commentary

As a review exercise, refer back to Chapters 2 and 5 in order to identify the appropriate management styles and ideologies together with the main arguments concerning the relationship between HRM and industrial relations.

We now examine three size categories of firm (small, medium and large) and describe research findings in relation to each.

Strategy and style in small firms

Research dealing with industrial relations in small firms is relatively limited, partly because the employment relationship has been assumed to be non-problematic on the grounds that harmony prevails (Scase, 2003). We have, however, made certain generalisations about small firms in the previous section in relation both to the extent of non-unionisation and to the limited research available concerning employment characteristics such as low pay, gender composition and degrees of informality within the employment relationship. In concentrating upon strategy and employee relations style, we now need to draw upon a few studies, such as that of Rainnie (1989), which deal with industrial relations in both unionised and non-unionised firms under the assumption that, for small firms at least, observations concerning strategy and style are appropriate to both categories. Rainnie provides a fourfold classification of small firms based upon their market context and the relationship between them and larger firms.

1. *Dependent firms*
   These are firms which have close relationships with larger enterprises upon whose economic success they depend. The dependency relationship often takes the form of subcontracting as in manufacturing, and licensing and franchising as in retailing. Subcontracting requires the larger firm to stipulate certain standards of quality and quantity of output within a strict, but negotiated, price regime and this will have cost implications for the smaller firm with regard to wages and other financial or fringe benefits, which in turn impact upon the employment relationship.

2. *Dominated firms*
   These firms, many of which operate within the retailing sector, compete against larger organisations by having lower operating costs in order to survive. Hence, they tend to be highly exploitative of their workforces by offering low rates of pay and poorer working conditions. They attract and usually demand, unskilled labour, hired on short-term contracts, usually on a part-time and temporary basis. Employees' bargaining position is usually weak or non-existent, and trade unions are normally not recognised. The nature of the employment relationship ranges from 'harmoni-

ous' (probably affecting only a small minority of firms) to subservient and fear inducing.

3. *Isolated firms*
   These are businesses trading in markets which larger firms have avoided for reasons mainly to do with long-term growth and profitability. Their business is normally local and of a specialist nature and, in order to compete effectively, their costs must be kept low. Main areas of business activity include leisure, hotel and catering sectors in which there are a very large number of isolated businesses. Survival means offering low prices to consumers and low wages to employees. Again there is a tendency to employ staff on a short-term and/or part-time basis; skill requirements are low or non-existent.

4. *Innovative firms*
   These businesses are to be found in 'high risk' areas and have a commitment to develop new products and services. Scase (2003) comments:

   > These are the enterprises that are given the greatest prominence in political debate and it is these which are seen to offer 'solutions' to macroeconomic problems ranging from unemployment to lack of industrial innovation and modernisation. They are viewed as capable of overcoming the so-called problems of large-scale enterprises because of their allegedly greater potential to respond to changing customer needs. In the 1980s, such small businesses were portrayed as the 'key' to Britain's economic rejuvenation when large sectors of manufacturing had been destroyed by a variety of global and national economic and political processes. (p. 475)

A minority of these firms exist independently and have established gaps and niches in the market for developing new products and services based on scientific, engineering and high technology specialisms. Many other enterprises, however, have close links with other larger concerns with whom they share licensing and funding arrangements, and to a certain extent are dependent upon them. In the latter case, the products and services developed by the innovative firm would be too expensive or unimportant for larger firms to pursue. Many larger firms benefit from the innovative firms' product developments should they have commercial potential and viability.

Before dealing specifically with employer strategy and style it is important to note that Scase (2003) makes a further distinction between 'high' and 'low' skill firms since each has distinctive patterns of employer–employee relations. High skill firms have been relatively under-researched, the main focus for industrial relations research being on low skill firms and the employment characteristics of low pay and other related factors. High skill firms tend to operate in areas such as pharmaceuticals, bioscience, computer software and electronics. Employees in these firms tend to be graduates 'who see themselves as relatively mobile within national and international labour markets and who often prefer a high level of working autonomy . . . [and exhibit] particularistic and protective professional cultures' (p. 593). All this differs markedly with the employment relationship existing within low skill firms. A number of categories of low skill firms based upon 'the nature of proprietorial roles' can be identified, each having its own particular pattern of employment relationship (Scase and Goffee, 1982) which we now briefly consider.

The **self-employed** category according the 2002 DTI small business survey makes up the largest proportion of small firm owners, they formally employ no labour and have no formal employment relations. They may constitute family-run businesses in the literal sense where work and domestic roles are intertwined (family businesses such as newsagents and fish and chip shops are examples).

Small employers constitute the second category identified by Scase and Goffee. Here, the employment relationship is more formal and yet the employer role is ambiguous and contradictory. On the one hand, employers often work alongside their employees which encourages interpersonal and face-to-face interaction, sometimes with adverse consequences (as noted in the previous section), while on the other, they act as employers and exercise their prerogatives as employers. In such situations 'there are often severe constraints to rational decision making and, potentially, there are tensions and interpersonal frictions associated with the exercise of proprietorial authority' (Scase and Goffee, 1982, p. 582). Occasionally, local community relations impinge upon work relationships. In a classic study of small firms in the waterproof garment-making industry which was located in the Manchester–Salford area, Cunnison (1966) states:

> The social organisation of waterproof garment production has demonstrated that workers, managers and employers were connected by common membership in a number of different systems of social relations which were localised in the same area: the industry was localised; kinship and affinity networks were localised; residence was localised; the Jewish community was localised. The systems thus overlapped one another in a number of different activities and interests other than work. . . . The economic relation between worker and employer in the work situation is [therefore] ambivalent, compounded both of conflicting and of common interests. . . . Thus when a dispute over some aspect of work occurred between an individual worker and his manager, interests and values from these other relationships might be drawn in, some of them stressing the common positions and interests of the two. Moreover, the attitude of other workers not personally involved in the dispute was liable to be influenced by their various and sometimes common interests with regard to the manager. Though such considerations did not necessarily modify the strength of the conflict, they did affect the way it was expressed, making it unlikely that workers would become involved in one another's disputes, and likely that such disputes would be conducted as particular, individual and situational issues. (p. 34)

Owner-controllers' source of authority lies in their personal management and financial expertise and not skills based on trades or crafts. They do not work alongside their employees and, being more responsible for the management and administration of their firms, 'they must devote more attention to the explicit development of employer-employee relations and with this, mechanisms of supervisory control' (Scase, 2003, p. 479). Tighter and more formal control systems and less informal relationships often create problems in the securing of employee commitment.

Owner-directors manage and control larger enterprises through the implementation of formalised management structures which determine the extent to which management functions are delegated to other managers. There will be considerable variation in employment relationship practices, ranging from the relatively formal with, for example, formal procedures in operation, to the relatively fluid, more personal relationships characteristic of the previous owner controller example.

Strategy and style

Scase identifies three types of personal-based strategies/styles whereby 'small business owners are able to obtain, or command the allegiance of their staff' (ibid., p. 584). These are termed paternalism, fraternalism and autocratic, and each is characterised by particular patterns of employer–employee relations governing work practices and rewards. We now consider each of these in more detail.

Paternalism

Self-Evaluation Activity 7.4
Attributes of the paternalist style
This SEA has no commentary

As a review exercise, identify the main attributes of the paternalist management style (see Chapter 2).

Paternalism as a management style is not confined to small firms. Variations of paternalism exist in large organisations such as Marks & Spencer and are more commonly referred to as 'neo-paternalism'. In relation to small firms, paternalism is characterised by employers' attempts to secure employee commitment through informal and interpersonal means. In some cases, the employee is assumed to be subservient and deferential to the employer. Scase (2003) argues that paternalistic strategies may be more commonly exercised in firms where 'there is relatively stable (and predictable) demand for their goods and where employees, for reasons ranging from the quality of their skills to geographical location, are unable to shift from one employer to another' (p. 585). Employees who possess particular skills essential to the firm's activities are more likely to be hired on a long-term basis and are often seen as relatively indispensable to the employer.

This can lead to a mutually reciprocal employment relationship which often extends beyond the workplace, with high levels of trust vested in the employee and a joint recognition of each other's obligations and responsibilities. This can be 'expressed in flexible working hours, employee use of employer resources (vehicles and equipment, and employer involvement in employees, personal welfare). In return, employees are expected to reciprocate through constantly giving priority to the interests of their employers, being "on call" to respond to emergencies and unexpected customer demands' (ibid., p. 586). This type of paternalism is commonly found in craft-based manufacturing and in much of the hotel and catering sector.

Instrumentalism and fraternalism
Scase (1995) points out that other firms operating in less stable market environments, and where demand for the product or service fluctuates and is relatively unpredictable, may require many relatively skilled employees whose skills, because of the nature of the work and product market, are highly transferable to other enterprises and not specific to the needs of the firm (these skills are termed universalistic). Paternalism under such circumstances 'becomes an inappropriate owner-manager strategy, since the relationship with employees will not be long term. Accordingly, there is less emphasis upon the need to establish more permanent relations of reciprocity and high trust' (p. 586). Employers, therefore, may adopt one of two strategies:

- The first, less commonly adopted strategy may be called instrumental or calculative, an approach intended to secure employee commitment by offering relatively high financial rewards. This strategy may not make much business sense as high wage costs may threaten the economic viability of the firm and may encourage operating inefficiencies.
- The second, more commonly adopted approach is termed fraternalism which is now examined in greater detail.

Fraternalism is both a strategy and a style which the owner-manager adopts, emphasising the need to identify with employees by, for example, working alongside them and developing interpersonal relationships. Employers attempt to demonstrate that by working at the same level of output as their employees 'they are not exploiting their staff for profit [and that] they can often pay themselves a similar level of wages (and) by giving employees a share in year-end profits identification with employees is reinforced' (ibid., p. 589). A further means of reinforcing strong identity with employees is by emphasising the importance of teamwork. Very often, the fact that some employers have previously been employees themselves will tend to emphasise the high degree of mutual understanding of work processes and the difficulties and constraints which workers often face in the accomplishment of their tasks. As Scase (1995) points out:

> It is these former self-employed workers who, if they become small employers, respond to the bargaining capacity of their employees by adopting fraternal strategies. This may be the only means whereby they can manage their staff and as such, this can inhibit further business growth since this would require them to withdraw from controlling their workers through their own day-to-day productive activities, that is by working alongside them. (p. 588)

Fraternalist employment relationships are, therefore, more likely to be found in those sectors where it is easier for employees to start their own businesses, where the costs of business start-ups is low and the amount of capital investment is minimised and where the ratio of labour to capital is correspondingly high. The traditional craft sectors such as painting, decorating, carpentry, hairdressing, pottery and interior design offer such opportunities. The building industry, characterised by 'highly fluctuating and unstable conditions of employment' (ibid., p. 588) is probably the best example, however:

> Here, workers are constantly shifting from one employer to another and such experiences of personal mobility interspersed by periods of unemployment, are likely, often by chance, to lead to many workers setting up businesses on a self-employed basis and then, because of customer demands for their work, to find themselves employing staff. (p. 588)

Cunnison (1966) describes a similar situation amongst her sample of waterproof garment workers where:

> Traditionally there has been considerable mobility within the industry, workers moving from one firm to another in search of employment, and this practice has had the effect of linking workers together in a unity wider than the single firm. [However,] competition between individual firms is intense, and in the short period, especially in slack times, the interests of workers and employers tend to draw together, whereas those of different firms diverge sharply. Moreover, the economic gap between worker and employer is small: it is fairly easy for a worker to become a boss. (pp. 6–7)

Autocratic styles

The market situation of employees which governs pay, skill levels, the extent to which labour can be substituted for other labour, together with supply and demand for that labour, in addition to other factors concerning the firm, such as the extent to which demand for its products or services fluctuates within a competitive market, will determine whether employers adopt either fraternal strategies or more autocratic styles. The reasons why employers may opt for autocratic styles within the employment relationship include the following:

- Low skill requirements of employers and the consequent absence of skills of employees make the latter highly vulnerable to the stipulations and commands of the former.
- In the absence of any trade unions, employees are unable to bargain with their employers and as a result employees endure low rates of pay and poor work and employment conditions as exist, for example, in clothing and textiles, many hotel and catering establishments and in retailing.
- 'Employees have low substitute value and, being readily expendable by their small business owners, they are compelled to accept the employment relation as this is determined by their employers' (Scase, 1995, p. 589).

Employers, according to Rainnie (1989), tend to legitimise autocratic styles by claiming that low levels of pay are outside their own personal control owing to the competitive pressures within certain industries, such as sections of the printing and clothing industries. Employees, therefore, are constrained to accept that, particularly during times of high unemployment, the choice is between low levels of remuneration or no jobs at all. Autocratic styles may range from exploitative autocracy or 'sweating', where the dominant employer treats weak employees as a commodity to be controlled according to market requirements and conditions, and benevolent autocracy, where employees are not so dependent on the employer that they cannot assert some degree of autonomy in the employment relationship. Within the printing industry there are two contrasting sectors in which small firms operate (Goss, 1991). In one sector, firms deal with high-quality, technologically-sophisticated work, have a strong craft base and are heavily dependent upon skilled, unionised labour. In the second sector, small firms are concerned with 'instant printing'. These enterprises have emerged mainly as a result of technological changes which have simplified and automated small-scale printing technology to create electronic and computerised methods of typesetting 'thereby eliminating the need for skilled labour' (p. 161). In this sector of printing, the use of younger workers is widespread; these workers 'are unable to bargain, or to protect their interests either through collective action or by effective labour legislation. They are highly vulnerable to the commands of their employers and as a result they are more compelled to comply to autocratic employer stipulations in terms of wages, work and employment conditions and quality of performance' (Scase, 1995, p. 590).

More recent research by Marlow and Patton (2002) sheds further light upon the vagaries of small-firm style within the manufacturing sector while not departing markedly from some of the approaches already identified. Taking a broadly 'labour process' perspective (see Chapter 2), the authors comment upon the somewhat contradictory approaches of employers towards the employment relationship. The authors note for example that there is a strong desire on the part of employers to create a common sense of purpose and 'harmony' based on a sense of joint risk and benefit taking (a type of 'unitarism' – see Chapter 2). The downside of this is the scapegoating of those employees who do not conform to the desired informal norms and who were identified as 'troublemakers' or 'misfits', hence:

Any resistance to work organization creates a dilemma for the owner, as it risks exposing the true nature of the employment relationship and undermining the social cohesion of the work group, which includes the owner. From this evidence, it would appear that the firm owners redefine individual challenges to authority as a personality or attitude defect in the transgressor. Consequently, the person who does not fit is excluded (p. 534).

In this type of situation, the employee would appear to be in a 'double bind' situation as the close proximity of the employer to employees engenders both a relationship based on fear and dependency within an informal employment context.

Concluding comments and summary: strategies and styles in small businesses

Small businesses are extremely diverse in composition of employment and within the product markets of the many industrial sectors in which they operate. They tend to experience highly fluctuating levels of performance and business fortunes, high rates of bankruptcies and set-ups. Collectively, they employ a high proportion of the workforce whose skills range from high and non-transferable (the minority), to low and highly substitutable (the majority). In order to accommodate this highly diversified sector of the economy, small business researchers have suggested a complex model of the management of small-firm employment relations based on type of ownership, market and product environments, skill requirements of employees, and the occupational characteristics of the various sectors in which small businesses operate. The styles and strategies which owner-employers use and which we have identified (paternalism, fraternalism and benevolent autocracy) would appear to be far more characteristic of non-union firms than unionised firms, although we would expect some overlap of styles between the two categories. The particular style adopted will vary according to the extent of the employer's economic dependence on employees and the ability of employees to resist the exercise of the employer's prerogative.

Self Evaluation Activity 7.5

Summarising the main strategies and styles
Response on website

Briefly summarise the three main strategies and styles which small firm employers have adopted.

Strategy and style in medium-sized firms

Medium-sized firms and establishments may be defined, in terms of employment size, as those which employ from 100 people to not more than 500 people. As with small businesses, medium-sized firms operate within diverse sectors of the economy and exhibit a range of management styles and practices concerning the employment relationship. Unlike small businesses, most will operate formal procedures and have varying degrees of hierarchically structured control systems. A number of factors have been considered as influencing the type of approach adopted by these organisations and establishments to the management of the employment relationship and include the following:

- The input of key individuals can shape an organisation at the early stages of its development by, for example, establishing a dominant organisational 'culture' (Purcell and Sisson, 1983).
- Marchington and Parker (1990) suggest that the extent to which the product market influences employment relations policies and styles depends upon the degree of competitive pressure and the degree of customer pressure.
- The degree of competitive pressure upon a firm measures the extent to which the company can dictate terms to the customer because of the absence of alternative suppliers (monopoly or oligopoly situations) or the extent to which the company is obliged to follow market trends. Competitive pressure tends to be greatest when demand for the company's products is falling, providing opportunities for new entrants to gain market shares. This may influence management styles as the company may have to make decisions affecting the workforce (possible redundancies, or at the very least a review of employee efficiency and payment systems). Competitive pressure is not likely to be so intense when demand in the market is growing and other firms find it difficult to enter the market. Under these circumstances there will be little pressure from the product market to influence how employee relations are managed.
- The degree of customer pressure, or monopsony (the opposite of monopoly) is indicative of the nature of customer demand (whether it is predictable or subject to fluctuations) and the nature of the customer profile. The greater the predictability and stability of demand, the greater the freedom enjoyed by management, while the greater the fluctuations in demand, the more market constraints are perceived to influence management's approach to the employment relationship.
- The nature of the company's product, employee behaviour and the absence or presence of trade unions are additional important influences.

Dimensions and types of management style in medium-sized firms

Notwithstanding these product market pressures, McLoughlin and Gourlay (1994) argue that management style in non-union settings can be considered along two dimensions:

1. *The degree of strategic integration* between individual personnel policies and between these and overall business strategy.
2. *The balance between individual and collective methods of regulation* in relation to substantive and procedural aspects of the employment relationship.

They add:

> *HRM type approaches would be those which exhibit high levels of strategic integration, and the variant most likely to be associated with non-union status would be 'traditional HRM' [or 'soft' HRM], although non-unionism may [also] occur as a result of the adoption of 'strategic HRM' [or 'hard' HRM]. . . . There are, therefore, strong links to a strategic orientation and a high level of individualisation of the employment relationship.* (pp. 37–9)

In their survey of non-unionism and management style in the 'high technology' sector in the South East of England, McLoughlin and Gourlay (1994) identify four management approaches or styles in the 23 non-union and seven of the unionised establishments surveyed. The results along the two dimensions are indicated in Figure 7.1. In seven of the 30 establishments, the dominant management style within the employer-employee relationship was identified as traditional HRM (high strategic integration/high individualisation). Four establishments had strategic HRM (high strategic integration/

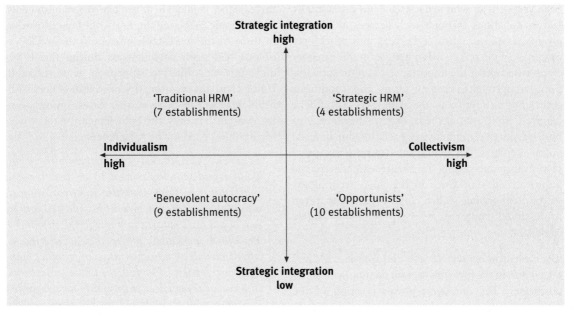

Figure 7.1 Positioning management styles
Source: McLoughlin and Gourlay, 1994, p. 45

high collectivisation) as the prevailing management style, while nine establishments were characterised by the benevolent autocracy style (low strategic integration/high individualism). A further ten establishments were classified as opportunists (low strategic integration/high collectivisation). High levels of individualisation were strongly associated with non-union status and 'all but one of the establishments where individual rather than collective modes of job regulation were dominant were non-union *and* part of a non-union firm' (p. 48). On the other hand, high levels of collectivisation were less likely to be associated with non-union status although seven of the fourteen establishments in this category did not recognise unions. McLoughlin and Gourlay conclude:

> *This underlines the point that it is the balance between individualism and collectivism that is important when considering management style and that the absence of unions does not in itself preclude some elements of the collective approach to managing aspects of the employment relationship. Significantly, the level of strategic integration did not appear to be strongly related to the presence or absence of unions, suggesting that, in itself, an HRM-type approach was not inevitably associated with non-union status.* (p. 48)

We will now examine these four management styles in relation to McLoughlin and Gourlay's survey (1994).

'**Traditional HRM**' is an approach and style that gives primacy to human resources and emphasises their central role in helping to meet organisational goals of competitive advantage by providing the means whereby the individual needs of employees are catered for. An important assumption here is that the securing of employee commitment and involvement will drastically reduce the demand for union services and hence make trade unions irrelevant to the needs of employees. The approach is not explicitly anti-union, but nevertheless seeks to substitute unions for high levels of individualisation in managing the employment relationship 'through policy devices such as single-status terms and conditions, employee profit-sharing and share-ownership schemes, performance-related pay and, in some cases the explicit linking of individual appraisal schemes to pay determination' (ibid., p. 50). There is also a strong commitment to employee training and development which often incorporates an appraisal process. Some companies in the sample had staff committees or joint consultative committees with elected employee representatives, but priority was always given to direct communication with employees both vertically down the hierarchy and horizontally 'across functions through such devices as briefing groups, employee attitude surveys and workforce meetings' (ibid., p. 51). All companies in this category emphasised either the importance of union substitution arrangements, keeping terms and conditions sufficiently attractive so that employees would be deterred from joining them, or the 'disinterest' of both parties to the employment relationship in trade union activities. An important deterrent to union organisation according to the researchers is the nature of the workforce in the 'high technology' sector, comprising skilled, highly paid and often professional employees who see unions as largely irrelevant.

'**Benevolent autocracy**' is a style and approach already referred to in the previous section dealing with small businesses. The dominant power position of the employer is established, but because of the particular skills and competencies of the employees (many of whom are manual) the latter can exert a measure of independence in the internal labour market of the establishment, and also the external labour market, particularly during times of labour scarcity. Because of this, management seeks a closer identity with employees. Other characteristics of this approach identified by the researchers include:

- low levels of strategic integration of personnel policies and practice with overall business policy; in some cases, establishments did not have a personnel presence;
- low priority given to training and development;
- none of the establishments in this category recognised trade unions, and all were part of non-union firms; and
- there was no evidence of any 'deep-seated' anti-union attitudes, however, and 'in most instances the issue appeared never to have arisen and no formal stance towards trade unions had ever been formulated' (ibid., p. 92).

'**Opportunists**' adopt 'fragmented' personnel policies and practices which lack formalisation. In some cases 'people' issues were lowly prioritised 'and training and development were often minimal'. Unlike the previous approach, there was, however, a greater collective orientation towards the regulation of the employment relationship. Nevertheless,

this category includes a 'mixed bag' of establishments. For example, McLoughlin and Gourlay report that in three of the ten establishments in this category, unions had been derecognised during the 1980s although a collective approach was retained. Unions had always been absent in four other establishments 'and in three further cases, unions were recognised, but only for one element of the workforce' (ibid., p. 56). The researchers add:

> In their various ways managements in all these establishments tended to be reactive and opportunist in their response to circumstances, although a marked degree of hostility to unions was sometimes evident in managerial utterances. Personnel specialists, where they were present, often acted in an administrative or 'conflict management' capacity. Overall, the management style in most of these cases is probably best regarded as a 'non-union variation' on the theme of the 'standard modern' or 'fire-fighting' approach identified as typical of larger British-owned manufacturing firms. (ibid., pp. 56–7)

'**Strategic HRM**' is an approach which demonstrates high levels of strategic integration and high levels of collectivism, and may be more commonly found in unionised organisations. The approach, as we have seen, requires high levels of integration of HRM policy with the business strategy of the organisation in order to secure the most efficient utilisation of the workforce in achieving the goals of maximising competitive advantage, optimising control and minimising labour costs. Within this scenario, trade union presence implying high levels of collectivisation is tolerated, provided the union input contributes positively towards realising these goals. Moves towards derecognition and increased individualisation are seen as necessary if this facilitates improvements to labour efficiency and productivity. All four establishments in this category actually recognised trade unions for significant proportions of their employees, and were amongst the largest surveyed by the researchers. All four establishments (three of which were American-owned) displayed relatively high levels of collective regulation of the employment relationship 'though an increased individualisation of hitherto predominantly collective employment relations as a part of a strategic response to new competitive conditions and/or business circumstances was in progress' (ibid., p. 59). Nevertheless, the evidence from two establishments indicates that adopting a strategic approach to HRM does not necessarily imply a reduction in the role of trade unions, suggesting that in some organisations HRM and collectivism not only co-exist, but may also complement each other.

Self-Evaluation Activity 7.6

Non-union approaches to the employment relationship
Response on website

Mini cases 7.1 and 7.2 are two examples of the approaches taken to the employment relationship by two non-union companies, one an American-owned company with an establishment of 300 employees (AZTEC), and the other, a British company with one establishment only, comprising 400 employees (IMPERIAL). Identify and comment on each of these approaches.

Mini cases 7.1 and 7.2
Case 7.1 The AZTEC approach

At AZTEC we take what we do very seriously, but we don't take ourselves too seriously. There is a sense of pride at AZTEC, professionalism is important. People are treated like and act like professionals. But people are professional without being stuffy. AZTEC people trust each other to do their jobs well and with the highest ethical standards. We take each other very seriously.

We have a strong sense of quality – quality in our products and services, of course; but also quality in our working environment, in the people we work with, in the tools that we use to do our work, and in the components we choose to make what we make. Economy comes from high value, not from low cost. Aesthetics are part of the quality. The effort to create quality extends to the communities in which we work and live as well.

The AZTEC approach is informal and non-bureaucratic. Verbal communication is key, not memos. 'Call don't write' is the watchword. People are accessible at all levels. People have fun working at AZTEC. There is laughing in the halls as well as serious discussion. More than anything else, the organisation is personable and approachable, but still dedicated to getting the job done. With informality, however, there is also a sense of confidence. AZTEC people feel like they are

on the winning side. They feel successful, and they are. It is this sense of confidence that generates the attitude to 'go ahead and try it, we'll make it work'.

AZTEC people like taking responsibility for what they do and thinking for themselves. At the same time, they are proud to share a single mission – making the world's best computers. Because the individual is key at AZTEC, there is real diversity in the view of what AZTEC really is. In fact, AZTEC is many things to many people. This consistency comes in providing those diverse people with the opportunity to fulfil themselves and experience achievement. The creativity, then, that emerges from the company comes from the many ideas of the individuals who are here. And that is the real strength of AZTEC.

Source: McLoughlin and Gourlay, 1994, p. 76

Case 7.2 The situation at IMPERIAL

Personnel policy and procedures at IMPERIAL are fragmented and largely unwritten. Links to overall business policy are tenuous and at best reactive. The personnel officer referred to personnel policy as 'a very grey area' with little 'written down'. Some attempts had recently been made to draft a formal written personnel policy. This contained a general statement about employment philosophy 'by the Chief Executive' which amounted to little more than a statement that the 'Directors' wish' was that 'employees would be able to look forward to full and rewarding long-term employment with the Company'. The document went on to explain elements of formal policies and procedures on matters such as consultation and grievances.

On the shop floor, work and the supervision of the work process was driven by concerns with maintaining continuity of production and improving productivity and output. Work was organised and controlled along classic Taylorist lines; assembly work was machine-paced and consisted of highly repetitive low-skilled tasks which required little training for line workers. Supervision was both direct and assisted by technological surveillance. For example, once a production job was running, hourly output was recorded on a 'master board' at the end of each assembly line. Along the lines were TV monitors which displayed production targets, the output achieved, and whether production was ahead (green) or behind (red). These devices were used by the production manager to motivate the staff, by encouraging lines to compete with each other.

There were basic attempts to 'humanise' the production environment to make the work more 'tolerable', for example by attempting to keep the same operators on each line in order that friends could sit next to each other and by arranging assembly-line work stations so that operators were seated close enough to enable conversation. There was also recognition that the quality of direct supervision required improvement and that there was a lack of 'people management' skills.

A few years ago, after a management 'buy-out', the decision was taken to derecognise the unions. The reason for the derecognition appeared to amount to taking advantage of a perceived weakness in the position of trade unions as a result of the Thatcher government's industrial relations reforms and a perception of a moderate tradition in the local labour market. According to the manufacturing manager, employee support for the unions had collapsed in the wake of the redundancy programme before the buy-out. After the new company had been formed, management, and, it was claimed, the remaining employees wanted a 'new start', 'free of history' and without the trade unions.

The linchpin of the approach to managing without unions to date had been a company council (a form of joint consultative committee), known as the 'staff association' comprising eleven elected employee members, which met monthly with the managing director in the chair and the personnel manager in attendance. This aspect of management's approach, therefore, incorporates a collective orientation to the employment relationship. The committee had no formal negotiating role and was intended as a means through which employee views could be gauged, grievances dealt with and information passed to the workforce. However, the employee representatives were prone to question the committee's value. In the view of one employee member, for example, management treated the employee representatives 'like puppets' and tried to use them as 'management mouthpieces'.

Source: McLoughlin and Gourlay, 1994, pp. 82–6

Guest and Hoque's typology

Guest and Hoque (1994) provide a classification of non-union establishments which 'goes beyond existing approaches' (p. 1). They then attempt to identify a number of consequences of 'belonging to a particular category of non-union establishment' for a range of industrial relations, HRM and performance outcomes. Finally, on the basis of their research, they consider whether non-union establishments represent the 'good, the bad or the ugly faces of the new industrial relations' (p. 1). Guest and Hoque argue that some classifications of non-union management styles and strategies are derived 'from the well-established traditions of industrial relations' with outcomes largely concerned with the 'propensity to unionise' or are based on original typologies of style (such as Purcell, 1987) developed 'in an earlier era when trade unionism was much more dominant' (McLoughlin and Gourlay, 1994, are cited as an example of this approach). Furthermore, the dimensions of 'individualism' and 'collectivism' have been demonstrated to be more complex than originally assumed (see Chapters 2 and 4) and 'require considerable unbundling' (p. 2). The rationale for adopting a different approach to this issue is explained in the following passage:

> Since non-unionism is the norm for new establishments, we have arguably reached the point where we should get away from studying non-union establishments in relation to unionism and propensity to become unionised. Indeed, the very term 'non-unionism' becomes a limiting definition of workplaces. Instead, we should be developing frameworks and dimensions which allow us to study aspects of employment relations and human resource management without distinctive reference to the union issue. It therefore follows that we need somewhat different ways of classifying non-union establishments. (p. 2)

Guest and Hoque base their typology on two dimensions. The first is whether or not firms have a human resource strategy, using the criterion of 'strategic integration'; and the second is the nature of human resource policy and practice, which includes employee involvement and communications, employee selection methods and training and quality improvements. Four types of non-union establishment were identified on the basis of these two dimensions (see Exhibit 7.1).

If we compare and contrast the above typology with that of McLoughlin and Gourlay (1994), it

Exhibit 7.1

Guest and Hoque's four non-union types

Type one: Establishments having a clear HRM strategy encouraging and achieving high levels of employee involvement and commitment, and representing the good face of non-unionism. This type is more formally labelled as the full utilisation, high involvement model.

Type two: Establishments having a clear strategy but which do not make much use of HRM practices, providing at best only minimum levels of employee rights. There may be a 'deliberate strategy to deprive workers of many of their traditional rights including a voice of any sort'. These establishments represent the ugly face of non-unionism and are more formally called the efficiency-driven model.

Type three: Establishments not having a clear HRM strategy, but which nevertheless have adopted many 'innovative' HRM practices which they have, fortunately for them, accidentally 'stumbled upon'. Managements in these establishments tend to 'latch on to' the latest fads without much thought as to how these may be applied successfully in practice. Ultimately, the adoption and implementation of practices without reference to broader strategic concerns may or may not be successful. This type of establishment is described as the lucky face of non-unionism, and more formally as opportunist.

Type four: Establishments having no HRM strategy and a low uptake of HRM practices. They are characterised by poor management practices which do not adequately consider human resource issues and represent the bad face of non-unionism. They could also be labelled (with qualifications) benevolent autocrats.

Source: Adapted from Guest and Hoque, 1994

would be possible to equate the latter's opportunist and benevolent autocracy categories with Guest and Hoque's type three (lucky) and type four (bad). But since Guest and Hoque ignore the collectivism-individualism dimension, they implicitly deny the possibility that collective employment relations can exist within a non-union context. Notwithstanding this criticism, it would probably be more appropriate to argue that we should not limit our conceptual framework by discounting either individualist or collectivist criteria, particularly for those firms which may have recently derecognised trade unions, and for those large organisations such as Marks & Spencer which regulate their employment relationships by using both collectivist and individualist means. Both typologies, therefore, may be regarded as complementing rather than mutually excluding each other.

The value of Guest and Hoque's research lies in their use of data from the WIRT survey of new and refurbished establishments owned mainly by UK, American, Japanese and German parents 'where management is effectively starting with a new establishment and is unconstrained by any local history

or tradition in the workplace . . . [and where] management is given the freest rein to introduce policies and practices of its choice' (p. 5). The other important aspect of the research is the quantification of outcomes concerning HRM, 'employee relations' and performance, and whether these vary for the four types of establishment.

HRM outcomes include: commitment of lower grade staff; quality of staff employed; quality of work of lower grade staff; quality of HR policies and practices; flexibility of staff; ability to move between jobs as needed; flexibility to adjust workforce size; line manager enthusiasm for HR policies. In assessing these outcomes across the four establishment types, Guest and Hoque reveal that the 'good' establishments report the most positive outcomes (with the 'ugly' also reporting good results), while the 'bad' report the worst outcomes.

'Employee relations' outcomes include: industrial dispute resolution; percentage labour turnover (1992); absenteeism (1992). The research findings for this category of outcomes reveal that the 'good' have the best pattern of results and the 'ugly' the worst.

Performance outcomes include: percentage of quality targets attained; how well the recession was weathered; productivity benchmarked against UK; quality benchmarked against UK; productivity benchmarked against the world; quality benchmarked against the world. From their analysis of this category of outcomes, Guest and Hoque conclude that 'the **good** claim the best performance outcomes with all the other categories emerging as significantly worse on at least one item' (p. 10).

Guest and Hoque's general conclusion based on results derived from an analysis of outcomes is predictable enough; that the 'good' 'consistently report the best results for HRM, employee relations and performance outcomes'. On the other hand, the 'bad' establishments 'consistently report the poorest outcomes'. Results for the 'ugly' establishments are mixed with 'distinct problems for employee relations'. Furthermore, the researchers suggest that:

> In this respect our results complement those obtained by Millward (1994) who found greater numbers of non-union establishments falling into what we have termed the bad or ugly categories in his larger WIRS 3 sample. On the other hand, the relatively positive HRM and performance outcomes suggest that on some criteria these establishments are quite successful. (p. 11)

A second important conclusion drawn by the researchers is that 'contrary to expectations, the UK-owned establishments claim to be in the vanguard of strategic human resource management. At the other extreme, the Germans are the least enthusiastic' (p. 10). These results need to be treated with caution until they are replicated by further and more extensive research. The researchers themselves admit that their findings are limited to new establishments and are heavily biased towards manufacturing (while acknowledging that the service sector remains a growth area within the economy, and contains the greatest proportion of non-union enterprises) and it would be 'dangerous to generalise them to older establishments or to the public sector' (p. 11). Nevertheless, this need not detract too much from their general conclusion that for their sample and within new manufacturing establishments, 'the adoption of an HRM strategy pays off' (p. 13).

A 'composite' approach

Dundon (2002) argues that the approaches such as those identified by Guest and Hoque (1994) which posit 'either–or' alternatives may be rather simplistic, reflecting 'ideal' rather than 'real' situations, given that management practices in non-union firms are 'remarkably diverse and complex' (p. 236). In similar vein Dundon intimates that the Flood and Toner (1997) 'substitution–suppression' dichotomy, considered below in relation to larger, multinational companies, is rather too general to be entirely meaningful. Nevertheless, while Flood and Toner deal exclusively with larger organisations where suppression and substitution are more likely to be part of a carefully thought out strategy aimed at excluding unions, five of the seven enterprises comprising Dundon's sample fall within the SME category where different criteria apply (see above). The typology of approaches adopted by Dundon and summarised in Exhibit 7.2, may, therefore, be applicable mainly, if not exclusively to the SME sector. However, it is important to note that these approaches are not (unlike that of Guest and Hoque) mutually exclusive, recognising as they do the complexities and dynamics of workplace employment relations.

Concluding comments and summary: strategy and style in medium-sized firms

In this subsection we have concentrated upon strategy and style in medium-sized non-union firms by reference to the two significant studies by McLoughlin and Gourlay (1994) and Guest and Hoque (1994). While it is difficult to generalise from this specific research, a few observations can safely be made:

- The human resource management approach in its two main guises is only one of several approaches to regulating the employment relationship in non-union firms.
- Newer establishments are more likely to be non-union than older establishments, irrespective of whether they are British or foreign owned.
- Firms that have recently derecognised unions within their workplaces and establishments are more likely to retain a collective orientation towards certain aspects of the employment relationship concerning, for example, employee

Exhibit 7.2

Non-union management control approaches

Approach	Type of anti-union behaviour and control
Fear stuff	*Union suppression*: Employer behaviour includes blatant intimidation of workers in order to instil fear of managerial reprisals to possible unionisation.
Sweet stuff	*Union substitution*: Management argue that unions are unnecessary, with better terms and conditions and sophisticated employee voice channels to resolve any grievances.
Evil stuff	*Ideological opposition to unions*: Management views unions as 'left wing militants' destructive to company performance.
Fatal stuff	*Blatant refusal*: Employer refuses to recognise a union or at best refuses to 'bargain in good faith'.
Awkward stuff	*Stonewalling*: Managers create what appear to be legitimate obstacles to union recognition, effectively employing 'delaying' tactics.
Tame stuff	*Damage limitation:* Employer behaviour can take the form of 'sweetheart' deals, partially recognising 'moderate' unions or creating internal (managerially controlled) staff associations.
Harm stuff	*Bypassing*: Employer behaviour seeks to effectively marginalise collective employee voice, often through specific non-union channels.

Source: Based on Dundon, 2002

representation and pay determination, albeit on management's terms.

- Firms and establishments which have been 'union-free' since their inception are likely to adopt one of two employer regimes:
  - a 'soft' or 'traditional' HRM approach whereby employees enjoy superior pay and conditions and have a measure of job security and therefore do not perceive any need for trade union representation; and
  - an approach which is overtly hostile to any trade union presence and representation which has much in common with the Dickensian *Bleak House* (Sisson, 1993) analogy where employers 'enjoy the flexibility of a disposable workforce and regulate by fear' (Hyman, 1997).

Strategy and style in large firms

Numerically, large non-union firms are in a minority, but have a high profile in the HRM and, increasingly, industrial relations texts and other publications (see, for example, Blyton and Turnbull, 1998). Companies such as Marks & Spencer and IBM 'have always been held up as exemplary non-union employers' (Gennard and Judge, 1997, pp. 107–8). More recently, companies such as Hewlett-Packard, Texas Instruments, Gillette, Mars, Eastman-Kodak, Polaroid, Digital Equipment Corporation, Wang Electronics BV and Verbatim have joined the ranks of large non-union organisations. In this section we examine in more detail the suppressionist and the substitutionist strategies of larger firms (Flood and Toner, 1997; Gall and McKay, 2001).

Generic characteristics of large non-union firms

Self-Evaluation Activity 7.7

Characteristics of non-union companies
The response is given below

Exhibit 7.3 gives an example of the traditional approach to managing some aspects of the employment relationship within International Business Computers (IBM) UK, before it was reorganised. From

Exhibit 7.3

Personnel policy at IBM

There are six important elements making up IBM's employment relations policy, according to Peach (1983, cited in Farnham and Pimlott, 1995, p. 336). These are:

1. The 'practice of full employment' whereby the company provides alternative employment for those whose jobs are displaced through technological change or economic circumstances, on condition that employees affected by these changes are willing to re-train, change jobs and move location. This policy was actually put to the test in the early 1990s, when internal restructuring initiated by the US parent company resulted in large-scale redundancies in IBM (UK). Obviously, the UK company did not anticipate job losses on this scale and re-deployment was not an option. Instead, the thousands of UK employees who became 'surplus to requirements' were offered generous inducements to leave the company voluntarily or to take early retirement.

2. The company is committed to 'single status', with all employees enjoying the same employee benefits and conditions of service irrespective of skill and other occupational attributes. According to IBM management, this approach reflects its willingness to 'judge people according to their contribution and not to a pre-defined pecking order – which is the essence of a company alert to, and willing to change' (Peach, 1983, p. 3).

3. The pay system is the same for the majority of employees and is based upon a job evaluation scheme 'with a monetary value placed on each job according to the company's policy of paying its employees favourably compared with other leading companies – in other words to occupy a high position in the market place' (ibid., p. 5).

4. There is a commitment to 'performance assessment and career counselling and planning', the main objective of which is the regular provision of 'a balanced statement of each employee's performance against objectives assessed by their manager and validated by his or her superior' (ibid., p. 6).

5. In common with many large non-union firms, IBM (UK)'s **downward communication** operates via company newspapers, annual statements, local newssheets, bulletin boards and video-taped messages from top management. **Upward communication** is facilitated by periodic employee attitude and opinion surveys and other employee relations audits.

6. Employee grievances are processed by:
   - the 'Speak-Up' programme which allows individuals and groups to request formal responses by management on issues and complaints about policy issues which affect them; and
   - the 'Open Door' system which enables employees who are dissatisfied with a decision by management to appeal against it either through the management hierarchy or to any level of management, bypassing the intervening levels. Peach suggests that around 25 per cent of appeals made in this way are upheld in favour of the employee.

These and other management approaches towards the employment relationship within IBM (UK) taken together are considered to be more than adequate as a method of union substitution.

this example (which is, of course, still relevant today), attempt to identify some of the main characteristics of large non-union companies.

Large non-union firms are generally characterised as:

- American and privately owned;
- operating mainly in non-manufacturing and service sectors;

- employing mainly non-manual, skilled or partially skilled workers;
- profitable or highly profitable and commercially successful in expanding product markets;
- having 'covertly non-union personnel policies' (Farnham and Pimlott, 1995, p. 337);
- justifying their non-union status by substituting alternative forms of employee representation and

providing higher rates of pay and better conditions of work than unionised organisations;

- claiming to have enlightened and progressive personnel and HRM policies and 'people-centred' managerial styles, making unions and collective bargaining irrelevant;
- having 'single status' for employees, employment security, promotion from within; and
- having careful selection and training for management, especially at supervisory level (Blyton and Turnbull, 1994, p. 235).

Flood and Toner (1997), in citing Toner's previous study of large US non-union companies in Ireland (1985), contend that:

This type of company often, although not exclusively, prefers to remain union-free in setting up greenfield branch plants outside the USA. In doing so, they attempt to develop a strong corporate culture built upon their employment practices which acts to reduce the perceived requirements for unionisation among their employees. (p. 261)

Gennard and Judge (1997) comment that:

To be a Marks and Spencer you need to be very people-oriented and to place great importance on respect for employees. This means highly developed and effective leadership skills, and that requires an investment in people. Gaining commitment and becoming a harmonious and integrated unitary workplace requires more than words: it can mean changing the established order. (p. 109)

Union substitution strategies in large non-union firms: benefits and costs

In their study of seven large non-union companies in the Republic of Ireland, Flood and Toner (1997) consider the question as to what advantage these companies following 'best practice' in HRM expect to achieve through union avoidance combined with union substitution. They go on to assert:

They do not, and perhaps cannot, take advantage of the absence of unions to reduce wages or benefits, ignore complaints and grievances or dismiss unsatisfactory workers at will. They do spend a

lot of money on communication procedures and fringe benefits. Is this a Catch-22 situation where, having kept unions out, they cannot do anything that could not be done in a union house, for fear of bringing unions in? (p. 261)

In order to understand the motives of non-union managements in keeping unions out of large organisations, Flood and Toner identify a number of perceived disadvantages on the part of management within three broad categories concerning communications, work organisation and conflict which are listed below.

Within the **communications** category, the following disadvantage was cited:

- the presence of unions makes communication more difficult, impedes personal contact and gives rise to bureaucracy.

The **work organisation** category included:

- unions make change more difficult;
- unions give rise to demarcation and inter-union argument;
- unions impose restrictions on production;
- unions cause a general lack of flexibility;
- unions impose higher manning levels;
- unions protect unsatisfactory workers; and
- unions inhibit individual reward systems.

The **conflict** category included:

- unions give opportunities for radicals to stir up trouble;
- unions promote an adversarial climate;
- unions encourage the pursuit of trivial grievances; and
- unions cause strikes and stoppages.

On the basis of these management perceptions and related opinions, Flood and Toner present a conceptual model which provides the rationale of a non-union strategy for large 'best practice' companies and which incorporates the following assumptions:

Firstly that these companies cannot hope to avoid many of the features of unionised companies such as good pay and benefits, and good complaints procedures; secondly that the absence of unions permits them, however, to build a more unitary and more individualistic culture than would normally be possible where a union is present, and thirdly that if they are successful in creating such a culture, they can reduce the likelihood of certain kinds of behaviour. (p. 267)

Their union-avoidance model is presented in Figure 7.2.

Union-avoidance models such as that of Flood and Toner (1997) tend to be based upon the original research of Kochan *et al.* (1986) into large non-union firms in the USA. They went on to identify ten substitution approaches managements adopted to ensure that unions were prevented from getting a foothold in these firms. The common characteristics of these firms can be identified by referring to columns (a) and (b) in Figure 7.2. The ten approaches comprise:

1. *Pay and conditions.* Pay and conditions, including fringe benefits should be equal or greater than those paid to workers in comparable industries and firms in order to pre-empt union organisation: column (a).
2. *Training and career development.* High rates of investment in training and development are regarded as beneficial to employees: column (a).
3. *Secure employment.* Significant efforts are made to provide secure employment and to avoid layoffs: column (a).
4. *Communications.* Sophisticated methods of communication and information-sharing are used to substitute those provided by trade unions and to forestall union organisation: column (a).
5. *Employee involvement.* Involvement in decision-making concerning the work itself is 'aimed at building a sense of partnership between management and workforce, with a view to creating a more unitary culture' (p. 271): column (b).
6. *Psychological climate.* The creation of a 'psychological climate' which encourages and rewards loyalty and commitment to the organisation within a unitary framework: column (b).
7. *Remuneration, appraisals and promotion.* The creation of a 'rational' system of administering pay, performance appraisal and promotions which rewards merit and acknowledges seniority with the objectives of:
   - ensuring that the pay system is fair and perceived to be fair: column (b); and
   - ensuring that the pay system encourages individual motivation and inhibits collectivism: column (b).
8. *Grievance procedures.* To ensure that the non-union grievance procedures and the monitoring of complaints are at least as good as those operating within unionised organisations without the need for 'third party' intervention and binding arbitration: column (b).
9. *'Greenfield' sites.* Setting up of new production facilities in areas where union organisation is sparse in order to avoid the creation of a 'union culture': column (b).
10. *Employee selection.* Employee selection devices are used in order to eliminate from consideration workers who might be 'pro-union': column (b).

Large non-union companies		
(a) Cannot hope to avoid these features of unionised companies:	(b) Can hope, in the absence of unions, to:	(c) If successful in building a unitary culture, can hope to reduce likelihood of:
• high wages and benefits • good complaints procedures • job security • good communications	• reduce platform for radicals • promote a 'unitary' culture • put individual reward systems in place • improve personal contact	• resistance to change • restrictions on production • work stoppages and strikes • inflexibility and excessive manning levels

Figure 7.2 Rationale of union-avoidance policy
Source: Flood and Toner, 1997, p. 268

Another large non-union organisation already referred to is the oft-quoted, albeit highly relevant, example of Marks & Spencer, who do not consider themselves as anti-union, cannot prevent any member of their staff from joining one, and even provide facilities for holding meetings in their stores. The company simply do not recognise trade unions for the purpose of any industrial relations activity and are confident that they provide their employees with everything (and more) that an active trade union could.

However, some non-union organisations such as QVC (see Main case 7.1) do not regard pay as an effective union substitution mechanism; while QVC claims to provide benefits for employees, the use of the pervasive 'Eaton Philosophy' is probably sufficient to justify union absence from the company's perspective.

Main case 7.1
QVC: Utopia or dystopia?

QVC, the satellite and cable-shopping channel, was founded in 1986 and is the leading global television channel retailer with sales in the region of $3.9 billion in 2001. In the UK QVC, which commenced trading in 1993, has over 2 million customers, a portfolio of over 15 000 products and revenues of £180 million. The main function of the company is to bring Quality, Value and Convenience (hence QVC) via television, internet and digital interactive services. QVC UK employs in the region of 1750 employees across two sites, the Knowsley, Merseyside, call centre and warehousing site and the Battersea, London, HQ. The Knowsley site employs 1500 workers who are mainly call centre agents, mainly female and part-time.

The parent company, QVC Inc., adopts both union-avoidance and substitution policies (the emphasis being on the former rather than the latter), as is typical of many US companies, and attempts to promote a working environment that negates the likelihood of employees joining unions. QVC UK adopts the anti-union stance of its parent and rationalises it by reference to the so-called 'Eaton Philosophy'. This is not so much a 'philosophy' but rather a persuasive individualist strategy of neo-unitarist (see Chapter 2) platitudes and was initially articulated by the Eaton Corporation, a major US manufacturing company.

The Eaton Philosophy: Excellence Through People

- *We expect the best of ourselves and each other*
- *We are committed to attracting, developing and keeping a diverse workforce that reflects the nature of our global business*
- *Our communications with one another are open, honest and timely*
- *We strive for active involvement of every employee in our continued success and growth*
- *We accept the challenge of lifelong learning*
- *We do our work with a sense of urgency*
- *We are accountable for our commitments and expect that our performance will be measured*
- *Compensation at Eaton is fair and competitive for performance that contributes to the success of the business*
- *We value employees' ideas, and we purposefully build an environment in which new ideas will flourish*

There would appear to be no formal statement concerning trade unions, but one ex-employee stated that: 'At the recruitment stage, you are given a very distinct impression – no, more than an impression – that unions are not tolerated.'

QVC UK has endorsed and adapted the 'Eaton Philosophy' for UK consumption and incorporated a number of 'principles' or commitments, known collectively throughout QVC as 'The Difference'. These include the 'commitment' to:

- teamworking;
- excellence;
- openness and trust;
- ethics and integrity;
- respect and concern;
- customer focus;
- pioneering spirit; and
- fun along the way.

The employment relationship at QVC is extremely individualised, and the above 'principles of commitment' are reinforced during staff appraisals. However, while the main methods of communication are downward, the company has introduced various initiatives over the years in an attempt to gain employee commitment. These include regular weekly team briefs, monthly 'one-to-one' appraisal meetings between employer and supervisor/team leader, staff forums to discuss issues relevant to staff, newsletters, suggestion schemes and a 'reward and recognition' programme. In addition, as a 'sop' to representation and a recognition that things 'may have to change' in the light of the EU Information and Consultation Directive, a company-wide 'Q Works Council' was formed comprising members of the management team and employees. Its function is to review changes in company policy and receive feedback 'from the floor' concerning issues affecting company performance.

QVC UK also offers certain 'benefits' that fall far short of the extensive substitution benefits offered by many other large non-union companies. These include:

- **Law Club:** for a small fee of 77p a month, advice is provided to employees concerning employment law, mortgages, personal injury etc.;
- **pension contributions:** The company contributes double the employee contribution (under review);
- **job-relevant education/training funding;**
- **staff discount on company products;** and
- **development programmes:** to assist employees who want to advance.

The QVC downside

QVC is a cost-minimising organisation, seeking to keep all costs, particularly labour costs, to a minimum. The parent company strategy to locate its call centre and warehouse in an impoverished area that has one of the highest unemployment rates in the country ensured that labour costs could be minimised, with call centre staff being paid little above the national minimum wage The fact that the workforce comprises mainly female and part-time labour is an added advantage as such labour is numerically flexible and disposable. Combined with the stresses and monotony of much call centre work, it is not surprising that labour turnover is remarkably high. High rates of turnover or 'churn' actually benefit QVC as employees rarely stay long enough to 'cause a nuisance', and the cost of training is minimal. The case concludes with a quote from a call centre employee (managers were unavailable to comment):

> *Working for QVC is the only choice for many Kirkby people, but most don't stick it for more than a year at most and a lot leave during the first few months. The pay is crap and they treat you like shit. All the things they say they have to benefit you like the benefits aren't worth a candle. You are treated like you were still at school. It would be different if there was a union because then we could express our grievances and would be treated with some respect. I've worked in other call centres in the past, but this is the worst.* (female, age 27)

Concluding comments and summary: strategy and style in large firms

Large non-union firms tend to adopt formalised approaches characterising their union substitution policies and strategies. These approaches are regarded as 'best practice' and indeed as exemplars of innovative HRM according to managerial accounts (Sieff, 1990, quoted in Turnbull and Wass, 1998). However, while it may be assumed that companies such as IBM, M&S and Hewlett-Packard have well-defined management styles and strategies, detailed, objective research into industrial and employment relations matters is sparse and inconclusive. The research undertaken by Turnbull and Wass is a welcome addition to our knowledge of the impact of union substitution strategies upon employees themselves and to some extent debunks the prevailing managerialist notion, that union substitution represents a 'happy house' situation in large companies while union suppression represents the 'bleak house' situation in many smaller companies.

Suppressionist strategies and union recognition: evidence from Gall and McKay, 2001

In Chapter 3 we examined the union recognition (UR) debate subsequent to the Employment Relations Act 1999 (ERA99). It is important to emphasise that overt or covert employer resistance to recognition of trade unions may reveal, within larger organisations, suppression and substitution strategies of varying degrees of sophistication, some of which we have already dealt with (substitutionist strategies are considered in more detail below). The UR provisions within the ERA99 enable requests for UR in non-union organisations to be put forward by unions if 50 per cent plus one or more of the workforce desire it. However, Gall and McKay (2001) provide some evidence, both statistical and anecdotal, which indicates varying degrees of resistance to UR, examples of which include:

- resistance to UR by companies in the newspaper, oil processing and transportation, and port sectors;
- the CBI and the Federation of Small Businesses are UR-antithetical, as a CBI Director of Employment Affairs stated: 'Any employer who is so deeply opposed to statutory union recognition that they will not under any circumstances entertain a trade union . . . will find a way of not entertaining a trade union' (quoted from Gall and McKay, 2001, p. 98);
- the TUC General Secretary (then its Deputy) in 1999 stated that union avoidance tactics ranging from softly-softly to blatantly aggressive 'might herald [some] employers introducing US-style union-busting' (ibid., p. 98); and
- surveys by the CBI, Dibb Lupton Allsop (1997–2002) and the Institute of Management all point to considerable levels of resistance to UR.

One of the most prominent methods of resistance to UR is suppression, or a suppressionist strategy to thwart existing or expected attempts and requests for UR. It is a strategy 'based on intimidation and creating an atmosphere of fear and trepidation' (Gall and McKay, 2001, p. 99). Tactics such as sackings, dismissals and redundancies or the threat of them are relatively common, and directed at 'activists' using pretexts such as minor infringements in time keeping, sickness absence and work performance. Once the 'activists' are dealt with, it is hoped that the UR claim will have dissipated. Other suppression tactics include the use of management 'plants' at union meetings 'to find out how and when the union is planning to organize its UR campaign in order to combat it' (ibid., p. 100); the use of CCTV and videos; and determining which employees speak to union organisers at the entrances to company premises.

Other more ominous examples of suppression include the use of US and UK anti-union consultants and legal firms that advise companies on the best suppression methods, including the use of meetings and other means of communications to warn about the 'union threat to the company's health and profitability and thus to wage levels and jobs' (ibid., p. 101). The cases reported in Exhibit 7.4 provide evidence of such tactics.

Exhibit 7.4

Examples of suppression tactics

One example is that of Regional Independent Media, a provincial English newspaper group. The management of this company made 250 employees redundant in 1998 and one consequence of this was the removal of union activists who would have been needed to mount a campaign to secure UR. The MD was quoted as saying 'my own observation is that we may not be so much over-staffed as wrongly staffed' while the HR director instructed managers to identify employees who were 'on side' for the creation of a 'continuity of production strike-breaking team' should the 'union problem get out of hand'. A steel company in Sheerness, Kent, is reported to have operated a 'termination programme' to weed out those employees deemed to be unhappy and at odds with the company's anti-union philosophy. Under this the ISTC branch secretary was reported to have been sacked. In the high profile case of Pricecheck supermarkets in London, the owner told staff: 'I will not recognise any union. . . . If staff don't like it then they don't have to work here.' At News International, the editors of the *Sun* and *The Times* wrote to their staffs in 1998 stating that the return of UR would see an end to the papers' era of growth and success as a result of 'flexible work practices' and co-operative attitudes, with the editor of the *Sun* stating that the return of UR 'cannot be good for your family, the paper, the company [or] the readers'.

General summary and conclusion: strategies and styles

Self-Evaluation Activity 7.8

Non-union strategies and styles

This SEA has no commentary

As a review exercise, briefly summarise the main approaches (strategies and styles) that we have considered so far, adopted by non-union firms in order both to suppress and to substitute trade union activities.

Apart from the main approaches thus far identified, the following observations are relevant.

Non-unionised firms have consistently outnumbered unionised firms, largely because of the very large number of small-to-medium size enterprises which fall into the non-union category. To this we must add the growing number of medium-sized firms which have derecognised unions in recent years. However, the amount of empirical research into non-union firms focusing on how these firms manage without unions and how employees perceive the employment relationship within them, is certainly disproportionate to the size of the phenomenon. Some of the research has been criticised because non-unionism is seen as 'problematic' in relation to those firms which are unionised: comparisons are made based on criteria concerning the propensity of employees to unionise and differences in management strategy and style in relation to unionised firms (Guest and Hoque, 1994; Turnbull and Wass, 1998; Dundon, 2002). Because of this, as Turnbull and Wass state:

> *The very term 'non-unionism' becomes a limiting definition of workplaces (Guest and Hoque) which tend to fall into either of two extreme types: the anti-union 'bleak house' where management deliberately seeks to deprive workers of their rights, most notably to trade union representation, or the more progressive 'happy house' where management lavish benefits on workers who, it would seem, simply fail to perceive any need to join a trade union.* (p. 98)

As we have seen earlier, the 'bleak house' scenario – also described as the 'ugly' face of non-unionism – or the 'black hole' (Guest, 1995; Guest and Conway, 1999) – is characterised by the relative absence of any formal procedures governing grievances, discipline, communication, etc.; the absence of personnel and other specialists; the tendency to dismiss employees rather than 'correct' their behaviour; low morale indicated by high rates of labour turnover and absenteeism; and low rates of pay, job insecurity and poor conditions of employment. The 'happy house' scenario has been described above and is characteristic of some medium-sized and a majority of larger non-union firms. Both 'bleak house' and 'happy house' categories correspond to the two dominant unitary types of management style identified in Chapter 2, namely the 'traditional paternalist' and the 'sophisticated paternalist' respectively. To be sure, many non-union firms will fall either within these categories, perhaps exhibiting characteristics of both, or outside this dichotomy altogether, showing patterns of employer–employee relations more typical of the small firms which we have previously considered.

The remainder of this chapter is devoted to a description of union substitution methods prevailing in the larger non-union companies, although it is important to note that these methods are also employed by unionised companies as part of their 'soft' HRM strategies and policies, the consequences of which may be to bypass traditional union communication routes and to sidestep collective bargaining arrangements and machinery. Before looking at these methods, attention should be drawn to an examination of existing research undertaken by Terry (1999). Essentially, Terry considers whether systems of employee representation in the non-union sector can provide effective substitutes for union-based systems, and argues that within the larger 'potentially unionisable' companies structures of collective employee representation 'closely resembling those associated with recognised trade unions . . . also represent explicit strategies of union avoidance' (p. 22). Terry goes on to argue that while there are pressures which may 'encourage' non-union firms to adopt forms of collective representation which are often called 'employee' or 'company' councils, the absence of any 'legally binding requirement' to do so may well render these forms of representation ineffective (see also Lloyd, 2001). Employee councils in non-union firms are, therefore, more likely to be used as a means to avoid unionisation in those areas which have a high potential for unionisation or where unions have already been derecognised.

EMPLOYEE INVOLVEMENT: A UNION SUBSTITUTION STRATEGY?

In Chapter 8, we contrast employee participation and involvement. Whereas employee participation stresses collective representation of employees in joint decision-making, employee involvement (EI) has an individualist focus and is part and parcel of 'soft' HRM approaches to managing the employment relationship, usually, but not necessarily, associated with a union-free environment in larger organisations.

Within a union-free environment EI is initiated and driven by employers, partly for union substitution purposes. EI is also used by managers to change employee attitudes and behaviour in order to secure greater commitment and raise employee output. Although the term 'employee involvement' first began to appear in the management literature during the late 1970s, and became a familiar part of management vocabulary in Britain during the 1980s, the concept dates back to the 1920s with the inception of the 'human relations' school of management and then during the 1950s and 1960s was associated with ideas concerning job enlargement, job enrichment and job design. During the 1980s, EI was increasingly utilised within an HRM context and framework, reinforced by the dissemination of Japanese management methods with which it is now associated. The forms and methods of EI tend to change, or at least change emphasis and labels, with a high turnover in usage. For example, the more formal method of *quality circles* is being replaced by a more all-embracing *total quality management* (TQM) concept entailing a process of 'continuous improvement' based on the Deming-inspired and Japanese adopted 'philosophy' of *kaizen* (Deming's philosophy is explained in more detail on pp. 376–7; see also the example of Nissan in Chapter 5).

Employee involvement in practice

The Workplace Industrial Relations surveys of 1980, 1984, 1990 and the WERS98, together with

other research conducted for the Department of Employment by Marchington *et al.* (1992), reveal the extent of EI practices in British workplaces – both union and non-union. The later surveys report significant growth since the early 1980s 'to the extent that it is now common parlance of most senior managers' (Marchington, 1995, p. 283). The findings of the WERS98 indicate that 'new' management practices and employee involvement schemes are fairly widespread in many of the workplaces surveyed. Although no comparisons as yet have been made with earlier data, we can safely assume that the growth in EI practices has been maintained. Table 7.6 identifies 16 frequently discussed management practices and employee involvement schemes together with the proportion of workplaces operating them. The table does not distinguish between sector, employment size and the type of union presence. Some of the practices identified are not considered in this chapter, and at least one (JCCs) is examined in Chapter 8.

The survey also found that over half of workplaces operated five or more of the 16 practices and that there are definite groupings of practices commonly used. For example, training, teamworking, supervisors trained in employee relations matters and problem-solving groups are all associated with one another.

A more optimistic picture of the extent of EI is provided by the IRS (2002) survey of 52 organisations. The more common methods used by these organisations include:

- **notice boards:** used by 96 per cent of organisations – the simplest way to communicate;
- **company intranet and emails:** 88 per cent of organisations use an intranet and 85 per cent use email to convey information to employees. This medium is also used for 'upward' communication;
- **team briefings/meetings:** used by almost 90 per cent of organisations;
- **company journal or newspaper:** 77 per cent of organisations use this method, representing a decline from 92 per cent in 1999;
- **attitude surveys:** undertaken annually, these are used by 73 per cent of organisations;
- **employee reports:** still one of the most unpopular methods, used by 35 per cent of organisations; and

Table 7.6 New management practices and employee involvement schemes

	Percentage of workplaces
Most employees work in formally designated teams	65
Workplace operates a system of team briefing for groups of employees	61
Most non-managerial employees have performance formally appraised	56
Staff attitude survey conducted in last 5 years	45
Problem-solving groups (e.g. quality circles)	42
Single status between managers and non-managerial employees	41
Regular meetings of entire workforce	37
Profit-sharing scheme operated for non-managerial employees	30
Workplace operates a just-in-time system of inventory control	29
Workplace-level joint consultative committee	28
Most supervisors trained in employee relations skills	27
Attitudinal test used before making appointments	22
Employee share ownership scheme for non-managerial employees	15
Guaranteed job security or no compulsory redundancies policy	14
Most employees receive minimum of five days' training per year	12
Individual performance-related pay scheme for non-managerial employees	11

Source: WERS 1998; First Findings
Note: Base all workplaces with 25 or more employees based on responses from 1926 managers

- **video presentations:** the least popular method with 19 per cent of organisations.

Table 7.7 provides a snapshot of EI over the past decade, according to the IRS EI surveys (1993–2002).

The survey report concludes that the passing of the EU Information and Consultation Directive, to be phased in to cover all organisations/enterprises employing at least 50 employees by 2008, should provide the impetus for employers before that date to implement, use and update the various EI practices referred to, and that 'employee relations and employee commitment and motivation are the areas most likely to benefit from employee involvement initiatives' (IRS, 2002, p. 14).

Types of employee involvement practices

Hyman and Mason (1995) identify four categories of EI comprising:

- downward communication to individual employees;
- downward communication to groups of employees;
- upward communication for individual employees; and
- upward communication for groups of employees.

Table 7.8 identifies these processes for selected methods of EI and the goal(s) to be achieved.

Downward communication from managers to employees is used to inform and 'educate' employees so that they are more likely to endorse management initiatives and plans. Methods used include briefing groups and team briefing, and other forms of structured and less formal communication such as employee reports, house journals or company newspapers. Downward communication is also justified if it is successful in concentrating employee attention on product market and 'quality' issues. Using Hyman and Mason's comprehensive classification, the following types of EI can be identified.

Table 7.7 Employee involvement over time: 1993–2002

Survey year	1993	1996	1999	2002
Survey sample	62	26	49	52
Organisations recognising a trade union	82%	88%	59%	67%
Rationale for introducing employee involvement initiatives	Builds and reinforces the bond between employees and organisation, enhances employee commitment	To engender a greater commitment to, and identification with, the goals of the business and to increase employee participation	Better working relationships to enhance wider corporate performance	To create sense of ownership in employees, and to ensure that employees understand the strategic direction of the business and their role in achieving success
Main employee involvement methods (% of respondents using)	Company newspaper (85%); health and safety committee (79%); team briefings (79%); collective bargaining (69%)	Team meetings (81%); company journal (81%); team briefings (81%); collective bargaining (77%)	Team meetings (92%); company journal (92%); team briefings (86%); email communications (82%)	Noticeboards (96%); team meetings (90%); company intranet (86%); team briefings (87%)
Effect of employee involvement initiatives on trade unions (% of those recognising at least one union)	Strengthened – 14%; weakened – 35%; no effect – 51%	Strengthened – 24%; weakened – 32%; no effect – 44%	Strengthened – 16%; weakened – 33%; no effect – 52%	Strengthened – 44%; weakened – 15%; no effect – 41%
Whether initiatives had been specifically designed to weaken role of trade union	Yes in a fifth of organisations	Yes in two organisations	Yes in five organisations	Yes in six organisations
Major barriers to employee involvement	Senior managers 20%; middle management 23%; supervisors 7%; trade unions 6%	Senior managers 21%; middle managers 14%; supervisors 21%; trade unions 5%	Senior managers 4%; middle managers 8%; supervisors 5%; trade unions 11%	Senior managers 7%; middle managers 2%; supervisors 2%; trade unions 7%
Key areas benefiting from employee involvement	Employee job satisfaction, productivity, effective decision-making	Quality, employee job satisfaction, employee commitment	Commitment/ motivation, employee relations, quality	Employee relations, management decision-making

Source: IRS, 2002

Table 7.8 Employee involvement processes

Methods	Communication	
	Flow	Goal
Group		
Briefing groups	Downward	Team communication
Chair's forums	Downward	Information dissemination
Semi-autonomous work groups	Upward	Group responsibility
Quality circles	Upward	Quality ethos, diagnostic improvements
Individual		
Counselling/mentoring	Upward	Employee welfare/development
Appraisal and development	Upward	Career development
Suggestion schemes	Upward	Diagnostic improvements

Source: Hyman and Mason, 1995, p. 77

Downward communication to individual employees

Self-Evaluation Activity 7.9

Examples of written downward communications
The response is given below

If you work within an organisation, identify examples of written downward communications used in your organisation. If you do not work in an organisation, contact a large organisation within your area in order to get this information.

Concentrating on written information, the following are examples of the more commonly used methods:

- *Employee handbooks* are sometimes issued to employees on joining the organisation but many organisations neglect to do this. The contents of handbooks vary but, provided they are updated regularly, the handbooks provide useful information on the organisation and its background, its objectives and purpose, its products or services, how the organisation operates, the main conditions of employment and employee benefits, and the 'rules' of the organisation including summaries of the main procedures such as grievances, discipline, redundancy and equal opportunities.

- *Employee reports* are provided by many larger organisations on an annual basis to employees, and provide up-to-date information on the company's activities concerning sales, production, financial, investment, sales, projections of company performance in the longer term, and other company-relevant material. By having this information in a readable, easily understood form, employees are better able to understand the company's sources of income, investment and expenditure, and with information presented to employees in a systematic, fair and easily understood manner, greater trust can be engendered between management and its workforce (Farnham, 2000).

- *Notice boards, letters, bulletins and briefing notes* are all fairly common, especially in larger organisations. Notice boards are an accessible and cheap method of providing current information, while letters may convey information concerning a single topic sent directly to employees. Regular bulletins and briefing notes are aimed mainly, but not exclusively, at middle and junior managers in order to update them on important matters.

- *Newsletters and house journals* have become widespread throughout Europe and are often used in conjunction with each other. They can be useful sources of information provided the issues are relevant and the material is produced in an interesting, professional fashion. It is, however, debatable as to whether this approach achieves its informational goals or whether management have adequately thought through the aims of written forms of communication. Hyman and Mason, citing a survey of 102 publications from the UK's 1000 largest companies undertaken by Spurr (1990), argue that, as only a handful of items (twenty-four out of some 4000 different news topics) were contributed by employees, it is questionable whether 'written, essentially downward communication methods might be considered a meaningful form of involvement' (p. 35).

Downward communication to groups of employees

There are two main methods used to communicate downwards to groups and they are identified below. The nature of the communication is predominantly oral, and the degree of interaction between management and employees varies depending upon the size of group, the nature and purpose of the communication and to whom it is directed.

Meetings/forums

These may take the form of departmental meetings, the purpose of which is to enable departmental heads to convey information from senior management to staff on a regular and largely informal basis (although written agendas and minutes may be used). Another form of meeting is the mass meeting, which is formalised, fairly infrequent and allows senior management to address all staff on specific topics at a particular location. Important announcements may be made and there is limited opportunity for discussion.

Team briefings

Group methods of downward communication have been popularised by team briefings which 'reflect the unitarist approach to employee involvement, placing great emphasis on "cascading information down the line", from executive management through to the shop floor' (Hyman and Mason, 1995, p. 79). Team briefings are used to:

- inform employees of high-level or strategic decisions;

- communicate general information concerning company goals and performance, together with other matters; and
- explain the reasons for decisions concerning aspects of change, for example, changes to production technology and how these affect local work arrangements, the work group and the department(s) concerned.

Team briefings therefore have a 'local flavour' and teams are composed of colleagues who normally work in close proximity to each other. The number of team members varies from about four to 16, and teams have a 'leader' or 'coach' who may be the supervisor. Briefing meetings are held regularly on a monthly or bi-monthly basis and ideally should be brief (no more than 30 minutes). Typically, a briefing meeting comprises each manager or supervisor (the 'leader' or 'coach') meeting his or her team face to face on a regular basis. Information is cascaded downwards and is directly relevant to 'performance indicators'; targets are identified, progress reports made and 'points of action' developed.

The aims of team briefings as far as the organisation is concerned are, firstly, to provide line managers and supervisors with a greater part to play in day-to-day employee relations and 'help make this level of management feel an integral and strategically important part of the organisation' (ibid., p. 79) and, secondly, to increase the level of employee commitment at workplace level. Securing employee commitment within the team-briefing context is regarded as desirable, if not necessary, in order to:

- decrease misunderstanding between management and employees;
- increase employee acceptance of organisational and technological change by explaining to them the reasons for these changes; and
- 'to improve upward communication in the long term, by making employees feel that they have the knowledge about the organisation that allows them to contribute positively to its decision making processes' (ibid., p. 79).

The system is designed to ensure that all employees from executive management down to the shop or office floor are fully informed of matters that affect their work. Gennard and Judge (1997) describe the system in the following way:

Leaders of each briefing session prepare their own briefs, consisting of information relevant and task-related to the employees in the group. The brief is then supplemented with information which has been passed down from higher levels of management. Any employee's questions raised which cannot be answered at the time are answered in written form within a few days. Briefers from senior management levels are usually encouraged to sit in at briefings being given by more junior managers, while line managers are encouraged to be available to brief the shop floor employees. Although team briefing is not a consultative process and is basically one-way, question-and-answer sessions do take place to clarify understanding. Feedback from employees is very important just as professional managers will explain management's view to the employees in a regular and open way, using examples appropriate to each work group. (p. 129)

Team briefing in theory may be regarded as a 'panacea', but in practice there may be a number of problems and pitfalls. For example, how are team briefings to be set up within a workplace which operates on a continuous shift-working basis, when employees are working all the time except for their rest breaks? Marchington and Parker (1990) identify a number of problems in one of their case study firms, Foodpack, a large food manufacturing company. Mini case 7.3 gives annotated extracts from this case example. Mini case 7.4 explores teamworking problems in a bank environment.

Mini case 7.3
Team briefing at Foodpack

Although the ground had been well prepared, the Personnel Manager was under no illusion that the team briefing offered a panacea for all the company's ills, and he was sensitive to its potential pitfalls. At the time of the launch he said: 'People can soon realise that they're being brought together and told a lot of crap. Also, they may develop into bitching sessions. . . . You have got to remember that this audience is not used to receiving information. But it is equally important not to talk down to the shop floor, only to talk in relevant language.'

There was a mixed reception from employees to the team briefing activities and on the positive side the researchers conclude: 'Clearly, therefore, team briefing seems to have had a direct, if minor effect on activity and also on attitudes to the company.' Less positively, 'departments such as baking and engineering were less convinced about the value of the sessions'. The bakers' foremen address their groups every month, but this 'gets squeezed in when there is a breakdown or at any other convenient moment, such as when we change commodities'. Because of the continuous nature of the process, and the extensive shift arrangements for this group of operators, it was not always possible for these supervisors to attend their brief by the Production Manager. One of these also indicated the difficulty he faced in trying to interest his staff, since much of the information is about 'market performance, management changes, company acquisitions, not just about Foodpack. That kind of information interests some, but not others . . . nine out of ten here are only interested if it affects their pockets.'

The engineers were also dubious about the benefits of more information of the type they had been given, and one of them described his feelings in this way: 'Whilst it gives you more interest in what is going on, I'm not dying to know. I'm not won over myself. I haven't bought shares or anything, though I might do when I've got a bit of money.' Proponents of new realism and an enterprise culture would do well to recognise that such a calculative orientation to work is not unusual on the shop floor. There are always likely to be problems in maintaining team briefing in an environment where workloads are highly variable over the course of the year, particularly during peak periods when continuity of production is paramount.

Source: Marchington and Parker, 1990, pp. 147–9

Mini case 7.4
Barkers Bank

Team briefing was introduced for the most popular and pressing of reasons, primarily to facilitate change (overcome resistance) and to tie in with the bank's strategy and longer-term objectives. As the bank was relocating, redundancies were inevitable, so it was essential that an effective structure of communication was in place.

The briefing process emphasised the role of the line manager who would be 'chief facilitator' as an alternative channel of communication to the traditional union one. Managers themselves became 'team leaders'. Briefings lasted between 15 and 30 minutes and took place after the main brief was received from head office.

One problem with briefing was the difficulty of communicating change positively in a climate of uncertainty. If staff were not told, this would cause suspicion and apprehension, and if staff were told, it would be in such vague terms that it merely served to reinforce fears. The position of managers was ambiguous, not only to staff but also to the managers themselves, and the nature of this 'role ambiguity' resulted in inconsistencies of approach as managers were not always able to deal with issues or queries raised by staff, either because of disagreements or because they did not have the answers.

Upward communication involves the use of what Hyman and Mason (1995) call 'diagnostic techniques' which aim at using employee knowledge of the process of production and other technological and organisational issues to 'maximise a zero-defects standard in production' (p. 81). This approach focuses upon the individual employee and the work group and includes the categories identified below.

Upward communication for individual employees

Three main techniques are in common use. These are attitude surveys, suggestion schemes and appraisal schemes.

Attitude surveys

These satisfy management's need to obtain the views and opinions of employees on issues of mutual importance. The feedback obtained should be acted upon rather than stored in personnel files to gather dust. Reasons for conducting attitude surveys include the need to diagnose any problems within the organisation; the assessment of the consequences of organisational change; the measurement of employee attitudes before and after the change programme; the provision of feedback on management policies, actions and plans; and the identification of issues which concern employees collectively.

Suggestion schemes

These have a long tradition in Britain, and may be considered to be the oldest form of EI, the first formal scheme of its type being introduced in the 1880s in the Scottish shipbuilding industry. Traditionally, suggestion schemes have been used to minimise costs, but more recently, particularly in Japanese companies, they have been used to encourage employee commitment and self-motivation. Employees are encouraged to contribute ideas concerning the improvement of working methods, cutting costs of production and improving other aspects of the organisation's activities. Ideas which are accepted are financially rewarded.

Appraisal and development schemes

Appraisal schemes have grown in popularity and are often linked with the total quality management (TQM) approach (see pp. 376–7). Coverage of appraisal schemes, once confined to managerial grades, is now increasingly extended to other non-manual and even manual grades. In essence, the appraisal process involves both the appraisee (the person to be appraised) and the appraiser (usually the immediate manager or supervisor) in a yearly assessment of past performance, the setting of goals for the next year and monitoring the extent to which these goals have been achieved. The 'development' aspect is concerned with allocating resources to the employee in order to enable him or her to achieve the agreed goals. While it is outside the scope of this book to consider appraisal schemes in any detail, it is important to note that there are a number of problems associated with them, a few of which are now identified:

- If the scheme is not properly resourced, then employees may not have the opportunity to improve their performance through the provision of training and educational facilities and may therefore regard appraisal as a means of reinforcing management control.
- If appraisal is linked to performance-related pay, then this can create tensions within the appraiser–appraisee relationship. For example, if promotion opportunities and pay are subject to performance appraisal, then the open relationship may be compromised by the reluctance of the appraisee to be frank about weaknesses, and the appraiser may be reluctant to provide too positive an assessment of performance.

- The complexity of many appraisal and development schemes requires, ideally, thorough training of both appraisers and appraisees in order to ensure that schemes are fully effective.

Upward communication for groups of employees

The purpose of 'upward communication' techniques and approaches is to exploit employees' knowledge and expertise of their jobs, particularly through the mechanisms of small groups and teams. The main approaches briefly considered here, teamworking and quality circles, are 'quality driven' and are geared towards improved methods of production and service delivery within a context which encourages co-operative relationships and change. The evolving 'philosophy' which is used to justify these approaches is known as total quality management (TQM) based on Deming's notion (1981) of total quality control

(TQC) adopted in Japan and then exported to western economies.

TQC and TQM

Production, not quality control must have primary responsibility for quality; and everybody, including top management, must participate in project-by-project quality improvement. (Shonberger, 1982, p. 82)

TQC concepts are based on the work of the American management scientist W.E. Deming. Shunned by the USA, his ideas were enthusiastically taken up in Japan where he is regarded as the father of Japanese quality control. (A prize named after him, the annual Deming prize, is awarded to the Japanese manufacturer exhibiting the most impressive quality performance.) The main TQC concepts and categories are identified in Table 7.9.

Table 7.9 Total quality control: concepts and categories

TQC category	TQC concept
1. Organisation	Production responsibility
2. Goals	Habit of improvement
	Perfection
3. Basic principles	Process control
	Easy-to-see quality
	Insistence on compliance
	Line stop
	Correcting one's own errors
	100 per cent check
	Project-by-project improvement
4. Facilitating concepts	QC as facilitator
	Small lot sizes
	Housekeeping
	Daily machine checking
5. Techniques and aids	Exposure of problems
	Foolproof devices
	Analysis tools
	QC circles

Source: Shonberger, 1982, p. 51

Production responsibility means assigning the primary responsibility for quality to production personnel thereby removing it from the quality control department. The initiative for this must come from the top of the organisational hierarchy. The *rate* of quality improvement can be accelerated by implementing items from TQC categories 2–5 (as shown in Table 7.9). As far as goals are concerned, the *habit of continuous improvement* is directed towards perfection which involves measurement of quality performance and the striving for perfect conformance to specifications (zero defects). Quality depends upon the integrated efforts of marketing, design engineering, purchasing, manufacturing engineering, production and service departments, and supports a quality strategy which presumes that ever-better quality will forever increase market share and the total market as well. The other categories and concepts listed support the TQC philosophy of continuous improvement. Within the TQC scheme of things, quality circles are just one of the 18 TQC concepts listed in Table 7.9. But as they became increasingly popular in Britain and the USA, we consider them briefly below.

TQM has become the more acceptable term in western economies, but the basic ideas are the same as those underpinning TQC. Essentially, TQM endorses the guiding philosophy and goal of continuous improvement (*kaizen*) and places considerable emphasis upon increasing employee work responsibilities, reorganising work and increasing employee involvement in problem-solving activities in order to achieve that goal. There is the same emphasis upon inter-departmental co-operation and integration in order to facilitate quality improvement where it matters, that is, by the production and service workers.

Teamworking and semi-autonomous working groups

This is a form of task-based involvement which focuses upon 'whole jobs' and is concerned with enlarging and extending the range and scope of tasks which comprise the job. The basic ideas behind teamworking date back to the 1960s when Herzberg *et al.* (1959) of the managerialist 'neo' human relations school developed the techniques of job enlargement and job enrichment, the former concentrating upon increasing the range and diversity of tasks making up a job, and the latter upon introducing more elements of responsibility into

work tasks. These techniques became integrated into a system of working which incorporated so-called principles of job design. Job design has been used to encourage group working, not only by enlarging and enriching jobs, but also by developing new 'user-friendly' production technologies as alternatives to Fordist assembly-line technology which, under certain circumstances, enable semi-autonomous work groups to make the product (cars, for example) 'on site'. In such situations, workers have considerable discretion, autonomy and responsibility over pace of work, how much to produce and when to produce, thereby maximising their EI potential. The 'experiments' in work group autonomy had very limited success in Britain and were dominated by 'high profile' examples mainly in Scandinavia.

Teamwork in teams of varying size from around seven upwards is now considered as incorporating both semi-autonomous working groups and the more prescriptive enlargement and enrichment approaches, and is often referred to as 'flexible specialisation'. Teamwork requires considerable investment in training, with benefits of improved employee commitment, morale and motivation. Geary (1994) in describing the range of teamworking techniques comments:

> In its most advanced form, team working refers to the granting of autonomy to workers by management to design and prepare work schedules, to monitor and control their own work tasks and methods, to be more or less self-managing ... At the other end of the spectrum, management may merely wish employees of comparable skill to rotate between different tasks on a production line or the integration of maintenance personnel to service a particular group of machines.

Quality circles

The quality circle (QC) is a Japanese development dating from around 1962. QCs comprise small voluntary groups of workers, both operatives and specialists such as engineers in the same circle. One of the main activities of QCs is concerned with the use of problem-solving techniques such as brainstorming, problem identification, data collection and analysis and presentation skills in order to reduce waste, improve performance and quality, increase competitiveness, promote self-development and group identity and to encourage communications.

In addition, 'morale-enhancing ideas – softball leagues, vending machines, repainting the lunch-room, and so on – are legitimate topics for QC discussion, and motivational benefits are expected to derive from the employee interaction and involvement that takes place in circles' (Shonberger, 1982, p. 185). Members are also trained in the use of simple statistical analysis in order to improve quality and meet quality objectives.

QCs flourished initially in the US where they 'sprouted . . . like dandelions in a spring lawn' (ibid., p. 181), and then became popular for a time in Britain during the 1980s. However, it is important to emphasise that circles are low on the priority list of important things to get accomplished and their impact as a method of employee involvement in western countries is relatively limited. Shonberger, for example, points out:

> It is a mistake to think of QCs – for all their morale and motivation advantages – as a ticket to achieving the quality levels that have been attained by the Japanese. In fact, QC circles founded on such a premise could do more harm than good in that they might delay for several years the introduction of a real quality control programme. (p. 185)

The success of QCs in Britain depends upon whether, as in Japan, they are regarded as an integral part of an organisation-wide quality management programme. Indeed, many circles have foundered because they were regarded as a panacea for certain organisational problems, or introduced as one more management 'fad'. The introduction of quality circles in Ford UK as a result of its doomed but well intentioned 'After Japan' initiative is a case in point. McKinlay and Starkey (1992) argue that 'the dismal failure of the labour relations element of the campaign was directly attributable to Ford's attempts to impose quality circles as a structural remedy for relatively poor productivity and quality, rather than introducing them as mechanisms for mobilising employee commitment to company goals' (p. 116).

A survey of manufacturing practices in a number of companies undertaken by Oliver and Wilkinson (1992) concluded that quality circles were the least favourably rated and the least successful. The reasons for this, they suggest, are:

> That quality circles were one of the first elements of Japanese practice to be emulated by British companies, so that there has been more chance for the 'honeymoon effect' to wear off . . . [and that] quality circles have been seen by many companies as a relatively low investment innovation and consequently have failed to attract the necessary commitment, being treated merely as 'bolt-on' accessories. (pp. 162–3)

Exhibit 7.5

Quality circles at Ford

The 'After Japan' campaign was a programme of productivity and quality improvement, a major part of which involved the introduction of quality circles to the shop floor of Ford's European car plants. The company invested substantial sums of money in the programme, which included the training of circle leaders and members in techniques of problem solving and analysis. Three people were appointed to coordinate the programme at company level, and plant managers were responsible for circle activities in their plants. There was a short pilot project, after which quality circles were launched across all plants in the UK. There was little consultation with unions or lower levels of management, as senior management considered quality circles to be a 'minor change for the better'. In the six months or so following their introduction, some successes were documented (for example, a 2.5 per cent saving in scrap at the Bridgend engine plant). However, union resistance was mounting, and in 1981, the trade unions withdrew their support from the programme. According to Guthrie's (1987) analysis, the programme was a 'resounding failure' in terms of its aims of improving work attitude and generating net cost savings.

Source: Oliver and Wilkinson, 1992, p. 169

The problems associated with quality circles, therefore, include the effects of transposing a Japanese-derived 'culture-bound' concept and method used successfully in Japanese companies into a western organisational context with no quality ethos and no traditions of group-based quality management. Another problem with QCs concerns their introduction into unionised organisations where, as in the Ford example (Exhibit 7.5), opposition may be encountered. Union opposition may be based upon perceptions of incompatibility between the essentially 'collective' orientation of industrial relations and the 'individualistic' preoccupations of HRM practices where QCs belong to the latter category.

Employee involvement: concluding comments

The take-up of EI has been fairly comprehensive and widespread in a growing number of organisations as the WIRS surveys and WERS98 suggest. Although EI can and has been regarded as a major union substitution practice, this is only one reason why managers have adopted it. A substantial number of larger unionised companies have integrated EI into their existing union channels without compromising the role of union representatives or altering collective methods of communication. Other companies use EI practices as an integral part of a wider HRM strategy geared towards increasing employee identification with, and commitment to, the organisation and are at least partially successful in this. However, yet other organisations, perhaps in a majority, have adopted EI as a 'fad', as with many other new management practices such as 'empowerment', and as we may expect, there is little integration of EI within HRM strategy. Within these and other organisations, EI may not work effectively in practice as line managers may 'lack the enthusiasm and commitment . . . and many employers have committed insufficient time and resources to training supervisors to deliver EI at the workplace' (Marchington, 1995, p. 301). However, the implementation of the EU Information and Consultation Directive (see Chapter 8) is likely to encourage organisations and enterprises to devise and incorporate effective EI approaches as part of their ongoing HR strategies.

A more fundamental criticism is posited by, for example, Hyman and Mason (1995) who argue that EI has had little or no effect upon the extent to which employees have influence within their organisations because:

- evidence that employees influence organisational decisions and other corporate matters is extremely limited. EI is confined either to immediate work and task issues or to facilitating communications;
- EI is concerned with securing employee commitment. With greater emphasis upon involvement practices, 'there is a danger that collective means to influence employer and managerial decisions will become further eroded' (p. 192); and
- EI is associated 'functionally and operationally' with employee flexibility and labour market deregulation 'which raises further doubts about the capability of involvement to serve as a vehicle for the expression of employee interests' (p. 192).

We conclude, therefore, that the impact of EI upon the employee has been marginal. In Britain employees, particularly in non-union organisations, are subject to management-initiated and directed involvement as the main, if not the sole, means of communication and information and for employees in these and other organisations, the EU Information and Consultation Directive cannot be implemented soon enough.

RELEVANT WEBSITES

www.dti.gov.uk (Department of Trade and Industry) Provides useful information and statistics concerning small and medium-sized enterprises (SMEs), together with information relating to its Small Business Service.

REFERENCES

Bassett, P. (1988) 'Non-unionism's growing ranks'. *Personnel Management*, March

Beaumont, P.D. and Harris, R. (1988) 'Subsystems of industrial relations: the spatial dimension in Britain'. *British Journal of Industrial Relations*, 26, 4, 397–407

Blyton, P. and Turnbull, P. (1994) *The Dynamics of Employee Relations*. London, Macmillan

Blyton, P. and Turnbull, P. (1998) *The Dynamics of Employee Relations*, 2nd edn. London, Macmillan

Brown, W. (1993) 'The contraction of collective bargaining in Britain'. *British Journal of Industrial Relations*, 31, 2, 189–200

Brown, W., Deakin, S., Hudson, M. and Pratten, C. (2001) 'The limits of statutory trade union recognition'. *Industrial Relations Journal*, 32, 3, 180–94

Claydon, T. (1997) 'Union derecognition; a re-examination' in Beardwell, I.J. (ed.) *Contemporary Industrial Relations: A Critical Analysis*. Oxford, Oxford University Press

Colling, T. (2003) 'Managing without unions: The sources and limitations of individualism', in Edwards, P. (ed.) *Industrial Relations Theory and Practice*, 2nd edn. Oxford, Blackwell

Cully, M., Woodland, S., O'Reilly, A. and Dix, G. (1998) *The 1998 Workplace Employee Relations Survey*. London, DTI

Cully, M., Woodland, S., O'Reilly, A. and Dix, G. (1999) *Britain at Work*. London, Routledge

Cunnison, S. (1966) *Wages and Work Allocation*. London, Tavistock Publications

Deming, W. (1981) 'What top management must do'. *Business Week*, July, 19–21

Dibb Lupton Allsop (1997–2001) *The Industrial Relations Survey*. London

Dickson, T. (1988) 'Big Blue and the unions: IBM, individualism and trade union strategies'. *Work, Employment and Society*, 2, 4, 506–20

DTI (Department of Trade and Industry) (2002) *Small and Medium Sized Enterprise (SME) Strategies 2001*. London, DTI

Dundon, T. (2002) 'Employer opposition and union avoidance in the UK'. *Industrial Relations Journal*, 33, 3, 234–45

Farnham, D. (2000) *Employee Relations in Context*, 2nd edn. London, CIPD

Farnham, D. and Pimlott, J. (1995) *Understanding Industrial Relations*. London, Cassell

Flood, P.C. and Toner, B. (1997) 'Large non-union companies: how do they avoid a Catch-22?' *British Journal of Industrial Relations*, 35, 2, 257–77

Freeman, R.B. and Medoff, J.L. (1984) *What Do Unions Do?* New York, Basic Books

Gall, G. and McKay, S. (1994) 'Trade union derecognition in Britain 1988–1994'. *British Journal of Industrial Relations*, 32, 3, 433–48

Gall, G. and McKay, S. (1999) 'Developments in union recognition and derecognition in Britain 1994–1998'. *British Journal of Industrial Relations*, 37, 4, 601–14

Gall, G. and McKay, S. (2001) 'Facing fairness at work: union perception of employer opposition and response to union recognition'. *Industrial Relations Journal*, 32, 2, 94–113

Gallie, D. (1996) 'Trade union allegiance and decline in British urban labour markets', in Gaillie, D., Penn, R. and Rose, M. (eds) *Trade Unionism in Recession*. Oxford, Oxford University Press

Gallie, D., Penn, R. and Rose, M. (eds) (1996) *Trade Unionism in Recession*. Oxford, Oxford University Press

Geary, J.E. (1994) 'Task participation: employees' participation enabled or constrained?' in Sisson, K. (ed.) *Personnel Management*. Oxford, Blackwell

Gennard, J. and Judge, G. (1997) *Employee Relations*. London, IPD

Goss, D. (1991) *Small Business and Society*. London, Routledge

Gregg, P. and Yates, A. (1991) 'Changes in wage setting arrangements and trade union presence in the 1980s'. *British Journal of Industrial Relations*, 29, 3, 361–76

Guest, D. (1995) 'Human resource management, industrial relations and trade unions', in Storey, J. (ed.) *Human Resource Management: A Critical Text*. London, Routledge

Guest, D. and Conway, N. (1999) 'Peering into the Black Hole: the downside of the new employment relations in the UK'. *British Journal of Industrial Relations*, 37, 3, 367–89

Guest, D.E. and Hoque, K. (1994) 'The good, the bad and the ugly: employment relations in new non-union workplaces'. *Human Resource Management Journal*, 5, 1, 1–14

Guthrie, G. (1987) 'After Japan and beyond'. *Production Engineer*, May, 29–31

Heery, E. (1997) 'The new, new unionism', in Beardwell, I.J. (ed.) *Contemporary Industrial Relations: A Critical Analysis*. Oxford, Oxford University Press

Herzberg, F., Mausner, B. and Synderman, B. (1959) *The Motivation to Work*. London, Granada

Hyman, R. (1997) 'The future of employee representation'. *British Journal of Industrial Relations*, 35, 3, 309–36

Hyman, J. and Mason, R. (1995) *Managing Employee Involvement and Participation*. London, Sage

IRS (2002) 'Employee involvement', *IRS Employment Trends*, No. 763

Jackson, M.P., Leopold, J.W. and Tuck, K. (1993) *Decentralisation of Collective Bargaining*. Basingstoke, Macmillan

Kelly, J. (1998) *Rethinking Industrial Relations*. London, Routledge

Knowles, K.G.J.C. (1952) *Strikes: A Study of Industrial Conflict*. Oxford, Basil Blackwell

Kochan, T.A., Katz, H.C. and McKersie, R.B. (1986) *The Transformation of American Industrial Relations*. New York, Basic Books

Lloyd, C. (2001) 'What do employee councils do? The impact of non-union forms of representation on trade union organisation. *Industrial Relations Journal*, 32, 4, 313–27

LPC (Low Pay Commission) (1998) *The National Minimum Wage: First Report of the Low Pay Commission*, Cmnd 3276. London, HMSO

Machin, S. (2000) 'Union decline in Britain'. *British Journal of Industrial Relations*, 30, 4, 631–45

Marchington, M. (1995) 'Involvement and participation', in Storey, J. (ed.) *Human Resource Management: A Critical Text*. London, Routledge

Marchington, M. and Parker, P. (1990) *Changing Patterns of Employee Relations*. London, Harvester Wheatsheaf

Marchington, M., Goodman, J., Wilkinson, A. and Ackers, P. (1992) *New Developments in Employee Involvement*. Research Series No. 2, Sheffield, Department of Employment

Marlow, S. and Patton, D. (2002) 'Minding the gap between employers and employees: the challenge for owner-managers of smaller manufacturing firms'. *Employee Relations*, 24, 5, 523–39

Mars, G. (1973) 'Chance, punters and the fiddle: institutionalised pilferage in a hotel dining room', in Warner, M. (ed.) *The Sociology of the Workplace*. London, Allen and Unwin

Martin, R., Sunley, P. and Wills, J. (1996) *Union Retreat and the Regions*. London, Jessica Kingsley

McKinlay, A. and Starkey, K. (1992) 'Competitive strategies and organisational change', in Salaman, G. (ed.) *Human Resource Strategies*. London, Sage

McLoughlin, I. and Gourlay, S. (1994) *Enterprise Without Unions: Industrial Relations in the Non-Union Firm*. Buckingham, Open University Press

Metcalfe, D. (1989) 'Trade unions and economic performance: the British evidence'. *LSE Quarterly*, 3, 21–42

Millward, N. (1994) *The New Industrial Relations*. London, Policy Studies Institute

Millward, N., Bryson, A. and Forth, J. (2000) *All Change at Work*. London, Routledge

Millward, N., Stevens, M., Smart, D. and Hawes, W.R. (1992) *Workplace Industrial Relations In Transition*. Aldershot, Dartmouth

Milner, S. (1995) 'The coverage of collective pay-setting institutions in Britain, 1895–1990'. *British Journal of Industrial Relations*, 33, 1, 69–91

Nolan, P. and O'Donnell, K. (1995) 'Industrial relations and productivity', in Edwards, P. (ed.) *Industrial Relations: Theory and Practice in Britain*. Oxford, Blackwell

Oliver, N. and Wilkinson, B. (1992) *The Japanisation of British Industry*. Oxford, Blackwell

Peach, L. (1983) 'Employee relations in IBM'. *Employee Relations*, 5, 3, 1–12

Penn, R. and Scattergood, H. (1996) 'The experience of trade unions in Rochdale during the 1980s', in Gallie, D., Penn, R. and Rose, M. (eds) *Trade Unionism in Recession*. Oxford, Oxford University Press

Phelps-Brown, H. (1959) *The Growth of British Industrial Relations*. London, Macmillan

Purcell, J. (1987) 'Mapping management styles in employee relations'. *Journal of Management Studies*, 23, 2, 205–23

Purcell, J. and Sisson, K. (1983) 'Strategies and practice in the management of industrial relations', in Bain, G.S. (ed.) *Industrial Relations in Britain*. Oxford, Blackwell

Rainnie, A.F. (1989) *Industrial Relations in Small Firms: Small Isn't Beautiful*. London, Routledge

Rose, M. (1996) 'Still life in Swindon: Case studies in union survival and employer policy in a "sunrise" labour market', in Gaillie, D., Penn, R. and Rose, M. (eds) *Trade Unionism in Recession*. Oxford, Oxford University Press

Scase, R. (1995) 'Employment relations in small firms' in Edwards, P. (ed.) *Industrial Relations: Theory and Practice in Britain*. Oxford, Blackwell

Scase, R. (2003) 'Employment relations in small firms' in Edwards, P. (ed.) *Industrial Relations Theory and Practice*, 2nd edn. Oxford, Blackwell

Scase, R. and Goffee, R. (1982) *The Entrepreneurial Middle Class*. London, Croom Helm

Scott, M., Roberts, I., Holroyd, G. and Sawbridge, D. (1989) *Management and Industrial Relations in Small Firms*. Research Paper 70, London, Department of Employment

Shonberger, R.J. (1982) *Japanese Manufacturing Techniques*. London, Macmillan

Sieff, M. (1990) *Marcus Sieff on Management: The Marks and Spencer Way*. London, Weidenfeld & Nicolson

Sisson, K. (1993) 'In search of HRM'. *British Journal of Industrial Relations*, 31, 2, 201–10

Smith, P. and Morton, G. (1993) 'Union exclusion and the decollectivisation of industrial relations in Britain'. *British Journal of Industrial Relations*, 31, 1, 97–114

Spurr, I. (1990) 'Are house journals just hot air?'. *Involvement and Participation*, 607, 14–17

Terry, M. (1999) 'Systems of collective employee representation in non-union firms in the UK'. *Industrial Relations Journal*, 30, 1, 16–30

Toner, B. (1985) 'The unionisation and productivity debate: an employee opinion survey in Ireland'. *British Journal of Industrial Relations*, 28, 1, 227–47

TUC (1998) *General Council Report*. London, Trades Union Congress

TUC (2002) *Annual Report*. London, TUC

Turnbull, P. and Wass, V. (1998) 'Marksist management: sophisticated human relations in a high street retail store'. *Industrial Relations Journal*, vol. 29, no. 2, pp. 98–111

WERS (1998) See Cully, M. *et al.* (1998)

WIRT (1990) See Millward, N. *et al.* (1992)

CHAPTER 8

EMPLOYEE VOICE, PARTICIPATION AND PARTNERSHIP

INTRODUCTION

The term 'employee voice' has been used in the wider context associated with trade union decline in Britain during the 1980s and 1990s as in: 'Have employees lost their voice?' (Millward *et al.*, 2000, ch. 4). It incorporates the formal mechanisms of employee participation and both the formal and informal activities of workplace representatives on the one hand, and direct means of communication on the other (see Chapter 7). Employee voice channels are also found in non-union organisations and workplaces, although not to the same extent as in unionised workplaces. In this chapter we use 'employee voice' not as a concept per se but as a 'catch-all' term used to cover a wide range of processes and structures which allow and even empower employees, directly or indirectly, to contribute to decision-making within the organisation.

Employee participation is concerned with the representation of worker interests within the organisation's decision-making process, the emphasis being upon representation and formality. In this book, and this chapter particularly, a clear distinction is made between employee participation on the one hand, and employee involvement on the other (the latter being considered in some detail in Chapter 7). It is necessary to make this distinction because, contrary to some views, there is in practice no staged process from involvement to participation which employers adopt in order to secure worker representation in the decision-making process, although ideally and normatively employers should practice both. More importantly, it is erroneous to extend the term employee or worker participation to practices which are more appropriately labelled 'involvement'. As a theoretical construct, the involvement–participation continuum has its uses, as we shall see. Indeed, we argue that most employers shy away from formal machinery which facilitates 'employee voice' and at best they are 'reluctant participators'.

'Partnership', 'social partnership' and 'partnership agreements' are relatively recent terms which have entered the lexicon of employment relations. Social partnership is characteristic of northern European countries such as Germany, Austria, the Netherlands and Scandinavia and denotes mostly formal arrangements and structures of negotiation and joint consultation between unions and employers at national, sectoral and workplace levels. At workplace level, probably the most salient example of partnership based on consensus is the works council, considered in greater detail later in the chapter. Despite the rhetoric of partnership which was manifested in the approach of the first New Labour government, the concept, as Terry (2003) points out, does not sit easily within the UK context in the absence of a legislative framework of the type that exists in some European nations, and without the requisite degree of 'shared commitment to commercial success, the balance between change (flexibility) and security, and the emphasis on dialogue and expertise' (p. 279). Nevertheless, the TUC endorsed the concept at national and organisational levels and encouraged the formation of partnership agreements between employers, unions and employees.

Within most work organisations in Britain, structures and mechanisms of formal employee participation do not feature very prominently. Apart from the machinery of collective bargaining and the 'pseudo' participation which often characterises joint consultative committees (see below), employees, more often than not, are unable to give voice to their collective interests through formal participative structures such as works councils, a situation exacerbated by the anti-collectivist ideology of 1980s' Thatcherism. Within the employment relationship in Britain, industrial action, as an expression of collective concern and power of employees, is often the only means of facilitating the bargaining process in order to achieve a favourable outcome to negotiations. The absence of democratic structures in many work organisations is at odds with the liberal democratic structures which exist within the wider European context, and is a problem which, arguably, should be addressed. Apart from adopting the European Works Council Directive, much more could have been done by the first Blair government through, for example, the introduction of legislation providing a statutory right to collective representation for all employees, possibly on the lines of the national works council system which operates in many EU countries. While formal participatory structures may not eliminate industrial action, the establishment of a general framework for informing and consulting employees might encourage employers and employee representatives to work 'in a spirit of co-operation' rather than conflict (EU Directive on worker information and consultation, 2001, partial implementation of which is expected by 2005).

Employee participation, according to Farnham (1997), is one of four policy choices open to managements in determining their industrial relations strategies 'including how work relations are structured, how work is organised and what emphasis they [management] should adopt in managing people at work' (p. 354). The other three choices are:

- worker subordination via managerial prerogative (see Chapter 2);
- union incorporation via collective bargaining (see Chapter 6); and
- employee commitment via employee involvement practices (see Chapter 7).

There is no satisfactory definition of participation partly because of the numerous and varied practices which are labelled 'participation', partly because there are normative and ideological connotations, and partly because there are semantic problems with 'participation' and related terms such as industrial democracy and employee involvement. At the most general level, participation can be unsatisfactorily defined as **the extent to which employees and their representatives should and do enter into joint decision-making with management and its representatives**. This definition says nothing about the extent or depth of participation, the motives of the parties concerned, the degree of influence the parties exert upon one another or the organisational structures most appropriate to the participation process.

Space does not permit a lengthy examination of these issues (see Hyman and Mason, (1995) and Marchington and Parker (1990), for a detailed analysis of these and other topics) and we shall confine ourselve to considering briefly the important terms relevant to participation before looking at the distinction between employee involvement (EI) and employee participation. We then go on to look at the extent of employee participation initiatives in Britain and why they have not been particularly successful. The relatively successful type of employee participation based upon the German system of 'co-determination' is considered in greater detail before dealing finally with European Works Councils. We then look at the empirical work which traces the extent of employee voice in the UK using the results of the Workplace Employment Relations Survey, 1998 (Cully *et al.*, 1999). Finally we look at the extent of the partnership ethos in Britain and the success or otherwise of partnership agreements concluded to date.

THE NATURE AND CONTEXT OF EMPLOYEE PARTICIPATION

There are two distinct approaches which have shaped participatory organisational structures in Western Europe during the post-Second World War period. The first approach concerns the rise of 'managerialism' (see Chapter 2) and the resurrection of managerial prerogatives during the 1980s together with the dominance of HRM practices. This approach considers employee influence in terms of 'involvement' in order to achieve certain organisational goals. The decision-making agenda, particularly concerning strategic issues, is set by management, as are the organisational goals and values to which employees are meant to be committed. While employees are denied influence over management decisions, Hyman and Mason (1995) assert that:

> In responding to the urgency of . . . market uncertainties and signals few employers can afford to be deflected by employee objections or encumbered by constitutional obstacles constructed by their unions. HRM seeks to find a solution to this conundrum by involving employees in task-based activities, but also alerting them to the precarious nature of paid work in a dynamic market environment through systems of communication and information provision. It might also be argued that HRM can serve to reduce or eliminate the potential of trade unions to materially interfere with management decision making processes or outcomes. (p. 6)

This, approach, therefore, emphasises employee involvement (EI) concerning job and task-based decisions rather than operational and strategic managerial decisions, and is dealt with in greater detail in Chapter 7. The second approach incorporates the strategy evidenced in most European Union countries and views participation as an employee right to question and influence organisational decision making. This has resulted in formalised structures of participation underpinned by legislation and based on representative democracy.

Self-Evaluation Activity 8.1

Main parties to employee participation
The response is given below

Identify the main parties concerned with employee participation together with the interests of each in the participatory process.

The main parties concerned are labour, employers and the democratic state. All three have different interests attributed to them of a largely ideological nature concerning the participatory process. These are considered in turn.

1. Employee interests
According to Hyman and Mason (1995), writers in the radical tradition contend that employees have little or no formal influence at work within a capitalist society. They argue for total democratisation of the workplace which implies, in a Marxist sense, partial or complete control over the means of production as a precondition.

Instead of 'employee or worker participation', radical theorists prefer to use the term industrial democracy, and in situations where workers have total control over the means of production (that is, in socialist states), workers' control. Industrial democracy as a concept is concerned with both direct and indirect representation. In the former situation, employees represent themselves individually, and directly influence and jointly determine decisions with management (management being assumed to be just as necessary a function within such organisations as within conventional organisations) without intermediaries or representatives. By definition, this can take place only within smaller organisations, the main examples of which are worker co-operatives. In the latter situation, employee representatives make decisions on behalf of their constituents, and it is here that we have the industrial equivalent of parliamentary democracy.

However, there is some debate as to what actually constitutes 'true' industrial democracy: should it, for example, be regarded as an ongoing process of 'encroaching control', whereby trade unions progressively gain experience of managerial functions and responsibilities through the extension of collective bargaining (see Chapter 6)? Or should it involve trade unions and/or employees appropriating and supplanting economic and political control of industrial organisations? Also, if industrial democracy is to emulate parliamentary democracy, there should be provision for the 'opposition' to become the 'government'. Moreover, in capitalist societies this analogy is inappropriate because the 'opposition' of employees and their unions is a permanent one, and despite degrees of joint decision-making, the more apposite analogy would be that of the one-party state.

2. Employer interests

Writers in what Hyman and Mason (1995) call the conservative tradition are associated with employers' interests and managerial needs 'to direct and control the labour of subordinates under conditions which can be alienating, insecure and poorly rewarded materially and motivationally' (p. 9). This does not preclude enhancing the motivational content of work, stressing employee involvement in task-related activities and management exercises in raising employee performance, as long as these produce positive outcomes for employers and contribute towards the economic success of the organisation. Most employers in Britain have not

been proactive in matters of participation. The main reasons for this state of affairs include the following:

- The need, perceived or real, to **reinforce and confirm the legitimacy of managerial power and decision-making**, particularly within a unitarist framework (see Chapter 2).
- The need to **manage and contain conflict in the interests of preserving harmonious relationships**; this, again, is part of the unitary ideology of management. Union avoidance is a major strategy; we may call this the push strategy, which involves pushing against trade unions and their activists. Another major strategy is the desire on the part of some employers to create an organisational environment in which employees do not feel the need for outside protection; this can be termed a pull strategy, which involves pulling employees towards employers by offering certain inducements such as rewarding individual effort and employee share-holding schemes. Ramsay (1977) has argued that there are certain patterns or 'cycles' which can be discerned over time (called the cycles of control thesis). During periods of economic growth and prosperity which have traditionally been accompanied by increased levels of trade union activity, Ramsay argues that employer efforts to harness greater employee involvement are intensified as the 'union threat' increases. Conversely, during periods of recession or economic stagnation, employer interest in involvement techniques wanes as trade union activity wanes. While Ramsey's argument would appear to be more applicable to the post-war period prior to 1979, it has been criticised by others such as Ackers *et al.* (1996), who argue that employee involvement techniques are introduced by employers for a variety of reasons apart from cyclical ones. They argue that during the 1980s and 1990s the greater demands upon companies generally to compete in, and respond effectively to, the increasingly stringent requirements of both national and global product markets has put employee involvement and HRM much higher on the managerial agenda.
- The need to **maintain, sustain and increase productivity** and to pursue **motivational objectives** has been of perennial concern to employers ever since F.W. Taylor's (1947) work on 'scientific management' and the growth of Fordist production systems enabled workers to maximise their incomes through

increased productivity (see Chapters 2 and 5). This was followed by the subsequent growth of the 'human relations' and 'neo-human relations' streams of management thought (encapsulated in the work of Argyris (1964), Herzberg (1974), Likert (1961) and McGregor (1960), to name but a few), which emphasised that greater motivation, higher levels of job satisfaction, appropriate leadership styles and effective teamworking could contribute to greater employee well-being and facilitate employee integration into the production process. Again, as Blyton and Turnbull (1998) point out:

> The human relations [and neo-human relations] view is consistent with a managerial orientation which is strongly unitarist in perspective. More than this, however, management's advocacy of certain types of participation represents an acknowledgement that employee commitment needs to be actively secured rather than passively assumed, and that involving employees in decision making is a means of achieving this. Management's support for [some forms of] participation is also an acknowledgement of the potential contribution of employee knowledge to the management of the organisation – in particular tapping valuable worker experience regarding the way work tasks are organised and performed. More generally this management orientation is an acknowledgement that many employees seek not only financial recompense from work but also a more extensive engagement with the institution in which they spend a large proportion of their waking hours. (p. 222)

- The need for **enterprise consciousness** among employees, according to Hyman and Mason (1995) 'echoes unitarist human relations principles [and] can be found within contemporary constructions of "human resource management"' (p. 11). Practices, which more accurately can be described as 'employee involvement', include team briefings, quality circles, *kaizen*-oriented activities and cascading communications (see Chapters 6 and 7).

3. The democratic state

Democratic institutions can only survive and prosper within a democratic state, but even so, apart from political democracy, fully democratic institutions and organisations are relatively rare, most often confined in

Britain to membership organisations which are largely voluntary, and to trade unions and related associations. We examined the role of government and the state in Chapter 4. In Britain and the United States, government has been relatively abstentionist in the industrial relations arena, but as we have seen in Chapter 6, rarely neutral: Labour governments before 1980 have tended to enact protective and enabling legislation favouring collective organisation often within a corporatist framework, while Conservative governments tended to favour employers and their organisations. Overall, before 1979, governments became more actively involved if the balance of power favoured one party over another. They often (but not always) acted upon recommendations of major government commissions such as the Whitley Commission in 1917, which established negotiating committees at national level, and the Donovan Commission in 1968, which confirmed the value of collective bargaining entered into freely by the parties concerned and underlined the view that collective bargaining between independent unions and employers constituted the most appropriate form of 'industrial democracy' within a pluralist society. The only government commission dealing specifically with employee participation and industrial democracy, the Bullock Commission which reported in 1977, produced recommendations which were not taken up by any subsequent government. Government inaction in the employee participation area contrasts sharply with the experience of other European countries, particularly those within the European Union, where legislation has been enacted to promote representative structures of participation, which in the case of Germany applies to the vast majority of organisations in both the public and private sectors.

Employee participation: an overview

We have already noted that there is considerable semantic confusion concerning the term 'employee participation'. We could, for example, opt for the all-embracing definition put forward by Wall and Lischeron (1977) as the 'influence in decision making exerted through a process of interaction between workers and managers' (p. 38). For our purposes, this definition is too general as it incorporates 'employee involvement', and also raises questions concerning complexities and variations in practice as pointed out by Blyton and Turnbull (1994, 1998). For example, there are issues relating to the:

- **depth of participation** concerning the extent to which employees or their representatives influence the final decision. This can range from *minimal* (little or no involvement) to *moderate* as with joint consultation, decision-making, collective bargaining and works councils, to *dominant* as with worker co-operatives;
- **range or scope** of decisions which are open to participation. This is determined by the willingness of the parties, particularly management, to broaden the scope (as with *co-operative bargaining*), the structure and size of the organisation and whether participation is required by legislation;
- **forms of participation structure**, of which there are many, ranging from suggestion schemes to board-level representation; there may be *formal* and *informal* mechanisms and activities, and *direct* or *indirect* methods;
- **levels at which participation takes place**; ranging from unit, or department to workplace where it is usually *direct*, often *informal*, and *task or work-based*; and
- **purpose and outcomes of participatory activity**, which may be merely to communicate and inform employees of a decision that has already been made (sometimes referred to as *pseudo participation*).

We are now in a position to place participation within the whole range of activities whereby employees may be able to influence managerial decisions. Blyton and Turnbull (1998), for example, have devised the model shown in Figure 8.1 which they call 'a continuum of employee participation'. Although useful in helping us to place different types of involvement and participation, it omits the other variables that we looked at above. The following headings incorporate the essential characteristics of

involvement and participation which extend from 'no involvement' to 'full employee control' and which are identified in Figure 8.2 below (we choose some, but not all of the above variables):

A. **Values and ideology** (attitudes and approaches to power and the employment relationship)
B. **Definitions of involvement/participation**
C. **Forms of involvement/participation**
D. **Levels of decision-making.**

The framework in Figure 8.2 incorporates many of the factors and characteristics that you may have considered. It demonstrates the theoretical logic of progression from one type of involvement or participation to another, and in this sense represents a more detailed continuum than that of Blyton and Turnbull. However, the evidence for such a progression either within capitalist or erstwhile socialist countries is slender indeed. It should also be pointed out that many of these examples are ephemeral as, for example, Yugoslav 'self-management', employee directors in British Steel and the Post Office, and the three large industrial co-operatives in Britain during the early 1970s (such as the Triumph Meriden co-operative). What Figure 8.2 does, however, is place employee participation firmly in the third category, with the main examples of collective bargaining and other forms of worker representation such as the German 'co-determination' example being relatively enduring features, especially when compared with most other forms of involvement and the 'industrial democracy' examples of the fourth category.

Employee involvement and employee participation contrasted

Having identified employee participation (EP) within the continuum detailed in Figure 8.1, we can now distinguish quite clearly between EI and EP.

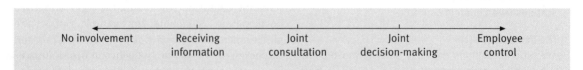

| No involvement | Receiving information | Joint consultation | Joint decision-making | Employee control |

Figure 8.1 Blyton and Turnbull's continuum of employee participation
Source: Blyton and Turnbull, 1998, p. 224

Values/ideology	Definitions	Forms of participation/involvement	Levels of decision-making
1. **Unitary view:** the enforcement and legitimisation of clear, hierarchical command in the interests of economic efficiency	1. No involvement or participation, apart from enjoying the economic benefits of the enterprise	1. Formal hierarchy and downward communication between management and shop floor	1. Possibly social and welfare (health and safety, recreational facilities, pension funds, etc.)
2. **Integrative:** the harmonisation of management/workforce objectives under the 'human relations' leadership of management. Strong but primitive HRM orientation	2. A process whereby the employee can and/or does individually exert some control over decision-making concerning the task and/or job. Typical 'employee involvement' techniques	2. Direct individual and group involvement through job enlargement, job enrichment, flexibility arrangements, team briefings, 'kaizen' arrangements, suggestion schemes. Some profit-sharing. The role of collective representation, where it exists, is minimised	2. Personnel and HRM: hiring and firing, apprenticeship, manning levels, etc.
3. **Distributive and pluralist:** the progressive or more sudden transfer of power from management to employee on a 'power-sharing' basis but where management retains ultimate control	3. A process whereby employees exert collective influence over decision-making and the labour process	3. Genuine 'employee participation'. Indirect collective participation either through: (a) trade unions and collective bargaining; or, (b) new forms of representation such as worker directors and works councils	3. Shared economic control or co-determination within the enterprise: (a) over technical matters such as methods of production; and (b) over business methods such as pricing, marketing, product choice and design, etc.
4. **Complete democratisation** of enterprises. New, democratic organisational forms	4. A process whereby employees exert full collective control over all decision-making and the labour process	4. (a) Direct democracy in smaller enterprises such as producer co-operatives (b) Indirect democracy in larger enterprises within a system of 'workers' control or 'self-management'	4. (a) Employee decision-making at all levels in co-operatives within capitalist society (b) Supra-enterprise policy-making (economic decisions at regional and national levels) within a 'socialist' society

Figure 8.2 Positioning employee participation

In this respect, the definitions of both EP and EI provided by Hyman and Mason (1995) are quite adequate for our purposes. They define EP as:

> state initiatives which promote the collective rights of employees to be represented in organ-isational decision making, or to the consequences of the efforts of employees themselves to establish collective representation in corporate decisions, possibly in the face of employer resistance. This

definition would include collective bargaining over terms and conditions of employment. (p. 21)

EI is defined as:

> practices and policies which emanate from management and sympathisers of free market commercial activity and which purport to provide employees with the opportunity to influence and where appropriate take part in the decision making on matters which affect them. (p. 21)

EI, then, is usually instigated and controlled by management often, but not always, espousing a unitary ideology concerning the employment relationship. Management sets the agenda which is consistent with requirements for a flexible and adaptable workforce within a competitive product market. Information disseminated by management concerning the enterprise as a whole is normally not subject to any decision-making input from employees, although employees are expected to respond positively towards it. Employee decision-making, as we have already noted earlier in this chapter, is normally confined to task-based activities.

Self-Evaluation Activity 8.2

Main characteristics of employee participation
This SEA has no commentary

We have identified the main characteristics of employee involvement. Attempt a short paragraph, similar to the one above, which describes the main characteristics of employee participation, and compare your efforts with what is included in Figure 8.3.

Rationale, approaches and initiatives of EP

Rationale

As we have seen, employee participation usually emerges from a collective employee interest, supported by political ideas, parties and governments receptive to such ideas and practices. Employers, on the other hand have usually resisted participatory ideas and practices. Hyman and Mason (1995) provide an example of employer prejudice to the participation proposals of the Bullock Committee of Inquiry on Industrial Democracy (1977):

> *Tensions between the contrasting interests of employers and labour became evident in the UK during the late 1970s: during this period, political expediency to mobilise union support was articulated by a strong (if patchy) union impetus towards participative arrangements which were capable of propelling employee interests beyond the areas bounded by collective bargaining alone. Together these movements manifested in proposals for worker directors, planning agreements and joint representative councils. The most ambitious of these initiatives was undoubtedly the*

Employee participation	Employee involvement
Mainly pluralist	*Mainly unitarist*
1. Inspired by government and/or workforce with some control delegated to workers	1. Inspired and controlled by management
2. Aims to harness collective employee inputs through market regulation	2. Oriented towards encouraging individual employee inputs through market regulation
3. Collective representation	3. Directed to responsibilities of individual employees
4. Management and organisational hierarchies chain of command broken	4. Management and organisational structures flatter but hierarchies undisturbed
5. Active involvement of employee representatives	5. Employees are often passive recipients of information and decisions already made
6. Decision-making at higher organisational levels	6. Decisions tend to be task-based
7. Plurality of interests recognised and machinery for their resolution provided	7. Assumes common interests between employer and employees
8. Aims to distribute strategic influence beyond management	8. Aims to concentrate strategic influence among management

Figure 8.3 Essentials of EI and EP
Source: Based on Hyman and Mason, 1995, p. 25

attempt to introduce a participative framework based on worker directors using the formula of a unitary board composed of equal numbers of shareholder and union appointees supplemented by a minority of 'neutral' directors. These proposals, made by a majority of members sitting on the Bullock Committee established by the Labour government, were subsequently frustrated by internal divisions in the union movement, a lack of political will by the then ruling but tottering government, and the concerted opposition of employers and Conservative politicians toward threatened erosion of managerial decision making and hierarchical prerogatives. In brief, the confrontational stances implicit in traditional voluntaristic industrial relations as expressed in a preference for collective bargaining were unable, ideologically or practically, to accommodate the joint concessions required by the parties for the adoption of alternative participative arrangements. The subsequent emergence and realisation of the 'Thatcherite' enterprise economy effectively removed any formal government policy attachment toward collective participation in the UK during the 1980s and early 1990s. (pp. 29–30)

Factors external to the organisation of work strengthened the rationale for employee participation during the 1960s and 1970s. For example, it was felt that rising levels of educational attainment would result in more critical questioning of the assumptions underlying everyday organisations and institutions and possibly lead to their restructuring on democratic lines. An increasingly intellectually sophisticated population would no longer accept the societal status quo unquestioningly, and as Salamon (1998) states: 'The period saw the demise of the "deferential society" and the rise of the "democratic imperative": that is those who will be substantially affected by decisions made by social and political institutions must be involved in the making of those decisions' (p. 358). Pressures for greater participation were also evident in order to counter the alienating tendencies of Fordist production systems (see Chapter 5) and this gave rise to various experiments in 'autonomous working groups', particularly in Norway and Sweden.

The British Labour governments of the 1960s and 1970s supported limited intervention to establish formal systems of employee participation, although it was not until the formation of the Bullock Committee itself that any serious attempt to establish a statutory national framework for employee participation became apparent: a White Paper published in 1978 recommended setting up Joint Representative Committees 'which, in organisations of over 2000 employees could instigate a ballot of employees to secure one-third employee representation on the board' (Salamon, 1998, p. 359). The Bullock Committee recommendations and the subsequent White Paper were not acted upon, and a change of government in 1979 ensured that they never would be. There were two significant attempts to introduce worker directors, into the British Steel Corporation in 1967 and the Post Office in 1977, but these 'experiments' were relatively short-lived and specific problems with them were experienced.

While national initiatives for employee participation petered out in Britain, government support for collective participation remained strong in individual European countries and within the European Union. Hyman and Mason (1995) identify the following conditions necessary for participation to thrive:

- A supportive political environment, enabling 'a balance of worker and employer influence through collective participation' to be achieved through supportive legislation.
- The important influence of stable social democratic governments, such as those in pre-1980 Germany (then West Germany) and Sweden. In the case of Germany, the ascendancy to power of the Christian Democrats under the Chancellorship of Kohl made no difference to the consensus between government, unions and employers in maintaining the statutory system of employee participation, or 'co-determination'.
- The maintenance of broad political consensus concerning the concept and practice of participation, seen as necessary 'for the regulation of an otherwise undisciplined labour market' (p. 30).
- Stability, encouraged through a 'sharing of responsibility for company performance by the individuals involved' and the belief that 'open confrontation between representatives of capital and labour is not necessarily the most beneficial approach to meet the longer-term interests of either party' (p. 30).

Approaches

Self-Evaluation Activity 8.3

Approaches to participation

The response is given below

Can you think of at least three approaches to participation which are practised in Britain and other European countries?

We can identify six approaches to participation (which, with the exception of collective bargaining, are described more fully in this chapter):

1. *Collective bargaining*

   Collective bargaining has been considered in Chapter 6, where it was argued that a broadening of the scope of bargaining from conjunctive to co-operative, or from distributive to integrative, would provide employees in unionised organisations with the appropriate means to participate in major areas of decision-making. In this context, partnership agreements are important (see below).

2. *Collective employee share schemes*

   These are schemes which encourage the accumulation of wealth through the collective ownership and administration of company shares 'which would offer institutional influence to union shareholders similar to that enjoyed by pension funds and other collective bodies' (Hyman and Mason, 1995, p. 37).

3. *Works councils*

   These are found in most European countries and while their structures vary both between and within countries, they are wholly representative bodies comprising employees and sometimes employer representatives who have both a right to receive company information concerning its policies and activities and a right to be consulted on issues prior to their implementation. Works councils often operate in both the public and private sectors of industry.

4. *Representation on company boards*

   Organisations which operate formally constituted works councils will also have higher-level representational bodies such as 'management' or 'supervisory' boards with roughly equal representation and, higher still, employee representation on company boards. Management boards meet less frequently than works councils and consider matters of longer-term and strategic importance. Their function is to monitor and sometimes help formulate company policy and strategy over a wide range of issues. Decisions made at this level are referred upwards to the company board on which a minority of employee representatives sit.

5. *Joint Consultative Committees (JCCs)*

   Joint consultation between employers and employees is concerned with the discussion of issues and 'matters of joint concern which are not the subject of negotiation with trade unions' (Donovan, 1968). Management tends to determine the issues for discussion and reserves the right to decide the final outcome without 'subjecting it to joint agreement with employees or their representatives' (Salamon, 1998). The forum for such discussions is known as the Joint Consultative Committee.

6. *European Works Councils*

   Not to be confused with company works councils, European Works Councils (EWCs) were formed as a result of the 1994 European Works Council Directive of the European Union. The Directive provides for EWCs to be set up in any multinational organisation employing at least 1000 employees where there are at least 150 employees in each of two member states. An EWC meets once a year to discuss strategic aspects of the company's activities including the structure, finance and economic policies of the company, production, sales and employment issues, introduction of new working methods or production processes, transfers of production, mergers, closures and redundancies.

Initiatives

The main initiatives in Europe have come from individual governments and the European Union itself. We confine ourselves here to the role of the European Union in encouraging the adoption and spread of employee representation systems. As long ago as 1970, before Britain's entry into the European Economic Community (as it was called then) in 1973, proposals for a 'European Company' with employee representation on a 'two-tier' board and works council were under discussion by the

Central Council of Ministers. These discussions were based on the so-called draft Fifth Directive introduced in 1972 dealing with company law, which included proposals for employee representation. The discussions were suspended amidst disagreement in 1982, and it was not until 1989 that a European Company Statute was introduced which included plans for employee participation compatible with the Fifth Directive (Hyman and Mason, 1995).

Brief history of the Fifth Directive

The Directive (see Exhibit 8.1)required that in companies employing more than 500 people there should be management board representation. Owing to opposition from employers and Conservative politicians in Britain, the draft directive was not ratified, and in 1983 the requirements were watered down: EU member states were invited to introduce employee participation either through management/supervisory board representation, or through works councils.

After the Fifth Directive

With the advent of the Single European Market, further proposals for employee participation were put forward in 1989 within the Statute for the European Company. These proposals had originally been put forward as a draft Regulation in 1970, then amended in 1975 and put to rest in 1982. This memorandum is even more defensive than the reconstituted Fifth Directive and no further action has been taken.

In 1980, the Vredeling Directive (named after the European Commissioner responsible for social affairs at the time) was introduced. It required public limited companies with complex structures, such as multinational companies, and with more than 100 employees to provide employees' representatives at local level with regular information concerning company-wide matters including its economic and financial position, its employment situation, its production and investment plans and its plans for introducing new working methods. Companies were also required to consult employee representatives when planning decisions might be detrimental to employees' interests; such decisions could involve closures, mergers and the like. If companies refused to provide such information, member states could impose penalties on the offenders, and employee

---

Exhibit 8.1

What the Fifth Directive says

The original version of 1972 would have guaranteed a measure of employee participation in certain circumstances. It would have required limited companies with 500 or more employees to set up a two-tier board system with supervisory and management functions. The supervisory board with minority employee representation would have had the right to nominate and dismiss members of the management board. The management board would have been required to submit a report every three months on the state of company affairs to the supervisory board. The authorisation of the supervisory board would have been needed for the closure or transfer of the company or substantial parts of it, for substantial curtailment or extension of the company's activities, for substantial changes of organisation within the company and for the establishment or termination of long-term co-operation with other companies.

The original proposal was watered down in 1975 and again in 1983, thus allowing for a more nebulous form of participation and a higher employment threshold level of 1000 employees or more. These later provisions 'represent considerable relaxation as compared to the earlier proposals and leave a great deal of latitude to Member States in the choice of management systems' (Vandamme, 1986, p. 143). However, the Commission's (and the European Parliament's) perseverance has not been rewarded, and in face of opposition from UNICE (the European employers' organisation) and the British Conservative government, negotiations dragged on aimlessly.

Source: Bridgford and Stirling, 1994, p. 144

representatives would also be entitled to seek more company information if that provided was deemed to be insufficient. Again, as a result of opposition, the Commission produced an amended version in 1983 which increased the threshold to 1000 employees, reduced the frequency with which information should be given, and restricted the type of information to be given.

As we saw in Chapter 4, the Community Charter of Fundamental Social Rights for Workers (signed by all member states except Britain in 1989 and commonly known as the Social Charter) emphasised the importance of information, consultation and participation of workers in companies or groups of companies with subsidiaries in two or more member states. Further decisions affecting employee rights were made at the inter-governmental conference in Maastricht in 1991 which resulted in the Treaty of European Union (known as the Maastricht Treaty). The treaty contained the so-called Social Chapter, which Britain initially refused to sign under the Conservatives but which was endorsed by the Labour government in 1998. The Social Chapter provides for 12 fundamental rights to workers. These have been translated into practical proposals for government action within the so-called Action Plan, and numbers 17 and 18 deal generally with rights to information, consultation and participation in decision-making. The proposals for information disclosure and consultation closely follow the Vredeling Directive outlined above. In December 1990 the Commission produced a Directive on European Works Councils (see pp. 404–411). We now go on to consider three forms of participation in greater detail. These are:

- joint consultation and JCCs;
- works councils, supervisory boards and employee directors;
- European Works Councils.

JOINT CONSULTATION AND JCCS

JCCs were recommended by Whitley in 1917 as a means of involving employees in management decision-making and controlling 'militant' trade unionism. Notwithstanding the general definition of JCCs given above, empirical evidence and theor-

etical contributions provide a more complex picture of their role and function. There is debate concerning the extent to which JCCs are institutional examples of either employee involvement or employee participation. As we shall see, the answer is 'a bit of both', bearing in mind the relationship which joint consultation has with collective bargaining and the ideological perspectives of the parties to the employment relationship. Joint consultation takes place mainly at the higher organisational and the lower establishment levels within both the public and private sectors of industry and in multinational and national enterprises (including inwardly-investing companies). The popularity of joint consultation and JCCs since their introduction in the early twentieth century has waxed and waned; they enjoyed greater popularity during the two high-consensus world war periods, and are well established in the public sector. There was some decline in joint consultation during the 1950s and 1960s, due partly to the trend towards 'domestic' bargaining (see Chapter 6) but overall, during the post-Second World War period, although the number of JCCs has gradually declined, the picture is one of overall stability. This is particularly so in the period since the 1980s, which also evidences a trend towards consultation in non-union organisations or organisations where unions are not recognised.

Joint consultation: involvement or participation . . . or both?

Self-Evaluation Activity 8.4

Joint consultation types
The response is given below

Read the description of the three types of joint consultation and indicate whether they are examples of EI or EP.

Three approaches to joint consultation have been identified (Farnham and Pimlott, 1995), known as pseudo consultation, classical consultation and integrative consultation.

Pseudo consultation is basically downward communication within the JCC, where management informs employee representatives of decisions already taken.

Employees and employee representatives are not empowered to influence management decisions. Pseudo consultation or 'information giving' is practised more commonly in organisations which are union-free or where unions are particularly weak and 'as a method of industrial relations, it merely seeks to maintain management's right to manage, neither to challenge it nor to legitimise managerial authority' (p. 52).

Classical consultation involves employee representatives discussing and considering matters which directly affect the workforce or sections of it. Employee representatives within such JCCs may be able to influence events before the final decision is taken by management. Farnham and Pimlott identify four characteristics of this type of joint consultation:

- matters of common interest to employees and employer are dealt with, with the exception of terms and conditions of employment which could be contentious;
- joint consultative machinery is separate from collective bargaining machinery;
- it is the responsibility of management to take and implement decisions arising from the consultative process; and
- the consultation process involves all employees, unionised and non-unionised and including supervisory and managerial staff.

Integrative consultation extends the range of issues subject to consultation, again of common concern to employers and employees, and can include matters such as introduction of new technology and other aspects of change, productivity and flexible working. The aim of the exercise is to arrive at a joint decision concerning problems arising from these matters, and is more similar to integrative or co-operative bargaining than to classical consultation or distributive bargaining. This type of joint consultation should reinforce rather than supplant collective bargaining (see below).

In looking at these three types of joint consultation, we could argue that pseudo consultation does not provide for any form of EI or EP. Employees are considered passive recipients of selective management information. Management makes the final decision at the end of the classical consultation process, but employee representatives get the opportunity to provide opinions and comments within a two-way communication process. This type of consultation process is more

indicative of EI than EP. EP features prominently within the integrative consultation process for reasons given above.

A refinement to the above typology is provided by Marchington (1987) who identified four different models or 'faces of consultation'. These are the non-union model, the competitive model, the adjunct model and the marginal model.

The **non-union model** is virtually identical to the pseudo consultation approach and aims to prevent workplace union organisation. Non-union JCCs are talking shops in which management sets the agenda. Employee representatives are informed of developments and are expected to endorse management thinking. The **competitive model** is somewhat similar to the classical consultation approach whereby in unionised organisations collective bargaining is seen as the 'competitor': the purpose of JCCs is to reduce the influence of collective bargaining by considering strategic issues and problems concerning, for example, the company's market position. Management is represented by senior line managers and non-managerial employees by a combination of shop stewards and other worker representatives. The **adjunct model** is similar to the integrative approach and the emphasis within JCCs is upon joint problem-solving concerning high-level, strategic information such as market prospects, business plans, quality and customer relations. Farnham and Pimlott (1995) add:

> *Managerial representation is provided by senior line management and members from the personnel team, with the workforce represented by shop stewards. The process is one of mutual influence between the management and union representatives. Within it, advance information provided to the members and management allows the union representatives to meet before the JCC takes place. This is to make the formal meetings more effective.* (p. 418)

This model is regarded as the 'best practice' model for pluralist management whereby both parties have a desire for the JCC to succeed. Finally, the **marginal model** is very low-key and JCCs consider relatively trivial matters concerning welfare and other peripheral issues.

Joint consultation and collective bargaining

In examining the developments in collective bargaining in Britain over the past 30 or so years (see Chapter 6), we noted that its scope had narrowed and its coverage had declined. Nevertheless, collective bargaining remains the single most important process of determining pay and working conditions for millions of employees. Clegg (1985) consistently argued that collective bargaining establishes the role of trade unions, within a system of industrial governance, of permanent opposition which prevents the development of autocracy in industry. In this sense, while collective bargaining remains central to trade union mobilisation, its adversarial essence should not be diluted by other less adversarial, oppositionary and, by implication, inferior forms of involvement/ participation such as joint consultation. Others, such as Marchington and Parker, 1990 (echoing Terry, 1986), argue that collective bargaining has been 'undermined by a resurgence and upgrading of JCCs [and that] its role [has been] progressively reduced to form without content' (p. 37). There are, therefore, two opposing views concerning the role of joint consultation in relation to collective bargaining. These are:

- **The upgrading or revitalisation perspective** whose proponents (Terry 1983; Batstone, 1984; Edwards, 1985) argue that managements have been introducing or upgrading their JCCs in order to deal with issues which were traditionally within the province of collective bargaining. These revitalised JCCs concern themselves with important strategic decisions of the plant or company and by doing so reduce the influence of shop stewards and other union officials within the collective bargaining process. To be sure, the JCCs will have shop steward representatives, who, from the standpoint of management, will gain a closer understanding of company problems and therefore come to accept the logic of management solutions. In this way, many of the issues previously dealt with by collective bargaining can be settled by consultative arrangements. Moreover, 'it is further assumed that managements are successful in their pursuit of such a strategy to the extent that they feel no need to confront trade unions "head on" via policies of a more aggressive nature' (Marchington and Parker, 1990, p. 40).

- **The downgrading or marginalisation perspective** whose supporters (Cressey *et al.*, 1985; MacInnes, 1985) argue that consultation has been downgraded, becoming marginal to the regulation of affairs in the workplace. JCCs deal with trivia to the point where one of the parties decides that there is no point in continuing with the dialogue. Moreover, committee members may 'find they have more pressing priorities which take precedence over their attendance at the JCC, and eventually someone not only forgets to organise a meeting, others forget they have even forgotten' (Marchington and Parker, 1990, p. 40).

Marchington and Armstrong (1986) proposed a third perspective:

> *in which consultation operates as an adjunct to negotiation (collective bargaining), as complementary to each other rather than working as competing processes in the regulation of workplace affairs. Negotiation is used for the determination of wages and working conditions, whereas consultation acts as a sounding board, helps to lubricate relationships, and generally fills the gaps needed to administer employee relations.* (p. 41)

This perspective conforms to the adjunct model which we considered in the previous section. Nevertheless, as Hyman and Mason (1995) assert, putting this unresolved debate to one side, JCCs are 'highly appropriate': firstly, where collective bargaining is centralised at industry or company level 'hence creating a need for a discussion forum at local level' (p. 125); secondly, in large organisations where there is often a lack of communication channels between management and employees; and, thirdly, 'where companies are seeking to reduce the importance of collective bargaining, and JCCs offer a viable alternative' (p. 125).

Joint consultation and JCCs: some empirical evidence

The WIRS and WERS98 survey findings (Millward *et al.*, 1992; Cully *et al.*, 1999; Millward *et al.*,

2000) remain the most authoritative. The findings concern JCCs at both workplace and higher organisational levels. With reference to Table 8.1, the surveys show that the overall incidence of workplace JCCs has been fairly stable since 1990 with 29 per cent of workplaces having a JCC on site. However, it is useful to draw a distinction between JCCs as 'window dressing' and those that are 'functioning consultative committees' (that is, those that meet at least once every three months). With regard to the latter category, there has been a long-term decline in their incidence from 30 per cent in 1980 to 23 per cent in 1998, affecting all sizes of establishments in all sectors of the economy, although it should be noted that the decline affected the public sector from 1990 to 1998 only.

The data also indicates that JCCs were much more prevalent in workplaces where unions were recognised than in workplaces where there was no recognised union, with the former category witnessing a decline accounted for by the decline in public sector JCCs amongst other factors. In workplaces with no recognised union, the picture is one of stability with JCC incidence varying by only three percentage points. Within private sector workplaces where unions are recognised, the decline in JCC incidence is steeper (35 per cent in 1980 to 24 per cent in 1998). Within industries, there were changes in the

Table 8.1 Incidence of workplace joint consultative committees by broad sector and by union recognition: 1980–98

	1980 %	1984 %	1990 %	1998 %
Any consultative committee				
All establishments	34	34	29	29
Functioning consultative committee				
All establishments	30	31	26	23
Size of establishment				
25–49 employees	21	21	18	14
50–99 employees	29	32	31	25
100–199 employees	39	47	37	32
200–499 employees	60	54	43	49
500 or more employees	66	70	61	58
Private sector	26	24	18	20
Private manufacturing and extraction	32	26	21	24
Private services	22	23	17	18
Public sector	39	42	45	32
Unions recognised	37	36	34	30
No recognised union	17	20	17	18
Private sector only				
Unions recognised	35	29	21	24
No recognised unions	16	20	17	18

Source: Millward *et al.,* 2000, p. 109

JCC incidence with JCCs becoming more common in private sector transport and communications and declining within the health services and energy. A further finding of significance is that JCCs are not as permanent an institution as might have been supposed, with 12 per cent of continuing workplaces abandoning their JCCs while 17 per cent established JCCs between 1990 and 1998. Two further findings concerning the incidence of JCCs are relevant:

- in workplaces with no recognised union, the existence of a fully functioning JCC did not increase the prospects for trade union recognition; and
- in workplaces that derecognised trade unions, 'the [subsequent] decline in employee voice . . . is not being offset by the introduction of consultative committees as alternative channels of representation' (Millward *et al.*, 2000, p. 111).

WERS98 also looked at the operation of JCCs in terms of influence over managerial decision-making. Around one-third of managers for the period 1990–8 rated their consultative committee as very influential. In relation to higher level consultative committees operating in organisations with several workplaces, the incidence of these increased during the period 1990–8 with 56 per cent of workplaces belonging to a larger organisation reporting a higher-level committee, up from 48 per cent in 1990. The increase in the number of such committees is at least partly due to the (then pending) impact of the transposition of the European Works Council Directive in 1999.

The conclusions that we can arrive at concerning JCCs in Britain during the past 30 years or so are, firstly, that while functioning JCCs remain a relatively important feature of industrial relations in many companies and workplaces, both within the private and public sectors, there has been a further decline in their incidence and representative voice during the 1990s. Secondly, given the variations in size and sector of establishments and workplaces, there appears to be greater informality in the operation of JCCs in the smaller service-based sectors; a more sophisticated and formalised approach in the declining but relatively larger manufacturing and public sectors where trade unions are generally stronger; and pressures for greater formalisation of communication and participatory structures, particu-larly in transnational organisations more sensitive to EU policies, directives and legislation.

Summary points

- The two main approaches which have influenced participatory structures within the European Union are, firstly, EI which is concerned with job and task-based decisions, and, secondly, EP which provides employees with the means to influence organisational decision-making.
- Employee interests within the decision-making process may theoretically extend to industrial democracy which challenges employer rights to manage, while employer interests are directed towards maintaining and reinforcing the legitimacy of managerial power and decision-making.
- Government initiatives to introduce a statutory form of EP in Britain came to nothing with the shelving of the Bullock Committee Report in 1979. This contrasts sharply with the experience of many EU countries where legislation has been introduced, and the European Commission itself which has encouraged participative structures to be developed in the EU member states.
- Approaches to participation include:
  - collective bargaining;
  - collective employee share schemes;
  - works councils;
  - employee representation on company boards;
  - joint consultative committees; and
  - European Works Councils
- JCCs are still fairly common in Britain, but there are reservations concerning the extent to which they are truly participative (see concluding comments above).

CO-DETERMINATION AND WORKS COUNCILS

We now consider works councils and management boards (including employee directors) within the formalised context typical of many European countries. As we have seen, works councils within the European Union often have statutory underpinnings and are formal structures having written constitutions dealing with election of representatives, frequency of meetings, issues for discussion and so on. There has been considerable opposition in Britain to the adoption of works councils on the European model. Employers have resisted them owing to their perceived threat to managerial authority and prerogatives, while unions are worried about the possible dilution of union representative functions and influence should non-union employees become council members, and the possible consequences of making unpopular decisions affecting the unionised workforce. However, there have been employer-led initiatives in situations where the union presence is weak or non-existent ('company councils' or 'employee councils' being examples), or where trade unions have been derecognised as in the privatised Northumbrian Water. Some Japanese inwardly-investing companies such as Nissan have introduced company councils within either a union-free environment or where single-union deals have been negotiated (see Chapter 5).

The German system of co-determination

The German system of co-determination (*Mitbestimmung*) is generally regarded as the 'best practice' model for employee participation in Europe. It comprises an employee-only works council (*Betriebsrat*) at workplace, company or group level, and employee representation on the supervisory/management boards (*Aufsichtsrat*) of companies. Works councils are underpinned by legislation but not mandatory (Van Ruysseveldt and Visser, 1996). There is no formal involvement by trade unions in the activities of the works council, but employers and works councils must co-operate with both unions and employers' organisations. Trade unions do, however, have representation rights at supervisory board level under the 1976 Co-determination Act, which applies to large companies. It is also quite common for the chairperson of a works council to have a seat on the supervisory board, establishing a direct link between these bodies. The works council system applies to all private sector companies with more than five employees, while the supervisory board system applies to private sector companies

with more than 500 employees. Parallel legislation provides for works councils in the public sector. The co-determination model (see below for different interpretations) is characterised by a high degree of formalisation and legal regulation, and for this reason the relationship between employer and employees at enterprise level is often described as 'institutionalised co-operation' (Van Ruysseveldt and Visser, 1996).

The term 'works council', as Frege (2002), points out has been subject to differing interpretations and is best understood within the context of co-determination. A number of models of co-determination have been devised, some of which are useful for possible application to the UK (Frege, 2002). These are outlined below:

1. The *democratisation/integration model* defines co-determination as 'the institutionalisation of social processes which allows for the positive integration of all participants' (Furstenberg, 1981, p. 31). It is a form of corporate governance underpinned by legislation.
2. The *surrogate/compensation model* sees co-determination as providing workers' rights not based on ownership but on legitimate democratic grounds.
3. The *counterpower/conflict model* regards co-determination as a means to restrict management power and control.
4. The *social control model* is a Marxist argument that co-determination supports the subordination of the working class and hides the real conflict of interest between workers and employers.
5. The *partnership model* sees co-determination as 'a participatory process leading to high trust, co-operation and compromise which are regarded as positive outcomes and not as a selling out to management' (Frege, 2002, p. 225).

Self-Evaluation Activity 8.5
Model applicability
This SEA has no commentary

In view of the pending transposition of the Information and Consultation Directive, which model would you select as being the most appropriate to the UK context (bear in mind that many of the models overlap).

Arguments for having works councils

Frege (2002) points out that many German academics put forward strong arguments for the co-determination and works council system. One strong argument is that co-determination improves the quality of local or workplace employment relations and the functioning of the organisation's internal labour market, thereby having a positive impact upon the company's economic performance. More specific arguments concerning the influence of works councils upon intra-organisation employment relations include:

1. The works council provides an employee voice for all employees, and not only trade union members, which reduces labour turnover and hence hiring and training costs.
2. The works council increases trust and co-operation between employer and employee. Employers know that they cannot get rid of works councils and therefore concentrate upon establishing co-operative methods of working.
3. Works councils increase the flow of information between management and workforce resulting in a greater equality of information exchange which in turn results in a more informed decision-making process and facilitates new and improved solutions.
4. The presence of works councils may well induce the diffusion of 'best practice' throughout the organisation in terms, for example, of improving production methods and working practices through the introduction of new technology and lessening the prospect of resistance to change.
5. Works councils can help improve quality of product and/or service.

Works council representation

The works council is the core of the German co-determination model (see Exhibit 8.2).

Works councils, as employee-only bodies, are directly elected by the workforce for an individual establishment (*Betrieb*). An 'establishment' could mean a company if it is small enough, an individual plant within a multi-plant company, one department store within a chain, or a distinct works on a single site characterised by several types of operation. Where a company comprises several establishments, each with its own works council, a works council for the company as a whole can be formed from delegates of existing works councils. Similarly, if the company is part of a group or consortium, a group (or combine) works council can be set up.

Exhibit 8.2

Historical development of co-determination

The idea of worker representation through works councils was first raised by the revolutionary Constitutional Assembly in Frankfurt in 1848 and was included in its draft constitution for a democratic German republic. By the end of the First World War a powerful, radical works council movement had developed which saw itself as the political basis of a post-war socialist order. Works councils became an important part of the structure of the Weimar Republic (1919–33). The councils in the Republic were incorporated into the liberal-democratic constitution and were legally authorised to represent workers and consult with employers. Collective bargaining was reserved for unions, operating at sectoral and national levels, while councils were bound to observe and implement agreements. This dual system of industrial relations, established in the Weimar Republic, continued nationally in West Germany after the Second World War. However, the trade unions initially opposed the early legislation (1951 and 1952) establishing works councils as the councils were perceived to be anti-union, did not provide sufficient rights for workers and threatened to weaken unions at plant level. It was only after collective bargaining was consolidated at industry level in the early 1960s that unions began to see works councils as legitimate devices for worker representation. Works council rights were considerably strengthened by the Social Democratic government under Willy Brandt in 1972, and it is this legislation, as amended by the Conservative-Liberal coalition in the 1980s, which governs the current structure and powers of works councils.

Works council size

Where the establishment employs five to 20 employees, only one representative may be elected. Five members may be elected in establishments with 51–150 employees, to 15 members where there are 1001–2000 employees, and to 31 members for workforces between 7001 and 9000 employees. In establishments having more than 9000 employees, two more members can be added for each additional 3000 employees. All manual and non-manual employees, together with trainees, are eligible for membership. The company's management board, owners and executives are ineligible for works council membership. Membership is dominated by DGB-affiliated trade unionists (DGB is equivalent to the TUC): in the 1994 elections, for example, DGB candidates won two-thirds of all seats, and accounted for three-quarters of all works council chairs, a success rate repeated in subsequent elections. The number of non-union works council members rose from 17 per cent in the mid-1970s to 25 per cent in the late 1990s. Coverage of the labour force by works councils is limited by a two main factors. Firstly, around a quarter of the labour force work in establishments that are too small to meet the size threshold, or are excluded because of the nature of their activities, or are in the public sector (which has its own arrangements). Secondly, while works councils are underpinned by legislation, they are not mandatory. Even so, around two-thirds of private sector employees work in establishments with a works council.

Their representative status, duties, rights and powers

Works councillors are elected for four years. In establishments with more than 300 employees, the employer may release a certain number of council members, on full pay, for works council activities. Members have a right to vocational and other training relevant to their duties, and are protected against dismissal, apart from offences relating to gross misconduct, while in office. Works councils are required to co-operate with the employer 'for the good of the employees and the establishment' (1972 Act), and cannot take industrial action, although informal sanctions do exist and act as a counter to employers' ability to grant or withhold a variety of concessions. The general statutory duties of works councils include:

- compliance with the law, with collective agreements and with works agreements for the benefit of employees;
- making recommendations to the employer on action to benefit employees and the establishment;
- promoting the rehabilitation and integration of people with disabilities, older workers and foreign workers; and
- calling meetings of employees at least four times a year, to which the employer is invited.

The rights of works councils range from information dissemination through participation in decisions, to joint decision-making. The main rights are:

- **The right to be heard,** by which councils have a right to express opinions on issues as well as to initiate proposals in some areas.
- **The right to information:** works councils have a general right to be informed concerning any issues relevant to management decision-making.
- **The right to consultation** where employers seek the views of works councils before making decisions.
- **The right to co-determination** whereby the employer cannot proceed with a course of action without the agreement of the works council on issues which are subject to joint determination.

The co-determination rights are the most important as they cover social policy issues such as payment methods and systems, bonus rates, piecework rates, premiums and performance-related pay, work and holiday schedules, overtime, reduced working hours and the 'humanisation' of work. Other issues about which works councils must be consulted include:

1. *Job design and the work environment*: Works councils must be informed of and consulted about changes to work arrangements and processes, changes to factory/plant and premises, and must be given the scope to make suggestions or express reservations. Works councils have a right of co-determination (joint decision-making) concerning the consequences of these changes and of mitigating their effects.

2. *Personnel matters*: Councils do exercise considerable influence over personnel management on matters which in Britain would be considered within the realm of managerial prerogative. Their influence therefore extends to major aspects of workplace relations and the internal labour market. Specifically, the rights concerning personnel include:

   - *Personnel planning* where there is a right to information and to make recommendations on the planning process itself, staff changes or movements and vocational training.

   - *Recruitment* whereby works councils can ask for vacancies to be advertised internally before external recruitment begins; failure to do this may lead to the council withholding consent to an appointment. Application forms require council approval as do guidelines for selection, transfer, regrading or dismissal of employees.

   - *Engagement, transfer and regrading* where, in establishments with more than 20 employees, the council must be informed about any engagement and movement of staff and shown any application or selection documents. The council can refuse to approve proposals concerning these matters if the employer breaches any agreed guidelines.

   - *Individual dismissal* where all dismissals must be notified, with the reasons for the dismissal, to the works council which has a statutory right to object. Any dismissal which is not notified is null and void.

3. *Financial and business matters*: In all companies having more than 100 permanent employees a subcommittee of the works council (the Economic Committee) can be formed to deal specifically with information given by the employer concerning the state of the business. Employers are required to give information on the financial state of the business supported by appropriate documentation as long as business confidentiality is not compromised. The information includes the economic and financial situation of the company, the product and market situation, investment, production and rationalisation plans, including new working methods, and reduction in activities, closures or transfer of operations. Employers in companies with more than 1000 employees must also inform employees individually, every three months in writing, concerning the state of the business. In firms with more than 20 employees, information can be presented verbally.

4. *Redundancies*: In companies with 20 or more employees, the employer must inform and consult the works council concerning any change to the business resulting in redundancies and must seek an agreement with the council about these changes. Works councils also have a right to negotiate levels of financial compensation for redundant employees.

5. *Works councils and trade unions*: German trade unions do not have a formal right to workplace representation and workplace bargaining is not recognised in the sense that it is in Britain. To be sure, shop stewards do exist, but mainly to provide lines of communication to the national union concerning pay claims. Since works councils are prevented from taking industrial action, shop stewards often take responsibility for co-ordinating official and unofficial strikes at plant level (although it has to be said that workplace-based disputes are rare occurrences). In practice, shop stewards work closely with works councils, reflecting the fact that a large proportion of councillors are union members.

Employee representation at board level

Participation at board level occurs within the two-tier board structure set up by the 1965 Joint Stock Companies Act. The structure comprises a supervisory board and a management board. The management board is responsible for conducting the business operations of a company, represents the enterprise legally, and is formally the employer. The supervisory board is legally required to appoint the management board or managing directors, depending on the type of organisation, and to oversee its activities. Employee representatives sit on the supervisory board which meets between two and four times a year. Only joint stock companies are required to have two boards as a matter of course. Other types of company are required to create a two-tier structure only if they are large enough to qualify for inclusion in one of the co-determination systems.

Supervisory board duties and rights

The supervisory board has a general right to request information from the management board on all aspects of the business, and this right also applies to individual members seeking information provided the request is supported by another member. Both supervisory boards and works councils are covered by confidentiality requirements. Information which must be provided as a matter of course includes:

- proposed corporate policies and other basic issues concerning the management of the enterprise;
- the profitability of the business, especially the return on equity;
- the general progress of the business; and
- operations which might be of considerable importance to the profitability or liquidity of the business.

Forms of board-level participation

There are three forms of board level participation. The first form covers joint stock and limited liability companies with more than 2000 employees under the provisions of the 1976 Co-determination Act, now extended to cover the former East Germany. In these companies the supervisory board comprises equal numbers of shareholder and employee members, with the size of the board varying according to company size. Some seats on the board are reserved for trade union representatives (if there is a trade union presence in the company), and the remaining seats are allocated to employees, with a guarantee of at least one seat for each of the manual, non-manual and managerial categories. Election is usually direct, by employee groups in enterprises with up to 8000 employees, and by electoral college in larger firms. The most important single activity of the supervisory board is to elect the management board, with the chair of the former board having a casting vote. From the union perspective, the 50–50 composition of the supervisory board is compromised by the presence of managerial staff on the employees' side who often support the shareholders' view on important issues. The board also elects a 'Labour Director' (sometimes against the wishes of the employee representatives) to the management board who oversees personnel and HRM matters.

The second type of supervisory board exists in enterprises with more than 1000 employees working in the coal, iron and steel industries under the co-determination legislation of 1951 and 1956. Here, as in the previous example, the board consists of an equal number of employee and shareholder representatives, but in contrast to the previous example, the chair of the board must be a neutral member, and the 'Labour Director' is appointed subject to the approval of the employee representatives. However, the number of boards and companies has fallen within these industrial sectors as, in common with other European and North American economies, the numbers employed in coal, iron and steel industries have declined, as have the industries themselves.

Supervisory boards in companies with 500–2000 employees constitute the third type whereby, under the 1952 Works Constitution Act (the predecessor to the 1972 Act), one-third of supervisory board members must be employee representatives. In other respects, the functions of the supervisory boards within these companies are identical with the first and second types which we have considered.

Works councils: conclusions and prospects

The 'best practice' German model is not without its critics. Strauss (1979) raises two important issues which are more than academic. The first issue is whether the prescriptions for participation match the realities of the participation process; the second issue is concerned with 'who benefits'? Are there, for example, positive benefits and outcomes such as higher productivity, increased employee satisfaction and fewer grievances for the parties involved in the co-determination process? Trade unions have often criticised the effectiveness of works councils by claiming that information provided by employers is insufficient and inadequate, and may arrive too late for any useful employee input. These issues affect all countries which have introduced works council arrangements (see Exhibit 8.3) and as Bridgford and Stirling (1994) comment: 'In certain countries, doubts about employee participation are so manifest that legislation has been introduced (in France and Belgium, for example), in order to remedy the situation' (p. 140). In Germany itself, there have been criticisms that trade unions as organisations

Exhibit 8.3

Some national works council systems

As in the UK, specific legislation providing for information and consultation of employees exists in areas covered by EU Directives – collective redundancies, transfers of undertakings, and health and safety. However, the right to be informed and consulted on an ongoing basis about more general company matters is a pivotal part of the role of works councils in many countries. All member countries of the EU, except the UK and Ireland, have legislated for the provision of information and consultation systems. The works council or equivalent is the most commonly used, but their nature and their ability to impact upon management decision-making differs from country to country. In most countries all companies or establishments over a certain size in terms of numbers of employees are required to set up a works council or similar body. In many member states the size of works council increases with the total number of employees. All member states have rules to protect confidential information. In general, works council members are bound by confidentiality requirements where the employer considers information to be commercially sensitive, and employers may be allowed to withhold information where disclosure would harm the company. In some member states such as France, Sweden and Italy, trade unions have a guaranteed involvement in works councils. In France and Germany there is a clear separation between the consultative and negotiating roles of trade unions.

The Netherlands: Has a system of information and consultation rights that applies to companies employing more than 50 people. The rights cover issues such as financial and employment situations, work organisation, information technology, mergers, closures, investment systems, recruitment and changes to the company's structure. Co-determination rights also exist in areas such as redundancies, recruitment, promotions, training, job evaluation, working time and holidays. In relation to productivity as compared with the UK, hourly productivity was 25 per cent and 26 per cent higher in the Netherlands for 1991 and 2001 respectively.

Austria: Information and consultation rights apply in companies with more than five employees and cover issues such as the financial and employment situation of the company, on which consultation must take place a minimum of four times a year. In addition, where a change to the business is planned, consultation must take place. As in the case of Germany, co-determination rights exist on such issues as rest breaks, daily working time, payment systems, recruitment of temporary workers, social plans for redundancy, and training and retraining. Austria's labour productivity figures per hour worked were 10 per cent above the UK's for 1992, rising to 16 per cent in 2001.

Finland: Information and consultation rights apply to companies employing more than 30 employees (20 if collective redundancies are proposed). The rights cover matters such as financial information (twice a year or immediately if changes are proposed), employment and training. Co-determination rights exist concerning changes that affect the workforce and proposed job cuts. Finland's productivity per hour was 8 per cent above that of the UK in 2001.

are unrepresented at works council level, and that the works councils are not permitted to discuss issues which unions consider as being central to the employment relationship, such as pay and the introduction of new technology. Most important in the German case is the prohibition of strike action under the Works Constitution Act 1952 which states that 'acts of industrial warfare between the employer and the works council shall be unlawful'. Perceptions of works councils and their effectiveness vary from organisation to organisation and by industry sector. For example, Bridgford and Stirling cite research reported in Berghahn and Karsten (1987) which identifies six 'perceptual categories' of works council (see also earlier arguments concerning advantages of works councils) These are:

- the works council which is respected but has an ambiguous position between workers and management;
- the works council which is firm in its representation of workers' interests and is respected by the employer;
- the works council which is co-operative but acts as a countervailing power;
- the works council which is an organ of management;
- the isolated works council; and
- the ignored works council.

Notwithstanding these criticisms, other evidence (Heller, 1986) suggests that employees do exercise some influence over management decision-making at enterprise level and that 'the existence of formal rules (within the German context) makes a substantial difference in promoting the actual participation of employees' (p. 82). In many cases, employee participation in decision-making is reinforced by the presence of works councillors on supervisory boards, although there is a danger that the loyalties of trade union and other employee representatives on such boards may be divided between the interests of the enterprise and its management and the interests of the employees whom they represent.

Frege (2002) concludes that, despite the challenges of German unification and European integration, the works council institution has not been weakened since the late 1980s and, if anything, councils are increasingly being included as 'co-managers' in new areas of decision-making such as technological and organisational restructuring. Empirical evidence, therefore, suggests that works councils remain a stable institution and that there is somewhat of a revival of interest in them, partly due to their importance being reinforced by the Information and Consultation Directive, 2002 (which we consider below in relation to the UK) and to the decentralising tendencies evident within European employment relations systems.

EUROPEAN WORKS COUNCILS

Introduction and background

The European Works Councils Directive was approved by the Council of Ministers in September 1994,

under the terms of the Maastricht Treaty, from which the UK initially 'opted out' but has now, under New Labour, 'opted in'. The EWC Directive 'represented one of the most far-reaching and controversial industrial relations measures ever passed into European law' (AEEU, 1997). With many companies now operating on a transnational scale, the Directive sought to ensure that employees in large and medium-sized multinational organisations are properly informed and consulted about the enterprise's progress and prospects. All EU member states, with the exception of the UK, had to transpose the Directive into national legislation by September 1996. Initial (EU) estimates suggested that the EWC Directive would affect up to 2000 enterprises or groups, with between 10 000 and 15 000 subsidiaries, and that 'upwards of 40 000 EWC representatives could be participating in 5000 meetings every year' (AEEU, 1997). Research by Wortmann (1994) indicated that 1500 large European firms would be affected, covering 5 million employees within the EU. However, Hall *et al.* (1995) suggested a more conservative estimate of 860 EU-based companies being affected, with 100–140 of them being UK firms.

A clause in the Directive (known as Article 13) provides for voluntary agreements, reached before September 1996, to continue in operation after the deadline for implementation. Trade unions and many companies have used this clause to press ahead with negotiations on voluntary EWC agreements, and according to an EU analysis (1996), over 100 companies had reached EWC agreements by January 1996. To date (2003) over 600 EWCs in multinational companies within the European Economic Area have been established (Gilman and Marginson, 2002), and the European Foundation for the Improvement of Living and Working conditions website www.eurofound.ie provides up-to-date information concerning details of agreements concluded.

What the Directive said

The aim of the Directive was to ensure that the opinions of employees are considered and included in the decision-making procedures of central management and 'to improve the right to information and consultation of employees in Community-scale undertakings . . . and groups of undertakings'

(Article 1). Article 2 of the Directive defines consultation as 'the exchange of views and the establishment of dialogue between employees' representatives and central management or any more appropriate level of management'.

The enterprises affected by the Directive are, firstly, 'community-scale undertakings', defined in Article 2 as 'an undertaking with at least 1000 employees within the 17 states covered by the Directive and at least 150 employees in two or more of the countries', and secondly, 'community-scale groups of undertakings', defined as groups with at least 1000 employees within EU countries which have two or more group undertakings in different countries within the EU with at least 150 employees. For example, a Dutch group consisting of a Dutch subsidiary employing 1100 people, and a separate French subsidiary employing 150 people would be covered by the Directive. The Directive also applies to undertakings and groups with headquarters outside the EU, provided they meet the workforce size thresholds.

The Directive allows for the level at which an EWC is established to be determined through negotiation. Generally, EWCs are likely to be established at group level in the controlling undertaking, a controlling undertaking being defined as one which can exert a 'dominant influence' over another by virtue of, for instance, ownership, financial participation or other criteria. The negotiating partners could also agree to create EWCs along product lines, or have a group-level EWC plus several others covering different sectors of the business. The responsibility for 'creating the conditions and means necessary' for the setting up of an EWC lies with the enterprise's central management team.

The procedure for creating an EWC comprises three main stages:

- **Stage one** of the procedure may be initiated by either the management team or at the request of at least 100 employees or their representatives from more than one of the 17 states covered. Trade unions are already using these provisions to initiate negotiations.
- **Stage two** involves the formation of a Special Negotiating Body (SNB) comprising between three and 17 members, with at least one coming from each of the member states in which the company has operations, in proportion to the number of employees. The composition of SNBs can include employee and trade union officials, and advisory 'experts' such as lawyers and economists.
- **Stage three** requires central management to open negotiations with the SNB with a view to reaching a written agreement on an EWC.

There are four possible outcomes to the negotiations between the SNB and central management. The first option is that the SNB decides not to proceed with negotiations, or to terminate negotiations in progress on a two-thirds majority vote. This option is not likely to be pursued by union representatives. The second option is the drawing up of a written agreement to establish an EWC arrangement, and covers the following issues:

- the undertakings or establishments covered;
- the composition of the EWC, the number of members, the allocation of seats and the term of office;
- the EWC's functions and the procedure for information and consultation;
- the venue, frequency and duration of meetings; and
- the duration of the agreement and the procedure for its renegotiation.

The agreement to establish an information and consultation procedure instead of an EWC is a third option which was included in the Directive after some employers had argued that an EWC was unnecessary because other methods for consulting and informing their workforces were in place. If, after three years, no agreement is reached, option four allows for the safety-net provisions laid out in the annex to the Directive to apply. These provisions are known as subsidiary requirements, which also come into play if management refuses to start negotiations within six months of a request to do so. Subsidiary requirements lay down what are effectively minimum standards concerning EWC roles and activities.

The subsidiary requirements

The subsidiary requirements provide that an EWC be established on the basis of standard rules governing its competence, composition and procedures. The competence of the EWC is limited to those matters which concern the enterprise as a whole or those which concern operations in at least two EU countries. The composition of the EWC ranges from three to 30 members (who must be employees of the enterprise) elected or appointed by and from the existing employee representatives or, where there are no such representatives, by the entire body of employees. The election and appointment of EWC members must be carried out in accordance with national practice and legislation, and EWC seats are allocated on the same numerical basis as laid down for the SNB. If size warrants, the EWC may elect a 'select committee' with a maximum of three members. The EWC will have the right to meet central management annually to be informed and consulted about:

- the structure of the enterprise and its economic and financial situation;
- the probable development of the business and of production and sales;
- the employment situation and probable trend;
- investments; and
- substantial changes concerning organisation, new working methods or production processes, transfers of production, mergers, cutbacks or closures of undertakings, establishments or important parts thereof, or collective redundancies.

The select committee or, where none exists, the full EWC, has the right to be informed and to meet with management concerning measures significantly affecting employee's interests (see last bullet point above). These meetings should take place as soon as possible on the basis of a report drawn up by management, on which the EWC may put forward an opinion. The EWC can adopt its own rules of procedure. For example, prior to any meeting with central management, the EWC, or the select committee, is entitled to meet without management being present. EWC members must inform employee representatives in the enterprise's various establishments of the content of the information and consultation procedures to be carried out. The EWC may be assisted in this by experts of its own choice. In addition, the operating costs, including the cost of organising meetings, interpretation and the accommodation and travelling expenses of members of the EWC and select committee are to be met by central management unless

otherwise agreed. Finally, four years after an EWC is established under the subsidiary requirements, it must decide whether to open negotiations with the management for an agreement covering a company-specific EWC arrangement or to continue to operate on the basis of the subsidiary requirements.

The initial UK opt-out

As a result of the Conservative government's opt-out from the Social Chapter of the Maastricht Treaty, Britain was excluded from coverage of the EWC Directive and was not forced to comply with its terms.

Self-Evaluation Activity 8.6

Consequences of the UK opt-out
Response on website

What do you think were the consequences of the opt-out for British employees and companies?

Voluntary agreements

Before the original deadline of 22 September 1996 (the date the EWC Directive was to come into force), there was nothing to prevent voluntary EWC agreements being concluded, and these would remain in effect after that date (Article 13). By 1996 over 100 UK companies had reached such agreements. The voluntary agreement approach found favour with employers' organisations such as the CBI and the EEF, but the danger of Article 13 agreements is that they are not fully protected by the law and there have been 'pre-emptive agreements proposed and signed that have sought to marginalise trade union representation' (Cressey, 1998). Marks & Spencer and BP both sought to get management appointees as representatives, and this exposed them to challenge in the courts. The reasoning behind this was that if trade unions or employee representatives representing at least one hundred employees in more than one member state felt that a voluntary agreement failed to meet criteria laid down in Article 13, they could, once the Directive came into force, ask for an SNB to be constituted in accordance with Article 5. If a company refused to set up an SNB on the grounds that it already had a voluntary agreement in line with Article 13, the matter could be referred to the courts.

Progress to date

Undoubtedly the principal development as far as the UK is concerned was the transposition and implementation by December 1999/January 2000 of the 'extension' Directive applying the original 1994 Directive, although some relatively minor amendments were made by a number of other member states. This mainly required the adoption of measures by the UK which had set out its transposition timetable involving:

- the use of Regulations under s.2(2) of the European Communities Act 1972;
- the launch of a consultation exercise towards the end of 1998;
- the submission of draft Regulations to Parliament before the 1999 summer recess; and
- the entering into force of the Regulations on 15 December 1999 and 17 January 2000.

The extension of the EWC Directive brought in at least another 125 UK-based multinationals within its scope (on top of the 114 companies already covered), plus some 175 multinationals based elsewhere. These groups had until 15 December 1999 to reach a voluntary 'Article 13-type' agreement before the legislation took effect. Before the process of transposing the extension Directive was completed, the original Directive had to be reviewed by the Commission who could propose 'suitable amendments to the Council where necessary'.

Those multinationals covered by the original Directive which *did not* conclude voluntary Article 13 EWC agreements before the 22 September 1996 deadline were compelled to set up SNBs under the procedures of Article 5 of the Directive (as transposed in national law), with a view to concluding EWC agreements under Article 6. By June 1998, 21 months after the first SNB requests could potentially have been submitted by employees or their representatives, the number of Article 5/6 deals appeared low, amounting to no more than 45 examples out of those 700–800 companies (see

the example of Cadbury, an Article 5/6 deal, in Exhibit 8.4) covered by the original Directive and without an Article 13 agreement (IRS, 1998). With regard to EWC agreements providing for information and consultation on transfers of production, mergers, closures and cutbacks, the European Parliament adopted a resolution in 2000 in which it called for the EWC Directive to be strengthened so as to ensure that information and consultation over restructuring is clearly provided for in formal terms.

As part of the process towards the 'Europeanisation' of employment relations (see Chapter 1), contact, liaison and co-operation is developing not only between trade unions organising in the various European operations of multinational companies, but also through direct contacts with EWCs, as Carley (2002) points out:

> It is in this area that EWCs appear to have developed a role in the Europeanisation of bargaining within multinationals, facilitating an exchange of information on working conditions, working hours, employment practice and sometimes pay between employee representatives from different countries. This information is relevant to local and national-level negotiations within the enterprise. (p. 4)

Debate concerning the wider EWC role in European-level bargaining is largely speculative. However, a fundamental stage within that process should take into consideration the factors which influence choices made by management and employee representatives in concluding agreements establishing EWCs (Gilman and Marginson, 2002). These include:

- a 'statutory model' effect whereby, scope for negotiations notwithstanding, agreements tend to conform with the provisions of the Directive's statutory model;
- a 'learning effect' under which innovatory features of earlier agreements are diffused to later agreements;
- a 'country effect' whereby, in their main features, EWCs resemble the national arrangements for employee information and consultation of the country in which an MNC is headquartered; and
- a 'sector effect', whereby in important respects EWCs within a given sector resemble each other,

Exhibit 8.4

An EWC agreement

Cadbury Confectionery Stream

European Employee Information and Consultation Forum

19/02/97

PRINCIPLES

This is an agreement between the Cadbury Schweppes Confectionery Stream group of companies in Europe, and its employee representatives on the provision of consultation and information sharing on transnational matters affecting employees within the Stream in Europe. The management and the representatives agree to co-operate in a spirit of constructive dialogue and exchange of ideas. By the provision of information and discussion, both agree to actively participate in the Forum. Members of the Forum are committed to acting in the best interests of the Stream and its employees. In general it is agreed that employee communications and involvement are best served within each of the Stream businesses and close to the workplace. The Forum shall not undermine existing consultative or information sharing channels at local level.

MEMBERSHIP AND REPRESENTATION
Covered by the Agreement

Stream	Country	No. Reps
Basset GmbH	Germany	–
Cadbury Ltd	UK	2
Cadbury Dulciora (including Chocolates Hueso Dulciora and Dulces Hispania)	Spain	1
Cadbury Faam BV	Netherlands	–
Cadbury France SA	France	1
Cadbury Ireland Limited (including Trebor Ireland Ltd)	Ireland	3
Cadbury Portugal – Produtos de Confeitaria LDA	Portugal	–
Piasten Schokladenfabrik Hofmann GmbH & Co KG	Germany	1
Trebor Bassett Group	UK	2
Central functions of Cadbury Schweppes Group and Stream Offices		1

REPRESENTATIVE ELIGIBILITY

Any current active employee of a Confectionery Stream business in the qualifying country can be nominated to attend the Forum subject to national law and local rules of eligibility. Employee representatives are elected to serve at the Forum meetings on the basis of nomination by Works Councils where relevant, or by secret ballot. Employee representatives are appointed to the Forum for four years. The appropriate members of management will attend the Forum according to the agenda items to be discussed. These will be from senior management such as MD, Regional MD, Business unit heads or functional heads as appropriate. In addition it will be usual for senior personnel management from the business units to be in attendance.

MEETINGS AND AGENDA

Forum meetings will take place annually. The duration of the meeting should provide a reasonable amount of time to conduct all business. Items on the agenda will be derived from the following list: the structure of the business; the economic and financial situation; the probable development of the business; employment trends; future trends; production and sales; substantial organisation changes; introduction of new working methods and production processes; transfers of production; mergers, cutbacks and closures; collective redundancies; health and safety; equal opportunities; environmental issues; capital expenditure; access for education and training for employees.

Source: www.eurofound.ie (accessed 6.1.2003)

possibly through the impact of the respective trade unions or European industry federations of trade unions.

A number of factors may influence the conduct of management and employee representative negotiators. These include:

- company-specific factors such as the nature of the business and employment relations arrangements;
- the terms of the Directive itself, including its provisions;
- different systems of industrial relations and employee representation arrangements found in the countries in which multinational corporations operating in the European Economic Area are headquartered; and
- the sector in which the companies concerned are located.

Gilman and Marginson conclude that there is indeed a multiplicity of factors which constrain the management and employee representatives in negotiating on the provisions of EWC agreements, with the influence of both country and sector factors significant. This seems to contradict the view of a homogenous 'Europeanisation' process and 'reflects a more general process of "converging divergences" under which growing divergence in industrial relations arrangements and practice within national systems is occurring alongside increased cross border convergence of practices within given sectors' (Gilman and Marginson, 2002, p. 50).

Concluding remarks

The growth in the number of EWCs (at least 1200 across the European Union to date) should facilitate the greater spread of information and consultation across transnational companies. However, the extent to which such practices are successful depends upon the degree to which managements are willing to broaden out the range of issues for discussion in accordance with trade union aspirations. In practice, different objectives have been sought from the Directive at EU level, with management bodies such as UNICE trying to limit discussion and scope while trade unions have sought to widen the net. Another important issue concerns certain procedural aspects. Cressey (1998) contends that:

There has been and will continue to be a series of negotiations in companies about whether they have adequate procedures concerning exemptions from the legislation and the ways to adapt to the directive. There will be variation across nations and a variety of processes put in place. In this sense the actual constitution of what is acceptable information, consultation and related participatory forms is still to be decided. (p. 78)

In a more positive vein, an effective EWC should provide managements with the opportunity to communicate corporate strategy, to allow discussion of change, to encourage international contact and to encourage an identity among staff of 'belonging' to an international company. Trade unions and employee representatives may regard EWCs as being useful as they gain access to company information which enables comparisons to be made which in turn facilitates their bargaining activities. A study by Marginson *et al.* (1999) of 386 voluntary agreements made by groups and undertakings *before* the EWC Directive came into force in 1996, involving one third of the 1200 multinational companies covered by the Directive, concluded that the Directive itself has provided a major impetus to European-level negotiations between the management of multinational companies and employee representatives. These 'Article 13' agreements have given rise to many active EWCs which 'have the potential to develop and sustain new and effective forms of employee-interest representation at European level' (IRS, 1998). However, as far as employees in Britain are concerned, EWC information and consultation is limited to group-level issues and, in the absence of any rights to consultation at domestic or 'local' level, for most British employees participation for the time being remains elusive.

Summary points

- The German system of 'co-determination' remains the most visible and important national example of EP in Europe.
- The co-determination system comprises:
  - works councils; and
  - a two-tier board structure consisting of a supervisory and a management board.

- European Works Councils (EWCs) are company-wide bodies which conform to the requirements of the EWC Directive of 1994 and affect 'community-scale undertakings' and 'community-scale groups of undertakings'.
- The UK initially opted out of the Social Chapter and so was excluded from coverage of the EWC Directive. The UK's subsequent endorsement of the Social Chapter meant that the UK transposed the Directive during December 1999/January 2000.

EMPLOYEE VOICE AND PARTNERSHIP

Here we consider certain aspects of 'employee voice' with particular reference to information and consultation, and partnership approaches. The term 'employee voice', as was pointed out in the introduction to this chapter, has entered the employment relations lexicon as a general term to include all varieties of participation, involvement and information-sharing within unionised and non-unionised contexts. The term itself is meaningless unless it is associated with a particular voice mechanism such as participation and/or involvement practices as, for example, demonstrated by Millward *et al.* (2000). In relation to the UK, there is, as we have seen in Chapter 3, a considerable amount of literature and research devoted to the decline in union representation, membership and influence during the 1980s, 1990s and into the 2000s (for example with regard to the case of joint consultative committees in unionised organisations). At the same time there has been an increase in the use of communication channels by employers, particularly regarding regular meetings between senior managers and workforce, and briefing groups (see Chapter 7). A crucial issue addressed by WERS98 and subsequent analysis (Cully *et al.*, 1999; Millward *et al.*, 2000) relates to the effectiveness of voice mechanisms from the employees' perspective. This reveals that with regard to assessments of how managers responded to employee concerns and suggestions there was a positive association with non-union or direct communication channels, but perceptions of fairness and fair treatment were positively associated with union channels of communication and a well-established union presence. This, in turn, has implications for

employment relations, government policy and union survival. No forms of direct involvement of the types considered in Chapter 7 were positively associated with fairness. As Millward *et al.* (2000) conclude:

> If 'fairness at work' is to remain one of the criteria by which labour market policy is judged (Department of Trade and Industry 1998), then the continuing decline of union representation must be a cause of concern. No amount of 'direct participation' – management dominated arrangements which were showed to be less durable than union representation – can be expected to encourage fair treatment for employees at work. (p. 230)

Millward *et al.* (2000) identify seven types of voice mechanism which have been dealt with in this book. These are:

1. one or more recognised trade unions (see Chapter 3);
2. a functioning consultative committee with representatives chosen through union channels (this chapter);
3. a functioning consultative committee with representatives not chosen through union channels (this chapter and Chapter 7);
4. regular meetings between senior management and workforce (Chapter 7);
5. briefing groups (Chapter 7);
6. problem-solving groups (Chapter 7); and
7. non-union employee representatives.

Table 8.2 provides a summary of union and non-union voice arrangements, 1984–98.

In relation to the EU Information and Consultation Directive

As mentioned earlier in the chapter, receptiveness on the part of UK governments to formalised systems of employee participation, such as those based on the co-determination and works council structures, has been lukewarm at best. The UK has, however, agreed to adopt the EU Information and Consultation Directive of 2002 in stages from 2005 to 2008. Details are provided in Exhibit 8.5.

Table 8.2 Percentages of workplaces having union and non-union voice arrangements: 1984–98

	1984	1990	1998
Type of voice arrangements (5 items)			
Union only	24	14	9
Union and non-union	42	39	33
Non-union only	16	28	40
Voice, but nature not reported	2	–	–
No voice	16	19	17
Type of voice arrangement (7 items)			
Union only	–	11	6
Union and non-union	–	42	37
Non-union only	–	33	46
Voice, but nature not reported	–	–	–
No voice	–	14	11

Source: Millward *et al.*, 2000, p. 122

Exhibit 8.5

What the Information and Consultation Directive says

Directive 2002/14/EC of the European Parliament and of the Council

Object

The purpose of the Directive is to establish a general framework setting out minimum requirements for the right to information and consultation of employees in undertakings or establishments within the Community.

Scope

The Directive applies to undertakings employing at least 50 employees in any one Member State, or establishments employing at least 20 employees in any one Member State.

Practical Arrangements and Coverage

It is up to Member States to determine the practical arrangements for exercising the right to information and consultation at the appropriate level. Information and consultation covers:

(a) information on the recent and probable development of the undertaking's or establishment's activities and economic situation;

(b) information and consultation on the situation, structure and probable development of employment and threat to employment (possible redundancy); and

(c) information and consultation on decisions likely to lead to substantial changes in work organization or contractual relations including those covered by legislation concerning collective redundancies and transfers of undertakings.

Consultation must take place with appropriate timing, method and content, at the relevant level of management and representation depending on the subject under discussion, on the basis of the information supplied by the employer, and in such a way as to enable employees' representatives to meet the employer and obtain a reasoned response to any opinion they may formulate. In addition, consultation should take place with a view to reaching agreement on decisions within the employer's powers concerning substantial changes in work organization or in contractual relations, including collective redundancies and transfers of undertakings.

Other Provisions

The Directive contains provisions on the protection of employee representatives, enforcement and sanctions, the handling of confidential information and the relationship with other employment legislation.

Implementation

The Directive will be transposed in phases, starting on 23 March 2005, with transitional periods of up to three years from 2005 for firms with fewer than 150 employees.

Source: www.dti.gov.uk (accessed 18.1.2003)

Responses of government, TUC and CBI to the Directive

Currently, UK law provides for the information and/ or consultation of employees or their representatives in the areas of collective redundancies (Chapter 13), transfers of undertakings (Chapter 13), collective bargaining (Chapter 6), occupational pensions, European Works Councils and the European Company Statute. UK developments in this area have been erratic and piecemeal, and progress has been hindered additionally by the conflicting interests of unions and the TUC on the one hand and of employers and CBI on the other. However, the Information and Consultation Directive imposes a general requirement that member states adopt appropriate structures to facilitate and enhance consultation and information-sharing, which, for the majority of EU states are already in place in the form of legislated-for works councils and other co-determination systems. Within the UK there is, as we have noted previously, no such comprehensive framework concerning information and consultation and, arguably, the tradition of vol-untarism in industrial relations and the ideological interests already referred to have militated against such a development. Notwithstanding this, the sec-ond Blair government will transpose the Directive in

2005, and to that end made its preliminary position clear in its report entitled: 'High performance work-places: The role of employee involvement in a modern economy' (DTI, 2002).

Self-Evaluation Activity 8.7

The government's position
The response is given below

Is it possible to gauge from the title of the government report the voice mechanism(s) it may favour?

The report emphasises the business case for infor-mation and consultation, but only in the context of encouraging 'high performance workplaces' (HPWs). HPWs are characterised by 'high levels of employee involvement and regard' (DTI, 2002, p. 11), valuing and motivating employees; adopting a joint approach to solving business problems involving everyone in the process; recognising the different rights, respons-ibilities and interests of different groups and indi-viduals; implementing change through involving, consulting and informing all stakeholders in the business; helping to improve work/life balance; and in some cases, coming to agreement whereby flexibility and employment security are traded. Clearly, then, information and consultation are regarded by government as one means of securing HPWs.

The report cites WERS98 in claiming that a wide diversity of practices exist aimed at 'involving people more closely in the workplace' (ibid., p. 16), but fails to mention one of its significant conclusions concerning employee voice: that no matter how much management-initiated involvement practices proliferate and are emphasised, employee perceptions of fairness in relation to decision-making depend heavily upon union recognition and representation. There is, therefore, a clear emphasis upon involvement rather than participation and an overriding concern for the business case which ignores fairness and full participation in decision-making. The main message of the report, however, is that there should not be a single model which is applicable to all organisations, but rather a diversity of approaches without legislative compulsion: 'Individual organisations should be able to develop their own arrangements tailored to their particular circumstances through voluntary agreements' (ibid., p. 18). This would apply particularly to small to medium-sized enterprises (SMEs):

> It is particularly important in the case of small and medium sized enterprises that legislation should only be imposed where absolutely necessary. This is why the Government opposed any reduction in the 50-employee threshold in the Information and Consultation Directive, and obtained derogations enabling us to delay applying the legislation to firms with less than 150 employees for up to 3 years (to March 2008). Once fully implemented, the Directive will only apply to 1% of companies in the UK – though 75% of employees stand to benefit (ibid., p. 25).

In response to the discussion document, the TUC presented its own submission and, to its credit, this is more of an academic document and therefore both more critical and more considered than the government document (TUC, 2002). While the TUC paper agrees with the main contention of the government paper (henceforth 'DTI') that there is no simple formula for high performance, there are a number of criticisms, some of omission, that it makes. Firstly, there is little causal analysis in DTI as to *why* a

positive attitude to employee involvement contributes to performance, much of the analysis residing within the HR literature to which little or no reference is made by DTI. The TUC report on the other hand cites numerous studies in support of straightforward arguments relating involvement positively with business gains. Secondly, the TUC rejects any notion advanced by many in the personnel profession that an exclusive focus on individual employee involvement is a recipe for success, together with the argument that the sole purpose of information and consultation is to align workers' aspirations with the goals of the business, which is essentially a 'unitarist' perspective. While there is evidence that direct participation or involvement can improve company performance, it is indirect (employee) participation that provides the best means for ensuring information-sharing and hence performance; it is, therefore, the 'collective voice to build commitment and trust [that is] likely to raise organisational performance' (TUC-CBI, 2001, para. 34). Hence the notion that direct and indirect participation conflict or mutually exclude each other is profoundly mistaken. Indeed, much research points to the probability that direct participation is more likely where there is a recognised union and some form of works council (TUC, 2002, p. 4), that direct and indirect involvement/participation are mutually reinforcing and can make important contributions to building HPWs.

Thirdly, given that handling information and the consultative process are learnt skills, often through experience as much as through instruction, the TUC posits the question: Are Britain's senior managers up to the job, given the argument that it is the quality of management that, at least in part, accounts for the poor productivity record of British firms and the 'productivity gap' between British and European, US and Far Eastern companies? Fourthly, the UK corporate governance model based on the 'shareholder economy' could mean that involving employees in corporate decision-making is a risky investment. The model also points to the relative weakness of other stakeholders in the organisation such as employees themselves. Most European countries, on the other hand, have a family of institutions (such as sectoral and/or regional collective bargaining machinery, arrangements for co-determination and social partner involvement in welfare and training systems) giving a well-established voice to all stakeholders. Fifthly, the TUC recommends a Code of Practice (not mentioned in DTI or the Directive) to make specific reference to subjects on which consultation should take place, and has produced a wide-ranging list:

- organisational changes;
- introduction of new working methods and production processes;
- transfers of production;
- mergers;
- cut-backs or closures of undertakings or establishments;
- collective redundancies;
- grievance and disciplinary procedures;
- pensions;
- payment systems;
- equal opportunities;
- training and workforce development;
- working hours and holidays;
- flexible working arrangements;
- environmental issues; and
- health and safety.

Sixthly, there should be a distinction drawn between consultation on the one hand and collective bargaining on the other at appropriate levels of representation. These functions should be kept separate as they are in most EU countries where formally legislated-for works councils exist. However, the paper identifies three practices which would be possible by agreement. These include:

- information and consultation via recognised unions with supplementary arrangements for non-union groups of employees, who must also be provided for by law, following judgements in the European Court of Justice on the UK Regulations implementing the Directive on Collective Redundancies and Transfers;
- an information and consultation body made up of representatives from unionised groups appointed by recognised unions and elected representatives from other non-union groups; and
- an information and consultation body for which elections are held for all seats. This is the most common current selection practice for JCCs.

Seventhly, the TUC has a preference for the Directive to apply to undertakings of at least 50 employees

on grounds of ensuring equal treatment for employees within multi-establishment undertakings and providing for consultation with higher-level management who are more likely to be responsible for decision-making. This understanding would also be more in keeping with the existing pattern of consultation arrangements within the UK and would also facilitate a 'single channel plus' or 'supplemented single channel' approach whereby union representatives in undertakings which recognise unions would be consulted primarily with other representatives consulted complementarily. Furthermore, within the UK context, the most viable approach to implementing the Directive would combine minimum standards with flexibility by:

- establishing a general duty on employers to carry out the necessary information and consultation procedures as directed by the Directive, where requested by employees;
- allowing employers and employees to determine the practical arrangements for information and consultation via negotiated agreements;
- in the absence of agreed information and consultation arrangements, enabling employees to seek the establishment of the necessary arrangements via some form of trigger mechanism; and
- making provision for a statutory fall-back framework to be enforced on employers who are unwilling to introduce the necessary information and consultation arrangements by agreement.

However, the TUC also argues that the government should try to promote information and consultation in small and medium-sized establishments (SMEs) and regrets the small firms' exclusion permitted by the Directive as small firms usually do not recognise unions and experience the vast majority of employment protection violations. The report goes on to argue:

> Giving workers a voice in their workplace will encourage workplace resolution of individual disputes. Such an approach is needed in the workplaces where the problems are greatest – small businesses. (p. 27)

Unlike the TUC, the CBI's position is more hostile to the Directive, although its website does not give much away to date, merely the statement:

CBI is deeply disappointed by the agreement of this dossier. Nonetheless the current text contains some useful flexibilities that will help limit its damaging impact. We will be pressing the Government to make full use of them during the implementation process. (www.cbi.org, accessed 18.1.2003)

In conclusion, while considerable pressure is being placed upon government by the TUC and CBI, the implementation of the Information and Consultation Directive, particularly if it incorporates modifications and refinements as, for example, suggested by the TUC, would represent a major impetus to the development of employee voice in the UK.

In relation to partnership

Definitions of partnership remain unsatisfactory and unclear, having different meanings and levels of analysis (Tailby and Winchester, 2000; Heery, 2002). The TUC has a headline definition: 'Partnership means a grown-up relationship between bosses and workers', while the DTI partnership website has a longer but more amorphous definition:

Partnership at work refers to the relationship between employers, employees and their representatives. Partnership is about developing better employment relationships at all levels, helping to build trust in the workplace, the sharing of information and working together to solve business problems. (www.dti.gov.uk/partnershipfund/index.html, accessed 18.1.2003)

The main pressure groups such as the TUC, CBI and Institute of Directors have, then, provided different interpretations of partnership, defining the term for their own ends (Ackers and Payne, 1998; Undy, 1999). The CIPD (Chartered Institute of Personnel and Development) views partnership as having 'more to do with an approach to the relationship between employers and employees individually, than it has to do with trade unions' (IPD, 1997). It is, therefore possible to define partnership in either pluralist or unitary terms (see Chapter 2), with the TUC view of partnership, for example (see below), being appropriately pluralist in nature. The Involvement and Participation Association (www.partnership-at-work.com, accessed 18.1.2003) has been instrumental in

providing a definition of partnership that is more workable than most, and which has been endorsed by a number of large enterprises and some trade unions (see below). Heery (2002) identifies four levels at which partnership operates. Firstly, at European level it can denote union involvement in the negotiation of framework agreements concerning, for example, parental leave and part-time work. Secondly, at national level, the TUC may be regarded as a partner in economic and social management. Thirdly, at sectoral level, the TUC works with a range of employer and management organisations in order to negotiate 'framework agreements' guaranteeing minimum employment standards. Finally, at company level social partnership can involve the negotiation of partnership agreements, normally between unions and management with the intention of creating a more harmonious and co-operative set of relationships within the organisation. Heery points out that, given the decentralised nature of UK employment relations, it is the growing numbers of partnership agreements that are the focus of attention.

Clearly, the two parties to the partnership agreement – trade unions and employers – will have both mutual and differing reasons for forming the agreement. For example, unions would hope to capitalise on the recognition procedures of the ERA99 by using partnership as a vehicle for the promotion of wider collective representation and collective bargaining while simultaneously sharing with management the concern for promoting performance and productivity in order to secure employment security. Hence unions would make certain concessions in return for enhanced employment protection, while employers would also make concessions in order to improve performance and productivity. As John Monks, the former General Secretary of the TUC, stated:

There is increasing evidence that partnership delivers. For employees it provides greater job security in satisfying, good quality jobs with access to training and influence over work organization. For employers the benefits include better quality decision-making and outcomes achieved by involving the whole workforce. A reduction in the amount of time spent on grievances and a more committed staff with a flexible approach to work. (TUC, 2001, p. 2)

The TUC rejects the view that partnership constitutes 'concession bargaining' or 'cosying up' to employers, or failing properly to defend the interests of members. Rather, the TUC argues that partnership is about *real* joint decision-making and problem-solving, about unions having more influence over employer behaviour and workers exercising greater control over their immediate working environment. Partnership, according to the TUC, depends on good employment relations and is more than traditional collective bargaining. The partnership agenda covers issues such as business strategy and how an organisation can meet the challenges of changing markets, technologies and customer requirements. It also embraces the development of a shared approach to training and the introduction of new forms of work. Partnership supplements and reinforces collective bargaining through greater openness and has a clear focus on issues affecting the quality of working life. The 'six principles of partnership' which the TUC endorses are:

- shared commitment to the success of the enterprise;
- recognition of legitimate interests;
- commitment to employment security;
- focus on the quality of working life;
- openness; and
- adding value.

Self-Evaluation Activity 8.8

Benefits to management
The response is given below

Identify the benefits to management/employer of partnership agreements.

Partnership at organisational level now involves working with rather than against employers, and as such requires management to accept the logic of some form of representation and communication through trade unions, this being the quid pro quo of the consultative style of management (Purcell, 1987) considered in Chapter 2. Apart from providing decisions with a degree of legitimacy they would otherwise not have, other alleged benefits to management include cost-effectiveness of communicating via representatives rather than individually, the value accrued to upward communication from staff and the stability such a relationship provides to managing employees (IRS, 1998).

History and background to partnership

The Involvement and Participation Association (IPA) was formed in 1896 in order to promote the idea of partnership and to bring together management and trade union representatives, hence the concept and practice of partnership per se is nothing new, despite the use of the terms 'social partners' and 'social partnership' during the 1980s and 1990s. Two long-standing examples of partnership are the multiple retailer The John Lewis Partnership, where individual employees are regarded as partners and receive a substantial share of the company's profits, and ICI, the chemical company, where partnership comprises an all-embracing joint consultation system with trade unions dating back to 1926. The IPA, then, has sought to disseminate best practice, provide guidance and advice and has established an underpinning set of partnership principles and practices (Martinez Lucio and Stuart, 2002).

During the 1980s a partnership dialogue was initiated by trade unions as part of the 'new realism' initiative (see Chapter 3). This focused upon challenges facing British industry and the need for a positive trade union response, which would include the development of a joint approach with employers to create economic success, improving quality, performance, cost and price competitiveness. It would also include considering issues such as training, investment, research and development, work restructuring, equal opportunities and health and safety. Partnership would also benefit from new forums for information and consultation such as works councils and an approach which stresses both 'individualism' (involvement and communication) and 'collectivism' (representative participation). In 1992 a joint statement of intent by employer and union representatives under the auspices of the IPA was issued which emphasised the following:

1. The parties to agree joint aims such as a joint commitment to the success of the organisation, a recognition to jointly build trust and a joint declaration recognising the legitimacy of the role of each party.

2. The areas where the parties need to rethink their approach. Management is asked to do more to ensure employment security, share the results of success with all who contribute to it and recognise the employee's right to be informed, consulted and represented. Unions are asked to promote job flexibility, to recognise that union and non-union members have a right to representation, giving up the right to single channel representation, and to accept management attempts to involve individual employees.

3. A summary of the benefits of the new approach enabling discussion on a range of subjects not featuring prominently in collective bargaining in the UK in the past, such as quality through improvement, training, education, investment, communication, equal opportunity, corporate values, company success, environment and health and safety.

4. Possibilities for representation channels or forums were to broaden the existing collective bargaining framework to include subjects of wider policy and the introduction of 'new' institutions such as works councils where a wide agenda of issues could be discussed by employers and employee representatives.

The TUC, as we have seen, has also developed its interest in partnership as a way of renewing and extending the role of organised labour within the workplace and moving beyond the traditions and legacies of adversarial employment relations. In 1999 it developed its six partnership principles (see p. 417) and then went on to form its own partnership consultancy and training body – the Partnership Institute – which aims to encourage the formation of partnership practices.

With the election of the first Blair government in 1997 there was an increased emphasis and impetus given to partnership as part of its 'modernisation' agenda. This was expressed in the white paper *Fairness at Work*, which stated: 'This White Paper is part of the Government's programme to replace the notion of conflict between employers and employees with the promotion of partnership' (DTI, 1998, p. 1). The substitution of conflict for partnership is problematic in itself since, on the one hand, collective voice and representation are undermined and de-emphasised, while on the other, many of the

partnership policies advocated by government in the public sector generally and the National Health Service in particular 'are concerned with new forms of individual-oriented human resource management practices and workplace strategies and not simply union-oriented ones' (Martinez Lucio and Stuart, 2002). The government's partnership agenda has been given substance via the DTI with the creation of the Partnership at Work Fund, 'an essential part of the Government's non-legislative approach to improve industrial relations in order to secure productivity improvements' (DTI, 2002, p. 12). The Fund, which encourages and finances joint working on matters such as involvement, bullying and the quality of working life, provides up to £50 000 of matched finance for each partnership project, and additional funding during 2002 was provided to support the planned expansion of the Fund. There were 49 Fund 'winners' in 2002, of which Barclays is an example (see Main case 8.1).

Main case 8.1
Partnership at Barclays

Setting the scene

During the 1990s, employment relations at Barclays was characterised by a sequence of strikes and other industrial action. Strike action threatened the bank's plans for restructuring, which meant streamlining its functions and making staff redundant. Moreover, industrial action was unwelcome publicity for the bank which was experiencing public dissatisfaction with branch closures. The catalyst for the move towards partnership relations was a series of branch strikes in 1997 over an unpopular performance-related pay scheme. The new management in the employee relations department realised that if the union, UNIFI, were to be brought into mainstream decision-making, conflict would be better managed and disagreements could be resolved outside the public glare. For their part, UNIFI was also looking for a change. In pre-partnership times the union was left out of decision-making and only informed of decisions that had already been made, and the only leverage UNIFI had in influencing decision-making was industrial action or the threat of industrial action. As an alternative means of dealing with the employment relationship,

UNIFI now argued that partnership meant that the union would not be contained by management and it could have a say before decisions were taken. Partnership provided an alternative to strike action, which had never been popular with the union membership, and also offered new membership recruitment opportunities.

The agreement

Following lengthy discussions at the partnership steering committee during the late 1990s, the ensuing agreement produced a three-year pay and benefits deal, and a commitment to improving relations between the bank and UNIFI, working together to rebuild trust and respect as the basis for future relationships through co-operation and joint problem-solving. Six principles of partnership were agreed to cement this new vision of employment relations:

1. To secure and promote the long-term success of Barclays.
2. To promote the interests of employees, customers and shareholders.
3. To ensure that Barclays meets customer expectations by having people with the right skills in the right place at the right cost.
4. To facilitate the management of change.
5. To ensure employees are managed fairly and professionally.
6. To promote equality of treatment and opportunity for all, valuing diversity.

The bank agreed to help the union influence the implementation of business strategy and plans, to facilitate UNIFI's role to promote the interests of its members, and to improve training, coaching and careers guidance for staff. In exchange, UNIFI endorsed the importance of co-operation with managers to develop shared agendas to promote the long-term success of the business. Whereas UNIFI traditionally rarely thought about the business case in negotiations, the partnership agreement commits the union to recognising business goals and objectives. As a result of a ballot, the agreement was accepted on a 20 per cent turnout.

To support the initiative, the bank established a partnership steering group to monitor progress and to recommend improvements to the new relationship. The steering group included senior figures from both sides, as well as lay representatives. In addition, nine joint working parties, with elected and jointly-trained representatives, were set up to examine company-wide issues such as change management, flexible working, performance management, pay, union facilities and representation, health and safety, equality and diversity, IT and job evaluation. The bank has also agreed to train 300 line managers and union staff representatives in partnership working (beginning in September 2002) in order to prevent it being regarded purely as a board-level initiative.

Outcomes of the Agreement

Working in partnership has had three key outcomes of particular significance to UNIFI. These concern culture, terms and conditions, and union organisation.

A new culture of employment relations

A successful bid in the second round of the DTI Partnership at Work Fund has resulted in a new leadership development programme for managers and union representatives, designed to encourage new ways of working based on trust. Part of this initiative involved a rolling programme of workshops across Barclays' various business units. The workshops focused upon:

- Developing a shared understanding of the business and its drivers, including the importance of diversity, work–life balance etc.
- Putting the partnership principles in local context.
- Putting partnership in the context of effective change.
- Building self-confidence and confidence in each other.
- Personal skills, for example, in the area of conflict resolution and communications.

'In the longer term, the aim is to integrate these workshops into the organisation's existing learning and development offering, which is centred upon the Barclays' University (the home for all learning and development for all employees). This step will help embed partnership with UNIFI even further into the Barclays' culture' (DTI, 2002).

New terms and conditions

Two, three-year pay deals, the most recent signed in 2002, signalling the end of annual pay bargaining negotiations, included a new performance pay system, harmonised terms and conditions, and private healthcare. In addition to a pre-existing agreement called

'HR Policies and Procedures for Managing Change' that provided a generous package in the event of redundancies, the bank has also agreed to give affected members of staff six months' notice, during which time they are paid to look for alternative work, provide career counselling, a job-swap scheme, retraining assistance and an augmented pension. The agreement of these was an important precursor to signing the partnership agreement, which the workforce endorsed with an overwhelming majority in a secret ballot in April 1999.

Union organisation

Partnership has brought a new system of union representation and extended recognition to new parts of the bank (in December 2002, six union representatives were seconded specifically to trade union recruitment for one month). Voluntary union representation at a local level is now formalised by a growing network of over 120 jointly accredited UNIFI lay representatives and six full-time health and safety representatives. Representatives also receive extensive training in discipline and grievance, union recruitment and the law, which conform to an agreed role profile. Representatives are also allocated appropriate resources and two days a month to handle union business.

Challenges

- Union officials now have to consider both a business case and employee welfare in joint decision-making. Part of the deal is that the union must also take ownership for controversial decisions.
- The union has a duty to communicate with its members on joint decisions, without undermining the trust of the bank in relation to confidential information or by appearing to be 'in bed with the boss'.
- The legitimacy of the union relies on its ability to convince members and non-members that their collective strength has a continuing impact on the nature of relations between bank and union.
- The credibility of the union relies on its ability to set and influence the business agenda and be prepared to exercise its power.
- Partnership has been slow to filter down the corporate hierarchy, particularly through the layers of line management and it has yet to be embedded throughout the company.

Self-Evaluation Activity 8.9

How successful is the Barclays partnership agreement?

Response on website

Based on your reading of the Barclays case, comment on the success or otherwise of the partnership agreement.

Issues and dilemmas: partnership as 'Janus-faced'?

Partnership agreements are varied and diverse, reflecting the specific needs and priorities of organisation, employees and unions. Often they are unwieldy compromises, which may not be in the long-term interests of either party. Here we consider in greater detail, through the research of Bacon and Storey (2000) and Oxenbridge and Brown (2002), the problem of *ambiguity* which is expressed in the two contrasting views of the partnership relationship (the term 'Janus-faced' is also appropriate, Janus being a Roman god who, as guardian of doorways and gates, is represented with two faces looking simultaneously forwards and backwards). The two contrasting views are essentially concerned with either the belief that partnerships represent a lifeline to unions after years of marginalisation, providing them with a legitimate voice in the wide-ranging affairs and issues of the organisations involved, or the argument that partnership agreements actually weaken unions and threaten and undermine workplace unionism. These views, as we have seen, are also ideological positions held by unions on the one hand and some employers on the other, often expressed in oppositional terms of 'collectivism v individualism' and 'pluralism v unitarism' (see Chapter 2). They also point to the motives of employers in pursuing partnership. As such, this dilemma raises more hypothetical questions and contentions than answers. Such questions include:

- Does the adoption of a partnership agreement/ arrangement signify a major change in management style including re-engaging with trade unions?
- Do partnership agreements require management to devise long-term strategies for managing the employment relationship?

- Do partnership agreements provide employers with the excuse for short-termism?
- Do partnership arrangements encourage the pursuit of 'individualism' of the type exercised in non-union firms at the expense of 'collective representation'?
- Or do new agreements manifest a mix and match of unitarism and pluralism where the two complement each other?

As a result of researching a number of large organisations such as Ford, Unilever, Cadbury-Schweppes and Royal Mail, Bacon and Storey (2000) arrive at the following conclusions. Firstly, there was little evidence that the agreements secured would provide stability in the longer term; hence partnership or 'framework' agreements may only be useful as 'stop-gaps' and short-term expediency. Secondly, while the motives of employers in securing agreements may have been to shift the emphasis in employment relations managements more towards individualism, any further motives amongst management to marginalise or even derecognise unions were not realised. In fact, agreements were made for highly pragmatic reasons in some organisations, 'even where unions were aggressively sidelined' (ibid., p. 423). Thirdly, there was no real evidence that firms were seeking genuine joint determination over any issue; indeed there was greater interest in attempting to overcome union resistance to management plans despite agreements emphasising joint approaches. Nevertheless, such agreements are not to be regarded as 'hollow shells', as some of them did 'in the main re-establish a role for trade unions and offered forums to establish joint rules and procedures, although the agreements were firmly management-driven' (ibid., p. 424).

Research by Oxenbridge and Brown (2002) in 11 case-study organisations, spanning a range of industry sectors, examined the motives and benefits to the parties (see above), the content of partnership arrangements and relationships, together with strategies of control vis-à-vis trade unions. With regard to arrangements and relationships, one major issue is whether union bargaining rights are enhanced or weakened by partnership agreements. It was found that, overall, the bargaining agenda was limited and negotiation over substantive issues restricted, with some firms providing unions with relatively extensive recognition rights while others within the service sector allowed only minimal rights. The situation concerning representation and consultation was equally varied, involving senior managers and full-time union officers in some organisations, and workplace representatives and management in other, mainly production organisations. Companies with consultative structures such as JCCs and works councils tended to be union dominated but recognised the need for non-union representation, while others had no or minimal consultative machinery.

In relation to control strategies, Oxenbridge and Brown (2002) found that the less formal the partnership arrangements, the more extensive were union rights. However, many firms used strategies to monitor unions after the partnership agreement was concluded. These include:

- Negotiating agreements or changes to existing agreements which explicitly limited union rights and activity in the workplace.
- Refusing to deal with 'difficult' trade union officials, and dealing only with officials perceived to be compliant.
- Endeavouring to reduce the number of unions the company dealt with.
- Taking steps to reduce union control over communication and consultative structures and increase management control of both. (p. 267).

Oxenbridge and Brown conclude that managements had various and varying reasons for entering into partnership agreements, and may use agreements as vehicles for either encouraging or inhibiting collective bargaining and representation, more usually the latter.

Concluding comments

The evidence to date is still patchy and inconclusive and research in the area is relatively uncritical (Kelly, 2001). Arguably, for partnerships to prosper and yield benefits to employer and unions/employees, there should be a long-term commitment by managers to working closely with unions (Bacon, 2001). Should this commitment be lacking, then partnerships are unlikely to be successful as managers may well take an opportunistic view of the costs and benefits of partnership to the organisation. A central assumption held by government and the CBI is that partnership is a model of co-operation in which adversarial industrial relations has no place and unions are required to be compliant. The TUC envisages a more proactive relationship with management, with unions being active partners in joint consultation and decision-making. Whatever assumption is made, a crucial issue is whether partnership agreements will deliver benefits and returns to both parties, and if these benefits do not materialise, or if costs outweigh benefits, then enthusiasm for partnership may well subside.

Summary points

- While there has been a decline in union voice since 1980 there has been an increase in the use of communication channels by employers, particularly regarding regular meetings between senior managers and workforce, and briefing groups.
- Perceptions of fairness and fair treatment are positively associated with union channels of communication and a well-established union presence.
- The Information and Consultation Directive which is to be phased in from 2005 will provide a legislative basis for union and non-union representation within larger organisations.
- Definitions of partnership vary, as do the type of partnership agreement, with some ambiguity in how the parties interpret them in theory and in practice.
- The 'six principles of partnership' which the TUC endorses are:
  - shared commitment to the success of the enterprise;
  - recognition of legitimate interests;
  - commitment to employment security;
  - focus on the quality of working life;
  - openness; and
  - adding value.
- Research suggests that a crucial issue for the long-term viability of partnership is whether partnership agreements will deliver benefits and returns to both parties, and if these benefits do not materialise, or if costs outweigh benefits, then enthusiasm for partnership may wane.

RELEVANT WEBSITES

www.dti.gov.uk/partnershipfund/index/html (Department of Trade and Industry) Good for information concerning partnership fund and case-study organisations concerning partnership; information and consultation and works councils.

www.eurofound.ie (European Foundation for the Improvement of Living and Working Conditions) Information concerning social partnership, European Works Councils, consultation and information.

www.partnership-at-work.com (Partnership at Work) An excellent site for all aspects of partnership.

www.tuc.org.uk/partnership (Trades Union Congress) Good for exploring the TUC's position on partnership and information and consultation.

REFERENCES

Ackers, P. and Payne, J. (1998) 'British trade unions and social partnership: rhetoric, reality and strategy'. *International Journal of Human Resource Management*, 9, 3, 529–550

Ackers, P., Smith, C. and Smith, P. (1996) *The New Workplace and Trade Unionism: Critical Perspectives on Work and Organisation*. London, Routledge

AEEU (1997) *European Works Councils*. London, AEEU

Argyris, C. (1964) *Integrating the Individual and the Organisation*. New York, Wiley

Bacon, N. (2001) 'Employee Relations' in Redman, T. and Wilkinson, A. (eds) *Contemporary Human Resource Management*. Harlow, Financial Times/Prentice Hall

Bacon, N. and Storey, J. (2000) 'New employee relations strategies in Britain: towards individualism or partnership?' *British Journal of Industrial Relations*, 38, 3, 407–27

Batstone, E. (1984) *Working Order*. Oxford, Blackwell

Berghahn, V.R. and Karsten, D. (1987) *Industrial Relations in West Germany*. Oxford, Berg

Blyton, P. and Turnbull, P. (1994) *The Dynamics of Employee Relations*. London, Macmillan

Blyton, P. and Turnbull, P. (1998) *The Dynamics of Employee Relations*, 2nd edn. London, Macmillan

Bridgford, J. and Stirling, J. (1994) *Employee Relations in Europe*. Oxford, Blackwell

Bullock Report (1977) *Report of the Committee of Inquiry on Industrial Democracy*, Cmnd 6706. London, HMSO

Carley, M. (2002) *Bargaining at European Level? Joint Texts Negotiated by European Works Councils*. Dublin, European Foundation for the Improvement of Living and Working Conditions

Clegg, H.A. (1985) 'Trade unions as an opposition which can never become a government', in McCarthy, W.E.J. (ed.) *Trade Unions*. Harmondsworth, Pelican

Cressey, P. (1998) 'European works councils in practice'. *Human Resource Management Journal*, 8, 1, 67–79

Cressey, P., Eldridge, J. and MacInnes, J. (1985) *Just Managing*. Milton Keynes, Open University Press

Cully, M., Woodland, S., O'Reilly, A. and Dix, G. (1999) *Britain at Work*. London, Routledge

Donovan (1968) *Report of the Royal Commission on Trade Unions and Employers' Associations 1965–1968*, Cmnd 3623. London, HMSO

DTI (Department of Trade and Industry) (1998) *Fairness at Work*, Cm 2968. London, HMSO

DTI (Department of Trade and Industry) (2002) 'High performance workplaces: the role of employee involvement in a modern economy. A discussion paper'. London, DTI

Edwards, P. (1985) 'Managing labour relations through the recession'. *Employee Relations*, 7, 2, 3–7

Farnham, D. (1997) *Employee Relations in Context*. London, IPD

Farnham, D. and Pimmlott J. (1995) *Understanding Industrial Relations*. London, Cassell

Frege, C.M. (2002) 'German works councils: a critical assessment'. *British Journal of Industrial Relations*, 40, 2, 221–48

Furstenberg, F. (1981) 'Zur Methodologie der Mitbestimmungsforschung' in Diefenbacher, H. and Nutzinger, H.G. (eds) *Mitbestimmung*. Frankfurt, Campus

Gilman, M. and Marginson, P. (2002) 'Negotiating European Works Councils: contours or constrained choice'. *Industrial Relations Journal*, 33, 1, 36–51

Hall, M., Carley, M., Gold, M., Marginson, P., and Sisson, K. (1995) *European Works Councils: Planning for the Directive*. London, IRS

Heery, E. (2002) 'Partnership v organising: alternative futures for British trade unionism'. *Industrial Relations Journal*, 33, 1, 20–35

Heller, F.A. (1986) 'Does formal policy or law as used in Europe contribute to improved employee information and participation?', in Vandamme, J. (ed.) *Employee Consultation and Information in Multinational Corporations*. Beckenham, Croom Helm

Herzberg, F. (1974) *Work and the Nature of Man*. London, Staples Press

Hyman, J. and Mason, B. (1995) *Managing Employee Involvement and Participation*. London, Sage

IPD (1997) *Employment Relations into the 20th Century*. London, IPD

IRS (1998) 'Works councils more prevalent than expected'. *IRS Employment Trends*, No. 664

Kelly, J. (2001) 'Social partnership agreements: who gains, who loses?' *Candid*, magazine of the GMB London Region, 5 July

Likert, R. (1961) *New Patterns of Management*. New York, McGraw-Hill

MacInnes, J. (1985) 'Conjuring up consultation'. *British Journal of Industrial Relations*, 23, 1, 93–113

Marchington, M. (1987) 'A review and critique of research on developments in joint consultation'. *British Journal of Industrial Relations*, 25, 3, 339–52

Marchington, M. and Armstrong, R. (1986) 'The nature of the new joint consultation'. *Industrial Relations Journal*, 17, 2, 158–70

Marchington, M. and Parker, P. (1990) *Changing Patterns of Employee Relations*. Hemel Hempstead, Harvester Wheatsheaf

Marginson, P., Gilman, M., Jacobi, O. and Krieger, H. (1999) *Negotiating European Works Councils: An Analysis of Agreements Under Article 13*. London, The Stationery Office

Martinez Lucio, M. and Stuart, M. (2002) 'Assessing partnership: the prospects for and challenges of, modernisation'. *Employee Relations*, 24, 3, 252–61

McGregor, P. (1960) *The Human Side of Enterprise*. New York, McGraw-Hill

Millward, N., Smart, D., Stevens, M. and Hawes, W.R. (1992) *Workplace Industrial Relations in Transition*. Aldershot, Dartmouth

Millward, N., Bryson, A. and Forth, J. (2000) *All Change at Work*. London, Routledge

Oxenbridge, S. and Brown, W. (2002) 'Two faces of partnership? An assessment of partnership and co-operative employer/trade union relationships'. *Employee Relations*, 24, 3, 262–76

Purcell, J. (1987) 'Mapping management styles in Employee Relations'. *Journal of Management Studies*, 24, 5, 533–48

Ramsay, H. (1977) 'Cycles of control: worker participation in sociological and historical perspective'. *Sociology*, 11, 3, 481–506

Salamon, M. (1998) *Industrial Relations: Theory and Practice*. London, Prentice Hall

Strauss, G. (1979) 'Workers' participation symposium introduction'. *Industrial Relations*, 18, 3, 247–61

Tailby, S. and Winchester, D. (2000) 'Management and trade unions: towards social partnership?' in Bach, S. and Sisson, K. (eds) *Personnel Management: A Comprehensive Guide to Theory and Practice*. Oxford, Blackwell

Taylor, F.W. (1947) *Scientific Management*. New York, Harper and Row

Terry, M. (1983) 'Shop stewards through expansion and recession'. *Industrial Relations Journal*, 14, 3, 49–58

Terry, M. (1986) 'How do we know if shop stewards are getting weaker?' *British Journal of Industrial Relations*, 24, 2, 169–80

Terry, M. (2003) 'Employee representation' in Edwards, P. (ed.) *Industrial Relations Theory and Practice*, 2nd edn. Oxford, Blackwell.

TUC (2001) *Partners for Progress: Winning at Work*. London, TUC

TUC (2002) TUC Submission on the Government's Discussion Document 'High Performance Workplaces' www.tuc.org.uk/law/tuc

TUC-CBI (2001) *The UK Productivity Challenge*. London, TUC-CBI

Undy, R. (1999) 'Annual review article: New Labour's "industrial relations settlement" the Third way?'. *British Journal of Industrial Relations*, 37, 2, 315–36

Vandamme, J. (ed.) (1986) *Employee Consultation and Information in Multinational Corporations*. Beckenham, Croom Helm

Van Ruysseveldt, J. and Visser, J. (1996) *Industrial Relations in Europe: Traditions and Transitions*. London, Sage

Wall, T.D. and Lischeron, J.A. (1977) *Worker Participation*. Maidenhead, McGraw-Hill

Wortman, M. and Dorrenbacher, C. (1994) 'An assessment of their qualitative impact of the proposed directive on European Works Councils'. Berlin, fast eV

CHAPTER 9

INDUSTRIAL ACTION

INTRODUCTION

Some writers argue that there has been a re-emergence of interest in conflict, this becoming, for whatever reason, more 'fashionable' in recent years (Danford and Stewart, 2003). However, in 'mature', democratic and pluralist societies, the potential for conflict in its many manifestations will always exist. The pluralist perspective legitimises conflict as a means whereby different interests may be articulated and resolved through normal democratic mechanisms. Moreover, it could be argued that democratic and participative processes within the wider society exist to ensure that conflicts do not pose a threat to the dominant class-based interests within the wider society. This argument, which provides the rationale for this chapter, is reinforced by Coser (1956) who asserts that employers and employees, as parties to conflict, engage in a process that neither side can win. The situation described by Coser is analogous to a 'game', which is played according to certain 'rules'. In this way, conflict becomes institutionalised in terms of an agreed set of rules and procedures endorsed by both parties. In similar vein, Dahrendorf (1959) argues that the legitimisation of trade unions by employers and the state constituted a major step towards industrial democracy and institutionalisation of industrial conflict. Manifestations of this phenomenon included:

- the consolidation of collective bargaining within a framework of agreed-upon rules and procedures thereby regulating and resolving conflicts between the parties;

- the implementation of institutionalised mechanisms for arbitrating and mediating between parties in dispute;

- the establishment of formal representation of employees' interests; and

- the tendency towards an institutionalisation of employee participation such as the national works councils established in many EU member states.

Within the employment relationship in Britain, industrial action, as an expression of collective concern and power of employees, is often the only means of facilitating the bargaining process in order to achieve a favourable outcome to negotiations.

As we noted in Chapter 1, the inequalities inherent in the social class structure of society and in the distribution of wealth and income are reflected in the inequalities in income, power and control relationships between managers and workers within the workplace. These inequalities manifest themselves in various forms of industrial conflict, some of which are overt, while others are hidden. The study of the employment relationship is partly concerned with analysing the causes and consequences of industrial conflict and the effectiveness of methods of conflict resolution by reference to its most overt forms – the strike and other types of overt industrial action.

We start by defining and identifying different types of industrial action before concentrating on the strike and the causes of strikes. We then go on to consider the pattern of strike activity in

Britain from 1946 until 2001. The extent to which the legislation of the 1980s and 1990s has affected the nature and scope of industrial action will then be examined. Finally, we consider the extent to which there is a new 'climate of conflict' within UK employment relations.

Learning objectives

When you have read this chapter, you should be able to:

1. Define industrial action.

2. Identify the main causes of industrial action.

3. Explain the basic patterns of strike activity in Britain from 1946–2001 in terms of duration and frequency of disputes, and number of worker days lost.

4. Assess the extent to which the recent legislation has affected industrial action.

DEFINITION AND TYPES OF INDUSTRIAL ACTION

Self-Evaluation Activity 9.1

Range of behaviours associated with industrial conflict
The response is given below

The following statement by Kornhauser *et al.* (1954) adequately sets the scene. What do you think is the 'total range of behaviour' to which Kornhauser *et al.* refer?

> *Complete work stoppages and outbreaks of violence due to industrial disputes are certainly the most dramatic expressions of industrial conflict. For the general public they are also the most disturbing. In the minds of many industrial conflict has come to mean strikes. . . . But a true understanding of industrial strife . . . demands consideration of related, less spectacular manifestations as well. It may even be suggested that the general object of study is not the labour dispute, the strike or the lockout, but the total range of behaviour and attitudes that express opposition and divergent orientations between industrial owners and managers on the one hand and working people and their organisations on the other. (p. 17)*

The statement by Kornhauser suggests that there are many types of industrial action, and the range of industrial action is suggested by Kerr (1964):

> *Its means of expression are as unlimited as the ingenuity of man. The strike is the most common and most visible expression. But conflict with the employer may also take the form of peaceful bargaining and grievance handling, of boycotts, of political action, of restriction of output, of sabotage, of absenteeism or of personnel turnover. Several of these forms, such as sabotage, restriction of output, absenteeism, and turnover, may take place on an individual as well as on an organised basis and constitute alternatives to collective action. Even the strike is of many varieties. It may involve all the workers or only key men. It may take the form of refusal to work overtime or to perform a certain process. It may even involve such rigid adherence to the rules that output is stifled. (p. 27)*

Industrial action, then, may be defined as **stoppages of work, instigated both collectively and individually by employees or trade unions on the one hand, or more rarely by management on the other.** The various forms of collective industrial action can now be described briefly:

- **The strike:** a situation where workers collectively withdraw their labour from the work situation for varying periods of time.
- **The lockout:** a situation where the employer refuses to allow workers to gain access to their workplaces and a stoppage of work results.

- **The go-slow:** a situation where workers who are in dispute with their employer decide literally to 'slow down' the pace of work.
- **The work to rule or contract:** observing contracts of employment to the letter; interpreting procedures, job specifications and the content of collective agreements in their fine detail, and getting management to issue precise instructions concerning issues such as health and safety procedures.
- **The removal of overtime:** a situation where workers decide not to work any overtime hours thereby working only those hours specified in the contract of employment with a view to slowing production.
- **The work-in and sit-in:** situations where workers continue to work and to 'occupy' the place of work, often as a protest against company closures, while refusing management access to the production process.

The strike, being the most overt form of industrial action, is also the most popular and demonstrative manifestation of the collective solidarity of a unionised workforce. The other, often less popular forms of industrial action identified above are taken *either* as action preceding a strike, and if that action is successful a strike will then be unnecessary, *or* as action which is just as important as a strike and which may even be preferred to strike action because it is cheaper to the union (no strike pay) and may not be regarded as a breach of contract (even though employees could be subject to disciplinary action). Non-strike industrial action was more popular during the 1960s partly because employees in buoyant labour markets receiving relatively high pay during periods of 'full' employment were not prepared to sacrifice pay for strike action, and partly because these forms of industrial action were more effective in securing pay increases and other concessions from management (Hyman, 1984). During the 1970s and 1980s, there was a decline in these forms of industrial action as research by Brown (1981), Edwards (1995) and the WIRS and WERS98 demonstrate. The suggested reasons for the decline include the weakening of the effectiveness of workplace union organisation which made it more difficult to co-ordinate such action, together with the increasing propensity for managements to

resist and sustain production during times of non-strike activity. Manifestations of individual industrial action include:

- **Labour turnover:** one of the most direct ways of reacting to the deprivations within the work situation is to leave the job.
- **Absenteeism:** grievances or dissatisfactions felt by individuals may manifest themselves in higher rates of absenteeism.
- **Pilfering and fiddling:** part of a 'counter-culture' set up by workers in the work situation which represents a challenge and opposition to the dominant interests and values of the employer.
- **Sabotage:** 'the deliberate disruption of work flows within an organisation or the undermining of the conditions whereby dominant management purposes are readily achieved' (Watson, 1995, p. 306).

The distinction between organised and unorganised conflict has been used to categorise workers' responses to work situations which cause dissatisfaction or deprivation. Unorganised conflict represents situations whereby workers respond to the 'oppressive situation in the only way open to them as *individuals*: by withdrawal from the source of discontent, or, in the case of certain forms of individual sabotage or indiscipline, by reacting against the immediate manifestation of oppression' (Hyman, 1984, p. 56). Unorganised conflict is mainly spontaneous, rarely calculative and the manifestations of conflict are mainly individual, although some forms of spontaneous unofficial collective strike action could be placed in this category. Organised conflict, on the other hand, is more likely to be collective and to 'form part of a conscious strategy to change the situation which is identified as the source of discontent' (ibid., p. 56). The legal definition of industrial action or 'trade dispute' is contained in TULRCA 1992, s. 218 and is:

any dispute between employers and workers, or between workers and workers which is connected with one or more of the following matters:

(a) terms and conditions of employment, or the physical conditions in which any workers are required to work

(b) engagement or non-engagement, or termination or suspension of employment or

the duties of employment of one or more
workers

(c) allocation of work or the duties of employment between workers or groups of workers

(d) matters of discipline

(e) the membership or non-membership of a
trade union on the part of a worker

(f) facilities for officials of trade unions; and

(g) machinery for negotiation or consultation,
and other procedures, relating to any of the
foregoing matters, including the recognition
by employers or employers' associations of the
right of a trade union to represent workers
in any such negotiation or consultation or in
the carrying out of such procedures.

The legal definition is used mainly to determine
whether the industrial action or trade dispute is
lawful or unlawful according to certain criteria
laid down in the legislation and which we shall
consider later in this chapter. As Farnham (1997)
argues:

*The state takes an active role in regulating indus-
trial conflict. If the state cannot achieve industrial*
peace by persuasion, argument or third party
intervention, it provides certain legal backstops
to contain and constrain what it defines to be
legitimate industrial action. These are aimed at
protecting those damaged by industrial action,
keeping the sanctions within acceptable constitutional bounds and discouraging what the state
defines as politically destabilising employee relations conflict. (p. 366)

Self-Evaluation Activity 9.2

Motives for taking industrial action
Response on website

Identify what the main motives for taking industrial
action might be.

A framework which can be used to analyse industrial conflict in both its individual and collective
manifestations in the widest possible range of employment situations is provided by Watson (1995,
pp. 294–6) and is summarised in Exhibit 9.1.

Exhibit 9.1

A framework for the analysis of industrial conflict

1. In a world where valued resources are scarce, people form coalitions of interest to help in the pursuit or defence of interests with regard to these resources.
2. Over time, some groups win out over others in the competition for scarce resources and attempt to consolidate their advantage through their control of institutions and through the propagation of ideologies.
3. Industrial capitalism emerged as 'bourgeois' groups became successful in pursuing their interests in certain societies, but the advantages which accrue from their use of such formally rational means as bureaucracy, technical division of labour, wage labour, advanced technology and the rest are constantly threatened. The threat comes not only from challenges on the part of less privileged groups but also as a result of various con-tradictory tendencies in the industrial capitalist system itself.
4. The relationship between the employer and employee centres on an *implicit contract*. This is an agreement between unequal parties in which the employee, in the light of his or her particular motives, expectations and interests, attempts to make the best deal possible, given his or her personal resources (skill, knowledge, physique, wealth, etc.). The bargain which is struck involves a certain relationship (in part explicit but largely, owing to its indeterminacy, implicit) between the employee inputs of effort, impairment and surrender of auto-nomy and employee rewards of cash payment and fringe benefits, job satisfactions, social rewards, security, power status, career potential.
5. The bargain is essentially unstable, especially as a result of the market context in which it is made. Market viability on the part of the employer creates a constant pressure to minimise costs – this in turn leading to

pressure to either cut the rewards or increase the efforts of the employee – either way to the employees' disadvantage. However, employees are bound to defend themselves, especially since they buy the goods and services on the same market. Paradoxically, the advertising and marketing efforts of employing organisations create a pressure on their employees to increase, or at least hold stable, their rewards (employees and customers being ultimately the same people).

6. To increase efficiency or market viability, employers introduce various organisational and technological changes, but any such change, however minor it may seem, potentially invites opposition from employees whose implicit contracts may be seen to be threatened. This may be because of a tendency to reduce 'rewards' like job satisfaction or the opportunity to use craft skills or because of a tendency to call for increased employee 'inputs' in the form of increased effort or a further reduction in the amount of autonomy which the employee has at work. Potential conflict, we can see, arises with practically any kind of managerial initiative in employment situations.

7. Both to improve their market position and to defend themselves, employees tend to form various coalitions of interest to present the kind of group challenge which is necessary to have any effect in the face of the greater power of the employer. Thus we get, within the employing organisations, trade union organisation, 'professional' group mobilisation and 'informal' office and shop floor groupings. All of these present challenges to the managerial prerogative.

8. In every workplace there is a constantly renegotiated agreement about what goes on and what rewards accrue. Only a fraction of this negotiating process is formal and much of the agreement is tacit. External conditions are never constant and therefore there are always threats to the stability of arrangements. The underlying conflicts of interest between employer and employee may become overt and apparent at any time and will tend to centre on two main issues: the amount of material rewards available to the employee and the extent of control over employees conceded to the employer.

9. We can say that a grievance situation arises whenever a particular implicit contract is perceived to go out of balance. The grievance may lead to any of a range of employee reactions, from striking to absenteeism and from obstructive behaviour to resigning. A grievance can be settled or accommodated not only by a return to the prior status quo but by a rebalancing of the implicit contract in a new form; an increase in cash being agreed to compensate for a loss in autonomy resulting from technical change, for example.

Source: Adapted from Watson, 1995, pp. 294–6.

STRIKES AND THEIR CAUSES

'A strike has been defined as a **temporary stoppage of work by a group of employees in order to express a grievance or enforce a demand**' (Hyman, 1984, p. 17). Within the context of this definition, the term *temporary* makes it clear that workers intend to return to their jobs when the strike is over. The term *stoppage of work* distinguishes the strike from other forms of industrial action undertaken by a *group* of employees thereby emphasising its collective nature. The strike is also a calculative act, which is specifically designed to express grievances, to seek a solution to problems and to apply pressure to enforce demands. The Office for National Statistics (ONS), which is the central institution for the collection and collation of strike data in Britain, has its own definition of strikes for statistical purposes as being: **all stoppages of work due to industrial disputes involving ten or more workers and lasting for at least one day.** Where the total days lost exceed 100 working days, a strike is included in the ONS data even if it fails to count under the criteria of its own definition. Whether this measure is an accurate reflection of strikes in British industry is difficult to judge. Brown (1981), for example, estimates that since Britain has historically been particularly affected by short and small-scale stoppages, especially in the manufacturing sector of the economy, as many as half the actual strikes may be excluded from the statistics in any one year. It has been more conventional to assume that the statistics covered around 66 per cent of the total number of strikes and 95 per cent of the days lost. The disparity really relates to the ease with which long stoppages are recorded and the difficulty of accounting for the 'lightning strikes' that existed and persisted in particular industries such as car manufacturing.

The main types of strike

Before looking at the actual causes and reasons given for taking industrial action in the form of strikes, it is important to note that six main types of strike have been identified, but it should also be noted that these categories are not mutually exclusive:

1. *The trial of strength*: has become 'the classic stereotype of the industrial dispute – the only sort which is ever likely to make the history books' (Hyman, 1984). These strikes tended to be long-drawn-out affairs involving considerable costs to employers, the workforce and the unions concerned, invoking the metaphor of industrial relations as 'trench warfare'. These protracted disputes have, historically, comprised a small minority of stoppages within a given period.
2. *The demonstration stoppage*: Hyman contends that 'the great majority of strikes fall in the category of demonstrations in force' (p. 24). The stoppage is often spontaneous although the underlying causes of this type of strike may be of long standing. Hyman adds: 'The spontaneous or demonstration strike is usually both small in scale and quickly settled. It is true that such strikes sometimes spread . . . and occasionally they prove unexpectedly protracted . . . but these cases are very unusual' (p. 24).
3. *The official strike*: is one where a union 'officially' supports its members according to the union rules governing the conduct of disputes.
4. *The constitutional strike*: is one which takes place *after* all relevant procedures have been exhausted and the parties acknowledge that they have failed to agree.
5. *The unofficial strike*: is one which has not been recognised by the union leadership. Traditionally, unofficial strikes tended to be spontaneous, informal, short in duration and involving relat-

ively few people. During the 1960s and 1970s, the vast majority of strikes in any one year were recorded by the Department of Employment as being unofficial simply because the large majority of disputes were over before the unions which might have had members involved had even heard of them, 'the matters at issue having been settled by direct negotiation between management and workers concerned' (Turner, 1969, p. 22). In recent years, the number of unofficial disputes has declined significantly.
6. *The unconstitutional strike*: is one which takes place *before* all relevant procedures have been exhausted.

Self-Evaluation Activity 9.3
Decline in unofficial strikes
Response on website

Why do you think the number of unofficial strikes has declined in recent years?

Main case 9.1
Anatomy of a strike and its causes:
1 The Thatcher legacy

The Magnet dispute

Magnet is a British subsidiary of the American conglomerate Berisford International and manufactures kitchen storage cupboards and worktops. Its Darlington factory has been at the centre of Britain's longest-running strike. In August 1996, 350 of Magnet's Darlington workers stopped work over pay; they voted decisively, via their four unions, for an entirely legal, official stoppage. Early that September, the company resolved the dispute by sacking the 350 strikers, and they have since been replaced by non-unionised workers, and that, as far as Berisford is concerned, is the whole story. These days, its official press releases refer to bringing 'the legacy of the 1996 dispute to an end', or at most, to 'a small legacy of a picket line outside the Darlington factory'. Its spokesperson adds: 'The jobs at Darlington have been filled. There never has been any question of reinstatement.'

The picketing rituals at Magnet have long turned automatic. Besides the shouting and staring (and drivers looking down at their steering wheels), there is the coffee-fetching, the stacking and unstacking of firewood, the tabloid rustling in quiet moments – and there are a lot of those. But the slow, old-fashioned quality of all this is deceptive. The Magnet strike is encrusted with allegations and counter-allegations: strikers harassed by private detectives, workers harassed by strikers, petrol poured over picket's caravans, nails poured under the wheels of delivery.

After two decades of legislation to make them rarer, modern strikes tend to be like this: bitter, fought at the fringes of the law, neither side really recognising the other as legitimate at all. The Magnet dispute seems to echo the Liverpool dockers strike and the 1993 stoppage at Timex in Dundee. However, the backdrop to the dispute has changed somewhat, and although the 'New' Labour government is not noted for its support of employees against chief executives, its white paper *Fairness at Work* (1998) suggests that Magnet-style industrial relations have had their day. The white paper proposals for reinforcing the individual and collective rights of employees has made the dispute a potential test case and a symbol to represent the old, soon-to-be-outdated way of doing things. In particular the proposal to change the law in line with the government's belief 'that in general those dismissed for taking part in lawfully organised official industrial action should have the right to complain to a tribunal of unfair dismissal' (p. 45) should deter employers from taking extreme measures against employees.

Roots of the dispute

Until the 1980s, the Magnet factory was a recognisably pre-Thatcherite enterprise: 'You could walk out when the coffee wasn't hot enough' said a long-term employee, only half-joking. Then, in 1989, there was a management buy-out just in time for the recession. As the market for houses shrank, so did the demand for kitchens to put in them and by 1993, with no dividend paid to shareholders for four years, Magnet decided to take drastic action. The workers would have to take a pay cut.

Pay cuts varied from between £5 and £50 a week. The best-paid employee received only £260; the vote for a strike was overwhelming. Before the strike commenced, the company abandoned the pay cuts. In return, the unions agreed that wages would be frozen for three years. A senior convenor and leader of the strike committee said: 'The company was not making money and we all agreed to help out.' It seemed that the idea of 'partnership' which New Labour currently

supports, existed in embryonic form at Magnet. But a sourness lingered. Shop floor 'perks' such as time off for bereavement began to disappear. In 1994, Berisford International bought Magnet and, as the business pages of newspapers approvingly noted, 'outlets were closed' and 'the workforce was cut back'. Darlington veterans muttered about the 'worst management of the lot'.

Berisford was not, in reality, a 'partnership' business, but a more common sort of employer. Before buying Magnet, it had traded in commodities and sugar refining, lost a lot of money in American property, and tried and failed to take over Clark's shoes. By 1996, Magnet was profitable again and the pay freeze was due to end. The unions asked for a 3 per cent pay increase. The management agreed to give the money to three-fifths of the workforce; the rest, better paid and longer serving, would get 'improvements' to shifts and overtime and a 'productivity bonus'. By the end of August the pickets were out on the grass and *The Northern Echo* was already using the word 'deadlock'. By March 1998, the pickets were still active even though 52 of the original 350 strikers went back to work before Magnet's deadline to do so – the 12th day of the strike – expired. The remainder have challenged their sacking with pickets of Magnet's showrooms, shouting in shareholders meetings, a march through Darlington, and collaboration with a number of external interested parties. There have been competing claims concerning the extent to which the factory has been profitable; while the Magnet management claim that profits have risen by 25 per cent, the strikers claim that fewer trucks are entering the gates with lesser loads. Such warring claims seem the sum of the dispute these days. Javelin PR put out their triumphant management faxes; the pickets count number plates, and watch the forklifts beep and slalom behind the gates. Specially installed security cameras peer at each picket. Just as the strikers stare at the factory instead of working in it, so the management watch the strikers instead of negotiating with them.

Self-Evaluation Activity 9.4
Causes of the Magnet dispute
This SEA has no commentary

Identify the main causes of the Magnet strike, then compare your list with the causes given below (pp. 435–7).

Main case 9.2
Anatomy of a strike and its causes: 2 The Blair legacy

The firefighters' dispute 2002–3

Since the late 1970s firefighters' pay increases have been determined by a formula linking the pay of a fully qualified firefighter to the earnings of the top quarter of adult male manual workers. This formula has led to a 20 per cent increase in firefighters' pay since 1997 and was strongly defended by the Fire Brigades Union (FBU) until 2001. Andy Gilchrist, General Secretary of the FBU, said in the July 2000 issue of the FBU's *Fire Fighter* magazine that 'our wages remain ahead of other essential public sector workers precisely because we have maintained the formula'. Negotiations on pay and conditions of service for fire brigade personnel are conducted in the National Joint Council for Local Authorities' Fire Brigades. This is a voluntary organisation covering England, Wales, Scotland and Northern Ireland on which employing authorities, through the Local Government Association and the Convention of Scottish Local Authorities, and the Fire Authority of Northern Ireland are represented, together with the FBU.

Negotiations begin

The negotiating process began in May 2002 and the FBU lodged a claim for a 40 per cent pay increase for firefighters. The employers responded by indicating that any significant pay increase had to be matched by modernisation of the fire service. The employers offered the FBU an unconditional interim 4 per cent pay increase from 7 November 2002 in advance of any agreement on a new pay formula. The employers also invited the FBU to join them in asking for an independent review (subsequently called the Bain Report Review) into firefighters' pay and conditions. This was rejected and in September 2002 the FBU issued a strike ballot. On 18 October 2002 the FBU announced support from its membership for strike action in pursuit of its claim for £30 000 for firefighters and control room staff.

The employers' initial offer and the Bain Report

The initial employers' offer was for an immediate 4 per cent pay increase linked to talks about reforming working practice plus, another 7 per cent from November 2003 if all reforms had been agreed. This offer was made on 12 November, and according to the employers, the full offer amounted to 11.3 per cent over two years at a time when inflation stood at 2.1 per cent. The offer was based on the recommendations of the independent review by Sir George Bain.

Run up to Bain

In July 2002, during negotiations with the FBU, the UK employers proposed a joint approach to government to establish an independent review. The FBU refused, so the employers approached the government alone. In early September, after negotiations within the Joint National Council broke down, the government decided it would be helpful to establish an independent review. The Bain Review was launched on 20 September and its remit was to review current issues surrounding the fire service fairly and objectively and make recommendations accordingly. The Review published an interim position paper on 11 November and this was followed by the final Report, published on 17 December 2002.

UK firefighters set to walk out as talks fail

The first firefighters' strike in more than 20 years looks certain to go ahead on Wednesday after the government told employers that there was no more money on the table and talks with unions collapsed. Barring a last minute pay deal which few in Whitehall expect, ancient army Green Goddess fire engines will take to the streets . . . when more than 50 000 firefighters are due to walk out. Calling the strike 'unjustified, dangerous and wrong', Tony Blair insisted that modernisation of the fire service had to go hand in hand with higher pay. Whitehall officials told employers no additional funding was available to improve on the recommendations from Sir George Bain, who has reviewed firefighters' pay, for an 11 per cent pay rise linked to changes in working practices. A senior representative on the employers' side said that when he saw the Bain Review's position paper, he knew the strike would take place, given the FBU's demand for a no-strings pay increase of 40 per cent. The Treasury is refusing to sanction the extra money, fearing that an overly generous award could trigger a wave of claims across the public sector. Mr Gilchrist (FBU leader) called the pay offer 'derisory and insulting' and he accused 'dark forces' in the Labour government of trying to provoke a strike rather than pay a fair wage. After Wednesday's 49 hour walkout the union plans a series of three eight-day stoppages on November 22, December 4, and December 16.

Several employers confirmed they had received strong indications from ministers that, while the government would back the Bain Review's recommendations, it would not offer any more – curtailing employers' freedom to offer more than an extra percentage point or so given their tight finances. (Adams, C., Turner, D. and Odell, M., *Financial Times*, FT.com site, accessed 13 November 2002)

What the Bain Report says

The main theme of the Report is that the fire service needs to be changed from top to bottom and every aspect of its work needs to be reformed. The focus needs to change from dealing with fire incidence to greater emphasis on fire prevention together with a modern, flexible, risk-based approach to allocating resources. The Bain Report is confident that, given the scope for reform, the move to a modern fire service would pay for itself over time and that in addition more lives will be saved and property losses reduced and communities will be more secure as a result. The main points the Report makes are:

- There has been a lack of leadership throughout the fire service at political, institutional and operational levels.
- There must be a new policy-making body, led by ministers, to set a clear framework of what the government requires from the service and the ways in which it should be modernised.
- A new system is needed that deploys resources to deal with most likely risks of fire in the most cost-effective way, based on risk assessment.
- New primary legislation is needed to put the fire service on a proper, modern basis.
- The review does not recommend regionalisation of the fire service but does recommend that fire authorities should increasingly collaborate where increased efficiencies and economies could result.
- New policy structure needs to be complemented by new institutions within the fire service – the Fire Service College must become the focus for the intellectual leadership of the service and the Fire Service Inspectorate should become a major engine of change and should help drive through the reforms proposed.
- There is a need for a new collective group to be engaged in policy work, bringing together Chief Fire Officers and central and local government.

- An improved programme of HR management should be put in place as a matter of high priority.
- A new pay structure should be based around an Integrated Personnel Development Scheme (IPDS) with the need to encourage mobility and flexibility. The system should be competence-based. The Report's findings indicate that there is no case for significant increases in pay based on the existing pay system. The employers' offer is based on the Bain recommendations.
- Comprehensive modernisation of the current pensions scheme is required.
- The Grey Book (conditions of service) needs to be amended so managers are free to manage others locally, such as flexible shift systems, part-time working and different crewing trends at different times of day. The Appointments and Promotions Regulations should be replaced by a core set of national requirements. The Discipline Regulations should be replaced with a system based on ACAS Code of Practice and the current negotiating machinery should be replaced. Non-compulsory redundancies may be necessary.

Reactions to Bain

The employers: In favour of the Bain recommendations: 'The LGA believes the Bain recommendations form the basis of delivering the changes required as long as all parties, Government, fire and local authorities and the staff play their full part.'

The FBU: Major objections concerning pay: 'Despite claims that Bain was acting independently, the recommendation of a 4% increase payable effective [from] November 2002 was exactly the rate of rise previously offered by the Fire Service Employers when negotiations officially broke down in September, and which led to the ballot for strike action being conducted by the FBU'; and modernisation, which is viewed as cost-cutting exercises involving 'further reductions in firefighter and control staff numbers'.

Academic commentary: The FBU website contains a condemnatory commentary on Bain by Seifert (2003a). This states that the final Report confirms the views expressed by the FBU that the Report is not independent of government, it usurps the views of employers, 'embraces the more extreme reforming instincts of members of the government', and its rhetoric is couched in managerialist terms as is its ideology. The Report's authors have a narrow vision which focuses upon 'costs' and 'cost-effectiveness' rather than safety and quality of service. Its view of pay is parsimonious and it parrots government policy relating to, inter alia, 'affordability'. There is a paucity of evidence presented to substantiate the Report's pay recommendations which 'mimic government thinking elsewhere in the public sector' (p. 2). Seifert concludes that the government missed an opportunity 'to use the goodwill, professional knowledge and dedication of public sector workers as the starting point for reforms. By embracing crude private sector models of employment – specifically Taylorisation through deskilling – alongside discredited ideas of efficiency – see the case for the privatisation of the railways for example – the report and the government have signed the warrant which may end the most successful provision of fire protection and safety in Europe' (p. 3).

Subsequent developments

1. Modernisation: As far as 'modernisation' is concerned – a catch-all term used by government to justify the introduction of cost-effective measures justified by job cuts, new or modified pay structures, de-centred decision-making and arguably a 'managerialist' ideology – the FBU (2003) maintains, albeit by adopting a different interpretation of the term, that 'modernisation is ongoing and receives the general support of the FBU. Indeed, we have pioneered new approaches to fire cover, fire safety and fire prevention whilst arguing for the increased funding necessary to upgrade training and equipment. We are happy to co-operate with necessary changes to training and skill acquisition as well as the more flexible use of resources in order to further improve the service given to the public. Our only caveat is that change be agreed with our members, not imposed by employers or unelected managers' (Andy Gilchrist, FBU 2003).

2. Government intervention: Between September and December 2002, the government intervened on three occasions between the FBU and the employers. The most serious intervention came after tentative agreement was reached, including a staged increase in pay amounting to 16 per cent by November 2003. Intervention in the form of the Office of the Deputy Prime Minister 'effectively blocked this opportunity to make progress' (FBU, 2003). Contrary to the government's argument, the employers confirmed that the

proposals in the draft agreement were fully costed and all figures were available to the government throughout the talks.

The last offer and perhaps the final one

A further offer by the employers was received by the FBU on 18 March 2003 and included a five-stage pay process with a 16 per cent increase by July 2004 and from that point increases in pay for 2005 and 2006 in line with a pay formula yet to be decided. The Executive Council of the FBU agreed to recommend the offer to the membership. A recall of Annual Conference on 19 March 2003 recommended that the membership reject the offer, which it proceeded to do. Professor Frank Burchill suggested some amendments which have been rejected by the government and employers. The dispute finally ended on 12 June 2003. A compromise 16 per cent pay deal tied to limited changes in working practices was accepted by a 3 to 1 margin at a special conference in Glasgow.

Source: Based on Bain Report, 2002; FBU, 2003; LGA, 2003; Seifert, 2003a, 2003b – websites accessed 23.3.2003; 25.4.2003

Self-Evaluation Activity 9.5
Differing perspectives on the conduct of the firefighters' dispute
This SEA has no commentary

Read the three annotated views relating to the conduct of the parties involved in the firefighters' dispute. Which of these do you think is the most valid? Justify your choice.

View 1 (Seifert, 2003b)

The local authority employers 'continue to dance to the tune of public sector policy dogma' which believes that private sector service provision is more efficient than what the public sector can produce and is therefore more akin to nineteenth-century free market dogma. The employers' offer has to be seen in the context of delegated business units making decisions without reference to central authority, and free of collective union voice: 'Such is the thinking behind "foundation" hospitals, Best Value in local government, education reforms and, of course, the "modernising" agenda for the fire service.' The offer bypasses existing collective bargaining machinery at local and national level and seeks to impose operational and employment decisions upon the firefighters. The current National Joint Committee (NJC) will be replaced by a 'working group representing all fire service stakeholders' but we do not know who will select them. Associated with this is the government Ad Hoc Forum functioning outside the NJC which influences the agreement. Seifert goes on to say:

> So where does the decision-making power lie? With whom is the FBU negotiating? Why does central government intervene so actively in a dispute between independent employers and an independent union? Why should either side be bound by the secret ruminations of something with such a Kafkaesque name as Ad Hoc Forum? At the end of this the employers are so unable to decide for themselves that the government insists that implementation will be audited to make sure that the new local leaders of the fire service are doing their job properly. These appear to be the same senior managers entrusted with the entire future of the service, unworried by bargaining with the unions, unaccountable to local communities, and eventually answerable only to the board of directors of the highly modern FirePlc. (Seifert, 2003b, p. 2)

View 2 (Metcalf, 2003)

The employers are incompetent and divided and they are bargaining with an intransigent union and this has always been a recipe for disaster. There is a lack of bargaining experience as the firefighters' pay has been determined by a formula agreed in the late 1970s and 'this lack of experience in bargaining is well evidenced by the cack-handed, stupid way the parties have conducted themselves in this dispute'. The FBU conjured the 40 per cent claim apparently 'out of thin air' but came down to 16 per cent as soon as 'Gordon Brown said "boo" to the union'. The employers are worse as they went 'cap in hand' to the Treasury with uncosted proposals asking the Chancellor to sign a blank cheque. This boils down

to a lack of HR expertise: 'are there any HR professionals in the employers' negotiating team? If so, what on earth is their role? If not, the employers should get some in now.' The four principles that should determine public sector pay – comparability, recruitment, retention and productivity (couched in the buzzwords of 'modernisation'; 'flexibility' and 'restructuring') give different responses to the 'right settlement'. Metcalf goes on to assert: 'Assuming collective bargaining is to continue we cannot be put through this shambles again. There should be compulsory arbitration using final offer [pendulum] arbitration.'

View 3 (Burchill, 2003)

The independent chairman of the NJC, Frank Burchill, counters Metcalf concerning the latter's assertion that there are no HR professionals in the employers' negotiating team. The team is serviced by the Employers' Organisation which provides advice in negotiations across local government. In addition, the general secretary and deputy general secretary of the TUC were involved. Burchill states that there is no shortage of HR and industrial relations experts willing to give advice and comment, and 'none of this fits with his [Metcalf's] picture of "incompetent, divided employers", "intransigent union", "lack of experience in bargaining", "cack-handed, stupid behaviour of the parties" and so on. The negotiators on both sides are highly intelligent people trying to reconcile conflicting interests . . . ideal outcomes are easier to perceive than achieve.'

Causes of strikes in general

Strikes have not been spread evenly throughout the labour force. For example, from 1966 to 1970 the number of days lost through strikes, relative to the size of workforce in particular industries, was greatest in the docks industry, followed by the car industry, shipbuilding and coal mining. These are some of the traditional, strike-prone industries which tended to distort the strike picture during the 1960s and 1970s. A number of explanations have been put forward in order to account for this distortion, and these are identified below.

Community integration

Kerr and Siegel (1954), in a study of strikes in 11 countries, found that miners, dockers and seamen had the highest strike records. They argue that community integration is the key to explaining the level of strike activity in these occupations. They also point out that miners, dockers and seamen tended to live in occupational communities which are relatively isolated and insulated from the wider society. In such communities, a consciousness of kind develops which involves a strong awareness of shared grievances, a close emotional commitment to trade unionism and a high level of working-class solidarity. Shared grievances and worker solidarity, set in the context of a close-knit community, tend to make strike action more likely. However, Kerr and Siegel's argument does not appear to have much empirical validity today, as most of the traditional industries around which occupational communities were based have declined and the communities themselves have fragmented. This is particularly the case in Britain with regard to the coal, shipbuilding and steel industries, all of which have experienced dramatic decline in their workforces and hence a decline in trade union membership and density.

Technological determinism

A second traditional explanation for variation in strike activity emphasises the role of technology, and has been used to explain the traditionally high frequency of strikes in the car industry. The work of Blauner (1964) was used to demonstrate that there was a direct correlation between the type of technology used in the production process and worker 'alienation'. Basically, Blauner hypothesised that assembly-line technology produces high levels of alienation amongst assembly-line workers and this leads to the development of hostile relations between workers and management. Strikes, as an expression of industrial conflict, will therefore be more likely in industries employing this type of production technology. Blauner's explanation has been criticised on a number of counts, not least for the assumption that there is an inevitability about the relationship between technology as determining behaviour and attitudes amongst workers. More fundamentally, Hyman (1984) points out that explanations based on Blauner's assumptions do not account for variations in strike activity within the same industries in different countries and posits the question: 'Why does the strike record for the British motor industry contrast so markedly with the comparative harmony in Germany or Japan, when the technology of car assembly is internationally uniform?' Research by Gallie (1978, 1988), and the early WIRS analyses (Daniel and Millward, 1983) do not lend support to Blauner's hypothesis, as technology is but one factor amongst many which may predispose workers to take strike or any other type of industrial action. The example of the 2002–3 firefighters' dispute, which commenced as a pay dispute but became embroiled in 'modernisation' – changing working practices based on technology and flexibility – and the possible threat of redundancies, is a case in point (see Main case 9.2).

Negotiating procedures

A third explanation for variation in strike activity deals with the effectiveness of the negotiating machinery available for resolving disputes. An early study by Ross and Hartman (1960) compared strike activity levels in 15 countries from 1900 to 1956. The study concluded that strikes are least likely to occur when there are well-established industry and organisational procedures for consultation and negotiation. If procedures exist whereby grievances can be speedily formulated and efficiently channelled into negotiating machinery, strikes are less likely to result. This view was supported by findings within the Devlin Report (1965), a government-sponsored investigation into the British docks industry. Devlin argued that a major reason for the high level of strikes in the industry (apart from casualisation of dock labour) was the ineffectiveness and cumbersome nature of the machinery for resolving disputes.

Strikers' definition of the situation

Hyman (1984) provides a critique of the above explanations for variations in strike levels between different industries. He contends that these explanations largely ignore the strikers' definition of the situation. For example, workers in one industry may define strikes as a last resort, while those in another may see strikes as a routine and even natural part of industrial life. Hyman argues further that workers do not simply react to production technology or negotiating machinery and predictably strike or not strike as the case might be; they define their work situation and the act of striking in a particular way. Hyman does not deny that factors such as production technology can influence behaviour, but maintains that they are translated into action via the meanings given to them by the workforce. Thus an explanation of the strike-prone British car industry and the relatively strike-free situation in the same industry in Japan and Germany requires a knowledge of the meanings and definitions workers give to industrial life.

Causes of strikes in particular

The biggest single cause of strikes has traditionally been disputes over wages. Tables 9.1 and 9.2 indicate that disputes over pay remain a very important cause of strikes. However, disputes concerning redundancy have become more important in five of the ten years from the period 1987–97 and in 1992–3 involved more than four times as many workers as disputes over pay. Since 1993, redundancy issues, while still important, loomed less large than pay.

In 2001, however, with regard to working days lost, disputes relating to working conditions were more significant than those caused by both pay and redundancy issues owing to ongoing staffing problems in the railway industry.

Issues causing disputes concerning pay are fairly varied and can include union demands for pay increases and bonuses, the restoration of pay differentials, rates for particular jobs and conditions in which the work is undertaken, guaranteed payments, changing payment systems and re-grading affecting pay, 'perks' and fringe benefits and reductions in earnings.

In 2001, 33 per cent of working days lost were due to disputes over working conditions and supervision but accounted for only 6 per cent of all stoppages. On the other hand, staffing and work allocation issues comprised 15 per cent of total days lost and 24 per cent of all stoppages. Pay accounted for 27 per cent of days lost and 36 per cent of all stoppages, while redundancy issues accounted for 17 per cent of the total days lost, and 12 per cent of stoppages. It is important to note that, as Table 9.2 indicates, there are considerable fluctuations from year to year with totals being distorted by larger strikes. Nevertheless, the trend from 1991 to 1999, with the exception of 1996, is

Table 9.1 Stoppages, workers involved and working days lost by main cause: 1998, 2001

Cause	Stoppages		Workers involved (000s)		Working days lost (000s)	
	1998	2001	1998	2001	1998	2001
Pay: wage rates and earnings levels	61	63	40.6	50.0	146.8	140.5
Pay: extra wage and fringe benefits	12	6	6.1	1.5	18.1	2.6
Duration and pattern of hours worked	5	10	1.4	7.3	2.2	13.2
Redundancy questions	19	24	19.9	23.8	54.5	88.1
Trade union matters	6	3	1.7	0.7	1.9	5.8
Working conditions and supervision	13	11	4.1	38.4	13.8	172.9
Staffing and work allocation	31	46	6.2	41.6	16.2	79.0
Dismissal and other disciplinary measures	19	31	12.6	16.7	28.0	23.0

Source: *Labour Market Trends*, June 1999 and November 2002

Table 9.2 Working days lost by main cause in all industries and services: 1991–2001 (000s)

	1991	1992	1993	1994	1995	1996	1997	1998	1999	2000	2001
Wage rates and earnings	306	182	145	154	119	1028	103	147	159	375	141
Extra wage and fringe benefits	3	14	5	6	83	34	26	19	8	7.8	2.6
Duration and pattern of hours worked	16	3	34	8	39	52	7	2	5	6.3	13.2
Redundancy questions	248	193	391	14	72	39	69	54	35	56.1	88.1
Trade union matters	4	10	4	1	3	6	2	2	2	0.4	5.8
Working conditions and supervision	66	49	3	2	1	91	8	14	15	10.9	173
Staffing and work allocation	62	52	62	62	88	35	18	16	6	23.4	79
Dismissal and other disciplinary matters	56	24	6	6	18	18	4	28	14	18.3	23
All causes	761	528	649	278	415	1303	235	382	242	499	525

Source: *Labour Market Trends*, November 2002, p. 598

downwards, with totals for 2000 and 2001 showing some increase.

PATTERNS OF STRIKE ACTIVITY IN THE POST-WAR PERIOD

In order to understand the pattern of strike activity, it is necessary to describe the main measures of strikes used in compiling the strike data collected by the Office for National Statistics (ONS). Tables and analyses of the data appear in the monthly statistical journal *Labour Market Trends*. Until September 1996 the raw data was collected from the Employment Service local office network, some public sector organisations, newspapers and other sources, but since 1996 information has been collected directly from the employer or trade union involved after the ONS has been notified of a dispute from press reports. All reported data must conform to the official definition of stoppages. The main measures used are working days lost, number of stoppages and workers involved. We now look at these measures, but first of all, a more detailed description of the ONS definition of stoppages is given (we looked at this briefly in the previous section). The descriptions

given are adapted from *Labour Market Trends* (2002, p. 602).

Definition of stoppages

The statistics cover stoppages of work in progress in the UK during a year caused by labour disputes between employers and workers, or between workers and other workers, connected with terms and conditions of employment. The statistics exclude disputes that do not result in a stoppage of work. Stoppages involving fewer than ten workers or lasting less than one day are also excluded unless the total number of working days lost in the dispute is 100 or more. Stoppages over issues not directly linked to terms and conditions between workers and employers are omitted, although in most years this is insignificant. The statistics include 'lockouts', that is where an employer prevents their employees from working by refusing entry to the place of work, and 'unlawful', that is, unlawfully organised strikes. However, no distinction is made between a 'strike' and a 'lockout' or between 'lawful' and 'unlawful' stoppages. This is mainly because of the practical difficulty in deciding into which category a particular stoppage falls. It was for similar reasons that a distinction between 'official' and 'unofficial' disputes was no longer made after 1981.

Main measures of strikes

Working days lost

In measuring the number of working days lost, account is taken only of the time lost in the *basic working week*. Overtime and weekend working are excluded and no allowance is made for absence from work. Where strikes last less than the basic working day, the hours lost are converted to full-day equivalents, as are days lost by part-time workers. The number of working days lost in a stoppage reflects the actual number of workers involved at each point in the stoppage. The calculation is arrived at by multiplying the duration of the stoppage by the total number of workers involved in the stoppage.

Number of stoppages

There are difficulties in ensuring complete recording of stoppages, in particular for short disputes lasting only a day or so, or involving only a few workers. Because of this recording difficulty and the cut-off applied, the number of working days lost is considered to be a better indicator of the impact of labour disputes than the number of recorded stoppages.

Workers involved

The figures for workers involved are for workers both *directly* and *indirectly* involved at the establishment where the dispute occurred. Workers indirectly involved are those who are not themselves parties to the dispute but are laid off because of the dispute. However, the statistics exclude workers at other sites who are indirectly affected. Workers involved in more than one stoppage during the year are counted in the statistics for each stoppage in which they take part. Part-time workers are counted as whole units. Given in Exhibit 9.2 is the method by which the number of workers involved at any time in the stoppage are recorded.

Britain's strike pattern

Self-Evaluation Activity 9.6

Identifying patterns and trends
The response is given below

Examine the strike statistics in Table 9.3 and attempt to identify any patterns or trends in relation to the three variables described above (working days lost, number of stoppages and workers involved). What conclusion can you arrive at with regard to larger stoppages involving the loss of 100 000 working days or more from 1977?

Exhibit 9.2

Recording numbers involved in stoppages

The statistics try to record the number of workers that are involved at any time in the stoppage. For example, consider a three-day strike where there are 200 workers involved on the first day; 300 on the second day, of whom 100 were involved for the first time; and 200 on the third day, of whom 50 were involved for the first time. The total number of workers involved in the dispute is 350 – the sum of all those involved on the first day, and those joining for the first time on subsequent days. However, the number of workers taking strike action for the first time cannot always be easily ascertained. In such cases the statistics record the highest number involved at any one time (300 in the above example). Take another example, where there are 200 workers involved in a stoppage on each of days one, two and three. It may be necessary to assume that there was a total of 200 workers involved, although it is possible, but unlikely, that as many as 600 workers could have been involved. For this reason, the statistics may underestimate the number of workers involved in a dispute. However the estimate of the number of working days lost is unaffected by this consideration.

Source: Labour Market Trends, 2002

Table 9.3 Stoppages in progress, United Kingdom: 1946–2001

Year	Working days lost (000s)	Workers involved (000s)	Stoppages	Stoppages involving loss of 100 000 working days or more
Annual averages				
1946–52	1 888	444	1 698	
1953–59	3 950	790	2 340	
1960–68	3 189	1 451	2 372	
1969–73	12 497	1 581	2 974	
1974–79	12 178	1 653	2 412	
Annual figures				
1977	10 142	1 166	2 737	12
1978	9 405	1 041	2 498	7
1979	29 474	4 608	2 125	15
1980	11 964	834	1 348	5
1981	4 266	1 513	1 344	7
1982	5 313	2 103	1 538	7
1983	3 754	574	1 364	6
1984	27 135	1 464	1 221	11
1985	6 402	791	903	4
1986	1 920	720	1 074	2
1987	3 546	887	1 016	3
1988	3 702	790	781	8
1989	4 128	727	701	6
1990	1 903	298	630	3
1991	761	176	369	1
1992	528	148	253	–
1993	649	385	211	2
1994	278	107	205	–
1995	415	174	235	–
1996	1 303	364	244	2
1997	235	130	216	–
1998	282	93	166	–
1999	242	141	205	–
2000	499	183	212	1
2001	525	180	194	1

Source: *Labour Market Trends*, November 2002

Main trends in the pattern of strike activity

The main trends are summarised from Waddington (2003) and are as follows:

- During the late **1940s and early 1950s** there were, in relative terms, fewer strikes than in many subsequent periods on all three measures of strikes. Wages and issues of trade union principle were the main causes of stoppages.
- During the early **1950s onwards** there were a number of large national strikes which occurred for the first time since 1926 in industries such

as engineering, shipbuilding, printing and dock working with pay and trade union principles being the main causes.

- During the **1960s** there was a substantial increase in the number of small strikes in the car industry and related sectors reflecting a growth in unofficial shop-floor disputes, while at the same time there was a continuation of the larger national disputes and 'this produced a peak of strike numbers in 1970 when 3906 strikes were recorded' (1995, p. 439). Docks, motor vehicles, shipbuilding, aircraft, non-electrical engineering, electrical engineering, locomotives and iron and steel accounted for half of non-coal stoppages and around 75 per cent of days lost and workers involved. Overall, however, up to 1968 the increase in the total number of strikes as compared to the previous period was slight.
- During the **1970s** the numbers of strikes began to fall slightly, but again the picture is distorted by the presence of large disputes which kept the numbers of workers involved and working days lost on the high side. As Table 9.3 indicates, there were several large disputes from 1977 to 1979, including stoppages in engineering and public sector disputes, culminating in the 'Winter of Discontent'.
- During the **1980s** all the main measures of strikes recorded falls, albeit with fluctuations. The large number of working days lost in 1984 is attributed to the coal strike of that year.
- During the **1990s and early 2000s** there were further substantial falls on all three indices and the number of large disputes fell significantly although there were some increases in 2002 and early 2003 (unofficial data).

For the period **1977–2001**, we can illustrate the extent to which large disputes distort the underlying trends by pointing to the high number of days lost in 1979 and 1984. This was also evident in 1997 when two disputes and stoppages in transport manufacturing accounted for some 22 per cent of working days lost. Tables 9.1 and 9.2 show a substantial decline in strike activity in the 1990s, while Table 9.3 shows that the number of strikes has been on a general downward trend throughout the last 20 years. Turning to working days lost we see a similar

downward trend but with some increases from 2000 onwards. Interestingly, the 234 700 working days lost in 1997 (equivalent to 10 days lost per 1000 employees) was the lowest on record for strike rates. The longer-term trend in strike activity, taking the base year as 1980, remains downward and it is still too premature to comment on recent years, statistics which may indicate an end to this trend.

However, a report in IRS (2002) is less circumspect and points to the upsurge in industrial disputes during the early part of 2002 (see Exhibit 9.3). Its analysis is speculative rather than academic in nature and is based on the apparent deterioration in relationships between government and unions. Much of the industrial action has taken place within the privatised rail network where there are wide variations in pay between different companies and between drivers and other staff. Safety has often been compromised and this factor has been an ongoing source of dispute between guards and their employers. Labour market factors, such as the shortage of train drivers, has strengthened the bargaining power of this particular group, and unions have had the upper hand in negotiations. However, it is premature to argue that the 'upsurge' in industrial action represents the beginnings of a longer-term upward trend, but it is nevertheless significant particularly as it may be a reflection, in part at least, of the deterioration in relationship between the Labour government and the unions (see Chapters 3 and 4). The industrial action itself has affected relatively few sectors and there has not been a general trend, although underlying tensions within the public sector, the eruption of the firefighters' dispute, the ongoing strife in the railway network and pay negotiations affecting local government workers made 2003 a livelier prospect.

Snapshot for 2001

- Around 525 000 working days were lost through labour disputes which is more than the average for the past ten years and the highest annual total since 1996. One dispute accounted for 30 per cent of working days lost in 2001.
- There were 194 stoppages of work, fewer than the average of 232 for the ten years from 1991.

Exhibit 9.3

2002: Where the action was?

January: Rail disputes involving the RMT staging first of a series of two-day strikes over pay and discipline issues, signalling the start of sustained industrial unrest on the railways. Overtime ban by ScotRail drivers represented by ASLEF with numerous one-day stoppages following. Two-day strike by RMT at Arriva Trains Northern followed by further strikes.

February: Blair says NHS reforms including planned foundation hospitals will not be stopped by 'wreckers'. TUC General Secretary calls Blair's comments 'juvenile'. First of a series of strikes by security guards at Manchester Airport takes place. Communication Workers Union (CWU) votes 2–1 in favour of strike action at Royal Mail.

March: After company sets up in-house job centre for disgruntled employees, workers at MG Rover reject strike action in ballot. TUC General Secretary warns government that an 'explosive cocktail of issues could lead to a haemorrhaging of trade union support'. Teachers' one-day strike in protest at London allowances. Four-day strike at Manchester Airport by 500 security staff. CWU announces a £500 000 reduction in donations to Labour Party over three years.

April: First North Western rail operator hit by strike action. Three main teaching unions threaten action concerning workloads. One-day strike by 1750 naval support workers at Faslane and Coulport over proposed transfer to private sector. Members of TGWU reject local government pay offer by 20–1. Fire Brigades Union calls for an end to its 24-year-old national pay formula.

May–December: Continuing chronic unrest in the rail network and growing disquiet concerning the pensions issue. The firefighters' industrial action commences in November.

- Working days lost through strikes accounted for just one in every 10 100 potential working days in the year, and of working days lost 41 per cent were from 22 stoppages in public administration, 20 per cent were from 94 stoppages in transport, storage and communication and 14 per cent from 12 stoppages in health and social work.
- The regions with the highest number of days lost per 1000 employee jobs were the West Midlands and the North West; the regions with the lowest were Northern Ireland and the South East.
- Stoppages over pay were less significant during 2001 compared with previous years and accounted for 27 per cent of working days lost. Working conditions and supervision accounted for 33 per cent of working days lost.
- Around 48 per cent of all stoppages lasted less than one working day. There were also 19 stoppages involving the loss of more than 5000 working days and accounting for 82 per cent of the total number of working days lost.

The evidence from WERS98

The WIRS/WERS98 series spans 23 years from 1980 to 2003 with a further WERS reporting imminently. Reliable data concerning industrial action within workplaces therefore includes the earlier period when industrial action was more prominent and widespread than during the latter period. It is, unsurprising that the WIRS/WERS98 data reflects the trend reported in successive ONS publications such as *Labour Market Trends* (see Table 9.4). Between 1980 and 1990 the decline in industrial action at workplace level was due largely to a reduction in non-strike action, with strike action being as common in 1990 as it was in 1980. During the 1990s both non-strike and strike action declined, with the former affecting 3 per cent of unionised workplaces in 1998 (9 per cent in 1990), and the latter affecting 2 per cent of unionised workplaces in 1998 (16 per cent in 1990). At sectoral level, industrial action features more prominently within the public than in the private sector, but overall, by

Table 9.4 Industrial action in workplaces with recognised unions: 1980–98

	1980 %	1984 %	1990 %	1998 %
All workplaces				
None	75	69	80	96
Non-strike action only	10	8	4	2
Strike action only	9	11	11	2
Both strike and non-strike action	7	11	5	–
Private sector manufacturing				
None	62	70	88	95
Non-strike action only	11	14	10	5
Strike action only	15	9	*	0
Both strike and non-strike action	12	7	3	0
Private sector services				
None	89	85	93	97
Non-strike action only	5	4	1	1
Strike action only	5	8	1	2
Both strike and non-strike action	1	3	5	1
Public sector				
None	73	61	67	95
Non-strike action only	12	7	4	2
Strike action only	8	14	23	2
Both strike and non-strike action	8	17	6	–

Source: Millward *et al.*, 2000, p. 178

1998, all forms of collective industrial action had virtually disappeared in all but a few workplaces.

Distribution of strike activity by industry sector

Self-Evaluation Activity 9.7

Identifying trends

The response is given below

As we have seen, certain industries have been more strike-prone than others. Table 9.5 shows working days lost per 1000 employees in mining, manufacturing and services sectors for the period 1977–2001. What trend or trends can you identify?

The distribution of strikes between the three sectors of mining, manufacturing and services has changed since 1960. Edwards (1995) comments: 'The most dramatic trend was a rise in the role of services, which were virtually strike-free during the early 1960s, and by the late 1980s they accounted for a fifth of all strikes' (p. 441).

The 'working days lost per 1000 employees' measure is the standard method that has been used to convert working days lost into a strike rate that takes account of the size of the labour force. This also enables comparisons to be made across industries and regions that differ in size. Since the number of employee jobs has not changed dramatically over the last 20 years, the rates for the UK show the same pattern of general decline and occasional

Table 9.5 Working days lost per 1000 employees, United Kingdom: 1977–2001

Year	Mining, energy and water	Manufacturing	Services	All industries and services
1977	251	1 101	124	448
1978	372	1 135	77	413
1979	232	3 347	422	1 272
1980	259	1 691	42	520
1981	374	396	117	195
1982	649	352	211	248
1983	2 212	345	39	178
1984	38 425	529	114	1 278
1985	7 518	183	86	299
1986	293	220	46	90
1987	482	124	181	164
1988	536	339	116	166
1989	165	156	199	182
1990	245	228	44	83
1991	87	52	30	34
1992	97	23	24	24
1993	91	28	31	30
1994	2	15	13	13
1995	6	17	20	19
1996	8	24	70	58
1997	9	21	8	10
1998	1	8	13	12
1999	–	14	7	10
2000	17	13	20	20
2001	141	11	22	20

Source: Labour Market Trends, June 1999 p. 304 and November 2002, p. 594

peaks that can be seen in the working days lost measure. Between 1982 and 1993 the mining, energy and water supply industries had the highest rate in each year except 1989, when there was a large strike in the public administration sector. Up until the late 1980s the rate for the manufacturing industries had been significantly higher than that of the service sector. However, over the 1990s, the rates have been fairly similar with the exception of 1996, when the service sector rate was almost three times the rate for the manufacturing sector. During 2000 and 2001, the rate of working days lost increased in services and in mining, energy and water.

International comparisons

It is useful to compare the UK strike rate with those of other countries in order to establish whether other countries display similar trends to those in the UK. We could argue, for example, that as there are similar trends between countries, then economic factors may constitute the most likely explanation for decline in strike activity, since most of the EU countries have experienced high rates of unemployment and similar economic conditions. In historical terms, we could explain the similarity in trends by reference to 'long wave' theory (see below). In the

British context the claims of the previous Conservative governments that the reductions in strike activity was the result of its industrial relations legislation are largely unfounded, given similar strike patterns in other EU countries where there has been little or no such legislation.

An analysis of strike data for EU and Organisation for Economic Co-operation and Development (OECD) countries for the period (Monger, 2003a, 2003b) reveals some similarities and some variations in strike activity both within the EU and OECD countries as shown in Table 9.6 and Figures 9.1 and 9.2. In 2001, the UK had the 11th lowest strike rate (defined as the number of working days lost due to labour disputes per 1000 employees) in the OECD, the same ranking as in 2000. As we have already seen, the UK strike rate doubled between 1999 and 2000 and then remained at that level for 2001, and this is also a feature within the EU and OECD. The OECD average strike rate of 29 days in 2001 is the lowest in the Labour Market Trends series and the lowest since 1983, but it should be noted that this statistic is slightly distorted by the high US figure. Notwithstanding this, the UK strike rate has been below both OECD and EU averages since 1991, with the exception of 1996. More specifically, the average UK strike rate for the period 1997–2001 was 52 per cent lower than the previous five-year period (1992–6) with equivalent falls for the OECD and EU being 45 per cent and 23 per cent respectively.

Looking at Table 9.6 and Figures 9.1 and 9.2 in more detail, Table 9.6 shows the number of working days lost through labour disputes for the ten-year period 1992–2001 for each of the OECD countries. For the latest period (1997–2001), the UK ranked eighth lowest out of 23, which compares with sixth lowest for 1992–6 and seventh lowest for the whole ten-year period. Within 14 EU countries (Greece is not considered), the UK has the seventh lowest strike rate (Figure 9.1), and for each year from 1992 to 2001 the UK rate has been significantly below the EU average with the exception of 1996. Over the ten-year period, Spain experienced consistently high rates, while Austria, Germany and Luxembourghave generally shown a low rate. In most countries, as for example in the case of Spain, France and Finland in 2000, there has been considerable yearly variation in strike rates with some years being dominated by

Table 9.6 Working days lost per 1000 employees, United Kingdom: 1977–2001

Average	1992–6	1997–2001	1992–2001
United Kingdom	24	21	22
(UK ranking)	6	8	7
Austria	2	1	2
Belgium	38	21	29
Denmark	46	292	172
Finland	170	58	112
France	97	73	84
Germany	17	1	9
Ireland	110	86	96
Italy	172	62	116
Luxembourg	13	1	6
Netherlands	30	5	17
Portugal	30	19	24
Spain	385	178	271
Sweden	54	6	30
EU average	84	46	64
Australia	107	69	87
Canada	174	192	183
Iceland	556	571	564
Japan	2	1	2
New Zealand	54	19	36
Norway	121	78	98
Switzerland	1	3	2
Turkey	175	28	95
USA	54	17	31
OECD average	61	47	54

Source: *Labour Market Trends*, April 2003

a small number of very large strikes. For example, there was a major dispute in the public sector in France in 1995, the private sector in Denmark in 1998, the health sector in Ireland in 1999 and transport in the UK in 1996. Six countries in the EU witnessed an increase in the strike rate between 1999 and 2000, with Finland, France and Spain showing the largest increases.

International definitions of strikes differ

A significant problem in collating international strike data is that definitions of strikes and other

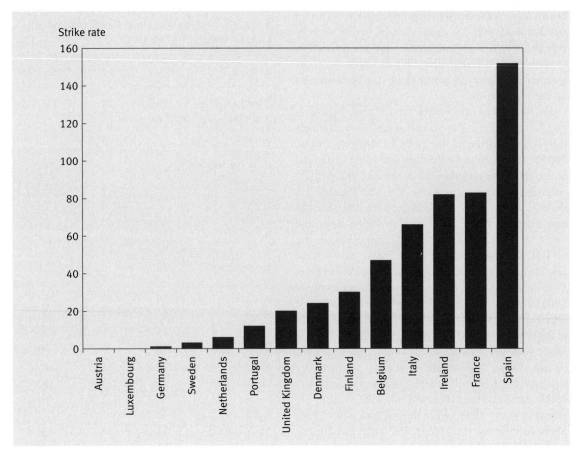

Figure 9.1 Working days not worked per 1000 employees (strike rate), EU: 2001
Source: *LMT*, April 2003

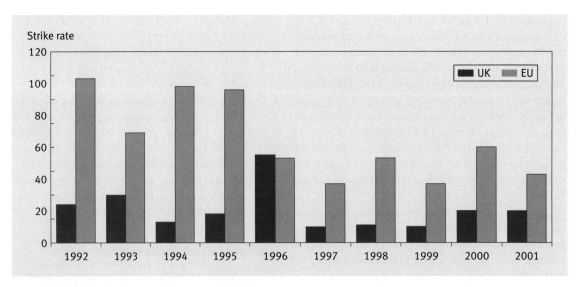

Figure 9.2 UK and EU average strike rates: 1992–2001
Source: *LMT*, April 2003

measurement criteria differ from country to country, as Table 9.7 indicates. Most countries rely on voluntary notification of disputes to a national or local government department, backed by media reports.

No country within the OECD aims to record the full effects of stoppages, neither are other forms of action such as work-to-rule and overtime bans included. There are differences in the criteria that

Table 9.7 Labour disputes: comparison of coverage and methodology

Country	Minimum criteria for inclusion in statistics	Are political stoppages included?	Are indirectly affected workers included?	Sources and notes
United Kingdom	Ten workers involved and of one-day duration unless 100 workdays not worked	No	Yes	Office for National Statistics collects information initially from press reports and then contacts employers and unions directly
Australia	Ten workdays not worked	Yes	Yes	Information gathered from Industrial Relations Department, employers, unions and press
Austria	No restrictions on size	Yes	No	Trade unions provide information
Belgium	No restriction on size. Excluding public sector stoppages	Yes	No	Questionnaires to employees following police or media coverage
Canada	Half-day duration plus 10 workdays not worked	Yes	No	Reports from Canada Manpower Centres, provincial Labour Departments' conciliation services and press
Denmark	100 workdays not worked. By employers' organisations	Yes	Yes	Voluntary reports submitted annually
Finland	One-hour duration	Yes	Yes	Principally returns from employers (90%); some reports from employees and press
France	One workday not worked. Excluding agriculture	Yes	Yes	Labour inspectors' reports
Germany	Ten workers involved and one-day duration unless 100 workdays not worked. Excluding public administration. From 1993 data covers entire FRG; earlier data covers West Germany only	Yes	No	Compulsory notification by employers to local employment offices
Iceland	Restrictions on size	Not known	No	No information
Ireland	Ten workdays not worked or one-day duration	Yes	Yes	Reports from Department of Enterprise and Employment, Department of Social Welfare and press

Table 9.7 (*Cont'd*)

Country	Minimum criteria for inclusion in statistics	Are political stoppages included?	Are indirectly affected workers included?	Sources and notes
Italy	No restrictions on size	Yes	No	No information
Japan	Half-day duration. Excluding unofficial disputes	Yes	No	Legal requirement to report to Labour Relations Commission
Luxembourg	No information	Not known	Not known	No information
Netherlands	No restrictions on size	Yes	Yes	Questionnaires to employers following a strike. National Dutch Press Bureau collects relevant news items on a contractual basis for Statistics Netherlands
New Zealand	Ten workdays not worked. Before 1988 excluding public sector stoppages	Yes	Yes	Information initially from press reports, employee and employer organisations and labour inspectors and subsequently from employer report forms
Norway	One-day duration	Yes	No	Employers' reports to the Ministry of Labour and Government Administration and press
Portugal	Strikes only. No restriction on size. Excluding general strikes at national level; excluding public administration	Yes	No	Legal obligation on trade unions to notify Ministry of Labour and Social Security
Spain	Strikes only before 1990. One-hour duration. Before 1989, excluding civil service	Yes	No	Legal obligation on party instigating strike to notify competent labour authority
Sweden	Eight hours not worked	Yes	No	Information gathered following press reports
Switzerland	One-day duration	Yes	No	Federal Office for Industry, Crafts, Occupations and Employment requests returns from employers and unions following press reports
Turkey	No restriction on size. Excluding energy services and most public services; excluding general strikes	No	Yes	Legal obligation on part of trade unions to notify Regional Directorates of Labour
United States	One-day or one-shift duration and 1000 workers involved	No	Yes	Reports from press, employers, unions and agencies

determine inclusion in statistics. Most countries exclude small stoppages, the threshold being defined in terms of the numbers involved, the length of the dispute, the number of days lost or a combination of all or some of these. Any difference in thresholds affects the number of days lost that are recorded. The USA and Denmark have particularly high thresholds, making comparison difficult. The USA, for example, includes only those disputes involving more than 1000 workers. Some countries exclude the effects of disputes in certain industrial sectors. Portugal, for example, omits public sector strikes and general strikes while Japan excludes days lost in unofficial disputes. Political stoppages are excluded for the UK, USA and Turkey. The inclusion or omission of those workers indirectly involved in a stoppage (those who are unable to work because others at their workplace are on strike) varies between countries. Half the countries listed in Table 9.7, including Australia, Belgium, France, the Netherlands, New Zealand, the UK and the USA, attempt to include them while Germany, Canada, Italy and Japan exclude them. This results in the latter category of countries recording a lower number of working days lost than those countries in the former category.

Explaining the strike trends

Edwards (1995) notes that there are five likely explanations for falling strike rates in the UK or indeed falling strike rates generally. These are:

- economic conditions;
- the shift of employment away from strike-prone industries and sectors;
- legal restrictions;
- improved means of dispute resolution; and
- 'better industrial relations'.

Economic conditions

Citing evidence from Davies (1979) for the period 1966–75, Edwards found that 'unemployment reduced the number [of disputes], but that it was not the high level of unemployment, but increases in the level of unemployment which reduced strikes' (p. 446). In addition, it was also found that high

levels of inflation tended to encourage strikes as concern with maintaining real income grew. By the same token, lower and declining inflation levels generally reduced employee expectations of higher pay increases.

Move away from strike-prone industries

As we noted earlier, many of the traditional strike-prone industries have declined both absolutely and in terms of numbers of employees. This in turn has reduced the bargaining power of trade unions representing workers in those industries. Nowhere is this more so than in the coal industry, which was one of the most strike-prone industries. Edwards (1995) comments:

> We may take its [the coal industry's] actual number of strikes per employee and calculate the number of strikes that it would have experienced had it stayed at the same size that it had in 1971 and in 1981. During the period 1986–1990, there would have been over 300 more strikes per annum on the 1971 employment level, and around 200 more on the 1981 level. This would have increased the number of strikes in Britain as a whole by two-fifths and a quarter respectively. (p. 446)

Role of the law

The trade union legislation of the 1980s and 1990s has restricted the definition of what constitutes lawful industrial action and has made it more difficult for workers to take industrial action as a result of balloting procedures and threats concerning the use of injunctions by employers. Research by Edwards (1992) suggests that there is no clear-cut relationship between the cumulative effects of legislative developments and industrial action. In attempting to 'measure the impact of the law once the effects of the labour market forces and structure of the economy have been taken into account, no consistent results for worker involvement or days lost have emerged, though the number of stoppages seems to have been reduced' (p. 446). The results, therefore, appear to be inconclusive, and there is, moreover, no evidence to suggest that the legislation has made workers less willing to take industrial action, but 'as part of a complex of other changes [the legislation] has indirectly shaped assumptions about the desirability and efficacy of action (p. 447)'.

Disputes and balloting procedures

According to Edwards (1995), the trend towards formalisation of procedures, including disputes procedures, occurred during the 1970s, and so would have had little impact upon strike incidence or working days lost during the 1980s and 1990s. Strike ballots have been legally required since 1984; evidence of ballots determining the outcome of a dispute is flimsy. This is partly because many strikes are of particularly short duration, with a high proportion lasting less than one day, and take place without a ballot being conducted. While this action is 'unlawful', these 'lightning' disputes are difficult to enforce and the law to all intents and purposes is irrelevant. Referring to research by Kessler and Bayliss (1995), who examined ACAS records containing data on strikes taken as a result of ballots, Edwards (1995) estimates that at least 60 per cent of strikes may take place without ballots in any one year and so we may only be generalising on the basis of the remainder of balloted strikes (40 per cent) and those disputes which were subjected to ballots but did not result in strike action; as Edwards puts it: 'the question is not whether some disputes are now settled without strikes but whether more ballots are now held, and whether the percentage of cases settled without a strike has increased' (p. 447).

'Better industrial relations'

This depends upon the nature or climate of industrial relations in the first place, and is a subjective as well as a relative evaluation. The climate and quality of industrial relations within an organisation is determined by many factors such as management style, union presence or absence, density of unionisation, technology, markets, skill requirements and so on. In similar fashion to Handy's typology of organisational culture (1993), 'good' or 'bad' industrial relations may be influenced by the nature of the power and control relationships between employer and employees such as the reassertion of managerial prerogatives over the past 20 years; the nature of the roles played by management and

individual managers which incorporates management style and ideology (see Chapter 2); the task culture and production process which includes technological changes and flexibilisation (see Chapter 5) and the extent to which individuals share the organisational goals, emphasising 'commitment', 'involvement', 'trust' and 'co-operation'. In general terms, if the industrial relations climate is 'poor', assuming a state of 'bad' industrial relations, then the greater the propensity for industrial action and strikes. Conversely, 'good' industrial relations would suggest industrial harmony rather than conflict. However, the deterministic nature of this simplistic cause–effect relationship belies a more complex interaction of factors.

Self-Evaluation Activity 9.8
The effects of Thatcherism
Response on website

If Thatcherism resulted in a deterioration in the general quality and climate of industrial relations, why did the number of strikes, workers involved and working days lost decline?

Long wave theory: a caveat

Kelly (1998) criticises industrial relations textbooks for being 'highly contemporary in their focus . . . the lack of adequate historical analysis opens up the danger of constructing future trends by simply projecting the recent past'. Essentially, long wave theory concerning strikes (developed initially by Kondratieff, 1979) looks at economic upswings and downswings over a period from around 1870 to 1974 within an international context. The basic conclusion from the research into strikes and long wave theory reported by Kelly is that towards the end of the Kondratieff upswings of 1869–75, 1910–20 and 1968–74 there were major strike waves which also coincided with periods of trade union growth; lesser strike waves can be detected towards the end of the Kondratieff downswings of 1889–93 and 1935–48. However, we argue that notwithstanding the validity of long wave theory, industrial relations textbooks should concentrate upon recent and contemporary data and trends while at the same time acknowledging the contribution of long wave theory (and mobilisation theory). Extrapolation from recent trends is a hazardous undertaking, especially if those trends are considered in isolation from the broader historical context. Unfortunately, space does not permit an examination of these issues which, as Kelly admits, remain contentious and problematic (1998, p. 107).

Summary points

- Industrial action is defined as work stoppages instigated either by management or trade union, and includes strikes, lockouts, go-slows, overtime bans, work-ins and sit-ins.
- Industrial action/conflict may be both individual and collective, organised and unorganised.
- The legal definition of industrial action (TULRCA) is necessary to determine whether industrial action is either lawful or unlawful.
- The main types of strike identified in the literature include:
  - the trial of strength;
  - the demonstration stoppage;
  - the official strike;
  - the unofficial strike;
  - the constitutional strike; and
  - the unconstitutional strike.
- Causes of strikes include the general categories of:
  - community integration;
  - technological determinism;
  - negotiating procedures; and
  - strikers' definition of the situation.
- More specific causes of strikes include:
  - pay;
  - hours of work;
  - redundancy;
  - trade union matters;
  - working conditions;
  - staffing; and
  - dismissal and disciplinary measures.
- Strike patterns are analysed using measures of:
  - working days lost;
  - number of stoppages; and
  - number of workers involved.

- Strike patterns and trends in the UK may be explained by:
  - economic conditions;
  - shift of employment from strike-prone industries;
  - legal restrictions;
  - improved means of dispute resolution; and
  - 'better industrial relations'.

STRIKES AND THE LAW

We now look in greater detail at the 1980s' and 1990s' legislation concerning industrial action which we considered in general terms in Chapter 4. The legislation restricted the definition of what constitutes lawful industrial action and narrowed the immunities which trade unions had gained under the 1906 Trades Disputes Act. Before looking at the specific provisions of the legislation, which we examine in chronological order in order to demonstrate the incremental progression of the various statutory provisions concerning industrial action, we consider briefly the situation that existed before 1980. McIlroy (1991) provides a clear and concise account which is reproduced in Exhibit 9.4.

The legislation examined

Employment Act 1980

Picketing
Concern about picketing as a result of the 'Winter of Discontent' was expressed in the Conservative Party manifesto and in the white paper which preceded the 1980 Act. Particular attention was paid to the 'secondary picketing' phenomenon (picketing of employers not directly involved in disputes and picketing affecting the general public and the violence and intimidation which accompanied picketing generally). The government wanted to limit the scale and scope of picketing which would limit action to the workplace directly involved. Secondary picketing, therefore, became unlawful and the regulation of picketing would be a matter for the police and the criminal law. Specifically the Act contained the following provisions:

Exhibit 9.4

The situation before 1980

If you go on strike then you are usually breaking your contract of employment. The courts have also found that a range of other industrial action . . . involves employees in breaking their contracts of employment. An employer often has little to gain financially by suing employees for breach of contract, apart from the unhelpful impact this is likely to have on future industrial relations. However, there is a civil wrong developed by the courts termed *inducement to breach of contract*. If employers could show the courts that it was the *union* that instigated, influenced or supported the industrial action then they might be able to convince the courts that the union was inducing the workers to break their contracts of employment.

In many cases judges were willing to do this and grant a legal order, an *injunction* instructing the union to call off the action. If the union did not do this it would be *in contempt of court* and could be fined large sums of money or eventually have its assets *sequestrated*. The courts also developed other civil wrongs – conspiracy, intimidation, and interference with contracts – which they used against union activities.

The position was made more difficult by the practice of the courts of issuing *interim injunctions*. An employer could within a matter of days secure a preliminary hearing of the case. The judge was only concerned as to whether, on the face of it, the employer had an arguable case, not whether it could be proved to the hilt, and whether looking at all the circumstances, the judge felt that it was more convenient to freeze the situation and restore the *status quo* by ordering the union to call off the industrial action until the full trial took place.

In the vast majority of cases the courts found for the employers, ignoring the problems this caused for unions and members who had to wait six months or a year before they could bring their bargaining power fully to bear on the employer. Of course, in most cases, the employers never returned to court for the full trial. The use of the interim injunction adequately met their purposes.

All of this meant, quite simply, that strikes and most forms of industrial action were unlawful. Trade unions, therefore, pressed parliament to *immunise* them from the impact of this judge-made law. If they were to carry out their functions of protecting their members, then they needed *specific immunities* from, for example, the civil wrong or tort of inducing breach of contract. Parliament decided unions would be protected where the industrial action is **'in contemplation or furtherance of a trade dispute'** (Trade Disputes Act, 1906). A *trade dispute* was defined quite widely as a dispute between employers and workers, which was related to, or connected with one or more of a long list of industrial matters. The list covered such issues as terms and conditions of employment, engagement, or dismissal of employees, allocation of work, discipline procedures and so forth.

If the industrial action fell within this definition of a trade dispute, then it was protected – or at least the trade unions were over the first hurdle. If the action did not fall within this definition, then the workers and their trade unions were in trouble. They then possessed no immunity and could be sued for committing one of the civil wrongs – most commonly inducement to breach of contract.

A major aim of the 1980 Act was to limit the immunities trade unionists possessed when taking industrial action.

Source: McIlroy, 1991, pp. 25–6

- workers to be protected when picketing at or near their own place of work, limiting pickets to the site on which they worked;
- there were provisions for mobile workers (such as lorry drivers) and workers whose location made picketing impracticable (such as oil rigs);
- there were protections for union officials and dismissed workers; and
- although not part of the Act, the Code of Practice on Picketing (1980) emphasised that picket numbers should not exceed six at any entrance to a workplace, that pickets should not

seek to halt essential supplies and that 'everyone has a right to decide for himself whether he will cross a picket line'.

Secondary action

The government now wanted to deal with the secondary boycott, the situation where workers taking industrial action requested workers employed by other employers such as customers, suppliers, contractors or transport workers, not to handle their product for the duration of the dispute. These forms of secondary action had been protected by the Trade Union and Labour Relations Act but were now restricted. The two main, rather complex provisions which defined secondary action are as follows:

1. Where workers, stewards or union officers induce a group of workers to break their contracts with their employer who is not himself a party to the dispute; or where workers, stewards or union officers interfer with the performance of contracts of employment or induce others or threaten to induce others to interfere with it.
2. If as a result of inducement to break or interfere with contracts of employment, a party to a commercial contract has been induced to break it, or its performance has been interfered with or threats to do so have been made.

For example, if workers on strike ask drivers not to remove finished goods from their plant and the drivers agree, thereby breaking their contract by refusing their employer's orders, and as a result their employer is in breach of his commercial contract with the struck employer then, on the face of it, there will be secondary action within the Act.

In summary, pure secondary action such as solidarity strikes where there was no contractual relationship between those involved in the primary strike and those seeking to help them was not protected and therefore unlawful (for example, miners taking action to support railway workers). Only secondary action where there was a contractual relationship between the primary and secondary employers would be lawful, and even then only within constraints. The provisions governing secondary action have proved complex and subject to a variety of interpretations.

The Employment Act 1982

Definition of trade disputes
The Act tightened up the definition of a trade dispute in three respects:

1. *Workers and their employer*: Before 1982 a trade dispute meant a dispute between employers and workers. The Act now changed this to workers and their employer. This would mean that in cases where trade unionists, in order to ensure basic terms and conditions were maintained, took industrial action against an employer *whose own employees were not taking action*, the dispute would not be protected.
2. *Workers and workers*: Before the 1982 Act disputes which to some extent involved conflicts between different groups of workers over, for example, demarcation, or the introduction of new technology, fell within the definition of a trade dispute. This type of action is now unlawful and the words *workers and workers* which appeared in the pre-1982 definition are omitted.
3. *Wholly or mainly*: Before the 1982 Act the definition of a trade dispute stated that the dispute taking place must simply *be connected with* one or more of:
   - terms and conditions of employment or the physical conditions in which workers are required to work;
   - engagement or non-engagement, or termination or suspension of employment or the duties of employment, of one or more workers;
   - allocation of work or the duties of employment as between workers or groups of workers;
   - matters of discipline;
   - the membership or non-membership of a trade union on the part of a worker;
   - facilities for officials of trade unions; and
   - machinery for negotiation or consultation, and other procedures, relating to any of the foregoing matters, including the recognition by employers or employers' associations of the right of a trade union to represent workers in any such negotiation or consultation or in the carrying out of such procedures.

The 1982 Act deleted *connected with* and replaced those words with *relate wholly or mainly* to one or more of these matters. This meant that where there were mixed elements in a dispute such as political factors as well as conditions of employment-related factors and where the political factors dominated, then there would be no protection by immunity. The intention here was to ensure that disputes are industrial and not 'political'.

Disputes outside the UK

Before the 1982 Act, the definition of a trade dispute stated: 'There is a trade dispute . . . even though it relates to matters outside Great Britain.' The Act made it unlawful for workers in Britain to take industrial action to support workers in dispute in other countries – unless the workers in Britain were likely to be affected by the outcome of the dispute taking place abroad in relation to one of the matters listed in the definition of a trade dispute.

Union liability; authorised/endorsed action; damages against unions

Industrial action was now more likely to be unlawful than in the past. The next step was to ensure that the union was financially responsible for unlawful industrial action. The Act changed the law so that trade unions could be sued in their own name for any action which fell outside the definition of a trade dispute or specific immunities. The union would be liable whenever unlawful industrial action was authorised or endorsed by a responsible person such as the union executive, anyone with power under the rule book to endorse or authorise the action, executive officers of the union or any other employed official of the union. The industrial action would not be regarded as 'authorised' or 'endorsed' if, for example, the union executive or executive officers repudiated the action.

The Act also set limits on the damages which could be awarded against unions in any one legal action. The limits are:

- £10 000 for unions with fewer than 5000 members;
- £15 000 for unions with between 5000 and 25 000 members;
- £125 000 for unions with between 25 000 and 100 000 members;
- £250 000 for unions with more than 100 000 members.

Dismissal of strikers

Under common law, employers could treat workers' action in going on strike as a repudiation of their contracts warranting dismissal. The Act permitted an employer to selectively re-engage strikers provided that more than three months had elapsed since the date of the worker's dismissal. If an employer follows this procedure other strikers dismissed and not re-engaged will have no right to a tribunal hearing. This provision thus strengthened the employers' position in a strike situation and undermined workers' rights.

Self-Evaluation Activity 9.9

Lessons that could be learnt from the Messenger dispute
Response on website

Minicase 9.1 is an account of the dispute between *Messenger* free newspapers and the National Graphical Association in 1983. What lessons could employers and unions learn from this dispute?

Mini case 9.1
The *Messenger* dispute

Eddie Shah ran a small group which published five *Messenger* free newspapers in the Lancashire and Cheshire area. He had problems with the National Graphical Association and when he opened a new typesetting plant at Bury he tried to exclude the union. The dismissal of six NGA members at the *Stockport Messenger* led the union to mount pickets at Bury and more importantly at Shah's Warrington plant to which most of the work done by NGA members had been transferred. For the NGA, the closed shop, control of membership and control of technology in the growing free sheet sector of the industry were key issues. They, therefore, asked all other NGA members not to work on, and all advertisers not to use the Messenger group's papers. This meant that for Eddie Shah his business was at stake.

In October 1983, Shah obtained injunctions against the print union and against the NUJ whose members had been asked not to handle copy. The two injunctions issued against the NGA under the 1980 and 1982 Acts ordered a halt to secondary picketing at Shah's

Bury and Warrington plants and the withdrawal of NGA instructions to members to boycott Messenger newspapers which under s. 14 of the 1982 Act constituted pressure to enforce 100 per cent membership. The NGA ignored the orders and, on 17th November 1983, the High Court found the NGA in contempt of court. A £50 000 fine was increased by a further £100 000 on 25th November as mass picketing of Shah's Warrington depot intensified and the judge also ordered the sequestration of the union's assets. In December the NGA was fined a further half a million pounds. An NGA strike in Fleet Street at the end of November produced further legal action by the Newspaper Proprietor's Association.

Source: McIlroy, 1991, pp. 69–73

According to Evans (1987), the number of injunctions sought by employers between May 1984 and April 1987 totalled 80, of which 11 concerned picketing, 16 concerned secondary action and 47 related to pre-strike ballots. A survey by Labour Research in 1987 reveals that from 1987 to 1988, there were 18 instances of legal action instigated by employers, seven of which concerned picketing and five of which concerned balloting. A further survey for Labour Research (1994) revealed that while the number of cases declined in 1992 and 1993, there was a marked increase in 1994 with 12 out of the 13 cases concerning changes to balloting arrangements as a result of the 1993 Act.

The Trade Union Act 1984

Ballots prior to industrial action
The balloting provisions apply not only to strikes but also to other industrial action, and state that the immunities protecting unions in taking lawful industrial action would continue to apply provided that unions adopt the following procedures:

- There had to be a ballot of all those whom the union reasonably believes will be called on to take part in the strike or other industrial action.
- The ballot must be secret, involve marking a paper and be conducted by post. The ballot could be conducted at the workplace if held immediately before, after, or during working hours.

- The ballot must be held not more than 28 days before the action begins or not more than 28 days before the action is authorised or endorsed where the union supported previously unofficial action. In other words, if a ballot was held, but strike action was delayed for more than 28 days because of continuing negotiation or because of the restraining effect of an injunction, another ballot would have to be held.
- The question on the ballot papers requires a straight 'yes' or 'no' about willingness to take industrial action, and must explicitly state that taking industrial action will involve a breach of employment contracts.
- The resulting action will only be protected by immunity if there is a straight majority in favour of the action. But there will then be no obligation on a union to support industrial action and no legal protection for members taking action against dismissal by their employer.

If the above procedures are not followed, then the Act gave a right to employers, customers and suppliers affected by the industrial action to take action for an injunction and damages.

The Employment Act 1988

Ballots on industrial action
The Act introduced three important changes to the 1984 Act:

1. **Union members.** The 1984 Act provided that unions would lose their immunity against legal action if they induced workers to take industrial action in breach of their contracts of employment without a ballot. The right to take legal action in these circumstances was given only to employers. The 1988 Act extended this right to union members. This was seen by government as extending the rights of the individual and increasing pressure on the union.

2. **Strike-breaking.** Unions sometimes took disciplinary action against members who worked normally during a strike or other industrial action, did the work of strikers, refused to pay a levy or cross picket lines. The Act now introduced a right not to be unjustifiably disciplined, and gave members the right to take a case to industrial tribunal where they had:

- not joined in or supported a strike or industrial action even if it was official;
- made allegations that the union or its officers acted contrary to union rules or broke agreements; and
- brought legal proceedings against the union.

3. **Separate ballots.** Where a ballot involved unions at different workplaces they could simply be counted to produce an overall result. Under the 1988 Act, this situation would prevail where all members involved share a 'common distinguishing factor' (where, for example, all those voting in the ballot represent all the union members in a particular grade or occupation employed by that employer). In all other instances there would be separate ballots for each workplace.

The Employment Act 1990

The main proposals concerning industrial action are based on the green paper *Unofficial Action and the Law* and include limits on secondary action, unofficial industrial action and dismissal of strikers.

Secondary action

The 1980 Act had given workers some protective immunity concerning taking industrial action to prevent or disrupt the flow of goods or services to or from a supplier or customer of the employer in dispute providing certain requirements were met. The 1990 Act removes immunity from all forms of secondary action so that workers at a struck plant seeking to get workers at the plant of a customer or supplier not to handle delivery would be open to legal action for damages as would any union authorising or supporting the action. This applies not only to those working under a contract of employment but also to independent contractors, freelance workers and the self-employed working under a contract of services.

Unofficial action

Provisions of the Act make unions responsible for the actions of anyone empowered by the rules to authorise or endorse industrial action whether they be the union executive committee, general secretary or president, any other committee of the union, any official of the union including lay shop stewards as well as paid officers. Responsibility and legal liability for the actions of all union personnel will apply, and a union cannot evade responsibility for the actions of its officials or other activists by changing its rules. The only way a union can escape being deemed to have authorised or endorsed industrial action is if it specifically repudiates the action.

Dismissal of strikers

Where industrial action is unofficial, the normal rules on dismissal identified in the Employment Act 1982 are relaxed. The main provisions are as follows:

- Any workers taking part in unofficial action such as the leaders or shop stewards may be selected out for dismissal and will have no right to take a case to industrial tribunal.
- Any industrial action in support of those selectively dismissed in unofficial action will be unprotected by the immunities and will be open to legal action by any employers or other persons affected.
- Action will not be deemed unofficial and covered by these provisions if all those taking part are non-trade unionists.

Trade Union Reform and Employment Rights Act 1993

The Act tightened up the provisions dealing with strikes in the following ways:

- All strike ballots had to be postal, thereby putting to an end the practice of workplace ballots established in 1984.
- Unions are required to provide employers with written notice of their intent to ballot members on industrial action at least seven days before commencement of the ballot, together with sample papers of the ballot at least three days before the start of the ballot.
- A union must ensure that it provides the employer with details of the ballot result and the names of those involved in the ballot.
- Strike ballots which involve 50 or more members must be independently scrutinised.
- A union must give the employer at least seven days' written notice of its intention to take official industrial action.
- Any individual who is deprived of goods or services as a result of unlawful industrial action can

bring proceedings before the High Court in order to restrain the unlawful act; such individuals can also apply to the new Commissioner for protection against unlawful industrial action for help and advice.

Employment Relations Act 1999

The Act makes substantial changes to the law in relation to the way legal action is conducted and the treatment of employees involved in disputes. The main changes are:

1. The simplification of ballots on industrial action. Where both parties agree, it will be possible to extend the 28-day period within which action must be taken before a ballot elapses to a maximum of eight weeks. This, it is hoped, will encourage further negotiation without the threat of legal action concerning ballot and notice provisions.
2. Those taking strike action will be offered greater protection from being dismissed. It is now 'automatically unfair' to dismiss an employee taking lawful industrial action for eight weeks (see also Chapter 13). Dismissal will then be fair only if the employer has taken 'all reasonable steps' to resolve the dispute.
3. While trade unions are no longer required to give employers a list of their members' names when an industrial action ballot or strike is held, they must still provide the employer with information concerning the group of employees to be balloted or asked to take strike action.

The legislation: summary and concluding comments

Self-Evaluation Activity 9.10

Union immunities and industrial action
Response on website

Before we assess the legislation on industrial action, attempt the following exercise that demonstrates the current position on trade union immunities concerning industrial action and which will assist you in reviewing that legislation. You should answer 'yes' or 'no' to the following questions:

In the event of strike action taking place:

1. Does the action constitute an inducement to breach, interfere with, conspiracy to break, or threat to break, a contract of employment?
2. Is the action taken in contemplation or furtherance of a trade dispute?
3. Is the dispute a trade dispute within the legal definition, that is:
   (a) between worker and employer
   (b) workers or ex-workers of the employer
   (c) in relation to a matter specified by law
   (d) is wholly or mainly connected with (c)?
4. Is the origin of the dispute within the UK?
5. Is the action primary action at the place of the original dispute?
6. Are pickets limited to the workplace of the original dispute and restricted in numbers?
7. Has a secret postal ballot been held in which a majority of those involved in the action have voted in favour of the action?
8. Has seven days' notice of the ballot and seven days' notice of the action been given to the employer?
9. Has the employer access to independent scrutiny of the strike ballot?
10. Have people involved in the strike ballot been identified?

The legislation dealing with strikes and industrial action in all the aspects described above is quite different now from what it was in 1979. As we have seen, strike activity is substantially lower than it was in the 1960s and 1970s and in 1997, for example, the DfEE recorded the lowest ever incidence of strikes since records began. We also considered some explanations attempting to account for this trend and concluded that government legislation could not, of itself, account for the declining trend. The apparent willingness of some employers to resort to litigation, while headline-provoking, tends to conceal the fact that most employers did not use the legislation, possibly for fear of prejudicing years of efforts and achievements in order to promote a constructive industrial relations climate and because 'normally the employer's aim is to stop industrial action rather than obtain damages' (Dickens and Hall, 2003).

However, it could be argued that the legislation governing strike and pre-strike activity, particularly with regard to balloting provisions, has resulted in changes which have influenced the negotiating behaviour of both parties. Balloting provisions have been accepted as a matter of routine by many union negotiators, despite initial opposition from unions and some employers. In the event of negotiations breaking down and subsequent industrial action being contemplated, ballots must be held. A very high proportion of ballots taken nationally (around 90 per cent in any one year) are decisively in favour of industrial action, and this tends to confer greater legitimacy upon the union's negotiating position than previous (now unlawful) practices, involving a 'show of hands' or site meetings, for demonstrating support for industrial action could provide. No longer can an 'active minority' be accused of orchestrating and manipulating industrial action for its own ends. In many cases, therefore, the legitimacy of the 'majority vote' in secret postal ballots may provide the impetus to further negotiation and resolution of the dispute without recourse to industrial action or the involvement of 'third parties' such as ACAS.

Progressive restrictions on unions' legal immunities, together with changes in picketing arrangements and curbs upon secondary action are more difficult to assess. Many of the 'high profile' disputes of the 1980s (such as the *Messenger* and *News International* disputes) demonstrated some employers' almost obsessive enthusiasm in resorting to court injunctions and other legal actions. On the other hand, disputes such as the miners' strike, even though it took place in the early years of the legislative onslaught, demonstrated the extent to which the new constraints on secondary action and picketing could be flouted. It may be, as Kessler and Bayliss (1998) suggest, that the low and declining level of industrial action in recent years has meant:

> that there have not been enough occasions on which the law might be tested for its practical significance to have emerged [and] if there were an upsurge in strike activity in the future, the significance of the changed legal framework might turn out to be greater than at present appears. (p. 252)

Moreover, the law has had relatively little impact upon the incidence of 'unofficial' disputes which

are deemed 'unlawful'. A significant proportion of unofficial stoppages are of very short duration (often less than a day and so do not fall within the official DfEE definition of stoppages), and are normally settled by negotiation at local level. There is little evidence that the provisions of the 1990 Employment Act concerning 'unofficial' strikes and the facility for employers to dismiss the 'leaders' of them have actually been used by employers; to do so would certainly be detrimental to 'good' industrial relations practice. The first Blair government accepted that dismissal of strikers taking lawful industrial action and the requirement to provide employers with the names of union members being balloted are unfair. The Employment Relations Act 1999 gave employees unfair dismissal rights for taking part in lawful industrial action and simplified the law and the Code of Practice on industrial action ballots and notice and, in particular, removed the provision concerning naming of union members. The TUC, not surprisingly, wanted the government to go further and is pressing for change in its response to the Government's review of the Employment Relations Act. As early as 1998, however, the TUC made its reservations known to the Government:

> The length of the Code [of Practice] illustrates the complexity of the framework of law on industrial action. The detailed obligations on unions provide enormous scope for employers to challenge any proposed industrial action. The test applied to applications for injunctions means that action can be halted on an allegation that there has been some infringement of the law, which is subsequently proved to be unfounded. This exacerbates disputes and we believe the emphasis should be on seeking a speedy resolution to the matter. As well as the unfairness of mischievous challenges to ballots, the TUC is concerned that unions can find themselves exposed to claims for damages even when every attempt has been made to comply with the obligations and it was understood that the action was lawful. Where an employer challenges the validity of the ballot after the action has taken place and shows that some aspect of the balloting requirements has not been met, then the union could face substantial claims for damages even though the action was considered to be

lawful at the time. We would urge the Government to examine aspects of the current legislation with a view to removing the anomalies whereby employers can frustrate the expressed wishes of a majority voting in industrial action ballots by resorting to legal technicalities. (1998, p. 12)

We have argued, therefore, that government legislation is one (but certainly not the main) reason for the decline in UK strike activity. As long as the incidence of strike action remains low, the impact of legislation upon such activity would seem to be slight at best, and 'legal changes were part of a much wider range of developments affecting strike activity' (Dickens and Hall, 2003).

RELEVANT WEBSITES

www.cipd.org.uk (Chartered Institute of Personnel and Development) Useful for members for access to 'People Management' online.

www.dti.gov.uk/er (Department of Trade and Industry) Access to strike data via *Labour Market Trends.*

www.fbu.org.uk (Fire Brigades Union) Good for the union perspective on the firefighters' dispute.

www.irfs.org.uk Useful material on the Bain Report.

www.lga.gov.uk (The Local Government Association) Useful for employer perspective on fire dispute.

www.tuc.org.uk (Trades Union Congress) Good student resources and links to other websites.

REFERENCES

Bain Report (2002) 'The future of the Fire Service'. www.irfs.org.uk

Blauner, R. (1964) *Alienation and Freedom.* Chicago, Chicago University Press

Brown, W.A. (ed.) (1981) *The Changing Contours of British Industrial Relations.* London, Heinemann

Burchill, F. (2003) 'Firefighters' dispute negotiators are no fools'. *People Management,* April, 22

Coser, L.A. (1956) *The Functions of Social Conflict.* London, Routledge and Kegan Paul

Dahrendorf, R. (1959) *Class and Class Conflict in Industrial Society.* London, Routledge and Kegan Paul

Danford, A. and Stewart, P. (2003) 'The rediscovery of conflict', in Hollinshead, G., Nicholls, P. and Tailby, S. *Employee Relations,* Harlow, Financial Times/Prentice Hall

Daniel, W.W. and Millward, N. (1983) *Workplace Industrial Relations in Britain.* Aldershot, Gower

Davies, R.J. (1979) 'Economic activity, incomes policy and strikes'. *British Journal of Industrial Relations,* 17, 2, 205–23

Devlin (1965) *Final Report of the Committee of Inquiry Under the Rt Hon. Lord Devlin into Certain Matters Concerning the Port Transport Industry,* Cmnd 2734. London, HMSO

Dickens, L. and Hall, M. (2003) 'Labour law and industrial relations: A new settlement', in Edwards, P. (ed.) *Industrial Relations Theory and Practice,* 2nd edn. Oxford, Blackwell

Edwards, P.K. (1992) 'Industrial conflict'. *British Journal of Industrial Relations,* 30, 3, 361–404

Edwards, P. (1995) 'Strikes and industrial conflict', in Edwards, P. (ed.) *Industrial Relations: Theory and Practice in Britain.* Oxford, Blackwell

Evans, S. (1987) 'The use of injunctions in industrial disputes'. *British Journal of Industrial Relations,* 25, 3, 419–35

Farnham, D. (1997) *Employee Relations in Context.* London, IPD

Fire Brigades Union (2003) 'Modernisation: the facts from the Fire Brigades Union'. www.fbu.org.uk/pay2003

Gallie, D. (1978) *In Search of the New Working Class: Automation and Social Integration in the Capitalist Enterprise.* Cambridge, Cambridge University Press

Gallie, D. (1988) *Employment in Britain.* Oxford, Blackwell

Handy, C.B. (1993) *Understanding Organisations.* London, Penguin

Hyman, R. (1984) *Strikes.* London, Fontana

IRS (2002) 'A spring of discontent?' *IRS Employment Trends,* No. 752, 27 May

Kelly, J. (1998) *Rethinking Industrial Relations.* London, Routledge

Kerr, C. (1964) *Labour and Management in Industrial Society.* New York, Doubleday

Kerr, C. and Siegel, A. (1954) 'The inter-industry propensity to strike', in Kornhauser, A., Dubin, R. and Ross, A.M. (eds) *Industrial Conflict*. New York, McGraw-Hill

Kessler, S. and Bayliss, F. (1995) *Contemporary British Industrial Relations*. Basingstoke, Macmillan

Kessler, S. and Bayliss, F. (1998) *Contemporary British Industrial Relations*, 2nd edn. Basingstoke, Macmillan

Kondratieff, N.D. (1979) 'The long waves in economic life'. *Economic Review*, 2, 4, 519–62 (first published in 1926)

Kornhauser, A., Dubin, R. and Ross, A.M. (eds) (1954) *Industrial Conflict*. New York, McGraw-Hill

LMT (Labour Market Trends) (1999) 'Labour disputes in 1998'. *Labour Market Trends*, June, 299–311

LMT (Labour Market Trends) (2002) 'Labour disputes in 2001'. *Labour Market Trends*, November, 589–603

LMT (Labour Market Trends) (2003) 'International comparison of labour disputes in 2000'. *Labour Market Trends*, January, 19–27

Labour Research Department (1987) 'Legal action instigated by employers'. October, p. 26

Labour Research Department (1994) 'Employers and litigation'. October, p. 31

Local Government Authority (2003) 'Commentary on the Bain Report'. www.lga.gov.uk

McIlroy, J. (1991) *The Permanent Revolution? Conservative Law and the Trade Unions*. Nottingham, Spokesman

Metcalf, D. (2003) 'A plague on both your houses'. *People Management*, March, 24–6

Millward, N., Bryson, A. and Forth, J. (2000) *All Change at Work*. London, Routledge

Monger, J. (2003a) 'International comparisons of labour disputes in 2000'. *Labour Market Trends*, 111, 1, 19–29

Monger, J. (2003b) 'International comparisons of labour disputes in 2001'. *Labour Market Trends*, 111, 4, 181–89

Ross, A.M. and Hartman, P.T. (1960) *Changing Patterns of Industrial Conflict*. New York, Wiley

Seifert, R. (2003a) 'Comments on the full Bain Report'. www.fbu.org.uk

Seifert, R. (2003b); 'Comments on the employers' offer of the 6th March 2003 in the 2002/2003 fire dispute'. www. fbu.org.uk

TUC (1998) *Response to Fairness at Work*. London, TUC

Turner, H.A. (1969) *Is Britain Really Strike-Prone?* Cambridge, Cambridge University Press

Waddington, J. (2003) 'Trade union organisation', in Edwards, P. (ed.) *Industrial Relations Theory and Practice*, 2nd edn. Oxford, Blackwell

Watson, T.J. (1995) *Sociology, Work and Industry*. London, Routledge

WIRS (1980) See Daniel, W.W. and Millward, N. (1983)

PART 4

THE EMPLOYMENT RELATIONSHIP: SKILLS, PRACTICES AND POLICY

CHAPTER 10

NEGOTIATION AND NEGOTIATING SKILLS

INTRODUCTION

Negotiation is a central, goal-directed activity pursued by two parties, the desired outcome of which is to arrive at an agreement that is acceptable to both parties. There is some semantic confusion concerning the terms *negotiation* and *bargaining*. Gennard and Judge (2002) point out that the process of collective bargaining between employers and employees is but one of a number of different forms of negotiation. This distinction is important if we regard negotiation as a general process, which encompasses a variety of different contexts, and as having a number of different variations and types. Another important point to make is that the skills required in any negotiation process are fairly general to all negotiating contexts, although the emphasis placed upon any particular category of skills will change according to the particular negotiating situation.

The chapter starts by looking at the purpose of and scope for negotiation, identifying the various types of negotiation situations. We then look at the stages of negotiation for all negotiating situations, and this is followed by an overview of the particular skills required for each stage of the negotiation process. The actual bargaining context of negotiations is then examined, together with relevant examples and activities.

Learning outcomes

When you have read the chapter, you should be able to:

1. Understand the purpose of negotiation and identify the different types of negotiating situations.

2. Explain the various stages in the negotiating process and determine the appropriate skills negotiators require for each negotiating stage.

3. Understand the 'psychology' of negotiation.

4. Appreciate the bargaining context of negotiations.

5. Use the negotiation skills we deal with to enrich your own negotiating behaviour.

THE NATURE AND PURPOSE OF NEGOTIATION

There are a number of principles or elements that facilitate our understanding of the basic process of negotiation. These are as follows (based on Fowler, 1992, 1996):

- The negotiation process involves the interaction, based on a common and shared interest, of at least two parties who wish to achieve a desired outcome.
- Despite the mutuality of interest, the parties start with different objectives, and these differences initially prevent the achievement of an outcome.
- The parties recognise that negotiation is the legitimate means for resolving differences, at least during the initial stages.
- Each party accepts that there is some possibility of persuading the other to modify the original position each initially adopted, and that it is therefore highly desirable that both parties compromise. Even if the parties initially are resolute about maintaining their opening positions, each must have some hope of persuading the other to change. Gennard and Judge (2002) call these processes purposeful persuasion and constructive compromise and point out:

  > Each party attempts to persuade the other by using arguments backed by factual information and analysis as to why they should accept their case (request). However the probability that one party can (purposefully) persuade the other to accept its case (request) completely is extremely low. If an agreement is reached, both parties must move closer towards each other's position. To achieve this, they must identify common ground within and between their positions. Constructive compromises can then be made within these limits. Compromise is only possible if sufficient common ground exists between the two parties. The overriding objective of any negotiation is for the parties to reach an agreement and not to score debating points or to save the face of one or both parties. (p. 298)

- Even when their ideal outcomes are not attainable, both parties retain some hope of an acceptable final agreement.

- Each party has some influence or power – real or assumed – over the other's ability to act. If one party is entirely powerless, there may be no point in the other party committing itself to a negotiating process. The party with 'absolute' power to act could settle the matter unilaterally. This power or influence may, however, be indirect and bear on issues which are the direct subject of negotiation.
- The negotiating process is dominated by verbal interchange and communication, and this introduces the 'human element' whereby all types of negotiation are influenced by socio-psychological factors such as emotion and attitudes.

We can now derive a general definition of negotiation from the elements identified above:

> *Negotiation is a process whereby two or more parties interact with each other in order to resolve their differences and who need to be jointly involved in an outcome which is mutually acceptable, the outcome being achieved by argument, persuasion and compromise.*

The purpose of negotiation, then, is to engage in joint problem-solving in order to reach an agreement satisfactory to both parties. This does not preclude the possibility of disagreement and conflict between the parties, as we shall see.

THE CATEGORIES OF NEGOTIATION

Self-Evaluation Activity 10.1

Categories and types of negotiation situations
The response is provided below

Within both the organisational context and the employment relationship, a number of different categories of negotiation or types of negotiation situation exist. Identify what these may be, providing examples of each.

Gennard and Judge (1997) identify four main types of negotiation situations represented in Figure 10.1.

The first negotiating situation identified by Gennard and Judge, that between individual members of management, is the most common one for industrial relations, personnel and human resource managers. They may negotiate amongst themselves or with managers from different specialisms such as finance or production.

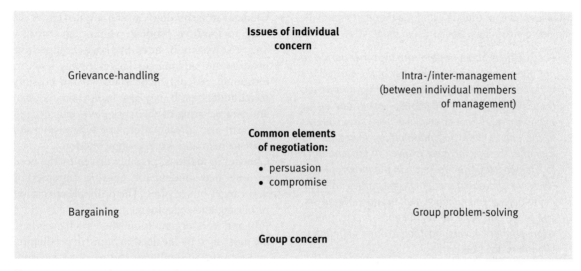

Figure 10.1 Types of negotiating situations
Source: Gennard and Judge, 1997, p. 146

Issues for negotiation include almost anything concerning the employment relationship such as introduction of new technology and working practices and procedures (for example, new shift working systems, revised payment systems and incentive schemes). Gennard and Judge comment:

> It is an activity in which all managers are involved daily. Negotiations take place day in and day out between managers of different and similar levels of executive authority and between different managers from different management functions. Nevertheless, some managers have difficulty in treating these intra- and inter-management relationships as negotiating situations and prefer to think of the process as 'influencing others'. (p. 147)

The second type of negotiating situation referred to by Gennard and Judge is grievance handling, which we consider in greater detail in Chapter 11. Grievances are complaints made by employees arising from the actions of management or because of the behaviour of other employees (with regard to, for example, sexual harassment) and are concerned with a range of issues stemming from conflicts of interest, misunderstandings and communication breakdown, organisational changes and work processes. Grievances can be both collective and individual, although most start off as complaints made by individual employees. Grievances are handled both formally through the organisation's grievance

procedure, which establishes an agreed set of rules for settling complaints, and informally, usually before the procedure is resorted to by the complainant's line manager. Gennard and Judge additionally point out that:

> In resolving an employee's grievances, management has to proceed on a one-by-one basis. It settles one person's grievance before moving on to resolve that of the next person. Management cannot offer to settle one person's grievance in exchange for getting other employees to agree to drop their grievances. In grievance handling neither management nor employee representative takes part in 'trading' (i.e. you drop that grievance and we shall accept another employee's grievance) . . . [they will be dealt with] sequentially, one at a time. (p. 148)

The third negotiating situation is the bargaining context, which is one of several types of negotiating situations managers and employees are concerned with. In dealing with collective bargaining in Chapter 6, we noted that there are both substantive and procedural issues that are the subject of negotiation, and this aspect will be dealt with later in this chapter. Normally, one party (the employee or trade union representatives) produces a 'shopping list' of demands concerning substantive issues such as pay, longer holidays, reductions in weekly hours worked, and so on, to which management are expected to make a response. In contrast to grievance handling, bargaining involves a certain amount of 'give and take' or trading without either party normally making concessions. Gennard and Judge add:

> Bargaining is about trading with the other party and not about conceding to the other party. Something is gained in return for trading something. However, there are bargaining situations – especially in the public sector – where an employer gives pay increases to the employees who trade nothing in return. For example, the pay increase is given to the workforce to compensate for an increase in the Index of Retail Prices. In a bargaining situation, the parties are seeking to defend and enhance their economic interests. The tenor and style of negotiations is likely to be relatively more adversarial than in other negotiating situations. (p. 148)

The final type of negotiating situation identified by Gennard and Judge is that of group/joint problem-solving, defined as 'a situation in which two or more parties negotiate the details whereon they will co-operate with each other to resolve a problem which is of common interest to them' (p. 149). The 'problem' may be either general or fairly specific. General problems may relate to various organisational changes brought about by competitive pressures in the market place and the need to make economies while improving organisational efficiency and effectiveness.

The organisational changes referred to above, and how they affect the workforce include the following:

- **Changes in ownership**, which may come about through takeovers, mergers, acquisitions and through privatisation of public services. This is the most fundamental change and the consequences for the workforce as a result of any subsequent 'rationalisation' include redundancies and changes to contracts of employment resulting in inferior working conditions.
- **Changes in management style** (see Chapter 2), which may be driven by recognition that the current approach is not appropriate. This may normally be accompanied by training and familiarisation programmes and briefings for all staff, and may also lead to some restructuring of patterns of supervision, allocations of responsibility and divisions of work.

- **Changes in technology**, which are driven by the need to improve product, volume and quality and to maintain and improve competitive position and advantage. This normally leads to retraining, redeployment, transfers and possibly to redundancies. It may also lead to the redesign and restructuring of the work environment, and this will also affect patterns of supervision and management and work group cohesion.
- **Changes in markets**, possibly driven by the need to seek new outlets for existing activities or new ranges of activities. The probable effects are retraining and redeployment.
- **Jobs and work organisation** whereby changes here are motivated by the need to improve production and output, and enhance the working environment. This normally means the creation of flexible patterns of work which could lead either to increased levels of employee responsibility consequent upon enlarging jobs and multi-skilling practices or it could lead to a larger proportion of the workforce employed on a temporary, fixed-term basis, performing mainly routine tasks.
- **Performance indicators and outputs** are important in that the assessment of these by managers may lead to drives for change if the operational indicators and/or the behavioural indicators give cause for concern. Operational indicators relate to the success and profitability of products and services; product mixes and portfolios; and productivity and output. Behavioural indicators relate to perceptual and staff management aspects; desired and prevailing attitudes and values; the extent of strikes and other disputes, absenteeism, labour turnover and accidents; harmony/discord, co-operation/conflict and the general climate of well-being). In these cases, the causes of each will/ should be assessed and addressed. They, in turn, lead to change programmes, which are designed to remedy the total performance of the whole organisation and the contribution of each department, division and function.

These changes, apart from the first, whether they require the diagnosis of consultants or not, are better facilitated with the co-operation of the workforce, given that both individual and collective resistance to change has negative consequences for individual employees and the organisation as a whole. This type of negotiation has also been termed integrative, which requires 'a potential for finding a common interest, a shared recognition that a problem exists and can be resolved by adopting a joint problem-solving approach aimed at finding a new rationale and mutually agreed solution' (Cairns, 1996, p. 8). Ideally, the resolution of such problems should result in a 'gain' for each party (or win-win situation), but where there is a financial cost incurred by the employer and a gain for the workforce, then it is a lose-win situation. Assuming the involvement of consultants, Gennard and Judge (1997) point out that:

> In group problem-solving negotiating situations, management is normally seeking the support and co-operation of its workforce to gain information upon which proposed action can be based and from which both will gain mutual advantage. The management negotiating style will not be adversarial. Management will offer 'carrots' to its employee representatives to gain their co-operation with its own proposed action. (p. 149)

THE NEGOTIATION STAGES

Self-Evaluation Activity 10.2
The stages of negotiation
The response is provided below

Negotiations in practice, which include the negotiating encounter, comprise a number of stages that negotiators have to consider if negotiations are to be effective. Can you identify what you think the important stages are?

Figure 10.2 illustrates the important stages of negotiation.

NEGOTIATING SKILLS

It is important to note that although there is a whole range of skills that are essential for the conduct of effective negotiations, emphasis should be placed upon particular skills required for each stage of the negotiation process. Figure 10.3 identifies the important skills for each of these stages.

We now consider the more important of these negotiating skills in greater detail. There is a tendency in the literature to group particular skills within a limited number of general categories. For example, Gillen (1995) includes all the skills in Figure 10.3 under the category 'positive influencing skills', while Fowler (1995) has two general skill categories of 'influence' and 'persuasion' and Kniveron (1974) identifies three categories of 'social interpersonal skills', 'information-handling skills' and 'discretionary judgement skills'. These general categories can be confusing unless they are used to describe a specific skill requirement relevant to a particular stage or development in the negotiation process. Wherever possible, we identify specific skills, and where terms such as 'persuasion' and 'influence' are used, they have specific connotations.

Persuasion

Effective negotiators achieve their results partly by exercising a range of skills that can be described as persuasion. Persuasion is based on approaches that respect the other person or persons within both negotiating teams, making it easier to understand, but not necessarily agree with, the other's point of view and argument. Persuasion should not be confused with manipulation, which is based on stealth whereby, intentionally or otherwise, the other person is tricked into accepting your way of thinking. For example, persuasive skills can be used by a union negotiating team to put forward the reasoning, facts and arguments to justify and support their demands. Similarly, the management negotiating team will persuade by reasoned argument concerning its offer. Cairns (1996) provides an example of persuasion within the public sector:

> For public sector unions in the 1980s, the depressive economic environment was compounded by the hostility of central government towards the public sector. Against this background, the unions launched a wage claim in 1985, the centrepiece of which was the assertion that local authority workers were not only low paid but had considerably slipped back in the national earnings

Stage	Requirements
Planning	Parties must be in a position to negotiate and the subject for negotiation must be endorsed by the parties as 'legitimate'
	Negotiating teams must be selected and the roles of negotiators determined, objectives of negotiation agreed with no dissent within the negotiating team
	Ensure that conditions and arrangements for negotiations are suitable
Preparation	Decide on the type of negotiations
	Selecting and briefing the negotiation team on tactics and strategy Apart from team size, agreement on who is to speak, on what subject and in what order is important. Anticipation of other side's arguments and how to counter them
	Researching, analysing and collating relevant information such as facts and data, rules and procedures, precedents and comparisons, attitudes of the parties to issues and whether some are 'tradable'
	Assessing the power positions of the parties
	Setting aims and objectives; what is 'ideal' – like to achieve; what is 'realistic' – hope to achieve; what is the 'fall-back' position – must achieve
Face-to-face negotiations	Setting the tone and climate of negotiation; each party putting all issues on the table from the outset
	Techniques for searching the 'common ground'
	Presentation of the case by each party
	Receiving the other side's response
	The argument and 'trade-off' stage; summarising, listening, anticipating
Closing negotiations	Have all the issues been discussed and agreed?
	That the 'final' offer is 'real' and not 'bluff'
	That the final offer is agreed formally by both parties
Writing the agreement	Clear up misunderstandings at the checking and drafting stage
	Ensure final ratification of the agreement
Implementing the agreement	Confirm timescale

Figure 10.2 The negotiation stages

'league table'. So powerful were the arguments in favour of these low-paid people that, despite tight financial curbs and penalising legislation, the employers shied away from the harsh light of continued public exposure on poverty pay. Central government did likewise. (p. 46)

Fowler (1995) identifies a number of specific skills which are linked to persuasion, all of which we deal with separately. These include:

- style (leadership and interpersonal skills);
- listening;
- probing and questioning;
- summarising; and
- body language.

Presentation skills

Both parties rely a great deal upon the spoken word and should take care to ensure that oral presentations in bargaining, for example, are well structured; including the initial explanation of the rationale behind offer or claim, summarising throughout the

Stage	Skills required
Planning	Leadership and interpersonal skills Skills of persuasion
Preparation	Information-gathering Analysis of data Judgemental skills
Face-to-face negotiations	Presentation skills Influencing skills Skills of persuasion and judgement Note-taking and summarising skills Interviewing skills (for grievance-handling) Interpersonal skills Listening and observing skills Questioning and probing skills Awareness of body language
Closing negotiations	Interpersonal skills Judgemental skills
Writing the agreement	Summarising and presentation skills
Implementing the agreement	Influence and persuasion in 'selling' the deal Time management

Figure 10.3 Most important skills required for each stage of the negotiating process

negotiations, and presenting or countering arguments during negotiations. This applies particularly to the opening presentation in face-to-face negotiations. Ideally, the opening presentation of either party should have an introduction which outlines the position and proposals, a main part, which details the position, backed up by data and examples, and a concluding summary which reinforces what has been explained. The presentation should be backed up by notes which should be referred to. Gennard and Judge (1997, p. 171) suggest a basic checklist which the parties should bear in mind before making the presentation:

Content – Have you said all you want to say?
Sequence – Is the presentation logical, and has each part been linked?
Balance – Does it have the right weight and emphasis?
Objective – Will it work to achieve this?

When face-to-face negotiations begin, it is usually up to the party that makes the claim to start presenting their case and it is the responsibility of the other party to respond to the claim. The nature of the response can have a crucial impact upon the course of negotiation (see the 'Bargaining context' on pp. 479–92).

Note-taking and summarising skills

This is an obvious but crucially important skill for both parties. Taking accurate notes will assist negotiators by providing a record of what has been said and to and by whom, identifying important arguments and amendments, and for checking the accuracy of salient contributions concerning what has been agreed, or what has yet to be agreed before and after adjournments. Clearly, it is not possible or advisable to attempt to produce detailed word-for-word accounts during face-to-face negotiations. However, during the writing-up stage accuracy is vital if the two parties are to agree on the wording of the agreement.

In a negotiation which involves a number of issues such as pay, working conditions, fringe benefits, holidays and overtime, it is fairly common for progress to be made more rapidly on some issues than others. In order to avoid subsequent disagreement and time-wasting involved in backtracking, it is useful to summarise periodically in order to secure agreement in the interim, on the basis of notes taken during the negotiation. Fowler (1992) illustrates this important point with reference to negotiation about working time:

> The discussion had reached the point at which it had become clear that levels of overtime were a key issue which now needed discussion. At this point, the management side's leader said: 'Before we go on to talk about overtime, I think we might all find it helpful to summarise where we have got to so far. The company has explained why it cannot consider a reduction in the working week. But we have accepted that some movement should be made on annual leave, and our proposition – which I take it you have agreed, at least in principle – is that the manual employees' entitlement should be harmonised with that of the clerical staff. Is everyone happy with that summary? If so, we'll just make a quick note of it so that we don't waste time later trying to remember what we said.' The effect of this summary was to lock both parties into an agreed approach to the annual leave issue, and prevent a possible dispute on overtime upsetting the progress which had already been made. (p. 76)

A summary may indicate that the two parties have different interpretations about each other's position and provides an opportunity to resolve these differences during the course of face-to-face negotiations.

Listening and observing

An obvious attribute which can be the key to a successful negotiation outcome, listening is important in attempting to identify verbal signals and clues, weaknesses and strengths in arguments and general errors in the other party's case. Listening carefully to what the other party is saying will reveal clues and ideas about how to move the negotiations forward and requires practice and skill. A good listener

may also be able to ascertain the real messages from apparently negative statements. For example, the statement: 'There is no possibility of my agreeing at this stage' could reveal the real message: 'Give me a little more time and I might be able to agree.'

Self-Evaluation Activity 10.3

What's the message?

This SEA has no commentary

Identify the real message of the following negative statement:

> *'Your proposals are unacceptable as they stand at the moment.'*

It is also essential to concentrate not only on the verbal message, but also on the way it is said. For example, we can detect how confidently or hesitantly statements are made, whether there are signs of irritation, boredom or impatience, and whether there is an immediate rejection of proposals being made or whether there is willingness to consider them. Cairns (1996), in considering the benefits of good listening skills, argues:

> The constant and conscious practice of listening skills during negotiations can develop them so that you are perceptive but not impressionable; you can take cognisance of what you have heard without being overly influenced; you become sensitive to the implications of what is being said but are not bowled over; and you become discerning and discriminatory about what you hear. This is the mark of the skilled negotiator. The ability to allow counter-arguments to be taken in, set alongside existing convictions and commitments, evaluated and responded to is a skill which must be learned and practised. (p. 98)

Effective listening requires concentration (for example, to sit where the speaker is visible and watch him or her closely), understanding/comprehension (preparing to 'think ahead' of the speaker) and absorption – retaining what has been said (Gennard and Judge, 2002). Practising these skills in face-to-face negotiations will, amongst other things, result in a keener 'questioning' approach being adopted by the parties.

Questioning and probing

During face-to-face negotiations, the parties will have certain objectives designed to probe the other side's position, test their commitment and willingness to move, uncover hidden blockages to progress and assess what reciprocal responses may be necessary. This tactical method of obtaining movement and influencing the outcome is common to all types of negotiation situation. According to Cairns (1996), 'The hypothetical nature of the questions or statements protects either side from being interpreted as having offered a concession' (p. 99). Management may wish to use this method constructively for the following reasons:

- They may not have the authority formally to concede their 'hypothetical' proposition.
- They may wish simply to test the water for a particular proposal.
- They may wish to add conditions before making a further formal offer.

Union negotiators will also find this method useful in probing the other side and in searching for agreement. The questioning/probing method relies heavily on 'what if' types of question, which, if misused 'have been exploited to adjourn negotiations and delay settlements' (Cairns, 1996, p. 99). Examples of 'risk-free', 'without commitment' questions/probes include: 'How would you feel if . . .'; 'Supposing you/we were to . . .'; 'Have you considered . . .'.

Another important aspect of the questioning/probing approach is to ask for information. There are a number of common mistakes which negotiators may make. These include:

- making factually incorrect statements;
- omitting relevant factual information;
- misusing statistics; and
- making statements that are faulty in logic or seem contradictory.

These mistakes should not be challenged directly by making statements such as 'You're wrong', it is better to probe by putting further questions such as: 'Can you explain your thinking about that more fully?', or 'I haven't fully grasped the logic of that: could you put it a different way?', or 'Could you explain the connection between that point and the one you have made earlier about . . . ?'. Faced with questions of this nature, the other party may realise for itself that its argument is flawed, rather than being told directly. As Fowler (1995) points out: 'Exposing flaws tactfully is a powerfully persuasive tool [the lesson being]: *probe the other person's/party's case with shrewd and tactful questioning for flaws of fact and logic*' (p. 26).

Finally, Cairns offers constructive advice to negotiators concerning questioning and probing, as outlined in Exhibit 10.1.

Leadership and interpersonal skills

The term 'leadership' is used here to describe the co-ordinating and influencing roles of principal negotiators. The term 'interpersonal skills' is concerned with handling informal and formal social relationships between the two parties as well as social relationships within the negotiating teams.

Self-Evaluation Activity 10.4

Activities associated with the lead negotiator role
Response on website

A leadership role, which the lead negotiator assumes, is concerned with a number of important activities at all stages of the negotiation process. Identify some of these activities and check your list with that given on the website.

Before considering some of these activities in greater detail, there are some relevant general issues to consider. Firstly, within the bargaining context, the way in which negotiations are handled by both teams (either skilfully or ineptly) can influence the climate of industrial relations within the workplace as well as the negotiation outcomes themselves. This dimension of negotiating skills has become increasingly important as a result of the general trend towards decentralisation of collective bargaining during the 1980s, 1990s and early 2000s (see Chapter 6). In this respect, Cairns (1996) points out:

Decentralisation of negotiations within industry, commerce and the public sector has brought more participants into the negotiation process

Exhibit 10.1

Advice to negotiators

1. You should brief your negotiating team that you are going to use this method and why, otherwise they may wonder what is going on and make damaging interruptions.
2. Do not commit the team members to agreeing something you have floated.
3. If either parties use this technique, be careful not to get 'bounced' into agreeing something. There is no reason for it, other than inexperience. Ask for a break/adjournment to consult others or make a telephone call etc. On the other hand, if you are in a position to respond – do it. If your response is positive it will encourage fluidity. If negative, it will stop management harbouring false hopes.
4. Union negotiators should avoid overplaying the 'we have no mandate or authority from the members to agree/discuss or negotiate this'. It can be used as a feint, but may be taken literally and opportunities may be lost. Equally, overuse can make union negotiators sound weak, not in command of the situation, unable to deliver final agreement, and to make concession-making more hazardous for the other side.
5. If management use this method to float 'conditional' offers, then invariably the condition will come first and the offer second. In doing so, the trick for management is to play down the conditions and play up the value of the concession. Union negotiators have to keep their eye on the ball with such offers. If necessary, split the conditions and the offer and evaluate them separately. If one heavily outweighs the other, there is more negotiating to be done.

Source: Adapted from Cairns, 1996, p. 101

from different backgrounds and with attitudes which inevitably impact upon the quality of negotiations. The development of additional tiers at a European level poses similar problems. When set alongside continuing intense domestic and international competition in the private sector and its transmission of pressures on to resources in the public sector, these issues have called for a reassessment of attitudes of all players in industrial relations negotiations. (p. 12)

We consider these aspects in greater detail later on. Secondly, it is reasonable to assume that members of both negotiating teams know each other fairly well and will therefore be familiar with the attitudes each member has towards the negotiating process. However, it is vitally important that the disposition and attitudes of members of the opposing team are considered, as this will increase the probability of influencing the outcome in a positive and constructive way. We now consider some of the more important leadership and interpersonal skills and activities.

Allocation of roles and tasks

The first task is to determine the size of the negotiating team. Cairns (1996) points out that trade union negotiators often have little choice about either the size or composition of a negotiating team as this is 'laid down constitutionally or forms part of a procedural agreement' (p. 57). However, Fowler (1992) argues that (presumably in the absence of constitutional constraints), 'it is not uncommon for the trade union side to field a sizeable team – a union official, perhaps, supported by a shop stewards' committee' (p. 35). Large teams can cause problems as this can result in greater formality than necessary, can be cumbersome and difficult to control and may lead to conflicting pressures on the lead negotiator. They can 'also lead to problems of confidentiality on negotiating strategy and potentially can make concessions more difficult to obtain' (Cairns, 1996, p. 57). On the other hand, large teams permit greater group representation 'and can lead to a broader base of support when it comes to ratifying the outcome of negotiations' (ibid., p. 57). Torrington *et al.* (2002) suggest that the different stages of negotiation may require different arrangements, and that 'relatively large numbers can be an advantage at the beginning, but are often a hindrance in the later stages' (p. 639). It is not essential that the management team is the same size as the union team as this will pose problems of co-ordination and differing views within the team. In view of the problems concerning too large a size of negotiating team, Fowler (1992) suggests that 'many experienced negotiators express a preference for three members in a team and certainly not more than five' (p. 35), while Cairns (1996) advises that, 'The only general guidance in democratic union organisation over negotiating team size and composition is: as small as possible, and as large as absolutely necessary' (p. 57).

Self-Evaluation Activity 10.5

Identifying negotiator roles
Response on website

The second task is concerned with the allocation of roles. Negotiators need specific roles within their teams. Identify the specific roles for members of each team and compare your list with that which appears on the website.

Co-ordinating activities of the team/handling information and expertise

These skills are extremely important during all stages of negotiation, particularly during the crucial preparatory stage. The 'ground rules' identified by Cairns (1996) for the preparatory stage include the following:

- **Understanding the process**: both negotiating teams must clearly understand all elements of the negotiating process including the nature of the opposing team, procedural arrangements for conducting negotiations and the team's negotiating objectives and priorities.
- **Understanding the roles**: each member of the negotiating team should be absolutely clear about the requirements of the roles they adopt, as described above.

- **Responsibility for speaking**: there should be agreement about who speaks and when. The lead negotiator assumes the responsibility for speaking with no other member of the team contributing unless requested to do so. 'It is bad practice to cut across the lead negotiator. You may inadvertently undermine your own case or bolster the other side. If someone feels strongly enough about something during negotiations, they should indicate to the lead negotiator that they would like to come in by raising their hand, or by passing a note to the lead negotiator, or they may ask for an adjournment in the same way' (ibid., p. 59).
- **Team decision-making**: 'The lead negotiator should secure the agreement of the team with regard to:
  - deciding tactics and strategy
  - deciding adjournments
  - deciding timings of meetings
  - deciding about reporting back to a wider committee or members (in the case of the union team) concerning an offer on the table; an impasse; a need to keep people informed about interim stages of negotiation; new issues introduced by the employer
  - checking and evaluating progress in the negotiation' (ibid., p. 59).

Assessing the other side's case

This should take place throughout the negotiation process, particularly if circumstances change, revised offers or claims are made, and during adjournments. Fowler (1992) identifies a number of salient points:

- Establish what the other party's case is and what they are seeking to achieve.
- Probe whether specific problems or cases lie behind generalised questions, claims or offers.
- Exchange factual data in advance of negotiations if this may helpfully influence the outcome or prevent delay and confusion during negotiation.
- Consider what facts and arguments the other party are likely to use in support of their case.
- Consider the possible existence of a hidden agenda – underlying issues that may influence the conduct and outcome of negotiations.

Resolving intra-group conflict

Conflict between group members, and between the lead negotiator and those he or she represents outside the formal negotiation process is quite common. In defining this activity from a trade union perspective, Cairns (1996) points out:

> *This part of the negotiating process does not form part of the formal negotiations. It takes place outside the particular negotiation – off-stage so to speak. It is a sub-process that can take place within a group, a union, or between unions, between negotiators and their members, or a negotiator and the union hierarchy. It can occur before the real negotiation begins, or be almost a continuous undercurrent shadowing the whole process ... the resolution of intra-group conflict can be decisive in terms of the efficiency and shape of the final negotiated outcome. For that reason the role of the negotiator in this part of the negotiating process is a crucial one.* (p. 24)

The lead negotiator will assume the role of counsellor/adviser to those he or she is representing, and in addition to operating in an informal capacity, may also be required during formal stages of the negotiation process, such as at the stage of the claim or grievance formulation; during adjournments in the negotiating process; during interim report-back stages; and during final settlement recommendation stages.

Similar problems will affect the management team from time to time, although they will be less marked, and if consensus is not achieved, then 'executive authority may decide' (ibid., p. 30).

Information-gathering and handling skills

Information-gathering and handling are important skills throughout the negotiation process. For example, during negotiations new information may be requested and this has to be analysed in relation to existing information and to the progress made so far in achieving negotiating outcomes. However, it is during the preparatory stage of negotiation that information-gathering is most important.

Self-Evaluation Activity 10.6
Pre-negotiation information
Response on website

What types of information do you think would be useful to both management and employee negotiating teams before 'face-to-face' negotiations begin? (Use the example of the annual pay negotiations.) Make a list and check your responses with the information categories provided on the website.

Information needed by the union team

Irrespective of whether the union's claim is based on increases of basic pay rates or total earnings, union negotiators need information that supports the validity of the claim. A claim which cannot be supported by reference to reliable statistical evidence is likely to be rejected by the management team. Union negotiators will therefore take the following criteria into consideration:

- **The cost of living/inflation criterion.** The 'fairness' of a claim will take into account annual changes in the Retail Price Index (RPI) as the basis for a 'living wage'. However, the RPI, and subsequent attempts by government to 'refine' it during the 1980s, can be regarded as only a very general indicator by negotiators and may not reflect the 'effect of inflation on a particular individual's or group's cost of living' (Salamon, 1998, p. 501). The cost of living element of the claim is more likely to be based on price and wage movements over the period since the last pay negotiations (usually 12 months) rather than any future movements, although sensible calculations of price and wage movements over the following 12 months are not precluded from consideration. Union negotiators should, therefore, be mindful of the fact that an underestimation of future inflation rates may put them at a disadvantage during the next pay round as there could be an element of 'catching-up' in order to restore wages for that interim period. Moreover, while some negotiations may provide for indexation in order to make pay increases 'inflation-proof', 'the amount of room left for negotiating "real" wage increases is very limited' (ibid., p. 502).

- **Information on relativities and differentials.** The term differentials is used to describe the extent to which pay levels differ within a single group of employees with differing skill attributes. Negotiators obviously require information which may concern the degree to which skill requirements and attributes have changed, or are likely to change, for example, as a result of work restructuring subsequent to the introduction of new technology. Torrington and Hall (1998) identify two types of relativities, which they term internal and external. Internal relativities exist in most unionised organisations where, for example, non-manual workers are represented by one union (or bargaining agent) and manual workers are represented by one or more other unions. Information concerning external relativities is required by negotiators where groups of workers in one organisation compare themselves with those in other companies, industries and services. Torrington and Hall point out that in the case of public sector pay bargaining:

  > There are large numbers of employees doing apparently similar work with pay scales that are broadly the same in all parts of the country. Every recipient of the pay is likely to make comparisons with friends and neighbours who are better off, or who seem to be better off. Public sector employees are extensively unionised and union research departments prepare detailed analyses of comparative pay rates, again picking those comparators that produce comparisons most favourable to their own cause. Any pay claim always has some comparator, as this is what gives it credibility. (p. 602)

Most organisations, as Salamon (1998) points out, conduct regular pay surveys that attempt to compare wages and salaries of their own employees with those in other companies with whom they are in competition. There are, however a number of problems with comparability information, apart from the obvious one of comparing 'like with like' in relation to jobs. Firstly, different organisations will have different approaches towards the organisation of production, work arrangements and flexibility issues which makes it difficult to compare jobs unless based on some form of job

evaluation. Secondly, pay should not be considered in isolation as the 'wage-work' bargain includes holidays, overtime and other earnings, fringe benefits, holidays and even pensions. Straight comparability with pay may ignore the 'trade-off' value of these other elements during negotiations. Much of the data concerning comparability can be obtained by union negotiators from their own trade unions. The larger unions in particular (such as UNISON and the TGWU) produce sophisticated analyses of wage movements in the industries and sectors where they have representation. The significance of comparability in determining pay claims has been emphasised by Mathieson (2000) who argues that, when linked to perceptions of 'fair pay', it may result in employee frustration or even industrial action (p. 182). However, perceptions of fair pay, being subjective and emotively-oriented, do not in themselves constitute an appropriate basis for devising, let alone pursuing, a pay claim.

- **Information concerning the 'going rate'.** Similar to the comparability argument, 'the comparison is made with the level of settlement achieved in recent negotiations either in the industry or more generally' (Salamon, 1998, p. 503). Information about this more general level of settlement, which often encompasses the industry as a whole, may be used by negotiators either as a substitute for more specific comparators, or as supplementary to that more detailed information.
- **Any other information** which the company will possess and which is considered necessary to assist the union team in the negotiating process (see section below dealing with disclosure of information).

Information required by the management negotiating team

Management may be seen to hold the 'trump card' as much information is internal to the organisation, and sensitive data and information concerning strategic decisions may be withheld unless required to be divulged by the disclosure requirements (see below). A major theme in a company's response to a union pay claim will be the 'ability to pay' having regard to past performance, current and future market trends and cost structures. Management's use of information needs to be carefully considered. For example, in difficult trading periods there is a clear requirement to stress the seriousness of the situation and point out the implications of cost burdens and the need to contain them, using the 'inability to pay' or 'inability to pay much' argument. If in poor years an inability to pay has been the theme, the 'ability' argument cannot be readily discarded when trading conditions turn round. On the other hand, a structuring of expectations by the use of a cautious approach during favourable times will help to create a more realistic scene for 'face-to-face' negotiations.

Great care needs to be taken to avoid a situation where, on the one hand, employees and their representatives are told of trading difficulties, thereby lowering expectations, while on the other hand, through external publicity, another rosier picture emerges designed to impress the public and keep up the share price. Any situation along these lines not only weakens the power of company negotiators to achieve a settlement but also throws into question the company's integrity in its relations with employees. There are both internal and external sources of information which the management team should have access to:

- **Internal management information.** Apart from information which a company might be requested, indeed required, to disclose to an independent recognised union for the purposes of collective bargaining, there is a range of basic items on which the management team should inform itself. Ideally, the system should be in place so that the information can be brought to bear on the proposed company response to a pay and conditions claim. Experience suggests, however, that many companies get into negotiation without fully recognising the way they are operating in the human resources field. The objective for the company and the management team is to have information available to meet any point the union team throws up in negotiation. This does not mean that the information has to be disclosed: it does mean that the union team's point can be dealt with on the basis of a full understanding. Basic information includes:
  - profitability which affects the 'ability to pay';
  - the total number of employees the company should employ, that is, the authorised complement as compared with the number of employees actually in post. If the former exceeds the latter then the company could be open to a productivity claim;

- structure and composition of the workforce including distribution by age, length of service, gender, ethnic origin of the company as a whole and by department;
  - wastage, recruitment, labour turnover and absenteeism;
  - payroll information to include levels of earnings by grade, department and individuals; incidence of overtime; comparison of base rates with overtime by grade, department and individual; control and allocation of overtime; union influence on overtime working; levels of allowances according to grade, department and individual;
  - investment, sales and general market position including current orders and new/future orders;
  - costings on pay rates and allowances including any proposed changes to rates, increments, allowances, bonuses and overtime.

- **External management team information.** Access to many of these sources are common to both management and union teams such as current movements in the RPI and related indexes and comparisons with similar employers regarding terms and conditions of service. Data from local pay and salary surveys of importance in local pay bargaining is usually collected and shared by many organisations. Of particular importance is information from employers' associations concerning the various types of agreement that exist within a particular industry. Associations also have data on the size of pay settlements recorded by member companies. Gennard and Judge (1997) point out that as many employer associations are also trade associations they have a wide variety of supplementary information concerning sales figures, import and export trends and unit labour costs.

Sources of information common to both parties

Both parties have access to a number of industrial relations and labour market sources. Gennard and Judge (1997) identify the following:

1. Industrial Relations Services (IRS) (formerly Industrial Relations Review and Report). This bi-monthly comprehensive publication contains data on employment trends and company

employment policies and practices 'which reviews trends in the general level of pay settlement and reports on pay deals concluded in private and public organisations as well as those involving a whole industry' (ibid., p. 227). There is also information on changes in the RPI and other indexes and on other bargaining statistics such as inflation, average earnings, productivity and labour costs, hours worked and employment and unemployment data. IRS also publishes a monthly pay updating service, which 'is the only regularly published source of pay statistics independent of employers, trade unions and the UK government' (ibid., p. 227). A related publication from the same stable is the *European Industrial Relations Review* which contains a comprehensive amount of information and data concerning developments within the European Union, which is particularly useful for negotiators in companies which have both outlets in the EU and European Works Councils.

2. The twice monthly report of Incomes Data Services Ltd (IDS) records changes to pay and conditions agreed at company and industry level in some detail and its *Pay Directory*, published three times a year, contains information on wage rates, holidays and shift premiums within a range of occupations across a variety of companies.

3. *Labour Market Trends* (LMT) is a monthly government publication, which includes information on most aspects of the national and regional labour markets and by industry sector concerning employment, unemployment, earnings and industrial disputes.

4. Another government publication, the *New Earnings Survey* 'is the most comprehensive source of earnings information in Great Britain' (ibid., p. 228). It surveys 1 per cent of employees in many different organisations and produces data on earnings and hours worked analysed by industry, occupation, age, region and collective agreement.

Disclosure of information

It is generally accepted that if negotiations are to be effective in achieving the aims of both parties it is both necessary and good practice for management to disclose relevant information to employee representatives concerning company activities, strategies and policies. Both the TUC and CBI have argued for disclosure. From a trade union perspective, financial information about the company's market position and prospects would be extremely useful as this would determine to some extent management's 'ability to pay' argument. As early as 1972, the TUC argued for disclosure on matters dealing with:

> *General ownership and organisational structure; manpower and personnel information; financial information covering sales, costs, incomes, 'performance indicators' and the value of the company's assets; prospects and plans including information on investment, sales and manpower.*
> (Farnham and Pimlott, 1995, p. 393)

The CBI has argued that disclosure is advisable in certain circumstances where if disclosure of information were withheld this would result in a deterioration in industrial relations. Possible areas for disclosure that the CBI recommends include information on how the company is organised, company financial information such as turnover, profits, dividends and directors' pay, and an account of the company's competitive situation and levels of productivity. Other areas include future plans for the company, information on policies concerning pay and conditions of employment and staffing matters.

Self-Evaluation Activity 10.7

Arguments against disclosure
Response on website

Given the weight of the argument for disclosure which the TUC and the CBI support (the latter to varying degrees), can you think of possible arguments against disclosure, and if so, what might they be?

The legislative requirements concerning disclosure of information were contained in the Employment Protection Act 1975 and incorporated into the Trade Union and Labour Relations (Consolidation) Act 1992, which contains a procedure enabling independent trade unions to obtain certain information from employers for the purposes of collective bargaining. The grounds for disclosure are that a trade union would be otherwise impeded in the conduct of bargaining and that disclosure would be in the interests of maintaining good industrial relations. The Act, however, specifically excludes the disclosure of certain types of information which:

- would be against the interests of national security to disclose;
- has been communicated to the employer in confidence;
- concerns an individual unless that individual has consented to disclosure;
- would cause substantial harm to the company for reasons other than its effect on collective bargaining; and
- has been obtained by the company for reasons of litigation.

In addition, with regard to the method of disclosure the employer cannot be required to produce, allow inspection of or copy any document or produce information that would incur an unreasonable amount of work or effort. Furthermore, Salamon (1998) points out that:

The onus is on the trade union representatives to ask for the information they require rather than on management to provide it automatically, and they must also know the manner in which management collects this information. [In addition] the amount of information that might legally be requested depends on the extent to which issues within the organisation are subject to joint regulation through collective bargaining; management is under no legal obligation to disclose information in respect of those issues which are simply a matter of joint consultation (except redundancy). Consequently as management withdraws elements from the scope of collective bargaining (for example, individualising pay) so it restricts the information that a union may demand. (p. 319)

ACAS issued a code of practice on disclosure of information to trade unions for bargaining purposes as early as 1977. The code provided practical advice to employers and trade unions on disclosure of information which would 'be in accordance with good industrial relations to disclose' and without which a trade union would be put in a disadvantageous position in a bargaining situation. It also recommended disclosure of information concerning pay and benefits, conditions of service, staffing, company performance and financial matters. The EU Information and Consultation Directive which was adopted in 2002 will require all employers with 50 or more staff to inform and consult with employees on any developments relating to the financial situation, structure and employment of staff. Its implementation in the UK is being phased in by 2008, and is likely to assist unions and employees in making more accurate assessments of what the employer can afford, and in what circumstances (Dix and Oxenbridge, 2003).

Summary points

- Although used interchangeably, the term 'bargaining' and 'negotiation' differ in that collective bargaining is but one of a number of different forms of negotiation.
- The 'desirable' outcome of any negotiation process should be compromise through both parties establishing common ground and persuading each other of the validity of their arguments.
- The different types of negotiation situations include grievance-handling, negotiation between members of management, bargaining and joint problem-solving.
- The negotiation process comprises several stages common to all types of negotiation and includes:
  - planning;
  - preparation;
  - face-to-face negotiation;
  - closing negotiations; and
  - writing-up and implementing the agreement.
- The most important skills required within the negotiation process include:
  - persuasion and influence;
  - information-gathering and analysis;
  - presentational skills;
  - judgemental skills;
  - note-taking and summarising;
  - listening and observing;
  - questioning and probing;
  - interpersonal and interviewing; and
  - awareness of body language.
- Leadership skills are of particular importance as they mainly concern the relationship between principal or lead negotiator and the other members

of the negotiating teams. The following activities are identified with the role of the lead negotiator:
- handling personal and working relationships within the negotiating team;
- allocation of roles and tasks to individual team members;
- co-ordinating activities of team members;
- handling information and expertise within the team;
- resolving any intra-group conflict;
- assessing the other side's case; and
- responsibilities for different aspects of the negotiation process.
- Information-gathering and handling skills are crucial to preparation, and good preparation is crucial to success. In a collective bargaining negotiation context concerning pay, for example, the union team will need information concerning:
  - cost of living and inflation;
  - pay comparabilities;
  - the 'going rate'; and
  - miscellaneous information relevant to pay negotiations.
The management team will require information concerning:
  - profitability;
  - structure and composition of the workforce;
  - labour turnover and absenteeism;
  - payroll information (including overtime and bonuses); and
  - investment, sales and market conditions and position.

THE BARGAINING CONTEXT

In the previous sections we have focused more generally upon negotiation as an 'umbrella' term which includes grievance-handling and bargaining. Bargaining between unions and management, irrespective of the level at which it takes place, is therefore one of several forms of negotiation (Gennard and Judge, 1997). This section concentrates upon the bargaining context and deals, firstly, with the nature of the power relationship in bargaining and the psychology of bargaining. We then concentrate on the bargaining encounter itself, identifying important factors which bargainers need to take into consideration in order to ensure a successful outcome. Before we look at these issues, however, we need to examine briefly what bargaining actually entails. Gennard and Judge define bargaining in the following way:

> Bargaining is one of a number of different forms of negotiation . . . defined as . . . the coming together of two parties to make an agreement by purposeful persuasion and constructive compromise. It is in a bargaining situation that the buyers and sellers of labour services are in their more adversarial relationship because their representatives are seeking to protect and advance the economic interests of their constituents. Bargaining is a situation in which the parties involved have a 'shopping list' of demands of each other. (p. 222)

Self-Evaluation Activity 10.8
Items to include in the 'shopping list'
Response on website

If you refer back to Chapter 6 in relation to collective bargaining, you should be able to distinguish between substantive and procedural aspects of collective bargaining and agreements. In a bargaining encounter, the 'shopping list' referred to by Gennard and Judge (1997) could include both substantive and procedural issues. If you were a union team bargainer, what items would you include in your shopping list?

Those items dealing with equal opportunities, harassment and bullying, and consultation on redundancies are procedural issues while the others are substantive. The management team will have a 'shopping list' as well, and may well include items such as:

- improvements to the efficiency of working arrangements;
- changes to shift-working patterns;
- increases in flexible working arrangements;
- an increase in the pay differential between skilled and non-skilled workers;
- an end to overtime payments; and
- additional costs arising from the current pay settlement to be recouped by efficiency and productivity improvements.

The 'shopping list' examples given above are fairly comprehensive, and it is most unlikely that all issues would be resolved in one bargaining session on a 'once a year' basis. As we have seen in Chapter 6, the range of issues subject to bargaining depends upon the nature of the bargaining relationship itself. If the bargaining relationship is conjunctive/distributive, then bargaining will be focused on one or two issues such as pay and working conditions often under adversarial conditions. Assuming the bargaining relationship is co-operative/integrative, the greater the number of issues that can be subject to bargaining throughout the year. Both types of bargaining relationship will involve both parties 'trading items in their respective shopping lists ... bargaining is about trading with the other party and not about conceding to the other party' (Gennard and Judge, 2002, p. 316).

Power relationships and the psychology of bargaining

We considered bargaining power as part of the institutional process and machinery of collective bargaining in Chapter 6. The relative power position of the parties to negotiation is a most important contextual factor. There are two aspects of the power relationship to consider: the first is the 'actual power' which the parties have; and the second is the perceptions of power held by each party. These two aspects of the power relationship are now considered in more detail.

'Actual' power

Walton and McKersie (1965) identify significant contextual factors which determine the extent of the power relationship between the parties and argue that there is a direct relationship between the power position of the parties, the threat of industrial action and the potential losses incurred by each party as a result of that action.

State of the economy
Economic conditions within specific industries will have an important bearing upon the relative power of the parties. Unions, for example, may enjoy a power advantage during 'good times' of relative prosperity.

Economic and market structure of the company
Bargaining power will reflect the parties' ability to sustain losses during strike action. Walton and McKersie argue that losses sustained through strike action depend upon the 'economic characteristics' of a company. If the company is highly integrated, losses to management will be higher than in a company with decentralised units where only one plant or workplace may be affected.

The nature of the technology
In industries that operate continuous process technologies, it may be possible for supervisors and managers to continue operations in the event of industrial action. In other industries, such as transport, the impact of such action is much greater.

Labour market structure
The structure of the labour market affects the power position of the union in that 'all the forces that influence the degree of attachment of an individual to a given employer also affect his ability to minimise strike costs' (ibid., p. 35).

Collective bargaining structure
A union negotiator may be in a favourable power position 'when he brings the resources of a large union to bear on a small company' (ibid., p. 35). Conversely, a management negotiator enjoys a power advantage when representing a large company bargaining with a small union.

In addition, the potential which exists for trade unions acting collectively to cause economic 'hurt' to the employer depends upon such factors as the elasticity of supply and demand for the product or service; the employer's market position; the length of the employer's production or service run and the availability of alternative labour or production. During the 1960s and 1970s these factors were much more to the fore than they were in the 1980s, 1990s and early 2000s for reasons we have explained in previous chapters. Another important factor affecting actual power relationships between the parties is 'public opinion'. Public opinion of itself does not guarantee the outcome of negotiations either for management or union, but in high profile and media-exposed situations it can bolster either case in the event of breakdown of negotiations, as Cairns (1996) explains:

> *Negotiations are not news, breakdowns are. Union negotiators then have to be prepared to explain to the public what they are asking for, how eminently reasonable and justified their members are in asking for it, and how they are not responsible for the breakdown and are willing to return to the negotiating table at any time. Shaping public opinion in this way serves four purposes: it helps to offset or neutralise adverse opinion or propaganda from other sources; it can bring pressure on the other side; it can bolster the commitment and morale of your own members; it can temper or neutralise opposition of 'silent partners' in a dispute.* (pp. 44–5)

Other factors that we have already considered which influence the actual power position of the parties include the power of argument and persuasion, and access to and use of information for the purposes of influencing the outcome(s) of negotiation.

'Perceived' power

The actual power of the parties is reinforced by the perceptions each party has of its own power vis-à-vis that of the other party. Both management and union teams will subjectively evaluate the costs and benefits, advantages and disadvantages to either of agreeing or not agreeing to each other's demands. For example, if the management team believes that the costs to the union and employees of not agreeing to its offer outweigh the costs to the union of agreeing to its offer, the management team has a perceived bargaining advantage over the union team – and vice versa. Costs are difficult to quantify, and Salamon (1998) points out that:

> *In addition to assessing the potential financial cost to union and employees of undertaking industrial action to secure an improved offer, management must also 'cost' such items as failure of the union negotiators to meet their members' expectations and their desire to maintain credibility with their members. It is possible, on this basis, for both sides to enter a negotiation with a perceived bargaining advantage over the other. These*

> *initial perceptions of bargaining advantage, and therefore the perceived relative bargaining power, will be refined during the course of the negotiations as more information regarding the objectives and strategies of both parties becomes available.* (p. 474)

The psychology of bargaining

Apart from perceptions of power, an important and related psychological process underscoring the bargaining relationship between the two parties is known as attitudinal structuring, which Walton and McKersie (1965) argue is the 'third result of the negotiation process' (p. 184), the other two results being the gains and concessions made by the two parties and the resolution of joint problems and integration of the interests of the parties. Attitudinal structuring is defined as '**a maintenance or restructuring of the attitudes of the parties towards each other which, taken together, define the relationship between them**' (adapted from ibid., p. 184). Walton and McKersie identify what they call four attitudinal dimensions which are:

1. **Motivational orientation and action tendencies** of each party towards the other. This is the most general category and can be subdivided as follows:
   - *Competitive orientation* where each party is motivated to defeat or win over the other and to maximise relative advantage over the other party; this is associated with the conflict/containment-aggression relationship patterns (see below).
   - *Individualistic orientation* where the parties pursue their own self-interests without wanting to help or hinder each other; this is associated with the accommodation relationship pattern (see below).
   - *Co-operative orientation* where each party is concerned about the other's welfare in addition to its own; this is associated with the co-operation and collusion relationship patterns (see below).
2. Beliefs about the other's **legitimacy**.
3. Feelings of **trust** toward the other party.
4. Feelings of **friendliness-hostility** toward the other party.

Walton and McKersie (1965) then go on to identify five patterns of relationship which stem from these attitudinal dimensions:

1. **Conflict:** This is characterised by a denial of the legitimacy of the other party's ends and means, where management deals with the union(s) only as a last resort. In this situation of extreme distrust and intense disliking of each other, the parties have no concern for each other's internal affairs and 'might be inclined to destroy the other organisation' (p. 186).

2. **Containment-aggression:** This is characterised by grudging acceptance of the other party with a competitive orientation where 'the union is determined to extend its scope of influence, and the company is insistent on containing the union's scope of action' (p. 186). There is little respect for each other and much suspicion and mutual antagonism concerning each other's motives. Negotiation tends to be confined to wages, hours and working conditions.

3. **Accommodation:** Here, the parties are *individualistic* in their orientation and recognise the legitimacy of the other's means and ends. Both parties accept the status quo and there is therefore no motivation to change the bargaining agenda in a situation where both have adjusted to each other and 'have evolved routines for performing functions and settling differences' (p. 187). There is a certain degree of mutual respect and little competition for allegiance of employees. Even so, the relationship is one of limited trust where the parties 'go about their business, interacting in a courteous but informal manner' (p. 188).

4. **Co-operation:** This is where the motivational orientation is co-operative and where there is complete acceptance of the legitimacy of the other party. The model of bargaining is described as *integrative* (Walton and McKersie, 1965) or *co-operative* (Chamberlain and Kuhn, 1965) – see Chapter 6. The range of issues subject to negotiation extends beyond pay, hours and working conditions to include other areas of common interest such as productive efficiency, financial concerns, employment security, technological and other work-related change, and so on. There is full mutual respect, trust and 'a friendly attitude between the parties generally' (Walton and McKersie, 1965, p. 188).

5. **Collusion:** Here, the parties form a coalition in which they pursue common ends which may be 'illegitimate'. 'For example, the parties may collude and agree to irresponsibly high wages in a product market which allows the employer to pass on the full cost to the consumer' (ibid., p. 188).

Figure 10.4 summarises the association between attitudinal dimensions and the patterns of relationship identified by Walton and McKersie.

These relationships and the attitudes which define them have implications for the parties and their joint dealings. Consequently, a party's preference for a particular relationship pattern may become an important objective of that party. Some of the above relationship patterns, such as accommodation, may be seen to be more appropriate as a goal than others, such as conflict, but sometimes a party will actually prefer a more conflictual pattern, perhaps for purposes of preserving internal cohesion. Three basic models of negotiating behaviour based upon the above framework are now considered.

Models of negotiating behaviour

Most models tend to assume that relationship patterns exhibit varying degrees of containment/aggression, accommodation or co-operation and may not necessarily reflect the complexities of a 'real life' bargaining encounter. Their use, however, lies in demonstrating what options are open to the parties, and the behaviour the parties adopt in order to achieve their ends. It is important to note that much of bargaining behaviour is ritualistic, defined as 'a behaviour which the parties feel obliged to carry out even though they are fully aware that such behaviour is for the benefit of their constituents and the other party is not taken in by it' (Gennard and Judge, 1997, p. 152). The bargaining ritual serves two main purposes. Firstly, for the union, the claim and the method by which it pursues the claim through negotiation must be seen as credible by the membership. This may mean portraying the opposition as intransigent and unreasonable in order to gain membership approval of bargaining objectives. Similarly, management, in order to legitimise its bargaining role in relation to its constituents will react appropriately to the union's offer 'when it publicly expresses "surprise and disappointment" at the union's claim'

Attitudinal dimensions	Pattern of relationship				
	Conflict	*Containment-aggression*	*Accommodation*	*Co-operation*	*Collusion*
Motivational orientation and action tendencies toward other	Competitive tendencies to destroy or weaken		Individualistic policy of 'hands off'	Co-operative tendencies to assist or preserve	
Beliefs about legitimacy of other	Denial of legitimacy	Grudging acknowledgement	Acceptance of 'status quo'	Complete legitimacy	N/A
Level of trust in conducting affairs	Extreme distrust	Distrust	Limited trust	Extended trust	Trust based on mutual blackmail
Degree of friendliness	Hate	Antagonism	Neutralism-courteousness	Friendliness	Intimacy – 'sweetheart relationship'

Figure 10.4 Association between attitudinal dimensions and relationship patterns within the bargaining context

Source: Walton and McKersie, 1965, p. 189

(ibid., p. 152). The reality, of course is that negotiations will, in all probability, be conducted amicably in the search for a compromise solution. Secondly, there may be an expectation on the part of both parties' constituents that the negotiations should last a minimum length of time (albeit unspecified) in order to safeguard their respective economic interests. Gennard and Judge point out that:

> *If an agreement is made relatively quickly, the management negotiators are likely to be accused by their colleagues of having made unnecessary trading concessions or of trading before it was necessary to do so. Union negotiators would face the same accusations from their members with the added danger that where wage agreements have to be accepted by the members in a ballot, the members may reject the proposed agreement perhaps despite its being highly beneficial. When this happens, the two sides have to return to the bargaining table for a period of time which reassures their constituents that their economic interests have been properly protected. The reopening of negotiations often brings only marginal amendments to the original deal rejected by the party's constituents. However, the deal is then accepted and praise is showered on their respective negotiators by the employer and employees.* (p. 153)

The ritualistic element of bargaining is normally present in the 'build-up' to the formulation and presentation of the union claim and is implicit in the three models of negotiating behaviour we now briefly consider.

The Warr model

This simple model is provided by Peter Warr (1973). The scenario is one where the union negotiating team demands an increase on basic pay rates of 5 per cent. The management team responds with an offer of 1 per cent, and they eventually settle at 3 per cent. Relevant factors include the following:

- Each team has a bargaining range. For management, this may extend from 1 per cent to 3.5 per cent. For the union team, the range is 2.5 per cent to 5 per cent.
- Within each team's bargaining range, there is a minimum point of resistance (as far as each will

go) and an ideally obtainable target (which may be around 4 per cent for the union team and 1.5 per cent for the management team).
- As the parties rarely or ever get what they ask for in a distributive bargaining situation, negotiators are likely to add something to their target when making the first demand, which Warr terms the demand point.

Figure 10.5 represents the model diagrammatically.

The bargaining range, which is between the demand and resistance points, also contains the target point. Each party know that the initial demand will not succeed (this is part of the bargaining ritual) and that its target may not be achieved. But although some movement away from the target may be required, there are naturally points beyond which each party will concede no more. These are the resistance points – as low as the union team will go and as high as the management team will go before each finally digs its heels in. So, in many cases the settlement range (within which the agreement will be reached) is between the two resistance points.

How, then, do the parties set their resistance, target and demand points; how do they discover the level of their opponent's points, and how do they persuade and coerce each other until agreement is reached? Warr suggests that this is done by:

- information-gathering by both parties (we have already looked at this aspect); and
- learning about the opponent in terms of how important the other party perceives the issues to be.

There is a related need to estimate the cost and consequences of not yielding as far as the other's resistance point – the minimum acceptable settlement and when a breakdown in negotiations or a strike is a preferred option for the management team rather than yielding to the union 'bottom-line' demand. Warr goes on to stress that:

> *All of this is complicated by the fact that the requirements and costs change as negotiations develop. It is quite customary for target points to be raised or new issues to be introduced as negotiations proceed and original demands are not met. This comes about partly because the necessary detailed study of the situation under discussion leads to discovering new points of conflict, but particularly because of negotiators'*

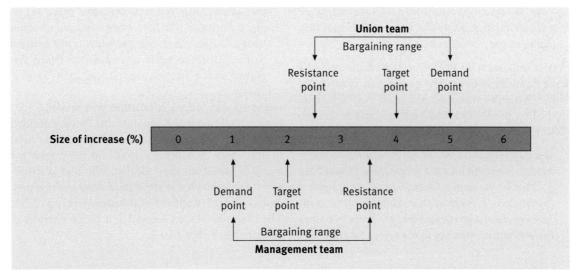

Figure 10.5 Warr's distributive bargaining model
Source: Warr, 1973, p. 21

increasing emotional investment in the negotiations and the increasing costs (in terms of money and of respect from others) that an unsatisfactory outcome would involve. Furthermore, as the conflict progresses so may group cohesiveness and aggressiveness develop to a point where the initial demands seem to group members to have been paltry ones. (p. 24)

When each party has a clear idea of the other's target and resistance points, the bargaining process then becomes one of *mutual persuasion* and *attitude change*.

The Magenau and Pruitt model

The model proposed by Magenau and Pruitt (1979) contains three basic elements:

- The **motivation** of the negotiating teams to maintain a **demand** (MD).
- The **motivation** of the negotiating teams to reach an **agreement** (MA).
- The **level of trust** between the negotiators.

The main assumptions concerning negotiating behaviour are:

1. That the strength of either party's motivation to maintain a demand is determined by:
   (a) the parties' perception of their relative bargaining power; and

   (b) the extent to which the parties themselves wish to achieve the demand.
2. That the strength of either party's motivation to reach an agreement is determined by:
   (a) the parties' perception of the value of the agreement to themselves; and
   (b) the urgency by which both parties seek an agreement.
3. 'It is the balance between these two motivations, related to the level of trust between the negotiators, which produces different negotiating behaviour' (Salamon, 1998, p. 475).

The main propositions stemming from these assumptions are:

If the motivation to maintain a demand clearly exceeds the motivation to reach an agreement, expressed as MD > MA, the outcome is likely to be a situation where either one party coerces the other or both parties coerce each other, with threat or use of industrial action a clear prospect. This is a characteristic feature of distributive bargaining behaviour.

If the motivation to reach an agreement clearly exceeds the motivation to maintain a demand, expressed as MA > MD, the outcome is likely to be a situation where concessions are made by both parties. This is a characteristic feature of co-operative bargaining behaviour. Even in this case, the threat of industrial sanctions cannot be excluded, particularly if a low trust relationship between the parties exists.

It is important to note that both high and low trust relations between the parties can exist in the above instances, although low trust may dominate in the first proposition and high trust in the second. Salamon also suggests that:

It is in the middle area, where motivation to maintain the demand and the motivation to reach an agreement are approximately equal, that neither distributive behaviour nor simple concession-making seems appropriate, and the bargainer takes co-ordinative initiatives to the extent that he trusts

the other. Most negotiations take place in, or move towards, this centre area and are medium trust relationships. Consequently it is not unusual to find all three types of behaviour being displayed within a single negotiation. (p. 475)

Gennard and Judge's aspiration grid model

Both management and union teams, having decided upon their negotiating aims and objectives, need to anticipate each other's aims and objectives 'for example, what do they idealistically and realistically want, and what is the minimum for which they would settle?' (Gennard and Judge, 1997, p. 229). The example which Gennard and Judge provides is described in Exhibit 10.2.

Exhibit 10.2

Aspiration grid example

As in a grievance-handling situation, the management bargaining team can now construct an aspiration grid which sets out the parameters for the expected outcome of the negotiations (see Table 10.1). The grid shows that ideally management would like to trade no items with the employees. However, it knows this is unrealistic and has established a realistic position of wishing to trade increases in pay and childcare facilities for changes in working practices and tightening of the conditions surrounding the sick-pay scheme. Management's fall-back position is to improve its pay offer, to provide childcare facilities and reduce the restrictions surrounding the sick-pay scheme in return for obtaining changes in working practices. The bottom line for the management negotiating team is to trade pay, childcare facilities and aspects of the sick-pay scheme in return for no change in holidays and working hours but alterations in working practices.

The aspiration grid shows what management expects are the negotiating objectives of its employees' representatives. It expects ideally the employees' representatives will want to change every item on the list. Management knows that the employees' representatives will view this as unrealistic. The grid therefore shows that the management expects the employees' realistic position to be one of seeking a deal around increases in pay and childcare facilities, and lesser restrictions on the sick-pay scheme in return for no changes in holidays and working hours and some changes to existing working practices. The grid shows that management anticipates that the bottom line for the employees' representatives is likely to be to trade increases in pay and childcare facilities in return for no changes in holidays and hours of work but acceptance of management's desire for changes in working practices and in the details of the sick-pay scheme.

The grid shows that there is a basis for agreement between the parties. This is indicated in that the fall-back positions of the two parties do not have two Xs against the same issue. Management is not prepared to trade holidays, working hours and changes in working practices, but anticipates the employees' representatives are prepared to trade these issues. The employees are expecting management not to be prepared to concede some pay increases and increased child facilities. However, management has evaluated that it can live with trading these issues. The management negotiating team now has a structure of how the bargaining can be expected to develop and evolve. In the face-to-face sessions with the employees' representatives it will have to pass information to them on what issues management is prepared to trade and at the same time seek to gain information from the employees' side which confirms management's expectations of what employees are prepared to trade.

Table 10.1 Aspiration grid model of bargaining

Possible resolution to grievance	Management			Union		
	Ideal	Real	Fall-back	Fall-back	Real	Ideal
Increased holidays	X	X	X	0	0	X
Reduced working week	X	X	X	0	0	X
Increased pay	X	0	0	X	X	X
Improved childcare facilities	X	0	0	X	X	X
Greater task flexibility	X	X	X	0	0	X
Tightening sick-pay scheme	X	X	0	0	X	X

Source: Gennard and Judge, 1997, p. 230

Tips for negotiators in the bargaining context

Here we consider what union and management team negotiators should do and what they should be aware of during the various stages of negotiation that we identified earlier in the chapter.

Planning and preparation stage

Selection of negotiating team members
We considered this aspect earlier in the chapter.

Assessment of bargaining strengths and weaknesses
You will find the material dealing with power and attitudinal structuring earlier in this section useful.

Information-gathering and the bargaining agenda or 'shopping list'
This has already been dealt with earlier in the chapter.

Establishment of bargaining aims
You can use any or all of the three models considered above.

Planning tactics and strategy for face-to-face negotiations
This is essential if both parties are to achieve their aims: 'Failure to prepare is preparing to fail' (Gennard and Judge, 2002, p. 321).

Other pre-negotiation business
A reasonable assumption to make is that management, usually through the personnel department, has a reasonable working relationship with shop stewards provided there is mutual trust and respect and, in the pre-negotiation period, stewards may volunteer a view about what they expect by way of settlement – which could be construed as a 'softening-up' exercise. In addition, it is important for management to assess the mood of the union membership.

Criteria for the good conduct of negotiations

These are 'normative' criteria, or conventions, stressing what 'ought' to take place rather than what actually does take place. Nevertheless, adherence to these criteria will result in 'best practice' for both negotiating teams.

Equality between the parties
Although each party has powers, perceived or actual, which are important factors in shaping the outcome of negotiation, both parties at the negotiating table nevertheless have equality in the context of the right to put arguments and claims and to have them dealt with fairly.

Negotiation in good faith
Both parties have to be genuine in what is being put forward. Nothing must be deliberately hidden behind the proposals which have been tabled, and the parties must mean what they say.

No splitting the union

In negotiation, speaking is done party to party. Neither management nor union negotiators should exploit any actual or potential divisions in either team. If, for example, management were successful in exploiting divisions in the union team in order to get the union into disarray and extract a 'good' settlement from the ruins it does not follow that the membership will accept the settlement.

No reference to informal discussions

Where lead negotiators of both teams have built up mutual confidence and trust, informal talks often take place between them before and during formal negotiation. This process of 'sounding out' can be of great importance in sensing where a settlement might lie. Informal contacts of this kind must be handled with great care, sensitivity and confidentiality. What must never be said is that 'what is now put forward is on the basis of my informal talk with X who indicates that it will lead to a settlement'. This will destroy any goodwill and rupture the whole negotiation process. The correct way is to table the points as if they were new and the result of formal consideration of current business.

No withdrawal of offers

The convention is that once an offer has been tabled then it is done in good faith and, unless some condition is attached to it, it is an open offer, is on the table and cannot be withdrawn. The same principle applies to any modification of any claim. Negotiation can therefore be likened to a ratchet movement. Once matters have been moved on, there is no going back and the new position provides the basis for resumed discussion. The only exception to this principle is when a condition is attached. For example: 'We are prepared to increase the offer from y per cent to y per cent plus 2 per cent provided you agree the [specified] productivity proposal.' If no agreement is forthcoming, then the offer remains at y per cent. In the unusual circumstance of the union team insisting on adding items to a claim, their having given an earlier assurance that what they had tabled was the totality of the claim, it would not be unreasonable for the management team to say that all existing offers were off the table. Negotiations would then have to start again.

Use of procedure not sanctions

The parties agree to take neither industrial action nor lockout until the disputes procedure has been exhausted. This does not mean that from the union's perspective no threats of industrial action can be made. If a union is sure of its strength through its assessment of the membership mood, then threatening industrial action can be a negotiating ploy.

No propaganda while negotiations continue

In negotiations, nothing is clear until agreement has been reached. As part of the bargaining ritual, the parties may have exaggerated and unrealistic claims and proposals. However, for the negotiating teams it is important that during face-to-face negotiations the negotiators keep the business to themselves. In practical terms, and usually over an adjournment period of a few days, the union team may well take soundings from the membership. If the offer from the management team so far is 'down the wrong road', the union team will arm itself with a membership view, and the management team would be well advised to take this fully into account. Similarly, the management team should not attempt to 'sell' the deal direct to employees, as this will be regarded by the union as exerting undue and unfair pressure.

Maintenance of credibility

Although most agreements represent improvements and are the result of 'trading' issues which neither side necessarily regard as satisfactory, some negotiating outcomes may be weighted heavily in favour of one party or the other. If management come out of it badly due to poor preparation, inept handling or for any other reason, the union may or may not make capital out of it to the detriment of the company. The convention is not to act so as to destroy the credibility of one party or the other, and this responsibility lies particularly heavily upon management. For example, after an unsuccessful strike and union capitulation concerning its claim, there is a temptation to 'take it out on the union and their negotiators'. In this type of situation, the convention requires management to rebuild the situation and maintain a good working relationship with the union and its representatives. It is a sound approach always to give the other party a face-saving way out of any untenable position.

Implementation of agreements

Agreements must be put into operation as agreed. Any significant agreement should be put into writing and each clause examined to ensure clarity and unambiguity.

Face-to-face negotiations

Prior to face-to-face negotiations, both union and management teams will have refined claims and responses to them. The management team may require that the claim(s) be notified in writing and subsequently request clarification of the claim from the union team. Ideally, the management team would need to satisfy itself as to what items of the claim the union team attach importance to, and what items, if any, can be dropped. Similarly, the union team needs to satisfy itself that the claim is based on adequate information concerning the company's activities and market position. The management team's first offer is derived from the analysis of the union claim based on costings of items within the claim and the priorities concerning items within the claim. The company offer may be put forward on the basis of a package deal, all items of which will have been costed and the savings likely to accrue taken as offsets against the costs of concessions elsewhere. It should be made clear that the union cannot 'pick and choose' which items to accept or reject in the proposed deal which must be seen as an entity in itself. The package approach does not mean that negotiations are inhibited, as the union team will certainly indicate which parts of the package are unacceptable in their present form. It will then be a matter for the management team to adjust the shape of the package. The main point of the approach is that the agreement, when it comes, covers all the business.

Putting the claim and offer forward

The union team will have prioritised items within its claim. Exhibit 10.3 is an example from the hotel industry, showing the items that might appear.

The question for the management team is whether there might not be advantage in changing the order in replying to the claim so that the most positive response is left until last. It may be that the union team under disclosure provisions has asked for financial information to support its claim. On the other hand, the company may have kept the union informed about market conditions. In either case the company has the opportunity to provide an overall assessment of its position concerning income and costs, profitability, investment plans, market forecasts and so on. This will, of course, not only be of benefit to the union team (as it will want to know what the offer is), but will also be helpful to the management team in establishing how realistic the offer is, and in communicating the offer in such a way that it contains enough information to support the case and is simple enough to be readily understood.

Room for manoeuvre

Given that union claims are seldom solely related to an increase in pay (even though the negotiations are described as 'the annual pay round'), the management team's response should obviously take account of other tradeable issues. Negotiation is about movement on the part of both parties, but it does not

---

Exhibit 10.3

Claim items

1. That there will be a 10 per cent or £10 per week across-the-board increase on all basic rates of pay whichever is the greater.
2. That there will be a minimum rate of £170 per week (experienced rate).
3. That the 50p shift premium will be increased by a minimum of 5 per cent.
4. Housekeeping (room persons). Increase the existing £2.00 per extra room serviced to £2.75 per extra room serviced.
5. Maternity. Full holiday entitlement applicable to all maternity leavers.

have to be equal movement (see negotiating models described above). The 'bargaining ritual' notwithstanding, the initial offer should be pitched at a realistic figure that can be fully supported by arguments about ability to pay. If the ability to pay is 5 per cent then a first offer of 2 per cent which, under pressure from the union team, is improved until 5 per cent is reached, this tends to weaken the employer's position. The union team will contend that if the arguments about ability to pay were genuine and only supported 2 per cent then how does it come about that the same arguments support a figure of 5 per cent? If the employer can be pushed that far, why stop there? An initial offer in these circumstances should be 3.75–4 per cent, which still gives room for manoeuvre.

Rejecting union claims

Within the company response the negotiating team will be dealing with a union claim that may be rejected wholly or partly. The main reasons for rejection may be:

- **Tactical**, in that the company may wish at a later stage to bring the item back into negotiation by making it the subject of an offer.
- **Related to cost.** An inability to afford a claim is a very good reason for rejecting it, but judgement has to be exercised when this particular justification is used. For example, a claim for the introduction of an occupational pension scheme would be very expensive, however it may be phased in, and the 'cannot be afforded' response would be appropriate. On the other hand, a claim for a few days' paid paternity leave may in actual cost terms be less than significant against the total wage bill. To dismiss claims like this on the grounds of 'cannot be afforded' tends to weaken the general application of the argument and may well expose the company to ridicule.
- **Assessed as unreasonable in the circumstances.** In the event of a paternity leave claim, for instance, and given that the employer has already introduced a generous scale of holiday entitlements, the employer may argue that within that benefit all absences should be accommodated. The employer may have the same view concerning paid leave for other domestic situations.

- **A reluctance to go beyond minimum legal requirements.** In dealing, for example, with a claim for extended maternity leave, pay and 'job back' rights, an employer may feel that the company should not move beyond statutory entitlements.

Form of rejection

The management team must express the company response clearly and emphasise areas where they feel able or unable to move. There is, however, a need to reject claims in a way that is definite but not necessarily categorical. During a period of negotiation agreement is often reached on many items, which earlier on were thought as being fixed for all time. Rejection of claims should not be so categorical that it precludes renegotiation in the immediate future as circumstances require. The union team and the membership often see categorical and absolute rejection of claims as grounds for challenge and a hardening of attitude.

Union consideration of offers

If the management team has prepared its case properly then the reasons for rejecting claims will have been explained, the general financial situation will have been set out and the offers themselves will relate to the company trading situation. Under these circumstances a summary dismissal by the union team should not be accepted. The management team must emphasise that their response needs proper consideration and should not react to a rejection by increasing the offer, as this would undermine management's case.

Subsequent offers and business

Union response to first company offer

On resumption of negotiation, the management team will have a clearer idea of where the union team priorities lie, based on the nature of its response to the offer and its views in the subsequent discussion. This phase of negotiation will be concerned with argument and counter-argument, probing and listening, and persuading the other party to accept the logic of arguments put forward. It is also the phase where attitudes are hardened or restructured. During the course of discussion the task of both parties will be to indicate which elements of the claim are tradeable and which are not.

Adjournments

Adjournments can be called by either party and usually take place when:

- an offer or response has been made and the other side wishes to reassess its position or when the party insists that this should be done;
- a party is in disarray as to its approach and arguments;
- a party (usually both) is physically and mentally tired and needs a break;
- the business appears to be getting nowhere and it is jointly in the parties' interests to have a break and start afresh.

Frequency and length of adjournments

The majority of adjournments take place on the basis that one party or both parties wish to assess their positions in the light of movement in negotiation, the arguments put by either side, and assess what should be done next. Frequent adjournments may indicate that divisions within teams have emerged or that one party wishes the other to press harder in negotiation. It may also indicate that the team has momentarily lost its authority: it may be that the management team needs to report back to senior management to get a fresh mandate for discussions about to be reopened, or the union team needs to consult with the wider union membership and union hierarchy. In such situations, management may use the advisory services of specialists and consultants who are not part of the negotiating team. The length of adjournment depends upon circumstances such as the following:

- If negotiations are progressing satisfactorily, or towards the end of business when an agreement is within reach, then adjournments need not be longer than a few hours in order to maintain the momentum of negotiations.
- If negotiations proceed over prearranged days, then natural adjournments present themselves as a matter of course.
- If business becomes heated, as sometimes happens, an adjournment should be long enough to enable the parties to regain their equilibrium.

The practical approach to adjournments is this: does the time interval permit one or both parties to consider fully the next stage of business? Is that interval going to be short enough to keep up the momentum of negotiation in favour of a settlement, or is it going to be long enough to permit attitudes to harden, thus making the next round more difficult?

Informal business during negotiations

While all negotiations proceed on a formal basis, there may be occasions when the ability to talk 'off the record' would facilitate progress. Team representatives, usually the lead negotiators, may wish to meet informally in order that a much easier and fuller exchange of views can take place so that when formal negotiations are resumed outstanding earlier difficulties can be removed.

Working parties

Some issues during negotiations may be too complex or controversial to be adequately dealt with around the table. The solution to this is to convene a joint working party in order to make progress while negotiations continue with new issues. Points to consider and agree include: composition and size of working party; terms of reference and date for report.

Closing negotiations: writing-up, ratifying and implementing agreements

It is particularly important for lead negotiators to summarise the state of the business from time to time during the negotiation process, which helps to establish the common ground between the two parties and ultimately to clarify the 'final offer'. Both teams need to be satisfied that all the issues have been discussed and agreed and that they understand what has been traded and accepted. Nevertheless, union negotiators may have problems in ascertaining whether the final offer is just that or whether there may still be room for manoeuvre. In any event, the final offer must be demonstrated to be better than existing conditions, credible to both parties. Gennard and Judge (1997) point out that 'where increases in pay and other conditions are being given in return for changes in working practices, etc., the last item to be decided is what will be the amount of increase in pay' (p. 234) *before* any final offer is made. The pay issue is likely to be the major sticking point in negotiations and, in order not to risk deadlock, should not be considered too early in negotiations. Therefore, the prospect of the parties agreeing on the pay issue is much higher if all other issues have been agreed beforehand. Cairns (1996) identifies four main forms of closing negotiations used by management. These are:

- **The final offer close**, where a final offer is linked to getting agreement across the whole range of issues negotiated.
- **The listing and valuation close**, where management negotiators 'list in full detail the concessions they have made during negotiations . . . and emphasise the total value of what's on offer in relation to individual members, cost to the employer and, at times, value to the union' (p. 118).
- **The conditional close**, where, for example, management 'links a final concession to a condition that the union recommends acceptance of the whole offer' (p. 119).
- **The put-up or shut-up final offer**, where management negotiators categorically threaten that unless the union accepts the offer, the plant will close/the contract will be cancelled/work will be relocated/the union will be derecognised.

The resulting agreement, having been checked thoroughly by both negotiating teams, must then be formally drafted and signed by the negotiators. It is possible even at this late stage that misunderstandings can occur, perhaps owing to differences in perception of the outcome of negotiations which may then require further refinement and fine tuning. The agreement then requires ratification, without which there can be no implementation. Ratification meetings 'confirm who is covered, how they will be affected, when the agreement will apply, what it contains, why settlement is being recommended . . . and reflect the context of negotiations and explain the process' (ibid., p. 130). Positive feedback to management principals and union membership will increase the chances of approval and facilitate implementation, which is largely a management responsibility.

Do human resource practitioners lack basic negotiation skills?

On the whole, the 1980s, 1990s and early 2000s were, with notable exceptions, progressively peaceful on the employment relations front. With the declining incidence of industrial disputes, the decline in the number of days lost due to strikes and the tendency for employers to derecognise unions for the purposes of collective bargaining, many HR managers grew accustomed to dealing with unions at arm's length, and many more had no contact with unions whatsoever. However, in view of the increase in trade union recognition agreements, a significant proportion of HR managers may not possess the requisite negotiation skills. As we saw in Chapters 3 and 6, the growth of recognition agreements covering full recognition including at least pay, hours and holidays means that, as Roberts (2002) asserts, 'bargaining is back on the agenda'. For many organisations this will mean retraining or training anew HR staff in the skills identified above, while their union counterparts have maintained their negotiating skills on courses offered by the TUC, with larger unions having established their own training colleges. Many union negotiators can be quite frustrated by the lack of expertise and experience amongst HR managers, as one union officer cited by Roberts indicates:

> 'It makes my job very difficult' says Kevin Egan, airports officer for Amicus-MSF. He has worked with several companies that have new recognition deals. At Saudi Arabian Airlines, he found himself negotiating pay with the global HR director based in Saudi. 'There is no experience of British unions and how they work. We have to call on ACAS expertise to smooth the way when bargaining breaks down', Egan says. (p. 39)

There is, therefore, a clear need for HR practitioners to be trained in the finer, and not so fine, points of negotiation.

THE ANNUAL PAY ROUND: AN INTERACTIVE CASE

This case is based on an actual bargaining situation. All names and dates have been changed. The background to the pay negotiations is described, and this is followed by a number of possible tactics and strategies which you are invited to follow up during face-to-face negotiations between the management and union teams, using what you have learnt in this chapter as a guide to good practice in order to secure a mutually acceptable outcome. Because of space considerations, a number of details have, of necessity, been omitted, although sensible assumptions can be made.

Background

The company Wear and Suspender Ltd manufactures fashion clothing for the department store market, and its fortunes are bound up with the success of the stores it services. During the 1990s, the market was buoyant but competitive. However, during the period 2001–4, owing to a general downturn in world markets which affected consumer demand in Britain, the demand for Wear and Suspender's products began to decline, and at least one department store chain was cutting down on its requirements. Profits are average for the industry, although productivity has been declining over the past five years. The company employs 700 production workers on two similar sites in the Medway area, 75 per cent of whom are unionised being members of the TGWU. The annual pay negotiations take place during November and are concluded by 1 December. The union negotiating team comprises five senior shop stewards from both sites and the management team includes the personnel manager, two works managers, the production manager, and the finance director. Members of both teams know each other well, although relations between them are not always amicable.

Preparatory talks are usually held in October and these are followed by more formalised meetings prior to the actual negotiations. The range of topics for bargaining has extended over the years to include virtually all terms and conditions of employment. With the exception of one large pay increase in 1999, subsequent awards have been moderate, barely keeping up with inflation but nevertheless comparing well with the rest of the industry. In accordance with the 2000 agreement, the production department workforce, comprising 90 per cent of the total manual workforce, receive average weekly earnings of £375 gross, including bonuses, for a standard working week of 39 hours, and 20 days holiday a year (excluding statutory holidays) paid at base rate, rising to 22 days after five years' service. No one has been made redundant for the past nine years and,

apart from a small increase in 1997, the numbers of employees have remained fairly constant since then.

A changing situation

For the first time in many years, the trading situation has now begun to deteriorate. Many department stores have reported falls in profits during the course of 2003, and sales in the months leading up to Christmas have been disappointingly low. It is predicted that consumer confidence will continue to remain low for at least the whole of 2004, despite cuts in interest rates. This has led some stores to reduce prices of many clothing items, and this in turn has led to many supplier companies, including Wear and Suspender, having either to cut their overheads or to contemplate making redundancies in order to remain competitive. In the case of Wear and Suspender, the following circumstances apply:

- a lower level of sales than hitherto for the foreseeable future at least;
- the trend towards lower productivity 'which needs to be reversed';
- overtime has 'regrettably' been cancelled except for urgent and outstanding orders with the prospect of less or even no overtime in future months; and
- the possibility of redundancy has been privately contemplated by management if new business is not forthcoming.

Prior to 'talks about talks', the Wear and Suspender JCC met in October, and committee members were informed of the deteriorating market situation and the possibly gloomy future ahead partly stemming from the housing market crash. Management provided no specific information, and certainly no information concerning possible redundancies was divulged. Rumours of 'bad times ahead' began to spread amongst the workforce. At a subsequent union branch meeting that was unusually highly attended, members expressed their concern that, despite the seasonal nature of the trade, the situation this time was gloomy and that management were not bluffing prior to negotiation. Moreover, it was felt that if the situation was as bad as management had suggested, then more detailed information from management was required before any pay claim could be formulated and submitted. The senior convenor undertook to seek the advice of the district union officer in order to confirm what types of information a trade union could request from the company for the purposes of collective bargaining. It was felt that without this information, the union bargaining team would be put at a considerable disadvantage in face-to-face negotiations. As one shop steward put it: 'We are fed up with having to take management's word for it every time we ask about the position of the company, whether it's orders or profits.'

Self-Evaluation Activity 10.9

Drafting a letter

Response on website

We are essentially at the planning and preparation stage of the negotiation for both parties. In order to clarify the position of the company on a number of matters and also for the purpose of negotiating effectively, draft a letter to the Managing Director requesting the relevant information.

A suggested sample letter is provided in Exhibit 10.4.

Exhibit 10.4

The Transport and General Workers' Union

Medway District Office

15 October 2003

Mr V. Fudge
Managing Director
Wear and Suspender Ltd
Bull Grove Industrial Park
Lepton
Medway
Kent

Dear Mr Fudge

At the last union branch meeting the members present voiced their concern about the position the company now faces, with the downturn in sales and declining orders. In order to formulate our pay claim in preparation for next month's negotiations, we need certain information so that we can enter into sensible negotiation about pay and other terms and conditions of members' employment. Our district official, Ron Fallows, has advised us that we are legally entitled to company information that will assist us in our negotiations with the management team. Over recent years, and as far back as I can remember, we have gone along with the information you have verbally provided us and we have both negotiated in good faith on a basis of trust and honesty. However, on this occasion the branch committee felt that, given the present unprecedented situation, we should have more information than what you have traditionally given us.

We therefore urgently request the following specific information:

- a breakdown of earnings for all employees including bonuses, overtime payments and other allowances
- weekly hours worked by all employees for the past year
- labour turnover statistics
- manpower plans for 2004
- state of orders projected for 2004
- investment plans, including any expenditure planned and for what purpose
- financial information concerning profitability, margins, earnings, etc.

I look forward to your prompt reply.

Yours sincerely
E. Rose
Senior Steward

There are two possible scenarios from here on. The first scenario is one where management responds positively to the letter, which indicates that there is a willingness to co-operate in negotiations on the basis of shared information and that management has nothing to hide and no hidden agenda. The second scenario is one where management does not reply to the letter and may indicate a more 'Machiavellian' approach to negotiation. We could, of course, assume that management was surprised to receive such a letter as the stewards had not made such a request on previous negotiating occasions and that the best strategy would be to address the issue during negotiations. Management did, in fact, ignore the letter and prepared for negotiation in the usual way by obtaining information on pay through the employers' association and by contacting other firms in the locality as well as consulting other statistical sources. The union team similarly obtained local information through its contacts and used the not inconsiderable resources of the TGWU research department to compile a detailed pay portfolio from which to formulate its claim.

A further development, however, annoyed the workforce and did not inspire confidence in management. Its effect was to compound and reinforce the suspicions and growing negative feelings which the union team had towards management. In the October edition of the company newsletter *Wear and Suspender Titbits* an item appeared which expressed the Managing Director's view concerning the company's situation, an extract of which is reproduced in Exhibit 10.5.

Informal enquiries for more information about the company's situation were met with polite rebuffs. At a meeting of the shop stewards committee, there was a prevailing view that management were attempting to create an atmosphere of gloom and despondency in order to lower the expectations of the workforce concerning pay increases and that the information contained in the newsletter was therefore an attempt to influence negotiations before they had actually begun. Moreover, the information was so general as to be virtually useless as a basis for negotiation and it was decided to write to the Managing Director to ask him once again to

Exhibit 10.5

Wear and Suspender Titbits

Living within our means

October 2003

In the past, I have always been perfectly frank and honest with you, the employees of *Wear and Suspender Ltd*, and will continue to be so as I value the trust you place in me to steer the company through stormy waters.

We have now hit a stormy sea and our boat is being rocked. As far as the company is concerned, the outlook, I am sad to say, is for further storms ahead. As you know, the economic situation affecting the retail sector is now affecting us mainly because of the housing market downturn and less disposable income of customers as a result. Orders are down and margins are being squeezed to an unprecedented extent. We still face stiff competition at home and overseas and some of our department store customers are demanding that our prices are more realistic in future contracts.

We now have to ensure that we live within our means and tighten our belts in order to survive and prosper. All of us will have to make sacrifices in order to secure our jobs, and pull together more now than we have ever done in the past.

We also need to modernise our equipment and machinery in order to keep abreast of the competition. All this costs money, but if we economise now, we can release investment funds to purchase new technology.

Finally, I would like to express my thanks and gratitude to all of you in making this firm as successful as it has been. Even more effort is required now in order to weather the storm and ensure a prosperous future. I know that I can count on your commitment, as I have done in the past.

provide specific information in order to clarify the situation (Exhibit 10.6).

Self-Evaluation Activity 10.10

Shopping list for the 2004 claim

Response on website

At the same committee meeting, it was decided to formulate the pay and conditions claim for 2004. Suggest what the 'shopping list' should include (assuming a rate of inflation of 3 per cent) and whether the claim should be influenced by the company's alleged plight.

The eve of negotiations

The reaction of management to the latest letter from the shop stewards committee has been one of stalling and 'playing for time'. (Note that the management team will not know about the union claim until face-to-face negotiations begin.) Many managers are unconvinced that the approach adopted by the MD was the right one, and that more specific information should have been disclosed to the union team prior to the start of negotiations. The management team therefore anticipate that the union team will not take the company's plight into consideration when

---

Exhibit 10.6

The Transport and General Workers' Union

Medway District Office

27 October 2003

Mr V. Fudge
Managing Director
Wear and Suspender Ltd
Bull Grove Industrial Park
Lepton
Medway
Kent

Dear Mr Fudge

We have all read your article in the October Company Newsletter. At a recent meeting of the shop stewards committee, concern was raised about some of the issues you identify in the Newsletter. The concern is not confined to the committee, and many of our members have raised similar concerns. You seem to suggest that the firm is experiencing difficult times and that changes will have to be made. As a union, we feel very strongly that we should be more involved in any discussions concerning the company's apparent problems right at the start if these affect our members.

In particular, you mention lack of orders, increased competition, lower profits, improving efficiency and a hint (frankly insulting to our members) of slack working and people not pulling their weight. As a union, we wish to see the firm succeed and we have always endeavoured to achieve that end in a spirit of partnership and co-operation. To that end, we as a union are seeking clarification on these issues, and in conjunction with my earlier letter requesting information, ask you to supply us with information on these matters.

We anticipate your early reply.

Yours sincerely

E. Rose

Senior Steward

formulating its claim and that the gap between claim and offer will be wide indeed! The management team has, therefore, decided to be openly candid with the union team at the outset of negotiation (but will not release any of the specific information that has been requested) in the hope that management's position will be appreciated even at this late stage.

Shop stewards have been fairly active in the wake of the article in the newsletter, and have raised various grievances and complaints on behalf of employees using the grievance procedure as a bargaining lever. Technically, grievances and complaints should be addressed to the immediate supervisor or line manager, rather than to the employee representative, and bypassing this formal channel has caused aggravation. The nature of the complaints and grievances concern safety issues, accompanied by veiled threats of what might happen if nothing was done about the problem. Management's response to this sudden spate of complaints has been to listen politely and take notes, but secretly they believe that the union's involvement here is a delaying tactic in the event that, if face-to-face negotiations become protracted, the possible backlog of grievances which require a management response within a time limit in order to progress to the next stage would become a serious issue and dispute in itself, the consequence of which would be to jeopardise the pay negotiations themselves.

Soundings taken by supervisors have revealed a groundswell of concern amongst production workers concerning the security of their jobs, together with the need to secure improvements to the bonus scheme as a means of improving individual earnings to a greater extent than hitherto. This information has been passed on to senior management.

Another development, which could profoundly influence the course of negotiation, came to the attention of the senior convenor (the lead negotiator) in the form of a handwritten note delivered in person to the senior convenor. The note is reproduced in Exhibit 10.7.

The start of face-to-face negotiations

The negotiating committee met for the first time on 3 November, and after a few constrained pleasantries, Bob Davies made the opening statement addressed to the management team with the MD, Victor Fudge, in the chair.

Self-Evaluation Activity 10.11

An opening statement
The response is provided below

Prepare the sort of opening statement which Bob Davies might have made.

An example of such a statement is given in Exhibit 10.8.

Exhibit 10.7

Handwritten note to senior convenor

Dear Bob

I have some very important information to give you from a reliable source. A member of the office staff on our site was talking to her friend about a number of fax messages she was dealing with these last few days (28th and 29th October). This friend happened to be a cousin of mine (you probably know Jane as she's the only member of the office staff who is a member of the TGWU white collar section and attends branch meetings) and she passed on information to me in confidence.

Basically, the company appears to be in the process of contacting a large multinational shopping chain and seems to be in the advanced stages of negotiating a very large order with them. As good luck would have it, this information was confirmed in separate reports coming from the sales office!

As I'm not on the negotiating team, I thought I'd write this information down rather than talk to you informally.

Yours

Frank

Exhibit 10.8

Example opening statement

We have prepared the details of our claim which have been distributed to you at this meeting. The pay claim is based on current figures available for the Retail Price Index, which shows that inflation is currently running at 3 per cent. The information which we have obtained from local firms indicates that pay settlements for 2004 have been running at 5 per cent, and this is in firms which had a higher base rate than in Wear and Suspender Ltd. Our research also shows that many firms in the locality now have a base wage rate of £395 a week for operatives who also enjoy a 37-hour week and 22 days' holiday a year on average earnings.

On a related matter, the negotiating team, as advised by our shop stewards committee, note with great concern that the company has found it fit to start a campaign based on fear of job loss and that the company has not replied to two polite requests for information which we feel we are legally entitled to. Even though we are not privy to the state of the order book, we have it on good authority that there is a profitable order in the pipeline. In the absence of relevant facts and figures, we feel that we are at a disadvantage and cannot negotiate sensibly on these issues. We cannot negotiate on the basis of selective dissemination of information and again request access to the full range of data on which to make a balanced decision.

The lead negotiator of the management team replied as shown in Exhibit 10.9, and confirmed management's position as outlined in the newsletter.

The final statement to the meeting made by the union team lead negotiator followed immediately (Exhibit 10.10).

Both management and union team agreed to meet in three days' time. The production manager said that, as a final statement from management for that meeting, he would like to end on a positive note by saying that there was a need to improve productivity and this meant that there was room for increasing output-related bonuses if the union were prepared to negotiate improved working practices. However, this did not mean that there was any room for manoeuvre on base rates or anything that added to overall costs with no related increase in output.

Report back

The subsequent union meeting was a very stormy affair, as predicted by the senior convenor and lead negotiator. Most of the members present wanted the

Exhibit 10.9

Management reply

I can only reaffirm the position outlined in our house magazine. There is a definite downturn in orders and this is likely to continue for the foreseeable future. We cannot understand where you obtained the so-called information concerning new orders. I can assure you that there are no imminent new orders, much as we would like this to be the case. About the inflation rate, the figure you quote was for the previous year and the official predicted rate of inflation for 2004 is more likely to be 5 per cent. Also, our information on local pay settlements differs from your information. Only one firm has settled at 5 per cent and the reason for that is that it has just recovered from a very severe decline in business and is allowing for an element of catching up. The clothing trade has never been able to pay high rates because, as you know, the business is so competitive and open to foreign imports. The best we as a company can do is to hold on to what we have got and have a year in which everyone consolidates their position.

Exhibit 10.10

Union final statement

If, as seems to be the case, the management team cannot or are not able to make a specific offer which represents an improvement, then I will have to report to the union meeting tomorrow that management are not negotiating seriously. It will be very difficult for me to contain the reactions of the union members and I cannot be responsible for the problems that might follow on from this.

union negotiators to tackle the problem of base rates and holiday pay as a matter of priority, and a minority wanted a commitment from the meeting that, if management did not concede on base rates, the members should institute some form of industrial action. This latter concern was never put forward as a formal motion and was therefore not taken as anything other than a few members 'letting off steam', even though they had some support. The meeting ended with the stewards being instructed to pursue the claim on base rates as a priority.

On the day following the union meeting, supervisors from both sites heard stories about the real possibility of industrial action, and this information was passed on to senior managers. A further complication for management was that the large order that the union had received information on had now been finalised. The exact terms of the deal were known only to two senior sales managers and the Managing Director, but it was clear that the order which was not due to start for two months into the new year would provide work for the production unit for some considerable time, ensuring continuity and security of employment for the foreseeable future.

Self-Evaluation Activity 10.12

Were preparations adequate?

The response is provided below

To what extent do you think the union and management teams made adequate preparations for negotiation?

Considering the union team first, it would appear that they had done their homework and consulted various sources of information, including the TGWU research department, in order to ensure that the claim reflected the situation locally, taking inflation and other measures

of performance into consideration. The union team were not, however, prepared to be sympathetic to the company's situation owing to management's reticence in divulging relevant information, and could rightly claim to have been 'kept in the dark' on those and other issues. The union team also concluded that on this occasion they could not negotiate meaningfully on management's opening statement as this was far too vague. Normally the team would agree an 'ideal' aim for the negotiation (what they would like to achieve), a 'realistic' aim (what they would hope to achieve) and a 'fall-back' aim (what they must achieve), but this has been deferred until appropriate information (concerning the new order, for example) is received by them.

As far as the management team is concerned, we may safely assume that the appropriate analyses concerning pay movements, inflation and so on were made. However, it is not clear on what issues management are prepared to trade with the union team, although there may be some movement on the pay/productivity front if efficiencies are agreed. It is obvious that the management team are withholding information as part of a strategy to consolidate its bargaining power, according to the dictum 'he who has information has power', and would ideally like to 'dribble' information selectively during the course of negotiation. Clearly the tone of the negotiation has been set by management wishing to discuss the whole area of productivity and working practices, which may or may not be determined by the eventual introduction of new technology. The union team, on the other hand, sees the main priority as pay, and a possible focus for negotiation and agreement would be to concentrate on the possible 'trade-offs' for both union and management negotiators in trading pay increases for efficiency improvements. We could also argue that the management team has not clearly identified its negotiating objectives because of uncertainties in the market and the sensitivity of information concerning the new order. In this respect, Gennard and Judge (2002) caution:

> A management that enters negotiations without having firmly fixed objectives is increasing the possibility of reaching an unsatisfactory outcome or entering into a dispute. However, before establishing viable negotiating objectives, management should undertake a detailed analysis and then make an assessment of the relative balance of bargaining power between itself and groups of workers with whom it is to negotiate. . . . This involves considering such questions as whether the group has the power to inflict costs on the employer, and if it does, whether it appears willing to use that power. Consideration has also to be given to whether the work group has the leadership necessary to impose any industrial sanctions. Management's answer to these questions will be significant factors in determining its negotiating objectives. (p. 320)

It should also be emphasised that in some situations management negotiators may feel that they have more to gain by withholding until the right tactical moment. On the other hand, management negotiators, by keeping silent or shielding information, may allow unrealistic expectations to build up. Cairns (1996) points out that:

> In a trade union setting this can lead to a union and its negotiators being locked in a democratic decision that is being overrun by a newly emerging economic background to the negotiations. In such situations, union negotiators are frequently between a rock and a hard place. To support and explain the new economic rationale (to the membership) can seem like betrayal, not to do so can mean negotiations foundering. More dangerously, confrontation may follow in an environment in which the workers' power position is much less favourable than originally believed . . . With the right motivation and skills, management negotiators can have a constructive influence on claims as well as settlements. However, ritualistic pleadings of poverty can lead to cynicism on the part of negotiators and those they represent. (p. 96)

Management responses to multi-item claims should focus on the advisability of introducing any particular proposal, the projected cost of it, the aggregate cost of all items being claimed and any priority being attached to an item by the other side. The union team need to know how to deal with resistance in all four areas. If, for example, aggregate cost is the problem, then it may be necessary to prioritise or even drop items in the claim to make progress with the rest on an 'if we were to . . . , would you . . .' basis.

SEAs 10.13 and 10.14 are intended to be tackled in small groups with the help of a tutor. The case, which also explores additional aspects of negotiation, is reworked below as a negotiation exercise.

Self-Evaluation Activity 10.13

Actual and perceived power positions
This SEA has no commentary

At this stage of the bargaining encounter, how would you assess;

(a) both parties' actual power positions; and
(b) both parties' perceived power positions and bargaining advantage.

Self-Evaluation Activity 10.14

Models of negotiating behaviour
This SEA has no commentary

Comment on the relevance of the three models of negotiating behaviour to the current situation at Wear and Suspender Ltd.

Negotiation exercise

This section dealing with negotiation is divided into two parts. The first part outlines a negotiation exercise based on Wear and Suspender Ltd, the background to which is provided in the last section, and what is required of the negotiators. The second part provides one possible scenario for the negotiations. These are followed by a summary of negotiation theory relevant to the case.

The annual pay round at Wear and Suspender Ltd: a negotiation exercise

The negotiation exercise is based on an actual negotiation concerning the 'annual pay round' at Wear and Suspender Ltd, using the background information provided earlier. The exercise requires the negotiating teams to prepare for and conduct 'around-the-table' negotiations, the end result of which is the joint written agreement. The minimum requirements for a successful role-play are:

- two negotiating teams of five players per team;
- two rooms, one of which can be used for actual negotiations;
- one 'observer' for each team whose function is explained below;
- tutor to co-ordinate activities;
- adequate time to prepare and conduct negotiations (say, three hours for preparation and three hours for 'around-the-table' negotiation; and
- additional time to ensure adequate preparation, for individuals to familiarise themselves with their roles and to ensure that both teams work from a common information base.

Stage One: planning and preparation

Allocation of roles within teams: This should not present too many problems. The teams should allocate roles on the lines of those suggested earlier in the chapter. Each team should therefore have a lead negotiator, a note-taker, specialists such as finance and HR personnel for the management team, and union representatives for the union team. The lead negotiator should co-ordinate the activities of the team at each stage of the negotiation process, present the claim/offer, organise adjournments and deal with any problems as they arise. The other members of the team participate fully in the planning and presentation of its case. The note-taker role is important, as this will provide a record of what arguments have been used during face-to-face negotiations and enable the teams to summarise their respective arguments/positions. In addition to the team roles, an independent observer should be allocated to each team. The duties of the observer include an evaluation of the team's conduct of negotiations, the extent to which negotiation skills have been used by each team member and how the team performed overall in achieving its aims and objectives.

Gathering and assembling information common to both teams: It is important that both teams make the same assumptions concerning the information relevant to both claim and offer. In essence this means that both teams need to co-operate at this stage concerning the rate of inflation, wage movements within the industry and so on. If conflicting assumptions are made at this stage, then the ensuing negotiations are invalid. To be sure, some information may be retained by one or both parties in an attempt to secure a bargaining advantage as, for example with the rumoured new contract, details of which may not be revealed until negotiations are well under way.

Devising claim and offer: On the basis of information gathered both claim and offer are formulated. One or more bargaining models previously described may be used here. It would be useful, if not essential to consider ideal, realistic and fall-back positions. Remember that there are 'trade-offs', for example between pay and working hours, and that it would therefore be sensible to include these and other aspects as part of a 'shopping list' as long as the list is kept relatively short.

Stage Two: face-to-face negotiations

This requires both teams to present claim and offer and then to negotiate until a constructive compromise is reached. Permanent breakdown of negotiations leading to industrial action is not an option; it is the easy way out if agreement is not reached and devalues the role-play. The best outcome is a 'win-win' situation where both teams feel that significant progress has been made. As we saw earlier, this stage of the negotiation process incorporates:

- the unveiling of each side's opening position; followed by
- discussion or argument with each side testing the other's stance and attempting to protect and enhance its own position; and finally
- a search for 'common ground' providing a basis for agreement.

The whole process will involve a rationalisation of differing and conflicting perceptions concerning the nature of what is being negotiated. Peripheral issues should be sidelined either as non-negotiable or to be resolved at a later date. Success in negotiations therefore depends upon achieving a consensus as to what the parties are trying to agree upon.

Face-to-face negotiation involves the use of a number of tactical devices that include:

- the use of adjournments to consider new points, to reconsider and review bargaining positions, to summarise the position so far and to allow for 'cooling down' if the proceedings become too heated;
- ensuring that any statements made by the opposing team are fully understood. It may, therefore, be necessary to ask for clarification;
- encouraging the other side to talk. This may reveal the 'bottom line' or aspects of their argument which lacks conviction;
- identifying the benefits of either side's case and of what is on the table;
- avoiding any implication that the trade union side has lost or the management team has won;
- avoiding getting bogged down in detail. If there is deadlock, suggest putting the contentious issue aside and switch to a new topic;
- emphasising and summarising the areas of agreement and common ground in order to create a positive climate for tackling difficult issues; and
- ensuring that only one person (normally the lead negotiator) speaks at any one time. If the discussion becomes heated then a mutually acceptable adjournment must be sought.

The role-play during this stage of the negotiation process involves the use and deployment of particular skills by each member of the negotiating teams. Teamwork, managing time, note-taking, summarising and interpersonal skills are essential for successful and effective negotiation. Under these circumstances, the main skills that can be assessed are:

- presentation skills;
- influencing skills;
- skills of persuasion and judgement;
- note-taking skills;
- summarising skills;
- interpersonal skills;
- listening and observing skills;
- questioning and probing skills;
- awareness of body language; and
- time-management skills.

Stage Three: reaching and writing up the agreement

After reaching agreement, both teams jointly write up the agreement which will be mutually binding.

A negotiating scenario

It should be stressed that the scenario in Exhibit 10.11 is an example of what could happen and is not intended to be a guide to 'best practice'.

Exhibit 10.11

Wear and Suspender Ltd: a negotiating scenario

Management Negotiation Team
Finance Director
Production Manager
Chairman/Summariser
Lead Negotiator/Personnel
Note-taker

Union Negotiation Team
Senior Shop Steward/Note-taker
Lead Negotiator
Senior Shop Steward
Senior Shop Steward
Shop Steward

Initial meeting of negotiation teams

Union negotiation team table their claim:

1. 5% pay increase.
2. Working week to be reduced from 39 to 35 hours.
3. Greater communication/integration with management, with particular reference to exchange of financial information concerning the company's position.
4. Annual leave entitlement to be increased from 20 to 22 days a year for all staff with immediate effect.
5. Consolidation of bonuses into base rates for the purpose of calculating holiday pay.

Union criticises management for not providing previously requested information, but management refutes this and says they have provided information and are baffled as to why it has not been received, and promise to look into it. Management promises to consider the union's claim but points out that it is highly unlikely that they could respond favourably to an 5 per cent pay award, particularly taking into account current market trends and the serious economic situation facing the company. The management team made a commitment, however, to review the situation and take advice from its Board of Directors – particularly its Finance Director – before the meeting reconvenes.

Meeting adjourns to discuss union claim
Meeting reconvenes

Management's response is tabled:

1. The company is prepared to offer a 3 per cent pay award with effect from 1 April 2004 conditional on monthly pay being introduced for all manual staff at that date. To ease the transition, the company will make an interest-free advance of two weeks' pay, repayable by staff over a six-month period.
2. The company is prepared, at this stage, to consider reducing the working week to 36.5 hours from 1 April.
   The offer is conditional upon quality and productivity being maintained at the following levels:

   Quality: rejects percentage no greater than 5 per cent
   Productivity: 50 units per person per day (based on a weekly average)

   The situation will be monitored on a monthly basis and, subject to these quality and productivity levels being maintained and/or improved, a further review could take place at the next annual negotiations with a possible further reduction in hours.
3. Although the company recognises the effective communication channels which already exist through the JCC and would not wish to detract from its effectiveness, management would welcome the opportunity to enhance this further by the introduction of a Works Forum which could be convened as and when particular areas of mutual concern arose which required specialist knowledge.
4. The company is prepared to offer an across-the-board increase of one day's annual leave with effect from 1 April. This offer is conditional on certain amendments to the calculation of sick pay. Thus, if a member of staff has been absent for less than five days in the preceding year (April–March), full sick pay will be maintained. For anyone exceeding five days' sick leave in the preceding year, no sick pay will be made for the first two days' of absence.
5. Management is prepared to consider consolidation of bonuses into holiday pay calculations on the basis of a capped figure of not more than £14 per week for a maximum of two weeks' leave per year.

The union team is less than happy with management's response and request an adjournment.

Adjournment to discuss response
Meeting reconvenes

Management restate that the offer is 'good' in the present economic climate given that they are trying to avoid redundancies. Union responds, emphasising the need to protect members, that the offer is unsatisfactory and states that after consultation with the membership the following items are on the table:

1. Our members are prepared to consider a 4.5 per cent pay rise, but will not consider any transfer from weekly to monthly pay. (*Bear in mind that members have not had a pay rise which keeps abreast of inflation for a number of years and that many local firms have settled at around 8 per cent.*)
2. Our members will, in principle, accept the reduction of the working week to 36.5 hours, but would insist that the framework is in place prior to 1 April to consider the way quality and productivity measures are implemented. It would certainly seem an appropriate use of a specialist Works Forum to look at assessment, evaluation and monitoring of quality and productivity levels.
3. Our members also recognise the value of the JCC but feel they should have more input into the decision-making process and are pleased at management's response with regard to the introduction of a Works Forum and would suggest that a Working Party is established to get things moving as soon as possible.
4. Our members are not prepared to accept any change to sick-pay procedures and are still looking for an across-the-board increase of two days on annual leave.
5. Our members would insist on consolidation of bonuses being applied to ALL holiday pay calculations, i.e. four weeks, not two.

Management's response

(*Chairman suggests that the meeting looks at one issue at a time. What follows is an abbreviated transcript.*)

M. In acknowledgement of the strength of your case the company is now prepared to offer a 3.5 per cent pay award but only on the proviso that the transition to monthly pay is accepted.
U. Our members will find this revised offer totally unacceptable. Given that inflation is running at 6 per cent together with the remarkable restraint the workforce has shown in recent years, we feel that a 6 per cent pay increase is totally reasonable.
M. Perhaps it would be best if Clark Anderson, our Financial Director, provided some background information on the financial climate facing the company. (*Finance Director to expand on why the company cannot afford to meet the union's demand with respect to a 4.5 per cent pay increase. Financial/statistical information to be introduced at this point. Re-emphasise the need for monthly pay to be introduced.*)

Union request adjournment
Meeting resumes

U. We appreciate your frankness at this late stage in providing relevant financial and related information, information which should have been available to us at a much earlier stage in the negotiations. However, you are still being less than honest with us. We have information that there is a major new order in the pipeline, which will provide work and security for our workforce for the foreseeable future. Our information comes from a very informed and reliable source.
M. (*Clearly embarrassed and needs time to discuss this development.*)

Management request adjournment
Meeting resumes

M. We cannot at this stage confirm that a contract has been finalised, which is why we have not, as yet, revealed any details. However, we did receive a positive response to our tender and we expect that the contract will go ahead and be finalised within three months. I have received a summary of the details of the contract which I can now let you have sight of. We are also bidding for additional contracts and will keep you informed of developments here. In view of this development, and in recognition of the commitment shown by our workforce, we are prepared to offer you a 4 per cent increase – but only with the introduction of the proposed monthly pay scheme. We also undertake to pay a further 1 per cent subject to the order being confirmed, this additional 1 per cent to take effect on the date the order is finalised.

U. We will have to consult our membership on this and also on the transitional period over which loans have to be repaid as a result of going on to monthly pay. Six months is not sufficient time for our members. They don't earn enough to have savings to fall back on. We would therefore be looking for a 12-month repayment period. We have also received information that one of our local competitors, Klingon and Vulcan, have had a 4.5 per cent pay increase agreed and they have not had as good a performance record as we have over recent years.

M. There may be room for flexibility over the transitional loan repayment period. With the case of Klingon and Vulcan, OK they have a 6.5 per cent deal but they have also made significant redundancies in order to secure the deal. We are attempting to get the best deal without making anyone redundant. Can we move on?

   The next outstanding issue is sick-pay procedures and annual leave. We can only reiterate our offer of an increase of one day to annual leave entitlement but will reduce the penalty period for loss of sick pay to one day rather than two.

U. Our members are very reluctant to accept the sick-pay policy and are still looking for an increase of two days for holiday entitlements. One of the main areas of concern with regard to sick-pay arrangements are those special cases, e.g. accidents/long term illness?

M. This is obviously an issue to which both the company and the union membership will need to devote much more time and discussion than this meeting will allow and, rather than delay proceedings any further, perhaps this would be an ideal agenda item for a Works Forum to discuss – bringing in specialist guidance from our new HR manager and possibly from external bodies? We're also aware of a number of grievances that seem to have arisen during recent weeks and the need to look at them collectively if we can reach some agreement about the more important issues during these negotiations.

U. Yes, we are aware of the recent increase in grievances and would agree that further discussions are necessary to resolve the matter of sick leave and holiday entitlements.

M. That leaves us with the issue of consolidation of bonuses into sick pay. The company is prepared to agree to the capped bonus system across four weeks' holiday pay but only on the basis that, in the event of overtime being worked, the first four hours worked beyond the full week will be at plain time rates with effect from 1 April or as soon as practicable thereafter. You must understand that we need to balance the costs involved with this package against quality and productivity levels.

U. We will obviously have to report back and ballot our members.

(After a few more adjournments and more negotiation, the following agreement was reached.)

Wear and Suspender Ltd
Annual Pay Negotiations for 2004
The Agreement

1. Pay Increase – Agreed

Both management and union representatives have agreed on an initial pay increase of 4 per cent from 1 April. Although management acknowledge that this amount is above the current RPI rate of 3 per cent, a further 0.5 per cent has been promised to the workforce conducive of the successful confirmation of the new contract and assuming that no current substantial orders are lost in the process. This offer can only be made with the proviso that the workforce accepts changes to the pay structure.

Management feel that a move towards monthly pay, as opposed to weekly pay, would do much to free up working capital and allow this money to be invested on short-term deposit. In turn, the interest gained by month-to-month investment could be put towards the pay increase for staff members. To this end, management are prepared to allow an interest-free loan of two weeks' salary to each member of staff during the transitional period from weekly to monthly pay. Both management and union representatives are in agreement that the workforce should not be penalised unduly during the transition, and have thereby confirmed a 12-month payback time limit on the interest-free loan.

2. Reduction of Working Week – Agreed

After much discussion, management, in conjunction with union representatives have agreed that staff at Wear and Suspender Ltd, who are currently working a 39-hour week, are working in excess of local industry averages of 37.5 hours.

Management have offered to reduce working hours by half-an-hour per day, taking the working week for any one member of staff to 36.5 hours, on the condition that productivity and quality are maintained. By this, management expect the percentage of rejects to be no greater than 5 per cent and productivity to remain at 50 units per day/per person. Union representatives on behalf of members have accepted the reduction of working hours to 36.5 hours per week, and fully understand the implications involved, that staff will be required to show greater commitment in order to fulfil the necessary criteria.

3. Works Forum – Agreed

Both parties recognise and agree the need for greater communication within the company in the light of the EU Information and Consultation Directive. This course of action will enable management and the workforce to develop a greater understanding of one another and build mutual trust by which the company can be taken forward gaining greater commitment to the company in the process.

As a result of the growing need for more open channels of communication, emphasis has been placed on implementing a Works Forum by which staff and management come together as soon as possible to decide on which best course of action the company should take to maintain quality and productivity levels.

It is understood by both parties that the workforce may adopt a more sympathetic approach to the plight of management if management in the process imparts an equal measure of information, especially when staff are making financial demands which the company may find difficult to accede.

4. Sick Pay and Annual Leave – Still to be agreed

Management's final offer on sick pay and annual leave is:

1. One day's extra holiday entitlement available to all members of staff conditional upon:
2. Any member of staff exceeding five days' sick leave in the preceding year will lose one day of sick leave entitlement.
3. Special dispensation is given to those who are genuinely sick through long-term illness and accidents.

(It was envisaged by management that this course of action would sort out the wheat from the chaff – i.e. those wishing to gain from the extra day's holiday entitlement would be more committed by giving full attendance. Likewise those who are not committed and take odd days off will be penalised by the new sick-pay structure.)

However, this proposal proved to be a bone of contention with union representatives and something on which they would not readily agree. It was agreed by both parties that this matter should be raised for further debate at the first Works Forum meeting in the absence of any firm acceptance at this time.

5. Consolidation of Bonuses – Agreed

After lengthy discussion, both management and union representatives have reached an agreement on the consolidation of bonuses. The terms agreed are that management are prepared to allow consolidation of bonuses into holiday pay calculations for 4 weeks' holiday up to a 'capped' figure of £14 per week with a condition that the first four hours of any overtime worked will be paid at 'flat' rate.

This Agreement signed by both parties:

Note concerning financial and other information: Wear and Suspender Ltd

Manual workforce (90 per cent of total workforce)	630
Average weekly pay (inc. bonuses)	£375
Working hours	39 per week
Annual leave	20 days p.a. (increasing to 22 after 5 years)
Current wage bill	£750 750 p.m./£9 009 000 p.a.

Assumptions

According to union
- Inflation 3 per cent
- Local pay settlements averaging 5 per cent
- Industry norms suggest local base rate £395; 37-hour week and 22 days' annual leave

According to company
- Inflation 3 per cent
- Only one local firm settled at 5 per cent
- Downturn in world markets affecting consumer demand
- Productivity declining in recent years
- Trading situation has begun to deteriorate

Relevant information

- No dissemination of company information to union
- No redundancies for 9 years
- Moderate pay rises in line with inflation over last few years
- Major new order with multinational shopping chain now confirmed – due to start March 2004

Cost of salary increases

5%	£614 250
4%	£491 400
3%	£368 550
2%	£245 700
1%	£122 850

For example: 5% of £375 = 18.75 × 630 = 11 812.5 per week × 52 = 614 250

Any additional costs to the company would be difficult to bear, particularly in the existing economic climate. It would, therefore, be necessary to justify ways in which additional funding could be raised or, alternatively, savings made on existing outgoings.

Summary points

- Within the bargaining context, the power relationship and the psychology of bargaining are vitally important in determining the tactics and strategies of both parties.
- The two important aspects of the power relationship are the 'actual power' possessed, and the 'perceptions of power' held by each party.

- The power position of the parties depends upon:
  - the state of the economy;
  - the market and economic structure of the company;
  - the nature of the technology employed;
  - the labour market structure; and
  - the collective bargaining structure.
- Perceptions of power held by each party are concerned with securing perceived bargaining

advantage relating to the costs of agreeing and not agreeing with the other side's bargaining stance.

- The psychology of the bargaining relationship will include some element of 'attitudinal restructuring' concerning the motivation of the parties, beliefs about the other party's legitimacy, and feelings of trust and friendliness/hostility. The types of bargaining relationship which could emerge include:
  - a conflict relationship;
  - a containment-aggression relationship;
  - an accommodatory relationship;
  - a co-operative relationship; and
  - a collusive relationship.
- A number of models of bargaining behaviour have been identified and include:
  - the Warr model;
  - the Magenau and Pruitt model; and
  - Gennard and Judge's aspiration grid model.
- The criteria for the good conduct of bargaining/negotiations include:
  - ensuring equality between the parties;
  - negotiation in good faith;
  - no splitting the union;
  - no reference to informal discussions;
  - no withdrawal of offers;
  - use of procedure not sanctions;
  - no propaganda while negotiations continue;
  - maintenance of credibility; and
  - implementation of agreements.
- During face-to-face negotiations, and after successful planning and preparation, the first offer and claim should be put forward, making allowances for movement and flexibility which in turn permits subsequent revisions of offers and claims.

REFERENCES

Cairns, L. (1996) *Negotiation Skills in the Workplace*. London, Pluto Press

Chamberlain, N.W. and Kuhn, J.W. (1965) *Collective Bargaining*. New York, McGraw-Hill

Dix, G. and Oxenbridge, S. (2003) 'Information and consultation at work: from challenge to good practice'. London, ACAS: www.acas.org.uk

Farnham, D. and Pimlott, J. (1995) *Understanding Industrial Relations*. London, Cassell

Fowler, A. (1992) *Negotiation Skills and Strategies*. London, IPM

Fowler, A. (1995) *Negotiating, Persuading and Influencing*. London, IPD

Fowler, A. (1996) *Effective Negotiation*. London, IPD

Gennard, J. and Judge, M. (1997) *Employee Relations*. London, IPD

Gennard J. and Judge, M. (2002) *Employee Relations*, 3rd edn. London, CIPD

Gillen, T. (1995) *Positive Influencing Skills*. London, IPD

Kniveron, B.H. (1974) 'Industrial negotiating: some training implications'. *Industrial Relations Journal*, 5, 3, 27–37

Magenau, J. and Pruitt, D.G. (1979) 'The social psychology of bargaining', in Stephenson, G.M. and Brotherton, C.J. (eds) *Industrial Relations: A Social Psychological Approach*. Chichester, Wiley

Mathieson, H. (2000) 'Trade unions and reward', in Thorpe, R. and Homan, G. (eds) *Strategic Reward Systems*. Harlow, Pearson

Roberts, Z. (2002) 'A square deal'. *People Management*, September, 36–8

Salamon, M. (1998) *Industrial Relations: Theory and Practice*, 3rd edn. London, Prentice Hall Europe

Torrington, D. and Hall, L. (1998) *Human Resource Management*. London, Prentice Hall Europe

Torrington, D., Hall, L. and Taylor, S. (2002) *Human Resource Management*. Harlow, Pearson

Walton, R.E. and McKersie, R.B. (1965) *A Behavioural Theory of Labour Negotiations*. New York, McGraw-Hill

Warr, P. (1973) *Psychology and Collective Bargaining*. London, Hutchinson

DISCIPLINE AND GRIEVANCE: INCORPORATING AN OVERVIEW OF INDIVIDUAL EMPLOYMENT LAW

INTRODUCTION

The employment relationship is governed by the contract of employment containing the rules, procedures, duties and obligations which prescribe how all employees should behave. The contract of employment is, in theory, a legal relationship between equals, the employee, as an individual, and the employer, as a company or entity, whereby the employer undertakes to provide employment, remuneration and employment conditions in return for employee commitment to perform certain duties related to her or his job. In practice the relationship is based not upon equality of exchange but on varying degrees of inequality in the exercise of managerial power, authority and control, requiring the subordination of the employee to the employer in the fulfilment of obligations and performance of job-related duties.

The contract of employment can therefore be regarded as a legitimate method of maintaining managerial authority and prerogatives thereby ensuring employee obedience to rules, the transgression of which is normally regarded as a disciplinary matter. However, the contract of employment may not, in practice, prevent the abuse of managerial authority which can result in individual or collective grievances. Perceptions of unfair treatment and other inequities within the employment relationship, while not necessarily breaking the formal employment contract, may affect the 'psychological contract' which is based not on the formal discharge of duties and obligation, but upon the implications and expectations of behaviour which individual employees have of management and vice versa in different situations and contexts. The possibility of extreme and widespread abuse of managerial power and authority is checked to some extent by government legislation which provides employees with certain minimal statutory rights (also termed a 'statutory floor of rights'), such as the right not to be unfairly dismissed. The statutory floor of rights, which exists independently of the contract of employment, has been developed in piecemeal fashion by different governments over the post-war period. Most formal contracts of employment, irrespective of whether they concern permanent, temporary or fixed-term employment, draw attention to disciplinary rules and procedures and highlight arrangements for handling grievances. More detailed information concerning rules and procedures governing not only discipline and grievance, but also arrangements for equal opportunities, harassment and discrimination and redundancy, is provided by many companies and organisations in the form of a company employee 'handbook'. In this chapter we deal with the two most commonly used procedural issues of discipline and grievance. For convenience and ease of learning the chapter is correspondingly divided into two parts, each having its own learning outcomes: **Part One** deals with disciplinary matters and **Part Two** with grievances.

Discipline and grievance are issues which are affected by individual employment legislation, as are those of discrimination, unfair dismissal, redundancy and employment tribunals which are dealt with in Chapters 12 and 13. It is, therefore, appropriate at this juncture to present an overview of the areas covered by this legislation as part of the introductory section before we go on to consider discipline and grievance (note that the collective aspects of government legislation were dealt with in Chapter 4).

AREAS COVERED BY INDIVIDUAL EMPLOYMENT PROTECTION LEGISLATION AND STATUTORY INSTRUMENTS

Contract of employment

The contract of employment forms the basis of the relationship between employer and employee. Within two months of employment employees who work more than eight hours a week are entitled to receive a written statement containing details of their employment, payment information, terms and conditions relating to hours of work, holiday entitlement and holiday pay. They are also entitled to information concerning job titles, places of work and other specific or stated terms of employment. Other information which must be provided or be reasonably accessible include health and safety matters; pension arrangements; length of notice required; details of collective agreements by which the employee is to be bound; disciplinary rules applicable to the employee and the person to whom employees can apply if dissatisfied with a disciplinary decision or if they have a grievance about their employment and the procedure to be followed. The legislative provisions are now contained in the Employment Rights Act 1996.

Discrimination and equality of opportunity

Organisations are legally required to be 'equal opportunity' employers. It is illegal to discriminate between people when offering employment, promotion, pay, training and development or any other opportunity on grounds of racial or ethnic origin and religion; gender, including pregnancy, marital status, pay and retirement age; disability; spent convictions for previous offences (although there are exceptions); length of service or hours worked and membership or non-membership of a trade union. The main legislation covering most of these areas are the Equal Pay Act 1970; the Sex Discrimination Act 1975; the Race Relations Act 1976 and the Disability Discrimination Act 1995. Supplementary legislation includes the Sex Discrimination Act 1986; the Sex Discrimination (Gender Reassignment) Regulations 1999; the Race Relations Amendment Act 2000 and the Sex Discrimination (Indirect Discrimination and Burden of Proof) Regulations 2000 (see Exhibit 11.1).

Health and safety

An employer may not order or request an employee to carry out work that is hazardous or unsafe without first providing adequate protective equipment, clothing and training where necessary. An employer may not coerce, order or request an employee to carry out an unsafe or hazardous activity. It is the duty of employers to provide as far as reasonably practical a healthy and safe working environment and ensure that this is maintained by all concerned. The relevant legislation is the Health and Safety at Work Act 1974 and various regulations and EU Directives.

Maternity and time off

All female employees are entitled to 26 weeks' paid maternity leave regardless of length of service or hours worked. In addition to this, there is a right to a further 26 weeks' unpaid maternity leave (Employment Act 2002). Pregnant employees are allowed time off with pay for ante-natal care. On returning from maternity leave the employee has a right to return to her previous job or (if this has ceased) to suitable alternative work. A new right for adoptive parents to take statutory adoption leave with pay following the adoption of a child is introduced in the Employment Act 2002, as is two weeks' paid paternity leave for working fathers. These provisions came into force in 2003. Employers must allow reasonable time off from work in order to carry out public duties, trade union duties, looking for work and attending job interviews, retraining and career/occupational counselling after employees have been declared redundant and before they have left. Parents of children under 6 years or disabled children under 18 years have the statutory right to request flexible working arrangements.

Redundancy and transfers of undertakings

Employers may dismiss by making redundant those employees whose work no longer exists or where fewer employees are required to carry out existing levels of work. Employers must consult with any recognised trade unions as soon as it is known that redundancies are to occur. The main provisions concerning redundancy are contained in the Employment Rights Act 1996. The Transfer of Undertakings (Protection of Employment) Regulations (TUPE) protect employees' rights when there is a change of employer following a change of ownership, takeover, merger or privatisation. It also applies where there is a change of status – for

example, from public to private sector and from building society to bank.

Individual rights

The essential employee rights, clarified and strengthened in recent years by the adoption of EU Directives, by the Employment Relations Act 1999 and the Employment Act 2002, include:

- the right to fair and equal treatment regardless of length of service, hours worked or whether designated a full- or part-time employee;
- the right to employment protection from unfair dismissal after one year's continuous service regardless of hours or whether designated a full- or part-time employee;
- the right to join or refuse to join a recognised trade union and the right not to be penalised, victimised or harassed for joining or refusing to join;
- the right to adequate and continuous vocational and job training;
- the right to a healthy and safe working environment;
- the right to information, consultation and participation on key workplace issues and other matters of relevance and importance;
- the right of access to personnel files and other information held; and
- the right to be represented or accompanied in all dealings with the organisation, especially concerning matters of discipline and grievance where that right is statutory.

Exhibit 11.1

Summary of relevant employment protection legislation

1970 Equal Pay Act
1974 Health and Safety at Work Act
1974 Rehabilitation of Offenders Act
1975 Sex Discrimination Act
1976 Race Relations Act
1980 Employment Act (trade union rights for individual employees)
1981 Transfer of Undertakings (Protection of Employment) Regulations
1986 Sex Discrimination Act
1986 Wages Act (right to itemised pay statement and not to have unauthorised deductions from pay)

1988   Employment Act (right not to be unjustifiably disciplined by a trade union; right of recourse to employment tribunal if discriminated against or disciplined by an employer concerning trade union rights)

1993   Trade Union Reform and Employment Rights Act (right not to be dismissed for exercising statutory employment rights; maternity leave to 14 weeks; health and safety provisions; TUPE regulations extended to non-commercial undertakings; right of individuals to join union of choice)

1993   Industrial Tribunals Regulations

1995   Disability Discrimination Act

1996   Employment Rights Act (consolidates previous legislation concerning maternity rights, redundancy, contracts of employment and unfair dismissal)

1996   Employment Tribunals Act

1998   Data Protection Act

1998   Human Rights Act

1998   Employment Rights (Dispute Resolution) Act (ACAS scheme for voluntary resolution of unfair dismissal applications)

1998   National Minimum Wage Act

1998   Employment Rights (Dispute Resolution) Act (functions of employment tribunals)

1999   Employment Relations Act ('family-friendly' provisions such as unpaid parental leave)

1999   Collective Redundancies and Transfer of Undertakings Regulations (compulsory consultation on redundancy with recognised unions)

1999   Working Time Regulations

1999   Sex Discrimination (Gender Reassignment) Regulations (protection for transsexuals under discrimination legislation)

1999   Maternity and Parental Leave etc. Regulations (new provisions covering maternity and parental leave)

2000   Part-time Workers (Prevention of Less Favourable Treatment) Regulations (provides for equal treatment of part-time workers compared to full-time workers on similar contracts within the same organisation)

2000   Regulation of Investigatory Powers Act (ensures that investigatory powers are exercised within confines of human rights)

2000   Telecommunications (Lawful Business Practice – Interception of Communications) Regulations (specifies circumstances when telephone calls and emails may be monitored in workplace)

2000   Race Relations Amendment Act (imposes duty on public authorities to promote equality in carrying out all their activities)

2000   Sex Discrimination (Indirect Discrimination and Burden of Proof) Regulations (shift of burden of proof from complainant to respondent)

2001   Employment Protection (Continuity of Employment) Regulations (preservation of continuity where employee is dismissed and subsequently reinstated or re-employed)

2001   Employment Tribunals Regulations (Constitution and Rules of Procedure) (amends the 1993 Regulations)

2002   Employment Rights (Increase of Limits) Order (increased compensation on limits for unfair dismissal, guaranteed pay and statutory redundancy pay)

2002   Employment Act (containing provisions relating mainly to dispute resolution and maternity rights). The following regulations stem from this Act:

2002   Fixed Term Work Regulations

2003   Maternity/Paternity/Adoption Leave and Pay Orders (new rates introduced)

2003   Tribunal Reform (ongoing)

2003   Dispute Resolution (unfair dismissal rules)

2003   Equal Pay Questionnaires (introduction of questionnaire procedures to assist all parties to a claim for equal pay)

2003   Flexible Working Arrangements

PART ONE: DISCIPLINE

Learning outcomes

When you have read Part One of this chapter, you should be able to:

1. Identify the main concepts concerned with discipline.

2. Describe and distinguish between disciplinary rules and disciplinary procedures.

3. Assess how disciplinary rules and procedures operate in practice.

DISCIPLINE-RELATED CONCEPTS

In everyday usage, discipline is simple to understand. If A breaks a rule, he will be punished if found out. A basic cause–effect relationship is established: an offence is followed by retribution. The wider philosophical notions embodying questions such as: *Why have rules? (Because they are there to be broken)*, interesting though they are, need not concern us here. However, there are important ideas derived from sociology and psychology which assist our understanding of discipline within an organisational context, some of which we now consider.

Discipline and punishment

Michel Foucault (1977) argued that the notion of discipline as we know it stems from monasticism and since then has become universally accepted. A number of conditions needed to be fulfilled for its implementation. Firstly, Foucault argued that discipline is 'cellular' in that the space in which individuals are subjected to discipline is divided and subdivided into more or less self-contained units, the monastery and the monastic cell being the original models. The earliest factories emulated the cellular monastic model, the aim being to maximise output and reduce the incidence of theft, interruptions to work, disturbances and so on. Another obvious example provided by Foucault is the prison. Secondly, discipline required a control of activity so that a worker's day is compartmentalised into supervised set tasks and routines. Finally, discipline

is 'developmental' in that it encourages training in organisation-specific skills which create dependency upon that organisation. The stereotypical example of the Japanese worker within a paternalistic company is one of the most appropriate.

Foucault argued that discipline requires continuous surveillance to be effective; the perfect disciplinary apparatus would make it possible for everyone to be in full view of the observer. The high level of electronic surveillance within call centres referred to in Chapter 5 is a good case in point: 'Hierarchically-based, continuous surveillance became an integrated system, a multiple, automatic, anonymous power; for although it rests on individuals, it functions as a network, a piece of machinery' (Foucault, 1997, p. 153).

Self-Evaluation Activity 11.1
Workplace disciplinary offences
Response on website

The disciplinary system according to Foucault is punitive. In your opinion, what workplace disciplinary 'offences' would incur punishment?

Bureaucracy legitimises discipline

The employment relationship normally exists within a bureaucratic structure of managerial controls which, amongst other things, administers the disciplining, promotion, training and rewarding of employees. Without bureaucratic controls, there would be no check upon the indiscriminate use of power as coercion by management. The bureaucratic form of organisation therefore confers legitimacy upon the actions of management within a hierarchical system of authority, bounded by a set of rules and procedures acceptable to every employee. Weber's classic analysis (1947) of bureaucratic organisation contains the following elements common to all organisations:

• a continuous organisation of functions bounded by rules;
• specified spheres of competence (such as job specialisation, limited allocation of authority, and rules governing the exercise of that authority);
• a hierarchy of jobs (which Weber calls 'offices') where jobs at one level are subject to the authority of jobs at the next highest level;
• all appointments are made on the basis of technical competence and ability to do the job;
• the officials (managers) of the organisation are separated from its ownership; and
• rules, decisions and actions are made explicit and recorded in writing.

Weber emphasised the rational and seemingly efficient aspects of bureaucracy (although many studies of bureaucracy subsequently reveal inefficiencies and cumbersome constraints upon decision-making). Despite a number of criticisms made by subsequent researchers, Weber clearly established the importance of formal rules and procedures, and it is the latter which underpin the framework of discipline in contemporary organisations.

Behaviour modification and conformity to authority

Behaviour modification is a general term which refers to methods of changing behaviour through the use of feedback or reinforcement. It is based on the *behaviourist* approach to learning which argues that learning is the result of experience, and that learning cannot take place without appropriate feedback or reinforcement. The reinforcement may be positive or negative, that is, used as a reward or as a punishment, the assumption being that if a particular behaviour is rewarded, then it is more likely

to be repeated, and if that behaviour is punished, it is more likely to be avoided in future. It follows, then, that if an employee transgresses and commits an offence, then that offence should be punished (that is, negatively reinforced) in order to prevent a recurrence of the offence. The question we should ask ourselves, however, is: *Is negative reinforcement always the appropriate response to make when an employee breaches a disciplinary code?* One of the problems with punishment is that it may result in fear, resentment and hostility in the punished person. Consider the brief summary of research into rewards and punishment given in Exhibit 11.2.

Self-Evaluation Activity 11.2
Supervision and discipline
Response on website

As a supervisor, team leader or line manager, what approach (positive or negative reinforcement) would you take to deal with the behaviours listed in Exhibit 11.2?

Conformity to authority or obedience 'is the reaction expected of people by those in authority positions' (Torrington and Hall, 1998, p. 545) and is essential for the maintenance of discipline (Torrington *et al.*, 2002, p. 526). The nature and level of obedience to authority was examined by Milgram (1974) who conducted a series of controversial experiments based on the question: *Would you torture someone else simply because you were told to do so by a person in authority?* The experiments involved volunteers acting as 'teachers' (the subjects of the experiment) of those trying to learn word pairs. If the 'learner' got the pairs wrong the 'teacher' administered the electric shock (the punishment). The shocks increased in intensity the greater the number of mistakes that were made. In fact, no electric shocks were administered; the 'learner', as a member of the experimental team, and the 'experimenter' (the person in authority) colluded with each other. However, the volunteer 'teachers' believed that they were administering real electric shocks which increased in intensity the more the 'learner' failed to provide the correct answer. The point of the experiment was to determine the limits of obedience to authority of the 'teacher', and in carrying out the experiments Milgram found that

Exhibit 11.2

To reward or to punish?

Research by O'Reilly and Weitz (1980) analysed how 141 supervisors in an American retail chain store used punishments to control the behaviour of their subordinates. There were four sanctions which were commonly used:

- Informal spoken warnings
- Suspension from work
- Loss of pay
- Dismissal

Supervisors used these sanctions to stop 'incorrect' behaviours such as:

- slack timekeeping
- sloppy appearance at work
- low sales records
- discourtesy to customers

Source: Adapted from Huczynski and Buchanan, 1991, p. 123

two out of every three subjects tested administered the electric shocks up to a level which was clearly marked 'fatal' simply because an authority figure told them to do so – disturbing but true! Milgram's work therefore demonstrates that we all have a predisposition to obey instructions from those in authority, however 'unreasonable' those instructions may be. Torrington and Hall (1998) point out that:

> *Managers are positioned in an organisational hierarchy in such a way that others will be predisposed, as Milgram demonstrates, to follow their instructions. Managers put in place a series of frameworks to explain how they will exact obedience; they use discipline. Because individual employees feel their relative weakness, they seek complementary frameworks to challenge the otherwise unfettered use of managerial disciplinary power: they may join trade unions, but they will always need channels to present their grievances.* (p. 548)

Is there any justice?

As we shall see, every organisation has some sort of framework incorporating ways of dealing with problems and dissatisfaction causing grievance and

discipline, and in 1971, with the passing of the Industrial Relations Act, employees for the first time could complain to an industrial tribunal (renamed 'employment tribunals' in 1998) that they had been disciplined and unfairly dismissed as a result. As the 1971 Industrial Relations Act was repealed in 1974, provisions concerning discipline and dismissal were incorporated into the Employment Protection (Consolidation) Act of 1978 and, more recently, these and other provisions were consolidated within the Employment Rights Act of 1996. In addition, ACAS has produced a detailed guide entitled *Discipline at Work* (2000a), which provides practical advice and guidance, identifies 'best practice' and demonstrates how disciplinary issues should be dealt with. ACAS has also issued a *Code of Practice on Disciplinary and Grievance Procedures* (2000b) which was previously contained within section 199 of the Trade Union and Labour Relations (Consolidation) Act 1992 and which incorporates changes made by the 1999 Employment Relations Act (see below). With the passing of the Employment Act 2002, the government aims to reduce the amount of litigation normally involving the employment tribunal system (discussed in greater detail in Chapter 13) thereby encouraging the parties (employer and employee) to adopt and use appropriate *statutory* procedures governing the conduct of discipline and grievances (IDS, 2002). Such procedures, stemming from the 2002 Employment Act, were to be introduced in late 2003 or early 2004.

Before 1971, as Gennard and Judge (1997) indicate:

> Employers had almost unlimited power to discipline and dismiss individual employees and in many instances they were not slow to exercise this power. While it was possible for a dismissed employee to sue for 'wrongful dismissal' under the common law, this was rarely a practical option because of the time and heavy costs involved. The only time that employer power was likely to be restricted was where trade unions were present in the workplace and dismissal procedures were established through the collective bargaining process. (p. 175)

The concept of justice manifested by the employment tribunal system (which is a quasi legal institution) to some extent reflects the wider system of criminal justice within society as a whole whereby individuals should not be accused or tried until the matter has been investigated, and that evidence should be presented in court to substantiate the accusation. There should be considered judgment before sanctions are decided upon, and it is usually considered fair that there should be a right of appeal against the judgment. There are problems with this analogy, however, and Rollinson (1993) points out that:

> Criminal laws exist to protect all of society's members. Moreover they are drawn up in public (in Parliament) and society has an opportunity to choose the lawmakers every five years. Imperfect as the system is, it still contains features which are largely absent in organisations. Here, management are the lawmakers. They draw up the laws in private, and largely to protect their own interests rather than those of all the members of the organisation. It is hardly surprising, therefore, that discipline has been called a very private system of justice. (p. 133)

This 'private' system of justice has also been termed 'natural justice', the principles of which 'have emerged from ideas of equity, due process and model legal practice' (Farnham, 2000, p. 422). According to

Farnham, the following principles of natural justice apply within the employment context:

- a knowledge of the standards or behaviour expected;
- a knowledge of the alleged failure and the nature of the allegation;
- an investigation to establish a prima facie case should normally precede any allegation;
- the opportunity to offer an explanation and for this explanation to be heard and considered fairly;
- the opportunity to be accompanied or represented;
- any penalty should be appropriate to the offence and take account of any mitigating factors;
- the opportunity and support to improve behaviour, except when misconduct goes to the root of the contract, should normally be provided; and
- a right of appeal to a higher authority.

Farnham goes on to argue that:

> Disciplinary procedures should conform to the principles of natural justice. These principles have emerged from ideas of equity, due process and model legal practice. The incorporation of these principles into disciplinary procedures is likely to enhance the perceived equity of procedures and foster voluntary compliance with the rules. Any perceived unfairness may create resentment and militate against compliance. In order to command respect and support, and to operate effectively, disciplinary procedures must also be accepted as fair and equitable by managers and facilitate consistent managerial action. (pp. 421–2)

It is to these disciplinary rules and procedures that we now turn.

DISCIPLINARY RULES

Disciplinary rules are intended to let employees know the standard of conduct expected of them, and to provide managers with the necessary authority to carry out their managerial and supervisory tasks. In order to achieve these objectives, the content of disciplinary rules should be as comprehensive and specific as possible and effectively communicated to the workforce. They should also make a positive contribution to the employment relationship. Employers have considerable discretion concerning the types of behaviour they may wish to make the subject of disciplinary rules provided they are 'reasonable' and conform to common law obligations. If these rules are deemed to be unreasonable or unlawful, then 'rule enforcement will be vulnerable to legal challenge via complaints of unfair dismissal, allegations of racial or sexual discrimination, or actions for breach of contract' (James and Lewis, 1992, p. 5).

Disciplinary procedures lay down the procedural mechanisms through which the behaviour of employees can be brought into line with that behaviour expected of them. The process of formulating such procedures requires considerable thought and care if they are to perform this function both efficiently and lawfully. Procedures should, as we have already emphasised, conform to and reflect the principles of natural justice.

Disciplinary rules

Self-Evaluation Activity 11.3
Coverage of disciplinary rules
The response is given below

Bearing in mind the nature and purpose of disciplinary rules noted above, what issues and subject matter do you think these rules should cover and be concerned with?

The ACAS advisory handbook suggests that rules should normally cover issues such as: absence, health and safety (to include alcohol consumption), misconduct, substandard work, the use of company facilities including computer facilities (email and internet), timekeeping, holiday arrangements, racial and sexual harassment. The handbook also provides useful prompts which assist in the devising of rules, and include:

- **Timekeeping:**
  - Are employees required to 'clock in'?
  - What rules are applied to lateness?
- **Absence:**
  - Who authorises absence and holidays?
  - Who should employees notify when they are absent from work?
  - When should notification of absence take place?

- When is a medical self-certificate sufficient?
- When will a doctor's certificate be necessary?
- **Health and safety:**
  - Are there special requirements regarding personal appearance or cleanliness (length of hair, protective clothing, jewellery)?
  - Are there special hazards?
  - Are there non-smoking areas?
  - Is alcohol prohibited?
- **Use of company facilities:**
  - Are private telephone calls permitted?
  - Are employees allowed to be on company premises outside working hours?
  - Is company equipment generally available for personal use?
  - Are there restrictions on email and internet use?

You might have thought of other topics that may be covered by disciplinary rules such as:

- security (such as the right to search employees);
- the use of company vehicles for personal business;
- disclosure of confidential information;
- availability of overtime working;
- attendance at medical examinations;
- claiming travel and other expenses;
- ownership of patents and inventions;
- accepting gifts and hospitality;
- contact with media;
- gambling;
- fighting;
- misuse or theft of company property;
- engagement in outside work;
- posting of unauthorised notices; and
- disclosure of relationships with job applicants.

Drawing up rules and their consequences

The formulation and revision of rules will need to be based on a thorough knowledge of the organisation, its activities, the characteristics associated with the production process and the workforce. The ACAS code emphasises the importance of discussion and consultation during this process in order to ensure that the rules are not only comprehensive and realistic, but seen as fair and reasonable. Therefore, in order to be fully effective, both disciplinary rules and procedures need to be accepted as reasonable by those who are to be covered by them and by those who operate them and, to that end, ACAS recommends that management should aim to secure the involvement of employees, unions and all levels of management in drafting new, or revising existing rules and procedures. One of the chief possible dangers of unilateral rule-making is that their application may generate considerable ill-will and resistance amongst employees which can only be overcome by consultation and negotiation. In addition, it should be noted that 'dismissals based on rules agreed with employee representatives are less vulnerable to successful challenge before an employment tribunal' (James and Lewis, 1992, p. 10).

In any consultative or negotiation process, it is crucial that management consider all viewpoints seriously and provide explanations for rejecting any suggestions, whether they come from union/employee representatives or from managerial colleagues, otherwise what appear to be desirable rules may in practice make matters worse. For example, James and Lewis cite the study of a machine shop undertaken by Terry (1977) where it was informal practice of workers to clean not only machines but also the area around the machines. As a result of an agreement between management and union, there was a formal requirement that workers clean 'machine tools and associated equipment'. Workers subsequently adopted a narrow definition of this phrase and abandoned their informal practice.

Disciplinary rules should make it clear that failure to meet the standards laid down can lead to disciplinary action and it is desirable to reinforce the point by indicating the types of behaviour that will be viewed as constituting a disciplinary offence. This, of course, can be incorporated into the rules themselves and/or cross-referenced to the disciplinary procedure. Within the disciplinary rules and procedure of Lloyds TSB, the example of gross misconduct (which normally results in dismissal) includes:

- acts of dishonesty;
- forgery of signatures;
- failure to observe Lloyds TSB procedures for handling cash, goods or assets;
- refusal to obey a reasonable instruction issued by a supervisory or managerial member of staff;
- violent, abusive or threatening behaviour;
- deliberate damage to, or removal of, Lloyds TSB property;
- unauthorised disclosure of confidential information;
- serious abuse of official position; and
- conduct of such seriousness that it is likely to bring Lloyds TSB into disrepute.

In examining disciplinary rules and procedures undertaken by IRS in 1995, 1998 and 2001, within a number of public and private sector organisations, the most common offences in rank order were as shown in Table 11.1.

Table 11.1 Most common disciplinary offences: 1995, 1998, 2001

1995	1998	2001
1. Absenteeism	1. Absenteeism	1. Absenteeism
2. Performance	2. Performance	2. Performance
3. Timekeeping	3. Theft/fraud	3. Timekeeping
4. Refusal to obey instructions	4. Health and safety infringements	4. Theft/fraud
5. Theft/fraud	5. Timekeeping	5. Disobeying instructions
6. Sexual/racial harassment	6. Disobeying instructions	6. Aggression/abuse
7. Aggression/abuse	7. Assault	7. Health and safety infringements
8. Health and safety infringements	8. Aggression/abuse	8. Alcohol/drug abuse
9. Fighting	9. Alcohol/drug use	9. Assault
10. Alcohol/drug use	10. Sexual/racial harassment	10. Sexual/racial harassment

Source: IRS, 1995, 1998, 2001

However, a survey conducted by the Industrial Society in 1998 which yielded responses from 864 HR specialists revealed that poor performance was still the most common cause for using disciplinary procedures (79 per cent of respondents), followed by absence/frequent sickness (69 per cent of respondents). The survey also indicated that disciplinary action is slightly more commonly used in relation to poor performance in the financial sector than elsewhere; that cases of lateness were encountered more frequently in manufacturing than elsewhere; and that there were more instances of disciplinary action against harassment in the public/voluntary sector than elsewhere (Industrial Society, 1999).

The ACAS code stipulates that employees should be made aware of the likely consequences of breaking rules and given a clear indication of the type of conduct which may warrant summary dismissal (see the Lloyds TSB example above). The consequences of breaking rules will vary according to the offence, and in many cases counselling is sufficient. In other cases it may be necessary to apply sanctions. Some employers see the use of one or more stages of the disciplinary procedure as a sanction in itself which may include oral warnings, written warnings and final warnings. Other more directly punitive measures include penalties which adversely affect take-home pay. This may be done by cutting merit or bonus payments; by changing an individual's basic pay rate through downgrading; or by temporary loss of earnings, such as suspension without pay. According to the IRS survey of 2001, the two most common sanctions cited by organisations are transfer to other work and downgrading. Others include suspension with or without pay, termination of employment with notice and summary dismissal.

It is necessary to consider the impact of penalties upon individuals and the employment relationship generally. Certain penalties should be avoided:

- if they are unsuitable – for example, by demotion or transfer to other employment if no suitable alternative jobs are available;
- if they are not going to help resolve underlying problems giving rise to the disciplinary action in the first place;
- if they are arbitrarily imposed and inconsistent with the gravity of the offence; and

- if, by their imposition, they are unlawful (for example, suspension without pay, demotion or transfer can be imposed only if contractual authority has been secured in advance or if the individual employee agrees to accept them).

In addition, the ACAS code states that the dismissal sanction for first breaches of discipline should never be used except in cases of gross misconduct. Gross misconduct is not defined in the code, and organisations have some discretion as to what to include within this category, partly because of the varied nature of their activities (see the Lloyds TSB example given above). Types of behaviour common to most organisations and which are listed as constituting gross misconduct include theft, fighting, malicious damage to company property, flagrant breaches of safety regulations, intoxication by alcohol or drugs, and serious cases of racial and sexual harassment. New offences, which are increasingly being categorised as examples of serious or gross misconduct, include unauthorised use of software, failure to protect computer data and unauthorised entry into computer files (IDS, 1997). It is important to note that dismissal should not be made an automatic penalty in relation to acts of gross misconduct 'since unfair dismissal law still requires consideration to be given to whether it is an appropriate sanction in the circumstances . . . and care must be taken to ensure that managers are left with sufficient flexibility as to the precise penalty to be applied. Otherwise they may be forced into taking disciplinary action which is unreasonable in the circumstances of a particular case' (James and Lewis, 1992, p. 18).

Communicating and implementing rules

Under section 1 of the Employment Protection (Consolidation) Act (EPCA) 1978, employers were required to provide written particulars of terms and conditions of employment and, in enterprises of over 20 employees, a note specifying any disciplinary rules applicable to the employee, as well as changes to these rules. Section 1 of EPCA was incorporated within the Employment Rights Act 1996, sections 1–6. However, three points should be borne in mind:

1. If the employer has fewer than 20 employees on the date the employment commences, the statement need not refer to disciplinary rules or procedures.
2. Although the Employment Rights Act does not state that employers must have disciplinary rules, the ACAS code emphasises their desirability.
3. Rules, disciplinary decisions, grievances and procedures relating to health and safety at work are exempted because separate rules and procedures are thought to be appropriate in this area and should be referred to in the information provided by employers under section 2 of the Health and Safety at Work Act 1974.

Exhibit 11.3

The Benefits Agency Rules of Conduct (sample only)

Basic Rules of Conduct

You must:
- maintain at all times a high standard of integrity and conduct
- be honest and beyond all suspicion of dishonesty
- attend work consistently and regularly

Private interests and your work

You must not:
- put your private interests before your duty
- allow your duty and private interests to conflict
- make use of your official business to further your private interests

Official premises and property

You must not:
- damage or deface official premises
- exhibit or distribute notices or handbills on official premises without permission
- use official postage paid envelopes for private communications

Equal opportunities

- You must not discriminate against anyone based on your preconception about the capabilities or characteristics of any particular group

Computer Misuse Act 1980

Under the Computer Misuse Act it is a criminal offence to access computer material:
- knowingly and without lawful authority
- to use that access to commit or facilitate the commission of further offences
- to modify computer material

Confidentiality

You must not:
- disclose information unless it has been made officially available to the public
- discuss confidential matters if there is a risk of them being made public

Absences

- You must not be absent from duty without permission, except in the case of sudden domestic trouble
- If there is a serious breakdown in public transport, you must make every effort to reach your normal place of duty, unless otherwise instructed
- You must tell your line manager as early as possible on the first day of absence if you are sick or have had contact with an infectious disease
- You must tell your line manager if you are continuously sick for four days or more while on annual leave

Private interests and outside activities

- You must not use or appear to use your public position for private gain
- You must not do any outside activity, which requires your attendance at any time during normal official working hours
- If you are employed on visiting or interviewing duties you must not engage in the following activities without first obtaining official approval: licencee of public house/off licence; sales assistant; barman/barmaid; waiter/waitress

Betting or gambling

- You must not bet or gamble during official hours

Smoking

You must:

- take care in the disposal of cigarette ends
- not smoke in mandatory non-smoking areas
- not smoke during interviews with the public

Source: Benefits Agency: Rules of Conduct (1998)

The employer should not only provide disciplinary rules but should also ensure that every effort is made to ascertain that employees know and understand the rules which 'may best be achieved by giving every employee a copy of the rules and by explaining them orally. In the case of new employees this should form part of the induction programme' (ACAS, 2000a). Many larger organisations include the rules in their staff handbooks (see example of the Benefits Agency in Exhibit 11.3).

A growing responsibility for enforcing disciplinary rules rests with line managers. According to the IRS survey, 2001, line managers appear to be playing a greater part in enforcement and operation of disciplinary procedures. However, predictions of wholesale devolution of disciplinary and grievance functions to line management appear to be unfulfilled; much of the disciplinary workload is still vested in specialist HR staff. It is, however, important that line managers are adequately informed of any disciplinary responsibilities they may have and are provided with the skills and responsibility for carrying them out. Senior management should also demonstrate willingness to support subordinates on disciplinary issues, otherwise managers will see little point in taking their role seriously. The lack of such support is an all too common source of complaint among supervisors and junior managers (James and Lewis, 1992).

DISCIPLINARY PROCEDURES

The Employment Act 2002 now compels employers to devise statutory dismissal, disputes and grievance procedures in order to tackle the growing caseload of employment tribunals. Employers losing employment tribunal cases often do so because they have either deficient procedures or no procedures whatsoever. As a minimum, employers must now adopt the procedures as outlined in the Act and in consultation with ACAS (see below). In addition, the Employment Relations Act 1999 introduced the statutory right to be accompanied by a fellow worker or trade union representative at disciplinary and grievance hearings. This right applies to all workers, not only employees working under a contract of employment and is spelt out in section 3 of the revised ACAS code (2000b). The revised code also emphasises the need for greater involvement of managers and employees in the formulation of new, jointly authored discipline and grievance procedures, stressing the importance of:

- communicating all procedures within the organisation;
- making provision for confidential notes to be kept of investigations and hearings, including witness statements;
- the employee knowing in advance the complaint against him or her, and 'all the relevant evidence'; and
- employees being told of their statutory right to be accompanied at any procedure by a colleague or trade union official.

The management of discipline comprises a major part of the work of personnel and HRM practitioners, and according to the 1998 and 2001 IRS surveys there is an ever-increasing devolution of this responsibility to line managers. The same surveys report that employers dismiss, on average, 0.5 per cent of their workforce each year, and 1.7 per cent of employees in 1998 and 2 per cent of employees in 2001 faced disciplinary action short of dismissal. Discipline, therefore, remains an important issue for both employers and employees. According to the ACAS code as reported in the IRS 1998 survey:

Disciplinary rules and procedures are necessary for promoting fairness and order in the treatment of individuals and in the conduct of industrial relations. They also assist an organisation to operate effectively. Rules set standards of conduct at work; procedures help to ensure that standards are adhered to and also provide a fair method of dealing with alleged failures to observe them.

Employee perception of fairness is a crucial factor in determining whether disciplinary action itself is unjust and/or inconsistent or vice versa. If the former, employers can be subject to legal challenge. The potential for legal challenge and poor industrial relations emphasises the importance of having a written disciplinary procedure which is coherent and meets the criterion of natural justice. The absence of disciplinary procedures, procedures which are poorly drafted and ambiguously worded, and the lack of sensitivity and skill in dealing with disciplinary matters can have major repercussions upon, and implications for, industrial relations. For example, according to Labour Market Trends (2002), dismissal and disciplinary measures were the fourth most common cause of strike action in the year to June 2002, with some 20 stoppages involving 9900 employees arising over disciplinary action.

Interestingly, Martin (1995) argues that the best cure for discipline is prevention, and if the 'right' people are recruited, the problem does not arise. He recommends that employers should check references and use objective selection techniques, together with the operation of appropriate induction and mentoring techniques and practices. The IDS (1997) survey also reveals that in order to reduce the actual number of disciplinary cases, employers often stress counselling rather than punishment. As a result of examining 50 procedures, the survey revealed that:

- there is greater informality in the initial stages of disciplinary procedures;
- many organisations prefer to deal with issues such as harassment and performance under separate procedures;
- misconduct due to alcohol or drug abuse may also be dealt with under separate procedures, with support and counselling offered;
- employers wish to encourage employee performance by means other than punishment-centred or punitive approaches.

The nature and content of procedures

The ACAS Code of Practice makes clear that procedures should not be viewed as negative sanctions and be punishment-oriented, but should provide encouragement for individuals to improve their conduct, that is, provide positive reinforcement of good behaviour. To this end, the code suggests certain guidelines as to the nature of the disciplinary procedure. Procedures should:

- be in writing;
- specify to whom they apply;
- be non-discriminatory;
- provide for matters to be dealt with without undue delay;
- provide for proceedings, witness statements and records to be kept confidential;
- indicate the disciplinary actions that may be taken;
- specify the levels of management that have the authority to take various forms of disciplinary action, ensuring that immediate superiors do not normally have the power to dismiss without reference to senior management;
- provide for workers to be informed of the complaints against them and, where possible, supplied with all relevant evidence before any hearing;
- provide workers with an opportunity to state their case before decisions are reached;
- provide workers with the right to be accompanied;
- ensure that, except for gross misconduct, no worker is dismissed for a first breach of discipline;
- ensure that disciplinary action is not taken until the case has been carefully investigated;
- ensure that individuals are given an explanation for any penalty imposed; and
- provide a right of appeal – normally to a more senior manager – and specify the procedure to be followed.

The coverage of procedures, according to James and Lewis (1992), needs to take three main aspects into consideration. Firstly, the level at which procedures operate, particularly within larger multi-establishment organisations, can be problematic. Procedures can, and do, operate at workplace, establishment, departmental divisional and organisational levels; however, in line with the trend to devolve numerous management functions to unit or workplace level, a growing number of organisations confine procedural arrangements to that level. Workplace-based procedures have the advantage

that they are more responsive to local needs, involve fewer levels of decision-making and reinforce local management responsibility for disciplinary matters. Secondly, in the interests of fairness and consistency, it is important that disciplinary procedures should not discriminate between different types of worker. James and Lewis point out that 'as a general rule, it is undesirable to operate different disciplinary procedures for different groups of workers' (p. 29), even though they may be performing different types of jobs and possess different skills. In addition, according to the ACAS handbook, procedures should not vary according to an employee's length of service; to do so might suggest favouritism and/or inequity of treatment. Thirdly, the subject matter of disciplinary procedures can be problematic as the range of issues incorporated into a procedure can be extremely broad. However, in recent years there has been a tendency to differentiate between procedures on particularly sensitive issues such as gender and racial discrimination and harassment. Hence, there may be a procedure devoted entirely to sexual harassment, another to bullying and yet another to equal opportunities. Other areas identified for special treatment include absenteeism, alcohol and drug abuse and work capability. The reasons for a greater differentiation of procedures include:

- the emergence of unfair dismissal case law which identifies procedural steps employers should take if dismissals on grounds of ill health or poor work performance are to be regarded as fair. A similar situation exists with sexual and racial harassment;
- increased awareness of costs incurred by employers owing to absenteeism, drug and alcohol abuse; and
- the desirability of retaining experienced staff in whom substantial investment has been made.

An increasing number of organisations will resort to disciplinary procedures in these sensitive areas only when all else has failed (but probably excluding racial/sexual harassment which, if proved, could constitute 'gross misconduct'). In the case of alcohol abuse, for example, Liverpool City Council has produced a policy statement and procedure, the main elements of which are summarised in Exhibit 11.4.

Exhibit 11.4

Policy statement on alcohol/problem drinking

Objectives

1. To promote an awareness of the possible harmful consequences of excessive drinking.
2. To encourage employees to seek voluntary advice and assistance.
3. To help minimise the need to invoke disciplinary procedures.

Policy

1. The city council regards alcoholism or problem drinking as an illness which requires treatment. The council is therefore prepared to assist any employee who has a drink problem.
2. The council will make available to employees guidance, including appropriate literature, on the harmful effects of alcohol and on means of identification of those suffering from excessive drinking.
3. Any employee who suspects that they may have an alcohol problem will be encouraged to voluntarily seek advice and guidance and treatment if necessary. Such advice may be obtained from the Departmental Personnel Officer or Welfare Officer and all requests will be treated in the strictest confidence.
4. An employee's immediate supervisor and work colleagues may often be the first to notice signs of a drinking problem and should alert either senior management or the Personnel Officer.
5. If, during treatment, an employee is unable to attend for work, he/she will be considered to be on sick leave.
6. Where there is no reasonable prospect of an employee being able to continue/resume his/her duties, and where, accordingly, an employee is declared medically unfit to carry out the duties of their employment, an offer of suitable alternative employment will be made, if this is possible.
7. Disciplinary measures will not be involved unless treatment is refused, and if subsequent work performance is not satisfactorily maintained and this is proved to be due to continued drinking.
8. Employees who are identified as having a drinking problem and refuse treatment will be dealt with under the normal disciplinary procedure.
9. A problem drinker cannot be excused from complying with normal standards of conduct and safety required of council employees. Any employee who behaves contrary to those standards or is found to be intoxicated on duty will be subject to the agreed disciplinary procedure.
10. Having accepted help or treatment and resolved the alcohol-related problem, the employee's normal promotional prospects will not be impaired.
11. The policy is applicable to all employees irrespective of the position they hold and does not discriminate at any level.

The policy statement and procedures apply equally to other drug-related problems.

Source: Liverpool City Council: Policy Statement on Alcohol/Problem Drinking (1998)

Designing the formal disciplinary procedure

As with disciplinary rules, the drafting of disciplinary procedures should, ideally, be based on the consent and involvement of managers, employees and their representatives. The ACAS handbook *Discipline at Work* (2000a) contains a 'model' disciplinary procedure, shown in Exhibit 11.5, which comprises three main stages. These cover oral first warnings in the case of minor offences, and written warnings for more serious offences, followed by final written warnings for serious misconduct which, if not observed, would lead to the final step of disciplinary transfer, disciplinary suspension or dismissal, according to the nature of the misconduct.

Exhibit 11.5

Using the ACAS model disciplinary procedure

(1) Purpose and scope

This procedure is designed to help and encourage all workers to achieve and maintain standards of conduct, attendance and job performance. The company rules (a copy of which is displayed in the office) and this procedure apply to all employees. The aim is to ensure consistent and fair treatment for all in the organisation.

(2) Principles

(a) No disciplinary action will be taken against a worker until the case has been fully investigated.

(b) At every stage in the procedure the worker will be advised of the nature of the complaint against him or her and will be given the opportunity to state his or her case before any decision is made.

(c) At all stages of the procedure the worker will have the right to be accompanied by a shop steward, employee representative or work colleague.

(d) No worker will be dismissed for a first breach of discipline, except in the case of gross misconduct when the penalty will be dismissal without notice or payment in lieu of notice.

(e) A worker will have the right to appeal against any disciplinary penalty imposed.

(f) The procedure may be implemented at any stage if the worker's alleged misconduct warrants such action.

(3) The procedure

Stage 1 – First warning

If conduct or performance does not meet acceptable standards, the worker will normally be given a formal oral warning. The individual will be advised of the reason for the warning and that it constitutes the first stage of the disciplinary procedure. A note of the oral warning will be kept but it will be spent after . . . months, subject to achievement and sustainment of satisfactory conduct and performance.

Written warning – if the misconduct or poor performance is more serious the worker will receive a first formal written warning from their supervisor. This will give details of the complaint, the improvement or change in behaviour required, the timescale allowed for this and the right of appeal. A copy of this written warning will be kept by the supervisor but will be disregarded for disciplinary purposes after . . . months subject to achievement and sustainment of satisfactory conduct or performance.

The warning will also inform the worker of the right of appeal, and that a final written warning may be considered if there is no sustained satisfactory improvement or change.

Stage 2 – Final written warning

If the offence is serious, or there is a failure to improve during the currency of a prior warning for the same type of offence, a final written warning will be given to the worker. This will give details of the complaint, the improvement required and the timescale. It will also warn that failure to improve may lead to action under Stage 3 (dismissal or some other action short of dismissal) and will refer to the right of appeal. A copy of this written warning will be kept by the supervisor but it will be disregarded for disciplinary purposes after . . . months subject to the achievement and sustainment of satisfactory conduct or performance.

Stage 3 – Dismissal or other sanction

If there is still a failure to improve the final stage in the procedure may be dismissal or some other action short of dismissal such as demotion or disciplinary suspension or transfer (as allowed in the contract of employment). Dismissal decisions can only be taken by the appropriate Senior Manager, and the worker will be provided, as soon as reasonably practicable, with written reasons for dismissal, the date on which the employment will terminate, and the right of appeal. The decision to dismiss will be confirmed in writing.

If some sanction short of dismissal is imposed, the worker will receive details on the complaint, will be warned that dismissal could result if there is no satisfactory improvement, and will be advised of the right of appeal. A copy of the written warning will be kept by the supervisor but will be disregarded for disciplinary purposes after . . . months subject to achievement and sustainment of satisfactory conduct or performance.

(4) Gross misconduct

The following list provides examples of offences which are normally regarded as gross misconduct:

1. theft, fraud, deliberate falsification of records;
2. fighting, assault on another person;
3. deliberate damage to organisational property;
4. serious incapability through alcohol or being under the influence of illegal drugs;
5. serious negligence which causes unacceptable loss, damage or injury;
7. serious act of insubordination; and
8. unauthorised entry to computer records.

If you are accused of an act of gross misconduct, you may be suspended from work on full pay, normally for no more than five working days, while the alleged offence is investigated.

If, on completion of the investigation and the full disciplinary procedure, the organisation is satisfied that gross misconduct has occurred, the result will normally be summary dismissal without notice or payment in lieu of notice.

(5) Appeals

A worker who wishes to appeal against a disciplinary decision should inform . . . within five working days. The Senior Manager will hear all appeals and his/her decision is final. At the appeal any disciplinary penalty imposed will be reviewed but it cannot be increased.

Both the 1998 and 2001 IRS surveys into disciplinary practice in larger organisations and the findings of the Workplace Employee Relations Survey (WERS) 1998, confirm previous survey findings in terms of both the proportion of employers adopting procedures and, having adopted them, the extent to which they follow the ACAS guidelines. All the respondent organisations in the IRS survey have written disciplinary procedures which apply to all employees, while around 92 per cent of all the WERS workplaces have them, with the situation remaining unchanged since 1984. However, 98 per cent of unionised workplaces had formal disciplinary procedures in place in 1998 as compared with 99 per cent in 1990 (Millward *et al.*, 2000).

The latter survey reveals that both disciplinary and grievance procedures are more common in larger workplaces, but even in the smaller workplaces with 25 to 49 employees, 88 per cent operated a disciplinary procedure. Nearly all organisations and workplaces in both surveys followed ACAS advice in adhering to the stages of the procedure; only a small minority (3 per cent in the WERS survey) did not permit employees to be accompanied by a third party in actions taken to discipline or dismiss them, 'and a further 2 per cent only allow the option of bringing a supervisor or line manager along – of little comfort if the dispute is centred around relationships with them, as they often are' (ibid., p. 14). The WERS also found that:

Where they [the employees] can be independently accompanied, 41 per cent of workplaces allow the employee to choose whom to accompany them. The remainder have a variety of options, ranging from trade union representatives (45 per cent), to full-time union officials (27 per cent) and nearly all permit colleagues to join the employee (87 per cent). Almost all the cases where there is no right to be accompanied, or where the option is confined to the boss, are workplaces without any union presence at all. (ibid., p. 14)

In addition, the survey conducted by the Industrial Society (1999) confirms the widespread use of procedures by employers, with 99.5 per cent of organisations using them. This is good news for the vast majority of employers for whom the statutory minimum procedure is a very basic framework indeed. The standard dismissal and disciplinary procedure (DDP) is intended to cover most eventualities in a very rudimentary way, while the modified DDP is intended to be used for employees who have been summarily dismissed for gross misconduct. Both types of procedure are detailed in Exhibit 11.6.

Exhibit 11.6

Standard dismissal and disciplinary procedure (Employment Act 2002)

Step 1: statement of grounds for action and invitation to meeting

- The employer must set out in writing the employee's alleged conduct or characteristics, or other circumstances, which led him to contemplate dismissing or taking disciplinary action against the employee; and
- The employer must send the statement or a copy of it to the employee and invite the employee to attend a meeting to discuss the matter.

Step 2: meeting

- The meeting must take place before the action is taken, except in the case where the disciplinary action consists of suspension;
- The meeting must not take place unless
  (a) the employer has informed the employee what the basis was for including in the statement under Step 1 the ground or grounds given in it, and
  (b) the employee has had a reasonable opportunity to consider his or her response to that information;
- The employee must take all reasonable steps to attend the meeting;
- After the meeting, the employer must inform the employee of his decision and notify the employee of the right to appeal against the decision if he or she is not satisfied with it.

Step 3: appeal

- If the employee does wish to appeal, he or she must inform the employer;
- If the employee informs the employer of his or her wish to appeal, the employer must invite the employee to attend a further meeting;
- The employee must take all reasonable steps to attend the meeting; and
- The appeal meeting need not take place before the dismissal or disciplinary action takes effect.

Modified dismissal and disciplinary procedure

Step 1: statement and grounds for action

The employer must:

- Set out in writing – (i) the employee's alleged misconduct which has led to the dismissal, (ii) what the basis was for thinking at the time of the dismissal that the employee was guilty of the alleged misconduct, and (iii) the employee's right to appeal against dismissal, and
- Send the statement or a copy of it to the employee.

Step 2: appeal

- If the employee does wish to appeal, he or she must inform the employer.
- If the employee informs the employer of his or her wish to appeal, the employer must invite the employee to attend the meeting.
- The employee must take all reasonable steps to attend the meeting.
- After the appeal meeting the employer must inform the employee of his final decision.

Self-Evaluation Activity 11.4

A defective procedure
This SEA has no commentary

You will be able to attempt this exercise when you have completed the following part of this chapter dealing with the ACAS 'model' procedure and the minimal procedure laid down in the 2002 Employment Act. Exhibit 11.7 is an example of a less than adequate disciplinary procedure. You have been called in as a consultant to advise on redrafting this procedure. Redraft the procedure according to ACAS and other guidelines.

Other points to note concerning formal procedures

There are a number of other aspects to note concerning the devising and operation of formal procedures which we shall now briefly mention.

- Written warnings should be used to encourage employees to bring their conduct or performance up to the required standard and should be disregarded after a specified period of satisfactory conduct.
- To ensure that disciplinary procedures are consistently applied by line managers, some written procedures provide a monitoring role for personnel specialists. Where line management is expected to take responsibility for disciplinary matters, organisations may also offer training or written guidance to help managers fulfil their disciplinary role and to help avoid legal challenge or a collective grievance. Almost 90 per cent of organisations in the 1998 and 2001 IRS surveys provide such written guidance (see below).
- The ACAS recommended staged approach to handling disciplinary matters could be applied selectively in some cases. For example, specific procedures may specify whether one or more stages can be omitted if appropriate, and it is not always necessary to give three warnings before deciding upon dismissal. Gross misconduct is an instance where the staged approach can be discarded altogether, and procedures should also point out that one or more stages could be omitted for serious offences short of gross misconduct.
- The full procedure often does not apply to new employees who are undergoing a probationary period or are on 'trial'.
- The procedure should make it absolutely clear about who is to be involved in carrying out disciplinary hearings at different stages of the procedure. For example, a Stage 1 oral warning and verbal investigation as a result of unsatisfactory job performance or conduct may be conducted

Exhibit 11.7

Defectors Ltd's defective procedure

Disciplinary procedure

This procedure will be used for all cases of disciplinary action:

STAGE 1   A manager or immediate supervisor shall issue a verbal warning, specifying the behaviour that is unacceptable.

STAGE 2   If a verbal warning has been issued, and then if there is a further breach of discipline the manager or supervisor shall issue a final written warning.

STAGE 3   If there is a further breach of discipline or the employee has committed a serious breach of discipline the manager can dismiss that person.

Warnings shall be taken off the record if no further warnings are issued within 12 months of the issue of the previous warning.

by a line manager. More serious or repeated offences involving formal interviews and written warnings/investigations may be undertaken jointly by line and personnel managers.

- The right of employees to appeal against a disciplinary decision should be formally acknowledged within the disciplinary procedure, as it is in the statutory procedure, particularly in view of the possibility that a dismissal might be judged unfair if a right of appeal is not provided. James and Lewis (1992) point out that:

> In practice, appeals are lodged on two main grounds: that the finding of guilt was wrong; and/or that the penalty imposed was out of proportion to the offence. To avoid subsequent misunderstandings it is therefore advisable to make it clear in procedures that both types of appeal are allowed. It is also sensible to indicate that appeals can be resolved, where appropriate, by the substitution of a lesser penalty.

The consequences for the employer of being lax in disciplinary matters are highlighted in a survey for Department of Trade and Industry conducted by Earnshaw (1998). The study claims that the reason for employers losing employment tribunal cases relates almost without exception to shortcomings in the operation of disciplinary procedures. The factors most commonly cited in tribunal decisions were:

- employees not being given the opportunity to defend themselves or put forward their side of the story;
- an employee not being made aware of the evidence against him or her;
- no disciplinary hearing having been held;
- insufficient investigation of the misconduct;
- warnings given prior to dismissal not being made explicit;
- employers deliberately choosing not to have a disciplinary procedure.

Handling disciplinary matters

There are four identifiable stages with which all parties should be familiar, even though they may not all be used in most disciplinary cases. According to James and Lewis (1992) and ACAS (2000a), these are:

- counselling and informal action;
- conducting preliminary investigations;
- preparing for disciplinary hearings/interviews;
- conducting a disciplinary hearing or interview; and
- selecting an appropriate penalty.

Exhibit 11.8

Written guidance for managers

Organisations often provide (and should provide) detailed information explaining how to implement and operate the procedures, and will include:

(1) **Using the procedure appropriately:** at what stage should a manager initiate the procedure? Advice stresses that informal counselling will often be a more satisfactory way of dealing with routine misdemeanours than formal interviews.

(2) **Determining the level:** which level of disciplinary action should apply to which kind of misconduct? For example: repeated lateness – formal verbal warning; a first breach of health and safety policy – first written warning; swearing at line manager or refusing to follow a reasonable instruction – final written warning; repeated breach of health and safety policy – dismissal; theft, racial/sexual harassment – dismissal for gross misconduct.

(3) **The role of personnel** in providing advice and ensuring the proper application of procedures. In many organisations, personnel or HRM specialists act in an advisory role and support line managers through the disciplinary process by informing on legal obligations, procedural details and case preparation.

(4) **The rights of the employee** to be accompanied, to full information about the nature of the offence concerned, to a fair hearing.

(5) **Investigating a case and preparing for a disciplinary interview:** for example: 'The investigating officer will need to establish the facts by obtaining witness statements, checking records, interviewing staff as appropriate. Managers will need to establish not only what has happened but also why an incident has occurred. Investigation does not automatically lead to disciplinary action.'

(6) **Conducting a disciplinary interview**

(7) **Deciding on the disciplinary action**

(8) **Cases involving criminal offences:** 'An employee will not necessarily be subject to formal disciplinary action because of his/her arrest, charge or conviction for a criminal offence *outside his/her employment*. In such circumstances the criteria for determining whether the disciplinary procedure should be invoked will be the extent to which the alleged offence is one which makes the employee unsuitable for his/her type of work, or which, if it becomes widely-known, would be detrimental to the authority's/company's interests or would in any way weaken public confidence in the conduct of the authority's/company's business.'

Source: Adapted from IRS, 1998

Counselling / informal action

In many cases it is not advisable to take formal action at the outset. Timely counselling may be all that is required to rectify matters which require sensitivity and empathy.

Self-Evaluation Activity 11.5

To discipline or not to discipline?
Response on website

The example in Mini case 11.1 may present a dilemma for an inexperienced supervisor. Advise her as to how to deal with the situation.

Mini case 11.1
The drowsy employee

John has been arriving at his desk unusually tired and, because of this, he has been rather short-tempered. On more than one occasion during the past three weeks or so he has shouted at colleagues, and in so doing has resorted to the use of the occasional four-letter expletive. This behaviour is generally regarded as out of character, and most would agree with a close colleague who said of John: 'He is normally so obliging, friendly and efficient so this behaviour is really out of character.' On a number of occasions throughout the day, John has been caught napping when he should have been working. Not surprisingly, John's productivity has dipped, although his timekeeping has been as good as usual. One or two of John's close colleagues are aware that John's wife Sarah had given birth to a healthy child about a month ago. However, they do not know that Sarah has been suffering from post-natal depression and that John has been helping with baby-related chores.

John's supervisor, Alice, has noticed the deterioration in his performance, but because of his good employment record does not want to put him on a disciplinary charge. She has only been in post for six months and does not want to make the wrong decision about John, so desperately needs some good advice.

A private conversation may elicit explanatory information concerning a problem with a worker who has been performing satisfactorily under normal circumstances. Additional training, advice and/or coaching may be needed, or appropriate assistance that the employee may have been unaware of could

be provided. In any event, any criticism should be constructive but the employee should nevertheless be warned that if within a specified timescale whatever aspect of her or his work, attendance, timekeeping etc. does not improve, then the next stage will be the formal disciplinary procedure. A written record of this and of any counselling and informal advice given, together with any action taken if necessary, should be made for reference purposes but will not be considered as part of a disciplinary record. The specific example of the approach adopted by Barclays is given in Exhibit 11.9.

Conducting preliminary investigations

Before action is taken, any alleged breach of conduct should be fully investigated. This may take the form of collecting documents, witness statements, observation of the place where the event is said to have occurred, and possibly searching employees or their property. The employee whose conduct is

---

Exhibit 11.9

Barclays' advice on informal disciplinary action

If informal action is required, give advice and counselling.

- In all cases hold the discussion out of the hearing of other employees. It should be a two-way discussion aimed at endeavouring to resolve any shortcomings in conduct or performance and encouraging improvement. Criticism should be constructive and the emphasis should be on finding ways in which the employee can remedy any shortcomings;
- Listen to any explanations put forward. If it becomes evident that there is no case to answer, this should be acknowledged and confirmed to the employee;
- Where an improvement is required, make sure that the employee understands what needs to be done, how performance or conduct will be reviewed, and over what period. A detailed action plan should be drawn up and agreed with the employee. He/she should be informed that, if required improvement is not achieved and maintained, the formal disciplinary procedure will be implemented;
- Where it appears that there may be a drug- or alcohol-related problem, the matter should be referred, in the first instance, to human resources;
- Be aware that many physical and mental health issues can cause a problem in the workplace. Where it appears that this may be a factor affecting the employee's conduct or capability, refer to human resources;
- Take care that a counselling discussion does not turn into a formal disciplinary interview, as this can deny the employee certain rights allowed under the formal procedure. If during the discussion it becomes obvious that the matter is more serious, the discussion should be adjourned. It should be made clear to the employee that the matter will be pursued under the formal disciplinary procedure;
- Make a note of any counselling discussion for reference purposes.

Source: Barclays Bank: Guidance on Procedures (1998)

under investigation must be told of the allegations against her or him. This should be done formally, making clear at this stage that it is purely an investigation that is being carried out and that the employee will have the opportunity to state his or her case. The investigative stage is extremely important because, should a case come to a tribunal, the tribunal will want to establish that the employer carried out a reasonable investigation into the alleged misconduct. Failure to do so will seriously prejudice the employer's case. In some situations, it may be considered necessary to suspend the employee while the investigation takes place. Suspension during investigations is not a disciplinary penalty and should be used when it is thought necessary to remove those concerned in an incident whilst investigations take place concerning cases such as alleged fraud, serious theft, fighting, drunkenness and other offences of similar gravity. An investigatory suspension should last for as short a period as possible and employees should be provided with a full explanation, ideally confirmed in writing. Suspension should be with pay unless the contract of employment allows for suspension without pay in such circumstances.

Preparing for a disciplinary hearing

The main aim of the disciplinary hearing/interview is to improve the employee's conduct or performance. The structure of the disciplinary interview should be planned and finalised, with attention being paid to timing of the interview and to the selection of appropriate accommodation where privacy and confidentiality can be maintained. All relevant facts should be assembled and if the complaint concerns absence, the pattern of absence for a period of months should be established and any special circumstances should be considered. The important rule here is that after the thorough investigation, all the relevant facts should be presented. Where necessary, written statements should be obtained from the person making the complaint, together with any witnesses, and the documentation shown to the employee well in advance of the interview so that the employee can prepare a defence and arrange for representation. The employee should therefore have full details of the nature of the complaint 'as it is a fundamental part of a fair disciplinary procedure that employees should know the case against them' (*Spink* v *Express Foods* (1990) IRLR 181). Employees should be reminded of their statutory right to be represented by a union representative or colleague who should also be provided with full details of the complaint. Finally, employees should be informed of where and when the interview or hearing will be held (see Exhibit 11.10).

Conducting the interview

A disciplinary interview or hearing will be convened only if the investigation reveals evidence of conduct

---

Exhibit 11.10
Notice of disciplinary interview

Dear_____   Date_____

I am writing to tell you that you are required to attend a disciplinary interview on_____at_____am/pm which is to be held in_____ At this interview the question of disciplinary action against you, in accordance with the company's discipline procedure, will be considered with regard to:

(Statement of alleged misconduct)

You have a statutory entitlement to be accompanied by another work colleague or your trade union representative.

Signed_____

Source: ACAS, 2000a

that may merit disciplinary action. Although conducting the interview too rigidly might inhibit constructive discussion, there is a greater danger that an unsystematic approach will cause the meeting to become confused and muddled. ACAS recommends the following procedure for conducting interviews:

1. The complaint against the employee is stated from the evidence that has been gathered either by the manager conducting the interview or by someone else deputising.
2. Any supporting witnesses make their statements.
3. The employee and representative have the chance to question the manager and witnesses about their statements.
4. The employee and/or representative give their side of the story and may call supporting witnesses.
5. The manager conducting the interview questions the employee and witnesses.
6. There may be a more general discussion in which both sides can raise any issues that were not covered earlier.
7. The employee is given a chance to highlight the aspects they wish to emphasise, including any mitigating circumstances. This opportunity for the employee to have a right of reply is extremely important. As Gennard and Judge (2002) put it: 'no right of reply – no natural justice' (p. 262).
8. The manager conducting the interview summarises and adjourns the meeting.
9. During the adjournment, the manager considers everything that has come out of the interview and decides what action to take. The length of the adjournment may be quite short in a straightforward case – say, half an hour – or longer if the issues are complex. In all cases management should avoid jumping, or even appearing to jump, to an immediate conclusion as soon as the interview ends.
10. The meeting is then reconvened and the manager announces the decision. This should then be confirmed in writing.

If during the hearing the employee refuses to give his or her version of events, the reason for not doing so should be explored, perhaps by inviting the employee to discuss the issue with a member of the personnel department. If the employee declines the invitation, it should be made clear that this will be to the detriment of the employee.

Caution must be exercised when criminal proceedings are being brought against the employee. As we noted earlier, minor offences committed outside company time may have little bearing upon the employee's work conduct, and even when brought to the attention of the employer could well be disregarded unless the offence and its consequences directly affect the performance of the employee's job. For example, if the employee is employed as a driver, is involved in a minor car accident outside working hours, is subsequently breathalysed and found just over the limit, then this will affect the employee's capability to do the job when the results of criminal proceedings are known.

Interviewing skills

Disciplinary interviews, in common with other types of interviews, require a number of skills, which are summarised in Exhibit 11.11.

Choosing the appropriate sanction

Although one or more stages of the disciplinary process itself may be regarded by many employers as sanctions in themselves, particularly for routine, non-repeatable offences, the more common sanctions range from the oral warnings to dismissal, as exemplified by the model procedure we looked at earlier. We also identified the common sanctions or penalties short of dismissal. James and Lewis (1992) point out that while there should be consistency of treatment, similar cases should not necessarily get the same treatment and individuals 'should be treated on their merits, with all relevant circumstances taken into account' (p. 69). These include:

- the employee's disciplinary record;
- the employee's position within the organisation, higher standards being expected from senior employees;
- the employee's length of service; employers may deal more leniently with those having long service; and
- the employee's age – young and inexperienced, or old enough to know better.

Exhibit 11.11

Disciplinary interviewing skills

The skills required when chairing other kinds of meetings are of value in disciplinary interviews. These include ensuring that everyone understands the purpose and procedure of the interview; keeping control firmly but constructively; preventing progress from becoming slowed by minor matters; ensuring that everyone (particularly the employee) leaves feeling they have said what they wanted to; using adjournments to maximum benefit; and summarising to prevent anyone from misunderstanding the key issues.

Handling the employee's anger skilfully can be very important. Employees charged with a disciplinary offence sometimes respond with personal accusations. Aspersions of this kind can be hurtful, and it is natural to want to refute them. Yet a manager who is provoked into an angry reaction may confirm in the employee's mind the very accusation that has been made. The manager must remain calm and make a reply on the lines of: *'I hear what you say, but I am not going to enter into an argument about it. Now let's move on.'*

Communication and questioning skills are vital. The employer must understand the issues and their possible consequences. The manager must state key points plainly, repeating them if necessary and check that they are understood. Communication is a two-way process, and managers must be just as careful to listen as to explain.

The questioning skills involved are similar to those in selection interviewing. Open-ended questions should be used, such as: *'What happened in the incident involving a customer last Friday?'* rather than closed or leading questions such as: *'Were you rude to a customer last Friday?'* Managers must avoid any line of questioning that could be seen as indicating a discriminatory attitude towards women or people from ethnic minorities.

Counselling skills may also be relevant. Even when disciplinary action is fully justified, there are often cases where it can be implemented with counselling. The best outcome of many disciplinary interviews is that the employee remains in employment and improves their conduct or performance. To achieve this, the manager may need to encourage the employee to see why faults have occurred and suggest improvements.

So, instead of saying: *'If you are late without good reason more than twice in the next three months, you will be dismissed,'* the counselling approach would be: *'Because you are now on a final warning, I think you should set yourself a timekeeping target. What do you think you should aim for over, say, the next three months?'* An employee who has ownership of an improvement target is far more likely to meet it than if one has been imposed without discussion.

Source: Fowler, 1996, p. 24

Self-Evaluation Activity 11.6

Choosing the appropriate sanction

Response on website

Which of the following sanctions do you think would be the most appropriate for each stage of the disciplinary procedure? 1. warnings; 2. withholding a pay rise; 3. deductions and fines; 4. suspensions; 5. demotion and transfer; 6. dismissal with notice; 7. dismissal without notice.

The tests of fairness and reasonableness

'Careful preparation and a well-conducted interview are not guarantees that individuals will not complain of unfairness, but they are essential if the test of reasonableness is to be satisfied' (Gennard and Judge, 2002, p. 263). The criterion of fairness must also be met when putting principles into practice. What, therefore, constitutes fair disciplinary practice and fair dismissal? There are two main categories of reasons for fairly disciplining and dismissing employees; these are: misconduct during employment and lack of capability.

Misconduct

As Gennard and Judge (1997) note, there are two types of misconduct: the first is persistent rule-breaking which can be dealt with quite straightforwardly, either informally, or if that does not work through the formal procedure. The employee will have no grounds for complaint 'provided that the disciplinary code is applied in a sensible and equitable manner' (p. 188). The second type is that of gross misconduct, and provided all the procedural mechanisms are adhered to, this should also be non-problematic. However, there are some instances where there is uncertainty concerning the case and how to deal with it. Examples here include suspected gross misconduct which cannot be readily proved because of lack of evidence and information, and where the employee concerned, assuming that he or she had been dismissed, could bring a complaint of unfair dismissal to the employment tribunal. The case of *British Home Stores* v *Burchell* (1978) IRLR 379, concerning alleged theft, was significant because of the judgment and the rules derived from it. Subsequently called the 'Burchell Rules', they contain a test of reasonableness for employers in cases where an employee is suspected of a dismissible offence. Basically, an employer must demonstrate:

- that the dismissal was for a bona fide reason and not on a pretext;
- that the employer's belief that the employee committed the offence was based on reasonable grounds of evidence indicating that in all probability the employee did commit the offence;
- that the employer's belief that the employee committed the offence was based on a reasonable investigation before dismissal.

Disobedience

Everyone working under contracts of employment has a duty to obey lawful and reasonable orders. This means that employees are *not* required to obey an order if to do so would break the law; nor are they obliged to follow instructions which fall outside the scope of the contract. There are a number of points to be stressed:

- Employees may have a contractual duty to perform tasks beyond the type of work they normally carry out, and refusal to do so would lead to disciplinary action.
- The reasonableness of disciplinary action is not to be determined solely by job description or contractual obligations. 'For example, employees may be disciplined for refusing to accept changes in job content or working hours if it can be demonstrated that the employer had a sound business reason for reorganising' (James and Lewis, 1992, p. 92). It is good practice, however, to consult individuals and union or workplace representatives before doing so.
- It is not automatically fair to dismiss a person for a clear breach of the employer's rules unless it can be shown that the discipline was a reasonable reaction to the circumstances. For example, if a cashier fails to record one sale on the till, it may be unreasonable to dismiss the cashier on the basis of one unexplained failure to comply with till procedure.
- Employers have a duty to act reasonably in health and safety matters, and where employees disobey orders on safety grounds, the matter should be investigated promptly before disciplinary action is taken.

Dishonesty

The contract of employment places an implicit obligation of mutual trust and confidence which dishonesty (stealing, fiddling expenses, falsifying time-keeping records, failing to disclose relevant information such as criminal convictions) can jeopardise. It is important to note:

- that dismissal will not be fair for relatively minor offences if a warning would have been more appropriate; and
- that the Burchell Rules will apply on reasonable grounds of suspicion.

Bad language

Again, the form of disciplinary action (dismissal or warning) appropriate for dealing with foul or abusive language will depend not only on the actual words used, but also on their context. In any event, disciplinary action for abusing a superior will normally be justified if managerial authority, trust and confidence are undermined. In this context, James and Lewis (1992) suggest that: 'In order to act reasonably, the events prior to the bad language should be examined as well as the incident which gave rise to the complaint. For example, a heat-of-the-moment outburst may be unlikely to recur and an apology may suffice' (p. 51).

Smoking

Employers have a duty to take reasonable care of the health and safety of their employees. Given the dangers of passive smoking, it may be appropriate and reasonable to take disciplinary action against employees who break no-smoking rules, but only if it is reasonable to do so under the circumstances. Moreover, a distinction should be made between the employee who deliberately breaks the non-smoking rule and the inexperienced employee who innocently smokes in a prohibited area. ACAS (1997) advises:

> If employees have been properly consulted and their views taken into account most organisations should find little difficulty in introducing and maintaining a smoking policy. Any problems that do arise can usually be dealt with by counselling. Where an employee persistently disregards a smoking policy, employers may wish to consider whether it is appropriate for this to be treated in the same way as other breaches of company rules and dealt with under the disciplinary procedure. (p. 12)

Therefore if the employer introduces no-smoking rules after consultation and fair notice of the change, and these rules are operated in reasonable fashion with fair procedures being followed in dealing with any breaches, then employers are likely to be found to have behaved reasonably.

Drinking and drugs

This has been dealt with adequately earlier in the chapter, using the example of Liverpool City Council.

Fighting

This may be considered as gross misconduct, but in some cases a warning will be adequate. Violence inflicted upon managers is assumed to amount to gross misconduct, and attacks by managers upon subordinates will be assumed to be equally serious. In considering a reasonable response to fighting, the following factors should be borne in mind:

- the employee's length of service;
- the employee's general work record; and
- the extent of any provocation and the nature of the employer's response to it.

Sexual and racial harassment

We consider this in more detail in Chapter 12. Harassment is generally viewed as gross misconduct; it is also an infringement of the anti-discrimination legislation whereby employers are liable for the acts of their employees committed in the course of employment. The extent to which these problems are taken seriously is indicated by the growing number of organisations with equal opportunities policies and separate procedures for harassment.

Disloyalty

Working during spare time is not normally subject to disciplinary action unless the activity causes serious harm to the employer or the contract of employment contains a prohibition. The obligation not to disclose confidential information varies according to the nature of the contract of employment, but in principle the leaking or misuse of confidential information may warrant disciplinary action.

Lack of capability

Capability is associated with an employee's ability to do his or her job because of, firstly, poor performance and, secondly, poor health or sickness as manifested by absenteeism.

Performance

Poor performance covers many circumstances and situations. Employers should encourage satisfactory levels of performance through training and other support. The ACAS handbook (2000a) also suggests that careful selection and training can minimise the risk of poor performance and that employers should heed the following principles:

- The standard of work required should be explained and employees left in no doubt about what is expected of them. Special attention should be paid to ensuring that standards are understood by employees whose English is limited and by young persons with little experience of working life.

- Job descriptions should accurately convey the main purpose and scope of each job and the tasks involved.
- Employees should be made aware of the conditions which attach to any probation period.
- The consequences of any failure to meet the required standards should be carefully explained.
- Where an employee is promoted, the consequences of failing 'to make the grade' in the new job should be explained.

The ACAS handbook (2000b) recommends that all cases of poor performance should be investigated, although it is not necessary to prove that the employee was incompetent. Line managers should be advised by personnel/employee relations specialists that no disciplinary action should be taken before:

- the employee has provided an explanation (which could concern domestic or health problems);
- the employee has been counselled appropriately;
- suitable, alternative work could be provided;
- length of service is considered;
- previous performance is considered; and
- the precise extent to which the performance is below standard is measured.

Any targets set during the period allowed for improvement must be realistic, and performance should be monitored. It is only when these 'best practice' measures have been taken, and despite this the outcome is unsatisfactory (that is, performance has not improved), that the disciplinary procedure can be invoked. James and Lewis (1992) suggest:

Warnings can be particularly valuable in distinguishing cases of genuine incapability from those where there is a failure to exercise to the full such talent as is possessed. Employees who are genuinely incapable will not improve simply because a warning has been issued. According to the Employment Appeals Tribunal (EAT), cases where people have not come up to standard through their own carelessness, negligence or idleness are much more appropriately dealt with as cases of misconduct than of incapability. (p. 89)

Absence

Authorised absence such as holidays and long-term absence due to ill-health are not disciplinary matters, although in the case of the latter, where there is little likelihood of the employee returning to work, it can be assumed and argued that the contract of employment has automatically terminated through 'frustration' (that is, no legally required dismissal and therefore no notice is due).

Unauthorised absence (that absence which can be explained by reasons other than illness, or other authorised absence) can constitute a serious breach of contract and, pending investigation and giving the employee an opportunity to explain, would normally be regarded as a matter justifying warnings rather than dismissal for a first offence. But if there is reasonable suspicion that a sick note is being abused (for example, an employee seen shopping while on sick leave), dismissal may be justified. Employees who take leave after having been refused permission, and warned of the potential consequences of doing so, can be fairly dismissed.

The problem for personnel and employment relations practitioners is that while unauthorised absence is a disciplinary matter, most absences are not categorised as 'unauthorised' and will be recorded as 'sickness', therefore raising the question as to whether sickness absence in every case is, in fact, genuine. If absence is monitored, and records of absences are kept which show frequency, duration, and any pattern based on time of week/month/year of absence, these will 'enable the manager to substantiate whether a problem of persistent absence is real or imagined' (Gennard and Judge, 2002, p. 267). The ACAS handbook (2000b) provides the following advice concerning the handling of frequent and persistent short-term absence:

- Absences should be investigated promptly and the employee asked to give an explanation.
- Where there is no medical advice to support frequent self-certified absences, the employee should be asked to consult a doctor to establish whether medical treatment is necessary and whether the underlying reason for absence is work-related.
- If after investigation it appears that there were no good reasons for the absences, the matter should be dealt with under the disciplinary procedure.

- In all cases the employee should be told what improvement in attendance is expected and warned of the likely consequences if this does not happen.
- If there is no improvement, the employee's age, length of service, performance, the likelihood of a change in attendance, the availability of suitable alternative work and the effect of past and future absences on the business should all be taken into account in deciding appropriate action.

If absence is due to illness and is supported by medical certificates, but there is nevertheless considerable doubt about the nature of the illness, the employee can be requested to be examined by an independent doctor appointed by the company; there is no compulsion to be examined by another doctor, although Gennard and Judge (1997) point out that:

> With the growth of occupational sick pay schemes, many organisations have overcome this problem by building compulsion into their scheme rules. Very often, advising an employee that such an examination will be required if attendance does not improve is sufficient to resolve the problem. (p. 193)

In cases where an employee has an unsatisfactory record of intermittent sickness absence, dismissal following a final written warning is fair, even though medical evidence may not be forthcoming (*Lynock v Cereal Packaging* (1988) IRLR 510).

Self-Evaluation Activity 11.7

Three disciplinary cases to consider
Response on website

Main cases 11.1–11.3 are three cases of fairly common examples of disciplinary offences. Answer the question(s) at the end of each case.

Main cases 11.1–11.3
Case 11.1 Accident-prone

John Smith is a heavy goods vehicle driver for a firm that supplies fresh fruit and vegetables around the Home Counties and has been employed with the firm as a driver since he joined it in 1970. John is a steady employee and has a good disciplinary record. He presently drives a large articulated lorry on runs from Kent and Sussex into London. In recent years the roads and motorways have become extremely busy and congested, lorries have increased in size and drivers seem to have become increasingly impatient and rattled. All this has contributed towards stress, and while John enjoys the job in that it gets him around, he dislikes the heavy traffic compared with the much quieter and more relaxed times he can remember during the 1970s.

About eight years ago, John had a major accident with his lorry during high winds. The empty lorry was blown into a ditch and was extensively damaged, but John was unhurt apart from shock effects and the company's insurers paid up. John was advised to travel in calmer weather in future. This accident was followed by many others, a few of them major. One accident which John did not report involved backing into a stationary car and, although the police were not involved, the car's owners contacted John's firm. The Transport Manager (TM) did not take formal disciplinary action against John but he was told that these incidents should stop.

In recent years there had been no improvement in John's accident record and the TM was increasingly reluctant to let John continue driving, especially as insurance costs were rising. But there was no other work which John could do, even if he wanted to. The annual renewal notice for the firm's vehicle insurance arrived which contained a letter from the insurance company's management with the following paragraphs:

> We have reviewed your insurance contract with us and there is a matter which I have to raise with you. Over a period of years, there has been a relatively large number of claims made which have resulted in our paying out considerable sums of money to settle these. Having analysed the details of the claims we find that the majority are due to one driver, Mr J. Smith.
>
> It is noticeable that the premium we have had to charge over the years has increased considerably due to loss of no claims discount and a loading for the high rate of accident claim. We have concluded that we can no longer issue insurance cover for your vehicles under the present arrangements. We would consider issuing cover providing that Mr J. Smith was no longer a driver, as we now consider him to be an uninsurable risk due to his accident proneness.

Despite having contacted the insurance company concerning the short notice between sending the letter and the actual renewal date, no compromise was possible: John was banned from driving **all** vehicles. The problem for the firm was compounded by the fact that no other insurance company would provide cover – except at a prohibitively high premium – unless John was released from all driving.

After consultations between the Managing Director and the TM it was decided that John should be told of the situation and that the firm had no option but to dismiss him. John was asked to see the TM next morning. The atmosphere was tense, particularly so since the two had known each other for most of their lives. John asked why he had not been informed of the problem before and the fact that the firm had paid hefty premiums because of the high number of accidents. The TM could not offer alternative employment and John did not pursue the matter, probably because he was too shocked and could not take in the situation. At last the TM told John that he would be dismissed from his job as driver from that day. John was offered a small, ex gratia severance payment over and above his pay in lieu of notice. This it was hoped would deter John from making a claim for unfair dismissal (employment tribunals were not mentioned just in case this would give John ideas). John went home and the TM sent a letter (see below) confirming the outcome of the meeting and enclosed a cheque for the amount due, which John received the next day.

I am writing to confirm the outcome of our meeting today and to enclose a cheque for the amount due to you. It is no longer possible to employ you as a driver and there is no other type of alternative employment you will take with us.

We request that you acknowledge receipt of the money and that it is accepted on the basis of a full and final settlement, precluding any future claims relating to the termination of your employment with this firm.

Questions

1. Comment on how the firm should have handled John's case.
2. Attempt a role-play of the dismissal meeting between John and the TM.

Case 11.2
The alcoholic

Computa Co. is a small computer firm specialising in producing modems and motherboards for 'whole system' producers. The firm has built up a reputation in the face of stiff competition for the quality of its products, and employs 40 people in production and despatch departments. The atmosphere is friendly and there is a sense of frenzied activity as the firm attempts to achieve its delivery dates.

The production section employs 20 people and is headed up by Chris who has been with the firm since it started up 17 years ago. Chris has seen many changes in technology during this period and the firm is very loyal to him for all the hard work and dedication he has shown. Chris has found things somewhat testing in recent years owing to the rapidity of change and the increased sophistication of the technology but, despite this, he is a good manager and can get the best out of people.

Owing to the increased complexity of technological developments, the firm created the position of Technical Manager six months ago and recruited Len Jones, a young hardware specialist with an MBA to the post. Len was to concentrate on the technical side, while Chris had the responsibility of managing the department. Len settled into the job quickly and proved extremely competent, having sorted out many technical problems and made some innovations. The firm was very pleased with Len and congratulated itself on the appointment.

Over a period of time, however, there was a discernible change in Len's demeanour and general attitude towards his job, and Chris was the first to notice this. Chris suspected that Len had a drink problem. Len developed a regular habit of drinking at lunchtime and coming back to the department incapable of doing much work. Chris often had to take Len home in his car in order to avoid trouble. The frequency of these occasions has now been noticed and commented upon by the other staff, but the matter has not been brought to the attention of anyone else. Chris feels rather protective towards Len because of the technical support and expertise Len offers and, if anything, Chris tends to cover up for Len in a sensitive and potentially embarrassing situation.

The situation has now deteriorated further with Len often taking Monday mornings off to recover from heavy weekend drinking sessions. Len tries to excuse himself by claiming he is unwell and certifies himself sick. Chris still feels protective towards Len but finds it increasingly difficult to justify this stance when Len comes to work still drunk. The other workers have mentioned nothing to Chris, but he detects considerable unease about the situation and is at a loss about what to do. Chris has, of course, spoken to Len about his drinking, but this does not prevent Len from falling back into his bad habits.

One morning, Jane, a new administrative assistant, sees Chris and tells him that her uncle from Australia, who is on holiday, is due to return to Australia later that day and requests to finish work two hours early so that she can accompany her uncle to the airport. Chris is in the middle of dealing with a large order which requires considerable and urgent paperwork and which Jane has been appointed to deal with. Chris tells Jane that the urgency of the job means that he cannot allow her to have time off and said that he was intending to ask Jane to work into the evening to finish it off. Jane is very annoyed and cannot help herself when she says: 'You can allow that lazy drunken Len of yours to have days off boozing, but you won't let any of us take an hour off. Don't think we haven't noticed you taking that drunkard home after lunch. I've had enough of this two-faced attitude of you lot!', whereupon she storms out of the office slamming the door behind her.

Jane returns to her work but finds she cannot concentrate, and during the break she tells her colleagues about the incident. Her colleagues are very supportive and offer to back her up. Still angry, Jane leaves work without mentioning anything to Chris, but tells her colleagues that they can inform Chris that she will be in the pub waiting to 'have a go' at Len for his drunken behaviour. The next day, Jane turns up for work as usual.

Questions

1. What advice would you give to the owner of the firm concerning the action that should be taken with regard to:
   - Len's situation
   - disciplinary action against Len
   - disciplinary action against Jane
   - Chris's managerial performance.
2. Role-play a meeting between Jane, Chris and the owner which has been called to discuss the incident of Jane leaving work.

Case 11.3
Playing games

In October 2003, the management of the Supa Dupa Company was made aware that certain staff members were using computer games on the internet during working hours. The accounts manager was concerned about the recent increase in the amount of overtime claimed for this department and decided to establish whether the allegation concerning computer misuse was valid. The IT department was requested to monitor each individual's use of the computer and asked to provide weekly reports to Accounts outlining when, and for how long, staff were using games packages during working hours. Monitoring was carried out over an eight-week period. Following receipt of initial reports from IT, it was clear that certain members of staff were abusing the system. Staff were permitted to use games packages during lunch breaks, but not in working hours. A memo was sent to all staff in Accounts informing them that they were not allowed to play games on computers during office hours, and warning that staff would be monitored. The consequences of not complying were also outlined in the memo.

Further monitoring by the IT department concerning computer use established that one employee in particular working in Accounts, Sonia Playstation, had, despite the warnings contained in the memo, continued to play games on her company computer during working hours. Furthermore, she had been working during recent weekends on overtime pay in order to catch up on a backlog of work, while continuing to play games on the company computer. In addition, it was discovered by her supervisor, Nina Tendo, that Sonia had outstanding orders in her desk drawer and had also been falsifying her daily performance indicator sheet. Nina spoke to Sonia informally, attempting to seek some sort of explanation but was met with sullen silence alternating with verbal abuse.

On 5 January 2004, Sonia was given a verbal warning in accordance with the company's disciplinary policy and procedure which was documented in her personnel records. Despite this and continued monitoring of her performance, Sonia's behaviour did not improve.

Question

Sketch a scenario outlining the likely course of the disciplinary process and indicating the likely outcome, making certain assumptions about the behaviour of Sonia as you proceed

Summary points for Part One

- The relevant concepts which assist our understanding of the practice of discipline include:
  - the concept of punishment;
  - the concept of bureaucracy which legitimises discipline and punishment;
  - the concept of behaviour modification which explains the nature and purpose of rewards (positive reinforcement) and punishments (negative reinforcement);
  - the concepts of conformity to authority and obedience; and
  - the concept of justice and natural justice.
- Disciplinary rules are essential in order to measure standards of conduct and provide managers with the authority to carry out their tasks. Rules should establish that failure to meet expected standards could lead to disciplinary action.
- Disciplinary procedures should be applied in order to help modify behaviour which falls short of the behaviour which is required.
- Ideally, rules and procedures should be applied in accordance with ACAS guidelines, while acknowledging the statutory nature of procedures.

- Failure to do so could result in complaints concerning unfair dismissal or unfair treatment.
- Surveys such as WERS (1998) reveal that the vast majority of organisations have disciplinary procedures although there are considerable variations in how they are operated.
- Proper handling of disciplinary matters will help to ensure fairness and 'reasonable behaviour' on the part of the employer, and should include:
  - conducting appropriate preliminary investigations;
  - adequate preparation for disciplinary hearings and interviews;
  - conducting a fair hearing or interview; and
  - selecting the appropriate penalty.
- The two main categories comprising potentially fair dismissal (assuming the employer acted fairly and reasonably and in accordance with the rules of natural justice) are:
  - misconduct during employment which includes disobedience; dishonesty; bad language; smoking; drinking and drugs; fighting; sexual and racial harassment and disloyalty; and
  - lack of capability concerning poor performance and absenteeism.

PART TWO: GRIEVANCES

Learning outcomes

When you have read Part Two of this chapter, you should be able to:

1. Determine the nature of grievances and why they exist.

2. Explain the importance of grievance procedures.

3. Explain how grievances are handled.

WHAT IS MEANT BY GRIEVANCE?

A grievance is the acquisition of a sense of injustice. Accompanying the sense of injustice is a feeling of dissatisfaction. We could argue that justice is the more important concept because, as Kelly (1998) suggests:

Dissatisfaction may be necessary to motivate collective action (and individual grievance) but it is not sufficient. For example, an employee may be unhappy with a pay freeze, but if he or she feels the measure was either fair (everybody suffered the same outcome) or unavoidable (the firm was facing bankruptcy) then behavioural consequences are unlikely. (p. 27)

Kelly goes on to argue that management groups seek to legitimise their actions:

- by conforming to national laws, European Directives and collective agreements;
- by reference to beliefs shared with subordinates such as 'fairness';
- by arguing that 'employee consent can be inferred from their actions, such as signing a contract or undertaking new duties' (ibid., p. 27).

Injustice therefore comes about when management violates established rules (for example, by instructing people to do work that is not part of their job), or when employer actions conflict with shared beliefs, or when employees withhold their consent because of actions which they deem unreasonable or unfair, or when employees attempt to assert their rights. All these instances can give rise to shared or collective grievances as well as grievances at an individual level. A grievance is, therefore, essentially **the articulation of a complaint arising from both a feeling of dissatisfaction and a sense of injustice.**

We should note that feelings of dissatisfaction at the level of the individual rarely turn into complaints and the 'few dissatisfactions that do produce complaint are also most likely to resolve themselves at that stage' (Torrington *et al.*, 2002, p. 530).

Self-Evaluation Activity 11.8

Complaints galore

This SEA has no commentary

After a brief summary provided by John Monks (the former TUC General Secretary), a number of examples of complaints to the TUC 'Bad Bosses' hotline are provided. Which of the categories identified by Kelly (1998) would you put them in? (The categories are: violation of established rules; conflict with shared beliefs; unreasonable/unfair actions; assertion of rights.)

The TUC 'Bad Bosses' hotline (see Exhibit 11.12) which was run for one week at the beginning of December 1997, received 4950 calls, many of them serious complaints about extremely bad practice. Three-quarters of the callers worked in small or medium-sized firms with less than 1000 employees. We may safely assume that most of the complaints made to the hotline would not have otherwise come to light as grievances in the callers' own organisations. Grievances, formally expressed, are a relatively rare

occurrence as employees may not question superiors' judgements, do not want to be considered as 'troublemakers', and 'believe that nothing will be done as a result of their complaint' (Torrington and Hall, 1998, p. 551).

The cases

Bullying (38 per cent of all calls)
David Anderson and his colleagues were subject to a campaign of public humiliation, verbal abuse and finally unfair dismissal by their boss at a media company in Northern Ireland. Mr Anderson said he had seen his boss make someone stand in a corner of the office wearing a dunce's hat, and had regularly seen and heard him shouting and swearing at staff in public areas. He said the boss frequently tried to chat up female members of staff and attempted to look up their skirts. He was also known to have been abusive about people's religions.

A manager in a national supermarket was verbally and physically abused by the store manager. When she stuck up for her staff, he pushed her into his office and threw things at her. She has been depressed and suicidal as a result and is unable to work.

Pay (25 per cent); long hours (13 per cent); no holidays (4 per cent)
A security guard from South Wales works a 65-hour shift with no break. He is expected to work 16-hour shifts on a normal working day. He does this job for £2.50 an hour and receives no overtime payments.

A foreign exchange bureau worker working for a major ferry operator on the south coast has to work 13-and-a-half-hour shifts without a break. There is no overtime pay, sick pay or holiday pay and union membership is not allowed.

Contracts (15 per cent)
A company in the North East have 'cancelled' Christmas. The firm are not allowing staff the time off that they had been promised following changes to their contracts. If staff do not work on Christmas Day or Boxing Day they have to use two days' annual leave to cover this time off. The company were making staff redundant who had been on sick leave even though doctors' notes had been provided.

Some people working at a manufacturing firm in the West Midlands are on contracts while others are not. Although their contract states staff are entitled to 15 days' sick leave, one woman employee said that in fact they are expected to take it as annual leave. This annual leave amounts to 10 days – unpaid.

Exhibit 11.12

The TUC view

It is hard to open any company annual report or pick up a management text book without reading that staff are a company's greatest asset. Many companies . . . do treat most of their staff fairly most of the time . . . but there is a rough end to life at work in Britain today. The technology and the jobs may have changed, but workplace relations can come straight from the pages of Dickens. The TUC's 'Bad Bosses Hotline' . . . revealed that many workplaces rely on bullying, exploitation and callous disregard for the welfare of employees. Much of this is the legacy of the 1980s. Encouraged by government moves to reduce rights at work, too many employers practised the worst kinds of macho-management. High unemployment and legal curbs on unions meant that many workers felt unable to resist.

Bosses are free to get rid of staff who have worked for them for less than two years with impunity. With many low paid sectors suffering high levels of staff turnover in any case, this gives bosses a free hand to treat their staff in the appalling ways we reveal in this report. More surprising to many will be the large number of calls received from managers and staff working for larger companies and organisations which reveal two further groups of bad workplaces:

- those that have 'rough treatment' built into their business plans with middle and junior managers given no choice but to treat their employees harshly;
- even in well-managed companies, individual managers can get away with bullying their staff and making their lives a misery.

Source: TUC 'Bad Bosses Hotline' (1998): www.tuc.org.uk/'bad bosses

Health and safety (11 per cent)
Female toilet cleaners for a city council in Scotland were increasingly worried following the latest round of cutbacks. It meant they now have to clean both men's and women's toilets at night as well as during the day. The women are scared of attacks in these toilets and complained to their employers. However, council officials seem not to have taken any notice. The caller will be spending Christmas Eve cleaning the toilets.

Employees of a Lincolnshire factory reported a list of health and safety abuses that made their working lives a misery. Top of their list was having to put their hand up and wait half-an-hour for permission to go to the toilet. A spokeswoman for the company said a continuous production line had to be kept going and that was why toilet breaks had to be ordered and staggered.

The IRS grievance survey (2002) revealed that up to 2001 the most common type of grievance formally processed using the individual grievance procedure was concerned with pay and grading (2001) and introduction of new working practices (1998).

However, during 2002 the issue of harassment and bullying has come into prominence (confirming the TUC hotline data), with 45 per cent of all complaints raised by employees being harassment and bullying related. The higher profile of harassment and bullying may suggest a greater awareness of these issues, together with greater support for employees from external sources such as the EOC, and internal policies concerning discrimination, diversity and harassment (see also Chapter 12). Other significant complaints raised by employees, according to IRS (2002) include discipline (27 per cent); new working practices (23 per cent); grading (22 per cent); discrimination (18 per cent); work allocation/staffing levels (17 per cent); non-pay terms and conditions (17 per cent); pay (15 per cent); health and safety (2 per cent) and 'miscellaneous' (18 per cent).

GRIEVANCE PROCEDURES

The current ACAS code of practice provides a checklist for handling grievances, in which it recommends that most routine complaints are best resolved informally in discussion with the worker's immediate line manager. Where grievances cannot be resolved informally, then the formal grievance procedure should be used. Worker's grievances should be dealt with quickly and equitably 'and at the lowest level possible within the organisation at which the matter can be resolved' (ACAS, 2000a). It is the responsibility of management to develop procedures which, if they are to be effective, need to be endorsed by both workforce and management. To that end, both parties, including trade unions, should be willing to participate fully in devising procedures and taking on the responsibility of joint authorship.

Legislative aspects and statutory procedures

In order to reduce the need for litigation by encouraging internal methods of dispute resolution, the Employment Act 2002 introduced statutory minimum internal grievance and disciplinary procedures. The Act also requires employees to raise grievances with their employers before applying to an employment tribunal. Two types of statutory procedure operate (see Exhibit 11.13). The first is the standard grievance procedure (SGP), which is used in the vast majority of cases, and the second is the modified grievance procedure (MGP), which applies where the employee has already left employment as in cases of constructive dismissal (see Chapter 13). The Act as yet contains no definition of what constitutes a grievance and relies upon both the existing vague definition contained in the Employment Relations Act 1999 as something which 'concerns the performance of a duty by an employer in relation to a worker' (section 13), and the more specific definition and examples contained in the ACAS handbook and code (ACAS, 2000a, b).

As with discipline, workers have a statutory right to be accompanied by a fellow worker or trade union official at grievance hearings as established by the 1999 Employment Relations Act. It has always been good employment relations practice to allow a worker to be accompanied or represented, and many organisations include such rights in contracts as a matter of course. Recognition agreements with trade unions will normally include rights for

members to be represented by either a lay or full-time official.

As in the case of discipline, most organisations have grievance procedures that go substantially beyond the statutory minimum SGP. The Workplace Employment Relations Survey (Cully *et al.*, 1999), indicates that around 91 per cent of all workplaces surveyed had a formal procedure in place for dealing with individual grievances. Not surprisingly, nearly all public sector workplaces (99 per cent) had formal grievance procedures. The method by which complaints are presented to management range from informal chats and discussion, to formal presentation of the complaint using the formal grievance procedure. In larger, unionised organisations arrangements for handling grievances are established by joint agreement within the existing negotiating machinery, as part of the existing collective agreement, which may be involved as part of the procedure if the grievance is not resolved during the earlier stages of the process (Gennard and Judge, 2002).

The way in which grievances are handled – or not handled – is partly influenced by the culture of an organisation. Farnham (2000) argues that:

> In a unitary or neo-unitary organisation there are assumptions that there are common values and common objectives and that management's right to manage is accepted by all. Therefore conflict within the organisation is seen as dysfunctional. Individuals may feel inhibited from raising a formal grievance because of the effect it may have on their career prospects and for fear of being labelled as a 'troublemaker' or a 'deviant'. In a pluralist organisation, conflict is seen as inevitable and it is assumed that employees have a right to question management decisions and management's application of policies and procedures. Employees therefore normally accept that they have a right to raise grievances where they feel that this is necessary and the formal grievance procedure is likely to be more commonly used. (p. 414)

Our previous examples of incidents described by employees on the 'bad bosses' hotline more than likely occur in organisations which adopt a unitary view of the employment relationship. These organisations may well have a grievance procedure, but

Exhibit 11.13

Employment Act 2002

Standard Grievance Procedure

Step 1: statement of grievance

- The employee must set out the grievance in writing and send the statement or a copy of it to the employer.

Step 2: meeting

- The employer must invite the employee to attend a meeting to discuss the grievance.
- The meeting must not take place unless (a) the employee has informed the employer what the basis for the grievance was when he or she made the statement under Step 1 above, and (b) the employer has had a reasonable opportunity to consider his response to that information.
- The employee must take all reasonable steps to attend the meeting.
- After the meeting the employer must inform the employee of his decision as to his response to the grievance and notify the employee of the right to appeal against the decision if the employee is not satisfied with it.

Step 3: appeal

- If the employee does wish to appeal, he or she must inform the employer.
- If the employee informs the employer of his or her wish to appeal, the employer must invite the employee to attend a further meeting.
- The employee must take all reasonable steps to attend the meeting.
- After the appeal meeting the employer must inform the employee of his final decision.

Modified Grievance Procedure

Step 1: statement of grievance

- The employee must: (a) set out in writing (i) the grievance, and (ii) the basis for it, and (b) send the statement, or a copy of it, to the employer.

Step 2: response

- The employer must set out his response in writing and send the statement or a copy of it to the employee.

the culture of fear which exists in some of them obviously discourages employees from taking their complaints further.

It should be noted that while the Employment Rights Act 1996 specifies that the contract of employment should contain 'a note specifying to whom the employee can appeal if he has a grievance and how to deal with this' and 'a note of any further steps available in the grievance or disciplinary procedures' (section 1), and that this applies to all organisations employing more than 20 employees, there is no specific legal requirement that all organisations should have a formal procedure. Guidance for employers on how to devise a grievance procedure and what it should contain is to be found in the ACAS code of practice (2000b), extracts of which are paraphrased in Exhibit 11.14.

Exhibit 11.14

Extracts from the ACAS code

- Grievance procedures enable individuals to raise issues with management about their work, or about their employers' 'clients' or their fellow workers' actions that affect them [such as] terms and conditions of employment; health and safety; relationships at work; new working practices; organisational change and equal opportunities.
- Procedures should be simple, set down in writing and rapid in operation. They should also provide for grievance proceedings and records to be kept confidential.
- Most routine complaints are best resolved informally in discussion with the worker's immediate line manager . . . this . . . can often lead to speedy resolution of problems and can help maintain the authority of the immediate line manager who may well be able to resolve the matter directly.
- Where the grievance cannot be resolved informally it should be dealt with under the formal grievance procedure. In larger organisations the procedure might contain all the following stages, but for smaller businesses the first and final stages might be sufficient.

First stage

Workers should put their grievance, preferably in writing, to their immediate line manager. Where the grievance is with the immediate line manager the matter should be raised with a more senior manager. Where the grievance is contested then the statutory right to be accompanied can be exercised. The manager should respond in writing within a specified time (say, within five days).

Second stage

Should the matter not be resolved at Stage 1, the worker should be permitted to raise the matter with a more senior manager who should arrange to hear the grievance within a specified period (say, five working days) and should inform the worker of the statutory right to be accompanied. The manager should respond to the hearing within a specified period (say 10 working days).

Final stage

Where the matter cannot be resolved at Stage 2, the worker should be able to raise their grievance in writing with a higher level of manager than for Stage 2. The subsequent process does not vary from that for the second stage of the process.

Special considerations

- Some organisations may wish to have specific procedures for handling grievances about unfair treatment, e.g. discrimination, harassment and bullying, as these subjects are particularly sensitive.
- Organisations may also wish to consider whether they need a whistle-blowing procedure in the light of the Public Interest Disclosure Act 1998. This provides strong protection to workers who raise concerns about wrongdoing (including fraud, dangers and cover-ups).
- Should a worker raise a grievance about the behaviour of a manager during the course of a disciplinary case, it may be appropriate to suspend the disciplinary procedure for a short period until the grievance can be considered.

Records

Records should be kept detailing the nature of the grievance raised, the employer's response, any action taken and the reasons for it. These records should be kept confidential and retained in accordance with the Data Protection Act 1998 which requires the release of certain data to individuals on their request. Copies of any meeting records should be given to the individual concerned although in certain circumstances some information may be withheld, for example to protect a witness.

Source: Adapted from ACAS, 2000b

The form that procedures take varies widely. Gennard and Judge (2002) point out that 'in a small non-union establishment, the procedure is likely to be found in the employee's contract of employment and expressed in a statement [such as]: *if you have a grievance relating to your employment, you should raise it with your immediate supervisor*' (p. 379). Some larger organisations will have a fully-fledged procedure, which may go into some detail, while others, such as local authorities, may have a 'minimalist' procedure for the authority as a whole, and a more detailed procedure for specific departments, perhaps focusing upon specific groups. For example, within the Liverpool local authority organisation, there is a specific complaints procedure within the Social Services Directorate aimed at 'carers and users', which is partly a requirement of the Children Act 1989. Most organisations distinguish between disputes procedures and grievance procedures and have separate procedures dealing with complaints concerning sexual and racial harassment.

Self-Evaluation Activity 11.9

'Best practice' procedures
The response is given below

Exhibit 11.15 is an example of a 'best practice' comprehensive grievance procedure. When you have read through it, identify in general terms the main characteristics of a grievance procedure applicable to that organisation.

Exhibit 11.15

Handle Organisation

These policies and procedures have been jointly agreed upon through a process of consultation between the company and senior stewards group for Port Sunlight and Warrington.

Grievance procedure

2.1 STAGES OF THE PROCEDURE
The Grievance Procedure provides all employees with the opportunity of drawing management's attention to any individual grievances they may have. The objective of the procedure is to settle all grievances as speedily as possible in a fair and equitable manner. A grievance once settled satisfactorily to all parties at any stage of the procedure shall not be reopened later. At all stages of the procedure the employee is entitled to be accompanied by an appropriate shop steward or representative. At each formal stage of the procedure a member of the Personnel Department will be present, and will prepare a written report of the proceedings.

The procedure will be invoked only when full informal discussion between the employee and his or her day/shift leader has failed to produce a mutually satisfactory solution.

STAGE 1   If the matter cannot be resolved by informal discussion between the employee and his or her day/shift leader, the employee may formally raise the grievance, in writing, within one week of the informal discussion. The written explanation of the grievance should be directed to his or her day/shift leader or Manager, as appropriate. He or she will arrange for a hearing to take place as soon as possible and will ensure that a decision will be passed to the employee and his or her representative within one week of the hearing.

STAGE 2   Should the matter not have been resolved at Stage 1, the employee may submit the grievance for further consideration within one week of the previous decision being made known to him or her. It should again be in writing, dated, and signed and directed via his or her line management to the next Manager in the line of seniority. This person, or his or her nominee, will arrange for a meeting to take place as soon as possible, and will ensure that a decision will be passed to the employee and his or her representative within one week of the hearing.

STAGE 3   Should the matter not have been resolved at Stage 2, the employee may submit the grievance for further consideration within one week of the result of the previous decision being made known to him or her. It should again be in writing, signed and dated, and should be directed, via the employee's line manager, to the Works Director.
   The Works Director or his nominee, will arrange for a hearing to take place as soon as possible, and will ensure that a decision will be passed to the employee and his or her representative within one week of the hearing.

Example:

Informal chat	Stage 1	Stage 2	Stage 3
Team Leader/Shift Leader or appropriate equivalent	Operations Manager Section/Technical Manager. Shift Manager or appropriate equivalent	Factory Manager or Operations Manager	Works Director or nominee

   If a trade union were involved for statutory representation purposes the appropriate representative at Stage 3 would be the senior shop steward or local branch official of that union. The Personnel Department representative will be the Personnel Manager Port Sunlight/Warrington or his or her nominee.
   If the matter concerns a member of a recognised trade union, and remains unresolved after Stage 3, the company and trade union may agree to deal with the matter in accordance with the disputes procedure in the appropriate agreement between the company and the trade union.

2.2 THE PROCEDURE IN OPERATION
In all respects, the preparation and conduct of a grievance interview should follow a similar pattern to the disciplinary situation, except that the onus is on the employee to present his or her case. It may be necessary to invite other employees to present their understanding of the facts of the situation – they in turn should be offered the opportunity to be accompanied by a representative.
   When the grievance procedure is being considered in conjunction with a concern related to a disciplinary decision it must be noted that:

(a) The grievance procedure may only be used if the employee wishes to take issue with the *procedure* used at the disciplinary meeting. Disagreement with the *result* of the disciplinary meeting should be expressed via the disciplinary appeals procedure.
(b) The disciplinary appeals procedure and the grievance procedure are therefore mutually exclusive. Only one forum may be used in the pursuit of a complaint and its decision is final.

The procedure outlined in Exhibit 11.15 provides the employee with the means for addressing a complaint concerning management behaviour, and indicates the steps that must be taken in order to process it. As the procedure has been jointly negotiated and agreed within a unionised company, there is an option for dealing with the complaint in the later stages of the procedure under the separate disputes procedure. An effective procedure is likely to have any or all of the following characteristics:

1. There will be a short overview which states the purpose of the procedure, stressing the need to settle as quickly as possible and as fairly and reasonably as possible. Representation rights and composition of hearings will be identified.
2. The procedure outlined has three stages, which is common for the vast majority of procedures although there is no recommended or 'ideal' number of stages. The staged approach is necessary to facilitate resolution of the complaint, and:
   - identify who is involved and present at each stage;
   - define the time limits for completion of each stage;
   - indicate what will happen if either the grievance is resolved or unresolved; and
   - often contains an explanation of any appeal mechanisms (although the example does not as there is a separate appeals section for that company) which could be inserted at the end of Stage 3 of the procedure. The following statement would be appropriate:

   > If the employee is not satisfied with the outcome of the matter at the end of Stage 3, he or she may appeal to the appeals panel. This should be in writing and made within five working days of the formal meeting with the department manager. This panel will be chaired by the personnel director and will meet within five working days of the appeal being received.

3. The complaint should be settled as soon as possible and as near as possible to the point of origin. Torrington *et al.* (2002) argue that:

   > Promptness is needed to avoid the bitterness and frustration that can come from delay. When an employee 'goes into procedure', it is like pulling

the communication cord in the train. The action is not taken lightly and it is in anticipation of a swift resolution. . . . The most familiar device to speed things up is to incorporate time limits between the steps. (p. 537)

4. As with discipline, representation can assist the employee who is either unwilling or too inexperienced to take on management individually. A shop steward or other employee representative will be relatively experienced in dealing with a variety of employee problems and will be able to act in an advisory capacity. Gennard and Judge (2002) stress that natural justice requires employee representation and that procedures should specify at what stage representation should be involved (Stage 2 in the above procedure). In any event the problem should be dealt with locally without representation, with representation desirable at the next stage if the employee requests it and 'if the employee is dissatisfied with the response from the immediate superior and wishes to appeal to higher management' (p. 206).
5. 'Fairness is needed not only to be just but also to keep the procedure viable' (Torrington and Hall, 1998, p. 537). The procedure must be seen to work effectively through even-handed treatment of the complaint and arguably the involvement of a third party such as ACAS at the appeals stage.

In summary, an effective procedure should:

- be in writing;
- specify to whom it applies;
- provide for issues to be dealt with quickly and specify time limits within which each stage should be complete;
- specify the levels of management dealing with the grievance; and
- have at least two stages and ideally three providing for further attempts to resolve the grievance.

DEALING WITH GRIEVANCES

The initial stage of a procedure is the most important as the first line manager or supervisor is involved and known to the person making the complaint. Sensitive handling of the complaint at this stage, which incorporates a preliminary informal meeting and interview, should result in the complaint being resolved (as the vast majority of them invariably are). There are, however, a number of factors to bear in mind at this crucial stage:

- Supervisors and first line managers, by dealing effectively with a complaint, have the opportunity to improve upon working relationships and reinforce mutual feelings of equity, justice and understanding.
- Supervisors and first line managers should resolve the complaint as quickly as possible and as close to the source of the complaint as possible.
- Supervisors and first line managers should be given as much autonomy and authority in handling grievances as considered practicable by superiors. This is important because interference by superiors at this stage could well undermine both the authority of the supervisor and the confidence of the employee in the ability of the supervisor to deal with the problem. In this context, Gennard and Judge (1997) point out:

> It causes the procedure to break down and the number of stages to be reduced. The effect is to remove the grievance from its source of origin, to slow down the process by having to go back through the correct stages, and to cause confusion and bad feeling. To avoid this, three things need to be clearly understood and accepted by management: everyone knows within the procedure the limits of their own and others' authority; the procedures are adhered to consistently; and first line managers have authority to settle grievances. (p. 208)

The grievance interview/hearing and subsequent developments

The grievance interview is handled relatively informally and corresponds to Stage 1 of the grievance procedure. The purpose of the interview is, firstly, for the manager to be clear about the nature of the grievance and, secondly, to get confirmation from the employee that this interpretation is correct and, thirdly, to deal with the complaint to the satisfaction of both parties. The grievance should be heard in an appropriate setting in a room where the complaint can be heard in privacy and free from any interruption. The interview should satisfy the following criteria:

1. In order to clarify the nature of the grievance, information must be gathered about the complaint. This will enable the employee to explain his or her side of the story in an open-ended way, with the aid of a few timely prompts when required. Listening skills are important here, as is a 'neutral' attitude which neither condemns nor sympathises, approves nor disapproves. Appropriate eye contact and body language are also important in encouraging confidence and a sense of importance in the employee. It is also useful for the manager to adopt what Gennard and Judge (1997) call the '5Ws technique' of obtaining information in a non-threatening way:
   - **What** is the grievance about?
   - **When** did the grievance happen?
   - **Where** did the grievance happen?
   - **Who** was involved in the grievance issue?
   - **Why** does what happened create a grievance for the individual employee and what does the individual want management to do about the grievance? (p. 212).

2. After all the necessary information has been obtained by the manager, the grievance should be restated. At this stage agreement is being sought on the facts and information only, and not on how the complaint should be resolved. Torrington *et al.* (2002, p. 550) summarise this phase of the interview in the following sequence:

Manager	Employee
1. States subject of grievance	
	2. Agrees with statement
	3. States case
4. Questions for clarification	
5. Restates grievance	
	6. Agrees or corrects

3. It is now important to put the management case concerning the grievance and what action has been taken together with the reasoning behind it. The manager should be prepared to explain the action taken in response to any questions from the employee. For example, if the grievance concerns bullying, the manager may say:

'*I have suspended X pending an investigation of his behaviour. Are you happy about that for now?*' The manager is attempting to persuade and justify to the employee the correctness of his or her action and decision. Of course, the manager may conclude, after hearing all the facts and ensuring mutual understanding of the employee's complaint, that the complaint cannot be justified on the grounds of personality clash or a misunderstanding of various rules, company policy, supervisory problems or administrative methods. The emphasis here, however, is to ensure that the employee understands the management position.

4. The employee's and manager's positions, now fully mutually understood by both parties, may well have established much common ground and also some areas of disagreement. At this stage, the grievance may well be settled if the disagreements are minor. However, management's approach to major areas of disagreement will be to make a decision and wait for the employee to submit the grievance for further consideration at Stage 2 of the procedure.

ACAS advice dealing with grievance interviews/hearings is paraphrased in Exhibit 11.16.

Exhibit 11.16

How should a grievance hearing be conducted?

- The hearing should be held in private.
- The worker should be told of her/his right to be accompanied.
- Ensure an open discussion of the issue.
- Adjourn hearing if further advice needs to be obtained.
- Don't make a snap decision unless the matter is very easy to rectify.

Preparing for the hearing

- Any hearing should be held in private.
- The worker has a statutory right to be accompanied at certain hearings.
- Management may find it useful to have someone take notes and act as witness to the proceedings.
- Management will normally already have a written statement of the grievance, and should find out before the hearing whether similar grievances have been raised before, how they have been resolved, and any follow-up action that has been necessary. This allows consistency of treatment in the procedure.

Conduct of the hearing

- Remember that a grievance hearing is not the same as a disciplinary hearing, and is an occasion when discussion and dialogue may fruitfully produce the answer.
- Make introductions as necessary.
- Invite the worker to restate her/his grievance and perhaps how he/she would like to see it resolved.
- Care and thought should go into resolving grievances, they are not normally issues calling for snap decisions, and the worker may have been holding the grievance for a long time. Make allowances for any reasonable 'letting off steam' if the worker is under stress.
- After summing up, management may find it useful to adjourn – they may need to explore possibilities with other managers about the resolution of the grievance, or they may themselves wish to take advice on how to proceed further.
- Tell the worker when they might reasonably expect a response if one cannot be made at the time, bearing in mind the time limits set out in the procedure.

Source: Adapted from ACAS, 2000a, p. 32

Negotiating a settlement

Grievance negotiations follow a similar approach to that outlined in Chapter 10 dealing with the important skills required (pp. 467–79). The informal grievance interview will have provided the opportunity for both parties to gather information, establish and understand mutual positions, and prepare for further encounters. Preparation for, and analysis of, the areas of disagreement will enable management to establish objectives for the following encounters with the employee and his representative. Gennard and Judge (2002) suggest that management should bear in mind the following questions (and this will apply equally for the employee):

- How would management/employee ideally like the grievance to be resolved? This is the ideal position.
- How do the parties realistically think the grievance can be resolved? This is the real position.
- What is the least for which management/employee will settle? This is the fall-back position.

The skills required of managers in the successful handling of grievances are very similar to those required in other negotiations.

Self-Evaluation Activity 11.10

Review exercise
This SEA has no commentary

As a review exercise, reread that part of Chapter 10 which deals with negotiation skills.

At this stage, the meeting with the employee and his or her representative and the management team should resolve the remaining disagreements. If, after negotiation, there is still disagreement, then the matter will be considered at Stage 3, and if the grievance is still unresolved, the employee has a right of appeal. After the grievance has been resolved, management, according to Gennard and Judge (1997) must:

- 'be convinced that the employee and his or her representative fully understand management's proposals' (p. 218); and
- ensure that 'once management has an oral agreement for the resolution of the employee's grievance, it should be written up' (p. 218).

Self-Evaluation Activity 11.11

Grievance handling
This SEA has no commentary

Main case 11.4 sets the scene for a grievance-handling situation. After you have read the case, discuss with your colleagues how you would handle this grievance. Role-play the initial meeting with Black. Assume that the outcome of this meeting is unsuccessful and that Black notifies you of his intention to lodge a formal complaint, thereby invoking the grievance procedure. Prepare for the Stage 1 grievance interview and role-play this. If the grievance has not been resolved at this stage, prepare for the Stage 2 hearing and set it up. If the grievance remains unresolved, prepare and enact Stage 3 and any subsequent appeals hearings as necessary. Write a short report dealing with the main issues arising from the process, and in particular:

- the information which both parties need;
- how the preliminary and Stage 1 interviews went (it would be useful to record the interviews);
- the cases of both parties; and
- how the grievance was finally resolved.

Main case 11.4
Regrading problems

Your organisation has just reorganised its departments into divisions in order to deal more effectively with the steady growth in its activities. Part of this reorganisation involved the combining of advertising, sales and marketing departments to form the marketing division. You, as Mr White, are manager of marketing operations for the North West. The reorganisation inevitably involved major changes in job descriptions, job evaluations and job redesign. As many of the jobs were different from the old ones, they were advertised internally and staff from the three 'old' departments were invited to apply for these new jobs. All staff were given a guarantee that their existing salaries would be protected should they not get their preferred job and took a job which was a grade or two lower. You have been busy interviewing candidates and the last interviews were held a few days ago.

On the whole, you are very satisfied with the appointments that have been made. In reorganisations such as this there are always fewer promotion opportunities than there are candidates to fill them, and there have been some disappointed people who had to take jobs other than their preferred ones. Today, you have received a request from Tom Black to see you and you have a good idea what it concerns.

Black was an advertising officer in the old advertising department and had applied unsuccessfully for two senior positions, both in marketing management, in the new structure. They were the only posts he had applied for, and he had subsequently been given the post of technical officer which was one grade lower (grade 6) than his previous post (grade 7), working for the 'brilliant' young man you had previously promoted above Black.

Black's last interview for the marketing management job, at which you were present, was the first of the day and did not go well. From the very beginning Black thought he was at a disadvantage because your boss, Mr Puce, who was on the interviewing panel, arrived 15 minutes late into the interview, despite the interview being delayed for 20 minutes owing to 'traffic problems'. Puce's interviewing style is abrasive, and was particularly so on this occasion. Black became flustered and gave a poor performance. The discussion after the interview was unflattering to Black who was described by Puce as a poor decision-maker and judge of character, with doubtful leadership qualities and who 'does not know who his friends are'. You suspect that Puce's attitude towards Black was related to a successful salary regrade claim, from grade 6 to grade 7, which Black had made nearly a year ago. Puce, who was on the grading appeals panel, had advised Black at the time that several vacancies were to be advertised immediately before the reorganisation, so 'why not wait until then and don't bother with the regrading claim'. Black had, evidently, ignored this advice and gone ahead with the claim.

You have been placed in an invidious position. You guess Black is disappointed with his drop in status, even though he has retained his salary. Puce obviously did not want Black to get the job, and you had to go along with Puce's opinion, especially since you had to make the decision not to appoint him. Obviously you do not want to annoy your boss, and you may have rationalised and now believe that Black has been treated fairly, especially as he has retained his salary. Not everybody could be promoted and you yourself had not been promoted even though you are managing a much larger section than prior to the reorganisation. Black has proved to be a keen, hard-working and loyal employee and you do not want to see him demotivated, especially now that, post-reorganisation, everyone's co-operation is essential. You ponder these issues as you wait for Black to see you.

Summary points for Part Two

- A grievance may be viewed as the acquisition and articulation of a sense of injustice and feeling of dissatisfaction as a result of management actions which are deemed to be unreasonable and unfair.
- Many grievances are not formally articulated as complaints but, as the TUC 'Bad Bosses' hotline reveals, they are real and fairly widespread, and concerned with:
  – bullying and harassment;
  – pay;
  – long working hours;
  – employment contracts; and
  – health and safety.
- Procedures for handling grievances exist in most organisations (WERS, 1998), but vary widely from organisation to organisation. Some firms (albeit a minority) have minimal policy statements while many others have comprehensive and staged procedures.
- The features of a comprehensive 'best practice' procedure include:
  – an overview stating the purpose of the procedure;
  – a specified number of stages;
  – time limits for the completion of each stage; and
  – an inbuilt appeals system.
- The complaint should be resolved quickly and as near to the point of origin as possible, underlining the importance of the initial, relatively informal stage of the procedure. It is at this stage that the grievance interview takes place, and the resolution of the complaint depends substantially upon how the interview is conducted.

RELEVANT WEBSITES

www.acas.org.uk (Advisory, Conciliation and Arbitration Service) Useful information on dispute resolution from the leading provider of such services.

REFERENCES

ACAS (1997) *Discipline at Work: The ACAS Advisory Handbook*. London, ACAS

ACAS (2000a) *Discipline at Work: The ACAS Advisory Handbook*. London, ACAS

ACAS (2000b) *Code of Practice on Disciplinary and Grievance Procedures*. London, ACAS

Cully, M., Woodland, S., O'Reilly, A. and Dix, G. (1998) *The 1998 Workplace Employee Relations Survey*. London, DTI

Cully, M., Woodland, S., O'Reilly, A. and Dix, G. (1999) *Britain at Work*. London, Routledge

Earnshaw, J. (1998) 'Industrial tribunals, workplace disciplinary procedures and employment practice'. *DTI Employment Relations Research Series No. 2*

Farnham, D. (2000) *Employee Relations in Context*, 2nd edn. London, CIPD

Foucault, M. (1977) *Discipline and Punish: the Birth of the Prison*. London, Allen Lane

Fowler, A. (1996) 'How to conduct a disciplinary interview'. *People Management*, November

Gennard, J. and Judge, G. (1997) *Employee Relations*. London, IPD

Gennard, J. and Judge, G. (2002) *Employee Relations*, 3rd edn. London, CIPD

Huczynski, A. and Buchanan, D. (1991) *Organisational Behaviour*. London, Prentice Hall

IDS (1997) 'Disciplinary procedures'. *IDS Study*, No. 640

IDS (2002) *Employment Act 2002*. London, Incomes Data Services

Industrial Society (1999) 'Managing discipline and grievance'. *Managing Best Practice*, No. 57

IRS (1995) 'Managing discipline at work'. *IRS Employment Trends*, No. 605

IRS (1998) 'Managing discipline at work'. *IRS Employment Trends*, No. 666

IRS (2001) 'Managing discipline at work'. *IRS Employment Trends*, No. 727

IRS (2002) 'Don't nurse a grievance: resolving disputes at work'. *IRS Employment Review*, No. 759

James, P. and Lewis, D. (1992) *Discipline*. London, IPD

Kelly, J. (1998) *Rethinking Industrial Relations*. London, Routledge

Lewis, D. and Sargeant, M. (2002) *Essentials of Employment Law*. London, CIPD

LMT (Labour Market Trends) (2002) 'Labour disputes in 2001'. *Labour Market Trends*, November, 589–603

Martin, D. (1995) *How to Deal with Discipline and Dismissal*. London, Gee Publishing

Milgram, S. (1974) *Obedience to Authority*. London: Tavistock

Millward, N., Bryson, A. and Forth, J. (2000): *All Change at Work?* London, Routledge

O'Reilly, C. and Weitz, B.A. (1980) 'Managing marginal employees: the use of warnings and dismissals'. *Administrative Science Quarterly*, 25, 3, 467–84

Rollinson, D. (1993) *Understanding Employee Relations*. Wokingham, Addison-Wesley

Terry, M. (1977) 'The inevitable growth of informality'. *British Journal of Industrial Relations*, 15, 2, 76–90

Torrington, D. and Hall, L. (1998) *Human Resource Management*. London, Prentice Hall Europe

Torrington, D., Hall, L. and Taylor, S. (2002) *Human Resource Management*. Harlow, Pearson

Weber, M. (1947) *The Theory of Social and Economic Organisation*. New York, Oxford University Press

WERS (1998) See Cully, M. *et al.* (1998)

CHAPTER 12

DISCRIMINATION AND DIVERSITY WITHIN THE EMPLOYMENT RELATIONSHIP

INTRODUCTION

Discrimination at work is concerned with the unequal and inequitable treatment of some employees irrespective of their ability to perform their jobs (but see more detailed definition below). The main types of discrimination are:

- sex or gender discrimination;
- discrimination on the grounds of sexual orientation or sexuality;
- race discrimination;
- religious discrimination;
- discrimination on grounds of disability;
- discrimination on grounds of age;
- discrimination on grounds of trade union status;
- discrimination against ex-offenders; and
- equal pay issues.

The traditional approach to the study of employment relations, as Liff (1995) points out, is overwhelmingly concerned with the white male worker, irrespective of fundamental changes in the labour market and the structure of work over the past few decades, thereby ignoring those groups which are prone to discrimination. The trade union movement, now amongst the foremost in fighting discrimination, used to be regarded as white and male-dominated, as evidenced by membership composition and the very small proportion of full-time officers and executive staff who were black or female. Moreover, most managements have traditionally been male-dominated (many still are) and white, and it is only in recent years that the proportion of women in management (and in trade unions for that matter) has risen, although very slowly.

Many of the changes in the labour market and patterns of working have been identified in Chapter 1. These changes have resulted in many more women entering the increasingly fragmented labour market. This, in turn, has raised the profile of 'equality' issues and influenced the emergence of equal opportunities and diversity initiatives and policies by both government and more 'progressive' managements during the past 30 years or so. The relevant legislation has been identified at the beginning of Chapter 11 and is considered in more detail in this chapter. Of particular and growing relevance to discrimination and equal opportunity issues is the direct and indirect influence and impact of European Union law, and this will be considered in some detail during the course of the chapter.

Discriminatory attitudes and practices impinge upon the employment relationship in a number of ways. For example, discrimination may be evident at the selection and recruitment stages of employment; opportunities for promotion may be restricted; there may be frequent instances of harassment and bullying within the workplace and equal opportunities policies, where they exist, may not be put into practice effectively enough. Occasionally, instances of discrimination may have more serious consequences both for employees and their organisation, and for the conduct of employment relations. The example of endemic racism at the Dagenham plant of the Ford Motor Company during October 1999, where workers staged a mass walkout after an Asian shop steward was pushed by a white foreman, is a case in point, and will be examined in greater detail later on in the chapter.

The main focus of the chapter will be upon the treatment of gender, race and disability discrimination both by legislative means and by action within the workplace. The equal pay issue will be dealt with mainly in connection with gender discrimination. We start by examining some of the main theoretical perspectives and contextual developments in relation to gender and race discrimination, accepting the argument that discrimination in the workplace is a reflection of the wider patterns of discrimination, racial and gender inequality inherent within the wider society. We then look briefly at the legal changes that have taken place, both at national and European Union level, which have sought to outlaw discrimination within the employment relationship. The chapter proceeds by looking at gender, race and disability discrimination in some detail, and the extent to which the relevant legislative and policy developments have influenced organisations in the adoption of equal opportunities and harassment policies and procedures.

Learning outcomes

When you have read this chapter, you should be able to:

1. Describe the basic explanations accounting for gender and racial inequalities within society as a whole.

2. Assess the extent to which these inequalities are reflected within the employment relationship.

3. Trace the development of national and European Union policies and legislation concerning gender, race, disability and equal pay.

4. Explain how organisations deal with discrimination through the operation of equal opportunities and diversity policies and procedures.

5. Identify the elements of other forms of discrimination based on age and trade union status and work through case examples of discrimination and harassment in the workplace.

EXPLAINING GENDER AND RACIAL DISCRIMINATION

Evidence of discrimination within the employment relationship is not hard to find, and points to the fact that members of ethnic minorities do less well in the labour market than whites, despite having similar levels of qualifications (Jones, 1993; Kirton and Green, 2001). Reporting on the results of successive surveys conducted by the Policy Studies Institute (PSI), Jones found that despite certain ethnic groups (such as Indian, Chinese and African Asian males) being reasonably well represented in certain jobs up to and including professional level, all ethnic groups were significantly under-represented in managerial grades. As Jones (1993) points out: 'men from certain minority groups have penetrated to a remarkable extent into certain professions, but to a much lesser extent into the management of large organisations' (p. 81). Later PSI surveys, such as that conducted by Modood *et al.* (1997) confirm the persistent labour market disadvantages faced by ethnic minorities. The extent of these disadvantages, or 'penalties' are revealed by Sly *et al.* (1998) who highlight certain factors based on their analysis of Labour Force Survey data. Information from the more recent Labour Force Survey (ONS 2002a) is also included:

- In 1997, 2.2 million people of working age belonged to ethnic minority groups (6.4 per cent of the total working-age population), half of them living in London.
- Black African men are most likely to have a higher qualification: Pakistani and Bangladeshi women tend to be the most poorly qualified.
- Economic activity rates for women vary widely between ethnic groups. In 1997, working-age black Caribbean and White women had economic activity rates of around three-quarters (75 per cent) compared with less than one-third for Pakistani/Bangladeshi women. However, by 2001 economic activity rates of black women had fallen to 57.6 while that of Indian women had risen to 60.1 per cent, with rates of white women fairly constant at 70.9 per cent.
- Nearly half of Indian self-employed and employee men are in the top two social or occupational categories compared with only a quarter of black Caribbean and Pakistani/Bangladeshi males. Black Caribbeans are the only group where women are more likely than men to be in the top two occupational categories. In 2001 around one-fifth of Pakistani/Bangladeshi people in employment were self-employed compared with only 10 per cent of white and 7 per cent of black people.
- The unemployment rate for Black African men was more than three times (25 per cent) that for white men (7 per cent) in 1997. Pakistani/Bangladeshi men also have high rates. Black African and Pakistani women had unemployment rates (24 per cent and 23 per cent respectively) four times that of white women (5.4 per cent) in 1997. The situation had not changed much by 2001 with black and Pakistani/Bangladeshi people having three times the unemployment rate of whites.
- The ratio of the ethnic minority unemployment rate to the white unemployment rate was higher in the 1990s than it had been in the mid to late 1980s – for example, it was 1.7 in 1987–9 compared with 2.4 in spring 1998 – and has been maintained into the early 2000s.

The Commission for Racial Equality, in commenting upon the rising ratio of black and Asian to white unemployment (CRE, 2002) stated that:

Some of this disparity can be explained by the different age profiles, qualifications and geographical distribution of the various ethnic groups, but these factors do not tell the whole story: there appears to be an undeniable, persistent overrepresentation of certain ethnic groups. (p. 5)

Women workers are still concentrated in poorly paid, routine occupations such as clerical and secretarial work. Far more women than men are in part-time occupations. To be sure, women have recently made some inroads into occupations defined as 'men's jobs' but only to a limited extent. Women are under-represented in all the higher managerial and professional grades. Those women who are successful economically have to fit into a world of 'maleness' and masculine value systems where they feel they do not fully belong. One of the major factors affecting women's careers is the male perception that, for female employees, work comes second to having children. A survey by Homans (1987), investigating the views of managers interviewing female applicants for positions as technical staff in the health services, revealed that the (male) interviewers routinely asked women applicants whether or not they had, or intended to have, children. Interviewers virtually never followed this practice with male applicants and, when asked why not, two themes ran through their responses:

- women with children may require extra time off for school holidays or if a child falls sick; and
- responsibility for childcare is seen as a mother's problem rather than a parental one.

Arguably, the bias in male attitudes may be less to do with the workplace itself than with the domestic responsibilities of parenting, and as long as it is taken for granted that parenting cannot be shared on an equal basis, the problems facing female employees will persist: 'it will remain a fact of life that women are severely disadvantaged, compared to men, in their career opportunities' (Cockburn, 1991, p. 123). The situation remains that, despite many advances in developing equality in the workplace, inequalities still exist. The EOC (1999, 2002a) draws attention to the following facts:

- 67 per cent of women and 78 per cent of men of working age were employed. In 2001, 69.3 per cent of women and 79.3 per cent of men of working age were employed.
- 43 per cent of women employees and 8 per cent of men employees work part-time. The situation remains unchanged for 2001.
- 52 per cent of employed women were in occupational groups in which more than 60 per cent of workers were women. These groups were: clerical and secretarial occupations; service occupations; and sales occupations.
- 54 per cent of employed men were in occupational groups in which more than 60 per cent of workers were men. These groups were: managers and administrators; craft and related occupations; and plant and machine operatives.
- Sexual harassment: in 2001, the EOC received more than 700 enquiries about sexual harassment.
- In 1998 women comprised 18 per cent of all executives (managers and directors); this compared with only 8.9 per cent in 1991. However, women comprised only 3.6 per cent of directors in 1998. In 2001 some 9 per cent of women in employment in the UK were managers and senior officials (this figure excludes executive directors).
- In 2001 female employment remained concentrated within a narrow band of occupations: administrative and secretarial (24 per cent), personal service occupations (14 per cent), and sales and customer service occupations (12 per cent). These three occupational groups accounted for only 12 per cent of employed men.

Moreover, persistent and institutional barriers to equality in the workplace remain. These include continuing job segregation in the labour market; the over-representation of women in part-time work and the inequality of treatment of part-time workers; women's over-representation in home working and the unequal treatment of home workers; women's under-representation in senior positions and the impact of discrimination generally on many women in the labour market.

Discrimination and prejudice

For our purposes, it is necessary to make a distinction between discrimination and prejudice. Discrimination refers to *actual behaviour* towards the other group. It can be seen in activities that disqualify members of one group from opportunities open to others, as when a black person is refused a job made available to a white person. Prejudice refers to *opinions or attitudes* held by members of one group towards another. A prejudiced person's preconceived views are often based on hearsay rather than on direct evidence, and are resistant to change even in the face of new information. Individuals may harbour favourable prejudices concerning groups with which they identify and negative prejudices against others.

Although prejudice is often the basis of discrimination, the two may exist separately. People may have prejudiced attitudes that they do not necessarily act upon. This is particularly the case within an organisation which acts upon discrimination legislation and equal opportunities policies and procedures. In such situations, an individual employee may have a predisposition to act in a prejudiced manner, but is constrained in doing so. However, the high incidence of racial and sexual harassment at work suggests that prejudiced attitudes are translated into action all too often, despite legislation and procedures.

Self-Evaluation Activity 12.1

Examples of discrimination
Response on website

Think of some examples of discrimination at work based on prejudiced attitudes.

THEORIES EXPLAINING GENDER INEQUALITIES AND DISCRIMINATION

There are a number of interesting and important theories which attempt to explain and justify differences between men and women. These theories can be placed into two categories. The first category is based on biology and the sexual division of labour, and the second category is based on the premise that gender roles are culturally rather than biologically produced and which we may label the social construction of gender roles.

There are also theories which examine the basis of inequalities between men and women. Inspired by the development of the Women's Liberation Movement, attention is focused upon the subordinate position of women in society and the feminist approaches which attempt to explain this type of inequality. There are three main feminist approaches which can be identified:

- Radical feminism.
- Marxist and socialist feminism.
- Liberal feminism.

We will now look briefly at these theoretical categories.

Biology and the sexual division of labour

Basically, the argument here is that biological differences between men and women lead them to occupy different social roles and exhibit different types of behaviours (the so-called socio-biological explanation). In terms of sexual behaviour, for example, men are more likely to be promiscuous, while women will be more circumspect in their pursuit of a 'suitable' male. Men will, in competing for the attention of women, be more assertive, physically stronger, more competitive and ultimately more dominant than women. Because of her biological function – that of childbearing – women are tied to the home base and, because of her physique, the woman is limited to less strenuous tasks. This sexual division of labour, it is claimed, is universal and accounts for the role of women in industrial society which is basically that of bearing and nursing children and providing them with warmth, security and emotional support in the home. In contrast to this, the male breadwinner spends his working day competing in an achievement-oriented society. The stress that this incurs in the male is relieved by the female through the provision of love, consideration and understanding. Socio-biological explanations of behaviour have been heavily criticised by feminists as a spurious attempt to provide 'scientific'

justifications for male power. More specifically, Oakley (1981) argues that:

- Gender roles are culturally rather than biologically determined.
- Evidence from a number of different societies shows that there are no tasks (apart from childbearing) which are performed exclusively by females.
- Biological characteristics do not bar women from particular occupations.
- The mother role is a cultural and not a biological construction. Evidence from several societies indicates that children do not require a close, intimate and continuous relationship with a female mother figure.

The social construction of gender roles

This explanation of male/female differences rests on the assumption that gender roles are culturally rather than biologically produced. In other words, humans learn the behaviour that is expected of males and females within their society. Gender is socially constructed in the sense that differences in the behaviour of males and females are learned rather than being the inevitable result of biology. Initially, the parent–child relationship is important, and Oakley (1981) identifies four ways in which socialisation into gender roles takes place:

1. The child's concept of himself or herself is affected by manipulation. For example, mothers tend to pay more attention to girls' hair and dress them in 'feminine' clothes.
2. Differences are achieved through the involvement and direction of boys and girls towards different objects and is particularly obvious in the provision of toys: girls are given dolls, soft toys and miniature domestic objects and appliances to play with, while boys are given toys which encourage more practical, logical and aggressive behaviour such as bricks and guns.
3. Parents and others such as primary school teachers will use verbal appellations such as 'You're a naughty boy', or 'That's a good girl'. This leads young children to identify with their gender and imitate adults of the same gender.

4. Male and female children are exposed to different activities. For example, girls are particularly encouraged to become involved with domestic tasks. In addition, much research has documented how stereotypes of masculinity and femininity are further reinforced throughout childhood and adult life. Portrayals by media advertising of men and women in traditional social roles have been criticised by feminists.

Theories of gender inequality

The feminist preoccupation with the position of women in society, which they argue is a subordinate one, has generated a vast, but by no means unanimous, literature which can be broadly categorised into the three approaches described below.

Radical feminism

Radical feminism supports the contention that men are responsible for the exploitation of women. Women are seen to be exploited because they undertake 'free' labour for men by carrying out childcare and housework, and because they are denied access to positions of power. Another argument that is commonly put forward is that society is regarded as patriarchal – dominated and ruled by men. This means that because men still dominate occupationally, politically and within society generally, it follows that society's values are male values and women's values are subordinate to them.

Marxist and socialist feminism

Women's exploitation is not attributed entirely to men, but to capitalism which is the main beneficiary. Housework and the 'job' of mother is 'oppressive' unpaid work from which capitalism benefits through the production of wealth. The exploitation of women in paid employment, and their generally subordinate position in the occupational hierarchy is held to be a consequence of the emergence of private property and the resultant lack of ownership of the means of production which deprives women of any power.

Liberal feminism

This approach suggests that gradual change in the social and economic systems of society will lead to an improvement in the position of women. According to this perspective, no one benefits from existing gender inequalities; both men and women are harmed as the potential of females and males alike is suppressed. For example, many women with the potential to be successful and skilled members of the workforce do not get the opportunity to develop their talents, while men are denied some of the pleasures of having a close relationship with their children. The explanation for this state of affairs lies not so much in the 'structures' and institutions of society, but in its culture and the attitudes of individuals. Socialisation into gender roles produces particular expectations of men and women, while discrimination prevents women from having equal opportunities. The liberal feminist agenda includes:

- the creation of equal opportunities in all spheres and particularly in education and work contexts;
- the aim of creating equal opportunities is pursued through the introduction of legislation and the changing of attitudes. Measures such as the Sex Discrimination and Equal Pay Acts help to tackle discrimination; and
- the elimination of sexism and stereotypical views of women and men from children's books and the mass media.

Although the least radical of feminist perspectives, the liberal agenda could still lead to considerable social change, and at the very least the changes it advocates could create the conditions whereby women have the same access as men to high status jobs.

Self-Evaluation Activity 12.2

Three questions about theories of gender difference
Response on website

1. Summarise the main theories which attempt to explain gender differences and gender inequality.
2. Identify what you think are the main characteristics of a 'patriarchal' (male-dominated) society.
3. To what extent do you think early twenty-first century Britain remains a patriarchal society?

Explanations for gender inequality within the employment relationship

Gender inequality within the employment relationship, as we have noted previously, comprises important disadvantages experienced by women as compared with men in paid employment. These include:

- lower levels of remuneration;
- greater likelihood of being in part-time work;
- higher concentration of employment at lower occupational levels; and
- employment in low status jobs.

A number of explanations for these inequalities, which we now briefly consider, focus upon the labour market and the employment relationship.

Human capital theory

Human capital theory argues that the apparent lack of commitment shown by women to paid employment is the cause of the disadvantages they suffer in the labour market. Because women are likely to abandon or interrupt their careers at an early age, they have less incentive to invest their time in lengthy programmes of training or education and are therefore of less value to employers than their more highly trained and more skilled male counterparts. For this reason, women will have less experience of their jobs than men which makes it difficult for women to be promoted to higher status and better-paid jobs. Women's lack of training, qualifications and experience resulting from the demands of childcare all contribute to their disadvantaged position in the labour market. The two main factors that have a positive influence upon women's career progression are a fully uninterrupted working life, without any break whatsoever, and being regarded as 'promotable' by 'having the ability and commitment to appear a long-term prospect, particularly through being able to work long hours' (Kirton and Green, 2001, p. 46). Thus women are seen as being at a considerable disadvantage when the model of employment is based on the full-time male employee.

Self-Evaluation Activity 12.3
Criticisms of human capital theory
Response on website

Can you think of any criticisms of human capital theory?

Dual labour market theory

Dual labour market theory distinguishes between the primary labour market which is characterised by high pay, job security, good working conditions and favourable promotion prospects, and the secondary labour market comprising lower paid jobs, poor job security, inferior working conditions and few opportunities for promotion. Both may exist within one organisation, but transfer from one to the other is difficult, if not impossible. Secondary sector workers are more dispensable and easily replaced and a high proportion of these workers are women. The relatively low status of women in society and their tendency not to belong to trade unions weakens their position further and makes it particularly difficult for them to get a foothold in primary sector employment. Once recruited to the secondary sector, women are likely to remain captives in it for the rest of their working lives. There are, however, some limitations and important exceptions which are not considered by the dual market approach:

- Some women in skilled manual jobs (for example, in the textile industry) are low paid even though their work may be very similar to primary sector men's jobs.
- Many women do have jobs in the primary sector, but not in manufacturing industry, as in the case of nurses, teachers and social workers.
- Dual labour market theory cannot adequately explain why women gain promotion less often than men, despite doing the same jobs.

Gender and post-Fordism

This approach may be considered as an extension to the dual labour market theory, but it takes into more detailed consideration the recent changes in the composition of the external and internal (to the organisation) labour market (see Chapter 1).

McDowell (1992), for example, uses the assumptions of post-Fordism (see Chapter 5) in order to explain the increased use of part-time female labour and the reduction in the employment of males in full-time permanent jobs.

Self-Evaluation Activity 12.4

Review of post-Fordism

Response on website

Look back over Chapter 5 in order to identify the types of changes postulated by post-Fordism.

Reserve army of labour

A Marxist explanation of the traditional role of women both within and outside the labour market argues that capitalism requires a spare pool of potential recruits to the labour force. Because of their inbuilt contradictions, capitalist economies experience cycles of boom and recession accompanied by increases in labour demand during the former and shedding of labour during the latter phase of the cycle. Improvements in the efficiency of production technology together with market demands to produce new products also requires a 'reserve army' to provide the necessary labour flexibility to deal with these changes.

One of the main functions of the reserve army is to reduce the wages of all members of the labour force as unemployed workers compete for jobs, thereby allowing employers to reduce wages and increase the rate and extent of exploitation. Beechey (1983) identifies a number of ways in which women have traditionally been particularly suited to the needs of this reserve army:

- Traditionally, women are less likely to be unionised and so are less able to resist redundancy than men.
- Women's jobs are least likely to be covered by redundancy legislation, making it more likely that women rather than men would be redundant at lower cost to the employer.
- Traditionally, unemployed women may not be eligible to state benefits if their husbands are working, and hence would not appear in the unemployment statistics: 'women who are made redundant are able to disappear virtually without trace back into the family' (p. 203).

- Traditionally, women were prepared to work for less pay than men, even in equivalent jobs, because they could rely upon their husbands' wages as the main source of income for the family.

While the reserve army explanation appears to take into account at least some of the fluctuations in the employment of women during the course of the twentieth century, for example in appearing to account for the increased employment of women during the two world wars, the theory may not adequately explain why a significant proportion of women are able to retain their jobs during periods of recession. Gardiner (1992), for example, argues that, according to substitution theory, there are advantages to the employer in allowing women to retain their jobs during times of recession and rising unemployment since they are a comparatively cheap substitute for male workers.

Gender, labour markets and occupations: an integrated approach

Crompton and Sanderson (1990) argue that it is the structure of the labour market which shapes people's career choices, and that men who choose to follow traditional masculine careers, and women who choose to follow traditional feminine careers, reinforce structural features of the labour market which produce gender differences, thereby making it difficult for other individuals to pursue careers which are not normally thought appropriate for their gender. Crompton and Sanderson identify a model of the labour market which takes into account these gender differences, making the following assumptions:

- The labour market and the position of individuals within it is partly determined by the presence or absence of qualifications.
- The value of qualifications is not fixed; occupational groups can attempt to increase the value of qualifications they hold by restricting access to the profession and creating artificial shortages of qualified workers.
- A distinction can be made between occupational labour markets which are external to the organisation, and organisational labour markets which are restricted to and controlled by firms or organisations.
- Amongst more skilled workers and professionals, there is movement between jobs and organisations;

they are not tied to the internal labour market of a particular organisation and therefore are not restricted in their efforts to improve their pay or secure promotion.

- Those skilled professional workers whose status and rewards depend partly upon their skills and partly upon their position within their employing organisation (such as company lawyers and accountants) belong to what Crompton and Sanderson describe as the occupational internal labour markets.

- Employees in firm internal labour markets depend almost wholly on their position in a particular organisation or firm for their status and rewards, and any mobility there is is limited to similar types of organisation (for example, senior local authority workers are unlikely, on the whole, to find jobs in any other type of organisation). In firm internal labour markets an employee is normally a highly trained generalist rather than the mobile specialist of occupational or occupational internal labour markets.

- Use is made of dual labour market theory to indicate that workers with few skills in the occupational labour market tend to end up in the secondary labour market.

For Crompton and Sanderson, gender segregation is:

A product of the past sex-stereotyping of occupations and conventional assumptions relating to the domestic role of women, formal and informal exclusionary (discriminatory) practices, and fluctuations in both the demand for labour and the nature of female labour available. (p. 46)

In some circumstances conventional expectations and exclusionary practices can be overcome, and women can break into those parts of the labour market to which they could not previously gain access. The researchers illustrate their theoretical assumptions by reference to four case studies within four areas of employment: pharmacy, accountancy, building societies and cooking and serving (see Exhibit 12.1).

Exhibit 12.1

Four examples

Pharmacy

Female membership of the Pharmaceutical Society increased dramatically during the course of the twentieth century, and by 1983 a majority of undergraduates studying pharmacy were women. Crompton and Sanderson argue that pharmacy has not been 'sex-typed' even though it involves high levels of scientific training usually associated with mainly male professions. However, flexible patterns of employment within the profession are usually associated with predominantly female professions. Regulations mean that a pharmacist has to be present if drugs are to be dispensed. This has led to the creation of considerable amounts of part-time work which is attractive to women seeking to combine work with childcare.

However, although women have a high profile within pharmacy, they tend to be concentrated within the lower levels of the profession. Until the 1980s part-time pharmacists in the NHS could not achieve promotion, and in companies such as Boots the requirement to be geographically mobile has discouraged women. Therefore, although women have been able to enter the occupational labour market in pharmacy, they have had limited success in gaining promotion within it.

Accountancy

There are a number of different professional qualifications and associations, and while the careers of some accountants are closely bound up with the firm internal labour market of particular organisations, other accountants are self-employed or work in small independent practices and have occupational rather than organisational careers. The proportion of women in accountancy is relatively low compared with pharmacy, and even by the mid-1960s less than 1 per cent of accountants were women, although by 1986 women comprised 36 per cent of those in accountancy training. Interviews with female qualified accountants revealed varying degrees of prejudice and discrimination amongst male colleagues and bosses as indicated by statements such as, 'I just think that that's where women are most fulfilled, at home having a family.' There were also few part-time opportunities in most firms which presented women accountants with a clear choice between their career or domestic childcare.

Building societies

In contrast to accountancy, most building society workers are female and in their particular survey Crompton and Sanderson established that 70 per cent of building society employees are women. (Since the study was published, many building societies have converted to banks, so while the building society sector has declined the same employment patterns exist within the 'new' banks.) The high concentration of women in building society employment has been attributed in part to the very rapid expansion of employment in these organisations during the 1970s, a time when many married women were deciding to seek employment or to continue in work despite having children.

As with accountancy, a large proportion of the female workforce tends to be concentrated at the bottom levels of the organisational hierarchy; clerical work is done by women, but senior managers are almost exclusively male. Crompton and Sanderson consider building societies as examples of *firm internal labour markets* with prospects largely tied to internal promotion opportunities. Men have been traditionally dominant in these labour markets and have used their dominance to exclude women. Women tend to lack the formal qualifications, the willingness to do irregular overtime and the ability to be geographically mobile, all of which are necessary prerequisites for securing promotion.

There are also unofficial practices which tend to block women's promotion opportunities. For example, senior managers who are invariably male occasionally act as 'sponsors' or 'mentors' for aspiring junior staff, assisting them with their careers. The process is discriminatory as the junior staff selected for mentoring are almost always male. Women also lack access to male-dominated informal networks and clubs which can provide the means to further career development. As a result of their interviews, Crompton and Sanderson revealed considerable evidence to suggest that exclusionary and discriminatory practices in building societies are widespread.

Cooking and serving

Work in catering and hotels has normally been considered 'women's work' because of its similarity to unpaid domestic work. Such work is generally low paid and low status, although in some areas there are limited career prospects. Crompton and Sanderson looked at work in hotels and the school meals service. Not surprisingly, it was found that almost all school meals workers were women, and since the school meals service is widely regarded as 'women's work' and is seen as unskilled, there is little competition from men for the jobs. As with other work of this nature, women are attracted to the job owing to the availability of part-time employment during school hours, making it relatively easy to combine work with looking after school-age children.

The hotel context is slightly different in that there are areas where men predominate. For example, most porters and many of the most senior and well-paid chefs are men. Management is fairly evenly split between males and females, but women predominate in housekeeping and personnel, as managers within institutional catering and as proprietors of small establishments. At the lower levels of the hotel hierarchy, women are employed as counter and kitchen hands, waitresses, chambermaids, etc.

Increasingly such workers are employed on a part-time and casual basis. The hotel trade is highly competitive and there is evidence from the case studies that employers are using greater numbers of casual workers who can be laid off during slack times in order to cut costs. Male employees therefore tend to have greater job security than female employees. Indeed, this is a classic example of women at the lower levels of hotel work being confined to a secondary labour market with little security and few prospects.

Source: Adapted from Crompton and Sanderson, 1990

Crompton and Sanderson's research, therefore, indicates that women continue to suffer considerable disadvantages within the labour market and employment relationship. However, the precise reasons for these disadvantages, the degree of inequality and extent of discriminatory practices between men and women varies from industry to industry. Crompton and Sanderson nevertheless suggest that there is some evidence from their work of a reduction in gender divisions within employment, and point out that:

> The decline in manual occupations, and the intensification of competition between different types of disadvantaged labour at the lower levels of service employment, might be expected to result in a decline in sex-typed occupations in the [occupational] structure as a whole. (p. 147)

At higher levels, more women have been using their educational success and the 'qualifications lever' to force their way into male strongholds, but while gender difference might become less oppressive and inegalitarian they will be a persisting feature within work and employment for the foreseeable future.

Summary points concerning discrimination and theories of gender inequality

- There is plenty of evidence of sex (and race) discrimination within society, the employment relationship and the workplace. Many women are still concentrated in low paid, routine and part-time occupations and work. Black workers are often discriminated against in relation to selection, recruitment and advancement.
- It is important to make the distinction between prejudice (attitudes and opinions) and discrimination (actual behaviour) since the former underpins the latter. Legislating against discrimination may have no effect upon the nature of an individual's prejudices.
- Theories explaining gender inequalities within society include:
  - socio-biological explanations (biological differences lead to different social roles and behaviours);

- social construction of gender roles through manipulation and social conditioning/engineering; and
- feminism, incorporating radical, Marxist and liberal feminism.
- Within the labour market, employment relationship and workplace, explanations for gender inequality include:
  - human capital theory (lack of commitment causes disadvantage at work);
  - dual labour market theory counterpoising the primary and secondary labour markets;
  - post-Fordist assumptions concerning flexible specialisation; and
  - reserve army of labour thesis concerning the substitutability of labour.
- The integrated approach suggested by Crompton and Sanderson (1990) argues that the labour market structure influences career choice, thereby reinforcing through the pursuit of traditional 'masculine' and 'feminine' careers the occupational gender inequalities.

ETHNICITY AND RACE

While Britain is becoming more ethnically diverse, divisions and inequalities between ethnic and racial groups continue to persist and are mirrored in the workplace. The term race is often used in an ambiguous and imprecise way, and there have been various attempts to establish racial categories based on biological differences; some researchers have distinguished four or five categories, while others have identified dozens. Obviously there are clear physical differences between human beings, and some of these differences are inherited. But the question of why some differences and not others become matters for social discrimination and prejudice has nothing to do with biology. Racial differences, therefore, should be understood as **physical variations singled out by the members of a community or society as socially significant** (Giddens, 1998). Differences in skin colour, for example, are treated as significant, whereas differences in colour of hair are not. Racism is prejudice based on socially significant physical distinctions. A racist believes that some individuals and groups are superior or inferior to others as a result of these racial differences.

Ethnicity refers to the cultural practices and outlooks of a given community of people that set them apart from others, that is, makes them culturally distinct from other groups in society: they are seen by others to be distinct. Different characteristics may serve to distinguish ethnic groups from one another, but the most usual are language, history/ancestry, religion, styles of dress or adornment. Ethnic differences are therefore entirely learned. There are many ethnic minority groups, and it is generally accepted that members of a minority group are disadvantaged as compared with the majority population and have some sense of group solidarity, of belonging together. The experience of being subject to prejudice and discrimination usually heightens feelings of common loyalty and interests. Members of minority groups often tend to see themselves as separate from the majority and are often physically and socially isolated from the larger community. Many minorities are both ethnically and physically distinct from the rest of the population, as, for example, West Indians and Asians in Britain.

Psychological interpretations of prejudice and ethnic inequality

There are two main explanations for ethnic differences and inequality of treatment. The first is based on stereotypes and scapegoats and the second is based on the authoritarian personality.

Stereotypes and scapegoats

Prejudice operates mainly through the use of stereotypical thinking, that is, thinking in terms of fixed and inflexible categories. Stereotyping is often closely linked to the psychological mechanism of displacement, in which feelings of hostility or anger are directed against objects that are not the real origin of those feelings; people vent their anger against 'scapegoats' (people blamed for things/events which are not their fault). Scapegoating is common when two deprived ethnic groups come into competition with one another for economic rewards. Those who direct racial abuse and attacks against blacks, for example, are often in a similar economic position; they blame blacks for grievances whose real causes lie elsewhere. Scapegoating is normally directed against

groups that are distinctive and relatively powerless, because they make an easy target (Protestants, Catholics, Jews, Italians, Black Africans and others have played the unwilling role of scapegoat at various times throughout western history). Finally, scapegoating frequently involves projection defined as the unconscious attribution to others of one's own desires and characteristics.

Self-Evaluation Activity 12.5

Stereotypes and scapegoating
This SEA has no commentary

Think of examples of stereotypes and scapegoating and discuss these with your colleagues and tutor.

The authoritarian personality

Adorno *et al.* (1950) argued that some individuals may possess certain personality traits which predispose them to stereotypical thinking and projection, and as a result of their research diagnosed a personality type which they termed the authoritarian personality. The researchers developed a number of scales which, they argued, could determine levels of prejudice. On one scale, for instance, interviewees were asked to agree or disagree with a series of statements expressing strongly anti-Semitic views. Those who were diagnosed as prejudiced against Jews also tended to express negative attitudes towards other minorities. People with an authoritarian personality tend to be rigidly conformist, submissive to their superiors and dismissive towards inferiors, and tend to be highly intolerant in their religious and sexual attitudes and beliefs.

The research has been criticised but, at the very least, the ideas of Adorno *et al.* are valuable in assisting understanding of authoritarian patterns of thought in general and the psychological bases of prejudiced attitudes in particular.

Sociological interpretations of prejudice and ethnic inequality

The psychological mechanisms of stereotypical thinking, displacement and projection are found amongst members of all societies, and help to explain why ethnic antagonism is such a common element in different cultures. However, they tell us little about the social processes involved in discrimination. Sociological concepts relevant to ethnic conflicts and disadvantage in society include:

- ethnocentrism;
- ethnic group closure; and
- resource allocation.

Ethnocentrism

Ethnocentrism is defined as a suspicion of outsiders combined with a tendency to evaluate the culture of others in terms of one's own culture. Combined with stereotypical thought, ethnocentrism can give rise to particularly virulent forms of racial prejudice or racism. Outsiders are conceptualised as aliens, barbarians or as being morally and mentally inferior.

Group closure

There is often a strong association between ethnocentrism and group closure. 'Closure' refers to the process whereby groups maintain boundaries separating themselves from others. These boundaries are formed by means of exclusion devices which accentuate the divisions between one ethnic group and another and include:

- limiting or prohibiting intermarriage between groups;
- restrictions on social contact or economic relationships such as trading; and
- physical separation of groups into 'voluntary' ghettos.

Resource allocation

Groups of equal power may mutually enforce lines of closure; their members keep separate from one another, but neither group dominates the other. More usually, however, one ethnic group occupies a position of power over the other, and in these circumstances group closure combines with resource allocation, with the dominant group controlling the distribution of wealth and material goods. Some of the fiercest conflicts between ethnic groups centre on lines of closure between them, precisely because

these lines signal inequalities in wealth, power and social standing. The concept of closure and unequal resource allocation assists our understanding of a whole range of differences, 'not just why the members of some groups get shot, lynched, or harassed, but also why they don't get good jobs, a good education or a desirable place to live' (Giddens, 1998, p. 215).

Race, labour markets and the employment relationship

As with gender, the existence of a dual labour market, where the secondary market comprises a relatively high proportion of ethnic minorities, is an important distinguishing factor. Workers of ethnic minority origin have also consistently suffered a disproportionately high level of unemployment. It would, however, be unhelpful to consider ethnic minorities as one homogeneous group, and the following factors suggest that there is a high degree of differentiation:

- With regard to unemployment, Pakistanis, West Indians and Guyanese do particularly badly, irrespective of their qualifications, while male Indians appear to be the most successful group in terms of using their qualifications to escape unemployment.
- Those with Indian origins are consistently better qualified than any other minority group, and as well qualified as, if not better qualified than, the white population.
- Those with Pakistani or Bangladeshi origins, and particularly the women from these two groups, are the least qualified of all.
- The West Indian and Guyanese population traditionally have the highest employment rate for any group.

Ethnic minority groups in common with a significant proportion of the female labour force are disadvantaged with regard to qualifications and employment opportunities, levels of pay, differential recruitment policies and practices, and trade union membership. Not only do ethnic minorities find access to organisations difficult, but once inside they generally find themselves discriminated against for reasons that are social rather than economic in origin, and for criteria that include not just skin colour but religious and political affiliation also (Doeringer and Piore, 1971). We now look briefly at two important sources of racial discrimination – selection and recruitment into employment, and trade unions and workers. In a survey concerning the distribution of the different ethnic groups between different types of employment undertaken in 1997 (Modood *et al.*, 1997, 2000), profound and enduring inequalities in employment were found to exist along a number of variables such as type of work and industry, hours, shifts and supervision.

Selection and recruitment

While a growing number of organisations in Britain undertake ethnic monitoring, it can, nevertheless, be difficult to estimate the extent of discrimination at the selection and recruitment stage. Modood *et al.* (1997) found that a quarter of all the ethnic minority persons who believed they had been discriminated against in a job application 'believed that it was for a mixture of reasons to do with their race and religion' (p. 233). Research by Jenkins (1988) indicates that managers involved in the recruiting process have a hierarchy of criteria for acceptability. The primary criteria involve appearance, manner and attitude, and maturity. Secondary criteria relate to 'gut feeling', employment history and experience, the ability to fit in, age, style of speech, literacy and marital status. Tertiary criteria concern references and English language competence.

In several areas minority workers are likely to face discrimination: they are less likely to fit the stereotypical 'married, two kids and a mortgage' pattern that recruiters seem to seek; their accent may well be regarded by white recruiters as inferior to white speech patterns; and they are less likely to 'fit in' to the existing organisation. Grint (1993) argues that:

> Minority workers suffer the ignominies commonly associated with disparaging racial stereotypes. In many ways it seems that a large number of recruiters do not perceive themselves to be racist but prefer white workers on the grounds of expediency: the white workforce is racist, therefore, irrespective of their own liberal notions of 'fairness', white recruiters fear the consequences of recruiting minority workers. Inevitably, the failure to challenge assumed racism actually facilitates its reproduction; thus self-proclaimed liberalism acts merely as a conduit for the perpetuation of racism. (p. 259)

Given the conventional recruitment procedures in many manufacturing firms – word of mouth and social networks – even conspicuously racist recruiters may never need to resort to racial discrimination in any open manner because the method of recruitment excludes ethnic minorities from the pool as a result of informal screening. The informal nature of this type of recruitment also implies that surveillance by state agencies is more difficult. Even where identically qualified individuals are interviewed, the emphasis placed upon the subjective assessment of the interviewer may ensure that the minority interviewee is not selected. A partial solution to this subjectivism is to formalise the procedure, and though this may not be the means to eliminate racial discrimination in the recruitment process it may be regarded as a means by which its effects can be reduced.

Mini case 12.1
Selection for temporary or permanent contract

Ms Sahay, who is of Indian origin, worked for the Post Office in Pushton on a casual basis from July 2003. In September of that year, she was asked to take an aptitude test, to decide whether she should continue on a temporary or permanent contract. She complained about this, because she knew that some white workers had not been asked to sit the test, but her concerns were not taken seriously.

It became clear during the tribunal hearing that three white workers – in fact whole batches of casuals – had been given contracts without having passed the test. The Post Office was unable to explain why some people had to sit for tests and not others. The tribunal was critical of the way the Post Office treated its Asian employees, and Ms Sahay in particular.

Ms Sahay was awarded £19 757 in compensation, including £10 000 for injury to feelings.

Self-Evaluation Activity 12.6
Methods of recruitment
Response on website

Can you think of one method whereby employers could recruit more employees from ethnic minorities?

Examples of discrimination in recruitment

Within the Civil Service in 1999 there were no ethnic minorities amongst the top three grades and within the top seven grades there were only 207 out of 18 644, representing 1 per cent of civil servants within these grades (CRE, 1999, p. 27). This is not because ethnic minorities have avoided work in the Civil Service; on the contrary, about 4 per cent of the total are minorities (Indians, Pakistanis and Bangladeshis, and West Indians make up about 1 per cent each with a further 1 per cent for all other minorities), marginally higher than the proportion for the total working population. These figures reveal a greater concentration of ethnic minorities within the lower reaches of the Civil Service (Grint, 1993). Within two areas of the Civil Service, comprising 'general fast-stream trainees' and 'examiners in insolvency', encouraging early trends were not maintained and 'in 1997 . . . there were no ethnic minority appointees in either area' (CRE, 1999, p. 28).

An investigation by the Commission for Racial Equality (CRE) into chartered accountancy (CRE, 1987) revealed that members of ethnic minorities were three and a half times less likely to be offered a job than white applicants, and the discriminatory practices occurred at all levels of the screening process. It was not until 1998 that the Association of Chartered Accountants concluded an agreement with the CRE to keep ethnic records of all its UK members. The picture is the same in many other occupations; around 2 per cent of probation officers and 1 per cent of police officers are from minority groups, while only around 1 per cent of solicitors come from minorities, mostly working in the smaller law firms.

These examples indicate the need for managers to devise a more formal and less prejudiced approach to recruitment. After all, if discrimination hinders the recruitment of the most qualified and suitable individual for the particular job, then it must be against the interests of the company both morally and economically. However, formality does contain its own problems, as Grint (1993) points out:

Formality can actually provide the cover for more rather than less, manipulation of the recruitment procedure. Concomitantly, reducing informal procedures may actually undermine some of the shop floor patterns of trust between managers and workers. Since there can never be a sufficiently universal rule book to cover all contingencies there clearly is a problem regarding the manipulation or misinterpretation of rules. However, the ordinarily superior record of public employment regarding ethnic minorities suggests that formality should not be cast aside because of its inevitable problems. (p. 264)

Finally, the CRE concluded a partnership agreement with the Ministry of Defence (MoD) which committed the MoD and the three armed services to certain equality aims and a 4 per cent target for ethnic minority recruits by 31 March 2001. The target was not achieved and some discrimination was still in evidence. Nevertheless 'all three services have made considerable effort to improve their performance on racial equality, for example through rigorous ethnic monitoring, positive action initiatives and new discrimination complaints procedures' (CRE, 2002, p. 27).

Trade union and employee discrimination

British trade unions have a long history of exclusionary tactics and strategies against ethnic minorities, and racism within the indigenous British workforce is nothing new. Documented reports of racist attacks by British workers upon Irish workers in the nineteenth century, then Jewish workers at the turn of the twentieth century are early examples. The TUC had, until relatively recently, often discriminated against minority workers. For example, as early as 1892 it made a declaration favouring the control of 'alien' labour. Grint (1993) identifies the following examples:

One of the earliest cases of official trade union hostility to their own minority members in Britain is that of the National Union of Seamen who were disinclined to support their minority members against the 1925 Special Restrictions (Coloured Alien Seamen) Order. Even Ben Tillet, an avowed socialist and radical union leader of the London dockers at the turn of the nineteenth century, was equivocal about the arrival of Jewish immigrants: 'Yes, you are our brothers and we will stand by you. But we wish you had not come'. . . . Similarly, the population as a whole seems to have been at best ambiguous about the status of the Jews. The Boer War was blamed by Keir Hardy [a trade unionist and founder of the Labour Party] and a substantial proportion of trade union leaders on the Army, composed as it allegedly was 'largely [of] Jews and foreigners'. Even during the Second World War indigenous anti-Semitism was ever present among the British working class, though they do not seem to have been as anti-Semitic as the government feared or the gutter press assumed. (pp. 266–7)

Interestingly enough, the influx of 'New Commonwealth' immigrants during the 1950s and 1960s during a period of full employment meant that labour shortages could be alleviated. For example, London Transport was active in recruiting bus conductors and drivers and underground railway staff through advertising and the provision of assisted passages for West Indians and their families. This ensured that there was little direct competition between white indigenous and minority workers. Similarly, in the North and Midlands where many Asian workers found manufacturing jobs, particularly in textiles, the general pattern was one where white employees left, leaving vacancies for Asian workers, rather than one where cheaper Asian workers pushed white workers out of the labour market. However, from the late 1960s onwards, with the increase in unemployment, there was a resurgence of racist attitudes by trade union members and white workers alike, based on the 'threat to jobs'. This type of 'occupational racism' was fuelled by the overt racism of some politicians, most notably Enoch Powell who gave his inflammatory 'rivers of blood' speech in 1968 which was supported by the London dockers. Even the Labour Party endorsed the establishment of immigration controls, while the TUC adopted policy statements explicitly linking the existence of immigrant workers to the issue of the 'coloured problem' and it was not until 1989 that the TUC at its annual conference supported the anti-racist resolution with a rule providing for expulsion of unions and members for 'deliberate acts of unlawful discrimination'.

Much empirical research suggests that, despite members of ethnic minorities being favourably inclined towards trade unions, white trade union members are generally less enthusiastic about anti-racist issues than their national officials (CRE, 1981; Lee, 1987). There is, therefore, a distinction to be made between racist attitudes of a proportion of white trade union members and workers, and the official anti-racist pronouncements of full-time union officers. But even at the upper levels of trade union hierarchies, there appears to be a mismatch between rhetoric and reality, particularly in relation to the staffing of trade unions, as Grint (1993) points out:

It is worth . . . acknowledging the extent to which trade union bureaucracies are themselves staffed by white employees. While there is little systematic evidence on this, because very few unions have ethnic monitoring, it is apparent that where studies do exist, they disclose a depressingly conservative picture of grossly under-represented ethnic minorities. The situation is worse than appears at first sight because the level of union density amongst ethnic minorities is substantially higher than the equivalent figure for white workers. In 1986 only thirteen of the main thirty-three British unions had any minority officials and many had only a token minority leader. Bill Morris . . . is the most senior minority union official. But although 56 per cent of minority employees were unionised in 1986, compared to 47 per cent of white employees, only 4 per cent of minority men held elected posts within their unions, compared to 11 per cent of white men. The figures were identical for white and minority women at 2 per cent (Policy Studies Institute, 1986).

In the face of declining union membership throughout the 1980s, 1990s and 2000s the TUC and unions generally have attempted, with varying degrees of success, to attract membership from diverse groups of employees. In order to do this, the TUC argues that positive and successful union initiatives in the areas of discrimination and equality will be 'major selling points' in the drive to recruit diverse members (TUC, 1997, 1998). Internal union structures and decision-making processes also need to be more open and representative of diverse groups in order to legitimise collective bargaining processes and other methods of joint regulation.

Summary points concerning race discrimination

- The distinction between race (physical variations considered as socially significant) and ethnicity (cultural practices and outlooks of one group which distinguish it from other groups), is important in understanding this type of discrimination.
- Prejudice is manifested by stereotypical thinking and scapegoating by, for example, targeting those groups that are 'distinctive' and/or powerless. Certain personality types such as the 'authoritarian personality' are, it is argued, more receptive to prejudice.
- Interpretations of prejudice and ethnic inequality include:
  - ethnocentrism (suspicion of 'outsiders');
  - group closure (groups segregating themselves from other groups); and
  - resource allocation (conflicts over scarce resources).
- Within labour markets and the employment relationship in Britain, ethnic and race inequality affects different groups in different ways, but in general they tend to be disadvantaged in terms of qualifications, employment opportunities, levels of pay, differential recruitment policies, trade union and employee discrimination.

AN OVERVIEW OF DISCRIMINATION LEGISLATION

With regard to the discrimination legislation, we firstly consider the national legislation and then any relevant Articles and Directives etc. emanating from the European Union. Amendments to existing legislation to implement a European Union common framework to tackle unfair discrimination on six grounds of sex, race, disability, sexual orientation, religion and age are also considered in greater detail where appropriate in the sections below. In May 2002 the government announced long-term plans to create a single Equality Commission to replace the three that already existed (the Equal Opportunities Commission, the Commission for Racial Equality and the Disability Rights Commission).

Sex discrimination

The national legislation recognises two important issues affecting men and women within the employment relationship:

- equal pay between men and women; and
- more general matters concerning sex discrimination.

We look at at each of these issues in turn.

Equal Pay Act 1970

This was the first piece of legislation with the aim of promoting equality at work between men and women. The Act, which came into full force in 1975, has been amended by the Sex Discrimination Acts of 1975 and 1986, by the Equal Pay (Amendment) Regulations of 1983 and the Pensions Act 1995. The Industrial Tribunals Rules of Procedure (Amendment) Rules 1996 amend the procedure used to deal with equal value claims.

The Act provides that a woman's contract is to have an equality clause implied into it if the contract does not specifically contain one. The effect of the equality clause is to modify the woman's contractual conditions so that they are no less favourable than those of a man who is engaged on like work or on work rated as equivalent.

Self-Evaluation Activity 12.7

Pay equality
Response on website

Identify some instances or circumstances where you think a woman's pay should be equal to that of a man.

In order to demonstrate equivalence, the woman must know who to compare herself with, that is, the comparator. The comparator needs to be of a different sex, employed by the same employer and at an establishment covered by the same terms and conditions. She may then take her case to an employment tribunal in order to seek redress. Should the job be considered equal by the tribunal (or subsequent courts of appeal), then she is entitled to receive equal pay backdated to a maximum of two years before the date at which she applied to tribunal. However, the employer, while accepting the principle of job equality could argue that the pay differential between the male and female employees concerned should be retained 'genuinely due to a material factor which is not the difference of sex' (s.1 (3) Equal Pay Act). A genuinely material factor (GMF) for the same work and work rated as equivalent under a job evaluation scheme could be cited by the employer from a range of examples including a difference of personal factors such as length of service, superior skill or qualifications and higher productivity.

Equal Pay (Amendment) Regulations 1983

The regulations provide a new criterion and test under which pay parity between the sexes can be claimed – where the man is on work of equal value to that of the woman. Equal value is defined in terms of the demands made by the job, and includes skill, effort and decision-making. An equal value claim is only relevant where the woman and her male comparator are not engaged in 'like work' or 'work rated as equivalent'. However, an important case, *Pickstone v Freemans plc* (1988) IRLR 357, established that an employer cannot defeat an equal value claim by showing that there is another man engaged on like work or equivalently rated work (see below) as long as the male comparator selected by the applicant (the woman bringing the case) falls outside those categories.

The effect of the amendment is threefold:

- It has opened up a far wider field for claims than existed under the old law. Comparisons can now be made between totally dissimilar jobs, in different pay structures and across different collective bargaining groups.
- It allows for an independent expert to evaluate and compare jobs even where the employer has no job evaluation scheme. The 1996 amendments to employment tribunal rules mean that the tribunal can now decide whether or not an independent expert should be appointed in the particular case.
- It allows an existing job evaluation scheme to be scrutinised by the tribunal to ensure that there is no discriminatory bias within the scheme itself.

For equal value claims the material factor defence which the employer may use allows the employer to justify a difference on non-sex-based grounds relating to personal differences or market forces. The amend-

ments apply equally to men who can, therefore, claim equality of terms with women on like work, work rated as equivalent, or on work of equal value.

Changes for 2003 and beyond

Equal Pay (Amendment) Regulations 2003

The new regulations drawn from the EU Equal Treatment Amendment Directive 2002 cover three areas:

Time limit for back pay: If an equal pay claim is successful, the Equal Pay Act entitled the complainant to receive back pay for up to two years before the date of the start of proceedings. The limit is now increased to six years in England and Wales and five years in Scotland.

No reasonable grounds: Up to 2003 an employer could argue that there were no reasonable grounds for an equal pay claim when, for example, work appears dissimilar in nature. This one-sided defence, which perpetuates stereotypes, is now not admissible under the regulations. However, an employment tribunal is now entitled to conclude that two jobs are not of equal value where they have already been rated differently on a job evaluation scheme, providing that the scheme is satisfactory.

Time limit for bringing equal pay claims: The existing time limit for bringing equal pay claims remains at six months but the limit can be extended where the employment tribunal or court considers that the employer concealed relevant facts from the complainant.

The Equal Pay Act and amendments cover the contractual aspects of discrimination concerning pay, while the Sex Discrimination Act of 1975 is designed to cover non-contractual discriminatory treatment.

Sex Discrimination Act 1975

The Sex Discrimination Act (SDA) promotes the equal treatment of women and men in employment, education and in the provision of goods and services, and deals with discrimination against women or men and on the grounds of marital status at all stages of the employment relationship concerning selection, the availability of opportunities for training and promotion, the provision of benefits and facilities, and dismissal. The SDA was passed following increased concern over, and interest in, women's rights. Subsequent to Britain's membership of the EEC in 1973, Article 119 and associated Directives concerning equal pay and treatment have had an important influence on discrimination law in the UK. The SDA established the Equal Opportunities Commission with a remit to:

- eliminate discrimination on the grounds of sex or marital status;
- generally promote equal opportunities between men and women; and
- monitor the implementation of the SDA and Equal Pay Act.

The Act covers both direct and indirect discrimination.

Direct discrimination

This is defined by section 1(1) in the following terms: 'A person discriminates against a woman in any circumstances relevant to the purposes of any provision of this Act if on the ground of her sex he treats her less favourably than he treats or would treat a man.' It is also unlawful to discriminate against married people of either sex if 'on the ground of (an employee's) marital status (an employer) treats that person less favourably than he treats or would treat an unmarried person of the same sex'. It is worth noting that while the Act does not mention discrimination against employees on the basis of their unmarried status – and so this is not unlawful – the EU Equal Treatment Directive prohibits discrimination on the grounds of 'marital or family status' and so would include single people. Direct discrimination, therefore, involves two key elements:

- there must be less favourable treatment; and
- the treatment must be because of sex or marital status.

Clarke (1995) points out that direct discrimination is frequently hidden or covert:

Many employers still discriminate against women by refusing to offer them jobs or promote them, but few employers admit that this is due to the woman's sex; some other reason will usually be given. It is the woman who has to prove that she has been discriminated against, and this is still a difficult task. (p. 9)

Self-Evaluation Activity 12.8
Equality of treatment
Response on website

Provide an example of each of:

(a) 'Less favourable treatment'.
(b) 'Treatment due to sex or marital status'.

In all cases of direct discrimination, it is necessary to compare a person's treatment with that of someone of the opposite sex. The comparison can be hypothetical – it is unnecessary for a woman, say, to show that a man was *in fact* treated more favourably than she was.

Indirect discrimination

Indirect sex discrimination takes place when a requirement or condition is applied equally to men and women. However, the condition has the effect that in practice it disadvantages a much larger proportion of one sex than the other, because they find it harder to fulfil, and it cannot be justified on grounds other than sex. In the same way, an employer may discriminate indirectly against a married person of either sex on the ground of their marital status. Clarke (1995) suggests that:

Indirect discrimination is a concept which enables individuals to challenge seemingly innocent practices, such as requiring certain educational qualifications, or setting age limits, or insisting on physical characteristics, which appear to be neutral but which in fact operate so as to disproportionately exclude one sex. However, unlike direct discrimination which can never be justified, the employer may be able to show that the practice has some business-related purpose, even though it has an adverse impact on one sex. (p. 9)

There are four criteria which must be satisfied in relation to indirect discrimination:

Requirement or condition: The employer must have made a 'requirement or condition', such as a stipulation 'that only full-time employees were eligible for redundancy on a last in, first out basis' (Clarke, 1995, p. 10) which could be deemed to be indirectly discriminatory to women. Another example is the insistence that job applicants be under a certain age which could be indirectly discriminatory since women are more likely than men to have taken a number of years out of the labour market to care for children.

Disproportionate effect: It should be established that the requirement, whatever it may be, indirectly discriminates against a larger proportion of women than men.

Detriment: A woman must demonstrate not only that she cannot comply with the requirement or condition, but also that this is to her detriment and that she is a real victim of the alleged discrimination.

Justification: Even if a woman can show that there is a discriminatory requirement or condition which operates to her detriment, the employer may be able to justify the existence of such a requirement. If the employer is shown to be indirectly discriminatory, then the courts (following the precedent of a 'benchmark' case *Bilka-Kaufhaus GmbH* v *Weber von Hartz* (1986) IRLR 317) must be satisfied that, in order to be justified, measures taken by the employer 'must correspond to a real need on the part of the undertaking and be appropriate and necessary to achieving the objectives pursued'.

Unlawful discrimination

Within the employment relationship, the Act makes it unlawful to discriminate on the basis of sex or marital status in relation to potential and present employees. In relation to potential employees, it is unlawful to discriminate in recruitment arrangements such as advertising and interviewing and in the terms and conditions of a job offer. It is also unlawful to discriminate in the adoption of selection criteria and selection methods. In relation to present employees it is unlawful to discriminate in the provision of opportunities for promotion, transfer or training, and in the provision of facilities or services such as study leave or company cars, and in unfavourable treatment such as dismissal.

There are some exceptions provided by the Act which permit lawful discrimination and these are termed genuine occupational qualifications (GOQs). These exceptions include occupations such as modelling, acting, or jobs such as toilet attendants. However, the Act does not permit positive discrimination where the employer may favour certain groups in the selection process. Nevertheless, the Act does allow positive action as in the example of the Metropolitan Police concerning race given earlier. Positive action, for example, would include situations whereby members of one sex have performed a job for the past 12 months and the employer feels that special training should be given exclusively for members of the opposite sex. Employers may also encourage applications from this group but not favour the applicants within the selection process.

The enforcement of the Act's provisions is through the following channels:

- The Equal Opportunities Commission (EOC) can, and does, take action concerning all aspects of discrimination considered above (the EOC *Code of Practice*, 1985, is dealt with later in the chapter).
- In instances which may lie outside the EOC's jurisdiction, individuals who feel they have been discriminated against can make a claim to the Employment Tribunal as detailed in the Equal Pay Act.

Social Security Act 1989; Pensions Act 1995

The Social Security Act provides for entitlement to equal treatment in the provision of employment-related benefit schemes after a period of paid maternity leave or during a period of paid family leave. The Pensions Act acknowledges the EU Directive on equal treatment for men and women in relation to occupational social security schemes and in particular to occupational pension schemes.

Employment Rights Act 1996

The Employment Rights Act (ERA) consolidated rights connected with pregnancy and maternity established by the Employment Act 1980, the Employment Protection (Consolidation) Act 1978 and the Trade Union and Employment Rights Act 1993. The rights concerning pregnancy and maternity are:

- **Time off for ante-natal care:** an employee who is pregnant and who has made an appointment to attend for ante-natal care on the advice of a medical practitioner, midwife or health visitor is entitled to take paid time off during working hours to keep the appointment.

- **Suspension on maternity grounds:** an employee is suspended on maternity grounds if she is suspended on the ground that she is pregnant, has recently given birth or is breast-feeding a child. As an alternative to suspension the employee has a right to be offered any suitable and appropriate alternative employment which the employer has available, and which is equivalent in terms and conditions. If an employee is dismissed in circumstances where she ought to be suspended under these provisions, she will be able to claim that her dismissal is automatically unfair.

- **Right to maternity leave for all employees:** there is a general right for employees to have 14 weeks' maternity leave regardless of the length of time for which they have been employed by their employer provided that they comply with all the notification requirements. Where an employee has a contractual right to maternity leave then she can 'pick and mix' her contractual and statutory rights to give herself the best composite right. If the employee is entitled, and wishes to exercise her right to return later than the end of the maternity leave period, within 29 weeks of the week of childbirth, then she must also inform her employer that she intends to exercise that right. If there is redundancy during the maternity leave period, then the employee is entitled to be offered any suitable alternative employment which is available on terms and conditions 'which are not substantially less beneficial' than those she enjoyed under her previous contract. Should the employer fail to provide suitable available alternative employment or if the employee is selected for redundancy because of any reason connected with her pregnancy or maternity leave, the employee will automatically be treated as having been unfairly dismissed.

- **Right to return to work after extended maternity leave:** the 'right to return' is the right of an employee to return to work at any time from the end of her maternity leave period up to 29 weeks after the beginning of the week in which childbirth occurs. To be entitled to this 'right to return', the employee must fulfil the requirements to be entitled to maternity leave; have notified her employer that she intends to exercise her right to return to work; and at the beginning of the 11th week before the expected week of childbirth she must have been continuously employed for at least two years.

- **The right to return to what?:** the employee's primary right to return is a right to return to work with the employer by whom she was employed at the end of her maternity leave period or his successor; in the job in which she was employed before she went on maternity leave on equivalent and no less favourable terms and conditions of employment and with seniority, pension and similar rights as if her employment up to the end of her maternity leave period was continuous with her employment after her return; otherwise on terms and conditions as if she had not been absent after her maternity leave period. If it is impracticable because of redundancy to permit the employee to return to work, she is entitled to be offered appropriate alternative employment; if the employer fails in this, the employee will be deemed to have been automatically unfairly dismissed. Failure to permit a woman to return after maternity leave is considered to be unfair dismissal. There are two exceptions to this general position:
  - where the employer employs five or fewer employees immediately before the end of her maternity leave period and it is not reasonably practicable for the employer to offer suitable alternative employment or to allow the woman to return to her original job, then the woman will not be treated as having been dismissed; and
  - if it is not reasonably practicable for reasons other than redundancy, for the woman to be allowed to return to her original job and the employer offers the woman suitable alternative employment and she accepts or unreasonably refuses that offer, then again, the woman will not be treated as having been dismissed by being refused the right to return to work.

- **Dismissal of a temporary replacement:** where a temporary replacement is engaged to do the work of an employee who is suspended on maternity grounds or absent because of pregnancy or confinement, then provided:
  - the replacement is informed of this fact when they take the job on; and
  - the replacement is dismissed to allow the woman to return to work,

the employer will still have to show that he acted fairly.

- **Right not to be dismissed because of pregnancy or childbirth:** an employee is considered to be automatically unfairly dismissed if she is dismissed for any reason related to her pregnancy; where her maternity leave period is ended by dismissal for any reason connected with:
  - the fact that she has given birth to a child; or
  - the fact that she took maternity leave or the benefits attached to it;
  - when she ought to have been suspended on maternity grounds;
  - where her maternity leave period, extended or otherwise, is ended by dismissal because of redundancy and she was not offered suitable alternative employment which was available; or
  - where she is ill at the end of her maternity leave, has given the employer a medical certificate covering the period of her illness (up to four weeks) and she is dismissed during the currency of the medical certificate.
- **Right to pay in lieu of notice whilst absent due to pregnancy or maternity:** employees who are given notice when they are away from work due to pregnancy or confinement are entitled to be paid in lieu of notice provided that their notice entitlement is not over a week more than the statutory minimum notice entitlement. Where it was the employee who gave notice, the requirement for the employer to pay for the notice period in such cases only applies if the employee actually leaves the employer's employment.
- **Automatic right to written reasons for dismissal in pregnancy and maternity cases:** a woman who is dismissed while pregnant or in trying to exercise her right to return to work is entitled to be given written reasons for dismissal without asking for them.

Employment Relations Act 1999

Based substantially upon the proposals contained in the 1998 *Fairness at Work* white paper, the 'family-friendly' provisions include:

- the extension of maternity leave to 18 weeks in line with maternity pay;
- giving employees rights to extended maternity absence and to (unpaid) parental leave after one year's service;

- provision for the contract of employment to continue during the whole period of maternity or parental leave, unless it is expressly terminated by either party, by dismissal or resignation;
- provision of similar rights for employees to return to their jobs after parental leave as currently apply after maternity absence;
- provision of the right to three months' parental leave for adoptive parents;
- provision of a right to reasonable (unpaid) time off work for family emergencies, which will apply to all employees regardless of length of service; and
- ensuring that employees are protected against dismissal or other detriment if they exercise their rights to parental leave and time off for urgent family reasons.

Sex Discrimination (Gender Reassignment) Regulations 1999

Transsexuals as medically defined are protected under the sex discrimination legislation and the 1999 Regulations now protect those undergoing gender reassignment.

Sex Discrimination (Indirect Discrimination and Burden of Proof) Regulations 2000

These Regulations implement the Burden of Proof in the EU Sex Discrimination Cases Directive 98/52. They amend the SDA and insert two new sections. First, the burden of proof has shifted from the complainant to the respondent who must show that no discrimination occurred. Second, the definition of indirect discrimination has widened from 'application of a condition or requirement' to 'application of a provision, criterion or practice, which is to the detriment of a considerably larger proportion of women than men'.

Employment Act 2002

The Act introduces new provisions governing maternity leave and pay, adoption leave and paternity leave.

- **Ordinary maternity leave (OML)** increased from 18 weeks to 26 weeks for all female employees, with the right to return to exactly the same job irrespective of whether it is full- or part-time, or the length of time worked for the current employer. Women in the same job for at least 26 weeks are entitled to unpaid **additional maternity leave (AML)** for 26 weeks;

- **Statutory maternity pay (SMP)** increased from 18 to 26 weeks and paid at a rate of 90 per cent of average pay for six weeks followed by a flat rate of £100 a week for 20 weeks whether or not there is a return to work. Those not entitled to SMP owing, for example, to a change of job during pregnancy may be entitled to **maternity allowance (MA)**, the standard rate being £100 a week.
- **Statutory paternity pay (SPP)** is introduced for the first time from April 2003 and paid at a flat rate of £100 per week for two weeks. This is additional to parental leave and must be taken in one single episode within 56 days from the date of birth or adoption;
- **Adoption leave** (paid) introduced in line with maternity leave. Adoption leave may only be taken by one parent; the other may take paternity leave.

Changes for 2003 onwards

Changes incorporate EU Council Directive 2000/78/EC, Equal Treatment Directive, establishing a general framework for equal treatment in employment and occupation, prohibiting direct and indirect discrimination and harassment on the grounds of religion or belief, disability, age and sexual orientation in the fields of employment, self-employment, occupation and vocational training. The specific provisions concern sexual orientation in the main and are contained in:

Employment Equality (Sexual Orientation) Regulations 2003
- Amendments to the discrimination acts (in this case the SDA) will make harassment unlawful in all cases, including sexual orientation harassment. Both harassment (unwanted conduct related to the sex of a person) and sexual harassment (any form of unwanted verbal, non-verbal or physical conduct of a sexual nature) are treated as forms of discrimination.

- The concept of positive action will cover sexual orientation.
- Discrimination after employment, where there is a clear link with former employment, is now unlawful.
- Discrimination is outlawed on grounds of heterosexual, homosexual or bisexual orientation. As the above terms are considered offensive by the lesbian and gay community, the Regulations define sexual orientation in terms of 'an orientation towards persons of the same sex, opposite sex, or both'.

Summary points concerning sex discrimination legislation

- National legislation is concerned primarily with equal pay between men and women and more general issues concerning sex discrimination.
- Equal pay legislation provides for an 'equality clause' to be included in the woman's contract of employment in respect of like work and equivalently-rated work.
- The employer could justify pay differentials on grounds of a 'genuinely material factor' (GMF) such as length of service, superior skill or qualifications. Legislation since 1983 also provides for equality of pay for work of equal value.
- The SDA which established the EOC covers both direct and indirect discrimination. Direct discrimination involves intentionally less favourable treatment because of sex or marital status. Indirect discrimination occurs where a requirement or condition affecting both sexes equally nevertheless has a disproportionate effect upon one sex.
- The SDA permits lawful discrimination in certain instances which the Act calls 'genuine occupational qualifications' (GOQs). The Act does not permit 'positive discrimination' but does not sanction 'positive action'.
- Other relevant legislation includes:
  - Social Security Act 1989
  - Pensions Act 1995
  - Employment Rights Act 1996 (pregnancy and maternity provisions)
  - Employment Relations Act 1999 ('family-friendly' provisions)
  - Employment Act 2002 (parental leave provisions).

Race discrimination

Legislation concerning discrimination on grounds of race and ethnicity is largely based on the Race Relations Act 1976 which makes discrimination unlawful on the grounds of colour, race, nationality or ethnic or national origin in employment and other fields. It is unlawful to discriminate against a person either directly or indirectly on these grounds. The Act does not, however, apply to the police or the public services.

Race Relations Act 1976

The Act has been amended slightly by the Employment Act 1989, the Further and Higher Education Act 1992, the Education Act 1993, the Race Relations (Remedies) Act 1994, and the Police Act 1997. The Act also established the Commission for Racial Equality (CRE) whose duties are:

- to work towards the elimination of racial discrimination;
- to promote equality of opportunity and good relations between persons of different racial groups generally; and
- to monitor the working of the Act and to make recommendations to the Secretary of State to amend the Act if and when necessary.

The CRE is given wide powers of investigation and power to draw up codes of practice to eliminate discrimination in employment (see pp. 602–7). An employee or applicant for a job who has been discriminated against may be awarded compensation by an employment tribunal.

It is important to note that the Race Relations Act (RRA) has not been directly subject to the European Community legislation which has so influenced the case law and statutory development of domestic sex discrimination law in the employment field. It is likely, however, that the EU will assume a more prominent role as a result of the inclusion of a general non-discrimination clause into the Treaty of Rome as a result of the Treaty of Amsterdam 1999. This will enable the Council of Ministers, acting unanimously on a proposal from the European Commission after consultation with the European Parliament, to take 'appropriate action to combat discrimination based on sex, racial or ethnic origin, religion or belief,

disability, age or sexual orientation'. In its report *An Action Plan Against Racism* (1999), the European Commission indicated its intention to legislate to combat race discrimination and this is contained in the EU Race Directive of 2000 (p. 580). In addition, the CRE in 1998 put forward a comprehensive set of proposals and recommendations to the Home Secretary which would, if adopted, substantially reform the RRA. The proposals focused on the following areas:

- increasing the duties on public bodies to promote racial equality and eliminate discrimination;
- tackling institutional discrimination;
- strengthening the law enforcement powers of the Act;
- compulsory ethnic monitoring for all private employers with more than 250 employees and for public bodies;
- clearer definitions of key concepts, such as positive action; and
- removal of some of the existing exceptions to the Act.

Many of these proposals were incorporated in subsequent legislation.

The basic structure of the RRA is to define discrimination in Part I. This covers:

- direct and overtly less favourable treatment on racial grounds;
- indirect or institutional discrimination which results from the imposition of apparently racially-neutral requirements or conditions which have a 'disproportionately deleterious' impact on a particular racial group and which cannot be objectively justified; and
- discrimination by way of victimisation (because, for example, an individual has previously brought proceedings under or makes allegations in relation to the RRA).

Having so defined what amounts to discrimination, the RRA goes on to say that discrimination of that kind, as manifested in certain separate fields, amounts to unlawful conduct. In relation to employment and recruitment for employment, the relevant provisions are contained in Part II of the Act. Later parts of the Act deal with the constitution and powers of the CRE, enforcement of the Act and remedies.

Direct discrimination

Direct discrimination occurs when, on the grounds of race, a person is treated less favourably, or would be treated less favourably, than other persons. Note that the difference in treatment has to be on grounds of race, although this does not have to be the sole reason, as long as it is a substantial or important factor.

Self-Evaluation Activity 12.9

Direct race discrimination

Response on website

Identify one or two examples of direct discrimination.

Indirect discrimination

Indirect discrimination occurs when a person applies to another a condition or requirement which he or she applies or would apply equally to persons not of the same racial group as that other but:

- which is such that the proportion of persons of the same racial group as that other who can comply with it is considerably smaller than the proportion of persons not of the racial group who can comply with it;

- which he or she cannot show to be justifiable irrespective of the colour, race, nationality or ethnic or national origins of the person to whom it is applied; and
- which is to the detriment of that other because he or she cannot comply with it.

Relevant examples are shown in Exhibit 12.2.

Victimisation

Victimisation occurs when an employer treats any person less favourably than others because that person threatens to bring proceedings, to give evidence or information, to take any action or make any allegation concerning the employer with reference to the RRA, or has already taken such actions.

Genuine occupational qualifications (GOQs)

Employers may lawfully discriminate in certain jobs where being a member of a particular racial group is a genuine occupational qualification (GOQ). The main GOQs are:

Authenticity: Relevant to the entertainment field, such as participating in a dramatic performance where it is necessary to have a person of a particular racial group to achieve an authentic act; modelling or photographic work, where it is necessary to use

---

Exhibit 12.2

Examples of indirect racial discrimination

In *Perera* v *Civil Service Commission* (1983) IRLR 166, the Employment Appeals Tribunal decided that, 'taking account of the fact that a larger proportion of "coloureds" are adult immigrants, placing an upper age limit of 32 on trainees for certain posts in the Civil Service made it harder for "coloured" immigrants to apply'.

In *Bohon-Mitchell* v *Common Professional Examination Board* (1978) IRLR 22, an industrial tribunal decided that the Board's requirement for non-law graduates from overseas universities to complete a two-year course of legal study before becoming barristers while only one year was required for non-law graduates from British and Irish universities was indirect discrimination. Fewer graduates from overseas countries could comply with this requirement.

Sara is a Muslim and wears traditional the Muslim headscarf, *hijaab*, to work at her local supermarket. She is well qualified for promotion to supervisor – a job which would involve managing the customer helpdesk. But the supermarket has a rule that no hats or scarves are to be worn by staff who deal with the public. Her manager has explained that all supervisors must present the same appearance to the public to seem approachable. When pressed, however, the manager admits that it would not detract from the company's image if Sara were to wear her headscarf with the rest of the uniform.

persons from particular racial/ethnic groups to provide authenticity for a work of art; the restaurant business, where it is necessary to have a person from a particular ethnic group, for example an Indian waiter in an Indian restaurant, to contribute to an authentic atmosphere.

Personal welfare or educational services: Where an employee's duties include providing individuals with personal services promoting their welfare or education, or similar personal services, and those services can most effectively be provided by a member of a particular racial group.

Racial harassment
Racial harassment constitutes unlawful racial discrimination and often also constitutes a criminal offence such as assault or incitement to racial hatred. Examples of harassment include personal attacks, verbal or written threats or insults, damage to property, victimisation and intimidation.

Race Relations (Amendment) Act 2000

The amended Act covers all employers, no matter how small or large, and gives protection to most employees, including vocational trainees and people who work for someone else on a contract. For the first time the Act imposes a general duty on all major public bodies to promote equality of opportunity and good race relations. Employers and employment agencies must not discriminate on racial grounds against people seeking work. The Act also applies to bodies responsible for conferring qualifications or authorisation to enter a particular profession. All aspects of employment are covered including recruitment, selection, promotion, transfer, training, pay and benefits, redundancy, dismissal and terms and conditions of work.

Changes for 2003 onwards

Changes incorporate the EU Directive concerning equal treatment irrespective of race or ethnic origin, the 'Race Directive'.

The Race Relations Act 1976 (Amendment) Regulations 2003
- Modified definition of indirect discrimination which now covers formal requirements, conditions

and provisions, as well as informal practices, thus widening the circumstances where indirect discrimination may be deemed to have occurred.
- New definition of harrasment which is defined as being unwanted conduct which is intended to, or which creates the effect of violating a person's dignity or creates an intimidating, hostile, degrading, humiliating or offensive environment for that person. This definition is extended to the field of employment and prohibits employers from harassing their employees or prospective employees.
- Modified genuine occupational requirement will apply where, having regard to the nature of employment, or the context in which it is carried out, being of a particular race or particular ethnic or national origins is a genuine and determining requirement and where that requirement is applied in an appropriate manner. It will apply to contract work, partnerships and trade unions.
- It is unlawful to discriminate against another party to the relationship on grounds of race or ethnic or national origins or harass that party once such a relationship has ended (for example after an employee has terminated her or his employment).
- Burden of proof in tribunal hearings allows the claimant to establish a prima facie case before the tribunal or court and places the onus on the respondent (employer) to prove that he or she did not commit an act of unlawful discrimination or harassment.

Disability discrimination

Disability Discrimination Act 1995

The Disability Discrimination Act (DDA) makes it unlawful for employers with more than 20 employees to discriminate against existing or prospective staff for a reason relating to their disability. A person has a disability 'if he has a physical or mental impairment which has a substantial and long-term adverse effect on his ability to carry out normal day-to-day activities'. The definition therefore covers impairments affecting the senses, such as hearing and sight, together with learning difficulties or a mental illness which is clinically well recognised. However, addictions, tattoos and body piercing are all excluded from the protection of the Act. For these purposes an impairment has a long-term effect only if it has lasted for at least 12 months, is likely to do so, or is likely to last for the rest of the life of a person. Day-to-day activities are normal activities carried out on a regular basis and must involve one of the following:

- mobility;
- manual dexterity (which covers the ability to use hands and fingers with precision);
- physical co-ordination;
- continence;
- the ability to lift, carry or move everyday objects;
- speech, hearing or eyesight;
- memory or ability to concentrate, learn or understand; and
- perception of the risk of physical danger.

Severe disfigurements are treated as disabilities although they have no effect on a person's ability to carry out normal day-to-day activities. Medication or equipment is not taken into account when assessing whether an impairment has a 'substantial effect' (one exception to this is when people wear glasses or contact lenses). Where a progressive condition has resulted in an impairment which has affected a person's day-to-day activities, but that effect is not yet substantial, it is to be treated as having a substantial effect if that is the likely prognosis. The examples given of progressive conditions are cancer, multiple sclerosis, muscular dystrophy and HIV infection. It should be noted that the DDA does not cover those with a latent genetic predisposition to disability, such as Huntington's chorea, unless the disability develops.

Direct discrimination by the employer

An employer discriminates against a disabled person if, for a reason relating to that person's disability:

- he or she treats him or her less favourably than he or she treats, or would treat, others to whom that reason does or would not apply; and
- he or she cannot show that the treatment in question is justified.

For example, where an advertisement might reasonably be understood to have indicated that a person might not get the job because of their disability or that an employer is unwilling to make adjustments for disabled people, and a disabled person who was not offered the post complains, the employment tribunal must take the advertisement into account. Unless it can be proved otherwise, the tribunal will assume that the reason the complainant did not get the job related to his or her disability.

Victimisation

It is unlawful for a person to victimise another for:

- bringing proceedings under the DDA;
- giving evidence or information in connection with such proceedings;
- doing anything under the DDA; or
- alleging that another person contravened the DDA (unless the allegation was false and not made in good faith).

As with race and sex discrimination, anything done by a person in the course of employment is treated as also done by the employer, whether or not it was done with the employer's approval. However, employers will not be liable if they can show that they took such steps as were reasonably practicable to prevent the employee's action.

The DDA established a National Disability Council with lesser powers than the EOC and CRE to advise government on ways to reduce or eliminate discrimination. However, the Council was abolished by the Disability Rights Commission Act 1999 (see below).

Disability Rights Commission Act 1999

The main purpose of the Act is to establish a Disability Rights Commission (DRC) for Great Britain. The Act makes provision as to the DRC's functions which are similar to those of the EOC and CRE. These functions are:

- to work towards the elimination of discrimination against disabled people;
- to promote the equalisation of opportunities for disabled people; and
- to keep under review the workings of the DDA and the DRC Act.

The DRC encourages good practice in the treatment of disabled people; advises ministers on existing and proposed legislation emanating from Britain and the European Union where issues arise which are connected with the elimination of discrimination against, or equalisation of opportunities for, disabled people; and provides information and advice to employers (among others) in particular sectors on, for example, making reasonable adjustments.

The DRC provides a central point of information and advice for employers, service providers and disabled people who will be able to go to the DRC for information about the law, their rights and responsibilities under it and advice about how best to comply with it. They may also seek help on good practice. The DRC will also have an important promotional role in spreading the message that discrimination is unacceptable and helping people to understand how it can be avoided.

With regard to unlawful discrimination, the DRC has the same power as the EOC and the CRE:

- to conduct a formal investigation in order to determine whether unlawful discrimination has taken or is taking place;
- to issue non-discrimination notices to those who have been subject to a formal investigation, where they are found to be discriminating unlawfully.

Like the CRE and EOC, the DRC will issue its own Code of Practice which will provide employers with practical guidance on how to avoid discrimination, promote the equalisation of opportunities and encourage good practice. Courts and tribunals will be able to take account of any provision of the Code which may be relevant to the particular case being scrutinised.

Changes from 2003 onwards

Changes incorporate EU Council Directive 2000/78/EC, 'Equal Treatment Directive', establishing a general framework for equal treatment in employment and occupation, prohibiting direct and indirect discrimination and harassment on the grounds of religion or belief, disability, age and sexual orientation in the fields of employment, self-employment, occupation and vocational training. That part of the Directive relating to disability comprises the new regulations.

Disability Discrimination Act 1995 (Amendment Regulations) 2003

- Ensure that formerly excluded employment is covered, such as employers with fewer than 15 employees, employment on ships, planes and hovercraft, firefighters, prison officers and specialised police forces, and widen the scope to cover police, partnerships, barristers, qualifications bodies, practical work experience, contract workers, occupational pensions and group insurance services.
- Ensure that treatment amounting to direct discrimination against disabled people cannot be justified because the Directive requires such protection on the ground that people have a particular disability.
- Identify harassment as a form of discrimination, defined in relation to disability as: 'conduct which, having regard to all the circumstances, should reasonably be considered as having the effect of violating the disabled person's dignity or creating an intimidating, hostile, degrading, humiliating or offensive environment . . .' (section 3B).
- Employers have a duty to make 'reasonable adjustments' to extend to any 'provision, criterion or practice' which causes more than a minor or trivial disadvantage to a particular disabled employee to the extent needed to remove the disadvantage, particularly in relation to indirect discrimination. For example, if it were reasonable to do so, an employer might have to vary a rule under which all employees have to work from 9am to 5pm in order to allow a disabled employee to work flexible hours to enable additional breaks to overcome fatigue arising from the disability.

Age discrimination

Age discrimination has been outside the scope of legislation, but the first Labour government's intention to initiate a consultation process and then to draft a non-statutory Code of Practice represented a first stage towards fulfilling its manifesto commitment that age discrimination would be made illegal (DfEE, 1998). Evidence of age discrimination is revealed in surveys undertaken by the Equal Opportunities Review (1993, 1998). The 1993 survey looked at discrimination in recruitment and found that around 25 per cent of advertisements contained a requirement that applicants should be under 45, and 50 per cent of these advertisements specified an age limit of 35 or under. The survey also discovered that discrimination in job advertisements is much more prevalent in the private than in the public sector. Discrimination is also rife in training and promotion/advancement within the organisation. The 1998 survey of over 7000 job advertisements found that the use of formal age barriers discriminating against older workers has dropped sharply since 1993, with 8 per cent of job advertisements in *The Sunday Times* stating a numerical age preference. While this is an improvement on 1993, the improvement may well conceal more subtle discriminatory changes in job advertisements:

> *However, some advertisements, while not specifying a numerical age range for candidates, used language that clearly signalled they were looking for someone from a particular age group. This was done in two main ways: by using language which either related to the preferred person, e.g. 'young' or 'articulate youngsters', or to the working environment, e.g. 'young, dynamic environment'.* (IRS, 1998a, p. 24)

The government's consultation process (IRS, 1998b) concluded that 'it is clear that age discrimination does exist against older workers [and occurs] across the whole spectrum of employment and can affect both old and young people'. The report emphasises that in common with sex, race and disability discrimination, both direct and indirect age discrimination exist within the employment context and occur more obviously where people 'hold strong, stereotypical views about a person's ability to do a job or to be developed because of their age'. The report identifies certain initiatives consistent with 'defeating unjustified age discrimination' including:

- 'the introduction of revised policy appraisal guidelines which highlight the need for all government departments to take account of equal opportunities issues – including age – when developing policy, and the introduction of monitoring arrangements to ensure departmental compliance;
- recognition of the need to take into account the views and concerns of older people before developing policies;

- setting a good example in the way the government takes account of age discrimination issues in terms of the employment and recruitment of its own staff, including issuing guidance on avoiding unfair age discrimination in employment within the Civil Service' (IRS, 1998b, p. 15).

While it is not, therefore, unlawful to discriminate on grounds of age, Clarke (1995) points out that age discrimination is a form of indirect sex or race discrimination:

> *So in Price v Civil Service Commission (1977), job applicants had to be between 17 and 28. It was held that this was a requirement or condition and that a smaller proportion of otherwise suitably qualified women could comply with the requirement in practice than the proportion of men who could comply, because of women's child-rearing responsibilities. Nor could the employer justify the requirement.*
>
> *However, it is not easy to successfully claim indirect discrimination based on age:*
>
> - *First, the employee must show that the age limit was an absolute bar, rather than simply a preference on behalf of the employer for employees under a particular age.*
> - *Secondly, the employee has to show that the proportion of people of a particular sex or racial group who can comply with the requirement or condition is considerably smaller than the proportion of people of the opposite sex or not of that racial group who can comply.* (p. 112)

Employers have been encouraged to operate in accordance with the government's voluntary *Code of Practice for Age Diversity in Employment* (DfEE, 1999), which deals with good practice in six stages of the employment cycle – recruitment, selection, promotion, training, redundancy and retirement. A summary of the survey into the effectiveness of the Code by IRS (2001) is given in Exhibit 12.3.

The UK, along with other EU member states, is obliged to implement legislation to prohibit age discrimination in employment by December 2006 (EU Equal Treatment Directive). The government will introduce legislation that is consistent with the regulations already in force concerning sexual orientation, sex, race, disability and religious discrimination and

Exhibit 12.3

Main findings of the DfEE research

- Employer awareness of the government Code was relatively low at 37 per cent.
- There were few examples of companies that had either changed their policies or practices as a direct result of the Code or intended to change their policies in the future.
- 90 per cent of older people believe employers discriminate against older people in the workplace, while 50 per cent of older people believe that younger people are discriminated against by employers.
- Around 25 per cent of older people believe they have experienced age discrimination in relation to an actual or possible job at some point in their working life.
- Both employees and line managers (apart from HR specialists) have little knowledge of age discrimination as an equality issue, and there is a tendency to believe that it refers only to disadvantage in relation to recruitment.
- There appears to be a general acceptance among younger and older employees and employers that it would be unusual for staff over the age of 50 to be promoted.

harassment. While no specific Regulations have been introduced, the aim would be 'to identify and prohibit unfair practice based on discriminatory attitudes or inaccurate assumptions, to remove the barriers which people of all ages face if they want to work' (DTI, 2001, p. 52).

Discrimination on grounds of religion or belief

Until 2003, there was no specific legal prohibition against discrimination on the ground of religious belief in Britain, although such discrimination was unlawful in Northern Ireland. However, the Race Relations Act (1976) contained provisions concerning discrimination against Sikhs and Jews. The EU Equal Treatment Directive 2000/78/EC established a general framework for equal treatment in the field of employment, which, as we have seen, covers sex, sexual orientation, race, disability and age discrimination and harassment. The Directive also includes discrimination on the ground of religion/belief. In line with other member states, the UK government has issued statutory Regulations – known as the Employment Equality (Religion or Belief) Regulations – which came into force in 2003. These Regulations are probably the least controversial as, compared with the other forms of discrimination, religion in the workplace is not a contentious issue. The British Social Attitudes Survey (ONS, 2002b)

found that only 2 per cent of the British public believed that employers discriminated against job applicants on grounds of religion or belief. This contrasts with around 10 per cent on grounds of sexual orientation and 20 per cent on grounds of race. The main regulatory provisions are:

- It is unlawful on grounds of religion or belief to discriminate directly or indirectly on the basis of less favourable treatment, the definitions of direct and indirect discrimination being similar to those contained in the sex, race and age regulations.
- It is unlawful to discriminate by way of victimisation and harassment, the definitions of which are similar to those within regulations governing sex, race and age discrimination.
- An employer is allowed, when recruiting for a post, to treat job applicants differently on grounds of religion or belief, if possessing a particular religion or belief is a genuine occupational requirement (GOR) for that post. An employer may also rely on that exception when promoting, transferring or training persons for a post where a GOR applies in respect of that post.
- As with the regulations governing sex, race and disability discrimination, the coverage of the Regulations is extended to all occupations and contract types, including police, barristers, advocates, partnerships, trade organisations, qualification bodies, pension schemes, insurance services, providers of vocational training and employment agencies.

Trade union status

Legislation prohibits discrimination owing to trade union status. The relevant legislative provisions are found in the Trade Union and Labour Relations (Consolidation) Act 1992 and the Employment Rights Act 1996. In the area of recruitment it is unlawful to deny a person employment on grounds of union membership or non-membership, and, as with sex and race discrimination, the job applicant must prove that they were refused employment on these grounds. It is also automatically unfair to dismiss an employee either for being or proposing to become a trade union member; for taking or proposing to take part in union activities; for not being a member, and for refusing to become a member or remain a member of a trade union (see Chapter 13). Finally, it is unlawful for an employer to victimise an employee on grounds of union membership.

Summary points concerning discrimination legislation on grounds of race, disability, age, religion and trade union membership

- The RRA established the CRE and, like the SDA, distinguishes between direct and indirect discrimination.
- Again as with the SDA, the RRA identifies instances where employers may lawfully discriminate on GOQ grounds.
- The DDA makes it unlawful for employers with more than 20 employees to discriminate on grounds of disability.
- The Disability Rights Commission Act, 1999, abolished the largely ineffective National Disability Council (set up by the DDA) and replaced it with a DRC with similar powers to those of the CRE and EOC.
- There is no legislation at the moment concerning age discrimination, although the government through a consultation process has drafted a non-statutory code of practice and legislation will come into force in December 2006.
- It is unlawful for employers to discriminate against employees and potential employees on grounds of trade union membership.

- New regulations which came into force during 2003 cover all forms of race discrimination in all organisations.

THE EUROPEAN UNION AND DISCRIMINATION

Since joining the European Economic Community in 1973, the British government, employers and employees have been increasingly affected by the various treaty provisions and Directives relating to equal rights for men and women. Much of European law is concerned with sex discrimination, but there has been increased concern about race discrimination.

Treaty provisions create rights enforceable by individuals which enable individuals to bring legal action in the national courts of member states. Hence, a person can initiate action concerning an equal pay claim against her employer by relying on Article 119 of the Treaty of Rome without having to resort to the Equal Pay Act 1970.

Directives, as we have seen in Chapter 4, operate as instructions to member states to introduce legislation giving effect to these Directives. If a member state does not introduce such legislation, then individuals can still enforce their rights under a particular Directive against their employer, provided that the employer is an organ of the state. An organ of the state is broadly defined as a result of the case *Foster v British Gas plc* (1990) IRLR 353 as '*a body, whatever its legal form, which has been made responsible by the State for providing a public service under the control of the State and has for that purpose special powers beyond those which result in the normal rules applicable in relations between individuals*'. So, for example, a person can rely on the Equal Treatment Directive (see below) in order to establish that it is unlawful for a local authority or a health authority to set different retirement ages for men and women employees. While Directives directly benefit public sector employees using the 'organ of the state' criterion, it is possible for private sector employees to claim damages from the British government where they have suffered some loss because of the government's failure to implement a Directive. There are two ways in which to do this:

1. Judge-made decisions in many cases will interpret British legislation so that it is congruent with the meaning of the relevant Directive.
2. Where a member state has failed to implement a Directive, an individual may be entitled to damages from the government provided:
   - the result required by the Directive includes conferring rights for the benefit of the individual;
   - the content of those rights can be determined by reference to the provisions of the Directive; and
   - there is a causal link between the breach of the obligation by the state and the damage suffered by the individuals so affected.

In addition, Clarke (1995) points out that it is possible to seek judicial review where European law is incompatible with domestic law:

> In R v Secretary of State for Employment ex parte EOC (1994), the EOC argued that the hours threshold contained in the Employment Protection (Consolidation) Act 1978 was contrary to Community law as it indirectly discriminated against women. The House of Lords held that the EOC was entitled to bring the action, and further held that the hours provisions were incompatible with Community law. As a result, the Government was forced to introduce the Employment Protection (Part-time Employees) Regulations 1995: the Regulations removed all hours qualifications for unfair dismissal, redundancy, maternity rights and other statutory rights. (p. 3)

Equal pay, equal treatment and other forms of discrimination

Article 119 of the Treaty of Rome as amended by the Maastricht Treaty, and replaced by a new Article 119 as a result of the Amsterdam Treaty 1999, enshrines the principle that:

> All member states should ensure and maintain the principle that men and women should receive equal pay for equal work.

Directive 75/117 (1975) deals directly with issues concerning equal pay for equal value, and this eventually resulted in the UK Equal Value Regulations 1984.

Directive 76/207 (1976) – Equal Treatment Directive deals with discrimination on the grounds of sex in all aspects of employment (access to employment, vocational training, promotion and working conditions). The corresponding UK legislation was the SDA (1975) and the Employment Act (1989).

Directive 79/7 (1979) – progressive implementation of the principle of equal treatment for men and women in matters of social security.

Directive 86/378 (1986) – implementation of the principle of equal treatment for men and women in occupational social security schemes.

Directive 86/613 (1986) – application of the principle of equal treatment between men and women engaged in an activity, including agriculture, in a self-employed capacity, and on the protection of self-employed women during pregnancy and motherhood.

Directive 92/85 (1992) – introduction of measures to encourage improvements in the safety and health at work of pregnant workers and those workers who have recently given birth or are breast-feeding.

Code of Practice concerning Implementation of Equal Pay for Work of Equal Value for Women and Men (COM(96) 336). The Code was introduced in 1996 to address the continuing problems concerning the still considerable differences in pay between men and women with the aim of eliminating sex discrimination in pay structures determined by job classification and job evaluation schemes.

Directive 96/34 (1996) – the result of the First European Framework Agreement introduced measures concerning parental leave, the provisions of which included:

- three months' unpaid leave for both parents before and after the birth or adoption of a child;
- protection from dismissal for requesting parental leave;
- the right to return to work after leave protected; and
- additional time off for reasons that cannot be avoided in order to reconcile family and personal life.

The Parental Leave Directive was implemented in Britain as part of the Employment Relations Act 1999.

Directive 97/81 (1997) – the result of the Second European Framework Agreement 'to provide for the removal of discrimination against part-time workers and to improve the quality of part-time work'. The main provisions are:

- that the conditions of employment for part-time workers should not be less favourable than for comparable full-time workers; and
- that the conditions of employment must be pro rata with those of full-time employees wherever appropriate.

Directive 98/52 (1998) concerns burden of proof in sex discrimination cases and provides that if the person bringing the complaint to an employment tribunal establishes 'facts from which it may be presumed that there has been direct or indirect discrimination' then the employer has to prove 'that there has been no breach of the principle of equal treatment' (IRS, 1999a, p. 32). The new regulations necessitated changes to the SDA regarding direct discrimination only; no amendments are required in relation to indirect discrimination and equal pay. The Directive was implemented in the UK on 12 October 2001.

Directive 2000/43 (2000) establishes a general framework for equal treatment in the field of employment as described above, and was incorporated into UK legislation during 2003, covering sex discrimination, sexual orientation, equal pay and disability. That part of the Directive dealing with age will not come into force as legislation until 2006.

Directive 2000/43 (2000) establishes a framework for equal treatment in the area of race and religious belief as described above, and was incorporated into legislation in 2003.

A change of government in 1997 heralded a more pro-European approach with New Labour endorsing a new Social Chapter arising from the Amsterdam Treaty. This emphasises, amongst other things, the commitment to achieve equality between men and women while Article 119 is amended by the Treaty to incorporate specific reference to work of equal value. Further EU Directives concerning discrimination on grounds of sex, race, ethnic origin or belief, disability, age or sexual orientation are in the process of being transposed into UK legislation.

DISCRIMINATION AND MANAGEMENT POLICIES

Having considered the extent of discrimination in Britain, with particular emphasis upon the employment relationship, and the UK and European Union legislation which seeks to eliminate discriminatory practices, we now consider what employers can and should do to achieve the aims of the legislation within the workplace. In relation to sex discrimination, we look in particular at some equal pay issues and at sexual harassment in the workplace, together with EOC prescriptions for 'best practice'. We then go on to consider other forms of related discrimination involving sexual orientation. The section continues with an overview of management policy and practice in relation to workplace sex and race discrimination. Finally, we place the entire issue of work-related discrimination within the context of equal opportunities policies and practices and the management of diversity.

Sex discrimination: the EOC Code of Practice 1985

The EOC Code of Practice adopts a procedural approach to managing equal opportunities which is based on efforts to control managerial behaviour by tightly specifying what management should do in order to avoid sex discrimination and encourage equal opportunities. While a failure to observe the Code cannot itself give rise to proceedings, in any proceedings before an industrial tribunal such a failure will be taken into account if it is relevant to the case. The first part of the Code deals with the role of good employment practices in eliminating sex and marriage discrimination while the second part deals with promoting equality of opportunity. The main elements of the Code are provided in Exhibit 12.4.

Self-Evaluation Activity 12.10

Effectiveness of discrimination legislation
Response on website

In your opinion, do you think that discrimination legislation and codes of practice are effective in eliminating workplace discrimination?

Exhibit 12.4

The EOC Code of Practice

(a) *Responsibilities of employers*: The primary responsibility at law rests with each employer to ensure that there is no unlawful discrimination. It is important, however, that measures to eliminate discrimination or promote equality of opportunity should be understood and supported by all employees. Employers are therefore recommended to involve their employees in equal opportunities policies.

(b) *Responsibilities of trade unions*: Trade unions should:
  - encourage and press for equal opportunities policies so that measures to prevent discrimination at the workplace can be introduced with the clear commitment of employers and trade unions;
  - pay careful attention to claims from members alleging discrimination;
  - ensure that deliberate acts of discrimination are treated as disciplinary offences;
  - train and inform all officials and representatives on their role and responsibilities for equal opportunity;
  - examine their own procedures to ensure they do not contain any discriminatory requirements or conditions.

(c) *Implementing an equal opportunities policy*: The Code states that the formulation and implementation of an equal opportunities policy 'will ensure the effective use of human resources in the best interest of both the organisation and its employees' and a statement clearly detailing the central relevance of equal opportunities to effective people and business performance will reinforce the organisation's commitment.

(d) *Code points for successful implementation are*:
  - the policy must be seen to have the active support of top management;
  - the policy should be clearly stated and, where appropriate, included in a collective agreement;
  - overall responsibility for implementing the policy should rest with senior management;
  - the policy should be made known to all employees and, where reasonably practicable, to all job applicants; and
  - trade unions have an important part to play in implementing genuine equality of opportunity and will obviously be involved in the review of established procedures to ensure they are consistent with the law.

(e) *Monitoring policy*: The policy should be monitored regularly to ensure that it is working in practice. In a small organisation or enterprise it may be quite adequate to assess the position of employees from personal knowledge. In a large, complex organisation a more formal analysis will be necessary, for example, by sex, grade and payment in each unit. This may need to be introduced by stages as resources permit. Sensible monitoring will show, for example, whether members of one sex:
  - do not apply for employment or promotion, or that fewer apply than might be expected;
  - are not recruited, promoted or selected for training and development or are appointed or selected in a significantly lower proportion;
  - concentrate their applications in certain jobs, sections or departments.

  A system of structured exit interviews and occasional skills audits will help assess the effectiveness of the equal opportunities programme.

(f) *Positive action*: The Code stresses that selection for recruitment and promotion must be on merit, irrespective of sex. However, it also refers to s. 48 of the SDA which allows certain steps to be taken by employers to redress the effects of previous unequal opportunities. The Act, where there have been few or no members of one sex in particular work in their employment for the previous 12 months, allows employers to give special encouragement to and provide specific training for the minority sex. Positive action measures suggested by the Code include:
  - training employees for work traditionally the preserve of the other sex;
  - positive encouragement to apply for management posts for which special courses may be required;

- advertisements which encourage applications from the minority sex, but make it clear that selection will be on merit, irrespective of sex; and
- notifying job agencies that as part of a positive action programme the employer wishes to encourage members of one sex to apply for vacancies, where few or no members of that sex are doing the work in question. In these circumstances job agencies should tell both men and women about the posts and, in addition, let the under-represented sex know that applications from them are particularly welcome.

The Code's warning is to be noted: that withholding information from one sex in an attempt to encourage applications from the opposite sex would be unlawful.

Source: EOC, 1985

Equal pay issues which employers should consider

Pay inequalities are deeply rooted. Special rates of pay for women doing the same job as men became illegal in 1975 when the Equal Pay Act of 1970 came into force in 1975. Many jobs, however, have traditionally been assigned to one sex or the other and in many areas this demarcation continues. Other factors contributing to the income gap include stereotyping and occupational segregation in other ways; for example, maternity leave can mean losing out on performance-related pay. The net effect has been to depress 'women's' rates. This is one factor which continues to produce a situation where overall women's earnings are still only around 70–80 per cent of male earnings (see Table 12.1) while women part-timers were paid a mere 58 per cent of men's full-time hourly pay (LRD, 1999). The fact that women tend to work in a sex-segregated labour market and the devaluation of skills traditionally associated with 'women's work' contributes to the problematic nature of pay inequity. The success of equal pay legislation needs to be measured against its effectiveness in tackling these problems but, as we have already noted, legislation inevitably has a marginal effect in changing what are primarily structural problems in pay systems. These problems and others concerning the processing of cases relate to:

Table 12.1 The pay gap: average gross weekly earnings of employees in selected occupations: 2001

Occupation	Women's earnings (£)	Men's earnings (£)	Percentage of men's earnings
General administrators and national government	501.00	563.40	88.9
Treasurers and company financial managers	680.10	1070.30	66.5
Medical practitioners	767.60	945.70	81.2
Solicitors	597.30	756.80	78.9
Nurses	366.40	391.20	93.7
Chefs/cooks	202.70	255.00	79.5
Bar staff	156.50	193.20	81.0
Care assistants and attendants	197.30	229.30	86.0
Sales assistants	184.00	229.40	80.2
Cleaners/domestics	181.40	221.20	82.0

Source: EOC, *Annual Report*, 2001

- overtime payments, bonuses and allowances for which many women may not be eligible, or may receive them at a lower rate;
- the discriminatory nature of payment systems themselves;
- part-time workers (of which over 4.5 million or around 85 per cent are women) often have limited pay and career prospects;
- discriminatory pay practices have traditionally been sustained by collective agreements;
- employees' lack of knowledge of their rights under UK and EU equal pay and equal value legislation; the legislation is relatively complicated and relies on the individual to take action; and
- delays in tribunal procedure may discourage genuine applicants; it is not unusual for a case to take three or four years through the tribunal and appeals system.

The extent of the problem

Tables 12.1, 12.2 and Figure 12.1 demonstrate gender pay inequalities and show that the aggregate pay gap between men and women actually widened from 2001 to 2002 (see also Exhibit 12.5). Pay data

from the New Earnings Survey (ONS, 2002c) reveals that women working full time earned 81 per cent of the average full-time earnings of men in 2002 and that the gender pay gap in hourly earnings was 19 per cent, widening to 25 per cent in weekly earnings owing to longer hours worked by men. Women working part-time earned only 59 per cent of the average hourly earnings of men who worked full-time, representing a gender pay gap of 41 per cent which has hardly changed since 1975. The gender pay gap is evident across occupations, being widest for managers and administrators, and within banking, insurance and pension provision.

An EOC briefing paper (1997a) argued that if the trend towards greater pay equality continues at its (then) present rate, it would be another 45 years before women achieve equal pay with men:

> It is over 20 years since the Equal Pay Act came into force yet there is still an average pay gap of 20 per cent. At this rate women will wait until the year 2040 to achieve equality in pay. There can be no equality of opportunity without equality in pay. Throughout their working lives women earn less than men, whether they are lawyers

Table 12.2 Average earnings and gender pay gaps: 2002

	Hourly	Weekly	Annual
Average earnings (£ per hour)			
Women:			
full-time	10.22	383.4	19 811
part-time	7.42	143.8	7 593
all	9.48	283.5	14 619
Men:			
full-time	12.59	513.8	27 437
part-time	8.82	165.3	9 845
all	12.46	484.1	26 020
Gender pay gaps (%)			
Women F/T and men F/T	18.8	25.4	27.8
Women P/T and men P/T	15.9	13	19.9
Women P/T and men F/T	41.1	72.0	72.3
All women and men	23.9	41.4	43.8

Source: ONS, 2002c

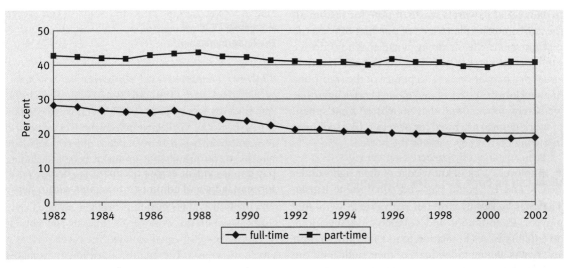

Figure 12.1 The gender pay gap: 1982–2002
Source: ONS, 2002c

Exhibit 12.5

Pay gap widens between sexes

The pay gap between men and women has widened, prompting a chorus of complaints from trade unions and equal opportunities activists. But business leaders strongly resisted renewed calls for a change in the law to force all companies to carry out equal pay audits. The average earnings of a woman in full-time work rose by 4.5 per cent in the year to April 2002, according to the Office for National Statistics. But male average earnings were up by 4.8 per cent, leaving female earnings at just 81.2 per cent of male earnings. Roger Lyons, joint general secretary of Amicus, Britain's largest manufacturing union, said: 'It will only change if companies of all sizes review the way that they pay their staff.' Mr Lyons condemned the Confederation of British Industry for opposing the demand by Amicus and the commission (EOC) for compulsory pay audits . . . Susan Anderson, director of human resources policy at the CBI, said the figures 'reflect the choices women take in their careers'.

Moreover, employers have no plans to conduct equality pay reviews despite the fact that the gap between women's and men's pay has hardly diminished in recent years (EOC, 2003). Some 55 per cent of large organisations do not intend to carry out pay reviews and only 18 per cent have conducted such an exercise or are in the process of doing so. Secrecy about pay remains widespread and more than 20 per cent of employers forbid staff from sharing information about their pay with colleagues.

Source: *Financial Times*, 18 October 2002, p. 3

---

or sales assistants. Unless significant changes are made in the way the pay gap is tackled, women face a future of continuing inequality. The EOC wants to see simplified and more effective equal pay legislation and greater recognition by employers that pay must be at the heart of their equal opportunity policies and practices.

The EOC's proposal (2001) for a new sex equality law contains recommendations aimed at closing the income gap, and the Commission is hopeful that pay equality can be achieved in the near future. However, a less optimistic view of the situation is provided by the argument that, despite some notable successes, attempts by individuals and trade unions to gain equal pay are a waste of time for behind all the convoluted explanations of unequal pay lies the real question: who is doing what and how do we rank their efforts? In addition, the essence of differential pay may lie in our acceptance of the traditions of a workforce so segregated along gender lines that we barely notice it and that no matter what sphere of work women are hired for or select, like sediment in a wine bottle they settle to the bottom.

What can be done about the problem?

The EOC seeks to work in partnership with employers, trade unions and voluntary organisations on equality issues in relation to income; and to raise awareness among individuals of their rights and the issues in relation to equal pay and other income.

Despite pessimistic views about the nature of pay inequality, a number of the larger trade unions have had some successes within the past decade in pursuing equal pay claims. This is borne out by survey data which reveals that for 1998 equal pay claims showed a record rise of 11 per cent and settlements were at an all-time high of £8 million (LRD, 1999). Successful claims concerning, for example, 250 UNISON members who won a £1.2 million settlement against St Helens Metropolitan Borough Council may encourage others to come forward. In the wake of this success, UNISON has launched its strategy to gain equal pay for 1 million women employed mainly within the local authority sector through negotiations, and if negotiation does not succeed, then through the courts. Similarly, Amicus-MSF (formerly MSF) initiated a claim on behalf of several thousand women employed in the NHS which is based on the successful claim of Pam Enderby, an equal pay for equal value 'benchmark' case (see Main case 12.1). Recent decisions of the European Court of Justice mean that women workers in different NHS professions can claim equal pay across the entire service, not just within trusts or authorities. The Amicus-MSF claim and other pay problems within the NHS has led to a government commitment to review and fundamentally restructure the NHS pay system, but whether this will satisfy equal pay campaigners such as Amicus-MSF remains to be seen. More recently UNISON lodged equal pay claims on behalf of nurses and other women health workers which were accepted by a tribunal-appointed panel in 2002.

Main case 12.1
The Enderby case

Enderby v Frenchay Health Authority and Secretary of State for Health (1991) IRLR 47–107 (1983–1994)
Pam Enderby was a senior speech therapist whose rate of pay was set by a collective agreement. Her union also negotiated with her employer, under a different collective agreement, on behalf of a group of people including pharmacists and physiotherapists. The latter's pay rates, at the same level of seniority, were significantly greater than Enderby's. She therefore brought an equal pay claim, based on the work of pharmacists and physiotherapists being of equal value to her own work as a speech therapist. The industrial tribunal dismissed Enderby's claim on a preliminary point – namely that the difference in collective bargaining machinery had given rise to the difference in pay, and that there had been no discrimination in the evolution of the separate collective bargaining machinery for two classes of employee.

The tribunal rejected the employer's alternative defence based on genuine material differences/material factors of 'market forces'. The health authority had argued that market forces justified the difference in pay: that pharmacists could work in the private sector and needed to be paid more to attract them. However, it was established that only some 10 per cent of the pay differential could be explained by the shortages of pharmacists and therefore the difference in pay was much greater than was required by market forces.

Enderby appealed to the Employment Appeals Tribunal (EAT) which upheld the tribunal's decision. Since the difference in pay arose from the different collective bargaining machinery used to negotiate pay, and since there was no discrimination in the setting up of the two collective bargaining structures, the pay differential was justified. On the question of the employer's alternative defence, the EAT overruled the tribunal and found for the health authority.

Enderby went to the Court of Appeal, which in turn sent a number of questions on the construction of the European equal pay legislation to the European Court of Justice.

The judgment of the European Court of Justice was based on the fact that once it is shown that there is a significant difference in pay between two jobs which are of equal value, one of which is carried out predominantly by men and one predominantly by women,

Article 119 of the Treaty of Rome (since amended by the Treaty of Amsterdam) shifts the burden of proving that the difference is objectively justified by factors which are unrelated to sex discrimination to the employer. If it were otherwise it would be impossible for employees to enforce their rights to equal pay. The fact that different rates of pay arose from separate negotiations between the same union and employers was not sufficient justification for the difference in pay between the two jobs, even though there was no discrimination within either sets of negotiation themselves. On the question of whether or not and to what extent the difference in pay could be justified by market forces, the European Court of Justice's answer was that it was up to the national court to quantify how much of the difference is attributable to market forces.

The relevant legislation considered here is:

1. Article 119 of the Treaty of Rome.
2. Article 1 of Directive 75/117/EEC which says: 'The principle of equal pay for men and women outlined in Article 119 of the Treaty of Rome . . . means, for the same work or for work to which equal value is attributed, the elimination of all discrimination on grounds of sex with respect to all aspects and conditions of remuneration.'
3. Equal Pay Act 1970 s. 1 (2c and 3) as added to by the Equal Pay (Amendment) Regulations 1983.

Self-Evaluation Activity 12.11

Effective employer equal pay policies
The response is given below

What steps should employers take in order to ensure that equal pay policies are effective? (A study of the Enderby case above will be useful.)

Employers bear much of the responsibility for ensuring equality of pay. The EOC's Code of Practice (1997b) recommends that employers should adopt an equal pay policy and provides detailed guidance on how employers should conduct internal pay reviews in order to eliminate pay inequality. The EOC Code is admissible as evidence in tribunal proceedings, but there is no legal obligation on employers to carry out a pay review or introduce an equal pay policy. The main points of the EOC Code of Practice on Equal Pay are:

1. Employers should study their pay structures 'to reveal any possible undervaluation of work typically carried out by women in comparison with that typically carried out by men and vice versa' (p. 11). The study should comprise three main stages. Firstly, the relevant information should be collected across the whole of the organisation's workforce. Secondly, the relevant information gained should be assessed and, thirdly, particular aspects of the pay system should be examined, especially those which might prove to be discriminatory.
2. The relevant information would include:
   - **Information about employees** such as gender, grade, job title, hours of work excluding breaks, required entry qualification, other relevant qualifications, length of service, basic pay, additional payments.
   - **Pay arrangements and practices** such as job descriptions, grading, classification and evaluation systems, job evaluation manual, performance pay handbook, rules concerning bonus and incentive schemes, piecework or contract work pay arrangements.
3. Assessing the relevant information. Key indicators of potential sex bias include:
   - women have lower average earnings than men with the same job title;
   - women have lower average earnings than men in the same grade;
   - women in female-dominated unskilled jobs are paid less than men in the lowest male-dominated unskilled job;
   - women are paid less than men with equivalent entry qualifications and length of service; and
   - the majority of men and women are segregated by different grading, classification and evaluation systems.
4. Particular aspects of the pay system. Practices which prove to be discriminatory include basic pay issues, bonus/performance pay and piece-rates, pay benefits, part-time workers, job classification, grading, evaluation and skills/competency-based systems. The example of basic pay discriminatory practices together with the advice given in the Code is given below:

Women are consistently appointed at lower points in a pay scale than men are.
   - Examine recruitment and promotion records to see if different treatment is objectively justifiable irrespective of sex.

- Are qualifications rewarded by allowances necessary for the posts? Is the way qualifications are defined adversely affecting women?

Women are paid less than male predecessors in the job.

- Check if job duties and responsibilities are the same or have changed. Do the changes justify any pay reduction?

Women progress more slowly through incremental scales and/or seldom reach higher points.

- Check whether service pay is linked to ability to do the job rather than length of service. Where women have broken or shorter periods of service because of family responsibilities, they may be less able to meet length of service criteria.
- Investigate criteria by which employees are progressed through a scale.

Men are paid more, by supplement or by a higher grading, because of 'recruitment and retention' policies.

- Adopt measures to deal with recruitment and retention problems, e.g. existing staff could be trained and then availed of development initiatives. The pool from which staff are normally drawn could be expanded. For example, clerical and non-manual staff might be considered for management training and apprenticeships through the use of positive action.

5. Once the pay structure study is completed, follow-up action is needed to tackle every instance of sexual discrimination detected in the pay structure. The follow-up action should then be evaluated to avoid perpetuating sexual discrimination.

The gender pay gap: problems and prescriptions

Notwithstanding the good intentions of the EOC Code of Practice (1997b), the reality concerning employer practice is far from satisfactory. EOC research (2001) uncovered a range of deep-seated problems associated with the wide and widening pay gap. As part of its 'Valuing Women' campaign intended to reduce those elements of the gender pay gap due to sex discrimination in pay systems, the EOC commissioned research by Rubery and

Grimshaw (2001) who identify problems associated with the current gender pay gap and go on to suggest policy implications and solutions which, they argue, should involve government, trade unions and, of course, employers.

Problems

Amongst the problems identified by Rubery and Grimshaw, the most significant are:

- women's concentration in many low-paid private services occupations is a major contributor to the overall gender pay gap: more than 60 per cent of women's employment is concentrated in just ten out of 77 occupations;
- current trends in public sector restructuring may be detrimental to women's employment and earnings prospects in the public services. These trends include employment policies which change the skills mix of an occupational group by substituting low-skilled for high-skilled employees; policies of subcontracting of services to the private sector, and growth of individualised payment systems (see Chapter 5);
- the large proportion of women in low-paid part-time employment (44 per cent) has a significant impact on gender pay inequality. Reasons for relative low pay of female part-timers include the relatively few part-time workers in high status jobs and the marginalisation of part-time workers within organisations;
- the UK has one of the highest gender pay gaps for hourly earnings in the EU (EUROSTAT, 1995);
- future trends in the UK gender pay gap could be intensified if there is:
  - further fragmentation of the public sector as a result of contracting out of services where work has been subcontracted, where franchises are operated and where employment agency staff are used;
  - further dismantling of career paths within organisations thereby widening the gap between the lifetime earnings of men and women (e.g. policies of delayering). This may mean that the difference between non-managerial and managerial posts is too great for internal promotion to be a real possibility;
  - further decline in collective bargaining coverage (see Chapter 6), accompanied by a rise in

the use of 'the market' to justify pay levels and differentials. This trend has decreased the transparency of labour markets, has granted employers greater discretion in pay decisions and may provide for the possibility of the reintroduction of gender pay discrimination, under the guise of individualised contracts;

– further transformation of payment systems with damaging consequences for women's pay. For example, the increased emphasis on the competencies of the individual worker rather than the nature of the job may lead to greater attention being paid to leadership skills which are often identified with 'masculine' characteristics. The increased use of performance awards can result in gender bias in assessment, confusion between performance and 'market value', and pressure to work additional unpaid hours.

Prescriptions

The mainstreaming of gender pay issues into the whole framework of policy-making is seen as essential if the gender pay gap is to be closed. The broad policy agenda would include raising the value attached to women's work; enabling women to participate in employment on a more equal and continuous basis; and the promotion of women's rights and participation as citizens. This policy agenda requires the active participation of government, employers and trade unions. The **government** needs to assess the impact of policies of restructuring on gender pay equality in the public services in relation to, for example, the Public Finance Initiative or Best Value. The undervaluation of women's work in the public sector needs to be addressed, and a long-term strategy to raise the relative level of the national minimum wage as a simple tool for closing the gender pay gap is required. **Employers** should introduce gender pay audits in order to increase the transparency of planned changes to work organisation, career structures or payments systems on gender pay equality. Employer commitment to provision of information on changing pay structures by gender may have a more beneficial effect than a commitment to establishing equal pay since many employers may not understand fully either the size or the causes of the gender pay gap within their own organisations. Finally, co-ordinated efforts should be made to create more formal and visible forms of training and qualifications in female-dominated areas of work – particularly in areas of part-time work. These would have positive repercussions on levels of relative pay and reduce the problems caused by the undervaluation of women's work. The **TUC and trade unions** should exert their collective pressure to goad government and employers into the actions identified above. Greater credence would accrue to TUC and union influence if greater attention were directed towards ensuring greater representation of women in their own organisations. Equal pay issues should be integrated into the collective bargaining agenda and the partnership approach by unions could be invigorated by the inclusion of equal opportunities as a core value.

Sexual harassment

Sexual harassment is one of the most offensive and demeaning experiences an employee can suffer. [It] can reduce the productivity or efficiency of an organisation and can have considerable cost implications where management fails to take appropriate action. Evidence also suggests that harassment can seriously affect employees' confidence and self-esteem as well as leading to absenteeism, poor morale and resignation. In addition, since sexual harassment is unlawful under the Sex Discrimination Act 1975, employers may find that, in certain circumstances, they are liable for the actions of employees who sexually harass other employees in the course of their work. (IRS, 1996)

Self-Evaluation Activity 12.12
Examples of sexual harassment
Response on website

Identify examples of what might constitute sexual harassment. How widespread do you think the phenomenon is?

Grounds and forms of harassment

Sexual harassment at work is unwelcome physical, verbal or non-verbal conduct of a sexual nature.

It includes demeaning comments about a person's appearance; indecent remarks; questions about a person's sex life; sexual demands by a member of the same or opposite sex; name-calling with demeaning terminology which is gender-specific; and unwelcome physical contact and other conduct of a sexual nature that creates an intimidating, hostile, or humiliating working environment. The essential characteristic of sexual harassment is that it is unwanted by the recipient. There is, however, a certain element of subjectivity in determining what behaviour is acceptable or offensive, but it is generally accepted that the following examples of unwanted behaviour are unwelcome and unpleasant (IRS 2002):

- physical contact;
- jokes, offensive language, gossip, slander, sectarian songs and letters;
- posters, graffiti, obscene gestures, flags, bunting and emblems;
- isolation or non-co-operation and exclusion from social activities;
- coercion for sexual favours and pressure to participate in political/religious groups; and
- intrusion by pestering, spying and stalking.

Legislation dealing with sexual harassment

The issue of harassment is being dealt with by the appropriate Regulations based on the EU Equal Treatment Directive referred to above and which became law from 2003 onwards. In any event, as we mentioned earlier, sexual harassment is unlawful under the SDA, which means that if an employee has been harassed, he or she can take the case to an employment tribunal. The tribunal will consider the SDA's criterion concerning 'less favourable treatment' and whether the applicant was dismissed or subjected to some other detriment. The principle underlying this criterion was established by *Strathclyde Regional District Council v Porcelli* (1986) IRLR 134 (Exhibit 12.6). Sexual harassment claims can be brought against the harasser and the employer. Under the SDA the employer is liable for the discriminatory acts of employees at the workplace, whether or not they were committed with the employer's knowledge and approval. Irrespective of liability, tribunals also expect employers to have

harassment policies in operation. If an employee is forced to quit his or her job as a result of harassment he or she may claim unfair (constructive) dismissal under the 1996 ERA provided he or she has been employed continuously for a period of two years. The tribunal can award compensation for losses resulting from the discrimination including wages and medical treatment costs. As a result of a ruling by the European Court of Justice (1993), there is no upper limit for compensation which, prior to 1993 was fixed at £11 000.

EU law

The EC Council of Labour and Social Ministers adopted a resolution relating to sexual harassment at work and, in 1991, as part of its third action programme on equal opportunities the EC adopted a Recommendation and Code of Practice on the protection of the dignity of women and men at work. The Recommendation asks member states to:

take action to promote awareness that conduct of a sexual nature, or other conduct based on sex affecting the dignity of women and men at work, including conduct of superiors and colleagues, is unacceptable if:

1. *such conduct is unwanted, unreasonable and offensive to the recipient*
2. *a person's rejection of, or submission to, such conduct on the part of employer or workers (including superiors or colleagues) is used explicitly or implicitly as a basis for a decision which affects that person's access to vocational training, access to employment, continued employment, promotion, salary or any other employment decisions; and/or*
3. *such conduct creates an intimidating, hostile or humiliating work environment for the recipient;*

and that such conduct may, in certain circumstances, be contrary to the principle of equal treatment within the meaning of [the Equal Treatment] Directive 76/207/EEC.

The Code of Practice recommends that senior management should develop and communicate a policy statement which should:

- expressly state that sexual harassment will not be permitted or condoned;

Exhibit 12.6

Strathclyde Regional District Council v Porcelli (1986) IRLR 134

This case was the first sexual harassment case to reach the appeal courts establishing that sexual harassment constituted direct discrimination under the SDA. The complainant, Mrs Porcelli, was a laboratory technician employed by the regional council in one of its schools. She claimed she had been unlawfully discriminated against when she had been compelled to seek a transfer to another school because of a deliberate campaign of vindictiveness against her by two male colleagues, some of it of a sexual nature. She claimed that the regional council was vicariously responsible for the behaviour of the two men.

The industrial (now employment) tribunal rejected Porcelli's application even though it accepted that the men's behaviour had been extremely unpleasant. However, the Employment Appeals Tribunal (EAT) rejected the decision of the industrial tribunal and allowed Mrs Porcelli's appeal. According to the court of appeal, even if only some of the treatment complained of was sexually-oriented, there was less favourable treatment on grounds of sex. What mattered was the treatment, not the motive for it, and therefore if any material part of the treatment included elements of a sexual nature to which the woman was vulnerable, but a man was not, then she had been treated less favourably on grounds of her sex. It was also held that conduct falling short of physical contact could still constitute sexual harassment.

Clarke (1995) comments:

Porcelli was important in establishing that unlawful sexual harassment encompasses more than simply a woman's being dismissed for refusing to have a sexual relationship with her boss. It is now clear that the existence of an unpleasant and intimidating work environment is sufficient detriment to establish a case. If the less favourable treatment is on the ground of sex, then this is unlawful, regardless of the motive for behaviour. It is also clear from the case law that whether a particular course of conduct amounts to sexual harassment depends upon how that conduct is viewed by the woman at whom it is aimed; comments and behaviour that some women find inoffensive can be highly intimidating to others. (p. 33)

- set out a positive duty on managers and supervisors to implement the policy and to take corrective action to ensure compliance with it;
- explain the procedure which should be followed by employees subjected to sexual harassment at work in order to obtain assistance;
- contain an undertaking that the allegation will be dealt with seriously, expeditiously and confidentially, and that the complainants will be protected against victimisation; and
- specify that disciplinary measures will be taken against employees guilty of sexual harassment.

Certain cases have established that employment tribunals will expect to see evidence of implementation of the Code of Practice on sexual harassment, and that any oversight on the part of the employer will not be considered favourably. The ET will also use the Code to help establish whether the conduct

to which the complainant was subjected amounted to sexual harassment.

Taking action on harassment: employers' responsibilities

The EOC (2002b) argues that dealing with sexual harassment is in the interests of employers as sexual harassment could damage business performance. Staff who are mistreating and harassing others are not using their time productively. Victims of harassment are likely to underperform as a direct result of stress and loss of self-esteem. Sexual harassment can also be expensive as employers can be held liable for the unlawful actions of those who work in their organisation, whether or not their actions were known. Employers can also be vicariously liable for what happens to agency workers. Claims can include compensation for personal injury, which may be substantial. Publicity associated with tribunal claims can also harm the image of an organisation.

In order to deal with harassment, employers should issue a policy statement demonstrating commitment to eliminating harassment; deal with complaints swiftly; provide advice and counselling; judiciously use the formal and informal complaints/grievance/harassment/disciplinary procedures where appropriate (IDS, 1999). Some of these issues are dealt with below.

The grievance procedure route

IRS (1996) found that in organisations without harassment policies 'a victim of sexual harassment is expected to lodge a complaint through the organisation's formal grievance procedure' and in many such organisations, resort to the grievance procedure is the only option open to complainants. The grievance procedure route has its limitations. Firstly, where the victim is expected to complain in the first place through her or his immediate line manager, women will normally be faced with approaching their immediate superior who may be a man: 'the embarrassment involved in raising a complaint with their line manager and the fear some women have of being taken seriously may dissuade them from pursuing a complaint through the organisation's formal grievance procedure' (IRS, 1996, p. 8). Secondly, grievance procedures often fail to take account of the fact or possibility that the accused harasser is often the immediate superior, so it is most unlikely that the victim will pursue her complaint via that channel. Nevertheless, Hawkins (1994) points out that 'requiring line managers to take on the role [of investigator] reinforces their day-to-day managerial responsibility for eliminating harassment . . . [although] allowing line managers to investigate complaints of harassment unassisted, particularly in the early stages of a policy, is likely to be very risky' (p. 28).

Counselling

In organisations with a harassment policy and procedure there will normally be provision for counselling support for complainants throughout the procedure. Where counsellors are included as a feature of the harassment policy, the role needs to be clear to the counsellors themselves, to supervisors and managers and to employees. Hawkins identifies two alternative counselling roles, depending upon the nature of the policy and procedure. These are:

- *Where the policy requires the complainant to take full responsibility for the complaint, the role may be restricted to one of pure counselling comprising an empathic ear, an explanation of procedural options, and, perhaps, behind-the-scenes support through assisting in the preparation of any written complaint or statement.*
- *Where the policy provides a higher level of support, the role must extend to accompanying the complainant at meetings with the alleged harasser or, less commonly, taking up the complaint on their behalf informally.* (p. 28)

Developing policies and procedures

Exhibit 12.7 is an extract from the EOC booklet *Consider the Cost: Sexual Harassment at Work* (1997c).

Self-Evaluation Activity 12.13

Why employers should implement sexual harassment policies
Response on website

Can you think of any reasons why employers should introduce sexual harassment policies?

Policy statements concerning sexual harassment should take the form of *either* a separate part of a general equal opportunities policy *or* a written policy statement dealing specifically with sexual harassment. Most firms in the IRS survey had both an equal opportunities policy and a separate policy for sexual harassment, although sexual harassment policies increasingly are part of a more general policy dealing with all types of harassment. The policy statement should incorporate all the points referred to in the EOC booklet, and in addition should make it clear that all employees have a right to be treated with dignity and respect; state that sexual harassment is unlawful and will not be permitted; define what is unacceptable behaviour; state that appropriate disciplinary action will be taken against those found guilty and point out that both sexes suffer harassment.

A specific complaints procedure for dealing with harassment cases should give employees confidence

Exhibit 12.7

Sexual harassment at work: what employers should do

1. Issue a policy statement concerning sexual harassment.
   The statement should:
   - define unacceptable behaviour
   - make clear that sexual harassment can be treated as a disciplinary offence
   - point out that both sexes can be subject to harassment
   - explain that it is for the person on the receiving end of any behaviour to decide whether she or he finds it unacceptable.
2. Lay down a procedure for dealing with complaints of sexual harassment.
   This can be included in the existing disciplinary and/or grievance procedures, but experience suggests that for most organisations a separate procedure for investigating complaints is needed. The procedure should:
   - specify to whom a complaint should be made, and provide an alternative
   - ensure that complaints are treated seriously and sympathetically
   - wherever possible provide for a manager of the same sex as the complainant to hear the complaint
   - ensure that any complaint is dealt with promptly and with due care. The investigation of the complaint should be carried out objectively and independently, and by someone with sufficient authority to be able to handle the matter effectively. If a complaint is upheld the harasser should be dealt with under the normal disciplinary procedure. If dismissal is a possible outcome, it is important that the usual procedures should be followed, i.e. an investigation and proper hearing at which the alleged harasser can comment on the case against them
   - ensure that any panel set up to investigate the complaint has at least as many women as men on it. Very often such panels include only one woman who is often of lower status than the men. A woman in this position will find it difficult to be effective
   - ensure that procedures set out a time frame for the investigation. The complainant and the alleged harasser should be told at the outset how long the investigation is likely to take, and who will be communicating with them. Complainants should be kept well informed at every stage.
3. Ensure that, if it becomes necessary, either during the investigation or afterwards, to separate the complainant and the alleged harasser, no pressure is put on the complainant to transfer. While it is acceptable to ask the complainant if they wish to move, they should not be presumed to do so. If there is a problem over them continuing to work together, it is the harasser who should be moved.
4. Introduce the policy statement and associated procedures in consultation with any workplace trade unions.
5. Ensure that the individual is not victimised either by line management or by their colleagues for having made a complaint.

Source: EOC, 1997c

that their allegations will be taken seriously and that complaints will be dealt with quickly and confidentially. It should also aim to provide a fair outcome to complaints, enforce penalties against harassers and protect against victimisation of the complainant. The formal procedure should be supplemented wherever possible with informal methods for dealing with the victim's situation. Provided in Exhibit 12.8 is the City of Liverpool local authority procedures for dealing with harassment, discrimination and bullying.

Finally, the successful implementation of a sexual harassment policy requires, firstly, the communication of the policy to the entire workforce in order to make employees aware of the company's procedures for tackling the problem; secondly, all managers concerned with the operation of the policy receiving training in all aspects of their role and, thirdly, a

Exhibit 12.8

Liverpool City Council

Complaints procedures

Informal procedures

1. Employees are strongly advised to keep a written record of the incidents including the following information: time, date and place the incident occurred, a full description of what happened, and name(s) if known of the alleged perpetrators and any witnesses.
2. All employees have the right to confidential support, advice and representation, and there are trained Advisory Officers in each directorate who can provide this. A current list of Advisory Officers will be displayed on notice boards and is available from the Equal Opportunities Team on . . .
3. There are a number of ways of dealing with incidents of harassment, discrimination and bullying which include:
   - telling the person(s) involved that the behaviour in question is offensive, unwanted and that it must stop immediately
   - enlisting the help of an Advisory Officer, personnel officer, trade union representative, specialist equalities officer or a colleague, for advice, assistance and support
   - reporting the matter to your line manager and asking him/her to respond informally by speaking to the alleged perpetrator. Consideration may also be given by line managers to dealing with the issue indirectly without mentioning that a complaint has been made and/or by rearranging desks or work allocations to reduce the risk of contact
   - managers may wish to provide training either for individuals or work groups
   - copies of this Policy, Code of Practice and publicity materials should be visible and available in the workplace
   - managers may wish to raise the complaint in an informal way and clearly inform the employee that harassment, discrimination and bullying are disciplinary offences.

Formal procedures

1. At all times, whether or not informal steps have been taken, any employee who feels that they or others have been harassed, discriminated against or bullied may make a formal complaint by using the Grievance Procedure.
2. Because of the sensitivity of such complaints and the need to resolve them speedily, the complaint should be made in writing and sent to your head of service or to an officer designated to deal with such complaints.
3. Should the complaint be made against a head of service, the complaint should be made to the relevant director. A complaint against a director should be made to the Chief Executive.
4. The first stage of the procedure (discussion with supervisor) may be omitted.
5. The investigating officer, together with a senior personnel officer or specialist Equality Officer, will conduct the investigation.
6. The complainant and the person against whom the allegations are made will be interviewed separately, and the proceedings will be confidential.
7. Both the complainant and the person against whom the allegations are made may be accompanied/ represented at all stages of the procedure by either an employee of their choice, a trade union representative, or a friend.
8. The investigation, which will include the interviewing of witnesses, should take a maximum of six weeks through investigation to conclusion.

9. An accurate record will be made of the investigation and its conclusion. The investigating officer will write to the complainant and the person against whom the allegations are being made, detailing the findings of the investigation and the action to be taken. The letter will contain an undertaking that the complainant will not be victimised or suffer any detriment. In the case of complaints concerning race and sex discrimination, complainants will be advised of their rights to apply to the Employment Tribunal for a decision on the matter.

10. If the complainant is dissatisfied with the outcome s/he must submit a written request to the directorate's personnel officer within seven working days. The matter will then be referred to the Chair and the decision here will be made in writing to both parties.

11. If the investigating officer or the Chair find that disciplinary action is justified then this decision will be notified to the complainant and the person against whom the allegations are being made. A disciplinary hearing normally will be convened within five working days and the person against whom the allegations are made will have the opportunity to challenge any of the evidence and/or make any submissions in mitigation.

12. During these proceedings it should not normally be necessary to repeat detailed interviews unless necessary in the interests of natural justice.

13. In some cases where it is considered appropriate to issue a disciplinary warning, it may be necessary to consider an alternative post or reallocation of work for the offender in order that s/he and the complainant do not continue to work in close proximity.

Conclusion

Employees will be protected from intimidation, victimisation, discrimination or bullying resulting from making a complaint or assisting in an investigation. Retaliating against an employee for making a complaint is a disciplinary offence. During an investigation, or where a complaint is upheld, counselling support must be offered to the complainant. Making false or unsubstantiated allegations with malicious intent will result in the disciplinary procedure being invoked.

Source: Liverpool City Council: Procedure for Dealing with Harassment, Discrimination and Bullying (1998)

review and monitoring of the policy regularly in order to develop and improve it.

Discrimination against lesbians, gay men and transsexuals

Most organisations are dominated by heterosexual men, and most organisationally-grounded studies of sexual harassment focus on heterosexuality (e.g. Burrell and Hearn, 1989), thereby neglecting the area of homosexuality in organisations. Within the heterosexualised workplace culture and context, surveys have revealed that a significant proportion of lesbian and gay employees conceal their sexual identity in order to avoid discrimination (Wilson, 2000; EOC, 2002a). Where sexual identities are revealed, then discrimination remains unacceptably

high, as indicated by a TUC report (2002) which revealed that 44 per cent of gay, lesbian and bisexual respondents who were union members experienced workplace discrimination. Some had been dismissed, while many were harassed, abused or threatened because of their sexuality.

The amendment to the SDA will now make discrimination on the grounds of sexual orientation illegal from 2003. Furthermore, the rights of transsexuals not to be discriminated against are now statutorily reinforced by the Sex Discrimination (Gender Reassignment) Regulations 1999. However, it should be noted that prior to surgery and during the 'real life test' (where transsexuals are required to present themselves as members of the opposite sex by wearing appropriate clothing, etc.) claims for discrimination may not necessarily be upheld by the employment tribunal (*Craft* v *Consignia plc* (2002)

IRLR 839, where the EAT held that an employee who was undergoing male-to-female gender reassignment treatment had not been constructively dismissed or discriminated against on the ground of sex because the employer would not let her use the female toilets). Prior to this, it was thought that the SDA did not provide any assistance for those discriminated against on grounds of sexual orientation or transsexualism as the SDA was confined to protection against gender-based discrimination. Early attempts to use the SDA against discrimination on grounds of sexual orientation had failed until the decision in the groundbreaking *P v S and Cornwall County Council* (1996) IRLR 610 case. In this case the applicant was employed as the general manager of a unit of an educational establishment operated by the county council. The applicant was taken on as a male employee but in April 1992 she informed her head that she proposed to have a gender reassignment. She wrote to her line manager explaining that she was to embark on a life test, which is a one-year period during which a patient planning to undergo an operation for gender reassignment lives in the mode of the proposed gender. The governors of the establishment were informed and during the summer P took sick leave for initial surgical treatment. However, at the beginning of September 1992 she was given three months' notice of dismissal. She was not permitted to return from sick leave in her female gender role. The final surgical operation took place before the notice of dismissal expired. The European Court of Justice held that:

> The Directive cannot be confined simply to discrimination based on the fact that a person is one or other sex. In view of its purpose and the nature of the rights which it seeks to safeguard, the scope of the Directive is also such as to apply to discrimination arising from the gender reassignment of the person concerned. Such discrimination is based essentially if not exclusively, on the sex of the person concerned.

Further cases confirmed the European Court of Justice ruling and would appear to protect transsexuals and presumably gays and lesbians employed in the private sector against discrimination. However, there still appears to be some inconsistency of judgment in cases of this type. For example in *Grant v South West Trains Ltd* (1998), the Advocate General found in favour of the lesbian railway clerk who complained that she had been discriminated against because her lover was refused the travel concessions from her employer, South West Trains, that she would be entitled to if her lover were of the opposite sex. The Advocate General said it would have been all right to limit concessions to an employee's married partner, but as South West Trains had made this concession available to common law partners, they had to include employee's homosexual partners. However, the European Court of Justice unexpectedly ruled that a lesbian employee was not entitled to the same employee benefits as a heterosexual employee and concluded that the scope of the Treaty of Rome could not be extended beyond the 'competencies of the Community'. The amendment to the SDA based on the Equal Treatment Directive now provide Regulations to outlaw this type of discrimination, the effects of which remain to be seen.

Employers' responsibilities concerning race and ethnicity

As happens under the SDA, an employer is vicariously liable under the RRA for the actions of his or her employees undertaken in the course of employment, whether or not the employer was aware of the racial discrimination. The RRA, as amended by the Race Relations (Amendment) Act 2000, makes it unlawful to discriminate against anyone on grounds of race, colour, nationality (including citizenship), or ethnic or national origin. The amended Act also imposes general duties on many public authorities to promote racial equality. All aspects of employment are covered by the amended Act including recruitment, selection, promotion, transfer, training, pay and benefits, redundancy, dismissal and terms and conditions of work. The employer can only avoid liability for acts or omissions of his or her employees undertaken in the course of employment if the employer can show that he or she has taken all reasonable steps to prevent unlawful race discrimination generally or of the type complained of. The existence of an equal opportunities policy covering all aspects of discrimination together with evidence that the policy is put into practice in appropriate ways will assist the employment tribunal in its proceedings and judgment. Similar remedies for those who are sexually discriminated against are also available to those who are subject to unlawful racial discrimination should they take their case to an employment tribunal.

Specific responsibilities of employers have been identified by the CRE and EOC Codes of Practice. Codes of practice, as we have seen, exist to encourage and promote effective management practices, and these practices need to be implemented and enforced in the following areas (CRE, 1984):

- ethnic monitoring;
- recruitment;
- selection;
- promotion, transfer, training and appraisal;
- employment conditions and pay;
- harassment and grievance-handling; and
- discipline, dismissal and redundancy.

Ethnic monitoring

The CRE Code recommends that employers regularly monitor the effect of selection decisions, personnel practices and procedures in order to ensure that the criteria within an equal opportunities policy are being met. The amended RRA 2000 extends to public authorities the general duty to promote race equality and good race relations. Public authorities also have a specific duty to monitor, by ethnic groups, all employees and all applicants for jobs, promotion and training. In public bodies employing more than 150 people, employers have to monitor, by ethnic groups, the numbers who receive training; benefit or suffer disadvantages as a result of performance assessments; are involved in grievances; have disciplinary action taken against them; and end employment with the body/authority. While the method of monitoring is left to each employer to determine, the CRE recommends comprehensive monitoring to include:

- the ethnic composition of the workforce of each workplace, section, shift and job category, and changes in distribution over periods of time;
- selection decisions for recruitment, promotion, transfer and training according to the ethnic group of candidates and reasons for these decisions;
- an estimation of the geographical areas from which employers expect to recruit different types

of employees and the proportions of the various minority ethnic groups within these areas;
- devising a suitable method for obtaining relevant information (self-assessment questionnaires for this purpose have been used successfully by many organisations);
- communicating the purpose for which the information is being collected.

Monitoring data should be collected from all applicants, since without this information employers may be unaware that they are discriminating against particular groups. The CRE recommends the use of nine categories comprising White, Black-African, Black-Caribbean, Black-Other, Indian, Pakistani, Bangladeshi, Chinese, Other. The information should be separate from other types of information required (for example, the application form) and should not be used as part of the recruitment or selection process.

Recruitment

Organisations committed to equality of opportunity should ensure that the recruitment (and selection) process itself is not discriminatory. It is unlawful to discriminate, outside of there being a genuine occupational qualification (GOQ) by mentioning or indicating the race of the preferred applicant in advertising; offering less favourable terms of employment; refusing the employment on grounds of race; affording less favourable terms in respect of promotion, training opportunities, facilities, benefits or services.

Assuming that there are no GOQs, employers should review job descriptions to ensure that they are based on current requirements and then draft a person specification containing objective criteria based on the actual qualifications, skills, experience and aptitude required from any person to be considered to fill the post, thereby ensuring that all candidates are compared against objective criteria rather than with one another. It is important to ensure that job advertisements are designed in such a way that they do not discriminate against specific groups. Specifically, employers:

- should not confine advertisements unjustifiably to those areas or publications which would exclude or disproportionately reduce the number of applicants of a particular ethnic group or groups;

- should review current employment advertising in order to attract applicants from the ethnic minority communities more effectively;
- should avoid recruiting by 'word of mouth', through existing employees where the workforce is predominantly white or black and the labour market is multi-racial;
- should avoid arrangements where applicants are mainly or wholly supplied through trade unions where this means that only members of a particular racial or ethnic group, or a disproportionately high number of them, come forward;
- should avoid prescribing requirements such as length of residence or experience in the UK, and where a particular qualification is required it should be made clear that a fully comparable qualification obtained overseas is as acceptable as a UK qualification; and
- should demonstrate their commitment to equality of opportunity by including a statement in literature sent to applicants that they are equal opportunity employers.

In cases where a particular race or ethnic group has been under-represented in the previous 12 months, the company should have a positive action programme whereby the advertisement can explicitly encourage applications from the ethnic minority population. If employment agencies are used, they should be told that such applicants are particularly welcome (provided that no applicant is excluded, denied information or the opportunity to apply). The employment agency itself should be fully aware of equal opportunities policies and ensure that it does not discriminate unlawfully in its recruitment process.

Selection

Selection criteria should be specifically related to the requirements of the job to be performed, and this should be made clear to the candidate. In addition, employers should not disqualify applicants because they are unable to complete an application form unassisted, unless personal completion of the form is a valid test of the standard of English required for the safe and effective performance of the job.

Employers should ensure that adequate records, including reasons for selection and rejection, are kept for each stage of the selection process, as this will be relevant if any unsuccessful applicant does bring a discrimination claim. Other selection methods such as tests should be carefully chosen to ensure that they do not discriminate unfairly. Concern has been expressed by both the EOC and CRE over the potential race and sex bias in certain forms of psychometric testing; for example it is claimed that in some tests questions are asked that lean towards knowledge and experience that would be more readily available to a white male. During the interview questions which could be interpreted as discriminatory should be avoided. If it is necessary to ask about qualifications or experience gained overseas 'this should not be done in a way that may make it appear that the qualifications or experience are being undervalued' (Clarke, 1995, p. 100). Finally, those responsible for selection should be made aware of the possible misunderstandings that can occur in interviews between persons of different cultural backgrounds.

Promotion, transfer, training and appraisal

It is unlawful to discriminate on racial grounds in affording access to promotion, transfer or training. Age limits for promotion, transfer or training should be questioned as they could lead to indirect discrimination. Many of the issues considered within the areas of selection and recruitment are also relevant here. Clarke (1995) refers to the following example:

> In 1990, the CRE carried out an investigation into promotion procedures at London Underground and found that they operated in a way which discriminated against ethnic minority staff. None of the 63 senior managers recently appointed had been from an ethnic minority; vacancies were not advertised internally or externally; and candidates for promotion were selected on the recommendation of their superiors. The employer could have used the provisions of section 38 of the RRA to actively encourage employees to apply for promotion. (p. 103)

With regard to promotion, employees should be made aware of promotion arrangements, job requirements and method of application; promotion systems should be closely examined to ensure that the criteria employed do not adversely affect employees on the grounds of race. Employers can usefully adopt monitoring arrangements analysing the results of promotion and appraisal systems. These arrangements should include analysis of the promotion success rates and length of time taken for people of differing ethnic groups to progress within the organisation. It is likely that most organisations will have concentrations of jobs in which employees of one racial group are concentrated and from which transfers are traditionally restricted. Efforts should be made to open up opportunities for more flexible career routes as, for example, with transfer skills training and work shadowing. Training records of employees should be kept to facilitate monitoring of the numbers of different racial groups who undergo training, day release and personal development; and where an imbalance is identified the causes should be analysed to ensure they are not discriminatory. Care should be taken to ensure that, as far as is practical, all eligible employees have the opportunity to attend training and development courses and it is important to ensure that the facilities available at the venue are suitable for people from differing ethnic backgrounds.

Employment conditions and pay

It is unlawful to offer employment on discriminatory terms by, for example, offering ethnic minorities employment on lower pay than whites or only to offer ethnic minorities jobs on the night shift. The CRE Code of Practice recommends that 'where employees have particular religious and cultural needs which conflict with existing work requirements, it is recommended that employers should consider whether it is reasonably practicable to vary or adapt these requirements to enable such needs to be met'. For example, orthodox Jewish employees are unable to work on Friday evenings and Saturdays and Sikhs, as part of their religious culture, are required to adopt certain dress codes.

Harassment and grievance-handling

Racial harassment can take the form of violence or ostracism and will amount to direct discrimination which is unlawful Mini case 12.2 illustrates the nature of racial harassment.

Mini case 12.2
Abuse in the 3rd Parachute Regiment

Mr Yazbeck, who is of Lebanese and Irish background, was a soldier with the 3rd Parachute Regiment. The abuse started on day one. He was called 'raghead', 'Jewboy', 'Jewpoof boy' and 'Arab' in a particularly nasty way. Other soldiers were given nicknames, but not on the basis of their race.

Mr Yazbeck was also severely physically abused by fellow officers. For example, about 15 to 20 times a week Lance Corporal Fisher would jab his fingers deep into Yazbeck's nostrils and yank his head back till he lost his balance, before finishing off with a string of vile racist expletives.

These incidents often took place in the presence of very senior officers. Mr Yazbeck told his sergeant and lieutenant what he was going through, but they did nothing about it. The abuse continued and Mr Yazbeck tried to take his life, soon after going absent without leave. He has since been treated for depression. The case was listed for hearing at Ashford employment tribunal in September 2001, but was settled before that for £20 000.

Many of the measures previously discussed that employers could take to prevent sexual harassment apply also to instances of racial harassment. However, the important issue of whether an employer can be held liable for the harassment of its employees by third parties who are not in its employment was raised in the case of *Burton* v *De Vere Hotels* (1996) as described in Mini case 12.3.

Mini case 12.3
Burton v *De Vere Hotels* (1996) IRLR 596

Miss Burton and Miss Rhule, who were of Afro-Caribbean origin, were employed by De Vere Hotels as casual waitresses. On the night in question they were waiting on 400 guests, all men, and the guest speaker was Bernard Manning. While clearing the tables the women heard Mr Manning make sexually explicit and racially abusive jokes and comments, some aimed directly at them. After Mr Manning's act was over, the guests started to make sexually and racially offensive remarks to both women. The next day the hotel manager apologised to the women for what had happened. The women alleged that their employer had discriminated against them on racial grounds by subjecting them to the detriment of racial abuse and harassment contrary to the RRA. Initially the industrial tribunal found that there was racial harassment but it was Mr Manning and the guests, not the employer, who had subjected the women to this and therefore their claims were dismissed. However, the EAT considered that the employer can be viewed as subjecting an employee to harassment if he or she causes or permits the harassment to occur in circumstances in which he or she can control whether it happens or not. The key question was whether the event was something which was sufficiently under the control of the employer that he or she could, by the application of good employment practice, have prevented the harassment or reduced the extent of it. If he or she could, then the employer had subjected the employee to harassment. Applying this to Miss Burton's case, it was held that the employer could have prevented or reduced the extent of the harassment but had failed to do so.

Source: Adapted from Painter and Puttick, 1998, p. 128

Discipline, dismissal and redundancy

> It is unlawful to discriminate in the operation of grievance, disputes and disciplinary procedures, for example by victimising an individual through disciplinary measures because he or she has complained about racial discrimination or given evidence about such a complaint. (CRE, 1984)

The employer must ensure that appropriate consideration concerning racial abuse or other racial provocation, communication and comprehension difficulties and differences in cultural background or behaviour are given in the operation of disciplinary procedures. Therefore discriminatory offences should be regarded as a disciplinary matter and extreme forms of discrimination (such as severe

harassment and racially motivated attacks) can often be regarded as gross misconduct carrying the penalty of summary dismissal.

It is also unlawful to discriminate on racial grounds in dismissal, and should there be any redundancies, selection criteria for redundancies (see Chapter 13) should not be indirectly discriminatory.

Self-Evaluation Activity 12.14
Managing ethnic diversity
This SEA has no commentary

Described below is a case which requires urgent action to be taken to rectify the situation. Indicate what action should be taken.

You are a newly-appointed HR manager in a company employing 850 people on one site, and have a special interest in the development of equal opportunities policies, which is one reason why you were appointed. The company, in its various policy statements, says it is committed to equal opportunities but as far as you can ascertain, very little, if anything has been put into practice. The company is located on the fringes of an inner city area which is ethnically diverse; in fact over 70 per cent of the inner city population is non-white. As one of your first tasks, you have decided to undertake an audit of the workforce, concentrating in the first instance on its ethnic composition. The initial results of the audit give you great cause for concern as they reveal, amongst other findings, that only 1.5 per cent of the entire workforce is non-white, and is almost wholly concentrated on the manual worker's night shift. There are no non-white employees on the manual day shift or amongst the non-manual or managerial staff.

After you report your initial findings to the managing director together with suggestions for remedial action, you have been told to 'get on with it'. Outline the action you would now take.

Racism at Ford's Dagenham plant

The incident related in Exhibit 12.9 demonstrates that one manifest example of racism can represent the 'tip of the iceberg' and that in many organisations racism is endemic. The particular incident was

Exhibit 12.9

Racism at Ford

During September and October 1999 a number of race and race-related incidents occurred at Ford's Dagenham plant. A dispute about shift work and rostering concerning Asian employees led to rioting, vandalism of vehicles and a walkout of night-shift workers. This incident was followed two days later by another walkout involving 800 workers after a complaint by an Asian shop steward that he was pushed by a white foreman. These incidents occurred only weeks after another Asian worker who claimed he was a victim of bullying won a case he brought to an employment tribunal. As a result of short-time working and demands for increased productivity, workers on the assembly line were feeling particularly pressurised by supervisors, the situation being compounded by the fact that whereas more than 40 per cent of assembly line workers are from ethnic minorities, only 10 per cent of their supervisors are. The Asian shop steward allegedly pushed by a white foreman was discussing racial harassment with a colleague when the incident took place. The situation at the Dagenham plant could be regarded as a failure of management to take its equal opportunities policies sufficiently seriously (see below). The alleged culture of institutional racism at the Dagenham plant had been reinforced in recent years by a number of revelations in the media detailing Ford's insensitivity towards its ethnic minority workforce. The main revelations are detailed below.

February 1996: Ford pays £1500 to four black workers after digitally altering a picture to give them white faces for an advertisement to be used in Poland. The company's claim that it was advised by its advertising agency to do this evoked little sympathy.

June 1996: £70 000 is paid to seven black and Asian workers after a 'kith and kin' policy is found to have existed. (A 'kith and kin' policy is an informal arrangement whereby jobs are allocated to certain groups of employees, in this case white employees.) The men were proved to have been unfairly denied jobs on the company's truck fleet.

March 1998: A TV advertisement spoofing *The Full Monty* is withdrawn by Ford following a complaint that, unlike in the film, no black actor is present in the line-up.

September 1999: An Asian assembly-line worker tells a tribunal how he had been banished to a 'punishment cell', refused protective clothing and found the word 'Paki' written on his payslip.

September 1999: Workers stage a mass walkout after an Asian shop steward was pushed by a white foreman.

In August 2000, a formal investigation of the incident by the CRE was suspended on the terms that Ford would:

- conduct a diversity and equality assessment review at all plants in Britain by April 2001; and
- implement and evaluate an effective monitoring system.

dealt with, but it was not possible to monitor the effectiveness of the remedy as Ford withdrew much of its investment in Dagenham shortly after.

Equal opportunities and managing diversity

As we have seen, legislation is extremely important as a means for combating discrimination and enforcing appropriate behaviour through the 'stick' of legal sanctions. The various commissions set up by the discrimination Acts, such as the CRE and EOC, play a significant 'overseeing' role in seeking to ensure that employers and others adhere to the legislation. Against the background of the discrimination legislation, the voluntary Codes of Practice developed by these commissions and by the European Union which concern equal pay, harassment and the development of equal opportunities policies, provide further encouragement for employers to adopt 'good practice'.

Self-Evaluation Activity 12.15
*Why should organisations develop
equal opportunities policies?*
Response on website

Apart from the legal and quasi legal reasons referred to
above, can you think of any other reasons why organisations should develop equal opportunities policies?

The evolution of equality: equal opportunities and managing diversity or 'the diversity of diversity'

Equal opportunities (EO) became established as both theoretical model and equality goal for most 'socially progressive' organisations during the 1970s and 1980s. The theoretical base for EO remains that of Jewson and Mason (1986), who distinguish between two EO approaches based on the liberal and radical traditions. The former stresses individual rights to have access to the employment, regardless of social category such as race, gender, sexual orientation, disability and age. Differences are minimised and competition is on the basis of merit only in that everyone should have the same opportunity for progression within a meritocracy. According to this approach, there is an emphasis on 'positive action' to remove obstacles to meritocratic competition. The UK discrimination legislation and EU Directives, together with the formalisation of procedures, are based on this model.

The radical approach to EO focuses on direct intervention to achieve not only equality of oppor-tunity but also 'equality of outcome' – that is, the fair distribution of rewards. Hence the absence of fair distribution is evidence of unfair discrimination. Policies associated with the radical perspective focus around 'positive discrimination' where employment practices are deliberately manipulated to obtain a fair distribution of those disadvantaged groups in the workplace and the imposition of quotas or the necessity to employ a minimum percentage of a certain group of workers. EO legislation in the UK, while based on the liberal 'sameness' approach, does also contain, to a much lesser extent, some elements of a radical 'difference' approach. These elements are visible, for example, in both the recognition of the existence of indirect discrimina-tion and in employer policies designed to improve the position of certain social groups.

Some criticisms of the EO 'sameness' perspective

Much of the criticism concerning EO has revolved around the effectiveness of the legislation and the mismatch between EO policies and rhetoric, on the one hand, and EO practice, on the other, within organisations. In particular, criticisms include the following:

- Given the persistence of both direct and indirect discrimination of all types within organisations, the prevalence of harassment and the widening of the gender pay gap, it could be argued that the legislation has not had the desired effect owing to a lack of political will underlying the legisla-tion and the institutional weakness of HRM and personnel managers who are largely responsible for implementation.
- The liberal EO approach itself promises more than it can deliver. For example, Webb (1997) demonstrates the extent to which equality proce-dures can be evaded (wittingly or unwittingly), indicating the limitations of formal procedures. A reliance upon procedures and bureaucratisa-tion may seem at odds with the trends towards deregulation and flexibility and has come to be seen as unfair and restrictive within a laissez-faire economy.
- The traditional approach to EO has been criti-cised for failing to deliver equality of outcome, and failing to look at the extent to which dis-crimination continues to exist: suitability criteria continue to be judged against the dominant white male norm.
- EO approaches based on 'sameness' only benefit a minority of workers from disadvantaged groups who can most easily meet the dominant norm. This is partly because EO perspectives rarely address themselves to the issues of wider societal and organisational structural inequalities.
- EO approaches have been criticised (Heilman, 1994) for the inadequacy of positive or 'affirmat-ive' action policies which may thus alienate large sections of the 'non-disadvantaged' workforce who perceive no advantages in the policies to themselves.

Managing diversity

The term 'managing diversity' (MD) had its origins in the USA when Johnston and Packer (1987) referred to the increasing diversity of the American workforce and the decline in the proportion of white males in the labour force, a trend which has been called the 'browning of America' (Abassi and Hollman, 1991). A popular definition of MD is provided by Kandola and Fullerton (2002):

> The basic concept of managing diversity accepts that the workforce consists of a diverse population of people. The diversity consists of visible and non-visible differences which will include factors such as sex, age, background, race, disability and work style. It is founded on the premise that harnessing these differences will create a productive environment in which everybody feels valued, where their talents are being fully utilised and in which organisational goals are met. (p. 8)

The basic idea is that organisations should recognise differences rather than deny or dilute them (Liff, 1996), thereby departing from the view that employees should be assimilated to meet an organisational norm or standard. Rather than difference being viewed negatively, there should be a celebration of difference, focusing on the benefits which would accrue to the organisation as a result of nurturing the inherent strengths of employees based on their cultural background, gender, age, disability or differential experience. A summary of the relevant EO and MD approaches is set out in Figure 12.2.

Kandola and Fullerton's 'validated strategic implementation model' (2002) is one of the better-known MD models, and is claimed to be 'the first ever to have been empirically tested and validated' (p. 91). The model comprises a 'strategy web' with eight 'strands' or components which comprise:

1. **Organisational vision:** 'If diversity is to become a business issue, then the organisation must have a clear vision of what it intends to achieve and why this vision is important' (p. 71).
2. **Top management commitment:** The securing of top management support is crucial to communicate a vision that motivates employees by focusing their energy on a common goal.
3. **Auditing and assessment of needs:** It is important to know the organisation, its culture, procedures

and human resources when embarking on MD, and this requires the collection of data and the auditing of key management processes.
4. **Clarity of objectives:** Having identified the areas that require attention, it is necessary to establish the objectives for implementation.
5. **Clear accountability:** It is important that diversity policies and strategies are understood by all if diversity is to be implemented effectively.
6. **Effective communication:** All information concerning the progress of the strategy should be shared throughout the organisation so that employees have a full understanding of the issues.
7. **Co-ordination of activity:** 'The implementation of the strategy needs to be co-ordinated either by individuals or groups at all levels of the organisation' (p. 85).
8. **Evaluation:** The review of progress is an ongoing process, continuous and rigorous.

The 'managing diversity' approach to managing discrimination demonstrated by the Kandola and Fullerton model claims that the traditional focus of equal opportunities policies is misplaced, and that rather than concentrating upon *groups* of employees who fall within particular categories (based on gender, ethnicity, and disability, for example), the focus of employers should be upon *all the individuals* within the organisation. Clarke (1995) argues that:

> The advantage of this approach is that it includes everybody within its scope and concentrates on the **diversity** of all individuals within the organisation, rather than just looking at a woman worker as a woman. Family-friendly policies, for example, should examine men's problems in reconciling work and family life, as well as women's. This approach can feed into a good equal opportunities policy by concentrating on the advantages to everyone rather than by simply avoiding disadvantages to particular groups. (p. 136)

Although it could be argued that MD could, and even should, be incorporated within an effective EO policy, there are important differences between the two approaches which we shall now briefly consider:

- EO approaches have sought to adopt a legislative solution to prevent discriminatory practices, while MD approaches emphasise the benefits of

View	Principle	Strategy	Operation	Type of equality	How driven	Focus orientation	Assumption, style and content
Liberal EO	Fair, equal opportunities	Level playing field	Policy statement, equality proof, recruitment/selection procedures	Equality of opportunity	Externally initiated, legally driven	Quantitative focus (improving numbers) and problem-focused	Assumes assimilation; reactive, race, gender and disability
	Positive action	Help to disadvantaged groups	Monitoring, pre-entry training, in-service training, special courses elevate EO within management	Equality of opportunity			
	Strong positive action	Give positive preference to certain groups	Family-friendly policies, improve access for disabled, make harassment a disciplinary offence	Moving towards equality of outcome			
Radical EO	Positive discrimination	Proportional equal representation	Preferential selection quotas	Equality of outcome			
MD	Maximise individual potential	Use diversity to add value	Vision statement, organisation audit, business-related objectives, communication and accountability, change culture	Equality means profit aligned with organisational objectives	Internally initiated and business driven	Qualitative focus, i.e. improving the environment, and opportunity focused	Assumes pluralism; proactive and considers all differences

Figure 12.2 Summarising approaches to equal opportunity and managing diversity

such approaches to the business and economic well-being of the organisation.

- EO approaches emphasise moral, social and ethical issues concerning individuals within society generally, while MD approaches argue that employers benefit economically 'if they invest in ensuring that everyone in the organisation is valued and given the opportunity to develop their potential and make a maximum contribution' (Torrington and Hall, 1998, p. 351).

- EO approaches aim to ensure an adequate and fair representation of disadvantaged groups in the workplace in order to reflect the distribution of those groups within the community and wider society through, for example, positive action

campaigns. MD approaches do not use positive action but focus upon improvement of opportunities of *all* employees, involving and benefiting everyone.

- EO policies are mainly the responsibility of personnel and HRM departments which are expected to put these policies into practice, while implementation of MD approaches is deemed to be the responsibility of every department and all managers.

- EO approaches are oriented towards equality of treatment of particular disadvantaged groups and ignore the needs of individuals, whereas MD approaches acknowledge that each and every individual is unique and should be treated accordingly.

MD approaches have been criticised for diverting attention from disadvantaged groups in the interests of business advantage and benefits for all. However, Ford (1996) suggests that the two approaches are not mutually exclusive and can co-exist within an integrated policy, the objective of which is the elimination of discrimination. One example of this is mainstreaming which is concerned with the integration of EO into all policy development, implementation, evaluation and review processes, thereby eliminating the need for specific equality policies. Equality issues are supposed to disseminate throughout the organisation which will facilitate a 'culture of diversity in which people of a much broader range of characteristics and background may confidently flourish' (Rees, 1998, quoted in Kirton and Green, 2001, p. 111). The example of Marks & Spencer's Equal Opportunities Statement, shown in Exhibit 12.10, reflects this integrated approach to some extent.

Elements of a good EO policy

Although organisations have different requirements depending upon the nature of the workforce, the product market, the size and complexity of structures and operations, there are, as Clarke (1995) points out, a number of key points applicable to all organisations. These are similar to those of the Kandola and Fullerton (2002) model.

As a first step in devising an EO policy, it is important to secure the commitment of all organisational participants to the aims of the policy, and not just the personnel or HRM department. 'Drafting an equal opportunities policy should not be left to the personnel or human resource division alone. Here the approach of focusing on managing diversity, rather than simple non-discrimination, can be important, as is awareness of the possible business advantages to the whole organisation' (Clarke, 1995, p. 137).

Secondly, Clarke suggests that the organisation should undertake an equal opportunities audit 'in order to see where any problems lie' which would include a consideration of all aspects of the employment relationship such as recruitment, training, promotion, dismissal, redundancy, staff turnover and pay structures.

Thirdly, on completion of the audit (which should then be undertaken regularly on an annual basis), potential problems may be revealed which should then be addressed:

In addition to developing an overall strategy, specific solutions should be sought for specific problems. For example, the company may have a very poor record of women returning to work after maternity leave. Why? What can be done to improve the position? Is turnover higher amongst women or ethnic minorities? In either case, is this because of a lack of opportunity for career development? Does the selection process produce fewer non-white applicants than would statistically be predicted for the locality? If so, is it because the company relies on word-of-mouth recruitment, or advertises in ways that do not reach ethnic

---

Exhibit 12.10

M & S Equal Opportunities Statement

Marks & Spencer is committed to an active Equal Opportunities Policy from recruitment and selection, through training and development, appraisal and promotion to retirement.

It is our policy to promote an environment free from discrimination, harassment and victimisation where everyone will receive equal treatment regardless of age, colour, disability, ethnic or national origin, gender, marital status, religion or sexual orientation. All decisions relating to employment practices will be objective, free from bias and based solely upon work criteria and individual merit.

The company is responsive to the needs of its employees, customers and the community at large and we are an organisation which uses everyone's talents and abilities where diversity is valued.

Source: Marks & Spencer plc: Equal Opportunities Statement (1998) *minorities, or has a poor reputation for employing non-whites? . . . There may be many other issues revealed by an equal opportunities audit. It is important to realise, furthermore, that monitoring should be continuous: the problems, and the solutions required, will change over time.* (ibid., p. 137)

Fourthly, to be effective, there should be a clear structure of responsibility for EO which should involve everyone, particularly those in managerial positions, in EO training.

Fifthly, the EO policy, having been introduced, should be continually reviewed and monitored in order to ensure that new problems are effectively dealt with. The policy itself should be modified where appropriate according to changes in legislation and in the internal labour market.

From policy to practice: rhetoric or reality?

Recent research by IRS suggests that employers are taking monitoring for equality more seriously than hitherto. In 2003, around 75 per cent of employers in the IRS (2003) survey undertook monitoring to check on EO indicators and 'the findings from the IRS research confirm that the need to ensure effect-ive equal opportunities policies and procedures is the most common reason for undertaking monitoring'. The most common characteristics on which monitoring is undertaken are, unsurprisingly enough, sex, ethnic origin, disability and age. Much of this activity is either in recognition or anticipation of existing and forthcoming legislation referred to earlier in the chapter (race relations and equality Directives). Nevertheless, many examples exist of organisations paying lip-service to the equality agenda (see Exhibit 12.11).

Self-Evaluation Activity 12.16

What more could Ford have done?

This SEA has no commentary

Reread the sections dealing with equal opportunities and managing diversity, with particular reference to the Kandola and Fullerton diversity model, and suggest what more Ford could have done to produce a credible EO/MD policy.

The evidence suggests that many organisations purport to have EO policies. Torrington and Hall,

---

Exhibit 12.11

Equal opportunities at Ford Dagenham?

The incidents concerning ethnic minorities at Ford's Dagenham plant in recent years have aroused suspicions concerning the operation of equal opportunities policies within Ford UK. A senior TGWU official stated that 'In Britain, "people problems" – racism, bullying and grievance problems – are not being treated as seriously as commercial and productivity problems' (Lamb, 1999). Although there is much talk of 'diversity in the workplace' at the top of the organisation, the policies do not appear to have filtered down to the shop floor. The workforce claim that management pays only lip-service to equal opportunities; bullying is one result and limited opportunity for promotion is another. The gap between policies as written and as implemented could be the result of poor promotion of these policies or the refusal of managers to embrace them, which in turn perpetuates and reinforces the workplace culture.

In October 1999, Ford's then global president Jac Nasser took personal control of the growing crisis over racism at Dagenham after flying in from Detroit to sign a comprehensive agreement with the unions to stamp out discrimination and harassment. The agreement, hailed by Bill Morris, leader of the TGWU as the 'fresh start that Dagenham needs', will set up joint equal opportunities committees at every Ford plant in Britain, backed by anti-racist policies for recruitment, promotion and corporate image-making.

However, while the agreement was generally endorsed, subsequent events and the closure of the Dagenham plant rendered the agreement ineffective.

however (1998), cite research conducted in 1994 when 89 per cent of their sample organisations had EO policies), a much smaller proportion put these policies into effect. The CRE (2002) found that while around 90 per cent of the large companies it surveyed had EO policies which specifically incorporated provisions for racial equality, only 45 per cent of them had taken any measures to implement the policy. However, more organisations are taking ethnic mainstreaming seriously as a result of the Race Relations (Amendment) Act 2000 and the MacPherson Report. Liff (1995) argues that there are three important factors which make implementation problematic: 'the relationship between line managers and personnel; the conflicts between EO and other priorities facing managers; and resistance from employees' (p. 480). We now look briefly at each of these factors:

1. *Line managers and personnel*: As we noted earlier, traditional EO approaches assume that the main responsibility for implementing EO policies rests with the personnel department, while the responsibility for MD lies with management in general. Liff cites a study by Collinson *et al.* (1990) which attempts to demonstrate that personnel managers' influence in implementing equality measures, particularly with regard to recruitment and selection matters, is limited owing to a lack of intervention in decisions involving line managers; undue deference shown to line management under the assumption that line managers had a better understanding of the situation; and reluctance to take responsibility for making 'wrong' decisions. The general problems besetting personnel management

discussed in Chapter 2 may well contribute to personnel's relative ineffectiveness in implementing EO policies.

2. *EO and other priorities*: Managers may regard the formal approaches recommended for adoption in the various Codes of Practice, concerning recruitment and selection for example, as unnecessarily time-consuming and costly, particularly when faced with production and staff shortage problems. It may therefore be tempting for managers to resort to informal methods of recruitment (which may include 'word of mouth') which are cheaper and quicker than formal methods, but also potentially discriminatory. Action based on economic expediency does not necessarily indicate that managers are opposed to EO practices; managers may, as Liff (1995) suggests, 'not be simply for or against equal opportunities. In some situations they may find it acceptable or may even be favourably disposed towards it. In other cases they may find it objectionable' (p. 481).

3. *Employee resistance*: Liff points out that 'groups who currently have a dominant position within the workforce are likely to feel threatened by EO initiatives' (p. 481). These groups normally comprise white male employees who may resent EO policies which favour minority groups who may be perceived to have been given 'special treatment' with regard to promotion and other opportunities for advancement.

A survey of NHS hospital trusts (Hurstfield, 1999) reveals that there is a considerable gap between formal policies and their implementation. Summary details of the survey are given in Exhibit 12.12.

Exhibit 12.12

NHS Trusts: a suitable case for treatment?

The survey was carried out by Industrial Relations Services Research (IRSR) in order to provide data on the extent to which NHS trusts have adopted EO policies and practices. During 1998, 420 or 99 per cent of all trusts in England were surveyed and case studies of 25 trusts were undertaken to examine issues in greater depth.

The findings

- Almost every trust has a general policy statement on EO, but there were wide variations in the extent to which trusts have introduced policies on specific subjects (see table below).

- Where subjects are covered, trusts prefer separate policies for different subjects rather than incorporating them in different policies (see table). For example, paternity leave is covered by a separate policy in 83 per cent of the trusts compared with 4 per cent that incorporate it in their general EO statement. The only exception to this is childcare.
- The majority of trusts collect monitoring data on their workforce by gender, ethnic origin, disability and full or part-time working, and nearly two-thirds also produce a report on the monitoring data for the trust board.
- Only a minority of trusts use their monitoring data to help produce forecasts or goals for the representation of women, ethnic minorities or disabled people in their workforces, with the highest proportion – one in three – setting targets for women, while 25 per cent had set targets for employing ethnic minorities and even fewer (13 per cent) for disabled people.
- The main initiatives the trusts identified for the previous two years were in the areas of disability (16 per cent of trusts) and gender (14 per cent of trusts), while only 10 per cent of trusts cited initiatives aimed at assisting ethnic minorities by increasing the proportion of ethnic groups in their workforces and senior management posts and strengthening links with local ethnic minority communities.
- While a high proportion of trusts operate EO policies, the case studies reveal the extent of the gap between the espousal of formal policies and their effective implementation, with poor communication and dissemination of policy details to staff, and inconsistent implementation of policies by line managers.

The survey indicates that there is considerable room for improvement when it comes to implementing EO policies in most hospital trusts.

Coverage and content of EO policies in NHS trusts

	Included in general EO policy %	Covered by specific policies %
Maternity pay/leave	5	96
Recruitment/selection	32	85
Adoption leave	3	84
Paternity leave	4	83
Carer leave	4	83
Harassment by staff	23	81
Jobsharing	9	73
Harassment by patients	12	59
Other special leave	3	55
Retainer schemes	3	38
Childcare	38	5

Source: IRS Employment Trends, 1999b

Equality policy update

As a result of increased expenditure by government, announced in 2002, and a 'modernisation' programme, the NHS has reinforced its commitment to promoting equality of opportunity in employment, and has launched a number of initiatives at both local (trust) and national level, to encourage the employment prospects of women, ethnic minority staff and disabled people. An equality framework for the health service – *The vital connection* – was launched in April 2000. It introduced a package of indicators, standards and monitoring arrangements, and set national targets on disability, tackling harassment, achieving a representative workforce and board-level training on equality and diversity. The targets are incorporated into both the HR Performance Framework for the NHS and the Improving Working Lives Standard (a commitment to improving the working lives of staff in the NHS).

Equality policies in the public services

In 2002 public authorities in Britain had a statutory authority to promote racial equality, but there was no similar requirement on them to promote gender equality. An EOC-commissioned study was undertaken by Escott and Whitfield (2002) to uncover evidence that could be used to support the introduction of a public duty on gender. The study examined practices in six public sector organisations comprising the Greater London Authority (GLA), the Scottish Executive, the Welsh Development Agency (WDA), City of Birmingham Council, West Midlands Police Authority, and various regional agencies in the North West Region. The key findings of the study concerned the legislative context, public policy-making, evidence of good practice, strategic approaches to gender mainstreaming and barriers to progress. These are considered in turn.

The legislative context

Apart from race, where there is a comprehensive duty to implement equality policies and practices, other equality duties tend to resemble a patchwork pattern. The authors state that 'There is a danger that if an equality duty is applied to public sector organisations individually and separately as and when the opportunity arises, there will be a fragmented approach and less emphasis on holistic equality strategies and gender mainstreaming' (p. iv)

Public policy-making

New Labour's modernisation agenda for public services has not taken sufficient account of the equality dimension. An important difference was identified between public sector organisations having a public duty applied to directly-provided services, and a public duty which has to be implemented by contract with a third party (subcontracted services, tendering, franchises, trusts). Clearly, the greater the extent of contracted-out services etc., the more problematic equality becomes within these services. Therefore, while the government preaches equality, its very policies in this respect will have the opposite effect.

Evidence of good practice

The six public authorities investigated have advanced gender equality strategies, mainly because:

- they have a corporate framework for gender equality with application to all policy-making, employment practices and service delivery;
- they enjoy political support and commitment of senior managers;
- they have institutional arrangements which place a corporate equalities strategy at the heart of policy-making, supported by sufficient resources;
- they have a budgetary process directly connected to the setting of equality standards and targets;
- they mainstream gender through policy development, performance management and service review and delivery;
- they apply the policy through key tools used to mainstream gender and specific programmes targeted at reducing inequality between men and women, including gender impact assessment; and
- they monitor and evaluate the application of equality policies at every level of the organisation and assess the equality impact of initiatives which provide greater service integration.

Strategic approaches to gender mainstreaming

The numerous gender initiatives undertaken in many public sector organisations generally do not represent a coherent or strategic approach. Gender mainstreaming remains the province of equalities specialists and is not yet a core part of moves to improve public policy-making.

Barriers to progress

A number of barriers were identified, and included:

- inconsistent and piecemeal application of gender-specific strategies within public sector organisations, reflected in the gulf which is often found between equalities statements and practical application;
- a lack of senior commitment to advancing gender policies;
- limited resources to fund improvements;
- a lack of data to enable the impact of policy and service delivery to be identified;
- the prioritisation of performance management and other modernisation strategies over equalities issues;
- the weakness of legislation to ensure that external contractors are fair employers and will

not introduce employment practices which are damaging to the position of women employees; and

- a lack of clarity over the application of gender equality policies to non-governmental organisations which are largely dependent on public funds.

Summary points concerning the management of equality

- The European Union, through Treaty Articles and Directives, has become increasingly influential in encouraging member states to introduce discrimination and equal pay legislation. Much of European law in this area is concerned with sex discrimination and equal rights for men and women.
- With regard to sex and race discrimination, employers should follow the procedural approaches suggested by the EOC and CRE Codes of Practice. The EOC Code deals with the importance of developing good employment practices in order to eliminate sex discrimination and promote equal opportunities.
- Pay inequality is an important ongoing issue as there is still a considerable pay gap between women and men which, at the current rate of progress will not be eliminated until 2040.
- The EOC Code of Practice concerning equal pay aims to provide concrete advice for employers and collective bargaining partners to ensure that the principle of equality between men and women performing work of equal value is applied to all aspects of pay and to eliminate sexual discrimination whenever pay structures are based on job classification and evaluation systems.
- Sexual harassment is common and widespread, but under-reported. Sexual harassment is unlawful under the SDA and under EU law. The EU Code of Practice concerning sexual harassment identifies measures which employers should take to deal with the problem.
- There are no statutory provisions expressly prohibiting discrimination on grounds of sexual orientation.
- The CRE has produced a Code of Practice which aims to encourage effective management practices in order to rectify and prevent race

discrimination. Areas covered include ethnic monitoring, recruitment, selection, promotion, transfer and appraisal, terms of employment, racial harassment, discipline, dismissal and redundancy.

- While we may distinguish between 'equal opportunities' and 'managing diversity', the two should be seen as complementary and as part of an overall approach which organisations should adopt to encourage and promote equality amongst employees.

RELEVANT WEBSITES

www.cre.gov.uk (Commission for Racial Equality)
www.drc.gb.org (Disability Rights Commission)
www.dti.gov.uk/er/equality (Department of Trade and Industry) Legislative and policy issues concerning equality.
www.eoc.org.uk (Equal Opportunities Commission)
www.equalitynet.org Information on discrimination issues.
www.statistics.gov.uk Office for National Statistics Source of statistical data re gender and race inequality.

REFERENCES

Abassi, S.M. and Hollman, K.W. (1991) 'Managing cultural diversity: the challenge of the '90s'. *ARMA Records Management Quarterly*, 25, 3, 24–32

Adorno, T.W., Frenkel-Bruswick, E., Levinson, D.J. and Sanford, R.N. (1950) *The Authoritarian Personality*. New York, Harper and Row

Beechey, V. (1983) 'The sexual division of labour and the labour process: a critical assessment of Braverman' in Wood, S. (ed.) *The Degradation of Work; Skill, Deskilling and the Labour Process*. London, Hutchinson

Burrell, G. and Hearn, J. (1989) 'The sexuality of organisation', in Hearn, J., Sheppard, D., Tancred-Sheriff and Burrell, G. (eds) *The Sexuality of Organisation*. London, Sage.

Clarke, L. (1995) *Discrimination*. London, IPD

Cockburn, C. (1991) *In the Way of Women*. London, Macmillan

Collinson, D.L., Knights, D. and Collinson, M. (1990) *Managing Discrimination*. London, Routledge

CRE (1981) *BL Cars Ltd . . . Report of a Formal Investigation*. London, CRE

CRE (1984) *Code of Practice for the Elimination of Racial Discrimination and the Promotion of Equality of Opportunity in Employment*. London, CRE

CRE (1987) *Chartered Accountancy Training Contracts*. London, CRE

CRE (1999) *Annual Report 1998*. London, CRE

CRE (2002) *Annual Report 2001*. London, CRE

Crompton, R. and Sanderson, K. (1990) *Gendered Jobs and Social Change*. London, Unwin Hyman

DfEE (Department for Education and Employment) (1998) *Action on Age: Report of the Consultation on Age Discrimination in Employment*. London, DfEE Publications

DfEE (Department for Education and Employment) (1999) 'Code of Practice for Age Diversity'. www.dfee.gov.uk/age diversity

Doeringer, P. and Piore, M. (1971) *Internal Labour Markets and Manpower Analysis*. Lexington, Mass. D.C. Heath

DTI (Department of Trade and Industry) (2001) *Towards Equality and Diversity: Implementing the Employment and Race Directive: Consultation Document*. London, DTI

Equal Opportunities Review (1993) 'Discrimination in recruitment'. EOR No. 4, May/June

Equal Opportunities Review (1998) 'Tackling age bias: code or law?'. EOR No. 80, July/August

EOC (Equal Opportunities Commission) (1985) *A Code of Practice for the Elimination of Discrimination on Grounds of Sex and Marital Status in Employment*. Manchester, EOC

EOC (Equal Opportunities Commission) (1997a) *Briefings on Women and Men in Britain*. Manchester, EOC

EOC (Equal Opportunities Commission) (1997b) *Code of Practice on Equal Pay*. Manchester, EOC

EOC (Equal Opportunities Commission) (1997c) *Consider the Cost: Sexual Harassment at Work*. Manchester, EOC

EOC (Equal Opportunities Commission) (1999) *Annual Report 1998*. Manchester, EOC

EOC (Equal Opportunities Commission) (2001) '*Just Pay': The Report of the Equal Pay Task Force*. Manchester, EOC

EOC (Equal Opportunities Commission) (2002a) *Annual Report 2001–2002*. Manchester, EOC

EOC (Equal Opportunities Commission) (2002b) *Dealing with Sexual Harassment*. Manchester, EOC

EOC (Equal Opportunities Commission) (2003) *The Gender Pay Gap*. Manchester, EOC

Escott, K. and Whitfield, D. (2002) *Promoting Gender Equality in the Public Sector*. London, Centre for Public Services

EUROSTAT (Statistical Office of the European Communities) (1995) 'European Structure of Earnings Survey'. www.unece.org/stats

Ford, V. (1996) 'Partnership is the secret of progress'. *People Management*, February

Gardiner, C. (1992) *Gender and Substitution Theory*. Cambridge, Polity Press

Giddens, A. (1998) *Sociology*. Cambridge, Polity Press

Grint, K. (1993) *The Sociology of Work*. Cambridge, Polity Press

Hawkins, K. (1994) 'Taking action on harassment'. *Personnel Management*, March

Heilman, M.E. (1994) 'Affirmative action: some unintended consequences for working women'. *Research in Organisational Behaviour*, 16

Homans, H. (1987) 'Man-made myth: the reality of being a woman scientist in the NHS', in Spencer, A. and Podmore, D. (eds) *In a Man's World: Essays on Women in Male-Dominated Professions*. London, Tavistock

Hurstfield, J. (1999) *Equal Opportunities and Monitoring in NHS Trusts*. IRS Research, Department of Health

IDS (Incomes Data Services) (1999) *Harassment Policies*. IDS, Study 662

IRS (1996) 'Sexual harassment at work'. *IRS Employment Trends*, No. 615

IRS (1998a) 'Government sets out its stall on tackling age discrimination'. *IRS Employment Trends*, No. 666

IRS (1998b) 'Tackling age bias: code or law?' *IRS Employment Trends*, No. 80

IRS (1999a) 'Burden of proof'. *IRS Employment Trends*, No. 671

IRS (1999b) 'Equal opportunities policies in NITS trusts'. *IRS Employment Trends*, No. 671

IRS (2001) 'Managing age diversity at work'. *IRS Employment Trends*, No. 729

IRS (2002) 'Sexual harassment: an EOR survey'. *Equal Opportunities Review*, 102, 8–21

IRS (2003) 'Monitoring for equality: a coming of age'. *IRS Employment Trends*, No. 770

Jenkins, R. (1988) 'Discrimination and equal opportunity in employment: ethnicity and "race" in the United Kingdom' in Gaillie, D. (ed.) *Employment in Britain*. Oxford, Blackwell

Jewson, N. and Mason, D. (1986) 'The theory and practice of equal opportunities policies: liberal and radical approaches'. *Sociological Review*, 34, 2, 307–34

Johnston, W. and Packer, A. (1987) *Workforce 2000: Work and Workers for the 21st Century*. Indianapolis, In., Hudson Institute

Jones, T. (1993) *Britain's Ethnic Minorities*. London, Policy Studies Institute

Kandola, A. and Fullerton, J. (2002) *Diversity in Action*. London, CIPD

Kirton, G. and Green, A-M (2001) *The Dynamics of Managing Diversity*. Oxford, Butterworth-Heinemann

Lamb, J. (1999) 'Race for a solution at Dagenham'. *People Management*, October, 20–1

Lee, G. (1987) 'Black members and their unions', in Lee, G. and Loveridge, R. (eds) *Manufacture of Disadvantage: Stigma and Social Closure*. Milton Keynes, Open University Press

Liff, S. (1995) 'Equal opportunities: continuing discrimination in a context of formal equality', in Edwards, P. (ed.) *Industrial Relations: Theory and Practice in Britain*. Oxford, Blackwell

Liff, S. (1996) 'Two routes to managing diversity: individual differences or social group characteristics'. *Employee Relations*, 19, 1, 11–26

LRD (Labour Research Department) (1999) *Pay Inequalities*. London, LRD

McDowell, L. (1992) 'Gender divisions in a post-Fordist era: new contradictions or the same old story?' in McDowell, M. and Pringle, R. (eds) *Defining Women: Social Institutions and Gender Divisions*. Cambridge, Polity Press

McPherson, Sir William (1999) 'The Stephen Lawrence Inquiry Report'. Cm. 4262-1, London Stationary Office

Modood, T., Berthoud, R., Lakey, J., Nazroo, J., Smith, P., Virdee, S. and Beishon, S. (1997) *Ethnic Minorities in Britain*. London, Policy Studies Institute

Oakley, A. (1981) *Subject Women*. Oxford, Martin Robertson

ONS (Office for National Statistics) (2002a) 'Employment by ethnic origin'. *Labour Force Survey*, ONS

ONS (Office for National Statistics) (2002b) 'British Social Attitudes Survey'. www.ons.gov.uk

ONS (Office for National Statistics) (2002c) 'New Earnings Survey'. www.ons.gov.uk

Painter, R.W. and Puttick, K. (1998) *Employment Rights*. London, Pluto Press

Policy Studies Institute (1986) *Black and White Britain*. London, Macmillan

Rees, T. (1998) *Mainstreaming Equality in the European Union*. London, Routledge

Rubery, J. and Grimshaw, P. (2001) *The Gender Pay Gap: A Research Review*. Manchester, EOC

Sly, F., Thair, T. and Risdon, A. (1998) 'Labour market participation of ethnic groups'. *Labour Market Trends*, December, 601–15

Torrington, D. and Hall, L. (1998) *Human Resource Management*. Hemel Hempstead, Prentice Hall Europe

TUC (1997) *Annual Report*. London, TUC

TUC (1998) *Annual Report*. London, TUC

TUC (2002) *Lesbian and Gay Equality at Work*. London, TUC

Webb, J. (1997) 'The politics of equal opportunity'. *Gender, Work and Organisation*, 4, 3, 159–67

Wilson, E. (2000) 'Inclusion, exclusion and ambiguity – the role of organisational culture'. *Personnel Review*, 29, 3, 21–38

CHAPTER 13

UNFAIR DISMISSAL, REDUNDANCY AND TRIBUNAL PROCEDURE

INTRODUCTION

To a great extent unfair dismissal, redundancy and tribunal hearings and machinery are related topics. Although unfair dismissal may be the result of the use of inadequate disciplinary procedures, there are other reasons for an employee being unfairly dismissed such as redundancy and misuse or misapplication of redundancy procedures. Whatever the reason for dismissal, an employee who considers that he or she has been unfairly dismissed may take the case to an employment tribunal which, after considering all the relevant evidence and arguments, will decide in favour of one of the parties. Accordingly, the chapter is in three parts: Part One deals with unfair dismissal while Parts Two and Three concern redundancy and employment tribunals respectively.

Learning outcomes

When you have read this chapter, you should be able to:

1. Explain the nature of, and describe the legislative provisions concerning unfair dismissal.

2. Identify the causes of, and legislative provisions for, redundancy.

3. Explain the operation of redundancy procedures and evaluate the criteria for redundancy selection.

4. Clarify the methods by which complaints can be processed by both ACAS and employment tribunals.

5. Prepare a case for, and explain the workings of, the employment tribunal.

PART ONE: UNFAIR DISMISSAL

Every employee has the right not to be unfairly dismissed, subject to certain exclusions and qualifications identified below. Over the past three decades or so, the legislation governing unfair dismissal has been subject to a number of changes. Amendments cover dismissal for non-union membership (Employment Act 1988), the extension of the application of the unfair dismissal rules to employees who have been dismissed while taking industrial action (Employment Relations Act 1999) and new provisions concerning procedurally unfair dismissals contained in the 2002 Employment Act. Over the years there have been variations in the length of the qualifying period necessary to claim for unfair dismissal, which was raised from 26 weeks in 1979 to two years in 1985, and has since been reduced by the Employment Relations Act 1999 (ERA99) to 12 months. In 1978 an attempt was made to consolidate the legislation in the Employment Protection (Consolidation) Act, but since then amendments have been made by a succession of Employment Acts, the Sex Discrimination Act 1986, the Trade Union Reform and Employment Rights Act 1993 and a number of other pieces of subordinate legislation. As a result, a further consolidation was necessary in the form of the Employment Rights Act 1996 (ERA). For the purposes of this section dealing with unfair dismissal, any references to 'legislation' will be assumed to relate to the ERA unless otherwise stated.

WHAT IS UNFAIR DISMISSAL?

It is usually quite obvious to both employer and employee when an employee has been dismissed. It occurs, for example, when:

- the employee's fixed-term contract expires and is not renewed;
- an employer does not allow an employee who qualifies to return to work after a period of maternity absence; and
- an employee has reason to resign because of certain conduct of the employer – known as *constructive dismissal* (see below).

The law on unfair dismissal does no more than give employees a legal right to be treated in the way in which a fair and reasonable employer would treat them anyway.

Self-Evaluation Activity 13.1

What is fair dismissal?

Response on website

In Chapter 11, we identified what was meant by fair dismissal. By reference to the relevant section in that chapter summarise what 'fair dismissal' means.

Those who may not complain of unfair dismissal

The legislation precludes certain categories of employees from complaining of unfair dismissal (unless employees are asserting a *statutory employment right* – see below). These are:

- those who are not employees (for example independent contractors or freelance agents);
- employees who have not completed one year's continuous employment with the same employer before their effective date of termination (although the qualifying period is not applicable to discrimination cases). This qualification is reduced to one month where an employee is dismissed on medical grounds in consequence of certain health and safety requirements or recommendations;
- employees who, before their effective date of termination, had reached the normal retiring age for their employment or, if there is no normal retiring age, had reached age 65;
- employees with fixed-term contracts for one year or more where the dismissal consists only of the expiry of the contract without renewal and the employee has previously agreed in writing to forego his or her right of complaint in such circumstances;
- employees who ordinarily work outside the UK under their contracts of employment. However,

most merchant seamen on British-registered ships and most employees working on offshore oil and gas installations in the British sector can complain of unfair dismissal;

- members of the police service and armed forces;
- masters and crew members engaged in share fishing who are paid solely by a share in the profits or gross earnings of a fishing vessel;
- employees who have reached a settlement with their employer, either by ACAS conciliation (see below) or on the basis of a 'compromise agreement' reached with the benefit of independent legal advice, in which they have waived their right to make a complaint in relation to the dispute to which the settlement relates; and
- employees covered by a dismissal procedures agreement which has been exempted from the unfair dismissal provisions by an Order made by the Secretary of State for Employment.

Constructive dismissal

The problems surrounding this form of dismissal have given rise to a great deal of case law over the years. Lewis and Sargeant (2002) define constructive dismissal as: 'the situation in which an employee terminates the contract with or without notice by reason of the employer's conduct' (p. 206). Consider also the following perspective on constructive dismissal provided by the DTI (1999):

> A tribunal may rule that an employee who resigns because of conduct by his or her employer has been 'constructively dismissed'. For a tribunal to rule in this way the employer's action has to be such that it can be regarded as a substantial breach of the employment contract indicating that he or she intends no longer to be bound by the contract. An example of this might be where the employer arbitrarily demotes an employee to a lower rank or poorer paid position. The contract is what has been agreed between the parties, whether orally or in writing or a combination of both, together with what must necessarily be implied to make the contract workable.

By virtue of the concept of constructive dismissal, the law treats some resignations as dismissals and therefore extends statutory dismissal rights to those employees who are forced to resign because of their employer's conduct. This form of dismissal may be extremely important in the context of reorganisations due to mergers/takeovers or downsizing or for other reasons, where employers may be seeking to introduce changes in terms and conditions of employment. Under the current definition, which applies to both unfair and redundancy dismissals, it does not matter whether the employee left with or without notice provided he or she was entitled to leave by reason of the employer's conduct. Some of the situations identified by Painter and Puttick (1998) where the employer is deemed to have broken the contractual obligation to the employee include:

- failing to respond to an employee's complaints about the lack of adequate safety equipment;
- undermining the authority of senior staff over subordinates;
- failure to provide an employee with reasonable support to enable him or her to carry out his or her job without disruption and harassment from fellow employees;
- a failure to investigate properly allegations of sexual harassment or to treat the complaint with sufficient seriousness;
- foul language by the employer;
- imposing a disciplinary penalty grossly out of proportion to the offence; and
- a series of minor incidents of harassment over a period of time which cumulatively amount to repudiation: the so-called 'last straw' doctrine.

Self-Evaluation Activity 13.2

Is this constructive dismissal?

Response on website

Consider the following case and suggest whether it warrants being treated as constructive dismissal:

Mr Akhtar was a junior-ranking and low-paid worker who had been employed by United Bank since 1978 in Leeds. A clause in his contract provided:

> The Bank may from time to time require an employee to be transferred temporarily or permanently to any place of business which the Bank may have in the UK for which a location or other allowance may be payable at the discretion of the Bank.

The employer required Mr Akhtar to transfer his place of employment from Leeds to Birmingham at short notice (six days) and with no financial assistance.

Types of unfair dismissal

Dismissal of an employee is held to be automatically or unquestionably unfair, and in most cases does not require the one-year's continuous employment qualifying period before claims are made, for the following reasons:

1. Because of dismissal for **trade union membership and activity,** or because of refusal to join a trade union or a particular trade union. Selection for redundancy on these grounds is also held to be unfair, as is dismissal for refusing to make a payment (for example, to a union or charity) in lieu of union membership, or for objecting to the employer deducting such a sum from wages.
2. Because the employee was dismissed or selected for redundancy on **maternity-related grounds** – that is, because she is pregnant or for a reason connected with her pregnancy or childbirth (see Chapter 11).
3. Because the employee was dismissed or selected for redundancy for taking or proposing to take certain specified types of action on **health and safety grounds.** For example by carrying out (or proposing to carry out) duties as a safety representative or as a member of a safety committee; by bringing to the employer's attention a concern about circumstances at work which they believe are harmful to health or safety; by leaving the place of work or refusing to return to it in dangerous circumstances which the employee reasonably believed to be serious or imminent and which could not be averted; by taking or proposing to take appropriate steps to protect themselves and other persons from the danger.
4. Because the employee was dismissed or selected for redundancy for having sought, in good faith, to assert a **statutory employment protection right** or had alleged an infringement of such a right. The relevant statutory rights are those

conferred by the ERA 1996 and relate to (as examples):
- written statement of employment particulars;
- itemised pay statement;
- remuneration during suspension on medical grounds;
- time off for ante-natal care;
- protection against unlawful deductions from pay; minimum period of notice;
- deduction of unauthorised or excessive union subscriptions;
- action short of dismissal on trade union grounds; and
- protection against detriment in cases relating to Sunday shop or betting work (see also point 8 below).

Similar protection is provided for employees who are dismissed for certain actions under the Transnational Information and Consultation of Employees Regulations 1999 or the Part Time Work Regulations 2000 or because they qualify for:
- the national minimum wage;
- working families tax credit;
- disabled person's tax credit

5. Because the employee was dismissed while **taking industrial action.** The provision in the ERA99 is that where an employee is dismissed by reason of the fact that he or she is taking part in 'protected' industrial action, then this dismissal will be automatically unfair. There is some difficulty with this provision because it has to be ascertained whether the union has protection from being sued for organising the action, which takes employment tribunals into new territory. Another difficulty is that some employees may be left without a remedy, 'namely those who have been dismissed by reason of their own breach of contract in taking strike action, rather than the fact of their participation in the collective action' (IDS, 1999).
6. Because the employee was dismissed arising out of a **conviction which is spent** under the terms of the Rehabilitation of Offenders Act 1974.
7. Because the employee was dismissed in connection with the **transfer of an undertaking** (see pp. 637–40). Essentially, where an undertaking or part of an undertaking is transferred from one employer to another (for example, through the

sale of the undertaking or part of the undertaking), if either the old or the new employer dismisses an employee solely or mainly because the undertaking has been transferred, the dismissal will be considered unfair. There is, however, a major exception to this, in that if a dismissal associated with the transfer, either by the old or new employer, is necessary for economic, technical or organisational reasons, entailing changes in the workforce, it may be considered fair if a tribunal finds that this is the main reason for dismissal and if it also finds that the employer acted reasonably in treating this reason as sufficient to justify dismissal.

8. Because the employee was dismissed, selected for redundancy or subjected to other detrimental action for refusing or proposing to refuse to do shop or betting shop work on Sundays. This applies to shop and betting shop workers who were in their current employment when the Sunday Trading Act came into force in 1994. It also applies to those subsequently employed who are contractually required to work on a Sunday, provided they have given three months' written notice of their intention to opt out of Sunday working at the end of the notice period but not before.

Did the employer act reasonably?

Apart from the unquestionably unfair dismissal categories identified above, an employment tribunal will have to consider whether the employer acted reasonably in relation to the disciplinary issues which we considered in Chapter 11 governing capability and conduct, in the circumstance of an employee who brings his or her case for unfair dismissal to that tribunal. (Reread the relevant section in Chapter 11 to remind yourself of the subcategories of capability and conduct.)

Before 1980, the burden of proof in unfair dismissal claims was on the employer. The Employment Act 1980 amended this provision (which was in the Employment Protection (Consolidition) Act 1978) so that the burden of proof became neutral. Another amendment by the 1980 Act required tribunals to consider the size and administrative resources of the organisation or company in assessing the reasonableness of a dismissal. This latter provision encouraged tribunals 'to be less exacting in their examination of the disciplinary standards and procedures of small employers' (Painter and Puttick, 1998, p. 194).

The test of reasonableness

In considering the test of reasonableness, the question is what a reasonable employer would have done in the circumstances and not what a particular tribunal would have thought right. In its present form the test is, specifically, whether the dismissal fell within 'band of reasonable responses to the employee's conduct within which one employer might take one view, another quite reasonably another' (*Iceland Frozen Foods* v *Jones*, 1982, IRLR 432). In relation to this, Painter and Puttick (1998) point out:

> *Provided the employment tribunal follows the 'band of reasonable responses' and does not substitute its own view, it will have considerable discretion in reaching its decision and it will only be in rare cases that its decision will be overturned on appeal. This is because the fairness of the dismissal is essentially a question of fact, and so long as the tribunal has properly directed itself as to the law then its decision will only be overturned if it was perverse – that is, if no reasonable tribunal could possibly have come to that decision on the particular facts.* (p. 194)

The tribunal in assessing the reasonableness of the dismissal, may also consider two further issues concerning:

• the substantive merits of the case; and
• procedural fairness.

Substantive merits

In relation to substantive merits, the employment tribunal will take into account mitigating factors such as the employee's length of service, previous disciplinary record and any explanation or excuse. It is also crucial to maintain consistency of treatment in the application of disciplinary rules so that employees who behave much in the same way as each other would receive much the same punishment.

Self-Evaluation Activity 13.3

Two dismissal incidents

Response on website

Consider the two incidents described below. What decision do you think the employment tribunal should have made in both these situations?

1. An employee of the Royal Mail was instantly dismissed following an assault on a fellow worker in the works canteen.
2. A hospital laundry worker was dismissed on grounds of misconduct for fighting with another employee while on duty. Mr Cain claimed that his dismissal was unfair because in the past other employees guilty of acts of gross misconduct, including fighting, had not been dismissed.

Procedural fairness

The second criterion concerns the fairness of procedures adopted by the employer in the events leading up to the dismissal. It has been argued that, as part of best practice, employers should develop a set of comprehensive formal procedures governing, *inter alia*, grievances and discipline (see Chapter 11). The Employment Act 2002 now places a legal obligation on all employers to adopt, as a minimum, statutory disputes and disciplinary procedures (DDPs) and grievance procedures (GPs), examples of which are contained in the Act. In addition, disciplinary rules may be regarded as preliminary warnings to employees that the employer regards certain types of offence seriously and that these will be likely to result in instant dismissal. However, it should be noted that 'there is no such thing as an "automatic" dismissal rule and employers must be prepared to exercise discretion, having allowed the employee to state his/her case and having considered such matters as the seriousness of the infringement of the rule, the employee's length of service and previous disciplinary record' (Painter and Puttick, 1998, p. 198). The following example illustrates this point:

> In Ladbroke Racing v Arnott (1983), the applicants were employed in a betting shop. The employer's disciplinary rules specifically provided that employees were not permitted to place bets or to allow other staff to do so. Two of the applicants had placed such bets, one for her brother on one occasion and the other occasionally for old-age pensioners; the third, the office manager, had condoned these actions. All three employees were dismissed and a tribunal found the dismissals to be unfair. This decision was upheld by the EAT and the Court of Session on the basis that rules framed in mandatory terms did not leave the employer free from the obligation to act reasonably and to take into account the relatively minor nature of the offences in this particular case. (ibid., p. 198)

A further example of procedural fairness relates to disciplinary hearings during which the person to be interviewed should be given the opportunity to state his or her case and be advised of any rights under the procedure including the right to be represented. Employees also have the right to be informed of the nature of the allegations made against them, that they should be allowed to state their case, and that those conducting the interview should be free from bias. The emphasis here is upon the person holding the inquiry who must be seen to be impartial and that justice must not only be done but also seen to be done. The following example cited by Painter and Puttick is relevant here:

> An illustration of the application of these principles is to be found in the decision of the EAT in Mayes v Hylton Castle Working Men's Social Club and Institute (1986), where two witnesses to an alleged act of sexual harassment by a club steward towards a barmaid were also members of the committee which dismissed the steward. The EAT held the dismissal to be unfair on the ground that it was a breach of natural justice for an apparently biased committee to decide the disciplinary matter. While the general rule is that if a person has been a witness s/he should not conduct the inquiry, the EAT did identify certain exceptions – for example, a firm which is owned and run by one person. (p. 199)

Procedurally unfair dismissals and the Employment Act 2002

The Employment Act 2002 has changed the law on unfair dismissal in two important respects where, firstly, an employer has failed to follow an applicable DDP and/or where, secondly, the employer has complied with the relevant DDP but has in some other way failed to follow a fair procedure. In the first respect, where an employee has been dismissed because the relevant DDP has not been completed, the employee will be treated as having been unfairly dismissed. Essentially, this creates another category of *automatically unfair dismissal* (see above), which arises where an employer has failed to comply with the statutory DDPs. For example, if the standard procedure applies but the employee is not invited to a disciplinary meeting, then the dismissal will be unfair regardless of whether the employer can demonstrate that the meeting would have made no difference and the employee would have been dismissed anyway. This strengthens the current position set out in the *Polkey* case (see Mini case 13.1) in which it was held that a failure to follow a fair procedure would render a dismissal unfair unless the employer could show that it would have been 'futile' in the circumstances of the case to follow a fair procedure. The 'futile' exception no longer applies where the employer has breached a DDP. It is important to note that this category of automatically unfair dismissal requires the employee to have completed one year's continuous service in order to qualify. In addition an employees right to be accompanied does not form part of the statutory DDP and a breach of that right will not render the dismissal automatically unfair.

Mini case 13.1
***Polkey* v *A.E. Dayton Services Ltd* (1987) IRLR 503**

Mr Polkey was one of four van drivers. The employer decided to cut costs, reduce the number of drivers to three and add salesman duties. Mr Polkey was called into the office and dismissed on grounds of redundancy without further ado. The employers had taken a view that he was unsuitable for the revised job and acted without consultation. At the employment tribunal, EAT and Court of Appeal the employers successfully pursued a line of argument given force in the earlier EAT case *British Labour Pump Co. Ltd* v *Byrne* (1979) IRLR 94 that lack of procedure (in the *Polkey* circumstances non-consultation) would have made no difference to the outcome. The case was then heard by the House of Lords which found the earlier decisions in favour of the employers' argument unacceptable. Their Lordships argued that:

The one question the industrial tribunal is not permitted to ask in applying the test of reasonableness posed by the EP(C)A 1978, s. 57(3) is the hypothetical question, whether it would have made any difference to the outcome if the appropriate procedural steps had been taken. On the true construction this question is simply irrelevant.

The point continued that in rare circumstances it might be argued and accepted that it had been reasonable not to use a procedure because it would have been 'utterly useless' or 'futile'. Otherwise lack of procedure would lead to a finding of unfair dismissal.

Compensation

However, *Polkey* also established that, when the tribunal comes to calculating compensation for the unfair dismissal, it could take into account the probability that – even if the employer had taken those steps which it failed to take before dismissing – a fair procedure would not have affected the outcome (that is, the decision to dismiss). Lord Bridge stated:

If it is held that taking the appropriate steps which the employer failed to take before dismissing the employee would not have affected the outcome, this will often lead to the result that the employee, though unfairly dismissed, will recover no compensation, or, in the case of redundancy, no compensation in excess of his redundancy payment.

Tribunals in subsequent cases have applied the Lords' decision concerning reductions in compensation, which became known as '*Polkey* reductions' defined by IRS (1999) as:

A percentage reduction, which may be made from any compensatory award for unfair dismissal, reflecting the chance that the employee would still have been dismissed even if the employer had carried out a fair procedure.

In the second respect, if the employer has followed a DDP but has not otherwise conducted a fair procedure (which may, for example, be set out in the employer's own company handbook or in the ACAS (2000) Code of Practice on Disciplinary and Grievance Procedures) then this does not make the dismissal necessarily unfair. The failure to follow a fair procedure will be one of the factors to consider in deciding whether, in the circumstances, the decision to dismiss fell outside the band of reasonable responses open to the employer (see Figure 13.1 concerning the steps involved in deciding an unfair dismissal case under the new provisions). The result is that an employer will not have to comply with a fair dismissal procedure on top of the DDPs if (and only if) he can show, first, that such a procedure would have made no difference to the outcome and, secondly, that the reason for the dismissal is substantively fair.

UNFAIR DISMISSAL REMEDIES

Many disputes concerning the fairness or unfairness of dismissals are settled through agreed voluntary procedures without the employee making a complaint to an employment tribunal. However, an employee can apply to an employment tribunal in order to bring his or her case to a tribunal hearing (we deal with tribunal procedure in Part Three of this chapter). Since the employee makes an application to the tribunal for a hearing, he or she is called

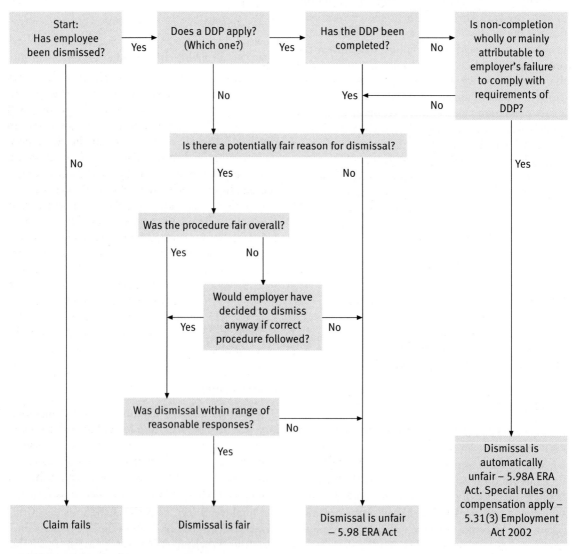

Figure 13.1 Unfair dismissal flow chart
Source: IDS, 2002, p. 93

the applicant. The tribunal must be satisfied that the applicant is qualified to make a claim and must therefore be satisfied on the following criteria:

- that the applicant is an employee;
- that the applicant's employment does not fall within an excluded category and has the requisite continuity of employment; and
- that the applicant has presented the claim in time.

Self-Evaluation Activity 13.4

Testing the validity of a claim for unfair dismissal/redundancy payments
Response on website

In order to determine whether a claim for unfair dismissal and/or redundancy payments is valid, the following questions should be asked. Answer 'yes' or 'no' to each question in order to find out whether the claim has been accepted or rejected by the tribunal.

1. Has a dismissal taken place?
2. Is the applicant qualified to make a claim?
3. Did the employer establish an admissible reason for the dismissal?
4. Was the dismissal reasonable in all the circumstances?
5. Was a statutory DDP procedure fully engaged?

The remedies

The remedies for unfair dismissal should the employee be successful in his or her claim are re-employment and compensation.

Re-employment

Employment tribunals will provide applicants with the alternatives of reinstatement and re-engagement and will ask them if they wish an order for either to be made. Reinstatement will involve the employee getting his or her old job back on the same terms and conditions of employment at the same level of pay and seniority, together with a compensatory payment for the period the employee was unemployed to the time the tribunal order was made. Re-engagement means that the employee obtains suitable alternative employment with the old employer under a new contract of employment plus compensation for any time out of work.

In deciding whether to make a reinstatement or re-engagement order, the tribunal will take into account:

- the employee's wishes;
- whether it is practicable for the employee to return to work for the employer (there may, for example, be circumstances in which this option is not practicable because relationships at the workplace have been seriously damaged); and
- in cases where the employee was partly to blame for the dismissal, whether or not it would be fair and just to make such an order.

If the employer fails to comply with the terms of an order for reinstatement or re-engagement the tribunal, on being notified of the failure, will make an award of compensation calculated in the usual manner provided for in the legislation. The tribunal will also make an additional award of compensation to be paid by the employer, unless the employer satisfies the tribunal that it was not practicable to comply with the order in the first place. In practice, the take-up rate for both reinstatement and re-engagement is extremely low. On average, between 1997 and 2003, around 1–2 per cent of unfair dismissal claims settled in favour of the applicant were resolved on the basis of the applicant being re-employed. The main reason for this is that the employee simply does not want his or her old job back (assuming it is still there to be taken back).

Compensation

The vast majority of awards are of a compensatory nature. Compensation for unfair dismissal will usually comprise a basic award and a compensatory award. However, where the main reason for dismissal concerned trade union membership or health and safety issues and if the employee has asked the tribunal to order reinstatement or re-engagement but is not, as a result, reinstated or re-engaged, a special award will be made. Finally, there is an additional award, which compensates the employee because of the employer's failure to comply with a tribunal order for reinstatement or re-engagement.

How the awards are calculated

The basic award

The basic award is calculated by adding up the following amounts. (It is important to note that only continuous employment subject to a maximum of 20 years can count.)

- One-and-a-half weeks' pay for each complete year of employment when an employee was between the ages of 41 and 65.
- One week's pay for each complete year of employment when an employee was between the ages of 22 to 40 inclusive.
- Half a week's pay for each complete year of employment when an employee was below the age of 22.

A week's pay is calculated according to the ERA 1996 provisions and is based on gross pay subject to a maximum of £250 (the 2002 figure) reviewed annually. For example, an employee aged 35 with 10 years' continuous service earning £300 gross a week will receive 1 week's pay, £250 multiplied by 10 years = £2500 basic award. The basic award can be reduced if the employee:

- contributed to some extent to the dismissal, or his or her conduct prior to the dismissal otherwise justified the reduction;
- has already been awarded or has received a redundancy payment;
- was within a year of age 65 at the effective date of termination;
- unreasonably refused an offer of reinstatement or unreasonably prevented the employer from complying with an order of reinstatement.

The minimum amount of basic award for unfair dismissal in 2003, however, was £3500.

The compensatory award

This award compensates the employee for the loss suffered as a result of the dismissal insofar as the employer is responsible for this loss. As well as covering loss of earnings between the hearing and an estimate of future loss, the tribunal will also consider matters such as loss of pension and other rights and any reasonable expenses incurred by the employee as a result of the dismissal. The compensatory award is an amount the tribunal 'considers just and equitable in all the circumstances having regard to the loss sustained by the complainant (employee) in consequence of the dismissal' (ERA 1996, s. 123). The maximum compensatory award was raised from £12 000 to £50 000 by ERA99 and in 2003 to £52 600 by the Employment Tribunals (Constitution and Rules of Procedure) Regulations. However, the tribunal will reduce the award if:

- it finds that the employee was partly to blame for the dismissal or the employee did not mitigate his or her loss (for example, by failing to make a reasonable effort to obtain another job);
- payments are made by the employer to the employee (for example, wages in lieu of notice or an ex gratia payment);
- the employee receives earnings from any other employment between dismissal and the tribunal hearing (for example, if the employee earns £500, then the award is reduced by that amount).

The compensatory award and 'Polkey reductions': the Employment Act 2002

(Before reading the following section, reread Mini case 13.1 dealing with Polkey.)

Following on from the *Polkey* decision is the principle that, in cases where the employer has dismissed for a substantively fair reason but has failed to follow a fair procedure, if he can show that a fair procedure would have resulted in dismissal anyway, then the compensatory award (but not the basic award) may be reduced – potentially to nil – because no injustice will have resulted to the employee. This 'Polkey reduction' principle remains in force alongside the provisions of the Act. It therefore appears that in cases where the relevant DDP has been followed, but the decision is found to be procedurally unfair in other respects, any Polkey reduction should not exceed 50 per cent, but reductions of up to 100 per cent are still possible. The examples in Exhibit 13.1 illustrate some of these aspects.

In calculating the compensatory award, taking the relevant provisions of the Employment Act 2002 (EA 2002) into consideration, the employee's loss as a result of the dismissal should be calculated and adjustments made as follows:

Exhibit 13.1

Three examples of Polkey reductions in relation to the Employment Act 2002

Example 1

Where an employer has dismissed without following the applicable DDP (for example, by failing to offer the right to an appeal), the dismissal will be automatically unfair. However, the employer can still argue that he had a substantively fair reason for dismissal and that following a fair procedure would therefore have made no difference to the outcome. The tribunal may reduce the compensatory award to nil if it concludes that the employee would have been dismissed anyway for the substantively fair reason or may reduce it by a percentage of between nought and 100 to reflect the chance that there would have been such a dismissal.

Example 2

Where an employer has followed the applicable DDP but has not in other respects followed a fair procedure, the dismissal will still be fair if the employer demonstrates on the balance of probabilities (that is, more than a 50 per cent chance) that dismissal would have resulted anyway.

Example 3

If, in Example 2, the tribunal finds a less than 50 per cent chance that dismissal would have resulted (that is, not sufficient to satisfy the balance of probabilities), then the dismissal will be unfair. However, the tribunal may reduce the compensatory award by a figure of between nought and 50 per cent to reflect the chance of dismissal.

- deduction of any payment already made by the employer as compensation for the dismissal (for example, an ex gratia payment), other than an enhanced redundancy payment;
- deduction of sums earned by way of mitigation, or to reflect the employee's failure to take reasonable steps in mitigation;
- percentage reduction under the Polkey principle;
- increase or reduction where the employer or employee failed to comply with an applicable DDP or GP (EA 2002);
- increase for the employer's failure to provide written particulars of employment (EA 2002);
- percentage reduction for the employee's contributory fault;
- deduction of any enhanced redundancy payment to the extent that it exceeds the basic award, and
- application of the statutory cap of £52 600.

The additional award

In most cases the additional award will be for an amount equivalent to not less than 13 weeks' pay and not more than 26 weeks' pay. Where, however, the dismissal was in breach of either the Sex Discrimination Act 1975 or the Race Relations Act 1976, then the additional award will be for an amount equivalent to not less than 26 weeks' pay and not more than 52 weeks' pay. The maximum week's pay used to calculate the award is £250. It is important to note that tribunals may exceed these limits if the total compensation awarded (apart from the basic award) would otherwise be less than the arrears of pay element of the original award with which the employer failed to comply.

The special award

As a result of amendments introduced by the EA 2002, the amount of compensation to be awarded to employees who are unfairly dismissed (or selected for redundancy), on the grounds of trade union membership and activities or non-membership is much higher than for other types of dismissal because a 'special award' is made in addition to the basic and compensatory elements. Also, where dismissal is union-related there is a minimum basic award which was set at £3500 in 2003. The special award can be made only where the employee (or applicant) requests the employment tribunal to make an order for reinstatement or re-engagement. Where reinstatement/re-engagement is sought by the dismissed employee, there are two different levels of compensation laid down depending on the following two circumstances:

- where reinstatement/re-engagement is requested but no such order is made by the tribunal, then the special award will comprise 104 weeks' pay subject to a minimum of £14 500 and a maximum of £29 000;
- where reinstatement/re-engagement is ordered by the tribunal but the order is not complied with. In this instance, unless the employer can satisfy the tribunal that it was not practicable to comply with the order, the special award will be 156 weeks' pay subject to a minimum of £21 800 and no maximum figure.

A tribunal can reduce a special award if, amongst other things, the employee's conduct before dismissal justifies a reduction, or if the employee has unreasonably refused an offer of reinstatement from the employer, or has unreasonably prevented the employer from complying with an order for reinstatement.

Interest on tribunal awards

Legislation provides that an employer who does not pay the compensation awarded by the tribunal within 42 days of the tribunal's decision, will be required to pay simple interest on the amount outstanding.

SOME CRITICISMS OF THE LAW OF UNFAIR DISMISSAL

Most of the criticisms concerning the law of unfair dismissal (Collins, 1992) have focused on the argument that it does not necessarily control effectively managements' perceived rights to dismiss employees. It could also be argued that as the employer does not have to comply with a fair dismissal procedure in addition to the DDP if that procedure could be shown to have made no difference to the outcome, and if the dismissal is substantively fair, the law existing before 2002 has effectively been reversed

(EA 2002, s. 98) and therefore represents a retrograde legislative step. Furthermore, judicial interpretation is often biased in favour of the employer. Painter and Puttick (1998) argue that:

> An explanation of the weakness of the law lies in the attitude of appeal court judges to the legislation. The judges are not happy with the unfair dismissal provisions because they are perceived to be 'corporatist' in that they overstep the boundary between matters which are suitable for state intervention and those which are not. The judges feel unhappy about meddling in affairs they have always thought should be left to individuals to resolve. Consequently the courts and tribunals are unwilling to substitute their own standards of fairness for management opinion and instead have the tendency to endorse the ordinary practices of employers. Once this occurs it is inevitable that the concept of fairness will tend to favour managerial control. (p. 222)

Painter and Puttick identify the following areas in order to demonstrate tribunal and judicial bias:

The concept of the reasonable employer: The main issue here is what actions the 'reasonable employer' would take in the circumstances, and *not* what the employment tribunal would have thought, and 'in this sense the courts do not set the norms of behaviour but merely reflect existing managerial standards' (p. 222). The authors cite the case shown in Mini case 13.2 as evidence.

Mini case 13.2
Saunders v Scottish National Camps Association Ltd (1980) IRLR 174

The employee was a maintenance worker at a children's camp. He was dismissed on the grounds of being a homosexual. The dismissal was held to be fair because a considerable proportion of employers would take the view that the employment of a homosexual should be restricted, particularly when required to work in close proximity to children. Instead of setting its own standards, the court in this case accepted the commonly held and highly prejudiced views of some employers.

Source: Painter and Puttick, 1998, p. 222

Overriding contractual rights: A dismissal may be held to be fair even though the employer breaks the contract. 'So the courts and tribunals have been prepared to hold as fair dismissals where the employee has refused to agree to a change in terms and conditions of employment in line with the employer's perception of business efficiency' (ibid., p. 223).

The dilution of procedural fairness: Another criticism of judicial and tribunal interpretation of the process of unfair dismissal has been the tendency for judges, at least from time to time, to de-emphasise the importance of the need to follow a fair procedure. However, 'since the *Polkey* decision it may well be that flouting procedures will result in a finding of unfair dismissal in a much increased proportion of cases. But employees in such cases may find they have achieved a Pyrrhic victory because the tribunal may reduce their compensation to nil if it is found that they were in any way at fault for their dismissal' (ibid., p. 223). For purposes of clarification, the *Polkey* case has been described briefly in Mini case 13.1.

Summary

- Many dismissals are 'unfair' if the employee has been dismissed owing to the unfair and unreasonable behaviour of the employer. However, some groups of employees are prevented by the legislation from complaining of unfair dismissal.

- Constructive dismissal may be regarded as a particular type of unfair dismissal where an employee feels compelled to resign owing to the conduct of the employer.
- Dismissal of an employee is automatically and unquestionably unfair on a number of statutory grounds.
- An employment tribunal in deciding whether a dismissal is unfair will take into consideration the 'test of reasonableness' in relation to the substantive merits of the case and the fairness of the procedures adopted by the employer.
- The Employment Act 2002 provides that, where an employee has been dismissed in circumstances where an applicable DDP has not been completed, and non-completion is wholly or mainly attributable to the failure of the employer to comply with the requirements of the DDP, the employee will be treated as having been unfairly dismissed. This creates a new category of automatically unfair dismissal, which arises where an employer has failed to comply with the statutory DDPs.
- The remedies for unfair dismissal are re-employment, which includes reinstatement and re-engagement, and compensation awarded. Special and additional awards are made in particular cases and situations.
- The law of unfair dismissal has been criticised for tribunal and judicial bias in favour of the employer.

PART TWO: REDUNDANCY

In general terms, redundancy means that the employer no longer requires the services of employees, whether it be one person or the entire workforce. One of the most important aspects of the traditional employment relationship, as we have pointed out elsewhere in this book, concerns the power of management (legitimised in terms of 'managerial prerogative') to 'hire and fire', more or less at will. Now circumscribed by the legislation that we have considered in this chapter and also in Chapters 11 and 12, employers find it more difficult to dismiss employees for the various reasons previously discussed. Those made redundant may be given very little explanation

of the reasons for it, which reflects the fact that the redundancy decision-making process in both legal and practical terms is almost entirely under the control of the employer.

In addition to the general definition of redundancy, redundancy has a specific legal meaning as set out in the ERA 1996 which defines a redundancy as a dismissal which is 'wholly or mainly attributable to':

- the fact that the employer has ceased, or intends to cease, to carry on the business for the purpose of which the employee was employed; or

- the fact that the employer has ceased, or intends to cease, to carry on that business in the place where the employee was employed; or
- the fact that the requirements of the business for employees to carry out work of a particular kind, or for employees to carry out work of a particular kind in the place where the employee was so employed, have ceased or diminished or are expected to cease or diminish permanently or temporarily and for whatever reason.

The key to the legal definition of redundancy 'is not the fact that the amount of work has diminished, but rather that the employer requires fewer employees' (IRS, 1998).

Self-Evaluation Activity 13.5

Reasons for making employees redundant
Response on website

Identify some of the possible reasons for making employees redundant.

The incidence of redundancies nationally normally reflects the trends in unemployment. For example, the number of officially recorded redundancies fell significantly during the late 1980s but increased sharply during the recession years of the early 1990s. From 1998 to 2001 the rate of redundancies slowed down somewhat but more recently, during the latter half of 2001, redundancies rose to 179 000, compared with 157 000 in the equivalent period of 2000. Moreover, the increase in redundancies during 2001 was the highest for any equivalent period since 1995 (IRS, 2001). There are, however, significant regional variations. For example, in the North West, ten in every 10 000 workers lost their jobs in the autumn of 1997, almost twice the rate at which posts were shed in the South East. In addition, jobs in certain industries are at greater risk than in others, with employment in construction being particularly unstable. On average during the autumn of 1997, construction workers were almost seven times more likely to lose their jobs than were employees in public administration, education and health. Over the same period personal and protective service jobs disappeared at the rate of five per 1000 employees. But in craft and related occupations,

they were lost at the rate of thirteen per 1000. Age is also a factor, with workers between 16 and 24 most likely to be made redundant, probably because they are the cheaper to dismiss and have the least experience. Among this group, jobs are lost at a rate of nine per 1000 employees. Conversely, the posts of those aged 45 to 54 and those over 55 appear to be the safest with jobs lost at the rate of six per 1000 employees (IRS, 1998). During the course of 2001, redundancies had increased significantly in manufacturing industry, the wholesale, retail and motor trade, and in transport and communication services, and this trend was reinforced during 2002 and 2003. There have also been more losses in hotels and catering as a result of sharp falls in overseas visitors (LMT, 2001).

THE LEGAL CONTEXT OF REDUNDANCY

As we noted earlier in the chapter, redundancy is one of the potentially fair reasons for dismissal. The law dealing with redundancy is contained in ERA which consolidated earlier redundancy law, including the first piece of redundancy legislation – the Redundancy Payments Act 1965, which introduced statutory compensation for redundancy and provided a measure of statutory protection for employees. One of the main objectives of the Redundancy Payments Act was to encourage labour mobility in response to employers' demands for labour and skills. The Act was also regarded as part of government policy to remove industrial relations conflict at the workplace (which the Donovan Commission in its report suggested was endemic), and has been criticised for individualising and 'judicialising' the employment relationship (Fryer, 1973). Furthermore, Painter and Puttick (1998) point out:

> *Despite its many elaborate provisions the legislation does not, in fact, do anything to give workers any greater job security; nor, arguably, has it in any way really restricted managerial power in redundancy situations. These, and other limitations in the present scheme were in fact quickly realised within a few years of the 1965 Act coming into operation. Arguably the rules we now have simply institutionalise redundancy as a relatively easy way of sacking unwanted workers.* (p. 228)

From the employee's perspective, the main characteristics of the present system, according to Painter and Puttick, are that:

- there is no such thing as a 'right' to a job;
- should a redundancy situation exist, employees may be dismissed without any comeback in a tribunal or court if the right procedural steps are taken;
- procedural rights, for example, to be given information, to be consulted, are generally limited, although the European Union has imposed certain procedural requirements in relation to 'mass' redundancies;
- compensation is limited; and
- collective action to fight redundancy can be punished by withdrawal of compensation rights.

The minimum rights laid down in the ERA can be improved through individual or collective negotiation, of which the latter is more effective, but do not normally guarantee job security. Negotiated improvements can include:

- regular provision by the employer of information on any aspect that may affect future job levels, such as profitability, plans for new technology and threats to the viability of the business;
- consultation and other procedural rights prior to redundancy decisions being made;
- agreed limits on redundancy dismissals on the circumstances in which jobs can be declared redundant; and
- enhanced compensation above statutory levels.

The basic statutory rights

These are the *minimum* rights which employees have, provided that the employee has been in continuous employment for two years, now reduced to one year by ministerial order stemming from the ERA99. In most cases the employee will need to show that he or she has been dismissed in much the same way as applies for unfair dismissal (see Part One of this chapter). For redundancy purposes as indicated by the ERA, an employee is 'dismissed' if the contract is terminated with or without notice; a fixed-term contract is not renewed; the employee decides to leave (with or without notice) in a situation in which

the conduct of the employer makes this permissible; the employer's business goes into receivership or liquidation or he or she dies. Most redundancy dismissals will have periods of notice which should be worked out in full, otherwise there is a risk of losing some or all of the redundancy pay.

Redundancy payments

The amount of redundancy pay depends entirely on the employee's contractual redundancy entitlement or, if no such provision exists, on the statutory scheme provided for in the ERA. Statutory redundancy pay is calculated by taking account of the age of the employee and his or her length of service. The number of weeks' pay will depend upon the employee's age at the time of the redundancy, although employment before the age of 18 is not included in calculations. The method of calculation is the same as that for the unfair dismissal basic award. Statutory payments are calculated in the following way:

- one and a half weeks' pay for each year of service in which the employer was over the age of 41 but below the normal retiring age (or 65, whichever is the lower);
- one week's pay for each year of service in which the employee was over age 22 and under 41; and
- half a week's pay for each year of service between the age of 18 and 22.

In calculating statutory entitlement, a week's pay cannot be more than £250 (the maximum applicable from 1 February 2002) and the maximum number of years of service which can be taken into account is 20. This means that the maximum statutory redundancy pay where the employee is aged 41 or over is currently £7500 The ERA stipulates that the employer is obliged to provide the employee and relevant trade union(s) with written details of how the redundancy pay is calculated. If there is any dispute or likelihood of non-payment, an employee who is to be dismissed as redundant must make a written claim for a redundancy payment from his or her employer within six months after the date of termination. If no payment is made, or the amount is in dispute, the employee may apply to an employment tribunal for a determination of the issue. Alternatively the employee could claim a redundancy payment by directly applying to an employment tribunal within six months of the date of termination.

Certain terms of any collective agreement may become incorporated into an individual employee's contract of employment, and will, therefore, become legally enforceable. Thus, redundancy terms might be a contractual entitlement on which an employee could sue if payment was not forthcoming or less than expected. Prior to 1990, the employer was statutorily entitled to reclaim from the government part of any redundancy payment made to an individual employee, which, as Gennard and Judge (1997) point out, 'was an important factor for an employer to take into consideration when considering an enhanced [redundancy] payment' (p. 248). Since 1990, when the rebate came to an end, the employer must now meet the total cost of the redundancy payment.

Instances of when a redundancy payment may be reduced or annulled

In certain situations and circumstances redundancy payments can be reduced or cancelled. These circumstances include:

- a reduction of the total payment by one-twelfth for each whole month in which the employee is over the age of 64;
- a reduction or loss of the total payment where the employee is dismissed for gross misconduct (other than taking part in a strike) during the obligatory notice period;
- no payment where the employee unreasonably refuses an offer of suitable alternative employment; and
- a reduction or no payment in circumstances where the employee is entitled to receive a pension on redundancy, or within 90 weeks of redundancy.

IMPORTANT STATUTORY AND JUDICIAL ISSUES

Apart from redundancy-related unfair dismissal, together with establishing both whether a redundancy actually took place and the right of the employee to

be compensated, the ERA establishes that a redundancy exists, firstly, if the dismissal is attributable 'wholly or mainly' to the fact that the employer has or intends to cease trading at the place where the employee is employed, or has or intends to cease trading altogether; and, secondly, due to the fact that the type of work normally done by employees at their normal workplace has ceased or diminished or is expected to do so. In the event of a closure of an employer's business, there is no question of not receiving redundancy pay, but there are problems with redundancy pay (and other pay-related factors) should the business become bankrupt. Bankruptcy or insolvency means either that a company is going into voluntary or compulsory liquidation; or that a receiver has been appointed; or that an 'administration' order has been made with an administrator running the company for the time being. Should an employer be made redundant during the course of the insolvency procedure, a redundancy claim can be made against the liquidator, receiver or equivalent. Failing that, a claim can be made on the National Insurance Fund. If a workplace closes, or an employee's work is no longer needed there, then that employee will normally be entitled to redundancy compensation. However, problems may arise if, rather than being made redundant, employees are asked to move to a different location. Such a move may be unacceptable to the employee for a variety of reasons and, in the absence of a mobility clause, there may be cause for a 'constructive dismissal' claim. However, in cases such as this, should an employee unreasonably refuse alternative work at another location, then that employee will not be eligible for redundancy compensation. If there is a mobility clause under such circumstances, redundancy claims will most certainly fail.

What if requirements for labour have been reduced or altered?

This can manifest itself, for example, in manpower reductions owing to a decline in the volume of work and orders or to technological changes resulting in a displacement of labour and/or changes in work arrangements and practices. The ERA defines these types of situations as diminishing requirements and it will be necessary for the employer to demonstrate that there has been a clear reduction in the need for the person to undertake work of the particular type which he or she is employed to do. The following criteria are important in determining whether a redundancy has taken place on the 'diminishing requirements' basis.

Changing the work requirements

The question to be asked here is whether there is a diminished need for the kind of work a claimant for redundancy does, and hence deciding whether a redundancy situation exists. Very often this involves looking at the contract in order to identify what an employee *should* be doing compared with what an employee is *actually* doing, which is what employment tribunals have considered when distinguishing between unfair dismissal and redundancy.

Self-Evaluation Activity 13.6

The 'contract test'

Response on website

Painter and Puttick (1998) cite the following example demonstrating the important issue of the 'contract test'. Was the outcome *unfair dismissal* or *redundancy*?

Mr Pink was employed at a shoe factory as a 'making and finishing' room operative, but in practice he spent most of his time specifically as a 'sole layer/pre-sole fitter'. While he had been away a trainee had been brought in to carry out sole laying work, and when redundancies were declared Mr Pink was selected rather than that person. (p. 234)

In recent years the contract test has not been the sole deciding factor. An EAT decision in 1997 stressed that tribunals should consider a three-stage approach involving the following questions:

- Was the employee dismissed?
- If so, had the requirements of the business for employees to carry out work of a particular kind 'ceased or diminished' (or were they expected to do so)?
- And, if so, was the dismissal *caused* wholly or mainly by that state of affairs?

Changing skill requirements

Changing skill requirements may prompt employers to dismiss staff surplus to requirements. It is questionable whether in such circumstances redundancy compensation is an adequate remedy when there is an element of unfairness in selecting employees for dismissal where the basis for selection includes dismissing people with a long service record or when employees are forced to make way for others who are less expensive to employ. In the following case, *Murphy* v *Epsom College* (1984) IRLR 271, again cited by Painter and Puttick (1998), the employment tribunal had to decide between unfair dismissal and redundancy.

Mr Murphy was a resident plumber at a college and his work included attending to and maintaining the heating system, and assisting with general plumbing work. Changes were made to the central heating system, and he was not technically qualified to deal with all the problems that might arise. He wrote to the employer saying he would refuse to undertake work not undertaken by a plumber, except under certain conditions. These included close supervision and the prior receipt of instructions detailing what was required.

The college's response was to appoint a 'heating engineer' and that person was also expected to do general plumbing work. Mr Murphy was thereupon sacked. The court held that this was not unfair dismissal but a 'redundancy' situation, despite obvious doubts as to how, exactly, a 'diminution' could be said to have occurred. Nevertheless the Court of appeal has in this case made it clear that tribunals dealing with similar circumstances in the future can, depending on the effects this has on the employer's overall employment requirements, conclude that such a reorganisation or 're-allocation of functions' amounts to a redundancy. (p. 235)

Workplace changes

Not all workplace changes and reorganisations result in redundancies and the courts have been traditionally reluctant to encumber employers with the expense and trouble of making redundancy payments as this may inhibit the change process.

The problem for tribunals to determine is whether there has been a diminution in the work required or whether the reorganised job has become so different as to replace the original job, thereby creating a possible 'redundancy situation'.

Displacement

There are two important circumstances concerning job displacement. The first derives from external factors such as existing employees being replaced by outside contractors. In this circumstance, employees will be able to claim redundancy compensation. The second circumstance involves displacement by another worker from within the organisation whose job has become redundant. The orthodox view was that the fact that an employer's requirement for employees to do work of a particular kind had diminished did not mean that the employees who did that work were necessarily the ones to go. It was believed that the employer could decide that there were special reasons for retaining those employees such as experience, skills, length of service, etc. and moving them to different jobs and, instead, making the employees who had been displaced by this process redundant and entitled to redundancy pay. This process of *bumping* or *transferred* redundancies was, however, held by the EAT in the case *Church v West Lancashire NHS Trust* (1998) IRLR 4 not to fall within the statutory definition of redundancy and that such 'bumped' employees may therefore not be entitled to redundancy compensation.

COLLECTIVE REDUNDANCIES

Employers wishing to dismiss as redundant 20 or more employees at one establishment within a period of 90 days or less must consult appropriate representatives about the dismissals. The consultation must begin 'in good time' and in any event:

- where the employer is proposing to dismiss 100 or more employees, at least 90 days; and
- otherwise, at least 30 days;

before the first of the dismissals take effect (TULRCA 1992). The 'appropriate representatives' can be elected employee representatives who are normally trade union representatives in unionised

establishments. It is a statutory requirement that employers allow representatives access to the employees whom it is proposed to dismiss. These employees need not be employed for any minimum number of hours a week, but those who work under a fixed-term contract are excluded unless the employment lasted for more than three months. 'Establishment' is not statutorily defined and the EAT has ruled that this is an issue to be determined by employment tribunal. More recently the European Court of Justice has indicated that the term 'establishment' must be understood as designating the unit to which the employees made redundant are assigned to carry out their duties.

Consultation

The consultation required must include consultation about ways of:

- avoiding the dismissals;
- reducing the numbers to be dismissed; and
- mitigating the consequences of the dismissal

and must be undertaken 'with a view to reaching agreement with the appropriate representatives'. According to the EAT, employers are required to begin consultation before they give notice of dismissal, but notices can be issued during the consultation period so long as the dismissals do not take effect until after the period has elapsed. Employers are required to disclose in writing a number of matters at the start of the consultation period. These are:

- the reason for the proposals;
- the number and description of employees whom it is proposed to dismiss;
- the total number of employees of any such description employed by the employer at that establishment;
- the proposed method of selecting the employees who may be dismissed;
- the proposed method of carrying out the dismissals with due regard to any agreed procedure, including the period over which the dismissals are to take effect; and
- the proposed method of calculating the redundancy payment if this differs from the statutory sum.

The above information must be delivered by the employer to each of the appropriate representatives by hand or by post, and in the case of union representatives, to the union head office. In the *Williams* v *Compair Maxam* case (1982, IRLR 83), the EAT suggested that, where a union is recognised, consultation should include discussion of, and where possible, agreement on, the criteria for redundancy selection.

Protective awards

Should the employer not comply with consultation requirements or fails to consult properly, employee representatives and the union can make a complaint to an employment tribunal. If a complaint is well founded the tribunal must make a declaration to that effect and may also make a protective award which refers to the wages payable for a protected period to employees who have been dismissed or whom it is proposed to dismiss. The protected period is limited in the following two ways:

• where it was proposed to make 100 or more employees redundant within 90 days, the period cannot exceed 90 days; and
• where it was proposed to make between 20 and 99 people redundant within 90 days the period cannot exceed 30 days.

The rate of compensation payable under a protective award is a week's pay for each week of the protected period, with proportionate reductions made concerning periods of less than a week. If, during the protected period, employees are fairly dismissed for a reason other than redundancy, or if they unreasonably resign, then their entitlement to the protective reward ceases on the day the contract was terminated. Similarly, employees who unreasonably refuse an offer of employment on the previous terms and conditions, or an offer of suitable alternative employment will not be entitled to a protective award in respect of any period during which, but for that refusal, they would have been employed. A DTI consultative document in 1998 recommended an improved level of sanctions including up to 90 days' pay in *all* cases of a failure to inform or consult on a 'transfer' or collective redundancy.

Notification

An employer proposing to make 100 or more employees redundant at one establishment within a period of 90 days, or more than 20 employees within 30 days, must notify the Secretary of State for Trade and Industry in writing of the proposal within 90 or 30 days respectively. There is no obligation, therefore, to notify if fewer than 20 employees are to be made redundant. In addition to notifying the Secretary of State, the employer is required to give a copy of the notice to the appropriate representatives.

Gennard and Judge (1997) point out that employers with well-established redundancy procedures will not fall foul of the law over either a failure to consult or notify. They add:

> *Notwithstanding this, the prudent employee relations specialist will keep the procedure under review in the light of any relevant tribunal decisions. The real problems arise for those organisations that do not have a procedure or who try to put together a procedure in a hurried and casual manner when redundancies are imminent. Such organisations might find that the price they pay for a lack of preparedness is extremely high. Tribunals have shown an increasing tendency to take a very narrow view of any special pleading by employers that there was no time to consult. To be acceptable, non-consultation (or notification) would have to be the result of some event that was quite out of the ordinary.* (p. 252)

TRANSFER OF UNDERTAKINGS

There has been a significant increase in the number and scale of business transfers in recent years; public sector compulsory competitive tendering (CCT) has contributed to this trend. At issue here is the impact of transfers upon employment conditions and possible enforced redundancies. The Transfer of Undertakings (Protection of Employment) Regulations 1981 (TUPE) was a step in the right direction in seeking to protect existing employee interests subsequent to transfer. The Regulations are supposed to implement the Acquired Rights Directive 77/187 whereby member states are required to ensure that apart from the normal employment protection which all employees should enjoy, there should be additional protection for employees in the event of a change of employer. The 'new' employer is not obliged to retain all the employees he or she has inherited, but equally he or she must provide good reason for dispensing with employees surplus to requirements. The regulations stipulate that existing employee's rights are maintained, and that redundancy rights concerning selection, representation and consultation are also retained. The development of TUPE case law is important as this makes it more difficult for employers to evade their responsibilities under the Regulations (see Exhibit 13.2).

Initially, the regulations applied to 'commercial' organisations and businesses, thereby potentially excluding employees in non-commercial sectors such as government departments, the NHS and local authority contexts, and it was not until 1993 that amendments made by the Trade Union Reform and Employment Rights Act finally included coverage of employees in those non-commercial sectors. Again this represented a belated adoption of the broader interpretation of organisations within the Acquired Rights Directive. The regulations refer to the *transferor* (the organisation relinquishing ownership of part of a business) and the *transferee* (the organisation acquiring that part of the business). The main provisions of the Regulations are:

- Employment contracts with the old employer (transferor) do not terminate at the time of transfer and will be treated as if they had been originally made with the new employer.
- All the transferor's rights, powers, duties and liabilities under or relating to such employment contracts are transferred to the new employer (transferee).
- Any action affecting the contract on the part of the transferor before the transfer is to be treated as if done by the transferee.

Liabilities

As a result of the House of Lords decision in *Litster* v *Forth Dry Docks and Engineering* (1989) IRLR

Exhibit 13.2

The TUPE saga

The TUPE Regulations 1981 should be interpreted in the light of the EC Acquired Rights Directive. In *Spijkers* v *Gebroeders Benedik Abattoir* (1986) ECR 1119 the European Court of Justice held that when deciding whether a relevant transfer has taken place for the purposes of the Directive, a national court must decide whether the 'economic entity' (company) has retained its identity. In doing so, the court must take account of all the factual circumstances of the transaction including the type of undertaking involved; the transfer or otherwise of assets; the transfer or otherwise of customers; whether the majority of staff are taken on by the new employer; and the degree of similarity between activities before and after the transfer and the duration of any interruption in those activities.

Some years later, in *Süzen* v *Zehnacker Gebäudereinigung GmbH Krankenhausservice* (1997) IRLR 255, the ECJ stated that the Directive does not apply to a change of contractor if there is no transfer of significant assets and the incoming contractor does not take a major part of the workforce previously assigned to the contract. The apparent effect of the *Süzen* case was that in labour-intensive activities where there are unlikely to be any significant assets to transfer, an incoming contractor could avoid obligations under the Directive simply by declining to take on the outgoing contractor's workforce.

The Court of Appeal (in the UK), however, has been reluctant to give the *Süzen* decision this strict interpretation. In *ECM (Vehicle Delivery Service) Ltd* v *Cox* (1999) IRLR 559 the Court found that there can, in some circumstances, be a TUPE transfer of a labour-intensive undertaking where the incoming contractor refuses to take on the outgoing contractors' employees in order to avoid the application of TUPE. Most recently in *RCO Support Services Ltd* v *UNISON & Others* (2000) IRLR 328, the Court affirmed the *Spijkers* test, holding that single factors such as the transfer of assets or employees must not be considered in isolation.

161, certain ground rules were established concerning the important issue of termination of employment *before* the transfer takes place. As Painter and Puttick (1998) put it: 'at what point in time must the employees be in the transferor's employment before they can come within the transfer rules' (p. 242) and secure the benefits of continuity of rights summarised above? If employees are unfairly dismissed immediately before the transfer their rights will not be affected. Specifically:

- Should employees be dismissed by the transferor before the transfer for a reason which is connected to the transfer, the employees must be treated as if they were still employed at the time of transfer.
- The TUPE regulations are therefore applied to any worker who was employed immediately before the transfer or would have been employed at that time had he or she not been unfairly dismissed for a reason connected with a transfer.
- Transferees will be responsible for unfair dismissals unless such can be shown to be for an 'economic, technical or organisational' reason entailing a change in the workforce.
- The principle that a person must be employed at the exact moment of transfer will now only apply if the reason for the dismissal is unconnected with the transfer; liability will then remain with the transferor.

The above ground rules do not, therefore, apply in situations where the dismissal was either for 'economic, technical or organisational' reasons or for redundancy reasons.

Self-Evaluation Activity 13.7

Two cases to consider
Response on website

Read Mini cases 13.3 and 13.4. What decision do you think the tribunal should make in each of these, that is, does TUPE apply or not?

Mini cases 13.3 and 13.4

Case 13.3 Continuity of employment

Mr Baxendale was employed from 1977, and Mr Meade from 1978, by the British Coal Corporation (BCC) or its subsidiary National Fuels Distributors Ltd (NFD). On 20 August 1992, BCC gave both men three months' notice of dismissal on the grounds of redundancy effective from 28 August. They received wages in lieu of notice and redundancy pay. Also on 20 August British Fuels Ltd (BFL), another subsidiary of BCC, offered the men employment with effect from 1 September 1992 on terms which were less favourable than those they enjoyed with NFD. They both accepted and began to work for BFL on 1 September. On the same day, the undertakings of NFD and BFL were merged. At the time of the men's dismissals and re-employment, it was not realised that there had been a transfer to which the TUPE Regulations and the EU Directive applied. On 22 January 1993 BFL notified both men that, for statutory purposes, their service with NFD would be treated as continuous with their service with BFL. They were given statutory statements incorporating this change into their existing terms which they accepted, Mr Meade on 23 April and Mr Baxendale on 14 May 1993.

On 23 September 1994 Mr Meade claimed before an employment tribunal under s. 11 of ERA that he was employed by BFL on the terms applicable to his employment with NFD. On 6 February 1995 Mr Baxendale was dismissed by BFL as being redundant. He also sought a declaration from an employment tribunal under ERA that, until dismissed, he was entitled to be employed by BFL on the terms of his employment with NFD.

Case 13.4 Change of contractor

The nine employees involved in this case were employed by C Ltd as scaffolders. Towards the end of 1999 they were performing a contract at a site owned by FO Ltd. In November 1999 C Ltd wrote to the employees informing them that they had lost the FO Ltd contract and, consequently, that the employees would cease working for C Ltd on 3 December. It further informed the employees that their employment would transfer under TUPE to P Ltd, the incoming contractor. However, P Ltd also wrote to the employees in November 1999, denying that TUPE would apply and refusing to take them on. It intended some of its existing staff, who had worked on a contract that P Ltd had recently lost, to perform the contract. The nine employees brought claims to the employment tribunal against both C Ltd and P Ltd, claiming payments in respect of unfair dismissal and redundancy. The tribunal conducted a preliminary hearing in order to determine whether TUPE applied to the change of contractor. The tribunal found that the employees had been dedicated to the contract, since they had worked at the FO site for a number of years and that there had been a 'stable economic entity' (in this case, the contract).

Changes to the Regulations

Proposals (DTI, 2001) to amend the Regulations include the following:

- in outsourcing situations there will be a relevant transfer if there is a change in service provision (that is, where one party arranges to contract out to another organisation the ongoing provision of a service or services, and can include the initial contracting out of the service or a change of contractors who provide it, and most importantly whether there are employees assigned to an organised group providing the service);
- there will be widespread application of transfer regulations to all potential transfers in the public sector;
- the employer transferring the service will be obliged to inform the new employer of all outstanding liabilities to be transferred;
- there will be safeguards to protect employees should businesses become insolvent; and
- an entitlement to pension provision should transfer.

REDUNDANCY POLICIES AND PROCEDURES

All organisations should face the possibility of making employees redundant and should, therefore, have an agreed redundancy policy in place together with appropriate procedures for handling collective redundancies. The redundancy policy and procedure should be part of the organisation's portfolio of employment policies and procedures which we have considered in this and previous chapters. The procedure for handling redundancies should permit redundancy situations to be handled fairly and

professionally. While most 'good' employers will develop policies and procedures which are guided by the organisation's overall corporate strategy and are seen to be appropriate for the type of business activity engaged in, it is increasingly likely, for reasons explained earlier, that these policies and procedures will be put into effect, if only to minimise the impact of redundancy situations upon employees. At the same time it should be emphasised that while reductions take place in the labour force for whatever reasons may be necessary, it is also important to ensure that the morale and goodwill of the remaining employees – the 'survivors' – are maintained to counter any feelings of insecurity and unease.

Self-Evaluation 13.8

Criteria for redundancy policies and procedures
Response on website

Detailed in Exhibit 13.3 is an example of a redundancy policy and procedure of a particular company. When you have read it, attempt to identify the important overall criteria which a 'good' policy and procedure should contain.

SELECTING FOR REDUNDANCY

In cases where redundancies are declared, it is the responsibility of the employer, ideally in consultation with employee/union representatives, to decide exactly who is going to lose their job, and the criteria to be used in this decision-making process. The IRS (2002) survey of redundancy reveals that the most important factors to be considered by employers in selecting people for redundancy are:

- requests for voluntary redundancy;
- the skill and competency level of the employee concerned;
- an assessment of past, current and potential performance;
- the ability to perform, or be trained for alternative jobs;
- the job of the employee concerned;
- the employee's attendance record;

Exhibit 13.3

Letugo Ltd

Policy for handling salaried staff redundancies

Scope

This policy applies to all clerical, technical and railway supervisory grades employed by LETUGO Ltd . . . It supersedes all previous contractual arrangements and agreements for handling salaried staff redundancies. This policy is not intended to alter protected staff travel benefits provided to displaced staff for the handling of salaried staff redundancies.

Policy

It is the policy of the company by careful forward planning to ensure as much security of employment as is reasonably possible for its employees. However, it is accepted that there will be occasions when redundancies may arise, for example, as a result of a reduction in business; from changes in technology; from reorganisation or changes in work methods; or where it is necessary to relocate business operations.

In the event of a surplus arising every effort will be made to enable staff to find alternative employment. When a reduction in the workforce is inevitable the company will handle the redundancy in a fair and consistent manner and will seek to minimise any hardship suffered by the staff concerned.

The company undertakes to consult with the appropriate trade union staff representatives at the earliest opportunity with a view to seeking agreement on ways of avoiding redundancies or reducing the surplus and mitigating consequences of redundancy where they are unavoidable.

The following information will be given during consultation:

- the reason for the redundancy
- the numbers affected by the redundancy
- the total number of staff employed
- the method of carrying out the redundancy including the period over which it will take place, and
- the agreed criteria for the selection of staff for redundancy.

The company will commit to make every effort to avoid and minimise redundancy and to seek alternative employment for the displaced employees. Employees affected by redundancy may be offered suitable alternative employment throughout the company which may require relocation and retraining. Where suitable alternative employment cannot be offered and other measures to avoid redundancy are unsuccessful, employees affected will be declared redundant in accordance with the provisions of employment legislation.

Redundancy payment will be based on the LETUGO standard redundancy terms. (However, this will not preclude special redundancy arrangements being offered to meet the particular needs of the business. Staff representatives will be advised when such special arrangements are being offered.)

Redundancy arrangements

Where a reduction in the number of salaried staff is necessary to meet the revised business requirements, the following arrangements will apply:

1. Staff in the activity affected by reduced workload will be informed of the reductions necessary and advised of vacant posts elsewhere within the company.
2. All displaced staff will be eligible to apply for consideration for vacant posts within the company. In accordance with the company's desire to mitigate the effects of redundancy, recruiting managers will give proper

consideration to applications from displaced staff in filling vacant posts. Displaced staff who are otherwise suitable will not be turned down for a vacancy purely on the basis that he or she will require training. Feedback will be provided to unsuccessful candidates on request.

3. Where displaced staff do not submit applications for 'suitable' vacancies they may nevertheless be offered these posts. Refusal to accept a 'suitable' alternative job may result in the employee being dismissed without redundancy pay.

Voluntary redundancy

4. The company will seek, where possible, to achieve redundancies through volunteers. With this objective in mind where it is established that there are insufficient or no suitable vacancies, volunteers will be sought for redundancy from amongst the staff directly affected by the redundancy. In the event that there are insufficient volunteers for redundancy from the staff affected, volunteers may be sought from other staff within the company. If there are more volunteers within the activity affected than are required, selection for redundancy will be determined with regard to retaining a balanced workforce with the requisite skills to meet future business needs. Selection from amongst the voluntary redundancy applicants will be decided by the departmental/functional manager against the criteria consulted with the staff representatives. Where there are insufficient volunteers for redundancy from amongst the staff directly affected, volunteers from other areas may be released providing this results in the subsequent appointment of a displaced member of staff. Volunteers will be advised in writing that they have been accepted for voluntary redundancy and of their leaving date.

5. Where there are insufficient volunteers for redundancy and the company considers that there is little prospect of suitable alternative work being found, salaried staff in the area affected will be placed under notice of redundancy. Staff will be selected for redundancy on the basis of the criteria consulted with the staff representatives. Staff made redundant will receive the benefits of the severance arrangements in place at the time. Statutory notice arrangements will apply.

6. The date of redundancy will be determined by the company, with regard to operational requirements and in consultation with staff representatives.

Alternative employment

7. *Employees transferred to a job with a lower rate of pay*
   When a member of staff accepts alternative employment in a job which is at the lower rate of pay as an alternative to redundancy, they will retain their base rate (for which staff on restructured salaries will be established at the time of consolidation) of pay for six months. At the end of the six-month period, the employee will be given the option of accepting the rate of pay for the post or leaving the company under redundancy. The existing pension arrangements will continue to apply to staff transferred to a position with a lower rate of pay.

8. *Retraining and redeployment*
   It is company policy to offer, wherever possible, opportunities to train for a job requiring different skills where this will assist in avoiding a potential redundancy situation. An individual who is otherwise suitable will not be turned down for a vacancy purely because he or she will require training.

Company support for displaced staff

9. The company will provide staff who are under notice of redundancy reasonable time off with pay to seek alternative employment. Consideration will be given to all applications for time off to seek alternative employment in accordance with statutory requirements and subject to the operational needs of the business. To ensure that this policy is consistently applied, the following procedure will be adopted:
   (a) time off must be agreed in advance by the relevant local manager
   (b) at least 48 hours' notice must be given wherever practicable
   (c) supporting evidence will be provided of the interview or appointment.

10. The company will provide redundancy counselling for displaced staff. Such counselling will include:
    - the identification of alternative employment (if any) within the company
    - the company will advise displaced employees regarding redundancy and pension entitlement. In addition, the company will make arrangements to provide guidance in other areas such as investment opportunities, tax, mortgages, state benefits and domestic budgeting
    - the company will provide additional assistance with CVs and interview techniques, and advice on training opportunities and details of unemployment or social security benefits.

LETUGO standard redundancy policy for salaried staff

LETUGO will apply a standard redundancy calculator for all staff leaving the company due to redundancy. The standard redundancy arrangements contained in this document will be implemented on 1 April 1998 or on the date of restructuring for staff whose salaries are restructured before that date. Provisions contained in the standard salaried staffs' terms and conditions to pay SERPS will fall on the implementation of this policy. This will not preclude the use of special enhanced redundancy arrangements from time to time to meet the particular needs of the business. The representatives of staff affected by the redundancy will be advised when special arrangements apply.

This policy outlines the standard redundancy pay arrangements.

Redundancy pay calculations

LETUGO will apply a standard calculator for determining redundancy pay based on length of service, the age band within which service falls, and the basic earnings of the member of staff affected. The annual salary used to determine redundancy pay will be that applicable at the date the member of staff leaves the company's employment. The matrix used to determine redundancy pay entitlement will be based on the formula of twice the statutory redundancy pay without the application of the upper salary limit. Basic 37-hour earnings (including the appropriate geographical allowances) will be applied to establish an individual's redundancy severance payment entitlement.

The matrix is configured as follows:

- one week's pay for each complete year of service between ages 16–21
- two weeks' pay for each complete year of service between ages 22–40
- three weeks' pay for each year of service between ages 41–65
- the last 20 years' service only will be counted for redundancy pay purposes
- redundancy pay will be limited for those staff approaching retirement, to basic earnings to be earned in the remaining period of employment.

Using the matrix

To establish redundancy pay entitlement an individual will refer to the matrix, using current age and length of service (only taking into account the last 20 years of service), to determine the number of weeks' severance pay. This figure will then be multiplied by basic weekly earnings to provide the individual's redundancy pay.

Basic weekly earnings, which will include for standard redundancy purposes any entitlements to geographical allowances, will be established by dividing the 37-hour week basic annual salary by 52.

Example

For example, an employee aged 50 with 16 years' service and a salary of £20 000 per annum will be entitled to 41 weeks' severance pay. Weekly pay will be determined by dividing £20 000 by 52 which provides a weekly salary of £384.62. The weekly salary is then multiplied by 41 to provide the severance payment, i.e. 41×384.62 = £15 769.42.

Notice entitlement

The company will seek to provide as much notice as is practicable of an impending redundancy. In the event that redundancy is unavoidable contractual notice will be provided. Leaving dates will be determined by operational requirements and, at the discretion of the company, staff may be released with pay in lieu of notice.

Counselling and support

The company will provide counselling and support services for redundant staff which will aim to assist them with finding new employment and in managing their financial affairs. The assistance will be tailored to meet individual circumstances and may include preparation for retirement, setting up a business or seeking alternative employment.

Source: Adapted from IRS, 1998, pp. 12–14

- the employee's length of service; and
- the employee's disciplinary record.

The IRS survey of employers within different industry sectors also indicated that, perhaps surprisingly, the most common approach to cutting posts is through compulsory redundancies (87 per cent), followed by natural wastage/freezing of posts (80 per cent), voluntary redundancy (75 per cent), early retirement (55 per cent) and redeployment (40 per cent). Regardless of whether redundancy selection criteria depend on performance, trainability and skill, employers pay very close attention to annual appraisals and to the knowledge and expertise of supervisors and line managers to choose employees. Performance, skills assessment and trainability criteria include annual appraisal, line manager's knowledge/expertise, competency assessment, enthusiasm and commitment, training records and skills tests and formal qualifications. Traditionally, employment tribunals look favourably on selection procedures in which points scores are allocated for several criteria such as attendance, disciplinary record and performance, with the points totals determining who goes and who stays (see below).

The criteria examined

As far as possible, objective criteria, precisely defined and capable of being applied in an independent way, should be used when determining which employees are to be selected for redundancy.

The purpose of having 'objective' criteria is to ensure that employees are not unfairly selected. Ideally, any areas of subjectivity should be agreed if possible with the appropriate trade union and employee representatives, and also be made known to the individuals concerned. Many organisations adopt a 'points system', which involves the allocation of points to the areas which the employer considers important. These areas may include the following criteria:

1. *Length of service*

   Selection on the basis of length of service, commonly known as 'last in, first out' (or LIFO) is a long-established and simple way of deciding which employees are to be made redundant. At its simplest, it means that employees with the least service are the first to lose their jobs when redundancies are declared. The IRS (2002) redundancy surveys revealed that, despite its simplicity, only 11 per cent of organisations surveyed actually used this method. Although being the easiest method of selection to administer, LIFO does not always address the precise needs of the employer. Where other factors are important, length of service may legitimately be regarded as only one consideration. The most commonly advanced reason for not applying the LIFO criterion revealed by the IRS surveys is that it is too crude and takes no account of the wider needs of the business, in particular the retention of the correct mix of skills. As one employer put it 'some of our more recent recruits are more effective than our older staff' (IRS, 2002, p. 6).

2. *Ability and performance*

It is potentially fair to select on these grounds but employers should ensure from the outset that the relevant areas are clearly defined. In applying this criterion, evidence of an objective employee appraisal, for example by reference to external praise or criticism of an employee's work, would be useful. The method of assessing performance and ability will vary from organisation to organisation. Many organisations will use annual appraisals; others will utilise the knowledge and expertise of supervisors and managers; while others will use competency assessments. Other methods of assessing ability include a willingness to adapt, skills tests and employee enthusiasm.

3. *Attendance records*

It is permissible to use attendance as a criterion for selection provided that the information is accurate. Before selecting on the basis of attendance it is important to know the reasons for and extent of any absences. The specific factors to be taken into account include:

- unauthorised leave;
- self-certified leave;
- leave covered by a doctor's certificate; and
- uncertified leave.

4. *Disciplinary record*

It is acceptable to use a person's disciplinary record as a criterion for redundancy selection, again, provided the information is consistent and accurate.

5. *An employee's age*

Selection on the basis of proximity to retirement and 'fitness' can be used, even though the result will, ironically, be the absolute reverse of the established LIFO principle. Tribunals generally recognise that employers might be under pressure to retain a younger workforce, while also appreciating that older employees sometimes have special skills. The case for retaining older employees with special skills has been established by tribunal judgments so employers must use the 'first in, last out' (FILO) principle sparingly. Similarly, redundancy decisions made on the basis of fitness should take into account 'capability' criteria, otherwise the redundancy could be considered to be an unfair dismissal. For example, in *Porter* v *Streets Transport Ltd* (1986) IRLR 420, Porter was selected for redundancy because he suffered from a gastric ulcer, while the other candidate for redundancy had shorter service but a clean bill of health. The EAT accepted that the selection on health grounds was reasonable, although in this case they found that more meaningful consultation would have revealed that Porter was willing to take another vacant position and this made the dismissal unfair.

6. *Qualifications and skills*

Assessment based on qualifications and skills is an objective criterion for redundancy selection and may be additional to the 'performance and ability' criterion, with the aim of maintaining a 'balanced' workforce appropriate to the future needs of the business.

7. *Value to the organisation*

An individual (and his or her position) within an organisation may be considered as a 'valued asset' and therefore may be used as a criterion. It must be established and clearly proved that an individual's contribution is essential to the future of the business, otherwise the criterion could be regarded as subjective.

8. *Social need*

This criterion requires that as part of the selection process, the 'employees' domestic circumstances be taken into account' (Salamon, 1998, p. 572), and may include a consideration of 'marital status, number of children and whether the employee is the sole family income' (ibid., p. 572).

Misapplication of, and discriminatory, criteria

Even though the criteria outlined above may be 'objective', selection will be unfair if the criteria areas are unreasonably applied. For example, in *Farmer* v *Ayrshire Metal Products* (1986) IRLR 211 the criteria were based on skills and ability with a points allocation system. Farmer was selected for redundancy having scored no points for skills. The employment tribunal stated that it was unfair as they could not understand how Farmer, with nine years' service and no written warnings, obtained no points, while another employee with short service amassed 21 points. The tribunal concluded that the criteria areas were reasonable, but they had been subjectively applied. In addition, employers who make redundancy selection on the basis of sex, race or disability are acting unlawfully. Extreme caution must be exercised in the selection and application of criteria in order to ensure that discrimination does not occur. For example, the use of LIFO in some cases which include the selection of women, the disabled and ethnic employees, can be considered as discriminatory. Any complaints arising from misapplication of and potentially discriminatory criteria should be dealt with through a redundancy appeals procedure which may require the establishment of a committee comprising senior management andtrade union or employee representatives in order to deal with individual grievances. Exhibit 13.3 provides an example of an existing points system.

Exhibit 13.4

Example of 'ReleaseU Ltd' selection criteria using the 'points system'

Personal details

(a) *Service record*

Points allocation for service up to present post and a points allocation in present post as follows:

Company service (up to present post)		Service in current post
0–2 years:	1 point	One point for each full year in post up to a maximum of 10 points
3–4 years:	2 points	
5–6 years:	3 points	
7–8 years:	4 points	
9–10 years:	5 points	
11–12 years:	6 points	
13–14 years:	7 points	
15–16 years:	8 points	
Over 16 years:	10 points maximum	

(b) *Discipline record*

Points are deducted, from a maximum of 15 points, in respect of an individual's disciplinary record and applies to current 'live' disciplinary actions: 12 months for warnings etc. and 2 years for final warnings.

Points are deducted as follows:

Verbal warnings:	1 point
Written warnings:	5 points
Suspensions:	10 points
Final warnings:	10 points

(c) *Sickness/attendance record*

Operating on a similar basis to that for disciplinary records, points are deducted from the points allocation of 15 points for this category. Sickness/attendance records for the past 2 years only apply.

Points are deducted as follows:

Absence

1 or 2 days:	1 point per period
3 days:	2 points per period
4 days:	3 points per period
1 week:	5 points per period
Up to 2 weeks:	6 points per period
Up to 3 weeks:	8 points per period
Over 3 weeks:	10 points per period

NB: Absences due to assaults, industrial injuries and maternity leave are not taken into account.

Lateness
1 point deducted per occasion

(d) *Qualifications*

GCSE subjects:	1 point per subject passed
A Levels:	3 points per subject
Institute of Supervisory Management:	5 points
Chartered Institute of Transport:	10 points

Other qualifications which are deemed to be pertinent to the job should be based on the institute qualification range of points. Other qualifications not relevant to the job should be based on GCSE and A Level points range. NVQs and GNVQs should be rated pro rata with GCSE and A Level subjects.

Assessments

(a) *Technical skills*

Assessment of the individual's knowledge of job-related tasks: for example in the case of a traffic operations person their knowledge of the service network, timetables, operational systems and ability to deal with passenger enquiries.

Points are subdivided up to 15 points maximum.

(b) *Supervisory skills*

Assessment of a number of items relating to an individual's employee management skills in dealing with his or her subordinates, ability to act independently and to deal with problems without reference to a higher authority. Also their ability to distinguish between minor and major matters that can be either dealt with by the individual or referred to a higher authority.

Points are subdivided up to 15 points maximum.

(c) *Interview*

An interview panel comprises an independent chairperson (employee relations manager or personnel services manager) and two general or departmental managers from the relevant discipline. A total of four standard questions are put to each candidate and an assessment is made of each individual's response, to a maximum of 5 points per question. The interview panel scores each question individually and the average number of points will be awarded.

Review panel

The interview panel are responsible for formulating the questions for the interview process and also for the items to be assessed in the technical and supervisory skills categories. Following the interviews the panel allocates the points for the various criteria and a recommendation on the selection(s) is put to a review panel.

The review panel comprises either the employee relations manager or the personnel services manager and a general manager or director (who has not been involved in the selection process). The review panel and interview panel meet to discuss the criteria process, how the points were allocated, conduct of the interviews, assessments, and the recommendations made.

The candidates are then informed of the results of the selection process. The details of the selection are discussed with the individual and the counselling stage of the redundancy procedure is introduced at this time.

WHAT HAPPENS AFTER REDUNDANCY?

The procedure outlined above gives some indication of the extent to which employers can help redundant employees, which will be in addition to the statutory requirement for employers to allow these employees to take time off for retraining or for seeking alternative employment. By law, employees under notice of redundancy who qualify for statutory redundancy payments are entitled to 'reasonable' time off to search for alternative work. In recent years, as the numbers of redundancies have increased, employers have paid more attention to the needs of redundant employees, particularly in relation to outplacement and counselling.

Outplacement

The meaning of outplacement is fairly specific and involves 'a process where an individual or individuals who have been made redundant by their employer are given support and counselling to assist them in achieving the next stage of their career' (Gennard and Judge, 2002 quoting Eggert, 1991, p. 432). Employers try to help employees to make the transition from redundancy to their next employment by providing practical assistance on a group or individual basis with regard to preparing CVs, researching the labour and jobs market, developing communication techniques and interview skills and presentation, and managing job searches. The use of outplacement services has grown in the past five years. The IRS survey (2002) found that 86 per cent of employers surveyed offer outplacement or counselling to help redundant employees find alternative work, compared with 67 per cent of employerssurveyed in 1998.

Counselling and support

In recognition of the fact that for many people redundancy can be a traumatic experience and can engender feelings of anger, guilt and resentment which may prevent employees, at least initially, from feeling positive about themselves, counselling plays an important role in encouraging employees to confront these emotions and in helping them to make decisions about future job options. Counselling is neither a panacea nor will it suit every employee; ideally counselling needs to be tailored to suit each individual employee's requirements and should be undertaken by professionals. Moreover, efforts should be made to reassure those employees who remain and who may be affected by 'survivor syndrome' – a condition which is characterised by feelings of insecurity, stress and disenchantment. Redundancy support includes:

- providing full details and advice about the redundancy terms;
- personal counselling to help employees come to terms with the situation;
- advice about matters such as pension benefits, income support, mortgages etc.;
- advice about job seeking concerning, for example, writing CVs and possible job choices;
- providing facilities to assist in job seeking such as typing and photocopying;
- advice about opportunities for further education or vocational training;
- providing facilities for local job centres to provide information and conduct interviews on employers' premises;
- circulating details of redundant employees to other employers; and
- providing advice and possibly direct assistance for redundant employees who decide to start their own business.

Managing the survivors

The immediate priority in a redundancy situation is the fair and sensitive handling of the employees who are losing their jobs, but once this has been achieved, the organisation's ongoing effectiveness is mainly dependent upon the morale of the surviving staff. A demoralised workforce which is concerned about its own job security and critical about the way the employer handled redundancies is unlikely to display the qualities of commitment, enthusiasm and initiative needed for business success. This aspect of redundancy should be taken into account as part of a much wider policy of open, honest and comprehensive employee information and communication. Sahdev (2002) argues that by failing to focus upon what comes next, employers are wasting a major opportunity to refocus their business and make the most of their new situation. She also points out that 'HR directors ought to be looking not just at redundancy packages and at how you deal with people who are leaving, but at survivor packages as well' (p. 36). The well-established CIPD Guide on redundancy (2002) summarises the primary objectives in managing the surviving workforce as:

- an effective two-way communication process with the qualities of openness, honesty and clarity, giving as positive a message as the situation allows;
- the demonstrable commitment of all managers to the necessity of change;
- the handling of the actual redundancy process in a way which demonstrates to the survivors that the organisation is behaving in a responsible, fair and effective manner, has done everything possible to minimise the redundancies and to support those who lose their jobs;
- providing clarity of direction for the future by fostering a positive, forward-looking attitude and showing survivors they have a valuable role to play in the organisation's future; and
- ensuring that managers have, or are assisted to develop, the necessary personal skills and attitudes to operate effectively during periods of potentially traumatic change.

Summary

- The causes of redundancy include the structural decline of industries; decline in levels of economic activity; technological change and work reorganisation.
- Statutory minimum rights concerning redundancy and redundancy payments are contained in the ERA 1996, but can be improved by individual and collective negotiation.
- The ERA provides instances of situations where redundancies are lawful, although there are important issues concerning 'diminishing requirements' including changed work and skill requirements, workplace changes and job displacement.
- Special provisions concerning redundancies apply on transfer of undertakings which the TUPE Regulations 1981 seek to enforce.
- All organisations should have adequate redundancy policies and procedures which should include a policy statement, measures to avoid redundancies, defining how the voluntary redundancy options may be used, defining appropriate selection criteria, devising suitable redundancy payments and redundancy support schemes.
- Selection criteria should include length of service, ability and performance, attendance records, disciplinary records, employees' age qualifications and skills.

PART THREE: EMPLOYMENT TRIBUNALS

Employment tribunals (ETs) are independent judicial bodies which were first established by the Industrial Training Act 1964 (when they were known as 'industrial tribunals'), suitable for hearing matters arising out of employment relations legislation. Tribunals comprise a legally qualified chair and two lay members drawn from panels, one with experience of industry from the employers' perspective and the other from the trade union or employee organisation's side. The composition of an ET will vary from case to case; for example, the same legally qualified chair (who must be a lawyer, barrister or solicitor of at least seven years' standing) may sit with different lay members on different days.

Although lay members are drawn from employer and employee-based panels, they are not expected to demonstrate any bias in deciding the case. Most decisions are unanimous, and there is an increasing tendency for the chair to sit alone where lay members' experience would have little to add.

The jurisdiction of employment tribunals is covered by the Employment Tribunals Act 1996 and concerns the various pieces of legislation that we have considered in this chapter and in Chapter 11 relating to matters which may form the subject of claims, complaints or representations derived from this legislation. The Employment Rights (Disputes Resolution) Act 1998 contains provisions governing

Table 13.1 Cases dealt with by ACAS and tribunals: 1997–2002

	1997	1998	2000	2002
Unfair dismissal	42 771	40 153	42 791	46 363
Protection of wages	24 972	24 981	30 845	36 205
Breach of contract	20 326	23 578	24 624	26 420
Sex Discrimination Act	6 587	6 882	5 904	6 325
Race Relations Act	2 886	3 173	3 200	3 697
Equal Pay Act	2 302	3 447	1 435	1 852
Disability Discrimination Act	1 408	2 758	2 916	4 065
Other	5 660	8 664	18 996	12 553
TOTALS	106 912	113 636	130 711	137 480

Source: ACAS Annual Report, 2002

the administration of traibunals. The cases dealt with by tribunals and ACAS have risen steeply. According to ACAS (1998–2002) to whom all cases are reported, the total caseload for 1992 was 72 000 rising to 106 912 in 1997. There were dramatic increases in caseloads, totalling 130 711 in 1999 and 137 500 in 2002. The distribution of cases dealt with by ACAS and employment tribunals from 1997 until 2002 is shown in Table 13.1.

The Employment Appeal Tribunal (EAT) was established by the Employment Protection Act 1975 and hears appeals against ET decisions in most, but not all, areas. The composition of the EAT is similar to that of ETs with a judge and two lay members. Its decisions are binding upon ETs, although appeals from its decisions on points of law can be made to the Court of Appeal and from there to the House of Lords.

Existing alongside the judicial structure of tribunals, there is a conciliation function which since 1974 has been role of ACAS. ACAS appoints a number of conciliation officers who are statutorily required to achieve settlements of cases without the need for a tribunal hearing. ACAS conciliates where a party requests it or where, even without such a request, they feel a settlement seems reasonably likely to be achievable. ET staff inform ACAS of applications which are made, and of the progress of cases. The ET procedural rules also provide for adjournments to be made in appropriate cases where ACAS conciliation could usefully take place. In 1997, ACAS conciliated 41 per cent of the 42 771 unfair dismissal cases, while in 2002, 49 per cent of the 46 363 cases were conciliated. Overall, the proportion of cases settled by ACAS has remained fairly constant over the years although there has been a tendency for the number of ACAS-settled cases to rise slightly over the past seven years. In 2002 these amounted to 42 per cent of cases cleared (as compared with 37 per cent in 1996 and 39 per cent in 1997).

LEGISLATIVE AND REGULATORY DEVELOPMENTS: 1998–2003

Important developments affecting the functions of ETs and the role of ACAS as an alternative to ETs include:

- Employment Rights (Dispute Resolution) Act 1998
- The ACAS unfair dismissal arbitration proposals, 1998
- The ACAS Arbitration Scheme (Statutory Instrument) 2001
- Employment Tribunals (Constitution and Rules of Procedure) Regulations 2001
- Employment Act 2002: Amendments to tribunal system
- Recommendations of the Employment Tribunal System Taskforce, 2002

Employment Rights (Dispute Resolution) Act 1998

The Act introduced a range of reforms of the tribunal system which we consider next.

Renaming

The renaming of industrial tribunals as 'employment tribunals' was deemed appropriate as it was claimed that:

The new name will better reflect the tribunals' modern role in dealing with employment rights disputes rather than their original purpose of considering appeals by employers against levies imposed under the Industrial Training Act. (CIPD, 2002, p. 12)

Attenuated hearings

Here, ETs are empowered to determine proceedings without a hearing, or without a full hearing, in a limited number of circumstances. These include:

- determination without any hearing and on written evidence alone (and in private) where both parties have given their written consent;
- determination hearing only the applicant or applicants (or his or her representatives) where:
  - the respondent has done nothing to contest the case; or
  - it appears from the application that the tribunal does not have the power to grant the relief claimed by the applicant or that he or she is not entitled to the relief he or she is claiming.
- determination hearing only the parties to the proceedings where:
  - the tribunal is 'on undisputed facts bound by a prior decision of a court in another case to dismiss the case' of either the applicant or the respondent; or
  - the hearing relates only to a preliminary jurisdictional issue about the entitlement of any party to bring or contest the proceedings before the tribunal.

Hearings by chair alone

The number of jurisdictions in which an ET chair *must* sit alone (without lay members) unless he or she decides otherwise is extended to cover:

- references to ETs concerning statutory redundancy payments;
- references to ETs concerning payment of liabilities of insolvent employers;
- references to ETs concerning written statements of employment particulars; and
- other payments to employees concerning issues such as 'medical suspension'; unauthorised deduction of union subscriptions; failure to pay a protective award made under redundancy consultation; failure to pay compensation for breach of the information and consultation requirements on the transfer of an undertaking.

'Legal officers' established

This is a new category of official who will carry out some of the more straightforward duties hitherto carried out by tribunal chairs. These duties could potentially cover any of the functions carried out by the chair alone (including granting postponements and extensions of time and making witness orders). A legal officer will not be able to carry out pre-hearing reviews or determine proceedings except where a case has been withdrawn or settled.

In addition, ACAS will now have a duty to conciliate in claims relating to statutory redundancy payments.

Alternative ACAS dispute resolution

The Act makes provision for a voluntary arbitration scheme to be drawn up by ACAS which will apply, initially at least, only to unfair dismissal disputes. Access to the ACAS scheme will have to be by written agreement following the intervention of an ACAS conciliation officer and in these circumstances the jurisdiction of the employment tribunals to hear the case in question will be excluded.

The ACAS Arbitration Scheme (Statutory Instrument) 2001

The scheme provides a voluntary alternative to the employment tribunal for the resolution of unfair dismissal disputes, in the form of arbitration. The resolution of disputes under the scheme is intended to be confidential, informal, relatively fast and cost-efficient. Procedures under the scheme are non-legalistic and far more flexible than the traditional model of the employment tribunal and the courts. For example, the scheme avoids the use of formal pleadings and formal witness and documentary procedures. Strict rules of evidence will not apply, and as far as possible, instead of applying the strict law or legal precedent, general principles of fairness and good conduct will be taken into account. Arbitral decisions, or 'awards' will be final with very limited opportunities for parties to appeal or otherwise challenge the result. The scheme also caters for legal requirements of other statutes such as the Human Rights Act 1998, existing law in the field of arbitration and EU law.

Employment Tribunals (Constitution and Rules of Procedure) Regulations 2001

Under these Regulations, tribunals have an overriding objective to deal with cases justly. Tribunals are under a duty to consider costs in certain circumstances and the maximum amount of costs that can be awarded without formal assessment or agreement is raised from £500 to £5000. The amount that tribunals can order a party to pay by way of deposit if the case appears weak is increased from £150 to £500. The rules previously referred to a party acting 'frivolously, vexatiously or abusively'. These terms are replaced with 'misconceived or unreasonably'. Crown employees including armed and security forces have the right to bring claims before tribunals. The Regulations amend provisions relating to the hearing of national security cases.

Employment Act 2002: amendments to tribunal system

The main provisions are:

- increasing or reducing awards between 10 and 50 per cent where the employer or employee has failed to comply with the statutory procedures prior to commencing proceedings;
- allowing a tribunal to disregard minor procedural errors if they do not affect the outcome of a case;

- introducing a fixed period of conciliation;
- amendment to the Employment Tribunals Act 1996 to introduce penalties for costs when parties have delayed procedures;
- regulations introduced permitting awards against representatives directly but costs should not exceed £10 000;
- amendment to Employment Rights Act to create a category of unfair dismissal where an employer has failed to comply with the statutory procedures. Compensation for such a failure will be four weeks' pay;
- amendments may be made to the current documentation used (IT1 and IT3) to require further details to be supplied with a view to assisting the parties to conciliate or reach a settlement;
- allowing the President of Employment Tribunals to make practice directions on the exercise and enforcement of discretionary powers to ensure consistency of approach; and
- tribunals will have greater powers at pre-hearing to strike out weak cases.

Recommendations of the Employment Tribunal System Taskforce, 2002

The Employment Tribunal System Taskforce, set up in 2001, made recommendations to the Secretary of State for Trade and Industry and the Lord Chancellor on how tribunal services can be made more efficient and cost-effective to users, against a background of rising caseloads (see Table 13.1). The Taskforce submitted its recommendations in 2002, and these include the following.

Greater coherence

The establishment of a high-level co-ordinating body to assist the system overall to move forward coherently, with a shared vision and key processes, was recommended. Greater coherence would bring benefits to both users and those working within the system. There is, for example, scope for improvement by greater co-ordination and better use of best practices across regions; key processes; continuous improvement mechanisms and benchmarking in particular against other jurisdictions.

Greater emphasis on the prevention of disputes

There should be greater emphasis on prevention of disputes. ACAS should do more in this area, particularly in promoting 'best practice' and alternative dispute resolution.

Earlier disclosure of information

There should be earlier disclosure of information by all parties, which ties in with the desire for greater dispute prevention methods. Earlier access to facts and an earlier understanding of the parties' positions would help:

- employees to understand if they do have a case with a reasonable prospect of success;
- employers to determine if they have behaved inappropriately;
- those advising parties to determine the merits of the case;
- each party to recognise the merits of the other's case and to consider reaching a settlement; and
- the judiciary to determine the most appropriate case-handling techniques.

The right infrastructure

The system cannot achieve its objectives without appropriate supporting resources such as developments in information technology resulting in improvements to internal procedures and in dealing with users, good IT links between ACAS and the rest of the ET system, more highly-skilled administrative staff in the ETs, appropriate resources for the workload, more training for all working in the system and appraisal and support procedures.

THE PROCEDURE FOR MAKING A COMPLAINT

The employee (called the applicant) can make an application to an employment tribunal on the form IT1 as soon as the employer (called the respondent) has given notice of the dismissal (if it is an 'unfair dismissal' case). This application should give particulars of the grounds of the complaint and must normally be received within three months of the employee's effective date of termination. If the application is late, the tribunal will consider the complaint only if there are circumstances making it not reasonably practicable for the employee to have made the application in time.

The Office of the Employment Tribunals dealing with the employee's application form will send the employer a copy of the application (form IT3) and a form called a *notice of appearance*. It is now possible for applicants and respondents to download an application or apply online (www.employment-tribunals.gov.uk). The employer should fill in this form, stating whether or not he or she wishes to contest the case and, if so, giving particulars of the grounds for doing so. The employer and employee may each request further particulars of the other's case. It is in the interests of both parties to complete these forms as fully as possible so that the tribunal does not have to come back to them for further details thereby ensuring that if the matter does come to a hearing both parties and the tribunal know exactly what is at issue.

Conciliation

Once a complaint has been made to ET, but before the hearing takes place, there is, as mentioned above, an opportunity for the case to be settled by conciliation. Copies of the completed IT1 and IT3 application forms and the notice of appearance by the employer are sent by the ET to ACAS who appoints a conciliation officer in order to help respondent and applicant make a voluntary arrangement to settle the complaint without having to go to tribunal. The conciliation officer usually begins by talking separately, and in confidence, to both applicant and respondent, encouraging them both to use any agreed voluntary appeals procedure where this has not already been done. The officer will discuss the case itself, help the parties understand any legal terms, points of law and qualifying conditions, and may draw attention to particular features of the case, including decisions taken in previous cases which may be similar. However, the officer will not offer any opinion on the merits of either side's case or 'take sides' in any way. Many dismissals are not clear-cut issues and quite often, in discussion with the conciliation officer, matters will be seen differently with the result that a voluntary solution will be reached through conciliation as an alternative to the case going to tribunal.

Where the applicant and respondent are willing, the officer will explore the possibility of the respondent's reinstatement of the applicant in the same job, or re-engagement in some other job. If an employee unreasonably refuses an offer of reinstatement, any eventual award of compensation made by a tribunal may be reduced. However, most conciliated settlements are those where the respondent pays the applicant a mutually agreed sum of money in compensation.

AFTER MAKING A COMPLAINT

A full tribunal comprising the chair and two lay members, or a chair sitting alone, may conduct a pre-hearing review of a case in advance of the full tribunal hearing. If it appears that the case has little prospect of success either party may be ordered to pay a deposit of up to £500 as a condition of continuing to proceed with, or defend the case. If the complaint is not settled or withdrawn at the pre-hearing stage, it proceeds to a full hearing by the ET. (Note that there are different types of hearing apart from the two main ones mentioned, details of which may be accessed on www.employmenttribunals.gov.uk.) At the hearing tribunals try to keep their proceedings as simple and informal as possible. Many applicants and respondents put their own cases to the tribunal, although some choose to have a representative who may be a lawyer, trade union official, representative of an employers' organisation, or simply a friend or colleague.

The procedure

The tribunal clerk explains the procedure to the parties. Normally the parties, or their representatives if they are represented, can expect to be called upon by the tribunal to make opening statements but there is no entitlement to do so. They are, however, entitled to address the tribunal at some stage in the proceedings. They can also call their witnesses, with the parties giving evidence themselves if they wish. Opportunities to cross-examine the other party's witnesses are provided.

Following the opening statements, witnesses for the respondent are called to give their evidence, which may be read out to the tribunal. A witness who has not provided a written statement of his or her evidence should be invited to explain in his or her own words the circumstances relating to the case. When the witness has finished his or her evidence, he or she will remain on oath for cross-examination by the applicant or representative and for questions to be put to him or her by the tribunal members. A similar right of cross-examination exists for the respondent or representative when the applicant's witnesses have given their evidence.

It is in the interests of both applicant and respondent to attend the hearing. If one party is neither present nor represented the tribunal may decide the case in their absence, after considering any written representations made. In some cases a tribunal finds it very difficult to reach a decision if a party does not attend, and may adjourn the case. A tribunal may dismiss an application if the applicant fails to attend without explanation.

Tribunal hearings are generally completed in one day, although some cases are heard over several days, or exceptionally several weeks. Decisions may be by majority vote, but in fact nearly all are unanimous. The tribunal usually announces its decision and the reasons for it straightaway. A written decision is also sent to the parties, generally within three to six weeks. Both parties have a right to ask for a review of the decision and a right to appeal against the tribunal's decision, on a question of law, to the EAT.

Financial assistance

Legal aid is not available at ETs, but some employees may be able to claim a limited amount of free advice under the legal advice and assistance scheme. This does not cover the cost of a legal representative at the hearing. Allowances are available from the tribunal office to cover costs of travel to a hearing and other expenses both to applicant and respondent, to the witnesses called and to representatives, so long as the representative is not a full-time official of an employers' organisation, a trade union, or a barrister or solicitor. Loss of earnings may also be paid up to a maximum.

PREPARATION OF CASES

The general principle of 'failure to prepare is preparing to fail' applies to anyone appearing before an ET, whether he or she is the applicant, respondent, representative or witness. Careful advance preparation of the available arguments and materials is essential if the case is to be adequately supported and dealt with.

To represent or not to represent?

It is extremely important for any employer who receives a notice of appearance form following an originating application to a tribunal to decide as soon as possible (if this has not already been done under the company's standard procedure) who is responsible for dealing with the matter on his or her behalf. He or she will, therefore, want to decide at the outset whether to handle the case himself or herself, delegate this responsibility to a senior manager (for example, personnel, employee relations or HRM), seek the advice of his or her employers' association (whether or not they provide representation before ETs as part of their service), or employ a lawyer.

To be legally represented or not is frequently a difficult problem. The persuasive value of other tribunal decisions or the binding nature of relevant higher court decisions may greatly assist a party's case, and the services of a lawyer or other practitioner knowledgeable in this area of employment law can be valuable in complex cases. It must be borne in mind that tribunals are arbiters of fact; they act as industrial juries, assessing the reasonableness of employers' actions, and detailed legal argument rarely has more than a limited place in these deliberations.

It is, therefore, a matter of judgement whether the employer or his or her staff handle ET cases, or whether outside representation is sought. Experienced HRM managers in larger firms, who are as familiar as possible about tribunal cases and judgments which may set precedents, should be capable of preparing and presenting most types of tribunal cases in which the employer may become involved. Small employers who do not have the relevant 'in company' expertise are most likely to benefit from the use of external representation.

Prerequisites for a well-prepared case

The prerequisites for adequate preparation include the following which we then consider in greater detail:

- Submission of a well-drafted **notice of appearance** within 14 days.
- Knowledge of the **burdens of proof**, which will have to be discharged, including those on the other party.
- Assembly of the available **documentary evidence** in support of the case to be presented.
- Preparing a **list of the documents** to be referred to in the proceedings and sending the list to the other side and to the tribunal about seven days before the hearing.
- Ensuring that the **necessary witnesses** will be available to attend the hearing.
- Knowledge of the **evidence** that each party's witnesses can give.
- **Anticipation** of the other side's case.
- In cases which are likely to involve complex questions, **access to a source of advice** and information on leading decisions.
- In unfair dismissal cases, **evidence** about the employee's financial loss and, if appropriate and available, his mitigation of it.

The notice of appearance

The notice of appearance which the respondent should deal with is the counterpart of the originating application (IT3), and should be submitted within 14 days of receipt of the originating application. Although the notice of appearance can include as much detail as the respondent wishes, it is not required by the rules of the tribunal to do more than outline the respondent's defence in general terms stating whether or not the respondent intends to resist the application and, if so, setting out 'sufficient particulars to show the grounds on which to resist the application'. The notice of appearance may state the respondent's objectives in presenting the case during the tribunal hearing and identify 'what main questions the respondent wishes the tribunal to decide and how it wishes the tribunal to decide them' (Greenhalgh, 1995, p. 125).

Knowledge of burdens of proof

If a party to ET proceedings does not know what he or she has to prove, it is impossible for his or her case to be adequately prepared. Furthermore, failure to provide evidence in support of an essential point (for example, how a selection for redundancy was made) means that the tribunal may conclude that an employer has not acted reasonably. The respondent should know what he or she has to establish and the 'burdens of proof' which are on the other party. For example, an applicant who has been dismissed must be able to prove this (that is, to discharge the burden of proof on himself or herself) in order to prevent the respondent from arguing that as the 'burden of proof' has not been discharged by the applicant, the applicant's case should therefore fail.

In addition, the general rule and tradition is that the party on whom the first onus of proof lies, presents his or her case first. In an unfair dismissal case, for example, if the respondent denies that the applicant was dismissed, the first onus or burden of proof – to show that there was a dismissal as statutorily defined – falls on the applicant, and the applicant's evidence would be called on first. If, on the other hand, the respondent admitted that the applicant had been dismissed but contended the dismissal was fair, the onus or burden of proving the reason for the dismissal and that it was one of the statutorily permitted ones, would fall on the respondent, and it would be the respondent's evidence which would normally be called on first.

Documentary evidence and lists of documents referred to

Each party should bring all original documents and relevant copies of letters, etc. Examples include:

- the written statement of reasons for dismissal;
- documents relating to the employee's pay (including fringe benefits);
- documents relating to pension/superannuation scheme applicable to the employee;

- letter of appointment; and
- formal warnings.

Tribunals may insist on the original documentation. Hence, if an original document such as a warning letter which one party wants to refer to in evidence is in the possession of the other party, he or she should, if possible, ask that party to make the document available for inspection and copying if necessary.

When sending out notices of hearings, ET offices advise that it may be helpful for the parties, well before the hearing date, to send each other lists of the documents which they respectively intend to refer to at the hearing. If complying with this suggestion, the parties are invited to send their lists to the ET office. The advice envisages that, on receipt of the other side's list, a party may then ask the other side to provide access to one or more of the documents on the list, or supply a copy of it. There is no statutory obligation on anyone to comply with these suggestions, but compliance with them is likely to speed up the proceedings and, in some circumstances, to avoid adjournments to examine the documents which have been produced to the surprise of the other party.

Professional advisers are requested by ET offices to prepare bundles containing all correspondence and other documents on which they intend to rely at the hearing. It seems sensible to suggest that, once such a bundle has been assembled (preferably in chronological order), numbered and listed, the documents in it should be copied and sent to the other side. Whilst ET offices specifically ask that documents (other than lists of documents) should not be sent to the tribunal in advance of the hearing, three sets of the documents should be prepared for the use of tribunal members and handed to them at the beginning of the hearing.

There may be circumstances, particularly when both sides are professionally represented, when the parties can agree in advance the documents to which they wish to refer during the proceedings. This will result in an agreed bundle of documents. Whilst this is desirable, there is no obligation on the parties to agree a bundle. Agreement to a bundle, or preparation of a bundle of documents by one side in advance of a hearing, does not inhibit a party from introducing other documents during the proceedings if this is considered necessary, or would be helpful to the tribunal or to the other side.

In practice, seven sets of documents need to be prepared – three for the tribunal, two for the other side and two for the use of the party preparing the bundle. As the original documents may have to be produced in evidence, there should in addition be a bundle of them which corresponds to the copies in the bundles distributed to those taking part in the proceedings. It is important to note, however, that there is no inference that written statements of the evidence to be given by witnesses should either be included in the lists of documents or in the bundles.

Attendance of witnesses

As in any other court of law, a party to tribunal proceedings can best discharge a burden of proof on him or her by calling evidence to establish the relevant facts. A failure to call a relevant witness when such a witness is available may result in the facts to which that witness could speak not being accepted by a tribunal, particularly if any assertion about those facts is challenged by the other party. As a result of an important case concerning this point, *Norfolk County Council* v *Bernard* (1979) IRLR 220, two points relevant to unfair dismissal cases emerged:

- In a dismissal case tribunals expect to hear evidence from a member of a disciplinary subcommittee, or from the person who took the decision to dismiss an employee, if the tribunal is to conclude that the employer acted reasonably.
- It is very difficult, if not hopeless, to expect to succeed in an appeal against an ET's decision in favour of an employee if there has been a lack of evidence by the employer at the tribunal hearing about his or her reasonableness in the handling of the dismissal.

Usually the parties to tribunal proceedings will themselves arrange for the attendance of witnesses, who will attend voluntarily. However, for unwilling witnesses an application can be made to a tribunal to require their attendance. If it is known in advance that an important witness will not be available on the date notified for the hearing, the tribunal should immediately be asked to arrange another date, the reason for the absence of the witness being given.

Evidence of witnesses

Apart from the essential consideration that the only witnesses to be called are those who are necessary to establish a case, it is important to try to ensure that witnesses confine their observations to the material facts, unless they are specifically asked by the tribunal or by the other side to express an opinion or are themselves experts called to give their professional opinions. A useful way to assess the potential value of the evidence of a particular witness can be to obtain from him or her in advance a written statement of his or her evidence. While this is not a process designed to 'put words into the mouth' of the witness, it is an important part of the preparation of any case. It focuses the attention of the witness on the factual evidence he or she can give and lets the party to the proceedings know whether the witness can cover from first-hand knowledge the points which the party is trying to prove. The best witness statements avoid excursions into irrelevant matters or unsolicited expressions of opinion. A sample witness statement could read as shown in Exhibit 13.5.

Anticipation of other side's case

Whilst the exchange of the originating application and the notice of appearance allows the parties in tribunal proceedings to have advance knowledge of the essentials of the points on which their cases will be founded, it is sensible for each party to try to assess in advance the strength and weakness of the other side's case. This should inevitably lead to an assessment of the weakness of one's own case and, through this, to try to find out how in earlier cases similar weaknesses have been regarded by ETs. For example, if there is doubt about whether a warning in a particular dismissal case has been sufficiently specific in conveying to the employee that his job was at risk, what arguments can the employer glean from previous cases where inadequate warnings had nevertheless been regarded by tribunals as sufficient to show that the employer had acted reasonably?

Source of advice on leading decisions

Because of the complexity and volume of case law which is relevant to tribunal proceedings, some

Exhibit 13.5

Sample witness statement

I am employed as the manager of the branch of X Ltd [with address]. I have held that post since October 1998. A staff of ten is employed at the branch of whom Mr Smith, the complainant, was one up to the time of his dismissal. He had been employed by the company since April 2001 and had worked at this branch throughout his service with the company. During the morning of 18 April this year (2003), I called Mr Smith into my office, and in the presence of my principal assistant, Ms Jones, I pointed out to Mr Smith that he had been half-an-hour late for work that morning and this had followed a number of previous late attendances by him during the preceding four months, on at least two of which I had told him that punctuality was essential for the effective conduct of the business and the proper performance of his contract of employment with the company. I produce a copy of the letter of appointment of Mr Smith and a copy of the written statement of particulars issued to him under the ERA 1996. I asked Mr Smith, 'Do you wish to offer an explanation for your late attendances?' Mr Smith replied, 'I have always told you why I have been late – slow buses and so on. Today was just another of those things.' I said, 'Is there anything you want to add about being half-an-hour late today?' He replied 'Only that I missed the bus this morning and could not get a lift. It's only a half-hour service from where I live, you know.'

I then told him that, particularly in view of his previous attendance record and the oral warnings given to him, I did not consider his explanation to be satisfactory and that therefore, in accordance with the disciplinary rules of the company, I would issue him with a formal written warning about his conduct. I told him that this would draw attention to the fact that further misconduct on his part could result in his dismissal.

Mr Smith then left my office. Later that morning, again in the presence of Ms Jones, I handed Mr Smith a formal written warning, the original copy of which I now produce. The letter was signed by me. I endorsed the copy at that time to record on it that I had handed the original to Mr Smith, and Ms Jones also endorsed the copy to the effect that she had witnessed the original being given to Mr Smith and that this is a true copy of it. I informed Mr Smith that under the disciplinary rules of the company, he had a right of appeal against the issue of a formal warning to him. Mr Smith did not exercise this right.

On 27 May this year (2003) Mr Smith was 50 minutes late for work. Upon his arrival I called him in to my office and again in the presence of Ms Jones asked him whether he wished to give an explanation for his late attendance on this occasion. He replied, 'Nothing that you would believe.' I said 'I am giving you the opportunity to offer an explanation. Whether you take it or not is up to you. I am going to report this latest occurrence to head office. Is there anything else you want to say?' Mr Smith replied 'No.' He left my office and returned to his work. I thereupon telephoned the Personnel Director of the company and reported the matter to him.

employers' organisations and unions provide advisory services designed to assist their members in preparing and presenting cases before tribunals. Many of these services do not involve the engagement of professional lawyers, of whom a relatively small number specialise in employment law, but they are intended either to help the parties themselves in the preparation of their cases, or to make available the services of officials with some experience of appearing before tribunals.

Evidence of an employee's loss

An applicant must be ready to provide evidence to the tribunal, if he or she succeeds in winning his or her case, of the loss which the employer's actions have caused him or her. When preparing his or her case for an unfair dismissal hearing, an employer must anticipate that, however good he or she believes his or her case to be, there will be a finding of unfair dismissal. The respondent should therefore be prepared to challenge any assessment provided by the applicant of his or her loss and, more specifically, to produce evidence about the limit of the employee's loss if this is available.

Summary

- Employment tribunals were established by the Industrial Training Act 1964, and their current jurisdiction is covered by the Employment Tribunals Act 1996. The rules governing how they are administered are contained in a number of regulations and the Employment Rights (Dispute Resolution) Act 1998. The EAT hears appeals against ET decisions, which may proceed to the Court of Appeal and the House of Lords.
- The caseload of tribunals has risen steeply and mainly concerns unfair dismissal and employment contract-related issues.
- ACAS performs an important conciliation function where cases may be settled without recourse to ETs.
- The Employment Rights (Dispute Resolution) Act 1998 introduced a number of reforms to the tribunal system including the renaming of tribunals, attenuated hearings, hearings by the chair alone and the establishment of 'legal officers'.
- The Employment Rights (Dispute Resolution) Act also provides for a voluntary arbitration scheme drawn up by ACAS, applying initially to unfair dismissal and phased in during the course of 1999.
- It is important that a case is adequately prepared by both applicant and respondent and preparation should take the following into consideration:
  - a well-drafted notice of appearance submitted in good time;
  - knowledge of discharging burdens of proof;
  - assembling available documentary evidence to support a case;
  - preparing a list and bundle of documents which may be referred to during the hearing;
  - ensuring attendance of witnesses and knowledge of evidence of witnesses; and
  - anticipation of the other side's case.

RELEVANT WEBSITES

www.acas.org.uk (Advisory, Conciliation and Arbitration Service)

www.employmenttribunals.gov.uk The Employment Tribunals website.

www.dti.gov.uk/er/redundancy.htm (Department of Trade and Industry) Document concerning redundancy arrangements.

REFERENCES

ACAS (1998–2002) *Annual Report*. London, ACAS (individual publication for each year)

ACAS (2000) *Discipline at Work: The ACAS Advisory Handbook*. London, ACAS

CIPD (Chartered Institute of Personnel and Development) (2002) *Redundancy*. London, CIPD

Collins, H. (1992) *Justice in Dismissal*. Oxford, Oxford University Press

DTI (Department of Trade and Industry) (1999) *Review of Tribunal Regulations*. London, DTI

DTI (Department of Trade and Industry) (2001) *Transfer of Undertakings (Protection of Employment) Regulations 1981: Government Proposals for Reform*. www.dti.gov.uk/er/tupe (accessed 15.7.03)

Eggert, M. (1991) *Outplacement*. London, IPM

Fryer, R.H. (1973) 'The myths of the Redundancy Payments Act'. *Industrial Law Journal*, vol. 2, pp. 1–12

Gennard, J. and Judge, G. (1997) *Employee Relations*. London, IPD

Gennard, J. and Judge, G. (2002) *Employee Relations*, 3nd edn. London, CIPD

Greenhalgh, R. (1995) *Industrial Tribunals*. London, IPD

IDS (Incomes Data Services) (1999) *Guide to the Employment Relations Act, 1999*. London, IDS

IDS (Incomes Data Services) (2002) Employment Act 2002. London, IDS

IRS (1998) 'The 1998 IRS Redundancy Survey Parts 1 and 2'. *IRS Employment Trends*, No. 659

IRS (1999) 'Polkey reductions'. *Industrial Relations Law Bulletin*, No. 608

IRS (2001) 'The 2001 IRS Redundancy Survey'. *IRS Employment Trends*, No. 728

IRS (2002) 'Managing downsizing and redundancy'. *IRS Employment Trends*, No. 759

Lewis, D. and Sargeant, M. (2002) *Essentials of Employment Law*. London, CIPD

LMT (Labour Market Trends) (2001) 'Labour market update'. *Labour Market Trends*, December, 531

Painter, R.W. and Puttick, K. (1998) *Employment Rights*. London, Pluto Press

Sahdev, K. (2002) *Managing Downsizing: Getting it Right*. Oxford, Chandos

Salamon, M. (1998) *Industrial Relations: Theory and Practice*, 3rd edn. Hemel Hempstead, Prentice Hall

PART 5

CONCLUSION

CHAPTER 14

THE RECENT PAST AND THE NEAR FUTURE

THE RECENT PAST

One of the main themes throughout the book is that of continuity and change. The problems and issues facing the main parties to employment relations (the employer, Chapter 2, the unions, Chapter 3 and the state, Chapter 4) have either changed in emphasis or changed altogether in recent years (see Chapter 1 for an overview). A casual analysis will reveal a bewildering variety of factors accounting for such change, all of which have been considered in the preceding chapters. The collective nature of employment relations institutions and processes such as collective bargaining and state regulation have been seriously undermined over the past three decades. For example, Millward *et al.* (2000) point to the dramatic fall in the coverage of collective bargaining with pay being a rare rather than a routine negotiated issue (Chapter 6), which itself is a consequence of the decline of the unionised sector and collective representation during the 1980s, 1990s and early 2000s. As collective representation declined so forms of direct communications with employees gained in prominence. The main developments over the period are identified as follows and are then discussed in turn:

- the increasing emphasis on market forces;
- the acceleration in the restructuring of British industry;
- the management of the employment relationship;
- the decline in collective bargaining;
- the increasing emphasis on communicating with the workforce;
- the plight of the trade unions;
- workplace representation of employees; and
- the decline in industrial action.

Market forces

With the advent of the Conservative governments during the 1980s until 1997, the emphasis upon market forces was to have a profound effect upon employment relations generally and the labour market in particular (Chapter 4). Employers' 'right to manage' was reinforced partly by restricting the powers and activities of trade unions and partly by encouraging fluidity and flexibility within the labour market. Individual employee rights were limited in some respects, with successive governments refusing to endorse the EU Social Chapter and Directives which would have extended employment protection in a number of significant areas. (However, in some cases legal decisions within the EU forced government to adopt certain measures. These included greater protection and consultation rights during transfer of undertakings, some widening of the legislation concerning race and sex discrimination to include equal pay, the introduction of legislation concerning disability discrimination and extension of the consultation regulations concerning health and safety – all considered in Chapters 12–14.) Many private sector employers were thus achieving greater control over the work and labour process, adopting anti-union strategies and shifting from pluralist to more unitarist styles (Chapter 2). In the public sector managers were appointed by government in order to prepare certain nationalised industries and concerns for privatisation and this was to have a profound effect upon the nature of employment relations within these industries. For example, the coal mining industry was decimated with dramatic reductions in the size of the workforce and a corresponding diminution in strength and power of the once proud NUM. In adopting HRM practices and strategies, managers reinforced the move away from collectivism to individualism.

The shift from collectivism to individualism was also assisted by the wide-ranging programme of legislation which was designed to erode the alleged 'monopoly power' of trade unions, while at the same time enhancing unilateral management control over the employment relationship. Specifically, during the early 1980s for example, support for trade union representation and collective bargaining diminished and restrictions were imposed upon secondary industrial action and picketing. Unions were made liable for unlawful industrial action. The incremental approach taken by government ensured that the legislation was palatable although not necessarily acceptable. By 1997, for example, protection against unfair dismissal was weakened by extending the qualifying period to two years, and all industrial action was considered unlawful if the necessary ballots and notice requirements were not met.

From 1997 to 2003, the retrograde developments instigated by previous Conservative governments were halted, and, despite the many instances of employment protection legislation enacted by the two New Labour governments, including statutory provision for union recognition and the minimum wage legislation, the intention was not to restore the collective union voice which lost so much ground during the 1980s and 1990s (Chapter 4).

The restructuring of British industry

The restructuring of British industry tended to accelerate during the 1980s and 1990s, the backdrop being the collapse of large sectors of traditional manufacturing industry and the shift towards an economy increasingly dominated by the service industries (the so-called 'post-industrial society' or 'service economy' – see Chapters 1 and 5). In addition, many sectors such as financial services, transport, telecommunications and broadcasting were subject to increased competition. These heightened competitive pressures were caused by the liberalisation of both internal markets and trade within the EU and were also linked to the increasingly global nature of markets. Another significant development was the rapid adoption of new computerised and information

technologies and the consequence of this development upon skills and work organisation in both the manufacturing and service sectors. The shift away from 'standard' forms of employment contract towards the increased use of non-standard contracts such as part-time and temporary work, together with a significant increase in labour market insecurity, have had a marked impact upon the employment relationship. The following areas were considered in greater detail by WERS98 (Cully *et al.*, 1999; Millward *et al.*, 2000).

Employment and contraction of the public sector

Since the 1980 WIRS survey which found that service industry workplaces outnumbered manufacturing industry workplaces by a ratio of two to one, both the 1990 and 1998 surveys have revealed an increase in the dominance of the service sector over manufacturing by a ratio of three to one. This is mainly, but not wholly due to the extensive privatisation and contracting-out of public sector services and industries. There was also a corresponding decline in employment in manufacturing more than matched by an increase in employment within the service sector. According to the 1998 WERS survey, workplaces within manufacturing account for 37 per cent of private sector employment and 25 per cent of all employees covered by the survey.

The contraction of the public sector has been such that by 1998 only Royal Mail and Transport for London were major employers still under state ownership. By 1998 the WERS revealed that the proportion of public sector workplaces had fallen to 28 per cent and accounted for 32 per cent of all employees in workplaces with more than 25 employees (down from 43 per cent of all employees in 1984).

Workplace size

No overall trend towards smaller workplaces has been revealed by the surveys since 1980. The 1998 survey revealed that workplaces employing between 25 and 49 employees still accounted for half the workplaces covered by the survey, while workplaces having between 50 and 99 employees accounted for a quarter of all workplaces. The 1998 survey also pointed to an increase in the proportion of 'stand-alone' sites (where the workplace and organisation are one and the same) which accounted for 27 per cent of workplaces with 25 or more employees. Within the private sector, there has been an increase in the number and proportion of foreign-owned or controlled workplaces which now comprise 13 per cent of workplaces in that sector (up from 6 per cent in 1980).

Nature of the labour force

The two important developments affecting the labour force during the 1980s, 1990s and early 2000s have been, firstly, a marked change in the proportion of the workforce employed on regular full-time contracts, which has resulted in an expansion of part-time work, and, secondly, an increase in labour market participation of women. The expansion of women's work has been almost entirely due to an expansion of part-time work and the explanation for the growth of this phenomenon has been subject to some controversy. The most plausible explanation is threefold:

1. Some employers may deliberately use part-time contracts in order to obtain a lower-paid workforce. As part-time work provides insufficient pay to support a family, it may lead to the recruitment primarily of female workers, thereby providing the basis for gender segregation of the workforce.
2. Part-time work may benefit employers as part-time labour is seen to be more flexible with regard to hours of work or the ability to dismiss employees. Part-time workers may be more willing to vary their hours of work, can be recruited to cover peak workloads, and could be more easily dismissed in times of economic difficulty because of their relatively limited coverage by employment legislation.
3. One important factor behind the growth of part-time work has been women's own preferences concerning working hours which reconcile employment with domestic circumstances.

Whatever the nature of the explanation, there are profound implications of this development for employment relations. For example, part-time work is often associated with inferior employment conditions and employment opportunities, and part-time workers are less likely than their full-time counterparts to be trade union members. This in itself may be sufficient to explain the decline in traditional systems of joint workplace regulation.

Other developments having important consequences for the conduct of the employment relationship include:

1. The phenomenal growth of temporary work from the mid-1990s which largely benefits employers where the emphasis is on low skill levels, poor employment conditions and acute job insecurity of such work. Temporary workers may, therefore, be regarded by employers as a favourable leverage in tipping the balance of power towards employers by encouraging a relatively cowed and docile workforce too afraid of joining trade unions.
2. The expansion of non-standard employment contracts may generate a distinct labour market segment in which the employment relationship is very different from that in the traditional employment model based on full-time work.
3. The extensive reduction in staffing levels and the frequent resort to large-scale redundancies has been a recurrent feature of employer policies from the late 1970s onwards and this continues to have implications for job stability and security.

WERS98 provides evidence for the increase in part-time work and the increased participation within the labour market of women. The proportion of workplaces with a high percentage of female employees rose from 22 per cent in 1984 to 29 per cent in 1998. WERS also records a substantial increase of part-time employees at workplace level in 1998 as compared to 1980 and 1984, particularly in those workplaces already having a proportion of part-time staff. The most significant finding here is that the proportion of those workplaces where at least 25 per cent of employees work part-time has grown significantly between 1990 (32 per cent of workplaces) and 1998 (44 per cent of workplaces). Overall, across the whole range of workplaces covered by WERS, 25 per cent of all employees worked part-time in 1998, compared with 18 per cent of all employees in 1990.

The management of the employment relationship

The management of the employment relationship has been dealt with in various parts of this book. Perhaps the most important change during the 1980s, 1990s and early 2000s was the shift in management thinking from an industrial relations to an HRM perspective (although we have maintained that the two approaches are not necessarily mutually exclusive – see Chapters 2, 5 and 7). Within both the large firm sector and the public sector, the traditional industrial relations model was based on collective bargaining and joint regulation of conditions of employment at both workplace and organisational levels. As we have seen, the weakening of the trade union power base, the haemorrhaging of union membership and the rise in the proportion of establishments and workplaces with no union presence during the 1980s provided some opportunity for British employers to reconsider the underlying pattern of relations with their employees. The precise nature and causes of these changes in management thinking have been considered in earlier chapters, although, the extent of their importance for the actual practice of employment relationships is still a matter for further research: there is patchy evidence concerning the growth and prevalence of HRM policies, with most studies examining only the formal commitment of employers to such policies. Of particular concern is whether such policies are viewed operationally by employers, managers and workers as methods of increasing and improving the dialogue between management and individual employees, improving the opportunities for employee involvement and relating more adequately reward to individual performance. On the other hand, these policies could be seen as an alternative mode of control of work performance leading to pressures for an intensification of work rather than to any liberation from control.

WERS98 does, however, provide us with some new evidence of how managements organise themselves in new ways to deal with the changing nature of employment relations. In particular, the survey considers the presence of specialists at the workplace, employment relations management in complex organisations and the changing role of the employment relations manager as identified below.

Workplace specialists

The presence of workplace personnel specialists (defined as 'managers whose job titles contain any of the terms "personnel, human resources or industrial, employee or staff relations" *and* who spend at least a quarter of their time on such matters', Cully *et al.*, 1999, p. 224), suggests that a workplace is 'devoting substantial resources to dealing with employment relations issues' (ibid., p. 224). The number and proportion of workplaces having personnel specialists satisfying this definition rose by 33 per cent during the 1990s and was accompanied by an increase in the responsibility of line and other managers for employment relations matters.

Complex organisations

Despite patchy evidence suggesting that where the employment relations function and personnel specialists are represented at board level and head offices respectively, the more likely employment relations issues are considered part of business strategy, WERS reveals that fewer head offices employed personnel specialists in 1998 than previously, the proportion falling sharply between 1990 and 1998 from 47 per cent to 36 per cent. In the private sector, the decline started earlier, from 1984 onwards, with the falling trend accelerating throughout the 1990s.

Changing role of employment relations managers/personnel specialists

WERS reveals that the employment relations functions of specialists in terms of the average number of tasks they performed has changed little since 1984 (Chapter 2) – the only significant change being reduced responsibility for payment systems. However, personnel specialists were devoting less time to these functions in 1998 than previously (86 per cent of their time in 1984; 69 per cent of their time in 1998). On the other hand, the responsibilities of non-specialists grew during the 1990s, with their involvement, on average, in almost five of the six job responsibilities in 1998. More non-specialists were engaged on these tasks in 1998 than in previous years, and their involvement was particularly pronounced concerning pay and conditions of employment (both of which are subject to increased unilateral management control), and also in the handling of grievances.

Management strategy and structure

While a strategic approach to management, whereby HRM is integrated with organisational aims and objectives, may be regarded as desirable, the reality for many organisations and workplaces suggests that such integration, where attempted, is severely constrained by structural factors. In examining the management function and approach to the management of employees across a whole range of functions, from recruitment to termination of employment, WERS revealed considerable management discretion and diversity concerning these functions. For example:

- Across workplaces there were wide variations in labour deployment.
- Many workplaces practised numerical flexibility which was often associated with low pay.
- Other approaches to flexibility included the use of non-standard forms of labour within the core workforce.
- 'High commitment' management practices were identified in workplaces having an active union presence.

Do these practices comprise a strategic approach? WERS98 found that around 66 per cent of workplaces claimed to have strategic plans which involved an HRM component, but only 57 per cent of workplaces had an 'integrated employee development plan'. In relation to the structure of the personnel function, 60 per cent of all workplaces had a personnel specialist, if not actually located at workplace level then at a higher level within the organisation. Taking strategy and structure together, while these are important determinants of management style, 'the diffusion of high commitment management practices was not particularly widespread. Most employers' approaches are geared towards retaining control while cutting labour costs, as witnessed by the widespread use of part-time contracts, contracted-out and agency workers and other forms of non-standard labour' (Millward *et al.*, 2000, p. 152). WERS also found that:

- Control and monitoring systems in most workplaces are fairly sophisticated, although the information on which these systems are based is not shared widely with employees.
- There was a relative absence of any devolution of authority from both senior to line management and from management to employees; line managers normally were not authorised to make decisions on matters such as recruitment, awarding pay increases or dismissals.

It appears that during the period of the surveys, there has been little evidence of any growth in strategic behaviour, the emphasis being on tight control systems and the selective adoption of high commitment practices largely on an ad hoc basis. Cully *et al.* (1999) conclude:

However, the evidence does justify the large amount of attention devoted to this area in recent years by demonstrating, from both a management and employee perspective, a close association between high commitment practices, committed employees and a superior climate of employment relations. As ever, though, a conundrum remains: why if this is the case, are such practices not more widespread? (p. 295)

The decline in collective bargaining

Collective bargaining, and in particular multi-employer bargaining, continued in seemingly inexorable decline throughout the 1990s and early 2000s. According to WERS98, multi-employer bargaining affected the pay of some or all employees in 34 per cent of workplaces with recognised trade unions in 1998, compared with 68 per cent in 1980 and 60 per cent in 1990. The decline was even more marked when the falling proportion of workplaces with recognised unions is considered. The only sector where multi-employer bargaining remains consistently high is the public sector with 41 per cent of public sector workplaces engaging at this level of bargaining (Chapter 6).

Communicating with the workforce

With the advent of HRM, much emphasis has been placed upon communicating with the workforce, not only through formal representative structures such as JCCs, but also through direct means or channels. Some of these are the regular use of the management chain, regular newsletters to all employees, regular meetings between management and workforce and suggestion schemes. Of these more direct forms of communication, WERS found that for the period 1984 to 1998:

- The most commonly reported method of direct communication, particularly in larger workplaces, was through the use of the management chain, with 60 per cent of workplaces using this method in 1998.
- The use of regular newsletters to all employees was the second most common method of direct communication, the use of which increased steadily throughout the 1980s and 1990s, from 34 per cent of all workplaces in 1984 to 50 per cent in 1990. The increase was much more pronounced in the manufacturing industry and in small organisations with fewer than 1000 employees.
- Regular meetings between senior management and all sections of the workforce also became more widespread during the 1980s and 1990s, affecting 34 per cent of all workplaces in 1984 and 48 per cent in 1998. The increase was more marked in smaller workplaces.
- Suggestion schemes also became more popular during this period, although the rate of increase in the use of this form of communication was slower than the other methods and affected fewer workplaces, with 33 per cent of workplaces operating them in 1998.

Information given to employees

Responses from management were sought concerning the following types of information given to employees or their representatives:

- **The financial position of the workplace.** Here, the proportion of workplaces where such provision was made rose from 55 per cent in 1984 to 66 per cent in 1998, with more substantial increases in small and medium-sized workplaces, particularly in the public sector.
- **The financial position of the organisation.** There was a very slight increase during the period in the proportion of workplaces where management

was willing to provide such information from 60 per cent of all workplaces to 61 per cent.
- **Investment plans.** Here, there was a substantial increase in providing this type of information from 27 per cent of all workplaces in 1980 to 53 per cent in 1998. The increase was more substantial within the public sector during 1990–8 as a result, for example, of agency operation in central government, trust status in the NHS and devolution of budgeting in many areas.
- **Staffing and manpower plans.** Responses reveal a substantial decline during 1984–90 from 67 per cent to 60 per cent of all workplaces and a slight rise during 1990–8 to 61 per cent of all workplaces. Again, it was more common to provide such information in the public sector and larger workplaces in the private sector.

The plight of trade unions

We have considered the plight of trade unions in the 1990s and early 2000s, particularly in relation to trade union membership and recognition. The decline in aggregate union membership slowed considerably in 1998–9 and there are some grounds for arguing that membership may increase slightly but significantly during 2000–1 partly as a result of recognition procedures contained in the ERA99. This does not mask the immensity of the change that has taken place since 1980 and which has been commented upon earlier in this chapter and throughout the book. WERS throws additional light on the nature of these developments, particularly at workplace level.

Union presence

By this is meant the presence of at least one union member at a workplace. After holding steady, union presence declined rapidly during the period 1984–98, from 73 per cent of workplaces in 1984 to 54 per cent in 1998, down by almost a third. There are variations by sector, with the public sector having a union presence in virtually every workplace, while in both private manufacturing and private services there was a rapid decline, with the former registering a fall from 77 per cent of workplaces in 1980 to

42 per cent in 1998. Measures of union density since 1998, such as those provided by successive Labour Force Surveys, have confirmed the decline in union presence. The slight increase in union membership for 2002–3 should not provide grounds for misplaced optimism.

Union membership density

As with union presence, overall union density across all workplaces fell steadily from 65 per cent in 1980 to 36 per cent in 1998. There are, however, significant variations across time and also between sectors of the economy. The period from 1980 to 1990 saw a fall in density of around 25 per cent in both private manufacturing and services with only a slight fall in the public sector. From 1990 to 1998, there was a much steeper decline in private services than in the other two sectors. There are also significant variations in union density across workplaces. For example, the proportion of workplaces with no union members increased substantially from 30 per cent of all workplaces in 1980 to 47 per cent in 1998. There was also a significant fall in workplaces with high levels of density, with the greatest rate of decline in those workplaces having 100 per cent membership, from 18 per cent of workplaces in 1980 down to 2 per cent of workplaces in 1998. Within the private sector the fall in membership density from 1980 to 1990 applied equally to all sizes of workplace and enterprise but, after 1990, the fall was much more marked within smaller workplaces and enterprises. The age of workplaces is significant, with older workplaces generally having higher union membership than younger ones.

Trade union recognition

The decline in trade union recognition for purposes of collective bargaining concerning pay and conditions of work (joint regulation) is examined in some detail by WERS. While there was no significant change in the public sector workplaces, private sector services and manufacturing workplaces of all types experienced a steep decline with the smallest workplaces having a greater rate of decline than larger ones. For example, the incidence of union recognition in workplaces having 25 to 49 employees fell from 30 per cent to 16 per cent during the period. The overall fall in recognition between 1990 and 1998 can be largely accounted for by the fact that newly-established workplaces were much less likely to recognise trade unions. Union recognition does not necessarily imply that all employees in a recognised workplace are affected by collective agreements. WERS identifies the proportion of employees in such workplaces who are actually covered by collective bargaining. Across all workplaces there was a decline in coverage from 70 per cent of all employees in 1984 to 41 per cent in 1998, the decline in coverage reflecting the decline in union recognition. It is still too early to gauge the effect of the statutory trade union recognition procedures but, as pointed out in Chapter 3, instances of recognition have increased and membership increases have been registered. Whether these increases are anything more than marginal remains to be seen.

Workplace representation

With the decline in union membership and recognition over the past 20 or so years the extent of collective representation of unionised employees becomes problematic. We have traced the relative decline of workplace representation of employees by shop stewards (Chapters 3, 5 and 8) and the WIRS surveys up to and including 1990 have confirmed this decline. However, a significant finding of WERS98 is that the decline bottomed out in 1990 and there was no further fall during the period 1990 to 1998. The private sector generally experienced the steepest decline in shop steward representation during the period; in 1980, 38 per cent of all private sector workplaces had a local union representative, while in 1998 only 17 per cent of these workplaces had one.

With regard to non-union representatives within the private sector, the proportion of non-union workplaces having these representatives remained virtually constant during the period 1990–8 (11 per cent of non-union workplaces in 1990 and 12 per cent in 1998). However, non-union representatives became more common in private sector services and less common in private sector manufacturing, and were more prevalent in larger workplaces.

Consultative committees

The proportion of workplaces with joint consultative committees (JCCs) did not decline substantially from 1980. After a fall from around 33 per cent of workplaces in 1980 to 29 per cent of workplaces in 1990, there was no further decline during 1990–8. The initial decline in the proportion of workplaces having JCCs is mainly attributed to the decline in the manufacturing sector generally during 1980 to 1990. Looking at JCCs by sector, WERS notes a slight decline in the public sector and a more substantial rise in the private sector, particularly within small and medium-sized workplaces, and where unions were recognised.

The decline in industrial action

In line with the national trend towards fewer industrial disputes involving fewer working days lost, WIRS confirms that the incidence of both official and unofficial *collective* industrial action fell by around 50 per cent during the period 1980 to 1990. Legal restrictions imposed by successive and incremental legislation during the 1980s together with the decline in union representations are common reasons given for the decline in industrial action. During that period, however, there had been some increase in individual conflict between employer and employee. For the period 1990 to 1998, WERS uses two indexes to measure both collective and individual conflict – the incidence of collective industrial action during the past year and the number of ET cases initiated by employees during the past year. The main findings are:

- A dramatic decline in the incidence of industrial action during this period, from 13 per cent of workplaces in 1990 to 2 per cent of workplaces in 1998.
- Strike action fell more steeply than non-strike action, with overtime bans and work-to-rules being the most common form of non-strike action.
- By 1998 'collective industrial action of any kind has thus virtually disappeared from British workplaces, a far cry from the situation at the start of our series, when around a quarter of workplaces experienced it in the course of a year' (Cully *et al.*, 1999, p. 171).

THE NEAR FUTURE

Prediction is risky, particularly in the volatile area of employment relations. The WERS98 data is already dated and the temptation is to play safe in predicting that established trends will continue for the remainder of the 2000s, to be confirmed or refuted by a subsequent WERS expected from 2005. There are problems with extrapolating from both theory and survey data. Concerning the former, competing and often conflicting theories imply multiple contrasting futures. For example, Marxist inspired theories are change-oriented (see mobilisation theory, Chapter 1) and predict the elimination of inequality between buyers and sellers of labour at work, while systems theory posits a future of equilibrium or 'steady state' where change at best is incremental and adaptive. Survey data is often inaccurate, incomplete and ambiguous and too specifically grounded to have general validity. Moreover, the interpretation of data is sometimes used to justify one or more trends and/or tendencies according to researchers' values. Even forecasting from existing known patterns using WERS and other survey data is fraught with uncertainty.

Nevertheless, it seems likely that many of the trends and developments concerning workplace employment relations will continue in the foreseeable future. At the 'macro' level there most certainly has been change which we have referred to throughout this book. However, the underlying patterns of continuity within the employment relationship persist, partly due to the many managers too conservative to embrace enlightened change and partly due to the structures and systems of control which enable inequalities within the employment relationship to persist, if not deepen. In considering the broader context of British employment relations, we look briefly at government policy, trade unions, collective bargaining, and the European Union.

Government policy

As mentioned earlier, prediction is problematic, but with the drawing to an end of the second term of a New Labour government, the emphasis remains upon continuity rather than drastic change and this is likely to continue into a third Labour term.

The main changes comprising the so-called 'lasting settlement' have been considered in some detail elsewhere in the book (the NMW; signing the EU Social Chapter and endorsement of Directives such as the EWC Directive; the Employment Relations Act 1999 with its provisions for individual and limited collective rights; the Employment Act 2002; and the imminent equality and information/consultation legislation). The emphasis will continue to be upon individual rather than collective rights, while still retaining Conservative legislation, which in terms of its severe regulation of trade unions is the most restrictive in Western Europe.

The balance of power between management and unions remains unchanged and probably will continue to favour the employer while the anti-union legislation remains on the statute book and as long as New Labour continues to appease the employers within the CBI. However, it would be fatuous to deny that despite the continuity with Conservative legislation there has not been a change in political direction, but it is a change that does not include employment relations as a significant part of New Labour's agenda, and in its incarnation as the 'Third Way' is subject to highly ambiguous interpretations. The so-called 'Third Way' (not as popular a term as it was during 1997–8) appears to embrace the move from collectivism to individualism, although acknowledging the need for government involvement and some regulation to promote 'fairness' and 'social partnership' within a national and EU context, while coming to terms with the economic and social dislocations caused by the globalising tendencies of international capitalism and the consequences of the ongoing and accelerating pace of information technology.

Moreover, New Labour's 'settlement' does not appear to represent a significant turning point for employment relations as it does not go far enough to redress the imbalances of power within the employment relationship. The British employment relations arena is still characterised by both the worst excesses of deregulated labour markets and the punitive curbs on collective action. Hence, despite the positive changes that New Labour has introduced, nothing short of a rolling programme of reforms aimed at improving the protection of collective and individual rights at work will suffice. As it stands at the moment the 'settlement' and the values and rhetoric it embraces are, at best, wholly inadequate. Two further developments may sour relations further between government and organised labour: the first is the government's 'modernisation' programme within public services (see Chapter 4) and the second is the marked reluctance to take the partnership ethos onto the national stage with the TUC and, at the danger of resurrecting 'tripartism', with the CBI.

Trade unions

As noted in Chapter 3, there has been a 20-year decline in union membership during which the percentage of the workforce covered by collective agreements fell from around 75 per cent to 40 per cent. However, there are reasons to believe that the prospects for a slight recovery of union membership and influence are better for the period 2003 and beyond than for many years:

- Unemployment has been declining for a number of years and with the October 2003 figure the lowest since 1980 the potential for increasing union membership will improve.
- The union recognition provisions in the Employment Relations Act 1999 will continue to assist union-organising drives, and although the relative complexity of the legislation has been a problem, many employers have concluded such agreements.
- Recent Labour Force surveys reveal a dramatic change in the composition of union membership. There is now little difference in the unionisation rates of men and women, while the gap between part-time and full-time employees is closing.
- Other factors which may encourage employees to join unions include a cumulative sense of grievance or injustice concerning their treatment in the workplace; their belief that management is either to blame for their problem or is unwilling to deal fairly with it; and their belief that a union would be able to take effective action to redress individual and collective grievances.

The prospects for increased union membership, and for unions themselves, have, therefore, certainly improved and unions and the TUC has responded to the challenge by identifying three broad strategies. The first of these incorporates the so-called *servicing model* which involves a move away from collective bargaining to servicing individual employees by devoting increased resources to the enforcement of individual legal rights. The second of these involves the *partnership approach* advocated by the TUC (see Chapter 8) and requires strong trade unions co-operating with employers to encourage the competitive success of the enterprise and the well-being of union members. By demonstrating that the union can 'add value' to the firm, the expectation is that employers will take unions seriously and agree to joint regulation of employment. Many successful attempts to secure partnership have, however, had the opposite effect as several 'partnership' companies have derecognised unions or threatened to do so. Elsewhere, a number of partnership companies have seen a weakening of workplace unionism as less time is spent by managers with workplace union representatives. The third strategy, the *organising model*, places much greater emphasis on gaining support among the workforce for a strong union presence and conflicts to some extent with the partnership approach (Chapters 3 and 8). This has been the more successful strategy, but the problem here is how unions and employers can cope with the hostility generated by these campaigns and move on to more stable bargaining relationships.

Should these strategies succeed, and the organising model seems best placed to do so, and if unions can devote enough resources to organising campaigns, then the prospects for union membership into the late 2000s seem more positive than hitherto.

Collective bargaining

The coverage of collective bargaining is directly related to the level of union membership. If, once more, the prospects for union membership are good, then collective bargaining will undoubtedly enjoy a renaissance. Earlier in the book we considered a number of developments affecting collective bargaining as a process and as an institution. These are:

- The continuing decline in multi-employer or industry-wide bargaining prevalent within private sector services and manufacturing and within the

privatised industries and services. This process is likely to continue within the foreseeable future.
- Some fragmentation of bargaining within the public and local authority sectors consistent with the contracting out of services and other changes.
- The decline in multi-employer bargaining accompanied by a decentralisation of bargaining to company level or single-employer bargaining.
- Some growth in the number of single-union agreements which is likely to be given some impetus as a result of the recognition provisions contained within the Employment Relations Act 1999. The development of partnership agreements (see below) will also result in more single-union deals.
- A reduction in the scope of substantive issues subject to bargaining as noted by WERS (see below). The supplanting or supplementing of collective pay determination by performance pay is now well established as is the extension of performance pay in new areas such as the teaching profession.

Partnership agreements are an outcome of the bargaining process. It is still too early to say whether these agreements will actually live up to the rhetoric espoused by government, the TUC and the partnership parties themselves, and we have already identified some reservations in this area. For the TUC, 'partnership' between employer and union is non-adversarial, placing consensus and co-operation high on the agenda. A significant benchmark development is the partnership project between Barclays Bank and UNIFI, commented upon in Chapter 8, which involves a three-year pay deal and other benefits for employees such as private health care and improved sickness benefits. An important element within the project is agreement on a system of jointly accredited union representatives. Optimism concerning the future of partnership agreements remains high within the TUC Partnership Institute and it may yet transpire that these optimistic predictions will come to pass.

The European Union

Throughout the book we have considered the impact of the EU upon various aspects of the individual and collective employment relationship. The most significant change since 1997 was the ending of the opt-out from the Social Chapter which enables the government to incorporate decisions and Directives within national legislation. The Employment Relations Act 1999 and the Employment Act 2002 contain EU-inspired provisions which improve individual rights at work. Other Directives such as the EWC Directive, the Directive concerning consultation on collective redundancies and TUPE, the equality Directives concerning age and religious discrimination and probably one of the most contentious and significant, the Information and Consultation Directive, have been or will shortly be enacted. It therefore seems highly likely that national legislation within the employment relations area will be increasingly influenced by the EU in some form or other, and this will help to redress the imbalances and inequalities within what is still one of the most deregulated labour markets in Europe. The extent to which, given the enlarged nature of the European Union, the process towards a more coherent 'Europeanisation' of employment relations will be achieved remains highly problematic.

REFERENCES

Cully, M., Woodland, S., O'Reilly, A. and Dix, G. (1999) *Britain At Work*. London, Routledge

Millward, N., Bryson, A. and Forth, J. (2000) *All Change at Work?* London, Routledge

LIST OF ABBREVIATIONS

KEY TRADE UNIONS: 2003

Amicus-AEEU	Amalgamated Engineering and Electrical Union half of Amicus
Amicus-MSF	Amicus half of Manufacturing Science and Finance Union
ATL	Association of Teachers and Lecturers
AUT	Association of University Teachers
BACM	British Association of Colliery Management
BAEA	British Actors Equity Association
BALPA	British Air Line Pilots Association
BECTU	Broadcasting, Entertainment, Cinematograph and Theatre Union
BMA	British Medical Association
CPSU	Civil and Public Services Union
CWU	Communication Workers Union
EETPU	Electrical, Electronic, Telecommunications and Plumbing Union
FBU	Fire Brigades Union
GMB	General Municipal and Boilermakers (now known simply as 'GMB')
GPMU	Graphical Paper and Media Union
ISTC	Iron and Steel Trades Confederation
MU	Musicians Union
NAHT	National Association of Head Teachers
NASUWT	National Association of Schoolmasters and Union of Women Teachers
NATFHE	National Association of Teachers in Further and Higher Education
NUJ	National Union of Journalists
NUM	National Union of Mineworkers
NUT	National Union of Teachers
PCSU	Public and Commercial Services Union
POA	Prison Officers Association
Prospect	Recruits from engineering, scientific, managerial and professional staff in agriculture, defence, electricity supply, energy, shipbuilding and transport
RCM	Royal College of Midwives
RCN	Royal College of Nursing of the United Kingdom
RMT	National Union of Rail, Maritime and Transport Workers
TGWU	Transport and General Workers Union
TSSA	Transport Salaried Staffs Association
UCATT	Union of Construction Allied Trades and Technicians
UDM	Union of Democratic Mineworkers
UNIFI	Financial and Banking Services
UNISON	The Public Service Union
USDAW	Union of Shop, Distributive and Allied Workers

OTHER RELEVANT ABBREVIATIONS

ABP	Associated British Ports
ACAS	Advisory Conciliation and Arbitration Service
BIM	British Institute of Management
BPIF	British Printing Industries Federation
CAC	Central Arbitration Committee
CBI	Confederation of British Industry
CCT	compulsory competitive tendering
CEEP	European Centre of Public Enterprises
CEGB	Central Electricity Generating Board
CIPD	Chartered Institute of Personnel and Development
CO	certification officer
CRE	Commission for Racial Equality
CROTUM	Commissioner for the Rights of Trade Union Members
DDA	Disability Discrimination Act 1995
DDP	dismissal and disciplinary procedure
DRC	Disability Rights Commission
EA2002	Employment Act 2002
EAT	Employment Appeals Tribunal
EC	European Commission
ECIA	Engineering Construction Industry Association
ECITB	Engineering Construction Industry Training Board
ECJ	European Court of Justice
EEF	Engineering Employers' Federation
EI	employee involvement
EMU	European Monetary Union
EO	equal opportunities
EOC	Equal Opportunities Commission
EP	employee participation
EPA	Employment Protection Act 1975
EPCA	Employment Protection (Consolidation) Act 1978
ERA	Employment Rights Act 1996
ERA99	Employment Relations Act 1999
ET	employment tribunal
ETUC	European Trade Union Confederation
EWC	European Works Council
FDI	foreign direct investment
FILO	first in, last out
FTO	full-time officer
GCHQ	Government Communications Headquarters
GMF	genuine material factor
GOQ	genuine occupational qualification
GP	grievance procedure
HPW	high performance workplace
HRM	human resource management
ICFTU	International Confederation of Free Trade Unions
IDS	Incomes Data Services
ILO	International Labour Organisation

IPA	Involvement and Participation Association
IPD	Institute of Personnel and Development
IRS	Industrial Relations Services
JCC	Joint Consultative Committee
JIC	Joint Industrial Council
JIT	just-in-time
JNC	Joint Negotiating Committee
LFS	Labour Force Survey
LGA	Local Government Association
LIFO	last in, first out
LMS	local management of schools
LMT	*Labour Market Trends*
LPC	Low Pay Commission
MCB	mass customised bureaucracy
MD	managing diversity
MNC	multinational corporation
MNE	multinational enterprise
NBPI	National Board for Prices and Incomes
NCB	National Coal Board
NDLS	National Dock Labour Scheme
NEC	National Executive Committee
NEDC	National Economic Development Council
NEDO	National Economic Development Office
NFU	National Farmers' Union
NHS	National Health Service
NIR	'new' industrial relations
NJC	National Joint Council
NMW	national minimum wage
OECD	Organisation for Economic and Co-operative Development
PFI	private finance initiative
PPP	public private partnership
PRB	pay review body
PRP	performance-related pay
PSBR	Public Sector Borrowing Requirement
PSI	Policy Studies Institute
QMV	qualified majority voting
RDW	registered dock worker
REH	rational expectations hypothesis
RPI	Retail Prices Index
RRA	Race Relations Act 1976
RWA	Regional Water Authority
SDA	Sex Discrimination Act 1975
SMES	small and medium enterprises
SNB	special negotiating body
STB	single-table bargaining
SUA	Single-Union Agreement
TEC	Training and Enterprise Council
TQM	total quality management
TUC	Trades Union Conference

TULRCA	Trade Union and Labour Reform (Consolidation) Act
TUPE	Transfer of Undertakings (Protection of Employment) Regulations
TURERA	Trade Union Reform and Employment Rights Act 1993
UMA	Union Membership Agreement
UNICE	Union of Industrial and Employers' Confederations of Europe
UR	union recognition
WERS	Workplace Employee Relations Survey
WIRS	Workplace Industrial Relations Survey

WEBSITE ADDRESSES FOR THE LARGER UNIONS

Amicus	www.aeeu.org.uk
	www.msf.org.uk
CWU	
Communication Workers union	www.cwu.org.uk
FBU	
Fire Brigades Union	www.fbu.org.uk
GMB	www.gmb.org.uk
GPMU	
Graphical, Paper and Media Union	www.gpmu.org.uk
RMT	
National Union of Rail, Maritime and Transport Workers	www.rmt.org.uk
NUT	
National Union of Teachers	www.teachers.org.uk
Prospect	www.prospect.org.uk
PCS	
Public and Commercial Services Union	www.pcs.org.uk
TGWU	www.tgwu.org.uk
UNIFI	www.unifi.org.uk
USDAW	
Union of Shop, Distributive and Allied Trades	www.usdaw.org.uk
UNISON	www.unison.org.uk

INDEX

A Companion Website accompanies *Employment Relations*, Second edition by Edward Rose

Visit the *Employment Relations* Companion Website at www.booksites.net/rose
to find valuable teaching and learning material including:

For Students:

- Learning objectives for each chapter
- Links to relevant sites on the web
- Glossary to explain key terms

Also: This site has a syllabus manager, search functions, and email results functions.